Foundations of Global Financial Markets and Institutions

Foundations of Global Financial Markets and Institutions

Fifth Edition

Frank J. Fabozzi and Frank J. Jones

With Francesco A. Fabozzi and Steven V. Mann

The MIT Press
Cambridge, Massachusetts
London, England

This book was set in Times Roman by Westchester Publishing Services. Printed and bound in the United States of America.

Library of Congress Cataloging-in-Publication Data

Names: Fabozzi, Frank J., author. | Jones, Frank Joseph, author.
Title: Foundations of global financial markets and institutions / Frank J. Fabozzi and Frank J. Jones ; with Francesco A. Fabozzi and Steven V. Mann.
Other titles: Foundations of financial markets and institutions
Description: Fifth edition. | Cambridge, MA : MIT Press, [2019] | Earlier editions published as: Foundations of financial markets and institutions. | Includes bibliographical references and index.
Identifiers: LCCN 2018026996 | ISBN 9780262039543 (hardcover : alk. paper)
Subjects: LCSH: Finance. | Financial institutions.
Classification: LCC HG173 .F29 2019 | DDC 332.1—dc22
LC record available at https://lccn.loc.gov/2018026996

10 9 8 7 6 5 4 3 2 1

To the memory of my sister, Lucy Fabozzi.
—FJF

To my wife, Sally.
—FJJ

Contents

Preface

The first edition of this book, published in 1994, was written by Frank Fabozzi and Franco Modigliani, the 1985 recipient of the Nobel Memorial Prize in Economic Sciences. In the Preface to the first edition, they wrote that the prior 30 years had been a time of profound, indeed revolutionary, change in the financial markets and institutions of the world. The hallmarks of that change were innovation, globalization, and deregulation. Since 1994, those forces have actually gathered more strength, and the financial landscape continues to undergo large and visible changes around the globe. Their purpose in writing the book was to instruct students about this fascinating revolution. They described the wide array of financial instruments that are now available for investing, funding operations, and controlling the wide range of financial risks. Each type of financial instrument was shown to be a response to the needs of borrowers, lenders, and investors, who manage assets and liabilities in a world of constantly changing interest rates, asset prices, regulatory constraints, and international competition and opportunities. The book devoted a considerable amount of space to explaining how the world's key financial institutions manage their assets and liabilities and how innovative financial instruments support that management. The focus on the actual practices of financial institutions was particularly beneficial to students who will inevitably have to respond to changes in those institutions and their environment.

This is the fifth edition of the book. The fourth edition was published in 2009. Given the significant changes in various aspects of the global financial markets, this edition is a substantial revision of the fourth edition. The table on pages xix–xxi compares the fourth edition to this new edition. The overriding emphasis when revising the book was to make it more global centric—hence the addition of the word "Global" in the book's new title. Consequently, the U.S. financial market is still covered in considerable detail, but we describe non-U.S. financial markets as well. For practical reasons, it is not possible for us to include a detailed discussion of every country's financial market. Instead, we show how the financial markets of other countries may be similar to or differ significantly from that of the U.S. market.

Frank J. Fabozzi
Frank J. Jones

Acknowledgments

We benefited greatly from the assistance of several individuals. Steven Mann and Francesco Fabozzi made major contributions. Steven Mann coauthored two chapters. Francesco Fabozzi provided research for several chapters, coauthored chapter 12, and prepared the end-of-chapter questions for more than half of the chapters. For this reason, they are given special recognition on the title page and book's cover.

Discussions with the following individuals were helpful in preparing some of the chapters: Michele-Leonardo Bianchi, Jeff Buetow, Jack Francis, Andy Jones, Andrew Kalotay, Jang Ho Kim, Woo Chang Kim, Svetlozar Rachev, and Stoyan Stoyanov.

Many chapters in the fifth edition were read by students who provided feedback that we found useful when revising some of the chapters. These students are

- Trey Aslanian (Princeton University),
- Matt Scarpill (St. Joseph's University),
- Aidan Young (University of Pennsylvania), and
- Desmond Young (University of Pennsylvania).

We are grateful to Professor Robert Shiller of Yale University, who has been supportive of all editions of this book. His endorsement of prior editions of this book is in his courseware video (Open Yale Course: https://oyc.yale.edu/economics/econ-252-08).

We also acknowledge some individuals who have helped us in numerous respects in the prior four editions of the book; they do not bear the burden of any errors or mistakes that may appear in the text. The following people, listed in alphabetical order, read some parts of the material that has gone into one of the editions of this text: Robert Arnott, Paul Asquith, Anand Bhattacharya, Helen M. Bowers, John H. Carlson, Bruce Collins, John Crockett, Henry Gabbay, Gary L. Gastineau, Gerald Hanweck, Arthur Hogan, Jane Howe, David P. Jacob, Frank Keane, Robert Kieschnick, Martin Leibowitz, K. C. Ma, Inayat U. Mangla, Ed Murphy, Mark Pitts, Richard Puntillo, Scott Richard, Manijeh Sabi, Dexter Senft, Richard Wilson, Eleanor Xu, Uzi Yaari, and Jot Yau.

Finally, Frank Fabozzi is grateful to his wife Donna for sacrificing social time to allow him to complete this three-year project and for her encouragement. Frank Jones is grateful to his wife Sally, whose limitless support was indispensable.

Overview of the Book

The emphasis on topic coverage is best explained by providing an overview of the book and how the current edition differs from the previous edition (the fourth edition). The book is divided into eight parts. Every chapter concludes with key points that are in bullet format so that the student can quickly review the concepts and principles covered in the chapter.

Part I: Financial Markets and Players

In this nine-chapter part, chapter 1 provides an introduction to financial markets, the attributes of financial assets, and the link between financial markets and the real economy. Chapter 2 (a new chapter) explains the role of governments in financial markets. Trying to understand the attributes of financial instruments without a thorough understanding of those who participate (the "players") in the financial market makes little sense. Understanding why private market participants actively buy certain types of financial instruments and avoid other types requires becoming familiar with the investment objectives of a wide range of investor types, as well as with any regulatory constraints that might be imposed. Chapter 3 covers the special role of financial entities called "financial intermediaries" and asset management firms. In chapter 4 (a new chapter), we provide an overview of private market participants. A key player in the financial market that we believe deserves its own chapter is the credit rating agencies, the subject of chapter 5 (a new chapter). Chapter 6 focuses on depository institutions, followed in chapter 7 (a new chapter) by the role of central banks. Insurance companies and the wide range of activities of investment banking firms are the subjects of chapters 8 and 9, respectively.

Part II: Understanding Risks and Asset Pricing

The five chapters in part II cover the risks that investors and issuers are exposed to when participating in financial markets and the implications for the pricing of assets. One of the objectives in the study of finance is to understand the trade-off between risk and return. The term "risk" carries many meanings in finance, depending on the context in which it is used. Rather than leave the concept of risk vague and describe its meaning in different contexts as they arise throughout the book, in chapter 10—a new chapter to this edition of the book—we provide an overview of risk. The chapter covers the difference between risk and uncertainty, the key elements of financial risk management and the identification of financial risks, the various types of investment risk faced by investors, and the various types of funding risk faced by entities seeking to raise capital.

The major topics in the balance of part II cover the properties and general principles in the pricing of financial assets (chapter 11), asset return distributions and the quantification of some risk measures (chapter 12), the selection of assets to include in a portfolio (chapter 13, a new chapter), and the theory of how assets are priced (chapter 14). These are the major theories in finance, and there is considerable debate as to whether these theories correctly describe the way investors should construct an investment portfolio (i.e., portfolio theory) and how assets should be priced (i.e., asset pricing theory).

Chapter 12, which describes return distributions and risk measures, is a new chapter to this book. The four principal topics covered in the chapter are the different types of distributions that financial asset returns can follow, different measures of dependence between asset returns, attributes of portfolio risk measures, and alternative ratios of reward to risk. This chapter precedes the chapters on portfolio theory and asset pricing, because the material presented is necessary to understand those theories and (just as important) the limitations of those theories. Although the topics draw on basic concepts in statistics, the coverage is at an elementary level. There are three important takeaways from chapter 12. The first is that substantial empirical evidence from real-world markets indicates that return distributions for financial assets do not follow the normal distribution, as assumed in much of finance theory. In fact, some market commentators believe that the failure of many financial models reported during the Great Recession of 2008–2009 is the result of relying on the assumption that returns follow a normal distribution, the principal distribution covered in introductory probability and statistics courses. The second takeaway is that a measure of dependence between financial asset returns as assumed in traditional portfolio theory, the covariance or correlation, is just one measure of dependence. For the purpose of both portfolio management and risk management, better measures can be employed. Finally, the measure of portfolio risk used in traditional finance theory is the variance or standard deviation. Other measures that offer a better means for capturing risk are available, and these measures affect the reward/risk ratios that should be used by investors when constructing portfolios.

Part III: Interest Rates, Interest Rate Risk, and Credit Risk

The structure of interest rates and interest rate and credit risks are the subjects of part III. Chapter 15, the first of two chapters in part III, focuses on the classical theory of interest rates, which, it is assumed, provides the anchor for all interest rates in an economy.

The classical theory of interest rates provides insight into what factors determine the level of interest rates in an economy. However, there is not a single interest rate. Rather there is a structure of interest rates. In chapter 16, we look closely at the structure of interest rates. We will see that there are a myriad of factors influencing the interest rates that investors seek on alternative investment products. These factors include the type of issuer, the characteristics of the debt obligation, and the state of the economy. The concepts introduced at the beginning of chapter 16 are used to demonstrate how debt obligations should be priced in the market, as well as how to determine the calculation of a bond's yield. In the last section of chapter 16, we explain the relationship between the yield on a debt instrument and its maturity, which is referred to as the "term structure of interest rates." The different economic theories that have been offered to explain the term structure of interest rates are described.

Part IV: Primary and Secondary Markets

The three chapters in part IV first cover the fundamentals of primary markets (chapter 17) and secondary markets (chapter 18). The characteristics of these markets and their regulation are covered in these two chapters. The chapters begin by discussing regulations in the U.S. market and then move on to regulation in other developed countries. The last of the three chapters, chapter 19, covers the foreign exchange market. Chapter 19 is a new chapter in the book. In the previous edition, this topic was covered in the chapter on foreign exchange derivatives.

Part V: Global Government Debt Markets

In the previous edition of the book, two chapters covered the government debt market: one on the U.S. Treasury market and the other on the municipal securities market. In this edition, the U.S. Treasury market is covered in chapter 20, but that chapter has been expanded to include non-U.S. sovereign debt markets. The U.S. municipal securities market is described in chapter 21. That chapter also covers subnational government debt markets and the importance of the development of that market for infrastructure financing in both developed and developing markets. Given the substantial expansion of the coverage in these chapters, they are basically new chapters.

Part VI: Corporate Funding Markets

The seven chapters covered in part VI describe the various financial markets that corporations and other business entities use to obtain funding. The first three chapters (chapters 22, 23, and 24) focus on equity markets. Chapter 22 describes the structure and trading venues of the U.S. equity market, and chapter 23 covers strategies that are used by investors in this market and the important topic of pricing efficiency. Non-U.S. equity markets, with emphasis on the relatively new and large Chinese market, are covered in chapter 24, a new addition to the book. The debt markets available to corporation and other business entities are covered in chapters 25–28. The global short-term funding market (more popularly referred to as the "global money market") is the subject of chapter 25; the intermediate- to long-term corporate notes and bonds are the subject of chapter 26.

Securitization is a tool for the creation of a corporate debt instrument backed by a pool of corporate-related assets, such as receivables and future revenue. Often one thinks of securitization being used for the creation of mortgage-backed securities that we discuss in the next part of the book. However, corporations use securitization for a variety of reasons, such as reducing funding costs and managing risk. The securitization process and the parties to a securitization are described in chapter 27.

A new addition to the book is the financial market for small and medium-sized enterprises and new entrepreneurial ventures, with emphasis on start-ups and venture capital. This coverage is in chapter 28, where the various types of financial instruments available to such entities—as well as the regulations pertaining to the issuance of those financial instruments—are discussed.

Part VII: Real Estate Markets

Real estate can be classified as either residential properties or commercial properties. Residential real estate includes one- to four-family properties. Chapter 29 describes the residential mortgage market where homeowners obtain funding to purchase a home and the types of mortgage loans. The pooling of residential mortgage loans to create a residential mortgage-backed security is the subject of chapter 30. In that chapter, agency residential mortgage-backed securities and residential private-label mortgage-backed securities are described. Also described in that chapter are mortgage derivative securities: collateralized mortgage obligations and stripped mortgage-backed securities.

Commercial real estate is income-producing properties and is the subject of chapter 31. The major commercial property types are multifamily housing, apartment buildings, office buildings, industrial properties (including warehouses), shopping centers, hotels, health care facilities (e.g., senior housing care facilities), and timberlands. Commercial real estate investments are classified as follows: private commercial real estate equity, public commercial real estate equity, private commercial real estate debt, and public commercial real estate debt. Each type is described in the chapter.

Part VIII: Collective Investment Vehicles and Financial Derivatives Markets

This last part of the book has eight chapters and begins with a description of collective investment vehicles (chapter 32), which is a new addition to the book. Collective investment vehicles are products that are managed by asset management firms. These investment vehicles involve the pooling of funds by asset management firms and the investment of those funds in certain financial assets. The major collective investment vehicles covered in this chapter are investment company shares (i.e., mutual funds/open-end funds and closed-end funds), exchange-traded funds, hedge funds, real estate investment trusts, and venture capital funds.

The seven remaining chapters focus on various types of financial derivatives, or simply, "derivatives." Chapters 33 and 34 describe financial futures and options, respectively. The pricing and applications of futures and options are the subjects of chapters 35 and 36, respectively. The various types of interest rate derivatives traded in the over-the-counter market (forward rate agreements, interest rate swaps, caps, and floors) are described in chapter 37. Foreign-exchange derivative markets are covered in chapter 38, and the market for credit risk transfer vehicles (the most important being credit default swaps) is the subject of the last chapter in the book, chapter 39.

Fifth Edition versus Fourth Edition

		Comments
Part I: Financial Markets and Players		
1	Introduction	Modified from chapter 1 to reflect the new structure of the book
2	Role of Governments in Financial Markets	New chapter
3	Financial Institutions, Financial Intermediaries, and Asset Management Firms	Update of chapter 2
4	Overview of Private Market Participants	New chapter
5	Credit Rating Agencies and Their Role in Financial Markets	New chapter
6	Depository Institutions: Activities and Characteristics	Update of chapter 3
7	Central Banks	New chapter
8	Insurance Companies	Update of chapter 6
9	Investment Banking Firms	Modification of chapter 7
Part II: Understanding Risks and Asset Pricing		
10	Overview of Risks and Their Management	New chapter
11	Properties and Pricing of Financial Assets	Chapter 9 in 4th edition

(continued)

Fifth Edition versus Fourth Edition (continued)

	Comments
12 Return Distributions, Risk Measures, and Risk-Return Ratios	New chapter
13 Portfolio Selection Theory	New chapter
14 Asset Pricing Theories	Revised chapter 12
Part III: Interest Rates, Interest Rate Risk, and Credit Risk	
15 The Theory of Interest Rates	Revised chapter 10
16 The Structure of Interest Rates	Revised chapter 11
Part IV: Primary and Secondary Markets	
17 Primary Markets	Revised chapter 13
18 Secondary Markets	Revised chapter 14
19 The Foreign Exchange Market	New chapter
Part V: Global Government Debt Markets	
20 Sovereign Debt Markets	New chapter
21 Subnational (Municipal) Government Debt Markets	New chapter
Part VI: Corporate Funding Markets	
22 The Structure and Trading Venues of the Equity Market	Revised chapters 17 and 18
23 U.S. Common Stock Market: Pricing Efficiency, Trading, and Investment Strategies	Revised chapters 17 and 18
24 Non-U.S. Equity Markets	New chapter
25 Global Short-Term Funding and Investing Markets	New chapter
26 Corporate Debt Markets	Revised chapters 19 and 20
27 Market for Asset-Backed Securities	Revised chapter 25
28 Financing Market for Small, Medium-Sized, and Entrepreneurial Enterprises	New chapter
Part VII: Real Estate Markets	
29 The Residential Mortgage Market	Updated chapter 22
30 Residential Mortgage-Backed Securities Market	Updated chapter 23
31 Commercial Real Estate Markets	New chapter

Fifth Edition versus Fourth Edition (continued)

	Comments
Part VIII: Collective Investment Vehicles and Financial Derivatives Markets	
32 Market for Collective Investment Vehicles	New chapter
33 Financial Futures Markets	Chapter 26 in 4th edition
34 Options Markets	Chapter 27 in 4th edition
35 Pricing Futures and Options Contracts	Chapter 28 in 4th edition
36 Applications of Futures and Options Contracts	Chapter 29 in 4th edition
37 Over-the-Counter Interest Rate Derivatives: Forward Rate Agreements, Swaps, Caps, and Floors	Chapter 30 in 4th edition
38 Market for Foreign Exchange Derivatives	Revised chapter 31
39 Market for Credit Risk Transfer Vehicles	Chapter 32 in 4th edition

I FINANCIAL MARKETS AND PLAYERS

1 Introduction

CONTENTS

Learning Objectives

After reading this chapter, you will understand:

- the components of the financial system;
- what a financial asset is and the principal economic functions of financial assets;

- the distinction between financial assets and tangible assets;
- what a financial market is and the principal economic functions it performs;
- the distinction between debt instruments and equity instruments;
- the various ways to classify financial markets;
- the differences between the primary and secondary markets;
- who participates in financial markets;
- the reasons for the globalization of financial markets;
- the distinction between an internal market and an external market;
- the distinction between a domestic market, a foreign market, and the Euromarket;
- the reasons entities use foreign markets and the Euromarkets;
- the differences among developed, emerging, and frontier stock markets;
- what is meant by an asset class;
- what a derivative instrument is and the two basic types of derivative instruments;
- the role of derivative instruments; and
- the link between financial markets and the real economy.

In a market economy, the allocation of economic resources is the outcome of many private decisions. Prices are the signals operating in a market economy that direct economic resources to their best use. The types of markets in an economy can be divided into (1) the markets for products (manufactured goods and services), called the **product markets**, and (2) the market for the factors of production (labor and capital), called the **factor markets**.

Our purpose in this book is to focus on one part of the factor markets, the market for financial assets, or more simply, the **financial market**. The financial market is one of the three major components of the **financial system**. The other two components are financial institutions and financial market infrastructure. **Financial institutions** are the entities that provide financial services to other entities in the financial system. They include depository institutions (e.g., banks), insurance companies, and securities firms. **Financial market infrastructure** is the component of the financial system that involves processing the payments of financial assets.

In this chapter, we will look at the role of financial markets, the "things" that are traded (i.e., bought and sold) in financial markets, the reasons for the integration of world financial markets, and the government's role in the regulation of these markets. Chapters that follow deal with the key financial institutions, and the financial market infrastructure will be discussed when we describe the different sectors of the financial market.

Financial Assets

We begin with a few basic definitions. An **asset**, broadly speaking, is any possession that has value in an exchange. Assets can be classified as tangible or intangible. A **tangible asset** is one whose value depends on particular physical properties—examples are buildings, land, or machinery. **Intangible assets**, by contrast, represent legal claims to some future benefit. Their value bears no relation to the form, physical or otherwise, in which these claims are recorded.

Financial assets are intangible assets. For financial assets, the typical benefit or value is a claim to future cash. With one exception (real estate, which is a tangible asset), this book deals with the various types of financial assets, the markets where they are traded, and the principles for valuing them. Throughout this book, we use the terms "financial asset," **financial instrument**, and **security** interchangeably.

The entity that has agreed to make future cash payments is called the **issuer** of the financial asset; the owner of the financial asset is referred to as the **investor**. Here are just seven examples of financial assets:

- a loan by Bank of America (investor) to an individual (issuer/borrower) to purchase a car
- a bond issued by the U.S. Department of the Treasury
- a bond issued by AT&T
- a bond issued by the City of New York
- a bond issued by the German government
- a share of common stock issued by Apple Inc.
- a share of common stock issued by Honda Motor Company, a Japanese automotive company

In the case of the car loan, the terms of the loan establish that over time, the borrower must make specified payments to the Bank of America. The payments include repayment of the amount borrowed plus interest. The cash flow for this asset is made up of the specified payments that the borrower must make.

In the case of a U.S. Treasury bond, the U.S. government (the issuer) agrees to pay the investor the bond interest payments every six months until the bond matures, and then at the maturity date, repay the amount borrowed. The same is true for the bonds issued by AT&T, the City of New York, and the German government. In the case of AT&T, the issuer is a corporation, not a government entity. In the case of the City of New York, the issuer is a municipal government. The issuer of the German government bond is a central government entity.

The common stock of Apple Inc. entitles the investor to receive dividends distributed by the company. In this case, the investor also has a claim to a pro rata share of the net asset value of the company in the case of the company's liquidation in a bankruptcy. The same is true of the common stock of Honda Motor Company.

Debt versus Equity Instruments

The claim that the holder of a financial asset has may be either a fixed amount or a varying, or residual, amount. In the former case, the financial asset is referred to as a **debt instrument**. The car loan, the U.S. Treasury bond, the AT&T bond, the City of New York bond, and the German government bond cited above are examples of debt instruments requiring fixed payments.

An **equity instrument** (also called a **residual claim**) obligates the issuer of the financial asset to pay the holder an amount based on earnings, if approved by the board of directors, after holders of debt instruments have been paid. Common stock is an example of an equity instrument. A partnership share in a business is another example.

Some securities fall into both categories. For example, **preferred stock** is an equity instrument, issued in the United States but not all countries, which entitles the investor to receive a fixed amount. This payment is contingent, however, and due only after payments to debt instrument holders are made.

Another "combination" instrument is a convertible bond, which allows the investor to convert debt into equity under certain circumstances. Both debt and preferred stock are called **fixed-income instruments**.

Certain types of financial instruments may seem odd at first. For example, there are bonds issued by life insurance companies where payments are made based on mortality rates or bonds issued by a mining company where the payments are based on the price of the natural resource being mined. Once you understand the needs of issuers and the risk/return relationships in financial markets to compensate investors for taking on certain risks, what may at first appear to be an odd or unusual financial instrument will make economic sense. Indeed, the purpose of this book is to help you understand the global financial markets and the players in the markets, so that you can understand why every type of financial instrument traded in the market fulfills the needs of issuers, investors, or both.

The Price of a Financial Asset and Risk

A basic economic principle is that the price of any financial asset is equal to the present value of its expected cash flow, even if the cash flow is not known with certainty. By **cash flow**, we mean the stream of cash payments over time. For example, if a U.S. government bond promises to pay $20 every six months for the next 30 years and $1,000 at the end of 30 years, then this is the bond's cash flow. In the case of the car loan by Bank of America, if the borrower is obligated to pay $500 every month for three years, then this is the cash flow of the loan. We elaborate on this principle throughout this book as we discuss several theories for the pricing of financial assets.

Directly related to the notion of price is the expected return on a financial asset. Given the expected cash flow of a financial asset and its price, we can determine its expected rate of return. For example, if the price of a financial asset is $100, and its only cash flow is $105 one year from now, then its expected return would be 5%.

The type of financial asset, whether debt instrument or equity instrument, as well as the characteristics of the issuer, determine the degree of certainty of the expected cash flow. For example, assuming that the U.S. government is not expected to default on the debt instruments it issues, the cash flow of U.S. Treasury securities is known with certainty. What is uncertain, however, is the purchasing power of the cash flow received.

In the case of the Bank of America car loan, the ability of the borrower to repay presents some uncertainty about the cash flow. But, if the borrower does not default on the loan obligation, the investor (Bank of America) knows what the cash flow will be. The same is true for the bonds of AT&T and the City of New York. In the case of the German government bond, the cash flow is known if the government of Germany does not default. However, the cash flow may be denominated not in U.S. dollars but in the German currency, the euro. Thus, although the cash flow is known in terms of the number of euros that will be received, from the perspective of a U.S. investor, the number of U.S. dollars is unknown. The number of U.S. dollars will depend on the exchange rate between the euro and the U.S. dollar at the time the cash flow is received.

The holder of Apple common stock is uncertain as to both the amount and the timing of dividend payments. Dividend payments will be related to company profits. The same is true for the cash flow of the common stock of Honda Motor Company. In addition, because Honda will make dividend payments in Japanese yen, there is uncertainty about the cash flow in terms of U.S. dollars.

We explain various types of risk in chapter 10, as well as in other chapters throughout this book, but we can see three of these risks in our examples in this chapter. The first is the risk attached to the potential purchasing power of the expected cash flow. This is called **purchasing power risk** or **inflation risk**. The second is the risk that the issuer or borrower will default on the obligation. This is called **credit risk**, or more specifically, as explained in chapter 10, **default risk**. Finally, for financial assets whose cash flow is not denominated in U.S. dollars, there is the risk that the exchange rate will change adversely, resulting in fewer U.S. dollars. This risk is referred to as **foreign-exchange risk** or **currency risk**.

Financial Assets versus Tangible Assets

A tangible asset, such as plant or equipment purchased by a business entity, shares at least one characteristic with a financial asset: Both are expected to generate future cash flow for their owner. For example, suppose a U.S. airline purchases a fleet of aircraft for $500 million. With its purchase of the aircraft, the airline expects to realize cash flow from passenger travel.

Financial assets and tangible assets are linked. Ownership of tangible assets is financed by the issuance of some type of financial asset—either debt instruments or equity instruments. For example, in the case of the airline, suppose that a debt instrument is issued to raise the

$500 million to purchase the fleet of aircraft. The cash flow from passenger travel will be used to service the payments on the debt instrument. Ultimately, therefore, the cash flow for a financial asset is generated by some tangible asset.

The Role of Financial Assets

Financial assets have two principal economic functions. The first is to transfer funds from those who have surplus funds to invest to those who need funds to invest in tangible assets. The second economic function is to transfer funds in such a way as to redistribute the unavoidable risk associated with the cash flow generated by tangible assets among those seeking and those providing the funds. However, as we will see, the claims held by the final wealth holders are generally different from the liabilities issued by the final demanders of funds because of the activity of financial intermediaries that seek to transform the final liabilities into the financial assets that the public prefers.

We can illustrate these two economic functions with three examples:

1. Richie Calbo has obtained a license to manufacture wristwatches with the logo for the U.S. Navy. He estimates that he will need $1.2 million to purchase plant and equipment to manufacture the watches. Unfortunately, he has only $300,000 to invest, and that is his life savings, which he does not want to invest, even though he has confidence that there will be a receptive market for the watches.

2. Amanda Santigo, an entrepreneur, has recently invented a product for the inexpensive and rapid processing of DNA samples for forensic science labs and has sold the rights for an amount that netted her $1 million after taxes. She plans to spend $150,000 to purchase a condominium, $50,000 on a car, and to invest the balance, $800,000.

3. Hasan Rahman, an associate at a major Los Angeles law firm, has received a bonus check that after taxes has netted him $280,000. He plans to spend $80,000 on a BMW and invest the balance, $200,000.

Suppose that, quite by accident, Richie, Amanda, and Hasan meet at a social function. Sometime during their conversation, they discuss their financial plans. By the end of the evening, they agree to a deal. Richie agrees to invest $200,000 of his savings in the business and raise the balance of the $1 million needed to purchase the plant and equipment as follows. Amanda agrees to buy a 50% interest for $800,000. Hasan agrees to lend Richie $200,000 for four years at an interest rate of 12% per year. Richie will be responsible for operating the business without the assistance of Amanda or Hasan.

Two financial claims came out of this meeting and the transactions that the parties agree to. The first is an equity instrument issued by Richie and purchased by Amanda for $800,000. The other is a debt instrument issued by Richie and purchased by Hasan for $200,000. Thus, the two financial assets allowed funds to be transferred from Amanda and Hasan, who had surplus funds to invest, to Richie, who needed funds to invest in tangible assets to manufacture the watches. This transfer of funds is the first economic function of financial assets.

That Richie is not willing to invest his life savings of $300,000 means that he wanted to transfer part of that risk. He does so by selling Amanda a financial asset that gives her a financial claim equal to one-half the cash flow from the business. He secures an additional amount of capital from Hasan, who is not willing to share in the risk of the business (except for credit risk), in the form of an obligation requiring payment of a fixed cash flow, regardless of the outcome of the venture. This shifting of risk is the second economic function of financial assets.

Financial Markets

A **financial market** is a market where financial assets are exchanged (i.e., traded). Although the existence of a financial market is not a necessary condition for the creation and exchange of a financial asset, in most economies, financial assets are created and subsequently traded in some type of financial market. The market in which a financial asset trades for immediate delivery is called the **spot market** or **cash market**.

The Role of Financial Markets

We previously explained the two primary economic functions of financial assets. Financial markets provide three additional economic functions.

First, the interactions of buyers and sellers in a financial market determine the price of the traded asset. Or, equivalently, they determine the required return on a financial asset. Because the inducement for firms to acquire funds depends on the required return that investors demand, it is this feature of financial markets that signals how the funds in the economy should be allocated among financial assets. This is called the **price discovery process**.

Second, financial markets provide a mechanism for an investor to sell a financial asset. Because of this ability, it is said that a financial market offers **liquidity**, an attractive feature when circumstances either force or motivate an investor to sell a financial asset. In the absence of liquidity, the owner would be forced to hold a debt instrument until it matures and an equity instrument until the company is either voluntarily or involuntarily liquidated. Although all financial markets provide some form of liquidity, the degree of liquidity is one of the factors that characterize different markets.

The third economic function of a financial market is that it reduces the cost of transacting. There are two costs associated with transacting: search costs and information costs.

Search costs represent explicit costs, such as the money spent to advertise one's intention to sell or purchase a financial asset, and implicit costs, such as the value of time spent locating a counterparty. The presence of some form of organized financial market reduces search costs. **Information costs** are costs associated with assessing the investment merits of a financial asset, that is, the amount and the likelihood of the cash flow expected to be generated. In a price efficient market, prices reflect the aggregate information collected by all market participants.

Classification of Financial Markets

Financial markets can be classified in many ways. One way is by the type of financial claim, such as debt markets and equity markets. Another is by the maturity of the claim. For example, there is a financial market for short-term debt instruments, called the **money market**, and one for longer-maturity financial assets, called the **capital market**.

Financial markets can be categorized as those dealing with financial claims that are newly issued, called the **primary market**, and those for exchanging financial claims previously issued, called the **secondary market** or the **market for seasoned instruments**.

Markets are classified as either **cash instrument markets** or **derivative instruments markets**. (The latter is described briefly later in this chapter and in more detail in chapter 39.)

A market can be classified by its organizational structure: It may be an **auction market**, an **over-the-counter market**, or an **intermediated market**.

All these classifications are summarized in table 1.1.

Market Participants

Participants in the global financial markets that issue and purchase financial claims include households, business entities (corporations and partnerships), national governments, na-

Table 1.1
Summary of classification of financial markets.

Classification by nature of claim:
- Debt market
- Equity market

Classification by maturity of claim:
- Money market
- Capital market

Classification by seasoning of claim:
- Primary market
- Secondary market

Classification by immediate delivery or future delivery:
- Cash (spot) market
- Derivatives market

Classification by organizational structure:
- Auction market
- Over-the-counter market
- Intermediated market

tional government agencies, state and local governments, and supranationals (such as the World Bank, the European Investment Bank, and the Asian Development Bank).

Business entities include nonfinancial and financial enterprises. Nonfinancial enterprises manufacture products (for example, cars, steel, and computers), provide nonfinancial services (including transportation, utilities, and computer programming), or do both. The roles in financial markets played by financial enterprises and a special type of financial enterprise known as a financial intermediary are described in chapter 2.

Finally, although we have focused on market participants that create and/or exchange financial assets, a broader definition of market participants would include regulators of financial markets.

Globalization of Financial Markets

Because of the globalization of financial markets, entities in any country seeking to raise funds need not be limited to their domestic financial market. Nor are investors in a country limited to the financial assets issued in their domestic market. Globalization means the integration of financial markets throughout the world into an international financial market.

The factors that have led to the integration of financial markets are (1) deregulation or liberalization of markets and the activities of market participants in key financial centers of the world; (2) technological advances for monitoring world markets, executing orders, and analyzing financial opportunities; and (3) increased institutionalization of financial markets.

Global competition has forced governments to deregulate (or liberalize) various aspects of their financial markets so that their financial enterprises can compete effectively around the world.

Technological advances have increased the integration and efficiency of the global financial market. Advances in telecommunication systems have linked market participants throughout the world, with the result that orders can be executed within milliseconds. Advances in computer technology, coupled with advanced telecommunication systems, allow the transmission of real-time information on security prices and other key information to many participants in many places. Therefore, many investors can monitor global financial markets and simultaneously assess how this information will impact the risk/return profile of their portfolios. Significantly improved computing power allows the instant manipulation of real-time market information, so that arbitrage opportunities can be identified. Once these opportunities are identified, telecommunication systems permit the rapid execution of orders to capture them.

The U.S. financial markets have shifted from domination by retail investors to domination by financial institutions. By **retail investors** we mean individuals. For example, when you or I buy a share of common stock, we are referred to as retail investors. Examples of financial institutions are pension funds, insurance companies, mutual funds, commercial banks, and savings and loan associations. We describe these financial institutions in the next eight chapters. Throughout this book, we will refer to these financial institutions as **institutional investors**.

The shifting of the financial markets from dominance by retail investors to institutional investors is referred to as the **institutionalization of financial markets**. The same thing is occurring in other industrialized countries. Unlike retail investors, institutional investors have been more willing to transfer funds across national borders to improve portfolio diversification or exploit perceived mispricing of financial assets in foreign countries.

The potential portfolio diversification benefits associated with global investing have been documented in numerous studies, which have heightened the awareness of investors about the virtues of global investing.

Classification of Global Financial Markets

Although there is no uniform system for classifying the global financial markets, an appropriate schematic presentation appears in figure 1.1. From the perspective of a given country, financial markets can be classified as either internal or external. The **internal market**, also referred to as the **national market**, is composed of two parts: the domestic market and the foreign market. The **domestic market** in a country is where issuers domiciled in that country issue securities and where those securities are subsequently traded.

The **foreign market** of any country is where the securities of issuers not domiciled in the country are sold and traded. The rules governing the issuance of foreign securities are those imposed by regulatory authorities where the security is issued. For example, securities issued by foreign corporations in the United States must comply with the regulations set forth in U.S. securities law. A non-Japanese corporation that seeks to offer securities in Japan must comply with Japanese securities law and regulations imposed by the Japanese Ministry of Finance.

Nicknames have developed to describe the various foreign markets. For example, the foreign market in the United States is called the "Yankee market." The foreign market in Japan is nicknamed the "Samurai market"; in the United Kingdom, the "Bulldog market"; in the Netherlands, the "Rembrandt market"; and in Spain, the "Matador market."

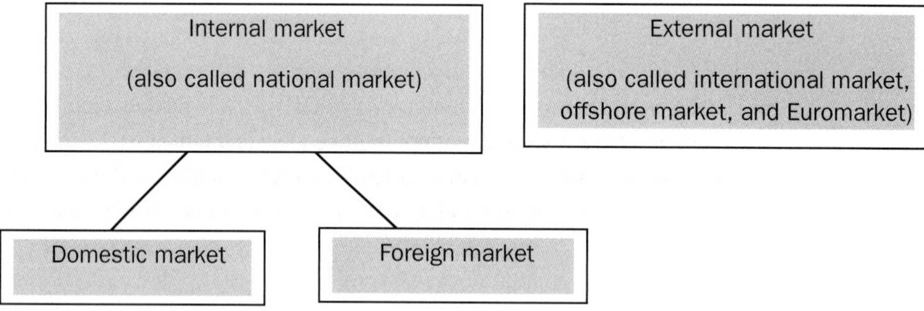

Figure 1.1
Classification of global financial markets.

The **external market**, also referred to as the **international market**, allows trading of securities with two distinguishing features: (1) at issuance, securities are offered simultaneously to investors in various countries; and (2) they are issued outside the jurisdiction of any single country. The external market is commonly referred to as the **offshore market**, or, more popularly, the **Euromarket**.[1]

Developed, Emerging, and Frontier Markets

Countries and their equity markets are typically divided into three categories: developed, emerging (developing), and frontier (pre-emerging). The differences among these three types are based mainly on two factors: the development of their economies and of their capital markets.[2] Their economic development refers mainly to their per capita income and potential growth. Developed countries have higher levels of per capita income but lower potential growth. The development of their capital markets refers to the size of their market capitalization (described next), the level of liquidity, and the development of their supporting regulatory and legal bodies. These two characteristics affect the growth potential, risk, and liquidity of investments in their markets. Developed countries are found mostly in North America, Western Europe, and Australasia, including the United States, Canada, Germany, the United Kingdom, Australia, New Zealand, and Japan.

An emerging (developing) market is a country that has some of the characteristics of a developed market but not all of them. Developing countries include Brazil, Russia, India, and China (as a group, popularly referred to as BRIC); Portugal, Ireland, Italy, Greece, Spain (PIIGS); and other countries. A frontier or pre-emerging market is a market that is too small and undeveloped to be considered an emerging market.

Asset Classes

In financial markets, participants talk about **asset classes**. In the financial markets of most developed countries, the **asset classes** are (1) common stocks, (2) bonds, (3) cash equivalents, and (4) real estate. How do market participants define their asset classes? There are two ways they do so.

One way is in terms of the investment attributes that the members of the asset class have in common. These investment characteristics include the major economic factors that affect the value of the asset class, and as a result, correlate highly with the returns of each member of the asset class, have similar risk and return characteristics, and have a common legal

1. The classification we use is by no means universally accepted. Some market observers and compilers of statistical data on market activity refer to the external market as consisting of the foreign market and the Euromarket.

2. "What Is the Difference between a Developed, Emerging, and Frontier Market?" May 11, 2012. http://www.nasdaq.com/article/what-is-the-difference-between-a-developed-emerging-and-frontier-market-cm140649.

or regulatory structure. Hence, based on this way of defining asset classes, the correlation between the returns of different asset classes would be low. Another way of defining an asset class is based simply on the characteristics of a group of assets that is treated as an asset class by asset managers.

Based on these two ways of defining asset classes, the traditional asset classes above can be extended to generate other such classes. From the perspective of a U.S. investor, for example, the traditional asset classes listed above have been expanded by separating foreign stocks and bonds into those issued by U.S. entities and those issued by foreign entities.

Moreover, common stocks and bonds are further divided into more asset classes based on the size of the corporation. Here, size refers to the **market capitalization** of the corporation's common stock. A corporation's market capitalization (or simply, "market cap") is equal to the total market value of its common stock outstanding. For example, suppose that a corporation has 50 million shares of common stock outstanding, and each share has a market value of \$400. Then this corporation's market cap is \$20 billion (50 million shares × \$400 per share).[3]

In the United States, one way of classifying asset classes is based on market cap:

- mega-cap stocks (greater than \$200 billion),
- large-cap stocks (\$10 billion to \$200 billion),
- mid-cap stocks (\$1 billion to \$10 billion),
- small-cap stocks (\$300 million to \$1 billion),
- micro-cap stocks (\$50 million to \$300 million), and
- nano-cap stocks (less than \$50 million).

Except for real estate, all the asset classes identified above are referred to as **traditional asset classes**. Real estate and all other asset classes that are not in the above list are referred to as **nontraditional asset classes** or **alternative asset classes**. They include commodities, private equities, hedge funds, venture capital, real assets, and currencies.

Derivatives Markets

So far, we have focused on the cash market for financial assets. With some contracts, the contract holder has either the obligation or the choice to buy or sell a financial asset at some future time. The price of any such contract derives its value from that of the underlying financial asset, financial index, or interest rate. Consequently, these contracts are called **derivative instruments**.

3. Another way of classifying stocks in terms of asset classes is growth stocks and value stocks. Although the market cap of a company is easy to determine given the market price per share and the number of shares outstanding, defining "value" and "growth" stocks is not simple to do at this point in the book. We'll describe value and growth stocks in chapter 23.

Types of Derivative Instruments

The two basic types of derivative instruments are **futures/forward contracts** and **options contracts**.

A futures or forward contract is an agreement whereby two parties agree to transact with respect to some financial asset at a predetermined price at a specified future date. One party agrees to buy the financial asset; the other agrees to sell the financial asset. Both parties are obligated to perform, and neither party charges a fee. The distinction between a futures and a forward contract and why this type of derivative is referred to as a risk-sharing type of derivative are explained in chapter 33.

An options contract gives the owner of the contract the right, but not the obligation, to buy (or sell) a financial asset at a specified price from (or to) another party. The buyer of the contract must pay the seller a fee, which is known as the option price. When the option grants the owner of the option the right to buy a financial asset from the other party, the option is a **call option**. If, instead, the option grants the owner of the option the right to sell a financial asset to the other party, the option is a **put option**. Options are more fully explained in chapter 34.

Derivative instruments are not limited to financial assets. Some derivative instruments involve commodities and precious metals. Our focus in this book, however, is on derivative instruments whose underlying asset is a financial asset or some financial benchmark, such as a stock index or an interest rate, a credit spread, or foreign exchange.

Moreover, other types of derivative instruments are basically packages of either forward contracts or option contracts. These include swaps, caps, and floors, all of which are discussed in chapter 37.

The Role of Derivative Instruments

Derivative instruments provide issuers and investors with an inexpensive way of controlling some major risks. While we describe most of these risks in chapter 10, here are three examples that clearly illustrate the need for derivative instruments:

1. Suppose that AT&T plans to obtain a bank loan for $700 million two months from now. The key risk here is that two months from now, the interest rate will be higher than it is today. Even if the interest rate were only one percentage point higher, AT&T would have to pay $7 million more in annual interest. Clearly, then, issuers and borrowers want a way to protect against a rise in interest rates.

2. IBM's defined benefit pension fund owns a portfolio consisting of the common stock of a large number of companies. (We describe defined benefit pension funds in chapter 4, but for now, the only salient point is that this type of pension fund must make periodic payments to the beneficiaries of the plan.) Suppose the pension fund managers know that two months from now, they must sell stock in its portfolio to pay beneficiaries $20 million. The

risk that the IBM pension fund faces is that two months from now when the stocks are sold, the price of most or all stocks may be lower than they are today. If stock prices do decline, the pension fund will have to sell off more shares to realize $20 million. Thus, investors, such as the IBM pension fund managers, face the risk of declining stock prices and may want to protect against this risk.

3. Suppose Coca-Cola Company plans to issue a bond in Switzerland and the periodic payments that the company must make to the bondholders are denominated in the Swiss currency, the franc. The amount in U.S. dollars that Coca-Cola must pay to receive the amount in Swiss francs it has contracted to pay will depend on the exchange rate at the time the payment must be made. For example, suppose that at the time Coca-Cola plans to issue the bonds, the exchange rate is such that 1 U.S. dollar is equal to 1.5 Swiss francs. So, for each 7.5 million Swiss francs that Coca-Cola must pay to the bondholders, it must pay U.S. $5 million. If at any time that a payment must be made in Swiss francs, the value of the U.S. dollar declines relative to the Swiss franc, Coca-Cola will have to pay more U.S. dollars to satisfy its contractual obligation. For example, if 1 U.S. dollar at the time of a payment changes to 1.25 Swiss francs, Coca-Cola would have to pay $6 million to make a payment of 7.5 million Swiss francs. This is U.S. $1 million more than when it issued the bonds. Issuers and borrowers who raise funds in a currency that is not their local currency face this currency risk.

The derivative instruments described in part VIII of this book can be used by the two borrowers (AT&T and Coca-Cola) and the one investor (IBM's defined benefit pension fund) in these examples to eliminate or to reduce the kinds of risks that they face.

As we will see in later chapters, derivatives markets may have at least three advantages over the corresponding cash (spot) market for the same financial asset. First, depending on the derivative instrument, it may cost less to execute a transaction in the derivatives market to adjust the risk exposure to new economic information than it would cost to make that adjustment in the cash market. Second, transactions typically can be accomplished faster in the derivatives market than in the cash one. Third, some derivatives markets can absorb a greater dollar transaction without an adverse effect on the price of the derivative instrument; that is, the derivatives market may be more liquid than the cash market.

The key point here is that derivative instruments play a critical role in global financial markets. A May 1994 report published by the U.S. Government Accountability Office (GAO) titled *Financial Derivatives: Actions Needed to Protect the Financial System* recognized the importance of derivatives for market participants. Page 6 of the report states:

> Derivatives serve an important function of the global financial marketplace, providing end-users with opportunities to better manage financial risks associated with their business transactions. The rapid growth and increasing complexity of derivatives reflect both the increased demand from end-users for better ways to manage their financial risks and the innovative capacity of the financial services industry to respond to market demands.

Unfortunately, derivatives instruments are too often viewed by the general public—and sometimes regulators and legislative bodies—as vehicles for pure speculation (that is, legalized gambling). Without derivative instruments and the markets in which they trade, the financial systems throughout the world would not be as integrated as they are today.

Financial Markets and the Real Economy

In the introduction to this chapter, we explained how a market economy can be divided into two markets, the product market and the factor market. We then explained the critical role of financial markets in the efficient allocation of capital. Another way of looking at a market economy is by dividing it into two markets: (1) the real economy and (2) the paper economy. The **real economy** refers to markets where products and services are produced and their prices are determined. The **paper economy** refers to markets where financial assets are traded (i.e., financial markets) and the prices of these assets are determined. The financial markets include not just the cash market but derivatives markets.

What is the linkage between the real economy and the paper economy? In the United States, there have been two well-known crises in the paper economy that have spilled over into the real economy, causing severe economic problems.

On October 29, 1929 ("Black Monday"), the stock market crashed. The most popular stock market index at the time, the Dow Jones Industrial Average, fell by 25% in two days and by 30% in one week. The decline in the value of U.S. stocks resulted in millions of Americans losing a major part, if not all, of their wealth. This loss of wealth reduced consumer purchasing, which in turn forced business firms to reduce operations. In turn, this led to a further loss of jobs. The end result was the Great Depression, which lasted from 1929 to 1939, representing the longest economic depression in the United States. During this period, unemployment reached 20%, the gross domestic product fell by 30%, industrial production fell by 47%, and the consumer price index fell by 33% (i.e., the country experienced deflation). In addition, because of the lack of confidence in the banking system, numerous banks failed as a result of a run on the banks (i.e., many individuals simultaneously withdrawing deposits) and borrowers being unable to repay their loans (e.g., resulting in foreclosure on residential properties). In the 1920s, an average of 600 banks failed each year. In 1930, however, 1,350 banks either suspended or terminated their operations.[4] The next year, 2,293 banks failed or suspended operations, and this number increased to almost 4,000 banks by 1933. It was during the Great Depression that major legislation involving bank regulation and financial markets were proposed by President Franklin Roosevelt and subsequently passed by Congress. Since then the legislation has been updated.

The next major legislative changes dealing with financial markets came in 2008 as a result of what has been referred to variously as the global financial crisis or the global recession. In the summer of 2007, the market collapsed for certain financial instruments (one type of mortgage-backed securities, which we discuss in chapter 30). There was a

4. FDIC, *Managing the Crisis: The FDIC and RTC Experience* (Washington, DC: Federal Deposit Insurance Corporation, n.d.), http://www.fdic.gov/bank/historical/managing/Chron/pre-fdic.

spillover from this market to the real estate market, which experienced a pricing bubble owing to low interest rates and buyers' belief in ever-increasing home prices. Banks and other financial institutions using excessive leverage[5] and derivative products (such as credit default swaps) faced liquidity problems as the credit markets dried up. The bankruptcy of a major investment bank, Lehman Brothers, in 2008 was a key event that triggered the global financial crisis. The crisis resulted in a slowdown in economic growth and a high unemployment rate. There were fears of another Great Depression, not just in the United States but worldwide. In fact, while the United States experienced its worst recession since the Great Depression, such countries as France, Germany, and Japan realized the slowest economic growth in decades. These events led to legislation in many countries to reduce the likelihood of a problem in the paper economy leading to a severe economic crisis in the real economy. In the United States, the major legislation seeking to accomplish this was the Dodd-Frank Wall Street Reform and Consumer Protection Act of 2010. As succinctly stated in this act, its intent is:

> To promote the financial stability of the United States by improving accountability and transparency in the financial system, to end "too big to fail," to protect the American taxpayer by ending bailouts, to protect consumers from abusive financial services practices, and for other purposes.

We describe various provisions of this act, referred to simply as the "Dodd-Frank Act," in later chapters.

What is interesting is that despite the linkage observed between the paper economy and the real economy when the stock market crashed in 1929 and during the Great Depression that followed, it seems that macroeconomic models did not focus on this linkage until the 2008 financial crisis. As noted in a 2012 report by Germany's central bank,[6] the Deutsche Bundesbank:

> Prior to the crisis, financial markets were generally not included in macro models, nor was this regarded as necessary because, for the most part, the financial markets were not themselves deemed to contain any potential to cause disruptions. In the wake of the crisis, however, financial markets have been increasingly integrated into empirical and theoretical macroeconomic models.[7]

Key Points

- The financial system is composed of three parts: financial markets, financial institutions, and market infrastructure.
- A financial asset (financial instrument or security) entitles the owner to the future cash flow to be paid by the issuer.

5. We discuss the risks associated with leverage in chapter 10.

6. Central banks and their role are described in chapter 7.

7. Deutsche Bundesbank, "National and International Financial Market Shocks and the Real Economy: An Empirical View," *Monthly Report* (March 2012): 35.

- The holder of a financial asset's claim can be either an equity or a debt claim.
- The value of any financial asset equals the present value of the expected cash flow.
- Three types of risk are associated with investing in financial assets: purchasing power or inflation risk, default or credit risk, and exchange-rate risk.
- The two principal economic functions of a financial asset are (1) to transfer funds from those who have surplus funds to invest to those who need funds to invest in tangible assets, and (2) to transfer funds in a way that redistributes the unavoidable risk associated with the cash flow generated by tangible assets among those seeking and those providing the funds.
- Financial markets provide the following three additional functions beyond that of financial assets themselves: (1) They provide a mechanism for determining the price (or, equivalently, the required return) of financial assets; (2) they make assets more liquid; and (3) they reduce the costs of exchanging assets.
- The costs associated with market transactions are search costs and information costs.
- Financial markets can be classified by type of financial claim (debt instrument versus equity claim), by the maturity of claims (money market versus capital market), by whether the security is newly issued or seasoned (primary market versus secondary market), and by the type of organizational structure.
- Derivative instruments derive their value from an underlying financial asset.
- Derivative instruments allow market players to more efficiently accomplish their financial goals.
- Globalization means the integration of financial markets throughout the world into an international financial market and allows (1) entities in any country seeking to raise funds to look outside their domestic financial market and (2) investors in a country to invest in financial assets issued outside their domestic market.
- The factors contributing to the integration of financial markets include (1) deregulation or liberalization of markets and the activities of market participants in key financial centers of the world; (2) technological advances for monitoring world markets, executing orders, and analyzing financial opportunities; and (3) the increased institutionalization of financial markets.
- The institutionalization of financial markets refers to the shifting of the financial markets from dominance by retail investors to dominance by institutional investors.
- From the perspective of a given country, financial markets can be classified as either internal (or national) or external.
- A country's internal market consists of its domestic market and foreign market.
- A country's domestic market is one in which issuers domiciled in the country issue securities and in which those securities are subsequently traded. In a country's foreign market, securities of issuers not domiciled in the country are sold and traded.

- In classifying countries and stock markets as developed, emerging, or frontier, two characteristics are used: (1) their economic development (such as their per capita income and potential growth) and (2) the development of their capital markets in terms of market capitalization, the level of liquidity, and supporting regulatory and legal bodies.
- Developed stock markets are in countries that have higher levels of per capita income but lower potential growth.
- Developed stock markets are found mostly in North America, Western Europe, and Australasia, including the United States, Canada, Germany, the United Kingdom, Australia, New Zealand, and Japan.
- An emerging (developing) market is a market in a country that has some of the characteristics of a developed market, but not all of them.
- Developing countries include Brazil, Russia, India, and China (BRIC) and Portugal, Ireland, Italy, Greece, and Spain (PIIGS).
- A frontier or pre-emerging market is a market in a country that is too small and undeveloped to be considered an emerging market.
- Financial assets are grouped together into asset classes.
- The traditional asset classes include stocks, bonds, and cash equivalents.
- Nontraditional asset classes or alternative asset classes include real estate, commodities, private equities, hedge funds, venture capital, real assets, and currencies.
- The real economy is the market where products and services are produced and where the prices of those products and services are determined.
- The markets where financial assets are traded (i.e., financial markets) are referred to as the paper economy.
- Financial markets are linked to the real economy.

Questions

1. What is the difference between a financial asset and a tangible asset?
2. What is the difference between the claim of a debtholder of Chevron Corporation and a common stockholder of Chevron Corporation?
3. What is the basic principle followed in determining the value of a financial asset?
4. Why is it difficult to determine the cash flow of a financial asset?
5. What factors affect the interest rate used to discount the cash flow expected from a financial asset?
6. Why are the characteristics of an issuer important in determining the price of a financial asset?

7. What are the two principal roles of financial assets?

8. In September 1990, a study by the U.S. Congress, Office of Technology Assessment, titled "Electronic Bulls & Bears: U.S. Securities Markets and Information Technology," included the following statement:

"Securities markets have five basic functions in a capitalistic economy:

1. they make it possible for corporations and governmental units to raise capital.

2. they help to allocate capital toward productive uses.

3. they provide an opportunity for people to increase their savings by investing in them.

4. they reveal investors' judgments about the potential earning capacity of corporations, thus giving guidance to corporate managers.

5. they generate employment and income."

For each of the functions cited above, explain how financial markets (or securities markets, in the parlance of this Congressional study) perform each function.

9. A U.S. investor who purchases the bonds issued by the Japanese government makes the following comment: "Assuming that the Japanese government does not default, I know what the cash flow of the bond will be." Explain why you agree or disagree with this statement.

10. Explain the difference between each of the following:

a. money market and capital market

b. primary market and secondary market

c. domestic market and foreign market

d. national market and Euromarket

11. Indicate whether each of the following instruments trades in the money market or the capital market:

a. General Motors Acceptance Corporation issues a financial instrument with four months to maturity.

b. The U.S. Treasury issues a security with 10 years to maturity.

c. Microsoft Corporation issues common stock.

d. The State of Mississippi issues a financial instrument with eight months to maturity.

12. A U.S. investor who purchases the bonds issued by the U.S. government makes the following statement: "By buying this debt instrument, I am not exposed to default risk or purchasing power risk." Explain why you agree or disagree with this statement.

13. Explain why liquidity may depend not only on the type of financial asset but also on the quantity one wishes to sell or buy.

14. In 2016, McDonald's issued in the Swiss bond market an eight-year bond denominated in Swiss francs (CHF). The par value was CHF 400 million. From the perspective of the

Swiss financial market, indicate whether this issue is classified as being issued in the domestic market, the foreign market, or the offshore market.

15. Give three reasons for the trend toward greater integration of financial markets throughout the world.

16. What is meant by the "institutionalization" of capital markets?

17. a. How is an asset class defined?

b. What are the traditional asset classes?

18. On August 25, 2017, the market capitalization of ExxonMobil was $324.73 billion. In terms of market cap, how would this company's stock be classified?

19. On August 25, 2017, Facebook's common stock closed at a price of $166.32 and the market cap of the company was $489.97 billion. What was the approximate number of shares outstanding?

20. What is the difference between an emerging stock market and a frontier stock market?

21. What are the two basic types of derivative instruments?

22. "Derivatives markets are nothing more than legalized gambling casinos and serve no economic function." Comment on this statement.

2 Role of Governments in Financial Markets

CONTENTS

Learning Objectives

After reading this chapter, you will understand:

- what is meant by macroprudential policy and microprudential policy;
- the link between macroprudential policy and systemic financial risk;
- the justification for the regulation of financial regulation;
- the various roles governments play in the financial system;
- what a country's central bank does;
- the role of monetary policy;
- what is meant by financial stability;
- the different forms of government bailouts, and the notion of "too big to fail";
- what is meant by moral hazard when a financial institution's management believes that the government will not allow it to fail;
- what systemically important financial institutions are, and the proposals for dealing with them;
- the objectives of the Bank for International Settlements, the Financial Stability Board, and supranational organizations; and
- the differing views on the degree of government intervention in the financial market.

Financial markets play a prominent role in many economies, and governments around the world have long deemed it necessary to participate in various aspects of these markets. This is clear from the history of financial crises and resulting economic recessions that have occurred in modern capitalist economies.

Governments play various roles in the financial system. They can do so in one or more of four ways. First, they can regulate financial markets, including financial intermediaries participating in the market. Second, they can act as financial intermediaries by making loans or guaranteeing loans to sectors or parts of the economy that are deemed to need assistance. Third, governments can influence financial markets at the macroeconomic level through the actions of their central banks. Finally, they can provide bailouts of or financial assistance to market sectors or corporations (financial and nonfinancial) during periods of market turmoil or distress.

In this chapter, we explain the role of governments and government policies regarding financial markets. There is considerable ideological debate about the proper role that governments should play in financial markets, and in the last section of this chapter, we discuss that debate. U.S. financial regulations are described in several chapters in this book.

Macroprudential versus Microprudential Government Policies

Government policy dealing with a country's financial system falls into two categories: macroprudential policy and microprudential policy. A government's macroprudential policy seeks to reduce the risk to the financial system as a whole. The risk to the financial system is referred to as **systemic financial risk** or simply **systemic risk**. In general, the term systemic risk refers to the probability that an entire system will collapse or fail. When applied to finance, systemic risk is referred to as systemic financial risk. The key here is the interconnectedness of the financial system's financial institutions and markets, as well as common exposures to economic factors, not only within a country but globally. In contrast to macroprudential policy, which focuses on the welfare of the entire financial system, microprudential policy seeks to control the risks associated with financial institutions. The interconnectedness of the financial institutions is not relevant here.

As a result of the 2008–2009 global financial crisis, policymakers throughout the world have focused on macroprudential policy, as it became apparent during that crisis that focusing only on the safety of individual financial institutions is not adequate to protect the financial system as a whole. The following four causes of the financial crisis showed policymakers that appropriate response tools are needed to deal with systemic risk: (1) excessive use of leverage and risk taking, (2) a bubble in the pricing of assets in a key sector of the financial market (residential property), (3) regulatory and supervisory failures, and (4) widespread failure of market discipline. We describe these causes in the chapters to follow.

As a result of this focus on macroprudential policy, the tools available to governments for implementing such policy and the impediments and challenges to the implementation of those tools by governments are now the subject of debate. The tools for implementing macroprudential policy are described later in this section. As for challenges, there are questions regarding whether governments should establish one supervisory entity to implement all macroprudential policy or share the responsibility among several supervisory entities. When a single supervisory entity is designated, that entity is typically the country's **central bank**.

Regulation of Financial Markets

In their regulatory capacities, governments greatly influence the development and evolution of financial markets and institutions. It is important to realize that governments, issuers, and investors tend to interact and affect one another's actions in certain ways. Thus, it is not surprising to find that a market's reactions to regulations often prompt a new response by the government, which can cause the institutions in the market to change their behavior further, and so on. A sense of how the government can affect a market and its participants is important for understanding the numerous markets and securities that will be described in the chapters to come.

Here we discuss regulations. Our purpose is not to provide a detailed account of the regulatory structures and rules. Rather, we provide a broad view of the goals and types of regulations, using the United States as our primary case, although we do mention regulations in other counties.

Justification for Regulation

The standard explanation or justification for governmental regulation of a market is that the market, left to itself, will not produce its particular goods or services in an efficient manner and at the lowest possible cost. Efficiency and low-cost production are hallmarks of a perfectly competitive market. Thus, a market unable to produce efficiently must be one that is not competitive at the time and will not gain that status by itself in the foreseeable future. Of course, it is also possible that governments might regulate markets that are viewed as competitive currently but are unable to sustain competition, and thus low-cost production, over the long run. A version of this justification for regulation is that the government controls a feature of the economy that the market mechanisms of competition and pricing could not manage without help. A shorthand expression used by economists to describe the reasons for regulation is **market failure**. A market is said to fail if it cannot, by itself, maintain all the requirements for a competitive situation.

The regulatory structure in the United States is largely the result of financial crises that have occurred at various times. Until the 2008–2009 financial crisis, most regulatory mechanisms were the products of the stock market crash of 1929 and the Great Depression of the 1930s. Some of the regulations may make little economic sense in the current financial market, but they can be traced back to some abuse that legislators encountered, or thought they encountered, at one time. Further, in addition to financial institution regulation, three other forms of regulation are most often a function of the federal government, with state governments playing a secondary role. For that reason, the present discussion of regulation concentrates on the central government and any agencies it creates.

Forms of Government Regulation of Financial Markets

A government's regulation of financial markets can take one or more of four forms: regulation of (1) disclosures, (2) financial activities, (3) financial institutions, and (4) foreign participants. Here we discuss each form of regulation.

Regulation of disclosures Regulation of disclosures requires issuers of securities to make public a large amount of financial information to current and potential investors. The standard justification for disclosure rules is that the managers of the issuing firm have more information about the financial health and future of the firm than do investors who own or are considering the purchase of the firm's securities. The cause of market failure here, if indeed it occurs, is commonly described as **asymmetric information**, which means investors and managers are subject to uneven access to or uneven possession of information. Also, the problem is said to be one of "agency," in the sense that the firm's managers, who act as agents for investors, may act in their own interests to the disadvantage of investors. The advocates of disclosure rules say that, in the absence of the rules, investors with comparatively limited knowledge about the firm would allow agents to engage in such practices.

The United States is firmly committed to disclosure regulation. The Securities Act of 1933 and the Securities Exchange Act of 1934 led to the creation of the Securities and Exchange Commission (SEC), which is responsible for gathering and publicizing relevant information and for punishing those issuers who supply fraudulent or misleading data. However, none of the SEC's requirements or actions constitutes a guarantee, a certification, or an approval of the securities being issued. Moreover, the government's rules do not represent an attempt to prevent the issuance of risky assets. Instead, the government's (and the SEC's) sole motivation in this regard is to supply diligent and intelligent investors with the information needed for a fair evaluation of the securities.

The need for disclosure regulation has been debated by economists. Some economists have denied the need and justification for disclosure rules, arguing that the securities market would, without governmental assistance, get all the information necessary for a fair pricing of new as well as existing securities.[1] In this view, the securities laws supposedly extracting key data from agent-managers are redundant. One way to look at this argument is to ask what investors would do if a corporation trying to sell new shares did not provide all the data investors wanted. In that case, investors either would refuse to buy that corporation's security, giving it a zero value, or would discount or underprice the security. Thus, a corporation concealing important information would pay a penalty in the form of reduced proceeds from the sale of a new security. The prospect of this penalty is potentially as much incentive to disclose as are the rules of a government agency, such as the SEC. Several studies have shown how management can benefit from voluntarily improved disclosure.[2]

Regulation of financial activities Regulation of financial activities consists of rules about traders of securities and trading on financial markets. A prime example of this form of regulation is the set of rules against trading by insiders who are corporate officers or others in positions to know more about a firm's prospects than the general investing public. Insider trading is another problem posed by asymmetric information. A second example of this type of regulation would be rules regarding the structure and operations of exchanges

1. See, for example, George J. Benston, "Required Disclosure and the Stock Market: An Evaluation of the Securities Exchange Act of 1934," *American Economic Review* 63 (1973): 132–155.

2. See, for example, Paul M. Healy and K. G. Palpeau, "Information Asymmetry, Corporate Disclosure, and the Capital Markets: A Review of the Empirical Disclosure Literature," *Journal of Accounting and Economics* 31 (2001): 405–440.

where securities are traded. The argument supporting these rules rests on the possibility that members of exchanges may be able, under certain circumstances, to collude and defraud the general investing public.

Like disclosure, financial activity regulation is also widely implemented in the United States. The SEC has the duty to carefully monitor the trades that corporate officers, directors, or major stockholders ("insiders") make in the securities of their firms. The SEC and another federal government entity, the Commodity Futures Trading Commission (CFTC), share responsibility for the federal regulation of trading in derivative instruments.

Regulation of financial institutions Regulation of financial institutions is the form of governmental monitoring that restricts these institutions' activities in the vital areas of lending, borrowing, and funding. The justification for this form of regulation is that these financial firms have a special role to play in a modern economy. Financial institutions help households and firms to save. Depository institutions also facilitate the complex payments among many elements of the economy, and they serve as conduits for the government's monetary policy. Thus, it is often argued that the failure of these financial institutions would severely disrupt the economy.

Historically, the U.S. government imposed an extensive array of regulations on financial institutions. Most of this legislation traces its historical roots to the Great Depression in the 1930s and deals with restrictions on the activities of financial institutions. (Later chapters explain some of the significant changes subsequently made to these regulations.) In recent years, expanded regulations restrict how financial institutions manage their assets and liabilities, typically in the form of minimum capital requirements for certain regulated institutions. These capital requirements are based on the various types of risk faced by regulated financial institutions and are popularly referred to as risk-based capital requirements.

Regulation of foreign participants Government regulation of foreign participants limits the roles that foreign firms can play in domestic markets and their ownership or control of financial institutions. Many countries regulate participation by foreign firms in domestic financial securities markets. Like most countries, the United States extensively reviews and changes its policies regarding foreign firms' activities in the U.S. financial markets on a regular basis.

Governments as Financial Intermediaries

Governments throughout the world have been the provider of loans or the guarantor of loans for sectors of the credit market that, in their view, are so critical to the operation of the economy that intervention is needed. In the United States, a federal loan guarantee provided by the federal government is a statutory commitment to pay either all or a specified part of the debt servicing (principal and interest) to a lender or to the holder of a debt security should the borrower default.

In providing loans and guarantees, a central government effectively acts as a nonprofit financial intermediary, borrowing money at the lowest possible rate and providing loans at a lower rate than a profit-oriented financial intermediary would, or guaranteeing loans on which it charges a reasonable guarantor rate. Governments can set up what is effectively a financial intermediary entity by creating either a government agency or a government-related financial entity. Before any government entity can grant any loans or provide loan guarantees, the central government must first authorize and allocate funding for the program run by the entity.

Governments will identify the credit sectors that need assistance. In the United States, for example, the government has provided loans or loan guarantees for qualified agricultural loans, residential housing loans, small business loans, and student loans for postsecondary education. For example, the U.S. Small Business Administration, a federal government agency, does not make direct loans to small businesses. Instead, it has several programs to help a small business obtain debt financing either through a guarantee of a loan provided by a third-party lender or through a guarantee of bonds issued by the small business.

Probably the best-known economic sector in which the government has established agencies or government-sponsored entities to provide credit support is the residential mortgage market. We describe the various entities that the U.S. government has established to facilitate the flow of credit to this critical market sector in later chapters. There is no doubt that government intervention in the housing finance market has resulted in a strong residential mortgage market in many countries.

However, as with any intervention, limits should be imposed. This was evident from the subprime mortgage crisis that began in the summer of 2007 in the United States, a crisis we describe in chapter 30. Critics of the government's role in the housing finance sector have argued that the government has effectively nationalized the country's mortgage system, with three government-related entities, the Federal National Mortgage Association (Fannie Mae), the Federal Home Loan Mortgage Corporation (Freddie Mac), and the Federal Housing Administration (discussed in chapters 29 and 30), insuring almost 90% of U.S. housing loans. It is argued that this emphasis on home ownership, along with low interest rates, fueled the housing bubble that burst in the summer of 2007. Moreover, government policies that fostered housing ownership for those who could not really afford the costs associated with owning a home, the so-called subprime borrowers, added to the problems in the housing finance market. Consequently, some U.S. congressional leaders are skeptical of the government's role in the housing finance market and are seeking a quick and significant reduction in the government's role in housing. Other congressional leaders feel that withdrawal of support by the government in the housing finance market will have a devastating impact on the housing sector and the economy.

Estimates of the cost of federal loans and loan guarantees have been made by economists. Some economists have argued that the government does not have the ability to accurately price the risk of loans and loan guarantees. Admittedly, a comprehensive estimate of the value of a federal loan guarantee, for example, is not simple.[3] Moreover, owing to political pressures, critics of government agencies operating such programs point out that the government routinely underestimates the risk to taxpayers of credit support programs.

In addition to government loans and loan guarantee programs, there are government-provided insurance programs. Effectively, the government is acting as a financial institution (an insurance company in this case), providing an insurance policy with no intent to realize a profit.

Government Influence on Financial Markets through the Actions of the Central Bank

Most countries have a government entity referred to as its **central bank**. This entity is responsible for the financial matters of that country, primarily through the implementation of monetary policy. **Monetary policy** is the set of tools that a government or its central bank can use to influence the economy and financial system for the purpose of achieving the country's economic objectives. Monetary policy tools are linked to the banking system, as described in chapter 7.

In the United States, monetary policy is carried out by the Board of Governors of the Federal Reserve (the Fed), and the statutory objectives of monetary policy are set forth in the Federal Reserve Act of 1913. Those objectives are stable prices, maximum employment, and moderate interest rates. Carrying out statutory monetary policy is the Fed's Federal Open Market Committee (FOMC). The FOMC issued a statement to explain its monetary goals following its meeting in January 2012. The statement indicated that with respect to stable prices (or equivalently, the rate of inflation), a 2% inflation rate was consistent with the long-run statutory objective of monetary policy, in the view of the Fed. Although monetary policy's statutory objective is the maximum level of employment, that level is principally determined by nonmonetary factors affecting the job market. Consequently, because those nonmonetary factors change over time, the FOMC does not state a specific number for this statutory objective. Estimates are that the long-run objective in terms of unemployment rate tends to be between 5.2% and 5.8%.

The tools available to the Fed for implementing monetary policy to accomplish its objectives are described in chapter 7. The main tool involves influencing key interest rates in the financial market.

In the United States, the Fed is also a lender of last resort, a role that it plays during turmoil in the financial markets. We discuss this role below. This is a function it performs in maintaining the country's financial stability. The central banks in most countries operate as if they had a policy of responsibility for maintaining financial stability.[4]

3. A study by the Organisation for Economic Co-operation and Development estimates the value of a loan guarantee to be 1% of the loan's value.

4. See "Roles and Objectives of Modern Central Banks," in *Issues in the Governance of Central Banks* (Basel: Bank for International Settlements, 2009), 25, http://www.bis.org/publ/othp04_2.pdf.

The objectives of a central bank vary from country to country. In most countries, price stability is typically the primary monetary policy objective. Here are three examples. The Bank of England, the central bank of the United Kingdom, states that its two core purposes are what it refers to as monetary stability, defined as follows: "Monetary stability means stable prices and confidence in the currency. Stable prices are defined by the Government's inflation target, which the Bank seeks to meet through the decisions taken by the Monetary Policy Committee (MPC)."[5] The European Central Bank (ECB), the central bank for the 17 European Union countries that use the euro as their currency, states that "the primary objective of the ECB's monetary policy is to maintain price stability."[6] The ECB defines price stability as "maintaining inflation rates of below, but close to, 2% over the medium term." Japan's central bank, the Bank of Japan, states that the bank's monetary policy should be "aimed at achieving price stability, thereby contributing to the sound development of the national economy."[7]

In addition, in most countries, central banks have supervisory authority over the country's banking system.

Financial Stability and Monetary Policy

As noted above, monetary policy is linked to the banking system. Financial stability is about avoiding an extreme event that could potentially impose large costs on the financial system and the real economy. It is here that the tools of macroprudential policy of a country are implemented, by (1) enhancing the financial system's liquidity regulation so as to reduce the frequency of unintended tightening of credit, which can freeze the efficient operations of markets, and (2) supervising the infrastructure of financial markets.

Financial stability is critical to the effective implementation of monetary policy. As William C. Dudley, then-president and chief executive officer of the Federal Reserve Bank of New York, said in 2013:

> In my mind, the biggest lesson of the financial crisis has been that monetary policy cannot work properly when there is financial instability. When financial instability occurs, it disturbs market functioning and can also impair bank balance sheets. The result can be disruption to the financial intermediation function with resulting constraints on the availability of credit for households and businesses. This, in turn, can lead to further reductions in aggregate demand that put additional stress on the weakened financial system. Obviously, this is not a favorable dynamic.[8]

5. For the Bank of England's statement on monetary stability, see the web page http://www.bankofengland.co.uk/MONETARYPOLICY/Pages/default.aspx.

6. For the ECB's statement on monetary policy, see the web page http://www.ecb.europa.eu/mopo/intro/html/index.en.html.

7. For the Bank of Japan's statement on monetary policy, see the web page http://www.boj.or.jp/en/mopo/outline/index.htm.

8. William C. Dudley, "Why Financial Stability Is a Necessary Prerequisite for an Effective Monetary Policy," Andrew Crockett Memorial Lecture, delivered before the BIS 2013 Annual General Meeting, Basel, June 23, http://www.newyorkfed.org/newsevents/speeches/2013/dud130624.html.

Unlike the quantitative objectives mentioned above for the primary goal of monetary policy of price stability of some targeted rate (e.g., 2%), it is difficult to express a financial stability objective in quantitative terms.

Government Bailouts

Governments throughout the world have used public (taxpayer) funds to provide financial support to prevent the failure of major industries, financial institutions, corporations, and subnational entities viewed as essential to a country's economy or financial system.

This practice followed by governments is referred to as a **government bailout**, or simply bailout. Table 2.1 lists the history of U.S. government bailouts by type of entity that was the beneficiary of financial assistance: nonfinancial corporations, financial corporations, industries, and one city. In the United States, the two entities responsible for the design and implementation of bailout plans are the U.S. Department of the Treasury and the Fed. The latter does so through its lending and credit programs.

Table 2.1
U.S. Government bailouts by type.

Type	Year
Nonfinancial corporations	
Penn Central Railroad	1970
Lockheed	1971
Chrysler	1980
Financial corporations	
Franklin National Bank	1974
Continental Illinois Bank and Trust	1984
Bear Stearns	2008
Fannie Mae and Freddie Mac	2008
American International Group (AIG)	2008
Citigroup	2008
Bank of America	2009
Industries	
Savings and loan industry	1989
Airlines industry	2001
Automobile industry	2008
Cities	
New York City	1974

Forms of Bailouts

Government assistance can come in various forms. As explained above, the government can make federal loans. For example, a federal loan of $1.75 billion was provided to Franklin National Bank in 1974. The Fed has provided a line of credit for bailouts to facilitate the acquisition of troubled entities. For example, when the investment banking firm of Bear Stearns nearly collapsed in June 2008, the Fed provided JPMorgan Chase with a $30 billion line of credit to support the purchase of Bear Stearns. Although the purchase price was $236 million, the potential obligations of Bear Stearns that JPMorgan Chase was assuming as a result of the acquisition required that such a line of credit be provided. In the case of American International Group (AIG), several forms of financial assistance were provided: an initial $85 billion line of credit with the Fed, followed by $110 billion in loans from the U.S. Department of the Treasury and the Federal Reserve Bank of New York ($40 billion of the Treasury's loan was through the Troubled Asset Relief Program (TARP), discussed later in the chapter).

The federal government can provide a loan and loan guarantee coupled with an equity position in the company seeking a bailout. The equity position typically comes in the form of a financial instrument called a **stock warrant**, allowing taxpayers to benefit from a recovery. Stock warrants were provided in both the AIG and Chrysler bailouts. In the case of AIG, the federal government effectively got a 79.9% equity interest (as well as the right to suspend dividends to stockholders) in that company in exchange for its $85 billion line of credit.

In the case of the savings and loan (S&L) industry, which had been having financial difficulties starting in the early 1980s,[9] Congress in 1989 passed taxpayer-financed bailout legislation, the Financial Institutions Reform, Recovery and Enforcement Act, which provided $50 billion to close failed S&Ls. For the purpose of liquidating insolvent S&Ls, the legislation established the Resolution Trust Corporation (RTC). The crisis was so severe that additional funding of $78 billion for the RTC was required by March 1990. In total, it has been estimated that the cost of bailing out the S&L industry during that episode was about $200 billion.

The Fannie Mae and Freddie Mac bailout shown in table 2.1 is the case of two government-sponsored enterprises (GSEs) established by Congress to provide credit to the housing sector in the form of mortgages. These two entities had $5 trillion in debt in the form of mortgage-backed securities and other debt. Both were placed under conservatorship of the U.S. government in 2008, and Congress is entertaining several plans for the future of these two corporations. The bailout plan for the two GSEs as provided for in an agreement with the U.S. Treasury was future support and capital investments of up to $100 billion per GSE, which called for the granting to the Treasury of (1) a form of stock (senior preferred stock) and (2) warrants giving the government a 79.9% ownership stake.

9. The S&L crisis is described in chapter 6.

Two banks, Citigroup and Bank of America, received several forms of aid. Both banks had a pool of troubled assets in the form of mortgage-backed securities. The federal government agreed to limit the losses realized on their pool of troubled assets: Citigroup's portfolio had a market value of $310 billion, and Bank of America's had a market value of $118 billion. In addition, for both banks, the Federal Deposit Insurance Corporation (FDIC) and the Fed committed additional amounts: Citigroup received $10 billion and $220 billion from the FDIC and the Fed, respectively, and Bank of America received $2.5 billion and $87.1 billion from the FDIC and the Fed, respectively. There was one more component to the bailout package for both banks: money from the program described next.

The largest government bailout was a special program established by Congress in October 2008, TARP, which was part of the Emergency Economic Stabilization Act. TARP authorized $700 billion to be used by the Treasury Department to deal with the adverse economic consequences resulting from the subprime mortgage crisis that began in the summer of 2007. The funds were to be used to purchase certain types of debt instruments as well as equity from financial institutions. Although the initial authorization was for $700 billion, subsequent legislation in 2010 (the Dodd-Frank Wall Street Reform and Consumer Protection Act) reduced that amount to $475 billion. Three of the financial institutions in table 2.1 received TARP money: AIG ($40 billion), Citigroup ($45 billion), and Bank of America ($45 billion, with $10 billion for Merrill Lynch).

In addition, governments get involved in negotiating deals for troubled entities or in assisting in their acquisition by financially sounder entities. For example, a large hedge fund, Long-Term Capital Management (LTCM), was heavily dependent on borrowed funds. Because of the Russian debt crisis in 1998, the positions taken by LTCM that turned on the fortunes of Russia's government debt resulted in losses that were large enough to make it impossible for LTCM to repay the amount it had borrowed from banks and other financial institutions. The amount owed was sufficiently large that a default would have had a ripple effect throughout the credit markets. As a result, a consortium of private financial entities was organized by the Federal Reserve Bank of New York for the purpose of buying LTCM so as to cover its debt obligations. Simultaneously, the Fed took pressure off the credit markets by taking action to make more credit available. The end result was that because of the actions by the consortium, the government did not make any payments in this bailout (and hence LTCM is not listed in table 2.1). No creditors realized losses, and the shareholders of LTCM realized no value for their equity interest.

Let's look at a bailout by a central government outside the United States. A good example is the Japanese government bailout and guarantees of its commercial banks due to the collapse of the Japanese stock and real estate markets. Since the end of 1989, the Japanese economy and stock markets have experienced an extended period of weakness. The major Japanese stock index, the Nikkei 225 stock market index, reached a high of 38,915.87 at the end of 1989. (As of year-end 2018, it remains less than 23,000.) The Japanese real estate bubble also peaked in late 1989 and collapsed after December 1989. There have been severe ramifications of this collapse in the stock and real estate markets. The first is the effect on the Japanese banking system. The collapse of the Japanese stock and real estate markets forced many major banks into bankruptcy. Many major banks became "zombies," defined as financial institutions with negative net worth. The Japanese government kept these banks marginally "alive" through guarantees and bailouts. These zombie banks had large amounts of nonperforming loans on their balance sheets, were neither dead nor alive, and could not support economic growth through loans.

Issues Associated with Government Bailouts

Advocates of government bailouts assert that in today's financial system, certain financial institutions or markets are just "too big to fail." More specifically, the interconnectedness of financial institutions throughout not only the U.S. financial market but also the global financial markets results in systemic risk that could have severe consequences for the financial system and the real economy. The determination of what financial institution is too big to fail is not always clear. For example, as explained earlier in this chapter, Bears Stearns was rescued in 2008 through guarantees and the purchasing of its assets by JPMorgan Chase. Yet a much larger financial institution, the investment banking firm of Lehman Brothers Holdings, with $615 billion in debt and with considerable global interconnectedness, was allowed to fail and file for bankruptcy.

The argument made by advocates for maintaining large banks is that the global economy and the global financial system are large and complex. To supply large amounts of capital to multinational corporations and to meet governments' needs require large banks that have the ability to operate globally and provide funding at a competitive rate. The economies of scale that can be achieved by large banks can make that operational efficiency possible. Moreover, no evidence suggests that smaller banks result in less systemic risk. For example, there can be just as much interconnectedness among many smaller banks as among big international banks. The financial meltdown leading to the Great Depression is an example of systemic risk arising from the failure of many small banks.

Ben Bernanke, then chair of the Fed, in remarks to the Federal Reserve Bank of Boston in October 2009, and in response to a question from the former Bank of England deputy governor, said that he preferred a "more subtle approach without losing the economic benefit of multi-function, international (financial) firms."[10] He also argued that banks would have to have plans—referred to as "living wills"—for breaking up once a certain size was reached. Although he did not support the breakup of large banks, he did believe that bank supervisors should impose restrictions on the growth of banks that fail to have good governance and risk management controls.

10. The Financial Services Roundtable on Systemic Risk, Prudential Measures, Resolution Authority, and Securitization Before the Financial Services Committee, United States House of Representatives, October 29, 2009 (statement of Scott Talbott, Senior Vice President of Government Affairs), https://financialservices.house.gov/media/file/hearings/111/talbott_-_fsr.pdf.

Opponents of the notion of too big to fail argue that a major risk is introduced into the financial system when the management of financial institutions believes the government will view those institutions as essential to the financial system and will not allow them to fail. This is known as a "Fed put." The risk associated with such a view is that a government safety net will encourage management to take on excessive risks. This is connected to a concept well known in the insurance industry: moral hazard. This concept is the tendency for the existence of an insurance policy (guarantee) to encourage risk taking by the insured and, as a result, enhance the probability of a payout of an insurance policy. Another concern is that banking regulators will be reluctant to prosecute entities that are viewed as too big to fail.

The question is whether too big to fail is too "too big to solve." Two solutions have been proposed. The first approach is a commitment by the government that it will no longer permit a bailout. This approach is not likely to be adopted by governments, or, even if adopted, not likely to be used. The second approach is to identify what is known as "systemically important" financial institutions and impose on any such firms a higher capital requirement than for other financial institutions (i.e., a capital surcharge). A **systemically important financial institution** (SIFI) is one that, in the view of regulators, is a large firm whose failure would cause a financial crisis. The notion of a SIFI was introduced as part of the banking capital requirement regulations set forth by the Basel Committee on Banking Supervision, which we discuss later in this chapter.

This second approach is the one that the United States is attempting to implement as part of its major legislation, the Dodd-Frank Act. Some economists have argued that the provisions of the Dodd-Frank Act have not reduced the systemic risk through contagion but have in fact exacerbated that risk.[11] As Glenn Hubbard points out, there were two effective ways that the Fed dealt with the financial crisis but are now of limited use as a result of provisions in the Dodd-Frank Act. First, at the height of the financial crisis, the Fed provided new borrowing facilities to supply badly needed liquidity. Instead of recognizing the importance of providing liquidity facilities during market turmoil (e.g., that during 2008–2009), the Fed had its lending authority reduced and its collateral requirements for emergency lending were increased (making it more difficult for an entity to borrow).[12] Second, the injection of public capital to fight a financial crisis, such as the government did by purchasing interests in banks through the TARP program, is barred by the Dodd-Frank Act.

Implementing this second approach requires identifying those entities that are SIFIs. This is not easy. Although the targeted candidates are typically large banks, the Fed has considered applying this approach to large asset management firms and traditional insurance companies. However, these market players do not impose systemic risk, and the cost

11. Glenn Hubbard, "Financial Regulatory Reform: A Progress Report," *Federal Reserve Bank of St. Louis Review* 95, no. 3 (2013): 181–197.

12. Hubbard, "Financial Regulatory Reform," 193.

of higher capital requirements on their lines of business would place them at a competitive disadvantage relative to their competitors who are not anointed with the title "SIFI."

The U.S. financial regulatory framework prior to the financial crisis of 2008 can best be described as one that for the most part limited its focus to individual financial institutions and financial markets. As a result, the responsibility for monitoring and addressing overall risks to financial stability did not reside with any single regulator, leaving gaps in the regulation of different types of financial institutions that operated across multiple financial markets. The Dodd-Frank Act addressed this problem through the creation of the Financial Stability Oversight Council (FSOC), which has the authority to constrain nonbank financial entities from what the FSOC views as excessive risk taking that threatens the stability of the financial system. An important role given to the FSOC is the authority to determine whether any action should be taken to break up those firms that it perceives as representing a "grave threat" to the financial stability of the United States. The FSOC is chaired by the secretary of the Treasury, guided by the expertise of the federal financial regulators, an independent insurance expert appointed by the president, and state regulators. Thus, the FSOC is chaired by a member of the executive branch, not the Federal Reserve.

Financial Regulators Outside the United States

Financial regulations in other countries have many similarities to their U.S. counterparts but some differences as well. Financial regulation in the United Kingdom and China are considered in later chapters. Here we briefly describe financial regulation in Germany, France, Switzerland, Singapore, and Japan.

Germany

The financial regulatory authority for Germany is the Federal Financial Supervisory Authority, which was formed in 2002. It is better known as "BaFin." It was formed by the merger of the Federal Banking Supervisory Office, the Federal Supervisory Office for Securities Trading, and the Federal Insurance Supervisory Office. This formation provides uniform national supervision of banks, insurance companies, brokers, stock exchanges, credit institutions, and others. All German financial activity is regulated under this umbrella.

France

The financial regulator in France is the Financial Markets Regulator (Autorite des Marches Financiers). Among its responsibilities are to safeguard investments in financial instruments and to maintain orderly financial markets. Autorite des Marches Financiers falls under the European regulatory authority of the Markets in Financial Instruments Directive (discussed in chapter 24).

Switzerland

The Swiss Financial Market Supervisory Authority (FINMA) is responsible for Swiss financial regulation. It supervises banks, stock exchanges, securities dealers, and insurance companies. FINMA is responsible for two of the world's largest banks, UBS and Credit Suisse. FINMA was founded in June 2007 by merging other Swiss regulatory bodies.

Singapore

The Monetary Authority of Singapore (MAS) is Singapore's central bank and is responsible for financial regulation, power granted to it by the MAS Act. In its capacity as financial regulator, it has the power to regulate and supervise financial institutions. Frameworks and guidelines are provided by MAS for various types of financial institutions.

Japan

The Japanese financial regulator is the Financial Services Agency (FSA). According to its annual report, FSA is "responsible for (i) ensuring the stability of the financial system; (ii) protecting the users of financial instruments and services, such as depositors, insurance policy holders, investors and the like; and (iii) facilitating the smooth function of financial services."[13] The pertinent bureaus are the Planning & Coordination Bureau, the Inspection Bureau, the Supervisory Bureau, Securities & Exchange Surveillance Commission Executive Bureau, and the Certified Public Accountants & Auditing Oversight Board Executive Division. Of particular interest is Securities & Exchange Surveillance Commission Executive Bureau, which is responsible for market "surveillance, inspection of securities companies, investigation of market misconduct, inspection of disclosure statements, investigation of criminal cases, etc."[14]

Other International Participants

Various entities provide direction, research, and advice to policymakers throughout the world. Here we describe two important international entities: the Bank for International Settlements and the Financial Stability Board.

13. http://www.fsa.go.jp/en/about/Annual_Reports/2014.pdf.

14. See the table "Fiscal 2014 Roles and Responsibilities of Bureaus … at the FSA," http://www.fsa.go.jp/en/about/Annual_Reports/2014.pdf.

Bank for International Settlements

An organization whose mission is to provide guidance to central banks in pursuing monetary and financial stability, to foster international cooperation in those areas, and to act as a bank for central banks is the Bank for International Settlements (BIS), located in Basel, Switzerland. Two primary operational roles of the BIS are acting as a counterparty in transactions between two central banks and serving as an agent or trustee in connection with international financial operations. In its role of providing guidance to policymakers of central banks, the BIS has four standing committees: (1) the Basel Committee on Banking Supervision, (2) the Committee on the Global Financial System, (3) the Committee on Payment and Settlement Systems, and (4) the Markets Committee. The objective of these committees is to oversee the adoption of best practices by central banks as they address the various issues they face.

The purpose of the Basel Committee on Banking Supervision is to educate policymakers on the key issues associated with the supervision of banks and by doing so to improve the quality of bank supervision throughout the world. In chapter 6 we discuss risk-based capital requirements for banks. These requirements are based on the various Basel Accords produced by this committee. In addition, the committee formulated a framework for identifying SIFIs, described earlier in this chapter. This committee has four task forces that deal with implementation issues: the Standards Implementation Group, the Policy Development Group, the Accounting Task Force Group, and the Basel Consultative Group.

The mandate of the Committee on the Global Financial System is the identification and assessment of potential sources of stress in global financial markets. The objective is to aid policymakers in understanding the structural underpinnings of financial markets so as to support central banks in the fulfillment of their responsibilities for monetary and financial stability. As an example of how it monitors markets to fulfill that purpose, in July 2011, a work group of the committee published a paper that examined "how insurance companies and pension funds are being affected by forthcoming accounting and regulatory changes in the current low-interest rate environment, and to investigate possible implications of changes in their investment strategies for the financial system."[15]

A key component of the global financial system is how the financial market infrastructure on payment and settlement systems deals with these infrastructure issues and sets standards for them both for domestic transactions and for cross-border and multicurrency settlement transactions.

Finally, the Markets Committee's purpose is to provide policy guidelines for enhancing market transparency, discussion of developments in finance markets, and an exchange of views on future developments that will have an impact on financial markets. In addition,

15. Bank for International Settlements, Committee on the Global Financial System, "Fixed Income Strategies of Insurance Companies and Pension Funds," CGFS Paper 44 (Basel: Bank for International Settlements, July 2011), iii.

this committee provides a forum for central bankers to discuss the specifics of their own market operations. The committee deals with topics relating to central banks' practices with respect to the eligibility of collateral because of the integral role of central banks in providing liquidity to the financial system on a day-to-day basis. The global crisis has highlighted the importance of this issue.

Supranational Organizations

A **supranational organization** is an entity created to promote economic development for its member countries. Two examples of supranational organizations are the International Bank for Reconstruction and Development, popularly referred to as the World Bank, and the Inter-American Development Bank. The general objective of the former is to improve the efficiency of the international financial and trading markets. The objective of the latter supranational is to promote economic growth in the developing countries of the Americas.

Financial Stability Board

Another international body that monitors the global finance system and makes policy recommendations to governments for enhancing the stability of financial institutions and financial markets is the Financial Stability Board (FSB). Several of the FSB activities that are part of its mandate are to

- assess vulnerabilities affecting the global financial system and identify and review on a timely and ongoing basis the regulatory, supervisory and related actions needed to address them, and their outcomes;
- promote coordination and information exchange among authorities responsible for financial stability;
- monitor and advise on market developments and their implications for regulatory policy;
- advise on and monitor best practice in meeting regulatory standards;
- undertake joint strategic reviews of the policy development work of the international standard setting bodies to ensure their work is timely, coordinated, focused on priorities and addressing gaps; …
- support contingency planning for cross-border crisis management, particularly with respect to systemically important firms.[16]

In November 2011, the FSB published a set of policy measures addressing the systemic and moral hazard risks associated with SIFIs described earlier in this chapter.

Views on the Degree of Government Intervention in Financial Markets

There are two contrasting views about the role of governments in financial markets. The first view is that there should be large-scale government interventions to solve problems

16. See the Financial Stability Board's web page, http://www.financialstabilityboard.org/activities/index.htm, dealing with sound and efficient payment, clearing, and settlement systems.

that involve massive market failures. The second view is that government intervention is the problem, not the solution, and in fact may lead to market failures by implementing policies that are not beneficial to financial markets.

In this debate on the degree of government intervention in financial markets, Joseph Stiglitz, the 2001 recipient of the Nobel Prize in Economic Sciences,[17] provides a middle-of-the-road view. He identifies four recurrent themes that have been observed about financial markets.[18] The first is that, historically, the occurrence of modern capitalism is the link between financial crises and economic recessions (e.g., the United States, Japan, and European countries). The debate centers on the actions that governments employ to minimize the risk of insolvency and ensure the stability of key financial institutions.

Throughout this book, we will discuss important financial innovations that have led to the creation of new financial instruments in the cash and derivatives markets, new investment strategies, and new technologies for implementing the trading of securities. These financial innovations may necessitate a re-evaluation of the role of government intervention, which is Stiglitz's second recurring theme.

The third recurrent theme is that as financial markets develop, there is development of a more sophisticated financial system. A prominent aspect of this is the formation of new types of financial institutions. The question is how governments should deal with the regulation of these entities.

Finally, as we will see in this book, there has been a pattern of regulation followed by liberalization of certain financial markets (i.e., deregulation). This, according to Stigliz, has been the dominant recurrent theme in policy discussions about the role of governments in financial markets. The deregulation of financial markets according to its proponents is that it enables the financial system to more efficiently allocate capital, thereby benefiting the economy.

Stiglitz disagrees with this view about the benefits of deregulation, arguing that

> the rationale for liberalizing financial markets is based neither on a sound economic understanding of how these markets work nor on the potential scope for government intervention. Often, too, it lacks an understanding of the historical events and political forces that have led governments to assume their present role. Instead, it is based on an ideological commitment to an idealized conception of markets that is grounded neither in fact nor in economic theory.[19]

Fundamentally, Stiglitz's view is one that is middle of the road. He rightly argues that financial markets are different from other types of markets, such as labor markets and nonfinancial product markets. And it is in financial markets where one might expect the potential for more market failures than in other types of markets. He argues that some forms of government regulation can produce a financial system that can lower the risk of market

17. He has also served as a member and chair of the U.S. President's Council of Economic Advisors and as senior vice president and chief economist of the World Bank.

18. Joseph E. Stiglitz, "Government, Financial Markets, and Economic Development," NBER Working Paper 3669 (Cambridge, MA: National Bureau of Economic Research, 1991).

19. Joseph E. Stiglitz, "The Role of the State in Financial Markets," *World Bank Economic Review* 7 (1993): 20.

failure and then identifies those circumstances. However, he argues that in some instances, government regulation (intervention) has caused a major financial crisis. That is, market failure occurred due to government failure, not market failure. The example of government failure he identifies—and the one we mentioned earlier in this chapter—is the S&L crisis.

Trump Administration's View on Bank and Financial Regulation

On February 3, 2017, President Trump signed an Executive Order identifying his "Core Principles for Regulating the United States Financial System."[20] These core principles are:

(a) empower Americans to make independent financial decisions and informed choices in the marketplace, save for retirement, and build individual wealth;

(b) prevent taxpayer-funded bailouts;

(c) foster economic growth and vibrant financial markets through more rigorous regulatory impact analysis that addresses systemic risk and market failures, such as moral hazard and information asymmetry;

(d) enable American companies to be competitive with foreign firms in domestic and foreign markets;

(e) advance American interests in international financial regulatory negotiations and meetings;

(f) make regulation efficient, effective, and appropriately tailored; and

(g) restore public accountability within Federal financial regulatory agencies and rationalize the Federal financial regulatory framework.

Key Points

- A government's macroprudential policy seeks to reduce systemic risk.
- A government's microprudential policy seeks to control the risks associated with financial institutions. The interconnectedness of the financial institutions is not relevant here.
- Governments play various roles in the financial system: regulating financial markets, including financial intermediaries participating in the market; acting as financial intermediaries by making loans or guaranteeing loans to sectors or groups of the economy that are deemed to need assistance; influencing financial markets at the macroeconomic level through the actions of their central banks; and providing bailouts or financial assistance for market sectors or corporations (financial and nonfinancial) during periods of market turmoil or distress.
- A useful way to organize the many instances of financial regulation is through four general forms: (1) regulation of disclosures, (2) regulation of financial activities, (3) regulation of financial institutions, and (4) regulation of foreign participants.

20. https://www.whitehouse.gov/the-press-office/2017/02/03/presidential-executive-order-core-principles-regulating-united-states.

- A country's central bank is responsible for the financial matters of a country, primarily through the implementation of monetary policy, which is the set of tools that can be used to influence the economy and financial system to achieve a country's economic objectives.
- In most countries, price stability is typically the dominant monetary policy objective.
- Financial stability is concerned with avoiding an extreme event that could impose potentially large costs on the financial system and the real economy.
- Government bailouts result in the use of public or taxpayer funds to provide financial support to prevent the failure of major industries, financial institutions, corporations, and subnational entities viewed as essential to a country's economy or financial system.
- Some policymakers argue that financial institutions or markets may be "too big to fail" because of their interconnectedness with other financial institutions and markets in the financial system, and that allowing such entities to fail would cause market turmoil that would adversely affect the real economy.
- Those who argue against the notion of institutions being too big to fail point out the moral hazard (i.e., excess risk taking) introduced into the financial system when the management of financial institutions believes that the government will view the institutions as too essential to the financial system and will not allow them to fail.
- A systemically important financial institution (SIFI) is a financial institution that, in the view of regulators, is a large firm whose failure would cause a financial crisis.
- The Bank for International Settlements (BIS) provides research, education, and guidance for central bankers to help improve various aspects of banking supervision, infrastructure market issues, and financial stability policies.
- The Financial Stability Board (FSB) monitors the global finance system and makes policy recommendations to governments for enhancing the stability of financial institutions and financial markets.

Questions

1. What is the economic rationale for the widespread use of disclosure regulation?
2. Why do some economists believe that disclosure regulation is unnecessary?
3. What is meant by "regulation of financial activities?"
4. What is meant by "systemic financial risk?"
5. An example typically given to illustrate systemic financial risk is a run on the bank (i.e., many bank depositors simultaneously withdrawing their funds from a bank). Explain why.
6. Reproduced below is table 3.5 from a publication of the BIS, which compares the macroprudential and microprudential perspectives. Explain each item in the table.

	Macroprudential	Microprudential
Proximate objective	[To] limit financial systemwide distress	[To] limit distress of individual institutions
Ultimate objective	[To] avoid output (GDP) costs	Consumer (investor/ depositor) protection
…	…	…
Correlations and common exposures across institutions	Important	Irrelevant
Calibration of prudential controls	In terms of systemwide risk; top down	In terms of risks of individual institutions; bottom up

Source: Claudio Borio, "Towards a Macroprudential Framework for Financial Supervision and Regulation?" BIS Working Paper 128 (Basel, Switzerland: Bank for International Settlements, February 2003).

7. In the same BIS working paper identified in the previous question, the following statement appears:

Although a commonly held view of systemic risk suggests that financial stability can be secured through a microprudential approach, an analysis of the origin of financial crises with significant macroeconomic costs suggests that a macroprudential perspective is important.

a. What is meant by "financial stability"?

b. Why is a macroprudential perspective important when dealing with financial stability?

8. a. In what ways does a government act like a financial intermediary?

b. What are the concerns when a government plays the role of a financial intermediary?

9. a. In setting forth monetary policy, certain objectives, such as price stability, can be quantified. Explain why.

b. In contrast to such objectives as price stability, monetary policy objectives dealing with financial stability cannot be quantified. Explain why.

10. a. What are the arguments in favor of government bailouts?

b. What are the arguments against government bailouts?

11. What are the different forms of support that government bailouts can take?

12. What was the purpose of the Targeted Asset Relief Program (TARP)?

13. How did the U.S. congress deal with the financial problems faced by Fannie Mae and Freddie Mac in 2008?

14. What is meant by a systemically important financial institution (SIFI)?

15. What two solutions to the "too big to fail" issue have been suggested?

16. In 2004, then chair of the President's Council of Economic Advisers, Gregory Mankiw, stated: "Expecting a government bailout if things go wrong creates an incentive for a company to take on risk and enjoy the associated increase in return." Explain whether you agree or disagree with this statement.

17. What is the purpose of the Basel Committee on Banking Supervision of the BIS?

18. What is the purpose of the Markets Committee of the BIS?

19. What does the Financial Stability Oversight Council (FSOC) have the authority to do?

20. What are the views held by economists on the degree of regulation needed for financial markets?

21. What have been the arguments for and against repeal of key financial regulation provisions of the Dodd-Frank Act?

3 Financial Institutions, Financial Intermediaries, and Asset Management Firms

CONTENTS

Learning Objectives

After reading this chapter, you will understand:

- the business of financial institutions;
- the role of financial intermediaries;
- the difference between direct and indirect investments;

- how financial intermediaries transform the maturity of liabilities and give both short-term depositors and longer-term, final borrowers what they want;
- how financial intermediaries offer investors diversification and so reduce the risks of their investments;
- the way financial intermediaries reduce the costs of acquiring information and entering into contracts with final borrowers of funds;
- how financial intermediaries enjoy economies of scale in processing payments from final users of funds;
- the nature of the management of assets and liabilities by financial intermediaries;
- how different financial institutions have differing degrees of knowledge and certainty about the amount and timing of the cash outlay of their liabilities;
- why financial institutions have liquidity concerns;
- the concerns that regulators have with financial institutions;
- the general characteristics of asset management firms; and
- the types of funds that asset management firms manage.

In this chapter, we discuss financial institutions and a special and important type of financial institution, the financial intermediary. Financial intermediaries include commercial banks, S&L associations, investment companies, insurance companies, and pension funds. The most important contribution of financial intermediaries is a steady and relatively inexpensive flow of funds from savers to final users or investors. Every modern economy has financial intermediaries, which perform key financial functions for individuals, households, corporations, small and new businesses, and governments. In the last part of this chapter, we provide an overview of asset management firm, organizations that manage funds for financial intermediaries as well as individual investors.

Financial Institutions

Business entities include nonfinancial and financial enterprises. Nonfinancial enterprises manufacture products (e.g., cars, steel, computers), provide nonfinancial services (e.g., transportation, utilities, computer services), or do both. Financial enterprises, more popularly referred to as **financial institutions**, provide services related to one or more of the following:

1. transforming financial assets acquired through the market and converting them into a different and more widely preferable type of asset;[1]
2. exchanging financial assets on behalf of customers;

1. The transformed assets then become the financial institution's liability. This is the function performed by financial intermediaries, the most important type of financial institution.

3. exchanging financial assets for their own accounts;
4. assisting in the creation of financial assets for their customers, and then selling those financial assets to other market participants;
5. providing investment advice to other market participants; and
6. managing the portfolios of other market participants.

Financial intermediaries include **depository institutions** (commercial banks, S&L associations, savings banks, and credit unions), which acquire the bulk of their funds by offering their liabilities to the public mostly in the form of deposits; insurance companies (life and property and casualty companies); pension funds; and finance companies. Deposit-accepting, or depository institutions, are discussed in chapter 6.

The second and third services in the list above are the broker and dealer functions, which are discussed in chapter 18. The fourth service is referred to as underwriting. As we explain in chapter 9, typically a financial institution that provides an underwriting service also provides a brokerage or dealer service.

Some nonfinancial enterprises have subsidiaries that provide financial services. For example, many large manufacturing firms have subsidiaries that provide financing for their parent company's customers. These financial institutions are called **captive finance companies**. Examples include General Motors Acceptance Corporation (a subsidiary of General Motors) and General Electric Credit Corporation (a subsidiary of General Electric).

Role of Financial Intermediaries

Financial intermediaries obtain funds by issuing financial claims against themselves to market participants and then investing those funds. The investments made by financial intermediaries—their assets—can be in the form of loans, securities, or both. These investments are referred to as **direct investments**. Market participants who hold the financial claims issued by financial intermediaries are said to have made **indirect investments**.

Two examples will illustrate this process. Most readers of this book are familiar with what commercial banks do. **Commercial banks** accept deposits and use the proceeds to lend funds to consumers and businesses. The deposits represent the obligation of the commercial bank and a financial asset owned by the depositor. The loan represents an obligation of the borrowing entity and a financial asset of the commercial bank. The commercial bank has made a direct investment in the borrowing entity; the depositor effectively has made an indirect investment in that borrowing entity.

As a second example, consider an **investment company**, a financial intermediary we focus on in chapter 32, which pools the funds of market participants and uses those funds to buy a portfolio of securities, such as stocks and bonds. Investment companies are more commonly referred to as "mutual funds." Investors providing funds to the investment company receive an equity claim that entitles the investor to a pro rata share of the outcome of the portfolio. The equity claim is issued by the investment company. The **portfolio** of financial assets acquired by the investment company represents a direct investment that it has made. By owning an equity claim against the investment company, those who invest in the investment company have made an indirect investment.

We have stressed that financial intermediaries play the basic role of transforming financial assets that are less desirable for a large part of the public into other financial assets—their own liabilities—which are more widely preferred by the public. This transformation involves at least one of four economic functions:

1. providing maturity intermediation,
2. reducing risk via diversification,
3. reducing the costs of contracting and information processing, and
4. providing a payments mechanism.

Each function is described below.

Providing Maturity Intermediation

Our example of the commercial bank has two notable features. First, the maturity of at least a portion of the deposits accepted is typically short term. For example, certain types of deposit are payable on demand. Others have a specific maturity date, but most are less than two years. Second, the maturity of the loans made by a commercial bank can be considerably longer than two years. In the absence of a commercial bank, the borrower would have to borrow for a shorter term or find an entity that is willing to invest for the length of the loan sought, or the investors who make deposits in the bank would have to commit funds for a longer length of time than they want. The commercial bank, by issuing its own financial claims, in essence transforms a longer-term asset into a shorter-term one by giving the borrower a loan for the length of time sought and the investor/depositor a financial asset for the desired investment horizon. This function of a financial intermediary is called **maturity intermediation**.

Maturity intermediation has two implications for financial markets. First, it provides investors with more choices concerning maturity for their investments; borrowers have more choices for the length of their debt obligations. Second, because investors are naturally reluctant to commit funds for a long period of time, they will require that long-term borrowers pay a higher interest rate than is required for short-term borrowing. A financial intermediary is willing to make longer-term loans, and at a lower cost to the borrower than an individual investor would, by counting on successive deposits to provide the funds until maturity (although at some risk—see below). Thus, the second implication is that the cost of longer-term borrowing is likely to be reduced.

Reducing Risk via Diversification

Consider the example of the investor who places funds in an investment company. Suppose that the investment company invests the funds received in the stock of a large number of companies. By doing so, the investment company has diversified and reduced its risk.

Investors who have a small sum to invest would find it difficult to achieve the same degree of diversification, because they do not have sufficient funds to buy shares of a large number of companies. Yet by investing in the investment company for the same sum of money, investors can accomplish this diversification, thereby reducing risk.

This economic function of financial intermediaries—transforming more risky assets into less risky ones—is called **diversification**. Although individual investors can do it on their own, they may not be able to do it as cost effectively as a financial intermediary, depending on the amount of funds they have to invest. Attaining cost-effective diversification to reduce risk by purchasing the financial assets of a financial intermediary is an important economic benefit for financial markets.

Reducing the Costs of Contracting and Information Processing

Investors purchasing financial assets should take the time to develop the skills necessary for understanding how to evaluate an investment. Once those skills are developed, investors should apply them to the analysis of specific financial assets that are candidates for purchase (or subsequent sale). Investors who want to make a loan to a consumer or business will need to write the loan contract (or hire an attorney to do so).

Although some people enjoy devoting leisure time to this task, most prefer to use that time for just that—leisure. Most of us find that leisure time is in short supply, so to sacrifice it, we have to be compensated. The form of compensation could be a higher return that we obtain from an investment.

In addition to the opportunity cost of the time to process the information about the financial asset and its issuer, there is the cost of acquiring that information. All these costs are called **information processing costs**. The costs of writing loan contracts are referred to as **contracting costs**. There is also another dimension to contracting costs: the cost of enforcing the terms of the loan agreement.

With this in mind, consider our two examples of financial intermediaries—the commercial bank and the investment company. People who work for these intermediaries include investment professionals who are trained to analyze financial assets and manage them. In the case of loan agreements, either standardized contracts can be prepared, or legal counsel can be part of the professional staff that writes contracts involving more complex transactions. The investment professionals can monitor compliance with the terms of the loan agreement and take any necessary action to protect the interests of the financial intermediary. The employment of such professionals is cost effective for financial intermediaries, because investing funds is their normal business.

In other words, there are economies of scale in contracting and processing information about financial assets because of the amount of funds managed by financial intermediaries. The lower costs accrue to the investor purchasing a financial claim of the financial intermediary and to the issuers of financial assets, who benefit from a lower borrowing cost.

Providing a Payments Mechanism

Although the previous three economic functions may not have been immediately obvious, this last function should be. Most transactions made today are not done with cash. Instead, payments are made using checks, credit cards, debit cards, and electronic transfers of funds. These methods for making payments, called **payment mechanisms**, are provided by certain financial intermediaries.

At one time, noncash payments were restricted to checks written against noninterest-bearing accounts at commercial banks. Similar check writing privileges were provided later by S&L associations and savings banks, and by certain types of investment companies. Payment by credit card was also at one time the exclusive domain of commercial banks, but now other depository institutions offer this service. Debit cards are offered by various financial intermediaries. A debit card differs from a credit card in that, in the latter case, a bill is sent to the credit card holder periodically (usually once a month) requesting payment for transactions made in the past. In the case of a debit card, funds are immediately withdrawn (that is, debited) from the purchaser's account at the time the transaction takes place.

The ability to make payments without the use of cash is critical for the functioning of a financial market. In short, depository institutions transform assets that cannot be used to make payments into other assets that offer that property.

Overview of Asset/Liability Management for Financial Institutions

In later chapters, we discuss the major financial institutions. To understand the reasons managers of financial institutions invest in particular types of financial assets and the types of investment strategies they employ, it is necessary to have a general understanding of the asset/liability problem faced. In this section, we provide an overview of **asset/liability management**.

The nature of the liabilities dictates the investment strategy that a financial institution will pursue. For example, depository institutions seek to generate income by the spread between the return that they earn on assets and the cost of their funds. That is, they buy money and sell money. They buy money by borrowing from depositors or other sources of funds. They sell money when they lend it to businesses or individuals. In essence, they are in the spread business—their objective is to sell money for more than it costs to buy money.

The cost of the funds and the return on the funds sold is expressed in terms of an interest rate per unit of time. Consequently, the objective of a depository institution is to earn a positive **spread** between the assets it invests in (what it has sold the money for) and the costs of its funds (what it has purchased the money for).

Life insurance companies—and to a certain extent, property and casualty insurance companies—are in the spread business. Pension funds are not in the spread business: They do not raise funds themselves in the market. They seek to cover the cost of pension obligations at a minimum cost that is borne by the sponsor of the pension plan. Investment companies face no explicit costs for the funds they acquire and must satisfy no specific liability obligations; one exception is a particular type of investment company that agrees to repurchase shares at any time.

Nature of Liabilities

By the **liabilities** of a financial institution, we mean the amount and timing of the cash outlays that must be made to satisfy the contractual terms of the obligations issued. The liabilities of any financial institution can be categorized according to four types, as shown in table 3.1. The categorization in the table assumes that the entity that must be paid the obligation will not cancel the financial institution's obligation prior to any actual or projected payout date.

The descriptions of cash outlays as either known or uncertain are undoubtedly broad. When we refer to a cash outlay as being uncertain, we do not mean that it cannot be predicted. There are some liabilities where the "law of large numbers" makes it easier to predict the timing or amount of cash outlays. This is the work typically done by actuaries, but of course even actuaries cannot predict natural catastrophes, such as floods and earthquakes.

As we describe the various financial institutions in later chapters, keep these risk categories in mind. For now, let's illustrate each one.

Type-I liabilities Both the amount and the timing of the liabilities are known with certainty. A liability requiring a financial institution to pay $5 million six months from now would be an example. For example, depository institutions know the amount that they are committed

Table 3.1
Nature of liabilities of financial institutions.

Liability Type	Amount of Cash Outlay	Timing of Cash Outlay
Type I	Known	Known
Type II	Known	Uncertain
Type III	Uncertain	Known
Type IV	Uncertain	Uncertain

to pay (principal plus interest) on the maturity date of a fixed-rate deposit, assuming that the depositor does not withdraw funds prior to the maturity date.

Type-I liabilities, however, are not limited to depository institutions. A major product sold by life insurance companies is a **guaranteed investment contract**, popularly referred to as a **GIC**. The obligation of the life insurance company under this contract is that, for a sum of money (called a premium), it will guarantee an interest rate up to some specified maturity date.[2] For example, suppose a life insurance company for a premium of $10 million issues a five-year GIC agreeing to pay 10% compounded annually. The life insurance company knows that it must pay $16.11 million to the GIC policyholder in five years.[3]

Type-II liabilities The amount of cash outlay is known, but the timing of the cash outlay is uncertain. The most obvious example of a Type-II liability is a life insurance policy. There are many types of life insurance policies that we shall discuss in chapter 8, but the most basic type is that, for an annual premium, a life insurance company agrees to make a specified dollar payment to policy beneficiaries upon the death of the insured.

Type-III liabilities With this type of liability, the timing of the cash outlay is known, but the amount is uncertain. An example is when a financial institution has issued an obligation in which the interest rate adjusts periodically according to some interest rate benchmark. Depository institutions, for example, issue accounts called **certificates of deposit (CDs)**, which have a stated maturity. The interest rate paid need not be fixed over the life of the deposit but can fluctuate. If a depository institution issues a three-year floating-rate CD that adjusts every three months and the interest rate paid is the three-month Treasury bill rate plus one percentage point, the depository institution knows it has a liability that must be paid off in three years, but the dollar amount of the liability is not known. It will depend on three-month Treasury bill rates over the three years.

Type-IV liabilities Numerous insurance products and pension obligations present uncertainty as to both the amount and timing of the cash outlay. Probably the most obvious examples are automobile and home insurance policies issued by property and casualty insurance companies. When, and if, a payment will have to be made to the policyholder is uncertain. Whenever damage is done to an insured asset, the amount of the payment that must be made is uncertain.

As we explain in chapter 9, sponsors of pension plans can agree to various types of pension obligations to the beneficiaries of the plan. There are plans whose retirement benefits depend on the participant's income for a specified number of years before retirement and the

2. A GIC does not seem like a product that we would associate with a life insurance company, because the policyholder does not have to die for someone to be paid. Yet as we shall see when we discuss life insurance companies in chapter 8, a major group of insurance company financial products is in the pension benefit area. A GIC is one such product.

3. This amount is determined as follows: $\$10{,}000{,}000 \times (1.10)^5$.

total number of years the participant worked. This will affect the amount of the cash outlay. The timing of the cash outlay depends on when the employee elects to retire and whether the employee remains with the sponsoring plan until retirement. Moreover, both the amount and the timing will depend on how the employee elects to have payments made—over only the employee's life or those of the employee and spouse.

Liquidity Concerns

Because of uncertainty about the timing or the amount of the cash outlays, a financial institution must be prepared to have sufficient cash to satisfy its obligations. Also keep in mind that our discussion of liabilities assumes that the entity holding the obligation against the financial institution may have the right to change the nature of the obligation, perhaps incurring some penalty. For example, in the case of a certificate of deposit, the depositor may request the withdrawal of funds prior to the maturity date. Typically, the deposit-accepting institution will grant this request but assess an early withdrawal penalty. In the case of certain types of investment companies, shareholders have the right to redeem their shares at any time.

Some life insurance products have a cash-surrender value: At specified dates, the policyholder can exchange the policy for a lump-sum payment. Typically, the lump-sum payment will penalize the policyholder for turning in the policy. Some life insurance products have a loan value, which means that the policyholder has the right to borrow against the cash value of the policy.

In addition to uncertainty about the timing and amount of the cash outlays, and the potential for the depositor or policyholder to withdraw cash early or borrow against a policy, a financial institution has to be concerned with possible reduction in cash inflows. In the case of a depository institution, this means the inability to obtain deposits. For insurance companies, it means reduced premiums because of the cancellation of policies. For certain types of investment companies, it means not being able to find new buyers for shares.

Regulations

Numerous regulations and tax considerations influence the investment policies that financial institutions pursue. When discussing the various financial institutions in later chapters, we will highlight the key regulations and tax factors.

In chapter 2, we discussed the role of the government in the regulation of financial markets. Here we provide a brief discussion of the risks that regulators have regarding financial institutions. These risks, several of which were described in the previous chapter, can be classified into the following sources of risk:

- credit risk,
- settlement risk,

- counterparty risk,
- liquidity risk,
- market risk,
- operational risk, and
- legal risk.

Credit risk is a broadly used term to describe several types of risk. In terms of regulatory concerns, credit risk is the risk that the obligor of a financial instrument held by a financial institution will fail to fulfill its obligation on the due date or at any time thereafter. According to the International Financial Risk Institute, **settlement risk** is the risk that when there is a settlement of a trade or obligation, the transfer fails to take place as expected. Settlement risk consists of counterparty risk (a form of credit risk) and a form of liquidity risk.

Counterparty risk is the risk that a counterparty in a trade fails to satisfy its obligation. The trade could involve the cash settlement of a contract or the physical delivery of some asset. In the context of settlement risk, **liquidity risk** means that the counterparty can eventually meet its obligation, but not at the due date. As a result, the party failing to receive timely payment must be prepared to finance any shortfall in the contractual payment.

Market risk is the risk to a financial institution's economic well-being that results from an adverse movement in the market price of assets (debt obligations, equities, commodities, currencies) it owns or the level or the volatility of market prices. Measures can be used to gauge this risk. One such measure endorsed by bank regulators is **value-at-risk** (VaR), a measure of the potential loss in a financial institution's financial position associated with an adverse price movement of a given probability over a specified time horizon.

Liquidity risk, in addition to being a part of settlement risk, has two forms, according to the International Financial Risk Institute. The first is the risk that a financial institution is unable to transact in a financial instrument at a price near its market value. This risk is called **market liquidity risk**. The other form of liquidity risk is **funding liquidity risk**. This is the risk that the financial institution will be unable to obtain funding to obtain the cash flow necessary to satisfy its obligations.

An important risk that is often overlooked but has been the cause of the demise of some major financial institutions is operational risk. Well-known examples in the past two decades include Orange County (1994, United States), Barings Bank (1995, United Kingdom), Daiwa Bank (1995, New York), Allied Irish Banks (2002, Ireland), Enron (2001, United States), MasterCard International (2005, United States), and the terrorist attack in New York on September 11, 2001.[4] **Operational risk** is defined by bank regulators as "the risk of loss resulting from inadequate or failed internal processes, people and systems, or

4. For a description of each of these examples, see chapter 1 in Anna Chernobai, Svetlozar T. Rachev, and Frank J. Fabozzi, *Operational Risk: A Guide to Basel II Capital Requirements, Models and Analysis* (Hoboken, NJ: John Wiley & Sons, 2007).

from external events."[5] The definition of operation risk includes **legal risk**. This is the risk of loss resulting from failure to comply with laws as well as prudent ethical standards and contractual obligations.

We will continue our discussion of the risks that financial institutions face and guidelines for dealing with them when we discuss depository institutions in chapter 6.

Asset Management Firms

Asset management firms manage the funds of individuals, businesses, endowments, foundations, and state and local governments. These firms are also referred to as **money management firms**, and those who manage the funds are referred to as **asset managers**, **money managers**, **fund managers**, and **portfolio managers**.

Asset management firms are either affiliated with some financial institution (such as a commercial bank, insurance company, or investment bank) or are independent companies. Larger institutional clients seeking the services of an asset management firm typically do not allocate all of their assets to one asset management firm. Instead, they typically diversify among several asset management firms, as well as possibly managing some portion of their funds internally. One reason for using several asset management firms is that firms differ in their expertise with respect to asset classes. For example, a client that seeks an asset manager to invest in common stock, bonds, real estate, and alternative investments (such as commodities and hedge funds) will use asset management firms that specialize in each of those asset classes.

As of January 2018, the largest asset management firm in the world is BlackRock with $6.2 trillion in assets under management, followed by the Vanguard Group ($4.9 trillion). Other asset management firms with more than $2 trillion in assets under management are UBS ($3.1 trillion), State Street Global Advisors ($2.8 trillion), Fidelity Investments ($2.4 trillion), and Allianz Asset Management ($2.3 trillion).[6] Of these six firms, four are U.S. based and two are European based—UBS (Switzerland) and Allianz Asset Management (Germany).

Asset management firms receive their compensation primarily from management fees charged based on the market value of the assets managed for clients. For example, if an asset manager manages $100 million for a client and the fee is 60 basis points, then the annual dollar management fee is $600,000 ($100 million × 0.0060). Management fees typically vary with the amount managed, the complexity of managing the asset class, whether the assets are actively managed or passively managed, and whether the account is an institutional account or individual account. Moreover, the management fee is typically higher for managing the assets of regulated investment companies than for other institutional clients.

5. This is the common industry definition that has been adopted by the BIS. See Basel Committee on Banking Supervision, *Operational Risk*, Consultative Document (Basel, Switzerland: Bank for International Settlements, January 2001).

6. https://www.relbanks.com/rankings/largest-asset-managers.

Although performance fees are common for hedge funds, which we discuss in chapter 32, asset management firms are increasingly adopting **performance-based management fees** for other types of accounts.[7] Many types of performance-fee structures are used in the asset management industry. The fee can be based solely on performance or on a combination of a fixed fee based on assets managed plus a performance-based fee. An example of the latter is a fee structure whereby the asset manager receives 80 basis points of the assets managed plus a fee of 20% of the return earned on those assets. The criterion for determining a performance-based fee varies. For example, the fee can be based on any positive return, the excess over a minimum return established by the client, or the excess over a benchmark (i.e., some index for the asset class) established by the client.

Types of funds managed by asset management firms include:

- regulated investment companies,
- insurance company funds,
- separately managed accounts for individuals and institutional investors,
- pension funds, and
- hedge funds.

Asset management firms typically are involved in managing the assets of several of the above.

Key Points

- Financial institutions provide various types of financial services.
- Financial intermediaries are a special group of financial institutions that obtain funds by issuing claims to market participants and use these funds to purchase financial assets. Intermediaries transform funds they acquire into assets that are more attractive to the public.
- Financial intermediaries do one or more of the following: (1) provide maturity intermediation, (2) provide risk reduction via diversification at lower cost, (3) reduce the cost of contracting and information processing, or (4) provide a payments mechanism.
- The nature of their liabilities, as well as regulatory and tax considerations, determine the investment strategy pursued by all financial institutions.
- The liabilities of all financial institutions will generally fall in different categories based on the degree of certainty of the amount and timing of the liability.
- The sources of risk of concern to regulators in their regulation of financial institutions include credit risk, settlement risk, market risk, liquidity risk, operational risk, and legal risk.

7. Robert D. Arnott, "Performance Fees: The Good, the Bad, and the (Occasionally) Ugly," *Financial Analysts Journal* 61, no. 4 (2005): 10.

• Several reports by regulators have recommended guidelines for controlling the risks of financial institutions.

• Asset management firms are involved in the management of funds for individuals, businesses, state and local government entities, and endowments and foundations.

• Asset managers generate income from fees based on the market value of the assets they manage, on performance fees, or on both.

Questions

1. Why is the holding of a claim on a financial intermediary by an investor considered an indirect investment in another entity?

2. The Insightful Management Company sells financial advice to investors. This is the only service provided by the company. Is this company a financial intermediary? Explain your answer.

3. Explain how a financial intermediary reduces the cost of contracting and information processing.

4. "All financial intermediaries provide the same economic functions. Therefore, the same investment strategy should be used in the management of all financial intermediaries." Indicate whether you agree or disagree with this statement. Explain your answer.

5. A bank issues an obligation to depositors in which it agrees to pay 3% guaranteed for one year. With the funds it obtains, the bank can invest in a wide range of financial assets. What is the risk if the bank uses the funds to invest in common stock?

6. Look at table 3.1 again. Match the types of liabilities to these four assets that an individual might have:

a. car insurance policy

b. variable-rate certificate of deposit

c. fixed-rate certificate of deposit

d. a life insurance policy that allows the holder's beneficiary to receive $100,000 when the holder dies; however, if the death is accidental, the beneficiary will receive $150,000

7. Each year, millions of American investors pour billions of dollars into investment companies, which use those dollars to buy the common stock of other companies. What do the investment companies offer investors who prefer to invest in the investment companies rather than buying the common stock of these other companies directly?

8. In March 1996, the Committee on Payment and Settlement Systems of the BIS published a report titled "Settlement Risk in Foreign Exchange Transactions" that offers a practical approach that banks can employ when dealing with settlement risk. What is meant by "settlement risk"?

9. The following appeared in the Federal Reserve Bank of San Francisco's *Economic Letter*, January 25, 2002:

Financial institutions are in the business of risk management and reallocation, and they have developed sophisticated risk management systems to carry out these tasks. The basic components of a risk management system are identifying and defining the risks the firm is exposed to, assessing their magnitude, mitigating them using a variety of procedures, and setting aside capital for potential losses. Over the past twenty years or so, financial institutions have been using economic modeling in earnest to assist them in these tasks. For example, the development of empirical models of financial volatility led to increased modeling of market risk, which is the risk arising from the fluctuations of financial asset prices. In the area of credit risk, models have recently been developed for large-scale credit risk management purposes.

Yet, not all of the risks faced by financial institutions can be so easily categorized and modeled. For example, the risks of electrical failures or employee fraud do not lend themselves as readily to modeling.

What type of risk is the above quotation referring to?

10. What is the source of income for an asset management firm?

11. What is meant by a performance-based management fee, and what is the basis for determining performance in such an arrangement?

4 Overview of Private Market Participants

CONTENTS

Learning Objectives

After reading this chapter, you will understand:

- who the private market participants in financial markets are;
- the role of households in the financial system and the types of risks they bear;
- how nonfinancial corporations participate in the financial market;
- what depository institutions and insurance companies are;
- what a pension fund is and the types of pension plans offered throughout the world;
- what a defined benefit pension plan is and how it differs from a defined contribution plan;
- the variations of the basic defined benefit plans;
- the reasons for the shift in preference in the private sector for defined contribution plans over defined benefit plans;
- the role of the Employee Retirement Income Security Act of 1974 (ERISA);
- what nonprofit organizations are and the types of nonprofit organizations;
- how foreign investors participate in a country's financial market;
- how central banks and supranational institutions act as foreign investors in a country's financial market; and
- the difference between foreign direct investments and portfolio investments.

In chapter 2, we discussed the government's role as a participant in the financial markets, and in chapter 3, we described how financial institutions and asset managers participate in the financial system. In this chapter, we describe other private market participants in financial markets. These players include the entities that issue financial assets and the entities that invest in financial assets. This chapter provides only an overview and leaves the details about particular players in the chapters to follow in this part of the book. We then focus on two particular financial institutions in chapters 6, 7, and 8. Chapters 6 and 7 cover depository institutions, and chapter 8 focuses on insurance companies. Another important market participant in the credit markets are credit rating agencies, the three most popular being Fitch Ratings, Moody's Investors Service, and Standard & Poor's. Because of their importance, we devote the next chapter to them.

Households

In chapter 1, we distinguished between the real economy and the paper (financial) sector of the economy. Households, along with nonfinancial corporations, are part of the real economy. For this reason, households play a key role in a country's economy. Through their investment of funds and through borrowing, households play a key role in the financial sector. Their savings and spending decisions affect asset prices and interest rates.

The balance sheet of a household has three components: (1) assets, (2) liabilities, and (3) equity or new worth. When households save, they use those funds to invest in financial assets. The asset side of the balance sheet of households can be divided into two components: assets invested in pension accounts and assets invested in nonpension accounts. As savers, then, households are investors. The investment made may be a direct or an indirect investment. An example of the former is a household's purchase of Apple Inc. stock or corporate bond. Indirect investments include collective investment vehicles and investments made through financial intermediaries, both of which are described in chapter 32.

Households are also issuers of debt obligations in the financial market. They do so when they borrow funds to finance consumer purchases on credit, purchase a home by borrowing funds, or obtain a student loan to pay for higher education. Those obligations appear on the balance sheet of households as liabilities. Finally, the difference between assets and liabilities is a household's net worth.

The behavior of households in the financial market is affected by government policies, such as tax policies that may provide a favorable tax treatment for certain types of investments and monetary policy, as we describe in chapter 7. When interest rates are altered by monetary policy, this action influences households in three ways. First, it affects the decisions of households as to how much to save and how much to consume. That is, a decline in interest rates has the effect of increasing consumption and therefore reducing saving; an increase in interest rates has the effect of decreasing consumption and increasing saving. Second, on the investment side, it affects the asset allocation of households between noninterest-bearing assets and interest-bearing assets. Finally, with respect to issuing debt (i.e., borrowing), it increases the amount borrowed when interest rates are lowered and decreases it when interest rates are increased.

The change in asset values also influences the behavior of households through what is termed the "wealth effect." As the portfolio value of the financial assets of households changes, households' net worth will also change. The change in net worth affects the amount a household is willing to borrow. More specifically, as net worth increases (decreases), households have more (less) collateral that can be used in a borrowing arrangement.

Households are the ultimate bearers of financial risk in the financial system. Although there are financial institutions and government programs that provide different forms of guarantees for the financial products that they issue, if the guarantors fail to fulfill their obligation, the risk is borne by households. On the issuance/liability side, as borrowers, households are a source of considerable credit risk in the financial system. Some loans by households are guaranteed by the central governments, agencies that they create, or subgovernment entities.

Nonfinancial Corporations

Nonfarm corporations are classified as financial corporations or nonfinancial corporations. **Financial corporations** include depository institutions, insurance companies, and investment companies. **Nonfinancial corporations** issue securities. They issue both common stock and debt obligations. In addition, corporations with excess cash to invest participate in financial markets by investing those funds on a short-term basis.

Some nonfinancial corporations have subsidiaries that are involved in the same activities as financial corporations and are referred to as **captive finance companies**. Three examples of U.S. captive finance companies are Ford Motor Credit (a subsidiary of Ford Motor Company) and General Electric Credit Corporation (a subsidiary of General Electric Company), and Caterpillar Finance Corporation (a subsidiary of Caterpillar Inc.). Many of the larger U.S. nonfinancial corporations have non-U.S. captive companies. For example, Ford Motor Company has Ford Credit Europe Bank Plc, Ford Capital B.V., Ford Credit Canada Ltd., Ford Credit Australia Ltd, Ford Credit de Mexico, Ford Credit Co. S.A. de C.V., Ford Motor Credit Co. of New Zealand Ltd. and Ford Motor Credit Co. of Puerto Rico. Hyundai Capital Services, a subsidiary of South Korea's Hyundai Motor Company, provides a wide range of financial products and services. Hyundai Motor Company has subsidiaries in other countries that are captive finance companies. For example, in the United Kingdom, there is Hyundai Capital UK Limited (a joint venture company established between Santander Consumer UK), Hyundai Motor UK, and Kia Motors UK.

Corporations make available various types of pension plans for their employees. In the case of defined benefit pension plans sponsored by corporations, the sponsor has the same choices as those of state and local governments that sponsor such plans: internal management, external management, or a combination of both.

Depository Institutions

Depository institutions include commercial banks, S&L associations, savings banks, and credit unions. Basically, with the funds that depository institutions raise through deposits and other funding sources, they make direct loans to individuals, nonfinancial and financial businesses, and state and local governments. They generate a profit, as explained in chapter 3, by earning a spread between the return realized on their investment and the cost of obtaining funds. Because of their important role in financial markets, they are highly regulated, and we devote chapter 6 to them.

Insurance Companies

Insurance companies provide insurance protection against the occurrence of future events that will adversely affect the insured and are therefore risk bearers. For providing this protection (i.e., accepting the associated risk), they receive an insurance premium. Between the time the insurance premium is paid to the insurance company and the time the company pays out claims to policyholders, the company can invest the premium in the financial market.

Insurance companies sell both investment-oriented and pure insurance products. The types of pure insurance products, and how they are classified in the insurance industry, are life insurance, health insurance, property and casualty insurance, liability insurance, disability insurance, and long-term care insurance. Certain insurance companies provide protection in the form of financial guarantees. The major participants in the financial system among the different types of insurance companies are life insurance companies. Although life insurance companies are risk bearers, there are some products they issue that are investment products. We devote chapter 8 to insurance companies.

Investment Companies

Investment companies are financial intermediaries that sell shares to the public and invest the proceeds in a diversified portfolio of financial assets. Each share represents a proportional interest in the net assets in which the funds are invested. Because the primary regulator of investment companies is the Securities and Exchange Commission (SEC), these companies are referred to as **registered investment companies**. Investment companies are divided into open-end companies and closed-end companies. While both types of investment companies are popularly referred to as "mutual funds," technically only open-end funds are mutual funds.

Investment companies are collective investment vehicles and are described in more detail in chapter 32.

Private Pension Funds

A pension fund is established for the purpose of providing benefits on retirement for designated groups of employees or professionals. The fund's pool of assets is purchased with the contributions to the pension plan for the exclusive purpose of financing pension plan benefits. The members of the pension fund or pension plan have a legal or beneficial right or some other form contractual claim against the pool of assets. A **pension plan sponsor** is the entity that designs, negotiates, and typically helps administer a pension plan for its members. A **private pension fund** is administered by an institution other than a government entity.

Many countries have created vehicles for their citizens to save funds in a pension plan in order to complement their private savings when they retire. Pension plans can be employee (occupational) vehicles or pension vehicles. The vehicles can be a pension fund, a pension insurance contract, or a product created by a bank of an investment company.

An **occupational pension plan** is linked to an employment or professional relationship between the plan member and the entity that establishes the plan (the plan sponsor). These plans are established by employers or groups of employers in the same industry (i.e., industry associations), professional associations, and labor associations. A pension plan that is not an occupational pension plan is a referred to as a **personal pension plan**. Some countries, such as the United States, have both types of pension plans, but others have only one type of plan.

Different private pension vehicles can be used to provide a pension. The three major ones are pension funds, pension insurance contracts, and book reserves.

A book reserves pension vehicle is one in which employers put money aside for their employees' retirement on their books. This type private pension vehicle exists in Germany.

For the private pension sector, there are pension insurance contracts, which we will discuss. For some countries, the largest ratio of pension-related assets to gross domestic product (GDP) is the largest part of private pension investments. In Denmark, where specialized insurance companies hold pension-related assets, the ratio is 67%.

To appreciate the importance of pension vehicles as investors in financial markets, a study by the OECD reported that the assets invested in 2015 by 35 OECD countries was US$39.6 trillion. In a survey of 45 non-OECD countries, the amount invested that same year was $1.3 trillion. In terms of investor share, pension vehicles were first, followed by depository institutions, investment companies, and insurance companies.

In terms of U.S. dollars, the five countries with the largest private pension fund total investment in 2015, accounting for 85% of total investments by OECD countries, were the United States, the United Kingdom, Australia, Japan, and the Netherlands. The number of pension funds varies greatly by country. For OECD countries, the five countries with the largest number of pension funds in 2015 were the United States (685,203), Australia (559,547), Ireland (67,840), the United Kingdom (43,690), and Canada (8,876).

The U.S. Private Pension System

In this section we look at the U.S. private pension system. The appendix to this chapter provides more information about the U.S. private pension system.

Individual retirement accounts An **individual retirement account** (IRA) is a tax-advantaged investment account that allows individuals to invest to accumulate retirement funds. The tax advantage of a qualified plan is that investment income (i.e., capital gains, dividends, and interest) is not taxed until funds are withdrawn. There is another tax advantage, depending on the type of IRA, whether traditional or Roth. In a **traditional IRA**, the amount invested (the maximum being specified by law) is deducted from taxable income for the year of the contribution. Thus, the individual is investing pre-tax income. When the funds are withdrawn by the individual, ordinary income, not capital gains, taxes are paid on the entire amount withdrawn. With a **Roth IRA**, the amount invested is not deducted from taxable income in the year contributed (i.e., the individual is investing after-tax income). Because taxes are paid on the amount invested, when the funds are withdrawn, no tax is paid on the amount that was invested or earned (no taxes at all).

The allocation of the funds in the IRA is determined by the individual. All of the financial risks are assumed by the individual. Funds can be allocated to individual stocks or bonds or invested in one of the collective investment vehicles described later.

Defined benefit plans With a **defined benefit plan**, the plan sponsor agrees to pay qualified employees covered by the plan benefits on retirement. The amount of the retirement benefit is determined by a formula that is based on a percentage of earnings and the number of years employed. The plan sponsor can be a single corporation; a union or a group of corporations, usually in a related industry; or a government entity.

Corporate-sponsored plans are referred to as **private plans**, whereas government-sponsored plans are referred to as **public plans**. Defined benefit plans sponsored by a union or a group of corporations are referred to as **Taft-Hartley multiemployer plans**. Defined benefit plans may be managed by the sponsor internally (i.e., with a portfolio management team composed of employees of the plan sponsor) or by an external asset management firm.

The liabilities of the pension plan are then those of the plan sponsor. So, for example, the obligations of General Electric's defined benefit plan are the liabilities of General Electric. From the employee's perspective, the financial risk associated with the future payments of a defined benefit plan are those of the sponsor. However, sponsors are corporations and state and local governments, and such entities can go into bankruptcy. For qualified private defined benefit plans, a federal government agency, the Pension Benefit Guaranty Corporation (PBGC), insures those plans. However, the PBGC's guarantee is not a guarantee by the U.S. government. Moreover, the likelihood is that without a bailout, the PBGC will not have sufficient funds to pay off the obligations that it has insured. This supports what was stated when we described households: The household is the ultimate risk bearer.

The number of U.S. defined benefit plans has been declining, as it has been in other countries. In 2011, of all private sector establishments that could sponsor a defined benefit plan, only 10% did so. Those private-sector defined benefit plans covered only 18% of workers in the private sector. In contrast to the private sector, state and local governments (i.e., public plans) covered 78% of their employees.[1] Not only is the number of plan sponsors in the private sector decreasing, but those corporations that had defined benefit plans are closing them to new employees. For example, General Electric announced in December 2010 that it was closing its defined benefit plan to new employees. Instead, employees would be given a different plan, the one we discuss next.

Defined contribution plans In a **defined contribution plan**, the plan sponsor is responsible only for making specified contributions to the plan on behalf of qualifying participants, not specified payments to the employee after retirement. The amount contributed is typically either a percentage of the employee's salary or a percentage of the employer's profits. The plan sponsor does not guarantee any specific amount at retirement. The payments that will be made to qualifying participants on retirement depend on the growth of the plan assets. That is, retirement benefit payments are determined by the investment performance of

1. William J. Wiatrowski, "The Last Private Industry Pension Plans: A Visual Essay," http://www.bls.gov/opub/mlr/2012/12/art1full.pdf.

the funds in which the assets are invested and are not guaranteed by the plan sponsor. The plan sponsor gives the participants various options as to the investment vehicles in which they may invest. Defined contribution pension plans come in several legal forms: 401(k) plans, money purchase pension plans, and employee stock ownership plans (ESOPs).

By far the fastest-growing sector of the defined contribution plan is the 401(k) plan or its equivalent in the nonprofit sector, the 403(b) plan, and in the public sector, the 457 plan. To the firm, this kind of plan offers the lowest costs and the fewest administrative problems. The employer makes a specified contribution to a specific plan or program, and the employee chooses how it is invested.[2] To the employee, the plan is attractive because it offers some control over how the pension money is managed. In fact, plan sponsors frequently offer participants the opportunity to invest in one or more families of mutual funds. More than half of all defined contribution plans offered by public institutions (such as state governments) use mutual funds, and the percentage of private corporations that use this approach is even higher.

Employees in the corporate, as well as the public, sector have responded favorably with almost half of all assets in defined contribution pensions now invested in mutual funds. Regulations issued by the U.S. Department of Labor require firms to offer their employees a set of distinctive choices, a development that has further encouraged pension plans to opt for the mutual fund approach, because families of mutual funds can readily provide investment vehicles offering different investment objectives.

Several fundamental differences separate defined benefit plans from defined contribution plans. In the defined benefit plan, the plan sponsor guarantees the retirement benefits, makes the investment choices, and bears the investment risk if the investments do not earn enough to fund the guaranteed retirement benefits. In a defined contribution plan, by contrast, the employer does not guarantee any retirement benefits but does agree to make specified contributions to the employee's account; the employee selects the investment options, and the employee's retirement payments come from the return on the investment portfolio, plus, of course, the employee and employer contributions.

Nonprofit Organizations

Nongovernmental entities can be classified as commercial enterprises or nonprofit (or not-for-profit) organizations. The distinction between the two entities is that commercial enterprises have as their primary objective the generation of a profit. **Nonprofit organizations** are not motivated by profit or any monetary gain but have as their primary objective financially supporting or actively engaging in activities that will benefit some specific public or private interest, such as humanitarian aid, education, the arts, or religion.

Nonprofit organizations include **foundations** and **endowments**. There are differences between the two regarding the requirements necessary for the tax-exempt treatment of

2. "Calling It Quits," *Institutional Investor* (February 1991): 125.

income generated from their investment funds. But the main difference between these two types of nonprofit organizations is that foundations are established with funds by a donor and no additional funds are added, whereas an endowment can continue to raise funds from the public on an ongoing basis. Foundations are established by wealthy individuals and families. Some foundations are company sponsored or linked to certain communities. Still others are termed **operating foundations**, because they award most of their gifts to their own units rather than to organizations outside the foundation. Endowment funds are commonly established by colleges and universities, hospitals, and religious organizations.

The five wealthiest foundations, corporate foundations, and community foundations are the Bill & Melinda Gates Foundation in the United States (endowment of about US$45 billion), the Wellcome Trust in the United Kingdom States (US$27 billion), the Howard Hughes Medical Institute in the United States (US$18 billion), the Garfield Weston Foundation in the United Kingdom (about US$16 billion), and the Stitchting INGKA Foundation in the Netherlands (about US$13 billion). The five universities with the largest endowments are Harvard (endowment of about US$38 billion), Yale (about US$26 billion), Princeton (about US$24 billion), Stanford (about US$23 billion), and the Massachusetts Institute of Technology (US$14 billion).

The board of trustees of the foundation or endowment specifies the investment objectives and the acceptable investment alternatives. The funds can be managed either in house or by external fund managers. Several universities with large endowments have formed their own asset management firms. For example, in 1974, Harvard University, the largest university endowment fund, formed Harvard Management Company to manage its endowment and related financial assets with the singular mission of producing "long-term investment results to support the educational and research goals of the University."[3]

Foreign Investors

Foreign investors that participate a country's financial market include individuals, nonfinancial businesses, and financial entities that are not domiciled in that country, as well as foreign central governments, supranationals, and sovereign wealth funds. Two types of investments can be made by foreign entities: foreign direct investments and foreign portfolio investments.

The OECD defines a **foreign direct investment** (FDI) as follows:

> FDI is defined as cross-border investment by a resident entity in one economy with the objective of obtaining a lasting interest in an enterprise resident in another economy. The lasting interest implies the existence of a long-term relationship between the direct investor and the enterprise and a significant degree of influence by the direct investor on the management of the enterprise. Ownership of at least 10% of the voting power, representing the influence by the investor, is the basic criterion used.[4]

3. See the web page http://www.hmc.harvard.edu/about-hmc/index.html.

4. See the web page http://www.oecd-ilibrary.org/sites/factbook-2013-en/04/02/01/index.html?itemId=/content/chapter/factbook-2013-34-en.

In contrast to an FDI, a **foreign portfolio investment** (FPI) is of a more temporary nature. Investment instruments, such as stocks and bonds, are normally traded in FPIs.

Central banks, supranationals, and sovereign wealth funds may participate in a country's financial market. A central bank may participate in another country's financial market through its central bank; we describe the role of central banks in chapter 7. A central bank participates by buying or selling financial assets in another country's financial market either to stabilize that country's currency relative to its domestic currency or as an investment vehicle (buying if an asset is perceived to be attractive and selling if a holding is perceived to be unattractive).

A **supranational institution** is an organization formed by two or more central governments through international treaties. These supranational institutions promote economic development for their member countries. Two examples of supranational institutions are the International Bank for Reconstruction and Development, popularly referred to as the World Bank, and the Inter-American Development Bank. The general objective of the former is to improve the efficiency of the international financial and trading markets. The objective of the latter is to promote economic growth in the developing countries of the Americas.

Sovereign wealth funds (SWFs) are country- or state-owned investment funds that countries establish. The funds for an SWF are obtained from proceeds from one or more of the following sources: (1) exports of natural resources, (2) privatizations of previously state-owned companies or enterprises, (3) government fiscal surpluses, (4) balance-of-payment surpluses, and (5) earnings from official foreign currency operations. Of course, the primary motive given for the establishment of an SWF has been to maximize returns available from investments outside the country that has established the SWF.

Since the establishment of the first SWF by Kuwait in 1953 (the Kuwait Investment Authority), motivated by that government's objective to protect the national standard of living from fluctuations in the price of its primary export (oil), the twenty-first century has seen significant growth in the number of SWFs. There are two reasons for the growth in the number and amount of assets accumulated by SWFs. The first is the commodity price boom in countries where either the government controls the exports or heavy taxes are imposed on the revenues received from such exports. The second reason is that the governments of many emerging market countries have run persistent current account surpluses greater than needed, thereby accumulating large stockpiles of international reserves with the intent of investing them in high-yield assets outside their country.[5]

According to the Sovereign Wealth Fund Institute, the five largest SWFs, based on assets under management as of June 2016, were Norway's Government Pension Fund ($873 billion), China's China Investment Corporation ($814 billion), the UAE's Abu Dhabi Investment Authority ($792 billion), Kuwait's Kuwait Investment Authority ($592 billion), and Saudi Arabia's SAMA Foreign Holdings ($582 billion).[6]

5. Joshua Aizenman, "Large Hoarding of International Reserves and the Emerging Global Economic Architecture," NBER Working Paper 13277 (Cambridge, MA: National Bureau of Economic Research, July 2007).

6. Information posted by the Sovereign Wealth Fund Institute on its website, http://www.swfinstitute.org/fund-rankings/.

The increase in the number of SWFs and their expanded role have prompted considerable debate as to the motives of these investment funds beyond that of enhanced return performance in several countries and the implications for the national security of countries where SWFs invest. One concern is that some SWFs have invested in technology companies that produce strategic military technology, allowing the SWFs to potentially obtain trade secrets. Another is that SWFs may hold a major interest in commercial enterprises of national concerns beyond the military sector. Because of the lack of transparency in SWF operations, some governments are concerned about such noncommercial motivations of SWFs. Yet the potential capital injections that can be provided to some essential industries in some countries appear to override any national security concerns.[7]

Key Points

- In addition to financial institutions, private market participants include households, nonfinancial corporations, depository institutions, insurance companies, nonprofit organizations, and foreign investors.
- Households are investors and debt issuers in the financial market whose behavior is influenced by interest rates and asset values.
- Households are a source of financial risk as borrowers and are the ultimate risk bearers as investors.
- Nonfarm corporations are classified as financial corporations or nonfinancial corporations.
- Some nonfinancial corporations have subsidiaries that are captive finance companies that are involved in the same activities as financial corporations.
- Insurance companies are risk bearers, with the largest sector in this industry being life insurance companies.
- Employer-sponsored pension plans are pension plans established by private entities (corporations) and public entities (state and local governments).
- Employer-sponsored pension plans can be either defined benefit or defined contribution plans.
- Defined benefit plans result in liabilities for the plan sponsor, and the management of those funds is the responsibility of the plan sponsor.
- For defined contribution plans, once contributions are made, the plan sponsor no longer has any liability, and plan participants make their own investment decisions.
- In the private sector, government regulation and the portability of pension funds have resulted in a decline in defined benefit plans in favor of defined contribution plans.
- In the public sector, defined benefit plans dominate.

7. For a further discussion of these issues, see Judith Goff, "Sovereign Wealth Funds: Stumbling Blocks or Stepping Stones to Financial Globalization?" *Federal Reserve Bank of San Francisco Economic Letter*, December 14, 2007.

• The Pension Benefit Guaranty Corporation (PBGC) is the federal government agency responsible for protecting the retirement benefits of workers of qualified private employer-sponsored defined benefit plans.

• The guarantee of the PBGC does not carry the guarantee of the U.S. government.

• Foreign investors who participate in a country's financial market include individuals, nonfinancial businesses and financial entities that are not domiciled in that country, as well as foreign central governments, supranationals, and sovereign wealth funds (SWFs).

• Foreign direct investments (FDIs) and foreign portfolio investments are the two ways in which investors can participate in the financial market.

• Central governments participate in the financial market of another country through their central bank's purchase and sale of that country's financial assets.

Questions

1. Explain how the household sector participates as both a borrower and a lender of funds in the financial market.

2. Explain why you agree or disagree with the following statement: "When a household purchases life insurance, there is no risk, insofar as the issuer of the policy guarantees a death benefit payment."

3. Why are households viewed as the ultimate risk bearers?

4. How do nonfinancial corporations participate in the financial markets?

5. Explain why some subsidiaries of a nonfinancial business can be classified as financial businesses.

6. What is the basic function of depository institutions?

7. What is the basic function of insurance companies?

8. Why does a defined benefit plan create a future liability for a plan sponsor?

9. a. What is the function of the PBGC?

b. Explain whether you agree or disagree with the following statement: "Workers whose pension plan is insured by the PBGC are guaranteed the full amount of their pension income."

10. Does ERISA require that a corporation establish a pension fund?

11. What are the stated objectives of SWFs?

12. What is the difference between FDI and foreign portfolio investment?

13. What is a central bank, and how does it participate in the financial market of another country as a foreign investor?

14. What is a supranational institute, and what is its general objective?

15. In an April 8, 2008, article in *Bloomberg Businessweek*, the following appeared: "China Investment Corp.'s chief risk officer denies allegations that the fund has hidden objectives in its investment strategy."

a. What is the "China Investment Corp."?

b. What types of allegations do you think the quotation is referring to?

Appendix: U.S. Pension Regulations and Issues

U.S. Pension Fund Regulation

The U.S. Congress passed comprehensive legislation in 1974 to regulate pension plans. This legislation, **the Employee Retirement Income Security Act of 1974** (ERISA), is fairly technical in its details. For our purposes, it is necessary only to understand its major provisions.

First, ERISA established **funding standards** for the minimum contributions that a plan sponsor must make to the pension plan to satisfy the actuarially projected benefit payments.

Prior to the enactment of ERISA, many corporate plan sponsors followed a pay-as-you-go funding policy. That is, when an employee retired, the corporate plan sponsor took the necessary retirement benefits out of current cash flow. Under ERISA, such a practice is no longer allowed. Instead, the program must be funded; that is, regular contributions to an investment pool along with investment earnings must be sufficient to pay the employee retirement benefits.

Second, ERISA established **fiduciary standards** for pension fund trustees, managers, or advisers. Specifically, all parties responsible for the management of a pension fund are guided by the judgment of what is called a "prudent man" in seeking to determine which investments are proper. Because a trustee is responsible for other people's money, it is necessary to ensure that the trustee takes the role seriously. To fulfill their responsibilities, trustees must act as reasonably prudent persons to acquire and use the information pertinent to making an investment decision.

Third, ERISA establishes minimum **vesting standards**. For example, the law specifies that, after five years of employment, a plan participant is entitled to 25% of accrued pension benefits. The percentage of entitlement increases to 100% after 10 years. Additional vesting requirements are noted in ERISA. Finally, ERISA created the PBGC to insure vested pension benefits. The insurance program is funded from annual premiums that must be paid by pension plans. We'll have more to say about the PBGC shortly.

Responsibility for administering ERISA is delegated to the Department of Labor and the Internal Revenue Service. To ensure that a pension plan is in compliance with ERISA, periodic reporting and disclosure statements must be filed with these government agencies. It is important to recognize that ERISA does not require that a corporation establish a pension plan. If a corporation does establish a defined benefit plan, however, it must comply with the numerous and complex regulations set forth in ERISA.

The Pension Benefit Guaranty Corporation

The U.S. government agency responsible for protecting the retirement benefits of workers of qualified private employer-sponsored defined benefit plans is the Pension Benefit Guaranty Corporation. Two separate insurance programs are under the PBGC's purview: single-employer and multiemployer plan insurance programs.

Created in 1974 as part of ERISA, PBGC has a threefold mission: (1) to encourage the continuation and maintenance of private-sector defined benefit plans, (2) to provide timely and uninterrupted payment of pension benefits, and (3) to keep pension insurance premiums at a minimum. By law, the PBGC must be self-financed. Moreover, as noted in the annual report of the PBGC, ERISA specifies "that the U.S. government is not liable for any obligation or liability incurred by PBGC." This point is critical, because if the PBGC fails, the workers whose pension it guarantees no longer have a guarantee.

Although the federal government does not stand behind the PBGC's obligations as explicitly stated under ERISA, an April 28, 2008, letter from the Congressional Budget Office to former congressman George Miller, then chair of the Committee on Education and Labor, stated that "an implicit expectation exists among many market participants and policymakers that taxpayers will ultimately pay for benefits should PBGC be unable to meet those obligations."[8]

To meet claims not covered by plan assets or obtained from terminated plan sponsors, no funding can be obtained from the federal government. This is because there are no appropriations from general revenues to cover any claims. Instead, funding sources are limited to investment returns, premiums received, and assets from terminated plans taken over by the PBGC. Premiums are set by Congress. In 1974, when the PBGC was established, the premium was set at $1 per participant for single-employer plans and $0.50 per participant for multiemployer plans. The per-participant rate has been raised over time, and it has also been adjusted for the financial health of the plan as measured by the amount of underfunding of the vested plan.

The PBGC can best be described as an insurer with little control over key financial decisions that might permit it to increase the likelihood of accomplishing its overarching mandate. Under ERISA, its mission is to preserve the defined benefit plans it insures and to protect the beneficiaries of those plans. The agency's inability to employ strategies available to private insurers and the influence of political issues associated with decisions made

8. Congressional Budget Office, Letter to the Honorable George Miller: A Review of the Pension Benefit Guaranty Corporation's New Investment Strategy, April 24, 2008, http://www.cbo.gov/sites/default/files/04-24-miller-pbgc_letter.pdf.

by Congress make the management of the PBGC one of the most challenging tasks faced by any financial institution.

The PBGC has acknowledged that, based on its current funded status and investment policy, the probability is high that it will have insufficient funds to pay all future benefits due current beneficiaries. For this reason, a reasonable goal for the PBGC would be to maintain the program as long as possible with the hope of eventually putting as small a deficit as possible on the U.S. government should the government agree to bail it out.

Consequently, it is not a surprise that the GAO highlighted the PBGC as a "high-risk" agency in its report to the U.S. Congress starting in 2003. In its February 14, 2013, update, the GAO acknowledged the progress made by the PBGC and actions by Congress to address the agency's weaknesses. Nonetheless, the GAO concluded: "Because of long-term challenges related to PBGC's governance and funding structure, PBGC's financial future is uncertain."[9]

One obvious way to reduce the likelihood of receiving the assets of terminated pension plans is for the PBGC to require one or more of the following: larger contributions, higher premiums for underfunded plans, or lower guaranteed payments. But such risk mitigation policies are currently unavailable to the PGBC's management. Unlike for an insurer, the first two requirements can have an adverse impact on the viability of current plans covered by the PBGC, whereas the last is a politically sensitive issue. Instead, it seems that the best that can be done is to prepare for the terminated plans, working with the sponsors of troubled plans, and, in the case of bankruptcy, litigating to obtain recovery of additional assets. These practices are currently being pursued by the PBGC's management.

Problems with Private-Sector Defined Benefit Pension Plans

The value of the liabilities of a defined benefit plan can be measured in terms of the present value of the projected payments to the plan's beneficiaries. The value of the plan's assets is equal to the market value of these assets. When the value of the assets exceeds the value of the liabilities, the plan is said to have a surplus. In the opposite case, that is, when the value of the liabilities exceeds the value of the assets, the plan is said to have a deficit. Typically, as an indicator of the ability of a plan to satisfy its liabilities, the funding ratio is calculated.

The funding ratio is the ratio of the plan's assets to its liabilities and is the primary measure of the plan's financial health (i.e., ability to meet plan obligations). When there is a surplus, this means that the funding ratio exceeds 100%, and the plan is said to be overfunded. The higher the funding ratio, the healthier the plan is. Concern arises when there is a deficit and the funding ratio falls below 100%. The plan in that case is underfunded.

The management of a plan by a sponsor should focus on meeting the liabilities. This means designing an investment policy and asset allocation strategy to satisfy liabilities.

9. U.S. Government Accountability Office, "GAO's 2013 High-Risk Series: An Update. GAO-13-359T" (Washington, DC: GAO, 2013): 26, http://www.gao.gov/assets/660/652166.pdf.

As indicated earlier, one of the responsibilities of plan sponsor consultants is to work with the plan sponsor to develop an investment policy and asset allocation strategy among the major asset classes to satisfy those liabilities. Unfortunately, it was not until plans realized substantial underfunding (i.e., funding ratios considerably below 100%) and huge deficits that there was acceptance of the major financial crisis that corporate defined pension plans faced. This crisis led to the passage on April 10, 2004, of the Pension Funding Equity Act, which gave corporate sponsors of defined benefit plans some "relief" from burdensome pension contributions and, as the 2004 act's summary stated, would "protect the retirement benefits of millions of American workers and help ensure that their pension benefits will be there when they retire." Unfortunately, the bandage placed on this major hemorrhage was not adequate. As Richard Ippolito, former chief economist of the PBGC, wrote after the passage of the 2004 act:

> Unfortunately, Congress has failed to adequately address the problems of the PBGC. In temporary legislation passed in April 2004, Congress reduced the required contributions companies must make to their defined-benefit pension plans by an estimated $80 billion over two years by changing the formula used to calculate pension liabilities. Congress also provided additional relief of approximately $1.6 billion to steel and airline companies with heavily underfunded pension plans.[10]

Congress subsequently modified and permanently extended the relief granted in the 2004 act with the passage of the Pension Protection Act of 2006.

The primary beneficiaries of these laws were the beneficiaries of plans sponsored by corporations in the steel and airlines industries. In fact, from 1975 to 2000, about 75% of the claims paid by the PBGC were made to employees in those two industries: Bethlehem Steel ($3.9 billion), LTV Steel ($1.9 billion), National Steel ($1.1.3 billion), Pan American Airlines ($800 million), and Eastern Airlines ($600 million). However, the pension problem goes beyond the steel and airlines industries. Examples of corporations with computed deficits based on December 31, 2003, accounting statements were Ford Motor, Allegheny Technologies, Goodyear, Navistar, Maytag, and Avon Products.[11] Moreover, the size of the deficit can be so large that it exceeds the value of the corporate sponsor.

Bernard Condon, writing in *Forbes* in August 2004, reported that although in 1999 more than half the companies in the S&P 500 had overfunded plans, only 51 were overfunded in 2004.[12] Moreover, based on pension fund accounting, which we describe later, strong arguments can be made that the number of pension funds identified as overfunded in 1999 might be far lower than was reported. To show the severity of the problem, Ippolito wrote in 2004:

> Pension plan underfunding stands at more than $350 billion, which increases the likelihood that more pension plans will go under and taxpayers will eventually be called upon to provide a bailout.[13]

10. Richard A. Ippolito, "How to Reduce the Cost of Federal Pension Insurance," *Cato Policy Analysis* 523 (2004): 1.
11. These figures were reported in *Analyst Accounting Observer,* June 24, 2004.
12. Bernard Condon, "The Coming Pension Crisis," Forbes.com, August 12, 2004.
13. Ippolito, "How to Reduce the Cost of Federal Pension Insurance," p. 1.

Some view this problem as the major financial crisis that the United States will face in future years and that will more than likely cause the phasing out of defined benefit plans in favor of defined contribution plans. Moreover, the same is also true for public-sector defined benefit plans. Although little had been mentioned in the press about the problems that state and local governments face until recently, the concern is the same. The question is: What caused this crisis?

Here we briefly present the reasons for the crisis.[14] However, the causes are not different from what we described with regard to the U.S. S&L crisis: poor regulatory supervision and poor asset/liability management. The additional contributing factor here is the inadequate accounting and actuarial treatment by the accounting and actuarial professions.

It is often denied by representatives of corporate plans and their consultants, but historically, the investment policy of plans focused on the growth of assets and not on the liability side. Plan sponsors made their asset allocation decisions among the major asset classes—common stock, bonds, real estate, and alternative assets—based on what was expected to be the better-performing assets, without consideration of the liabilities. Hence, during the period of rising equity prices in the 1990s, greater allocations were made to that asset class. Stock market returns in 1997 and 1998, for example, were 33% and 28%, respectively. Not only were plan sponsors not watching liabilities when evaluating the performance of the plan, but some accounting and actuarial rules allowed them to benefit from certain asset allocations.

To understand the root of the crisis, let's look at the liability side, so that we know how liabilities are valued. As just explained, the value of the liabilities is determined by the present value of the future liabilities. Simple enough, except when one asks what interest rate should be used to calculate the present value of the liabilities. The interest rate used to calculate any present value is called the **discount rate**. The basic property of the time value of money is that the lower the discount rate is, the higher the present value will be. When discussing the valuation of cash flows in later chapters, we will see another important property about the relationship between future cash flows and present value. Specifically, present value may be highly sensitive to the discount rate used. This sensitivity of the present value of cash flows is referred to as its **duration**. The duration measure applies to both assets and liabilities. It is not our purpose here to describe duration in any detail, but it is sufficient to understand its role in the pension crisis story by noting that duration is the approximate percentage change in the value of an asset or liability for a 100-basis-point change in the discount rate or interest rate. Typically, duration for a defined benefit plan is 15, so if pension liabilities are $1 billion, as determined by using a discount rate of, say, 10%, then if a discount rate of 9% is used instead, the liabilities will increase by 15%, to $150 million. Such a small change in the discount rate leads to a significant change in the value of the liabilities! Therefore, the question of who gets to establish the discount rate that is used for computing the liabilities is important.

14. For further discussion, see Frank J. Fabozzi and Ronald J. Ryan, "Reforming Pension Reform," *Institutional Investor*, January 2005, 84–88.

The answer to that question is that the rules for pension accounting for financial reporting purposes allow the plan sponsor to determine it in conjunction with actuaries. Basically, the sponsor should be using a discount rate that reflects the rate of return on assets that it can reasonably be expected to earn on the plan's assets in the future. This discount rate is referred to accordingly as the **return on assets**. Determining the return on assets is highly subjective in determining the economic well-being of the plan, yet the choice (subject to some guidelines) is left with the plan sponsor. In 2001, for example, the investor Warren Buffett had this to say about this aspect of pension accounting:

> Unfortunately, the subject of pension [return] assumptions, critically important though it is, almost never comes up in corporate board meetings. … And now, of course, the need for discussion is paramount because these assumptions that are being made, with all eyes looking backward at the glories of the 1990s, are so extreme. I invite you to ask the CFO of a company having a large defined-benefit pension fund what adjustment would need to be made to the company's earnings if its pension assumption was lowered to 6.5 percent. And then, if you want to be mean, ask what the company's assumptions were back in 1975 when both stocks and bonds had far higher prospective returns than they do now.[15]

Buffett goes on to warn that too high a return on assets risks litigation for a company's chief investment officer, its board, and its auditors. Yet overestimating return on assets is a hard-to-resist temptation, because it produces a lower value for the liabilities and a higher funding ratio (i.e., a seemingly healthier pension plan).[16]

We now have the background for understanding the pension crisis. In the 1990s, pension funds allocated more to common stock than to bonds, for the reason described earlier. Starting in 2000, two conditions in the financial markets moved against pension funds. First, the stock market declined, which had a significant impact on the value of plan assets. Second, the return on assets assumptions made by plan sponsors came under closer scrutiny. Interest rates had declined, and with a dismal outlook for the stock market, the return on assets assumption was lowered. The result was deterioration in funding ratios. In fact, some still argue that the return on assets assumptions that plan sponsors have adopted subsequently are still too aggressive and that if the liabilities of pension plans were assessed properly, funding ratios would be considerably lower.

To see how the selection of the return on assets trickles down to distort the plan sponsor's corporate earnings, consider the evidence provided by two Wall Street analysts, David Zion and Bill Carcache.[17] They estimated that if the accounting treatment required by accounting rules were replaced by what actually happened to the pension plans, the aggregate reported earnings for companies in the S&P 500 would have been reduced by 69% in 2001 and by

15. Warren Buffet and Carol Loomis, "Warren Buffett on the Stock Market," *Fortune*, December 10, 2001, http://archive.fortune.com/magazines/fortune/fortune_archive/2001/12/10/314691/index.htm.

16. There are other benefits. See Fabozzi and Ryan, "Reforming Pension Reform."

17. David Zion and Bill Carcache, "The Magic of Pension Accounting" (New York: Credit Suisse First Boston, September 27, 2002).

10% in 2000. Thirty companies would have seen a decline in earnings in excess of $1 billion, with seven companies seeing a decline of more than $5 billion.

Problems with U.S. Public-Sector Defined Benefit Pension Plans

Our discussion of the problems faced in the private sector for defined benefit plans also applies to the public sector. Defined benefit plans are far more common than defined contribution plans in this sector for the reasons noted in the chapter. As with private sector plans, these plans have been characterized by poor asset management, a failure to understand how to assess performance, and overly optimistic assumptions about asset returns. These problems have resulted in considerable underfunding of public-sector defined benefit plans. The "Milliman 2012 Public Pension Fund Study" found that for the 100 largest public-sector defined benefit plans, underfunding was $895 billion, with a funding ratio of 75.1%.[18] The rate of return on assets assumed in this calculation was 7.65%.

State and local governments have sought to deal with the underfunding problems in several ways.[19] First, some sponsors have issued new bonds with the sole purpose of refinancing current liabilities. This tactic has not proved to be satisfactory in dealing with the long-term problem faced by public-sector defined benefit plans. Second, the modification and the adoption of new types of defined benefit plans by state and local governments do nothing to reduce underfunding but instead add new risks for taxpayers. Finally, encouraging employees' early retirement does not deal adequately with the problem and is typically a costly solution.

In light of the failure of the so-called reforms that have been pursued by state and local governments, a call has been made for public-sector pension reform by freezing defined benefit plans and shifting to defined contribution plans, as has been done in the private sector. However, it should be remembered that despite the problems faced by the PBGC, there is no equivalent insurer for public-sector defined benefit plans.

18. Rebecca A. Sielman, "Milliman 2012 Public Pension Funding Study," http://publications.milliman.com/publications/eb-published/pdfs/2012-public-pension-funding-study.pdf.

19. For a more detailed discussion, see Richard C. Dreyfuss, "Fixing the Public Sector Pension Problem: The (True) Path to Long-Term Reform," Civic Report 74 (New York: Manhattan Institute, February 2013), http://www.manhattan-institute.org/html/cr_74.htm#.UpySiKMo7DB.

5 Credit Rating Agencies and Their Role in Financial Markets

CONTENTS

Learning Objectives

After reading this chapter, you will understand:

- the importance of credit ratings in the financial market;
- what a credit rating agency (CRA) is and what a nationally recognized statistical rating organization is;

- regulation of CRAs;
- the different credit rating systems of the three major rating companies;
- the difference between investment-grade bonds and noninvestment-grade (or high-yield) debt;
- what a rating transition matrix is;
- how regulators use credit ratings;
- what the nonregulatory uses of credit ratings are;
- the issuer-pay system for compensating CRAs and the potential conflicts that can arise;
- the concern about the overreliance of ratings by market participants; and
- factors considered in the rating of sovereign government debt, corporate bonds, and U.S. municipal bonds.

A major risk in the financial system is default risk, which is one form of credit risk. Default risk is the risk that the obligor will fail to satisfy the terms of the lending agreement. This would involve failing to make the contractual interest payments and the scheduled repayment of principal on a timely basis. Investors who do not have access to their own credit analysis staff use, to different degrees, opinions about default risk as provided by companies that perform credit analysis and cast their opinion in the form of a rating, referred to as a **credit rating**. These commercial rating companies are referred to as **credit rating agencies** (CRAs). Although the term "agencies" might suggest that they are somehow government-affiliated or government-related entities, they are not.

In this chapter, we look CRAs, their role in financial markets, their credit rating systems, the factors that they consider when assigning a credit rating, and the controversies associated with CRAs in the performance of what is expected of them.

The Role of CRAs in the Financial System

CRA ratings provide a critical function in the financial system by reducing information asymmetry in the market for debt obligations and private contracts. This role of CRAs has fostered the development of debt markets throughout the world, improving market efficiency and allowing a reliable interest rate structure[1] that can be used for determining compensation for exposure to different degrees of default risk.

The notion of information asymmetry is important to understanding how efficiently capital markets operate, so we'll start with a brief explanation. In a two-party transaction, one party may have more information than the other party.[2] For example, in the sale of a used car, the seller has more information about the car's condition that affects its value than the

1. The structure of interest rates is described in chapter 16.

2. Information asymmetry and its adverse impact on markets was set forth in George Akerlof, "The Market for 'Lemons': Quality Uncertainty and the Market Mechanism," *Quarterly Journal of Economics* 84, no. 3 (1970): 488–500.

potential buyer does. In the case of a debt obligation, at the time of issuance, information asymmetry exists because the issuer (i.e., the seller of the security) knows more about the creditworthiness of the debt obligation than does the buyer (i.e., the investor). Creditworthiness is not directly observable and therefore requires that the buyer acquire information about this attribute of a debt obligation. Buyers can do this by (1) performing their own analysis of creditworthiness based on information obtained from the issuer, (2) retaining the services of a third party to provide an assessment of the creditworthiness of a debt obligation, or (3) using ratings that a CRA provides to the public. The difference between the second and third alternatives is that the third party provides a private evaluation, whereas a CRA evaluation is available to the public and does not require that a fee be paid by the buyer. Instead, the issuer pays a fee, a practice that has raised the problem of a potential conflict of interest, as discussed later in this chapter.[3]

CRAs and Nationally Recognized Statistical Rating Organizations in the United States

Because CRAs play a critical role in credit markets by performing credit analysis on entities issuing securities or private contracts, in the United States, entities that have been recognized by the Securities and Exchange Commission (SEC) to assign ratings are referred to as **nationally recognized statistical rating organizations** (NRSROs). For an entity seeking to be classified as an NRSRO, the SEC's Office of Credit Ratings (created in 2006 by the Credit Rating Reform Act) reviews the entity's position in the market and operational capability. With respect to position in the market, the focus is on whether the entity is nationally recognized. For operational capability, the SEC looks at organizational structure, rating procedure and methodology, financial resources sufficient to maintain independence of the entities it rates, the size and quality of the staff, and independence from the companies that it rates. In addition to its role in the registration of NRSROs, the Office of Credit Ratings monitors the activities and performs periodic examinations of registered NRSROs.

When a CRA applies to the SEC for NRSRO status, it becomes registered with respect to one or more of the following five categories of ratings: (1) financial institutions, brokers, or dealers; (2) insurance companies; (3) corporate issuers; (4) issuers of asset-backed securities; and (5) issuers of government securities, municipal securities, or securities issued by a foreign government.[4] The 10 CRAs registered as NRSROs as of December 2015 and the date of their initial registration are[5]

3. At one time, buyers paid for the service of having a bond rated. However, with the invention of the photocopier and therefore the ability to easily distribute an opinion to those who did not pay for having the rating, the CRAs shifted to an issuer-pay system.

4. Credit Rating Agency Reform Act of 2006, Section 3, http://www.sec.gov/divisions/marketreg/ratingagency/cra-reform-act-2006.pdf.

5. Securities and Exchange Commission, "2015 Summary Report of Commission Staff's Examinations of Each Nationally Recognized Statistical Rating Organization," https://www.sec.gov/ocr/reportspubs/special-studies/nrsro-summary-report-2015.pdf.

NRSRO	Date of Registration
A.M. Best Company Inc. ("AMB")	September 24, 2007
DBRS Inc. ("DBRS")	September 24, 2007
Egan-Jones Ratings Company ("EJR")	December 21, 2007
Fitch Ratings Inc. ("Fitch")	September 24, 2007
HR Ratings de México, S.A. de C.V. ("HR")	November 5, 2012
Japan Credit Rating Agency Ltd. ("JCR")	September 24, 2007
Kroll Bond Rating Agency Inc. ("KBRA")	February 11, 2008
Moody's Investors Service Inc. ("Moody's")	September 24, 2007
Morningstar Credit Ratings LLC ("Morningstar")	June 23, 2008
Standard & Poor's Ratings Services ("S&P")	September 24, 2007

European Regulation of CRAs

CRAs did not perform well in assigning ratings to structured finance products such as subprime mortgage-backed securities. More specifically, these products, which had been awarded the highest credit rating, exhibited poor credit performance. In 2007 and 2008, this systematic overrating led to the collapse of the subprime mortgage-backed securities market and had a ripple effect on global credit markets and the global economy. Another concern was the downgrading of sovereign government debt of certain countries in the eurozone, which some market observers viewed as unjustified. As a result of the global credit crisis and the downgrading of certain sovereign debt, European regulators sought measures to strengthen the regulatory and supervisory framework for CRAs when operating in the European Union.

To so do, the following rules were established by the European Union. First, a regulatory framework and oversight structure was introduced in 2009. More specifically, registration of CRAs was required, they had to provide a sound methodological basis for deriving ratings that had to be transparent to market participants, and they were required to avoid conflicts of interest. When the European Securities and Market Authority was created in 2011, CRAs had to register with this entity, which then regulated the registered CRAs. To deal with regulator concerns about sovereign ratings, in 2013, the rules were amended to address what were perceived to be weaknesses with the CRA rating methodology.

Later in this chapter, we will discuss a major concern with credit ratings: the overreliance of investors on ratings. We will also discuss a major problem with CRAs: conflicts of interest in assigning ratings. The regulations of the European Securities and Market Authority seek to reduce overreliance on credit ratings and potential conflicts of interests of CRAs. In addition, the regulations seek to make the credit rating process more transparent, improve the reliability of ratings, and encourage more entities to participate in the credit rating business.

Credit Rating Systems

Each CRA assigns a rating to the entity or financial instrument being rated. The three major CRAs are Moody's, S&P, and Fitch. The rating systems used by these three rating companies are shown in table 5.1, along with a brief description of each rating.

In all three systems, the term **high grade** means low default risk; that is, there is a high probability of future payments. Moody's uses the symbol Aaa to designate the highest-grade debt obligations, but the other two major CRAs use AAA. The next highest grade is Aa (Moody's) or AA (S&P and Fitch). All CRAs use the symbol A to denote the third grade. The next three grades are Baa or BBB, Ba or BB, and B, respectively. There are also C grades. S&P and Fitch use plus or minus signs to provide a narrower credit quality breakdown within each class, and Moody's uses 1, 2, or 3 for the same purpose. These refinements in the ratings are referred to as rating "notches."

Debt obligations rated triple A (AAA or Aaa) are said to be **prime**; double A (AA or Aa) are of **high quality**; single A issues are referred to as **upper medium grade**, and triple B

Table 5.1
Summary of corporate bond ratings systems investment grade: high creditworthiness.

Moody's	S&P	Fitch	Brief Definition
Aaa	AAA	AAA	Gilt edge, prime, maximum safety
Aa1	AA+	AA+	
Aa2	AA	AA	Very high grade, high quality
Aa3	AA–	AA–	
A1	A+	A+	
A2	A	A	Upper medium grade
A3	A–	A–	
Baa1	BBB+	BBB+	
Baa2	BBB	BBB	Lower medium grade
Baa3	BBB–	BBB–	
Ba1	BB+	BB+	
Ba2	BB	BB	Low grade, speculative
Ba3	BB–	BB–	
B1	B+	B+	
B2	B	B	Highly speculative
B3	B–	B–	
	CCC+		
Caa	CCC	CCC	Substantial risk, in poor standing
	CCC–		
Ca	CC	CC	May be in default, extremely speculative
C	C	C	Even more speculative than those above
	CI		CI = Income bonds; no interest is being paid
		DDD	Default
		DD	
	D	D	

are **medium grade**. Lower-rated debt issues are said to have speculative elements or to be **distinctly speculative**.

If a debt obligation has a rating in the top four categories, it is said to be **investment grade**. When a debt obligation is assigned a rating below the top four categories, it is said to be **noninvestment grade** or more popularly referred to as **high-yield debt** or, unfortunately, misnamed a **junk debt**. Thus, the debt market can be divided into two sectors based on credit ratings: the **investment-grade market** and the **noninvestment-grade market**. This distinction is important, because investment guidelines of institutional investors may prohibit the purchase of noninvestment-grade debt obligations.

If a rated entity receives a different rating from two or more CRAs, the rating is said to be a **split rating**. For example, Moody's might assign a particular bond issue a AA rating, whereas S&P might assign the same issue an A rating.

After the initial rating is assigned, a CRA monitors the debt obligation or issuer. A CRA may announce that it is reviewing a particular credit rating, and it may go further and state that the outcome of the review may result in a **downgrade** (i.e., a lower credit rating being assigned) or an **upgrade** (i.e., a higher credit rating being assigned). The risk that there will be a change in a credit rating that results in a lower rating is referred to as **downgrade risk**. When this announcement is made by a rating agency, the issue or issuer is said to be under **credit watch**.

In addition, to help market participants make credit decisions, for certain types of debt instruments, the CRAs provide information for assessing potential rating downgrades and upgrades. They do so by periodically publishing a **rating transition matrix** or **rating migration matrix**. These tables are available for different transition periods (e.g., one year or five years).

Table 5.2 shows a portion of a hypothetical average one-year transition matrix for corporate bonds. In the table, the first row shows the start-of-the-year rating, and the first column shows the end-of-year rating. Look at the cell where the rating at the beginning of the year

Table 5.2
A hypothetical average one-year rating migration table.

From/To	Aaa	Aa1	…	A1	A2	A3	Baa1…	B1	B2	…	Ca-C	…	
Aaa	87	6.15	…	0.31	0.13	0.02	0.01	…	0.01	0	…	0	…
Aa1	2	74.9	…	1.6	0.53	0.13	0.17	…	0	0	…	0	…
…	…	…	…	…	…	…	…	…	…	…	…	…	…
A1	0.1	0.24	…	75.8	8.08	2.91	0.69	…	0.07	0.02	…	0	…
A2	0.06	0.04	…	5.24	76.11	5.99	2.87	…	0.05	0.04	…	0	…
A3	0.04	0.06	…	1.89	6.71	73.41	6.76	…	0.1	0.05	…	0.01	…
Baa1	0.03	0.04	…	0.26	1.83	6.8	72.55	…	0.38	0.07	…	0.02	…

Note: The top row is the starting rating; the first column is the rating at the end of one year.

is A1 and the rating at the end of the year is A1. This cell represents the percentage of issues rated A1 at the beginning of the year that did not change their rating over the year, that is, experienced no downgrades or upgrades. As can be seen, 75.80% of the issues rated A1 at the start of the year were rated A1 at the end of the year.

Now look at the cell where the rating at the beginning of the year is A1 and at the end of the year is A3. This shows the percentage of issues rated A1 at the beginning of the year that were downgraded to A3 by the end of the year, 2.91%. One can interpret this figure as a probability. In our example, it is the probability that an issue rated A1 will be downgraded to A3 by the end of the year. A rating transition matrix also shows the potential for upgrades. Again, in table 5.3, issues rated A2 at the beginning of the year have a 5.24% chance of being upgraded to A1 at the end of the year.

Use of Ratings by Regulators

Because of the perceived importance of the need for third-party credit analysis, U.S. regulators began to incorporate rating requirements for financial regulatory purposes in 1931. In that year, the Fed and another banking regulator, the Comptroller of the Currency, required that banks use ratings for distinguishing between investment-grade and noninvestment-grade bonds. For all bonds rated noninvestment grade, banks had to report their holdings in terms of market value, which was not the case for investment-grade bonds, where the holdings were reported in terms of the purchase price. The Fed and the Comptroller of the Currency, along with yet another banking regulator, the FDIC, banned the purchase of noninvestment-grade bonds by banks in 1936. The National Association of Insurance Commissioners used ratings for determining capital reserve requirements. Specifically, in 1951, insurers who invested in lower-rated bonds had higher capital reserve requirements imposed.

The term "NRSRO" was adopted in 1975 so that the SEC could determine how much capital brokerage firms and dealer firms must hold for different grades of debt instruments on their balance sheets. This requirement led to greater reliance on NRSROs to define creditworthiness in federal and state regulations. For example, when establishing the appropriate investments in which insurance companies may invest, several state insurance codes rely to different degrees on the ratings of NRSROs.[6]

The U.S. Congress relied on credit ratings when defining such terms as a "mortgage-related security." The Secondary Market Enhancement Act of 1984 stipulated that mortgage-related securities be rated in one of the two highest rating categories by at least one of the CRAs. Credit ratings were employed by the U.S. Department of Education for setting financial responsibility standards for entities that wished to participate in student financial

6. The concept of an NRSRO has been used in the securities law of other countries. El Salvador provides an example. In that country, if a CRA is recognized by the U.S. SEC, it can register as a "classifier of risk."

assistance programs under Title IV of the Higher Education Act of 1965. With greater use of credit ratings by the U.S. Congress in lawmaking and by regulators in monitoring financial institutions, institutional investors adopted ratings in their investment guidelines and mandates for both internal and external managers. Registered investment companies incorporated them into their prospectuses. For example, the SEC's Rule 2a-7 for money market funds, which we discuss in chapter 32, prohibits investment in certain types of securities if they do not have a credit rating.

Nonregulatory Use of Ratings

In addition to regulators' use of credit ratings, four other market participants benefit from the existence of ratings: issuers, asset management firms, brokerage firms and dealers, and transactors in private contracts.

Issuers of debt obligations typically must have at least one rating to market their securities. This is because investors, by investment guidelines or regulation, set forth permissible investments in terms of NRSRO ratings. When an entity issues a security, the yield at which it has to offer the security to the public is the cost of its funds. As explained in chapter 23, the higher the rating is, the lower the funding cost will be.

In chapter 3, we discussed asset management firms. These firms receive mandates from clients. For example (and what is relevant here), some firms have accounts in which they can invest only in debt obligations that receive a certain rating. For example, there are client funds that can be invested only in investment-grade bonds, whereas others can invest primarily in noninvestment-grade bonds. The investment guidelines that an asset management firm must comply with in managing client funds dictate the permissible credit-rated debt obligations. Asset management firms typically have a credit analysis group that performs independent research to analyze the issuer's creditworthiness. Typically the credit analysis group will use ratings as a screen to determine eligible debt obligations in which the firm can invest. As discussed later in this chapter, a major concern for regulators is that investors might rely too much on these ratings.

Brokerage firms and dealers utilize ratings in several ways. First, when offering debt instruments to clients (asset management firms and retail investors), they make sure that the securities offered are consistent with a buyer's investment guidelines. Second, when acting in their capacity as investment advisers for issuers of debt obligations, they discuss with their clients which CRAs to obtain a rating from. Third, as explained earlier, securities firms are required to use ratings for determining net capital requirements, which is the reason the SEC created the NRSRO designation for qualified CRAs.

Finally, private contracts can arise in the financial market between two parties. The most common example is the over-the-counter derivative contract. Ratings are used to determine acceptable counterparties. Brokerage firms and dealers determine the minimum rating for a counterparty using investment guidelines and, where applicable, regulatory requirements.

Concerns Regarding CRAs

Ratings are opinions and not guarantees. So it is not surprising that defaults have occurred despite a debt issue initially receiving a high investment-grade rating. However, some of the miscues by CRAs in the past suggested to regulators that greater oversight of CRAs was in order. In the 1980s, for example, new, legally untested bond structures were introduced into the U.S. municipal bond market. The best-known example is the Washington Public Supply System's revenue bonds (nicknamed "Whoops" bonds), issued for five nuclear power plants (Projects 1, 2, 3, 4, and 5) in 1980. S&P and Moody's rated the bonds for Projects 1, 2, and 3 triple A and the bonds for Projects 4 and 5 A– (by Moody's) and A+ (by S&P). Only one of the nuclear power plants was completed, the issuer defaulting on $2.5 billion, the largest municipal bond default at the time. In 1994, Orange County, California, defaulted on bonds it had issued that had been rated AA/Aa by both Moody's and S&P, leading to the bankruptcy filing of that county. At the time, it was the largest bankruptcy of a municipality in U.S. history.

In the 1990s, alternatives were considered by the SEC with respect to how to deal with the use of NRSRO ratings when implementing rules set forth by the SEC and the designation of entities as NRSROs. Basically, the SEC decided to continue the use of NRSRO ratings and the designation of NRSROs. The alternatives that the SEC considered were (1) eliminating reliance on NRSRO ratings and not designating an NRSRO and (2) putting into place more direct and expanded oversight of CRAs. In 1997, the SEC sought comments from market participants for the attributes of a rating organization to qualify as an NRSRO and also set forth a formal application process for a rating organization seeking NRSRO status. Three other issues for which comments were solicited by the SEC were whether to (1) prohibit an NRSRO from charging issuers a fee based on the issuance size of a transaction (because of concern that a size-based fee would compromise an NRSRO's objectivity); (2) mandate that an NRSRO make its ratings generally available to the public, not just to its subscribers; and (3) substitute under certain circumstances statistical models of default risk for ratings. The SEC did not act on these issues at that time.

The major concerns and increased awareness of the ratings assigned by CRAs began in the early 2000s as a result of the well-publicized bankruptcies of major corporations that were initially highly rated. The first was Enron Corporation, whose bonds carried an investment-grade rating just days before it filed for bankruptcy in 2001—the biggest corporate bankruptcy in U.S. history. In 2002, there was the bankruptcy of WorldCom. Its bonds were rated investment grade three months prior to its bankruptcy filing. In March 2002, the bonds of Global Crossing were rated investment grade; in July 2002, it defaulted on its loans. There were California utilities that were rated A—two weeks prior to defaulting. The bonds of AT&T Canada carried an investment-grade rating in February 2002; the company defaulted in September 2002.

As a result of the Enron bankruptcy in 2001, Congress reviewed the issues relating to CRAs. Two hearings were held in 2002 (January and March) by the Senate Committee on Governmental Affairs. The March 20 hearing, titled "Rating the Raters: Enron and the Credit Rating Agencies,"[7] focused specifically on the role of CRAs in the Enron bankruptcy. Testimony by one prominent legal expert argued that Congress should instruct regulatory authorities to discard the use of ratings, because ratings failed to provide useful or timely information about an issuer's creditworthiness. The conclusion of the Senate Committee on Governmental Affairs' staff report, titled *Financial Oversight of Enron: The SEC and Private-Sector Watchdogs*,[8] concluded that the CRAs exhibited a disappointing lack of diligence in their credit analysis of Enron.

More recently, attacks on the performance of ratings assigned by CRAs to structured products leading up to the 2007 subprime mortgage crisis have raised further concerns in the United States and other major countries. The focus of the investigations both in the United States and in Europe has been on two issues. The first is the influence of the issuer on the ratings assigned to securities that it issues. The second is investors' overreliance or exclusive reliance on ratings.

Influence of the Issuer on Ratings

When the credit rating business started, users/investors of ratings would pay the CRA. That is, the compensation was a **user-pay model**. The ratings were published monthly, and subscribers paid for the books. Enter that great innovation in the 1970s: the photocopier. Because all or portions of the ratings book could be copied and distributed, the user-pay model was no longer feasible for CRAs as a business model. To survive, the CRAs shifted from a user-pay model to **issuer-pay model**, wherein the payment for the assignment of a rating became the responsibility of the issuer. Although an issuer could refuse to obtain any rating, typically, they would obtain at least one rating from one of the CRAs, because it would be difficult to issue a debt obligation without a rating. But the issuer-pay model can result in a potential for conflicts of interest, which calls into question the objectivity of ratings. More specifically, it has been argued that issuers will select a CRA from which it can obtain the highest possible rating, and that, in an attempt to attract issuers, a CRA will compromise its rating criteria to the benefit of the issuer.

This potential conflict of interest has given rise to the **rating shopping hypothesis** about the behavior of issuers in their dealings with CRA. This hypothesis asserts that an issuer will search (i.e., shop) among the CRAs for the one that provides the best credit rating.[9] Another

7. "Rating the Raters: Enron and the Credit Rating Agencies: Hearings before the Senate Committee on Governmental Affairs," 107th Cong. 471 (March 20, 2002).

8. Report of the Staff of the Senate Committee on Governmental Affairs, *Financial Oversight of Enron: The SEC and Private-Sector Watchdogs* (October 7, 2002).

9. See, for example, Francesco Sangiorgi, Jonathan Sokobin, and Chester Spatt, "Credit-Rating Shopping, Selection and the Equilibrium Structure of Ratings," working paper, Carnegie Mellon University, Pittsburgh, PA, 2009; Patrick Bolton, Xavier Freixas, and Joel D. Shapiro, "The Credit Ratings Game," *Journal of Finance* 67

form of the rating shopping hypothesis relates to shopping for as many ratings as possible, even if it is at the same rating level. Moreover, there is a concern that when monitoring issuers that it has rated, a CRA may be hesitant to downgrade the debt of those issuers because in the future, downgraded issuers may be reluctant to have new debt rated by that CRA.

The counterargument is that CRAs have a strong "incentive to build and protect their reputations for being independent and objective."[10] A CRA's success in the marketplace depends in large part on the reputational capital that it builds, because the issuers will not continue to pay for ratings from a CRA that investors believe may have been biased in the past. Thus, a CRA's reputation for issuing honest and objective ratings is perhaps its greatest marketable asset, and reputational incentives to issue objective ratings are a strong countervailing force acting against any potential conflict of interest engendered by the issuer-pay model. In fact, an empirical study conducted by two members of the Federal Reserve Board found "no evidence consistent with rating agencies acting in the interests of issuers due to a conflict of interest" and that "instead, rating agencies appear to be relatively responsive to reputation concerns and so protect the interests of investors."[11]

Investors' Overreliance on Ratings

The increased adoption by regulators and market participants elevated the role of ratings. It has been argued that the unintended consequence is the overreliance on ratings by investors, asset managers, and regulators. There is growing concern that investors, particularly institutional investors, rely on ratings without performing their own credit analysis and that herd behavior results from relying solely on ratings. A report by the SEC acknowledged the growing dependence on ratings by investors and regulators not only for public debt offerings but also for private debt arrangements. For example, ratings are used in determining collateral requirements by counterparties for non-exchange traded derivatives and by dealers in lending transactions. Two studies suggest that overreliance on the ratings of emerging market sovereign bonds was a destabilizing factor in the 1997–1998 Asian financial crisis.[12]

In April 2008, a report by the Financial Stability Forum states: "Investors should address their over-reliance on ratings. Investor associations should consider developing standards

(2012): 85–111; Emmanuel Farhi, Josh Lerner, and Jean Tirole, "Fear of Rejection? Tiered Certification and Transparency," *Rand Journal of Economics* 44 (2013): 610–631; Christian C. Opp, Marcus M. Opp, and Milton Harris, "Rating Agencies in the Face of Regulation," *Journal of Financial Economics* 108 (2013): 46–61.

10. Daniel M. Covitz and Paul Harrison, "Testing Conflicts of Interest at Bond Rating Agencies with Market Anticipation: Evidence That Reputation Incentives Dominate," FEDS Working Paper 2003–68 (Washington, DC: Federal Reserve Board, 2003): p. 2, http://www.federalreserve.gov/pubs/feds/2003/200368/200368abs.html.

11. Covitz and Harrison, "Testing Conflicts of Interest," p. 23.

12. See Giovanni Ferri, L.-G. Liu, and Joseph E. Stiglitz, "The Procyclical Role of Rating Agencies: Evidence from the East Asian Crisis," *Economic Notes* 28 (1999): 335–355; Helmut Reisen and Julia von Maltzan, "Boom and Bust and Sovereign Ratings," *International Finance* 2 (1999): 273–293.

of due diligence and credit analysis for investing in structured products."[13] In response, in late 2008, such industry associations as the European Fund and Asset Management Association, the European Securitization Forum, and the Investment Management Association prepared industry guidelines to address the issue of overreliance on ratings for securitized products.

Proposals both in the United States and in Europe have sought to reverse the alleged overreliance or sole reliance on ratings. Section 939A of the Dodd-Frank Act resulted in the SEC "adopting amendments today to remove references to credit ratings in rules and forms promulgated under the Securities Act and the Exchange Act."[14] The SEC stated:

> While we recognize that credit ratings play a significant role in the investment decisions of many investors, we want to avoid using credit ratings in a manner that suggests in any way a "seal of approval" on the quality of any particular credit rating or rating agency, including any nationally recognized statistical rating organization ("NRSRO"). Similarly, the legislative history indicates that Congress, in adopting Section 939A, intended to "reduce reliance on credit ratings."

A similar tack has been taken for banks in the eurozone. In July 2011, the European Commission's internal markets commissioner, Michel Barnier, stated in a speech to the European Securities and Markets Authority, "To limit overreliance, we will be strengthening the requirement for banks to carry out their own analysis of risk and not rely on external ratings in an automatic and mechanical way."[15]

Factors Considered When Assigning Ratings

As discussed earlier in the chapter, CRAs rate a wide range of debt obligations by different issuers. Here we briefly describe the factors that they consider when rating the debt of sovereign governments, corporations, and U.S. state and local governments. All CRAs consider the same factors. They differ as to what weight they assign to each factor when determining their final rating.

Sovereign Government Debt

Sovereign debt is the obligation of a country's central government. For the reasons discussed subsequently, two sovereign debt ratings are assigned by credit rating agencies, a **local currency debt rating** and a **foreign currency debt rating**.

The three major CRAs all assign ratings to sovereign bonds. The two general categories of risk analyzed when assigning ratings are economic risk and political risk. The former category is an assessment of the ability of a government to satisfy its obligations. Both quantitative and qualitative analyses are used to assess economic risk.

13. "Report on Enhancing Market and Institutional Resilience" (Financial Stability Forum, 2008), 37.
14. SEC Releases 33-9245 and 34-64975; File S7-18-08, Washington, DC.
15. Available at http://europa.eu/rapid/press-release_SPEECH-11-514_en.htm.

Political risk is an assessment of the willingness of a government to satisfy its obligations. A government might be able to pay but unwilling to do so. Political risk is assessed based on qualitative analysis of the economic and political factors that influence a government's economic policies.

The reason for distinguishing between local debt ratings and foreign currency debt ratings is that historically, the default frequency differs by the currency denomination of the debt. Specifically, defaults have been greater on foreign currency–denominated debt. The reason for the difference in default rates for local currency debt and foreign currency debt is that if a government is willing to raise taxes and control its domestic financial system, it can generate sufficient local currency to meet its local currency debt obligation. This is not the case with foreign currency–denominated debt. A national government must purchase foreign currency to meet a debt obligation in that foreign currency and therefore has less control with respect to its exchange rate. Thus, a significant depreciation of the local currency relative to a foreign currency in which a debt obligation is denominated will impair a national government's ability to satisfy such obligations.

The implication is that the factors analyzed to assess the creditworthiness of a national government's local currency debt and foreign currency debt will differ to some extent. When assessing the credit quality of local currency debt, for example, S&P emphasizes domestic government policies that foster or impede timely debt service. For foreign currency debt, credit analysis by S&P focuses on the interaction of domestic and foreign government policies. S&P analyzes a country's balance of payments and the structure of its external balance sheet. The areas of analysis with respect to its external balance sheet are the net public debt, total net external debt, and net external liabilities.

Corporate Debt

To assess the default risk of a corporate issuer or a corporate debt obligation, CRAs generally look at three areas: (1) the protections afforded to debtholders that are provided by covenants limiting management's discretion, (2) the collateral available to the debtholder should the issuer fail to make the required payments, and (3) the ability of an issuer to make the contractual payments to debtholders.

There are covenants imposed on management. Covenants establish rules for several important areas of operation for corporate management. These provisions are safeguards for the debtholder. Indenture provisions are analyzed carefully when assigning a rating to a bond or loan. When assessing the ability of an issuer to service its debt (i.e., make timely payments of interest and principal), the ability of an issuer to generate cash flow goes considerably beyond the analysis of the myriad financial ratios and cash flow measures that can be used as a basic assessment of a company's financial risk. CRAs also look at qualitative factors, such as the issuer's business risk and corporate governance risk, to assess the issuer's ability to pay.

Business risk is the risk associated with generating operating cash flows. Operating cash flows are uncertain, because the revenues and the expenditures composing the cash flows are uncertain. Revenues depend on conditions in the economy as a whole and in the industry in which the company operates, as well as on the actions of management and its competitors. To assess business risk, the three major CRAs look at the same general areas. S&P states that when analyzing business risk, it considers country risk, industry characteristics, company position, product portfolio/marketing, technology, cost efficiency, strategic and operational management competence, and profitability/peer group comparisons.[16] Moody's investigates industry trends, national political and regulatory environment, management quality and attitude toward risk taking, and basic operating and competitive position.[17] Fitch reviews industry trends, operating environment, market position, and management.[18]

Corporate governance issues have to do with (1) the ownership structure of the corporation, (2) the practices followed by management, and (3) policies for financial disclosure. The eagerness of corporate management to present favorable results to shareholders and the market has been a major factor in several of the corporate scandals in recent years and is what is referred to as **corporate governance risk**. Chief executive officers, chief financial officers, and the board of directors are being held directly accountable for disclosures in financial statements and other corporate decisions. Certain mechanisms can mitigate the likelihood that management will act in its own self-interest. These mechanisms fall into two general categories. In the first category are mechanisms that more strongly align the interests of management with those of shareholders. Such an alignment can be accomplished by granting management an economically meaningful equity interest in the company. Also, manager compensation can be linked to the performance of the company's common stock.

In the second category are the company's internal corporate control systems, which can provide a way to effectively monitor the performance and decision-making behavior of management.

In addition to corporate governance, CRAs look at the quality of management when assessing a corporation's ability to pay. To assess management quality, Moody's examines the business strategies and policies formulated by management. The factors Moody's considers are strategic direction, financial philosophy, conservatism, track record, succession planning, and control systems.

Having achieved an understanding of a corporation's business risk and corporate governance risk, the CRAs move on to assessing financial risk. The analysis involves traditional ratio analysis and other factors affecting the firm's financing. These measures, which are described in most books on investment management, address interest coverage, leverage, cash

16. Standard & Poor's Corporation, *Corporate Rating Criteria* (New York, 2005), 20.

17. Moody's Investors Service, *Industrial Company Rating Methodology* (New York, July 1998), 3.

18. Fitch Ratings, *Corporate Rating Methodology* (New York, n.d.), 1–2.

flow, net assets, and working capital. Once these measures are calculated for the firm being analyzed, CRAs compare them with similar measures for other firms in the same industry.

U.S. Municipal Debt

The market for subgovernment debt is the subject of chapter 21. We'll describe here the factors that CRAs consider when assigning ratings to subnational entities in the United States, more specifically, the debt of state and local governments. As explained in chapter 21, there are two basic types of municipal security structures: tax-backed debt and revenue bonds. Tax-backed debt obligations are some form of tax revenue. The common type of tax-backed debt is a general obligation debt. The second basic type of security structure is found in a revenue bond. Such bonds are issued for either project or enterprise financings where the bond issuers pledge to the bondholders the revenues generated by the operating projects being financed. Examples include airport revenue bonds, college and university revenue bonds, hospital revenue bonds, single-family mortgage revenue bonds, multifamily revenue bonds, public power revenue bonds, resource recovery revenue bonds, toll road and gas tax revenue bonds, and water revenue bonds.

To evaluate tax-backed debt, the CRAs assess information in four basic categories. The first category includes information on the issuer's debt structure and overall debt burden. The second category relates to the issuer's ability and political discipline to maintain sound budgetary policy. The focus of attention here is usually on the issuer's general operating funds and whether the issuer has maintained balanced budgets over three to five years. The third category involves the specific local taxes and intergovernmental revenues available to the issuer, as well as historical information on both tax collection rates (which are important when looking at property tax levies) and the dependence of local budgets on specific revenue sources. The last category of information necessary for the credit analysis is an assessment of the issuer's overall socioeconomic environment. The determinations to be made for this category include trends of local employment distribution and composition, population growth, real estate property valuation, and personal income, among other economic factors.

Although numerous security structures can be used for revenue bonds, the key factor in rating such debt is whether the project being financed will generate sufficient cash flow to satisfy the obligation to bondholders. The analysis is comparable to the factors considered when rating corporate debt.

Key Points

- Credit rating agencies (CRAs) play a critical role in credit markets by performing credit analysis on entities issuing securities or private contracts and casting their opinions in the form of a credit rating.

- CRAs reduce information asymmetry in the market for debt obligations and private contracts.
- CRAs recognized by the SEC are classified as nationally recognized statistical rating organization (NRSROs).
- The three major CRAs are Moody's Investors Service, Standard & Poor's Rating Services, and Fitch Ratings.
- In terms of credit rating, the debt market is divided into two sectors: the investment-grade market and the noninvestment-grade market.
- A debt obligation is investment grade if its ratings are in the top four rating categories.
- A debt obligation assigned a rating below the top four categories is said to be noninvestment grade, or more popularly referred to as high-yield debt.
- The compensation system for assigning ratings has shifted from a user-pay system to an issuer-pay system.
- A major concern with the issuer-pay system is that it may result in conflicts of interest, because it can result in rating shopping and the reluctance of a CRA to downgrade an issuer.
- Because of the importance placed on credit ratings by regulators, a major concern is that investors overrely or exclusively rely on ratings rather than performing their own credit analysis.
- Sovereign debt, the obligation of a country's central government, is assigned two credit ratings, a local currency debt rating and a foreign currency debt rating, because historically, the default frequency differs according to the currency denomination of the debt.
- The CRAs analyze both quantitative and qualitative factors when assessing the economic risk and political risk of sovereign debt issues.
- When assigning a credit rating to corporate debt, the CRAs assess the protections set forth in the loan agreement, the collateral available for the debtholders should the issuer fail to make the required payments, and the capacity of the issuer to fulfill its payment obligations.
- When assessing the ability of a corporate issuer to service its debt, CRAs assess the issuer's business risk, corporate governance risk, and financial risk.
- When assessing business risk (the risk associated with operating cash flows), some of the main factors considered are industry characteristics and trends, the company's market and competitive positions, management characteristics, and the national political and regulatory environment.
- Assessing corporate governance risk involves assessing (1) the ownership structure of the corporation, (2) the practices followed by management, and (3) policies for financial disclosure.

• Assessing corporate financial risk involves traditional ratio analysis and valuation of other factors affecting the firm's financing.

• To assess the debt of municipal issuers in the United States, a different type of credit evaluation is used for tax-backed debt and revenue-backed debt.

• Four basic categories are analyzed when assigning a credit rating to tax-backed debt: (1) the issuer's debt structure and overall debt burden, (2) the issuer's ability and political discipline to maintain sound budgetary policy, (3) the specific local taxes and intergovernmental revenues available to the issuer, and (4) the issuer's overall socioeconomic environment.

• For revenue bonds, the key factor in rating such debt is whether the project being financed will generate sufficient cash flow to satisfy the obligation due bondholders.

Questions

1. What role does a CRA play in the financial market?

2. What is the relationship between a CRA and a nationally recognized statistical rating organization?

3. Explain whether you agree or disagree with the following statement: "A nationally recognized statistical rating organization is permitted to provide a credit rating for any type of debt obligation."

4. In January 2003, the U.S. SEC published a report on the role and function of CRAs in the operation of the securities markets. Part 2 of the report provides a background discussion of how credit ratings have become incorporated into the U.S. regulatory framework. The report states:

> During the past 30 years, regulators, including the Commission, have increasingly used credit ratings to help monitor the risk of investments held by regulated entities, and to provide an appropriate disclosure framework for securities of differing risks.[19]

Give at least two examples of how regulators have used credit ratings to do the stipulated activities.

5. Why is the distinction between investment grade and noninvestment important for investors?

6. What is meant by a rating "notch"?

7. What is a rating transition matrix, and how can it be used by an investor?

8. What is the concern with the issuer-pay model used by credit rating agencies?

19. U.S. Securities and Exchange Commission, "Report on the Role and Function of Credit Rating Agencies in the Operation of the Securities Markets: As Required by Section 702(b) of the Sarbanes-Oxley Act of 2002" (Washington, DC: January 2003), 5.

9. What is meant by the "rating shopping hypothesis"?

10. Why is there concern that investors overrely on credit ratings when making investment decisions?

11. Why do CRAs assign both a local currency debt rating and a foreign currency debt rating?

12. When assigning a credit rating, the CRAs analyze a company's business risk. What is meant by business risk?

13. What is meant by corporate governance risk, and why do credit rating agencies employ it?

14. a. Why do credit rating agencies evaluate municipal debt obligations of U.S. entities that are tax-backed and revenue-backed in a different way?

b. Which type of municipal debt is analyzed in a manner similar to corporate debt?

6 Depository Institutions: Activities and Characteristics

CONTENTS

Learning Objectives

After reading this chapter, you will understand:

- what a depository institution is;
- how a depository institution generates income;
- who the U.S. federal regulators of depository institutions are;
- the basic principles of the regulation of depository institutions;
- what the soundness and safety principle is for depository institutions;
- the rating of banks using the CAMELS system;
- the public backstops available to depository institutions;
- what the Basel Accords are, and the pillars on which they are based;
- what risk-based capital requirements are for depository institutions and how they are calculated;
- the regulation of systemic risk by federal banking agencies;
- the types of income-generating activities of depository institutions;
- how depository institutions obtain funds;
- the method for determining reserve requirements;
- the rationale for depository insurance, and how the insurance is priced;
- what thrifts are, and the differences between thrifts and banks; and
- what the shadow banking system is, and the concerns with this form of credit intermediation.

Depository institutions include commercial banks (or simply, "banks") and thrifts (savings associations and credit unions). These financial intermediaries accept deposits. Deposits represent the liabilities (debt) of the deposit-accepting institution. With the funds raised through deposits and other funding sources, depository institutions make direct loans to various entities and also invest in securities. Their income is derived from two sources: the income generated from the loans they make and the securities they purchase, and fee income.

Depository institutions are highly regulated because of the important role they play in the financial system. Deposit accounts at banks are the principal means by which individuals and business entities make payments. In all countries, banks are subject to government regulation that imposes specific requirements, restrictions, and guidelines. The basis for bank regulations are (1) licensing and supervision (the need to have a license to engage in the banking business), (2) minimum requirements (the most important of which is bank minimum capital requirements), and (3) market discipline (banks must disclose financial and other information to depositors and other creditors).

Governments implement monetary policy through their banking system. Because of their important role, depository institutions are afforded special privileges, such as access to some form of deposit insurance and access to a government entity that provides funds for liquidity for emergency needs. An important global banking practice is deposit insurance, which is practiced in many countries to protect bank depositors from losses resulting from a bank's inability to honor withdrawals. The International Association of Deposit Insurers, formed to enhance deposit insurance effectiveness, has 83 members globally. Special privileges, such as deposit insurance, are referred to as "public backstops."

As of year-end 2017, the 10 largest banks in the world as measured by the market value of their common stock in order of size were JPMorgan Chase & Co. ($376 billion), Bank of America Corp. ($313 billion), Industrial & Commercial Bank of China ($312 billion), Wells Fargo ($306 billion), China Construction Bank ($228 billion), HSBC Holdings ($205 billion), Citigroup ($200 billion), Bank of China ($166 billion), Royal Bank of Canada ($117 billion), and Commonwealth Bank of Australia ($108 billion).

In this chapter, we look at depository institutions, with a primary focus on banks. We focus on the U.S. banking system, because it reflects the banking systems in other advanced economies. At the end of the chapter, we discuss a sector of the financial system referred to as the "shadow banking system" and the concerns associated with the activities of that nontraditional banking system.

Regulators of U.S. Banks

Today we are aware of the role of the federal government in the regulation of commercial banks, but prior to 1863, the federal government played almost no role in their regulation. Instead, banks were regulated only at the state level. Realizing the need for a stronger banking system, the U.S. Congress passed the National Bank Act in 1863 authorizing the federal chartering of national banks. The Office of the Comptroller of the Currency (OCC) was created and empowered with providing national bank charters and regulation of national banks. As a result, there existed state and national banks, a structure popularly referred to as "dual banking." The dual banking structure still exists today, with every state having its own state banking department responsible for regulating banks chartered by the state.

Realizing the need for banks to obtain liquidity during periods of economic stress, the federal government wanted to establish a banking system that would have an entity that banks could borrow from, a sort of "lender of last resort." The U.S. Congress accomplished this with the passage of the Federal Reserve Act of 1913.This legislation established the Federal Reserve System (FRS) as the central banking system. Banks that were members of the FRS were entitled to all the services that the FRS was empowered to provide by the legislation. We discuss these services later in this section. The legislation required that all nationally chartered banks become members of the FRS. State-chartered banks had the option to become members. Most state-chartered banks elected not to become members.

Today, state-chartered banks can be classified as state banks that are members of the FRS and nonmember state banks. With the passage of the Depository Institutions Deregulation and Monetary Control Act of 1980, the capital requirements that we shall discuss for member banks were also applied to state-chartered nonmember banks.

Today, banks are regulated and supervised by several federal and state government entities. "Bank regulation" refers to a federal agency's authority to issue specific regulations and guidelines that govern the operations, activities, and acquisitions of banking organizations.

Once those regulations and guidelines are in place, bank supervision involves monitoring and examining the condition of individual banks and determining whether they are compliant with the regulations. Enforcement powers are granted to federal agencies if a bank fails to comply with regulations or is found to have financial difficulties. Below we discuss the three federal agencies that regulate banks: the Federal Reserve, the OCC, and the FDIC.[1] Before doing so, we discuss briefly the various types of bank structure.

The simplest form of bank structure is a national bank that has no subsidiaries. A more complex form is a national bank that has two subsidiaries, an operating subsidiary that performs typical bank activities (discussed later) and a financial subsidiary that undertakes activities that are financial in nature. There are two types of holding company structures. (A holding company is one that owns other companies.) In a bank holding company, the parent holding company has as part of its holdings a national bank and a state bank. In a financial holding company, the parent holding company has as its holdings a national bank and a securities company. Basically, financial holding companies are conglomerates that are allowed to engage in a wide range of financially related activities. Large banks are typically financial holding companies, and the activities performed by the securities company are the investment banking activities that we describe in chapter 9.

The Federal Reserve

The Board of Governors of the Federal Reserve System (or simply, the Fed) was established in 1913. Its objective is to regulate banks and certain other types of depository institutions through bank reserves so as to provide stability to the banking sector through its authority to conduct national monetary policy. In addition, the Fed has the authority to conduct safety and soundness examinations of bank holding companies, the U.S. branches of foreign banks, and state-chartered banks that are members of the FRS.

The responsibilities of the Fed were significantly expanded by the Financial Services Modernization Act of 1999 (also called the Gramm-Leach-Bliley Act) and the Dodd-Frank Wall Street Reform and Consumer Protection Act of 2010 (hereafter the Dodd-Frank Act). The former made the Fed the umbrella regulator for financial holding companies. The Dodd-Frank Act made the Fed the primary regulator of all financial firms (bank and nonbanks) that the Financial Stability Oversight Council (FSOC) designates as systemically significant,[2] as well as the safety and soundness authority over the payment, clearing, and

1. It is possible for different parts of a bank to be regulated by different regulators.

2. See chapter TK for a discussion of SIFIs.

settlement systems that the FSOC identifies as systemically important and that are not regulated by the Commodities Futures Trading Commission (CFTC) or the SEC. Consequently, not only does the Fed have the power of examining banks, it now also oversees the country's systemic risk.

Office of the Comptroller of the Currency

The OCC is an independent bureau of the U.S. Department of the Treasury.[3] The head of the OCC is the comptroller of the currency and is appointed by the president of the United States, with the advice and consent of the U.S. Senate. It is the responsibility of the OCC to charter, regulate, and supervise both national banks and federal savings associations. The Dodd-Frank Act made the OCC the primary regulator of federal savings associations. The OCC also supervises federal branches and agencies of foreign banks. The OCC's goal in supervising banks and federal savings associations is to "ensure that they operate in a safe and sound manner and in compliance with laws requiring fair treatment of their customers and fair access to credit and financial products."[4] To fulfill its responsibility, the OCC has examiners who are responsible for analyzing loan and investment portfolios, analyzing funds management, rating banks (using the system described later in this chapter), and determining compliance with consumer banking laws for national banks and federal savings associations with less than $10 billion in assets. Furthermore, the National Risk Committee of the OCC monitors the federal banking system to identify any potential or actual threats to the system's safety and soundness.

As with the Fed, the OCC's responsibilities include overseeing systemic risk. One way in which it does so is by surveying the underwriting practices of those it regulates—through the Survey of Credit Underwriting Practices—which identifies trends in lending standards and credit risk for the most common types of commercial and retail credit offered by national banks and federal savings associations.

Federal Deposit Insurance Corporation

The FDIC is an independent federal agency that (1) insures deposits, (2) examines individual banks, (3) supervises banks, and (4) resolves both troubled or failed banks and any financial institution (bank or nonbank) that is designated a SIFI. Funding for the FDIC comes from the insurance premiums paid by banks and thrift institutions for deposit coverage and from interest the FDIC earns on investing in U.S. Treasury securities.

The FDIC is given broad authority to utilize deposit insurance funds to assist depository institutions if a determination is made that there is systemic threat to the financial system. This authority was granted to the FDIC by the Federal Deposit Insurance Corporation Improvement

3. In chapter 20, we discuss the U.S. Department of the Treasury and the bureaus that compose it.

4. See the web page http://www.occ.gov/about/what-we-do/mission/index-about.html.

Act of 1991. The involvement of the FDIC as the 2008 financial crisis worsened serves as an example of its functions. In October 2008, the FDIC made a determination of an increase in systemic risk to the system. First, with the approval of Congress as provided for in the Emergency Economic Stabilization Act of 2008, the maximum amount of any deposit insured by the FDIC was temporarily increased to $250,000 from its previous level of $100,000. (Subsequently the Dodd-Frank Act made the $250,000 ceiling permanent.) Second, the FDIC agreed to temporarily guarantee both all noninterest-bearing accounts without consideration for the $250,000 insurance ceiling and certain newly issued debt by banks, thrifts, and certain holding companies. (Subsequently the Dodd-Frank Act explicitly authorized the FDIC to guarantee bank debt.)

FDIC resolution role for troubled banks One of the most critical roles of the FDIC is to provide a resolution when an FDIC-insured bank is about to fail. The resolution process followed by the FDIC is supposed to be executed in a manner that minimizes disruption to the banking system and maximizes value.

The FDIC assumes two roles in the resolution process. First, because it is an insurer, the FDIC protects all of the failing bank's depositors for the amount of their insured deposits by using one of the three resolution methods discussed later in this chapter. Second, the FDIC serves as the bank's receiver and administers the receivership estate for all creditors. These two roles played by the FDIC—protecting depositors in its insurer role and acting as receiver for all creditors—are functionally different.

The FDIC can employ three basic resolution mechanisms for failing insured banks: (1) purchase and assumption transactions, (2) deposit payoffs, and (3) open bank assistance transactions.

In a **purchase and assumption transaction**, a bank purchases some or all of the assets of a failed bank and assumes some or all of the liabilities, including all insured deposits. To complete the transaction, the acquiring (assuming) bank occasionally may receive some form of assistance from the FDIC.

In a **deposit payoff transaction**, the failing bank is closed, and the FDIC is appointed receiver. In its role as insurer, the FDIC immediately pays all depositors with insured funds the full amount of their insured deposits. Depositors whose deposits are uninsured and other general creditors of the bank do not receive any payment but instead receive from the FDIC in its role as receiver a certificate entitling the holder to a portion of the proceeds received by the FDIC when the failed bank's assets are liquidated. The certificate is called a receivership certificate.

In the third resolution method, an **open bank assistance transaction**, the FDIC in its role of insurer provides financial assistance to a bank that is in danger of failing. The FDIC does so by making loans to the bank, purchasing the assets of the bank, or placing additional deposits in the bank. This resolution method is no longer commonly used because of restrictions imposed by legislation in the early 1990s on what the FDIC can do.

FDIC resolution role for systemically important financial institutions Prior to 2008, the FDIC had the authority to resolve troubled insured banks and thrifts. However, it did not have the right to take any action against other financial institutions that were not insured banks or thrifts. So, for example, the FDIC did not have the authority to place into an FDIC receivership a holding company or an affiliate of an insured bank or any other nonbank financial company that might pose a systemic threat to the financial system.

The best-known example of these financial entities excluded from FDIC receivership is Lehman Brothers, whose failure caused major disruption to global financial markets. The resolution could potentially have been realized through the U.S. bankruptcy courts. However, the bankruptcy of Lehman Brothers in October 2008 clearly demonstrated that the bankruptcy system was not equipped to deal with the swift resolution of a financial institution whose failure posed a major threat to the financial system.

Because of this regulatory gap in the government's resolution authority, the Dodd-Frank Act extended the FDIC's receivership power and authority to allow it to effect an orderly liquidation of troubled financial institutions (banks and nonbanks) designated as **global systemically important banks** (G-SIBs) by the FSOC. The act requires that all bank holding companies with assets of more than $50 billion designated as G-SIBs prepare a resolution plan that could be achieved through the U.S. Bankruptcy Code. The plan—commonly referred to as a "living will"—must describe how, in the event of material financial distress or failure, the G-SIB would be resolved in a rapid and orderly manner under the U.S. Bankruptcy Code.

The U.S. Congress felt that bankruptcy would be the preferred procedure for resolving the failure of a G-SIB. However, it realized that it might be unrealistic to expect U.S. bankruptcy courts to do so in a manner that would reduce the risk of a systemic threat to the financial system. For this reason, it included in the Dodd-Frank Act a provision that grants the FDIC broad backup authority to place any G-SIB into an FDIC receivership process.

The FDIC can use this authority if (1) no reasonable private sector solution is available to avert the default of the G-SIB and (2) a resolution that could potentially be obtained through the bankruptcy process would have serious adverse effects on the financial system. This is not a blanket authority granted to the FDIC. Instead, the Dodd-Frank Act requires a two-thirds vote of the Federal Reserve Board and the board of the FDIC and a determination by the secretary of the Treasury to carry out this authority.

Bank Regulation

Bank regulation has three components: (1) safety and soundness, (2) deposit insurance, and (3) systemic risk. We described the role of bank regulators with respect to systemic risk earlier in the chapter. Our focus here is on the first two components.

Safety and Soundness Regulation

In broad terms, safety and soundness regulation and supervision involve assessing a bank's likelihood of defaulting and, if a default does occur, assessing the magnitude of the losses that will be realized by the bank's creditors and stockholders.

Bank ratings To measure the safety and soundness of a bank, an examiner conducts on-site examinations with a focus on reviewing and rating a bank's performance, financial condition, and regulatory compliance with regulations. The result of the on-site examination is a bank rating. The use of a bank rating system increases the likelihood that bank examiners will be consistent in their examinations of banks while allowing for differences that exist among banks owing to bank size and the complexity and riskiness of a bank's revenue-generating activities. The system used to rate banks that has been adopted by federal bank regulators is the CAMELS rating system, which stands for *c*apital adequacy, *a*sset quality, *m*anagement, *e*arnings, *l*iquidity, and *s*ensitivity to market risk. It has the elements shown in table 6.1.

Table 6.1
Elements of CAMELS bank ratings.

Element	Description
Capital adequacy	A capital adequacy assessment entails assessing a bank relative to its risks, such as credit risk, market risk, and other risks associated with the bank's financial position on both balance sheet and off-balance-sheet items.
Asset quality	An asset quality assessment entails assessing existing and potential credit risk associated with a bank's portfolio, as well as risks associated with the bank's off-balance-sheet items. Included in this analysis are recent changes in a bank's default rate on loans, exposure to counterparty risk, the performance of the portfolio, and changes in the marketability of assets.
Management	A management assessment involves assessing the corporate governance of a bank by its senior management team and board of directors. Management oversight and systems in place to deal with compliance and interaction with external auditors, for example, are examined.
Earnings	Current earnings and their sustainability are examined to rate a bank's earnings quantity and quality.
Liquidity	A bank's liquidity is assessed by looking at the bank's ability to fulfill its expected funding needs in a timely manner without incurring excessive losses that could result if the bank were forced to sell assets at a significant discount from market prices. Other liquidity factors that examiners assess are economic factors, such as the trend of deposits and the stability of deposits.
Sensitivity to market risk	Because a bank's assets and off-balance-sheet items are affected by changes in the factors that drive their values, bank examiners assess the market risk exposure to these factors. Also considered in assigning a rating is the ability of the bank's management to manage the portfolio's risk exposure to control a mismatch in the duration of assets and liabilities, as well as management's ability to monitor and control permitted trading activities.

Capital adequacy and capital requirements Later in this chapter we discuss the various activities undertaken by banks. Of course, these activities can result in the realization of losses. To protect depositors, a bank must have adequate capital to absorb such losses, as well as to mitigate the potential risk that widespread banking losses may occur that would adversely affect the credit market and the real economy. As part of its safety and soundness regulation, the amount of capital that a bank needs to have on hand to absorb losses must be determined. That amount, referred to as a bank's capital requirement, is determined by regulators relative to the bank's total assets and the risk attributes associated with the assets in which the bank has invested.

Minimum capital requirements are established by regulators and then applied by them in their supervisory role. However, there is not just one minimum capital requirement, because regulators have established several categories of capital. To establish a bank's minimum capital requirement, regulators must evaluate the trade-off between imposing a level that is reasonable to reduce the risk of default and maintain a bank's ability to remain solvent but at the same time is not so high that it would severely restrict the amount of capital available for credit to the different sectors of the economy.

For a business, the term "capital" refers to the amount of equity supplied by the stockholders of a firm, or in this case, a depository institution's stockholders. It is measured by the difference between the value of the assets and the value of the liabilities. When determining a bank's capital, the regulations mandate that total assets and liabilities be measured in different ways. This results in different definitions of capital.

Because the amount of capital required cannot be invested in higher-earning assets, capital requirements for a bank represent a cost of doing business. Capital requirements are constantly being revised. At one time, the rules were based solely on the view of U.S. regulators regarding capital adequacy. Since 1988, capital requirements have been established based on an international framework developed by the Bank for International Settlements (BIS) and referred to as the **Basel Accords**. Unlike the pre-1988 capital requirements, which in the United States were based on a bank's total assets, the various standards established by the Basel Accords (described later in this chapter) link capital requirements to the risks associated with a bank's assets, and hence the standards are referred to as **risk-based capital requirements**. The principle is simple: the riskier an asset is, the greater the capital required to protect against the risk of loss will be. Initially, the sole risk that was considered in the Basel Accords was credit risk. In later Basel Accords, capital requirements were based on market risk and operational risk in addition to credit risk.

The Basel Accords—referred to as Basel I (the first accord, published in 1988), Basel II, and Basel III—which establish a bank's capital requirements are constantly undergoing changes and modifications. It is impractical to delve into their nuances and calculations here. Instead, we will review some of the broader principles involved.

Under the Basel Accords, the calculation of risk-based capital requirements can be done in one of two ways. The first is based on an external assessment of the credit riskiness of a bank and is referred to as the **standardized approach**. In this approach, the assets held by a bank are grouped by type of financial instrument and are further grouped by the credit rating associated with the obligor. Examples of an external assessment would be the ratings assigned by the CRAs.

The second approach is based on a bank's internal credit risk models and internal rating system and accordingly is referred to as the **internal rating–based approach**. Banks that adopt this approach are permitted to apply their own internal measures for determining the key drivers of credit risk as primary inputs to the calculation of their capital requirement, with the stipulations that certain conditions must be satisfied and explicit supervisory approval is required. The credit risk models allow the bank to determine the probability of default of the borrowers in its portfolio and to construct an estimate of loss should a default occur. Once these risk measures are obtained from internal models, they are converted into risk weights, which are used to determine capital requirements using a formula set by the BIS.

The Basel Accords are built on what the BIS refers to as three "pillars": (1) minimum capital requirements, (2) supervisory review process, and (3) market discipline. Our focus here is on the first pillar, which deals with the calculation of the minimum capital requirement based on credit, market, and operational risk. The starting point is defining what is meant by "capital." At this stage of our understanding of capital markets, explaining the components is difficult. Suffice it to say that the BIS defines Tier 1 and Tier 2 capital, the difference lying in what components make up each.[5]

Tier 1 capital, also referred to as **core capital** or **basic equity**, includes two components. The first is permanent shareholders' equity. This is stock issued by the bank that is fully paid common stock and perpetual preferred stock. Perpetual preferred stock is preferred stock that does not mature and for that reason is considered permanent equity. The second component of Tier 1 capital is "disclosed reserves." This component is a little more difficult to grasp, but it is basically the amount of profits retained and any reserves that the bank has set aside for general or legal contingencies.

Tier 2 capital, also called **supplementary capital**, comprises several components; we mention only two here. The first is hybrid (debt/equity) capital instruments, a category that includes financial instruments that combine the characteristics of equity capital and debt. The second is subordinated debt, which includes conventional unsecured subordinated debt capital instruments with a minimum original fixed term to maturity exceeding five years and preferred stock that has a limited life (as opposed to perpetual preferred stock).

Regulatory capital is based on the liability/stockholders' equity side of the balance sheet. What must be determined next is how much weight to give to the different financial instruments in the bank's portfolio. This is needed because it is not the total assets of the bank but the risk-weighted assets that are considered in assessing regulatory capital. Thus, weights must be assigned to each financial instrument. The BIS determines what those weights

5. There is also Tier 3 capital, which we do not discuss here.

should be for each asset. There are weights based on credit risk, market risk, and operational risk, and the weights also depend on the method the bank chooses for calculating its capital requirement, the standardized approach or the internal rating–based approach, which we discuss later in this chapter.

Based on the definition of regulatory capital and risk-weighted assets, a capital ratio is calculated. A bank's total capital ratio may not be less than 8% of Tier 1 capital.

Deposit Insurance

Because of the important economic role played by banks, the U.S. government sought a way to protect banks against depositors who, because of what they thought were real or perceived problems with a bank, sought to withdraw funds in a disruptive manner. Bank panics occurred frequently in the early 1930s, resulting in the failure of banks that might have survived economic difficulties except for the massive withdrawals they experienced.

The federal government created a backstop, devised in 1933, to prevent a run on the bank: federal deposit insurance. This insurance was provided through a new agency, the FDIC. A year later, federal deposit insurance was extended to S&Ls with the creation of the Federal Savings and Loan Insurance Corporation. In 1933, federal deposit insurance covered accounts up to $2,500. Today the standard maximum deposit insurance amount is $250,000. The maximum coverage applies per depositor, per insured depository institution, for each account ownership category. Since federal deposit insurance was established in 1933, no depositor has lost any money on an FDIC-insured deposit.

Even though federal deposit insurance achieved its objective of preventing runs on banks, it unfortunately created incentives that encouraged managers of depository institutions to take on excessive risks. If highly risky investments work out, the benefits accrue to the stockholders and management; however, if they do not, it is the depositors who are supposed to absorb the losses. Yet depositors feel little concern about the risk that a depository institution is assuming, because their funds are insured by the federal government. From a depositor's perspective, as long as the amount deposited does not exceed the insurance coverage, one depository institution is as good as another.

The pricing of premiums imposed by the FDIC for its first 50 years in operation differed significantly from the current system. Basically, during this 50-year period, all insured depository institutions paid a premium for insurance coverage based on the institution's size. More specifically, an annual premium rate of 3.3 to 8.3 cents was paid for every $100 of insured deposits. Legislation in the 1980s and 1990s altered this system, effectively turning such premiums into penalties for violating risk-based capital requirements or acts violating the supervisory process rather than for insurance coverage per se. In the absence of any violations, the FDIC charged no premiums for deposit insurance coverage, regardless of the risk profile of an institution.

The Federal Deposit Insurance Corporation Improvement Act of 1991 mandated that the FDIC establish a risk-based deposit insurance assessment system. The FDIC complied with the mandate by adopting a regulatory system that classified insured depository institutions into nine risk categories. The classifications were based on a combination of two factors. The first was a capital evaluation, and the second was a supervisory rating. The capital evaluation was based on data contained in an insured depository institution's *Consolidated Reports of Condition and Income*, more commonly referred to as the **Call Report**. Based on these data, an insured depository institution was assigned a capital evaluation of either well capitalized (Group 1), adequately capitalized (Group 2), or undercapitalized (Group 3). A consolidation of the nine risk categories into just four risk categories was made by the FDIC in 2007, once again basing the categorization of an insured depository institution on capital evaluations and supervisory ratings.

In 2010, the FDIC was ordered by the Dodd-Frank Act to amend its methodology for assessing pricing for insured depository institutions. The final rules eliminated risk categories for large institutions; they also combined the CAMELS ratings described earlier in the chapter and forward-looking financial measures to obtain one of two scores. The first score was for what was classified as **highly complex institutions**. The second score was for all others classified as **large institutions**. For large and highly complex institutions, the two scores are (1) a performance-based score and (2) a loss severity score. These scores are then combined to obtain a total score.

The total assessment rate that determines the price of deposit insurance for an insured depository institution is obtained (after some adjustments) through calculations that convert the total score into the amount of the assessment obligation. However, these final amendments for assessing risk for the purpose of pricing deposit insurance are likely to be modified further to be more consistent with the standardized approach under the Basel III risk-based capital rules described earlier.

Bank Activities

Commercial banks are involved in numerous income-generating activities, which can be broadly classified as follows: (1) individual banking, (2) institutional banking, and (3) global banking. Of course, different banks generate more activity in some areas than in others. For example, money center banks (defined later) are more active in global banking.

Individual banking encompasses consumer lending, residential mortgage lending, consumer installment loans, credit card financing, automobile and boat financing, brokerage services, student loans, and individual-oriented financial investment services (such as personal trust and investment services). Mortgage lending and credit card financing generate interest and fee income. Mortgage lending is often referred to as "mortgage banking." Brokerage services and financial investment services also generate fee income.

Loans to nonfinancial corporations, financial corporations (such as life insurance companies), and government entities (state and local governments in the United States and foreign governments) fall into the category of **institutional banking**. Also included in this category are commercial real estate financing, leasing activities, and factoring (i.e., purchasing of accounts receivable of a business). In the case of leasing, a bank may be involved in leasing equipment as a lessor,[6] as a lender to lessors, or as a purchaser of leases. Loans and leasing generate interest income, and other services that banks offer institutional customers generate fee income. These services include management of the assets of private and public pension funds, fiduciary and custodial services, and cash management services (such as account maintenance, check clearing, and electronic transfers).

In the area of **global banking**, banks now compete head-to-head with another type of financial institution—investment banking firms. Global banking covers a broad range of activities involving corporate financing and capital market and foreign exchange products and services. Most global banking activities generate fee income rather than interest income. At one time, some of these activities were restricted by federal legislation. More specifically, the Banking Act of 1933 contained four sections barring commercial banks from certain investment banking activities. These four sections are popularly referred to as the **Glass-Steagall Act**. After decades of debate regarding the need for such restrictions, the Glass-Steagall Act was repealed with the enactment of the **Gramm-Leach-Bliley Act** in November 1999, which expanded the permissible activities for banks and bank holding companies.

Corporate financing involves two components. The first is the procuring of funds for a bank's customers, which can go beyond traditional bank loans to involve the underwriting of securities. When assisting their customers to obtain funds, banks also provide bankers' acceptances, letters of credit, and other types of guarantees for their customers. That is, if a customer borrows funds backed by a letter of credit or other guarantee, its lenders can look to the customer's bank to fulfill the obligation. The second area of corporate financing involves providing advice on such matters as strategies for obtaining funds, corporate restructuring, divestitures, and acquisitions.

Capital market and foreign exchange products and services involve transactions in which the bank may act as a dealer or broker in a service. For example, some banks are dealers in U.S. government or other securities. Customers who wish to transact in these securities can do so through the government desk of the bank. Similarly, some banks maintain a foreign exchange operation, buying and selling foreign currency. Bank customers in need of foreign exchange can use the services of the bank. In their role as dealers, banks generate income in three ways: (1) through the bid-ask spread; (2) from capital gains on the securities or foreign currency used in transactions; and (3) in the case of securities, through the spread between interest income earned by holding the security and the cost of funding the purchase of that security.

The financial products developed by banks to manage risk also yield income. These products include interest rate swaps, interest rate agreements, currency swaps, forward contracts, and interest rate options. We discuss each of these products in later chapters.

6. The bank buys the equipment and leases it to another party. The bank is the lessor, and the party that uses the leased equipment is the lessee.

Banks generate either commission income (i.e., brokerage fees) or spread income from selling such products.

Bank Funding

When describing the nature of the banking business, we focused on how a bank can generate income. We now look at how a bank can raise funds. The three sources of funds for banks are (1) deposits, (2) nondeposit borrowing, and (3) common stock and retained earnings. Banks are highly leveraged financial institutions, which means that most of their funds come from borrowing—the first two sources. Included in nondeposit borrowing are borrowing from the Federal Reserve through the discount window facility, borrowing reserves in the federal funds market, and borrowing through the issuance of instruments in the money and bond markets.

Deposits

Several types of deposit accounts are available. **Demand deposits** (checking accounts) not paying any interest or minimal interest can be withdrawn on demand. Savings deposits pay interest (typically below market interest rates), do not have a specific maturity, and usually can be withdrawn on demand.

Time deposits, also called **certificates of deposit**, have a fixed maturity date and pay either a fixed or a floating interest rate. Some certificates of deposit can be sold in the open market prior to their maturity if the depositor needs funds. Other certificates of deposit cannot be sold. If a depositor elects to withdraw the funds from the bank prior to the maturity date, the bank imposes an early withdrawal penalty. A **money market demand account** is one that pays interest based on short-term interest rates. The market for short-term debt obligations is called the **money market**, which is how these deposits get their name. They are designed to compete with money market mutual funds.

Reserve Requirements and Borrowing in the Federal Funds Market

A bank cannot invest $1 for every $1 it obtains in deposit. All banks must maintain a specified percentage of their deposits in a noninterest-bearing account at one of the 12 Federal Reserve Banks. These specified percentages are called **reserve ratios**, and the dollar amounts based on them that are required to be kept on deposit at a Federal Reserve Bank are called **required reserves**. The reserve ratios are established by the Federal Reserve Board (the Fed). The reserve ratio differs by type of deposit. The Fed defines two types of deposits: transactions and nontransactions deposits. Demand deposits and what the Fed calls "other checkable deposits" are classified as transactions deposits. Savings and time deposits are nontransactions deposits. Reserve ratios are higher for transactions deposits relative to nontransactions deposits.

To arrive at its required reserves, a bank does not simply determine its transactions and nontransactions deposits at the close of each business day and then multiply each by the applicable reserve ratio. The determination of a bank's required reserves is more complex. Here we give a rough idea of how it is done. First, to compute required reserves, the Federal Reserve uses an established two-week period called the **deposit computation period**. Required reserves are the average amount of each type of deposit held at the close of each business day in the computation period, multiplied by the reserve requirement for each type.

Reserve requirements in each period are to be satisfied by **actual reserves**, which are defined as the average amount of reserves held at the close of business at the Federal Reserve Bank during each day of a two-week reserve maintenance period, beginning on Thursday and ending on Wednesday two weeks later. For transactions deposits, the deposit computation period leads the reserve period by two days. For nontransactions deposits, the deposit computation period is the two-week period four weeks prior to the reserve maintenance period.

If actual reserves exceed required reserves, the difference is referred to as **excess reserves**. Because reserves are placed in noninterest-bearing accounts, an opportunity cost is associated with excess reserves. At the same time, the Fed imposes penalties on banks that do not satisfy the reserve requirements, giving banks an incentive to manage their reserves so as to satisfy reserve requirements as precisely as possible.

Banks temporarily short of their required reserves can borrow reserves from banks with excess reserves. The market where banks borrow or lend reserves is called the **federal funds market**. The interest rate charged to borrow funds in this market is called the **federal funds rate**. Because of the importance of this market, which is part of the interbank lending market, we discuss it further in chapter 25, where we cover the money market.

Borrowing at the Fed Discount Window

The Federal Reserve Bank is the banker's bank—or, to put it another way, the bank of last resort. Banks temporarily short of funds can borrow from the Fed at its discount window.

Collateral is necessary to borrow, but not just any collateral will do. The Fed establishes (and periodically changes) the types of eligible collateral. Currently it includes (1) Treasury securities, federal agency securities, and municipal securities, all with a maturity of less than six months, and (2) commercial and industrial loans with 90 days or less to maturity.

The interest rate that the Fed charges to borrow funds at the discount window is called the **discount rate**. The Fed changes this rate periodically to implement monetary policy. Bank borrowing at the Fed to meet required reserves is quite limited in amount, even though the discount rate generally is set below the cost of other sources of short-term funding available to a bank. The Fed views borrowing at the discount window as a privilege to be used to meet short-term liquidity needs and not as a device to increase earnings.

Continual borrowing for long periods and in large amounts is thereby viewed as a sign of a bank's financial weakness or as exploitation of the interest differential for profit. If a bank appears to be going to the Fed frequently to borrow relative to its previous borrowing pattern, the Fed will make an "informational" call to ask for an explanation for the borrowing. If no subsequent improvement in the bank's borrowing pattern occurs, the Fed then makes an "administrative counseling" call, in which it tells the bank that it must stop its borrowing practice.

Other Nondeposit Borrowing

Most deposits have short maturities. Bank borrowing in the federal funds market and at the discount window of the Fed is short term. Other nondeposit borrowing can be short term (in the form of issuing obligations in the money market) or intermediate to long term (in the form of issuing securities in the bond market). An example of the former is the repurchase agreement (or "repo") market, which we discuss in chapter 26. Examples of intermediate or long-term borrowing are floating-rate notes and bonds.

Banks that raise most of their funds from the domestic and international money markets, relying less on depositors for funds, are called **money center banks**. In contrast, a **regional bank** is one that relies primarily on deposits for funding and makes less use of the money markets to obtain funds. In recent years, the mergers of larger regional banks with other regional banks have formed so-called "superregional banks." With their greater size, these superregional banks can compete in certain domestic and international financial activities that were once the domain of money center banks.

Nonbank Depository Institutions: Thrifts

Thrifts are nonbank depository institutions; they include savings institutions and credit unions. As with banks, thrifts can operate under a federal or state charter and have their deposits insured by a federal agency. The federal insurer can be the FDIC for savings associations and the National Credit Union Administration (NCUA) for credit unions. All depository institutions are subject to periodic regulatory and federal insurance examination.

Although there are differences between banks and thrifts in terms of the activities in which they specialize and certain regulatory oversights, all depository institutions have become more like each other in the past two decades and their differences have become less distinct. The new regulatory structure as set forth in the Dodd-Frank Act and the slight expansion in the range of activities permitted for thrifts, as well as the adoption of the international capital standards required by the Basel Accords, have been the latest and most dramatic step toward blurring the distinction between thrifts and banks.

Savings Institutions

Savings institutions include S&Ls and savings banks. These thrifts are either mutually owned or operate under corporate stock ownership. "Mutually owned" means no stock is outstanding, so technically the depositors are the owners. The provision of funds for financing the purchase of a home motivated the creation of savings institutions, and accordingly, residential mortgages typically compose the principal assets of savings institutions.

The Home Owners' Loan Act of 1933 mandates that a federal savings association is required to be a **qualified thrift lender**. There is a test to qualify, the qualified thrift lender test, which requires that the thrift hold qualified thrift investments equal to at least 65% of its asset portfolio. The list of QTLs includes many home-related lending and other forms of retail lending (e.g., student loans, automobile loans). Examples of home-related lending are (1) loans to purchase, refinance, construct, improve, or repair domestic residential or manufactured housing; (2) home equity loans; and (3) securities backed by or representing an interest in mortgages on domestic residential or manufactured housing.

For funding, savings institutions offer accounts that look similar to demand deposits and that pay interest, called **negotiable order of withdrawal** accounts. They also offer money market deposit accounts, can borrow in the federal funds market, have access to the Fed's discount window, and can borrow from the Federal Home Loan Banks (which are called *advances*).

Larger S&Ls operate as holdings companies (SLHCs). According to the Home Owners' Loan Act, an SLHC includes any company that directly or indirectly controls either a savings association or any other company. As institutions, **savings banks** are similar to, although much older than, S&Ls..

With respect to regulation, the Dodd-Frank Act transferred regulatory responsibility for thrifts from the Office of Thrift Supervision to two federal banking agencies. More specifically, the OCC has enforcement authority over federal savings associations, but the FDIC has the same authority over state savings associations. The OCC and the FDIC have different enforcement policies from those that the Office of Thrift Supervision had. In addition, under the Dodd-Frank Act, SLHCs are regulated in almost the same manner as bank holding companies. The OCC and FDIC have the supervisory authority to limit activities that are legally permissible for savings associations.

Although major legislation dealing with depository institutions came about as a result of the 2008–2009 financial crisis, prior substantial legislation followed the financial problems faced by S&Ls in the 1980s, referred to as the **S&L crisis**. The appendix to this chapter describes this crisis. It is worthwhile reading about the S&L crisis, because it provides an excellent example of a poorly designed financial institution that was from the outset likely to fail and impose substantial costs on U.S. taxpayers.

Credit Unions

Credit unions are the smallest of the depository institutions. Credit unions can obtain either a state or a federal charter. The Federal Credit Union Act of 1934 authorized the formation of federally chartered credit unions in all states. Their unique aspect is the "common bond" requirement for credit union membership. According to the statutes that regulate federal credit unions, membership in a federal credit union "shall be limited to groups having a common bond of occupation or association, or to groups within a well-defined neighborhood, community, or rural district."

Credit unions are either cooperatives or mutually owned. No corporate stock ownership is permitted. The dual purpose of credit unions is therefore to serve their members' saving and borrowing needs. Technically, because credit unions are owned by their members, member deposits are called *shares*. The distribution paid to members is therefore in the form of dividends, not interest.

The National Credit Union Share Insurance Fund insures the shares of all federally chartered credit unions. State-chartered credit unions may elect to have National Credit Union Share Insurance Fund coverage; for those that do not, insurance coverage is provided by a state agency.

Federal regulations apply to federally chartered credit unions and state-chartered credit unions that elect to become members of National Credit Union Share Insurance Fund. Most states, however, specify that state-chartered institutions must be subject to the same requirements as federally chartered ones. Effectively, therefore, most credit unions are regulated at the federal level. The principal federal regulatory agency is the NCUA.

Credit unions obtain their funds primarily from deposits of their members. With deregulation, they can offer a variety of accounts, including share drafts, which are similar to checking accounts but pay interest. The Central Liquidity Facility, which is administered by the NCUA, plays a role similar to the Fed's as the lender of last resort. The Central Liquidity Facility provides short-term loans to member credit unions with liquidity needs.

Credit union assets consist of small consumer loans, residential mortgage loans, and securities. Regulations 703 and 704 of the NCUA set forth the types of investments in which a credit union can invest. They can make investments in **corporate credit unions**. What is a corporate credit union? One might think that a corporate credit union is a credit union set up by employees of a corporation. It is not. Federal and state-chartered credit unions are referred to as "natural person" credit unions, because they provide financial services to qualifying members of the general public. In contrast, corporate credit unions provide a variety of investment services, as well as payment systems, only to natural person credit unions.

Shadow Banking

What we have described above concerning depository institutions is referred to as the "traditional banking system" for providing credit. As explained, there is considerable regulation of the depository institutions because of the important role that credit plays in financial markets and the real economy. Moreover, public backstops are available to depository institutions to minimize risk to depositors and to the financial system in general.

An important contributor to the 2008–2009 financial crisis was a system that few market participants were aware of—the **shadow banking system**. We conclude this chapter with a discussion of shadow banks.

To put the shadow banking system into perspective, we can place it in the context of two common forms of credit intermediation:[7] (1) *nonintermediated, direct lending*, whereby borrower and lender interact directly, and (2) *intermediated lending through traditional banking*, whereby banks take in deposits and lend them to customers (consumers, businesses, and governments). **Shadow banking** is a form of credit intermediation, a market-based form of lending, that involves entities and activities that are outside the traditional banking system. It therefore lacks the regulation of and backstops available to banks.

As mentioned in chapter 3, financial intermediaries perform such functions as maturity intermediation and diversification. Traditional banks perform these functions and have been the primary form of credit intermediation. As explained in this chapter, this is done through a regulatory structure that examines banks for safety and soundness, allows for the control of credit, and provides a backstop for depositors when financial problems arise (through deposit insurance) and by providing a lender of last resort.

In the mid-1970s, new approaches to obtaining credit appeared that differed from both traditional banking and nonintermediated, direct lending. These new approaches, the result of the financial innovations occurring at that time, resulted in what has been referred to as shadow banking. The adjective "shadow" indicates that this form of credit intermediation was far less transparent to the public and to regulators than was traditional banking.[8] The legal entities created for the purpose of shadow banking transactions were called **special-purpose vehicles** (SPVs). As with traditional banking, shadow banking involved substantial leverage. In fact, because of the lack of regulation, the leverage available in shadow banking was much greater than that available in traditional banking. Despite the greater risks of liquidity and leverage associated with shadow banking compared to traditional banking, this form of credit intermediation took place in a system that lacked the public backstops that exist in traditional banking.

SPVs created for the purpose of shadow banking obtain their funding not through deposits, as is done by traditional banks, but through a chain of market-based transactions.[9] It is difficult to explain these transactions for funding for shadow banks at this stage of our study of financial markets, because they make use of some of the financial innovations and

7. Looking at shadow banking from this perspective is suggested in David Luttrell, Harvey Rosenblum, and Jackson Thies, "Understanding the Risks Inherent in Shadow Banking: A Primer and Practical Lessons Learned," Staff Paper 18 (Federal Reserve Bank of Dallas, November 2012).

8. Despite this type of credit intermediation being around since the 1970s, the term was first coined by Paul McCulley, who at the time was a managing director of the asset management firm PIMCO ("Teton Reflections, Global Central Bank Focus," PIMCO, Newport Beach, CA, September 2007).

9. When an SPV obtains a large amount of short-term borrowings from sources other than demand deposits to finance operations and activities, the process is referred to as "wholesale funding."

participation by parties described in later chapters of this book. The chain of transactions typically involves an SPV issuing commonly used debt obligations, such as commercial paper and repurchase agreements (see chapter 26). However, funding is not limited to those two common forms of borrowing. There are also relatively new forms of debt obligations, referred to as structured credit instruments, that use the securitization technology described in chapter 27. The debt obligations issued by SPVs are acquired by such market participants as collective investment vehicles (e.g., mutual funds), insurance companies, and pension funds. Effectively, these participants are the equivalent of depositors, but they are not protected by depository insurance.

Although our description makes it seem as though shadow banking and traditional banking are independent (i.e., the parties involved in shadow banking are separate from traditional banks), that is not the case. The SPVs created for shadow banking transactions are linked not only to major banks but also to major investment banking firms and insurance companies. The major risk with shadow banks is that because of the absence of public backstops available to banks (such as deposit insurance and a lender of last resort), the SPVs involved in this form of credit intermediation are susceptible to greater funding risk (i.e., the risk that the SPV is unable to obtain funding at a favorable interest rate to make lending profitable). This situation then leads to the liquidation of an SPV by its lenders and is the equivalent of a run on a bank.

From the inception of shadow banking up to 2008, investors viewed the credit instruments issued by SPVs as having very little credit risk, as well as having little funding risk. SPVs created by traditional banks were supported by the bank with a line of credit. Moreover, the view was that in times of credit stress, there would be indirect credit and funding backstops available to bank-created SPVs, because a bank could draw on the public backstops available to it through the Fed.

How important, as measured by liabilities, was the shadow banking system? A study by the Federal Reserve Bank of Dallas estimated that at its peak, in 2008, the liabilities were $20 trillion. The traditional banking system at the time had liabilities totaling $11 trillion.[10] Consequently, shadow banking was not a minor sector of the financial system. In fact, the same study estimated that the shadow banking system's liabilities had surpassed those of the traditional banking system as early as 1996!

Difficulties regarding liquidity and asset valuations did occur at various points after the inception of shadow banking. However, the difficulties were resolved without impairing the growth of the shadow banking system. By 2008, however, several conditions in the financial market had precipitated a major collapse of the shadow banking system. Specifically, asset valuation declined for mortgage-related assets, and because a large portion of the assets in which the SPVs invested consisted of such assets, the value of SPVs declined. As a result, SPVs found it difficult to generate positive returns on their asset portfolios. The problems in the financial market also resulted in the tightening of credit, making it

10. Luttrell, Rosenblum, and Thies, "Understanding the Risks Inherent in Shadow Banking," 6.

extremely difficult for SPVs to obtain new funding once their short-term debt matured. All these events underscored the vulnerability of the shadow banking system.

The conclusion of a study by the Federal Reserve Bank of Dallas had the following to say about the shadow banking system:

> The shadow banking system has its benefits. It serves the same function as traditional banking but in some areas maintains advantages due to superior market knowledge and specialization. Despite declining shadow banking system holdings following the crisis, these entities are unlikely to disappear soon. Given the continued presence, size, and risks, and the credit flows and economic growth benefits that shadow banking facilitates, the proper dose and measure of reform is crucial. Devising how to address vulnerabilities is no small task because of how the system has intertwined itself with traditional banking, particularly with the large global banks. Realigning incentives will not be easy.[11]

Key Points

- Depository institutions accept various types of deposits.
- With the funds raised through deposits and other funding sources, depository institutions make loans to various entities and invest in securities.
- Income is derived from investments (loans and securities) and fees.
- Because of the important role of depository institutions in financial markets and the real economy, they are heavily regulated.
- Bank regulation refers to a federal agency's authority to issue specific regulations and guidelines that govern the operations, activities, and acquisitions of banking organizations.
- Bank supervision entails monitoring and examining the condition of individual banks and determining whether they are in compliance with regulations.
- Bank regulation has three components: (1) safety and soundness, (2) deposit insurance, and (3) systemic risk.
- Safety and soundness regulation and supervision involve assessing the likelihood of a depository institution's defaulting and, if a default does occur, assessing the magnitude of the losses that will be realized by creditors and stockholders.
- Bank examiners conduct on-site examinations with a focus on reviewing and rating a bank's performance, financial condition, and regulatory compliance.
- The system used to rate banks that has been adopted by federal bank regulators is the CAMELS rating system, covering capital adequacy, asset quality, management, earnings, liquidity, and sensitivity to market risk.
- There are two types of holding company structures in the banking industry: (1) a bank holding company, in which the parent holding company has as part of its holdings a national bank

11. Luttrell, Rosenblum, and Thies, "Understanding the Risks Inherent in Shadow Banking," 20.

and a state bank, and (2) a financial holding company, in which the parent holding company has as its holdings a national bank and a securities company.

• Financial holding companies are conglomerates that are allowed to engage in a wide range of financially related activities.

• The Federal Reserve is the primary regulator of all financial firms (bank and nonbanks) designated as systemically significant; it also has safety and soundness authority over the payment, clearing, and settlement systems that are systemically important and are not regulated by other government agencies.

• The Office of Comptroller of the Currency (OCC) charters, regulates, and supervises both national banks and federal savings associations.

• The OCC examiners are responsible for analyzing loan and investment portfolios and funds management, rating banks, and determining compliance with consumer banking laws for national banks and federal savings associations with less than $10 billion in assets.

• The Federal Deposit Insurance Company (FDIC) is an independent federal agency that (1) insures deposits, (2) examines individual banks, (3) supervises banks, and (4) resolves both troubled or failed banks and any financial institution (bank or nonbank) that is designated as a systemically important financial institution.

• If the OCC makes a determination that there is systemic threat to the financial system, the FDIC has broad authority to utilize deposit insurance funds to assist depository institutions.

• An important role of the FDIC is to provide a resolution when a troubled FDIC-insured bank is about to fail.

• The FDIC assumes two roles in the resolution process: (1) as an insurer of deposits and (2) as a receiver and administrator of the receivership estate for all creditors.

• The FDIC basically can use one of three basic resolution methods: (1) purchase and assumption transactions, (2) deposit payoffs, and (3) open bank assistance transactions.

• The Dodd-Frank Act extended the FDIC's receivership power and authority to allow it to effect an orderly liquidation of troubled financial institutions (banks and nonbanks).

• As part of its safety and soundness regulation, the amount of capital that a bank needs to absorb losses must be determined. It is referred to as a bank's capital requirements.

• Minimum capital requirements are established by regulators and then applied by regulators in their supervisory role.

• A depository institution's capital is the amount of equity supplied by its stockholders and is measured as the difference between the value of the assets and the value of the liabilities.

• The various standards established by the Basel Accords link capital requirements to the risks associated with the assets; hence the standards are referred to as risk-based capital requirements.

- The underlying principle behind risk-based capital requirements is that the riskier an asset is, the more will be the capital required to protect against the risk of loss.
- Under the Basel Accords, the calculation of risk-based capital requirements can be determined using either the standardized approach or the internal rating–based approach.
- The Basel Accords are built on three pillars: minimum capital requirements, a supervisory review process, and market discipline.
- The Basel Accords stipulate two levels of capital requirements: Tier 1 (core capital or basic equity) and Tier 2 (supplementary capital).
- Federal deposit insurance serves as a public backstop to prevent a run on a bank.
- The three sources of funds for banks are deposits, nondeposit borrowing, and retained earnings and sale of equity.
- Banks are highly leveraged financial institutions, meaning that most of their funds are obtained from deposits and nondeposit borrowing (including borrowing from the Fed through the discount window facility, borrowing reserves in the federal funds market, and borrowing by the issuance of instruments in the money and bond markets).
- Banks must maintain reserves at one of the 12 Federal Reserve Banks, according to reserve requirements established by the Fed.
- Banks temporarily short of their required reserves can borrow reserves in the federal funds market or borrow temporarily from the Fed at its discount window.
- Income-generating activities of bank can be broadly classified as individual banking, institutional banking, and global banking.
- Thrifts are nonbank depository institutions; they include savings institutions and credit unions.
- As with banks, thrifts can operate under federal or state charter and have their deposits insured by a federal agency.
- Although there are differences between banks and thrifts in terms of the activities in which they specialize and certain regulatory oversight, all depository institutions have become more alike as a result of the Dodd-Frank Act and the adoption of the international capital standards required by the Basel Accords.
- Savings institutions include savings and loan associations (S&Ls) and savings banks.
- The Dodd-Frank Act of 2010 gave the OCC enforcement authority over federal saving associations and the FDIC authority over state savings associations.
- To obtain a charter as a savings association, a thrift must pass a qualified thrift lender test, which is based on the composition of the portfolio of its assets.
- The primary assets of savings associations are home-related loans.
- Credit unions are depository institutions that have a "common bond" requirement for membership and are owned by those members.

• The principal federal regulatory agency is the National Credit Union Administration (NCUA).

• The three forms of credit intermediation are (1) nonintermediated, direct lending, in which borrower and lender interact directly; (2) intermediated lending through traditional banking, in which banks take in deposits and lend them to customers (consumers, businesses, and governments); and (3) market-based lending, which involves entities and activities outside the traditional banking system.

• Market-based credit intermediation is referred to as shadow banking and until 2008 represented a large sector of the credit market.

• Unlike traditional banking, shadow banking lacks regulation and the backstops available to banks (deposit insurance, a lender of last resort) that prevent a run on banks and protect investors.

• The legal entities created for the purpose of shadow banking transactions are special-purpose vehicles (SPVs). These entities obtain their funding not through deposits, as is done by traditional banks, but through a chain of market-based transactions.

• The SPVs created for shadow banking transactions were often linked not only to major banks but also to major investment banking firms and insurance companies.

• The major risk with shadow banks is that because of the absence of public backstops available to banks, such as deposit insurance and a lender of last resort, SPVs are susceptible to greater funding risk, which can lead to the liquidation of an SPV by its lenders and is the equivalent of a run on the bank.

Questions

1. In a March 17, 2009, speech titled "Finance: A Return from Risk," delivered before the Worshipful Company of International Bankers in London, Mervyn King, governor of the Bank of England and chair of its Monetary Policy Committee, stated:

> Banks are dangerous institutions. They borrow short and lend long. They create liabilities which promise to be liquid and hold few liquid assets themselves. That though is hugely valuable for the rest of the economy. Household savings can be channelled to finance illiquid investment projects while providing access to liquidity for those savers who may need it.

Explain what Mr. King means.

2. Explain why you agree or disagree with the following statement: "Not only does the Fed have the power to examine banks, it now oversees the country's systemic risk."

3. Explain why you agree or disagree with the following statement: "Risk-based capital requirements for banks consider only credit risk."

4. Explain the ways in which a bank can accommodate withdrawal of deposits.

5. Why do you think a debt instrument whose interest rate is changed periodically based on some market interest rate would be a more suitable investment vehicle for a depository institution than a long-term debt instrument with a fixed interest rate?

6. Explain each of the following types of deposit accounts:

a. Demand deposits

b. Certificates of deposit

c. Money market demand accounts

d. Share deposits

e. Negotiable order of withdrawal accounts

7. Describe the current system for charging premiums for federal deposit insurance and how it differs from the way premiums were charged up until 1980.

8. Consider this headline from the *New York Times* of March 26, 1933: "Bankers Will Fight Deposit Guarantees. … Bad Banking Would Be Encouraged."

a. What do you think this headline is saying?

b. Discuss the pros and cons of whether deposits should be insured by the U.S. government.

9. Explain what is meant by each of the following:

a. Reserve ratio

b. Required reserves

c. Excess reserves

10. Explain what is meant by each of the following:

a. Individual banking

b. Institutional banking

c. Global banking

11. What are the primary assets held by S&Ls?

12. Explain why you agree or disagree with the following statement: "In recent years, the differences in regulatory treatment and activities of banks compared to thrifts have increased."

13. The following passage appeared in the *Final Report of the National Commission on the Causes of the Financial and Economic Crisis in The United States*, submitted to Congress in January 2011:

> In the early part of the 20th century, we erected a series of protections—the Federal Reserve as a lender of last resort, federal deposit insurance, ample regulations—to provide a bulwark against the panics that had regularly plagued America's banking system in the 19th century. Yet, over the past 30-plus years, we permitted the growth of a shadow banking system—opaque and laden with short-term debt—that

rivaled the size of the traditional banking system. Key components of the market—for example, the multitrillion-dollar repo lending market, off-balance-sheet entities, and the use of over-the-counter derivatives—were hidden from view, without the protections we had constructed to prevent financial meltdowns. We had a 21st-century financial system with 19th-century safeguards.

Explain what this passage means.

Appendix: The S&L Crisis

As indicated in main text of this chapter, although major legislation dealing with depository institutions came about as a result of the 2008–2009 financial crisis, prior substantial legislation followed the financial problems faced by S&Ls in the 1980s, referred to as the **S&L crisis**. This appendix describes this crisis. It is worthwhile reading about the S&L crisis, because it provides an excellent example of a poorly designed financial institution that was from the outset likely to fail and cause substantial costs to U.S. taxpayers.

The details of the growth of the S&L industry since the late 1960s and the ensuing S&L crisis would fill an entire book, so only the basics of the problems of this industry are presented here. Until the early 1980s, S&Ls and all other lenders financed housing through traditional mortgages at interest rates fixed for the life of the loan. The period of the loan was typically long, frequently up to 30 years. Funding for these loans, by regulation, came from deposits having a maturity considerably shorter than the loans. Such a situation creates the funding risk of lending long and borrowing short. It is extremely risky, although regulators took a long time to understand it.

No problem arises, of course, if interest rates are stable or declining. But if interest rates rise above the interest rate on the mortgage loans, a negative spread results, eventually leading to insolvency. Regulators at first endeavored to shield the S&L industry from the need to pay high interest rates without losing deposits by imposing a ceiling on the interest rate that would be paid by S&Ls and by their immediate competitors, the other depository institutions.

However, the approach did not and could not work.

With the high volatility of interest rates in the 1970s, followed by the historically high level of interest rates in the early 1980s, all depository institutions began to lose funds to competitors exempt from ceilings, such as the newly formed money market funds; this development forced some increase in ceilings. The ceilings in place since the middle of the 1960s did not protect the S&Ls, which began to suffer from diminished profits and increasingly from operating losses. A large fraction of S&Ls became technically insolvent as rising interest rates eroded the market value of their assets to the point where assets fell short of liabilities.

Regulators, anxious to cover up the debacle of their empire, let these S&Ls continue to operate, worsening the problem by allowing them to value their mortgage assets at book value. Profitability worsened with deregulation of the maximum interest rate that S&Ls could pay on deposits. Even though deregulation allowed S&Ls to compete with other financial institutions for funds, it also raised funding costs. Banks were better equipped to cope with rising funding costs, because bank portfolios were not dominated by old, fixed-rate mortgages, as S&Ls were. A larger portion of bank portfolios consisted of shorter-term assets and other assets whose interest rates reset to market interest rates after short periods.

The difficulty of borrowing short and lending long was only part of the problem faced by the industry. As the crisis progressed and the situation of many S&Ls became hopeless, fraudulent management activities were revealed. Many S&Ls facing financial difficulties also pursued strategies that exposed the institution to greater risk in the hope of recovering if these strategies worked out. What encouraged managers to pursue such high-risk strategies was that depositors were not concerned with the risks associated with the institution where they deposited funds, because the U.S. government, through federal deposit insurance, guaranteed the deposits up to a predetermined amount. Troubled S&Ls could pay existing depositors through attracting new depositors by offering higher interest rates on deposits than financially stronger S&Ls offered. In turn, to earn a spread on the higher cost of funds, troubled S&Ls had to pursue riskier investment policies.

7 Central Banks

CONTENTS

Learning Objectives

After reading this chapter, you will understand:

- what a central bank is and the role of central banks;
- the structure of the Federal Reserve System and the nature of the Fed's instruments of monetary policy;
- the meaning of required reserves for banks and the fractional reserve banking system of the United States;
- the implementation and impact of open market operations and of open market repurchase agreements;
- the role of the Fed's discount rate;
- the different kinds of money and the definitions of key monetary aggregates;
- the money multiplier and how it generates changes in the monetary aggregates from changes in the banking system's reserves;
- how banks and investors participate with the Fed in changing the level of the monetary aggregates;
- the goals of monetary policy, including price level stability, economic growth, stable interest rates, and stable foreign exchange rates;
- the operating targets of Fed policy (those monetary and financial variables that are affected by its tools in a predictable way);
- the intermediate targets of Fed policy (economic variables that the Fed can affect indirectly through its work with operating targets);
- why the federal funds rate and bank reserves have often been operating targets of monetary policy;
- how the broad monetary aggregates have sometimes served as intermediate targets, as have certain interest rates; and
- several aspects of global central banks.

In economies or groups of economies, the process by which the supply of money is created is a complex interaction among several economic agents that perform different functions at different times. The agents are business firms and households who both save and borrow, depository institutions that accept savings and make loans to firms, government entities, individuals and other institutions, and the nation's central bank, which also lends and buys and sells securities.

In this chapter, we explain the role of central banks in the complex process of creating the money supply. To do this, we use the example of the U.S. central bank (the Federal Reserve Bank or simply "the Fed") in the creation of the supply of money to highlight its interaction with banks and other units of the economy. We also explain the tools that the

Fed can use to manage the rate of growth in the money supply. We then examine the goals of monetary policy; that is, the conditions in the economy that the Fed seeks to bring about. Although the Fed cannot directly cause these conditions to exist, it can follow policies to target variables that it can influence with its tools. We begin with a brief description of the role of central banks in general and then focus on the U.S. central bank. We conclude with a discussion of the issues related to global central banks.

Central Banks and Their Purpose

The primary role of a **central bank** is to maintain the stability of the currency and money supply for a country or a group of countries. To be a little more specific, let's look at the central bank of the United Kingdom, the Bank of England. On its website, it identifies its role in financial stability as follows:

> **Risk assessment**: monitoring current developments both in the United Kingdom and abroad—including links between financial markets and the wider economy and, within financial markets, between different participants—to identify key risks to the financial system. For example, the Bank examines the overall financial position of borrowers and lenders; the links between financial institutions; and the resilience and vulnerability of households, firms, financial institutions, and international financial systems to changes in circumstances. The Bank also conducts risk assessment and research on the major developed countries and the main emerging-market economies.
>
> **Risk reduction**: reducing vulnerabilities and increasing the financial system's ability to absorb unexpected events. This can involve the promotion of codes and standards over a wide field, ranging from accounting to improving legal certainty, and management of countries' external balance sheets.
>
> **Oversight of payment systems**: oversight of the main payment and settlement systems in the UK that are used for many types of financial transaction—from paying wages and credit card bills to the settlement of transactions between financial institutions.
>
> **Crisis management**: developing and coordinating information sharing within the Bank, with the FSA and HM Treasury, and with authorities internationally to ensure future financial crises are handled and managed effectively. In undertaking this work, the Bank advises on and implements policy measures to mitigate risks to the financial system.[1]

One of the major ways that a central bank accomplishes its goals is through monetary policy. For this reason, a central bank is sometimes referred to as a **monetary authority** (e.g., Monetary Authority of Singapore, Hong Kong Monetary Authority, and Bermuda Monetary Authority). In implementing monetary policy, central banks require private banks to maintain and deposit the required reserves with the central bank (we discuss reserve requirements later in this chapter). For this reason, a central bank is also referred to as a **reserve bank** (e.g., Reserve Bank of Australia, Reserve Bank of India, and South African Reserve Bank).

1. http://www.bankofengland.co.uk/financialstability/functions.htm. In the quote, "FSA" is the Financial Services Authority, and "HM Treasury" is Her Majesty's Treasury.

When discharging its responsibilities during a financial crisis or to avert a financial crisis, central banks perform the role of lender of last resort for the banking system. For example, the Bank of England states the following for its role as lender of last resort:

> In exceptional circumstances, as part of its central banking functions, the Bank may act as "lender of last resort" to financial institutions in difficulty, in order to prevent a loss of confidence spreading through the financial system as a whole.

The central banks of the 19 member countries of the Group of Twenty (G20) countries are listed in table 7.1. Established in 1999 as an international forum for finance ministers and central bank governors of developing economies to discuss key issues of the global economy, the G20 includes 19 member countries plus the central bank of the European Union (the **European Central Bank**, ECB). The ECB, which came into being on January 1, 1999, is responsible for implementing the monetary policy for the member countries of the European Union. The European System of Central Banks consists of the ECB and the central banks of the member countries. Also listed in the second column of table 7.1 are the names of the 19 major central banks.

There is widespread agreement that the central bank should be independent of the government so that decisions of the central bank will not be influenced for short-term political purposes, such as pursuing a monetary policy to expand the economy but at the expense of inflation.[2] As stated in a speech by Frederic Mishkin, a former governor of the U.S. Federal Reserve Board of Governors, on April 3, 2008: "Evidence supports the conjecture that macroeconomic performance is improved when central banks are more independent."[3] He provides examples from the Bank of England and Bank of Canada.[4] Moreover, this view is supported by several studies of central banks of industrialized countries.

In 1975, as a result of the oil crisis and economic recessions being faced throughout the world, the United States formed an informal meeting of senior financial officials from five countries in addition to the United States: the United Kingdom, France, Germany, Italy, and Japan. The group, which became known as the **Group of 6** (G6), decided to meet annually thereafter. The following year, Canada joined the group, which then became known as the **Group of 7** (G7). In 1998, Russia joined the group and it became known as the **Group of 8** (G8). In 2014, Russia was suspended from the G8 and it once again became known as the G7. Although the G7 can concur on economic and financial policies and establish objectives, compliance is voluntary.

2. Further analysis and discussion regarding the issue of central bank independence can be found in James Forder, "Central Bank Independence and Credibility: Is There a Shred of Evidence?" *International Finance* 3 (April 2000): 167–185, and Alex Cukierman, "Central Bank Independence and Monetary Policy Making Institutions: Past, Present, and Future," *Journal Economía Chileña* 9 (April 2006): 5–23.

3. "Central Bank Commitment and Communication," presentation at the Princeton University Center for Policy Studies, http://www.federalreserve.gov/newsevents/speech/mishkin20080403a.htm#f19.

4. Further evidence is provided in Frederick S. Mishkin and and Niklas J. Westelius, "Inflation Band Targeting and Optimal Inflation Contracts," NBER Working Paper 12384 (Cambridge, MA: National Bureau of Economic Research, July 2006).

Table 7.1
The 19 central banks of the member countries of the G20.

Member State	Name of Central Bank	Ratio of Countries Public Debt to GDP (2017)*
Argentina	Central Bank of Argentina	53.7
Australia	Reserve Bank of Australia	47.1
Brazil	Central Bank of Brazil	78.4
Canada	Bank of Canada	98.2
China	The People's Bank of China	18.6
France	Bank of France	96.1
Germany	Deutsche Bundesbank	65.7
India	Reserve Bank of India	50.1
Indonesia	Bank Indonesia	33.1
Italy	Bank of Italy	131.2
Japan	Bank of Japan	223.8
Mexico	Bank of Mexico	51.5
Russia	Central Bank of Russia	11.8
Saudi Arabia	Saudi Arabian Monetary Agency	30.0
South Africa	South African Reserve Bank	43.3
South Korea	Bank of Korea	38.2
Turkey	Central Bank of the Republic of Turkey	29.6
United Kingdom	Bank of England	90.4
United States	Board of Governors of the Federal Reserve System	77.4

* *Source* for this column is *The World Factbook* (Washington, DC: United States Central Intelligence Agency, 2017).

The Central Bank of the United States: The Federal Reserve System

The most important agent in the money supply process is the Federal Reserve System, which is the central bank of the United States and is often called the Federal Reserve or "the Fed." Created in 1913, the Fed is the government agency responsible for the management of the U.S. monetary and banking systems. Most large commercial banks in the United States are members of the Federal Reserve System. The Fed is managed by a seven-member **Board of Governors**, who are appointed by the president and approved by the Congress. These governors have 14-year appointments (with one appointment ending every two years), and one governor is the board's chair. The **Chairmanship of the Fed** is a highly visible and influential position in the world economy. The Federal Reserve System consists of 12 districts covering the entire country; each **district** has a Federal Reserve Bank that has its own president.

An important feature of the Fed is that, by the terms of the law that created it, neither the legislative nor the executive branch of the federal government should exert control over it. From time to time, critics charge that the Fed guards this autonomy by accommodating either the White House or Congress (or both) far too much. The Fed has substantial regulatory power over the nation's depository institutions, especially commercial banks.

It is worth noting here, before we discuss the Fed's tools for monetary management, that financial innovations over the past two decades have made the Fed's task more difficult. The public's increasing acceptance of money market mutual funds has funneled a large amount of money into what are essentially interest-bearing checking accounts. (See chapter 32 for more information on mutual funds.) Another relevant innovation is the practice of asset securitization, which we discuss in chapter 27. Securitization permits commercial banks to change what once were illiquid consumer loans of several varieties into securities. Selling these securities in the financial markets gives the banks a source of funding that is outside the Fed's influence. The many hedging instruments to be analyzed in part VIII of this book have also affected banks' behavior and their relationship with the Fed. In general, that transformation amounts to reduced Fed control of banks and increased difficulty in implementing monetary policy.

The Fed and the Supply of Money

Tools of Monetary Policy to Influence the Money Supply

The Fed has several tools by which it influences, indirectly and to a greater or lesser extent, the amount of money in the economy and the general level of interest rates. These tools are reserve requirements (whose use is somewhat constricted by congressional mandate), open market operations, open market repurchase agreements, and the discount rate. These instruments represent the key ways that the Fed interacts with commercial banks in the process of creating money. Our discussion of these tools explains the impact of their use on a generally specified money supply. Later in this chapter we describe the money supply in more detail.

Reserve requirements Bank reserves play an important role in the U.S. banking and monetary system and are directly linked to the growth in the money supply. Generally, the higher the growth rate in reserves, the higher the rate of change in the money supply. Later in this chapter, we discuss this linkage in some detail. At this point, we want to focus on the meaning and function of reserve requirements.

The United States has a **fractional reserve banking system**, which means that a bank must hold or "reserve" some portion of the funds that savers deposit in a form approved by the Fed. As a result, a bank may lend to borrowers only a fraction of what it takes in as deposits. The ratio of mandatory reserves to deposits is the **required reserve ratio**. For many years, the Fed had the authority to set this ratio. In the Depository Institutions Deregulation and Monetary Control Act (DIDMCA) of 1980, Congress assumed much of that responsibility, establishing new rules regarding this ratio to be applied to all depository institutions, including commercial banks, thrifts of various types, and credit unions.

In a key provision of the DIDMCA, Congress adopted a basic ratio of 12% for what are termed checkable or transactional accounts, that is, **demand deposits**, or accounts on which checks may be written often. For nontransactional but short-term deposit accounts—known as **time deposits**—the required reserve ratio is 3%. The 1980 law also authorizes the Fed to change the required reserve ratio on checking accounts to any level between 8% and 14%, and to raise it to 18% under certain conditions. In early 1992, the Fed reduced the ratio to 10% for banks with total checkable accounts at or above $46.8 million. For banks with smaller totals in these accounts, the required reserve ratio is 3%. A bank must maintain the required reserves as either currency on hand (that is, cash in the bank) or deposits in the Federal Reserve itself. The more important form is the deposit, which serves as an asset for the bank and as a liability of the Fed.

A bank has **excess reserves** if its reserves amount to more than the Fed requires. A bank's **total reserves** equal its required reserves plus any excess reserves. A bank whose actual reserves fall short of required levels can borrow excess reserves from other banks (see chapter 25 for more on the federal funds market), or it can borrow reserves from the Fed itself, which we discuss later in this chapter.

Open market operations The Fed's most powerful instrument is its authority to conduct **open market operations**, which means that the Fed may buy and sell, in open debt markets, government securities for its own account. These securities may be U.S. Treasury bonds, Treasury bills, or obligations of federal agencies. The Fed prefers to use Treasury bills, because, in that large and liquid market, it can make its substantial transactions without seriously disrupting the prices or yields of bills. When it buys or sells, the Fed does so at prices and interest rates that prevail in these debt markets. The parties to the Fed's transactions may be commercial banks or other financial agents who are dealers in government securities.

The unit of the Fed that decides on the general issues of changing the rate of growth in the money supply, by open market sales or purchase of securities, is the **Federal Open Market Committee** (FOMC). The FOMC consists of the Board of Governors, the president of the Federal Reserve Bank of New York, and presidents of some of the other district Fed banks. This committee meets approximately every six weeks to analyze economic activity and levels of key economic variables. The variables may include short-term interest rates (such as the federal funds rate), the U.S. dollar's rate of exchange with important foreign currencies, commodity prices, and excess reserves, among other things.[5] After this analysis, the committee sets the direction of monetary policy until the next meeting. This direction is summarized in a brief "directive" at the time of the announcement after the meeting. The minutes of these meetings are published at a later time.

5. D. S. Batten, M. P. Blackwell, I.-S. Kim, S. E. Nocera, and Y. Ozeki, "The Conduct of Monetary Policy in the Major Industrial Countries," Occasional Paper 70 (Washington, DC: International Monetary Fund, July 1990), p. 24.

The implementation of policy, through open market operations, is the responsibility of the **trading desk of the Federal Reserve Bank of New York**. The desk transacts, in large volume, with large securities firms or commercial banks that are dealers, or market makers, in Treasury securities. Although the desk does not buy and sell for profit, it functions as a rational investor, buying at the lowest prices and selling at the highest prices offered at the time of the transactions.

Fed purchases augment the amount of reserves in the banking system. If the seller is a commercial bank, it alters the composition, but not the total, of its assets by exchanging the securities for reserves at the Fed. If the seller is not a bank, much or all of the check with which the Fed pays will probably be deposited in a bank. The bank receiving the deposit would experience an increase in liabilities (the customer's deposit) and in assets (the growth in its reserve account at the Fed). In either case, the proceeds from selling the securities to the Fed raise the banking system's total reserves. Such an increase in reserves typically leads to an increase in the money supply. Individual banks whose reserves rise will generally make new loans, equal to the new deposit less required reserves, because loans earn interest whereas reserves do not. New loans represent growth in the money supply.

Conversely, the Fed's sale of Treasury securities reduces the money supply (or its rate of growth), because the funds that security dealers pay for the securities come from either deposits at banks or, if the dealers are banks, from the banks' own accounts. A reduction in deposits reduces reserves and leaves the banks less to lend.

Open market repurchase agreements The Fed often employs variants of simple open market purchases and sales, and these are called the repurchase agreement (repo) and the *reverse repo*. The Fed conducts these transactions, which are actually more common than the outright purchases or sales,[6] with large dealers in government securities and, occasionally, with central banks of other countries.

In a repurchase agreement, the Fed buys a particular amount of securities from a seller that agrees to repurchase the same number of securities for a higher price at some future time, usually a few weeks. The difference between the original price and the repurchase price is the return earned by the Fed for letting the dealer have the cash for the life of the agreement and, also, the cost to the dealer of borrowing from the Fed. In a reverse repo (also known as a **matched sale** or a **matched sale-purchase transaction**), the Fed sells securities and makes a commitment to buy them back at a higher price later. The difference in the two prices is the cost to the Fed of the funds and the return to the buyer for lending money.

An example illustrates some of the features in a Fed repurchase agreement. (A detailed analysis of repos appears in chapter 25.) Suppose the Fed wants to increase bank reserves for some reason over a short period of time, and it seeks out a financial institution that has $20 mil-

6. David M. Jones and Ellen Rachling, "Monetary Policy: How the Fed Sets, Implements, and Measures Policy Chokes," in *Handbook of Portfolio Management,* ed. Frank J. Fabozzi (Hoboken, NJ: John Wiley, 1998), chapter 2.

lion in Treasury securities but no excess reserves. Suppose further that the institution wants to lend $20 million for seven days to a borrower. After some discussions, the Fed agrees to "buy" the securities from the institution at a price that reflects the current repo rate, and to "sell" them back in seven days, when the institution's borrower pays off that loan. The current annualized rate is 4.3%. The transaction would look like this: The Fed would buy the securities for approximately $19,983,292 and sell them back, seven days later, to the institution at the principal value of $20 million. The difference of nearly $16,708 is the interest the institution pays for the seven-day financing and the return to the Fed for lending that money. And for those seven days, the financial institution and the entire banking system can enjoy an increase in reserves, if, of course, the bank keeps the roughly $20 million in its account at the Fed.

The Fed uses repos and reverse repos to bring about a temporary change in the level of reserves in the system or to respond to some event that the Fed thinks will have a significant but short-lived effect. A particularly good example of such an event is a large payment by the U.S. Treasury (as in tax refunds or Social Security benefits) that sharply but temporarily raises reserves at the banks. Of course, these temporary changes in the system's reserves alter the banks' ability to make loans and, ultimately, to prompt growth in the money supply for a short period.

Discount rate As mentioned in chapter 6, the Fed makes loans to banks that are members of the system. A bank borrowing from the Fed is said to use the **discount window**, and these loans are backed by the bank's collateral. The rate of interest on these loans is the **discount rate**, set at a certain level by the Fed's Board of Governors. As the rate rises, banks are understandably less likely to borrow; a falling rate tends to encourage them to borrow. Proceeds from discount loans are also reserves and increase the banks' capacity to make loans. Banks generally do not prefer to gain reserves in this way, because the loans cost money as well as invite increased monitoring of the borrowing banks' activities. Accordingly, the flow of this borrowing has a very slight impact on the money banks have and can lend and, therefore, on the supply of money.

There is general agreement that the discount rate is the least effective tool at the Fed's disposal, and its use in monetary policy has diminished over time. Today, changes in the discount rate function largely as the Fed's public signals about its intention to change the rate at which the money supply is growing.

Different Kinds of Money

Until now, we have spoken in general terms about the money supply. But we can be more precise and identify several different meanings of the word "money" and several different types of money.

First of all, money is that item which serves as a **numeraire**, or unit of account—in other words, the unit that is used to measure wealth. In the United States, the numeraire is the dollar; in Japan, it is the yen; and so on. Second, we call money any instrument that serves as a medium of exchange, that is, anything that is generally accepted in payment for goods, services, and capital transactions. In the United States, the medium of exchange encompasses currency, which is issued by the Treasury or the Fed, and demand deposits, which support payment by means of checks and are held at depository institutions, such as commercial banks. The medium of exchange also performs the function of being a store of value, which means that the exchange medium can be used to carry resources over from the present to the future. Obviously, this function is impaired in times of high and unpredictable inflation.[7] Other accounts that resemble demand deposits include the NOW account (or Negotiable Order of Withdrawal account) and share drafts of credit unions.

Other assets that do not function in the role of medium of exchange have many properties in common with the numeraire. These properties include safety, divisibility, and high liquidity (which is the capacity to be transformed into the medium of exchange promptly and at negligible cost). Because of these properties, these assets are good substitutes for money, in particular, as stores of value. The assets of this type include *time deposits* at commercial banks or thrifts. These accounts earn interest over their specified lives, and the investor may not draw on the money in the account for a transaction, without incurring a penalty, until the deposit's maturity date. Other assets that are substitutes for money include balances in money market mutual funds.

Money and Monetary Aggregates

Monetary policy and the actions of the Federal Reserve System often concentrate on what are called **monetary aggregates**. The purpose of the aggregates is to measure the amount of money available to the economy at any time.

The most basic monetary aggregate is the **monetary base**. Also termed "high-powered money," the base is defined as currency in circulation (or coins and Federal Reserve notes held by the public) plus the total reserves in the banking system. It is important to note that reserves make up the bulk of the base, which is under the control of the Fed. Thus, this aggregate is the one that the Fed is most able to influence with its various monetary tools.

The instruments that serve the role of **medium of exchange**—currency and demand deposits—are included in a monetary aggregate that is sometimes referred to as the narrow measure of the money supply and is labeled M_1. Thus, M_1 measures the amount of the medium of exchange in the economy. M_2 is a more inclusive aggregate, because it takes into account all the instruments that substitute for money in the capacity of storing value. Therefore, M_2 is defined as M_1 plus all dollars held in time and savings accounts at banks

7. The **giro payment**, an alternative to the check, is used in many foreign countries. The giro payment is a direct order to the payer's bank to make a payment to a seller of some good or service. The check, of course, is an order to pay that is drawn on an account at the payer's bank and that the payer gives to the seller.

and thrift institutions, plus all dollars invested in retail money market mutual funds, plus some additional accounts (such as overnight repurchase agreements). Some analysts also watch developments in two other monetary aggregates, which are labeled M_3 and L (for liquid assets). These aggregates (M_3 and L) equal M_2 plus certain other financial assets, including long-term time deposits, commercial paper, bankers' acceptances, and some Treasury securities.

The ratio of the money supply to the economy's income (as reflected by the gross national product or some similar measure) is known as the **velocity of money** in circulation. Velocity measures the average amount of transactions carried by a dollar. If the economy's velocity were stable, monetary policy could achieve any desired level of income by simply targeting the aggregate. Unfortunately, velocity is not a stable relationship, and in fact, the linkages between the economy's income and the various aggregates vary considerably over time.

Typically, the monetary aggregates move in somewhat similar patterns, rising and falling at roughly the same rates and at roughly the same times. A major question in Fed policymaking (which we discuss below) has revolved around choosing the most appropriate definition of the money supply.

The Money Multiplier: The Expansion of the Money Supply

Our discussion of how the supply of money is created focuses on the linkage between the banking system's reserves and the aggregate M_1. The process we describe, the **money multiplier**, can be generalized to the other monetary aggregates, but the complexities involved in those processes are not relevant to our task now.

We begin by restating that the creation of the money supply and changes in it are the result of complex interactions of four parties: the Fed, banks, savers, and borrowers. The Fed provides reserves to banks and also requires banks to hold, as reserves, a portion of the deposits that the public holds at the banks. The banks, playing their key role in the money multiplier, lend the remainder of the deposits (or most of it) to borrowers at an interest rate that exceeds that of demand deposits. For any one bank, the remainder equals deposits less required reserves, which can be expressed as deposits times (1 – required reserve ratio). Clearly, the funds one bank lends to a borrower can become the borrower's deposits in another bank. The borrower's decision to hold wealth as deposits rather than cash also affects the money multiplier. Then, that second bank must keep a fraction of those new deposits as reserves and can lend out to other borrowers an amount equal to the deposits less required reserves.

We illustrate this process with an extended example. Suppose the Fed's required reserve ratio is 12%, and deposits at Bank A are $100 million, and those at Bank B are $50 million. Bank A has reserves of $12 million and outstanding loans of $88 million, and Bank B has reserves of $6 million with loans to borrowers of $44 million. For Bank A, the loan amount to $88 million equals either $100 million of deposits less $12 million of reserves, or $100 million times (1 – 0.12). For Bank B, loans of $44 million equal $50 million minus the 12%

required reserves of \$6 million. Thus, neither Bank A nor Bank B has any *excess reserves* (which equal total less required reserves). The level of reserves in the banking system has caused M_1 to reach the level of (let us say) \$900 billion, which equals \$250 billion in currency and \$650 billion in demand deposits. For this example, we assume that the amount of currency in the system does not change.

The Fed can increase the reserves by either lending to the banks or by purchasing government securities from the banks or other investors. (We ignore here the Fed's authority to change the required reserve ratio.) In this example, suppose that the Fed buys \$5 million of U.S. Treasury securities from a dealer who deposits the check, which is drawn on the Fed, with Bank A. Bank A's reserve account with the Fed has increased by \$5 million, and so have its (demand) deposits, its total reserves, and the overall level of M_1. But required reserves have risen only by \$600,000. This leaves an additional \$4.4 million that the bank is free and eager to invest in order to improve its income.

We continue by assuming that a machinery manufacturing firm borrows all of the \$4.4 million in a one-year loan, then buys equipment from a company that places all of that money in a checking account (or demand deposit) at another bank, which is Bank B. Bank A must transfer reserves for the amount of the loan to Bank B. The situation regarding Bank A is this: Its level of deposits remains unchanged at \$105 million; its loans have increased by \$4.4 million to \$92.4 million; its reserves have fallen by \$4.4 million (from \$17 million to \$12.6 million); so its ratio of reserves to deposits is again the required 12%, and it has reached its capacity for making loans because Bank A's deposits are unchanged from their level of \$900.005 billion.

After the transaction, Bank B's deposits have risen by \$4.4 million, an increase that raises the amount by an additional \$4.4 million (or \$9.4 million altogether, so far) to \$900.0094 billion. Bank B has total reserves of \$10.4 million and excess reserves equal to 88% of the \$4.4 million in new deposits. Thus, Bank B can lend \$3.87 million, keeping \$528,000 as required reserves. If loans of \$3.87 million are made to borrowers who place those loans as deposits with other banks, the process of creating money, in the form of M_1, will continue. Where will the process end, and what amount of new money, in the form of new demand deposits, will arise from the new reserves? In other words, what is the money multiplier?

In this example, the Fed's open market purchase of \$5 million of U.S. Treasury securities, along with the banks' incentive to make as many loans as they are permitted to, has created demand deposits of \$9.4 million at the first two banks involved. Still more deposits can be created at other banks. This process will continue as long as other banks use the ever smaller increases in demand deposits to make loans, which become additional demand deposits and excess reserves at still other banks, and so on. Although the process has no set limit in terms of time, there is a maximum number of dollars in new demand deposits that will spring from the new reserves.

This process is a form of a multiplier series that can be expressed in an algebraic formula. If we let ΔTDD be the total demand deposits created, ΔR be the reserves injected into the system by the Fed's purchase of Treasury securities, and REQ be the required reserve ratio, then the total of new deposits generated by the expansion of the initial injection of reserves would equal:

$$\Delta TDD = \Delta R + (1 - REQ) \times \Delta R + (1 - REQ)^2 \times \Delta R + (1 - REQ)^3 \times \Delta R + (1 - REQ)^4 \times \Delta R + \ldots \tag{7.1}$$

Because there are many potential elements in this series, which can get cumbersome, it is best to use this simple version of it:

$$\Delta TDD = \Delta R / REQ. \tag{7.2}$$

In the example, REQ equals 12%, and ΔR equals $5 million. Hence, new total demand deposits (if banks lend as much as they can and keep no excess reserves) amount to $5 million/0.12, or $41.67 million. The money multiplier is, therefore, 8.33 ($41.67/$5). As a result, total will reach $900.04167 billion when the process is completed, which equals the original $900 billion plus $41.67 million in new deposits. Equation (7.2) clearly shows that the eventual amount of the new demand deposits is negatively related to the required reserve ratio: As REQ falls, the change in TDD rises; and as REQ increases, the change in TDD declines. Thus, if everything in the example were the same, but REQ were 10% instead of 12%, the new demand deposits would reach $50 million.

Obviously, the process of reducing the money supply works in the opposite way. That is, if the Fed wants to drain reserves from the system and reduce the banks' lending ability, it sells securities. The reduction in reserves, as the public trades deposits for marketable securities, allows banks to make fewer new loans or to renew fewer old ones.

The Impact of Interest Rates on the Money Supply

In chapter 15, we explain how changes in the money supply affect interest rates. We note here only that interest rates actually influence the change in the money supply. This point emerges from an evaluation of two key assumptions made above.[8] First, banks are assumed to want to make all the loans they can. If, however, banks were to keep some excess reserves, they would make fewer new loans and generate fewer deposits at other banks, which would affect the amount of M_1 that the Fed's purchase of securities would generate.

One of the important factors in a bank's decisions about excess reserves is the level of market interest rates. High rates make excess reserves costly, because they represent loans not made and interest not earned. If rates are low, banks may keep some excess reserves. Hence, the level of interest rates positively influences the amount of M_1 that any increase

8. Lucas Papademos and Franco Modigliani, "The Supply of Money and the Control of Nominal Income," in *Handbook of Monetary Economics,* ed. Benjamin M. Friedman and Frank H. Hahn (Amsterdam: North-Holland, Elsevier, 1990), chapter 10.

in reserves will create. Moreover, interest rates can also positively (but probably only slightly) affect the amount of reserves in the system: High market rates may prompt banks to borrow at the discount window in order to make loans, and these borrowed funds are part of reserves.

By the second assumption, borrowers retain none of their loans in cash, but rather deposit all cash flows—proceeds from sold securities, loans, and so on—into checking accounts. In contrast, if borrowers took some of their borrowings in cash, banks would receive fewer deposits and would have fewer reserves from which to make new loans. Accordingly, the public's demand for cash as a portion of its liquid wealth has an impact on the amount of M_1 that arises from the Fed's injection of new reserves.

The level of market rates shapes decisions about cash holdings. Many deposit accounts pay interest, so holding cash imposes an opportunity cost. The higher the rate is, the greater the cost will be, and the more money investors will shuttle into deposits. But the rate on deposits is not the only relevant interest rate. The desired amount of deposits, from which transactions can be easily made, also reflects the rates of return from other assets. As those returns rise, investors would hold more in deposit accounts. For these reasons, the level of interest rates positively affects the size of the money multiplier and, hence, the amount that any increase in reserves will produce.

An example illustrates this point about the impact of rates on the money multiplier and the change in the money supply arising from an infusion of reserves by the Fed. The money multiplier from the previous example was 8.33 or 1/REQ, where REQ was 0.12. Let us now assume that the behavior of banks and depositors responds to interest rates. First, we will assume that the rate of return on bank loans is such that banks do not make all the loans they can but rather want to hold 1% of their deposits (TDD) in excess reserves (ER), with the result that the ratio ER/TDD equals 0.01. Second, let us suppose that the interest rate is at the level where the public will hold only 75% in checkable deposits (rather than 100% as before) and 25% in cash or currency. This means that the ratio C/TDD is 0.33. With these assumptions, the formula for the multiplier is now:

$$\frac{1+(C/TDD)}{REQ+(ER/TDD)+(C/TDD)}.$$

Plugging in the actual values, we have a much lower multiplier, which is:

$$\frac{1.33}{0.12+(0.1)+0.33}=2.89.$$

Remember, this multiplier is reduced because households and banks do not deposit or lend, respectively, all that they can, and these drains from the money creation process reduce the multiplier effect of any increase in reserves.

The Money Supply Process in an Open Economy

Our discussion so far describes central bank activity in what economists call a *closed economy*. A closed economy is one in which foreign transactors—of either goods or financial assets—play a negligible role. In the modern era, almost every country has an **open economy**, where foreign firms and investors account for a large and increasing share of economic activity. This is especially true of the world's largest economy, that of the United States. An understanding of the money supply process therefore must include the influence of the foreign sector.

Monetarily, the crucial fact of significant foreign participation in the U.S. economy is that foreign central banks, firms, and individuals hold a substantial number of U.S. dollars. They do so for transactional reasons—buying and selling goods and services in the United States—and for investment purposes—treating the dollar as a financial asset. What makes the foreign holdings of dollars important is that the dollar's exchange rate with currencies of most developed countries floats according to demand and supply in the market. (As explained in this chapter, most central banks, including the Fed, try to keep exchange rates within politically acceptable ranges.)

Shifts in the dollar's exchange rates affect the prices of domestic and imported goods, the revenues of U.S. companies, and the wealth of all investors in the country. As a result, the Fed accepts responsibility for maintaining some stability in the exchange rates. A major way to discharge this duty is to *intervene in the foreign exchange markets*. (See chapter 19 for more detail on foreign currency markets.) The Fed intervenes by buying and selling foreign currencies for its own account. (Most central banks of large economies own, or stand ready to own, a large amount of each of the world's major currencies, which are considered **international reserves**.)

If the Fed thinks the dollar's value is too high and a foreign currency's is too low, it can purchase some of the foreign currency with its own supply of dollars. A purchase involves increasing the outstanding number of dollars and thereby the monetary base. If the Fed thinks the dollar has too low a value relative to some other currency, it might sell some of its holdings of that currency for dollars. Thus, selling foreign currency entails a reduction in the monetary base. Intervention in the currency market is often a response to a particular international event. Moreover, the intervention usually involves a transaction with other central banks, which consists of an immediate exchange of currencies and an agreement for a future offsetting exchange. Thus, this kind of action allows the Fed to know the terms by which the currency deal will terminate and the time when it will terminate.

Our discussion of the elements of monetary policy in this chapter makes it clear that the dollar's exchange rates with important foreign currencies function as a major goal of monetary policy. That is, when forging and implementing policy, the Fed considers the effect of a change in the money supply on the relative value of the dollar in the foreign exchange market.

Dramatic evidence of the growing importance of international policy coordination on monetary matters occurred in two meetings of central bankers of the large industrial nations in the mid-1980s. In 1985, central bank chairpersons and directors of the United States, Great Britain, France, Germany, and Japan (known as the Group of Five) met at the Plaza Hotel in New York. This is known as the **Plaza Agreement**. They agreed to coordinate policies to bring down the value of the U.S. dollar and to stabilize international exchange rates and trade. In 1987, at the Louvre Museum in Paris, central bankers from these five countries and Canada agreed to work together to keep exchange rates at their current levels. These efforts at international cooperation on monetary and exchange issues are generally seen as successful.[9]

Goals of Monetary Policy

By using such tools as open market operations (which change the reserves in the banking system), the Fed can prompt the banking system and depositors to implement desired changes in the money supply and in its rates of growth. The Fed manages the money supply to achieve certain economic goals. In this section, we identify some of the more commonly cited goals of Fed policy.[10]

Stability in prices is a major goal of the Fed. The standard way of measuring inflation is the change in a major price index. Based on the historical experience with inflation, policymakers and economists came to appreciate how unstable price levels retard economic growth, provoke volatility in interest rates, stimulate consumption, deter savings, and cause capricious redistribution of income and wealth with attendant social disturbances.

However, inflation in advanced economies is seldom (if ever) the result of excessive demand due to monetary or fiscal policy. A more important source of inflation is an economic shock in the supply of a crucial material, such as the oil shocks of the 1970s, which affected almost all countries. Evidence that the inflation at the end of the 1970s was not related to excessive demand for goods and services is that it occurred with high unemployment and gave the world a period of **stagflation**, which is a condition of both inflation and recession.

It is important to note that, when confronted with a supply shock, a central bank such as the Fed has two choices. First, the banking authorities can refuse to accommodate the higher price levels that follow the shock by matching them with an increase in the money supply. The results of nonaccommodation will initially tend to be higher interest rates and a decline in economic activity. For this reason, central banks and political authorities frequently have opted for the second choice, which is a policy of accommodation and increased growth in the supply of money. Unfortunately, this kind of policy permits the inflation to continue unchecked or possibly to accelerate.

9. Frederic S. Mishkin, "What Should Central Banks Do?" *Federal Reserve Bank of St. Louis Review* 82, no. 6 (November/December 2000): 1–13.

10. Ben S. Bernanke and Frederic S. Mishkin, "Central Bank Behavior and the Strategy of Money Policy: Observations from Six Industrialized Countries," NBER Working Paper No. 4082 (Cambridge, MA: NBER, May 1992): 1–77.

High employment (or low unemployment) of the civilian labor force represents a second major goal of the Fed. Although politicians often speak of the U.S. government's commitment to promoting "full employment," most people understand that an unemployment rate of zero is not possible. The reason is that **frictional unemployment**—the temporary unemployment of those changing jobs or seeking new or better ones—is both unavoidable and helpful to an economy. It is unavoidable, because people do change jobs and are likely to do so more readily as employment levels rise, and because workers are always leaving or entering the labor market. Frictional unemployment is helpful, because it allows a constant reallocation of labor and leads to increased efficiency in the workforce.

Given that zero unemployment is not a feasible goal, the appropriate goal of the Fed and other governmental policymakers is actually a high level of employment. But economists and policymakers cannot agree on a suitable definition or specification of high employment. It does not help to specify a high level of employment as one that approaches 100% less the level of frictional unemployment, because there is also little agreement on the true rate of frictional unemployment. For practical purposes, many observers consider that a civilian unemployment rate between 4% and 5% indicates an economy operating at or near a level of high employment.

It is important to realize that high employment is one of the Fed's goals because, in certain circumstances, the Fed's policy can indirectly influence the level of employment. When the economy is operating sluggishly or below capacity, increases in the money supply can bring about economic expansion and employment, because those increases can reduce interest rates, stimulate investment, encourage consumption, and lead to the creation of new jobs. A policy of expansion of the money supply is frequently described as an "easy money policy," because the Fed is said to ease the way for banks to acquire reserves and extend loans. But when the economy's output is close to capacity (given its stock of productive assets and population), easy money policies can be disadvantageous, because they may kindle inflation and raise interest rates. Policymakers must often wrestle with the tough question of whether easing monetary policy will create higher employment or simply ignite inflation, or an undesirable combination of higher unemployment and higher inflation.

Economic growth, the third goal of the Fed, is the increase in an economy's output of goods and services. Clearly, this goal is closely related to the goal of high employment. As would be expected, there is little agreement about the exact rate of growth that policymakers should try to achieve. Variously described as "sustainable" or "steady" or "reasonable," the economy's appropriate rate of growth has to be substantial enough to generate high employment in the context of an expanding workforce but low enough to ward off inflation. The goal of stabilizing interest rates is directly related to the goal of growth and the Fed's responsibility for the health of the nation's financial and banking system.

Note that the goal is to stabilize rates, not to prevent changes in them. Interest rates move up and down with changes in economic conditions. Those movements can provide signals of important economic developments, and it would be a mistake for the Fed to try to prevent such changes in rates. However, the Fed may help economic conditions by trying to moderate the impact of large moves in rates. Some increases in rates may reflect temporary or reversible developments, and the Fed can appropriately respond to these changes in a way that eliminates or greatly reduces such increases.

Stability in foreign currency exchange rates is the final Fed goal that we will discuss. The foreign exchange market has become much more important in recent years, as the economies of the world have become more integrated, and foreign currency exchange rates have begun to affect ever larger segments of the economy. Because exchange rates are clearly dependent in some ways on the monetary policies of the major countries, the Fed has accepted the goal of stabilizing foreign exchange rates.[11] Of course, some fluctuations in exchange rates arise for economically sound reasons that monetary policy in one country cannot influence or control. A prime example is a pronounced difference in the fiscal policies between two countries. In general, an important explanation of unstable rates among most of the world's major currencies has been the failure of the large industrial economies to coordinate their fiscal and monetary policies.

A chief disadvantage of unstable foreign currency exchange rates is that volatility in the prices of currencies inhibits the international trade that offers a host of benefits to all participating countries. Furthermore, both high and low exchange rates for the dollar are considered detrimental to the U.S. economy. High exchange rates (i.e., a "strong" dollar or one with high value in terms of foreign currencies) reduce demand for U.S.-made products abroad and stimulate the import of foreign goods; the result is a trade imbalance. A "weak" dollar contributes to inflation, as U.S. buyers pay more for the many goods they do import. For these reasons, the Fed's goal of stability in the currency market often amounts to keeping the value of the dollar, in terms of the major foreign currencies, within some range that is considered politically acceptable and helpful for international trade, especially exports.

Trade-Offs and Conflicts among Policies

This account of the widely accepted goals of monetary policy reveals a profound problem in the conduct of monetary policy. The goals are numerous, but the Fed's capabilities are limited to the simple menu of (1) trying to raise the rate of growth in the money supply by providing more reserves to banks, and (2) trying to reduce the rate of monetary expansion by reducing the reserves in the banking system. As a result, often one goal may require a monetary policy that is inconsistent with some other goal. In other words, a monetary policy that furthers progress toward one goal may actually make attaining another either difficult or impossible.

For example, an easy money policy of expanding the money supply (that is, stimulating higher growth rates for one or more monetary aggregates) might appear to promote growth and low interest rates, but it might also raise the prospect of inflation, affect the exchange

11. Bernanke and Mishkin, "Central Bank Behavior and the Strategy of Money Policy," p. 11.

rate disadvantageously, and increase interest rates. Another example concerns the goal of price stability and the Fed's responsibility for the health of financial institutions. Suppose that, at a time of high inflation, many such institutions have invested according to inflationary expectations and have made many loans to firms dealing in real assets. Suppose, too, that the Fed decides it needs to take steps to curb current inflation. In such a situation, the tight monetary policy that accomplishes this goal—a policy of reducing the rate of growth in the money supply—actually may imperil the institutions, because the policy might well weaken the financial health of the firms that borrowed from the financial institutions.

Economists frequently describe this problem in this way: The Fed's policy necessarily represents trade-offs among its various goals, which have different levels of relative importance at different times, depending on the state of the economy. In other words, the Fed, like any monetary policymaker, has numerous goals, but at any given time, it focuses on the goal that is most in danger of not being achieved.

Goals and Types of Targets

A second problem in the implementation of monetary policy is that the Fed has no direct control over the goals that are the final objectives of its policies. The Fed cannot, with any of its monetary tools (open market operations, discount rates, etc.), directly influence such complex economic variables as the prices of goods and services, the unemployment rate, the growth in GDP, and foreign exchange rates. We know the Fed can affect the rate of growth in the money supply only by means of its control of reserves in the banking system. As discussed in chapter 6, the Fed cannot fully determine changes in the money supply. The growth in the money supply depends to a substantial degree on the preferences, actions, and expectations of numerous banks, borrowers, and consumers.

The Fed seeks to achieve its goals through a form of chain reaction, which has the following chronology and structure. The Fed first employs one or more of its tools to affect what are called **operating targets**, which are monetary and financial variables whose changes tend to bring about changes in **intermediate targets**. Intermediate targets, which may include interest rates or monetary aggregates, are variables that have a reasonably reliable linkage with the variables, such as output or employment, that constitute the Fed's goals or **ultimate objectives**. Thus, the Fed exerts whatever influence it has on the intermediate targets in an indirect way, by means of its control over the operating targets. So its power over the variables that make up its goals is quite indirect and dependent on the linkages among the various targets and goals.

Although economists have argued many years about the identity of appropriate operating and intermediate target variables, there is no dispute about the chief characteristics of a suitable operating or intermediate target.[12] The first characteristic is *linkage:* An operating target

12. A formal treatment of the requirements for targets is available in Benjamin M. Friedman, "Targets and Instruments of Monetary Policy," in *Handbook of Monetary Economics*, ed. Benjamin M. Friedman and Frank H. Hahn (Amsterdam: North-Holland, 1990), chapter 22.

must have an expected connection with the intermediate target, which itself must eventually affect the economy in a way that is consistent with the Fed's goals. The second characteristic is *observability:* Both operating targets and intermediate targets must be readily and regularly observable economic variables, so that the Fed can monitor its success in influencing their levels or rates of change. The third and final characteristic is *responsiveness:* To function as an operating target, a variable must respond quickly and in an expected way to the Fed's use of one or more of its tools; and an appropriate intermediate target is one that reacts, in an anticipated way and a meaningfully short time, to changes in the operating target.

Choosing the operating target In some countries, a key foreign currency exchange rate may well function as an operating target. Although the Fed has become more conscious of foreign exchange developments in the past 15 years or so, it has not adopted the dollar's exchange rate with any currency or group of currencies as an operating target. Instead, the Fed's monetary policy has directly targeted either short-term interest rates or some measure of bank reserves.

An important point about the operating target is that the Fed must choose either a short-term rate or the level of some reserves and cannot choose to target both kinds of variables.[13] To understand why the Fed must make a choice, remember what the Fed's tools allow it to do. Those tools—whether the secondary ones of discount loans and management of reserve requirements, or the primary tool of open market operations—enable the Fed to change only the level of reserves in the banking system. Obviously, a change in reserves also changes short-term rates, because they are determined in the interbank market for excess reserves. Under most circumstances, the change in reserves is negatively related to the change in interest rates: As the Fed supplies more reserves and banks gain more ability to make more loans and buy other assets, the short-term rates fall; as the Fed withdraws reserves and reduces the banks' lending capacity, the short-term rates rise.

Because of this inverse relationship, it might seem possible for the Fed to view each of these variables as a target and to set them all simultaneously. But, in fact, that is impossible. The reason is that the Fed cannot know or predict the public's **demand for money**, which is the aggregate demand for holding some of its wealth in the form of liquid balances, such as bank deposits. The public's desire to hold money depends on many factors, especially preferences and anticipation about future income and price inflation, among other things. Unexpected changes in those factors may well shift the public's desired holdings in significant ways. Therefore, the Fed cannot be certain how much impact any change in reserves will have on short-term rates. Without knowledge of what the rate will be for a given change in reserves, the Fed cannot simultaneously determine both the rate and the level of reserves.

By choosing its operating target, then, the Fed makes the decision to let the other variable fluctuate in response to changes in the public's demand for money. When an interest rate is

13. William Poole, "Optimal Choice of Monetary Policy Instrument in a Simple Stochastic Macro Model," *Quarterly Journal of Economics* 84, no. 2 (1970): 197–216.

the target, the Fed must let the growth in reserves vary as it strives to keep that interest rate at a certain level or to smooth its transition to a new (higher or lower) level. When some aggregate of reserves is the target, the Fed is forced to allow interest rates to change substantially, so that it can try to bring the level of reserves to that dictated by the Fed's policy. Of course, the Fed can change its target from time to time in order to rein in the variable that has fluctuated while the Fed focused on the other. But however often the Fed might change targets, it remains a fact that, at any given time, the Fed cannot target both rates and reserves.

Choosing the intermediate target The best known of the intermediate targets is the money supply, measured by one of the more inclusive monetary aggregates that we described in chapter 6. In the 1970s, many countries began to target the growth rates of one or more aggregates. The policy, at least as publicly stated, was to supply reserves at a pace that would lead to a selected rate of growth in the aggregates. The idea behind this policy was that the goals of central bank activity—growth, stable prices, and so on—would be realized if the money supply were to grow at a known and steady rate. Over time, other intermediate targets have been specified, and they include foreign exchange rates, the level of national output (such as the gross domestic product), and the level of actual or expected inflation.[14] Furthermore, the array of interest rates—including rates available to consumers and investors—may also function as a target variable. We have said that a prime characteristic of a suitable intermediate target is that it is readily observable. Some of the candidates mentioned above do not fit that rule: Information on the GDP, for example, is available only on a quarterly basis, and measures of actual or expected inflation may be subject to considerable dispute.[15]

Interestingly, in recent years, many central banks have adopted inflation, despite certain problems in measurement, as a key intermediate variable. The reason is that the monetary aggregates have not had the kind of reliable and persistent relationship either with target variables or with goals that policymakers require. In most European countries, policymakers follow price indexes for sensitive commodities and make decisions about short-term rates and bank reserves on the basis of actual and expected inflation. In the United States, it is commonly said that former Fed chairman Alan Greenspan carefully monitored the price of gold, among other commodities. Thus, the purchasing power of the domestic currency and the foreign exchange rate of the currency have become far more typical intermediate targets than have monetary aggregates.

Global Central Banks

We conclude this chapter with a brief description of several aspects of global central banks. The investigation of global bank regulation and supervision was motivated by the global

14. Bernanke and Mishkin, "Central Bank Behavior and the Strategy of Money Policy," p. 41.

15. Friedman, "Targets and Instruments of Monetary Policy," p. 1203.

Table 7.2
Some basic differences in banking systems around the world.

Characteristic	Brazil	China	United Kingdom	United States	High	Low	Median
Total bank assets/GDP (%)	105	189	607	84	1,942	18	78
Total bank claims on private sector/GDP (%)	53	N/A	206	57	206	6	39
Number of banks per 100,000 people	0.1	0.02	0.5	2.1	437.5	0.01	0.4
Share of total assets for the five largest banks (%)	71	63	68	47	100	12	73
Share of total bank assets that are government owned (%)	44	N/A	26	0	74	0	8.5
Share of total bank assets that are foreign owned (%)	18	N/A	18	N/A	100	0	49
Professional supervisors per bank	2.1	N/A	0.8	0.3	25.3	0.1	2.7
Percent of 10 largest banks rated by international agencies (%)	100	N/A	100	100	100	0	70

Source: This table was created from data in table 1 in James R. Barth, Gerard Caprio, and Ross Levine "Bank Regulation and Supervision in 180 Countries from 1999 to 2011," NBER Working Paper No. 18733 (Cambridge, MA: National Bureau of Economic Research, 2013).

Note: Columns 3 and 7 represent absolute numbers; the other six columns represent percentages.

banking crisis of 2008. These banking problems still plague many countries. Systemic banking crises have continued to destabilize global economies since 1990.[16]

Measuring bank regulation and supervision around the world is, however, difficult. Hundreds of laws and regulations, emanating from different components of national and local governments, define policies regarding bank capital standards, the entry requirements of new domestic and foreign banks, bank ownership restrictions, and loan provisioning guidelines.

Table 7.2 provides information on the global commercial banking system for four selected countries: Brazil, China, the United States, and the United Kingdom. The information provided is the number of banks, the proportion of assets in government-owned banks, the proportion of banking assets in foreign-owned banks, the number of official bank supervisors per bank in the country, and the percentage of the 10 largest banks in a country that are rated by one of the major international rating agencies. The high, low, and median values for each characteristic shown in the table's last three columns are for 180 countries. As can be seen, the range of these characteristics for the global banking is significant.

Table 7.3 shows the factors that countries consider when assessing systemic risk in the banking sector. The factors that regulators in most countries consider most important are bank capital ratios and bank liquidity ratios, whereas the least-often mentioned factor is stock market prices.

16. James R. Barth, Gerard Caprio, and Ross Levine, "Bank Regulation and Supervision in 180 Countries from 1999 to 2011," NBER Working Paper 18733 (Cambridge, MA: National Bureau of Economic Research, 2013), http://www.nber.org/papers/w18733.

Table 7.3
Bank supervisory criteria for assessing systemic risk.

Criterion	Number of Countries Reporting
Bank capital ratios	113
Bank liquidity ratios	104
Sectoral composition of bank loan portfolios	101
Growth in bank credit	100
Bank nonperforming loan ratios	99
Bank profitability ratios	93
Bank provisioning ratios	92
Bank leverage ratios	84
Foreign exchange position of banks	79
Housing prices	48
Stock market prices	46

Source: This table was created from data in figure 15 in James R. Barth, Gerard Caprio, and Ross Levine, "Bank Regulation and Supervision in 180 Countries from 1999 to 2011," NBER Working Paper 18733 (Cambridge, MA: National Bureau of Economic Research, 2013).

Among the major findings for the 180 countries covering the period from 1999 through 2011 is the substantial heterogeneity of bank regulatory and supervisory policies across countries. And, although there has been some convergence for some types of banking sector policies, bank regulatory and supervisory policies remain quite diverse. The diversity in regulatory regimes provides an excellent opportunity for research examining the causes of these policy differences, the impacts of banking policies on the performance of banks, and the related effects on the overall financial sector and real economy. The last column in table 7.1 provides the ratio of public debt to its GDP for the 19 countries whose central banks are shown in the table.

Key Points

- The central bank of a country plays a key role in that country's economic and financial markets by implementing policies to stabilize the currency and controlling the money supply.
- The central bank may also act as a lender of last resort to the bank system in order to avert a financial crisis.
- Evidence suggests that a central bank can act more effectively by being independent of the government.
- The Federal Reserve System is the U.S. central bank.
- The Fed's tools of monetary policy include required reserves, open market operations and repurchases, and discount loans to banks.
- The Fed supplies reserves to the banking system, which participates, along with investors, in generating the money supply.

- The chief means of supplying reserves is open market operations: The Fed's purchase of government securities provides reserves, and the Fed's sale of securities reduces reserves.
- The money supply is composed of various types of money as well as demand and time deposits, which can be grouped into monetary aggregates.
- The fundamental aggregate is the monetary base, composed of currency plus total reserves in the banking system.
- M_1 equals currency plus all checkable deposits; other aggregates include various time deposits.
- The money multiplier is the process by which changes in bank reserves generate larger changes in the money supply.
- Banks use added reserves to buy assets or to make loans; the seller or borrower redeposits these proceeds, which then support additional loans, and so on.
- The value of the multiplier depends on the required reserve ratio, the public's demand for cash, the banks' willingness to make loans, and the level of interest rates.
- The growing international integration of economies requires that the Fed, along with other central banks, consider the impact of its monetary operations on foreign currency exchange rates.
- The goals of monetary policy include a stable price level, economic growth, high employment, stable interest rates, and predictable and steady currency exchange rates.
- Monetary policies involve difficult trade-offs, and policies that help achieve one goal may make another goal less attainable.
- Because the Fed has no direct control or influence on the complex economic variables that constitute the goals, it must identify intermediate targets that influence these variables and are, in turn, influenced by operating targets that are variables the Fed can control to a substantial extent.
- The Fed's intermediate targets may be interest rates, monetary aggregates, or possibly exchange rates.

Questions

1. What is the role of a central bank?
2. Why is it argued that a central bank should be independent of the government?
3. Identify each participant and its role in the process by which the money supply changes and monetary policy is implemented.
4. Describe the structure of the Board of Governors of the Federal Reserve System.
5. a. Explain what is meant by the statement "the United States has a fractional reserve banking system."

b. How are these items related: total reserves, required reserves, and excess reserves?

6. What is the required reserve ratio, and how has the 1980 Depository Institutions Deregulation and Monetary Control Act constrained the Fed's control over the ratio?

7. In what two forms can a bank hold its required reserves?

8. a. What is an open market purchase by the Fed?

b. Which unit of the Fed decides on open market policy, and which unit implements that policy?

c. What is the immediate consequence of an open market purchase?

9. Distinguish between an open market sale and a matched sale (which is the same as a matched sale–purchase transaction or a reverse repurchase agreement).

10. What is the discount rate, and to what type of action by a bank does it apply?

11. Define the monetary base and M_2.

12. Describe the basic features of the money multiplier.

13. Suppose the Fed were to inject $100 million of reserves into the banking system by an open market purchase of Treasury bills. If the required reserve ratio were 10%, what is the maximum increase in M_1 that the new reserves would generate? Assume that banks make all the loans their reserves allow, that firms and individuals keep all their liquid assets in depository accounts, and no money is in the form of currency.

14. Assume the situation from question 13, except now assume that banks hold a ratio of 0.5% of excess reserves to deposits and that the public keeps 20% of its liquid assets in the form of cash. Under these conditions, what is the money multiplier? Explain why this value of the multiplier is so much lower than the multiplier from question 13.

15. Name three widely accepted goals of monetary policy.

16. What keeps the Fed from being able to achieve its goals in a direct way?

17. Comment on this statement by an official of the Federal Reserve:

> [The Fed] can control nonborrowed reserves through open market operations [but] it cannot control total reserves, because the level of borrowing at the discount window is determined in the short run by the preferences of depository institutions.[17]

18. Why is it impossible for the Fed to target simultaneously both the Fed funds interest rate and the level of reserves in the banking system?

19. It is often said that you cannot hit two targets with one arrow. How does this comment apply to the use of monetary policy to "stabilize the economy"?

20. What are the tools and responsibilities of the Fed for monitoring and affecting the level of activity in the stock market?

17. Alfred Broaddus, "A Primer on the Fed," in *The Financial Analyst's Handbook*, ed. Sumner N. Levine (Homewood, IL: Dow Jones–Irwin, 1988), p. 194.

8 Insurance Companies

CONTENTS

Learning Objectives

After reading this chapter, you will understand:

- the role of insurance companies as risk bearers;
- the different types of insurance companies;
- the fundamentals of the insurance industry;
- the nature of the business of insurance companies;
- how insurance companies generate income;
- the structure of the insurance industry;
- what reinsurance companies and captive insurance companies are;
- the difference between a stock company and a mutual company, and the advantages and disadvantages of each type;
- the types of life insurance policies;
- investment-oriented products offered by life insurance companies (guaranteed investment contracts and annuities);
- the difference between general account products and separate account products;

- the reasons insurance companies fail and whether they should be treated as globally systemic important financial institutions;
- the regulation of insurance companies in the United States and the European Union;
- the debate and evidence about whether insurers pose significant systemic risk;
- catastrophic risks faced by insurers, and strategies to mitigate those risks;
- what catastrophe bonds and insurance-linked securities are;
- insurance company investment strategies;
- the expansion of insurers into the pension fund area and banks (bank insurance model); and
- what insurance-based investment banking is.

Insurance companies provide (sell and service) insurance policies, which are legally binding contracts. According to the insurance contract, insurance companies (or simply, "insurers") promise to pay specified sums contingent on the occurrence of some specified future event or events, such as death or an automobile accident. Thus, insurers are risk bearers. They accept or underwrite the risk in return for a fee, referred to as an insurance premium, paid by the policyholder.

Insurers are key participants in a country's economy not only as suppliers of risk management products for a country's households, businesses, and governments, but also as major investors. With the funds available to invest from the premiums received, insurers are major buyers of the investment products described in later chapters, as well as participants in the financial derivatives markets described in part VIII of this book. They also provide investment-oriented products that we describe later in this chapter. In addition to their importance in a country, they are major players in the global financial markets with the concern that insurers pose a significant systemic risk and whether major insurers should be considered globally systemically important financial institutions (SIFIs). We'll address this issue later in this chapter.

Types of Insurance

Countries have different types of insurance policies that insurance companies may issue. The classification of insurance companies in the United States are life insurance, health insurance, property and casualty (P&C) insurance, liability insurance, umbrella insurance, disability insurance, long-term care insurance, and structured settlements.

Life Insurance

For life insurance, the risk insured against is the death of the insured. The **life insurance company** pays the beneficiary of the life insurance policy in the event of the death of the insured. There are several types of life insurance policies, which will be examined later in this chapter.

Health Insurance

In the case of health insurance, the risk insured is medical treatment of the insured. The **health insurance company** pays the insured (or the provider of the medical service) all or a portion of the cost of medical treatment by doctors, hospitals, or others. This type of insurance has undergone significant changes in the past two decades in many countries. As a result, the health industry has been significantly restructured, so that the largest health insurance companies specialize in health insurance rather than sell health insurance in addition to other products, such as life insurance.

Property and Casualty Insurance

The risk insured against by a P&C insurance company is damage to various types of property. Specifically, it is insurance against financial loss caused by damage, destruction, or loss to property as the result of an identifiable event that is sudden, unexpected, or unusual. The major types of such insurance are (1) a house and its contents against such risks as fire, flood, earthquakes, and theft (homeowners insurance and its variants) and (2) a vehicle against collision, theft, and other damage (automobile insurance and its variants)

Liability Insurance

With liability insurance, the risk insured against is litigation, or the risk of lawsuits against the insured due to actions by the insured or others. Liability insurance offers protection against third-party claims, that is, payment is usually made to someone who experiences a loss and who is not a party to the insurance contract, not to the insured.

Umbrella Insurance

Typically, umbrella insurance is pure liability coverage over and above the coverage provided by all the policies beneath it, such as homeowner, automobile, and boat policies. The name "umbrella" refers to the fact that it covers liability claims of all the policies underneath it. In addition to providing liability coverage over the limits of the underlying policies, it provides coverage for claims that are excluded from other liability policies, such as invasion of privacy, libel, and false arrest. Typically, users of umbrella policies have a large amount of assets that would be placed at risk in the event of a catastrophic claim.

Disability Insurance

Disability insurance insures against the inability of employed persons to earn an income in either their own occupation ("own occ" disability insurance) or any occupation ("any occ"). Typically, "own occ" disability insurance is written for professionals in white-collar occupations (often physicians and dentists) and "any occ" is for blue-collar workers. Another distinction in disability insurance is the sustainability of the policy, which can be of two types. The first is guaranteed renewable (or guaranteed continuable), whereby the issuer has to sustain the policy for the specified period of time, and the issuer cannot make any changes in the policy except to change the premium rates for the entire class of policy (but not for an individual policyholder). The other type is noncancelable and guaranteed renewable (or simply noncancelable), whereby the issuer has no right to make any change in any policy during the specified period. Disability insurance is also divided into short-term disability and long-term disability, with six months being the typical dividing time.

Long-Term Care Insurance

As average life expectancies rise, older individuals have become concerned about outliving their assets and being unable to care for themselves as they age. In addition, custodial care for the aged has become very expensive and in many countries may not be covered by some form of government-provided insurance for the aged. Thus, demand has surged for insurance to provide custodial care for the aged who are no longer able to care for themselves. This care may be provided in either the insured's own residence or a separate custodial facility. Many types of long-term care insurance are available.

Structured Settlements

Structured settlements are fixed, guaranteed periodic payments over a long period of time, typically resulting from a settlement on a disability policy or other type of insurance policy.

For example, suppose an individual is hit by an automobile and, as a result, is unable to work for the rest of his or her life. The individual may sue the P&C company for future lost earnings and medical care. To settle the suit, the P&C company may agree to make specified payments over time to the individual. The P&C company may then purchase a policy from a life insurance company to make the agreed-on payments.

Fundamentals of the Insurance Industry

A major task for the insurers is deciding which applications for insurance they should accept and which ones to reject. The process of deciding which application to accept or reject is referred to as the **underwriting process**. The insurance company must also determine how much to charge for the insurance if it accepts the application. This activity is referred to as **policy pricing**.

Because insurance companies collect insurance premiums initially and make payments later *when* or *if* an insured event occurs, insurance companies maintain the premiums collected in an investment portfolio that generates a return. Thus, the two sources of income for insurance companies include the underwriting income (the insurance premium) and the investment income earned. The investment returns from the investment of the insurance premiums accumulate until the funds are paid out on the policy. The premium provides a fairly stable type of revenue. Investment returns may vary considerably with the performance of the investment strategy pursued by the insurer's management. Consequently, an insurance company's profits result from the difference between its revenue (i.e., insurance premiums collected plus investment returns) and its operating expenses and insurance payments or benefits. The type of risk insured against, which determines the level of premium collected and benefit paid, defines the insurance company.

A fundamental aspect of the insurance industry results from the relationship between its revenues and costs. A baker purchases ingredients, uses these ingredients to make assorted bakery products, and then sells those products, all in a fairly short time frame. Therefore, a bakery's profit margin can be relatively easily calculated. In contrast, an insurance company collects premium payments and invests them. The payments to a policyholder on the insurance policy occur later and, depending on the type of insurance, often in an unpredictable manner. Consequently, the payments are contingent on potential future events. For example, for life insurance, it is certain that everyone will die. However, it is not known when any specific individual will die. The timing of the payment on any specific insurance company that sells insurance on an individual's life is not known with certainty. Although the payments on any single life insurance policy are uncertain, actuaries can predict the pattern of deaths on a large portfolio of life insurance policies, making the aggregate much more predictable in terms of the patterns of death using standard actuarial tables.

At the other extreme, not only are payments on home insurance against hurricanes singularly uncertain, but the payments on a portfolio of homes remains uncertain as well. If one house in some geographical region is destroyed by a flood, it is likely that many other homes will also be destroyed. Thus, two important differences distinguish calculating the profitability of bread manufacturers and of insurance companies. The first is that the timing and magnitude of the payments are much less certain for an insurance company. The second is the long lag between the receipts and payments made by an insurance company, which introduces the importance of the investment portfolio and the generation of investment income.

These differences in the providers of a baked goods and insurance lead to differences in the way consumers of bread and insurance view their providers. Purchasers of baked goods are not harmed if the bakery goes bankrupt the day after they buy the baked goods. The purchaser of baked goods receives the product immediately, but the owner of an insurance policy receives a payment on the insurance policy in the future only if an insured event occurs, so the policy owner must be concerned about the continued viability of the insurance company. Therefore, the credit rating of an insurance company is important to a purchaser of insurance, especially for the types of insurance that may be paid well into the future.

Structure of Insurance Companies

Based on the previous discussion, insurance companies are really a composite of three companies. First, there is the "home office" or actual insurance company. This company designs the insurance contract ("manufactures" the contract) and provides the backing for the financial guarantees on the contract, that is, assures the policyholder that the contract will pay off under the conditions of the contract. This company is called the **manufacturer** and **guarantor** of the insurance policy. Second, there is the investment component that invests the premiums collected in the investment portfolio. This is the **investment company**.

The third component of an insurance company is the **distribution component** or the sales force. Distribution forces come in different types. First, there are the agents who are associated with the company. Agents sell only or mainly the company's own manufactured products. These agents typically are not employees of the company (although some companies also use employees as salespeople) but are entrepreneurs financially associated with the company. There are also **brokers** who are not associated with any company but sell the insurance products of many companies. Brokers have traditionally operated individually but are increasingly operating in groups called **producer groups**. In many countries, changes in regulations have allowed commercial banks to become distributors of insurance products. We describe this bank insurance model later in this chapter. The Internet has also been used by some insurance companies to distribute insurance products directly to clients. Internet distribution is very new and has considerable potential but is still in its infancy. This mode of distribution has been most successful in the more commodity-like insurance products, such as term life insurance and automobile insurance.

These three components of insurance companies traditionally have been combined in one overall company, but they are increasingly being separated, and the three functions are being provided by different companies. First, as previously mentioned, many insurance companies use independent brokers or producer groups to distribute their products rather than use their own agents. Many companies no longer have their own agents and sell all their products exclusively through brokers, producer groups, or on the Internet. Second, insurance companies are increasingly outsourcing parts of their investment portfolio or even the entire portfolio to external independent investment managers. Investment managers are also increasingly diversifying, that is, not specializing in managing any one type of assets (such as pension fund assets, mutual funds, or insurance company assets) but are managing several or all of them. Third, although the home office component of an insurance company seems to be the core of the insurance company, some home offices use external actuarial firms to design their contracts. And, more importantly, they may reinsure some or all of the liabilities they incur in providing insurance.

Reinsurance Companies

To reduce risk, insurance companies may reinsure some or all of the liabilities they incur in providing insurance. Companies established for that purpose are called **reinsurance companies** or **reinsurers**. According to the reinsurance transaction, the initial (primary) insurer transfers the risk of the insurance policy to the reinsurer. The guarantee on the insurance policy is thus provided by the reinsurer rather than by the primary insurance company.

The five largest reinsurers in the world are Munich Reinsurance Company; Swiss Reinsurance Company Limited; Hannover Re; Berkshire Hathaway Inc.; and Lloyd's. The two larger reinsurers in Asia are Korean Reinsurance Company and China Reinsurance (Group) Corporation.

Captive Insurance Companies

In chapter 2, we described how a company may decide to retain certain risks. To insure against these risks, companies have established insurance companies that they wholly own. The insurance companies created for this purpose are referred to as **captive insurance companies**. These insurers provide their owners a form of self-insurance and can provide for insurance protection against any type of commercial risks that are provided for by P&C insurance companies, as well as life insurance. In the United States, the majority of Fortune 500 companies have established captive insurance companies. In recent years, smaller companies have also created captives. Worldwide there are about 5,000 captives. Even a government can set up a captive. For example, the government of China created captive and marine cargo specialties to establish captives for a few of its state-owned enterprises.

There are several types of captives. Some of the alternative captives are single-parent captives, association captives, industry captives, and diversified captives. Most captives are **single-parent captives**—the captives provide pure self-insurance for the parent company that created them. **Association captives** are created by a trade association or members of an industry to provide insurance coverage for their members. Typically, association captives insure against liability risks, such as medical malpractice lawsuits. When companies in the same industry jointly create a captive to deal with a specific insurance problem faced by the industry, the captives created are referred to as **industry captives**. Captives that underwrite unrelated risks in addition to the parent company's business are referred to as **diversified captives**.

There are legal jurisdictions where most captives have been domiciled outside of the home country of the company or association creating the captive. These legal jurisdictions offer favorable tax laws, as well as requirements regarding capitalization requirements, investment restrictions, fees, and financial reporting requirements. The major ones are Anguilla, Barbados, Bermuda, Cayman Islands, Ireland (Dublin), Guernsey, Isle of Man, and Luxembourg. In the United States, states have developed their own regulations regarding captives for medical insurance as a result of The Patient Protection and Affordable Care Act (commonly known as "Obamacare").

Stock versus Mutual Insurance Companies

Focusing on the United States, the two major forms of insurance companies are stock and mutual. A **stock company** is similar in structure to any corporation or public company. Shares (of ownership) are owned by independent shareholders and are traded publicly. The shareholders care only about the performance of their shares (i.e., the stock appreciation and the dividends). Their holding period, and thus their view, may be short term. The insurance policies are simply the products or business of the company, and management is evaluated in terms of performance.

In contrast, a **mutual company** has no stock and no external owners. The policyholders are the owners. The owners, that is, the policyholders, care primarily or even solely about the performance on their insurance policies, notably the company's ability to pay on the policy. Because these payments may occur considerably into the future, the policyholders' view may be long term. Thus, whereas stock companies answer to two constituencies (their stockholders and policyholders), mutual companies deal with only one, because their policyholders and their owners are the same.

The reason for the existence of both forms of insurance structures has been examined by economists. Organizational theory is the field in management that tries to identify the organizational structure that provides the most effective solution to the risk that a firm's managers will seek to make decisions based on their own self-interest at the expense of the firm's owners. This is the principal-agent problem in financial economics: Agents in the form of managers act in their own interest rather than that of the principals in the form of owners of the company. One study that has looked at the reason for the existence of the two structures for life insurance companies notes the following:

> The coexistence of stock and mutual companies in the property-casualty insurance industry suggests that at least one of three hypotheses is true: the two organizational forms have competing advantages; the market may be rich enough that different organizational forms can survive in different niches; and the market may not have reached its final equilibrium (or perhaps history may influence the equilibrium).[1]

At one time in the United States, the largest insurers operated as mutual companies, but a number of mutual companies have converted to stock companies, a process referred to

1. Patricia Born, William M. Gentry, W. Kip Viscusi, and Richard J. Zeckhauser, "Organizational Form and Insurance Company Performance: Stocks versus Mutuals," in *The Economics of Property-Casualty Insurance*, ed. David F. Bradford (Chicago: University of Chicago Press, 1998), chap. 6, 168–192.

as **demutualization**. The motivation for demutualization is the need to obtain funding to support growth. When a mutual company converts to a stock company, shares can be sold to the public to raise funds, and stock can be used as currency to acquire or merge with other insurance companies.

Types of Life Insurance Policies

Table 8.1 shows the five largest life companies in the United State, Europe, and Asia as measured by total assets. Although different types of life insurance policies are sold in different countries, we focus our description on policies sold in the United States. For this reason, it is important to understand the impact of the U.S. tax code on certain types of insurance production. The U.S. tax code allows for favorable tax treatment of certain types of life insurance policies that have an investment feature. Specifically, the buildup of investment income from certain types of policies is not taxed. Neither is the beneficiary of the death benefit of a life insurance policy subject to an income tax. Finally, the death benefit of the policy may or may not be subject to estate tax, depending on how the ben-

Table 8.1
Largest life insurers in the United States, Europe, and Asia.

Rank	Company	Total Assets as of December 31, 2017 (US$ billion)
United States		
1	Prudential Financial	821
2	Met Life	721
3	Berkshire Hathaway	682
4	American International Group (AIG)	503
5	TIAA	294
Europe		
1	Allianz (Germany)	1,047
2	AXA (France)	1,038
3	Prudential plc (United Kingdom)	645
4	Legal & General (United Kingdom)	643
5	Assicurazioni Generali (Italy)	642
Asia		
1	Ping An (China)	926
2	Japan Post Insurance (Japan)	699
3	Nippon Life Insurance Co (Japan)	661
4	Zenkyoren[a] (Japan)	513
5	Dai-Ichi Life Insurance (Japan)	476

Source: Data https://www.relbanks.com/top-insurance-companies/world.

[a]As of March 31, 2017.

eficiary status is structured. Consequently, life insurance products offer considerable tax advantages.

The two fundamentally different types of life insurance are term insurance and cash value life insurance. In addition, other investment-oriented products are sold by life insurers.

Term Insurance

Term insurance is pure life insurance. If the insured dies while the policy is intact, the beneficiary of the policy receives the death benefit. If the insured does not die within the designated period, the policy is invalid and holds no value. No cash value or investment value accrues to a term insurance policy. In addition, the policyholder cannot borrow against the policy.

Cash Value or Permanent Life Insurance

A broad classification of life insurance includes cash value or permanent or investment-type life insurance, usually called "whole life insurance."[2] In addition to providing pure life insurance (as does term insurance), whole life insurance builds up a cash value or investment value inside the policy. This cash value can be withdrawn and can also be borrowed against by the owner of the policy. Or, if the owner wishes to let the policy lapse, he or she can withdraw the cash value. Growth in the cash value of the life insurance policy is referred to as the "inside buildup." A major advantage of this and other insurance products that offer a cash or investment value is that the inside buildup is not subject to taxation.

Life insurance products can be complex. Only an overview is provided in this chapter. The first of the two categories of cash value life insurance policies discretizes whether the cash value is guaranteed or variable. The second category deals with whether the required premium payment is fixed or flexible. The four possible combinations, shown in table 8.2, are discussed here.

Guaranteed cash value life insurance Traditional cash value life insurance, whole life insurance, provides a guaranteed buildup of cash value based on the general account portfolio of the insurance company. The insurance company guarantees a minimum cash value at the end of each year. This guaranteed cash value is based on a minimum dividend paid on the policy. In addition, the policy can be either participating or nonparticipating. For **nonparticipating policies**, the dividend and the cash value on the policy are the guaranteed

2. Most whole life insurance policies pay death benefits when one specified insured dies. An added dimension of whole life policies insures two people (usually a married couple) jointly and pays the death benefit not when the first person dies but when the second person (usually the surviving spouse) dies. This type of policy is called "survivorship insurance" or "second-to-die insurance." The survivorship feature can be added to standard cash value whole life, universal life, and variable universal life policies. Thus, each of the four policies in table 8.2 could also be written on a survivorship basis. Survivorship insurance is typically sold for estate planning purposes.

Table 8.2
Classification of cash value insurance.

	Guaranteed Cash Value Policies	Variable Life Policies
Fixed premium	Whole life insurance	Variable life insurance
Flexible premium	Universal life insurance	Variable universal life insurance

amounts. For **participating policies**, the dividend paid on the policy is based on the realized actuarial experience of the company and its investment portfolio.

The cash value may be above but not below the guaranteed level for participating policies. Thus, the actual performance of the policy can be substantially affected by the actual policy dividends over the guaranteed amount.

Variable life insurance Unlike the guaranteed or fixed cash value policies, which are based on the general account portfolio of the insurance company, **variable life insurance policies** allow the policy owners, within limits, to allocate their premium payments among separate investment accounts maintained by the insurance company and also to shift the policy cash value among the separate accounts. As a result, the amount of the policy cash value and the death benefit depend on the investment results of the separate accounts selected by the policy owner. Thus, this policy offers no guaranteed cash value or death benefit, which depends instead on the performance of the selected investment portfolio.

The types of separate account investment options offered vary by insurance company. Typically, the insurance company offers a selection of common stock and bond fund investment opportunities, managed by the company itself and other investment managers. If the investment options perform well, the cash value buildup in the policy will be significant. However, if the policyholder selects investment options that perform poorly, the variable life insurance policy will perform poorly, resulting in little or no cash value buildup, or, in the worst case, the termination of the policy.

Universal life and variable universal life insurance The key element of **universal life insurance** is the flexibility of the premium for the policyholder. This flexible premium concept separates pure insurance protection (term insurance) from the investment (cash value) element of the policy. The policy cash value is set up as the cash value fund (or accumulation fund), to which the investment income is credited and from which the cost of term insurance for the insured (the mortality charge) is debited. Expenses are also debited.

This separation of the cash value from the pure insurance is called the **unbundling** of the traditional life insurance policy. Premium payments for universal life are at the discretion of the policyholder, except for a minimum initial premium to begin the coverage and then at least enough cash value in the policy each month to cover the mortality charge and other expenses. If not covered, the policy will lapse. Both guaranteed cash value and variable life can be written on a flexible- or a fixed-premium basis.

Other Investment-Oriented Insurance Products

Life insurers increasingly offer products with a significant investment component in addition to their insurance component: guaranteed investment contracts and annuities.

Guaranteed investment contracts Insurance companies have increasingly sold products that have a significant investment component in addition to their insurance component. The first major investment-oriented product developed by life insurance companies was the **guaranteed investment contract** (GIC). According to a GIC, a life insurance company agrees, in return for a single premium, to pay the principal amount and a predetermined annual crediting rate over the life of the investment, all paid at the maturity date of the GIC. For example, a $10 million, five-year GIC with a predetermined crediting rate of 10% means that at the end of five years, the insurance company pays the guaranteed crediting rate and the principal. The risk to the customer is that the return of the principal depends on the ability of the life insurance company to satisfy the obligation, just as in any corporate debt obligation. The risk that the insurer faces is that the rate earned on the portfolio of supporting assets is less than the guaranteed rate paid to the customer.

The maturity of a GIC can vary from one year to 20 years. The interest rate guaranteed depends on market conditions and the rating of the life insurance company. The interest rate will be higher than the yield of the country's risk-free rate for the same maturity. These policies are purchased by individuals and by pension plan sponsors as a pension investment and, as explained in chapter 9, by one type of pension fund, a defined pension fund, to "derisk" their obligations.

A GIC is nothing more than the debt obligation of the life insurance company issuing the contract. The word "guarantee" does not mean that there is a guarantor other than the life insurance company. Effectively, a GIC is a zero-coupon bond issued by a life insurance company and, as such, exposes the investor to the same credit risk. This credit risk has been highlighted by the default of several major issuers of GICs. The two most publicized in the United States were Mutual Benefit, a New Jersey–based insurer, and Executive Life, a California-based insurer, which were both seized by regulators in 1991.

Annuity Another insurance company investment product is an annuity. In the United States, an annuity is often described as "a mutual fund in an insurance wrapper." (Mutual funds are discussed in chapter 32.) What does this mean? To answer this question, assume that an insurance company investment manager has two identical common stock portfolios, one in a mutual fund and the other in an annuity. For the mutual fund, all income (that is, the dividend) is taxable, and the capital gains (or losses) realized by the fund are also taxable, although at potentially different tax rates. The income and realized gains are taxable whether they are withdrawn by the mutual fund holder or reinvested in the fund. There are no guarantees associated with the mutual fund; its performance depends solely on the portfolio performance.

Because of the insurance wrapper, discussed below, an annuity in the United States is treated as an insurance product; as a result, it receives preferential tax treatment. Specifically, the income and realized gains are not taxable if not withdrawn from the annuity product. Thus, the "inside buildup" of returns is not taxable on an annuity, as it is also true for other cash value insurance products. At the time of withdrawal, however, all the gains are taxed at ordinary income rates.

The insurance wrapper on the mutual fund that makes it an annuity can be of various forms. The most common wrapper is the guarantee by the insurance company that the annuity policyholder will get back no less than the amount invested in the annuity (there may also be a minimum period before withdrawal to get this benefit). Thus, if an investor invests $100 in a common stock–based annuity, and at the time of withdrawal (or at the time of death of the annuity holder) the annuity has a value of only $95, the insurance company will pay the annuity holder (or its beneficiary) $100. Many other types of protection or insurance features have also been developed.

Of course, insurance companies impose a charge for this insurance benefit—an insurance premium for the insurance component of the annuity. Thus, whereas mutual funds have an expense fee imposed on the fund's performance, an annuity has a **mortality and expense fee** imposed. Therefore, annuities are more expensive to the investor than are mutual funds. In return, annuity policyholders get the insurance wrapper, which provides the tax benefit. Annuities can be either fixed annuities (similar to GICs) or variable annuities whose performance is based on the return of a common stock or bond portfolio.

General Account and Separate Account Products

The general account of an insurance company refers to the investment portfolio of the overall company. Products "written by the company itself" generally carry a "general account guarantee," that is, they are a liability of the insurance company. When the credit rating agencies (e.g., Moody's, Standard & Poor's, Fitch) provide a credit rating, they do so on products written or guaranteed by the general account. Such ratings are on the claims-paying ability of the company. Typical products written or guaranteed by the general account are whole life, universal life, and fixed annuities (including GICs). Insurance companies must support the guaranteed performance of their **general account products** to the extent of their solvency.

Other types of insurance products receive no guarantee from the insurer's general account, and their performance is not based on the performance of the insurance company's general account but solely on the performance of an account separate from the general account, often an account selected by the policyholder. These products are called **separate account products**. Variable life insurance and variable annuities are separate account products. The policyholder chooses specific portfolios to support these products. The performance of the insurance product depends almost solely on the performance of the portfolio selected, adjusted for the fees or expenses of the insuring company.

Participating policies The performance of separate account products depends on the performance of the separate account portfolio chosen and is not affected by the performance of the overall insurance company's general account portfolio. In addition, the performance of some general account products is not affected by the performance of the general account portfolio. For example, disability income insurance policies may be written on a general account, and even though their payoff depends on the solvency of the general account, the policy performance (e.g., its premium) does not participate in the investment performance of the insurance company's general account investment portfolio.

Other general account insurance products participate in the performance of the company's general account investment portfolio. For example, a life insurance company provides the guarantee of a minimum dividend on its whole life policies, but the policies' actual dividends may increase if the investment portfolio performs well. This "interest component" of the dividend exists in tandem with the expense and mortality components. Thus, the performance of the insurance policy participates in the overall company's performance. Such a policy is called a **participating policy**, in this case, a participating whole life insurance policy.

Captive Reinsurance Arrangements by Life Insurers

Earlier we described captive insurance companies. Although the original captives were created by noninsurance entities, life insurers have been creating captives to circumvent some recent regulatory requirements. In contrast to the use of captives by noninsurance entities for providing a form of self-insurance, captives owned by life insurers are simply risk transfer vehicles for a given life insurer.[3] The structures created by life insurers are referred to as reinsurance captives, even though the risk is not transferred to an independent insurer. As a result, there has been considerable debate about such captives. In a report by the New York State Department of Financial Services published in June 2013, they are referred to as "shadow insurance" arrangements, because they hide the financial weakness of the sponsoring life insurer and increase the broader financial system's systemic risk.

There are two views on the use by life insurers of captive reinsurance arrangements. One view is that captive reinsurance arrangements are an efficient vehicle for a life insurer to manage statutory capital for some its products. The benefit to the consumer is that it results in lower premiums than would be possible in the absence of such an arrangement and more insurance protection without the insurer increasing the risk of insolvency. The other view is that insolvency risk is significantly higher for life insurers using a captive reinsurance arrangement than implied by the parent insurer's current credit ratings, producing a substantial expected cost of default for the industry. This view is supported by an empirical study by Koijen and Yogo.[4]

3. For this reason, they are referred to as special purpose vehicle captives.

4. Ralph S. J. Koijen and Motohiro Yogo, "The Cost of Financial Frictions for Life Insurers," *American Economic Review* 105, no. 1 (2015): 445–475.

Regulation of Insurance Companies

Every country has its own system for regulating insurers. In fact, even within a country, regional regulators may have their own regulatory system. The United States is the prime example of this, with each state regulating insurance companies. In the European Union, every member country has its own regulatory system.

International Association of Insurance Supervisors

Before describing the U.S. insurance regulatory system, it is worthwhile to describe global efforts to regulate the insurance industry. The International Association of Insurance Supervisors is a voluntary membership organization representing insurance regulators and supervisors from 140 countries that make up 97% of the world's insurance premiums. Formed in 1994, the two objectives of the International Association of Insurance Supervisors are to

- Promote effective and globally consistent supervision of the insurance industry in order to develop and maintain fair, safe and stable insurance markets for the benefit and protection of policyholders; and to
- Contribute to global financial stability.[5]

Three activities are undertaken by the International Association of Insurance Supervisors to achieve its objectives. The first activity is to establish principles, standards, and guidance for effective insurance supervision. The second is to promote the implementation of its supervisory principles and standards by international organizations, regional groups, and supervisors. The third is to play a key role in financial stability issues, which includes developing a methodology for the identification of global systemically important insurers and policy measures to address their systemic risks.

One of the principal objectives of regulation of insurers is to reduce the risk of insolvency. So we begin with a brief history of reasons for failures of insurers, limiting our discussion to U.S. insurers.

Reasons for Failures of Insurers

For insurers, failure means to (1) default, (2) be liquidated, (3) be taken over by regulators, or (4) obtain external support to avoid the first three kinds of failure. The causes of failure were reported in a study by Standard & Poor's in an effort to improve on the way in which the rating company formulates its criteria for rating insurers.[6] The study, which looked at failure since the 1980s throughout the world, found that the following key factors were present:

5. From http://www.iaisweb.org/home.

6. Michelle Brennan, Rodney A. Clark, and Michael J. Vine, "What May Cause Insurance Companies to Fail—and How This Influences Our Criteria" (New York: Standard & Poor's Rating Services, June 13, 2013).

- poor liquidity management,
- underpricing and underreserving,
- a high tolerance for investment risk,
- management and governance issues,
- difficulties related to rapid growth and/or expansion into noncore activities, and
- sovereign-related risks.[7]

The first two factors listed were the principal reasons for the failure of U.S. insurers.

Poor liquidity management led to the failure of some U.S. life insurance companies from 1991 to 1994, including First Executive Corporation, Executive Life Insurance Company of California, First Capital Holdings Corporation, Mutual Benefit Life Insurance Company, Monarch Life Insurance Company, Kentucky Central Life Insurance Company, and Confederation Life Insurance Company. The liquidity problem for these failed companies arose from an overconcentration in illiquid assets that could not be used to satisfy the insurer's liabilities.

The overconcentration in illiquid assets for some of the failed life insurers were:

- Mutual Benefit: real estate developments;
- Executive Life Insurance Company: illiquid high-yield bonds and hybrid capital securities;
- Monarch Life: Real estate equity investments; and
- Kentucky Central and Confederation: mortgage loans on commercial real estate, including construction loans on new developments and high loan-to-value mortgages.

The liquidity issue faced by these life insurers was much like the run-on-the-bank scenario faced by depository institutions.

Liquidity-driven problems were also faced in 1999 by life insurers that issued GIC policies, which we described earlier. As explained, most GIC products allow policyholders to surrender or cash out their policy. The surrender rate for GICs was so high in 1999 that it led to the failure of five life insurers: GenAmerica Financial Corporation, General American Life Insurance Company, ARM Financial Group Inc., Integrity Life Insurance Company, and RGA Reinsurance Company.

From 1984 to 1989, several U.S. insurers, mostly P&C insurers, became insolvent for the second reason listed: the loss reserves proved deficient following a period of inadequate pricing. The insurers included Mission Insurance Company and Transit Casualty Insurance Company.

Of course, there were also the "near misses"—instances in which external support prevented the collapse of an insurer. The best-known case of external support was the federal government's bailout of the American International Group (AIG). AIG had followed an overly

7. Brennan, Clark, and Vine, "What May Cause Insurance Companies to Fail," p. 3.

aggressive investment strategy using the leverage provided by credit derivatives, a derivative product described in chapter 39. We described the 2008 federal government bailout of AIG in chapter 2.

U.S. Regulatory System

Regulation of U.S. insurers is governed by the McCarran-Ferguson Act of 1945, which grants states the right to regulate the business of insurance. There is a state-based regulatory system of insurers. Insurance companies whose stock is publicly traded are also regulated by the SEC.

Although the primary insurance regulators are at the state level, the federal government is also involved. The main involvement relates to federal programs for dealing with risks that are difficult for private insurance companies to insure.

The current state-based regulatory system All states have an insurance department that is either part of a state financial regulatory department or an independent state agency. The head of the insurance regulatory department, typically referred to as the insurance commissioner, is either appointed by the state's governor or elected. For example, in the state of Michigan, the regulatory agency responsible for insurance (as well as for banking and securities markets) is the Office of Financial and Insurance Regulation, which is part of that state's Department of Energy, Labor and Economic Growth, and the commissioner is appointed by the governor. In the state of New York, the Insurance Division is part of that state's Department of Financial Services. Before October 2011, New York State had a stand-alone agency, the New York State Insurance Department. The state's Department of Financial Services was formed by combining the New York State Insurance Department and the New York State Banking Department.

Insurance regulation deals with solvency regulation and consumer protection. Solvency regulation is the same as what we discussed in chapter 6 with respect to bank regulation—safety and soundness regulation. State laws regarding solvency regulation deal with (1) capital requirements and reserves, (2) permissible investments, and (3) general and separate accounts. Licensing of and standards of conduct for participants in the insurance business and the approval of products developed by insurers are the focus of consumer protection regulation.

The relationship between the premium revenues and the eventual contingent contractual insurance policy payments bears on an important aspect of evaluating insurance companies. Accountants and auditors, credit rating agencies, and government regulators all monitor insurance companies. These monitors watch the financial stability of the insurance companies based on, among other things, the level of synchronicity between the premiums and insurance policy payments and also the volatility of the payments. To ensure an insurer's financial stability, these monitors require insurance companies to maintain reserves or surplus, consisting of the excess of assets over liabilities. Regulators and accountants define these reserves or surpluses differently and refer to them by different names. Because state statutes establish the treatment of both assets and liabilities for insurance companies, a surplus is also known as **statutory surplus** (or **reserves**), or STAT surplus. Generally accepted accounting principles surplus (or reserves) is defined by accountants for their purposes. Statutory and GAAP reserves are measured differently, but their purposes are similar, though not identical. Statutory surplus is important because regulators view it as the ultimate amount that can be drawn on to pay policyholders. The growth of this surplus for an insurance company also determines how much future business it can underwrite.

Defining assets is straightforward; defining liabilities is more difficult. The complication in determining the value of liabilities arises because the insurance company commits to making payments at some time in the future, and those future payments are recorded as contingent liabilities on its financial statement. The reserves are simply an accounting entry, not an identifiable portfolio.

Model laws and regulations are developed by the National Association of Insurance Commissioners (NAIC), a private voluntary association composed of state insurance commissioners. Adoption of a model law or regulation by the NAIC is not binding on any state. However, states typically use these guidelines when writing their own laws and regulations. The NAIC seeks to foster uniformity of regulation, the lack of which in the current system has drawn major criticism and provided one of the arguments for moving primary regulation from the states to the federal government. Although the adoption of model laws is not binding, the NAIC does have some power granted to it by every state and by the federal government. For example, every state has adopted a law that requires insurers to file financial statements prepared on forms developed by the NAIC and to use the NAIC's calculation methodology to compute risk-based capital requirements.

Insurance companies are typically rated by credit rating agencies (e.g., Moody's, Standard & Poor's, A. M. Best Company, Fitch) with respect to both their ability to pay claims and their outstanding debt, if any. Equity analysts who work at investment banks and broker-dealers also evaluate the attractiveness of the outstanding common stock of publicly traded insurance companies.

Current and potential regulation by the federal government As with depository institutions, regulators impose capital requirements on insurance companies. As just explained, in the case of insurers, capital requirements are set by state regulators; consequently, capital requirements vary by state. This is in stark contrast to the regulatory framework dealing with insurers in other countries, developed and emerging, where regulation takes place at the national level. Moreover, there is no actual authority or governmental power requiring states regulators to act on the NAIC model laws and regulations.

Proposals have been made to change the current system of regulation at the state level and to add greater regulation at the federal level, making a federal agency the lead insurance regulator. The argument for doing so is that it could eliminate regulatory inconsistencies across states. Proponents point out that this form of regulation would allow coordination with other federal agencies, such as the Federal Reserve Board and the SEC. Proponents of the current system of state regulations point to the stellar performance of insurers during the 2008–2009 financial crisis. Whereas federally regulated banks required a bailout, with the exception of the American International Group, whose actions required a government bailout (described in chapter 2), the insurance industry fared well.

The need for regulatory reform of the insurance industry was recognized by the Dodd-Frank Wall Street Reform and Consumer Protection Act, which took the first step toward federal oversight. Title V (Insurance) of this act established the Federal Insurance Office (FIO) as a branch of the Treasury Department. The FIO is responsible for all insurance except health care and most long-term care. The FIO was given limited authority to eliminate duplicative state regulation, coordinate with international authorities on insurance matters, and to report to Congress on attributes of the current U.S. regulatory system and how it could be modernized.

In executing its charge to assess and recommend ways to modernize insurance regulations, the FIO drew on a 2011 study titled "Modernizing Insurance Regulation in the United States,"[8] popularly referred to as the Cluff Fund Report. The recommendations in that report dealt with the problems inherent in the current state-based system, which was described as "fragmented, inconsistent and inefficient" and something that could only be dealt with by regulation at the federal level. The near-term recommendations for changes in the regulatory structure are for a better coordinating role for the FIO and improvements to state regulations. The mid- to long-term recommendations for a regulatory framework for national standards are the following:

- Keep the existing state-based regulatory framework, but foster through state action more uniform national standards.
- Establish federally enforced state "passports," whereby states would be limited in their ability to refuse recognition of an insurer domiciled in another state.
- Establish direct federal oversight and regulation of insurance.

EU Regulatory Approach

The first insurance regulations for members of the European Union were enacted in 1994. The primary concern of the regulation was protecting consumers by focusing on insurance products and pricing policies. Solvency was not officially addressed by the EU legislative program, Solvency I Directive, which sought to harmonize the insurance regulatory regime for EU members.

8. L. Charles Landgraf, John S. Pruitt, and Tom Baker, "Modernizing Insurance Regulation in the United States," prepared for the Anthony T. Cluff Research Fund of the Financial Services Roundtable (New York: Dewey & LeBoeuf LLP, October 11, 2011), http://www.fsround.org/fsr/pdfs/cluff/CluffFundInsuranceModernizationStudy.pdf.

On January 1, 2016, the European Union adopted new regulations, Solvency II Directive, that replaced 14 insurance directives. The principal objectives of the Solvency II Directive (in addition to providing enhanced consumer protection) are to give policyholders greater confidence in the products of insurers, harmonize regulatory regimes, and modernize supervision. The "Supervisory Review Process" required by the Solvency II Directive shifts the focus of regulators from compliance monitoring and capital to evaluating the risk profiles and the quality of insurers' risk management and governance systems. Thus, the Solvency II Directive was not just about capital requirements for insurers but also about authorization, corporate governance, supervisory reporting, public disclosure, risk assessment and management, and solvency and capital reserves.

When comparing the EU and U.S. approaches to insurance regulations, the authors of one study argue that the EU approach is more "fluid and principles-based" than the approach taken by the United States.[9] By a "flexible" approach, the authors mean that risk-based capital standards imposed on insurers are used as guidelines for insurers rather than as absolute standards.[10] By providing greater flexibility, it is argued that insurers can develop strategies to deal with risk that can reduce the possibility of the insurance industry adding to systemic risk. Moreover, the authors of the study point out that the EU approach has been more successful in promoting an insurance industry that is financially strong according to empirical studies.

Insurers and Global SIFIs

There has been a debate as to whether the importance of large insurers can cause systemic risk events that adversely impact a country's financial market or even the global financial market. The potential for insurers to create systemic risk events was brought to light by one major life insurer, America International Group (AIG), because of its losses in the financial derivatives markets, more specifically, credit default swaps (the subject of chapter 39).

A report by the Geneva Association consists of several papers on the differences between banks and insurers and what the differences mean for systemic risk and other implications for regulators.[11] Despite both banks and insurers being financial intermediaries willing to accept the transfer of risks from other market participants, the risks faced by banks and insurance companies differ. In discussing the role of banks and their activities in chapter 6,

9. The information in this section draws from Martin Eling, Robert W. Klein, and Joan T. Schmit, "Insurance Regulation in the United States and the European Union: A Comparison" (Oakland, CA: Independent Institute, November 2009).

10. Martin Eling and Thomas Parnitzke, "Dynamic Financial Analysis: Conception, Classification, and Implementation," *Risk Management and Insurance Review* 10, no. 1 (2007): 33–50; Martin Eling, Hato Schmeiser, and Joan T. Schmit, "The Solvency II Process: Overview and Critical Analysis," *Risk Management and Insurance Review* 10, no. 1 (2007): 69–85.

11. "Anatomy of the Credit Crisis," in *The Geneva Reports Risk and Insurance Research*, ed. Patrick M. Liedtke (Zurich: Geneva Association, January 2013).

we will see that two of the major risks that banks accept are credit risk resulting from their lending activities and liquidity risk due to the mismatch between borrowing short term and lending long term. These two risks can result in difficulties for one major bank that can spill over to another bank, causing a "run on banks." Avoiding such runs is one of the motivations for bank deposit insurance and regulation of banks. This is not the nature of the risks faced by insurers in their core business activities. Hence the argument is that the insurance industry is not prone to systemic risk.

Support for this view is provided in a report of the Group of Thirty, an international body of leading experts in finance and economics, whose mission is to study economic and financial issues facing the global economy.[12] The authors of the study conclude that even under stress conditions, with respect to insurance companies, it would be "unlikely to cause widespread insolvencies in the primary insurance market and would have only a limited effect on the financial system and the real economy generally."[13] Harrington's study of the bailout of AIG by the federal government concluded that the financial problems of that insurer were not the result of the insurance products it sold but of its trading activities in a financial derivative product and its securities lending program.[14]

Several studies have investigated whether insurers pose systemic risk. None have found that to be the case. For example, investigating the issue of whether U.S. insurers have the potential to cause systemic risk for the U.S. economy, Cummins and Weiss looked at (1) the primary indicators that determine whether insurers are systemically risky and (2) the contributing factors that add to the vulnerability of the economy to systemic risk.[15] Although the principal conclusion reached by the authors is that no systemic risk is posed by U.S. insurers' core activities, the study did identify potential concerns. They find that both life insurers and property-casualty insurers are vulnerable to reinsurance crises and that life insurers are vulnerable to intrasector crises. Noncore activities, such as financial guarantees and derivatives trading, may cause systemic risk. Cummins and Weiss conclude that to reduce systemic risk that might result from noncore activities, efforts to strengthen mechanisms for insurance group supervision must be continued.

Catastrophic Risk and Its Management

Insurers face extreme risks or catastrophic risk in their business, or what is also referred to as "tail risk." The types of events and the resulting payout by the insurer can threaten solvency.

12. Group of Thirty, *Reinsurance and International Financial Markets* (Washington, DC, 2006), pp. 31–39.

13. Group of Thirty, *Reinsurance and International Financial Markets*, p. 5.

14. Scott E. Harrington, "The Financial Crisis, Systemic Risk, and the Future of Insurance Regulation," *Journal of Risk and Insurance* 76 (December 2009): 785–819. We discuss the specific financial derivative in chapter 39 and securities lending in chapter 9.

15. David Cummins and Mary A. Weiss, "Systemic Risk and the U.S. Insurance Sector," *Journal of Risk and Insurance* 81 (2011): 489–528.

That is, the insurer may not have sufficient capital to satisfy the claims of all policyholders. For P&C insurers, catastrophic risk encompasses the potential damages associated with natural disasters (hurricanes, windstorms, and earthquakes). In the case of life insurers, the catastrophic risks are extreme mortality risk or longevity risk, depending on the life insurance product.

Extreme Mortality Risk and Longevity Risk

Extreme mortality risk is the risk of an extreme event leading to more deaths than predicted from a mortality table. Extreme mortality events include disease-related deaths, natural catastrophe–related deaths (e.g., earthquakes, floods), war-related deaths, or terrorism-related deaths.[16] Because of their impact on the global population, disease-related events appear to be the main extreme mortality event faced by life insurers. An influenza pandemic is considered the most serious disease-related event. Extreme mortality risk is a concern for pure life insurance products, because death benefits must be paid out sooner than expected when the insurer established the policy premium.

In contrast, **longevity risk** is the risk of policyholders living longer than expected when the cost of the insurance (the premium) was established. This occurs when mortality rates decrease. Longevity risk is the risk associated with investment products, such as annuities. The longer a policyholder lives, the greater the payout will be relative to what it was expected to be when the premium was determined. Longevity risk is a concern not only for annuity-type products offered by life insurers but also for defined benefit plans.

Catastrophe Bonds and Insurance-Linked Securities

Although insurance companies are risk bearers, these institutional investors have pursued strategies to share risks using reinsurance. Other catastrophic risk management strategies involve structured finance technology, described in chapter 27, to create **catastrophe bonds** (nicknamed "cat bonds") issued by insurers that can provide them with a level of protection against catastrophic risk that may not be available in the reinsurance market.

The securities created by life insurance companies and P&C insurance companies to transfer catastrophic risk are called **insurance-linked securities**. These securities, which are issued by insurers, provide a good example of the convergence between the insurance industry and the financial markets using structured finance technology. We do not cover structured finance here. Instead, we just discuss one type of insurance-linked securities, catastrophe bonds.[17]

16. For a more detailed discussion of extreme mortality risk, see Dale Hagstrom, Chris Lewis, Scott Mitchell, and Steven Schreiber, "Quantifying and Managing Extreme Mortality Risk of Life Insurers," Milliman White Paper, May 2013, http://www.milliman.com/uploadedFiles/insight/life-published/pdfs/managing-extrememortality-risk.pdf.

17. For a discussion of the use of securitization technology to transfer risk by insurers, see Chris van Heerden, "Life Insurance Reserve Securitization," in *Structured Products and Related Credit Derivatives: A Comprehensive*

Cat bonds are issued by P&C insurers and reinsurers for the purpose of transferring catastrophic risk. In some ways, they are structured like standard bonds: they have a maturity value, a maturity date, and an interest rate. They differ from a standard bond in that if losses of the insurer (i.e., the bond issuer) exceed a specified amount, the amount paid to the bondholder at the maturity date is reduced. A formula specifies how much less the maturity value will be based on the excess loss. The incentive for investors to purchase cat bonds is that the interest rates they offer exceed those of otherwise similar bonds with the same credit rating.

Cat bonds were first issued in 1996, triggered by two super catastrophes in the United States: Hurricane Andrew (category 5), which struck South Florida and Louisiana in 1992, causing an estimated $26 billion in damage, and the 1994 earthquake (magnitude 6.7) in Northridge, California, which caused $15 to $20 billion in damage. For the first cat bond issue, the interest rate was 400 basis points higher than that paid by otherwise comparable bonds. That is, for the risk of losing some or part of the principal at the maturity date, investors in the first cat bond received compensation of 4% per year above what otherwise comparable bonds offered.

Life insurers issue catastrophe mortality bonds that are structured such that the payment depends on the change in a designated mortality index. For that mortality index, there is a base mortality index set. If at the maturity date the mortality index exceeds that base mortality index, then the principal amount paid at issuance is a reduced amount that is determined by a specified formula. The first catastrophe mortgage bond issued was in late 2003 by the reinsurer Swiss Reinsurance Group (Vita Capital Ltd.).

Insurance Company Investment Strategies

In general, the characteristics of insurance company investment portfolios should reflect their liabilities, that is, the insurance products they underwrite. There are many differences among the various types of insurance policies. Among them are the following:

- the expected time at which the average payment will be made by the insurance company (technically, the "duration" of the payments); and
- the statistical or actuarial accuracy of estimates of when the event insured against will occur and the amount of the payment (that is, the overall risk of the policy).

In addition, the taxes vary across different types of insurance policies and companies.

The key distinction between life insurance and P&C insurance companies lies in the difficulty of projecting whether a policyholder will be paid off and how much the payment will be. Although this is no easy task for either a life or a P&C insurance company, it is easier from an actuarial perspective for a life insurance company. The amount and timing

---

Guide for Investors, ed. Brian Lancaster, Glenn Schultz, and Frank J. Fabozzi (New York: John Wiley & Sons, 2008), chapter 20.

of claims on P&C insurance companies are more difficult to predict because of the randomness of natural catastrophes and the unpredictability of court awards in liability cases. This uncertainty about the timing and amount of cash outlays to satisfy claims has an impact on the investment strategies of the funds of P&C insurance companies compared to life insurance companies.

Without investigating the details for the differences in the portfolios of different types of insurance products, the major differences in the portfolios of life companies and P&C companies are as follows. Life companies on average have less common stock, more private placements, more commercial mortgages, fewer municipal bonds, and longer maturity bonds. (These securities and financial assets are discussed in later chapters.) The difference in municipal bond holdings is due to the tax-exempt characteristic of these securities. The larger holdings of private placements and commercial mortgages indicate the yield orientation of life companies. This yield orientation is also consistent with the low holding of common stock for life insurance companies.

Insurance Company Expansion into Other Financial Services

In many countries, the regulators of the insurance industry have given increased latitude to insurers to sell noninsurance products or provide financial services traditionally supplied by other financial institutions (such as banks and investment banks). Here we describe three ways that insurance companies have expanded into other financial services for individuals and businesses.

Bank Insurance Model

As just explained, the distribution channels of insurance companies have been changing. One of the major changes involves some sort of relationship between a bank and an insurance company. Banks are averse to manufacturing insurance products because of their inexperience and regulatory issues; the risk borne by manufacturing insurance products; and the long payback period of some insurance products. However, insurance companies are attracted by the commercial bank customer base. As a result, commercial bank distribution of insurance company products has grown considerably. This bank insurance model is called "bancassurance."

The arrangements made between banks and insurance companies can be (1) a strategic alliance arrangement, (2) a mixed arrangement, or (3) a full integration model. With a **strategic alliance**, the relation involves solely the bank marketing a company's insurance products. The **mixed arrangement** calls for all marketing to be performed by the insurance company with the bank's only duty being to provide leads from its customer base. The **full integration arrangement** involves the bank using its own insurance brand and providing customized solutions to its customers for their financial needs. Banks would also require insurance regulatory approvals. The bank's activities associated with the full integration arrangement are the marketing of insurance and servicing of claims.

Depending on the type of bank insurance arrangement, the benefits to the bank are:[18]

- The potential to reduce reliance on interest rate spreads (particularly during low interest rate periods), increase income, and obtain a more stable stream of income by diversifying into insurance.
- Offer a wide range of financial services to current bank clients and by doing so increase customer retention.
- Improve integration of financial services provided to customers tailored to their life cycle.
- Capitalize on the bank's customer base.
- Get access to funds that would otherwise be invested with life insurers, who sometimes benefit from tax advantage.

From the perspective of an insurance company, the following are potential benefits, depending on the type of arrangement:

- Reduce reliance on the use of traditional agents to sell their products by making use of the channels owned by the bank partner.
- Obtain access to the bank partner's customer base.
- Jointly develop new financial products with the bank partner and market those products via the bank network rather than a network of agents.
- Share the cost of servicing policies with the bank partner.
- Use the partner bank's capital to improve the insurer's solvency and expand business.

From a regulatory perspective, the integration of banks and insurers is challenging. The favorable impact is that the diversification offered by the bank insurance model may lower systemic risk, because it potentially (1) reduces the volatility of bank income and (2) provides insurers with access to additional capital that improves solvency.

In the United States, the bank insurance model was permitted following the repeal in 1999 of a restriction on banks to use this model (i.e., the Glass-Steagall Act). In contrast, bancassurance has long been a practice in Europe and by 2007 had made significant penetration in many European countries, particularly France, Italy, Portugal, and Spain.[19] In such developing countries as Brazil and Malaysia, there has been significant use of bancassurance. China had no restrictions on selling non-life policies but that was not the case for life

18. The advantages for banks and insurers based on the type of arrangement is described in C. Wong and L. Cheung, "Bancassurance Developments in Asia—Shifting into a Higher Gear Bancassurance," *Sigma* 7 (2002): 3–38 (Swiss Re Institute).

19. See Swiss Re, "Bancassurance: Emerging Trends, Opportunities and Challenges," *Sigma* 5 (2007): 11.

insurance. The Chinese government removed several regulatory obstacles impeding the adoption of bancassurance in 2003.

Pension Funds and Insurance Companies

At one time, three distinct types of products were available for individuals: insurance, savings/investment, and retirement. The specific products in each distinguishable category were as follows. Insurance products included term life and whole life. Savings/investment products included stocks, bonds, and collective vehicles (such as mutual funds and exchange-traded funds). Private retirement products included defined benefit and defined contribution plans (provided by employers and the subject of chapter 4), and individual retirement accounts (IRAs) (provided by investment companies).

Over the past three decades, many products have been developed that fit into two or even three of these categories. Into which of these three categories, for example, does an IRA sold to a customer by a life insurance agent fit? Arguably, the correct answer to this question is all three categories. Figure 8.1 provides a summary of some of the products on the insurance/savings/retirement spectrum, which are really hybrids. We have discussed the various insurance products in this chapter. Retirement products are discussed in chapter 4. Mutual funds and other collective investment products are discussed in chapter 32. This section discusses products that are hybrid retirement and savings products but are often manufactured and distributed by insurance companies.

In the United States, the products that are a hybrid of retirement and investment products and are often distributed by insurance companies and agents are 401(k)s, Roth 401(k)s, and variable annuities. These products are also often distributed by many insurers, and the

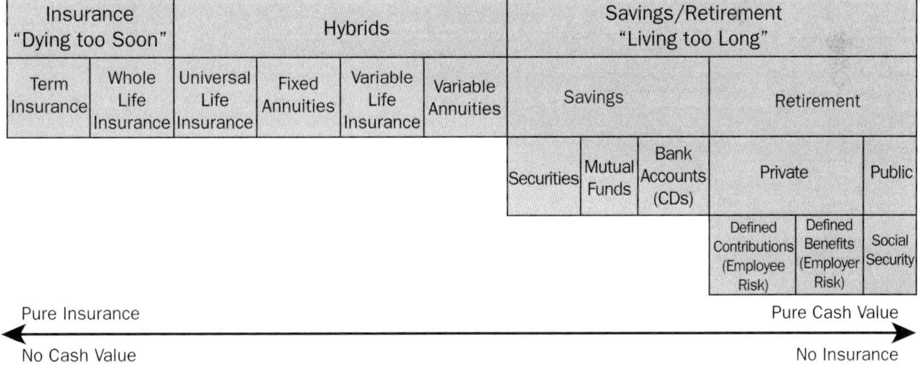

Figure 8.1
Insurance/savings/retirement vehicles.
Source: Frank J. Jones, "An Overview of Institutional Fixed Income Strategies," in *Professional Perspectives on Fixed Income Portfolio Management*, volume 1 (Hoboken, NJ: John Wiley & Sons, 2000).

insurance companies often include some of their own products in these categories. Because these plans are retirement plans, they have tax advantages for the investor.

Insurance-Based Investment Banking

As will be explained throughout this book, many of the financial risks faced by participants in the capital markets are being transferred from financial institutions to the public market. We will see in later chapters how this transfer has been done via the securitization mechanism. In the insurance industry, debt instruments (such as bonds) have been created allowing businesses and governments that need protection against the occurrence of certain events to go directly to the capital market to obtain that protection through the public issuance of securities rather than by purchasing traditional insurance. That is, rather than an insurance company absorbing the risk of some event, an entity that needs insurance protection can issue a bond whose payoff at the bond's maturity date depends on whether an adverse event occurs and the amount of the loss if it does. The compensation to investors who purchase the bond is a higher interest rate than on an otherwise comparable bond.

The area of finance in which publicly issued securities are used as a substitute for traditional insurance policies is referred to as **insurance-based investment banking**. Two examples help illustration how the public markets (here the bond market) can be used to circumvent traditional insurance.

For our first example, consider the operator of Tokyo Disneyland, Oriental Land Company. In 1999, the company issued $200 million of bonds to insure against the risk of a Tokyo earthquake. We have already discussed earlier cat bonds issued by a P&C insurer or reinsurers, which were the first such bonds issued by a noninsurance company. There were two issues of five-year bonds sold with a maturity value of $100 million each. For investors in the first bond issue, the entire principal and interest would be lost if an earthquake occurred. The proceeds would then be used by Oriental Land to repair damages to the park resulting from the earthquake. Investors would pay off the holders of the second bond issue in full, even if an earthquake occurred. However, the maturity of the bond issue would increase from five years to 8.5 years if there were an earthquake. This second bond issue basically provided Oriental Land with emergency funding for 3.5 years should that entity have any difficulty obtaining financing. Thus, not only were investors in the bond market providing earthquake protection, they were also providing future financing protection.

For our second example, consider the use of securities by the Fédération Internationale de Football Association (FIFA) to provide protection against acts of terrorism that might have canceled the 2002 World Cup competition in Asia. Because of the terrorist attacks on the World Trade Center in New York City, on the Pentagon in Washington, DC, and in midair over Pennsylvania on September 11, 2001, insurance for events canceled as a result of acts of terrorism was becoming difficult to obtain. The insurance company that was supposed to provide cancellation insurance, AXA, decided against providing the insurance because of the attacks on September 11, 2001. Without the cancellation policy, the 2002

World Cup could not take place. To resolve this problem, FIFA, working with the investment banking firm Credit Suisse First Boston, created and then issued in September a bond (referred to as a "cancellation bond") that would be sold in the bond market, thereby transferring terrorism risk to investors in the financial market. The amount of the bonds issued was $260 million.

Key Points

- In general, insurance companies bear risk from parties who wish to avert risk by transferring it to the insurance companies. The party seeking to transfer the risk pays an insurance premium to the insurance company. Insurance companies pay the insured if and when the insured event occurs.
- The types of insurance include life insurance, health insurance, property and casualty (P&C) insurance, liability insurance, umbrella insurance, disability insurance, and long-term health care insurance.
- An insurance company has three components: guarantor component, investment component, and distribution component.
- The revenue for insurers is derived from the premiums received and from investment returns when premiums are invested until a claim is paid out.
- To reduce risk, a primary insurer can transfer some of its risk to a reinsurance company.
- If an insurance company decides to retain certain risks, it can self-insure against these risks by establishing a captive insurance company that it wholly owns.
- Captive insurance companies are classified as single-parent captives, association captives, industry captives, and diversified captives.
- In the United States, an insurance company is structured either as a stock company (which is similar in structure to any corporation or public company) or as a mutual company (whose owners are the policyholders rather than external investors).
- Because of funding needs for growth, many mutual companies have converted to stock companies, a process referred to as demutualization.
- There are two fundamentally different types of life insurance: term insurance (pure insurance protection) and cash value life insurance (combined insurance protection and investment vehicle).
- Insurance companies increasingly offer products with a significant investment component in addition to their insurance component: guaranteed investment contracts and annuities.
- Insurance products are classified as general account and separate account products.
- The general account of an insurance company refers to the investment portfolio of the overall company, and products usually carry a "general account guarantee" (i.e., are a liability of the insurance company).

• Separate account products receive no guarantee from the insurer's general account, and are guaranteed based on the performance of an account that is separate from the general account of the insurance company, often an account selected by the policyholder.

• Insurance regulation deals with solvency regulation and consumer protection.

• The two principal reasons for the failure of an insurance company are poor liquidity management and underpricing and underreserving.

• In the United States, insurance companies are regulated at the state level, leading to inconsistencies and inefficiency in regulatory oversight.

• The arguments for making the federal government the lead insurance regulator are to eliminate any regulatory inconsistencies across states and to allow better coordination with other federal agencies, such as the Federal Reserve and the SEC.

• In the European Union, the Solvency II Directive has shifted focus from compliance monitoring and capital to evaluating the risk profiles and the quality of their risk management and governance systems.

• There has been considerable debate as to whether large insurers can cause systemic risk events that adversely impact a country's financial market and the global financial market.

• Valid arguments have been made that unlike large banks that are categorized as global SIFIs, the core products of insurers are sufficiently different from those of banks so that they should not be classified as global SIFIs.

• Several studies conclude that insurers do not pose systemic risk to national or global financial markets, although the insurers' noncore activities that may cause systemic risk.

• Insurers of extreme or catastrophic risks night face solvency-threatening events.

• Insurers have entered into other areas of finance: banking and pension funds.

• For P&C insurers, catastrophic risk encompasses the potential damages associated with natural disasters (for example, hurricanes, windstorms, and earthquakes). For life insurers, the catastrophic risks are extreme mortality risk and longevity risk, depending on the life insurance product.

• In addition to reinsuring, insurers have created insurance-linked securities to transfer risk through securitization from insurers to the investing public. These bonds include catastrophe bonds and catastrophe mortality bonds.

• Insurance-based investment banking involves the creation of bonds that can be used in lieu of traditional insurance by those seeking insurance.

Questions

1. Why are insurance companies referred to as "risk bearers"?
2. With respect to insurance companies, what is meant by the "underwriting process"?
3. What are the major sources of revenue for an insurance company?

4. How are the profits of an insurance company determined?

5. How do the portfolios of life and health insurance companies differ from those of P&C insurance companies?

6. The following quote is from a publication by the law firm of Paul/Weiss:

> Worldwide, banks and insurance companies have made a compelling case for operating in a more integrated manner than had historically been the case. Bancassurance has been an extremely successful business model in Europe, and banks and insurers are eager to repeat this success story in Asia.[20]

What is bancassurance?

7. In the bank insurance model, what types of arrangements can be made between an insurer and a bank?

8. Comment on the following statement: "All insurance activities pose no threat of systemic risk."

9. New York Life, the largest mutual life insurance company in the United States (as well as one of the 100 largest U.S. corporations), explains on its website why it has not converted to a stock company:

> The question really comes down to this: What's in the best interests of our policyholders and the company—remaining a mutual or becoming a stock company? The answer for us is absolutely clear: Being a mutual allows us to maintain our focus on serving our policyholders by delivering high performing whole life insurance policies through the best-trained financial professionals in the industry. Over the years we've made innovations in our products and investments in our people to ensure that we'll continue to meet the long-term needs and requirements of our policyholders. We believe this approach is in the best interests of both our clients and our company—today and for the years ahead.[21]

a. What is the difference between a stock and a mutual insurance company?

b. Explain why you agree or disagree with the arguments put forth by New York Life for not converting to a stock company.

10. What problems are associated with the current state-based system of government regulation in the United States?

11. Why should a purchaser of life insurance be concerned about the credit rating of his or her insurance company?

12. What are term insurance, whole life insurance, variable life insurance, and universal life insurance?

13. a. What is a guaranteed investment contract (GIC)?

b. Does a GIC carry a "guarantee" like that carried by a government obligation?

20. "Regulatory Foundations for Bancassurance in China" (New York: Paul/Weiss, July 2003), https://www.paulweiss.com/media/1864576/bancassurance.pdf.

21. "The Mutual Advantage," January 20, 2009, http://www.newyorklife.com/nyl/v/index.jsp?vgnextoid=5b1ece94229d2210a2b3019d221024301cacRCRD.

14. What is the statutory surplus, and why is it an important measure for an insurance company?

15. What is meant by an insurance company reinsuring its liabilities?

16. Whose liabilities are harder to predict, those of life and health insurers or those of P&C insurers? Explain why.

17. In an article in *Forbes*, the following statement appeared, contrasting the management of stock insurance companies and mutual insurance companies:

> With their survival on the line, publicly traded insurers are scrambling for cash by cutting dividends and issuing new shares (diluting existing investors), begging regulators for a relaxation of capital requirements and lobbying Washington for a cut of the $700 billion Wall Street bailout. Their mutually owned rivals haven't asked for a dime. Their statutory surpluses (the regulatory counterpart to book value) have held steady or even increased. Some are announcing plans to pay out near-record dividends to policyholders.[22]

What message is being conveyed in this statement, and how does it relate to the principal-agent problem?

18. What type of strategies have insurers employed to deal with catastrophic risk?

19. For what type of investment product are life insurers concerned with longevity risk?

20. The following statement is from an article by Christopher Kampa and Paul Siegert:

> Insurance-linked securities, once considered to be an alternative form of risk transfer, have become a mainstream method of transferring risk from insurers to the capital markets. With greater attention being paid to risk at the institutional level and the search for portfolio diversification at the investment level, insurance-linked securities seem poised to further facilitate the convergence between the capital and insurance markets.[23]

Why do such products as insurance-linked securities represent the convergence of capital markets and insurance markets?

22. Bernard Condon and Daniel Fisher, "Mutual Respect," *Forbes*, December 4, 2008, p. 1.

23. Christopher Kampa and Paul Siegert, "Alternative Risk Transfer: The Convergence of the Insurance and Capital Markets," July 19, 2010.

9 Investment Banking Firms

CONTENTS

Learning Objectives

After reading this chapter, you will understand:

- the nature of the investment banking business;
- the revenue-generating activities of investment banks;

- the activities of investment banking firms that require them to commit their own capital;
- the role investment bankers play in the underwriting of securities;
- the different types of underwriting arrangements;
- the difference between riskless arbitrage and risk arbitrage;
- what proprietary trading is, and the Volcker Rule;
- the various roles investment bankers play in mergers and acquisitions;
- what is meant by merchant banking; and
- why investment banking firms create and trade risk control instruments.

Investment banking firms play a key role in capital markets by performing two general functions. For corporations, U.S. government agencies, state and local governments, and foreign entities (sovereigns and corporations) that need funds, investment banking firms assist in obtaining those funds. For investors who wish to invest funds, investment banking firms act as brokers or dealers in the buying and selling of securities. Thus, investment banking firms perform a critical role in the primary market and the secondary market that we describe in chapters 17 and 18.

Investment banking firms are highly leveraged companies, that is, the amount of borrowed funds relative to the amount of equity is high. The activities in which they are engaged dictate that this be the case. Historically, the increasing need for capital resulted in the consolidation of firms in the industry and a change in many firms from a partnership structure to a corporate structure, which gives firms easier access to public funds. Investment banking firms generate revenue from commissions, fee income, spread income, and principal activities. Specifically, these activities can be classified as follows:

- public offering of securities,
- private placement of securities,
- securitization of assets,
- mergers and acquisitions,
- merchant banking,
- advising on financial restructuring,
- trading of securities,
- prime brokerage,
- trading and creation of derivative instruments, and
- asset management.

In this chapter, we describe each of these activities performed by investment banking firms, but before doing so, we describe the way investment banks are classified.

Investment Banking Industry

In the United States, prior to 1999, federal legislation in the form of the Glass-Steagall Act separated the activities of commercial banks, investment banks, and insurance companies. The Glass-Steagall Act restricted the types of securities that commercial banks in the United States could underwrite—an important investment banking activity, as explained in this chapter. This act had regulated the industry since the Great Depression. The Gramm-Leach-Bliley Financial Services Modernization Act of 1999 supplanted the Glass-Steagall Act and eliminated the restrictions on the activities conducted by companies in each financial sector. Now commercial banks as well as insurance companies can underwrite securities.

As a result, the firms that are involved in the activities of investment banking fall into two categories. The first category comprises investment banks that are affiliated with large financial services holding companies. Most such firms are affiliated with large commercial bank holding companies, which the Federal Reserve, the regulator of bank holding companies, refers to as "nonbanking investments."[1] Examples of commercial bank holding companies that have an investment banking affiliate are Bank of America, Barclays Bank, Citigroup, Credit Suisse, Goldman Sachs, JP Morgan Chase, Morgan Stanley, and UBS. These investment banks are referred to as **bank-affiliated investment banks**. In the second category are investment banking firms that are independent of a large financial services holding company and for that reason are referred to as **independent investment banks**. Examples are the Blackstone Group, Greenhill & Company, Houlihan Lokey, Raymond James, and Morgan Keegan.

Investment banking firms are also classified according to the investment banking activities they perform into full-service investment banks and boutique investment banks. **Full-service investment banks** are basically involved in the wide range of activities described in this chapter. The bank-affiliated investment banks fall into this category. The larger full-service investment banking firms—which are viewed as the premier investment banking firms because of their size, reputation, presence in key markets, and customer base—are referred to as "bulge-bracket" firms. **Boutique investment banks** specialize in limited areas of investment banking.

Since the financial crisis of 2008, the market share of U.S. investment banks has been dominated by U.S. firms, and the market share of European investment banks has declined.[2]

1. The Federal Reserve defines nonbanking activities that are closely related to banking as "mortgage banking, consumer and commercial finance and loan servicing, leasing, collection agency, asset management, trust company, real estate appraisal, financial and investment advisory activities, management consulting, employee benefits consulting, career counseling services, and certain insurance-related activities." See the Federal Reserve's web page, http://www.fedpartnership.gov/bank-life-cycle/grow-shareholder-value/bank-holding-companies.cfm.

2. Charles Goodhart and Dirk Schoenmaker, "The United States Dominates Global Investment Banking: Does It Matter for Europe?" Bruegel Policy Contribution (Brussells: Bruegel, March 2016), http://bruegel.org/wp-content/uploads/2016/03/pc_2016_06-1.pdf.

According to several commentaries, small, medium, and large European countries would find European-based global investment banking firms difficult to support and, should there be financial difficulties faced by such firms, it would cause major problems for any European country.[3] The expectation is that in the near future, it is likely that European-based global investment banks' role will continue to decline. Since 2015, the market share of Chinese investment banks in the Asia-Pacific region has surpassed the market share of both U.S. and European investment banks.

Goodhart and Schoenmaker believe that with the declining role of a European-based global investment banks, the result will be a four-tier investment banking system with the first tier being the U.S.-based bulge-bracket firms.[4] Strong regional investment banks throughout the world will be in the second tier. In Europe, these firms would include Barclays Bank and NM Rothschild in the United Kingdom and Deutsche Bank in Germany. In the Asia-Pacific region, they would include CITIC in China. The Hongkong and Shanghai Bank (HSBC), the largest bank in Hong Kong, has roots in both the European and Asia-Pacific regions. The third tier, according to Goodhart and Schoenmaker, consists of bank-affiliated investment banking firms that support corporations and governments but are not involved in global investment banking activities. Examples would be Australian and Canadian banks. Finally, boutique firms that specialize in advisory and wealth management activities described later in this chapter represent the fourth tier.

Public Offering of Securities

The traditional role associated with investment banking is the underwriting of securities. In the United States, the traditional process for issuing new securities involves investment bankers performing one or more of the following three functions:

- advising the issuer on the terms and the timing of the offering,
- buying the securities from the issuer, and
- distributing the issue to the public.

The adviser role may require investment bankers to design a security structure that is more palatable to investors than a particular traditional instrument. Seeking to reduce the cost of borrowing for their clients, investment bankers have designed innovative security structures with characteristics that are more attractive to investors while not being onerous to issuers. We will give several examples of these financial innovations in later chapters.

3. See, for example, Martin Wolf, "Top European Bankers Warn of US Threat to Their Future," *Financial Times*, October 12, 2015; Martin Wolf, "Europe Will Always Need Investment Banking," *Financial Times*, October 16, 2015; John Gapper, "A Global Retreat for European Banks," *Financial Times*, October 22, 2015; and "European Banks: Banking and Nothingness," *The Economist,* October 17, 2015.

4. Goodhart and Schoenmaker, "The United States Dominates Global Investment Banking."

When selling new securities, investment bankers need not undertake the second function of buying the securities from the issuer. An investment banker can merely act as an adviser or distributor of the new security. The function of buying the securities from the issuer is called **underwriting**. When an investment banking firm buys the securities from the issuer and accepts the risk of selling the securities to investors at a lower price, the firm is referred to as an **underwriter**. When the investment banking firm agrees to buy the securities from the issuer at a set price, the underwriting arrangement is referred to as a **firm commitment**. The risk that the investment banking firm accepts in a firm-commitment underwriting arrangement is that the price it pays to purchase the securities from the issuer may be less than the price it receives when it reoffers the securities to the public. In contrast, in a **best-efforts underwriting arrangement**, the investment banking firm agrees only to use its expertise to sell the securities; it does not buy the entire issue from the issuer.

The fee earned from underwriting a security is the difference between the price paid to the issuer and the price at which the investment bank then offers the security to the public. This difference is referred to as the **gross spread**, or the **underwriter discount**. Numerous factors affect the size of the gross spread. Two important factors are the size of the offering and the type of security. Generally, the larger the offering size is, the smaller the gross spread will be. In general, the gross spread on bonds is less than for common stock.

A new common stock offering is classified as an initial public offering or a secondary common stock offering. An **initial public offering** (IPO) is a common stock offering issued by companies that have not previously issued common stock to the public. A study Ritter on IPOs from 1999 to 2013 found that, with few exceptions, gross spreads for moderate-sized IPOs were about 7%, but megadeals had gross spreads of far less than 7%:[5] Facebook, for example, had a 1.1% gross spread on a $16 billion IPO in 2012, Twitter had a 3.25% gross spread on a $10 billion IPO in 2013, General Motors had a gross spread of 0.75% on a $15.8 billion IPO in 2010, and Visa had a gross spread of 2.8% on a $17.9 billion IPO in 2008.

A **secondary common stock offering** is an offering of common stock that had been issued in the past by the corporation. The range for the gross spread as a percentage of the amount raised is 3% to 6%. Because of the risk associated with pricing and then selling an IPO to investors, the gross spread is higher than for a secondary common stock offering. For traditional bond offerings, the gross spread as a percentage of the principal is around 50 basis points. This smaller gross spread compared to that for common stock offerings reflects the lower risk associated with such underwritings.

The typical underwritten transaction involves so much risk of capital loss that for a single investment banking firm to undertake it alone would expose it to the danger of losing a significant portion of its capital. To share this risk, an investment banking firm puts together

5. Table 10 in Jay R. Ritter, "Initial Public Offerings: Updated Statistics," December 4, 2014, http://bear.warrington.ufl.edu/ritter/IPOs2013Statistics.pdf.

a group of firms to underwrite the issue. This group of firms is known as an **underwriting syndicate**. The gross spread is then divided among the lead underwriter(s) and the other firms in the underwriting syndicate. The lead underwriter manages the deal ("runs the books" for the deal). In many cases, more than one firm may act as lead underwriter, in which case the lead underwriters are said to "co-lead" or "co-manage" the deal. In a bond transaction, the lead underwriters customarily receive 20% of the gross spread as compensation for managing the deal.

To realize the gross spread, the entire securities issue must be sold to the public at the planned reoffering price, which usually requires a great deal of marketing muscle. Investment banking firms attempt to sell the securities to their investor client base (retail and institutional). To increase the potential investor base, the lead underwriter puts together a **selling group**. This group includes the underwriting syndicate plus other firms not in the syndicate. Members of the selling group can buy the security at a concession price (a price less than the reoffering price). The gross spread is thereby divided among the lead underwriter, members of the underwriting syndicate, and members of the selling group.

The underwriting of securities is not limited to offerings in the United States. An issuer can select among many foreign securities markets to identify the one in which to offer securities and so reduce its cost of funds. Indeed, some securities are offered simultaneously in several markets throughout the world.

Investment bankers also may assist in offering the securities of government-owned companies to private investors. This process is referred to as **privatization**. An example is the IPO of the U.S. government–owned railroad company Conrail in March 1987. More than 58 million shares were sold, raising a total of $1.65 billion. It was the largest IPO in the history of the United States. Other examples from outside the United States are the United Kingdom's British Telecom, Chile's Pacifica, and France's Paribas. In the case of British Telecom (the government-owned telephone company of the United Kingdom), the amount raised was $4.7 billion. This global offering was offered simultaneously in several countries. In the 1990s, investment bankers increased their role in placing the securities of government-owned companies into the hands of private investors. Eastern Europe, for example, followed a major program of privatization.

In the industry, investment banking firms that underwrite securities in the different areas are ranked by some measure of market share, referred to as the "league tables." Investment bankers view this rating as a key indicator of their importance in a market sector. Market share can be measured by the number of deals done in a year or by the total dollar volume of all deals done in a year.[6]

6. *The Financial Times* provides detailed information on league tables; see the web page http://markets.ft.com/investmentBanking/dealMap.asp.

Private Placement of Securities

In addition to underwriting securities for distribution to the public, investment banking firms place securities with a limited number of institutional investors, such as insurance companies, investment companies, and pension funds.

Investment banking firms assist in the private placement of securities in several ways. They work with the issuer and potential investors on the design and pricing of the security. Investment bankers first design many of the new security structures in the private placement market. Field testing of the innovative securities described in this book most often occurs in the private placement market. For example, zero-coupon corporate bonds were first publicly issued by corporations in April 1981, and the first issue was by J. C. Penney. Prior to that time, a private offering was made by PepsiCo.

An investment banker may be involved with lining up investors as well as designing the issue. Or, if the issuer has already identified the investors, the investment banker may serve only in an advisory capacity. Work as an adviser generates fee income, as does arranging the placement with investors. An investment banker may also participate in the transaction through a best-efforts underwriting arrangement.

The fees for arranging a private placement vary, depending on the issuance amount and the complexity of the transaction. Moreover, when raising venture capital for clients, investment bankers are frequently offered the opportunity to share in the prosperity of the company. This opportunity typically comes in the form of an option to buy a specified number of shares at a price set at the time the funds are raised. An arrangement that allows the investment banking firm to benefit from the company's success is referred to as an "equity kicker."

Securitization of Assets

The "securitization of assets" refers to the issuance of securities using a pool of assets as collateral. The securitization of home mortgage loans to create mortgage-backed securities was the first example of this process. After 1985, investment bankers worked with corporations to either securitize a wide range of loans and receivables or to buy loans and receivables in the market and issue securities backed by them.

Securities backed by a pool of loans or receivables are called **asset-backed securities** and are discussed in chapter 27. When an investment banker works with a corporation to issue an asset-backed security, the sale of the security generates revenue from the bid-ask spread. When an investment banker buys loans and receivables and then issues securities, a profit is generated on an asset-backed security transaction, derived as follows: the price that the security is sold for minus the price that the investment banker paid to purchase the collateral (i.e., the cost of buying the loans and receivables) minus the interest cost of "warehousing" the collateral purchased until the securities are sold.

Mergers and Acquisitions

Investment banking firms are active in mergers and acquisitions (M&As). Also included under M&A activities are leveraged buyouts (LBOs), restructuring and recapitalization of companies, and reorganization of bankrupt and troubled companies.

Investment bankers participate in M&A activity in one of several ways: (1) by finding M&A candidates; (2) by advising acquiring companies or target companies with respect to price and nonprice terms of an exchange, or by helping target companies fend off an unfriendly takeover attempt; and (3) by assisting acquiring companies in obtaining the necessary funds to finance a purchase.

The fees charged by investment bankers in M&A work depend on the extent of their participation and the complexity of the activities they are asked to perform. An investment banker may simply receive an advisory fee or retainer. More likely, an investment banker will receive a fee based on a percentage of the selling price. The fee structure in this case may be one of three types: (1) the percentage may decline with increasing selling price; (2) the percentage may be the same regardless of the selling price; or (3) the percentage may be fixed, with addition of an incentive fee if the price is better than a specified amount. An example of the first fee structure is what is called the 5–4–3–2–1 "Lehman formula." In this fee structure, which some firms have adopted, the fee is set at 5% of the first $1 million, 4% of the second $1 million, 3% of the third $1 million, 2% of the fourth $1 million, and 1% for any excess amount. A typical flat percentage is 2% to 3% of the selling price.

Participating in an LBO can generate several fees. LBOs call for a firm to be acquired using mostly debt funds and taken private. The debt raised is from one of two sources: senior bank debt and unsecured junior debt (called subordinated debt, or mezzanine financing). An investment banking firm can earn fees from (1) proposing the acquisition, (2) arranging the financing, (3) arranging bridge financing (i.e., temporary funds lent until permanent debt financing is completed), and (4) other advisory fees.

An investment banking firm may provide its own capital for bridge financing. This type of merchant banking is discussed in the next section.

Under "other advisory fees" are the fees charged by investment banking firms for providing a valuation of a firm that is the subject of a takeover or a merger, and for rendering a "fairness opinion." The question of fairness arises in such a transaction based on the issue of whether the purchasers of the company might have had access to information that allowed them to acquire the firm at a price less than its true market value. This situation is of increasing concern in LBOs, particularly management-led LBOs (that is, where the current management of the firm makes an offer to purchase the company). An investment banking firm is typically engaged by the board of directors of the company that is the subject of the takeover to render an independent and expert opinion as to the fairness of the price being offered for the shares. The need for a fairness opinion, as well as advising, has increased as a result of the Sarbanes-Oxley Act. The board of directors will want to have a third party review some of its major business transactions before it approves them. Fees for a fairness opinion range from $50,000 for a transaction involving a few million dollars to $1 million or more for large transactions.

Merchant Banking

When an investment banking firm commits its own funds by taking either an equity interest or a creditor position in companies, this activity is referred to as **merchant banking**. Investment banking firms have divisions or groups that undertake merchant banking through a series of private equity funds. As described by one boutique investment banking firm, Noble Capital Markets, merchant banking activities include:

- Targeting domestic companies within our areas of focus and expertise
- Analyzing a company's opportunities and assessing its risks within their respective industry
- Structuring, negotiating and executing the transaction
- Work in assessing the appropriate time and manner in which to harvest the investment.[7]

The work of the merchant banking team does not stop after the transaction. As noted by Noble Capital Markets, the firm assists the "management team and Board of Directors to create value and grow their businesses to facilitate long-term shareholder value."

Advising on Financial Restructuring

Financial restructuring involves a significant modification of a corporation's capital structure, operating structure, or corporate strategy with the objective of improving efficiency. Financial restructuring may be undertaken to (1) avoid bankruptcy or problems with creditors or (2) reorganize the firm under Chapter 11 of the U.S. Bankruptcy Code.[8] Investment bankers advise corporations on financial restructuring in order to generate fee income.

Here are two examples of financial restructuring situations advised by the boutique investment banking firm Greenhill & Co. as reported on the firm's website. In 2011, the firm advised a natural gas–fired power plant located in Texas, Bosque Power Company, on its negotiations with lenders and restructuring. In the same year, the firm advised a U.K. listed multichannel retailer, Findel plc, on the "restructuring of its balance sheet comprising an equity capital raising and refinancing of its debt and pension obligations."[9]

7. https://noblecapitalmarkets.com/investmentbanking.
8. We discuss the U.S. Bankruptcy Code in chapter 26.
9. http://www.greenhill.com/business/transactions/region/united-kingdom/target/restructuring.

Trading of Securities

A successful underwriting of a security requires a strong sales force. The sales force provides feedback on advance interest in the deal, and the traders (or market makers) provide input into pricing the deal as well. It would be a mistake to think that once all the securities are sold, the investment banking firm's ties with the deal are ended. In the case of bonds, those who bought the securities will look to the investment banking firm to make a market in the issue. Therefore, the investment banking firm must be willing to take a principal position in secondary market transactions. Revenue from this activity is generated through (1) the difference between the price at which the investment banking firm sells the security and the price paid for the securities (called the "bid-ask spread") and (2) appreciation of the price of the securities held in inventory. Obviously, if the securities depreciate in price, revenue will also be reduced.

To protect against a loss, investment banks engage in hedging strategies. The various strategies employed by traders to generate revenue from positions in one or more securities include riskless arbitrage, risk arbitrage, and speculation. Below we discuss the first two strategies.

Riskless Arbitrage

In the finance industry, the term "arbitrage" is used to refer to two types of transactions: riskless arbitrage and risk arbitrage. The first type of arbitrage transactions, **riskless arbitrage**, calls for a trader to find a security or package of securities trading at different prices. For example, some common stocks of companies trade in more than one location in the United States. Also, the common stock of some multinational companies trades in both the United States and on an exchange in one or more foreign countries. If price discrepancies occur in the various markets, it may be possible to lock in a profit after transaction costs by selling the security in a market where it is priced higher and buying it in a market where it is priced lower. In the case of a security priced in a foreign currency, the price must be converted based on the exchange rate.

Traders do not expect such situations to occur, because they are rare. Although they do occur periodically in financial markets, riskless arbitrage opportunities of the type described are short lived. In some situations, however, packages of securities and derivative contracts, combined with borrowing, can produce a payoff identical to that of another security, even though the two are priced differently. The key point is that a riskless arbitrage transaction does not expose the investor to any adverse movement in the market price of the securities in the transaction.

Because the concept of riskless arbitrage provides the underlying process by which assets are priced, we will provide an example. The following table shows three securities, A, B, and C, that can be purchased today; one year from today, we assume they can experience only two possible outcomes, state 1 and state 2:

Security	Price ($)	Payoff in State 1 ($)	Payoff in State 2 ($)
A	70	50	100
B	60	30	120
C	80	38	112

In this example, we use the following notation. Let W_A and W_B be the quantity of security A and B, respectively, in the portfolio. Then the payoff (i.e., the terminal value of the portfolio) under the two states can be expressed mathematically as follows:

Payoff if state 1 occurs: $\$50W_A + \$30W_B$;

Payoff if state 2 occurs: $\$100W_A + \$120W_B$.

Can we create a portfolio consisting of A and B that will reproduce the payoff of C regardless of the state that occurs one year from now? That is, we want to select W_A and W_B such that:

If state 1 occurs: $\$50W_A + \$30W_B = \$38$;

If state 2 occurs: $\$100W_A + \$120W_B = \$112$.

The dollar payoff on the right-hand side of the two equations is the payoff of C in each state.

We can solve these two equations algebraically, obtaining a value of 0.4 for W_A and 0.6 for W_B. Thus, a portfolio consisting of 0.4 of security A and 0.6 of security B will have the same payoff as security C. How much will it cost us to construct this portfolio? As the prices of A and B are \$70 and \$60, respectively, the cost is

$0.40(\$70) + 0.60(\$60) = \$64$.

Note that the price of C is \$80.Thus, for only \$64, an investor can obtain the same payoff as C. This riskless arbitrage opportunity can be exploited by buying A and B in the proportions given above and shorting (selling) C. (Short selling is discussed in chapter 23.) This action allows the investor to lock in a profit of \$16 today regardless of what happens one year from now. By selling C, the investor must pay \$38 if state 1 occurs and \$112 if state 2 occurs. The investor will obtain the amounts necessary to make the payments in either state that occurs from the payoff resulting from A or B.

Risk Arbitrage

Certain trading strategies are believed to carry a low level of risk. Because of the risk exposure, such trading strategies are unfortunately labeled **risk arbitrage**. Of the two types of risk arbitrage, the first arises in the case of exchange offers for securities of corporations coming out of a bankruptcy proceeding. For example, suppose that company A is being reorganized, and one of its bonds is now selling in the market for $200. If the trader believes that the outcome of the bankruptcy proceedings will be the exchange of three securities with an estimated value of $280 for the existing bond worth $200, then the trader will buy the existing bond. The trader will realize a profit of $80 if in fact the final exchange offer is as anticipated, and the value of the package is worth $280.

The spread between the $280 potential package and the $200 price for the bond reflects two risks: the risk that the exchange will not take place on the terms that the trader believes, and the risk that the value of the package of three securities that will be received will be less than $200. The "risk" in this risk arbitrage transaction reflects these two risks.

The other type of risk arbitrage occurs when a merger or acquisition is announced, referred to as **merger arbitrage**. The merger or acquisition can involve a cash exchange, an exchange of securities, or a combination of both. We'll first consider a cash exchange. Suppose that company X announces that it plans to make an offer to buy company Y's common stock for $100 per share at a time when company Y's common stock is selling for $70. One would expect that the market price of Y's common stock would rise to about $100.The risk, however, is that company X will, for whatever reason, withdraw its planned purchase of the stock. The price of company Y's common stock consequently may rise to, say, $90 rather than $100. The $10 difference is the market's assessment of the likelihood of the planned purchase not being completed. An investor who buys the common stock of Y can lock in a profit of $10 if the purchase occurs at $100.The risk is that it will not occur and that the price will decline below $90.

The various attempts of UAL Corporation (the parent company of United Airlines) provide a classic example of the risk associated with this type of risk arbitrage. In September 1989, a group consisting of pilots and management made a $300 per share bid for UAL's stock. Even though the board of UAL approved the offer, the bidders could not obtain the necessary financing to complete the transaction. During this time, the stock reached a peak of $296 per share. In mid-October, when the bidding group acknowledged that the transaction would not take place, the stock fell by almost 50% in a matter of a few days. In January 1990, another bid for UAL Corporation for $201 per share was made by the union. Once again, the financing for the takeover could not be obtained, resulting in a plunge in the market price. Industry experts estimated these failed takeover attempts resulted in losses to risk arbitrageurs of more than $1 billion.

When a transaction involves the exchange of securities rather than cash, the announced terms of the exchange will not be reflected immediately in the price of the securities involved. For example, suppose that company B announces that it plans to acquire company T. Company B is called the "bidding" or "acquiring" firm, and company T is the target firm. Company B announces that it intends to offer one share of its stock in exchange for one share of company T stock. At the time of the announcement, suppose that the prices of the stock of B and T are $50 and $42, respectively. If the acquisition does take place as announced, a trader who acquires one share of company T for $42 can exchange it for stock worth $50, a spread of $8. This spread reflects three risks: (1) the acquisition may not be consummated for one reason or another, and then T's stock may have to be sold, possibly at a loss; (2) the time delay means a cost is involved in financing the position in T's stock; and (3) the price of company B's stock can decline in value so that when T's stock is exchanged for B's, less of a spread is realized.

The way to protect against this last risk is for the trader to buy shares of T and sell short an equal number of shares of B (recall that the transaction is a one-for-one share exchange) so as to lock in a spread of $8 if the transaction is consummated. Let's look at what happens now if the price of company B's stock changes at the time the transaction is consummated. At that time, the price of the stock of company B and company T will be the same.

Suppose the price of company B's stock falls from $50 to $45. Then, when the trader exchanges one share of stock T for stock B, there will be a profit of $3 at the purchase price of $42 for stock T. The short sale of one share of stock B for $50 can now be covered by buying it back for $45, realizing a profit of $5. The trader's overall profit will be $8, the spread that the trader wanted to lock in.

Suppose instead that at the time the exchange is consummated, one share of stock B is worth $60 per share. By exchanging stock T, which was purchased at $42, for one share of stock B, which is now worth $60, a trader can realize a profit of $18 on this leg of the transaction. However, because stock B was sold short for $50 and must now be purchased for $60 to cover the short position, a loss of $10 is realized on the second leg of the transaction. Overall, a profit of $8 is still realized. Thus, risk arbitrage to lock in a spread, if the *exchange is consummated on the announced terms*, involves buying the shares of the target company and shorting the shares of the acquiring or bidding company. The number of shares depends on the exchange terms. Our example assumes a one-for-one exchange, so one share of company B was shorted for every share of company T purchased. Had the exchange been one share of company B for every two shares of company T, then one share of company B would have been shorted for every two shares of company T purchased.

The first risk remains: the risk that the deal will not be consummated. To reduce this risk, the trader or research department must carefully examine the likelihood of a successful takeover or merger.

Proprietary Trading

Proprietary trading, or "prop" trading, occurs when the trader positions the capital of the investment banking firm to take advantage of a specific anticipated movement of prices or a spread between two prices. The benefits of being right, particularly with a highly leveraged position, are rewarding. We read in the popular press that some investment banking firms have reaped millions of dollars from some specific speculative position; it should be remembered, however, that just as often we read about large trading losses from speculative strategies.

Here are just a few notable examples of major financial debacles from prop trading:

- In April and May 2012, JPMorgan Chase lost approximately $6 billion from trades on complex derivatives in its London office.[10]
- The now bankrupt Lehman Brothers lost $32 billion in 2008 from prop trading and other transactions when the bank acted as a principal. The company's common equity at the time was only $18 billion.
- Merrill Lynch and Citigroup lost $20 and $15 billion, respectively, in structured products known as collateralized debt obligations (see chapter 39).
- In the fourth quarter of 2007, Morgan Stanley lost $4 billion in prop trading.
- In February 1995, a derivatives trader for Barings Bank, Nick Leeson, speculated in Nikkei 225 stock index futures and Japanese government bonds, resulting in losses so great that it brought down the bank. Although the trades were unauthorized, it highlights that proprietary trading must be accompanied by risk control systems.

Economists, regulators, and market participants have argued that prop trading at bank-affiliated investment banks was a leading cause of the global financial crisis that began in 2007. Because of the financial debacle arising from prop trading by bank-affiliated investment banks, the Obama Administration proposed, as part of regulatory reform, prohibiting financial institutions that benefit from government support (such as the insuring of deposits by the federal government) from engaging in certain activities that would place the bank's capital at risk. One such activity is prop trading. This prohibition or limitation of prop trading by banks is popularly referred to as the **Volcker Rule**, so named after the adviser to President Obama and former Federal Reserve chair Paul Volcker, who proposed it.

Subsequent to the proposal in 2011 of the Volcker Rule, debates followed as to its merits. One of the major concerns with implementing the Volcker Rule is drawing the line between prop trading and market making. That is, it may be difficult to define prop trading in some instances because of the similarity of that activity to the normal market-making activity of bank-affiliated investment banks. In his letter to the Fed, Volcker also warned regulators to be careful when defining market making. He said that holding "substantial securities in a trading book for an extended period obviously assumes the character of a proprietary position, particularly if not specifically hedged,"[11] and that is what the Volcker Rule tries to prevent.

Banks opposed any such restrictions, because historically, a significant share of their profits was generated from prop trading, as well as from other activities involving principal transactions. However, among the major supporters of the Volcker Rule were some who

10. The bets were made by the firm's chief investment officer and his trader, Ina Drew (nicknamed "the London Whale"), on credit derivatives, the subject of chapter 39. The SEC and regulators in the United Kingdom fined the firm about $900 million for inadequate supervision and control.

11. This is a statement made by Paul Volcker in his February 13, 2012, comment letter to several government agencies on prohibitions and restrictions on proprietary trading.

had formerly held key positions in the financial industry. For example, in a comment letter to the SEC, John Reed, the CEO of Citigroup from 1984 to 2000, described the rule as a "critical response" to prop trading, and went even further to state that the penalties for its violations were not severe enough. He noted, "When a firm is focused on market gain, it will employ every available device to achieve those gains—including taking advantage of clients and putting the firm at risk." It is interesting to note in that in the 1990s, Mr. Reed was a key driver in passing legislation for the separation of commercial and investment banking (the Glass-Steagall Act).

In a *Wall Street Journal* editorial, Roger Vasey, who managed the global debt markets group at Merrill Lynch, disputed the claims of opponents of the Volcker Rule that it would impair the ability of the banks to generate profits.[12] He argued that based on his experience, banks could be successful without proprietary trading, noting that this was the case before Merrill Lynch became a bank-affiliated investment bank. After the repeal of the Glass-Steagall Act in 1999, banks that did have government-guaranteed deposits took on riskier positions.

In addition to officials of investment banking firms who attacked the Volcker Rule, others expressed concern regarding the rule's impact on market-making activities. A January 16, 2012, comment letter to the SEC by Darrell Duffie of Stanford University focused on the adverse impact on market making that would be an unintended consequence of the Volcker Rule:

> [The] proposed implementation of the Volcker Rule would reduce the quality and capacity of market-making services that banks provide to U.S. investors. Investors and issuers of securities would find it more costly to borrow, raise capital, invest, hedge risks, and obtain liquidity for their existing positions. Eventually, non-bank providers of market-making services would fill some or all of the lost market-making capacity, but with an unpredictable and potentially adverse impact on the safety and soundness of the financial system.

The letter goes on to identify and then explain the two major unintended consequences of the proposed Volcker Rule:

1. Over the years during which the financial industry adjusts to the Volcker Rule, investors would experience higher market execution costs and delays. Prices would be more volatile in the face of supply and demand shocks. This loss of market liquidity would also entail a loss of price discovery and higher costs of financing for homeowners, municipalities, and businesses.
2. The financial industry would eventually adjust through a significant migration of market making to the outside of the regulated bank sector. This would have unpredictable and potentially important adverse consequences for financial stability.

Other important players in the financial market expressed concern about the Volcker Rule's impact on market making in non-U.S. government bonds. The Volcker Rule did exempt U.S. government bonds, but not the bonds of other countries. In an interview on Bloomberg

12. Roger Vasey, "Banks Don't Need to Gamble with Taxpayer Money," *Wall Street Journal Online*, April 16, 2012, http://online.wsj.com/news/articles/SB10001424052702304356604577337484269627406.

Television on January 30, 2012, Mark Carney, governor of the Bank of Canada (the central bank of Canada), expressed concern about how the failure to clearly distinguish between prop trading and market making could have an adverse impact on the market for foreign government bonds. Governor Carney, an important financial policymaker, pointed out that because the Volcker Rule did not exempt the government bonds of other countries, a market in which U.S.-based banks played a key role, "there is a potential for real liquidity change."[13] The same concern was expressed in a Bloomberg interview on January 25, 2012, with respect to Canada's federal and provincial government bonds, by Ontario's finance minister Dwight Duncan. Objections were also raised by the Japanese central bank that the cost of trading its country bonds would increase as a result of the Volcker Rule. The internal commissioner of the European Union, Mark Barrier, also expressed similar concern to the U.S. Treasury.

After two years of debate and fine-tuning of the Volcker Rule, initially proposed in November 2011, the final rule was approved in December 2013 with an effective implementation date of April 2014. In general, the Volcker Rule as adopted prohibits a banking entity from (1) engaging in short-term proprietary trading and (2) acquiring or retaining an ownership interest in or sponsoring a hedge fund or private equity fund. A banking entity is defined as an insured depository institution and companies affiliated with insured depository institutions. The Volcker Rule does expressly permit certain trading activity, such as underwriting activities, market-making-related activities, risk-mitigating hedging activities, trading in government obligations, undertaking insurance company activities, and organizing and offering hedge funds or private equity funds. However, larger banks and bank affiliates (size being based on the amount of total assets) that conduct proprietary trading of the sort permitted by the Volcker Rule are subject to compliance reporting to ensure they are conforming to the rule.

As a result of the Volcker Rule, 1 bank-affiliated investment banks have closed down their prop trading desks, and some have spun off their prop trading desks as independent ventures (specifically, hedge funds, which are described in chapter 32). For example, Credit Suisse spun off its internal hedge fund (an entity that did prop trading) to create the entity Credit Value Partners. UBS created an Australian-based hedge fund, MST Capital, which does proprietary trading.

Execution of Trades for Clients

Commissions are generated by executing trades for investors, both retail and institutional investors. Two common institutional trades that investment bankers are called on to execute are block trades and program (or basket) trades. These trades are discussed in chapter 23.

13. Christine Harper and Greg Quinn, "Bank of Canada's Carney Says Volcker Rule Might Damage Markets," *Bloomberg Businessweek*, February 6, 2012, http://www.businessweek.com/news/2012-02-06/bank-of-canada-s-carney-says-volcker-rule-might-damage-markets.html. The rules may be found on the SEC's website, http://www.sec.gov/rules/final/2013/bhca-1.pdf.

Prime Brokerage

An investment banking firm can provide a package of services to hedge fund and large institutional investors. This package of services, referred to as prime brokerage, includes securities finance (i.e., securities lending and the financing of securities), global custody, operational support, and risk management systems. Prime brokerage is a fee-driven service, except in the case of securities finance, where interest income is earned.

With respect to securities lending, in the secondary market for securities and the various trading strategies employed by institutional investors, market participants may have to borrow funds to purchase securities or to borrow securities. Because some investors need to borrow securities, other investors who own securities may be willing to lend them. Institutional investors usually look to an investment banking firm that is operating in the secondary market to provide these services. Investment banking firms generate fee income and interest income for their participation in these activities.

Trading and Creation of Derivative Instruments

Futures, options, swaps, caps, and floors are examples of instruments that can be used to control the risk of an investor's portfolio, or, in the case of an issuer, the risk associated with the issuance of a security. These instruments are referred to as **derivative instruments** and allow an investment banking firm to realize revenue in several ways. First, customers generate commissions from the exchange-traded instruments they buy and sell. This process is no different from the commissions generated by the brokerage service performed for customers when stocks are bought and sold.

Second, certain derivative instruments are created by an investment banking firm for its clients when it acts as a counterparty to the agreement. These products are called **over-the-counter instruments** or **dealer-created derivative instruments**. An example is a swap, which we describe in chapter 37. The risk of loss of capital is present when an investment banking firm is a counterparty, because the investment banker becomes a principal to the transaction. To protect against capital loss, an investment banking firm will seek another party to take the other side of the transaction. When this occurs, spread income is generated.

Derivative instruments are also used to protect an investment bank's own position in transactions. Here are just two examples. Suppose an investment banking firm underwrites a bond issue. The risk that the firm is exposed to is a decline in the price of the bonds purchased from the issuer, which are to be reoffered to the public. Using either interest rate futures or options (the subject of chapters 34 and 37), the investment banking firm can protect itself. As a second example, an investment banking firm has many trading desks with either long or short positions in a security. Derivative instruments can be used by the trading desks to protect the firm against an adverse price movement.

Asset Management

Full-service investment banks have divisions that manage assets for various clients, such as insurance companies, endowments, foundations, corporate and public pension funds, and high-net-worth individuals. These asset management divisions may also manage regulated investment companies. Examples include Goldman Sachs Asset Management (a division of Goldman Sachs & Co.) and Morgan Stanley Investment Management (a division of Morgan Stanley). Money management activities generate fee income based on a percentage of the assets under management.

Key Points

- Investment banking firms distribute newly issued securities and are involved in the secondary market as market makers and brokers.
- Before 1990, the Glass-Steagall Act separated the activities of commercial banks, investment banks, and insurance companies, thereby restricting the types of securities that commercial banks in the United States could underwrite, an important investment banking activity.
- The Gramm-Leach-Bliley Financial Services Modernization Act of 1999 supplanted the Glass-Steagall Act and eliminated the restrictions on the activities conducted by companies in each financial sector, so that commercial banks as well as insurance companies can underwrite securities.
- Firms involved in the activities of investment banking fall into two categories: bank-affiliated investment banks and independent investment banks.
- Investment banking firms are highly leveraged companies.
- The services performed by investment banking firms include the public offering (underwriting) of securities, trading of securities, private placement of securities, securitization of assets, mergers and acquisitions, merchant banking, advising on financial restructuring, securities finance, prime brokerage, trading and creation of derivative instruments, and asset management.
- Full-service investment banking firms engage in many activities associated with investment banking; boutique investment banking firms specialize in one or a few of these activities.
- In the United States, the traditional process for issuing new securities involves (1) advising the issuer on the terms and the timing of the offering, (2) buying the securities from the issuer, and (3) distributing the issue to the public.
- Underwriting is the function of buying the securities from the issuer, with the investment banking firm accepting the risk of selling the securities to investors at a lower price.
- In a firm-commitment underwriting arrangement, the investment banking firm agrees to buy the securities from the issuer.

- In a best-efforts underwriting arrangement, the investment banking firm does not buy the entire issue from the issuer but instead agrees only to use its expertise to sell the securities.
- The gross spread earned by an investment banker is the difference between the price paid to the issuer and the price at which the investment bank then offers the security to the public.
- A new common stock offering is classified as an initial public offering (IPO) or as a secondary common stock offering.
- An IPO is a common stock offering issued by companies that have not previously issued common stock to the public. A secondary common stock offering is an offering of common stock that had been issued in the past by the corporation.
- To share the risk of capital loss that may be incurred by a single investment banking firm's underwriting of an issue, an investment banking firm puts together an underwriting syndicate.
- A selling group is put together for an underwriting to increase the potential investor base.
- Various strategies are employed by traders to generate revenue from positions in one or more securities: riskless arbitrage, risk arbitrage, and speculation.
- A riskless arbitrage trade calls for a trader to find a security or package of securities trading at different prices.
- Certain trading strategies are believed to carry a low level of risk, and because of the risk exposure, such trading strategies are unfortunately labeled risk arbitrage.
- Proprietary trading (prop trading) involves a trader positioning the firm's capital to take advantage of a specific anticipated movement of prices or a spread between two prices.
- The Volcker Rule as adopted prohibits a banking entity from (1) engaging in proprietary trading and (2) acquiring or retaining an ownership interest in or sponsoring a hedge fund or private equity fund.
- Exceptions to the Volcker Rule are defined for certain trading activities, such as underwriting activities, market making-related activities, and risk-mitigating hedging activities.
- There is a concern that the Volcker Rule might have an unintended adverse impact on the liquidity of certain types of securities.
- Investment banking firms assist in the private placement of securities as opposed to the public offering of securities.
- Investment banking firms create asset-backed securities or work with clients to create such securities.
- Investment banking firms generate revenue from mergers and acquisitions (M&As), which include leveraged buyouts (LBOs), restructuring and recapitalization of companies, and the reorganization of bankrupt and troubled companies.

- Investment bankers may participate in M&A activity in one of several ways: (1) by finding M&A candidates; (2) by advising acquiring companies or target companies with respect to price and nonprice terms of an exchange, or by helping target companies fend off an unfriendly takeover attempt; and (3) by assisting acquiring companies in obtaining the necessary funds to finance a purchase.
- Merchant banking refers to an investment banking firm committing its own funds by either taking an equity interest or a creditor position in companies.
- Financial restructuring involves a significant modification of a corporation's capital structure, operating structure, or corporate strategy with the objective of improving efficiency.
- Securities lending is an activity whereby an investment banking firm puts together borrowers and lenders of securities.
- Securities lending is part of the more general area known as securities finance.
- Prime brokerage is a fee-driven activity whereby an investment banking firm provides a package of services to hedge fund and large institutional investors. The services may include securities finance (i.e., securities lending and the financing of securities), global custody, operational support, and risk management systems.
- Investment banking firms generate revenue from derivatives markets from (1) commissions on the trading of exchange-traded instruments by clients and (2) income from being counterparties to clients that want to take a position in an over-the-counter or dealer-created derivative instrument.
- Full-service investment banks have divisions that manage assets for various clients, such as insurance companies, endowments, foundations, corporate and public pension funds, and high-net-worth individuals.

Questions

1. In what four ways can investment banking firms generate revenue?
2. In what three ways can an investment banking firm be involved in the issuance of a new security?
3. What is meant by the "underwriting function"?
4. The market share of investment banking is dominated by European-based investment banks. Explain whether you agree or disagree with this statement.
5. It has been suggested that in the future, the investment banking system will have four tiers. What are those tiers?
6. What is the difference between a firm-commitment underwriting arrangement and a best-efforts arrangement?
7. Describe at least three activities in which investment banking firms must commit their own capital.

8. In a typical underwriting, why is it necessary to form an underwriting syndicate and a selling syndicate?

9. a. What is meant by the "underwriting spread"?

b. How is the underwriting spread distributed among the lead manager, the members of the underwriting syndicate, and members of the selling syndicate?

10. "Gross spreads on moderate-sized IPOs for common stock range from 2% to 4%." Explain why you agree or disagree with this statement.

11. What is meant by "riskless arbitrage"?

12. Suppose that one year from now, the following two outcomes are possible for securities X, Y, and Z:

Security	Price ($)	Payoff in State 1 ($)	Payoff in State 2 ($)
X	35	25	40
Y	30	15	60
Z	40	19	66

Indicate whether a riskless arbitrage opportunity is possible.

13. Explain why an attempt to profit from a merger is not a riskless arbitrage.

14. What is merchant banking?

15. What is meant by "securitization of assets"?

16. In its 2013 Form 10-K report filed with the SEC, the Goldman Sachs Group made the following statements about its business activities:

> Investment Banking serves corporate and government clients around the world. We provide financial advisory services and help companies raise capital to strengthen and grow their businesses.

What investment banking services does Goldman Sachs provide in a financial advisory capacity?

17. "The Volcker Rule does not permit a bank entity to engage in market-making activity." Explain why you agree or disagree with this statement.

18. In its 2013 Form 10-K report, the Goldman Sachs Group stated that "in March 2012, we began redeeming certain interests in our hedge funds and will continue to do so." Why?

19. On May 7, 1999, the investment banking firm Goldman Sachs converted from a partnership to a corporation and completed an IPO in which it sold 51 million shares of common stock.

a. Why do you think Goldman Sachs converted to a corporation?

b. Why was the sale of its common stock referred to as an IPO?

20. Fortis Private Equity is an international provider of banking and insurance services to personal, business, and institutional customers. Its website states the following:

> Is your organisation family-owned and in need of support to resolve succession issues? A privately held company looking for funds to finance expansion? A management team requiring capital to fund a buyout? Fortis Private Equity provides finance and support to the management teams of profitable small and medium-sized enterprises in diverse sectors that have a focused strategy, a strong market position and a growth potential.

What type of investment banking service is Fortis referring to, and what are the risks in this activity for Fortis?

21. What does prime brokerage encompass?

22. What is meant by "securities lending"?

23. What does securities finance involve?

II UNDERSTANDING RISKS AND ASSET PRICING

10 Overview of Risks and Their Management

CONTENTS

Learning Objectives

After reading this chapter, you will understand:

- the general meaning of risk;
- the distinction between risk and uncertainty;
- the difference between systematic risk and idiosyncratic risk;
- the relationship between systematic risk (nondiversifiable risk) and idiosyncratic risk (diversifiable risk);
- the three activities of financial risk management: identifying financial risks, quantifying each identified risk, and evaluating how to deal with each identified risk;
- the risk retention decision and the choices for dealing with each risk: retaining a risk, neutralizing a risk, and transferring a risk;
- the three general categories of financial risk: investment risk, funding risk, and systemic financial risk;
- what is meant by investment risk and the different types of investment risk: price risk, credit risk, reinvestment risk, inflation risk, liquidity risk, and foreign exchange-rate risk;
- the role of derivatives, asset securitization, and structured finance in managing financial risk;
- the different forms of credit risk and how credit risk is measured and controlled;
- what price risk is and the role of factor models in quantifying price risk;
- the two major factors that affect the price sensitivity of a bond;
- what funding risk (or financing risk) is and the different types of funding risk: leverage risk, funding liquidity risk, timing risk, and fixed-floating financing risk;
- what systemic risk is and the various ways to define it; and
- how financial innovation can be classified and how the classifications relate to managing the various forms of risk.

Read any publication dealing with a topic in finance, and undoubtedly you will see the term "risk" used. Listen to any business program on television or radio, and it is highly likely that you will hear the term "risk" used in different ways. The reason is that the term is a general concept that has different meanings in finance. As we will explain in this chapter, there are different types of risks that arise in different contexts. So unless one qualifies what type of risk one is referring to, what is meant by the term will be unclear. For example, we will see that financial markets have a wide range of market participants with varying tolerances for different types of risk. The risk one market participant is willing to accept is not necessarily the risk acceptable to another participant. The development of well-functioning financial markets involves the creation of risk-reducing instruments to transfer some form of risk from one market participant who wants to reduce or eliminate the exposure to that risk to another who is willing to accept that same risk.

In this chapter, we provide an overview of the different types of financial risk that will be referred to throughout this book and the general principles of managing risk, referred to as "risk management." This chapter covers a wide range of topics, some of which were mentioned earlier in this book and some of which will be taken up in more detail in later chapters.

Defining Risk

There is no shortage of definitions of risk. The word "risk" is derived from the Italian verb *riscare*, which means "to dare." In Chinese, risk or venture (fēng xiǎn) is expressed as two symbols, the first meaning danger and the second meaning opportunity. In everyday parlance, risk is often viewed as something that is negative, such as a danger, a hazard, or a loss. But we know that some risks lead to economic gains, whereas others have purely negative consequences. For example, although the purchase of a lottery ticket involves an action that results in the risk of losing an amount equal to the cost of the ticket, it potentially has a substantial monetary reward. In contrast, the risk of death or injury from a random shooting is a purely negative consequence.

Businesses recognize that accepting risk is necessary to obtain the competitive advantage that leads to the generation of profits. Introducing a new product or expanding production facilities involves both return and risk. When a business is exposed to an event that can cause a shortfall to a targeted financial measure or value, this is a financial risk that it faces. The financial measure or value could be some measure of the company's profit, such as earnings per share or return on the amount invested by the company's owners. The financial goals for households are monetary objectives, such as accumulating a target dollar amount from saving and investing to purchase a car or home, financing the costs of a child's college education, or funding retirement at some target age. When seeking to achieve financial goals, households must accept the risk associated with the financial assets in which they invest and the risks associated with the investment strategies that they employ.

Risk versus Uncertainty

When formulating theories about how assets are valued in the financial market, the assumption made is that when facing risk, investors pursue plausible decision rules to select assets. Theories in corporate finance likewise assume that when facing risk, management will follow rules that are plausible as it makes key financial decisions that have an impact on the firm's value. The rules that are applied in decision making by both investors and managers are based on their beliefs regarding the set of outcomes that can result from a decision. In formulating those beliefs about outcomes, theories in finance assume that investors and managers can draw on probabilities to quantify the risk associated with outcomes.

We often refer to risk as the uncertainty regarding what may happen in the future. But is risk equivalent to uncertainty? Economists have argued this question of "risk as uncertainty" or "risk versus uncertainty." The distinction between risk and uncertainty was first made in 1921 by two economists, Frank Knight[1] and John Maynard Keynes.[2] The distinction that Knight made between risk and uncertainty is as follows. He argued that "risk" applies to decision making in which the outcome of the decision is unknown, but the decision maker can fairly accurately quantify the probability associated with each outcome that may arise from that decision. Knight referred to this risk as "measurable risk" or "risk proper." In contrast, Knight viewed uncertainty as applying to decisions in which the decision maker cannot know all the information needed to determine all probabilities associated with the outcomes. This situation gives rise to what is referred to as **Knightian uncertainty** and what Knight referred to as "unmeasurable uncertainty" or "true uncertainty."

Knight provides the following example to help distinguish between risk and uncertainty. Consider an urn that includes red and black balls. Two individuals are drawing from the urn. The first individual has no information about the number of red and number of black balls in the urn and assumes there is an equal probability of drawing a ball of either color. In contrast, the second individual has information that the urn contains three red balls for each black ball. This means that the second individual knows that for every four balls in the urn, three are red and, therefore, the probability of drawing a red ball is 75% and the probability of drawing a black ball is 25%. According to Knight, the second individual faces risk, whereas the first individual faces uncertainty.

John Maynard Keynes made a similar distinction, arguing that there is risk that can be calculated and another sort of risk he labeled "irreducible uncertainty." Keynes recognized that in some decisions, the risks cannot be calculated, because attempting to do so would require relying on assumptions about the future that have no basis in probability theory.

In practice, is the distinction between risk and uncertainty made by Knight and Keynes of importance in decision making? This is a long-running debate among economists: Some have argued that the two concepts are the same, but others argue that the distinction is crucial. The global financial crisis of 2008–2009, however, provided support for the Knight-Keynes view of the distinction between risk and uncertainty. One of the major factors that contributed to the financial crisis was the failure of risk management models to warn about

1. Frank Knight, *Risk, Uncertainty, and Profit* (New York: Houghton Mifflin, 1921).

2. John Maynard Keynes, *Treatise on Probability* (New York: Macmillan & Co., 1921).

the financial problems leading to the financial crisis. It appears that the management of financial entities thought they had adequate risk models to prevent a major collapse in the financial system. That is, management of financial entities failed to recognize that they were dealing with situations that involved Knightian uncertainty or Keynes's irreducible uncertainty.

More recently, Nassim Taleb has popularized the term *black swan event* to characterize a high-impact, hard-to-predict, and rare event that is beyond the realm of normal expectations based on historical events in financial markets, technology, and the sciences.[3] In the context of financial markets, a "high-impact event" means that the event has a large monetary impact. Basically, a black swan event is a surprise to the decision maker and after the event has occurred, the failure to consider such an event is inappropriately rationalized. Linking this to Knightian uncertainty, black swan events are presumed not to exist.

Systematic Risk versus Idiosyncratic Risk

In the study of financial markets, one of the key issues covered in this book is asset pricing. To determine the fair value of an asset and how an asset's value will change over time, the factors that drive (i.e., affect) asset valuation must be determined. Because the factors affect asset valuation, they are referred to as "risk factors." However, for simplicity in our discussion here, we will refer to them as simply "factors."

Because the factors are assumed to affect the valuation of all assets in an asset class, they are referred to as **common risk factors** or **systematic risks**. In addition to systematic risks, there are factors that may be unique to the issuer of a particular asset. This risk is referred to as **idiosyncratic risk**. For example, in later chapter 14 we discuss systematic factors for common stock. Examples of idiosyncratic risk for a company would be a prolonged strike by its employees, an uninsured natural disaster that destroys a principal manufacturing plant, the expropriation of major overseas manufacturing facilities by the government of the country in which the facilities are located, or a patent infringement by the company.

In chapter 14, we review theories about the pricing of assets. These theories tell us that in markets that operate efficiently when pricing assets, investors should only be compensated for accepting systematic risks. In other words, assets price only systematic risks. The reason is that, according to one of the major theories in finance, idiosyncratic risk can be eliminated through the proper selection of assets so as to create a diversified portfolio. In contrast, one cannot eliminate systematic risks by creating a diversified portfolio. Hence, systematic risks are referred to as **nondiversifiable risks**, and idiosyncratic risk is referred to as **diversifiable risk**.

3. See Nassim N. Taleb, *The Black Swan: The Impact of the Highly Improbable*, 2nd ed. (New York: Random House, 2010), and Nassim N. Taleb, *Foolishness by Randomness: The Hidden Role of Chance in Life and in the Markets* (New York: Random House, 2005).

Financial Risk Management

Financial risk management involves the following activities:

- identifying financial risks,
- quantifying each identified risk, and
- evaluating how to deal with each identified risk.

Identifying Financial Risks

Not all risks faced by households, financial entities, and businesses are easy to identify. Some risks, unfortunately, are identified only after a financial problem or financial crisis occurs. The three general categories of financial risk that businesses, financial entities, and households face are (1) investment risk, (2) funding risk, and (3) systemic financial risk. We describe each of these risks in later sections of this chapter.

Quantifying Risks

Not all risks can be quantified. In finance, financial metrics have been used to quantify many of the risks described later in this chapter. These metrics draw on concepts in the fields of probability and statistics. This is the principal reason that it is critical for students interested in the study of finance to have a strong background in probability and statistics.

All models used in finance to measure risk are based on assumptions and estimated parameters. Some market observers argue that it was the failure of risk models used for quantifying risk of financial institutions that resulted in the 2008–2009 global financial crisis. This is why it is critical to understand the underlying assumptions of the risk measures and models discussed throughout this book. The Knight-Keynes distinction between risk and uncertainty should always be kept in mind when using and applying a risk measure when managing financial risk.

Evaluating How to Deal With Each Identified Risk

Once the relevant risks are identified, corporate and household risk management involves evaluating how to deal with each risk. This is the **risk retention decision**, because it involves determining which risks to retain. The choices for dealing with each risk are:

- retaining the risk,
- neutralizing the risk, or
- transferring the risk.

Of course, each identified risk can be treated differently. For each of the three choices—retention, neutralization, and transfer—there are in turn further decisions as to how the risk should be handled.

Retained risk The decision as to which identified risks a business or a household should retain is based on an economic analysis of the expected benefits versus expected costs associated with bearing that particular risk. Aggregating all the risks across any risk that a business or household has elected to bear produces what is called its **retained risk**. Any retained risk realized will have a potential adverse economic impact. In the case of a business, it may adversely impact earnings, cash flow, and the value of the business; for a household, it may have an adverse impact on income and net worth.

With respect to businesses, an **unfunded retained risk** is a retained risk for which potential losses are not financed until they occur. In contrast, a **funded retained risk** is one for which an appropriate amount is set aside up front (either as cash or as an identified source for raising funds) to absorb the potential loss. The management of retained risk is referred to as **risk finance**.

Risk neutralization If a business or household elects not to retain an identified risk, there are two alternatives: neutralize the risk or transfer the risk. **Risk neutralization** is a risk management policy whereby a business or household acts on its own behalf to mitigate the outcome of an expected loss from an identified risk without transferring that risk to a third party.

A risk neutralization strategy can involve mitigating the probability of the identified risk occurring or reducing the severity of the loss should the identified risk in fact occur. For a business, a risk neutralization strategy for some risks may be a natural outcome of the business itself or of financial factors affecting the business. For example, suppose that a company projects an annual loss of $100 million to $150 million from returns because of product defects, and this amount is material relative to the company's profitability. A company could introduce improved manufacturing processes to reduce the probability of defect for each item produced. This would reduce both the variance of the number of defective products and the expected number of defective products. Alternatively, the company could implement an exchange policy to reduce the loss per defective product. Either strategy could reduce the upper range of the potential loss.

As an example involving a financial factor, a Japanese-headquartered company operating in both Japan and in countries in the Eurozone will likely have cash inflows and outflows in euros. As a result, the company faces one of the investment risks discussed later in this chapter, foreign exchange-rate risk: the risk that the exchange rate moves adversely to the company's exposure in that currency. But this risk has offsetting tendencies if there are both cash inflows and outflows in the same currency. Assuming that the currency is the euro, the cash inflows are exposed to a depreciation of the euro relative to the Japanese yen;

the cash outflows are exposed to an appreciation of the euro relative to the Japanese yen. If the company projects future cash inflows over a certain period of €80 million and a cash outflow over the same period of €70 million, then the company's net currency exposure is a €10 million cash inflow. That is, €70 million exposure is hedged naturally.

Risk transfer For certain identifiable risks, a company may decide to transfer the risk to a third party. This can be done either by entering into a contract with another party willing to take on the risk or by embedding that risk in some type of security (i.e., creating a market instrument whose payoff depends on the outcome of the risk).

Let's consider households first. The most common risk transfer vehicle used is an insurance policy. For example, home and auto insurance sold by P&C companies are vehicles used by households to obtain both asset protection resulting from some event and protection of a household's wealth that potentially could be put at risk from a lawsuit in which a home or auto was involved. Life insurance policies are available to provide a guaranteed sum of money to the beneficiaries as a result of the loss of income due to the death of the household's principal wage earner; annuities, discussed in chapter 8, can be used to provide an income stream for retirement. There are other types of insurance, such as medical insurance and disability insurance. Basically, insurance policies transfer risks from households to insurance companies.

Businesses also use insurance companies to protect assets and mitigate the damage that can be done by those assets. There are capital market instruments called "financial derivatives" (or simply "derivatives") that provide for the efficient transfer of risk. Although derivatives are too often mischaracterized in the popular press as speculative vehicles that can cause havoc in the financial markets, when properly utilized by market participants, they can reduce the types of risks already mentioned and described later in this chapter.

In addition to derivatives, capital market instruments have been created using structured finance technology to transfer risk that was previously taken on by financial institutions (such as banks and insurance companies) to the investing public. A few examples will illustrate this type of instrument. At one time, depository institutions originated commercial loans to corporations and consumer loans to individuals to purchase a home (residential property); these institutions retained those loans in their portfolios. The risks associated with the loans were borne by the depository institution. Because the loans were held in the portfolio of depository institutions, they tied up much needed capital. It is expected that regulatory capital requirements[4] for depository institutions (i.e., how much capital a

4. Although in later chapters we discuss "capital" for financial institutions (such as banks and insurance companies), the term is sometimes confused with the term "physical capital," which is used in the production of goods and services by a manufacturing firm (e.g., for machinery, equipment, facilities). Simply put, when referring to the "capital" of a financial institution, the term means the difference between the institution's assets and liabilities. Sounds simple to figure out, except that (as discussed in chapter 7) regulators of financial institutions have different ways in which they measure capital for regulatory purposes.

depository institution must have) will increase over time due to changing regulations. As a result, it is expected that the world's depository institutions will not have sufficient capital to provide loans to governments, businesses, and consumers throughout the world. One of the solutions that depository institutions have adopted is to sell bonds that are backed by a pool (i.e., package) of loans that they originated. The investors in these bonds then look for their payment not from the depository institution that created the bonds but from borrowers whose loans are in the pool of loans. The bonds created are referred to as "securitized products" or "asset-backed securities," and the process of creating them is referred to as **asset securitization**.

The asset securitization process, which we describe in much more detail in chapter 27, transfers the risks associated with the pool of loans from the depository institution that created the asset-backed securities to the investors who purchase these securities. However, it has been argued that asset securitization was responsible for the financial crisis that began in the summer of 2007. As a result, asset securitization is viewed, much like derivatives, as an "evil" capital market mechanism that seeks to exploit the general public. We discuss the merits of this view in chapter 27. Here we only note that governments throughout the world have either adopted or proposed legislation that would foster the development of asset securitization.

Although asset securitization is often used by depository institutions, operating companies use this process to remove the risks associated with the loans they grant to customers. For example, automobile manufacturers make loans to customers for the purpose of purchasing an automobile. Automobile manufacturers can retain those loans and bear the risk associated with them. By pooling automobile loans to create asset-backed securities, automobile manufacturers transfer those risks to the investors who buy the securities.

Asset securitization is not the only type of capital market instrument for transferring risk. Asset securitization is a type of **structured finance vehicle**, which we describe in chapter 27. Here is one example of the type of capital market instruments that insurance companies have created to transfer specific risks.

P&C companies are concerned with catastrophic events that can cause major losses. For example, the heavy rainfalls in France at the beginning of June 2016 resulted in insured losses that were expected to be as much as €600 million (U.S.$682 million). It is estimated that more than 1,000 natural catastrophes occurred in 2015, resulting in overall insured losses of $31 billion.[5] To transfer the risk of such catastrophes to investors willing to accept this insurance risk by potentially earning a higher interest rate, P&C companies created catastrophe bonds (nicknamed "cat bonds"). The payoff to an investor in a cat bond depends on whether a qualifying catastrophe or event occurs. If it does, the bondholders will lose part or all of the principal they invested, and the P&C company that issued the cat bond can use the funds not paid to bondholders to recoup some or all of the losses from the event.

5. Insurance Information Institute, "Catastrophes: Global," http://www.iii.org/fact-statistic/catastrophes-global.

Investment Risk

In very general terms, **investment risk** refers to the likelihood that an investment or an investment strategy will have a performance outcome that is less than what the investor expected. In the general category of investment risk are various types of risk that can result in below-expected performance. These risks include

- credit risk,
- price risk,
- reinvestment risk,
- inflation risk,
- liquidity risk, and
- foreign exchange-rate risk.

Credit Risk

Credit risk is a major risk in the financial system. This type of risk encompasses many forms of risk, and there is no standard definition as to what it means.

Most market participants refer to credit risk in the context of the failure of a borrower in a lending agreement to satisfy the contractual obligation to make timely payments of interest and repayment of principal. Lending agreements include loans and bonds. Used in this way, credit risk refers to **default risk**. For example, when an individual borrows money from a bank to purchase a home, the lending arrangement exposes the lending bank to default risk—the risk that the borrower will fail to repay the loan. When in April 2013, Apple issued $17 billion of bonds, the purchasers of those bonds were exposed to default risk—the risk that Apple would not be able to make the interest payments or repay the principal when it comes due.

Although the term "credit risk" is most commonly used in the context as just described, credit risk in a broader sense means the failure of a counterparty to a transaction to fulfill its obligation. This form of credit risk, referred to as **counterparty risk**, exists not only in financial market transactions but also in many transactions in everyday life. Here are two examples of such transactions. When an individual purchases a one-year subscription to a magazine and pays for that subscription fee upfront, there is the risk that the magazine publisher will go out of business and therefore not fulfill its obligation to deliver the magazine. When an individual pays for a service prior to its performance, there is the risk that the service provider will fail to perform. Service providers often request "advances" or "deposits" before undertaking a service.

Many transactions in financial markets involve counterparty risk. We will see this when we discuss private transactions throughout this book. For example, suppose that on May 1,

2014, an investor enters into a transaction with a financial institution in which the two parties agree to the following. For a sum of \$264,000 paid by the investor to the financial institution at the time the agreement is entered into, the financial institution agrees to allow the investor to purchase 10,000 shares of company X for \$200 per share on May 1, 2018. As explained in chapter 34, this transaction is a special type of derivative transaction called an "option." At the time of the transaction, suppose that on May 1, 2014, the price of a share of company X's stock was \$132. Hence, this agreement allows the investor to benefit from a rise in the price of company X's stock above \$200. No matter what happens to company X's stock four years later on May 1, 2018, the investor forgoes the \$264,000 payment. On May 1, 2018, suppose Company X's stock price was \$448 per share. This transaction would generate a profit for the investor as follows. The investor would purchase the company X's stock from the financial institution at the agreed-on price of \$200 per share. This would require the payment for 10,000 shares of \$2,000,000 (=\$200 × 10,000). The total cost of acquiring the 10,000 shares would be \$2,264,000, which is the \$2,000,000 needed to purchase the stock plus the \$264,000 to enter the agreement on May 1, 2014. The value of the 10,000 shares on May 1, 2018 would be \$4,480,000 (=\$448 × 10,000), resulting in a profit of \$2,216,000. However, suppose that when the investor requests that the financial institution perform its part of the agreement, this counterparty does not have the financial ability to do so. This is counterparty risk.

Derivative transactions of the sort described above are very common in financial markets, and there is a major concern about counterparty risk in the financial system. An extreme example of counterparty risk that underscores its critical importance was the bankruptcy of a major financial institution, Lehman Brothers Holding Inc., in September 2008. At the time, this firm was the counterparty in many private transactions involving derivative instruments, and its bankruptcy resulted in the failure to satisfy its obligations in these transactions. Moreover, the firm also borrowed funds so the firm's creditors realized default risk, because Lehman was unable to repay its debt obligations.

Admittedly, default risk and counterparty risk seem very much like the same type of risk, namely, the risk that one party to a transaction will fail to perform, and, in fact, many market participants do use the terms interchangeably. If one wanted a way to distinguish between the two risks, the examples above should serve. The term "default risk" is commonly used to describe a lending arrangement in which the borrower fails to perform. "Counterparty risk" is the term typically used when the failure occurs in a derivative transaction that is not a lending or a funding arrangement. Some market participants refer to counterparty risk as "counterparty default risk."

Credit risk encompasses one more type of risk, which might best be explained with an illustration. Let's consider once again the Apple bonds. At the time that they were issued, the price of those bonds reflected the default risk as perceived by market participants. As discussed in chapter 11, by "price," we mean the interest rate that Apple will have to pay to bondholders when it issues the bonds. The greater the perceived default risk, the higher the interest rate Apple will have to pay. That interest rate is made up of at least two components. The first component is the interest rate that investors want for holding a bond that has no default risk. The second component is compensation for the default risk perceived by investors. That additional compensation for default risk above the interest rate on a default-free bond is referred to as the **credit spread**. That credit spread is not constant over the life of the bond. The risk that an investor in Apple bonds faces is that sometime in the future, the market will view Apple as having a greater default risk and as a result will require a greater credit spread, which will have an adverse impact on the price of the bond. This aspect of credit risk is referred to as **credit spread risk**.

Measuring credit risk The measurement of default risk and counterparty risk requires an analysis of the ability of the issuer or counterparty to meet its obligations. Professional asset managers analyze an issuer's financial information and the specifications of the debt instrument itself to estimate the ability of the issuer to live up to its future contractual obligations. This activity is known as **credit analysis**. Most large institutional investors have their own credit analysis department not only to assess the credit risk of an issuer/counterparty but also to determine limits on how much exposure to that issuer or counterparty is acceptable. Banks maintain credit departments for assessing credit risk. The credit analysts in these departments develop **internal ratings** that are used when making lending decisions.

Investors who do not have access to their own credit analysis use, to different degrees, opinions about default risk as provided by the credit rating agencies who perform credit analysis and cast their opinion in the form of a credit rating. As explained in chapter 5, the three major rating agencies are S&P, Moody's, and Fitch, although more firms have entered the rating business over the past few years.

Criticism of the performance of credit rating agencies have led to service providers formulating credit scoring models and credit risk models for evaluating credit risk. Let's look first at credit scoring models.

A **credit scoring model** takes information about the attributes of a borrower and through statistical analysis derives a **credit score**. Based on the credit score, a lender may decide to grant a loan or to classify lenders into different credit risk classes. For individuals, the best-known credit scoring model is one used to construct the FICO score. The model assigns a percentage weight to such factors as length of credit history and amount owed, all information provided by credit bureaus, to derive the FICO score. The FICO score, which ranges from 300 to 850 (with higher scores indicating a better credit rating), is used to measure credit risk for consumer credit decisions, such as mortgage lending, auto loans, and credit card lines of credit. For corporations and governments, **credit risk models** have been developed to determine the probability of default and, if a default does occur, how much will be recovered.

Market instruments for controlling credit risk Because of the importance of controlling credit risk, several credit risk transfer vehicles are available in the market. Some of these vehicles are derivatives, referred to as "credit derivatives," with the type most commonly used by investors called "credit default swaps." In addition, securitized products (known as collateralized loan obligations) have been created that are issued by banks, and there are bonds (known as credit-linked notes) issued by corporations that use structured finance. These credit risk transfer vehicles are the subject of chapter 39.

Price Risk

The price of an asset will change over time. That is, the price can increase or decrease. The concern to an investor who owns an asset is that the price will decrease. For example, suppose an investor purchased the stock of General Electric Company on November 12, 2015, for $30.41 per share. The price risk that this investor faces is that the price per share would decline below $30.41. On August 1, 2018, the price for the stock was $13.63, which would have resulted in a loss of $16.78 per share.

One might be tempted to say that price risk is the risk of a decline in the price of an asset. However, that is not true because of a position that one can take in an asset. Buying an asset does in fact result in a loss if the price declines. When an investor buys an asset, the investor is said to be "long the asset," or to be in a long position for that asset. However, an alternative position is to be "short the asset," which means that the investor has sold an asset, even though the investor did not own the asset sold. This may sound like a criminal act. However, the ability to sell an asset that is not owned, referred to as "selling short," is a critical aspect of financial markets that allows asset prices to reflect their true values. We'll have more to say about the mechanisms available in the market for short selling and the economic role of short selling in later chapters. What is important here is that for a short position, price risk is the risk that the price will increase. Let's consider once again the stock of General Electric on November 12, 2015, for $30.41 per share. Now suppose that instead of buying that stock, the investor sold the stock short for $30.41 per share. On April 19, 2016, the stock price was $31.14. This means that if the investor had to produce the stock on that day (which is referred to as "covering the short position"), the investor would have had to pay $31.14 to buy the stock. Because the investor sold the stock for $30.41, this investor would have realized a loss of $0.73 per share.

So now we see that **price risk** is the risk of an adverse movement in the price of a stock, which could result from either an increase or a decrease in an asset's price, depending on the investor's position. A long position's price risk is that the price will decline; a short position's price risk is that the price will increase. In general, we can say that price risk is the risk of an unfavorable movement in an asset's price.

What causes price risk? The starting point for answering this question is to understand what factors cause an asset's price to change. Basically, this means determining what drives an asset's price. So, to determine price risk, we must at least understand qualitatively what variables drive an asset's price. The variables that affect an asset's price are referred to as "risk factors" or simply "factors." In the case of a stock, one might believe that the price of the stock is affected by the earnings of a company, the growth of those earnings, and the level of interest rates. It is reasonable to expect that the factors driving the price of a bond are the level of interest rates in the market and the issuer's credit rating.

Measuring price risk Given the factors that one would expect to drive an asset's price, one must develop a model that links an asset's price sensitivity to the factors. Such models are referred to as "asset pricing models." Given an asset pricing model, one can measure an asset's price risk exposure to each factor. That is, there may not be one measure of price risk for an asset but one for each factor. The exposure of an asset to a factor is referred to as its **factor beta**. The factor beta is estimated using various statistical models incorporating historical returns for the asset.

In the case of debt obligations, such as bonds, the key drivers of the change in a bond's price are the level of interest rates and the issuer's credit risk. The level of interest rates is measured by the interest rate on what is viewed as a default-free security, securities issued by the U.S. Department of the Treasury. As mentioned earlier, the component of the interest rate that reflects compensation for the issuer's credit risk is the credit spread

A mathematical relationship between the bond's price and these two factors (i.e., Treasury rates and credit risk) can be developed to estimate the exposure of a bond to each of these factors. In general, the term **duration** is used to quantify the exposure of a bond's price to changes in Treasury interest rates. We describe this measure in more detail in chapter 16. The exposure of a bond's price to changes in the issuer's credit risk is referred to as **credit spread duration**, because it refers to the exposure to changes in the credit spread.

Market instruments for controlling price risk There are many derivative instruments in the marketplace for controlling the price risk of an individual asset and a portfolio of assets. We describe derivatives to control price risk for common stock and derivatives to control exposure to interest rate risk in part VIII of the book.

Reinvestment Risk

Reinvestment risk is the risk that when proceeds are received from an investment, they will have to be invested at an interest rate that is less than when the original investment was made.

Investors in bonds face reinvestment risk. First, when a bond is purchased, one can compute the potential yield for that bond, as explained in chapter 11. The yield calculated assumes that the bond is held to maturity and that any interest payments can be reinvested from the time the interest payment is received from the bond issuer until the bond matures. Here is an example. Suppose that in May 1984, an investor purchased a bond issued by the U.S. Treasury that matured in 30 years (i.e., it would have matured in May 2014). The yield on that bond would have been approximately 13%. That is, if one of those bonds had been purchased for $1,000, the annual interest rate that would have been paid by the U.S. Department of the Treasury was $130 per year or $65 every six months. An investor would typically say that a 13% yield was being earned. However, as explained in chapter 11, this is the case only if (1) the interest received every six months can be reinvested at an annual interest rate of 13%, and (2) the bond is held to maturity (May 2014 in our example). A little knowledge of the history of interest rates since the 1980s will make it clear why it is unlikely that the interest payments received from the U.S. Treasury would not have allowed for reinvestment at 13%. For example, 10 years after the bond was purchased (i.e., in May 1994), the interest received would had to have been reinvested in 20 years Treasury bonds, which at the time offered 7.5%, far less than the reinvestment rate needed to generate a 13% yield. Moving forward another 10 years to May 2004, when the interest received would had to have been reinvested for another 10 years, the 10-year Treasury interest rates were about 3.5%. Five years later, the interest received would have been reinvested at 2.13%. Hence, one can see the reinvestment risk faced by an investor who purchased the U.S. Treasury bonds in May 1984. How serious is reinvestment risk? The amount of interest from the reinvestment of the bond's interest to generate the expected 13% yield is substantial, as is demonstrated in chapter 11. In contrast, if an investor in May 2014 purchased a 30-year Treasury bond, the yield at that time was only 3.4%, and expectations were that the interest rate would not fall far below that rate. Hence, the reinvestment risk would have been far less.

Another example of reinvestment risk faced by a bond investor arises when the bond has a feature that allows the issuer to repurchase the bond from the investor at some future date. This provision, referred to as a **call provision**, is a benefit to the issuer, because it allows the issuer to retire the bond issue if interest rates have declined since the time the bond was issued and then issue new bonds at the lower interest rate. This call provision results in reinvestment risk for the investor, who will then have to reinvest the proceeds received from the issuer at a lower interest rate than when the bonds were purchased.

Inflation Risk

Inflation occurs when the prices of most goods and services rise, resulting in a reduction in purchasing power. When income rises at a rate less than the inflation rate, then the standard of living of households declines. Failing to take into account inflation when planning for retirement can result in a retirement income supporting a lower standard of living than was expected. When an investor invests in assets to generate retirement income, the **real return** that the investor realizes is the return after adjusting for the inflation rate. **Inflation risk**, also referred to as **purchasing power risk**, is the risk that the nominal return earned (i.e., the return without considering inflation) will be less than the inflation rate. Put differently, inflation risk is the risk of earning a negative real return.

When investing in different asset classes, an investor is exposed to different degrees of inflation risk. For example, historically, stocks and real estate have been observed to expose investors to less inflation risk than do bonds. Given that each asset class has a different exposure to inflation risk, a portfolio composed of different asset classes will have an exposure to inflation risk that depends on the allocation to each asset class.

Although the typical bond may have greater inflation risk than common stock and real estate, there are bonds issued by the U.S. Department of the Treasury, financial institutions, and nonfinancial corporations that have protection against inflation risk. These bonds are referred to as **inflation-adjusted bonds** (also called "linkers"). For such bonds, the interest rate or the principal is indexed to the inflation rate. In addition, some derivatives allow for the control of inflation risk.

Liquidity Risk

Liquidity allows investors the flexibility to rebalance a portfolio (i.e., by buying and selling assets) in order to implement an investment strategy. Liquidity can be viewed in terms of the potential loss that an investor may realize if the investor wishes to sell immediately instead of engaging in a costly and time-consuming search to identify a buyer willing to pay a higher price. A financial asset's liquidity may depend on the quantity that the investor wishes to sell (or buy). Although an investor may wish to sell a small quantity of an asset that is liquid, there may be illiquidity if a large quantity of the asset is to be sold.

As explained in chapter 9, although an asset's liquidity serves an important function, there is no uniformly accepted definition of what liquidity is. Several studies have defined liquidity in terms of the ability of an investor to trade an asset at short notice at a low cost and without having a significant adverse impact on the asset's price. **Liquidity risk** for an asset can then be defined as the risk that when an investor executes a trade for that asset, prevailing market conditions will be such that the cost will be higher and there will be a significant adverse impact on the price at which the trade is executed.

Foreign Exchange-Rate Risk

When an investor acquires an asset whose cash flows are not denominated in the investor's domestic currency, the investor is really taking two positions—a position in the asset and a position in the currency. If the investor has a long position, there is the risk that the currency will change at the time of receipt of the cash flow such that fewer units of the domestic currency are realized. More specifically, the risk is that the currency in which a cash flow is paid (i.e., the foreign currency) will depreciate relative to the domestic currency. This risk is referred to as **foreign exchange-rate risk** or **currency risk**. Certain foreign exchange derivative products—the subject of chapter 38—can be used to control the degree of an investor's foreign exchange-rate risk exposure.

There is potentially another risk associated with investing in an asset whose cash flows are denominated in a foreign currency. A foreign government may prevent its currency from being fully converted into a convertible currency. (A convertible currency is one that can be freely exchanged into another currency.) The risk of loss associated with an action taken by a foreign government to make its currency inconvertible is called **convertibility risk**.

Funding Risk

Funding risk, also referred to as **financing risk**, is the risk associated with obtaining funds. There are four types of funding risk: leverage risk, funding liquidity risk, timing risk, and fixed-floating financing risk.

Leverage Risk

When individuals or businesses borrow funds, they are said to be using **financial leverage**, or simply, “leverage.” Benefits and risks are associated with the use of leverage by businesses. To understand them, we take as an example the chief financial officer (CFO) of a corporation who is considering borrowing $400 million at a cost of 6% per year. The corporation will deploy the proceeds received in various business activities with the purpose of generating a rate of return that exceeds the cost of borrowing (6% per year). The corporation benefits in terms of adding to its profitability by the difference between the rate of return earned and the cost of borrowing. For example, if the corporation earns 8% on the $400 million borrowed, then the cost of the borrowed funds for the year is $24 million (6% × $400 million), and the amount received from deploying the funds in the business is $32 million (8% × $400 million). The difference of $8 million adds to the corporation’s profit. If the CFO borrowed even more funds, the amount of profit added would have been even greater as long as the corporation earned more than 6% per year.

What we have just described is the benefit of using leverage. The risk should be obvious: it is the risk that the corporation fails to earn a return on the amount borrowed greater than the cost of borrowing. In our illustration, suppose that the corporation earns only 2% per year on the borrowed funds. It thus paid $24 million for the borrowed funds but generates only $8 million, reducing its profitability as a result of the borrowing by $16 million. If the amount of leverage employed is such that the cost of all the borrowed funds by the corporation results in the inability of the firm to pay its contractual debt obligations, creditors will force the firm into bankruptcy.

Leverage risk is the adverse financial impact resulting from the use of leverage. The degree of leverage of a corporation can be measured in two ways: the debt ratio and the debt-to-equity ratio. The **debt ratio** is the amount of funds provided by the corporation’s creditors (referred to simply as “debt”) divided by the total amount of funds that the corporation has available to invest (i.e., total assets). The basic financial accounting identity is:

Total assets = Equity + Debt.

Then total assets represent the amount of funds available for the corporation to invest. The debt-to-equity ratio is:

$$\text{Debt ratio} = \frac{\text{Debt}}{\text{Total assets}}.$$

The higher the debt ratio is, the greater will be the leverage used by the corporation. For firms in the same industry, the higher the debt ratio is, the greater the leverage risk will be.

The second way to calculate the degree of leverage is by computing the **debt-to-equity ratio**:

$$\text{Debt-to-equity ratio} = \frac{\text{Debt}}{\text{Equity}}.$$

The higher the debt-to-equity ratio is, the greater the leverage will be, and therefore for firms in the same industry, the greater the leverage risk will be.

The decision regarding the amount of debt relative to equity that a corporation should have (i.e., the degree of leverage) is referred to as its "capital structure decision." There are various financial theories that suggest the factors a corporation should consider when determining its optimal capital structure.

In chapter 6, we described depository institutions, which include banks. These financial institutions are highly leveraged. That is, the percentage of funds they invest represents predominantly borrowed funds relative to the equity raised from stockholders. The debt ratio for depository institutions is roughly 92% (expressed as a percentage). The profitability of depository institutions depends primarily on management's ability to invest in loans and other debt obligations so as to earn a higher return than its cost of borrowing.

Households also borrow funds and thereby create leverage and face leverage risk. The benefits associated with the use of leverage by households are not as easy to quantify as those for corporations and depository institutions. Households borrow to accelerate the purchase of goods and services rather than to postpone any purchase until sufficient funds are available for an outright purchase without borrowing. Certain purchases do have economic benefits that households believe will accrue by borrowing. Two examples are borrowing for college education and purchasing a home. In the former case, the expectation is that the cost of borrowing for college will generate lifetime future earnings that warrant the cost. In the case of the purchase of a residence using borrowed funds, the belief is that ownership of a home rather than renting will provide a benefit as a result of the potential price appreciation of the home purchased. This was a belief shared by many households prior to the bursting of the housing bubble in 2007.

Funding Liquidity Risk

It is not uncommon for participants in financial markets to be forced to settle financial obligations immediately at the request of the lender. For example, a bank's depositors for some reason may want to withdraw funds from a bank at the same time. The bank must have the ability to satisfy those obligations immediately. Another example is a highly leveraged investor whose borrowing agreement grants the lender the right to request the immediate payment of the amount borrowed. The ability of the borrower to settle its debt obligations immediately is referred to as **funding liquidity**. **Funding liquidity risk** is then the risk that over a specific horizon, an entity will not be able to settle its obligations with immediacy.

Timing Risk

Timing risk is the risk associated with the timing of raising capital. More specifically, it is the risk that the cost of obtaining funds will be higher than expected at some future date when the funds are needed.

As an example of timing risk, consider a corporation that wants to raise funds by borrowing in the marketplace. Suppose that in September 2008, a corporation with a credit rating of BBB (the meaning of which we explain in chapter 5) wanted to issue a $400 million 20-year bond. The person in a corporation responsible for determining how much to raise and when to raise those funds is the CFO. Suppose that the CFO has determined that the $400 million is not needed immediately. Instead, the CFO was considering either issuing the bonds that day or sometime over the next five months. Let's look at this CFO's decision using actual market interest rates. According to interest rate data published by the Federal Reserve, the interest rate for such a corporation seeking to borrow for 20 years and whose credit rating was BBB would have been about 7.31% in September 2008. By issuing immediately, the CFO would have locked in a cost of 7.31% for the next 20 years. Here is what the Federal Reserve reported as interest rates for the next four months: October 2008, 8.38%; November 2008, 9.21%; December 2008, 8.49%; and January 2009, 8.19%. This was a period of considerable interest rate volatility in the financial markets, as can be seen by the large movement in interest rates over this five-month period. The timing risk faced by the CFO was that by not issuing the bonds that day, the CFO placed the company at risk of having to issue the bonds over the next four months at a higher interest rate than it would have paid in September 2008. Indeed, that is what happened, because the interest rates were higher for each of the four months following September 2008.

Suppose the CFO decided not to issue the bond in September 2008, but seeing that interest rates rose from 7.31% to 8.38% in one month and then again in the following month (from 8.38% to 9.21%), the CFO decided to issue the bonds in November 2008 at 9.21%. The timing risk that the CFO faced when the decision was made to issue the bonds in November 2008 was losing the opportunity to benefit from a decline in interest rates, which did in fact occur in the next two months (8.49% and 8.19% in December 2008 and January 2009, respectively).

State and local governments share the same timing risk as businesses. They raise funds and are concerned with the interest rate that they must pay. Because interest rates fluctuate, the risk is that they may have to raise funds at a time when interest rates are higher than they currently are.

Although our illustration of timing risk involves raising funds in the form of borrowed money (bonds in our example), the CFO faces timing risk when a decision must be made to raise funds by issuing common stock. To understand this, suppose the CFO of a corporation wants to raise $200 million by issuing common stock at a time when the common stock is $100 per share. The funds are not needed immediately but sometime over the next 60 days. Ignoring the cost of issuing the common stock, this means that if the CFO issues immediately, then two million shares ($200 million/$100) would have to be issued. By postponing the issuance to take advantage of a rise in the price of the corporation's common stock, the CFO takes the risk that the stock's price will decline, forcing the corporation to issue more than two million shares of common stock. By issuing more shares, the corporation will have more shares outstanding, diluting corporate earnings more than if it issued the common stock today.

Households face timing risk, particularly with the purchase of a home. A household that has the capacity to purchase a home now with borrowed funds at prevailing interest rates faces two forms of timing risk. The first is that the interest rate at which it must borrow to purchase a home is known today (called the mortgage rate), but postponement of the purchase may result in having to pay a higher mortgage rate. The second is that if the purchase is postponed to a future date, housing prices may increase, resulting in the household having to borrow more to purchase a home.

Fixed-Floating Financing Risk

Another form of funding risk involves the decision to pay a fixed interest rate over the entire time period for which the funds are borrowed (referred to as **fixed-rate borrowing**) or to pay an interest rate that varies periodically (**variable-rate borrowing** or **floating-rate borrowing**). This form of funding risk is referred to as **fixed-floating financing risk**.

With floating-rate borrowing, the interest rate is reset (i.e., changes) at designated times and is reset according to a formula. The formula has two components: a reference rate plus a constant amount. The **reference rate** is some market interest rate that changes over time. For example, the most common reference rate is the London interbank offered rate (LIBOR), a rate we discuss further in chapter 25. The constant amount is referred to as the **margin**. So, as an example, the interest rate formula on a floating-rate debt obligation that resets every year might be one-year LIBOR plus 150 basis points. In the formula, one-year LIBOR is the reference rate and the margin is 150 basis points. Because the one-year LIBOR changes every year, the rate that the borrower would pay varies every year while the debt obligation is outstanding.

Let's consider a CFO of a U.S. corporation deciding whether to issue a $400 million bond that pays a fixed interest rate of 6% per year for the next 20 years. Alternatively, the CFO can issue a $400 million floating-rate bond whose interest rate resets every year based on the formula: one-year LIBOR plus 150 basis points. Suppose that for the first year, one-year LIBOR is 3%. Then for the first year, the borrowing cost for the $400 million will be 4.5% (3% + 150 basis points). This would be a clear advantage to borrowing on a floating-rate basis. However, the risk is that over the next 19 years, one-year LIBOR might rise above 4.5%, which would make borrowing on a fixed-rate basis more advantageous. If the CFO selects the fixed-rate borrowing alternative, then the risk is that one-year LIBOR will fall below 4.5%, so that floating-rate borrowing would be more advantageous.

Fixed-floating financing is faced not only by businesses when determining the form of financing that they will use but also by households when they purchase a home with borrowed funds. When borrowing funds to purchase a home, a household can select a loan that has a fixed rate over its life or a floating rate over its life. A floating-rate loan to purchase a home is referred to as an "adjustable-rate loan" and is described in chapter 29.

Systemic Financial Risk

In general, the term **systemic risk** refers to the probability that an entire system will collapse or fail. When applied to finance, systemic risk is referred to as **systemic financial risk**.[6] The example typically given to illustrate systemic financial risk is a run on a bank (i.e., bank depositors simultaneously withdrawing their funds from a bank). Prior to the protection offered to bank depositors in the United States through federal deposit insurance, the inability of one bank to meet the demands for the withdrawal of deposits caused not only the failure of that bank but also triggered a chain reaction that produced runs on other banks, causing them to fail.

In 2007 the U.S. Congress, following the problems faced in certain sectors of the financial market in that year, held hearings under the title "Systemic Risk: Examining Regulators' Ability to Respond to Threats to the Financial System." Yet despite the concern about systemic financial risk threat to the global financial system, there is no universally accepted definition of what that risk is. In a 2007 speech, then governor of the Federal Reserve Board Frederic Mishkin defined systemic financial risk as follows:

> When we speak of systemic risk, we mean the risk of a sudden, usually unexpected, disruption of information flows in financial markets that prevents them from channeling funds to those who have the most productive profit opportunities.[7]

6. Do not confuse systematic risk described earlier in the chapter with systemic risk as described here.

7. Speech titled "Systemic Risk and the International Lender of Last Resort," given at the Tenth Annual International Banking Conference, Federal Reserve Bank of Chicago, Chicago, Illinois, September 28, 2007. Available at http://www.federalreserve.gov/newsevents/speech/mishkin20070928a.htm#pagetop.

He then went on to say:

We have seen how systemic risk, when it becomes especially severe, can result in financial crises—the seizing up of financial markets—which can have potentially important economic consequences.

The Bank for International Settlements (BIS) provides the following definition of systemic financial risk:

The risk that the failure of a participant to meet its contractual obligations may in turn cause other participants to default with a chain reaction leading to broader financial difficulties.[8]

Although there is no universally accepted definition of systemic financial risk, the basic notion is clear. The interconnectedness of financial institutions throughout the world can, by contagion, cause major disruptions to the global financial system. In chapter 2, we gave examples of this concern when we discussed government intervention in the financial market.

Financial Innovation

Since the 1960s, there has been a surge in the number of significant financial innovations. Observers of financial markets categorize these innovations in different ways. Below we describe just two possible ways of classifying these financial innovations. With an understanding of the risks described in this chapter, the reasons for financial innovation should be clear.

The Economic Council of Canada classifies financial innovations in the following three broad categories:[9]

- **Market-broadening instruments**, which increase the liquidity of markets and the availability of funds by attracting new investors and offering new opportunities for borrowers.
- **Risk management instruments**, which reallocate financial risks to those who are less averse to them or who have offsetting exposure, and who are presumably better able to shoulder them.
- **Arbitraging instruments and processes**, which enable investors and borrowers to take advantage of differences in costs and returns between markets, and which reflect differences in the perception of risks, as well as in information, taxation, and regulations.

Another classification system of financial innovations based on more specific functions has been suggested by the BIS: price risk-transferring innovations, credit risk-transferring instruments, liquidity-generating innovations, credit-generating instruments, and equity-generating instruments.[10] **Price risk-transferring innovations** provide market participants

8. Bank for International Settlements, *64th Annual Report* (Basel, Switzerland: BIS, 1994), p. 177.

9. Economic Council of Canada, *Globalization and Canada's Financial Markets* (Ottawa: Supply and Services Canada, 1989), p. 32.

10. Bank for International Settlements, *Recent Innovations in International Banking* (Basel: BIS, April 1986).

with more efficient means for dealing with price or exchange-rate risk. Reallocating the risk of default is the function of credit risk-transferring instruments. Liquidity-generating innovations do three things: (1) they increase the liquidity of the market; (2) they allow borrowers to draw on new sources of funds; and (3) they allow market participants to circumvent capital constraints imposed by regulations. Instruments to increase the amount of debt funds available to borrowers and to increase the capital base of financial and nonfinancial institutions are the functions of **credit-generating innovations** and **equity-generating innovations**, respectively.

As you read the chapters on the various sectors of the financial markets that we review in this book, it is important to understand the factors behind any innovations in that market.

Key Points

- Many forms of risk are faced by participants in the financial markets.
- There is a difference between risk and uncertainty, as was first pointed out in 1921 by two economists, Frank Knight and John Maynard Keynes.
- Knight argued that risk applies in situations where the decision maker can fairly accurately quantify the probability associated with each outcome that may arise from that decision; he referred to this risk as "measurable risk" or "risk proper."
- Knightian uncertainty exists when the decision maker cannot know all the information needed to determine all the probabilities associated with the outcomes of a decision. This form of uncertainty was referred to by Knight as "unmeasurable uncertainty" or "true uncertainty."
- Keynes made a similar distinction between risk and uncertainty, referring to the latter as "irreducible uncertainty."
- The risks that affect the value of an asset can be classified as systematic risks and idiosyncratic risks.
- Systematic risks or common risk factors are those risks that affect the valuation of all assets in an asset class. Because they cannot be diversified away, they are also referred to as "nondiversifiable risks."
- Idiosyncratic risk is a risk that is unique to an issuer. Because it can be diversified away in a portfolio, it is referred to as "diversifiable risk."
- The financial risks faced by businesses, financial entities, and households are (1) investment risk, (2) funding risk, and (3) systemic financial risk.
- Broadly speaking, investment risk refers to the probability that the outcome realized by an investment or an investment strategy will be below what the investor expected.
- Financial risk management involves (1) identifying financial risks, (2) quantifying each identified risk, and (3) evaluating how to deal with each identified risk.

- Once the relevant risks are identified, risk management involves assessing which risks to retain, with the choices being (1) retaining a risk, (2) neutralizing a risk, or (3) transferring a risk.
- Retained risk is the aggregate of all risks that a business or household has elected to bear.
- An unfunded retained risk is a retained risk for which potential losses are not financed until they occur; a funded retained risk is a retained risk for which an appropriate amount has been set aside up front (either as cash or as an identified source for raising funds) to absorb the potential loss.
- There are two alternatives for dealing with risks that are not retained: neutralize the risk or transfer the risk.
- Risk neutralization is a risk management policy whereby a business or household acts on its own behalf to mitigate the outcome of an expected loss from an identified risk without transferring that risk to a third party.
- An entity may decide to transfer the risk to a third party by either entering into a contract with another party willing to take on the risk that an entity wishes to transfer or by taking a position in a market instrument whose payoff depends on the outcome of the risk that the entity wishes to transfer to the public.
- Capital market instruments have been created using structured finance technology to transfer risk that was previously taken by financial institutions, with asset securitization being one example.
- Investment risk includes price risk, credit risk, reinvestment risk, inflation risk, liquidity risk, and foreign exchange-rate risk.
- Credit risk encompasses default risk and credit spread risk.
- Several credit risk transfer vehicles are available in the market.
- Price risk is the risk of an adverse movement in the price of an asset that could result from an increase or decrease in an asset's price, depending on the investor's position: A long position's price risk is that the price will decline, and a short position's price risk is that the price will increase.
- Risk factors (or simply, "factors") are the variables that affect an asset's price. A model that shows how these factors affect an asset's price is called an "asset pricing model."
- Given an asset pricing model, one can measure an asset's price risk exposure to each factor, which is referred to as an asset's "beta factor."
- Duration is a measure of a bond's price sensitivity to changes in the general level of interest rates. Credit spread duration is a measure of a bond's price exposure to changes in the credit spread.
- Many derivative instruments are available for controlling the price risk of an individual asset and a portfolio of assets.

- Reinvestment risk is the risk that when proceeds are received from an investment, they will have to be reinvested at an interest rate that is less than when the original investment was made.
- Inflation risk (also referred to as "purchasing power risk") is the risk that the nominal return earned will be less than the inflation rate; that is, inflation risk is the risk of earning a negative real return.
- An asset's liquidity risk is the risk that when an investor executes a trade for that asset, prevailing market conditions will be such that the cost will be higher and there will be a significant adverse impact on the price at which the trade is executed.
- Foreign exchange risk (also referred to as "currency risk") is the risk that the currency in which a cash flow is paid (i.e., the foreign currency) will depreciate relative to the domestic currency.
- Funding risk, or financing risk, is the risk associated with obtaining funds and includes leverage risk, funding liquidity risk, timing risk, and fixed-floating financing risk.
- Leverage risk is the adverse financial impact resulting from the use of leverage.
- The degree of leverage of a corporation can be measured by its debt ratio (the ratio of the debt to total assets) or its debt-to-equity ratio.
- Funding liquidity is the ability of a borrower to settle its debt obligations immediately. The risk that an entity cannot do so is called "funding liquidity risk."
- Timing risk is the risk associated with the timing of raising capital resulting in a funding cost higher than expected at some future date when the funds are needed.
- A funding risk associated with the decision as to whether to borrow on a fixed-rate or floating-rate basis is referred to as a "fixed-floating financing risk."
- In general, the term "systemic risk" refers to the probability that an entire system will collapse or fail. When applied to finance, it is referred to as "systemic financial risk."
- Financial innovations can be classified in terms of the type of financial instrument (market-broadening instruments, risk management instruments, and arbitraging instruments and processes) and according to more specific functions (price risk-transferring innovations, credit risk-transferring instruments, liquidity-generating innovations, credit-generating instruments, and equity-generating instruments).

Questions

1. In an article, Pablo A. Guerron-Quintana explains the difference between risk and uncertainty as follows:

Consider the experiment of flipping a fair coin (Case A). In this experiment, the unknown is whether the coin will land heads or tails. Because we are dealing with a fair coin, we know that the odds of heads after each flip are 50–50. That is, if we were to flip the coin let's say 100 times, the coin would land, on average, 50 times heads and 50 times tails. The crucial insight from this experiment is the observation that we know exactly the odds of each of the possible events: 50 percent heads and 50 percent tails. Furthermore, we have this knowledge before starting the experiment. …

Now let's consider an alternative experiment (Case B). As before, we are interested in learning the result of flipping a coin. The key difference is that we know the coin is no longer fair, but we do not know the odds of obtaining heads. Furthermore, the coin is replaced by a new (and unfair) coin after each flip. Under this scenario, the only thing we know is that the coin will land either heads or tails. If we were thinking about flipping the coin 100 times, we could not (before we start the experiment) tell how many times the coin will land on heads.[11]

a. Which of the two experiments is an example of Knightian uncertainty? Explain why.

b. Which of the two experiments is an example of Knightian risk? Explain why.

2. The following quote is from Donald Rumsfeld, Secretary of Defense under President George W. Bush from 2001 to 2006:

Reports that say that something hasn't happened are always interesting to me, because as we know, there are known knowns; there are things we know we know. We also know there are known unknowns; that is to say we know there are some things we do not know. But there are also unknown unknowns—the ones we don't know we don't know.

Discuss this quote in the context of risk and uncertainty.

3. The quote below is taken from a description of risks by and methods for dealing with risks faced by a financial entity, Goldman Sachs. The three blanks are intentional. In addition to liquidity risk, the quote below discusses another form of risk. What is that risk?

The Goldman Sachs _________ plan sets out the plan of action we would use to fund business activity in crisis situations and periods of market stress. The _________ plan outlines a list of potential risk factors, key reports and metrics that are reviewed on an ongoing basis to assist in assessing the severity of, and managing through, a liquidity crisis and/or market dislocation. The _________ plan also describes in detail the firm's potential responses if our assessments indicate that the firm has entered a liquidity crisis, which include funding our potential cash and collateral needs as well as utilizing secondary sources of liquidity.

4. Explain the risk management policy followed by an individual who purchases a home insurance policy that has a large deductible (i.e., an amount of loss that the homeowner absorbs before the insurance company makes a payment).

5. The following is from the University of British Columbia Board of Governors' Policy No. 125 regarding major capital projects:

The University manages risk on major capital projects through a variety of strategies incorporated into its project planning, delivery and procurement processes. Risk management strategies include the avoidance, reduction and transference of risk away from the University, as appropriate. However,

11. Pablo A. Guerron-Quintana, "Risk and Uncertainty," *Business Review* (Federal Reserve Bank of Philadelphia) Q1 (2012): 10.

some types of risk cannot be fully or economically managed through these means and in those cases, it is prudent and cost efficient to retain and self-insure against such risks.

The document then goes on to describe the establishment of funds for major capital projects to protect against overruns "to manage risk in a prudent and cost-efficient manner, including through the avoidance, reduction or transference of risk away from the University, as appropriate" and to explain how each fund is to be financed. Discuss the general elements of this risk management policy.

6. The following excerpt is taken from various filings of Kimberly-Clark Corporation (manufacturer of well-known products, such as Huggies, Kleenex, and Pull-Ups):

Selected insurable risks are retained, primarily those related to property damage, workers' compensation, and product, automobile and premises liability based upon historical loss patterns and management's judgment of cost effective risk retention.

Describe this corporation's risk management policy.

7. Suppose that your car needs a major repair that will cost $3,000. You sign an agreement with the car repair shop to perform the services. The repair shop must order the necessary parts and estimates that it will take one week for the parts to be acquired. The repair shop requires that you provide an upfront payment of $1,500 as a deposit before the parts are ordered. What is the financial risk to which you are exposed?

8. "Because idiosyncratic risk cannot be diversified away, it is referred to as systematic risk." Explain whether you agree or disagree with this statement.

9. In a speech in 2009, Ben Bernanke, then chair of the Federal Reserve, concluded:

In the wake of the ongoing financial crisis, governments have moved quickly to establish a wide range of programs to support financial market functioning and foster credit flows to businesses and households. However, these necessary short-term steps must be accompanied by new policies to limit the incidence and impact of systemic risk.[12]

a. What is meant by systemic risk?

b. Why does systemic risk impede the flow of credit available to businesses and households?

c. Why is government intervention needed to reduce systemic risk rather than relying solely on individual market participants to do so without intervention?

10. The following excerpt is from a paper by Neil Adrian S. Cabiles of the University of Bologna:

Bank engagement in securitization [re]lies on two rationales. One is that securitization provides the bank with an additional funding source and the other is that it can be a risk management tool.[13]

12. Ben Bernanke, "Financial Reform to Address Systemic Risk," speech to the Council on Foreign Relations, March 10, 2009, Washington, DC.

13. Neil Adrian S. Cabiles, "Credit Risk Management through Securitization: Effect on Loan Portfolio Choice," working paper, University of Bologna.

a. What is securitization?

b. Why is asset securitization a risk management tool?

11. The following excerpt is from an article by Georges Dionne:

The creation of structured finance was mainly motivated by the transfer of credit risk, through the use of credit derivatives (e.g., CDSs) and banks' securitization of loans, to investors. For example, the selling of bank loans to trusts serves to transfer banks' credit risk via structured products to various groups of investors such as pension funds, industrial and service corporations, hedge funds or even other banks.[14]

a. What is meant by "structured finance"?

b. Give two examples of applications of structured finance to risk management other than securitization.

12. What is the relationship between systematic risk and common risk factors?

13. Why is the duration of a bond a common risk factor?

14. a. What is credit spread risk?

b. Why might one expect that credit spread duration would be a quantitative measure of credit spread risk?

15. Mr. Bennett wants to invest $100,000 for the next 10 years with the following investment strategy. The amount will be invested in a default-free U.S. government security that matures every month. Every time the security matures, the investor will use the proceeds to invest in another government security with one month to maturity. Suppose further that one-month government securities today pay an interest rate of 5%. In Mr. Bennett's view, this investment strategy has little risk, because one-month securities have no price risk if held to maturity and he can lock in at least a 5% return over the next 10 years. Discuss this investment strategy and the risks associated with it.

16. Ms. Callan, a citizen of the United States who resides in the country, wants to invest in a U.K. government bond that matures in 10 years. The government bond in which she will invest pays interest once a year in British pounds, and the principal repayment is also in British pounds. The government bond she is considering pays 4%, and she believes that interest rates over the next 20 years in the United Kingdom will not fall below 4%. In the opinion of Ms. Callan, she will be able to earn at a minimum a 4% return on her investment. What is your opinion regarding the risks of realizing at least a 4% return?

17. In the early 1980s, when interest rates were at historic highs, investment banking firms introduced a security backed by U.S. government bonds that paid no annual interest (referred to as zero-coupon bonds) with all of the interest being paid at the bonds' maturity

14. Georges Dionne, "Structured Finance, Risk Management, and the Recent Financial Crisis," *Ivey Business Journal* (October 2009), http://iveybusinessjournal.com/topics/strategy/structured-finance-risk-management-and-the-recent-financial-crisis#.U8qcF2cg_IU.

date. The securities were given such names as TIGRS (Treasury Income Growth Receipts, a Merrill Lynch product), CATS (Certificates of Accrual on Treasuries, a Salomon Brothers product), and LIONS (Lehman Investment Opportunity Notes, a Lehman Brothers product).

a. Why do you think securities with this feature were introduced at that time?

b. Too often it was stated that these securities had no risk. What risks does an investor face when purchasing these securities?

18. The following excerpt is from an article by Lucy Meakin and David Goodman:

> Germany is planning to auction its longest-maturity inflation-linked bonds to date, a sign that the slowest pace of consumer-price increases in the euro region for more than four years isn't deterring investors.[15]

a. What is an inflation-linked bond?

b. Why do you think that investors are not deterred from buying these bonds despite low rates of inflation in recent years?

c. What is meant by a "credit rating"?

d. What commercial entities provide credit ratings?

e. What is an internal credit rating?

19. What is the purpose of a credit scoring model?

20. What financial market instruments can be used to control credit risk?

21. a. What is meant by a "call provision" in a bond?

b. Why does a call provision in a bond increase reinvestment risk?

22. In 2006 and 2007, because of concerns about the South Korean currency (the won) appreciating, export companies in that country entered into a derivatives contract called a "knock-in, knock-out contract." Basically, this was an agreement to hedge against an appreciation of the won. Why would South Korean exporters want to hedge against the won appreciating?

23. The following excerpt is from a 2010 article by Shah Gilani:

> In today's multinational corporations, managing foreign-currency exposure has evolved into one of the key responsibilities of the chief financial officer (CFO). Former Microsoft Corp. (Nasdaq: MSFT) CFO John Conners recently lamented that foreign-currency management is one of the most-difficult and least-understood jobs in finance. If CFOs struggle with currency exposure, we're all in trouble.[16]

What can the CFO do to deal with foreign exchange risk?

15. Lucy Meakin and David Goodman, "Lowflation No Bar to Linker Sales as Germany Plans 2030 Bond," *Bloomberg News*, April 1, 2014, http://www.bloomberg.com/news/2014-04-01/lowflation-no-bar-to-linker-sales-as-germany-plans-longest-bond.html.

16. Shah Gilani, "Exchange-Rate Risk: The Unseen Enemy of U.S. Investors," *Money Morning*, September 29, 2010, http://moneymorning.com/2010/09/29/exchange-rate-risk/.

24. The CFO of a corporation faces timing risk when raising funds, via the issuance of either bonds or common stock. Explain why.

25. Two corporate treasurers are arguing about the cheapest form of long-term debt financing: fixed-rate or floating rate. They ask for your opinion. Provide it.

26. The CFO of a U.S. corporation is considering borrowing £500 million at a cost of 4% per year. The corporation will deploy the proceeds received to expand its lines of business.

a. Explain what will happen to corporate earnings if the proceeds invested from the funds raised can earn 7% per year.

b. Explain what will happen to corporate earnings if the proceeds invested from the funds raised can earn 1% per year.

c. Based on your answers to (a) and (b), describe the advantages and disadvantages of the use of financial leverage.

27. a. Banks are highly leveraged entities. Suppose that the debt ratio of a bank is 92% (expressed as percentage). What does this mean?

b. If a bank has a debt ratio of 92%, what is the debt-to-equity ratio?

28. A security has been created by pooling loans to individuals who will use the proceeds to purchase a home. The securities that are backed by the pool of loans are called "mortgage-backed securities." If the borrowers in the pool of loans have an impaired credit history (i.e., a poor credit history), then the mortgage-backed securities created are called "subprime mortgage-backed securities." Typically, each loan is for 30 years. One of the major risks faced by an investor in this security is credit risk. This risk is that the borrower will default on the loan, resulting in the loss by investors of principal and interest. To assess this risk, investors would have to forecast how many borrowers would default each year over the next 30 years, as well as how much will be recovered if the borrower defaults. The default and recoveries over the next 30 years depends on a myriad of factors. Two obvious ones are the state of the economy and conditions in the housing market. So forecasting what would be received by an investor over the next 30 years in order to value subprime mortgage-backed securities would require forecasting the state of the economy and the conditions in the housing market. Adding to this problem, the history of defaults of borrowers classified as subprime is limited, because these are relatively new types of loans. Despite the complexities of making the required forecasts and the limited information about default, the risks associated with subprime mortgage-backed securities were calculated by market participants and relied on when assessing the risks of institutional portfolios that contained them and of the trading desks of banks that held them in inventory.

Why does this type of risk modeling fall into the category of Knight's unmeasurable uncertainty and Keynes's irreducible uncertainty?

11 Properties and Pricing of Financial Assets

CONTENTS

Learning Objectives

After reading this chapter, you will understand:

• the many key properties of financial assets: moneyness, divisibility and denomination, reversibility, cash flow, term to maturity, convertibility, currency, liquidity, return predictability or risk, complexity, and tax status;

• the components of an asset's discount rate or required rate of return;

• what is meant by a basis point;

• how the discount rate is structured to encompass the components of an asset's risk;

• the principles of valuing complex financial assets;

• the inverse relationship between an asset's price and its discount rate;

• the principles that reveal how the properties of an asset affect its value, either through the discount rate or through its expected cash flow;

• what factors affect the price sensitivity of a financial asset to changes in interest rates; and

• what duration means, and how it is related to the price sensitivity of an asset to a change in interest rates.

Financial assets have certain properties that determine or influence their attractiveness to different classes of investors and issuers. This chapter introduces these properties in preparation for a more detailed exposition in later chapters. The chapter also provides the basic principles of the valuation or pricing of financial assets and illustrates how several of the properties of financial assets affect their value.

Properties of Financial Assets

The 11 properties of financial assets are (1) moneyness, (2) divisibility and denomination, (3) reversibility, (4) cash flow, (5) term to maturity, (6) convertibility, (7) currency, (8) liquidity, (9) return predictability, (10) complexity, and (11) tax status.[1]

Moneyness

Some financial assets are used as a medium of exchange or in settlement of transactions. These assets are called **money**. In the United States, money consists of currency and all forms of deposits that permit check writing. Other assets, although not money, are very close to money in that they can be transformed into money at little cost, delay, or risk. They

1. Some of these properties are taken from James Tobin, "Properties of Assets," undated manuscript, Yale University, New Haven, CT.

are referred to as **near money**. In the case of the United States, these include time and savings deposits and a security issued by the U.S. government called a "Treasury bill."[2] Moneyness is clearly a desirable property for investors.

Divisibility and Denomination

Divisibility relates to the minimum size in which a financial asset can be liquidated and exchanged for money. The smaller the size, the more the financial asset is divisible. A financial asset (such as a deposit) is typically infinitely divisible (down to the penny), but other financial assets have varying degrees of divisibility depending on their denomination, which is the dollar value of the amount that each unit of the asset will pay at maturity. Thus, many bonds come in $1,000 denominations, commercial paper in $25,000 units,[3] and certain types of certificates of deposit in $100,000 or more. In general, divisibility is desirable for investors but not for borrowers.

Reversibility

Reversibility refers to the cost of investing in a financial asset and then getting out of it and back into cash again. Consequently, reversibility is also referred to as **turnaround cost** or *round-trip cost*.

A financial asset (such as a deposit at a bank) is obviously highly reversible, because usually there is no charge for adding to or withdrawing from it. Other transactions costs may be unavoidable, but these are small. For financial assets traded in organized markets or with **market makers** (discussed in chapter 18), the most relevant component of round-trip cost is the so-called **bid-ask spread**, to which might be added commissions and the time and cost, if any, of delivering the asset. The spread charged by a market maker varies sharply from one financial asset to another, reflecting primarily the amount of risk the market maker is assuming by "making" a market.

This market-making risk, which is discussed in more detail in chapter 18, can be related to two main forces. One is the variability of the price as measured, say, by some measure of dispersion of the relative price over time. The greater the variability is, the greater the probability of the market maker incurring a loss in excess of a stated bound between the time of buying and that of reselling the financial asset. The variability of prices differs widely across financial assets. For example, Treasury bills have a very stable price for the reason explained at the end of this chapter, but a speculative stock will exhibit much larger short-run variations.

The second determining factor of the bid-ask spread charged by a market maker is what is commonly referred to as the **thickness of the market**: essentially, the prevailing rate at

2. U.S. Treasury bills are discussed in chapter 20.

3. Commercial paper is described in chapter 25.

which buying and selling orders reach the market maker (that is, the frequency of transactions). A **thin market** is one that has few trades on a regular or continuing basis. Clearly, the greater the frequency of order flows, the shorter the time that the security will have to be held in the market maker's inventory, and hence the smaller the probability of an unfavorable price movement while held.

Thickness, too, varies from market to market. A three-month U.S. Treasury bill is easily the thickest market in the world. In contrast, trading in stock of small companies is not thick but thin. Because Treasury bills dominate other instruments both in price stability and thickness, their bid-ask spread tends to be the smallest in the market. A low turnaround cost is clearly a desirable property of a financial asset, and as a result, thickness itself is a valuable property. This explains the potential advantage of larger over smaller markets (economies of scale), along with a market's tendency to standardize the instruments offered to the public.

Cash Flow

The return that an investor will realize by holding a financial asset depends on all the cash distributions that the financial asset will pay its owners; this includes dividends on shares and coupon payments on bonds. The return also considers the repayment of principal for a debt security and the expected sale price of a stock. When computing the expected return, noncash payments—such as stock dividends and options to purchase additional stock, or the distribution of other securities—must also be accounted for.

In a world of nonnegligible inflation, it is also important to distinguish between nominal expected return and real expected return. The expected return that we described above is the nominal expected return. That is, it considers the dollars that are expected to be received but does not adjust those dollars to take into consideration changes in their purchasing power. The net real expected return is the nominal expected return after adjustment for the loss of purchasing power of the financial asset as a result of anticipated inflation. For example, if the nominal expected return for a one-year investment of $1,000 is 6%, then at the end of one year, the investor expects to realize $1,060, consisting of interest of $60 and the repayment of the $1,000 investment. However, if the inflation rate over the same period of time is 4%, then the purchasing power of $1,060 is only $1,019.23 ($1,060 divided by 1.04). Thus, the return in terms of purchasing power, or the real return, is 1.923%. In general, the expected real return can be approximated by subtracting the expected inflation rate from the expected nominal return. In our example, it is approximately 2% (6% minus 4%).

Term to Maturity

Term to maturity is the length of the period until the date at which the instrument is scheduled to make its final payment or the owner is entitled to demand liquidation. Instruments for which the creditor can ask for repayment at any time, such as checking accounts and many savings accounts, are called "demand instruments." Maturity is an important characteristic of financial assets (such as bonds) and can range from one day to more than a half of a century. Bonds with no maturity date, called "perpetual bonds," have been issued to lock-in law interest rates. In the United Kingdom, there is one well-known type of bond issued by the Bank of England called a "consul." Many other instruments, including equities, have no maturity and are thus a form of perpetual instrument.

Note that even a financial asset with a stated maturity might terminate before its stated maturity. This may occur for several reasons, including bankruptcy or reorganization, or because of **call provisions** entitling the debtor to repay in advance, usually at some penalty and only after a number of years from the time of issuance. Typically, perpetual bonds have a call provision, allowing the issuer to call the bond five years after issuance. Sometimes the investor may have the privilege of asking for early repayment. This feature is called a **put option**. Some assets have maturities that may be increased or extended at the discretion of the issuer or the investor. For example, the French government issues a six-year *obligation renouvelable du Trésor*, which allows the investor, after the end of the third year, to switch into a new six-year debt. Similar bonds are issued by the British government. All these features regarding maturity are discussed in later chapters.

Convertibility

As the preceding discussion shows, an important property of some assets is that they are **convertible** into other assets. In some cases, the conversion takes place within one class of assets, as when a bond is converted into another bond. In other situations, the conversion spans classes. For example, a corporate convertible bond is a bond that the bondholder can change into equity shares. Preferred stock may be convertible into common stock. It is important to note that the timing, costs, and conditions for conversion are clearly spelled out in the legal descriptions of the convertible security at the time it is issued.

Currency

We have noted throughout our discussion that the global financial system has become increasingly integrated. In light of the freely floating and often volatile exchange rates among the major currencies,[4] this fact gives added importance to the currency in which the financial asset will make cash flow payments. Most financial assets are denominated in one currency, such as U.S. dollars or yen or euros, and investors must choose among them with volatile exchange rates in mind.

Some issuers, responding to investors' wishes to reduce **currency** risk, have issued *dual-currency securities*. For example, some Eurobonds[5] pay interest in one currency but principal

4. Exchange rates and the foreign exchange market are the subject of chapter 19.

5. Eurobonds are discussed in chapter 26.

or redemption value in a second. U.S. dollars and yen are commonly paired in these cases. Furthermore, some Eurobonds carry a currency option that allows the investor to specify that payments of either interest or principal be made in either one of two major currencies.

Liquidity

Liquidity is an important and widely used notion, although at present no universally accepted definition of liquidity exists. A useful way to think of liquidity and illiquidity, proposed by Professor James Tobin,[6] is in terms of how much sellers stand to lose if they wish to sell immediately as opposed to engaging in a costly and time-consuming search.

An example of a quite illiquid financial asset is the stock of a small corporation or the bond issued by a small school district. The market for such a security is extremely thin, and one must search for one of a very few suitable buyers. Less suitable buyers, including speculators and market makers, may be located more promptly, but they will have to be enticed to invest in the illiquid financial asset by an appropriate discount in price.

For many other financial assets, liquidity is determined by contractual arrangements. For example, ordinary deposits are perfectly liquid, because the bank has a contractual obligation to convert them at par on demand. In contrast, financial contracts representing a claim on a private pension fund may be regarded as totally illiquid, because they can be cashed only at retirement.

Liquidity may depend not only on the financial asset but also on the quantity one wishes to sell (or buy). Although a small quantity may be quite liquid, a large lot may run into illiquidity problems. Note that liquidity is again closely related to whether a market is thick or thin. Thinness always has the effect of increasing the turnaround cost, even of a liquid financial asset. But beyond some point, thinness becomes an obstacle to the formation of a market, and it has a direct effect on the illiquidity of the financial asset.

Return Predictability

Return predictability is a basic property of financial assets, in that it is a major determinant of their value. Assuming investors are risk averse, the riskiness of an asset can be equated with the uncertainty or unpredictability of its return. We will see in chapter 12 how the unpredictability of future returns can be measured and how it is related to the variability of past returns. But whatever measure of volatility is used,[7] it is obvious that volatility varies greatly across financial assets. There are several reasons for this variability.

First, as illustrated later in this chapter, the value of a financial asset depends on the cash flow expected and on the interest rate used to discount this cash flow. Hence, volatility will

6. Tobin, "Properties of Assets."

7. Proxy measures for volatility include the standard deviation of expected returns or the range in which the outcome can be expected to fall with some stated probability.

be a consequence of the uncertainty about future interest rates and future cash flow. The future cash flow may be contractual, in which case the sole source of its uncertainty is the reliability of the debtor with regard to fulfilling the obligation. The cash flow may be in the nature of a residual equity claim, as is the case for the payments generated by the equity of a corporation. The cash flows from U.S. government securities are the only cash flows generally regarded as altogether riskless. Corporate debt and corporate stock cash flows are generally riskier than cash flows of U.S. government securities. Corporate equities represent a wide range of risk, from public utilities to highly speculative issues.

As for a change in interest rates, it will in principle affect all prices in the opposite direction, but the effect is much larger in the case of the price of a financial asset with a long maturity than one with a short remaining life, as illustrated later in this chapter. Thus, on this account also, short-term U.S. government securities, such as Treasury bills, tend to be the safest assets, except for cash (if properly insured). For individual stocks, the interest effect is generally swamped by cash flow uncertainty, although movements in interest rates have the characteristic of affecting all stocks in the same direction, whereas a change in expected cash flow is largely dependent on a firm's particular financial situation. In general, uncertainty about returns and future prices can be expected to increase as the investment horizon lengthens.

What has been said so far relates to the predictability of nominal returns, although the relevant measure, of course, is real returns—returns corrected for gains or losses of purchasing power attributable to inflation. Of course, if inflation is absent or small, the determinants of real and nominal uncertainty and risk coincide. But in the presence of highly unpredictable inflation (which is usually the case with high inflation), real returns may be drastically harder to predict than nominal returns.

Complexity

Some financial assets are complex in the sense that they are actually combinations of two or more simpler assets. To find the true value of such an asset, one must break it down into its component parts and price each separately. The sum of those prices is the value of the complex asset. A good example of a complex asset is the **callable bond**, that is, a bond whose issuer is entitled to repay the debt prior to the maturity date. When investors buy such a bond, they in effect buy a bond and sell to the issuer an option that allows the issuer to redeem the bond at a set price prior to the issue's scheduled maturity. Therefore, the correct or true price of a callable bond is equal to the price of a similar noncallable bond less the value of the issuer's right to retire the bond early.

A complex asset can be viewed as a bundle or package of cash flows and options belonging to either the issuer or the holder, or both. Other examples of a complex asset include a convertible bond, a bond that has payments that can be made in a different currency at the option of the bondholder, and a bond that can be sold back to the issuer at a fixed price (that is, a **putable bond**).

In some cases, the degree of complexity is high: Many convertible bonds are also callable, and some bonds give their issuers the right either to extend the asset's maturity or to redeem it early. Also, some Japanese firms have issued bonds that are convertible into Japanese stock (denominated in yen, of course) but that are sold for, and make coupon and principal payments in, another currency, such as U.S. dollars.

Tax Status

An important feature of any asset is its **tax status**. Governmental regulations for taxing the income from the ownership or sale of financial assets vary widely, if not wildly. Tax rates differ from year to year, from country to country, and even among regional and local governments (states and municipalities in the United States) within a country. Moreover, tax rates may differ across financial assets, depending on the type of issuer, the length of time the asset is held, the nature of the owner, and so on. For example, in the United States, pension funds are exempt from income taxes (see chapter 4 for more details), and coupon payments on municipal bonds are generally free of taxation by the federal government (see chapter 21).

Principles of Pricing Financial Assets

The fundamental principle of finance is that the true or correct price of an asset equals the **present value** of all cash flows that the owner of the asset expects to receive during its life. In general, the correct price for a financial asset can be expressed as follows:

$$P=\frac{CF_1}{(1+r)^1}+\frac{CF_2}{(1+r)^2}+\frac{CF_3}{(1+r)^3}+\ldots+\frac{CF_N}{(1+r)^N},$$

where

P = the price of the financial asset,

CF_t = the cash flow in year t ($t = 1, \ldots \ldots, N$),

N = maturity of the financial asset, and

r = appropriate discount rate.

The Appropriate Discount Rate

The appropriate **discount rate**, r, is the return that the market or the consensus of investors requires on the asset. A convenient (but approximate) expression for the appropriate discount rate is:

$$r = RR + IP + DP + MP + LP + EP,$$

where

RR = the real rate of interest, which is the reward for not consuming and for lending to other users;

IP = the inflation premium, which is the compensation for the expected decline in the purchasing power of the money lent to borrowers;

DP = the default risk premium, which is the reward for taking on the risk of default in the case of a loan (or bond) or the risk of loss of principal for other assets;

MP = the maturity premium, which is the compensation for lending money for long periods of time;

LP = the liquidity premium, which is the reward for investing in an asset that may not be readily converted to cash at a fair market value; and

EP = the exchange-rate risk premium, which is the reward for investing in an asset that is not denominated in the investor's home currency.

Obviously, the price of an asset is inversely related to its discount rate: If the discount rate rises, the price falls; and if the rate declines, the price increases.

Illustration

Let us construct a simple example to illustrate the pricing of a financial asset. We can then use the hypothetical financial asset to illustrate some of the properties explained earlier in this chapter.

Suppose a bond has a maturity of four years and pays annual interest of \$50 at the end of each year plus a principal of \$1,000 at the conclusion of the fourth year. Because this bond pays \$50 per \$1,000 of principal, the periodic coupon rate is 5%. This rate is commonly and simply referred to as the **coupon rate**. Thus, using the previous notation, we have

$$N = 4 \; CF_1 = \$50 \; CF_2 = \$50 \quad CF_3 = \$50 \quad CF_N = \$1{,}050.$$

Furthermore, assume that the market thinks the real rate is 2.5%, the inflation premium is 3%, the bond's default risk justifies a premium of 2%, the maturity premium is 0.5%, and the liquidity premium is 1%. Because the cash flows are denominated in U.S. dollars, the foreign-exchange rate premium is zero. That is,

$$RR = 2.5\%, \; IP = 3.0\%, \; DP = 2.0\%, \; MP = 0.5\%, \; LP = 1.0\%, \; EP = 0\%.$$

Thus, we have the following value for the discount rate:

$$r = 2.5\% + 3.0\% + 2.0\% + 0.5\% + 1.0\% + 0\% = 9.0\%, \text{ or } 0.09.$$

Using the formula for price, the price of this bond is

$$P = \frac{\$50}{(1.09)^1} + \frac{\$50}{(1.09)^2} + \frac{\$50}{(1.09)^3} + \frac{\$1{,}050}{(1.09)^4}.$$
$$= \$870.41$$

Price and Asset Properties

We can use this hypothetical financial asset to illustrate the effect of some of the properties of financial assets on price or asset value. First, it should be clear that the price of a financial asset changes as the appropriate discount rate, r, changes. More specifically, the price changes in the opposite direction to the change in the appropriate discount rate. An illustration of this principle appears in table 11.1, which shows the price of our hypothetical financial asset for various discount rates.

Let's look at how reversibility affects an asset's value. Suppose a **broker's commission** of $35 is imposed by brokers to buy or sell the bond. The price of the four-year bond is then

$$P = -\$35 + \frac{\$50}{(1.09)^1} + \frac{\$50}{(1.09)^2} + \frac{\$50}{(1.09)^3} + \frac{\$1{,}050 - \$35}{(1.09)^4}.$$
$$= \$810.62$$

Notice that the initial commission of $35 is subtracted on an undiscounted basis, because that payment is made at the time of purchase.

Suppose also that a government entity imposes a transfer tax of $20 on each transaction. Because this rise in the cost of reversing an investment diminishes its reversibility

Table 11.1
Price of a four-year bond for various discount rates.

Cash Flow: $CF_1 = \$50$ $CF_2 = \$50$ $CF_3 = \$50$ $CF_4 = \$1{,}050$	
Appropriate Discount Rate (%)	**Price ($)**
4	1,036.30
5	1,000.00
6	965.35
7	932.26
8	900.64
9	870.41
10	841.51
11	813.85
12	787.39
13	762.04
14	737.77

to some extent, the present value of all cash flows associated with owning the bond now looks like:

$$P = -\$35 - \$20 + \frac{\$50}{(1.09)^1} + \frac{\$50}{(1.09)^2} + \frac{\$50}{(1.09)^3} + \frac{\$1{,}050 - \$35 - \$20}{(1.09)^4}$$
$$= \$776.45.$$

The change in price is significant and demonstrates why financial markets adjust so sharply (and rapidly) when governments impose restrictions on, or raise the cost of, capital market transactions.

To see how default risk affects the price of an asset, assume that, right before you bought the bond, a news story convinced investors that this bond is less risky than they had thought. So, the default risk premium falls from 2% to 1%, and the appropriate discount rate thus declines from 9% to 8%. Ignoring commissions and transfer fees, table 11.1 shows that the price would increase from $870.41 to $900.64.

What about liquidity? Suppose immediately after the purchase of this bond, factors in the market for this bond cause its liquidity to decline. An investor buying this asset would plan for such a possibility by raising the liquidity premium. Assume that the liquidity premium increases from 1% to 3%. The appropriate discount rate then increases from 9% to 11%. Ignoring the commission and the transfer fee, table 11.1 shows that the price would be $813.85. The fall in price, from the original $870.41 to $813.85, shows how important liquidity can be.

Now, let's tackle the notion of complexity by assuming that the bond is convertible into a fixed number of shares of common stock of the company that issued the bond. The price of our four-year bond would then be greater than $870.41 by an amount equal to the value that the market assigns to the right to convert the bond into common stock. For example, suppose we observe that the price of our hypothetical bond with the conversion privilege is $1,000.41. This means that the conversion privilege is valued by the market at $130.

The unresolved question is whether $130 is a fair value for this conversion privilege. Valuation techniques to determine the fair value of any type of option (such as a conversion privilege) are available. It is sufficient to understand why a knowledge of how to value an option is important. Because many financial assets have options embedded in them, failure to assess the options properly may lead to the mispricing of financial assets.

Now, let's turn our attention to currency. Suppose that this bond was issued by a German firm and that all payments are in euros. The cash flow in U.S. dollars that a U.S. investor will receive is uncertain, because the dollar-euro exchange rate will fluctuate over the four years. Suppose that the market assigns an exchange premium of 3%. As a result, the appropriate discount rate increases from 9% to 12%, and the price would be $787.39 (see table 11.1). To continue with the effect of currency risk, suppose that immediately after the purchase of this bond, the market expects that the exchange rate between the U.S.

dollar and the euro will become more volatile. The market will adjust for this volatility by increasing the foreign currency risk premium, which, in turn, increases the appropriate discount rate and decreases the price.

It is easy to illustrate the impact of taxes. Suppose that our bond is granted a favorable tax treatment such that the interest and any capital gain from this bond would not be taxed. Suppose that the marginal tax rate on otherwise equivalent taxable bonds is 33.33%, and the appropriate discount rate is 9%. Then the after-tax discount rate would be approximately 6%, as shown below:

$$\text{Pretax discount rate} \times (1 - \text{marginal tax rate}) = 0.09 \times (1 - 0.3333) = 6\%.$$

Because our hypothetical bond is free of taxes, the appropriate discount rate would be adjusted to compensate for this feature. The discount rate that would be used is 6%, because it is the equivalent of a 9% discount rate and a 33.33% marginal tax rate. From table 11.1, we see that the price of the bond would be \$965.35.

Continuing with the importance of tax features to the price of a financial asset, suppose that immediately after the purchase of this bond, the market comes to expect that the U.S. Congress will raise the marginal tax rate. This expectation would increase the value of the tax-exempt feature by decreasing the discount rate based on the anticipated rise in the marginal tax rate. The opposite would occur if the market came to expect that the U.S. Congress would lower the marginal tax rate.

Although we have used a single discount rate to discount each cash flow, theoretical reasons suggest that this is inappropriate. Specifically, in chapter 18, we will look at the relationship between a bond's maturity and yield. In addition, a financial asset should be viewed as a package of cash flows. Each cash flow should be treated as if it were an individual asset with only one cash flow, and that cash flow has its own discount rate that depends on when it will be received. Consequently, a more general formula for pricing a financial asset is

$$P = \frac{CF_1}{(1+r_1)^1} + \frac{CF_2}{(1+r_2)^2} + \frac{CF_3}{(1+r_3)^3} + \ldots + \frac{CF_N}{(1+r_N)^N},$$

where r_t is the discount rate appropriate for period t.

Price Volatility of Financial Assets

As table 11.1 makes clear, a fundamental pricing principle is that a financial asset's price changes in the opposite direction of the change in the required rate of return. We refer to the required rate of return as the **required yield**. This principle follows from the fact that the price of a financial asset is equal to the present value of its cash flow. An increase (decrease) in the yield required by investors decreases (increases) the present value of the cash flow and, therefore, the financial asset's price.

The price sensitivity of a financial asset to a change in the required yield will not be the same for all assets. For example, an increase in the required yield of one percentage point may result in a decline in one asset's price of 20%, but only of 3% for another. In this section, we will see how the characteristics of a financial asset and the level of interest rates affect the price responsiveness of a financial asset to a change in the required yield. We also present a measure that can be used to gauge the approximate price sensitivity of a financial asset to changes in the required yield.

Note that the analysis in this section applies fully and directly to bonds and other financial assets that have known expected cash flows and known expected maturities. An analysis of the price sensitivity of other major financial assets, such as preferred stock and common stock (which are perpetuals and have uncertain cash flows), must be postponed to a later chapter.

In our discussion, we will refer to changes in the required yield. It is convenient to measure a change in yield in terms of what market participants refer to as a **basis point** rather than in terms of a percentage change. One basis point is defined as 0.0001, or equivalently, 0.01%. Therefore, 100 basis points is equal to one percentage point, and a yield change from 9% to 10% represents a 100 basis point change in yield. A yield change from 7% to 7.5% is a 50 basis point change, and a yield change from 6% to 8.35% is a 235 basis point change in yield.

The Effect of Maturity

An asset's maturity is a factor that affects its price sensitivity to a change in yield. In fact, a bond's price sensitivity to a change in the discount rate is positively related to the bond's maturity. Consider the case of two bonds that have the same coupon rate and the same required yield but different maturities. If the required rate were to change, the price sensitivity of the bond with the longer maturity would be greater than that of the bond with the shorter maturity.

An illustration of this link between maturity and price change appears in table 11.2, which shows the price of a bond that pays $50 annually and $1,000 at maturity—a 5% coupon rate—for various maturities and discount rates. Table 11.3, which is based on table 11.2, shows the differences across maturities in a bond's dollar price decline and percentage price decline for an increase in the discount rate of 100 basis points. For example, if the discount rate rises from 9% to 10%, the price of a four-year bond falls from $870.41 to $841.51, which represents a price decline of $28.90 and a percentage price decline of 3.32%. In contrast, a similar rise in the discount rate causes the price of a 20-year bond to fall considerably more, from $634.86 to $574.32, which represents a price decline of $60.54 and a percentage price decline of 9.54%.

Table 11.2
Price of a bond paying $50 annually and $1,000 at maturity for various discount rates and maturities.

	Bond Price ($)			
	Number of Years to Maturity			
Discount Rate (%)	4	10	15	20
4	1,036.30	1,081.11	1,111.18	1,135.90
5	1,000.00	1,000.00	1,000.00	1,000.00
6	965.35	926.40	902.88	885.30
7	932.26	859.53	817.84	788.12
8	900.64	798.70	743.22	705.46
9	870.41	743.29	677.57	634.86
10	841.51	692.77	619.70	574.32
11	813.85	646.65	568.55	522.20
12	787.39	604.48	523.24	477.14
13	762.04	565.90	483.01	438.02
14	737.77	530.55	447.20	403.92

The Effect of the Coupon Rate

A bond's coupon rate also affects its price sensitivity. More specifically, for two bonds with the same maturity and required yield, the lower the coupon rate is, the greater the price responsiveness will be for a given change in the required yield.

To illustrate this, consider a 5% coupon bond and a 10% coupon bond, each of which has a maturity of 15 years and a principal of $1,000. If the required yield for both bonds is 9%, the price of the 5% coupon bond would be $677.57, and the price of the 10% coupon bond would be $1,080.61. If the required yield increases by 100 basis points, from 9% to 10%, the price of the 5% coupon bond would fall to $619.70, whereas the price of the 10% coupon bond would fall to $1,000. Thus, the 5% coupon bond's price declines by $57.87 or 8.5% ($57.87/$677.57), and the 10% coupon bond's price declines by $80.61 or by 7.5% ($80.61/$1,080.61). Although the dollar price change is greater for the higher-coupon bond, the percentage price change is less.

In later chapters, we will discuss a special type of bond, one with no coupon rate. This is called a **zero-coupon bond**. The investor who purchases a zero-coupon bond receives no periodic interest payment. Instead, the investor purchases the bond at a price below its principal and receives the principal at the maturity date. The difference between the principal and the price at which the zero-coupon bond is purchased represents interest earned by the investor over the bond's life. For example, consider a zero-coupon bond with a principal of $1,000 and a maturity of 15 years. If the required yield is 9%, then the price of this bond would be $274.54.[8] The difference between the principal of

8. The price is the present value (which is $1,000) 15 years from now discounted at 9%.

Table 11.3
Price decline if the discount rate increases 100 basis points for a bond paying $50 annually and $1,000 at maturity for various discount rates and maturities.

	Price Change ($)			
	Number of Years to Maturity			
Discount Rate Change (%)	4	10	15	20
From 4 to 5	−36.30	−81.11	−111.18	−135.91
From 5 to 6	−34.65	−73.60	−97.20	−114.70
From 6 to 7	−33.09	−66.87	−85.04	−97.18
From 7 to 8	−31.62	−60.83	−74.62	−82.66
From 8 to 9	−30.23	−55.41	−65.65	−70.60
From 9 to 10	−28.90	−50.52	−57.87	−60.54
From 10 to 11	−27.66	−46.12	−51.15	−52.12
From 11 to 12	−26.40	−42.17	−45.13	−45.06
From 12 to 13	−25.35	−38.58	−40.23	−39.12
From 13 to 14	−24.27	−35.35	−35.81	−34.12
	Percentage Price Change (%)			
From 4 to 5	−3.50	−7.50	−10.01	−11.96
From 5 to 6	−3.47	−7.36	−9.71	−11.47
From 6 to 7	−3.43	−7.22	−9.42	−10.98
From 7 to 8	−3.39	−7.08	−9.12	−10.49
From 8 to 9	−3.36	−6.94	−8.83	−10.01
From 9 to 10	−3.32	−6.80	−8.54	−9.54
From 10 to 11	−3.29	−6.66	−8.25	−9.08
From 11 to 12	−3.25	−6.52	−7.97	−8.63
From 12 to 13	−3.22	−6.38	−7.69	−8.20
From 13 to 14	−3.18	−6.25	−7.41	−7.79

$1,000 and the price of $274.54 is the interest that the investor realizes at the maturity date.

A zero-coupon bond will have greater price sensitivity than a bond with a coupon rate selling at the same required yield and with the same maturity. For example, consider once again the 15-year zero-coupon bond. If the required yield increases from 9% to 10%, the price of this bond would fall to $239.39, a percentage price decline of 12.8% ($35.15/$274.54). This percentage change is greater than the declines in price for the 15-year maturity 5% coupon and 15-year 10% coupon bonds.

The Effect of the Level of Yields

Tables 11.2 and 11.3 also bring out another interesting property about asset prices. Notice that, for a given maturity, the dollar price change and the percentage price change are higher for the lower initial discount rates than for the higher initial discount rates. For example, consider the 15-year bond when the discount rate is 5%. The price of the bond falls from $1,000 to $902.88 when the discount rate increases from 5% to 6%, a price decline of $97.20 and a percentage price decline of 9.72%. In contrast, a rise in the discount rate of 100 basis points from 13% to 14% reduces the same bond's price by $35.81 (from $483.01 to $447.20) and by the percentage of 7.41%.

The implication is that the lower the level of yields is, the greater the effect a change in interest rates will have on the price of a financial asset.

Measuring Price Sensitivity to Interest Rate Changes: Duration

From our discussion thus far, we see that three factors affect the price sensitivity of an asset to changes in interest rates: the maturity, the coupon rate, and the level of interest rates. When managing the price sensitivity of a portfolio, market participants seek a measure of the sensitivity of assets to interest rate changes that encompasses all three factors.

A useful way to approximate an asset's price sensitivity to interest rate changes is to examine how the price changes if the yield changes by a small number of basis points. To do this, we use the following notation:

Δy = change in yield (in decimal),

P_0 = initial price of the asset,

P_- = asset's price if the yield is decreased by Δy, and

P_+ = asset's price if the yield is increased by Δy.

Then, for a small decrease in yield, the percentage price change is

$$\frac{P_- - P_0}{P_0}.$$

The percentage price change per basis point change is found by dividing the percentage price change by the number of basis points (Δy times 100). That is,

$$\frac{P_- - P_0}{P_0(\Delta y)100}.$$

Similarly, the percentage price change per basis point increase in yield is

$$\frac{P_0 - P_+}{P_0(\Delta y)100}.$$

The percentage price change for an increase and decrease in interest rates will not be the same. Consequently, the average percentage price change per basis point change in yield can be calculated. This is done as follows:

$$\frac{1}{2}\left[\frac{P_{-}-P_0}{P_0(\Delta y)100}+\frac{P_0-P_{+}}{P_0(\Delta y)100}\right],$$

or equivalently,

$$\frac{P_{-}-P_{+}}{2P_0(\Delta y)100}.$$

The approximate percentage price change for a 100-basis-point change in yield is found by multiplying the previous formula by 100:

$$\frac{P_{-}-P_{+}}{2P_0(\Delta y)}.$$

For example, the price of a 5% coupon bond with a principal of $1,000 and a maturity of 15 years is $677.57. If the yield is increased by 50 basis points from 9% to 9.5%, the price would be $647.73. If the yield is decreased by 50 basis points from 9% to 8.5%, the price would be $709.35. Thus, we have the following values:

$\Delta y = 0.005$,

$P_0 = \$677.57$,

$P_{-} = \$709.35$, and

$P_{+} = \$647.73$.

The application of the foregoing formula provides this number:

$$\frac{\$709.35-\$647.73}{2(\$677.57)(0.005)}=9.09.$$

This measure of price sensitivity is popularly referred to as **duration**—a concept we introduced in chapter 6 when discussing the interest rate risk of a depository institution. Table 11.4 shows how the duration is determined for a 5% coupon bond with different maturities when the interest rate is initially at 9%.

Table 11.5 shows the duration for three coupon bonds with different maturities, assuming different initial yields. As can be seen from this table, the relative magnitude of duration is consistent with the properties described earlier. Specifically, (1) for bonds with the same coupon rate and the same yield, the longer the maturity is, the greater the duration will be; (2) for bonds with the same maturity and at the same yield, the lower the coupon rate is, the greater the duration will be; and (3) the lower the initial yield is, the greater the duration will be for a given bond. Thus, duration picks up the effect of all three factors: maturity, coupon rate, and initial level of yield.

Duration is related to the price sensitivity as follows:

Table 11.4
Determination of duration for a 5% coupon bond with a principal of $1,000 and an initial required yield of 9%.

	Number of Years to Maturity			
	4	10	15	20
Price at 9% (P_0)	$870.41	$743.29	$677.57	$634.86
Price at 9.5% (P_+)	$855.80	$717.45	$647.73	$603.44
Price at 8.5% (P_-)	$885.35	$770.35	$709.35	$668.78
Duration	3.40	7.12	9.09	10.29
Duration $= \dfrac{P_- - P_+}{2(P_0)(0.005)}$	3.40	7.12	9.09	10.29

Table 11.5
Duration for various bonds by maturity, coupon rate, and yield level.

		Duration			
		Number of Years to Maturity			
Coupon Rate (%)	Yield (%)	4	10	15	20
5	5	3.55	7.73	10.39	12.48
5	9	3.40	7.12	9.09	10.29
5	12	3.29	6.67	8.16	8.79
10	5	3.36	6.93	9.15	10.95
10	9	3.21	6.30	7.91	8.97
10	12	3.10	5.85	7.05	7.69
0	5	3.81	9.53	14.30	19.08
0	9	3.67	9.18	13.77	18.38
0	12	3.57	8.93	13.40	17.88

Approximate percentage change in a financial asset's price $= -\text{Duration} \times (\text{Yield change in decimal form}) \times 100$.

For example, suppose that the required yield on the 5% coupon, 15-year bond increases from 9% to 10% (0.01 in decimal form). Then, because this bond's duration is 9.09:

Approximate percentage change in price $= -9.09 \times (0.01) \times 100 = -9.09\%$.

We showed earlier that the actual percentage change in price if the required yield increases from 9% to 10% would be a fall of 8.5%. Thus, duration is a close approximation of the percentage price change. The approximation is better for smaller changes in the required yield. For example, if the required yield changes by 20 basis points (0.002 in decimal form) from 9% to 9.20% rather than 100 basis points, then based on duration, the approximate percentage change in price would be −1.82%. The actual price if the required yield increased by 20 basis points is \$665.41, a decline of \$12.16 from the price of \$677.57 at 9%. The actual percentage price change is therefore −1.79%(−\$12.16/\$677.57). Duration does an excellent job of approximating the percentage price change in this case.

In general, one can interpret duration as follows: *the approximate percentage change in price for a 100-basis-point change in interest rates around the prevailing yield.* Duration does a good job of approximating the price change for a small change in yield (on the order of 50 basis points in either direction). The larger the yield change is, the poorer will be the approximation that duration provides.

Although we have developed duration in the context of bonds, note that the basic principle applies equally to other financial assets. For example, consider a financial asset whose cash flow is as follows:

Year	Cash Flow
1	\$30
2	\$75
3	\$120
4	\$140
5	\$200
6	\$250
7	\$300

Suppose that the appropriate discount rate is 7%. Then the price of this financial asset would be \$794.31. If the yield were decreased by 50 basis points to 6.5%, the price would be \$812.82. If the yield were increased by 50 basis points to 7.5%, the price would be \$776.36. Thus, for this financial asset, we know that

$\Delta y = 0.005$,

$P_0 = \$794.31$,

$P_- = \$812.82$, and

$P_+ = \$776.36$.

The duration is then 4.59, calculated as follows:

$$\frac{\$812.82 - \$776.36}{2(\$794.31)(0.005)} = 4.59.$$

Although we have focused on the price sensitivity of individual financial assets to changes in interest rates, we can extend the principle to a portfolio of financial assets. The duration of a portfolio of assets is simply the weighted average of the duration of the individual assets. The weight used for each asset is its market value in the portfolio.

Moreover, the principle can be extended to a liability stream. A liability can be viewed as a financial asset with a negative cash flow. The present value of the cash outlays is equal to the value or price of the liability stream. When interest rates change, the value of the liability stream changes. A duration of a liability stream can be calculated in the same way as the duration of a financial asset.

Importance of Measuring Price Sensitivity to Interest Rate Changes

The importance of being able to measure the sensitivity of an individual asset, a portfolio of assets, and a liability cannot be overemphasized. To control interest rate risk, it is necessary to be able to measure it. An investor with a portfolio of assets wants to be able to measure her exposure to interest rate changes in order to assess whether the exposure is acceptable. If it is not, she can alter the exposure. Various instruments that we describe later in this book provide a means for doing so. Financial institutions manage assets against liabilities. The interest rate risk exposure of a financial institution is the difference between the duration of its assets and the duration of its liabilities.

From our discussion, it may seem simple to calculate the duration of an asset. Unfortunately, this is not the case, because for most assets, the cash flow can change when interest rates change. In our illustrations, we have assumed that when interest rates change, the cash flows are unchanged. However, as we describe the various financial instruments in later chapters, we will see that as interest rates change, either the issuer or the investor can alter the cash flow. Consequently, if a change in the cash flow is not considered when interest rates change, the duration calculation can be misleading.

When a duration is calculated under the assumption that the cash flows do not change when interest rates change, the resulting duration is called **modified duration**. In contrast, a duration calculated assuming that the cash flow changes when interest rates change is called **effective duration**. For some assets, the difference between modified duration and effective duration can be quite dramatic. For example, with some of the more complex financial instruments discussed later in this book, the modified duration could be four, whereas the effective duration could be 25! In this case, an investor might believe that the price of the asset will change by approximately 4% for a 100 basis point change in interest rates (modified duration) when, in fact, it would change by approximately 25% for a 100-basis-point change in interest rates (effective duration).

Macaulay Duration

The term "duration" was first used in 1938 by Frederick Macaulay as a measure of the weighted average time to maturity of a bond.[9] It can be shown that the measure Macaulay developed is related to the price sensitivity of a bond to interest rate changes. Unfortunately, too many market participants interpret duration as some measure of average life instead of a measure of price sensitivity to interest rate changes. This misinterpretation has been a key factor in several financial blunders. For example, for some complex financial assets, the effective duration is greater than the **Macaulay duration**. Market participants who interpret duration as a measure of the average life of an asset find this difficult to believe.

Consequently, when you hear the term "duration" used, interpret it as a measure of price sensitivity to rate changes, not some measure of the asset's average life. In addition, understand what type of duration measure is being used, effective duration or modified duration. Effective duration is the appropriate measure. Finally, if someone you know thinks that Macaulay duration means something for managing a portfolio or the asset/liability position of a financial institution, photocopy this page and tell them to review this discussion!

Key Points

- A financial asset has many properties, and each affects the asset's value in a distinctive and important way.
- Some properties are intrinsic to the asset, such as its maturity or promised cash flow.
- Other properties are features of the market for the asset, such as the costs of trading the asset.
- Still other properties reflect decisions by government about the asset's tax status.
- A complex asset is one that provides options for the issuer or the investor, or both, and so represents a combination of simpler assets.
- An asset's price is the present value of its expected cash flows, discounted at an appropriate rate.
- The appropriate discount rate for an asset's cash flows depends on the properties of the asset.
- The appropriate discount rate can often be approximated as the sum of rewards for the various risks an asset poses to its buyer.
- The price of an asset moves in the opposite direction of a change in its discount rate.
- The price of a complex asset is the sum of the prices of its component parts.
- Assets have different degrees of price sensitivity to a change in the discount rate or required yield.

9. Frederick R. Macaulay, *Some Theoretical Problems Suggested by the Movements of Interest Rates, Bond Yields, and Stock Prices in the United States Since 1865* (New York: National Bureau of Economic Research, 1938).

- Factors that influence an asset's price sensitivity include its maturity, its coupon rate, and the initial level of the required yield.
- The longer an asset's maturity is, the greater will be its price sensitivity to a change in the discount rate, other things being equal.
- The larger an asset's coupon rate is, the lower will be its price sensitivity to a change in the discount rate, other things being equal.
- The lower the initial discount rate is, the greater will be the price sensitivity of most assets to a change in that rate.
- Duration is a measure of price sensitivity that incorporates maturity, coupon, and level of yield; it provides an approximation of the percentage price change for small changes in yield.
- It is important to be able to measure the price sensitivity of an asset or liability to interest rate changes, and the appropriate measure is the effective duration.

Questions

1. Your broker is recommending that you purchase U.S. government bonds. Here is the explanation: "Listen, in these times of uncertainty, with many companies going bankrupt, it makes sense to play it safe and purchase long-term government bonds. They are issued by the U.S. government, so they are risk free."

How would you respond to the broker?

2. You just inherited 30,000 shares of a company you have never heard of, ABD Corporation. You call your broker to find out whether you have finally struck it rich. After several minutes, she comes back on the telephone and says: "I don't have a clue about these shares. It's too bad they are not traded in a financial market. That would make life a lot easier for you." What does she mean?

3. Suppose you own a bond that pays $75 yearly in coupon interest and is likely to be called in two years (because the firm has already announced that it will redeem the issue early). The call price will be $1,050. What is the price of your bond now, in the market, if the appropriate discount rate for this asset is 9%?

4. Your broker has advised you to buy shares of Hungry Boy Fast Foods, which has paid a dividend of $1.00 per year for 10 years and will (according to the broker) continue to do so for many years. The broker believes that the stock, which now has a price of $12, will be worth $25 per share in five years. You have good reason to think that the discount rate for this firm's stock is 22% per year, because that rate compensates the buyer for all pertinent risks. Is the stock's present price a good approximation of its true financial value?

5. You have been considering a zero-coupon bond, which pays no interest but will pay a principal of $1,000 at the end of five years. The price of the bond is now $712.99, and its required rate of return is 7.0%. This morning's news contained a surprising development.

The government announced that the rate of inflation appears to be 5.5% instead of the 4% that most people had been expecting. (Suppose most people had thought the real rate of interest was 3%.) What would be the price of the bond, once the market began to absorb this new information about inflation?

6. State the difference in basis points between each of the following:

a. 5.5% and 6.5%

b. 7% and 9%

c. 6.4% and 7.8%

d. 9.1% and 11.9%

7. a. Does a rise of 100 basis points in the discount rate change the price of a 20-year bond as much as it changes the price of a four-year bond, assuming that both bonds have the same coupon rate and offer the same yield?

b. Does a rise of 100 basis points in the discount rate change the price of a 4% coupon bond as much as it changes the price of a 10% coupon bond, assuming that both bonds have the same maturity and offer the same yield?

c. Does a rise of 100 basis points in the discount rate change the price of a 10-year bond to the same extent if the discount rate is 4% as it does if the discount rate is 12%?

8. During the early 1980s, interest rates for many long-term bonds were above 14%. In the early 1990s, rates on similar bonds were far lower. What do you think this dramatic decline in market interest rates means for the price volatility of bonds in response to a change in interest rates?

9. a. What is the cash flow of a 6% coupon bond that pays interest annually, matures in seven years, and has a principal of $1,000?

b. Assuming a discount rate of 8%, what is the price of this bond?

c. Assuming a discount rate of 8.5%, what is the price of this bond?

d. Assuming a discount rate of 7.5%, what is the price of this bond?

e. What is the duration of this bond, assuming that the price is the one you calculated in part (b)?

f. If the yield changes by 100 basis points, from 8% to 7%, by how much would you approximate the percentage price change to be, using your estimate of duration in part (e)?

g. What is the actual percentage price change if the yield changes by 100 basis points?

10. Why is it important to be able to estimate the duration of a bond or bond portfolio?

11. Explain why you agree or disagree with the following statement: "Determining the duration of a financial asset is a simple process."

12. Explain why the effective duration is a more appropriate measure of a complex financial instrument's price sensitivity to interest rate changes than is modified duration.

12 Return Distributions, Risk Measures, and Risk-Return Ratios

CONTENTS

This chapter was coauthored with Francesco A. Fabozzi.

Learning Objectives

After reading this chapter, you will understand:

- how an asset's rate of return is calculated;
- what is meant by a random variable;
- what a probability distribution is, and the difference between a discrete and a continuous probability distribution;
- the four moments that are used to describe a probability distribution;
- why it is important to understand the distribution of asset returns;
- what information is contained in the tails of a probability distribution;
- the stability property of a probability distribution, and why it is important for portfolio management and risk management;
- the statistical properties of the normal distribution;
- why the normal distribution has been criticized as a probability distribution for asset return distributions;
- why nonnormal stable distributions are favored over the normal distribution for describing asset return distributions;
- stylized facts about asset return distributions;
- what joint probability distributions are and why they are needed in portfolio management and risk management;
- the use of covariance/correlation to measure the joint randomness of random variables;
- the three basic features that an investment risk measure should be able to take into consideration: (1) relativity of risk, (2) multidimensionality of risk, and (3) asymmetry of risk;
- the difference between an arithmetic average return and a geometric average return;
- what a reward-risk ratio is, and the different types of such ratios that can be calculated.

In the chapters 13 and 14, we discuss two important theories: the theory of portfolio selection and asset pricing theories. These theories are based on assumptions regarding the probability distribution for asset returns, a measure of risk, and a reward-risk ratio for constructing and selecting among alternative portfolios. For example, chapter 13 discusses the theory of portfolio selection assuming that the probability distribution of returns is normally distributed and that the measure of risk is the variance. If investors construct portfolio as the theory suggests, using the Sharpe ratio (one type of reward-risk ratio explained in this chapter), then one theory of asset pricing can be derived.

The purpose of this chapter is not only to explain the statistical concepts needed to understand the theories covered in the next chapter but also to briefly review alternative probability distributions for returns, alternative risk measures, and alternative reward-risk ratios that have been used by practitioners to overcome the drawbacks of the theories explained in the next two chapters. The coverage here is at a basic level. Courses in financial theory and risk management provide a more extensive discussion of these concepts.

What is critical to understand is that the quantitative measures of risk described here are driven by assumptions and by the estimation of parameters required to calculate the selected risk measure. Therefore, a major risk associated with measuring risk is **model risk**, or the risk that the models are subject to forecasting errors.

Measuring the Rate of Return

An asset's rate of return (or simply, "return") over a given time interval is equal to the change in the asset's price plus any distributions received from holding the asset, expressed as a fraction of the asset's price at the beginning of the time interval. When computing the asset's return, it is important to include any income distributions made to the investor, or the measure of return will be deficient. The income distribution can be interest income in the case of a debt obligation or dividend income in the case of a stock.

An asset's return, designated by R, is given by:

$$R = \frac{p_1 - p_0 + C}{p_0},$$

where

p_0 = price at the beginning of the time interval,

p_1 = price at the end of the time interval, and

C = cash distribution.

For example, if an asset's price increased from \$100 on January 1 to \$105 by December 31 of the same year, and on December 31 a cash distribution of \$1 was made, then the asset's return for the year would be

$$R = \frac{\$105 - \$100 + \$1}{\$100} = 0.06 = 6\%.$$

Return Distributions

When studying financial markets, it is critical to understand the distribution of the returns of an asset. Moreover, it is necessary to make some assumption about asset return distributions when building models for selecting assets to be included in a portfolio. With the exception of a risk-free asset, the return on an asset is a random variable.

A random variable is a function that assigns a numerical value to the potential outcomes of an experiment. For example, in the experiment of tossing a die, we could define the random variable x as the number of dots on the face of the die that shows. The possible outcomes (i.e., the numerical values) are 1, 2, 3, 4, 5, and 6. When tossing a coin, there are two possible outcomes: head and tail. The numerical value of 1 can be assigned to the outcome of a head occurring and a numerical value of 2 can be assigned to the outcome of a tail occurring. A random variable can be discrete or continuous. As the name suggests, a **discrete random variable** limits the outcomes so that the random variable can only take on discrete values. A **continuous random variable** can take on any possible value in the range of possible outcomes. When a random variable is the return on an asset, the random variable is assumed to be continuous. Our focus in this chapter is on continuous random variables.

Describing a Probability Distribution

A **probability distribution** assigns a probability to each numerical value of a random variable. For example, in the tossing of a die, each numerical value of this random variable is assigned a probability of 1/6. For the coin tossing, the numerical value for a 1 occurring (an outcome of a head) is 1/2, and the numerical value for a 2 occurring (an outcome of a tail) is also 1/2. Throughout most of this book, we will use probability distributions to describe the probability distribution for asset returns.

There are discrete and continuous probability distributions. Because our focus is on continuous random variables, we will look at the properties of various continuous probability distributions.

The information that can be obtained from the continuous probability distribution of an asset's expected return is critical when pricing assets (explained in chapter 14) and when constructing portfolios (described in chapter 13). Four measures are commonly used to describe a probability distribution: location, dispersion, asymmetry, and concentration in tails. In statistical terminology, these measures are referred to as the **statistical moments** (or simply, "moments") of a probability distribution.

The **location** of a probability distribution is a measure of its central value. The three measures used to describe **central value** are the mean (or average), the median, and the mode. There is a relationship among these three measures that depends on the skewness of a probability distribution, to be described later. The most commonly used measure of location in finance is the mean, which is typically denoted by the Greek letter μ ("mu"). The mean is the **first moment** of a probability distribution and is also referred to as the **expected value**. In practice, when computing the central measure for a random variable from a **sample** of size n, the sample mean is used and is computed as:

$$\bar{x} = \left(\frac{1}{n}\right)\sum_{i=1}^{n} x_i, \tag{12.1}$$

where $\bar{x}$ is equal to the mean of the sample, and x_i is the ith observation.

Dispersion is a measure of how spread out the potential outcomes are that can be realized. Although there are various measures of dispersion—variance, mean absolute deviation, and range—the most commonly used measure in finance is the variance. The **variance** measures the dispersion of the outcomes that can be realized relative to the mean and is referred to as the **second moment** of a probability distribution. For a sample of size n ($i = 1, 2, \ldots, n$) for random variable x, the variance, denoted by var(x), is computed as follows:

$$\text{var}(x) = \left(\frac{1}{n}\right)\sum_{i=1}^{n} x_i(x_i = \bar{x})^2.$$

Basically, the variance is the average of the squared deviations from the mean. Because the variance is in squared units, the standard root of the variance is typically used. The square root of the variance is called the **standard deviation.**

In statistics, the lowercased letter σ ("sigma") of the Greek alphabet is used to denote the standard deviation, and σ^2 is used to denote the variance. The same notation is also used in finance.

When we discuss portfolio selection theory in chapter 13, we will see how, according to this theory, investors who select assets for inclusion in a portfolio take into consideration only the first two moments of the probability distribution of return on assets: the mean and variance.[1] For this reason, portfolio theory is often referred to as **mean-variance analysis** or **mean-variance optimization**. The other measures or statistical moments described below are ignored. More recent approaches to portfolio theory seek to include moments higher than the second moment.

A probability distribution can be symmetric or asymmetric around its mean. A commonly used measure for the asymmetry of a distribution is its **skewness**, which is the **third moment** of a probability distribution. An asymmetric distribution can exhibit either negative or positive skewness. Negative skewness indicates that the distribution is skewed to the left; that is, compared to the right tail, the left tail is elongated (see figure 12.1, top panel). Positive skewness indicates that the distribution is skewed to the right; that is, compared to the left tail, the right tail is elongated (see figure 12.1, bottom panel).

A probability distribution's skewness measure is denoted by β ("beta") and ranges from -1 to $+1$.[2] A probability distribution that is symmetric around its mean has a β equal to zero. Nonsymmetric probability distributions (i.e., skewed distributions) have a nonzero β. The value of β can range from -1 to $+1$. A positive β means that the probability distribution is skewed to the right; a negative β means that the probability distribution is skewed to the left. Unlike the calculation of the mean and the variance, which have a uniform formula for calculating the value of the moment of a probability distribution, the definition of skewness does not. The two most common measures of skewness used are Fisher's skewness and Pearson's skewness, the latter being equal to the square of the Fisher's skewness.

1. Also considered is the correlation of returns between assets, which we describe later in this chapter.

2. We will use the Greek letter β in a different way in the chapters that follow. The notation here is just to describe the moments of a probability distribution.

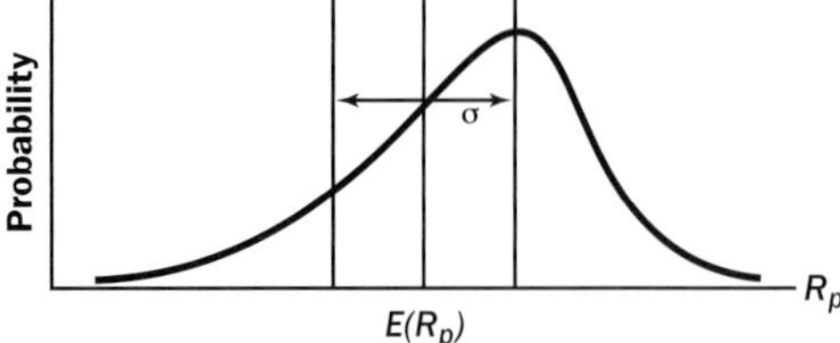

Probability distribution skewed to right

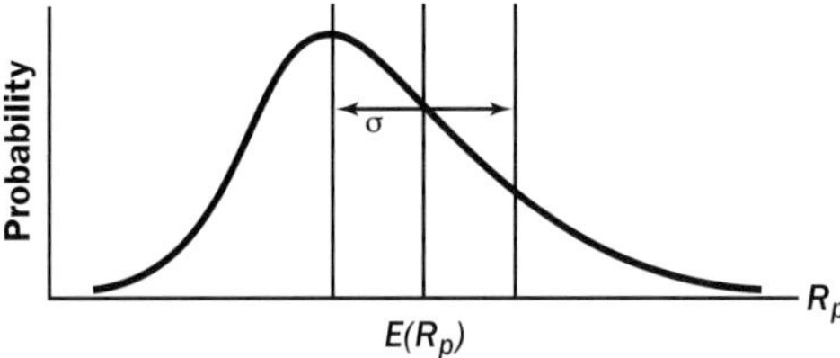

Figure 12.1
Negative (top panel) and positive (bottom panel) skewed probability distributions.

The tails of a probability distribution contain important information about potential outcomes. The **tails** of a probability distribution are the portion of the distribution that holds information about extreme outcomes that may arise for the random variable.[3] The "fatness" of the tails of a probability distribution is related to the peakedness of the distribution around its mean. The joint measure of peakedness and tail fatness is called **kurtosis**. Kurtosis, denoted by α, is the **fourth moment** of a probability distribution and determines the tail weight. As for skewness, there is no standard measure for kurtosis. Fisher's kurtosis and Pearson's kurtosis are two commonly used measures. Fisher's kurtosis, also referred to as **excess kurtosis**, is found by subtracting three from Pearson's kurtosis.

In addition to the four commonly used moments just explained for describing a probability distribution, a concept called an α-quantile is also used. The **α-quantile** provides information about where the first α% of the probability distribution is located. Given an arbitrary observation of some probability distribution, this observation will be less than the α-quantile, denoted by q_α, in α% of the cases and will exceed it in $(100-\alpha)$% of the cases. There are special names given to some quantiles: quartiles and percentiles. The 25%, 50%, and 75% quantiles are referred to as **quartiles**, with the 25% quantile being the first quartile, the 50% quantile being the second quartile, and the 75% quantile being the third quartile. The 1%, 2%, … , 98%, and 99% quantiles are called **percentiles.**

3. Extreme events are referred to as "black swan events" by Nassim Taleb, an options trader, in his book *The Black Swan: The Impact of the Highly Improbable* (London: Penguin, 2007).

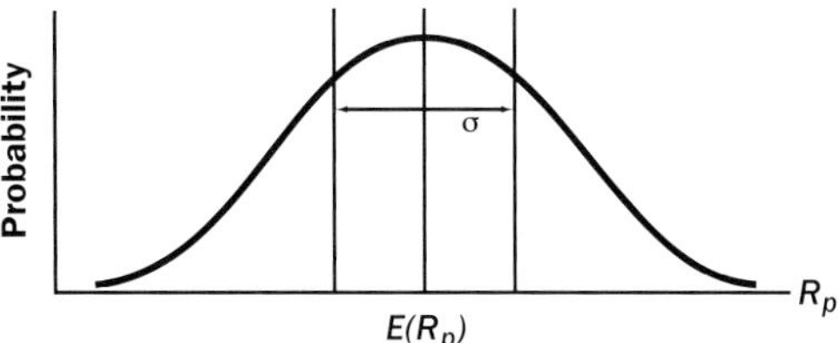

Figure 12.2
Normal (Gaussian) probability distribution; σ denotes the standard deviation.

Continuous Probability Distributions Used to Describe Returns

Numerous probability distributions have been used to describe asset returns. We limit our discussion to distributions that have a specific desirable property for the purpose of portfolio theory, the **stability property**. The family of probability distributions that possess the stability property is the **stable distribution**. A special case of the stable distribution is the **normal distribution**, the distribution that dominates portfolio theory and much of financial theory. We first describe the normal distribution and then discuss the family of stable distributions.

Normal distribution The normal distribution, also referred to as the Gaussian distribution, is a bell-shaped distribution (see figure 12.2). The normal distribution is symmetric around the mean. This means that half of the probability distribution is below the mean (i.e., to the left of the mean in figure 12.2) and half is above the mean (i.e., to the right of the mean in figure 12.2). Another well-known characteristic of the normal distribution is that approximately 68% of the probability is given to values that lie in an interval of one standard deviation around the mean, and the probability is about 95% when the interval is two standard deviations around the mean. Nearly all the probability is assigned to values within three standard deviations around the mean (99%).

In terms of the four moments of a continuous probability distribution, the normal distribution can be described as follows. First, the measure of central value, the location parameter, equals the mean of the distribution (μ), and the measure of dispersion is the variance (σ^2). Because the normal distribution is symmetric, the skewness measure (β) is equal to zero. The Fisher kurtosis (excess kurtosis) measure for the normal distribution is 3.

With respect to kurtosis, figure 12.3 shows the difference between a normal probability distribution and a probability distribution that is symmetric but not normally distributed. For both distributions, the mean is zero and the variance is equal to 1.[4] As can be seen, the

4. When a normal distribution has a mean of 0 and a variance of 1, it is referred to as a "standard" normal distribution.

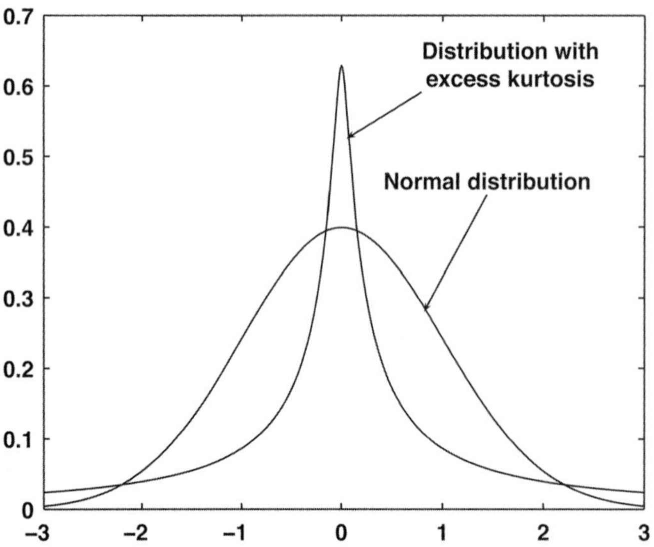

Figure 12.3
Difference between a standard normal distribution and a distribution with high excess kurtosis.

symmetric nonnormal distribution is characterized by a higher peak at the mean (i.e., zero is the mean) than the normal distribution. A probability distribution with this characteristic is said to be a **leptokurtic distribution**.

Figure 12.3 shows the implications for the tails of the distribution for the nonnormal symmetric distribution compared to the normal distribution as a result of the former's greater peakedness. The greater peakedness causes the tails of the symmetric nonnormal distribution to be fatter than those for the normal distribution. When a probability distribution has this characteristic, it is said to be a "fat-tailed distribution" or a "heavy-tailed distribution." Because the Fisher (excess) kurtosis measure for a normal distribution is 3, the same measure for a fat-tailed distribution will be greater than 3. If instead of having greater peakedness than a normal distribution, a probability has less peakedness, the probability distribution is said to be a **platykurtic distribution**. For such probability distributions, there is less probability in the tails than in the normal distribution, and they will have a Fisher kurtosis measure that is less than 3.

Let's look at actual returns distributions for the major stock market indices of several countries: the United States in figure 12.4 (Standard & Poor's 500, S&P 500), Germany in figure 12.5 (Deutscher Aktienindex, DAX), Japan in figure 12.6 (Nihon Keizai Shinbun, Nikkei 225), and the United Kingdom in figure 12.7 (Financial Times Stock Exchange 100, FTSE 100).[5] Although a visualization of the figures for all indices and all periods

5. We discuss each of these stock market indexes in chapter 22.

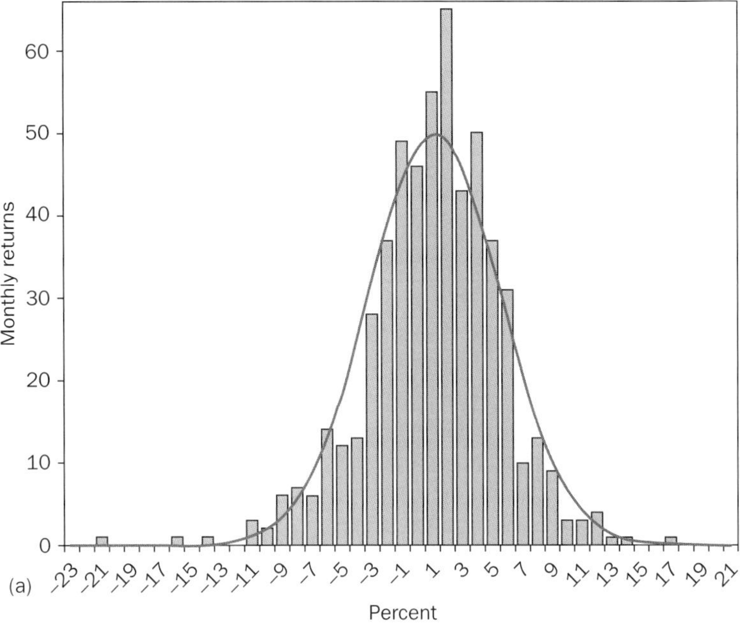

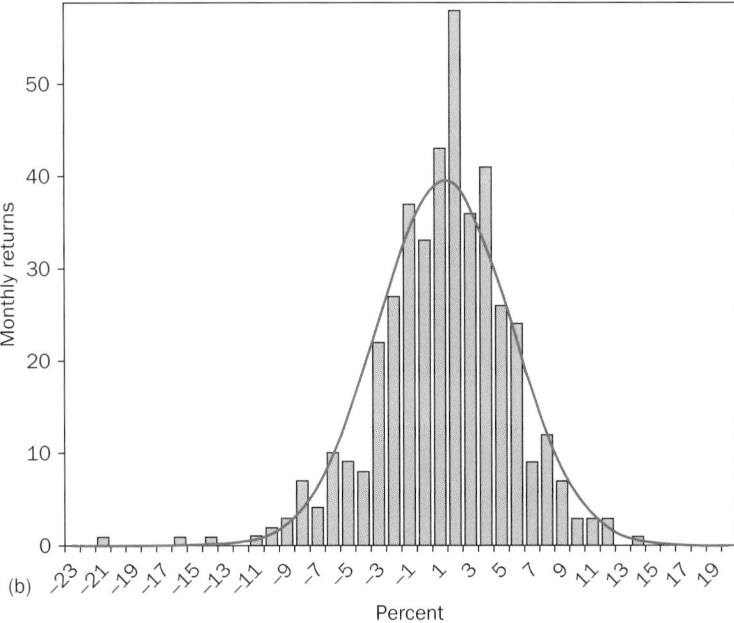

Figure 12.4
S&P 500 monthly returns plotted against a normal distribution: (a) S&P 500 monthly returns from 1970 to 2015; (b) S&P 500 monthly returns from 1980 to 2015; (c) S&P 500 monthly returns from 1990 to 2015.
Source: This figure was created for the authors by Jang Ho Kim of Kyung Hee University using CRSP data.

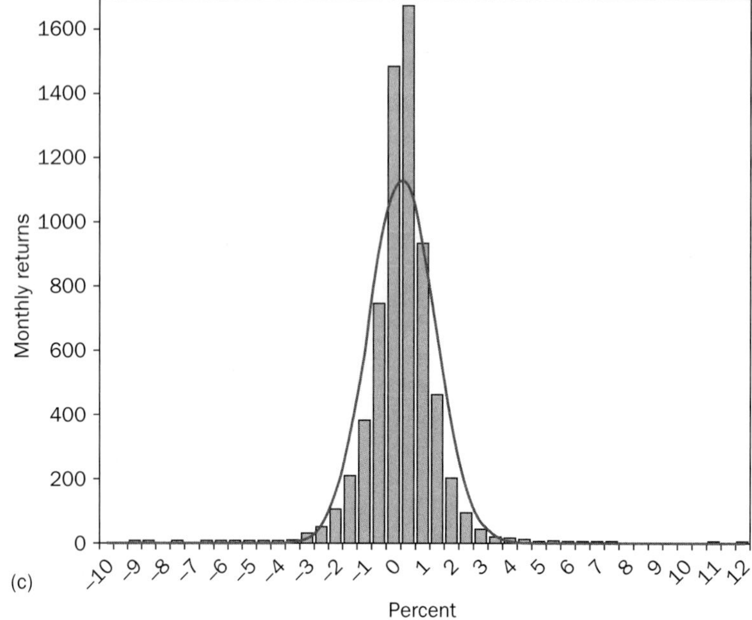

Figure 12.4 *(continued)*

suggests that the distributions are not normal, a more rigorous analysis is required to make that determination. Statistical tests are used to determine whether a distribution is normal. We will not discuss these tests here, but they are the Jacque-Bera test, the Anderson-Darling test, and the Kolmogorov-Smirnov test. In general, these tests reject the hypothesis that the distributions are drawn from a normal distribution.

Stability property There is a highly desirable property of the normal distribution that makes it attractive in dealing with asset returns for the purpose of portfolio theory as well as risk management.[6] The property, referred to as the "stability property," states that the sum of a number of N random variables that follow a normal distribution will again be a normal distribution, provided that the random variables behave independently of one another.

The stability property is important for two reasons in portfolio theory and risk management. First, suppose that an investor has a portfolio of 80 stocks, and each of those 80 stocks is assumed to follow a normal distribution and behave independently of every other one. The stability property of the normal distribution means that the portfolio return (where the

6. See Svetlozar T. Rachev and Stefan Mittnik, *Stable Paretian Models in Finance* (Chichester, UK: John Wiley & Sons, 2000).

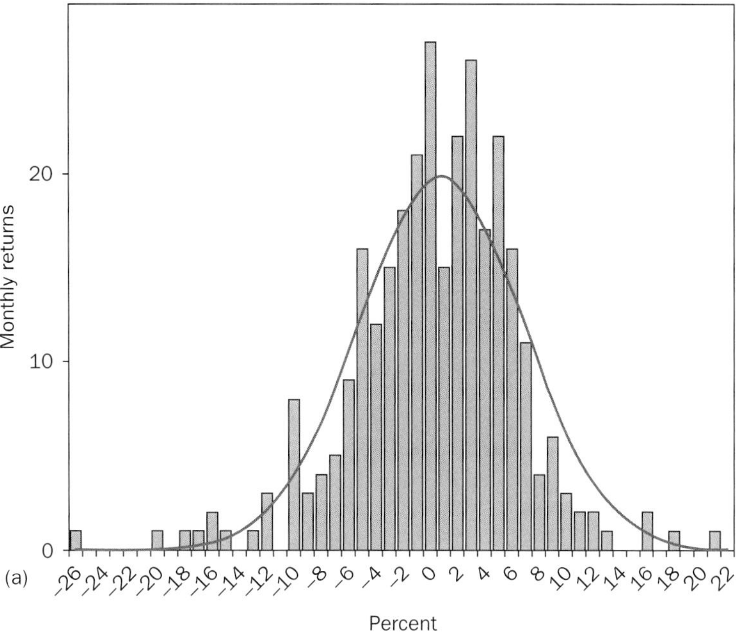

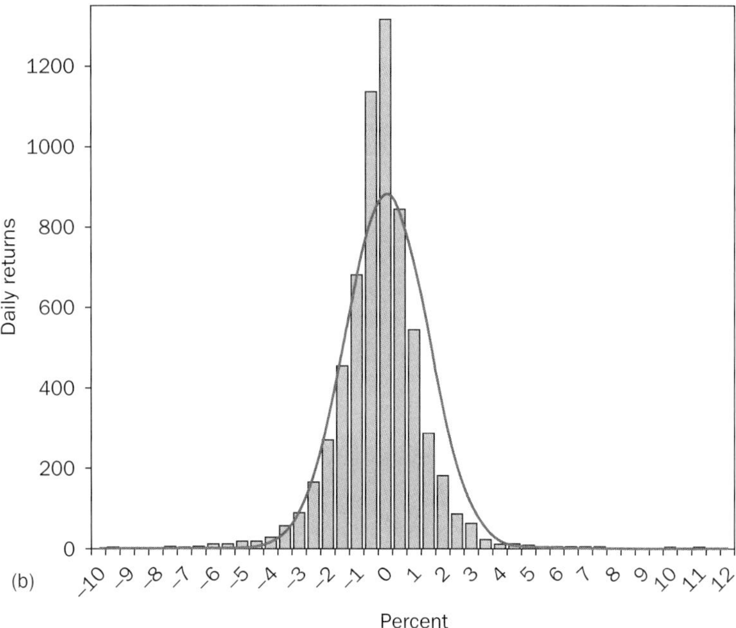

Figure 12.5
DAX returns plotted against a normal distribution, 1991–2015: (a) DAX monthly returns; (b) DAX daily returns. *Source:* This figure was created for the authors by Jang Ho Kim of Kyung Hee University using data from Yahoo! Finance.

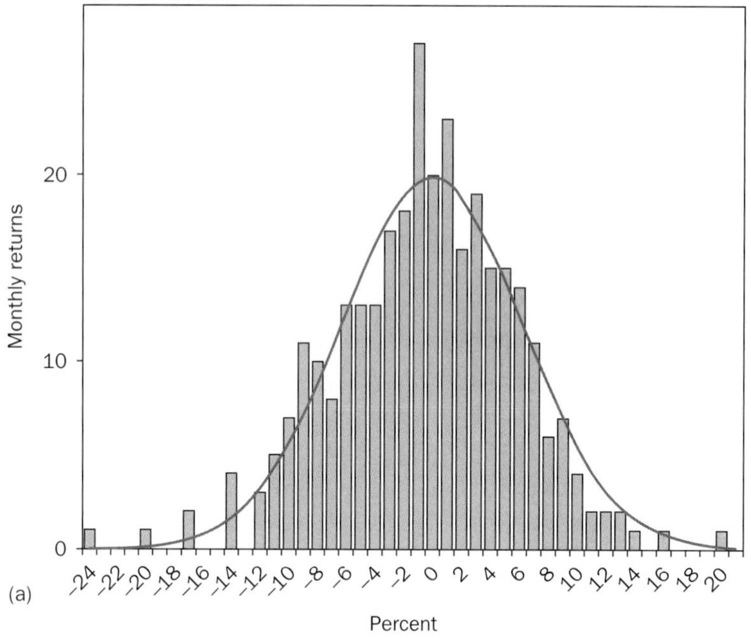

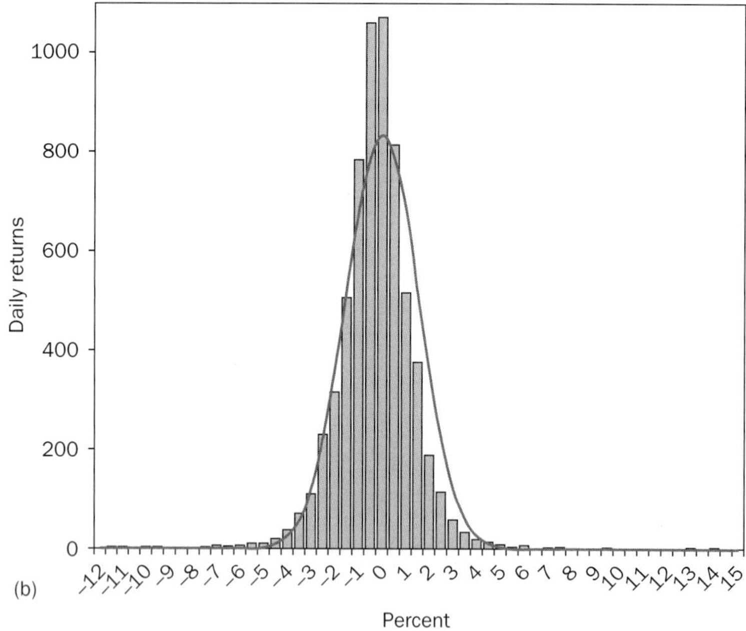

Figure 12.6
Nikkei 225 returns plotted against a normal distribution, 1990–2015: (a) Nikkei 225 monthly returns; (b) Nikkei 225 daily returns.
Source: This figure was created for the authors by Jang Ho Kim of Kyung Hee University using data from Yahoo! Finance.

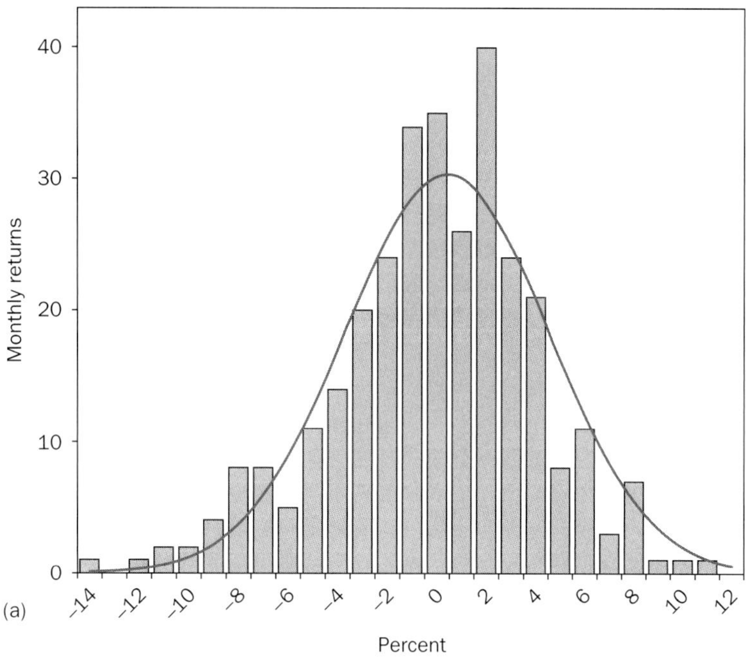

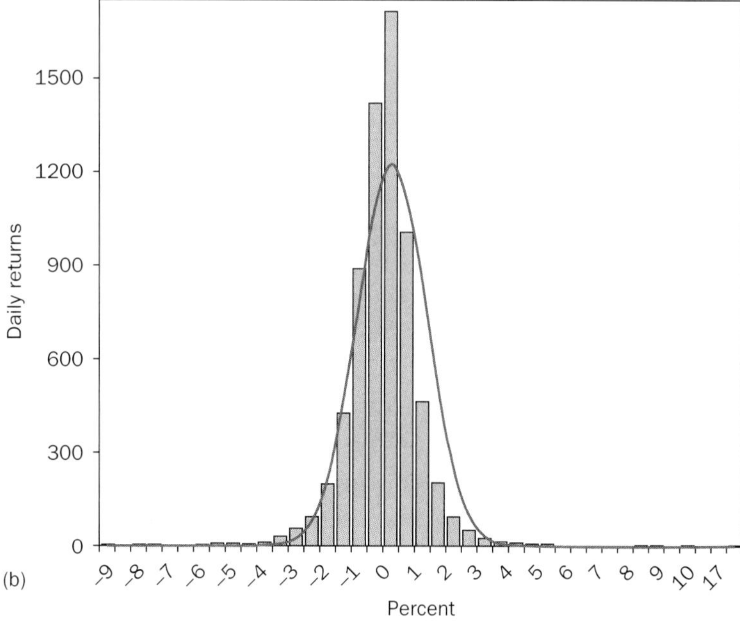

Figure 12.7
FTSE 100 returns plotted against a normal distribution, 1990–2015: (a) FTSE 100 monthly returns; (b) FTSE 100 daily returns.
Source: This figure was created for the authors by Jang Ho Kim of Kyung Hee University using data from Yahoo! Finance.

portfolio is composed of those 80 stocks) will follow a normal distribution. In our discussion of probability distributions below, the discussion is restricted to those distributions that satisfy the stability property. The second reason is that the stability property allows aggregation of asset returns over time. An example is the daily returns of some stock. If the daily return for the stock is assumed to be normally distributed, and if an investor aggregates the daily returns to obtain a weekly return for that stock, then by the stability property, the weekly return is also normally distributed.

Attacks on the normal distribution The use of the normal distribution has been criticized on empirical grounds. According to the normal distribution, holding an asset will expose an investor to small-percentage daily losses and small-percentage daily gains much more often than it will expose the investor to negligible or extreme fluctuations. However, a preponderance of empirical evidence based on observed returns for various asset classes and for different countries leads to rejection of the hypothesis that return distributions are normally distributed.[7] The empirical evidence from many countries has shown that asset returns exhibit fat tails relative to the normal distribution. The implication is that the extreme values (i.e., the values found in the tails of a distribution) are more likely to occur (i.e., have a higher probability of occurrence) than predicted by the normal distribution. This means that between periods in which the market for an asset exhibits relatively modest changes in price, there will be periods in which the changes are much greater (i.e., market crashes and market booms) than predicted by the normal distribution. In the case of stocks, the presence of fat tails can help explain larger price fluctuations for stocks over short periods than can be explained by changes in fundamental economic variables, as Robert Shiller has observed.[8]

The extreme losses that occurred during the financial crisis of 2008–2009 raised the question of whether existing models and practices, largely based on the normal distribution, represent an adequate and reliable framework for portfolio management and risk management. However, empirical attacks on the use of the normal distribution are not solely of recent vintage. Empirical studies on the properties of asset return distributions date back to the pioneering work of Benoit Mandelbrot[9] and Eugene Fama.[10] Shortly after the publication of their research rejecting the normal distribution, Paul Cootner expressed his concern regarding the implications of that finding for their statistical tests, stating:

7. See Svetlozar T. Rachev, Christian Menn, and Frank J. Fabozzi, *Fat-Tailed and Skewed Asset Return Distributions: Implications for Risk Management, Portfolio Selection, and Option Pricing* (Hoboken, NJ: John Wiley & Sons, 2005), chapter 5.

8. Robert Shiller, "Do Stock Prices Move Too Much to Be Justified by Subsequent Changes in Dividends?" *American Economic Review* 71 (1981): 421–436.

9. Benoit Mandelbrot, "The Variation of Certain Speculative Prices," *Journal of Business* 26 (1963): 394–419.

10. Eugene F. Fama, "Mandelbrot and the Stable Paretian Hypothesis," *Journal of Business* 36 (1963): 420–429; Eugene F. Fama, "The Behavior of Stock Market Prices," *Journal of Business* 38 (1965): 34–105.

> Almost without exception, past econometric work is meaningless. Surely, before consigning centuries of work to the ash pile, we should like to have some assurance that all our work is truly useless. If we have permitted ourselves to be fooled for as long as this into believing that the Gaussian assumption is a workable one, is it not possible that the Paretian revolution is similarly illusory?[11]

Despite the Mandelbrot-Fama findings, as well as numerous other studies, the "normality" assumption remains the cornerstone of many leading theories used in finance.

Family of stable distributions Alternative probability distributions to describe asset returns have been proposed and empirically tested. Testing of these alternative probability distributions is necessary, because there is no fundamental theory that can suggest a distributional model for asset returns, and hence the problem remains largely a statistical one. Our focus here is on the class of probability distributions known as the stable distribution.

Mandelbrot and Fama not only rejected the assumption of normality based on their empirical work, they also proposed an alternative probability distribution to replace the normal distribution, the stable Paretian distribution. A major drawback to all the alternative probability distribution models tested is their failure to satisfy the stability property, which is a highly desirable property for asset returns in the context of portfolio management. Only for the class of stable distributions does one obtain the property that portfolio returns follow a stable distribution. By "class" of a probability distribution, we mean that there are probability distributions that fall into the category of the distribution (i.e., they have the general statistical properties of the distribution).

The class of stable distributions is a large and flexible class of probability distributions that also allows skewness and heavy tails for asset returns. The normal distribution turns out to be one particular case of the class of stable distributions that is symmetric. To distinguish between the normal distribution and nonnormal distributions that are in the class of stable distributions, Mandelbrot referred to nonnormal stable distributions as **stable Paretian distributions** or **Lévy stable distributions**.

A stable distribution is described by four parameters:

1. a location parameter (μ),
2. a scale parameter (σ),
3. a skewness parameter (β), and
4. a kurtosis parameter (α).

When $\beta \neq 0$, the stable distribution is skewed and is characterized by fat tails. That is, there is a high probability that an extreme outcome may occur relative to what could occur for a normal distribution when the kurtosis parameter (α) has a value that is less than 2. The value for α, also referred to as the **index of stability**, is positive but cannot exceed 2. The range

11. Paul H. Cootner, *The Random Character of Stock Market Prices* (Cambridge, MA: MIT Press, 1964), 337.

for the skewness parameter, β, is from -1 to $+1$. The stable distribution is skewed to the right if β is positive and skewed to the left if β is negative.

The normal distribution and the Lévy distribution are special cases of the stable distribution.[12]

From a computational perspective, the major drawback to the stable nonnormal distributions (i.e., stable Paretian distributions) is that the variance equals infinity because of the tail behavior of the stable nonnormal distribution. The implication for portfolio theory will be clear when we discuss the theory in chapter 13, where we explain the critical role of the variance. A second problem involves another technical point regarding the ability to estimate the probability function. Basically, with the exception of the normal distribution and Lévy distribution,[13] there is no closed-form expression (i.e., analytical solution) for a stable Paretian distribution. Although this may have been a valid problem with the use of stable distributions at one time, that is no longer the case, because significant advances in computational finance over the past 25 years have made it fairly straightforward to fit observed returns to determine a stable Paretian distribution's parameters.

Although observed stock returns exhibit tails thicker than those of the normal distribution, they are still inconsistent with the size of the tails predicted by the stable Paretian distribution. More recently, **tempered stable distributions** have been suggested for modeling the distribution of stock returns; such distributions address not only the issue of tail thickness being more consistent with observed stock returns but also the problem of infinite variance. The mathematics of the tempered stable distribution is beyond the scope of this chapter, but the basic idea is simple. Tempered stable distributions are obtained from the class of stable distributions through a process called "tail tempering." Tail tempering is accomplished by modifying only the tails of stable distributions so that they remain thicker than the tails of the normal distribution but do not lead to an infinite volatility.[14]

Some Stylized Facts about Stock Returns

An extensive body of empirical research on stock returns in the stock markets of many countries has accumulated since the early 1960s. A fair conclusion from these studies leads to several stylized facts. As used here, the expression "stylized facts" refers to empirical findings that are consistent for different times and different country stock markets investigated. They are (1) skewness, (2) fat tails, (3) volatility clustering, (4) autoregressive behavior, and (5) the temporal behavior of tail thickness.[15]

12. The only other special case of the stable distribution is the Cauchy distribution, which has much fatter tails than the normal distribution.

13. This is also true for the Cauchy distribution.

14. The technique is described in Michele Leonardo Bianchi, Svetlozar T. Rachev, Young Shin Kim, and Frank J. Fabozzi, "Tempered Infinitely Divisible Distributions and Processes," *SIAM: Theory of Probability and Its Applications* 55 (2010): 59–86.

15. Stoyan V. Stoyanov, Svetlozar T. Rachev, Boryana Racheva-Yotova, and Frank J. Fabozzi, "Fat-Tailed Models for Risk Estimation," *Journal of Portfolio Management* 37, no. 2 (2011): 107–117.

The first two stylized facts were discussed earlier. **Skewness** of stock returns means that asymmetry exists in the upside and downside potential of price changes. There can be negative or positive skewness. Negative (positive) skewness means that price behavior is such that more negative (positive) stock price changes are exhibited than would be suggested by a symmetric distribution. **Fat tails** means that the probability of extreme price movements (up and down) is much larger than predicted by the normal distribution. **Volatility clustering** means that large price changes tend to be followed by large price changes, and small price changes tend to be followed by small price changes. **Autoregressive behavior** means that price changes depend on price changes in the past (e.g., positive price changes tend to be followed by positive price changes). Finally, the **temporal behavior of tail thickness** means that the probability of extreme price changes through time is smaller in normal markets and much larger in turbulent markets.

Joint Probability Distributions

Thus far we have discussed the probability distribution of a single random variable, the return on an asset. A probability distribution that involves only a single random variable is referred to as a **univariate probability distribution** and helps us understand the attributes of the returns for an individual asset. However, in chapters 13 and 14, we will be considering a portfolio of assets and therefore will be interested in the probability distribution for multiple assets. This requires that we expand our understanding of probability distributions from univariate probability distributions to **multivariate probability distributions**, or what is referred to as **joint probability distributions**.

To understand the concept of a joint probability distribution using asset returns, suppose that an investor has constructed a portfolio consisting of the common stock of two companies, company ABC and company XYZ. There is a univariate probability distribution for the return on the common stock of company ABC and a univariate probability distribution for the return on the common stock of company XYZ. The return distribution for the common stock of each company is called the **marginal probability distribution**. Suppose an investor is interested in the return on a portfolio consisting of the common stock of these two companies. The portfolio return of interest is known as a **joint probability distribution**.

When dealing with joint probability distributions, an investor is faced with the interdependence between the two return distributions. For example, in the case of the returns for the common stock of companies ABC and XYX, do large returns for company ABC imply large returns for the stock of company XYZ or small returns for the common stock of company XYZ? This property is referred to as the **dependence of random variables**. When there is no dependence between two random variables, the two random variables are said to be **independently distributed**. Although there is a technical definition of what is meant by independently distributed, the basic idea is simple in the special case of only two random variables. The two random variables are said to be independently distributed if the value of one random variable does not provide any information about the value of the other random variable.

Although the field of statistics offers several ways to measure the dependence between two random variables, the measure used in finance is the covariance or equivalently, correlation.

Covariance and Correlations

The **covariance** of two random variables is a measure of the joint variation of the random variables, where the association is assumed to be a linear one. In the case of two random variables, the covariance is calculated with sample data as follows. Let x and y be two random variables, and denote their sample means by $\bar{x}$ and $\bar{y}$, respectively. Assuming that there are n observations for the two random variables, then the covariance between the two random variables x and y, denoted by cov(x, y), is

$$\operatorname{cov}(x, y) = \left(\frac{1}{n}\right)\sum_{i=1}^{n}(x_i - \bar{x})(y - \bar{y}). \tag{12.2}$$

In words, the covariance is calculated by (1) calculating for all observations for each random variable the deviation from its respective mean, (2) multiplying for each observation the deviation for each random variable, (3) summing the product of the deviations, and (4) dividing by the number of observations. The sample covariance is then the average of all joint deviations.

A problem with the covariance is that it is affected by the scale of the random variables. In other words, the covariance is *scaling variant*. As a result, it is not possible to compare any pair of covariances, and it is difficult to interpret their values. For example, suppose that for our two random variables, x and y, the computed covariance is 30. Suppose that x is measured in a different way, such as $20 + 10x$. A mathematical property of the covariance is that the covariance would be 10 times the original covariance. That is, the covariance would be 300.

To deal with this problem, an alternative but related measure can be developed by dividing the covariance by the variance of the two random variables. The resulting measure is called the **Pearson correlation coefficient**, or simply the **correlation coefficient**. That is, the correlation coefficient, denoted by cor(x, y), is

$$\operatorname{cor}(x, y) = \frac{\operatorname{cov}(x, y)}{\operatorname{var}(x)\operatorname{var}(y)}, \tag{12.3}$$

where var(x) and var(y) are the sample variances as computed using equation (12.2).

The correlation coefficient can then be shown to have a value between −1 and 1, where −1 means the two random variables are perfectly negatively correlated, and 1 means they are perfectly positively correlated. Unlike the covariance, the correlation coefficient is not affected by the scale of the two random variables and is therefore said to be *scale invariant*.

Portfolio Risk Measures

In portfolio theory, which we describe in chapter 13, the variance of a portfolio's return has historically been the most commonly used measure of investment risk. However, investors have developed different investment strategies in their attempt to realize their investment objectives. Consequently, financial theorists, practitioners, and regulators have come to believe that it is difficult to accept the view that there is only one definition of investment risk. Moreover, the variance or standard deviation as a risk measure may no longer be suitable if returns are not normally distributed.

Before exploring alternative measures of risk, let us discuss the basic features of investment risk measures. Leslie A. Balzer has argued that a risk measure is investor specific, and therefore there is "no single universally acceptable risk measure."[16] He proposed three basic features that an investment risk measure should be able to take into consideration: (1) relativity of risk, (2) multidimensionality of risk, and (3) asymmetry of risk.

Relativity of risk means that the risk should be related to performing worse than some alternative investment or benchmark. Several proposals in the literature have suggested that investment risk be measured by the probability of the investment realizing a return that is less than an investor's designated risk benchmark.[17] In addition, an investor could have multiple investment objectives, which would call for multiple risk benchmarks. This is what Balzer means by **multidimensionality of risk**. The key is identifying a suitable benchmark that reflects an investor's investment objectives. Finally, **asymmetry of risk** means that it is reasonable to expect that risk is an asymmetric concept related to downside outcomes. Consequently, any realistic candidate for an investment risk measure should value upside and downside differently. Although the standard deviation considers positive and negative deviations from the mean as a potential risk, for this measure, outperforming relative to the mean is penalized just as much as underperforming.

Value-at-Risk Measure

The **value-at-risk** (VaR) measure is defined as the minimum level of loss at a given, sufficiently high, confidence level for a predefined time horizon. Figure 12.8 illustrates the VaR measure graphically.

A VaR's predefined time horizon could be a time period of any length. The confidence level that is often used in practice is either 95% or 99%. Banks, for example, calculate a daily VaR. For example, suppose a portfolio has a one-week 95% VaR equal to $10 million. This means that over the horizon of one week, the portfolio may lose more than $10 million with

16. Leslie A. Balzer, "Investment Risk: A Unified Approach to Upside and Downside Returns," in *Managing Downside Risk in Financial Markets: Theory, Practice and Implementation*, ed. Frank Sortino and Stephen Satchell (Oxford: Butterworth-Heinemann, 2001), 103–156.

17. See, for example, Balzer, "Investment Risk."

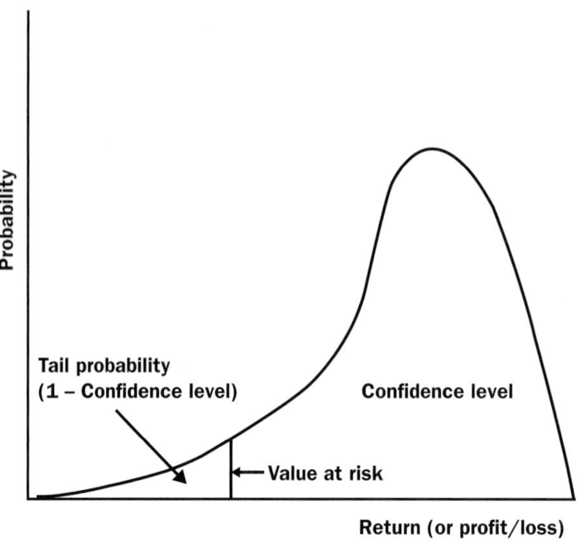

Figure 12.8
Illustration of the value-at-risk (VaR) measure.

probability equal to 1 minus the confidence interval, 5% in our example. The probability of 1 minus the confidence level is called the **tail probability**. Although this example is in terms of a portfolio's dollar loss, the VaR for a portfolio can be calculated in terms of percentage returns. Suppose that the market value for a portfolio is $100 million. If the one-week 95% VaR of the return distribution is 2%, then over the time horizon of one week, the portfolio may lose more than 2% ($2 million) of the portfolio's market value with probability equal to 5%.

As with all quantitative risk measures described here, VaR is heavily dependent on the probability distribution assumed for the returns. A VaR can be computed assuming a normal distribution, a *t*-distribution, or a stable distribution, for example. VaR varies with the assumed distribution, because the tails of the distribution are different. An assumption about the return distribution that does not reflect the true distribution can lead to an under- or overestimation of VaR for a given confidence level. As we discuss in chapter 13, where we cover portfolio theory, if VaR is used as the measure of the risk that is to be minimized in selecting an optimal portfolio, then the portfolio constructed based on the optimization process will not in fact be optimal, because the risk measure fails to reflect the true portfolio risk.

The calculation of VaR is not as simple as calculating the dispersion measures discussed earlier. Various methods have been employed to calculate VaR. The three most common methods in practice are the RiskMetrics method, the historical method, and the Monte Carlo method. An explanation of these methods and their underlying principles is beyond the scope of this chapter. What is important to understand now is that the VaR is more complex to calculate than the dispersion measures, but because of the importance of identifying the true risk of a portfolio, computational complexity is not a reason to shy away from difficult calculations of a risk measure.

Bank regulators throughout the world have adopted VaR as a measure of risk for banks. One of the advantages of VaR is that it is easily understood. However, that does not mean that it is the risk measure of choice for all market participants. VaR has a well-known deficiency because it fails to satisfy one of the theoretical properties of what is referred to as a "coherent" risk measure. The four properties of a coherent risk measure are monotonicity, positive homogeneity, subadditivity, and translation invariance. The problem with the VaR is that it does not always satisfy the subadditivity property (i.e., the property dealing with diversification). It turns out that the VaR for a portfolio may be greater than the sum of the VaRs of the assets composing the portfolio. Thus, the VaR could show more risk if assets were combined into a portfolio than if the assets were held in isolation.

VaR provides a good opportunity to illustrate the notion of model risk that we discussed in the introduction to this chapter. JPMorgan Chase developed its own VaR for measurement of firmwide risk and risk for its trading operations. In its filings with the SEC, it reports daily VaR, using a 95% confidence interval. In April 2012, JPMorgan Chase reported that the bank changed the model it was using to compute VaR. According to the new model, the VaR was $115 million, an amount 24% less than under the previous VaR model used at the beginning of 2012. This was the first of several changes to JPMorgan Chase's VaR model beginning in January 2012 that significantly changed the bank's VaR.[18] These changes to JPMorgan Chase's VaR model and the impact on the daily VaR came to light as a result of the bank's trading loss of more than $6.2 billion in 2012, a number inconsistent with a daily VaR of anything in the range of $100 million. In testimony before the U.S. Senate Banking Committee, it was alleged by JPMorgan Chase's chief executive officer, Jamie Dimon, that the trading loss was attributable to the adoption of a new VaR that understated risks. The key takeaway from JPMorgan Chase's use of its VaR model is that these models are far from perfect.

Conditional Value-at-Risk Measure

There is another limitation to the use of VaR as a measure of risk, which brings us to our next related risk measure: **conditional value-at-risk** (CVaR). For a given tail probability, CVaR is defined as the average of the VaRs that are larger than the VaR at that tail probability. Therefore, CVaR focuses on the losses in the tail that are larger than the corresponding VaR level. Because CVaR indicates the magnitude of such losses, it is also referred to as the **average value-at-risk** (AvaR) measure.[19]

Like the VaR, the CVaR has an intuitive interpretation. Unlike the VaR, however, the CVaR is a coherent risk measure: It satisfies all four required properties discussed earlier.

18. Dawn Kopecki and Michael J. Moore, "JPMorgan Switches Risk Model Again after Whale Loss," Bloomberg.com, April 12, 2013, http://www.bloomberg.com/news/2013-04-12/jpmorgan-switches-risk-model-again-after-whale-loss.html.

19. A related measure also used to refer to CvaR: "expected tail shortfall" (ETL). There are slight technical differences between CVaR and ETL.

Moreover, it overcomes one other drawback of the VaR: It is not informative about the magnitude of the losses larger than the VaR level.

There are convenient ways for computing and estimating CVaR that permit its application to optimal portfolio design and risk management. However, a discussion of these methods is beyond the scope of this chapter.

Reward-Risk Ratios

In portfolio theory, an important metric is a measure of the return realized relative to the risk accepted. Typically, these metrics are referred to as **reward-risk ratios** and are widely used as a criterion for selection among alternative portfolios and as metrics for evaluating the performance of a portfolio manager or the performance of an asset class. The higher the ratio is, the better the performance will be. The numerator of the ratio is some measure of return, and the denominator is some measure of risk.

Reward Measures

For applications in finance where the reward-risk ratio is presented in terms of the return on an asset or the return on a portfolio, the reward is the realized return. The realized return is an average return realized over a time interval. For example, if the time interval is a month and there are five years of monthly returns, then the realized return is the average monthly return. The average return can be computed in one of two ways: as an arithmetic average return or as a geometric average.

The **arithmetic average return** is an unweighted average of the returns achieved during a series of such measurement intervals. The general formula is

$$R_A = (R_{P1} + R_{P2} + \cdots + R_{PT}) / T,$$

where

R_A = the arithmetic average return,

R_{Pk} = return in period k ($k = 1, \ldots, T$), and

T = number of time periods.

For example, let's consider an investor who realized the following portfolio returns: −10%, 20%, and 5% in July, August, and September, respectively. The arithmetic average monthly return is 5%.

The arithmetic average return for a portfolio can be thought of as the mean value of the withdrawals (expressed as a fraction of the initial portfolio value) that can be made at the end of each interval while maintaining the initial portfolio value intact. In the preceding example, the investor must add 10% of the initial portfolio value at the end of the first month, can withdraw 20% of the initial portfolio value at the end of the second month, and then can withdraw 5% of the initial portfolio value at the end of the third month.

The **geometric average return**, also referred to as the **time-weighted average return**, measures the compounded rate of growth of the initial value, assuming that all cash distributions are reinvested. The general formula is

$$R_G = [(1 + R_{P1})\,(1 + R_{P2})\,\ldots\,(1 + R_{PT})]^{1/T} - 1,$$

where R_G is the geometric average return and R_{Pk} and N are as defined for the arithmetic average return.

For example, if the portfolio returns were −10%, 20%, and 5% in July, August, and September, as in the preceding example, then the geometric average return would be

$$R_G = [(1 + (-0.10))\,(1 + 0.20)\,\ldots\,(1 + 0.05)]^{1/3} - 1 = 0.043.$$

As the geometric average return is 4.3% per month, $1 invested in the portfolio at the end of June would have grown at a rate of 4.3% per month during the three-month period.

In general, the arithmetic average and geometric average returns do not provide the same answers, because computation of the arithmetic average return assumes the initial amount invested is maintained (through additions or withdrawals) at its initial portfolio value. In contrast, the geometric average return is the return on a portfolio that varies in size because of the assumption that all proceeds are reinvested.

An example shows how the two averages fail to coincide. Consider a portfolio with a $100 million market value at the beginning of 2017, a $200 million value at the end of 2017, and a $100 million value at the end of 2018. The annual returns are 100% and −50%. The arithmetic average return is 25%, whereas the geometric average return is 0%. The arithmetic average return consists of the average of the $100 million withdrawn at the end of 2017 and the $50 million replaced at the end of 2018. The rate of return is clearly zero; however, the 100% return in 2017 is exactly offset by the 50% loss in 2018 on the larger investment base. In this example, the arithmetic average return exceeds the geometric average return. This outcome always proves to be true, except in the special situation where the returns in each interval are the same, in which case the averages are identical

Now that we know that the realized return should be computed using the geometric average return, let's look at how the reward (i.e., numerator) is calculated for a reward-risk ratio. The reward can be measured on an absolute or relative basis. Reward-risk ratios that use *absolute* rewards use in the numerator the difference between the realized return and the risk-free rate, or zero. When the reward is measured on a *relative* basis, it is the difference between the realized return and a benchmark selected by a client.

The most popular reward-risk ratio that measures the reward on an absolute basis is the **Sharpe ratio**.[20] The risk-free return is used to reduce the realized return in this reward-risk ratio:

20. William F. Sharpe, "Mutual Fund Performance," *Journal of Business* 39 (suppl.) (1966): 119–138.

$$\text{Sharpe ratio} = \frac{\text{Realized return} - \text{Risk-free rate of return}}{\text{Standard deviation of the realized returns}}.$$

Two well-known reward-risk ratios that measure reward on a relative return basis (i.e., a return in excess of the benchmark) are the Sortino ratio and the information ratio:

$$\text{Sortino ratio} = \frac{\text{Realized return} - \text{Minimum acceptable return}}{\text{Standard deviation of returns below the minimum acceptable return}}.$$

$$\text{Information ratio} = \frac{\text{Realized return} - \text{Return on the benchmark}}{\text{Standard deviation of the excess return returns}}.$$

Risk Measure

The denominators of these three ratios all represent a different measure of risk. The Sharpe ratio has come under attack by researchers and practitioners because of its use of the standard deviation (variance) as a measure of risk, which fails to recognize that the return distribution is likely to be skewed. The Sortino ratio addresses this criticism of the Sharpe ratio by using the standard deviation of only the realized returns that are less than the minimum acceptable return. The information ratio uses a risk measure that is calculated by first computing the realized return minus the benchmark return and using those observations to compute the standard deviation. This standard deviation measure is more popularly referred to in the investment management community as "tracking error."

Key Points

- An asset's return over a given time interval is equal to the change in the asset's price plus any distributions received from holding the asset, expressed as a fraction of the asset's price at the beginning of the time interval.
- With the exception of a risk-free asset, the return on an asset is a random variable.
- When constructing a portfolio of assets, it is necessary to make some assumption about asset return distributions.
- A random variable is a function that assigns a numerical value to the potential outcomes of an experiment.
- A discrete random variable limits the outcomes such that the random variable can only take on discrete values. When the random variable can take on any possible value within the range of possible outcomes, it is a continuous random variable.
- When the random variable of interest is the return on an asset, the random variable is assumed to be continuous.
- Probability distributions are used to describe the potential outcomes of a random variable.

- Four commonly used measures to describe a probability distribution (and referred to as the "statistical moments" of a distribution) are location, dispersion, asymmetry, and concentration in tails.
- A probability distribution's location is a measure of its central value (the first moment), and the measures used to describe this moment are the mean (or average), the median, and the mode.
- The most commonly used measure of location in finance is the mean or value.
- A measure of the variability of the outcomes that can be realized is the second moment of a probability distribution: dispersion. The three most commonly used measures of dispersion are the variance, mean absolute deviation, and range.
- Variance is a measure of the dispersion of the outcome that can be realized relative to the mean and is basically the average of the squared deviations from the mean. The square root of the variance is the standard deviation.
- The asymmetry of a probability distribution around its mean is its skewness and is the third moment of a probability distribution. An asymmetric distribution can exhibit either negative skewness (skewed to the left) or positive skewness (skewed to the right).
- The two most commonly used measures of skewness are Fisher's skewness and Pearson's skewness, the latter being equal to the square of Fisher's skewness.
- The tail of a probability distribution is the portion of the distribution that contains information about extreme outcomes that may arise for the random variable.
- The peakedness of a probability distribution affects how fat the tails are.
- The fourth moment of a probability distribution is measured by its kurtosis, which is the joint measure of peakedness and tail fatness.
- Two measures of kurtosis are Fisher's kurtosis (also referred to as excess kurtosis) and Pearson's kurtosis.
- The α-quantile of a probability distribution provides information about where the first α% of the probability distribution is located.
- A desirable property that a probability distribution should possess when used in portfolio and risk management is the stability property. The class of probability distributions that have this property is known as the stable distribution.
- The normal distribution or Gaussian distribution is a bell-shaped distribution that is symmetric around the mean. It is a special case of a stable distribution.
- Only the first two moments, mean and variance, are needed to describe a normal distribution. A symmetric nonnormal distribution characterized by a higher (lower) peak at the mean than the normal distribution is said to be a leptokurtic (platykurtic) distribution and has a fatter (thinner) tail than the normal distribution.
- The stability property that a normal distribution satisfies is that the sum of N random variables that follow a normal distribution will again be a normal distribution, provided that the random variables behave independently of one another.

- The stability property is important in portfolio theory and risk management. The stability property means that (1) the portfolio return (where the portfolio is composed of assets whose returns are normally distributed) will follow a normal distribution and (2) its use allows the aggregation of asset returns over time.
- Empirical evidence does not support the assumption that real-world asset return distributions are best described by a normal distribution; instead, they exhibit fatter tails than predicted by the normal distribution.
- Because there is no fundamental theory that can suggest a distributional model for asset returns, alternative distributions must be empirically tested.
- Because of its desirable characteristics with respect to the stability property, the stable distribution has been suggested to describe asset return distributions.
- The class of stable distributions is a large and flexible class of probability distributions, which also allows for skewness and heavy-tailedness for asset returns. Because this class includes as a special case the normal distribution, a nonnormal stable distribution is referred to as a "Paretian stable distribution."
- A stable distribution is described by four parameters: a location parameter, scale parameter, skewness parameter, and kurtosis parameter (called the "index of stability").
- In the past, certain computational aspects made it difficult to use the Paretian stable distribution for portfolio management (e.g., an infinite variance), but advances in computational finance and modeling (i.e., the tempered stable distribution) have eliminated those problems.
- Five stylized facts have been observed for asset return distributions: (1) skewness, (2) fat tails, (3) volatility clustering, (4) autoregressive behavior, and (5) temporal behavior of tail thickness.
- In portfolio management and risk management, the probability distribution of interest is the joint probability distribution.
- Covariance/correlation is the commonly used way to measure the dependence between two random variables.
- A measure of the joint variation of two random variables that are assumed to be in a linear association is the covariance and its related measure, the correlation.
- The correlation measure overcomes the limitation of the covariance measure, which depends on the scale used to measure the random variable. The range of the correlation is −1 to 1.
- The three basic features that an investment risk measure should be able to take into consideration are (1) relativity of risk, (2) multidimensionality of risk, and (3) asymmetry of risk.
- Relativity of risk means that risk should be related to an asset's performing worse than some alternative investment or benchmark.
- Because an investor could have multiple investment objectives, multiple risk benchmarks are necessary, which underscores what is meant by the multidimensionality of risk.

- Asymmetry of risk means that because it is reasonable to expect that risk is an asymmetric concept related to the downside outcome, any realistic candidate for an investment risk measure has to value upside and downside outcomes differently.
- Two alternative risk measures proposed are value-at-risk (VaR) and conditional value-at-risk (CvaR).
- VaR is defined as the minimum level of loss at a given, sufficiently high confidence level for a predefined time horizon.
- A limitation of the use of VaR as a measure of risk is that it ignores the amount of losses larger than the VaR at that tail probability.
- CVaR (also called "average value at risk") for a given tail probability is defined as the average of the VaRs and hence focuses on the losses in the tail that are larger than the corresponding VaR level.
- An average return can be calculated as either an arithmetic average return or a geometric average return, with the latter being the preferred method.
- Reward-risk ratios measure the reward on a relative or absolute basis.
- The best-known and most commonly applied reward-risk ratio in finance is the Sharpe ratio, but because of the Sharpe ratio's drawbacks, the Sortino ratio is preferred.
- Reward-risk ratios can be calculated based on different reward measures and different risk measures.

Questions

1. Suppose an investor acquires an asset for $20 and sells that asset for $22 one year later. During that period, a cash distribution of $1 was received by the investor just prior to the sale of the asset. What is the investor's one-year rate of return?

2. Explain why the return on an asset that does not pay a cash distribution over the time interval it is held is equal to the ratio of its selling price to its purchase price, then subtracting 1 from the computed ratio.

3. Why are measures of risk dependent on the probability distribution assumed for returns or profits and losses?

4. A portfolio manager is working with the firm's quantitative team to develop a risk model for the firm. The portfolio manager suggests (based on experience) building the model based on a certain probability distribution of returns. A member of the quantitative team points out that the problem with the probability distribution proposed is that it does not satisfy the stability property. The portfolio manager does not understand the objection. Explain the issue to the portfolio manager.

5. Some practitioners and researchers believe that risk cannot be captured in a single number. How does this statement relate to one of the three features of a risk measure as suggested by Leslie Balzer?

6. When a normal distribution is assumed for the return distribution, why are observations three standard deviations above the mean viewed as representing "tail risk"?

7. A study of daily returns for the S&P 500 by Cook Pine Capital LLC investigated returns from December 30, 1927, through November 21, 2008.[21] For the 20,319 daily returns, the following information was reported:

Mean: 0.026%,

Standard deviation: 1.182%,

Kurtosis: 18.347,

Skewness: −0.098,

Maximum daily return: 16.61%, and

Minimum daily return: −20.47%.

The table below shows the daily return distribution as observed over the period and what the normal distribution would predict. The distribution is in terms of the number of standard distributions above the mean.

Number of Standard Deviations from Mean	Actual Distribution		Normal Distribution	
	Observed	Percentage	Predicted	Percentage
$+6\sigma$	26	0.13	0	0.00
$+5\sigma$	13	0.06	0	0.00
$+4\sigma$	34	0.17	1	0.00
$+3\sigma$	89	0.44	27	0.13
$+2\sigma$	276	1.36	435	2.14
$+1\sigma$	1,393	6.86	2,761	13.59
0σ	16,603	81.71	13,872	68.27
-1σ	1,377	6.78	2,761	13.59
-2σ	325	1.60	435	2.14
-3σ	100	0.49	27	0.13
-4σ	43	0.21	1	0.00
-5σ	19	0.09	0	0.00
-6σ	21	0.10	0	0.00
Total	20,319	100	20,319	100

21. Cook Pine Capital LLC, "Study of Fat-Tail Risk," November 26, 2008, http://www.cookpinecapital.com/pdf/Study%20of%20Fat-tail%20Risk.pdf.

What does the information in the table suggest about the daily return distribution for the S&P 500?

8. One vendor of risk models, FinAnalytica, publishes daily risk measures. The following extracts are from the company's website:[22]

As an industry standard, Value at Risk (VaR) measures the worst expected loss of a portfolio over a specific time interval at a given confidence level. Most commercial risk analytics products today measure VaR based on the thin-tailed and symmetric normal, "bell-shaped" distribution curve. As demonstrated by the current crisis, these normal distribution assumptions result in overly optimistic VaR estimates and they inadequately account for extreme events.

a. Explain what is meant by the above excerpt.

FinAnalytica's Cognity risk management software platform uses fat-tailed, asymmetrical distributions throughout, and incorporates the most advanced statistical methods to model extreme events, volatility clustering, regime switching and correlation shifts in times of market crisis.

b. In the above excerpt, what is meant by "extreme events"?

c. What is meant by "volatility clustering"?

d. Why do you think it is important to model "correlation shifts in times of market crisis"?

Cognity risk analytics provide more accurate fat-tailed VaR estimates that do not suffer from the over-optimism of normal distributions.

e. In the above excerpt, what is meant by "the over-optimism of normal distributions"?

But Cognity goes beyond VaR and also provides the downside Expected Tail Loss (ETL) measure—the average or expected loss beyond VaR. As compared with volatility and VaR, ETL, also known as Conditional Value at Risk (CVaR) and Expected Shortfall (ES), is a highly informative and intuitive measure of extreme downside losses.

f. In the above excerpt, explain what each of the concepts of risk means.

9. Nicholas Taleb, a trader and the author of a body of work attacking risk measures used by financial institutions, wrote an article titled "Ten Principles for a Black Swan–Proof World." One of the principles listed in the article is the following:

Do not let someone making an "incentive" bonus manage a nuclear plant—or your financial risks. Odds are he would cut every corner on safety to show "profits" while claiming to be "conservative." Bonuses do not accommodate the hidden risks of blow-ups. It is the asymmetry of the bonus system that got us here. No incentives without disincentives: capitalism is about rewards and punishments, not just rewards.[23]

a. How does this principle apply to the issue of measuring risks that banks must report to regulators?

22. FinAnalytica, http://www.finanalytica.com/daily-risk-statistics.

23. Nicholas Taleb, "Ten Principles for a Black Swan–Proof World," *Financial Times*, April 7, 2009, FT.com.

b. How does this principle relate to the 2012 trading loss of \$6.2 billion by JPMorgan Chase bank?

10. Suppose that the monthly returns for two investors is as follows:

Month	Investor 1 (%)	Investor 2 (%)
1	9	25
2	13	13
3	22	22
4	−18	−24

a. What is the arithmetic average monthly return for the two investors?

b. What is the geometric average monthly return for the two investors?

c. Why does the arithmetic average monthly return diverge more from the geometric monthly return for investor 2 than for investor 1?

11. The following statements appeared in an article by James Picerno:[24]

It's easier to identify weak points in a given risk metric than to offer solutions. So, fairly or not, the Sharpe ratio's various flaws have been dissected in numerous studies over the years. Its leading drawback is arguably the fact that financial market returns don't follow a normal statistical distribution.

a. In the above excerpt, why is the drawback related to the use of the normal distribution?

Standard deviation can be used to analyze data for any distribution curve, but it's not particularly well suited for profiling the nonnormality of investment returns.

b. Explain why.

Those who assume that returns are normally distributed, then, run the risk of underestimating the potential for big losses, particularly over short periods of time. That's because financial markets exhibit what are known as fat tails.

c. Explain why.

12. Explain each of the measures of reward that can be used in a reward-risk ratio.

13. How does the Sortino ratio overcome the limitations of the Sharpe ratio?

14. If the minimum acceptable return that is established by a client is the risk-free rate of return, is the Sortino ratio equivalent to the Sharpe ratio?

15. Why is it important to understand the tails of an asset return distribution?

16. The problem with the normal distribution is that it does not satisfy the stability property. Explain whether you agree or disagree with this statement.

24. James Picerno, "Building a Better Sharpe Ratio," *Financial Advisor Magazine*, March 30, 2012, http://www.fa-mag.com/news/building-a-better-sharpe-ratio-10199.html.

17. In terms of the four moments of a continuous probability distribution, what is the measure of

a. central value

b. dispersion

c. skewness

d. kurtosis

18 a. If the asset return distribution for a stock has excess kurtosis, are the tails of this distribution more or less than the normal distribution?

b. What is the name of an asset return distribution for a stock that has excess kurtosis?

19. a. What is meant by a stable Paretian distribution?

b. What is meant by the index of stability for a stable Paretian distribution?

20. What are the four stylized facts that have been observed for asset return distributions?

21. What does tail probability mean?

22. Why is conditional value-at-risk a superior risk measure than value-at-risk?

23. In studies of asset return distributions, one often sees information about the Jarque-Bera test, the Anderson-Darling test, and the Kolmogorov-Smirnov test. What is the purpose of these tests?

24. Given the following information:

Realized return = 8.5%

Risk-free rate of return = 3.2%

Standard deviation of realized returns = 5%

Minimum acceptable return = 4.2%

Standard deviation of below the minimum acceptable return = 3%

Calculate the following ratios:

a. Sharpe ratio

b. Sortino ratio

c. Information ratio

13 Portfolio Selection Theory

CONTENTS

Learning Objectives

After reading this chapter, you will understand:

- the concept of portfolio diversification;
- how to calculate the expected return and risk of a single asset and a portfolio of assets;
- portfolio theory's assumptions about how investors make decisions and about return distributions;

- the importance of the correlation between two assets when measuring a portfolio's risk;
- what is meant by a feasible portfolio and a set of feasible portfolios;
- what is meant by the Markowitz efficient set or efficient frontier;
- what is meant by an optimal portfolio, and how an optimal portfolio is selected from all the portfolios available on the Markowitz efficient frontier;
- the criticisms of portfolio theory;
- what behavioral finance is, and how it differs from standard finance theory; and
- the issues associated with the implementation of portfolio theory in practice.

The development of the theoretical relationship between risk and expected return is built on two economic theories, the portfolio selection theory and capital market theory. **Portfolio theory** deals with the selection of portfolios to maximize expected returns consistent with individually acceptable levels of risk. **Capital market theory** deals with the effects of investor decisions on security prices. More specifically, it shows the relationship that should exist between security returns and risk if investors construct portfolios as indicated by portfolio theory.

Together, portfolio theory and capital market theory provide a framework to specify and measure investment risk and to develop an economic equilibrium relationship between risk and expected return (and hence between risk and the required return on an investment). These theories have revolutionized the world of finance by allowing portfolio managers to quantify the investment risk and expected return of a portfolio and by allowing corporate treasurers to quantify the cost of capital and risk of a proposed capital investment.

In this chapter, the focus is on portfolio theory, which covers how, under assumed conditions, investors select the assets to be included in a portfolio. The theory presented is referred to by various names—modern portfolio theory, Markowitz portfolio theory, and mean-variance theory. The theory draws on the concepts described in chapter 12. Prior to the development of the portfolio theory presented in this chapter, investors would often speak of risk and return, but the failure to quantify these important measures made constructing a portfolio of assets highly subjective and provided no insight into the return investors should expect. Moreover, investors would focus on the risks of individual assets without understanding how combining them into a portfolio could affect the portfolio's risk. The theories we present here and in chapter 14 quantify the relationship between risk and expected return. In October 1990, as confirmation of the importance of these theories, the Alfred Nobel Memorial Prize in Economic Science was awarded to Harry Markowitz,[1] the developer of portfolio theory, and to William Sharpe, who is one of the developers of capital market theory.[2]

1. Harry M. Markowitz, "Portfolio Selection," *Journal of Finance* 7, no. 1 (1952): 77–91; and Harry M. Markowitz, *Portfolio Selection*, Cowles Foundation Monograph 16 (New York: John Wiley & Sons, 1959).

2. William F. Sharpe, "Capital Asset Prices," *Journal of Finance* 19, no. 3 (1964): 425–442.

Although these theories are the cornerstone of much of finance, they have been under constant attack. This should not be surprising in the intellectual development of any field. Portfolio theory was formulated in 1952 by Markowitz and is still referred to as "modern" portfolio theory. Today, special issues of journals are devoted to describing the extension of portfolio theory as formulated by Markowitz. These extensions are not a criticism of the intellectual contribution by Markowitz but indicate how to modify the assumptions and deal with issues associated with implementation. Consequently, the chapter begins with portfolio theory as formulated by Markowitz, and the balance of the chapter is devoted to a brief description of the extensions and implementation issues. The topic of portfolio theory goes far beyond what is covered here and is typically reserved for a course in investment management.

The Concept of Portfolio Diversification

Investors often talk about "diversifying" their portfolio. An investor who diversifies is one who constructs a portfolio in such a way as to reduce portfolio risk without sacrificing return. This goal is certainly one that investors should seek. However, the question is how to do it in practice.

Some investors would say that including assets across all asset classes could diversify a portfolio. For example, an investor might argue that a portfolio should be diversified by investing in stocks, bonds, and real estate. Although that might be reasonable, two questions must be addressed to construct a diversified portfolio. First, how much should be invested in each asset class? Should 40% of the portfolio be in stocks, 50% in bonds, and 10% in real estate, or is some other allocation more appropriate? Second, once the allocation is determined, which specific stocks, bonds, and real estate should the investor select?

Some investors who focus only on one asset class, such as common stock, argue that these portfolios should also be diversified. By this they mean that an investor should not place all of his or her investment funds in the stock of one corporation but should invest in the stocks of many corporations. Here, too, several questions must be answered to construct a diversified portfolio. First, which corporations should be represented in the portfolio? Second, how much of the portfolio should be allocated to the stocks of each corporation?

Before the development of portfolio theory as presented in this chapter, although investors often talked about diversification in general terms, they did not have the analytical tools with which to answer the questions posed above.[3] For example, in 1945, Dickson Leavens wrote:

> An examination of some fifty books and articles on investment that have appeared during the last quarter of a century shows that most of them refer to the desirability of diversification. The majority, however, discuss it in general terms and do not clearly indicate why it is desirable.[4]

3. For a detailed discussion of the history of portfolio theory, see Harry M. Markowitz, "The Early History of Portfolio Theory: 1600–1960," *Financial Analysts Journal* 55, no. 4 (1999): 5–16.

4. The excerpts here and below are from Dickson H. Leavens, "Diversification of Investments," *Trusts and Estates* 80 (1945): 469–473.

Making the assumption that risks are independent, he then shows how an investor can benefit from diversification. What is noteworthy is his final paragraph, in which he cautions investors that the assumption that risks are independent for each security is important but in practice is not likely to hold:

> Diversification among companies in one industry cannot protect against unfavorable factors that may affect the whole industry; additional diversification among industries is needed for that purpose. Nor can diversification among industries protect against cyclical factors that may depress all industries at the same time.

Seven years later, Harry Markowitz formulated portfolio theory, which quantified the notion expressed in Leavens's insights using the basic statistical concepts explained in chapter 12.[5] As we will see, the Markowitz diversification strategy discussed in this chapter is primarily concerned with the degree of covariance between asset returns in a portfolio as a measure of portfolio risk, rather than with the risk of each asset in isolation.

Markowitz Portfolio Theory

When constructing a portfolio of assets, investors seek to maximize the expected return from their investment, given some level of risk they are willing to accept. (Alternatively stated, investors seek to minimize the risk they are exposed to given some target expected return.) Portfolios that satisfy this requirement are called **efficient portfolios**. Portfolio theory tells us how to achieve efficient portfolios. Because Markowitz is the developer of portfolio theory, efficient portfolios are sometimes referred to as "Markowitz efficient portfolios."

To construct an efficient portfolio of risky assets, it is necessary to make some assumption about how investors behave when making investment decisions. A reasonable assumption is that investors are **risk averse**. When faced with two investments with the same expected return but two different risks, a risk-averse investor will prefer the one with the lower risk. Given a choice of efficient portfolios from which an investor can select, an **optimal portfolio** is the one most preferred.

To construct an efficient portfolio, an investor needs to be able to estimate the expected return for each asset that is a candidate for inclusion in the portfolio, and not only to specify some measure of risk but also measure that risk for each asset. As explained in chapter 12, there are different quantitative measures of risk. The one selected in Markowitz portfolio theory is the standard deviation (variance).

5. A similar framework for portfolio theory was set forth at the same time Andrew D. Roy, "Safety First and the Holding of Assets," *Econometrica* 20 (1952): 431–449.

Expected Portfolio Return

The expected value of a portfolio's return (or simply, "the expected portfolio return") is the weighted average of the expected value of the return for each asset over the time period. Mathematically,

$$E(R_p) = w_1 E(R_1) + w_2\, E(R_2) + \cdots + w_K\, E(R_K), \tag{13.1}$$

where

$E(R_p)$ = expected portfolio return,

$E(R_k)$ = expected return for asset k ($k = 1, \ldots, K$),

w_k = the weight of asset k in the portfolio (i.e., the market value of asset k as a proportion of the market value of the total portfolio) at the beginning of the period, and

K = number of assets in the portfolio.

In the actual implementation of the theory, the mean return from historical returns, adjusted where necessary by the investor, is used in equation (13.1).

As can be seen from equation (13.1), the calculation of the expected portfolio return is simple once the expected return for each asset is estimated: It is simply a weighted linear combination of the assets making up the portfolio. Measuring the portfolio's risk, however, is not as straightforward.

Measuring Portfolio Risk

The measure of risk used in Markowitz portfolio theory is the variance, and hence the theory is also referred to as "mean-variance" theory. Chapter 12 explained how to calculate an asset's return variance from a sample of historical returns. Moving from the variance of individual assets to the portfolio variance that will be the measure of portfolio risk is not as simple. Let's begin with the simple case of the portfolio variance of a two-asset portfolio (assets 1 and 2), which is

$$\sigma^2(Rp) = w_1^2 \sigma^2(R_1) + w_2^2 \sigma^2(R_2) + 2(w_1)(w_2)\operatorname{cov}(R_1, R_2), \tag{13.2}$$

where

$\sigma^2(Rp)$ = portfolio variance,

$\sigma^2(R_1)$, $\sigma^2(R_2)$ = variance of asset 1 and asset 2, respectively,

w_1, w_2 = portfolio allocation (weight) of assets 1 and 2, respectively, and

$\operatorname{cov}(R_1, R_2)$ = covariance between the return for assets 1 and 2.

As can be seen from equation (13.2), the covariance between the two assets is introduced. As explained in chapter 12, covariance is a measure of the dependence structure or covariability between two random variables. In our application, these variables are the returns for assets 1 and 2.

An alternative to measuring the covariability of two random variables is to determine the correlation. As explained in the previous chapter, the correlation between random variables is the covariance of the two random variables divided by the product of their standard deviations. Applying this formula to the returns for assets 1 and 2, we have:

$$\text{cor}(R_1, R_2) = \text{cov}(R_1, R_2)/[\sigma(R_1)\sigma(R_2)],$$

where $\text{cor}(R_1, R_2)$ is the correlation between the returns of assets 1 and 2. Solving for the covariance, we have:

$$\text{cov}(R_1, R_2) = \sigma(R_1)\sigma(R_2)\ \text{cor}(R_1, R_2). \tag{13.3}$$

Substituting equation (13.3) into equation (13.2) for the covariance, the portfolio variance can be rewritten as

$$\sigma^2(Rp) = w_1^2\sigma^2(R_1) + w_2^2\sigma^2(R_2) + 2(w_1)(w_2)\sigma(R_1)\sigma(R_2)\,\text{cor}(R_1, R_2). \tag{13.4}$$

The General Case

The mathematics for the two-asset case is not complicated. Moving from the two-asset case to the general case in which there are more than two assets gets a little trickier. For example, the three-asset case (i.e., assets 1, 2, and 3) where the portfolio variance is defined in terms of variances and covariances is as follows:

$$\begin{aligned}\sigma^2(R_p) = {} & w_1^2\sigma^2(R_1) + w_2^2\sigma^2(R_2) + w_3^2\sigma^2(R_3) + 2(w_1)(w_2)\,\text{cov}(R_1, R_2) \\ & + 2(w_1)(w_3)\,\text{cov}(R_1, R_3) + 2(w_2)(w_3)\,\text{cov}(R_2, R_3).\end{aligned} \tag{13.5}$$

In general, for a portfolio with K assets, the portfolio variance is given by

$$\sigma^2(R_p) = \sum_{k=1}^{K}\sum_{h=1}^{K} w_k w_h\,\text{cov}(R_k, R_h). \tag{13.6}$$

In equation (13.6), the K variances are the cases in which $k = h$ results, and the covariance between every pair of assets is when $k \neq h$ results.

The Role of Correlation in Determining Portfolio Risk and the Diversification Effect

Let's consider the expected portfolio return and portfolio variance using a simple two-asset portfolio. This allows us to assess the role that the correlation plays in determining portfolio risk. Suppose we have the following information for the two assets, 1 and 2:

Asset	$E(R)$	$\sigma(R)$
1	12%	30%
2	18%	40%

Let's assume that the portfolio has equal weights for both assets (i.e., $w_1 = w_2$). Based on this information, the expected portfolio return from equation (13.1) is

$$E(R_p) = 0.50(12\%) + 0.50(18\%) = 15\%.$$

From equation (13.4), the portfolio variance is

$$\begin{aligned}\sigma^2(R_p) &= (0.5)^2(30\%)^2 + (0.5)^2(40\%)^2 + 2(0.5)(0.5)(30\%)(40\%)\,\text{cor}(R_1, R_2)\\ &= 625 + 600\,\text{cor}(R_1, R_2).\end{aligned}$$

Taking the square root of the above equation, we obtain the standard deviation:

$$\sigma(R_p) = [625 + 600\,\text{cor}(R_1, R_2)]^{0.5}.$$

We can now see how portfolio risk changes for our two-asset portfolio with different correlations between the returns of the two assets. We know that the correlation ranges from −1 to +1. Let's examine the following three cases for $\text{cor}(R_1, R_2) = -1$, 0, and 1. Substituting into the equation above for the correlations for these three cases of $\text{cor}(R_1, R_2)$, we get:

$\text{cor}(R_1, R_2)$	−1	0	+1
$\sigma(R_p)$	5%	25%	35%

As the correlation between the expected returns on assets 1 and 2 increases from −1.0 to 0.0 to 1.0, the standard deviation of the expected portfolio return increases from 5% to 35%. Note that although the portfolio risk changes with the correlation, the expected portfolio return remains 15% for each case.

This example clearly illustrates the effect of Markowitz diversification. The principle of Markowitz diversification states that as the correlation (covariance) decreases between the returns for assets that are combined in a portfolio, so does the variance (hence the standard deviation) of the return for the portfolio. This is the result of the degree of correlation between the asset returns.

As can be seen, investors can construct a portfolio to maintain expected portfolio return but lower portfolio risk by combining assets with lower (and preferably negative) correlations. However, in practice, very few assets have small to negative correlations with other assets. The problem, then, becomes one of searching among large numbers of assets in an effort to identify the portfolio with the minimum portfolio risk for a given level of expected portfolio return, or, equivalently, the highest expected portfolio return for a given level of portfolio risk.

Constructing Portfolios

Constructing a portfolio (i.e., selecting the assets and the amount allocated to each asset), as suggested, results in portfolios that have the highest expected return for a given level of risk. Portfolios that have this attribute are referred to as "efficient portfolios." To construct efficient portfolios, the following assumptions about how investors select assets are made:

- **Mean-variance assumption**: Only the expected value and the variance are used by investors when making asset selection decisions.
- **Risk-aversion assumption**: Investors are risk averse, which means that when faced with a decision about which of two assets to invest in, when both have the same expected return but different risks, investors will prefer the asset with the lower risk.
- **Homogeneous expectations assumption**: All investors have the same expectations regarding expected return, variance, and covariance for all risky assets.
- **One-period horizon assumption**: All investors have a common one-period investment horizon.
- **Optimization assumption**: When constructing portfolios, investors seek to achieve the highest expected return for a given level of risk.

The construction of efficient portfolios given the universe of potential assets requires a massive number of calculations. For a universe of G assets, there are $(G^2 - G)/2$ unique covariances to calculate. Hence, for a portfolio of just 50 assets, 1,224 covariances must be calculated. For 100 securities, 4,950 covariances must be calculated. Moreover, identifying the portfolio that minimizes risk for each level of return requires use of an optimization algorithm, and more specifically, quadratic programming.

Although the algorithm used to solve a quadratic programming problem is covered in a course in management science (operations research), it is unnecessary for appreciating how efficient portfolios are constructed. Instead, we will just consider an example to show the results of the optimization process. To do so, we will use our earlier two-asset portfolio illustration, assets 1 and 2. Recall that for two assets, $E(R_1) = 12\%$, $\sigma(R_1) = 30\%$, $E(R_2) = 18\%$, and $\sigma(R_2) = 40\%$. In the earlier example, we did not make any assumption about the correlation between the two assets. Here, however, we will assume that $\text{cor}(R_1, R_2) = -0.5$. The expected portfolio return and the standard deviation for five different portfolios (A, B, C, D, and E) made up of varying proportions of assets 1 and 2 are shown in table 13.1.

Table 13.1
Portfolio expected returns and standard deviations for five asset allocations for assets 1 and 2.

Portfolio	Weight of Asset 1 (%)	Weight of Asset 2 (%)	$E(R_p)$ (%)	$\sigma(R_p)$ (%)
A	100	0	12.0	30.0
B	75	25	13.5	19.5
C	50	50	15.0	18.0
D	25	75	16.5	27.0
E	0	100	18.0	40.0

Note: $E(R_1) = 12\%$, $\sigma(R_1) = 30\%$, $E(R_2) = 18\%$, $\sigma(R_2) = 40\%$, and $\text{Cor}(R_1, R_2) = -0.5$.

Feasible Portfolios

Any portfolio that an investor can construct given the universe of candidate assets is referred to as a **feasible portfolio**. The five portfolios shown in table 13.1 are all feasible portfolios in which the risk is measured in terms of the portfolio's standard deviation. The collection of all feasible portfolios is called the set of feasible portfolios, or simply the **feasible set**.

In our illustration, where only two assets are candidates for inclusion in a portfolio, it is easy to graphically show the set of feasible portfolios. The feasible set, shown in figure 13.1, is a curve that represents those combinations of portfolio risk and expected portfolio return that are attainable by constructing portfolios from all possible combinations of asset 1 and asset 2. The five portfolios in table 13.1 are identified on the curve representing the feasible set. Beginning with portfolio A and proceeding to portfolio E, the allocation to asset 1 goes from 100% of the portfolio to 0%, and the allocation to asset 2 goes from 0% to 100%—therefore, all possible combinations of asset 1 and asset 2 lie between portfolios A and E (i.e., on the curve labeled AE in figure 13.1). In the case of two assets, any other asset allocation to the two assets not lying on this curve is not attainable, because there is no mix of assets 1 and 2 that can be created. It is for this reason that curve AE is the feasible set.

Figure 13.1 shows the feasible set for the two-asset case. The general case, in which there can be more than two assets, is shown in figure 13.2.[6] For the general asset case, the feasible set is not a curve as shown in figure 13.1 for the two-asset case but instead is an area as shown by the shaded area in figure 13.2. The reason is that unlike in the two-asset case, it is possible to create portfolios that result in combinations for the expected portfolio return and portfolio risk that not only lie on curve I-II-III in figure 13.2 but also in the shaded area.

6. Note that figure 13.2 is for illustrative purposes only. The actual shape of the feasible set will depend on the expected return and standard deviation of returns for the assets chosen and the correlation between all pairs of asset returns.

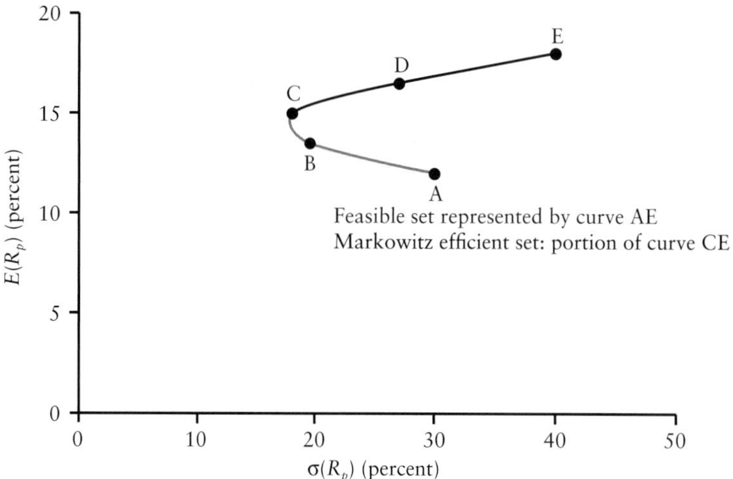

Figure 13.1
Feasible and efficient portfolios for assets 1 and 2.

Efficient Portfolios

An **efficient portfolio** is one that gives the highest expected return for the feasible set of portfolios with the same risk. It is also referred to as a **Markowitz efficient portfolio** and a **mean-variance efficient portfolio**. For each level of portfolio risk, there is an efficient portfolio, and the collection of all efficient portfolios is referred to as the "set of efficient portfolios," or simply the **efficient set** or **Markowitz efficient set**. The efficient set is also referred to as the **efficient frontier**.

Figure 13.1 shows that part of the feasible set for our two-asset case that represents the efficient set. Although the feasible set is shown by the curve AE, the efficient set is the portion of the curve CE, which is part of the feasible set. Portfolios on this portion of the curve offer the highest expected portfolio return for a given level of portfolio risk. Of the five portfolios shown in table 13.1, only three, portfolios C, D, and E, are part of the efficient set. The reason for excluding the remaining two portfolios of the feasible set from the efficient set—portfolio A, with $E(R_p) = 12\%$ and $\sigma(R_p) = 20\%$, and portfolio B, with $E(R_p) = 13.5\%$ and $\sigma(R_p) = 19.5\%$—is because there is at least one portfolio among the efficient set (e.g., portfolio C) that has a higher expected portfolio return and a lower portfolio risk than either portfolio A or portfolio B. Also, portfolio D has a higher expected portfolio return and a lower portfolio risk than portfolio A. In fact, the entire portion of the feasible set represented by curve AC is not efficient, because for any portfolio representing a combination of expected portfolio return and portfolio risk, there is a portfolio among the efficient set that has the same portfolio risk and a higher expected portfolio return, or the same expected portfolio return and a lower portfolio risk, or both. In other words, for any

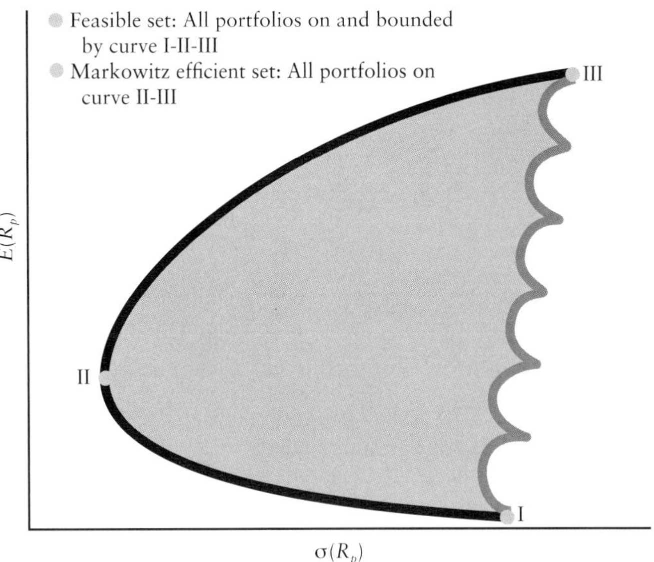

Figure 13.2
Feasible and efficient portfolios with more than two assets.

portfolio among the portion of the feasible set given by curve AC (excluding portfolio C), there exists a portfolio that *dominates* it by having the same expected portfolio return and a lower risk, or the same portfolio risk and a higher expected portfolio return, or a lower portfolio risk as well as a higher expected portfolio return. For example, portfolio D dominates portfolio A, and portfolio C dominates both portfolios A and B.

Again, figure 13.1 represents the special case of only two assets. Figure 13.2 shows the general case. As can be seen, the efficient set is given by curve II-III, because it can be easily observed that all feasible portfolios represented on that portion of the curve dominate the portfolios in the shaded area. Note that any portfolio above the efficient set cannot be constructed, given the expected return and risk for each asset and their correlations.

Selecting the Optimal Portfolio

It makes economic sense that the portfolio that should be selected by an investor is one on the efficient set (i.e., lies somewhere on the efficient frontier). The efficient portfolios represent a trade-off between expected portfolio return and portfolio risk. How does the investor select which portfolio in the efficient set is the best one? Intuitively, it would seem that one key element missing from the framework described thus far is the investor's tolerance for risk. Well, that is precisely what is missing, and for an investor to select the best portfolio given his or her risk tolerance, risk must be introduced. Remember that in the Markowitz mean-variance framework, risk is the portfolio's variance (or standard deviation) of returns.

In the economic "theory of choice," the concept used to represent a trade-off is an investor's utility function. This concept, first developed by John von Neumann and Oskar Morgenstern,[7] comes to prominence when a decision maker is faced with a set of choices. The decision maker in our case is an investor, and the choices are the efficient portfolios contained in the efficient set. So before we discuss how an investor can select a portfolio from the efficient set, let us review the concept of a utility function.

A **utility function** assigns a (numerical) value to all possible choices faced by a decision maker, and the larger the assigned value of a particular choice is, the greater will be the utility derived from that choice. The objective is to maximize the decision maker's utility subject to one or more constraints. In introductory microeconomics, utility functions are used to describe the trade-off between different consumer goods with the object of maximizing utility subject to a budget constraint.[8] It is clear in our application to portfolio theory that the trade-off is between a portfolio's expected value and that portfolio's risk. The constraint imposed is that the allocation of the portfolio's funds must be such that the weights (i.e., the w_i in the above equations) sum to 1.

The efficient portfolios offer different levels of portfolio expected return and portfolio risk such that the greater the portfolio's expected return is, the greater will be the portfolio risk. Investors are faced with the decision of choosing one of the efficient portfolios when the portfolio's expected return is a desirable commodity that increases the level of utility, and risk is an undesirable commodity that decreases the level of utility. Therefore, investors obtain different levels of utility from different combinations of expected portfolio return and portfolio risk. The utility obtained from any possible such combination is expressed by the utility function. Put simply, the utility function expresses the preferences of investors for different combinations of perceived portfolio risk and expected return.

Utility functions can be expressed mathematically. However, that is unnecessary for our purpose, which is to understand conceptually the general idea about how the decision is made by an investor. So instead of mathematically expressing a utility function, we will show it graphically. Figure 13.3 shows three curves, labeled u_1, u_2, and u_3. By convention, the horizontal axis measures portfolio risk, and the vertical axis measures the portfolio expected return. Each curve represents a set of portfolios with different combinations of portfolio risk and expected portfolio return. All points on the same curve identify combinations of portfolio risk and expected portfolio return that, based on the investor's preferences, offer the same level of utility. Because they offer the same level of utility, each curve is referred to as an **indifference curve**. For example, on the indifference curve u_1 in the figure, two points, P_1 and P_2, are shown. The two points represent two portfolios, with the portfolio corresponding to P_1 having a higher portfolio expected return than the portfolio

7. John von Neumann and Oskar Morgenstern, *Theory of Games and Economic Behavior* (Princeton, NJ: Princeton University Press, 1944).

8. In chapter 15, which describes the theory of interest rates, we will see another application of utility functions.

corresponding to P_2 but also having a higher risk. Because the two portfolios lie on the same indifference curve, the investor has an equal preference for (or is indifferent to) the two portfolios—or, for that matter, any portfolio on the curve.

Notice two things about the indifference curves. First, the slope of the indifference curve is positive, and this is so for a rational economic reason: At the same level of utility, the investor requires a higher expected portfolio return in order to accept higher portfolio risk. Second is the positioning of each indifference curve. The utility the investor receives is greater the farther the indifference curve is from the horizontal axis, because that indifference curve represents a higher expected portfolio return at every level of portfolio risk. Thus, for the three indifference curves shown in figure 13.3, u_3 has the highest utility and u_1 the lowest.

Given a choice from the set of efficient portfolios, the **optimal portfolio** is the one that is preferred by the investor, where preference is represented by the investor's utility function. Figure 13.3 demonstrates graphically how this is done. The figure shows three indifference curves representing an investor's utility function. Also shown is the (Markowitz) efficient frontier. From this display, it is possible to determine the optimal portfolio for the investor with the indifference curves shown. Remember that the investor wants to get to the highest indifference curve achievable given the efficient frontier. In light of that requirement, the optimal portfolio is represented by the point where an indifference curve is tangent to the efficient frontier. In figure 13.3, that point is portfolio P^*_{MEF}. For example, suppose that P^*_{MEF} corresponds to portfolio D in figure 13.1. We know from table 13.1 that this portfolio is made up of 25% of asset 1 and 75% of asset 2, with $E(R_p) = 16.5\%$ and $\sigma(R_p) = 27.0\%$.

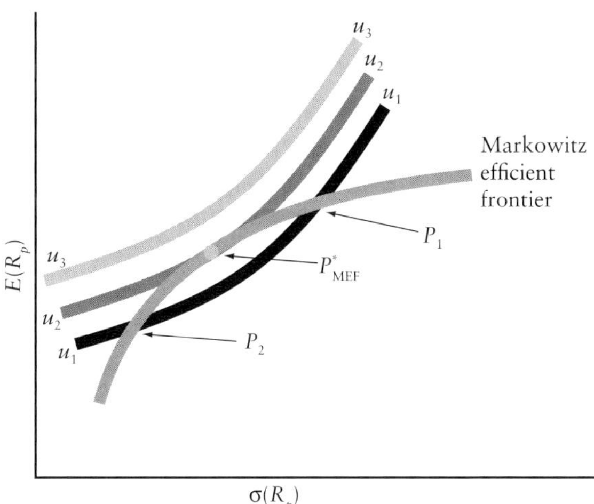

Figure 13.3
Selection of the optimal portfolio.

Consequently, for the investor with preferences with respect to portfolio expected return and portfolio risk as determined by the shape of the indifference curves represented in figure 13.3 and expectations for asset 1 and 2 inputs (expected returns and variance-covariance) represented in table 13.1, portfolio D is the optimal portfolio, because it maximizes the investor's utility. If this investor had a different preference for portfolio expected return and portfolio risk, there would have been a different optimal portfolio. For example, figure 13.4 shows the same efficient frontier but with three indifference curves assumed by a different investor. In this case, the optimal portfolio is P^{**}_{MEF}, which has a lower portfolio expected return and portfolio risk than P^{*}_{MEF} in figure 13.3. Similarly, if the investor had a different set of input expectations, the optimal portfolio would be different.

At this point in our discussion, it is natural to ask: How do we estimate an investor's utility function so that the indifference curves can be determined? Unfortunately, there is little guidance about how to construct a utility function. In general, economists have not successfully estimated utility functions. The inability to estimate utility functions does not mean that the theory is flawed. What it does mean is that once an investor constructs the efficient frontier, the investor will subjectively determine which efficient portfolio is appropriate in relation to his or her tolerance for risk.

Criticisms of Portfolio Theory

As formulated by Markowitz and described in the previous section, portfolio theory is a normative theory. That is, it is a theory that describes a norm of behavior investors should pursue when constructing a portfolio. And if investors do follow that norm of behavior when making portfolio allocation decisions, the portfolio selected should be an efficient

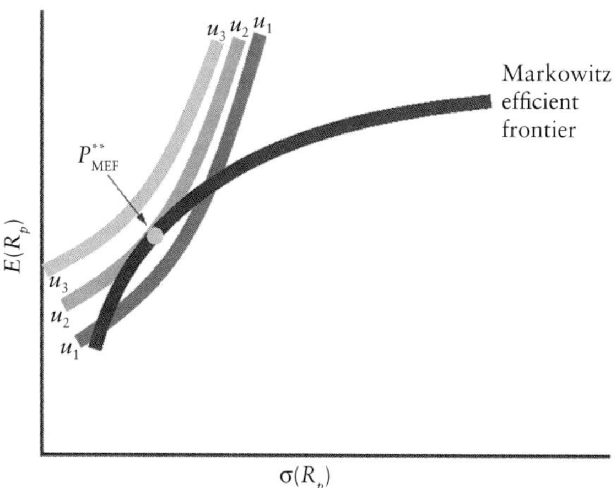

Figure 13.4
Selection of the optimal portfolio with different indifference curves (utility function).

portfolio. So the criticisms of portfolio theory focus on the assumptions on which the theory is built. After we discuss these criticisms, we'll look at the issues associated with implementing modern portfolio theory.

Certain assumptions made in portfolio theory have been identified earlier in the chapter: the mean-variance, risk aversion, homogeneous expectations, one-period horizon, and optimization assumptions. The mean-variance, homogeneous expectations, and one-period horizon assumptions have come under most attack. We discuss these criticisms, and then describe an alternative view of the investment decision-making process known as **behavioral finance**.

The mean-variance assumption states that the appropriate measure of risk considered by an investor is the variance of the distribution of portfolio returns. The limitations on the use of variance as a measure of risk were thoroughly described in chapter 12.

The homogeneous expectations assumption holds that every investor has the same expectations about the inputs: means, variances, and correlations of returns. Insofar as investors typically do not have access to the same data, it is unlikely that this assumption holds. With regard to the one-period assumption, the theory does not specify what that period is.

In addition to theoretical issues, there are practical issues associated with implementing the mean-variance model. Specifically, estimation errors in the forecasts significantly affect the resulting portfolio weights. Studies have shown that estimation errors for the expected returns tend to exert more influence than estimation errors for the variances and covariances.[9] Furthermore, it turns out that errors in the variances are about twice as important as errors in the covariances.[10] Hence, some portfolio managers refer to mean-variance optimization techniques as "error maximizers"[11] that can produce extreme or nonintuitive weights for some assets in the portfolio.

Because of estimation errors, studies have raised concerns as to whether simply weighting each security equally in a portfolio would do as well as a portfolio constructed by applying the Markowitz framework for determining optimal weights. Several studies since the early 1980s have found that naive diversification (i.e., an equally weighted portfolio) often outperforms portfolios created by employing mean-variance analysis.[12]

Behavioral Finance Theory and Investor Decision Making

One of the earliest attacks on the foundations of economic principles that financial economists use when formulating financial theories came in the late 1970s from Daniel Kahneman

9. See, for example, Michael J. Best and Robert T. Grauer, "The Analytics of Sensitivity Analysis for Mean-Variance Portfolio Problems," *International Review of Financial Studies* 4 (1991): 315–342.

10. See, for example, Vijay K. Chopra and William T. Ziemba, "The Effect of Errors in Means, Variances, and Covariances on Optimal Portfolio Choice," *Journal of Portfolio Management* 19 (1993): 6–11.

11. Richard Michaud, *Efficient Asset Allocation: A Practical Guide to Stock Portfolio Optimization and Asset Allocation* (Boston: Harvard Business School Press, 1998).

12. See, for example, Victor DeMiguel, Lorenzo Garlappi, and Raman Uppal, "Optimal versus Naive Diversification: How Inefficient Is the 1/*N* Portfolio Strategy?" *Review of Financial Studies* 22 (2009): 1915–1953.

and Amos Tversky. In numerous experiments, these two psychologists demonstrated that the actions of decision makers are inconsistent with the assumptions made by economists. They then formulated a theory, known as "prospect theory," that attacks expected utility theory.[13]

Other attacks on the assumptions of standard financial theory from the field of psychology led to the specialized field in finance known as behavioral finance. **Behavioral finance** looks at how psychology affects investor decisions and the implications not only for the portfolio theory we describe in this chapter but also for asset pricing theory (explained in chapter 14), option pricing theory (explained in chapter 34), and market efficiency. The foundations of behavioral finance lie in the research of Kahneman, Paul Slovic, and Tversky.[14]

Hersh Shefrin notes the following three themes in the behavioral finance literature:[15]

Behavioral Finance Theme 1: Investors err when making investment decisions, because they rely on rules of thumb.

Behavioral Finance Theme 2: Investors are influenced by form as well as substance when making investment decisions.

Behavioral Finance Theme 3: Prices in the financial market are affected by errors and decision frames.

The first behavioral finance theme involves **heuristics**. This term means a rule-of-thumb strategy or a good guide to follow to shorten the time it takes to make a decision. For example, here are three rules of thumb provided on the *MSN Money* website for increasing the likelihood of success when investing in common stock: (1) ignore guru predictions, (2) avoid cheap stocks, and (3) follow the big players.[16] For retirement planning, a rule of thumb that has been suggested for having enough to retire is to invest 10% of annual pretax income. As for what to invest in to reach that retirement goal (i.e., the allocation among asset classes), a suggested rule of thumb is that the percentage an investor should allocate to bonds should be determined by subtracting the investor's age from 100. So, for example, a 45-year-old individual should invest 55% of his or her retirement funds in bonds.

These are examples of heuristics, and in some circumstances, such rules of thumb or quick guides can work fairly well. However, the psychology literature tells us that heuristics can also lead to systematic biases in decision making, or what psychologists refer to as **cognitive biases**. In the context of finance, these biases lead to errors when making investment decisions. Shefrin refers to these biases as **heuristic-driven biases**.

13. Daniel Kahneman and Amos Tversky, "Prospect Theory: An Analysis of Decision under Risk," *Econometrica* 47, no. 2 (1979): 236–291. See also Daniel Kahneman and Amos Tversky, "Advances in Prospect Theory: Cumulative Representation of Uncertainty," *Journal of Risk and Uncertainty* 5 (1992): 297–323.

14. Daniel Kahneman, Paul Slovic, and Amos Tversky, *Judgment under Uncertainty: Heuristics and Biases* (New York: Cambridge University Press, 1982).

15. Hersh Shefrin, *Beyond Greed and Fear: Understanding Behavioral Finance and the Psychology of Investing* (New York: Oxford University Press, 2002), 4–5.

16. Harry Domash, "10 Rules for Picking Stock Winners," *MSN Money*, September 27, 1997.

Let's recall the assumptions about investor behavior underlying modern portfolio theory, which we referred to earlier. The first assumption, the mean-variance assumption, is that an investor computes the mean and variance of the return of financial assets and constructs an optimal portfolio based on that statistical information. Behavioral finance, however, finds that investors do not make such mean-variance calculations but instead rely on heuristics to guide their portfolio choice.

The second behavioral finance theme involves the concept of framing. The term **framing** as used here refers to the way in which a situation or choice is presented to an investor. Behavioral finance asserts that the framing of investment choices can result in significantly different assessments by an investor as to the risk and return of each choice and therefore the ultimate decision made.[17] Hersh Shefrin and Meir Statman provide an example of faulty framing coupled with a cognitive bias.[18] Individual investors often fail to treat the value of their stock portfolio at market value. Instead, investors have a "mental account," in which they continue to mark the value of each stock in their portfolio at the purchase price despite the change in the market value. The reason they are reluctant to acknowledge any losses on stocks they own is that it keeps alive the hope that those stocks will turn around to realize a gain. When they finally sell their losing stocks, they close the mental account, and only at that time acknowledge a loss that had hitherto occurred only on paper. Hence, investment decisions are affected by this mental accounting rather than being based on the true economic impact that an investment decision would have on the investor. Behavioral finance assumes that such "frame dependence" plays a role in making investment decisions, and hence the second theme of behavioral finance carries that name. In contrast, standard finance theory assumes frame independence. Frame independence means that investors "view all decisions through the transparent, objective lens of risk and return."[19]

Finally, the third theme of behavioral finance shows how errors caused by heuristics and framing dependence affect the pricing of assets. In chapter 18, we discuss the pricing efficiency of markets. According to behavioral finance, asset prices do not reflect their fundamental value because of the way investors make decisions. That is, markets will be price inefficient. Hence, Shefrin labels the third behavioral finance theme "inefficient markets."

Behavioral finance can explain investor behavior that is inconsistent with what mean-variance analysis would suggest. Here is one example. It is estimated that if investors follow the mean-variance framework, they should hold more than 300 stocks. Yet it is reported that the average investor holds only three or four stocks. This puzzle, labeled the

17. See Amos Tversky and Daniel Kahneman, "The Framing of Decisions and the Psychology of Choice," *Science* 211 (1961): 453–458; and Amos Tversky and Daniel Kahneman, "Rational Choice and the Framing of Decisions," *Journal of Business* 59, pt. 2 (October 1986): S251–S278.

18. Hersh Shefrin and Meir Statman, "The Disposition to Sell Winners Too Early and Ride Losers Too Long: Theory and Evidence," *Journal of Finance* 40, no. 3 (1985): 777–790.

19. Shefrin, *Beyond Greed and Fear*, 4.

diversification puzzle, can be explained in the context of behavioral finance. More specifically, the theory of portfolio selection as set forth by behavioral finance theorists, called "behavioral portfolio theory," asserts that investors construct their portfolios as layered pyramids. The objective of the pyramid's bottom layers is to provide downside protection, and the objective of the pyramid's top layers is to provide upside potential. In lieu of traditional risk aversion, in behavioral portfolio theory, the motivation when constructing portfolios is not the attitude of investors toward risk but rather the aspirations of investors. In the context of behavioral portfolio theory, investors place at the top of the pyramid a few stocks of an undiversified portfolio; other investors operationalize aspirations by buying lottery tickets. Either type of behavior on the part of investors—maintaining an undiversified portfolio or buying lottery tickets—can be explained by behavioral portfolio theory, not by mean-variance analysis.

That leaves us with two theories. Who is right, supporters of standard finance theory or supporters of behavioral finance theory? In fairness, we have not provided the responses of the supporters of standard finance theory to the criticisms of those who support behavioral finance. Nor have we presented the attacks on behavioral finance. Fortunately, David Hirshleifer does provide that analysis. He describes the common objections to both approaches. He refers to the standard finance theory as the "fully rational approach" and behavioral finance as the "psychological approach."[20] A criticism of both approaches is that they can go "theory fishing" to find theories in market data to support their position. Objections to the fully rational approach are (1) the calculations needed to implement this approach are extremely difficult to do, and (2) the empirical evidence in the finance literature does not support rational behavior by investors. Objections to the psychological approach, according to Hirshleifer, are (1) alleged psychology biases are arbitrary, and (2) the experiments performed by researchers that find alleged psychological biases are arbitrary.

Key Points

- Portfolio theory, developed by Harry Markowitz, explains how investors should construct efficient portfolios and select the best or optimal portfolio from among all efficient portfolios.
- Markowitz portfolio theory differs from previous approaches to portfolio selection in that Markowitz demonstrated how the key parameters to the portfolio selection problem should be measured.
- Only two statistical moments are used to construct a portfolio, expected return and risk as measured by the variance (or standard deviation) of returns, and hence the technique is referred to as "mean-variance analysis."

20. See table 1 in David Hirshleifer, "Investor Psychology and Asset Pricing," *Journal of Finance* 56, no. 4 (2001): 1533–1597.

- A basic assumption of portfolio theory is that an investor's preferences for portfolios with different expected returns and variances can be represented by a function (the utility function). Another basic assumption is that investors are risk averse.
- The goal of diversifying a portfolio is to reduce a portfolio's risk without sacrificing its expected return.
- The goal of portfolio selection can be cast in terms of not just the expected return and variance of returns but also the correlation (or covariance) between assets.
- A portfolio's expected return is simply a weighted average of the expected return of each asset in the portfolio, with the weight assigned to each asset being equal to the market value of the asset in the portfolio relative to the total market value of the portfolio.
- The risk of an asset is measured by the variance or standard deviation of its return. Unlike the expected return, a portfolio's risk is not a simple weighting of the standard deviation of the individual assets in the portfolio.
- Portfolio risk is affected by the correlation between the assets in the portfolio: the lower the correlation is, the smaller the portfolio risk will be.
- A criticism of the mean-variance framework is that it ignores such moments as skewness and fat tails that have been observed for asset returns in real-world financial markets.
- Proponents of behavioral finance have attacked mean-variance analysis because in their view, investors do not make investment decisions in the manner assumed by portfolio theory.
- In practice, the Markowitz framework has been extended to take into account transaction costs, tax effects when rebalancing a portfolio, constraints, and short selling.
- One of the most serious difficulties encountered when implementing the Markowitz framework (as it would be for any framework requiring estimates) is the impact of forecasts for the individual means, standard deviations, and pairwise correlations on the portfolios generated.

Questions

1. Professor Harry Markowitz, corecipient of the 1990 Nobel Prize in Economics, wrote the following:

> A portfolio with 60 different railway securities, for example, would not be as well diversified as the same size portfolio with some railroad, some public utility, mining, various sorts of manufacturing, etc.[21]

Why is this true?

2. Two portfolio managers are discussing modern portfolio theory. Manager A states that the objective of Markowitz portfolio analysis is to construct a portfolio that maximizes

21. Harry M. Markowitz, "Portfolio Selection," *Journal of Finance* 7, no. 1 (1952): 89.

expected portfolio return for a given level of portfolio risk. Manager B disagrees, believing that the objective is to construct a portfolio that minimizes portfolio risk for a given level of expected portfolio return. Which portfolio manager is correct?

3. What is meant by a "risk-averse investor"?

4. What is meant by a "Markowitz efficient frontier"?

5. Explain why not all feasible portfolios are on the Markowitz efficient frontier.

6. What is meant by an "optimal portfolio," and how is it related to an efficient portfolio?

7. a. How does an investor select an optimal portfolio?

b. Explain the role of an investor's preference when selecting an optimal portfolio.

8. Explain the critical role of the correlation between assets when determining the potential benefits from diversification.

9. "The maximum diversification benefits will be achieved if asset returns are perfectly correlated." Explain why you agree or disagree with this statement.

10. Investment advisers who argue for investing in a portfolio consisting of both stocks and bonds point to the fact that the correlation of returns between these two asset classes is less than 1, and therefore such a portfolio provides the benefits of diversification.

a. What does the correlation of the returns between two asset classes measure?

b. In what sense would a correlation of return of less than 1 between stocks and bonds suggest potential diversification benefits?

11. Suppose we have the following information for two assets, 1 and 2:

Asset	$E(R)$ (%)	$\sigma(R)$ (%)	Weight (%)
1	8	20	60
2	11	28	40

a. What is the portfolio variance and standard deviation if the correlation between the two assets is −1?

b. What is the portfolio variance and standard deviation if the correlation between the two assets is 0?

c. What is the portfolio variance and standard deviation if the correlation between the two assets is 1?

d. Comment on what happens to the portfolio standard deviation as the correlation increases from −1 to 1.

e. What is the portfolio expected return if the correlation between the two assets is −1, 0, or 1?

12. The following excerpt is from Warren Bailey and Rene M. Stulz:

> Recent international diversification literature uses monthly data from foreign stock markets to make the point that American investors should hold foreign stocks to reduce the variance of a portfolio of domestic stocks without reducing its expected return.[22]

a. Why would you expect that the justification of diversifying into foreign stock markets would depend on empirical evidence regarding the ability to "reduce the variance of a portfolio of domestic stocks without reducing its expected return"?

b. Typically in research papers that seek to demonstrate the benefits of international diversification through investing in a foreign stock market, two efficient frontiers are compared. One is an efficient frontier constructed using only domestic stocks, the other is an efficient frontier constructed using both domestic and foreign stocks. If benefits can be realized by diversifying into foreign stocks, should the efficient frontier constructed using both domestic and foreign stocks lie above or below the efficient frontier constructed using only domestic stocks? Explain your answer.

13. The following excerpt is from John E. Hunter and T. Daniel Coggin:

> The extent to which investment risk can be diversified depends upon the degree to which national markets were completely dominated by a single world market factor (i.e., if all cross-national correlations were 1.00), then international diversification would have no benefit. If all national markets were completely independent (that is, if all cross-national correlations were zero), then international diversification over an infinite number of countries would completely eliminate the effect of variation in national markets.[23]

a. Why are the "cross-national correlations" critical in justifying the benefits from international diversification?

b. Why do Hunter and Coggin argue that no benefit results from international diversification if these correlations are all 1.00?

14. Indicate why you agree or disagree with the following statement: "Because it is difficult to determine an investor's utility function, Markowitz portfolio theory cannot be employed in practice to construct a Markowitz efficient portfolio."

15. The following is an excerpt from Marshall E. Blume regarding the Prudent Man Rule:

> According to this rule, a trust manager must invest in each asset on its own merit. If each asset is safe, then the total portfolio will be safe. For example, futures cannot be used under the Prudent Man rule because they are inherently risky—even though investment managers now know that when futures are combined with other assets, they can reduce portfolio risk.
>
> ....

22. Warren Bailey and Rene M. Stulz, "Benefits of International Diversification: The Case of Pacific Basin Stock Markets," *Journal of Portfolio Management* 16, no. 4 (1990): 57–61.

23. John E. Hunter and T. Daniel Coggin, "An Analysis of the Diversification from International Equity Investment," *Journal of Portfolio Management* 17 (1990): 33–36.

Markowitz focused on the portfolio as a whole, not explicitly on the individual assets in the portfolio, which was clearly at odds with the Prudent Man rule for personal trusts. In fact, under the Employee Retirement Income Security Act passed in the mid-1970s, investing in derivatives to reduce the risk of a portfolio was, for the most part, legally imprudent.[24]

Why is the prudent man rule for investing personal trusts in conflict with the way to construct a portfolio as suggested by Markowitz portfolio theory?

16. How does the behavioral finance approach differ from the standard finance theory approach?

17. What is meant by the “diversification puzzle”?

18. What have been the major impediments to applying the mean-variance framework in practice?

24. Marshall E. Blume, “The Capital Asset Pricing Model and the CAPM Literature,” in *The CAPM Controversy: Policy and Strategy Implications for Investment Management*, ed. Diana R. Harrington and Robert A. Korajczyk (Charlottesville, VA: Association for Investment Management and Research, 1993), 5.

14 Asset Pricing Theories

CONTENTS

Learning Objectives

After reading this chapter, you will understand:

- the assumptions underlying capital market theory;
- the capital market line and the role of a risk-free asset in its construction;
- why the capital market line dominates the Markowitz efficient frontier;
- what the security market line is;
- the difference between systematic and unsystematic risk;
- the capital asset pricing model (CAPM), the relevant measure of risk in this model, and the limitations of the model;
- what the market model is;
- the findings of empirical tests of the CAPM and the difficulties of testing this model;
- the arbitrage pricing theory model;
- the different types of factor models used in practice: statistical, macroeconomic, and fundamental; and
- some fundamental principles concerning risk and return that are valid regardless of the asset pricing model used.

In chapter 13, we explained portfolio selection theory. In this chapter, we describe capital market theory and the implications of both that theory and portfolio theory for the pricing of financial assets. Most of this chapter focuses on asset pricing models that are equilibrium models. Given assumptions about the behavior and expectations of investors, and assumptions about capital markets, these models predict the expected return an investor should require. Thus, the models provide an answer to the question of what risk premium an investor should demand. Knowing the expected cash flow and the expected return, one can determine the theoretical value of an asset; therefore, these models are referred to as "asset pricing models."

Economic Assumptions

Economic theories are an abstraction of the real world and as such are based on some simplifying assumptions. These assumptions simplify matters a great deal, and some of them may even seem unrealistic. However, they make economic theories more tractable from a mathematical standpoint. Some of the assumptions discussed in this chapter are precisely those criticized by proponents of behavioral finance. It should be noted that although we call these assumptions "behavioral assumptions," they are the behavioral assumptions made by standard finance, or what we mentioned in the previous chapter as the fully rational approach. They are not the assumptions of those who advocate behavioral finance.

Assumptions about Investor Behavior

When constructing a portfolio of risky assets, capital market theory makes the following assumptions about the behavior of investors.

Behavioral Assumption 1: Capital market theory assumes that investors make investment decisions based on two parameters: the expected return and the variance of returns. Portfolio theory, described in chapter 13, is sometimes referred to as a mean-variance model. This assumption tells us what investors use as inputs when making their investment decisions. Their specific behavior follows from the assumption that to accept greater risk, they must be compensated by the opportunity of realizing a higher return. We refer to such investors as risk averse. This definition is oversimplified. A more rigorous definition of risk aversion is described by a mathematical specification of an investor's utility function. However, this complexity need not concern us here. What is important is that an investor who faces a choice between two portfolios with the same expected return will (it is assumed) select the portfolio with the lower risk.

Behavioral Assumption 2: Capital market theory assumes that the risk-averse investor subscribes to the method of reducing portfolio risk by combining assets with counterbalancing correlations, as explained in chapter 13.

Behavioral Assumption 3: Capital market theory assumes that all investors make investment decisions over some single-period investment horizon. The length of that period (six months, one year, two years, etc.) is not specified. In reality, the investment decision process is more complex, with many investors looking at more than one investment horizon. Nonetheless, the assumption of a one-period investment horizon is necessary to simplify the mathematics of the theory.

Behavioral Assumption 4: Capital market theory assumes that all investors have the same expectations with respect to the inputs that are used to derive the Markowitz efficient portfolios, namely, asset returns, variances, and correlations. This is the homogeneous expectation assumption.

Assumptions about Capital Markets

The four behavioral assumptions listed above deal with the behavior of investors when making investment decisions. It is also necessary to make assumptions about the characteristics of the capital market in which investors transact. The three assumptions in this regard are as follows.

Capital Market Assumption 1: Capital market theory assumes that the capital market is perfectly competitive. In general, the number of buyers and sellers is sufficiently large, and all investors are small enough relative to the market, that no individual investor can influence an asset's price. Consequently, all investors are price takers, and the market price is determined where supply equals demand.

Capital Market Assumption 2: Capital market theory assumes that no transaction costs or impediments interfere with the supply and demand for an asset. Economists refer to these various costs and impediments as "frictions." The costs associated with frictions generally result in buyers paying more than they would in the absence of frictions and sellers receiving less. In the case of financial markets, frictions include commissions charged by brokers and the bid-ask spreads charged by dealers. They also include taxes and government-imposed transfer fees.

Capital Market Assumption 3: Capital market theory assumes that a risk-free asset exists in which investors can invest. Moreover, it assumes that investors can borrow funds at the same interest rate offered on that risk-free asset. That is, it assumes that investors can lend and borrow at some risk-free rate.

Capital Market Theory

According to portfolio theory as formulated by Markowitz, an investor should create a portfolio with the highest expected return for a given level of risk, where risk is measured by the portfolio's variance. In chapter 13, we did not consider the possibility of constructing efficient portfolios in the presence of a risk-free asset, that is, an asset whose return is known with certainty.

In the absence of a risk-free rate, portfolio theory tells us that Markowitz efficient portfolios can be constructed by using expected portfolio return and portfolio variance. Once a risk-free asset is introduced, and assuming that investors can borrow and lend at the risk-free rate (capital market assumption 3), the conclusion of portfolio theory can be qualified as illustrated in figure 14.1. Every combination of the risk-free asset and the Markowitz efficient portfolio M is shown on the tangent line in the figure. This line is drawn from the vertical axis as the risk-free rate tangent to the Markowitz efficient set, also referred to as the "efficient frontier." The point of tangency is denoted by M. All portfolios on the line are feasible for the investor to construct. Portfolios to the left of M represent combinations of risky assets and the risk-free asset. Portfolios to the right of M include purchases of risky assets made with funds borrowed at the risk-free rate.

Now let's compare a portfolio on the line to the portfolio on the Markowitz efficient frontier with the same risk. As an example, we'll compare portfolio $P_{A,}$ which is on the Markowitz efficient frontier, with portfolio $P_{B,}$ which is on the line and therefore has some combination of the risk-free rate and the Markowitz efficient portfolio M. Notice that for the same risk, the expected return is greater for P_B than for P_A. In fact, this dominance is true for all but one portfolio on the line, portfolio M, which is on the Markowitz efficient frontier.

Recognizing this preference, we must modify the conclusion from portfolio theory that an investor will select a portfolio on the Markowitz efficient frontier, depending on the

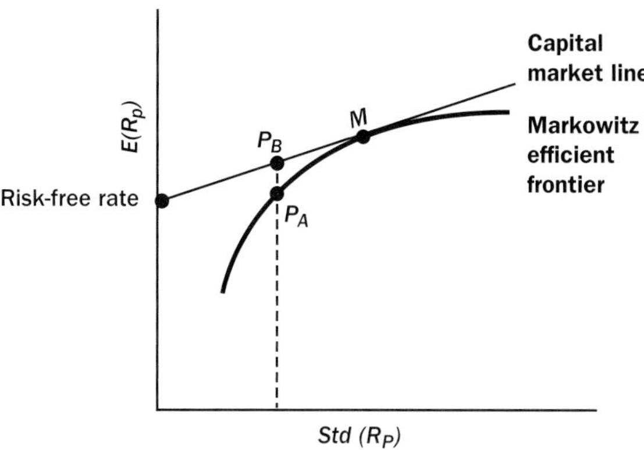

Figure 14.1
The capital market line.
Note: Portfolios to the right of *M* are leveraged portfolios (borrowing at the risk-free rate to buy a market portfolio). Portfolios to the left of *M* are combinations of the risk-free asset and the market portfolio.

investor's level of risk aversion. With the introduction of the risk-free asset, we can now say that an investor will select a portfolio on the line representing a combination of borrowing or lending at the risk-free rate and purchases of the Markowitz efficient portfolio *M*. The particular efficient portfolio that the investor will select on the line depends on the investor's risk preference.

Several studies have demonstrated that the opportunity to borrow or lend at the risk-free rate implies a capital market in which risk-averse investors will prefer to hold portfolios consisting of combinations of the risk-free asset and some portfolio *M* on the Markowitz efficient frontier.[1] Sharpe called the line from the risk-free rate to portfolio *M* on the efficient frontier the **capital market line** (CML), the name adopted by the industry.

One more key question remains: How does an investor construct portfolio *M*? Eugene Fama answered this question by demonstrating that *M* must consist of all assets available to investors, and each asset must be held in proportion to its market value relative to the total market value of all assets.[2] So, for example, if the total market value of some asset is $500 million and the total market value of all assets is $X, then the percentage of the portfolio that should be allocated to that asset is $500 million divided by $X. Because portfolio *M* consists of all assets, it is referred to as the **market portfolio**.

1. William F. Sharpe, "Capital Asset Prices: A Theory of Market Equilibrium under Conditions of Risk," *Journal of Finance* 19, no. 3 (1964): 425–442; John Lintner, "The Valuation of Risk Assets and the Selection of Risky Investments in Stock Portfolio and Capital Budgets," *Review of Economics and Statistics* 47, no. 1 (1965): 3–37; Jack L. Treynor, "Toward a Theory of Market Value of Risky Assets," unpublished paper, Arthur D. Little, Boston, 1961; and Jan Mossin, "Equilibrium in a Capital Asset Market," *Econometrica* 34 (1966): 768–783.

2. Eugene F. Fama, "Efficient Capital Markets: A Review of Theory and Empirical Work," *Journal of Finance* 25, no. 2 (1970): 383–417.

Now we can restate how a risk-averse investor who makes investment decisions as suggested by portfolio theory and who can borrow and lend at the risk-free rate should construct efficient portfolios. This process combines an investment in the risk-free asset with the market portfolio. The theoretical result that all investors will hold a combination of the risk-free asset and the market portfolio is known as the **two-fund separation theorem**,[3] with one fund consisting of the risk-free asset and the other consisting of the market portfolio. Although all investors will select a portfolio on the CML, the optimal portfolio for a specific investor is the one that will maximize that investor's risk preference.

Deriving the Formula for the CML

Figure 14.1 graphically shows us the CML, but we can derive a formula for the CML algebraically as well. This formula will be key to achieving our goal of showing how a risky asset should be priced.

To derive the formula for the CML, we combine the two-fund separation theorem with the assumption of homogeneous expectations (behavioral assumption 4). Suppose an investor creates a two-fund portfolio: a portfolio consisting of w_F invested in the risk-free asset and w_M invested in the market portfolio, where w represents the corresponding percentage (weight) of the portfolio allocated to each asset. Thus,

$$w_F + w_M = 1, \text{ or } w_F = 1 - w_M.$$

What are the expected return and the risk of this portfolio? As we explained in chapter 13, the expected return is equal to the weighted average of the two assets. Therefore, for our two-fund portfolio, the expected portfolio return, $E(R_p)$, is equal to

$$E(R_p) = w_F R_F + w_M E(R_M).$$

Because we know that $w_F = 1 - w_M$, we can rewrite $E(R_p)$ as follows:

$$E(R_p) = (1 - w_M)R_F + w_M E(R_M),$$

which can be simplified to

$$E(R_p) = R_F + w_M [E(R_M) - R_F]. \tag{14.1}$$

Now that we know the expected return of our hypothetical portfolio, we turn to the portfolio's risk as measured by the variance of the portfolio. We know from equation (13.4) how to calculate the variance of a two-asset portfolio. We repeat equation (13.4) here:

$$\sigma^2(R_p) = w_1^2 \sigma^2(R_1) + w_2^2 \sigma^2(R_2) + 2(w_1)(w_2)\sigma(R_1)\sigma(R_2)\,\mathrm{cor}(R_1, R_2),$$

3. James Tobin, "Liquidity Preference as Behavior toward Risks," *Review of Economic Studies* 25, no. 2 (1958): 65–86.

We can use this equation for our two-fund portfolio. Asset 1 in this case is the risk-free asset F, and asset 2 is the market portfolio M. Then,

$$\sigma^2(R_p) = w_F^2\sigma^2(R_F) + w_M^2\sigma^2(R_M) + 2(w_F)(w_M)\sigma(R_M)\sigma(R_F)\,\mathrm{cor}(\mathrm{R}_F, R_M),$$

We know that the variance of the risk-free asset, σ^2 (R_F), is equal to zero, because no possible variation in the return results when the future return is known. The correlation between the risk-free asset and the market portfolio, cor (R_F, R_M), is zero, because the risk-free asset has no variability and therefore does not move at all with the return on the market portfolio, which is a risky asset. Substituting these two values into the formula for the portfolio's variance results in the following:

$$\sigma^2(R_p) = w_M^2\sigma^2(R_M).$$

In other words, the variance of the two-fund portfolio is represented by the weighted variance of the market portfolio. We can solve for the weight of the market portfolio by substituting standard deviations for variances.

Because the standard deviation is the square root of the variance, we can write:

$$\sigma(R_p) = w_M\,\sigma(R_M)$$

and therefore

$$w_M = \sigma(R_p)/\,\sigma(R_M)$$

Now let's return to equation (14.1) and substitute for w_M the result we just derived:

$$E(R_p) = R_F + \frac{\sigma(R_p)}{\sigma(R_M)}[E(R_M) - R_F].$$

Rearranging, we get

$$E(R_p) = R_F + \frac{E(R_M) - R_F}{\sigma(R_M)}\sigma(R_p). \tag{14.2}$$

This equation yields the CML.

Interpreting the CML Equation

Capital market theory assumes that all investors hold the same expectations for the inputs into the model (behavioral assumption 4). With homogeneous expectations, σ (R_M) and σ (R_p) are the market's consensus for the expected return distributions for the market portfolio and portfolio p. The slope of the CML is given by

$$\frac{E(R_M) - R_F}{\sigma(R_M)}.$$

Let's examine the economic meaning of the slope. The numerator is the expected return of the market beyond the risk-free return. It provides a measure of the risk premium, or the reward for holding the risky market portfolio rather than the risk-free asset. The denominator is the risk of the market portfolio. Thus, the slope measures the reward per unit of market risk. Because the CML represents the return offered to compensate for a perceived level of risk, each point on the line is a balanced market condition, or equilibrium. The slope of the line determines the additional return needed to compensate for a unit change in risk. For this reason, the slope of the CML is also referred to as the **market price of risk**.

The CML says that the expected return on a portfolio is equal to the risk-free rate plus a risk premium. As noted in chapter 13, we seek a measure of the risk premium. According to capital market theory, the risk premium is equal to the market price of risk times the quantity of risk for the portfolio (as measured by the standard deviation of the portfolio). That is,

$$E(R_p) = R_F + \text{Market price of risk} \times \text{Amount of portfolio risk.}$$

The Capital Asset Pricing Model

Up to this point, we know how a risk-averse investor who makes decisions based on two parameters, risk and expected return, should construct an efficient portfolio: by using a combination of the market portfolio and the risk-free rate. Based on this result, we can derive a model that shows how a risky asset should be priced. In the process of doing so, we can refine our thinking about the risk associated with an asset. Specifically, we can show that the appropriate risk that investors should be compensated for accepting is not the variance of an asset's return but some other quantity. To illustrate, we need to take a closer look at portfolio risk.

Systematic and Unsystematic Risk

In Markowitz portfolio theory, variance of return is the measure of risk used. This risk measure can be decomposed into two general types of risk: systematic risk and unsystematic risk.

Systematic risk is the portion of an asset's return variability that can be attributed to a common factor. It is also called **undiversifiable risk**. Systematic risk is the minimum level of risk that can be obtained for a portfolio by means of diversification across a large number of randomly chosen assets. Thus, systematic risk results from general market and economic conditions that cannot be diversified away.

The portion of an asset's return variability that can be diversified away is referred to as **unsystematic risk**. It is also sometimes called **diversifiable risk**, **residual risk**, **idiosyncratic risk**, or **company-specific risk**. This is the risk that is unique to a company, such as a strike, an unfavorable outcome of litigation, or a natural catastrophe. Some examples of this type of risk in real life are the product tampering involving Tylenol capsules (manufactured by Johnson & Johnson) in October 1982 and the chemical accident at the Union

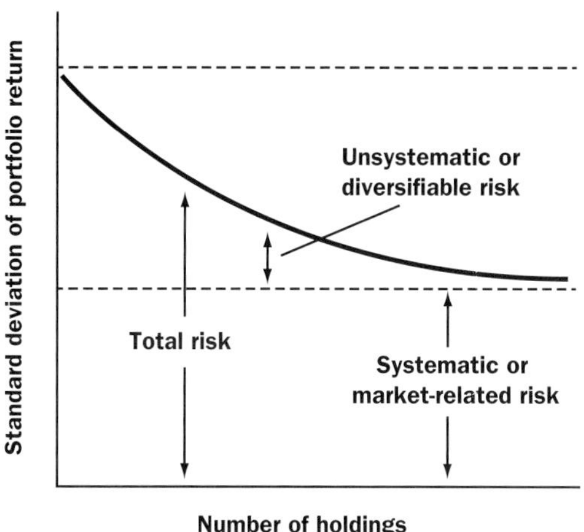

Figure 14.2
Systematic and unsystematic portfolio risk.

Carbide plant in Bhopal, India, in December 1984. Both of these unforeseeable and hence unexpected tragedies negatively affected the stock prices of the two companies involved.

Figure 14.2 depicts how diversification reduces unsystematic risk for portfolios as more securities are added to a portfolio. It shows total portfolio risk declining as the number of holdings increases. Increasing diversification gradually tends to eliminate unsystematic risk, leaving only systematic risk. The remaining variability results from the fact that the return on nearly every security depends to some degree on the overall performance of some common factor, and that common factor is the general market. Consequently, the return on a well-diversified portfolio is highly correlated with the market, and its variability or uncertainty is basically the uncertainty of the market as a whole. For this reason, systematic risk is also referred to as **market risk**. Investors are exposed to market risk no matter how many stocks they hold, which is why systematic risk is referred to as "nondiversifiable risk."

Empirical studies of returns from investing in common stocks support these statements about systematic and unsystematic risk. The major findings of the studies on the impact of diversification on the risk of a portfolio of common stock are as follows:

1. The average return is unrelated to the number of issues in the portfolio, yet the standard deviation of return declines as the number of holdings increases.

2. At a portfolio size of about 20 randomly selected common stocks, the level of total portfolio risk is reduced such that what is left is systematic risk.

3. For individual stocks, the average ratio of systematic risk to total risk is about 30%.

4. On average, approximately 40% of the single-security risk is eliminated by forming randomly selected portfolios of 20 stocks.

5. The return on a diversified portfolio follows the market closely, with the ratio of systematic risk to total risk exceeding 90%.

Quantifying systematic risk Systematic risk can be quantified by dividing security return into two parts: one part perfectly correlated with and proportional to the market return and a second part independent from (uncorrelated with) the market. The first component of return is usually referred to as "systematic return" and the second as "unsystematic return" or "diversifiable return." Thus we have the following:

$$\text{Security return} = \text{Systematic return} + \text{Unsystematic return}. \qquad (14.3)$$

As the systematic return is proportional to the market return, it can be expressed as the symbol beta (β) times the market return, R_M. The proportionality factor beta is a **market sensitivity index**, indicating how sensitive the security return is to changes in the market level. (How to estimate beta for a security or portfolio will be discussed later.) The unsystematic return, which is independent of market returns, is usually represented by the symbol epsilon followed by a prime (ε'). Thus, the security return, R, may be expressed as

$$R = \beta R_M + \varepsilon'. \qquad (14.4)$$

For example, if a security has a beta of 2.0, then a 10% market return will generate a 20% systematic return for the stock. The security return for the period would be the 20% plus the unsystematic component. The unsystematic component depends on factors unique to the company, such as labor difficulties, higher than expected sales, and so on.

The security returns model given by equation (14.4) is usually written in such a way that the average value of the residual term, ε', is zero, by adding a factor, alpha (α), to the model to represent the average value of the unsystematic returns over time. That is, we set $\varepsilon' = \alpha + \varepsilon$ so that[4]

$$R = \alpha + \beta R_M + \varepsilon, \qquad (14.5)$$

where the averages over time should tend to zero.

The model for security returns given by equation (14.5) is usually referred to as the **market model**. Graphically, the model can be depicted as a line fitted to a plot of security returns against rates of return on the market index, as shown for a hypothetical security in figure 14.3.

The beta factor can be thought of as the slope of the line. It gives the expected increase in security return for a 1% increase in market return. In figure 14.2, if a security has a beta of 1.0, a 10% market return will result, *on average*, for a 10% security return.

4. The equation here is the one used in William F. Sharpe, "A Simplified Model for Portfolio Analysis," *Management Science* 9, no. 2 (1963): 277–293. Some vendors and academics use as the variables the excess returns in calculating beta. The excess return is found by subtracting a suitable risk-free rate from the asset's return and from the market's return. This is referred to as the "risk-premium" form of the market model.

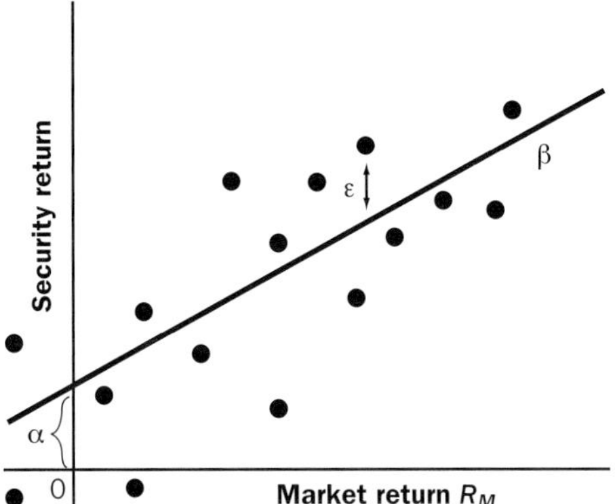

Figure 14.3
Graphical depiction of the market model.
Note: Beta (β), the market sensitivity index, is the slope of the line. Alpha (α), the average of the residual returns, is the intercept of the line on the security axis. The epsilon primes (ε'), the residual returns, are the perpendicular distances of the points from the line.

The alpha factor is represented by the intercept of the line on the vertical (security return) axis. It is equal to the average value over time of the unsystematic returns (ε') on the stock. For most stocks, the alpha factor tends to be small and unstable.

Using the definition of security return given by the market model, the specification of systematic and unsystematic risk is straightforward—they are simply the standard deviations of the two return components.[5]

The systematic risk of a security is equal to beta times the standard deviation of the market return:

$$\text{Systematic risk} = \beta\sigma(R_M). \tag{14.6}$$

The unsystematic risk equals the standard deviation of the residual return factor, ε:

$$\text{Unsystematic risk} = \sigma(\varepsilon). \tag{14.7}$$

Given measures of individual security systematic risk, we can now compute the systematic risk of the portfolio. It is equal to the beta factor for the portfolio, β_p, times the risk of the market index, $\sigma(R_M)$:

$$\text{Portfolio systematic risk} = \beta_p\, \sigma(R_M). \tag{14.8}$$

5. The relationship between the risk components is given by $\sigma^2(R_p) = \beta^2\, \sigma^2(R_M) + \sigma^2\,(\varepsilon')$.
This follows directly from equation (14.5) and the assumption of statistical independence of R_M and ε'. The R^2 term previously discussed is a ratio of systematic to total risk (both measured in terms of variance):

$$R^2 = \frac{\beta^2\sigma^2(R_M)}{\sigma^2(\varepsilon')}$$

The portfolio beta factor in turn can be shown to be simply an average of the individual security betas, weighted by the proportion of each security in the portfolio:

$\beta_p = w_1\beta_1 + w_2\beta_2 + \cdots + w_n\beta_n$,

or more concisely:

$$\beta_p = \sum_{i=1}^{n} w_i\beta_i, \tag{14.9}$$

where

w_i = the proportion of portfolio market value represented by security *i*,

n = the number of securities.

Thus, the systematic risk of a portfolio is simply the market value weighted average of the systematic risk of the individual securities. It follows that the beta for a portfolio consisting of all securities is 1. If a stock's beta exceeds 1, it is above the average. If the portfolio is composed of an equal dollar investment in each security, the β_p is simply an unweighted average of the component security betas.

The unsystematic risk of the portfolio is also a function of the unsystematic security risks, but the form is more complex.[6] The important point is that with increasing diversification, this risk approaches zero.

With these results for portfolio risk, it is useful to return to the studies of the impact of diversification on risk. One study compared the standard deviation for 20-stock portfolios with the predicted lower limits based on average security systematic risks.

The lower limit is equal to the average beta for the portfolio times the standard deviation of the market return. The standard deviations in all cases studied were close to the predicted values. These results support the contention that portfolio systematic risk equals the average systematic risk of the component securities.

The implications of these results are substantial. First, we would expect realized rates of return over long periods to be related to the systematic risk as opposed to the total risk of

6. Assuming the unsystematic returns (ε') of securities to be uncorrelated (reasonably true in practice), the unsystematic portfolio risk is given by

$$\sigma^2(\varepsilon'_p) = \sum^{n} w_i^2\,\sigma^2(\varepsilon'_j),$$

where $\sigma^2(\varepsilon'_i)$ is the unsystematic risk for stock *i*. Assume that the portfolio is made up of an equal percentage invested in each security and that $\sigma^2(\varepsilon')$ is the average value of the $\sigma^2(\varepsilon'_j)$. Then $w_i = 1/n$, and

$$\sigma^2(\varepsilon'_p) = \frac{1}{n}\sigma^2(\varepsilon'),$$

which—assuming $\sigma^2(\varepsilon')$ is finite—obviously approaches zero as the number of issues in the portfolio increases.

securities. As the unsystematic risk is relatively easily eliminated, we should not expect the market to offer investors a "risk premium" for bearing such risk. Second, because security systematic risk is equal to the security beta times $\sigma(R_M)$, which is common to all securities, beta is useful as a *relative* risk measure. The β gives the systematic risk of a security (or portfolio) relative to the risk of the market index. Thus, it is often convenient to speak of systematic risk in relative terms, that is, in terms of beta rather than beta times $\sigma(R_M)$.

Estimating beta The beta of a security or portfolio can be estimated by estimating the market model given by equation (14.5) using regression analysis applied to historical returns. The estimated slope for the market model is the estimate of beta. A series of returns is computed over some time interval for some broad market index (such as the S&P 500 stock market index) and for the stock (or portfolio).[7] For example, monthly returns can be calculated for the past five years, providing 60 return observations for both the market index and the stock or portfolio. Or weekly returns can be calculated for the past year. Nothing in financial theory indicates whether weekly, monthly, or even daily returns should be used. Nor does theory indicate any specific number of observations, except that statistical methodology indicates that more observations give a more reliable measure of beta.[8]

Beta estimates are available on the Internet from Yahoo Finance and Google Finance for individual stocks. Table 14.1 shows the estimates of beta from the Yahoo Finance web site for five stocks as reported on August 3, 2018. Yahoo Finance uses monthly price changes for the company's stock and the monthly change of the S&P 500 index. Three years of returns (36 months) are used (when available).

Our purpose here is not to provide an explanation of the mechanics of calculating beta but to point out the practical problems in estimating beta. (Other econometric issues are involved, but we do not focus on these.) The difference in the calculated beta will depend on the following factors:

- the length of time over which a return is calculated (e.g., daily, weekly, monthly);
- the number of observations used (e.g., three years of monthly returns or five years of monthly returns);
- the specific period used; and
- the market index selected (e.g., the S&P 500 stock market index or an index consisting of all stocks traded on exchanges, weighted by their relative market value).

Moreover, the question arises of the stability of beta over different time intervals. That is, does the beta of a stock or portfolio remain relatively unchanged over time, or does it change? The interesting question concerns the economic determinants of the beta of a

7. We discuss several broad market indexes in chapter 22.

8. This assumes that the economic determinants that affect the beta of a stock do not change over the measurement period.

Table 14.1
Beta estimates for five stocks on August 3, 2018, from Yahoo Finance.

Company (Ticker Symbol)	Yahoo Finance
Apple Inc. (APPL)	1.14
Coca-Cola Co. (KO)	0.53
General Dynamics (GD)	0.85
Netflix Inc (NFLX)	1.39
Fedex Corp (FDX)	1.53

stock. The risk characteristics of a company should be reflected in its beta. Several empirical studies have attempted to identify these macroeconomic and microeconomic factors.

The Security Market Line

The CML represents an equilibrium condition in which the expected return on a *portfolio* of assets is a linear function of the expected return on the market portfolio. A directly analogous relationship holds for *individual security* expected returns:

$$E(R_i) = R_F + \frac{E(R_M) - R_F}{\sigma(R_M)}\sigma(R_i). \tag{14.10}$$

Equation (14.10) simply uses risk and return variables for an individual security in place of the portfolio values in the equation for the CML given by equation (14.2). This version of the risk-return relationship for individual securities is called the **security market line** (SML). As in the case of the CML, the expected return for an asset is equal to the risk-free rate plus the product of the market price of risk and the quantity of risk in the security.

Another more common version of the SML relationship uses the beta of a security. To see how this relationship is developed, let's look back at equation (14.3). In a well-diversified portfolio (i.e., Markowitz diversified), the unique or unsystematic risk is eliminated. Consequently, it can be demonstrated that

$$\sigma^2(R_i) = \beta_i^2\sigma^2(R_M),$$

and the standard deviation is

$$\sigma(R_i) = \beta_i\,\sigma(R_M).$$

Therefore,

$$\beta_i = \frac{\sigma(R_i)}{\sigma(R_M)}.$$

If β_i is substituted into equation (14.10), we have the beta version of the SML, as shown in equation (14.11), popularly referred to as the **capital asset pricing model** (CAPM):[9]

$$E(R_i) = R_F + \beta_i\,[E(R_M) - R_F]. \tag{14.11}$$

This equation states that, given the assumptions of capital market theory described earlier, the expected (or required) return on an individual asset is a positive linear function of its index of systematic risk as measured by beta. The larger beta is, the higher will be the expected return. Notice that it is only an asset's beta that determines its expected return.

Let's look at the prediction of the CAPM for several values of beta. The beta of a risk-free asset is zero, because the variability of the return of a risk-free asset is zero and therefore it does not covary with the market portfolio. So, if we want to know the expected return for a risk-free asset, we would substitute zero for β_1 in equation (14.11):

$$E(R_i) = R_F + 0[E(R_M) - R_F] = R_F.$$

Thus, the return on a risk-free asset is simply the risk-free return, as expected.

The beta of the market portfolio is 1. If asset *i* has the same beta as the market portfolio, then substituting 1 into equation (14.11) gives

$$E(R_i) = R_F + 1[E(R_M) - R_F] = E(R_M).$$

In this case, the expected return for the asset is the same as the expected return for the market portfolio. If an asset has a beta greater than the market portfolio (i.e., greater than 1), then the expected return will be higher than for the market portfolio. The reverse is true if an asset has a beta less than the market portfolio. A graph of the SML is presented in figure 14.4.

The SML, CML, and Market Model

In equilibrium, the expected return of individual securities will lie on the SML and not on the CML because of the high degree of unsystematic risk that remains in individual securities, a

9. The model is sometimes stated in risk premium form. Risk premiums, or excess returns, are obtained by subtracting the risk-free rate from the rate of return. The expected security and market risk premiums—designated $E(r_i)$ and $E(r_M)$, respectively—are given by

$$E(r_i) = E(R_i) - R_F,$$
$$E(r_M) = E(R_M) - R_F.$$

Substituting these risk premiums into equation (14.11), we obtain:

$$E(r_i) = \beta_i[E(r_M)].$$

In this form, the CAPM states that the expected risk premium for the investor's portfolio is equal to its beta value times the expected market risk premium. Or, equivalently stated, the expected risk premium should be equal to the quantity of risk (as measured by beta) and the market price of risk (as measured by the expected market risk premium).

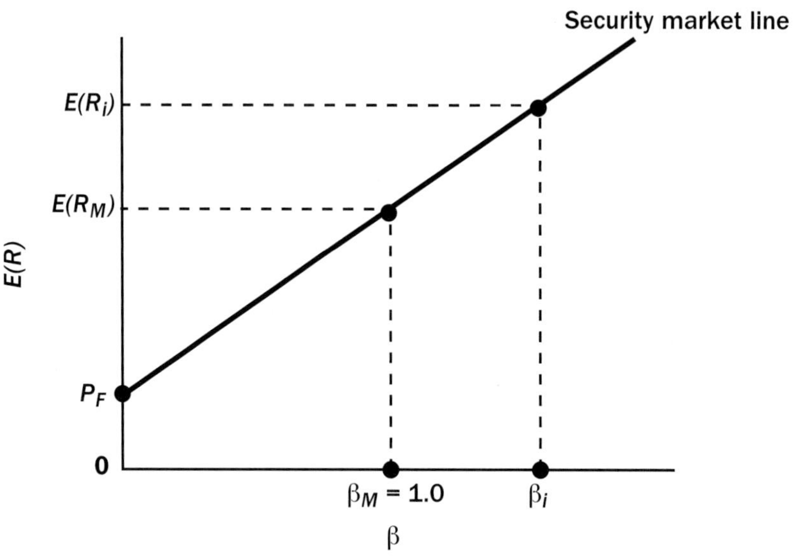

Figure 14.4
The security market line.

risk that can be diversified out of portfolios of securities. It follows that the only risk investors will pay a premium to avoid is market risk. Hence, two assets with the same amount of systematic risk will have the same expected return. In equilibrium, only efficient portfolios will lie on both the CML and the SML, which underscores the fact that the systematic risk measure, beta, is most correctly considered to be an *index* of the contribution of an individual security to the systematic risk of a well-diversified portfolio of securities.

It is important to point out the difference between the market model and the CML and SML. The CML and the SML represent a predictive model for expected returns. The market model is a descriptive model used to describe historical data. Hence, the market model makes no prediction of what expected returns should be.

Tests of the CAPM

The CAPM is indeed a simple and elegant model, but these qualities do not in and of themselves guarantee that it will be useful for explaining observed risk/return patterns. Here we briefly review the empirical literature on attempts to verify the model.

The major difficulty in testing the CAPM is that the model is stated in terms of investors' expectations and not in terms of realized returns. To test the CAPM, it is necessary to convert the theoretical CAPM given by equation (14.11) to a form that can be tested empirically. We will not go through this exercise here but will simply provide the model that is typically tested. Nor will we delve into the econometric problems associated with testing the CAPM, although we discuss later in this chapter an important theoretical issue that raises serious questions about the testability of the CAPM and therefore the empirical findings of researchers.

The empirical analogue of equation (14.11) asserts that over the period of time analyzed, (1) a linear relationship exists between the average risk premium return on the market and the average risk premium return on a stock or portfolio, and its slope is β_i; and (2) the linear relationship should pass through the origin. Moreover, according to the CAPM, beta is a complete measure of a stock's risk. Consequently, alternative risk measures that might be proposed (the most common being the standard deviation of return) should not be significant contributors to the explanation of a stock's return. Recall that the standard deviation measures a stock's total risk, which includes both systematic and unsystematic components.

The CAPM holds for both individual securities and portfolios. Therefore, the empirical tests can be based on either. Tests based on individual securities, however, are not the most efficient method of obtaining estimates of the magnitude of the risk/return trade-off, for two reasons.

The first problem is called the "errors in variables bias" and results from the fact that the beta of a stock typically is measured by correlating the stock's return over some sample of historical data. The slope of the resulting line (the regression coefficient) is the estimate of beta. It is subject to errors from various sources. These errors are random in their effect; that is, some stocks' betas are overestimated and others are underestimated. Nevertheless, when these estimated beta values are used in the test, the measurement errors tend to attenuate the relationship between average return and risk. By carefully grouping the securities into portfolios of securities with similar betas, much of this measurement error problem can be eliminated. The errors in individual stocks' betas cancel out, so that the portfolio beta can be measured with much greater precision. In turn, tests based on portfolio returns will be more efficient than tests based on security returns.

The second problem relates to the obscuring effect of residual variation. Realized security returns include a large random component, which typically accounts for about 70% of the variation of return (the diversifiable or unsystematic risk of the stock). By grouping securities into portfolios, we can eliminate much of this "noise" and thereby get a much clearer view of the relationship between return and systematic risk.

It should be noted that grouping does not distort the underlying risk/return relationship. The relationship that exists for individual securities is exactly the same for portfolios of securities.

The major results of the empirical tests conducted in the early 1970s are summarized as follows:

1. The evidence shows a significant positive relationship between realized returns and systematic risk as measured by beta. The average market risk premium estimated is usually less than predicted by the CAPM, however.

2. The relationship between risk and return appears to be linear. The studies give no evidence of significant curvature in the risk/return relationship.

3. Tests that attempt to discriminate between the effects of systematic and unsystematic risk do not yield definitive results. Both kinds of risk appear to be positively related to

security returns, but substantial evidence supports the proposition that the relationship between return and unsystematic risk is at least partly spurious—that is, partly a reflection of statistical problems rather than the true nature of capital markets.

Obviously, we cannot claim that the CAPM is absolutely right. But the early empirical tests do support the view that beta is a useful risk measure and that high-beta stocks tend to be priced so as to yield correspondingly high rates of return.

In 1977, however, Richard Roll wrote a paper criticizing the previously published tests of the CAPM.[10] Roll argued that although the CAPM is testable in principle, no correct test of the theory had yet been presented. He also argued for the practical impossibility that a correct test would ever be accomplished in the future.

The reasoning behind Roll's assertions revolves around his contribution that only one potentially testable hypothesis is associated with the CAPM, namely, that the true market portfolio lies on the Markowitz efficient frontier (i.e., it is mean-variance efficient). Furthermore, because the true market portfolio must contain all worldwide assets, the value of most of which cannot be observed (e.g., human capital), the hypothesis is in all probability untestable.[11]

Since 1977, some studies have purported either to support or to reject the CAPM. These tests attempt to examine implications of the CAPM other than the linearity of the risk/return relation as the basis of their methodology. Unfortunately, none provides a definitive test, and most are subject to substantial criticism, suffering from the same problem of identifying the "true" market portfolio.

The Arbitrage Pricing Theory Model

An alternative model to the CAPM was developed by Stephen A. Ross in 1976.[12] This model is based purely on arbitrage arguments and hence is called the **arbitrage pricing theory (APT) model**.

The APT model postulates that a security's expected return is influenced by a variety of factors, as opposed to just the single market index of the CAPM. Specifically, look back at equation (14.5), which states that the return on a security is dependent on its market

10. Richard Roll, "A Critique of the Asset Pricing Theory: Part 1. On the Past and Potential Testability of the Theory," *Journal of Financial Economics* 4 (1977): 129–176.

11. The hypothesis tested in the traditional tests of the CAPM cited earlier—namely, that a linear relationship exists between average security returns and beta values—sheds no light on the question. This result follows, because an approximately linear relation between risk and return would be achieved in tests involving large, well-diversified common stock portfolios, irrespective of whether securities were priced according to the CAPM or some totally different model. The result is tautological. The fact that a positive relationship between realized returns and betas is typically found simply indicates that the returns on the proxy indexes used for the true market portfolio are larger than the average return to the global minimum-variance portfolio.

12. Stephen A. Ross, "The Arbitrage Theory of Capital Asset Pricing," *Journal of Economic Theory* 13, no. 3 (1976): 343–360; and Stephen A. Ross, "Return, Risk and Arbitrage," in *Risk and Return in Finance*, ed. Irwin Friend and James Bicksler (Cambridge: Ballinger, 1976).

sensitivity index and an unsystematic return. In contrast, the APT states that the return on a security is linearly related to H "factors." The APT does not specify what these factors are, but it is assumed that the relationship between security returns and the factors is linear.

To illustrate the APT model, let us assume a simple world with a portfolio consisting of three securities with two factors (otherwise, more complicated mathematical notation must be introduced). The following notation is used:

$\tilde{R}_i$ = the random rate of return on security i ($i = 1, 2, 3$),

$E(R_i)$ = the expected return on security i ($i = 1, 2, 3$),

F_h = the hth factor that is common to the returns of all three assets ($h = 1, 2$),

$\beta_{i,h}$ = the sensitivity of the ith security to the hth factor, and

$\tilde{\varepsilon}_i$ = the unsystematic return for security i ($i = 1, 2, 3$).

The APT model asserts that the random rate of return on security i is given by the following relationship:

$$\tilde{R}_i = E(R_i) + \beta_{i,1} F_1 + \beta_{i,2} F_2 + \tilde{\varepsilon}_i. \tag{14.12}$$

For equilibrium to exist among these three assets, the following arbitrage condition must be satisfied: using no additional funds (wealth) and without increasing risk, it should not be possible, on average, to create a portfolio to increase return. In essence, this condition states that no "money machine" is available in the market. Ross showed the following risk and return relationship results for each security i:

$$E(R_1) = R_F + \beta_{i,F1}[E(R_{F1}) - R_F] + \beta_{i,F2}[E(R_{F2}) - R_F], \tag{14.13}$$

where

$\beta_{i,Fj}$ = the sensitivity of security i to the jth factor,

$E(R_{Fj}) - R_F$ = the excess return of the jth systematic factor over the risk-free rate and can be thought of as the price (or risk premium) for the jth systematic risk.

Equation (14.12) can be generalized to the case that includes H factors as follows:

$$E(R_i) = R_F + \beta_{i,F1}[E(R_{F1}) - R_F] + \beta_{i,F2}[E(R_{F2}) - R_F] + \cdots + \beta_{i,FH}[E(R_{FH}) - R_F]. \tag{14.14}$$

Equation (14.14) is the APT model. It states that investors want to be compensated for all the factors that *systematically* affect the return of a security. The compensation is the sum of the products of each factor's systematic risk, $\beta_{i,Fh}$, and the risk premium assigned to it by the market, $E(R_{Fh}) - R_F$. As in the case of the two other risk and return models described earlier, an investor is not compensated for accepting unsystematic risk.

Comparison of the APT Model and CAPM

Examining the equations, we can see that the CAPM, equation (14.11), is a special case of the APT model, equation (14.14):

CAPM: $E(R_i) = R_F + \beta_i[E(R_M) - R_F]$.
APT: $E(R_i) = R_F + \beta_{i,F1}[E(R_{F1}) - R_F] + \beta_{i,F2}[E(R_{F2}) - R_F] + \cdots + \beta_{i,FH}[E(R_{FH}) - R_F]$.

Advantages of the APT Model

Supporters of the APT model argue that it offers several major advantages over the CAPM. First, it makes less restrictive assumptions about investor preferences concerning risk and return. As explained earlier, the CAPM theory assumes that investors trade off risk and return solely on the basis of the expected returns and standard deviations of prospective investments. In contrast, the APT model simply requires some rather unobtrusive bounds be placed on potential investor utility functions.

Second, no assumptions are made about the distribution of security returns. Finally, because the APT model does not rely on the identification of the true market portfolio, the theory is potentially testable.

Factor Models in Practice

Thus far we have presented the APT, which tells us how a security should be priced based on its exposure to various types of risk. In practice, three types of factor models are used to evaluate common stock: statistical factor models, macroeconomic factor models, and fundamental factor models.[13]

Statistical Factor Models

As just discussed, identifying the factors presents certain difficulties. In a **statistical factor model**, historical and cross-sectional data on stock returns are tossed into a statistical model. The statistical model used is principal components analysis, which is a special case of a statistical technique called "factor analysis." The goal of the statistical model is to best explain the observed stock returns with "factors" that are linear return combinations and are uncorrelated with one another.

For example, suppose that the monthly returns for 1,500 companies for 10 years are computed. The goal of principal components analysis is to produce factors that best explain the observed stock returns. Let's suppose that six factors provide explanations. These factors

13. Gregory Connor, "The Three Types of Factor Models: A Comparison of Their Explanatory Power," *Financial Analysts Journal* 51, no. 3 (1995): 42–57.

are statistical artifacts. The objective in a statistical factor model then becomes to determine the economic meaning of each of these statistically derived factors.

Because of the problem of interpretation, it is difficult to use the factors from a statistical factor model to obtain expected returns. Instead, practitioners prefer two other models, which allow them to prespecify meaningful factors and thus produce a more intuitive model.

Macroeconomic Factor Models

In a **macroeconomic factor model**, the inputs to the model are historical stock returns and observable macroeconomic variables called "raw descriptors." The goal is to determine which macroeconomic variables are pervasive in explaining historical stock returns. Those variables that are pervasive in explaining the returns are then the factors included in the model. The responsiveness of a stock to these factors is estimated using historical time series data. The sensitivity of the factors is estimated so that they are statistically independent. Then there will be no double counting.

An example of a macroeconomic factor model for the U.S. equity market is the Burmeister, Ibbotson, Roll, and Ross model.[14] This model has five macroeconomic factors that reflect unanticipated changes in the following macroeconomic variables: investor confidence (confidence risk), interest rates (time horizon risk), inflation (inflation risk), real business activity (business cycle risk), and market index (market timing risk).

Fundamental Factor Models

Probably the most popular models are fundamental factor models, which use company and industry attributes and market data as raw descriptors. Examples of the descriptors used include price/earnings ratios, book/price ratios, estimated economic growth, and trading activity. The inputs into a fundamental factor model are stock returns and the potential raw descriptors about a company. Those fundamental variables about a company that are pervasive in explaining stock returns and make economic sense are then the factors retained in the model. The sensitivity of a stock's return to a factor is estimated using statistical analysis.

There are several third-party vendors who have created fundamental factor models. In a series of academic papers, Eugene Fama and Kenneth French have shown that the following five factors should be included in a factor model. In their original paper, they showed that a three-factor model that included the market (as measured by beta and as suggested by the CAPM), size (as measured by market capitalization), and value (as measured by the book-to-value ratio) explained the returns on stocks better than the CAPM did.[15] That is,

14. Edwin Burmeister, Roger Ibbotson, Richard Roll, and Stephen A. Ross, "Using Macroeconomic Factors to Control Portfolio Risk," unpublished paper.

15. Eugene Fama and Kenneth French, "Common Risk Factors in the Returns on Stocks and Bonds," *Journal of Financial Economics* 33 (1993): 3–56.

they added two factors to the CAPM. More recently, they showed that by including two additional factors—measures of profitability and investment—their five-factor model outperformed their three-factor model in explaining returns.[16] Several asset management firms have suggested additional factors.[17]

Some Principles to Take Away

In this chapter and the previous one, we have covered the heart of what is popularly called "modern portfolio theory" and APT. We pointed out the assumptions and their critical role in the development of these theories and explained the empirical findings. Even though you should now understand the topics covered, you might still be uncomfortable as to where we have progressed, given the lack of theoretical and empirical support for the CAPM and the difficulty of identifying the factors in the APT model. You are not alone: A good number of practitioners and academics feel uncomfortable with these models, particularly with the CAPM.

Nevertheless, comfort comes from several general principles about risk and return derived from these theories that few would question:

1. Investing has two dimensions, risk and return. Therefore, focusing only on the actual return that an investor achieves without looking at the risk that was accepted to achieve that return is inappropriate.
2. It is also inappropriate to look at the risk of an individual asset when deciding whether it should be included in a portfolio. What is important is how the inclusion of an asset in a portfolio will affect the risk of the portfolio.
3. Whether investors consider one risk or 1,000 of them, risk can be divided into two general categories: systematic risk (which cannot be eliminated by diversification) and unsystematic risk (which can be diversified away).
4. Investors should only be compensated for accepting systematic risks. Thus, when formulating an investment strategy, it is critical to identify the systematic risks.

Key Points

- Capital market theory is based on a set of behavioral assumptions and market assumptions.
- If investors select portfolios as assumed by portfolio theory, and if a risk-free asset is introduced, a new set of efficient portfolios can be constructed that represents a combination of a risk-free asset and the market portfolio.

16. Eugene Fama and Kenneth French, "A Five-Factor Asset Pricing Model," *Journal of Financial Economics* 116 (2015): 1–22.

17. See, for example, Andrea Frazzini and Lars Pedersen, "Betting against Beta," *Journal of Financial Economics* 111 (2014): 1–25.

- The risk of an asset's return as measured by its variance can be broken down into systematic risk and unsystematic risk.
- The portion of an asset's return variability that can be attributed to a common factor is its systematic risk.
- Because systematic risk cannot be diversified away, it is referred to as "undiversifiable risk," and in the case where this is one source of risk, it is called "market risk."
- Because a portfolio's systematic risk cannot be eliminated, it is the minimum level of risk that can be obtained by means of diversification across many randomly chosen assets.
- Unsystematic risk is the portion of an asset's return variability that can be diversified away and is referred to as "diversifiable risk." Other names for unsystematic risk are residual risk, idiosyncratic risk, and company-specific risk.
- The beta of an asset is a measure of sensitivity to the market and therefore is a relative measure of systematic risk.
- An asset's beta is estimated using regression analysis on data obtained from historical returns for the asset and some market index.
- The capital asset pricing model (CAPM) is an economic theory that describes the relationship between risk and expected return. Equivalently, it is a model for the pricing of risky securities.
- The CAPM asserts that the only risk priced by rational investors is systematic risk, because that risk cannot be eliminated by diversification.
- Essentially, the CAPM says that the expected return of a security or a portfolio is equal to the rate on a risk-free security plus a risk premium.
- The risk premium in the CAPM is the product of the quantity of risk times the market price of risk.
- The beta of a security or portfolio is an index of the systematic risk of the asset and is estimated statistically.
- Beta is calculated from historical data on both the asset's return and the market's return.
- Numerous empirical tests of the CAPM, in general, fail to fully support the theory.
- Richard Roll criticized studies of the CAPM because of the difficulty of identifying the true market portfolio and argued that such tests are not likely to appear soon, if at all.
- The CAPM assumes that investors are concerned with only one source of risk: the risk having to do with the future price of a security. However, other risks include the capacity of investors to consume goods and services in the future.
- The arbitrage pricing theory (APT), developed purely from arbitrage arguments, postulates that the expected return on a security or a portfolio is influenced by several factors.
- Proponents of the APT model cite its less restrictive assumptions as a feature that makes it more appealing than the CAPM.

- Testing the APT model does not require identification of the "true" market portfolio. But it does require empirical determination of the factors, because they are not specified by the theory.
- The APT model replaces the problem of identifying the market portfolio in the CAPM with the problem of choosing and measuring the underlying factors.
- One of the most popular factor models is the Fama-French five-factor model.
- Although the theories presented are controversial or difficult to implement in practice, several principles are not controversial and can be used to understand how to price financial assets.

Questions

1. a. Explain why the CML assumes a risk-free asset and that investors can borrow or lend at the risk-free rate.

b. Using a graph, demonstrate why the CML dominates the Markowitz efficient frontier.

2. How should an investor construct an efficient portfolio in the presence of a risk-free asset?

3. a. What is meant by two-fund separation?

b. What do the two funds consist of?

4. Indicate why you agree or disagree with the following statement: "As a percentage of the total risk, the unsystematic risk of a diversified portfolio is greater than that of an individual asset."

5. In the CAPM, why is systematic risk also called "market risk"?

6. Indicate why you agree or disagree with the following statement: "An investor should be compensated for accepting unsystematic risk."

7. a. Suppose that a stock has a beta of 1.15. How do you interpret that value?

b. Suppose that a stock has a beta of 1.00. Can one mimic the performance of the stock market by buying shares in only that stock?

8. a. What is the market model?

b. What input into the CAPM is estimated from the market model?

9. Assume the following: expected market return = 15%, risk-free rate = 7%. If a security's beta is 1.3, what is its expected return according to the CAPM?

10. The following is an excerpt from the article "Risk and Reward," published in the *Economist* of October 20, 1990:

> Is the CAPM supported by the facts? That is controversial, to put it mildly. It is a tribute to Mr Sharpe (co-winner of the 1990 Nobel Prize in Economics) that his work, which dates from the early 1960s, is still argued over so heatedly. Attention has lately turned away from beta to more complicated ways of carving up risk. But the significance of CAPM for financial economics would be hard to exaggerate.

a. What are the general conclusions of studies that empirically investigated the CAPM?

b. Summarize Roll's argument on the problems inherent in empirically verifying the CAPM.

11. What are the fundamental principles underlying the APT model?

12. What are the advantages of the APT model relative to the CAPM?

13. What are the difficulties in practice of applying the APT model?

14. Does Richard Roll's criticism of the CAPM also apply to the APT model?

15. "In the CAPM, investors should be compensated for accepting systematic risk; in the APT model, investors are rewarded for accepting both systematic risk and unsystematic risk." Explain why you agree or disagree with this statement.

16. What are the difficulties of using a statistical factor model?

17. How does a macroeconomic factor model differ from a fundamental factor model?

18. Indicate why you agree or disagree with the following statement: "There is considerable controversy concerning the theories about how assets are priced. Therefore, the distinction between systematic risks and unsystematic risk is meaningless."

19. Indicate why you agree or disagree with the following statement: "The theories of the pricing of capital assets are highly questionable. Basically, there is only one type of risk, and investors should seek to avoid it when they purchase individual securities."

20. Explain the Fama-French factor model.

III INTEREST RATES, INTEREST RATE RISK, AND CREDIT RISK

15 The Theory of Interest Rates

CONTENTS

Learning Objectives

After reading this chapter, you will understand:

- Fisher's classical approach to explaining the level of the interest rate;
- the role of individual preference when choosing current and future consumption in the determination of interest rates;
- the role of the loan market in the determination of interest rates;
- the role of production opportunities in the determination of interest rates;
- how the market equilibrium interest rate is determined;
- what is meant by Pareto optimality;
- the meaning of equilibrium, and how changes in the demand and supply function affect the equilibrium level of the interest rate;
- the loanable funds theory, which is an expansion of Fisher's theory;
- the meaning of liquidity preference in Keynes's theory of the determination of interest rates;
- Böhm-Bawerk's positive theory of capital;
- the factors that determine the real rate of interest in an economy;
- what is meant by the real rate of interest and the nominal rate of interest;
- the relationship between the real rate of interest and the nominal rate of interest and inflation (Fisher's law);
- the basic feature of Treasury Inflation Protection Securities;
- how the expected rate of inflation can be estimated using U.S. Treasury securities;
- what the natural rate of interest is;
- the controversy involving the existence of a safe asset;
- why a safe asset is needed in an economy;
- the economic reason that a negative interest rate can exist in an economy;
- what is meant by a quantitative easing monetary policy and a negative interest rate policy; and
- the historical interest rate levels in the United States.

An **interest rate** is the percentage of the amount loaned that the borrower agrees to pay the lender in a loan agreement each year. For example, suppose that a bank agrees to loan a consumer $20,000 for four years and the lending arrangement calls for an interest rate of 5% per year and repayment of the loan amount ($20,000) at the end of the four years. Then each year, the consumer pays interest to the bank of 5% times the $20,000, or $1,000, per year. Basically, an interest rate is the cost of borrowing money from a lender and the compensation to the lender for loaning money. This concept of an interest rate is not new to modern economies. Interest rates have a long history. Here is a sample of estimated interest rates over the past 5,000 years: 20% in Mesopotamia (around 3000 BC), Babylon (1772 BC), and Italian cities (about AD 1150); about 8% in Rome in 443 BC, Athens and Rome ca. 300–200 BC, Holland in the 1570s, and the United States in the 1870s. Since 2008 (the beginning of the global financial crisis), interest rates around the world have been at historically low levels. In fact, in some countries, interest rates have been negative! That is, the borrower is charging the lender for holding money.

In this chapter, we describe a theory of interest rates that offers an explanation of what determines the level of interest rates. In doing so, we focus on the one interest rate that can be said to provide the anchor for other rates—the short-term, riskless, real rate. By **real rate**, we mean the rate that would prevail in the economy if price levels remained constant and were expected to be constant indefinitely. We then look at three important issues. The first is what is meant by a riskless interest rate. Is there a financial instrument that provides a positive interest rate without any risk? Second, we look at negative interest rates and discuss whether there is a lower bound on that rate. Finally, we look at alternative interest rates measures that can be used as the benchmark interest rate in the economy. In chapter 16, we describe the structure of interest rates. There is no single interest rate for all loan arrangements in an economy. The interest rate offered on a particular loan depends on a myriad of factors related to the type of borrower (the issuer in the case of a bond), the characteristics of the loan arrangement, and the state of the economy.

Fisher's Theory of Interest Rates

To understand what determines the basic rate, we must inquire why some people might decide not to consume all their current resources (i.e., to save) and why others want to invest. Those desirous of borrowing might want to use the proceeds either to make further loans (i.e., acquire financial assets) or to invest (i.e., acquire income-yielding physical assets, such as a plant, equipment, or residential structures). In our discussion, we abstract from financial intermediaries and assume that all loans directly or indirectly end up being transferred to an investor.

Economists have developed theories of interest rates. The major theories were formulated in the books written by two economists: an Austrian economist, Eugen Böhm von Bawerk, in 1884,[1] and an American economist, Irving Fisher, in 1930.[2] We'll start with the theory of interest rates as set forth by Fisher and then explain Böhm-Bawerk's theory.[3]

1. Actually, Böhm-Bawerk's writings on the theory of interest rates appear in two books. His 1884 book, *Geschichte und Kritik der Kapitalzins-Theorieen*, translated by William Smart as *Capital and Interest* (North Charleston, SC: Createspace, 1989) described the various practical and theoretical opinions about interest rates. The book laid the foundation for his book (translated by William Smart in 1989), *The Positive Theory of Capital* (North Charleston, SC: Createspace, 1989). The 1989 translated book is available at https://mises.org/system/tdf/The%20Positive%20Theory%20of%20Capital.pdf?file=1&type=document.

2. Irving Fisher, *The Theory of Interest Rates* (New York: Macmillan, 1930).

3. The two theories are described in Paul A. Samuelson, "Two Classics: Böhm-Bawerk's Positive Theory and Fisher's Rate of Interest through Modern Prisms," *Journal of the History of Economic Thought* 16, no. 2 (1994): 202–228.

To begin, let's define what is meant by "saving." Saving reflects primarily the choice between current consumption and future consumption. To understand that choice (and all consumer choices), we need to consider two fundamental concepts: preference and opportunity.

Preferences for Current versus Future Consumption

Consider first the representation of preferences. Suppose that our consumer is to choose among a variety of "baskets" (or "bundles"), where each basket consists of a certain quantity of current consumption and a certain quantity of future consumption.

Preferences (or tastes) can then be described fully by a complete preference ranking of all the relevant baskets. Insofar as the amount of current and future consumption can vary by any small dose, some choices among the possible baskets will be ranked equally; that is, the consumer will be indifferent as to certain choices among baskets.

This consideration makes it possible to obtain an effective representation of preference, as shown in figure 15.1. The figure measures current consumption (C_1) along the horizontal axis and future consumption (C_2) along the vertical axis. Hence, any point in the diagram represents a commodity basket, such as H. Some other point, H^*, represents an indifferent choice to H; more generally, a curve from H to H^* and beyond consists of baskets indifferent to both H and H^*. Such a curve is called an **indifference curve**. The indifference curve in figure 15.1 is labeled u.

Note that an indifference curve goes through every point in the diagram, although the indifference curves cannot intersect, because that would imply that a given basket is ranked both higher and lower than another—a clear inconsistency. The indifference curve u here falls from left to right, because both consumption now and consumption later can be taken

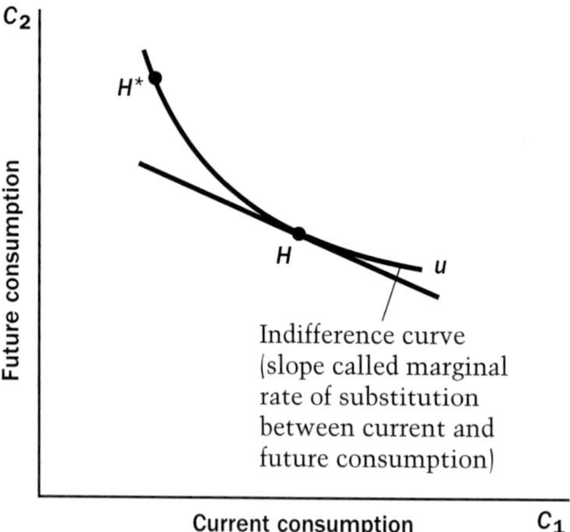

Figure 15.1
Indifference curve between current and future consumption.

to be desirable. As basket H in figure 15.1 includes more current consumption than basket H^*, for it to be indifferent from basket H^*, basket H must have less future consumption, C_2.

The reason the curve is drawn convex with respect to the origin is the assumption that, as the consumer gives up successive equal amounts of current consumption, more future consumption will be needed to make up for the loss of an additional unit. This assumption appears reasonable, although a complete justification of it is beyond the scope of this chapter

At any point on an indifference curve, we can draw a tangent to the curve. Fisher refers to the slope of this tangent as the **marginal rate of time preference**. It measures how much additional consumption next period is needed to compensate the consumer for the loss of a unit of consumption now. That is, the slope of the tangent measures the marginal rate of substitution between current and future consumption.

We might conjecture that a particular person would be impatient to consume now rather than later, and therefore it would take more than one unit tomorrow to induce that person to give up the enjoyment of one unit today. In other words, the marginal rate of time preference, or the slope of the indifference curve, would be larger than 1. For this reason, Fisher proposed labeling the excess of the slope over unity a "measure of impatience."

It turns out, however, that this conjecture about the slope is wrong. It is easy to verify that the slope of the indifference curve changes as we move along it, and therefore that it is most unlikely to be everywhere greater than unity. On the left side of the diagram, where today's endowment is small, the slope can be counted on to be larger than unity. However, as we move to the right, and the current endowment grows larger relative to the future one, the slope must become smaller than 1, meaning that the consumer may be willing to give up a unit of today's abundant supply for less than one unit to add to tomorrow's scarce supply. This insight is important for understanding why interest rates can in principle be negative.

Opportunity in the Loan Market

To understand saving behavior, we need to look at how preferences interact with opportunities. Let's first consider a case in which the opportunities (or baskets among which a person can choose) are defined by (1) an initial endowment of the commodity now and later and (2) a loan market where individuals are free to exchange this initial or current endowment for a different one by lending or borrowing at a fixed exchange rate of $R = 1 + r$ units of the commodity in the next period (i.e., the future in our illustration) per unit of the commodity loaned in the current period. R is the gross return (principal plus interest), and r is the net return, or interest rate. For example, if a unit of current consumption is loaned at 5%, then $r = 0.05$ and $R = 1.05$.

We represent this opportunity locus in figure 15.2 by means of the negatively sloped straight line mm going through the endowment basket at point B (with current endowment as Y_1 and future endowment as Y_2). We refer to the opportunity locus in the loan market as the "market line." It slopes downward, because to get more C_1, you must reduce C_2. It is

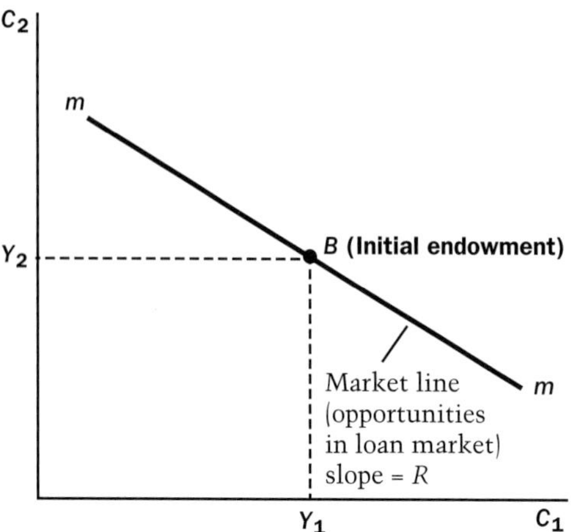

Figure 15.2
Representation of opportunity locus in the loan market (the market line).

a straight line, because at any point on it, by giving up one unit of current consumption, we can get the same additional amount, *R*, of future consumption. And it goes through *B*, because if no lending made current consumption equal to the current endowment of Y_1, then future consumption would equal the future endowment of Y_2. Thus, the opportunity locus must include point *B*.

Now let us add to the diagram a family of indifference curves, as shown in figure 15.3. One curve in the diagram is tangent to the market line, such as curve u_4 at point *D*. The consumption basket corresponding to point *D* can be shown to be the preferred one among all those available, given the market line; hence it will be the chosen basket.

Following this logic, suppose the consumer started by considering point *H* on indifference curve u_2, where current consumption is greater than at *D*. Suppose next he considered giving up some current consumption in favor of more future consumption along his market opportunity line. He would first reach point *F* and would find it a preferable choice, being on a higher indifference curve, u_3. Continuing, he would reach point *D* on u_4, offering yet higher utility. But beyond *D*, he would immediately start reaching lower and lower utility curves, such as curves u_2 and u_3. We see that the point of tangency of the market line to an indifference curve provides the best of all feasible choices.

Recalling that the slope of an indifference curve at any point measures the marginal rate of substitution between current and future consumption, we see that at the chosen point, the marginal rate of substitution is equal to the market rate *R* (or the marginal rate of impatience, equal to *r*). It is an important property of a perfect market that, because everybody is confronted with the same market rate *r*, everybody at the chosen point must exhibit the same degree of impatience. In particular, if *r* is positive (as it generally is in our type of

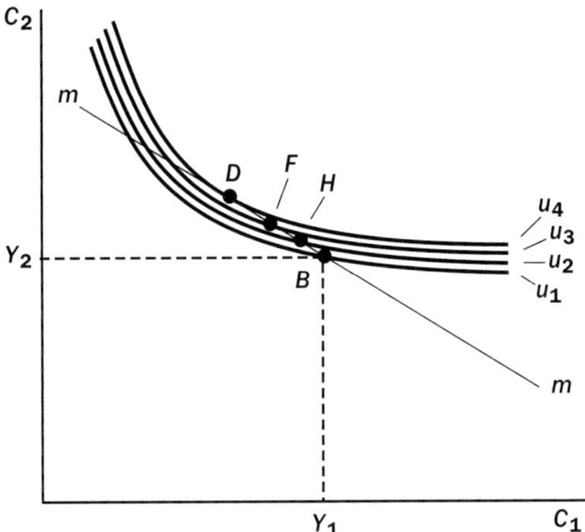

Figure 15.3
Family of indifference curves and the market line.

economy), everybody will be impatient; that is, everybody will be willing to give up a unit of current consumption to lend more only if they can get $1+r$ units later, with $r>0$, because that opportunity is offered by the market.

Economic Forces Affecting the Market Rate

So far, we have assumed that the market rate r is a given. But what in fact determines r in this simple economy? The answer, of course, is demand and supply. For any given market rate, R, each person will decide how much to consume now and how much to save or dissave (the difference between the current endowment and consumption). In this simple economy, saving or dissaving is the same as lending or borrowing. By summing up the net lending of each participant, for each R, we obtain a supply curve for loans, such as the one graphed in figure 15.4. We draw it as initially rising from left to right, on the commonly held assumption that net lending will rise as R rises. For sufficiently low R, net lending is negative, because borrowing would exceed lending. We'll suppose zero investment at the outset. Then market equilibrium requires that net lending be zero. It therefore occurs at point E, where the curve cuts the horizontal axis. (Note that we draw the net lending curve as declining in the rightmost section. We discuss the reason for this behavior later.)

The market rate R reflects two major forces: the time preferences of participants and their endowments. More impatience tends to make for a smaller supply of loans (saving) at any given R and to lower the supply curve in figure 15.4, thereby shifting E to the right. A large endowment of the current commodity relative to the future makes people more eager

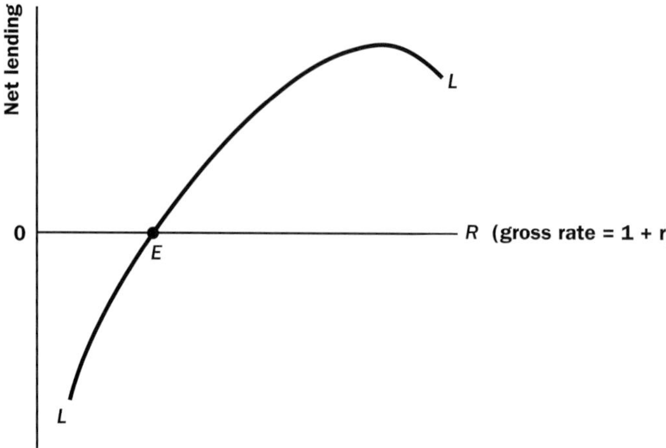

Figure 15.4
Supply curve for loans.

to lend, raises the curve, and thus reduces R. If the curve is raised sufficiently, E may be pushed to the left until it is less than unity, and therefore r will become negative. This point may seem paradoxical, but it is important to understand that no opportunity of transferring resources to the future through investment (or money, which is disregarded) exists outside of lending and borrowing.

Carryover through Investment

We now enlarge the model to allow for the possibility of investments—a productive process through which, by using current resources as an input, we obtain an output of future commodities. An investment opportunity locus might look something like the curve *tt* in figure 15.5, which is referred to as the **transformation curve** or the **production function**. It rises from left to right on the assumption that as more is invested, more future output will result. It is convex from below on the customary assumption of decreasing returns to scale (although increasing returns are possible in some regions without changing the argument). The slope of the transformation curve measures the **marginal productivity of capital**.

Consumer Choices

The consumer faces several decisions regarding (1) how much to invest, (2) how much to lend (or borrow), and (3) how much to consume now and later. But only two of these choices are independent: Because current resources are given, once a person has decided how much to consume and invest, net lending will be determined uniquely by income minus

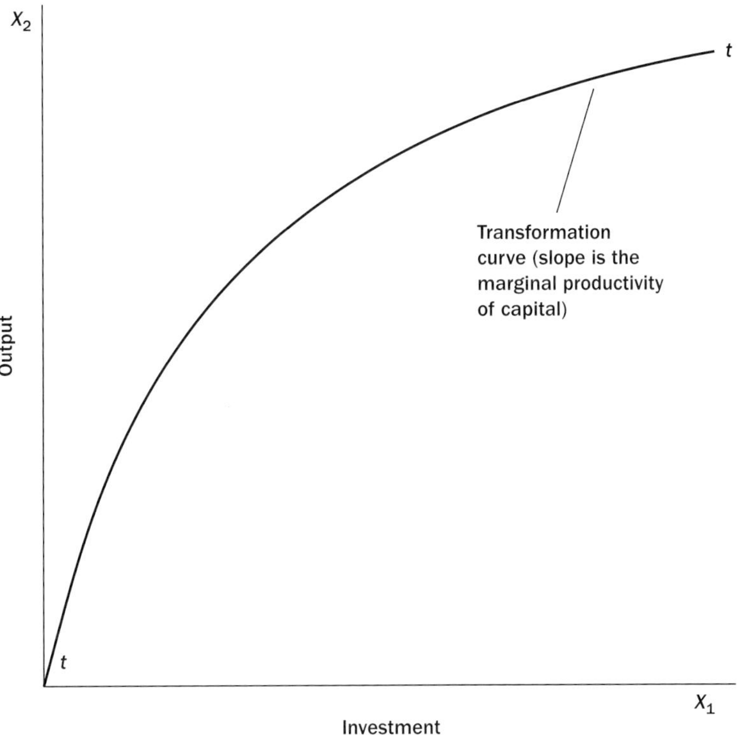

Figure 15.5
Opportunity locus from investment (transformation curve or production function).

the two other expenditures. Similarly, net borrowing and investment, together with the future endowment, uniquely fix future consumption.

Let's consider first the decision as to how much to invest. As the consumer's "income" (or what she has available to spend on consumption now and later) is limited by the sum of her endowment and any profits she may derive from her production opportunity, a necessary condition to achieve the best feasible consumption is to ensure for herself as large a profit as possible. To see how this result can be achieved, look again at figure 15.5. Recall that profit at any output (or input) is the difference between the output produced with the input (or investment) and the cost of the input. The output for any investment is given by the curve *tt* in figure 15.5.

What about the cost? Let us suppose initially that the owner of a firm must borrow the entire amount needed to finance the investment. In that case, clearly the cost of any given investment will be what is to be repaid next period, namely, the amount borrowed times the gross market rate R. This cost can be represented in figure 15.6 by a straight line with slope R going through the origin, and as shown in figure 15.6 by the line *MM*. Thus, the profit for

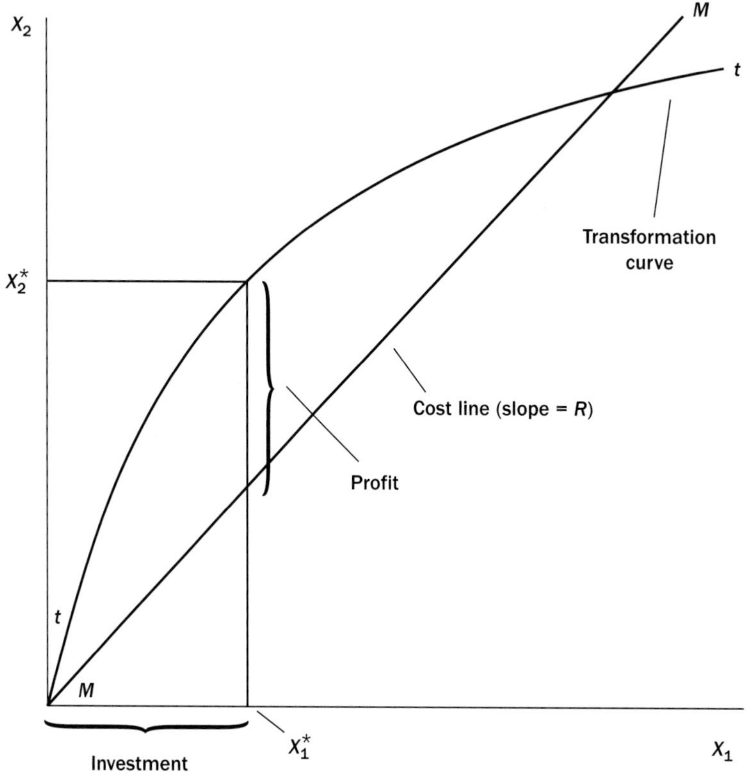

Figure 15.6
Measuring the profit from investing.

any output is the difference between the curve *tt* and the line *MM*, which is illustrated in figure 15.6 for an assumed investment of X_1^*. We refer to the line *MM* in the figure as the "cost line." Because it represents the cost of borrowing, however, it has the same slope (in absolute value) as the market line in figure 15.2.

As the consumer increases investment from an investment of zero (at the origin), we can see from the graph that profits initially rise (provided there are profits at all). The additional profit attributable to increased investment gets smaller and smaller, though, until it reaches a point in the figure of no more incremental profit. This point is shown as point *A* in figure 15.7. If the consumer continues to expand investment still further, the profit (as measured by the vertical distance between the cost line *MM* and the transformation curve *tt*) becomes smaller and smaller. Point *A*'s one distinguishing characteristic is that it is where the curve *tt* has precisely the same slope *R* as the cost curve *MM*, as shown in figure 15.8. We draw through *A* a line *mm* with the same slope as *R* (and hence parallel to *MM*). This line is tangent to *tt* at *A*.

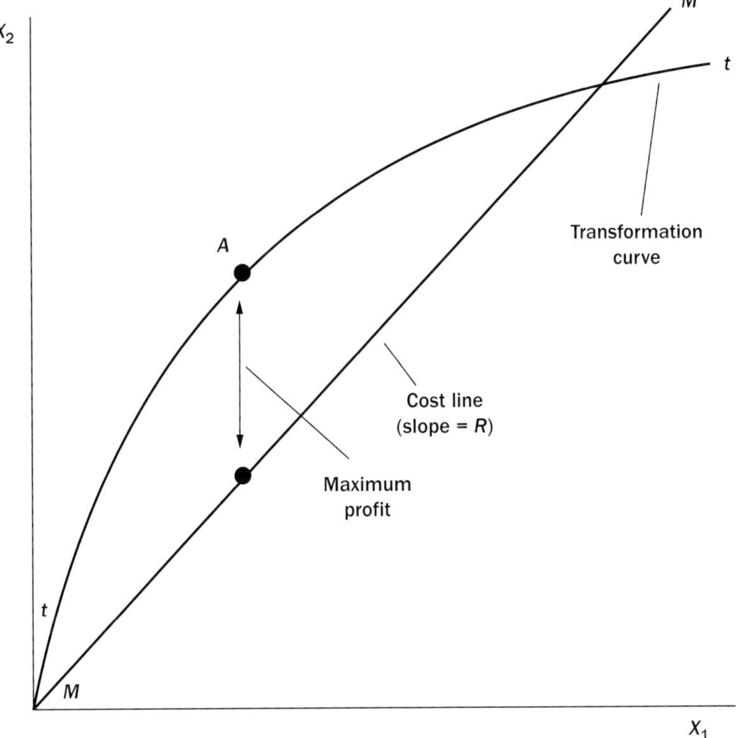

Figure 15.7
Profit maximization point.

Because the slope of *tt* represents the marginal productivity of capital, we can conclude that the optimum rate of investment for the firm is where the marginal productivity of capital *M* equals the market gross rate *R* or, equivalently, where the additional output that can be obtained from an additional unit of input is just equal to the cost of borrowing that additional unit of input (and the amount obtained by further increases in investment is less than the cost of borrowing).

We can now proceed to examine the consumption decision and its interaction with the investment decision. To this end, we first show in figure 15.9 how the transformation curve, curve *tt* in figure 15.5, would be represented if graphed on the earlier figures 15.1 through 15.3. We obtain the transformation curve (production function), curve *tt*, in figure 15.9 by rotating the curve *tt* in figure 15.5 by 180 degrees and shifting the origin to point *B*, which represents the initial endowment as in figure 15.2. The resulting curve is the locus of all achievable baskets of current and future commodity available to the person through a combination of the initial endowment and the transformation opportunity.

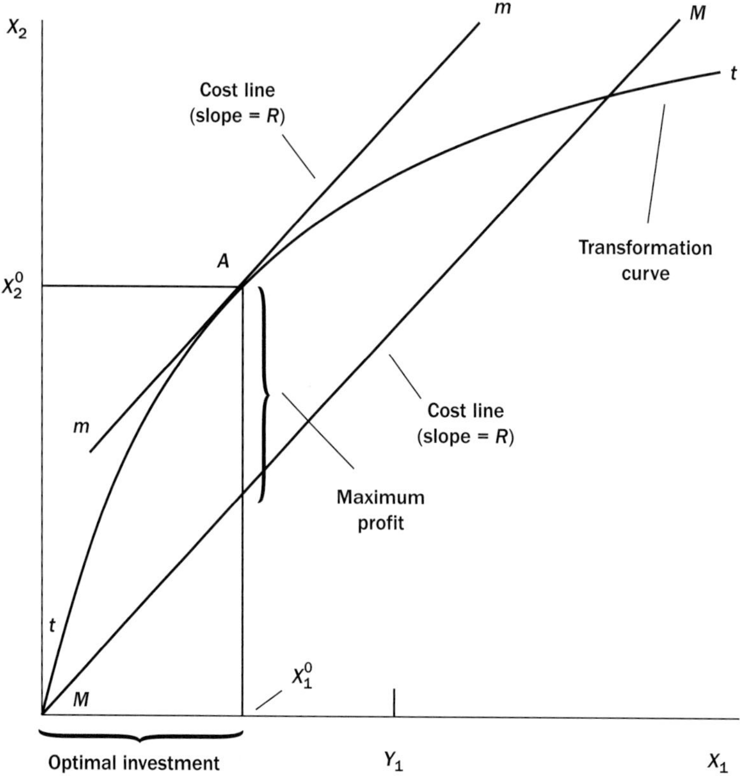

Figure 15.8
Profit maximization and the cost line.

The amount invested is shown in figure 15.9 along the horizontal axis by the difference between the current endowment Y_1 and the point on the horizontal axis corresponding to any point on the transformation curve, which is illustrated in figure 15.10. At point W, the corresponding value on the horizontal axis is I^W, and the amount of the investment is the difference between Y_1 and I^W. Future consumption corresponding to the point W on the transformation curve is C_2^W, which consists of the future endowment Y_2 plus the profit from the investment as measured by the difference between C_2^W and Y_2.

Suppose for a moment that no market permitted an exchange of C_1 with C_2. Then the curve tt in figure 15.10 would represent the household opportunity locus. The person's best choice, the basket (C_1, C_2), would then be found at a point of tangency of that curve with an indifference curve. But in a market economy, the budget constraint does not come from the initial endowment B in figure 15.2, or from the initial endowment enlarged by the transformation function, as in figure 15.9, but instead from the endowment plus the profit that can be earned through the production and sale of C_2. It follows that to maximize

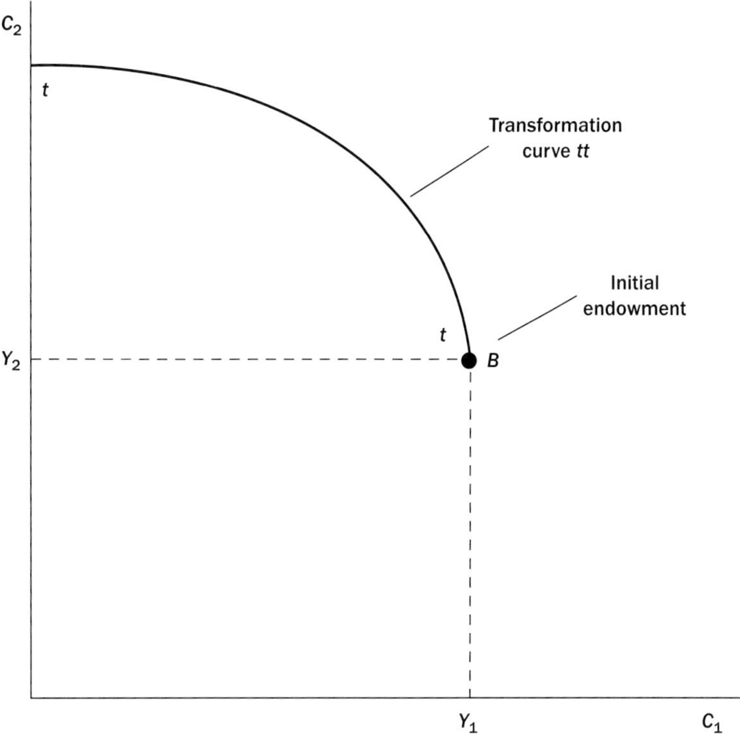

Figure 15.9
Transformation curve imposed on current and future consumption graph.

satisfaction, the individual's should, to begin with, maximize the profits obtained from the transformation activity. This maximization will yield a new budget equation that includes the best choice of basket (C_1, C_2).

This optimal decision is shown graphically in figure 15.11. Point A on the transformation function curve tt is such that the slope is equal to the slope of the market line mm. We know that this point (which corresponds to point A in figure 15.8) represents the amount of investment ($Y_1 - X_1^0$) and output (X_2^0) that will maximize profits. Through point A, a new budget line mm (again tangent to tt at A) represents the outcome of adding maximum profits to the endowment in figure 15.11. The utility-maximizing basket will then be at a point of tangency of this profit-augmented budget line to an indifference curve, such as point C^0.

A most important property resulting from the existence of a perfect loan market, together with a transformation, is that it separates the current consumption decision from current income by opening up the possibility of saving and dissaving through transformation and net lending. Similarly, it frees the investment from the saving decision, as the person can bridge the gap between saving and investment through lending and borrowing. In the specific case graphed in

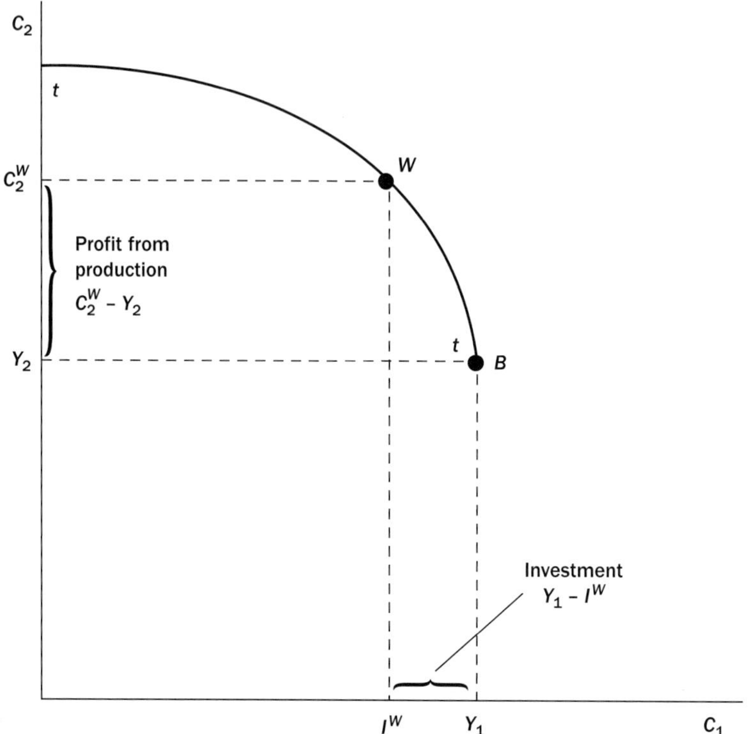

Figure 15.10
Measuring investment and profit from investment.

figure 15.11, we find that the chosen consumption C_1^0 is less than the initial endowment Y_1, so the person saves an amount shown in the figure. But that amount is not sufficient to finance an optimal investment equal to the distance between Y_1 and I_A of the chosen production. Hence the difference $(C_1^0 - I_A)$ is made up by borrowing, as indicated in the figure.

Figure 15.11 illustrates how a rational person can both save and borrow. Many other combinations can work out by varying the position of the chosen points A and C^0 relative to each other and to the endowment basket B as well. For example, if A falls between C^0 and B, the person ends up saving more than she needs for her investment, and thus she will save, invest, and lend. However, if C^0 falls to the right of B, the person will dissave, but she can invest at the same time by borrowing the sum of her investment and dissaving.

Incidentally, it should be apparent by now that we can drop our initial assumption that the investment is financed entirely by borrowing, because, if it were financed by the owner's own saving, the cost to the investor of the funds would still be R per unit, which is the amount of interest that would have to be forgone to shift funds from making loans in the market to financing the investment (the opportunity cost).

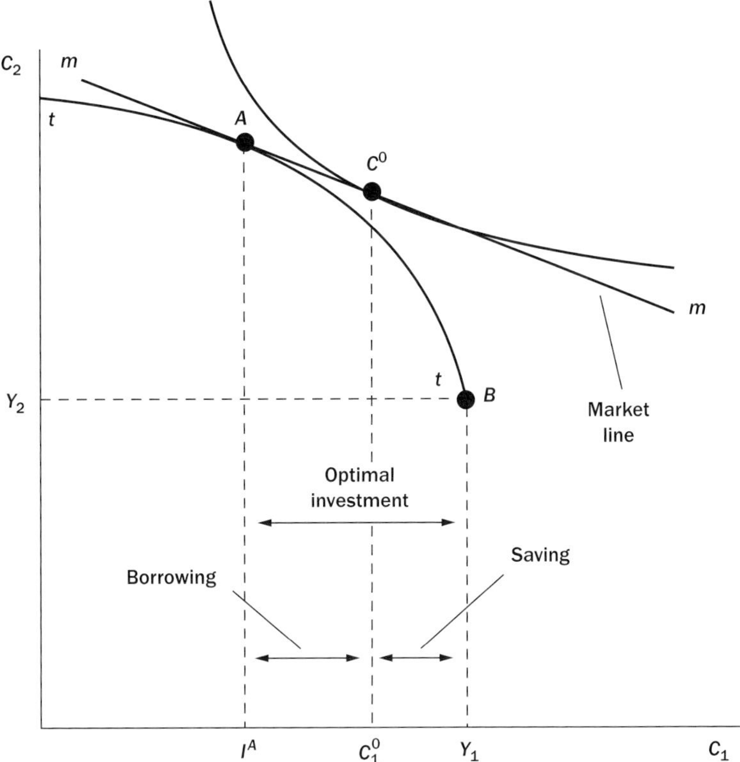

Figure 15.11
Optimal investment and borrowing decisions.

Market Equilibrium

So far, we have discussed how a person responds in terms of saving, investing, and borrowing to a given market R. But what determines R itself? The answer once again is demand and supply; that is, the price must be such as to clear the market. The situation we described needs to clear two markets. The first market for loans R must be such that gross lending equals gross borrowing, or, equivalently, that net borrowing is zero. The second market is the market for the current commodity. The two sources of demand for it are consumption and investment, and R must be such that aggregate consumption (C) plus aggregate investment (I) equals the given endowment (Y). Thus, $C+I=Y$, or, equivalently, $I=Y-C=S$.

Consequently, R must be such that the demand for investment equals the economy's net saving, denoted by S. But how can R clear two markets at the same time? One variable cannot satisfy two equations at the same time, *unless* one is redundant in the sense that the two provide identical solutions. Indeed, it happens that the two market-clearing conditions here are

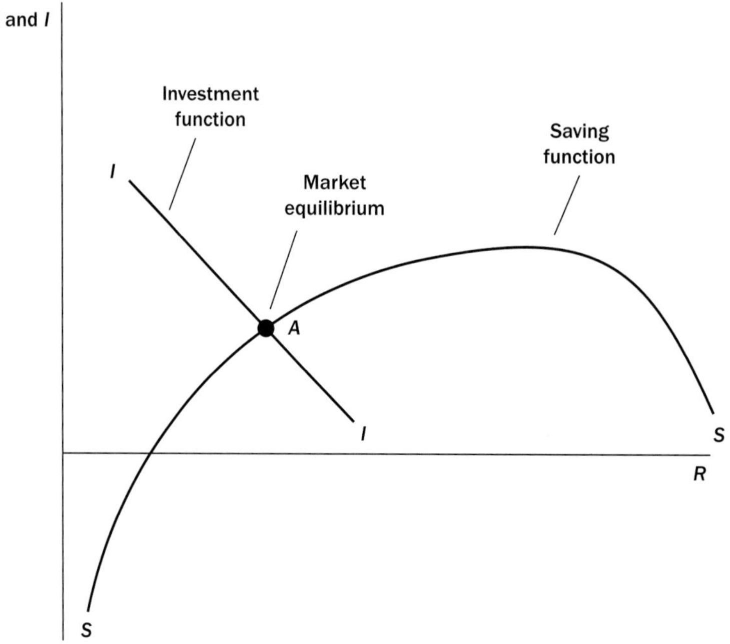

Figure 15.12
Market equilibrium.

redundant. To see why, recall that the decisions of each individual must satisfy a "budget constraint"; that is, a person's net lending must equal the excess of her saving over her investment. If we sum up this constraint over the entire market, we get $L=S-I$, where L is net lending.

It is apparent from this equation that if an interest rate clears the commodity market by making $S=I$, then that same rate makes $L=0$, or clears the loan market. Thus, we can conclude that the equilibrium R must equate the supply of saving and the demand for investment, or, equivalently, the demand for and supply of loanable funds. If we want to graph the mechanism determining R, it will be more enlightening to use the commodity market (i.e., saving equals investment).

Equilibrium in this market is represented graphically in figure 15.12, where the rising curve plots the supply of saving, analogous to LL in figure 15.4. The investment function is drawn to decline uniformly with R. The justification for this choice can be found in figure 15.8. We have shown that the investment chosen is at the point where the transformation curve has slope R. If R rises to R_1, then the investment must shift to a point where the slope is R_1; and because R_1 is larger than R, the transformation curve at R_1 must be steeper. But because of the convexity of the transformation curve, it can occur only if investment is to the left of the initial level, that is, smaller. The market-clearing interest rate is then at the intersection of the saving and investment functions, where the two are equal.

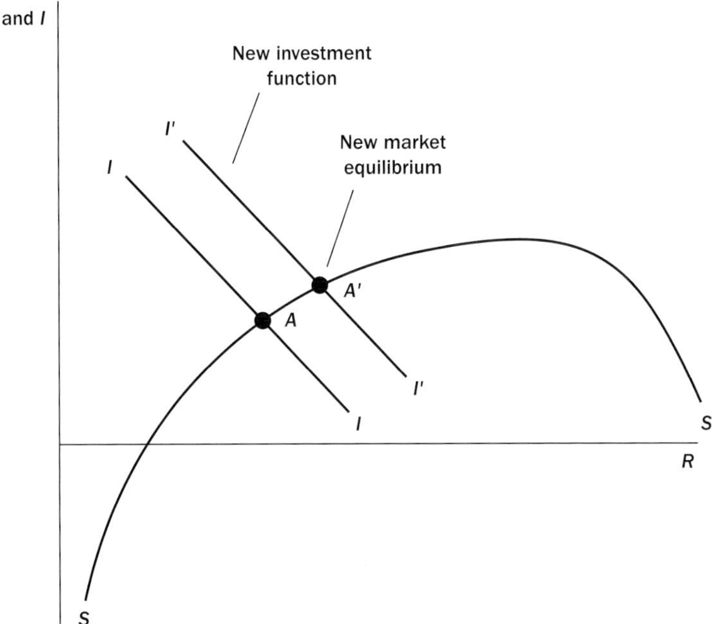

Figure 15.13
Change in I, S, and R if investment function increases.

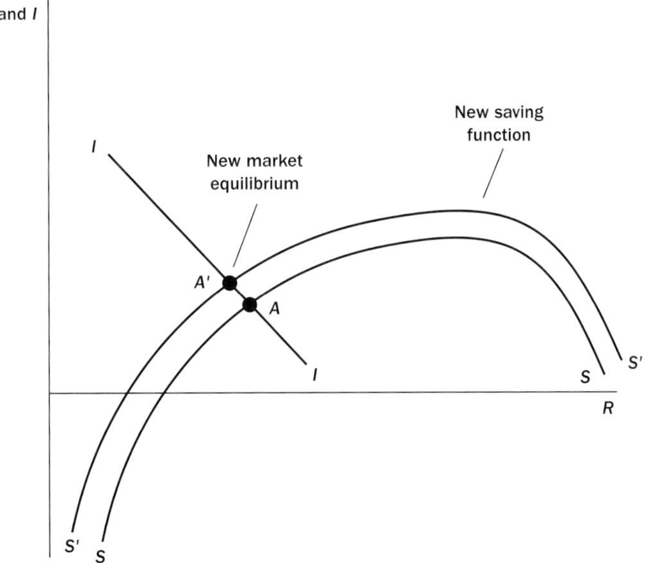

Figure 15.14
Change in I, S, and R if saving function increases.

It is also apparent from figure 15.12 that, as long as the intersection occurs in a region where the saving rises with R, the market-clearing interest rate will be higher, the higher the investment function is. As can be seen in figure 15.13, a shift of the investment function up and to the right (meaning more demand for investment at any given R) will raise the interest rate and result in increased saving and investment. Similarly, an increased propensity to save—a shift of the saving curve up and to the left, as shown in figure 15.14—will reduce the interest rate and result in saving and investment, although by less than the shift, because the lower R will have a depressing effect on saving.

The basic conclusion is that the interest rate reflects a complex set of forces that controls the demand for investment and the supply of saving. These forces are discussed extensively elsewhere, and we do not examine them here except for setting out a representative catalog of relevant factors: the rate of growth of population and productivity; fiscal policy, including incentives to save and invest; demographic variables; the role of bequests; the nature of technological progress; and the openness of international capital markets.

The Loanable Funds Theory of Interest Rates

Fisher's theory is a general one and obviously neglects certain practical matters, such as the power of the government (in concert with depository institutions) to create money and the government's often large demand for borrowed funds, which is frequently immune to the level of the interest rate. Also, Fisher's theory does not consider the possibility that individuals and firms might invest in cash balances. Expanding Fisher's theory to encompass these situations produces the **loanable funds theory of interest rates**.

This theory proposes that the general level of interest rates is determined by the complex interaction of two forces. The first is the total demand for funds by firms, governments, and households (or individuals), which carry out a variety of economic activities with those funds. This demand is negatively related to the interest rate (except for the government's demand, which frequently may not depend on the level of the interest rate). If income and other variables do not change, then an increase in the interest rate will reduce the demand for borrowing on the part of many firms and individuals, as projects become less profitable, and consumption and holding cash grow more costly. The second force affecting the level of the interest rate is the total supply of funds by firms, governments, banks, and individuals. Supply is positively related to the level of interest rates, if all other economic factors remain the same.

With rising rates, firms and individuals save and lend more, and banks are more eager to extend more loans. (A rising interest rate probably does not significantly affect the government's supply of savings.) In an equilibrium, the intersection of the supply and demand functions sets the interest rate level and the level of loans. In equilibrium, the demand for funds equals the supply of funds. In this case, all agents are borrowing what they want, investing to the desired extent, and holding all the money they wish to hold. In other words, equilibrium extends through the money market, the bond market, and the market for investment assets.

As in Fisher's theory of interest rates, shifts in the demand and supply curves may occur for many reasons: changes in the money supply, government deficits, changed preferences by individuals, new investment opportunities, and so on. These shifts affect the equilibrium level of the interest rate and of investment in predictable ways. Finally, the expectation of inflation can affect the equilibrium rate through the supply of funds curve, as savers demand higher rates (because of inflation) for any level of savings. Note that this analysis has excluded the question of default on loans: the rate discussed is the risk-free rate, either in its nominal rate or real rate (nominal and real rates are discussed below).

The Liquidity Preference Theory of Interest Rates

The liquidity preference theory, originally developed by John Maynard Keynes,[4] analyzes the equilibrium level of the interest rate through the interaction of the supply of money and the public's aggregate demand for holding money. Keynes assumed that most people hold wealth in only two forms: "money" and "bonds." For Keynes, "money" is equivalent to currency and demand deposits, which pay little or no interest but are liquid and can be used for immediate transactions. Bonds represent a broad Keynesian category and include long-term, interest-paying financial assets that are not liquid and that pose some risk, because their prices vary inversely with the interest rate level. Bonds may be liabilities of governments or firms. (Default risk is not considered here, and the rate is the risk-free rate, in real or nominal form.)

The public (consisting of individuals and firms) holds money for several reasons: ease of transactions, precaution against unexpected events, and speculation about possible rises in the interest rate. Although money pays no interest, the demand for money is a negative function of the interest rate. At a low rate, people hold a lot of money, because they do not lose much interest by doing so and because the risk of a rise in rates (and a fall in the value of bonds) may be large. With a high interest rate, people desire to hold bonds rather than money, because the cost of liquidity is substantial in terms of lost interest payments and because a decline in the interest rate would lead to gains in the bonds' values. The negative linkage between the interest rate and the demand for money appears as curve *D* in figure 15.15, which relates the interest rate to the amount of money in the economy, given the level of income and expected price inflation.

For Keynes, the supply of money is fully under the control of the central bank (the Fed in the United States). Moreover, the money supply is not affected by the level of the interest rate. Thus, the supply of money appears, in figure 15.15, as the vertical line, *MS*, and the line above the *MS* indicates a quantity that does not vary with the interest rate. Of course, equilibrium in the money market requires that the total demand for money equals total supply. In figure 15.15, equilibrium implies an interest rate of *i*. Furthermore, equilibrium in the money market implies the equilibrium of the bond market.

4. John Maynard Keynes, *The General Theory of Employment, Interest and Money* (New York: Harcourt, Brace & World, 1936).

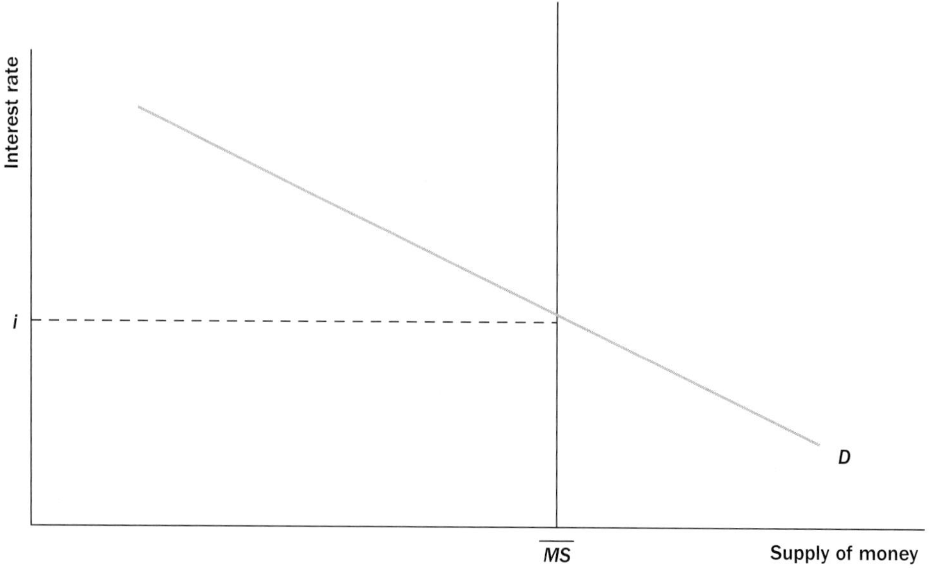

Figure 15.15
Equilibrium in Keynes's market for money.

The equilibrium rate of interest can change if there is a change in any variable affecting the demand or supply curves. On the demand side, Keynes recognized the importance of two such variables: the level of income and the level of prices for goods and services. A rise in income (with no other variable changing) raises the value of money's liquidity and shifts the demand curve to the right, increasing the equilibrium interest rate. Because people want to hold amounts of "real money" (or monetary units of specific purchasing power), a change in expected inflation would also shift the demand curve to the right and raise the level of interest.

The money supply curve can shift, in Keynes's view, only by actions of the central bank. The central bank's power over interest rates arises because of its ability to buy and sell securities (open market operations), which can alter the amount of money available in the economy. Generally, Keynes thought that an increase in the money supply would, by shifting the supply curve to the right, bring about a decline in the equilibrium interest rate. Similarly, he reasoned that a reduction in the money supply would raise rates. However, there is now widespread recognition that the question of linkage between the money supply and the level of the interest rate is rather more complex than that.

In a comprehensive analysis of this theory, it can be shown that the impact of a change in the money supply can affect the level of interest rates through a liquidity effect, an income effect, and a price expectations effect. Their impact on interest rates will depend on relative magnitudes, based on the level of economic activity at the time of the change in the money supply.

Böhm-Bawerk's Positive Theory of Capital

Forty years before Irving Fisher formulated his theory of interest rates as described in this chapter, the Austrian economist Eugen Böhm von Bawerk set forth his theory of interest rates and why interest rates must be positive. It would seem to make sense that his theory should be presented first. However, in the almost 500 pages of his book *Positive Theory of Capital*, only two figures appear, and both have limited value in understanding his theory. This is the reason that Robert Shiller, when describing the Böhm-Bawerk's theory, wrote: "This was not Mathematical Economics. It was Literary Economics."[5] And when contrasting the theory by Böhm-Bawerk and Fisher, Paul Samuelson wrote that Böhm-Bawerk "was not quite able to formulate his intuitive vision in terms that would satisfy today's persnickety jury of theorists."[6]

We will now describe Böhm-Bawerk's theory of the determinants of interest rates and why they must be positive.[7] The theory set forth by Böhm-Bawerk, as with the theory by Fisher, emphasizes the importance of time as the primary factor affecting interest rates. Böhm-Bawerk offered three reasons. His first two reasons have to do with what economists refer to as **positive time preference**. The first reason Böhm-Bawerk offers is that over time, an individual's marginal utility declines because an individual expects higher income in the future. Appealing to psychology, his second reason is that the marginal utility of a product/good declines over time. Taken together, positive time preference—according to Böhm-Bawerk—results in individuals who want to borrow to pay a positive interest rate and for those who are willing to lend to require compensation in the form of a positive interest rate. This idea of positive time preference is consistent with the theoretical framework of Fisher.

In addition to time preference, like Fisher, Böhm-Bawerk recognized the importance of technology and argued that technology is the third reason for positive interest rates. His explanation of technology, which may be a little more difficult to understand, is what he refers to as the "roundabout" nature of production or what he simply refers to as "roundaboutness," which involves a time-consuming production process.

To understand what Böhm-Bawerk meant by "roundaboutness," we can use the concept of "goods of higher order," a term originated by Carl Menger, another Austrian economist.[8] He begins with "goods of lowest order," which are goods that can be directly consumed. Crops produced by a farmer would be an example of goods of lower order. Then there are the tools that are used in production, and those tools would be of higher order than goods that can be

5. Robert Shiller, http://oyc.yale.edu/transcript/1076/econ-252-11.

6. Samuelson, "Two Classics: Böhm-Bawerk's Positive Theory and Fisher's Rate of Interest through Modern Prisms," p. 228.

7. Admittedly, we are not doing justice to the important contribution of his work not only to capital theory but also to how his theory disputes the view of social theory as set forth by Karl Marx.

8. This is described in chapter 3 ("The Principle Determining the Value of Goods of Higher Order") of his 1871 book, *Grundsätze der Volkswirtschaftslehre*. The book was translated by James Dingwall and Bert F. Hoselitz, *Principles of Economics* (Auburn, Alabama: Ludwig von Mises Institute, 1976).

directly consumed. So, a hoe and tractor would be examples of such goods. Going up an order higher, we have capital goods, which are used to produce tools. The manufacturing of steel that is needed to produce a hoe or a tractor and the manufacturing of rubber for the tires of a tractor would be an example of capital goods. The further those goods that are of higher order are from the production of the goods of lowest order, the more time is needed.

Now let's return to Böhm-Bawerk's theory. The production process begins with the production of capital goods, and then once those capital goods are produced, they are used to help produce goods of lower order desired by the economy. As a result, for the same amount of input, a roundabout production process will generate a greater amount of output. In other words, productivity can be increased if some production is allocated to create goods of higher order that can be used to more efficiently create goods of lower order.

Böhm-Bawerk illustrates roundaboutness with an example of a person who is seeking to obtain water from a spring. The simplest way to obtain the water is to go to the spring each time water is desired. A more efficient production process, however, would be to either use a pail to carry water from the spring to that person's home or use a pipe to draw water from the spring to the person's home. The manufacturing of a pail or the creation of a conduit system to get water from the spring to the person's home are examples of roundaboutness. The creation of the pail and the pipe involves the creation of capital goods, but such creation take times time. One could think of other examples, such as the production of steel or wood products that a farmer can use to create tools to make farming more efficient.

The implication of roundaboutness is that it not only increases capital goods but also affects interest rates. If capital goods generate higher levels of output for a given level of inputs, there must be a reward for doing so. This increase in output takes the form of a rate of return, which is referred to as "net productivity," and it can be measured terms of a percentage per year. It is a "net" measure, because it is net of the costs of producing capital goods. Producers of capital goods will create them only if doing so is expected to result in a positive net productivity (and therefore will lead to a positive interest rate) and will do so even if the two positive-time preference theories do not hold.

Efficiency Properties of Markets

The equilibrium achieved with the intermediation of the loan markets contributes an important property from the point of view of the efficiency of the economy in producing and allocating resources. Economists refer to this property as **Pareto optimality**. Instinctively we think of economic efficiency as implying the absence, or minimization, of waste. Pareto optimality makes that notion precise and conceptually operational: An allocation is Pareto optimal if it is not possible to reallocate the goods (inputs and outputs) in such a way that some will be better off while nobody will lose.

Clearly, if an allocation is not Pareto optimal, some slack or waste is present; conversely, if slack is present, the allocation cannot be Pareto optimal. In our simplified economy, Pareto optimality is ensured by profit maximization plus the fact that, at market equilibrium, both the marginal productivity of capital and the marginal rate of time preference equals R for every firm and for every consumer. Thus, it is impossible to increase output by reshuffling inputs among firms; the additional output by those who would gain inputs is offset precisely by the output lost by those losing inputs. By similar reasoning, we can infer that no welfare gain can come from reshuffling the given output among consumers.

Although this result is logically important, it turns out we cannot make too much of it with respect to existing free market economies. First, the result presupposes a perfectly competitive market, which free competition may fail to ensure because of restrictive practices. Second, it ignores transaction costs, information costs, and the consequences of incomplete information. Third, it presents an issue of externalities or effects—negative or positive—that production may have on people other than the buyer of the product. Finally, society may value things other than efficiency, such as the distribution of welfare. Therefore, some non-Pareto optimal solution may trade efficiency for some other property. All these considerations are incentives to make markets more perfect and allow valuing externalities through the price mechanism.

Real and Nominal Interest Rates: Fisher's Law

The interest rate we have used in our discussion so far is the real rate, which would prevail in the absence of inflation. This rate measures the amount of the commodity next period that can be exchanged for one unit of the commodity now. It generally differs from the nominal rate, which measures the amount of money to be repaid next period per unit borrowed now. The two rates are connected by a simple relation known as **Fisher's law**. It rests on the principle that an exchange of money now for money later must imply the same rate of exchange between the commodity now and the commodity later, as implied by the real rate.

Suppose the real rate is $1+r$. Then by delivering one unit of the commodity now, we can obtain $(1+r)$ units next period. Alternatively, we could sell the commodity now at the spot price, p_1, and invest the proceeds in a loan at the nominal rate $(1+i)$, obtaining $p_1(1+i)$ units of money next period.

How many units of the next-period commodity does that equation represent? To find the answer, we must divide by the second-period price of the commodity, p_2. Thus, the second-period quantity is $p_1(1+i)/(p_2)$. This quantity must equal the real rate $(1+r)$:

$$(1+r)=\frac{1+i}{1+p^*}, \tag{15.1}$$

where the denominator of equation (15.1) is from

$$\frac{p_1}{p_2}=\frac{1}{p_2/p_1}=\frac{1}{1+\left[(p_2-p_1)/p_1\right]},$$

and $(p_2-p_1)/p_1=p^*=$ the percentage rise in the price level over the period of the loan.

Equation (15.1) can be restated in the form

$$(1+i)=(1+r)(1+p^*).$$

Therefore, the nominal gross rate is the product of the gross real rate and 1 plus the rate of inflation. The equation, in turn, implies that

$$i=r+p^*+rp^*.$$

For the most common values of r and p, the product of r and p is small enough to be neglected, and the equation can be written as

$$i\approx r+p^*,$$

or

$$r\approx i-p^*. \tag{15.2}$$

Equation (15.2) is the formula commonly used to compute the ex post real rate of interest, which cannot be observed directly in the market. It is equally common to measure the anticipated or ex ante real rate of interest by replacing p by anticipated inflation. The ex ante rate differs from the ex post rate because of errors of expectation. It should be clear that the real rate so computed is not necessarily the same as the rate that would clear markets in the economy without inflation, because market imperfections (including taxation and possibly inflation illusion) can alter the real rate. For instance, in the early phase of unanticipated inflation, the real rate typically falls. In other words, besides reflecting fundamental forces (such as saving and productivity), the real rate may also be affected by other forces (such as inflation), especially in the short run.

Estimating the Market's Expected Inflation Rate

Economists often make forecasts of the future rate of inflation over some period of time. Prior to 1997, these forecasts were often used by market professionals to estimate what interest rate adjustment should be made to compensate for inflation when considering the purchase of a bond or making a loan. Since 1997, however, it is far more common for market professionals to use the yield on certain U.S. government securities to obtain an estimate of the market's consensus of the expected rate of inflation.

The U.S. Treasury Inflation Protected Securities (TIPS) are used for this purpose. These securities are a specific type of inflation-adjusted securities or inflation-linked bonds that are issued by the U.S. Department of the Treasury. They are described in more detail in chapter 20. For our purpose here, the details about the mechanics of TIPS are unimportant. Basically, TIPS are issued via an auction process, in which their yield is determined. The investor in a TIPS receives the yield, which is determined through the bidding process plus an adjustment for the rate of inflation lagged by two months. The rate of inflation is measured by the Consumer Price Index (CPI). The yield that the investor bids for is the real interest rate, which (as explained earlier) is the difference between the nominal yield and the expected rate of inflation. So, if an investors bids 0.50%, then the investor receives 0.50% plus the rate of inflation measured by the CPI with a two-month lag.

To estimate the expected inflation rate, an investor compares the yield on a TIPS with that of the yield on a traditional Treasury security with the same maturity. That yield is a nominal interest rate. Because we know from Fisher's law that the nominal yield minus the expected rate of inflation is the real yield, we can back out the expected rate of inflation. This is done by subtracting the real yield for the TIPS of the same maturity from the nominal yield of a Treasury security with a given maturity. On August 29, 2017, the yield quote on a traditional 10-year Treasury note was 2.17%, and the yield quote for a 10-year TIPS was 0.42%. Thus, the expected annual inflation rate over the next 10 years would be 1.75% (i.e., 2.17% – 0.42%).

Natural Rate of Interest

The **natural rate of interest** (also called the "neutral rate of interest") is the real short-term interest rate that would prevail if there were no transitory financial disturbances. That is, it is interest rate that would prevail for stable economic output and a constant inflation rate. The natural interest rate provides a benchmark for the conduct of monetary policy. Monetary policy would be judged to be expansionary if the short-term real rate were below the natural rate, and contractionary in the opposite case. The natural rate of interest is used in policy discussions and decisions.

Closely related to the natural interest rate is the natural rate of unemployment. The unemployment rate is also of paramount importance to policymakers, such as the Fed. The "natural rate of employment"—technically, the non-accelerating inflation rate of unemployment (NAIRU)—is the rate of unemployment arising from all sources except fluctuations in aggregate demand. Even in good times, a healthy, dynamic economy will have at least some unemployment as workers switch jobs (called "frictional unemployment") and as new workers enter the labor force and other workers leave it. The Fed makes monetary policy decisions to foster the lowest level of unemployment consistent with stable prices. In June 2017, the Federal Open Market Committee (FOMC) estimated that the long-run normal rate of unemployment was between 4.5% and 5.0%.[9]

There have been four major findings on the natural rate of interest covering four advanced economies (the United States, Canada, the Eurozone, and the United Kingdom).[10] The findings are consistent across the four economies studied. The first major finding is evidence of

9. "What is the Lowest Level of Unemployment That the U.S. Economy Can Sustain?" Available at https://www.federalreserve.org/faqs/economy_14424.htm.

10. Kathryn Holston, Thomas Laubach, and John C. Williams, "Measuring the Natural Rate of Interest: International Trends and Determinants," *Journal of International Economics* 108 (2017): 59–75.

time variation in the natural rate of interest. The second finding is a downward trend in the natural rate of interest, with the natural rates of all four economies being at historically low levels. The third finding is a substantial co-movement in the natural rate of interest across the four economies. Finally, the estimates of the natural rates of interest are very imprecise.

Risk-Free Interest Rate and the Existence of a Safe Asset

The risk-free interest rate is the theoretical interest rate an investor would require from a risk-free investment over a specified time. Here "risk free" means that all the risks described in chapter 10 do not exist in an investment that is classified as riskless.

For example, a three-month Treasury bill has often been referred to as a "risk-free investment" and therefore as a safe security for investors who want to avoid any risk, assuming that investors hold it for three months. However, it would have price risk if it were held for either one month or six months. If the investment was for a one-month holding period, the three-month Treasury bill would have to be sold before maturity at an initial unknown price, thus exposing the investor to price risk. With a six-month holding period, at the end of three-months, the investor would have to invest in a new three-month investment at an initially unknown yield. In either case, the investor is faced with an unknown risk over a three-month holding period. Thus, many investors would consider a three-month U.S. Treasury bill to be risk-free rate for U.S. investors who plan to hold it over a three-month holding period. However, two implicit assumptions are made when classifying a three-month Treasury bill as a risk-free security. First, it is assumed that the U.S. government will not default on its obligations (i.e., no credit risk). Second, it is assumed that inflation is insignificant (i.e., no inflation risk). Moreover, for an investor whose home currency is not the U.S. dollar, an investment in a three-month Treasury bill would expose the investor to foreign-exchange rate risk.

There is an ongoing controversy—the **safe asset controversy**—that in real-world financial markets there is a shortage or absence of a risk-free asset offering a meaningful positive riskless rate. There are several definitions of what a safe asset is. Gary Gorton defines a safe asset as "an asset that is (almost always) valued at face value without expensive and prolonged analysis."[11] Safe assets play several critical roles in a financial market. First, safe assets are used by certain financial entities to satisfy regulatory requirements. Second, they are used as a pricing benchmark. Third, they are used as collateral in financial transactions. Finally, the development of asset pricing theory and derivatives pricing relies on the existence of a safe or riskless asset. However, as Peter Fisher, former undersecretary of the U.S. Treasury, states in an article about the meaning of the riskless rate: "The idea of risk-free sovereign bonds is best thought of as an oxymoron or as an anomaly of recent history. It is not a useful, necessary or an enduring feature of the financial landscape."[12]

11. Gary B. Gorton, "The History and Economics of Safe Assets," *Annual Review of Economics* 9 (2017): 547–586.

12. Peter R. Fisher, "Reflections on the Meaning of 'Risk Free'," in *Sovereign Risk: A World without Risk-Free Assets* (Basel, Switzerland: Bank for International Settlements, 2013), pp. 65–72.

Several studies have focused on the challenges for monetary policy and global financial stability when there is a shortage of a safe asset.[13] Other studies have investigated how asset pricing (discussed in chapter 14) would be impacted when either there is no meaningful riskless asset offering a positive interest rate or if for some reason market participants (such as investors and traders) elect not to invest in a riskless asset. One of the earlier investigations of the role of a riskless asset in financial theory is by Fischer Black, who confirmed that the CAPM holds even in the absence of a risk-free asset (referred to as "Black's zero-beta CAPM").[14]

Negative Interest Rates

In recent years, some countries have realized nominal negative interest rates for some periods. The economic reason for the realization of negative nominal interest rates is as follows. When weak economies cause deflation (a decline in price levels), investors tend to conserve spending and save, instead of spending and investing. They plan to spend in the future when prices are lower due to inflation. This leads to a further decrease in aggregate demand, leading to further deflation. An expansionary monetary policy—that is, lower interest rates—is often used to combat what economists refer to as "stagnation." Monetary easing by the Fed (in the case of the United States) is accomplished by the Fed buying outstanding debt securities to reduce Treasury yields, which is the standard way of dealing with deflation. According to this method, the Fed funds rate is the interest rate target. This method is called **qualitative easing**. However, if deflationary pressure is sufficiently weak, even reducing the Fed's interest rate to zero may not provide sufficient stimulus to the economy. A negative interest rate may therefore be necessary. When the Fed employs this method, it is referred to as a **negative interest rate policy**.

With a negative interest rate, the Fed and, subsequently, individual commercial banks charge negative rates to their lenders. That is, depositors in banks, instead of receiving money on deposits, pay to keep their money in the bank. This provides an incentive for depositors to spend the money rather than pay interest for keeping it as deposits. For example, according to a negative interest rate policy, if the negative interest rate were –0.2%, bank depositors would have to pay 0.2% on their deposits instead of receiving a positive interest rate.

When the financial crisis of 2008–2009 struck, the central bank of the United Kingdom (the Bank of England) and other large central banks cut their overnight rate for bank borrowing to almost zero. When their economies still did not recover, they began to experiment with other tools. One of these tools was quantitative easing, to be explained shortly. A negative interest rate policy has also been used by several other countries. The European

13. See, for example, Gauti B. Eggertsson and Paul Krugman, "Debt, Deleveraging, and the Liquidity Trap: A Fisher-Minsky-Koo Approach," *Quarterly Journal of Economics* 127 (2012): 1459–1513; and Pierre-Oliver Gourinchas and Jeanne Olivier, "Global Safe Assets," BIS Working Paper 399 (Basel, Switzerland: Bank for International Settlements, December 2012).

14. Fischer Black, "Capital Market Equilibrium with Restricted Borrowing," *Journal of Business* 45 (1972): 444–453.

Central Bank (ECB) introduced negative rates in 2014 on behalf of its member countries, to prevent the Eurozone from falling into a deflationary spiral. Non-Eurozone countries, such as Denmark, Sweden, and Switzerland, have also used negative rates for different purposes.

After 2008, the Fed found that even very low or negative interest rates were insufficient to stimulate the economy, so rather than decreasing interest rates to manage monetary policy, the Fed began to increase its balance sheet holdings by buying outstanding long-term bonds. This type of easing was called "quantitative" easing (QE). According to QE, the focus is on the size of the Fed's balance sheet that results from the Fed purchasing U.S. government and other securities, rather than Fed-influenced interest rates, which is the focus of qualitative easing monetary policy. QE in the U.S. began on November 25, 2008, when the Fed announced that it would purchase up to $600 billion of agency mortgage-backed securities and agency debt. The Fed initiated a second round of quantitative easing, QE2, in the fourth quarter of 2010, and subsequently conducted several other rounds of QE. The Bank of Japan and the ECB also eased in this way.

In addition, in 2007, the U.S. economy was further weakened by federal government budgetary problems, which involved cutbacks. Specifically, no stimulative fiscal policy was in place, further weakening the economy. By September 2017, the economy had strengthened, and the Fed began unwinding the QE plan implemented in 2008 by then-Fed chairman Bernanke to stimulate the weak economy. During this QE period, the Fed had more than quadrupled the size of its balance sheet to $4.5 trillion. This plan for unwinding was a sign of confidence in the economic recovery.

Historical Interest Rates in the United States

Thus far we have described two types of what is referred to as "interest rates": nominal interest rates and real interest rates. Here we take a brief look at historical nominal and real interest rates in the United States based on yields on U.S. Treasury bills, notes, and bonds. Treasury bills are short-term instruments issued by the U.S. government with a maturity of no more than one year. U.S. Treasury notes and bonds have a maturity in excess of one year. Treasury notes have a maturity of up to 10 years, and bonds have a maturity greater than 10 years. Treasury bills, notes, and bonds are guaranteed by the U.S. government.

From 1870 until 1978, the yields on U.S. Treasury securities varied between 2% and 7% most of the time. Therefore, the historical yields on U.S. Treasury securities were quite simple during this 109-year period. But from 1970 to 1979, the economy experienced stagnation, which is a combination of slow economic growth and accelerating inflation. This stagnation was induced by the 1973 oil crises and the 1979 energy crisis. The resulting inflation was of significant concern to federal government policymakers, including the Fed and then-president Jimmy Carter. This concern was the basis for what was referred to as the "Volcker tightening." Paul Volcker became the Fed chairman during August 1979 and remained until August 1987. Volcker instituted a series of Fed tightenings of the Fed funds rate beginning in 1979 to eliminate inflation. Under Volcker, the Fed funds rate reached highs of 20% during 1979 and 1980. This series of tightenings also caused two recessions in 1980 (six months) and 1981–1982 (16 months). In addition, during 1981, the 30-year Treasury bond yield increased to more than 14%.

Although that was the bad news at the time, the good news resulting from these tightenings and recessions was that they unleashed a period of economic growth, reduction in the inflation rate, and a decline in bond yields. They also induced a stock market rally, which continued into mid-2018 (but also included two major equity bear markets in 2000–2002 and 2007–2009, discussed below). Ten-year Treasury yields declined to approximately 1.50% in 2015 and remained slightly over 2% in 2017.

Returning to the Fed tightening period during 1979–1981, prior to this period, during 1979, inflation was 13.31%, and long-term corporate bonds returned –4.18%. After the Fed tightening began, the Fed funds rate exceeded 19%, the one-year Treasury bill yield exceeded 10%, the 10-year Treasury note yield exceeded 15%, and the inflation rate was more than 11% (in early 1980).[15]

The economy recovered quickly from the two recessions. Inflation, which had annual rates of 13.3% and 12.4% in 1979 and 1980, respectively (it peaked at 14.8% in March 1980), declined to 8.9% in 1981 and 3.9% in 1982. After real GDP growth rates of –0.04%, 1.29%, and –1.40% in 1980, 1981, and 1982, respectively, real GDP growth grew by 7.83% (1983), 5.63% (1984), and 4.28% in 1983 (1985). The rest of the 1980s and the beginning of the first half of the 1990s exhibited moderate growth—with the exception of 1991, which experienced a short (8-month), mild (–0.17% real GDP growth) recession due to a real-estate based recession.

Then from 1995 to 1999, one of the strongest stock market periods in U.S. history occurred. This was a large-cap growth, technology sector-led rally and ended in what was called the tech "bubble." The years 2003–2006 constituted a period of economic and financial moderation—in fact, it was called the "Great Moderation" due to its low macroeconomic volatility.

In 2007–2008, another speculative period—this time due mainly to subprime mortgages—called the Great Recession (as opposed to the Great Depression in 1929) followed. This was the most severe recession since the Great Depression. The Great Recession has had a continuing effect on the bond market. In 2008, yields on U.S. Treasury bills fell from slightly over 3.0% at the beginning of the year to almost zero by the end of the year. In the wake of the 2008–2009 financial crisis, investors' behavior could be described as an extreme flight to safety—investors were willing to accept little (if anything) risk in return for the assurance that they would get their principal back. In other words, the return of capital took precedence over the return on capital.[16] From 2009 to 2017, 10-year Treasury note yields

15. Marvin Goodfriend and Robert G. King, "The Incredible Volcker Disinflation," *Journal of Monetary Economics* 52 (2005): 981–1015.

16. Goodfriend and King, "The Incredible Volcker Disinflation."

remained near historical lows at 2.3%. From 2009 to 2015, the yield on 90-day Treasury bills did not exceed 0.12%.

These movements have led to a current conundrum in the bond market as of year-end 2017. Many bond market observers ask when bond yields will return to their "normal" higher yields of 5% and more, using the period of 1970–2000 as the basis for what is normal in the bond market. In contrast, many bond market observers look at the period after 1970–2000 and conclude that 10-year Treasury bond yields are currently normal at slightly more than 2%, where they have been for more than a decade. The proponents of the post-2000 low yield as being normal argue that the 1970–2000 period was an anomalous period and therefore does not represent what market participants should expect for future interest rates.

Key Points

- Interest is the price paid for the temporary use of resources, and the amount of a loan is its principal.
- Irving Fisher's theory of interest analyzes the equilibrium level of the interest rate as the result of the interaction of savers' willingness to save and borrowers' demand for investment funds.
- In Fisher's terms, the interest rate reflects the interaction of savers' marginal rate of time preference and borrowers' marginal productivity of capital.
- The loanable funds theory is an extension of Fisher's theory and proposes that the equilibrium rate of interest reflects the demand and supply of funds, which depend on savers' willingness to save, borrowers' expectations regarding the profitability of investing, and the government's action regarding money supply.
- The liquidity preference theory is Keynes's view that the rate of interest is set in the market for money balances.
- In the liquidity preference theory, the demand for money reflects the liquidity of money by comparison with long-term financial instruments; demand depends on the interest rate, income, and the price level.
- In the liquidity preference theory, changes in the money supply can affect the level of interest rates through the liquidity effect, the income effect, and the price expectations effect; their relative magnitudes depend on the level of economic activity at the time of the change in the money supply.
- Eugen Böhm von Bawerk set forth his theory of interest rates and why interest rates must be positive: positive time preference, declining marginal utility of a product/service over time, and technology (roundaboutness).
- Fisher's law states that the observable nominal rate of interest is composed of two unobservable variables: the real rate of interest and the premium for expected inflation.

- The real rate of interest is the interest rate that would prevail in the absence of inflation.
- It can be shown that the nominal rate of interest is approximately equal to the real rate of interest plus anticipated inflation, a relationship referred to as "Fisher's law."
- The yield offered on Treasury Inflation Protected Securities (TIPS) is the market's real rate.
- The expected annual rate of inflation can be estimated from the yield on TIPS and the yield on traditional Treasury securities of the same maturity.
- The natural rate of interest (or neutral rate of interest) is the real short-term interest rate that would prevail if there were no transitory financial disturbances.
- Safe assets play four critical roles in a financial market: (1) they are used by certain financial entities to satisfy regulatory requirements; (2) they are used as a pricing benchmark; (3) they are used as collateral in financial transactions; and (4) the development of asset pricing theory and derivatives pricing relies on the existence of a safe or riskless asset.
- Negative interest rates can exist in an economy, and central bank policies can produce that outcome.

Questions

1. Explain what these terms mean in Fisher's theory of interest rates:

a. the marginal rate of time preference;

b. the marginal productivity of capital; and

c. the equilibrium interest rate.

2. How does the loanable funds theory expand Fisher's theory of interest rate determination?

3. How do the assets—money and bonds—differ in Keynes's liquidity preference theory?

4. What did Böhm-Bawerk mean by "roundaboutness" in his theory of why interest rates must be positive?

5. What is meant by "the real rate of interest"?

6. What is meant by "the nominal rate of interest"?

7. According to Fisher's law, what is the relationship between the real rate and the nominal rate?

8. Why is it difficult to measure an economy's real rate of interest?

9. On July 30, 2017, the following information was available to an investor:

Yield on 10-year TIPS: 0.58%

Yield on 10-year Treasury notes: 2.31%

What was the expected annual rate of inflation over the next 10 years as of June 30, 2017?

10. Explain whether you agree or disagree with the following statement: "The riskless interest rate is the real short-term interest rate that would prevail if there were no transitory financial disturbances."

11. What is the controversy involving the existence of a safe asset?

12. Explain at least two important roles played by a safe asset in a financial market.

13. Explain why you agree or disagree with the following statements:

a. "A bond issued by a corporation of the highest credit rating can qualify as a risk-free asset."

b. "A five-year U.S. Treasury note would qualify as a risk-free asset because of its guarantee by the U.S. government."

14. Explain why you agree or disagree with the following statement: "Negative real interest rates cannot exist in an economy that is properly functioning."

15. What is meant by a "negative interest rate policy"?

16. What can be said about future normal interest rates?

16 The Structure of Interest Rates

CONTENTS

Learning Objectives

After reading this chapter, you will understand:

- why historically the yields on securities issued by the U.S. Treasury have been used as the benchmark interest rates throughout the world;
- what is meant by a "risk premium";
- what factors affect the yield spread between two bonds;
- what the swap curve is and why it is used as an interest rate benchmark;
- what is meant by the "term structure" of interest rates;
- what the yield curve is;
- the different shapes the term structure can take;
- what is meant by a "spot rate" and a "spot rate curve";
- how a theoretical spot rate curve can be determined from the U.S. Treasury yield curve;
- what is meant by an "implicit forward rate," and how it can be calculated;
- how long-term rates are related to the current short-term rate and short-term forward rates;
- the different shapes that have been observed for the U.S. Treasury yield curve;
- the different theories about the determinants of the shape of the term structure: the pure expectations theory, the liquidity theory, the preferred habitat theory, and the market segmentation theory; and
- the risks associated with investing in bonds when interest rates change: price risk and reinvestment risk.

In chapter 15, we explained interest rate determination in a simple economy. However, no economy has just one interest rate; instead, there is a structure of interest rates. The interest rate that a borrower must pay depends on a myriad of factors, which we describe in this chapter. We begin with a discussion of the structure of interest rates, explaining the factors that affect the yield spread or risk premium for non-U.S. Treasury securities (i.e., why debt obligations not issued by the U.S. Treasury offer a higher potential yield than U.S. Treasury securities offer). We then focus on one particular relationship: the relationship between the yield offered on a debt obligation and its maturity. This relationship is referred to as the "term structure of interest rates."

The Structure of Interest Rates

The numerous debt obligations issued by public and private entities throughout the world offer different interest rates. When an entity agrees to pay an interest rate on a debt obligation that it has issued, the interest rate is not randomly determined. Instead, certain factors affect the interest rates that determine what interest rate an entity will have to pay if it wants to borrow money. We refer to these factors that determine the interest rate that borrowers must pay as the "structure of interest rates." The starting point in determining the interest rate that a borrower must pay is the base interest rate.

The Base Interest Rate

The securities issued by the U.S. Treasury, popularly referred as to **Treasury securities**, or simply **Treasuries**, are backed by the full faith and credit of the U.S. government. Consequently, market participants throughout the world view them as having no credit risk. As a result, historically the interest rates on Treasury securities served as the benchmark interest rates throughout the U.S. economy, as well as in international capital markets. Other important benchmarks have developed in the international capital markets, and we will discuss one of these.

Treasury securities are used to develop benchmark interest rates. The two categories of U.S. Treasury securities are discount securities and coupon securities. The fundamental difference between the two types results from the form of the stream of payments that the holder receives, which in turn reflects the prices at which the securities are issued. Coupon securities pay interest every six months, plus principal at maturity. Discount securities pay only a contractually fixed amount at maturity. Treasury securities are typically issued on an auction basis according to regular cycles for securities of specific maturities. The current Treasury practice is to issue all securities with maturities of one year or less as discount securities, called **Treasury bills**. All securities with maturities of two years or longer are issued as **Treasury coupon securities**.

The most recently auctioned Treasury issues for each maturity are referred to as **on-the-run issues** or **current coupon issues**. Issues auctioned prior to the current coupon issues are typically referred to as **off-the-run issues**; they are not as liquid as on-the-run issues and therefore offer a higher yield than the corresponding on-the-run Treasury issue. Note that every day, the U.S. Department of the Treasury estimates the yield for Treasury securities based on the yield for on-the-run and off-the-run issues.

The minimum interest rate or **base interest rate** that investors demand for investing in a non-Treasury security is the yield offered on a comparable maturity for an on-the-run Treasury security. So, for example, if an investor wanted to purchase a 10-year bond on a particular day at the time that the 10-year on-the-run Treasury is 4.49%, then the minimum yield the investor would want is 4.49%. The base interest rate is also referred to as the **benchmark interest rate**.[1]

1. The term "benchmark interest rates" has also been used to describe nearly risk-free short-term reference interest rates, such as the "IBORS" that we describe in chapter 25—the three major ones being the London Interbank Offered Rate (LIBOR), Euro Interbank Offered Rate (EURIBOR), and Tokyo Interbank Offered Rate (TIBOR).

The Risk Premium

Market participants talk of interest rates on non-Treasury securities as "trading at a spread" to a particular on-the-run Treasury security (or at a spread to any particular benchmark interest rate selected). For example, if the yield on a 10-year non-Treasury security is 5.89% when the on-the-run 10-year Treasury yield is 4.49%, then the spread would be 140 basis points. This spread reflects the additional risks the investor faces by acquiring this security that is not issued by the U.S. government, and therefore the spread can be called a **risk premium**. Thus, we can express the interest rate offered on a non-Treasury security as

Base interest rate + Spread,

or equivalently,

Base interest rate + Risk premium.

We have already discussed the factors that affect the base interest rate in chapter 15. One of the factors is the expected rate of inflation. That is, the base interest rate can be expressed as

Base interest rate = Real rate of interest + Expected rate of inflation.

How can the real rate of inflation required by market participants be estimated? The U.S. Department of the Treasury issues securities indexed to the CPI. These securities are called **Treasury Inflation Protected Securities** (TIPS), and we discuss them in chapter 20.

There are factors that affect the interest rate by which a security offers above an otherwise comparable benchmark security. This additional interest rate is referred to as the **yield spread** or simply **spread**. The factors that drive the yield spread include

1. the type of issuer,
2. the issuer's perceived creditworthiness,
3. the term or maturity of the instrument,
4. provisions that grant either the issuer or the investor the option to do something,
5. the taxability of the interest received by investors, and
6. the expected liquidity of the issue.

Typically, the benchmark interest rate used is a U.S. Treasury security. However, it is important to emphasize that yield spreads must be interpreted relative to the benchmark interest rate used, particularly in relation to the second and last factors, which affect the spread when the benchmark interest rate is other than the yield on U.S. Treasury securities.

Types of issuers A key feature of a debt obligation is the nature of the issuer. The bond market is classified by the type of issuer, and groups of securities of the various kinds of issuers are referred to as **market sectors**. The spread between the interest rates offered in two sectors of the bond market on obligations with the same maturity is referred to as an **intermarket sector spread**.

Excluding the Treasury market sector, the other market sectors include a wide range of issuers, each with different abilities to satisfy their contractual obligations. For example, in the corporate market sector, issuers are classified as follows: (1) utilities, (2) industrials, (3) finance, and (4) banks. The spread between two issues in a market sector is called an **intramarket sector spread**.

Perceived creditworthiness of issuer As explained in chapter 10, credit risk encompasses two forms of risk: default risk and credit spread risk. The risk that the issuer of a bond may be unable to make timely principal or interest payments is called "default risk" and is gauged by the issuer's credit rating, as assigned by credit rating agencies (the three major ones being Moody's Investors Service, Standard & Poor's Corporation, and Fitch Ratings).

In all systems, the term **high grade** means low credit risk, or conversely, a high probability of future payments. The highest-grade bonds are denoted by Moody's by the symbol Aaa, and by S&P and Fitch by the symbol AAA. The next highest grade is denoted by the symbol Aa (Moody's) or AA (S&P and Fitch). For the third grade, all rating systems use A. The next three grades are Baa or BBB, Ba or BB, and B, respectively. There are also C grades. Moody's uses 1, 2, or 3 to provide a narrower credit quality breakdown within each class, and S&P and Fitch use plus and minus signs for the same purpose.

Bonds rated triple A (AAA or Aaa) are said to be **prime**, double A (AA or Aa) are of **high quality**, single-A issues are called **upper medium grade**, and triple-B issues are **medium grade**. Lower-rated bonds are said to have speculative elements or to be **distinctly speculative**.

Bond issues assigned a rating in the top four categories are referred to as **investment-grade bonds**. Issues that carry a rating below the top four categories are referred to as **noninvestment-grade bonds**, or more popularly as **high-yield bonds** or **junk bonds**. Thus the bond market can be divided into two sectors, the investment-grade and noninvestment-grade markets.

Another form of credit risk that we did not describe in chapter 10 (because we did not discuss credit ratings) is the risk that the issuer's credit rating will be lowered. This risk is referred to as **downgrade risk**.

The spread between Treasury securities and non-Treasury securities that are identical in all respects except for credit quality is referred to as a **credit spread**. For example, suppose that the yield for corporate bonds with 10 years to maturity on a particular day is 5.39% for AAA-rated bonds and 5.66% for AA-rated bonds. Suppose also that the 10-year on-the-run Treasury rate is 4.49%. Hence, the yield spread for 10-year AAA-rated corporate bonds is 90 basis points (5.39% − 4.49%), and for AA-rated corporate bonds the yield spread is 117 basis points (5.66% − 4.49%). In this illustration, we see that the lower the credit quality is, the larger the yield spread will be. This is the typical relationship observed in real-world debt markets.

Term to maturity As explained in chapter 11, the price of a financial asset fluctuates over its life as yields in the market change. As we demonstrated, the volatility of a bond's price depends on its maturity. More specifically, holding all other factors constant, the longer the maturity of a bond is, the greater will be its price volatility resulting from a change in market yields. The spread between any two maturity sectors of the market is called a **maturity spread**, or **yield curve spread**. (The graphical relationship between the yield and maturity for a sector of the market is called the "yield curve" and is discussed in more detail later in this chapter.) Although this spread can be calculated for any sector of the market, it is most commonly calculated for the Treasury sector.

In the corporate bond market, a maturity spread can be similarly calculated, but the issues must have the same credit quality. For example, suppose that on a given day the following yields are observed for AA-rated corporate bonds:

2-year AA corporate bonds: 4.67%

5-year AA corporate bonds: 5.07%

10-year AA corporate bonds: 5.66%

The maturity spreads are then:

2-year/5-year maturity spread: 5.07% − 4.67% = 0.40% = 40 bps

2-year/10-year maturity spread: 5.66% − 4.67% = 0.99% = 99 bps

5-year/10-year maturity spread: 5.66% − 5.07% = 0.59% = 59 bps

The relationship between the yields on comparable securities but different maturities is called the **term structure of interest rates**. The term-to-maturity topic is of such importance that we devote the last section of this chapter to it.

Inclusion of options It is not uncommon for a bond issue to include a provision that gives either the bondholder or the issuer an option to take some action against the other party. An option that is included in a bond issue is referred to as an **embedded option**.

The most common type of option in a bond issue is a **call provision**. This provision grants the issuer the right to retire the debt, fully or partially, before the scheduled maturity date. The inclusion of a call feature benefits issuers by allowing them to replace an old bond issue with a lower-interest-cost issue should interest rates in the market decline. Effectively, a call provision allows the issuer to alter the maturity of a bond. A call provision is detrimental to the bondholder, because the bondholder will be uncertain about maturity and might have to reinvest the proceeds received at a lower interest rate if the bond is called and the bondholder wants to keep his or her funds in issues with a similar risk of default.

An issue may also include a provision that allows the bondholder to alter the maturity of a bond. An issue with a **put provision** grants the bondholder the right to sell the issue back to the issuer at par value on designated dates. Here the advantage to the investor is that, if interest rates rise after the issue date and result in a price that is less than the par value, the investor can force the issuer to redeem the bond at par value.

A **convertible bond** is an issue giving the bondholder the right to exchange the bond for a specified number of shares of common stock. This feature allows the bondholder to take advantage of favorable movements in the price of the issuer's common stock.

The presence of these embedded options affects the spread of an issue relative to a Treasury security and the spread relative to otherwise comparable issues that do not have an embedded option. In general, market participants require a larger spread over a comparable Treasury security for an issue with an embedded option that is favorable to the issuer (e.g., a call option) than for an issue without such an option. In contrast, market participants require a smaller spread over a comparable Treasury security for an issue with an embedded option that is favorable to the investor (e.g., a put option or a conversion option). In fact, for a bond with an option that is favorable to an investor, the interest rate on an issue may be less than that on a comparable Treasury security!

A major part of the bond market is the mortgage market. A wide range of mortgage-backed securities is discussed in chapters 30 and 31. But as explained in chapter 10, these securities expose an investor to a form of call risk known as "prepayment risk." Consequently, a yield spread between a mortgage-backed security and a comparable on-the-run Treasury security reflects this call risk. To see how, let's consider a basic mortgage-backed security called a "Ginnie Mae pass-through security." This security is backed by the full faith and credit of the U.S. government. Consequently, the yield spread between a Ginnie Mae pass-through security and a comparable Treasury security is not to the result of credit risk. Instead, it is primarily the result of call risk.

Taxability of interest Unless exempted under the federal income tax code, interest income is taxable at the federal level. In addition to federal income taxes, state and local taxes may apply to interest income.

The U.S. federal tax code specifically exempts the interest income from qualified municipal bond issues from taxation at the federal level. **Municipal bonds** are securities issued by state and local governments and by their creations, such as "authorities" and special districts.

The large majority of outstanding municipal bonds are tax-exempt securities. Because of the tax-exempt feature of municipal bonds, the yield on municipal bonds is less than that on Treasuries with the same maturity. The difference in yield between tax-exempt securities and Treasury securities is typically measured not in basis points but in percentage terms. More specifically, it is measured as the percentage of the yield on a tax-exempt security relative to the yield of a comparable Treasury security.

The yield on a taxable bond issue after federal income taxes are paid is:

$$\text{After-tax yield} = \text{Pre-tax yield} \times (1 - \text{Marginal tax rate}).$$

For example, suppose a taxable bond issue offers a yield of 3% and is acquired by an investor facing a marginal tax rate of 35%. The after-tax yield would then be:

$$\text{After-tax yield} = 0.03 \times (1 - 0.35) = 0.0195 = 1.95\%.$$

Alternatively, we can determine the yield that must be offered on a taxable bond issue to give the same after-tax yield as a tax-exempt issue. This yield is called the **equivalent-taxable yield** and is determined as follows:

$$\text{Equivalent-taxable yield} = \frac{\text{Tax-exempt yield}}{(1 - \text{Marginal tax rate})}.$$

For example, consider an investor facing a 35% marginal tax rate who purchases a tax-exempt issue with a yield of 1.95%. The equivalent-taxable yield is:

$$\text{Equivalent-taxable yield} = \frac{0.0195}{(1 - 0.35)} = 0.03 = 3\%.$$

Note that the lower the marginal tax rate is, the lower the equivalent-taxable yield will be. Thus, in our previous example, if the marginal tax rate were 25% rather than 35%, the equivalent-taxable yield would be 2.6% rather than 4%, as shown here:

$$\text{Equivalent-taxable yield} = \frac{0.0195}{(1 - 0.25)} = 0.026 = 2.6\%$$

In the United States, state and local governments may tax interest income on bond issues that are exempt from federal income taxes. Some municipalities exempt interest income paid on all municipal issues from taxation; others do not. Some states exempt interest income from bonds issued by municipalities in the state but tax the interest income from bonds issued by municipalities outside the state. The implication is that two municipal securities of the same quality rating and the same maturity may trade at some spread because of different tax policies and hence the relative demand for bonds of municipalities in different states. For example, in a high-income-tax state, such as the State of New York, the demand for bonds of municipalities drives down their yield relative to the yield of bonds issued by municipalities in low-income-tax states, such as the State of Florida.

In the United States, municipalities are not permitted to tax the interest income from securities issued by the U.S. Treasury. Thus, part of the spread between Treasury securities and taxable non-Treasury securities of the same maturity reflects the value of the exemption from state and local taxes.

Expected liquidity of an issue Bonds trade with different degrees of liquidity. The greater the expected liquidity with which an issue trades, the lower will be the yield that investors require.

As noted earlier, Treasury securities are the most liquid securities in the world. The lower yield offered on Treasury securities relative to the yield on non-Treasury securities reflects, to a significant extent, the difference in liquidity. Even in the Treasury market, however, some differences in liquidity occur, because on-the-run issues have greater liquidity than do off-the-run issues. An important factor that affects the liquidity of an issue is the size of the issue. One of the reasons U.S. Treasury securities are highly liquid is the large size of each individual issue.

An Alternative Benchmark Interest Rate: The Swap Rate

Let us return to the interpretation of the yield spread on a non-U.S. Treasury security that is used as the benchmark interest rate. Because the U.S. Treasury securities are viewed by market participants as having minimal credit risk, the yield spread between a non-U.S. Treasury security and that on a U.S. Treasury security reflects credit risk, as well as liquidity risk and the risk associated with any embedded options. Several alternative benchmarks have been suggested. The attributes of a benchmark interest rate are that (1) the market for the financial instrument should be viewed as having minimal credit risk, and (2) it should be highly liquid.

Of the several alternative benchmarks suggested, the one that has been used most frequently is the interest rate swap rate. We describe an interest rate swap and the swap rate in more detail in chapter 37. Here we briefly explain a generic interest rate swap, which is a derivative instrument.

The parties to an interest rate swap exchange interest rate payments on specified dates: One party pays a fixed rate and the other party a floating rate over the life of the swap. In a typical swap, the floating rate is based on a reference rate, and the reference rate is typically LIBOR. LIBOR is the interest rate at which prime banks in London pay other prime banks on U.S. dollar certificates of deposits.

The fixed interest rate that is paid by the fixed-rate counterparty is called the **swap rate**. Dealers in the swap market quote swap rates for different maturities. For example, the fixed interest rate may be the 10-year Treasury rate. So a 10-year treasury rate would be "swapped for" the LIBOR. The relationship between the swap rate and the maturity of a swap is called the **swap rate yield curve**, or more commonly, the **swap curve**. Because the reference rate is typically LIBOR, the swap curve is also called the **LIBOR curve**.

There is a swap curve for most countries. For euro interest rate swaps, the reference rate is the euro interbank offered rate (Euribor), which is the rate at which bank deposits in EU countries that have adopted the euro currency are offered by one prime bank to another prime bank.

The swap curve is used as a benchmark in many countries outside the United States. Unlike a country's government bond yield curve, however, the swap curve is not a default-free yield curve. Instead, it reflects the credit risk of the counterparty to an interest rate swap. Because the counterparty to an interest rate swap is typically a bank-related entity, the swap curve reflects the average credit risk of representative banks that provide interest rate swaps. More specifically, a swap curve is viewed as the **interbank yield curve**. It is also referred to as the **AA-rated yield curve**, because the banks that borrow money from one another at LIBOR have credit ratings of Aa/AA or above. In addition, the swap curve reflects liquidity risk. However, the liquidity of the interest rate swap market has increased to the point where it is now a more liquid market than the market for some government bonds.

One would expect that if a country has a government bond market, the yields in that market will be the best benchmark. That is not necessarily the case. Using a swap curve has several advantages over using a country's government securities yield curve.[2] First, it may be advantageous for technical reasons: In a government bond market, some of the interest rates may not be representative of the true interest rate but instead be biased by some technical or regulatory factor unique to that market. For example, market participants may need to cover a short position in a particular government bond, and the actions to cover a short position would push up the demand for that particular government bond and drive down its yield. In the swap market, nothing has to be delivered, so technical market factors have less of an impact. Also, there may be government bonds selling above or below their par value. As explained earlier, government tax authorities might tax such bonds differently if they are purchased and held to maturity. As a result, the yields at which these bonds trade in the marketplace will reflect any tax advantage or disadvantage.

Although it may be difficult to appreciate these factors at this point in our study of financial markets, the key is that the observed interest rate on government securities may not reflect the true interest rate because of these factors. This is not the case for swap rates. This market is not regulated, and hence swap rates represent true interest rates. However, swap rates do reflect credit risk and liquidity risk.

Second, to create a representative government bond yield curve, a large number of maturities must be available. However, in most government bond markets, securities with only a few maturities are issued. For example, as will be seen when we discuss U.S. Treasury securities in chapter 20, the U.S. government issues only four securities with a maturity of two years or more (2, 5, 10, and 30 years). Although plenty of off-the-run issues are available from which to construct a government bond yield curve, the yields on such issues may not be true interest rates for the reasons just noted. In contrast, in the swap market, a wide range of maturities is quoted. In fact, in the United States, the issuance of 30-year bonds was suspended for a time, and as a result, 30-year Treasury rates were unavailable. Yet swap dealers quoted 30-year swap rates.

2. For a further discussion, see Uri Ron, "A Practical Guide to Swap Curve Construction," in *Interest Rate, Term Structure, and Valuation Modeling,* ed. Frank J. Fabozzi (New York: John Wiley & Sons, 2002), chapter 6.

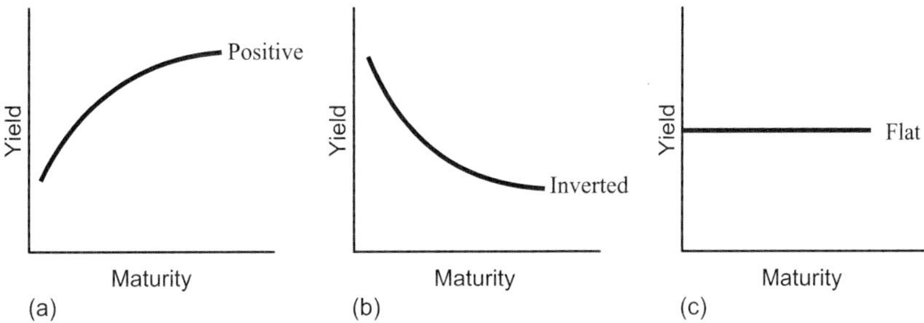

Figure 16.1
Three hypothetical yield curves.

Finally, the ability to compare government yields across countries is difficult because of differences in the credit risk for every country. In contrast, as explained earlier, the swap curve is an interbank yield curve, which facilitates cross-country comparisons of benchmark interest rates.

The Term Structure of Interest Rates

Now we will look at the relationship between the yield on a bond and its maturity. Because the maturity of a bond is referred to as its **term to maturity** or simply its **term**, the relationship between yield and maturity is referred to as the **term structure of interest rates**. Here we explain the various theories about the determinations of the term structure of interest rates.

The graphic that depicts the relationship between the yield on bonds of the same credit quality but different maturities is known as the **yield curve**. Market participants tend to construct yield curves from observations of prices and yields in the Treasury market. Two reasons account for this tendency. First, Treasury securities are free of default risk, and differences in creditworthiness do not affect yield estimates. Second, as the largest and most active bond market, the Treasury market offers the fewest problems of illiquidity or infrequent trading.

Figure 16.1 shows the general shape of three hypothetical Treasury yield curves observed from time to time in the United States. Daily yield curve information is available from a variety of sources on a real-time basis. Historical information about daily yield curves from 1990 on can be obtained from the U.S. Department of the Treasury's website.[3]

As we explained in chapter 15, from a practical viewpoint, the Treasury yield curve functions mainly as a benchmark for pricing bonds and setting yields in many other sectors of the debt market—bank loans, mortgages, corporate debt, and international bonds. More recently, market participants have come to realize that the traditionally constructed Treasury

3. See http://www.ustreas.gov/offices/domestic-finance/debt-management/interest-rate/yield_historical_main.shtml.

yield curve is an unsatisfactory measure of the relationship between required yield and maturity. The key reason is that securities with the same maturity may actually provide different yields. As we will explain, this phenomenon reflects the role and impact of differences in the bonds' coupon rates. Hence, it is necessary to develop more accurate and reliable estimates of the Treasury yield curve. In what follows, we show the problems posed by traditional approaches to the Treasury yield curve and offer an innovative and increasingly popular approach to building a yield curve. The approach consists of identifying yields that apply to zero-coupon bonds and therefore eliminates the problem of nonuniqueness in the yield-maturity relationship.

Spot Rates

As explained in chapter 11, the price of any financial asset is the present value of its cash flow. However, in our illustrations and discussion to this point in the book, we have assumed that one interest rate should be used to discount all cash flows from a financial asset. In chapter 15, we indicated that the appropriate interest rate is the yield on a Treasury security with the same maturity as the financial asset, plus an appropriate yield premium or spread.

As just noted, however, there is a problem with using the Treasury yield curve to determine the appropriate yield at which to discount the cash flow of a bond. To illustrate this problem, we'll use the following two hypothetical five-year Treasury bonds, A and B. The difference between these two Treasury bonds is the coupon rate, which is 12% for A and 3% for B. The cash flow for these two bonds per $100 of par value for the 10 six-month periods to maturity would be:

Period	Cash Flow for A ($)	Cash Flow for B ($)
1–9	6.00	1.50
10	106.00	101.50

Because of the different cash flow patterns, it is not appropriate to use the same interest rate to discount all cash flows. Instead, each cash flow should be discounted at a unique interest rate that is appropriate for the time period in which the cash flow will be received. But what should the interest rate be for each period?

The correct way to think about bonds A and B is not as bonds but as packages of cash flows. More specifically, they are packages of zero-coupon instruments. A **zero-coupon instrument** is one that is purchased at an amount below its maturity value and pays no interest periodically. Instead, the interest is earned at the maturity date, when the investor receives the maturity or principal value. Thus, the interest earned is the difference between the maturity value and the price paid. For example, bond A can be viewed as 10 zero-coupon instruments: one with a maturity value of $6 maturing six months from now, a second with a maturity value of $6 maturing one year from now, a third with a maturity value of $6 maturing 1.5 years from now, and so on. The final zero-coupon instrument matures 10 six-month periods from now and has a maturity value of $106.

Likewise, bond B can be viewed as 10 zero-coupon instruments: one with a maturity value of $1.50 maturing six months from now, one with a maturity value of $1.50 maturing one year from now, one with a maturity value of $1.50 maturing 1.5 years from now, and so on. The final zero-coupon instrument matures 10 six-month periods from now and has a maturity value of $101.50. Obviously, in the case of each coupon bond, the value or price of the bond is equal to the total value of its component zero-coupon instruments.

In general, any bond can be viewed as a package of zero-coupon instruments. That is, each zero-coupon instrument in the package has a maturity equal to its coupon payment date or, in the case of the principal, the maturity date. The value of the bond should equal the value of all the component zero-coupon instruments. If this does not hold, it is possible for a market participant to generate riskless profits. Because no one can pass up riskless and certain profits, the market must drive these two prices to equality, and our discussion here assumes that equality.

To determine the value of each zero-coupon instrument, it is necessary to know the yield on a zero-coupon Treasury with that same maturity. This yield is called the **spot rate**, and the graphical depiction of the relationship between the spot rate and its maturity is called the **spot rate curve**. As demonstrated next, this curve is derived from theoretical considerations of the yields of the actually traded Treasury securities. Such a curve is called a **theoretical spot rate curve**.

Constructing the theoretical spot rate curve Let's see how the theoretical spot rate curve is constructed from the yield curve that is based on the observed yields of Treasury bills and Treasury coupon securities.

The process of creating a theoretical spot rate curve in this way is referred to as **bootstrapping**.[4] To explain this process, we'll use the data for the hypothetical price, annualized yield (yield to maturity), and maturity of the 20 Treasury securities shown in table 16.1. (In practice, all coupon rates are estimated so that the price of each bond is par.)

4. In practice, the Treasury securities that are used to construct the theoretical spot rate curve are the most recently auctioned Treasury securities of a given maturity (i.e., the on-the-run Treasury issues). As we explain in chapter 20, there are actual zero-coupon Treasury securities with a maturity greater than one year that are outstanding in the market. These securities are not issued by the U.S. Treasury but are created by certain market participants from actual coupon Treasury securities. It would seem logical that the observed yield on zero-coupon Treasury securities could be used to construct an actual spot rate curve, but this approach has problems. First, the liquidity of these securities is not as great as that of the coupon Treasury market. Second, some maturity sectors of the zero-coupon Treasury market attract specific investors who may be willing to trade off yield in exchange for an attractive feature associated with that particular maturity sector, thereby distorting the term structure relationship.

Table 16.1
Maturity and yield to maturity for 20 hypothetical Treasury securities.

Maturity (years)	Coupon Rate (%)	Yield to Maturity (%)	Price ($)
0.50	0.0000	0.0800	96.15
1.00	0.0000	0.0830	92.19
1.50	0.0850	0.0890	99.45
2.00	0.0900	0.0920	99.64
2.50	0.1100	0.0940	103.49
3.00	0.0950	0.0970	99.49
3.50	0.1000	0.1000	100.00
4.00	0.1000	0.1040	98.72
4.50	0.1150	0.1060	103.16
5.00	0.0875	0.1080	92.24
5.50	0.1050	0.1090	98.38
6.00	0.1100	0.1120	99.14
6.50	0.0850	0.1140	86.94
7.00	0.0825	0.1160	84.24
7.50	0.1100	0.1180	96.09
8.00	0.0650	0.1190	72.62
8.50	0.0875	0.1200	82.97
9.00	0.1300	0.1220	104.30
9.50	0.1150	0.1240	95.06
10.00	0.1250	0.1250	100.00

Throughout the analysis and illustrations to come, it is important to remember that the basic principle underlying bootstrapping is that the value of the Treasury coupon security should be equal to the value of the package of zero-coupon Treasury securities that duplicates the coupon bond's cash flow.

Let's start by considering the six-month Treasury bill in table 16.1. As we explained earlier in this chapter, a Treasury bill is a zero-coupon instrument. Therefore, its annualized yield of 8% is equal to the spot rate. Similarly, for the one-year Treasury, the cited yield of 8.3% is the one-year spot rate.[5] Given these two spot rates, we can compute the spot rate for a theoretical 1.5-year zero-coupon Treasury. The price of a theoretical 1.5-year zero-coupon Treasury should equal the present value of the three cash flows from an actual 1.5-year coupon Treasury, where the yield used for discounting is the spot rate corresponding to the cash flow. Using $100 as par, the cash flow for the 1.5-year Treasury with the 8.5% coupon rate is computed as follows:

0.5 years: $0.085 \times \$100 \times 0.5 = \$4.25$.

1.0 years: $0.085 \times \$100 \times 0.5 = \$4.25$.

1.5 years: $0.085 \times \$100 \times 0.5 + 100 = \$104.25$.

5. The U.S. Treasury no longer issues a one-year Treasury bill. We will assume its existence for the purpose of this illustration.

The present value of the cash flow is then:

$$\frac{\$4.25}{(1+z_1)^1}+\frac{\$4.25}{(1+z_2)^2}+\frac{\$104.25}{(1+z_3)^3},$$

where

z_1 = one-half the annualized six-month theoretical spot rate,

z_2 = one-half the one-year theoretical spot rate,

z_3 = one-half the 1.5-year theoretical spot rate.

Because the six-month spot rate and the one-year spot rate are 8.0% and 8.3%, respectively, we know these facts:

$z_1 = 0.04$ and $z_2 = 0.0415$.

We can compute the present value of the 1.5-year coupon Treasury security as follows:

$$\frac{\$4.25}{(1.0400)^1}+\frac{\$4.25}{(1.0415)^2}+\frac{\$104.25}{(1+z_3)^3}.$$

Because the price of the 1.5-year coupon Treasury security (from table 16.1) is \$99.45, the following relationship between the market price and the present value of the cash flow must hold:

$$\$99.45=\frac{\$4.25}{(1.0400)^1}+\frac{\$4.25}{(1.0415)^2}+\frac{\$104.25}{(1+z_3)^3}.$$

We can solve for the theoretical 1.5-year spot rate to obtain a value of z_3 of 0.04465.

Doubling this yield, we obtain the bond-equivalent yield of 0.0893 or 8.93%, which is the theoretical 1.5-year spot rate. That rate is the rate that the market would apply to a 1.5-year zero-coupon Treasury security if, in fact, such a security existed.

Given the theoretical 1.5-year spot rate, we can obtain the theoretical two-year spot rate. The cash flow for the two-year coupon Treasury in table 16.1 is

0.5 years: $0.090 \times \$100 \times 0.5 = \$4.50$.

1.0 year: $0.090 \times \$100 \times 0.5 = \$4.50$.

1.5 years: $0.090 \times \$100 \times 0.5 = \$4.50$.

2.0 years: $0.090 \times \$100 \times 0.5 + 100 = \$104.50$.

The present value of the cash flow is then:

$$\frac{\$4.50}{(1+z_1)^1}+\frac{\$4.50}{(1+z_2)^2}+\frac{\$4.50}{(1+z_3)^3}+\frac{\$104.50}{(1+z_4)^4}$$

where z_4 is half of the two-year theoretical spot rate. Because the six-month spot rate, the one-year spot rate, and the 1.5-year spot rate are 8.0%, 8.3%, and 8.93%, respectively, then

$z_1 = 0.04$, $z_2 = 0.0415$, and $z_3 = 0.04465$.

Therefore, the present value of the two-year Treasury security is

$$\frac{\$4.50}{(1.0400)^1} + \frac{\$4.50}{(1.0415)^2} + \frac{\$4.50}{(1.04465)^3} + \frac{\$104.50}{(1+z_4)^4}.$$

Because the price of the two-year coupon Treasury security is \$99.64, the following relationship must hold:

$$\$99.64 = \frac{\$4.50}{(1.0400)^1} + \frac{\$4.50}{(1.0415)^2} + \frac{\$4.50}{(1.04465)^3} + \frac{\$104.50}{(1+z_4)^4}.$$

Solving for the theoretical two-year spot rate, we would find that z_4 is 0.046235. Doubling this yield, we obtain the theoretical two-year spot rate bond-equivalent yield of 9.247%.

One can follow this approach iteratively to derive the theoretical 2.5-year spot rate from the calculated values of z_1, z_2, z_3, and z_4 (the six-month, one-year, 1.5-year, and two-year rates, respectively), and the price and coupon of the bond with a maturity of 2.5 years. Furthermore, one could derive the theoretical spot rates for the remaining 15 half-yearly rates. The spot rates thus obtained are shown in table 16.2. They represent the term structure of interest rates for maturities up to 10 years, at the particular time to which the bond price quotations refer.

Column 2 of table 16.2 reproduces the calculated yield to maturity for the coupon issue listed in table 16.1. A comparison of this column with the last column giving the yield to maturity of a zero-coupon bond is instructive: It confirms that bonds of the same maturity can have different yields to maturity. That is, the yield of bonds of the same credit quality does not depend on their maturity alone. Although the two columns do not change much at the beginning, they diverge more after the third year, and by the ninth year, the zero-coupon yield is nearly 100 basis points higher than that of the same maturity with a coupon of 13% and selling at a premium.

Using spot rates to value a bond Given the spot rates, the theoretical value of a bond can be calculated by discounting a cash flow for a given period by the corresponding spot rate for that period. This is illustrated in table 16.3.

The bond in our illustration is a 10-year, 10% coupon Treasury bond. The second column of table 16.3 shows the cash flow per \$100 of par value for a 10% coupon bond. The third column shows the theoretical spot rates. The fourth column is simply one-half of the annual spot rate of the previous column. The last column shows the present value of the cash flow in the second column when discounted at the semiannual spot rate. The value of this bond is the total present value, \$85.35477.

Table 16.2
Theoretical spot rates.

Maturity (years)	Yield to Maturity (%)	Theoretical Spot Rate
0.50	0.0800	0.08000
1.00	0.0830	0.08300
1.50	0.0890	0.08930
2.00	0.0920	0.09247
2.50	0.0940	0.09468
3.00	0.0970	0.09787
3.50	0.1000	0.10129
4.00	0.1040	0.10592
4.50	0.1060	0.10850
5.00	0.1080	0.11021
5.50	0.1090	0.11175
6.00	0.1120	0.11584
6.50	0.1140	0.11744
7.00	0.1160	0.11991
7.50	0.1180	0.12405
8.00	0.1190	0.12278
8.50	0.1200	0.12546
9.00	0.1220	0.13152
9.50	0.1240	0.13377
10.00	0.1250	0.13623

Forward Rates

Thus far we have seen that we can extrapolate the theoretical spot rates from the Treasury yield curve. In addition, we can extrapolate what some market participants refer to as the "market's consensus regarding future interest rates." To see the importance of knowing the market's consensus regarding future interest rates, let's consider the following two investment alternatives for an investor who has a one-year investment horizon:

Alternative 1: Investor buys a one-year instrument.

Alternative 2: Investor buys a six-month instrument; when it matures in six months, the investor buys another six-month instrument.

With alternative 1, the investor will realize the one-year spot rate, and that rate is known with certainty. In contrast, with alternative 2, the investor will realize the six-month spot rate, but the six-month rate six months from now is unknown. Therefore, for alternative 2, the rate that will be earned over one year is not known with certainty. This is illustrated in figure 16.2.

Suppose that this investor expected that six months from now, the six-month rate will be higher than it is today. The investor might then feel alternative 2 would be the better

Table 16.3
Illustration of how to value a 10-year, 10% Treasury bond using spot rates.

Maturity (years)	Cash Flow ($)	Spot Rate	Semiannual Spot Rate	Present Value ($)
0.5	5	0.08000	0.04000	4.8077
1.0	5	0.08300	0.04150	4.6095
1.5	5	0.08930	0.04465	4.3859
2.0	5	0.09247	0.04624	4.1730
2.5	5	0.09468	0.04734	3.9676
3.0	5	0.09787	0.04894	3.7539
3.5	5	0.10129	0.05065	3.5382
4.0	5	0.10592	0.05296	3.3088
4.5	5	0.10850	0.05425	3.1080
5.0	5	0.11021	0.05511	2.9242
5.5	5	0.11175	0.05588	2.7494
6.0	5	0.11584	0.05792	2.5441
6.5	5	0.11744	0.05872	2.3813
7.0	5	0.11991	0.05996	2.2128
7.5	5	0.12405	0.06203	2.0274
8.0	5	0.12278	0.06139	1.9274
8.5	5	0.12546	0.06273	1.7774
9.0	5	0.13152	0.06576	1.5889
9.5	5	0.13377	0.06689	1.4613
10.0	105	0.13623	0.06812	28.1079
Total				**85.35477**

investment. However, this expectation is not necessarily true. To understand why, and to appreciate why it is necessary to know what the market's consensus regarding future interest rates is, let's continue with our illustration.

The investor will be indifferent to the two alternatives if they produce the same total dollars over the one-year investment horizon. Given the one-year spot rate, there is some rate on a six-month instrument six months from now that will make the investor indifferent between the two alternatives. We denote that rate by f.

The value of f can be readily determined given the one-year spot rate and the six-month spot rate. If an investor places \$100 in a one-year instrument (alternative 1), the total amount in dollars that will be generated at the end of one year is:

Total dollars at the end of year for alternative $1 = \$100\,(1 + z_2)^2$,

where z_2 is the one-year spot rate. (Remember, we are working in six-month periods, so the subscript 2 represents two six-month periods, or one year.)

The proceeds from investing at the six-month spot rate will generate the following total dollars at the end of six months:

Total dollars at the end of six months for alternative $2 = \$100\,(1 + z_1)$,

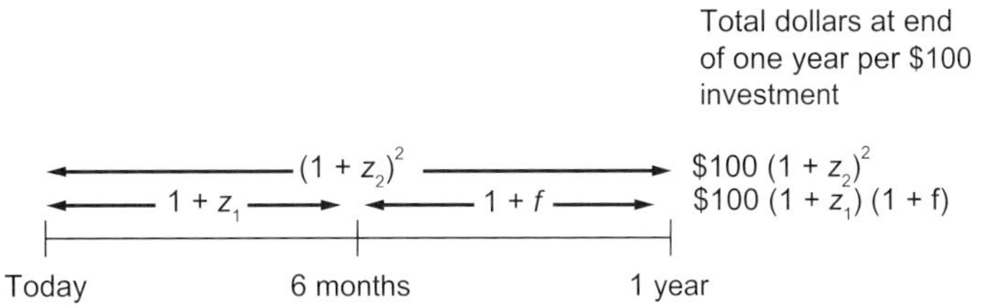

Figure 16.2
Two alternative one-year investments.

where z_1 is the six-month spot rate. If this amount is reinvested at the six-month rate six months from now, which we denoted by f, then the total dollars at the end of one year will be:

Total dollars at the end of year for alternative 2 = \$100 $(1+z_1)(1+f)$.

The investor will be indifferent between the two alternatives if the total dollars are the same. Setting the two equations for the total dollars at the end of one year for the two alternatives equal, we get:

$$\$100\,(1+z_2)^2 = \$100\,(1+z_1)(1+f).$$

Solving the preceding equation for f, we get:

$$f = \frac{(1+z_2)^2}{(1+z_1)} - 1.$$

Doubling f gives the bond-equivalent yield for the six-month rate six months from now that we are interested in.

We can illustrate the calculation of f using the theoretical spot rates shown in table 16.2. From that table, we know that:

Six-month spot rate = 0.080; therefore, $z_1 = 0.0400$.

One-year spot rate = 0.083; therefore, $z_2 = 0.0415$.

Substituting into the formula, we have:

$$f = \frac{(1.0415)^2}{(1.0400)} = 0.043.$$

Therefore, the forward rate on a six-month security, quoted on a bond-equivalent basis, is

8.6% (= 0.043 × 2).

Here is how we use this rate of 8.6%. If the six-month rate six months from now is less than 8.6%, then the total dollars at the end of one year would be higher by investing in the one-year instrument (alternative 1). If the six-month rate six months from now is greater than 8.6%, then the total dollars at the end of one year would be higher by investing in the six-month instrument and reinvesting the proceeds six months from now at the six-month rate at the time (alternative 2). Of course, if the six-month rate six months from now is 8.6%, the two alternatives give the same total dollars at the end of one year.

Now that we have the rate f in which we are interested and we know how that rate can be used, let's return to the question posed at the outset. From table 16.2, the six-month spot rate is 8%. Suppose that the investor expects that six months from now, the six-month rate will be 8.2%. That is, the investor expects that the six-month rate will be higher than its current level. Should the investor select alternative 2 because the six-month rate six months from now is expected to be higher? The answer is no. As explained in the previous paragraph, if the rate is less than 8.6%, then alternative 1 is the better alternative. Because this investor expects a rate of 8.2%, then he or she should select alternative 1, even though he or she expects the six-month rate to be higher than it is today.

This result is somewhat surprising for some investors. But the reason is that the market prices its expectations of future interest rates into the rates offered on investments with different maturities. Knowing the market's consensus regarding future interest rates is critical. The rate that we determined for f is the market's consensus for the six-month rate six months from now. A future interest rate calculated from either the spot rates or the yield curve is called a **forward rate** or an **implied forward rate**.

Similarly, borrowers need to understand what a forward rate is. For example, suppose a borrower must choose between a one-year loan and a series of two six-month loans. If the forward rate is less than the borrower's expectations of six-month rates six months from now, then the borrower would be better off with a one-year loan. If instead the borrower's expectations are that six-month rates six months from now will be less than the forward rate, the borrower would be better off by choosing a series of two six-month loans.

The forward rate consists of two elements. The first is when in the future the rate begins. The second is the length of time for the rate. For example, the two-year forward rate three years from now means a rate three years from now for a length of two years. The notation used for a forward rate, f, will have two subscripts, one before f and one after f, as shown: ${}_tf_m$.

The subscript before f is t and is the length of time that the rate applies. The subscript after f is m and is when the forward rate begins. That is, the length of time of the forward rate f when the forward rate begins.

Remember our time periods are still six-month periods. Given the preceding notation, here is what the notation means:

Notation	Interpretation for the Forward Rate
${}_{1}f_{12}$	six-month (1-period) forward rate beginning six years (12 periods) from now
${}_{2}f_{8}$	one-year (2-period) forward rate beginning four years (8 periods) from now
${}_{6}f_{4}$	three-year (6-period) forward rate beginning two years (4 periods) from now
${}_{8}f_{10}$	four-year (8-period) forward rate beginning five years (10 periods) from now

It can be demonstrated that the formula to compute any forward rate is

$${}_{t}f_{m} = \left[\frac{(1+z_{m+t})^{m+t}}{(1+z_{m})^{m}} \right]^{1/t} - 1.$$

Notice that if $t = 1$, the formula reduces to the one-period (six-month) forward rate.

To illustrate, for the spot rates shown in table 16.2, suppose that an investor wants to know the two-year forward rate three years from now. In terms of the notation, $t = 4$ and $m = 6$. Substituting for t and m into the equation for the forward rate, we have:

$${}_{4}f_{6} = \left[\frac{(1+z_{6+4})^{6+4}}{(1+z_{6})^{6}} \right]^{1/4} - 1.$$

This expression means that the following spot rates are needed: z_6 (the three-year spot rate) and z_{10} (the five-year spot rate). From table 16.3, we know:

z_6 (the three-year spot rate) = 9.9787%/2 = 4.894% = 0.04894,
z_{10} (the five-year spot rate) = 13.623%/2 = 6.812% = 0.06812.

Then we have

$${}_{4}f_{6} = \left[\frac{(1.06812)^{10}}{(1.04894)^{6}} \right]^{1/4} - 1.$$

Therefore, ${}_{4}f_{6}$ is equal to 9.755%, and doubling this rate gives 19.510%, the forward rate on a bond-equivalent basis.

We can verify this result. Investing \$100 for 10 periods at the semiannual spot rate of 6.812% will produce the following value:

$\$100(1.06812)^{10} = \$193.286.$

Investing \$100 for six periods at 4.894% and reinvesting the proceeds for four periods at the forward rate of 9.755% gives the same value:

$$\$100(1.04894)^6\,(1.09755)^4 = \$193.286.$$

Relationship between spot rates and short-term forward rates Suppose an investor purchases a five-year, zero-coupon Treasury security for \$58.48 with a maturity value of \$100. The investor could instead buy a six-month Treasury bill and reinvest the proceeds every six months for five years. The number of dollars that will be realized will depend on the six-month forward rates. Suppose that the investor can actually reinvest the proceeds maturing every six months at the implied six-month forward rates.

Let us see how many dollars would accumulate at the end of five years. The implied six-month forward rates were calculated for the yield curve given in table 16.2. Letting f_t denote the six-month forward rate beginning t six-month periods from now, the semiannual implied forward rates using the spot rates shown in table 16.2 are:

$$f_1 = 0.043000,\quad f_2 = 0.050980,\quad f_3 = 0.051005,\quad f_4 = 0.051770,$$
$$f_5 = 0.056945,\quad f_6 = 0.060965,\quad f_7 = 0.069310,\quad f_8 = 0.064625,$$
$$f_9 = 0.062830.$$

By investing the \$58.48 at the six-month spot rate of 4% (8% on a bond-equivalent basis) and reinvesting at the foregoing forward rates, the number of dollars accumulated at the end of five years will be

$$\$58.48(1.04)(1.043)(1.05098)(1.051005)(1.05177)(1.056945)(1.069310)$$
$$(1.064625)(1.06283) = \$100.$$

Therefore, we see that if the implied forward rates are realized, the \$58.48 investment will produce the same number of dollars as an investment in a five-year, zero-coupon Treasury security at the five-year spot rate. From this illustration, we can see that the five-year spot rate is related to the current six-month spot rate and the implied six-month forward rates.

In general, the relationship between a t-period spot rate, the current six-month spot rate, and the implied six-month forward rates is:

$$z_t = [(1+z_1)(1+f_1)(1+f_2)(1+f_3)\ \ldots\ (1+f_{t-1})]^{1/t-1}.$$

To illustrate how to use this equation, let's look at how the five-year (10-period) spot rate is related to the six-month forward rates. Substituting into the preceding equation the relevant forward rates just given and the one-period spot rate of 4% (half of the 8% annual spot rate), we obtain:

$$z_{10} = [(1.04)(1.043)(1.05098)(1.051005)(1.05177)(1.056945)\,(1.060965)(1.069310)$$
$$(1.064625)(1.06283)]^{1/10} - 1 = 5.51\%.$$

Doubling 5.51% gives an annual spot rate of 11.02%, which agrees with the spot rate given in table 16.2.

Forward rate as a hedgeable rate A natural question to ask about forward rates is: How well do they predict future interest rates? Studies demonstrate that forward rates do not do a good job of predicting future interest rates.[6] So why do we emphasize understanding forward rates? The reason, as we demonstrated in our illustration of how to select between two alternative investments, is that the forward rates indicate how an investor's expectations must differ from the market consensus for the investor to make the correct decision.

In our illustration, the six-month forward rate may not be realized, which is irrelevant. What is important is that the six-month forward rate indicated to the investor that if expectations about the six-month rate six months from now are less than 8.6%, the investor would be better-off with alternative 1.

For this reason, as well as for others explained later, some market participants prefer not to talk about forward rates as being market consensus rates. Instead, they refer to forward rates as **hedgeable rates**. For example, by buying the one-year security, the investor was able to hedge the six-month rate six months from now.

Historical Shapes Observed for the Treasury Yield Curve

If we plot the term structure—the yield to maturity, or the spot rate, at successive maturities against maturity—what is it likely to look like? Figure 16.1 shows three generic shapes that have appeared for the U.S. Treasury yield curve with some frequency over time. Table 16.4 shows five selected daily Treasury yield curves in tabular form.

Panel A of figure 16.1 shows an upward-sloping yield curve; that is, the yield rises steadily as maturity increases. This shape is commonly referred to as a **positively sloped yield curve**. Market participants differentiate positively sloped yield curves based on the steepness or slope of the curve. The slope is commonly measured in terms of the maturity spread, where the maturity spread is the difference between long-term and short-term yields. Although there are many maturity candidates to use as proxies for long-term and short-term yields, we'll use the maturity spread between the six-month and the 30-year yield in our example.

The first two daily yield curves shown in table 16.4 are positively sloped yield curves. The three- and six-month yields are roughly the same for both dates. However, the steepness of the slope is different. The maturity spread between the 30-year and six-month yield (i.e., the three-month/six-month spread) was 195 basis points (5.73% – 3.78%) on April 23, 2001, and 401 basis points (7.89% – 3.88%) on April 10, 1992. The convention in the marketplace is to refer to a positively sloped yield curve whose maturity spread as measured

6. Eugene F. Fama, "Forward Rates as Predictors of Future Spot Rates," *Journal of Financial Economics* 3 (1976): 361–377.

Table 16.4
U.S. Treasury yield curve for five dates.

Date	3 Month	6 Month	1 Year	2 Year	3 Year	5 Year	7 Year	10 Year	20 Year	30 Year	Shape
4/23/2001	3.75	3.78	3.75	3.77	4.15	4.38	4.78	5.06	5.84	5.73	Normal
4/10/1992	3.74	3.88	4.12	5.16	5.72	6.62	7.03	7.37	N/A	7.89	Steep
8/14/1981	N/A	N/A	16.71	16.91	15.88	15.34	15.04	N/A	14.74	13.95	Inverted
1/3/1990	7.89	7.94	7.85	7.94	7.96	7.92	8.04	7.99	N/A	8.04	Flat
1/4/2001	5.37	5.20	4.82	4.77	4.78	4.82	5.07	5.03	5.56	5.44	Humped

Sources: The data for 4/23/2001, 4/10/1992, 1/3/1990, and 1/4/2001 are from the daily yield curves provided by the U.S. Treasury. The data for 8/14/1981 are from various Treasury yield tables published by the U.S. Treasury.

by the six-month and 30-year yields as a **normal yield curve** when the spread is 300 basis points or less; when the maturity spread is more than 300 basis points, the yield curve is said to be a **steep yield curve**.

When a yield curve's maturity spread increases (or in the parlance of the market, it "widens"), the yield curve is said to *steepen;* when the maturity spread decreases (i.e., "narrows"), the yield curve is said to *flatten.*

Panel B of figure 16.1 shows a downward-sloping or **inverted yield curve**, where yields in general decline as maturity increases. There have not been many instances in the recent history of the U.S. Treasury market of the yield curve exhibiting this characteristic. The most notable example occurred in August 1981. Table 16.4 shows the daily yield curve for one day in that month, on August 14. Treasury yields at the time were at historical highs. The yield on the two-year was 16.91% and declined for each subsequent maturity until it reached 13.95% for the 30-year maturity.

Finally, panel C of figure 16.1 shows a **flat yield curve**. Although the figure suggests that for a flat yield curve, the yields are identical for each maturity, that is not what is observed. Instead, the yields for all maturities are similar. The yield curve on January 3, 1990, reported in table 16.4, is an example. Notice the very small six-month/30-year maturity spread: 10 basis points. A variant of the flat yield is one in which the yields on short-term and long-term Treasuries are similar but the yield on intermediate-term Treasuries is lower.

Determinants of the Shape of the Term Structure

Two major theories evolved to account for these observed shapes of the yield curve: **expectations theory** and **market segmentation theory**.

The expectations theory includes several forms: **pure expectations theory**, **liquidity theory**, and **preferred habitat theory**. All share a hypothesis about the behavior of short-term forward rates, and they also assume that the forward rates in current long-term contracts are closely related to the market's expectations about future short-term rates. These three theories differ, however, on whether and how other factors also affect forward rates.

The pure expectations theory postulates that no systematic factors other than expected future short-term rates affect forward rates; the liquidity theory and preferred habitat theory assert that other factors are also involved. Accordingly, the last two forms of the expectations theory are sometimes referred to as **biased expectations theories**.

Pure expectations theory According to the **pure expectations theory**, the forward rates exclusively represent the expected rates. Thus, the entire term structure at a given time reflects the market's current expectations of the family of future short-term rates. According to this view, a rising term structure, as in panel a of figure 16.1, must indicate that the market expects short-term rates to rise throughout the relevant future. Similarly, a flat term structure reflects an expectation that future short-term rates will be mostly constant, whereas a falling term structure must reflect an expectation that future short rates will decline steadily.

We can illustrate this theory by considering how an expectation of a rising short-term future rate would affect the behavior of various market participants so as to result in a rising yield curve. Assume an initially flat term structure, and suppose that economic news subsequently leads market participants to expect interest rates to rise.

1. Those market participants interested in a long-term investment would not want to buy long-term bonds, because they would expect the yield structure to rise sooner or later, resulting in a price decline for the bonds and a capital loss on the long-term bonds purchased. Instead, they would want to invest in short-term debt obligations until the rise in yield occurred, permitting them to reinvest their funds at the higher yield.
2. Speculators expecting rising rates would anticipate a decline in the price of long-term bonds and therefore would want to sell any long-term bonds they own and possibly to "short sell" some they do not now own.[7] (Should interest rates rise as expected, the price of longer-term bonds will fall. If the speculator sells these bonds short and then purchases them at a lower price to cover the short sale, a profit is earned.) The proceeds received from the selling of long-term debt issues that the speculators now hold or the shorting of longer-term bonds will be invested in short-term debt obligations.
3. Borrowers wishing to acquire long-term funds would be pulled toward borrowing now, at the long end of the market, by the expectation that borrowing at a later time would be more expensive.

All these responses would tend either to lower the net demand for, or to increase the supply of, long-maturity bonds, and two of the responses would increase the demand for short-term obligations. Clearing of the market would require a rise in long-term yields in relation to short-term yields; that is, these actions by investors, speculators, and borrowers would tilt the term structure upward until it was consistent with expectations of higher

7. "Short selling" means selling a security that is not owned but borrowed. The process for selling stocks short is described in chapter 22.

future interest rates. By analogous reasoning, an unexpected event leading to the expectation of lower future rates would result in the yield curve sloping downward.

Unfortunately, the pure expectations theory suffers from one shortcoming, which, qualitatively, is quite serious. It neglects the risks inherent in investing in bonds and similar instruments. If forward rates were perfect predictors of future interest rates, then the future prices of bonds would be known with certainty. The return over any investment period would be certain and independent of the maturity of the instrument initially acquired and of the time at which the investor needed to liquidate the instrument. However, with uncertainty about future interest rates and hence about future prices of bonds, these instruments become risky investments in the sense that the return over some investment horizon is unknown.

Similarly, from a borrower's or issuer's perspective, the cost of borrowing for any required period of financing would be certain and independent of the maturity of the instrument initially sold if the rate at which the borrower would have to refinance debt in the future were known. But with uncertainty about future interest rates, the cost of borrowing is uncertain if the borrower must refinance at some time over the periods in which the funds are initially needed.

In the following section, we examine more closely the sources and types of risk that the pure expectations theory ignores.

Risks associated with bond investment Two risks cause uncertainty about the return over some investment horizon. The first is the uncertainty about the price of the bond at the end of the investment horizon. For example, an investor who plans to invest for five years might consider the following three investment alternatives: (1) invest in a five-year bond and hold it for five years, (2) invest in a 12-year bond and sell it at the end of five years, or (3) invest in a 30-year bond and sell it at the end of five years. The return that will be realized for the second and third alternatives is not known, because the price of each long-term bond at the end of five years is not known. In the case of the 12-year bond, the price will depend on the yield on seven-year debt securities five years from now, and the price of the 30-year bond will depend on the yield on 25-year bonds five years from now. Because forward rates implicit in the current term structure for a future 12-year bond and a future 25-year bond are not perfect predictors of the actual future rates, the price for both bonds five years from now remains uncertain.

The risk that the price of the bond will be lower than currently expected at the end of the investment horizon is called **price risk**. An important feature of price risk is that it is greater the longer the maturity of the bond. The reason should be familiar from our discussion in chapter 15: the longer the maturity is, the greater will be the price volatility of a bond when yields rise. Thus, investors are exposed to price risk when they invest in a bond that will be sold before the bond's maturity date.

The second risk has to do with uncertainty about the rate at which the proceeds from a bond that matures before the end of the investment horizon can be reinvested until the investment horizon. For example, an investor who plans to invest for five years might consider the following three alternative investments: (1) invest in a five-year bond and hold it for five years; (2) invest in a six-month instrument and, when it matures, reinvest the proceeds in six-month instruments over the entire five-year investment horizon; and (3) invest in a two-year bond and, when it matures, reinvest the proceeds in a three-year bond. The risk in the second and third alternatives is that the return over the five-year investment horizon is unknown, because the rates at which the proceeds can be reinvested until maturity are unknown. This risk is referred to as **reinvestment risk**.

Interpretations of pure expectations theory Several interpretations of the pure expectations theory have been put forth by economists. These interpretations are not equivalent; nor are they consistent with one another, in large part because they offer different treatments of the two risks associated with realizing a return that we have just explained.[8]

The broadest interpretation of the pure expectations theory suggests that investors expect the return for any investment horizon to be the same, regardless of the maturity strategy selected.[9] To illustrate, let's consider an investor with a five-year investment horizon. According to the pure expectations theory, it makes no difference whether a five-year, 12-year, or 30-year bond is purchased and held for five years because the investor expects the return from all three bonds to be the same over five years. A major criticism of this broad interpretation of the theory is that, because of price risk associated with investing in bonds with a maturity greater than the investment horizon, the expected returns from these three different bond investments should differ in significant ways.[10]

A second interpretation, referred to as the **local expectations** form of the pure expectations theory, suggests that the return will be the same over a short-term investment horizon starting today. For example, if an investor has a six-month investment horizon, buying a five-year, 10-year, or 20-year bond will produce the same six-month return. Studies demonstrate that the local expectations formulation, which is narrow in scope, is the only one of the interpretations of the pure expectations theory that can be sustained in equilibrium.[11]

The third and final interpretation of the pure expectations theory suggests that the return that an investor will realize by rolling over short-term bonds to some investment horizon will be the same as the return from holding a zero-coupon bond with a maturity identical to the investment horizon. (A zero-coupon bond has no reinvestment risk, so future interest rates over the investment horizon do not affect the return.) This variant is called the **return-to-maturity expectations** interpretation. For example, let's once again assume that

8. These formulations are summarized by John Cox, Jonathan Ingersoll, Jr., and Stephen Ross, "A Re-examination of Traditional Hypotheses about the Term Structure of Interest Rates," *Journal of Finance* 36 (1981): 769–799.

9. F. Lutz, "The Structure of Interest Rates," *Quarterly Journal of Economics* 55 (1940): 36–63.

10. Cox, Ingersoll, and Ross, "A Re-examination of Traditional Hypotheses," 774–775.

11. Cox, Ingersoll, and Ross, "A Re-examination of Traditional Hypotheses."

an investor has a five-year investment horizon. By buying a five-year zero-coupon bond and holding it to maturity, the investor's return is the difference between the maturity value and the price of the bond, all divided by the price of the bond. According to return-to-maturity expectations, the same return will be realized by buying a six-month instrument and rolling it over every six months for five years. The validity of this interpretation is subject to considerable doubt.

Liquidity theory We explained that the drawback of the pure expectations theory is that it does not consider the risks associated with investing in bonds. Nonetheless, we have just shown that risk is indeed involved in holding a long-term bond for one period, and that risk increases with the bond's maturity, because maturity and price volatility are directly related.

Given this uncertainty, and the reasonable consideration that investors typically do not like uncertainty, some economists and financial analysts suggest a different theory. This theory states that investors will hold longer-term maturities if they are offered a long-term rate higher than the average of expected future rates by a risk premium that is positively related to the term to maturity.[12] Put differently, the forward rates should reflect both interest rate expectations and a "liquidity" premium (really a risk premium), and the premium should be higher for longer maturities.

According to this theory, which is called the **liquidity theory of the term structure**, the implicit forward rates will not be an unbiased estimate of the market's expectations of future interest rates, because they embody a liquidity premium. Thus, an upward-sloping yield curve may reflect expectations that future interest rates either (1) will rise or (2) will be flat or even fall, but with a liquidity premium increasing fast enough with maturity so as to produce an upward-sloping yield curve.

Preferred habitat theory Another theory, known as the **preferred habitat theory**, also adopts the view that the term structure reflects the expectation of the future path of interest rates as well as a risk premium. However, the habitat theory rejects the assertion that the risk premium must rise uniformly with maturity.[13] Proponents of the habitat theory say that the latter conclusion could be accepted if all investors intend to liquidate their investment at the first possible date, and all borrowers are eager to borrow long, but that assumption can be rejected for two reasons.

First, it is obvious that many investors wish to carry resources forward for appreciable periods of time—to buy a house, for example, or to provide for retirement. Such investors are concerned with the amount available at the appropriate time and not the path by which that goal is reached. Hence, risk aversion dictates that they should prefer an instrument

12. John R. Hicks, *Value and Capital,* 2nd ed. (London: Oxford University Press, 1946), 141–145.

13. Franco Modigliani and Richard Sutch, "Innovation in Interest Rate Policy," *American Economic Review* 56 (1966): 178–197.

with a maturity matching the period for which they wish to invest over shorter-term investment vehicles. If these investors buy a shorter-term instrument, they will bear reinvestment risk—the risk of a fall in the interest rates available for reinvesting the proceeds of the shorter-term instrument. Investors can avoid that risk only by locking in the current long rate through a long-term contract. Similarly, if they buy an instrument with a maturity longer than the time they wish to invest for, they will bear the risk of a loss in the price of the asset (price risk) when liquidating it before its maturity, because of a rise in interest rates. Entirely analogous considerations apply to borrowers: Prudence and safety call for borrowing for a maturity by matching the length of time for which funds are required.

Second, a lot of the demand for and supply of securities these days come from financial intermediaries, which have liabilities with specified maturities. These institutions seek to match as closely as possible the maturity of their liabilities with the cash flow of a portfolio of assets. When constructing such a portfolio, a financial institution will restrict its investments to certain maturity sectors.

To illustrate this preference for maturity sectors, let's consider a life insurance company that issues a five-year guaranteed investment contract.[14] The insurance company will not want to invest in six-month instruments because of the associated reinvestment risk. As another example, assume a thrift borrows funds at a fixed rate for one year with the proceeds from the issuance of a one-year certificate of deposit. The thrift is exposed to price (or interest rate) risk if the borrowed funds are invested in a bond with 20 years to maturity. Clearly, then, either of these institutions faces some kind of risk if it invests outside its preferred maturity sector.

The preferred habitat theory asserts that, to the extent that the demand and supply of funds in a given maturity range do not match, some lenders and borrowers will be induced to shift to maturities showing the opposite imbalances. However, they need to be compensated by an appropriate risk premium whose magnitude reflects the extent of aversion to either price or reinvestment risk.

Thus, this theory proposes that the shape of the yield curve is determined by both expectations of future interest rates and a risk premium, positive or negative, to induce market participants to shift out of their preferred habitat. Clearly, according to this theory, yield curves sloping up, down, flat, or humped are all possible.

Market segmentation theory The **market segmentation theory** also recognizes that investors' preferred habitats dictate saving and investment flows. It also proposes that the major reason for the shape of the yield curve lies in asset/liability management constraints (either regulatory or self-imposed) and/or creditors (borrowers) restricting their lending (financing) to specific maturity sectors.[15] However, the market segmentation theory differs

14. See chapter 8 for a discussion of guaranteed investment contracts.

15. This theory was suggested in J. M. Culbertson, "The Term Structure of Interest Rates," *Quarterly Journal of Economics* 71 (1957): 489–504.

from the preferred habitat theory in that it assumes that neither investors nor borrowers are willing to shift from one maturity sector to another to take advantage of opportunities arising from differences between expectations and forward rates.

Thus, for segmentation theory, the shape of the yield curve is determined by the supply of and demand for securities within each maturity sector. This formulation seems untenable: It presupposes the prevalence of absolute risk aversion, but the evidence does not support that proposition. Thus, market participants must be expected to shift away from their habitat when sufficiently large discrepancies occur between market and expected rates. This potential shifting ensures that the differences between market and expected rates will not grow too large, and this consideration leads back to the preferred habitat theory.

Key Points

- Every economy operates not just with one interest rate but rather with a structure of interest rates.
- The yield spread is the difference between the yield on any two bonds and reflects the difference in their risks.
- A country's government bond market can be used as the base or benchmark interest rate for that country.
- The base interest rate is equal to the real rate of interest plus the expected rate of inflation.
- The risk premium is the yield spread between a nongovernment security and a comparable government security.
- The factors that affect the yield spread include (1) the type of issuer (agency, corporation, or municipality), (2) the issuer's perceived creditworthiness as measured by the rating system of credit rating agencies, (3) the term or maturity of the instrument, (4) the embedded options in a bond issue (e.g., call, put, or conversion provisions), (5) the taxability of interest income at the federal and municipal levels, and (6) the expected liquidity of the issue.
- The swap rate yield curve also provides information about interest rates in a country.
- The swap rate yield curve, or simply "swap curve," is not a default-free yield curve but rather reflects interbank credit risk.
- In many countries, market participants use the country's swap curve as the benchmark interest rate rather than the country's government bond yield curve.
- The term structure of interest rates refers to the relationship between yield and maturity for comparable bonds.
- The yield curve is the graphical depiction of the relationship between the yield on bonds of the same credit quality but different maturities.
- Historically, the yield on Treasury securities is the benchmark rate used for the yield on nongovernment bonds; consequently, the most commonly constructed yield curve is the Treasury yield curve.

- A problem arises with using the Treasury yield curve to determine the one yield at which to discount all the cash payments of any bond.
- Each cash flow in a bond's total pattern of cash flows should be discounted at a unique interest rate that is applicable to the period when the cash flow is to be received.
- Any bond can be viewed as a package of zero-coupon instruments, so its value should equal the value of all the component zero-coupon instruments.
- The spot rate is the rate on a zero-coupon bond.
- The rate on a zero-coupon security can be estimated from the Treasury yield curve using a method known as bootstrapping.
- Under certain assumptions, the market's expectation of future interest rates can be extrapolated from the theoretical Treasury spot rate curve. The resulting forward rate is referred to as the implicit forward rate.
- The spot rate is related to the current six-month spot rate and the implicit six-month forward rates.
- A knowledge of the forward rates implicit in the current long-term rate is relevant when formulating both investment strategies and borrowing policies.
- Several theories have been proposed as to the determination of the term structure.
- The pure expectations theory hypothesizes that the one-period forward rates simply represent the market's expectations of future actual rates; thus, the long-term spot rate would itself be explained fully by the market expectations of future short rates.
- According to the pure expectations theory, the term structure might be positive, negative, or flat, depending on whether the market expects rising, falling, or unchanged short-term rates, respectively.
- The pure expectations theory fails to recognize the risks associated with investing in bonds—price risk and reinvestment risk—when investors buy bonds whose maturity is different from the time for which they plan to hold the bond.
- The price risk of investing in long-term bonds, and the fact that the risk increases with maturity, gives rise to an alternative: the liquidity theory of the term structure.
- According to the liquidity theory of the term structure of interest rates, forward rates are the sum of expected future rates and a risk premium that increases for increasingly distant future rates and, hence, rises with the maturity of a bond.
- The liquidity theory of the term structure of interest rates has shortcomings, because it presupposes that all lenders want to lend short and all borrowers want to borrow long; if so, long borrowers must offer lenders a premium, rising with maturity, to accept the risk of going long.
- In reality, both lenders and borrowers vary substantially in their maturity preferences, with each market participant being able to eliminate risk not by borrowing or lending short but by lending (or borrowing) for a period coinciding with his or her preferred habitat. But

at the same time, agents could presumably be induced to depart from their preferred habitat with the availability of a risk premium.

• Although the preferred habitat version of the expectations theory suggests, like the liquidity theory, that forward rates are the sum of a component reflecting expected future rates and a risk premium, that premium will not rise continuously with maturity but will materialize in any maturity neighborhood where supply exceeds demand.

• According to the preferred habitat theory, a negative premium or discount would be expected if supply exceeded demand.

• One theory of the term structure explains the shape of the term structure by the concept of market segmentation.

• In common with the preferred habitat theory, the market segmentation theory recognizes that participants in the bond market have maturity preferences; however, it postulates that these preferences are absolute and cannot be overcome by the expectation of a higher return from a different maturity, no matter how large the return.

• Proponents of the market segmentation theory argue that each maturity is a separate market and that the interest rate in every such market is determined by the given demand and supply; consequently, the interest rate at any maturity is totally unrelated to expectations of future rates.

• This market segmentation theory is of doubtful use in reality, because it implies highly irrational, implausible, and counterfactual behavior.

Questions

1. a. What is the credit risk associated with a U.S. Treasury security?

b. Why is the U.S. Treasury yield considered the base interest rate?

c. What is meant by "on-the-run" Treasuries?

d. What is meant by "off-the-run" Treasuries?

2. Consider the following five corporate bonds and trading information about them:

Issuer	Rating	Yield (%)	Spread (bps)	Treasury Benchmark
Corporation A	Triple A	7.87	50	10
Corporation B	Double A	7.77	40	10
Corporation C	Triple A	8.60	72	30
Corporation D	Double A	8.66	78	30
Corporation E	Triple B	9.43	155	30

a. Which of the five bonds has the greatest credit risk?

b. What is meant by "spread"?

c. What is meant by "Treasury benchmark"?

d. Why does each spread reported reflect a risk premium?

3. For the corporate bond issues reported in question 2, answer the following questions:

a. Should a triple-A-rated bond issue offer a higher or lower yield than a double-A-rated bond issue of the same maturity?

b. What is the spread between the corporation A's issue and corporation B's?

c. Is the spread reported in part (b) consistent with your answer to part (a)?

d. The yield spread between these two bond issues reflects more than just credit risk. What other factors would the spread reflect?

e. Corporation B's issue is not callable. However, corporation A's issue is callable. How does this information help you understand the spread between these two issues?

4. The following yields were reported on August 4, 2014, for U.S. Treasury securities, corporate bonds, and tax-exempt bonds (i.e., municipal bonds):

Issuer	Rating	2-Year	5-Year	10-Year
Treasury	—	0.52	1.75	2.56
Corporate	AAA	—	1.87	2.92
Corporate	AA	0.52	2.02	3.26
Corporate	A	0.65	2.12	3.42
Tax exempt	AAA	0.42	1.15	2.15
Tax exempt	AA	0.43	1.30	2.44
Tax exempt	A	0.63	1.47	2.42

a. Why is the yield on a tax-exempt security less than the yield on a Treasury security of the same maturity and credit rating?

b. Why is the yield on a tax-exempt security less than the yield on a corporate security of the same maturity and credit rating?

c. What appears to be the relationship between yield and maturity for corporate bonds?

d. For an investor in the 40% marginal tax bracket, compare the yield on the two-year AA-rated corporate bond and the tax-exempt bond on an equivalent-taxable yield basis.

5. a. What is meant by an "embedded option" in a bond?

b. Give an example of an embedded option that might be included in a bond issue.

c. Does an embedded option increase or decrease the risk premium relative to the base interest rate?

6. a. What is meant by the "swap rate"?

b. What is meant by the swap curve?

7. Why do market participants in some countries prefer to use the swap curve rather than the government bond yield curve?

8. a. What is a yield curve?

b. Why is the Treasury yield curve closely watched by market participants?

9. What is meant by a "spot rate"?

10. Explain why it is inappropriate to use one yield to discount all the cash flows of a financial asset.

11. Explain why a financial asset can be viewed as a package of zero-coupon instruments.

12. Why is it important for lenders and borrowers to have knowledge of forward rates?

13. You are a financial consultant. At various times, you hear the following comments on interest rates from clients. How would you respond to each comment?

a. "The yield curve is upward sloping today. This suggests that the market consensus is that interest rates are expected to increase in the future."

b. "I can't make any sense out of today's term structure. For short-term yields (up to three years), the spot rates increase with maturity; for maturities greater than three years but less than eight years, the spot rates decline with maturity; and for maturities greater than eight years, the spot rates are virtually the same for each maturity. There is simply no theory that explains a term structure with this shape."

c. "When I want to determine the market's consensus regarding future interest rates, I calculate the implicit forward rates."

14. You observe the Treasury yield curve on page 411 (all yields are shown on a bond-equivalent basis). All securities maturing from 1.5 years on are selling at par. The six-month and one-year securities are zero-coupon instruments.

a. Calculate the missing spot rates.

b. What should the price of the six-year Treasury security be?

c. What is the implicit six-month forward rate starting in the sixth year?

15. a. Using the theoretical spot rates in table 16.2, calculate the theoretical value of a 7%, six-year Treasury bond.

b. Using the theoretical spot rates in table 16.2, calculate the two-year forward rate four years from now.

Year	Yield to Maturity (%)	Spot Rate (%)
0.5	5.25	5.25
1.0	5.50	5.50
1.5	5.75	5.76
2.0	6.00	?
2.5	6.25	?
3.0	6.50	?
3.5	6.75	?
4.0	7.00	?
4.5	7.25	?
5.0	7.50	?
5.5	7.75	7.97
6.0	8.00	8.27
6.5	8.25	8.59
7.0	8.50	8.92
7.5	8.75	9.25
8.0	9.00	9.61
8.5	9.25	9.97
9.0	9.50	10.36
9.5	9.75	10.77
10.0	10.00	11.20

c. Verify your answer to part b by assuming an investment of $100 is invested for six years.

16. "Forward rates are poor predictors of the actual futures rates that are realized. Consequently, they are of little value to an investor." Explain why you agree or disagree with this statement.

17. An investor is considering two alternative investments. The first alternative is to invest in an instrument that matures in two years. The second alternative is to invest in an instrument that matures in one year and at the end of one year, reinvest the proceeds in a one-year instrument. The investor believes that one-year interest rates one year from now will be higher than they are today and therefore is leaning in favor of the second alternative. What would you recommend to this investor?

18. a. What is the difference between a normal yield curve and a steep yield curve?

b. What is meant by a "humped" yield curve?

19. What is the common hypothesis about the behavior of short-term forward rates that is shared by the various forms of the expectations theory?

20. a. What are the types of risks associated with investing in bonds, and how do these two risks affect the pure expectations theory?

b. Give three interpretations of the pure expectations theory.

c. What are the two biased expectations theories about the term structure of interest rates?

d. What are the underlying hypotheses of the two biased expectations theories of interest rates?

IV PRIMARY AND SECONDARY MARKETS

17 Primary Markets

CONTENTS

Learning Objectives

After reading this chapter, you will understand:

- the difference between primary and secondary markets;
- the principles for regulating a primary market;
- three critical issues dealing with the regulation of the primary market: how a "security" is defined, disclosure requirements when securities are issued, and the solicitation of funds;
- the major federal securities laws dealing with the issuance of a new security in the United States;

- variations in the underwriting of securities;
- what a bought deal is and why it is used by issuers;
- the use of an auction to issue a security;
- what a preemptive rights offering is and why a standby underwriting arrangement may be needed;
- what is meant by an "integrated and segmented world capital market" and the implications for raising funds; and
- why firms may seek to raise funds outside their local capital market.

With an initial investment from various private investors, in September 1998, Larry Page and Sergey Brin raised $1 million to start Google Inc.; that is, they did not offer Google's common stock to the public. On April 29, 2004, Google Inc. filed an initial public offering (IPO) (a first-time offering of a private company of its common stock to the public) with the U.S. Securities and Exchange Commission (SEC). On August 19, 2004, shares were sold to the public, making Google a public corporation. As explained in chapter 1, financial markets can be categorized as those dealing with financial claims that are newly issued, called the **primary market**, and those for exchanging financial claims previously issued, called the **secondary market**, or the market for seasoned securities. It was in the primary market that Google, as well as other startup companies, raised funds through an IPO. The primary market involves the distribution to investors of newly issued securities or seasoned securities issues issued by a corporation to the public. This market also includes the offering of securities of government-owned companies to private investors, a process referred to as **privatization**.

The participants in the marketplace that work with issuers to distribute newly issued securities are investment bankers, entities described in chapter 9. In that chapter, we described the traditional process of underwriting of securities and how investment bankers perform at least one of three functions: (1) advising the issuer on the terms and the timing of the offering, (2) buying the securities from the issuer, and (3) distributing the issue to the public.

In this chapter, we explain primary markets, focusing on the regulations followed by many developed countries and the various ways in which new securities are issued. In chapter 28 we describe the various financial instruments that can be used by start-up companies to raise funds. We begin with a description of the regulation of the primary market in the United States and then discuss regulation in other countries. In chapter 18, we cover the secondary market.

Regulation of the Primary Market

Entities seeking to raise funds in every developed country are required to comply with that country's securities laws. In the United States, for example, there are two principal pieces of federal legislation regarding securities, the Securities Act of 1933 (Securities Act) and the Securities Exchange Act of 1934 (Exchange Act). Subsequent legislation has amended various regulations of both acts, with major amendments with respect to fundraising resulting from the major financial crises that have occurred in the intervening years. These amendments include the Sarbanes-Oxley Act of 2002, the Dodd-Frank Wall Street Reform and Consumer Protection Act of 2010 (Dodd-Frank Act), and the Jumpstart Our Business Startups Act of 2012 (the JOBS Act).

In Japan, the Securities and Exchange Law of 1948 is the counterpart to the U.S. Securities Act and Securities Exchange Act. This act and Japan's Commercial Code and Civil Codes are the principal regulations dealing with securities in Japan.

The U.S. federal agency responsible for administrating federal securities laws as set forth in these 1933 and 1934 acts is the SEC. State laws, also referred to as "blue sky laws," are administered by a designated agency responsible for regulating the sales of securities in the state. The Financial Industry Regulatory Authority is the self-regulating entity in the United States, which in 2007 replaced the National Association of Securities Dealers. In Japan, the Ministry of Finance is the key regulator; the Securities Dealer's Association, an entity composed of member security companies, is the second most powerful regulator. The Canadian Securities Administrators (Canada), Financial Services Authority (United Kingdom), Australian Securities and Investment Commission (Australia), and Comision Nacional del Mercado de Valores (Spain) are examples of the principal regulators in other countries.

In all countries, securities laws dealing with the primary market cover three critical issues:

- how a "security" is defined,
- disclosure requirements when securities are issued, and
- the solicitation of funds.

Defining a Security

The securities law of all countries begins with defining what a security is. It is natural to think of the financial products that we describe in later chapters in this book as securities (stocks and bonds). Although the term "security" has been used throughout this book interchangeably with "financial instrument," in terms of security law, it has a far broader meaning than just stocks and bonds. The decision in a 1946 landmark Supreme Court case (SEC v. W. J. Howey Co.) involving land sales contracts has been used to determine whether a transaction falls in the realm of a "securities" transaction. The court ruled that "an investment contract for purposes of the Securities Act means a contract, transaction or scheme whereby a person invests his money in a common enterprise and is led to expect profits solely from the efforts of the promoter or a third party." It does not make a difference whether there is a formal certificate or nominal interests in the physical assets that may be used by the entity obtaining funds.

The definition of a security as provided by the Supreme Court in the Howey decision has been applied in the analysis of whether a transaction is a security transaction in matters involving shares in fishing boats, sale of franchises, sale of cemetery lots, and housing cooperative shares. In fact, a 2004 Supreme Court decision in a matter involving the public sale of pay phones by ETS Payphones Inc. found the arrangement to be a security transaction. The transaction involved the sale and leaseback arrangement for pay phones. Although lower courts indicated that this type of transaction was not a security transaction, the Supreme Court ultimately ruled that it was, thereby reaffirming the Howey decision. The U.S. courts have ruled that when an investment is made in an entity for a reason other than for profit or financial gain, the investment instrument is not a security. For example, in a 1975 case involving an investment by certain individuals in a cooperative housing project (United Housing Foundation, Inc. v. Foreman), the court ruled that the investment by the individuals was for the purpose of obtaining a residence and not for financial gain or profit.

Disclosure Requirements

There are two basic objectives of the U.S. Securities Act, and they are typically also the objectives in other countries. The first objective deals with the disclosure of information about the securities that an entity is planning to issue. Disclosure is accomplished by the issuance of a **prospectus** that provides "full and fair disclosure of the character of securities sold in interstate and foreign commerce and through the mails." The second objective of the Securities Act is to prevent the sale of securities as a result of deceit, misrepresentation, and other fraud. These two objectives of the Securities Act deal with the initial distribution of securities and the registration of those securities, whereas the Exchange Act deals with the secondary market for securities by mandating ongoing periodic reporting of financial information to investors.

In other countries, the securities laws dealing with the primary market regarding disclosure are similar to those of the United States. The prospectus for a new offering is required for entities seeking to issue securities in the European Union (EU), for example. Under the EU rules, when an issuer obtains approval of its prospectus by a member country in the EU, it is valid for the issuance of securities in all EU countries. This is popularly referred to as a "single passport for issuers," and the rationale is that it ensures at least minimum protection of investors regardless of the EU country where the securities are purchased.

Regulators of the primary market throughout the world periodically revise their prospectus requirements. In fact, many countries have regulations for simplified and "plain language" disclosure rules that should be followed by issuers (i.e., the creation of a plain language prospectus). The SEC adopted plain English disclosure rules in 1998 in public offerings by domestic and foreign issuers. Specifically, the SEC expects that issuers comply with six principles of plain English when preparing the summary and factor sections provided on the front and back cover pages of a prospectus: use short sentences; use definite, concrete, and everyday language; use an active voice; use when possible a tabular presentation or bullet points; avoid using legal jargon or business terms that are highly technical;

and avoid double negatives. For the prospectus as a whole, the rules require that the issuer be "clear, concise and understandable." There are much more detailed rules than described here, but the key is just better communication about the company, its business, and its risks.

In the same year that the United States adopted its plain language prospectus rules, several other countries followed suit. For example, Hong Kong's Securities and Futures Commission published "Project on the Use of Plain Language: How to Create a Clear Prospectus" that contained sample prospectuses.[1]

A study conducted by the European Commission in 2015 (referred to as a "consultation") identified the shortcomings of the EU prospectus requirements. For issuers, the study reported that the rules constitute a considerable amount of legal paperwork and, particularly for smaller firms, it was costly to prepare a prospectus. The study also indicated that investors found it difficult to read through the hundreds of pages of a prospectus that followed these rules. As a result, in June 2017, the EU adopted Regulation (EU) 2017/1129 to mitigate these problems.

SEC filing requirements Unless an exemption can be obtained or special rules apply (such as for smaller reporting companies), the SEC requires that a company file the documents described in box 17.1. The Securities Act provides for penalties in the form of fines, imprisonment, or both if the information provided is inaccurate or material information is omitted. Moreover, investors who purchased the security are entitled to sue the issuer to recover damages if they incurred a loss as a result of misleading information. The underwriter may also be sued if it can be demonstrated that the underwriter did not conduct a reasonable investigation of the information reported by the issuer.

One of the most important duties of an underwriter is to perform due diligence. The following excerpt is taken from a court decision that explains the obligation of an underwriter to perform due diligence:

> An underwriter by participating in an offering constructively represents that statements made in the registration materials are complete and accurate. The investing public properly relies upon the underwriter to check the accuracy of the statements and the soundness of the offer; when the underwriter does not speak out, the investor reasonably assumes that there are no undisclosed material deficiencies. The representations in the registration statement are those of the underwriter as much as they are those of the issuer.[2]

The filing of a registration statement with the SEC does not mean that the security can be offered to the public. The registration statement must be reviewed and approved by the SEC's Division of Corporate Finance before the security can be offered to the public. Typically, the staff of this division will find a problem with the registration statement. The

1. See http://www.sfc.hk/web/EN/assets/components/codes/files-current/web//project-on-the-use-of-plain-language-how-to-create-a-clear-prospectus/project-on-the-use-of-plain-language-how-to-create-a-clear-prospectus.pdf.

2. *Chris-Craft Industries, Inc. v. Piper Aircraft Corp.*, 1973.

Box 17.1
Required Filings with the SEC

Registration statement: The initial registration filing with the SEC, Form S-1, must contain financial accounting information, as well as a description of the business, the securities, the risk factors faced by investors, and how the proceeds received will be used. The financial statements that are required to be included are audited balance sheets for each of the two most recent fiscal years, audited statements of income and cash flows for each of the three fiscal years preceding the date of the most recent audited balance sheet being filed or such shorter period as the company has been in existence, and interim financial statements.

10-K report: Form 10-K must be filed on an annual basis with the SEC within 90 days after the end of the company's fiscal year. Form 10-K consists of the following three sections: (1) a business summary, (2) management discussion and analysis, and (3) audited financial statements (balance sheet, income statement, statement of cash flow, and statement of changes in stockholders' equity).

10-Q report: Form 10-Q is similar to Form 10-K but must be filed quarterly, not just annually, and much less detailed information is required. The financial statements are unaudited but subject to a review.

8-K report: Form 8-K is an occasional filing; it must be filed if a certain event occurs. Examples of such events are entering bankruptcy or receivership, completion of an acquisition or disposition of assets, the departure of directors or principal officers, election of directors or the appointment of principal officers, and changes in control. Form 8-K must be filed within four business days of the event.

Proxy statement: Information about the issues to be voted on by shareholders and management's recommendation are provided in the proxy statement issued by a company.

Forms 3, 4, and 5: Forms 3, 4, and 5 are filings with the SEC that contain information on the ownership of securities by corporate insiders (i.e., officers and directors) and any beneficial owners (i.e., owners of more than 10% of the company's equity securities), and how that ownership changes over time.

Schedule 13D and Schedule 13G reports: The "beneficial owner" of a company is defined by the SEC as any person who directly or indirectly shares voting power or investment power (the power to sell the security). Schedule 13D, commonly referred to as the "beneficial ownership report," must be filed when a person or group of persons acquires beneficial ownership of more than 5% of a voting class of a company's equity registered within 10 days after the purchase. Schedule 13G is similar to Schedule 13D but requires less information when the person acquiring the shares is only a passive investor with no intention of altering or influencing the control of the issuer.

staff then sends a "letter of comments" or "deficiency letter" to the issuer explaining the problem it encountered. The issuer must then remedy any problem by filing an amendment to the registration statement. If the SEC staff is then satisfied, it will issue an order declaring that the registration statement is "effective," and the underwriter can solicit sales. The approval of the SEC, however, does not mean that the securities have investment merit or are properly priced or that the information is accurate. It merely means that the appropriate information appears to have been disclosed.

The time interval between the initial filing of the registration statement and the time the registration statement becomes effective is referred to as the "waiting period." During the waiting period, the SEC does allow the underwriters to distribute a preliminary prospectus. Because the prospectus is not effective, the cover page of the prospectus states this status in red ink, and as a result, the preliminary prospectus is commonly referred to as a "red herring." During the waiting period, the underwriter cannot sell the security, nor may it accept written offers from investors to buy the security.

A closely related concept is the "quiet period." The SEC prohibits management teams or their marketing staff from making forecasts or expressing opinions about the value of the company prior to an IPO. In addition, for publicly traded stocks, for four weeks before the close of the business quarter, corporate insiders cannot speak to the public about the company's business, usually to avoid the appearance of inside information.

Self-registration rule In 1982, the SEC approved **Rule 415**, which permits certain issuers to file a single registration document indicating that it intends to sell a certain amount of a certain class of securities at one or more times in the next two years. Rule 415 is popularly referred to as the **shelf registration rule**, because the securities can be viewed as sitting on a "shelf" and can be taken off that shelf and sold to the public without obtaining additional SEC approval.

In essence, the filing of a single registration document allows the issuer to come to market quickly, because the sale of the security has been preapproved by the SEC. Prior to the establishment of Rule 415, a lengthy period was required before a security could be sold to the public. As a result, in a fast-moving market, issuers could not come to market quickly with an offering to take advantage of what it perceived to be attractive financing opportunities. For example, if a corporation felt that interest rates were attractive and wanted to issue a bond, it had to file a registration statement and could not issue the bond until the registration statement became effective. The corporation then took the chance that during the waiting period, interest rates might rise, making the bond offering more costly.

U.S. exemption rules In most countries, unless an exemption is set forth in a country's securities law, an entity seeking to raise funds through a transaction that is defined as a security must register that security with regulators. Even if an entity can find an exemption to registering the security with regulators, the country's securities law still will have restrictions with respect to general solicitation or general advertising in connection with the offering of securities.

In the United States, the JOBS Act facilitated raising funds by requiring that the SEC amend Rule 144A of the Securities Act, which is a private offering exemption for a nonpublic offering of securities. This exemption from registration applies to the resale of securities to what the SEC classifies as qualified institutional buyers (QIBs). The SEC defines a QIB as a large, sophisticated organization with the primary responsibility of managing large investment portfolios with at least $100 million in securities and that is recognized by regulators as needing less protection from issuers than the typical public investor. Prior to the JOBS Act, Rule 144A required that securities be offered for resale only to QIBs. With the JOBS Act, Rule 144A was amended so that offers of securities can be made to investors who are not QIBs as long as the securities are sold only to persons whom the seller reasonably believes are QIBs.

In the United States, two other exemptions are provided for in the Securities Act: the intrastate offering exemption and the private offering exemption. The Securities Act allows an exemption for securities sold within a state (i.e., intrastate), which is accordingly referred to as the "intrastate offering exemption." The three conditions that must be satisfied to qualify for the intrastate offering exemption are (1) the issuer must be incorporated in the state where the securities are to be offered; (2) the issuer must do a significant amount of its business in the state where the securities are to be offered; and (3) the securities must be offered and subsequently sold only to bona fide residents of the state. The private offering exemption, also referred to as the "nonpublic offering exemption" or the "private placement exemption," exempts transactions by an issuer not involving any public offering. Three requirements must be satisfied by the buyers. They must (1) either be capable of evaluating the investment risks and attributes of the security or be able to bear the economic risks associated with the security, (2) have access to the type of information typically provided in a prospectus for a registered security, and (3) agree not to resell or distribute the security to the public.

Private placement of securities Public and private offerings of securities differ in terms of the regulatory requirements that must be satisfied by the issuer. The Securities Act of 1933 and the Securities Exchange Act of 1934 require that all securities offered to the general public be registered with the SEC, unless given a specific exemption. The securities acts allow three exemptions from federal registration. First, intrastate offerings—that is, securities sold only within a state—are exempt. Second, a small-offering exemption (Regulation A) specifically applies if the offering is for $1 million or less, in which case the securities need not be registered. Finally, Section 4(2) of the 1933 Act exempts from registration "transactions by an issuer not involving any public offering." However, the 1933 act does not provide specific guidelines to identify what is a private offering or placement.

In 1982, the SEC adopted Regulation D, which sets forth the specific guidelines that must be satisfied to qualify for exemption from registration under Section 4(2). The guidelines require that, in general, the securities not be offered through any form of general advertising or general solicitation that would prevail for public offerings. Most important, the guidelines restrict the sale of securities to "sophisticated" investors. Such "accredited" investors are defined as those (1) with the capability to evaluate (or who can afford to employ an adviser to evaluate) the risk and return characteristics of the securities and (2) with the resources to bear the economic risks.[3]

The exemption of an offering does not mean that the issuer need not disclose information to potential investors. The issuer must still furnish the same information deemed material by the SEC. This information is provided in a private placement memorandum, as opposed to a prospectus for a public offering. The distinction between the private placement memorandum and the prospectus is that the former does not include information deemed by the SEC to be "non-material," whereas such information is required in a prospectus. Moreover, unlike a prospectus, the private placement memorandum is not subject to SEC review.

In the United States, one restriction imposed on buyers of privately placed securities is that the securities may not be resold for two years after acquisition. Thus, the market contains no liquidity for that time period. Buyers of privately placed securities must be compensated for the lack of liquidity, which raises the cost to the issuer of the securities.

In April 1990, however, SEC Rule 144A became effective. This rule eliminates the two-year holding period by permitting large institutions to trade securities acquired in a private placement among them without having to register these securities with the SEC. Under Rule 144A, a large institution is defined as one holding at least $100 million of the security. Private placements are now classified as Rule 144A offerings or non-Rule 144A offerings. The latter are more commonly referred to as "traditional private placements." Rule 144A offerings are underwritten by investment bankers.

Rule 144A encourages foreign corporations to issue securities in the U.S. private placement market for two reasons. First, it will attract new large institutional investors into the market who were unwilling previously to buy private placements because of the requirement to hold the securities for two years. Such an increase in the number of institutional investors may encourage foreign-based entities to issue securities. Second, foreign entities had been unwilling to raise funds in the United States prior to the establishment of Rule 144A, because they had to register their securities and furnish the necessary disclosure set forth by U.S. securities laws. Private placement requires less disclosure. Rule 144A also improves liquidity, reducing the cost of raising funds.

Solicitation of Funds

When an issuer seeks to raise funds, it must use one or more methods for soliciting potential investors, such as direct mailing, advertising, or Internet postings. Securities laws typically cover the methods that may be used by issuers for the solicitation of funds.

3. Under the current law, an accredited investor is one who satisfies either a net worth test (at least $1 million, excluding automobiles, home, and home furnishings) or an annual income test (at least $200,000 for a single individual, $300,000 for a couple for the last two years, with expectations of such income to continue for the current year).

In the United States, for example, SEC Rule 502(c) provides guidance on what types of activity constitute general solicitation and advertising; they include placing advertisements in newspapers and magazines, advertising on television and radio broadcasts, and sponsoring seminars to which attendees have been invited by general solicitation. Even with the general guidance provided by the SEC, it is still not simple to determine what constitutes general solicitation and advertising, and it is the SEC's position that what constitutes general solicitation is a matter of particular facts and circumstances.

In the United States, a common exemption that may be used by an entity to avoid the ban on general soliciting and advertising is Rule 506 of Regulation D of the Securities Act. This rule allows an issuer to raise an unlimited amount of capital from up to 35 accredited investors and up to 35 nonaccredited investors. The term "accredited investor" has a specific meaning, defined in Regulation D. There are individual accredited investors and institutional accredited investors. An **individual accredited investor** is an individual who meets certain annual income and/or net worth thresholds.[4] An **institutional accredited investor** includes such entities as banks, insurance companies, mutual funds, and venture capital funds.

In July 2013, the SEC was forced to adopt a new set of rules that removed, under special circumstances, the ban on general solicitation and advertising. This was the result of the JOBS Act of 2012, which was passed by Congress to stimulate economic recovery in the United States by making it easier for small companies and startups to find investors, with the expectation that employment opportunities would increase. Although the JOBS Act directed the SEC to remove the ban on general solicitation and advertising for securities offerings, it still placed two obligations on entities seeking to raise funds. First, sales had to be limited to accredited investors. Second, the issuer of the security had to undertake "reasonable steps" to verify that all buyers of the security were, in fact, accredited investors. This second responsibility of the issuer sounds simple, but its implementation was not, because it came with a complicated set of principles established by the SEC to determine what constitutes "reasonable steps" to ensure that one is soliciting an accredited investor. Despite the difficulty of implementation in practice, the JOBS Act removed restrictions on the soliciting of investors so long as those investors are accredited investors.

Variations in the Underwriting of Securities

In our discussion in chapter 9 of the role of investment bankers, we described the traditional syndication process; however, not all deals are underwritten using this process. Variations include the "bought deal" for the underwriting of bonds, the auction process for both stocks and bonds, and a rights offering for common stock.

4. The U.S. Congress has delegated to the U.S. Government Accountability Office (GAO) the responsibility for determining the rules for individuals to qualify as an accredited investor.

Issuance via a Bought Deal

A **bought deal** refers to the offering of a security (stock or bond) whereby an underwriter agrees to purchase all of the security from the issuer at a fixed price without premarketing the deal before purchasing it from the issuer. The bought deal was introduced in the Eurobond market in 1981, when Credit Suisse First Boston (now Credit Suisse) purchased from General Motors Acceptance Corporation a $100 million issue. Although initially used for public bond offerings, the bought deal is now also commonly used for the public offering of equity.

The mechanics of a bought deal are as follows. The lead manager, or a group of managers, offers a potential issuer of a security a firm bid to purchase the entire offering of the security. The issuer is given a short period of time to accept or reject the bid. If the bid is accepted, the underwriting firm has "bought the deal." It can in turn sell the securities to other investment banking firms for distribution to their clients or distribute the securities to its own clients. Typically, the underwriting firm that buys the deal will have presold most of the issue to its institutional clients.

When used in the case of common stock, it is not for an IPO. Instead it is for the public offering of a seasoned equity offering. That is, the company already has common stock outstanding and seeks to raise funds. One method is the marketing of the common stock prior to its offering, which involves a marketing process that can be quite lengthy. The bought deal, which is referred to as an "accelerated seasoned common stock offering," is now the predominate issuance method in North America, and the traditional firm commitment for seasoned offerings of common stock is rare.[5] Studies also indicate that it has become the predominate issuance method in Europe.[6]

For example, in June 2017, Cantor Fitzgerald Canada Corporation, a subsidiary of the U.S. investment banking firm Cantor Fitzgerald, agreed to buy on a bought deal basis 31,250,000 common shares of the Canadian company Prometic Life Sciences for a price $1.70 per share for gross proceeds of $53,125,000.

Issuance of a Security via an Auction Process

Another variation for the issuance of securities is the auction process, in which the issuer announces the terms of the issue, and interested parties submit sealed bids to receive an

5. See Erdal Gunay and Nancy Ursel, "Underwriter Competition in Accelerated Seasoned Equity Offerings," Working Paper, University of Windsor, Ontario. Available at https://ssrn.com/abstract=2138215. The following study reports that by 2003, accelerated offerings exceeded traditional seasons equity offerings in the United States: Don Autore, Raman Kumar, and Dilip Shome, "The Revival of Shelf-Registered Corporate Equity Offerings," *Journal of Corporate Finance* 14 (2008): 32–50. The following study finds that from 1993 to 2005, 69% of Canadian seasoned equity offerings were accelerated bought deal offerings: J. Ari Pandes, "Bought Deals: The Value of Underwriter Certification in Seasoned Equity Offering," *Journal of Banking and Finance* 34 (2010): 1576–1589.

6. See, for example, Bernardo Bortolotti, William L. Megginson, and Scott Smart, "The Rise of Accelerated Seasoned Equity Underwritings," *Journal of Applied Corporate Finance* 20 (2008): 35–37.

allotment or all of the securities auctioned. The U.S. Department of the Treasury uses an auction system for the allocation of its massive offering of securities. The auction process is also used by state and local governments in the issuance of bonds and by public utilities. This process is referred to as a "competitive sale." In the case of bonds, the bidders are individual underwriters and underwriter syndicates. The winning underwriter (syndicate) is the one that bids the lowest interest cost and, on winning the entire offering, reoffers the bonds to its client base.

Use of auction for an IPO The auction process has also been used for an IPO offering. In a traditional IPO offering, an investment banking firm uses its team of equity analysts and its sales force to determine from its institutional client base at what price a firm going public can sell its shares. For example, the Twitter IPO on November 7, 2013, was priced at $26 per share, as determined by investment bankers, Twitter's lead underwriters (Goldman Sachs, Morgan Stanley, and Bank of America). An alternative for an IPO is an auction. Starting in the mid-1990s, several firms in the technology sector used this form of IPO issuance, among them Yahoo, Overstock.com, and Google Inc.

Let's first discuss the mechanics of an auction and how the price that winning bidders must pay is determined, and then look at the relative merits of a traditional issuance of an IPO versus an auction. Suppose there are 30 million shares to be issued for an IPO, and the bids and the number of shares are as in table 17.1.

The first column in the table shows all the bids, with bid price shown in the second column. So, "A" represents all investors who bid $50.00, and the number of shares they bid for in the aggregate is three million. Because there are 30 million shares to be allotted,

Table 17.1
Illustration of an auction for an IPO.

Investor	Bid Price per Share ($)	Aggregate Number of Shares Bid	Remaining Shares to Be Allocated
A	50.00	3,000,000	27,000,000
B	48.00	3,000,000	24,000,000
C	46.00	7,000,000	17,000,000
D	44.00	5,000,000	12.000,000
E	42.00	2,000,000	10,000,000
F	40.00	2,000,000	8,000,000
G	38.00	2,000,000	6,000,000
H	36.00	2,000,000	4,000,000
I	34.00	2,000,000	2,000,000
J	32.00	3,000,000	−1,000,000
K	30.00	4,000,000	0
L	28.00	3,000,000	0
M	26.00	4,000,000	0
N	24.00	5,000,000	0

the remaining number of shares (shown in the last column) is 27 million. Looking now at Investors I, at a bid price of $34.00, only two million shares remain to be allocated. Investors J bid at $32.00 for three million of the remaining two million shares. So at a price of $32.00, the market has cleared (i.e., the total number of shares will be sold).

The question then is what price the winning bidders (Investors A through J) will pay. The price will be that of the lowest winning bidder, $32.00. That is, a single price will be paid by all bidders. This type of auction is called a **Dutch auction**. So, even though Investors A bid for three million shares at $50.00 per share, they will pay only $32.00 per share. Investors K through N will receive no shares. How much will be allocated to Investors J, who bid for three million of the two million remaining shares? All those who bid $32.00 will receive a proportionate allocation. For example, if Mrs. Chen bid for 3,000 shares at $32.00, she will be allocated only 2,000 shares.

For our hypothetical IPO issuer, the amount that will be raised before any fees is $960 million.

In August 2004, Google Inc. used a Dutch auction for its IPO, raising $2.7 billion. The question is: What is the best method for an IPO: traditional issuance using the underwriting process with investment bankers or a Dutch auction? Let's consider the Twitter IPO on November 7, 2013, priced at $26 per share as determined by the firm's investment bankers. The valuation for the firm based on $26 per share was $15.2 billion. The opening price at which it traded on the New York Stock Exchange was $45.00 per share, and the closing price was $44.90 per share. At a share price of $45.00, the valuation of the company was $31.8 billion. Thus, the investment bankers felt the company was worth $15.2 billion and the market thought it was worth $31.8 billion. Somebody's valuation model was off!

Of course, investment bankers argue that their direct purchase of the stock in an IPO offering as intermediaries adds value, because they search their institutional client base, making it likely that the issuer will get the highest price (proceeds) after adjusting for the underwriting fees. However, since the 1990s, the measure of a good underwriting seems not to be the proceeds received by the firm for its IPO but rather the jump in the stock price at the time of issuance. For example, in the case of Twitter, the pricing considerably below what the market suggested on the opening day (about $45) resulted in substantially less proceeds to Twitter. The beneficiaries were those who were fortunate enough to get an allocation of shares from their broker—primarily institutional investors. One of the reasons Google Inc. selected the Dutch auction was because it was viewed as more "democratic": It allowed retail investors to participate in the IPO offering.

One argument put forth by investment bankers as to the advantage of the traditional underwriting process is that the syndicate involved in the underwriting process can support the market price for a period of time after issuance. This is because in most such underwritings, the investment banking firm agrees to stabilize the price in the secondary market to keep it from falling below the price at which it was sold to the public. One might think that this constitutes market manipulation. However, it is permitted by SEC Rule 10b-7, where the SEC sets forth the activities it considers to constitute market stabilization of a new issue and what it considers market manipulation.

Preemptive Rights Offering

A corporation can issue new common stock directly to existing shareholders through a **preemptive rights offering**. A preemptive right grants existing shareholders the right to buy some proportion of the new shares issued at a price below market value. The price at which new shares can be purchased is called the **subscription price**. A rights offering ensures that current shareholders can maintain their proportionate equity interest in the corporation. In the United States, the practice of issuing common stock by means of a preemptive rights offering is uncommon. In other countries, it is much more common; in some countries, it is the only means by which a new offering of common stock may be sold.

For the shares sold through a preemptive rights offering, the underwriting services of an investment banker are not needed. However, the issuing corporation may use the services of an investment banker for the distribution of common stock that is not subscribed to. A **standby underwriting arrangement** will be used in such instances. This arrangement calls for the underwriter to buy the unsubscribed shares. The issuing corporation pays a **standby fee** to the investment banking firm.

World Capital Markets Integration and Fundraising Implications

An entity may seek funds outside its local capital market with the expectation of doing so at a lower cost than if its funds were raised in its local capital market. Whether lower costs are possible depends on the degree of integration of capital markets. At the two extremes, the world capital markets can be classified as either completely segmented or completely integrated.

In the former case, investors in one country are not permitted to invest in the securities issued by an entity in another country. As a result, in a **completely segmented market**, the required return on securities of comparable risk traded in different capital markets throughout the world will be different even after adjusting for taxes and foreign exchange rates. An entity may be able to raise funds in the capital market of another country at a lower cost than raising funds in its local capital market.

At the other extreme, a **completely integrated market** contains no restrictions to prevent investors from investing in securities issued in any capital market throughout the world. In such an ideal world capital market, the required return on securities of comparable risk will be the same in all capital markets after adjusting for taxes and foreign exchange rates. This situation implies that the cost of funds will be the same regardless of where in the capital markets throughout the world a funds-seeking entity elects to raise funds.

Real-world capital markets are neither completely segmented nor completely integrated but fall somewhere in between. A **mildly segmented market** or **mildly integrated market** implies that world capital markets offer opportunities to raise funds at a lower cost outside the local capital market.

Motivation for Raising Funds Outside the Domestic Market

A corporation may seek to raise funds outside its domestic market for four reasons. First, in some countries, large corporations seeking to raise a substantial amount of funds may have no other choice but to obtain financing in either the foreign market sector of another country or the Euromarket, because the fundraising corporation's domestic market is not sufficiently developed to be able to satisfy the fundraiser's demand for funds on globally competitive terms. Governments of developing countries use these markets when seeking funds for government-owned corporations in the process of privatizing.

The second reason is the opportunity to obtain a reduced cost of funding (taking into consideration issuing costs) compared to that available in the domestic market. As we explained in chapter 16, in the case of debt, the cost will reflect two factors: (1) the risk-free rate, which is accepted as the interest rate on a U.S. Treasury security with the same maturity or some other low-risk security (called the **base rate**), and (2) a **spread** to reflect the greater risks that investors perceive as being associated with the issue or issuer.

A corporate borrower who seeks reduced funding costs is seeking to reduce the spread. The integration of capital markets throughout the world diminishes such opportunities. Nevertheless, imperfections in capital markets throughout the world prevent complete integration and thereby may permit a reduced cost of funds. These imperfections, or market frictions, occur because of differences in security regulations in various countries, tax structures, restrictions imposed on regulated institutional investors, and the credit risk perception of the issuer. In the case of common stock, a corporation seeks to gain a higher value for its stock and to reduce the market impact cost of floating a large offering.

The third reason to seek funds in foreign markets is a desire by corporate treasurers to diversify their source of funding in order to reduce reliance on domestic investors. In the case of equities, diversifying funding sources may encourage foreign investors who have different perspectives on the future performance of the corporation. Two additional advantages of raising foreign equity funds, from the perspective of U.S. corporations, are the following: (1) some market observers believe that certain foreign investors are more loyal to corporations and look at long-term performance rather than short-term performance as do investors in the United States,[7] and (2) diversifying the investor base reduces the dominance of U.S. institutional holdings and its impact on corporate governance.

The fourth reason is that a corporation may issue a security denominated in a foreign currency as part of its overall foreign currency management. As an example, consider a

7. "U.S. Firms Woo Investors in Europe and Japan," *Euromoney Corporate Finance,* March 1985, 45; and Peter O'Brien, "Underwriting International Corporate Equities," in *Capital Raising and Financial Structure*, ed. Robert L. Kuhn, vol. 2 in The Library of Investment Banking (Homewood, IL: Dow Jones–Irwin, 1990), chapter 4.

U.S. corporation that plans to build a factory in a foreign country where the construction costs will be denominated in the foreign currency. Assume that the corporation plans to sell the output of the factory in the same foreign country. Therefore, the revenue will be denominated in the foreign currency. The corporation then faces exchange rate risk: The construction costs are uncertain in U.S. dollars, because during the construction period, the U.S. dollar may depreciate relative to the foreign currency. Also, the projected revenue is uncertain in U.S. dollars, because the foreign currency may depreciate relative to the U.S. dollar. Suppose that the corporation arranges debt financing for the plant, in which it receives the proceeds in the foreign currency and the liabilities are denominated in the foreign currency. This financing arrangement can reduce exchange rate risk, because the proceeds received will be in the foreign currency and will be used to pay the construction costs, and the projected revenue can be applied to service the debt obligation.

Corporate Financing Week asked the corporate treasurers of several multinational corporations why they used nondomestic markets to raise funds.[8] The treasurers' responses reflected one or more of the reasons just cited. For example, the director of corporate finance of General Motors said that the company used the Eurobond market with the objective of "diversifying funding sources, attract[ing] new investors and achiev[ing] comparable, if not cheaper, financing." A managing director of Sears, Roebuck stated that the company "has a long-standing policy of diversifying geographical [funding] sources and instruments to avoid reliance on any specific market, even if the cost is higher." He stated further that "Sears cultivates a presence in the international market by issuing every three years or so."

Key Points

- The primary market involves the distribution to investors of newly issued securities and seasoned offerings.
- Entities seeking to raise funds in every developed country are required to comply with that country's securities laws.
- In the United States, there are two principal pieces of federal legislation regarding securities: the Securities Act of 1933 (Securities Act) and the Securities Exchange Act of 1934 (Exchange Act).
- The Securities and Exchange Commission (SEC) is the U.S. federal agency responsible for administrating federal securities laws as set forth in the Securities Act and the Exchange Act.
- In all countries, securities laws dealing with the primary market cover three critical issues: (1) how a "security" is defined, (2) disclosure requirements when securities are issued, and (3) the solicitation of funds.

8. Victoria Keefe, "Companies Issue Overseas for Diverse Reasons," *Corporate Financing Week,* November 25, 1991, Special Supplement, 1, 9.

• There are typically two basic objectives of the securities laws in countries: (1) the disclosure of information about the securities that an entity is planning to issue and (2) the prevention of the sale of securities as a result of deceit, misrepresentation, and other fraud.

• Disclosure information is accomplished by the issuance of a prospectus that provides "full and fair disclosure of the character of securities sold in interstate and foreign commerce and through the mails."

• Unless an exemption is allowed, an issuer of a new security must file certain documents with regulators. In the United States, the following documents must be filed with the SEC: 10-K report; 10-Q report; 8-K report; proxy statement; Forms 3, 4, and 5; and Schedule 13D and Schedule 13G reports.

• In the United States, SEC Rule 415, the shelf registration rule, permits certain issuers to file a single registration document indicating that it intends to sell a certain amount of a certain class of securities at one or more times in the next two years.

• Variations in the underwriting process include the bought deal for the underwriting of bonds and seasoned equity offerings, the auction process, and preemptive rights offering for underwriting common stock.

• A private placement is different from the public offering of securities in terms of the regulatory requirements that must be satisfied by the issuer. Certain provisions in federal securities law allow issuers to be exempt from registering a new issue with the SEC.

Questions

1. Why must a country's securities law provide guidance as to what a security is?

2. Why is it critical for the securities law of a country to set forth what a public offering of securities is?

3. "In the United States, the federal government—not the states—regulate the issuance of securities." Explain whether you agree or disagree with this statement.

4. What is the purpose of a prospectus?

5. In the Eurozone, the public offering of securities are carried out under the European Prospectus Directive and allows an issuer that has had a prospectus approved in an European Union member state to use the same prospectus for the securities in any other European Union member state. What is the rationale for the European Union allowing this—which is referred to as the "passport" mechanism?

6. The Securities Act of 1933 and the Securities Exchange Act of 1934 require that all securities offered to the general public be registered with the SEC unless granted a specific exemption. The Securities Act provides for exemptions from federal registration. Describe some of these exemptions.

7. In an article published in 2009, Donald Langevoort argues that U.S. securities regulation has historically focused on retail investors rather than on institutional investors. He goes on to observe that foreign entities wanting to sell securities in the United States should only be required to comply with the laws of their home countries, as long as those laws are "reasonably responsive to institutional investor interests."[9] Explain why you agree or disagree with this view.

8. In September 2013, Twitter Inc. acquired MoPub (a mobile ad startup). The acquisition occurred a few days prior to Twitter's announcement that the company was going public. What document did Twitter Inc. have to file with the SEC as a result of the acquisition?

9. The following was included in a filing by Facebook Inc. on April 26, 2013:

What items of business will be voted on at the Annual Meeting?

The items of business scheduled to be voted on at the Annual Meeting are:

- Proposal One: the election of eight directors;
- Proposal Two: a non-binding advisory vote on the compensation program of our named executive officers as disclosed in this proxy statement;
- Proposal Three: a non-binding advisory vote on the frequency with which we will conduct a non-binding advisory vote on the compensation program for our named executive officers; and
- Proposal Four: the ratification of the selection of Ernst & Young LLP as our independent registered public accounting firm for the fiscal year ending December 31, 2013.

What is the name of the document filed by Facebook Inc. with the SEC that contains this information?

10. a. What is meant by a "bought deal"?

b. Why do corporations seeking to raise funds of seasoned common stock prefer to use a bought deal rather than a firm commitment arrangement?

11. When comparing a bought deal for seasoned equity offerings to a traditional offering via a firm commitment, the latter is referred to as a "marketed" offering. Explain why.

12. On July 29, 2010, Panasonic Corporation announced that its board of directors resolved to file a Shelf Registration Statement in Japan for offerings of shares of common stock. The planned issuance period was within one year of the effective date of the Shelf Registration Statement (i.e., from August 12, 2010 to August 2011) for a planned amount of issues of up to ¥ 500 billion. The common stock would be issued via a public offering in Japan, and the proceeds would be used to repay short-term interest-bearing debt. Why would the board of directors want to use a shelf registration?

9. Donald Langevoort, "The SEC, Retail Investors, and the Institutionalization of the Securities Markets," *Virginia Law Review* 95 (2009): 1079.

13. The FewerSearches.Net company is using a Dutch auction to do an IPO of its stock. Ten million shares are to be issued. The table below lists the bids and number of shares at each bid price:

Investor	Bid Price per Share ($)	Aggregate Number of Shares Bid
A	70.00	2,000,000
B	60.00	1,000,000
C	55.00	3,000,000
D	54.00	2,000,000
E	50.00	1,000,000
F	49.00	2,000,000
G	44.00	3,000,000
H	42.00	3,000,000
I	41.00	4,000,000
J	40.00	3,000,000
K	33.00	2,000,000
L	28.00	4,000,000
M	20.00	4,000,000
N	14.00	7,000,000

a. Who are the winning bidders?

b. How much will each winning bidder pay for a share of FewerSearches.Net?

c. How much of the security will be allocated to each winning bidder?

d. How much will FewerSearches.Net receive in proceeds before fees are paid?

14. Indicate whether you agree or disagree with the following statement: "A preemptive rights offering always requires the issuer to use the services of an investment banker to underwrite the unsubscribed shares."

15. The following statements come from the December 24, 1990, issue of *Corporate Financing Week*:

> As in the public market, growth in the private placement market was slowed this year by a rise in interest rates that pushed many issuers to the sidelines, by the Mideast crisis and by a flight to quality by investors.… Foreign private placements saw a marked increase due to Rule 144A.

a. What are the key distinctions between a private placement and a public offering?

b. Why would Rule 144A increase foreign private placements?

16. What is meant by a "completely integrated world capital market"?

17. How can the integration of world capital markets best be described, and what are the implications for fundraising?

18. Why might a corporation seek to raise funds outside its local capital market even if it results in a higher cost of funds?

18 Secondary Markets

CONTENTS

Learning Objectives

After reading this chapter, you will understand:

- the definition of a secondary market;
- the need for secondary markets for financial assets;
- the difference between a continuous and a call market;
- the requirements of a perfect market;
- what short selling is and the importance of short selling for pricing securities in financial markets;
- frictions that cause actual financial markets to differ from a perfect market;
- why brokers are necessary;
- the role of a dealer as a market maker and the costs associated with market making;
- what is meant by the "operational efficiency" of a market;
- what is meant by the "pricing efficiency" of a market;
- the implications of pricing efficiency;
- the different forms of pricing efficiency; and
- the implications of pricing efficiency for market participants.

In chapter 1, we described the various functions of financial markets. We noted in that chapter that financial markets can be divided into primary and secondary markets. In the secondary market, already issued financial assets are traded. The key distinction between a primary market (as described in chapter 1) and a secondary market is that, in the secondary market, the issuer of the asset does not receive funds from the buyer. Instead, the existing issue changes hands in the secondary market, and funds flow from the buyer of the asset to the seller.

In this chapter, we explain the various features of secondary markets. These features are common to the trading of any type of financial instrument. We take a closer look at individual markets in later chapters.

Function of Secondary Markets

It is worthwhile to review once again the function of secondary markets. In the secondary market, an issuer of securities—whether it is a corporation or a governmental unit—can obtain regular information about the value of the asset. The periodic trading of the asset reveals to the issuer the consensus price that the asset commands in an open market. Thus, firms can discover what value investors attach to their stocks, and firms or noncorporate issuers can observe the prices of their bonds and the implied interest rates investors expect and demand from them. Such information helps issuers assess how well they are using the funds acquired from earlier primary market activities, and it also indicates how receptive investors would be to new offerings.

The other service that a secondary market offers issuers is the opportunity for the original buyer of an asset to reverse the investment by selling it for cash. Unless investors are confident that they can shift from one financial asset to another as they deem necessary, they would naturally be reluctant to buy any financial asset. Such reluctance would harm potential issuers in one of two ways: Either issuers would be unable to sell new securities at all, or they would have to pay a higher rate of return, because investors would increase the discount rate in compensation for the expected illiquidity in the securities.

Investors in financial assets receive several benefits from a secondary market. Such a market obviously offers them liquidity for their assets as well as information about the assets' fair or consensus values. Furthermore, secondary markets bring together many interested parties and thereby reduce the costs of searching for likely buyers and sellers of assets. Moreover, by accommodating many trades, secondary markets keep the cost of transactions low. By keeping the costs of both searching and transacting low, secondary markets encourage investors to purchase financial assets.

Architectural Structure of Secondary Markets

Different architectural structures can be used when establishing a secondary market for a financial asset.[1] The two general architectural structures are order-driven and quote-driven markets. Real-world financial markets use a blend of these structures for different types of financial assets. To understand the difference between an order-driven and a quote-driven market, we must make clear who the potential parties are.

Potential Parties to a Trade

The potential parties to a trade include (1) natural buyers, (2) natural sellers, (3) brokers, and (4) dealers. The **natural buyers** and **natural sellers** want to take a position for their own portfolios. They can be retail investors or institutional investors.

A **broker** is a third party in a trade that acts on behalf of a buyer or seller who wishes to execute an order. In economic and legal terms, a broker is said to be an "agent" of one of the parties to the trade. The brokerage activity does not require the broker to buy and hold in inventory or sell from inventory the financial asset that is the subject of the trade. Instead the broker receives, transmits, and executes a customer's orders. In exchange for this service, the broker receives an explicit commission.

1. For a more detailed discussion of secondary market structures, see Robert A. Schwartz and Reto Francioni, *Equity Markets in Action: The Fundamentals of Liquidity, Market Structure, and Trading* (Hoboken, NJ: John Wiley & Sons, 2004).

A **dealer** is an entity that acts as an intermediary in a trade by buying and selling for its own account. Basically, a dealer buys a financial asset to place in its inventory or sells a financial asset from its own inventory. A dealer is said to "take a position" in an asset. Notice the distinction between a dealer buying and selling for its own account, which is acting as an intermediary in a trade, and a natural buyer and natural seller purchasing or selling for their own accounts. When acting in this capacity, a dealer commits its own capital to accommodate a trade sought by other parties. Hence, in contrast to a broker, a dealer acts as a **principal** in a trade. The potential income earned from this intermediary activity is the difference between the price at which a dealer is willing to offer a financial asset to investors (the ask price) and the price at which a dealer is willing to buy a financial asset from investors (the bid price). The difference is referred to as the **bid-ask spread**.

A special type of dealer is called a **market maker**. This term describes a dealer that has a special obligation in the secondary market. That special obligation is to use its capital to make an orderly market for designated financial assets.

Order-Driven Markets and Quote-Driven Markets

Now let's explore what is meant by an "order-driven market" and a "quote-driven market." The difference is based on how trading takes place and how the price is determined. In its purest sense, an **order-driven market** is one in which all of the participants in the trade are natural buyers and natural sellers—no dealer is acting as an intermediary. The clearing price is determined by the flow of buy and sell orders. Another term used to describe an order-driven market is an **auction market**.

In a **quote-driven market**, rather than the price being determined by the interaction of natural buyers and natural sellers, it is determined by the dealer and is based on prevailing market information. The dealer then stands ready to buy and sell a financial asset at the prices it quotes. Because of the role played by the dealer in a quote-driven market, this market structure is also is also referred to as a **dealer market** or **dealership market**.

Types of Order-Driven Markets

An order-driven market can be further classified as a continuous order-driven market or a periodic call auction.

In a **continuous order-driven market**, prices are determined continuously throughout the trading day as buyers and sellers submit orders. For example, given the order flow at 10 a.m., the market-clearing price of a financial asset may be $70; at 11 a.m. of the same trading day, the market-clearing price of the same financial asset, but with different order flows, may be $70.75. Thus, in a continuous market, prices may vary with the pattern of orders reaching the market and not because of any change in the basic situation of supply and demand. We return to this point later in this chapter.

The other type of order-driven market structure is the **periodic call auction**, in which orders are batched or grouped together for simultaneous execution at preannounced times. For example, a periodic call auction can occur at the opening of the trading day, at the close of the trading day, or at designated times during the trading day. The auction may be oral or written. In either case, the auction will determine or "fix" the market-clearing price at a particular time of the trading day. This use of the word "fix" is traditional and is not pejorative or suggestive of illegal activity. The price obtained for a periodic call auction can be determined through a price scan auction or a sealed bid auction.

In a **price scan auction**, an auctioneer announces tentative prices and the participants physically present respond indicating how much they would be willing to buy and sell at each tentative price. The market-clearing price is then determined by the price that will balance the buy and sell orders. In a **sealed bid/ask auction**, the bid price/ask price and the quantities a participant is willing to transact are submitted. Information about the order of a party who participates in the auction is not disclosed to the other participants involved in the auction. Buy and sell orders are then cumulated by price: from the highest bid price to the lowest bid price for buyers and from the lowest ask price to the highest ask price for sellers. The market-clearing price is the price at which the cumulated buy orders equal the cumulated sell orders.

Trading Locations

In chapter 22, we describe the different types of trading venues for stocks, bonds, and derivative instruments. Trading venues can be divided into exchanges, over-the-counter (OTC) markets, and off-exchange markets, which mean trading venues that are not exchanges or OTC. Here we briefly describe the first two venues.

In all countries, there are secondary markets that are legally established as national securities exchanges, which we will refer to simply as **exchanges**. The products traded on an exchange are approved by the directors of the exchange and are referred to as "listed products." For example, in the case of common stock, the product is the stock of a company. However, not all companies' common stock in a country is listed on a stock exchange. The stock exchange will specify requirements for a company to be traded on that exchange. Such a company is said to be a "listed company." Other products that can be traded on an exchange are certain types of derivative products, such as options and futures. In fact, as explained in chapter 33, by definition, a futures contract is an exchange-traded product. Only those who are members of an exchange are permitted to trade on the exchange. The general public cannot trade on an exchange and must trade through an exchange member. The rules for trading on an exchange are set forth by the exchange. Exchanges used to be physical, in-person locations but have evolved to be electronic forums.

The **OTC market** is simply the market where non-exchange-traded products are traded.

Trading in the OTC market is done by geographically dispersed traders linked to one another by telecommunications systems. In the case of common stock, unlisted stocks are traded in the OTC market. Non-exchange-traded derivatives are traded in the OTC market. (We explain OTC derivatives in chapter 37.) Although some bonds are traded on an exchange, such trading of bonds is extremely rare. Bonds are a good example of a product that can be traded on an exchange but for which the majority of trading is in the OTC market. Foreign exchange (currency) is primarily traded in the OTC market. Derivatives are traded on both exchanges and the OTC market.

The architectural structure of an exchange market can be either order driven or quote driven. The New York Stock Exchange (NYSE) is an order-driven market and is a hybrid continuous order-driven/periodic call auction market. In contrast, the Nasdaq is an exchange that is a quote-driven market but has an element of an order-driven market. This is because the opening of the Nasdaq is a periodic call auction.[2] All OTC markets are quote-driven markets.

Theoretically Perfect Market Characteristics

To explain the ideal characteristics of secondary markets, we first describe a **perfect market** for a financial asset. Then we can show how common occurrences in real markets keep them from being theoretically perfect.

In general, a perfect market results when the number of buyers and sellers is sufficiently large, and all participants are small enough relative to the market so that no individual market agent can influence the commodity's price. Consequently, all buyers and sellers are price-takers, and the market price is determined where there is equality of supply and demand. This condition is more likely to be satisfied if the commodity traded is fairly homogeneous (for example, corn or wheat). But a market is not perfect only because market agents are price-takers. A perfect market is also free of transactions costs and any impediment to the interaction of supply and demand for the commodity. Economists refer to these various costs and impediments as **frictions**. The costs associated with frictions generally result in buyers paying more (or sellers receiving less) than in the absence of frictions.

In the case of financial markets, frictions include:

- commissions charged by brokers;
- bid-ask spreads charged by dealers;
- order handling and clearance charges;
- taxes (notably on capital gains) and government-imposed transfer fees;
- costs of acquiring information about the financial asset;
- trading restrictions, such as exchange-imposed restrictions on the size of a position in the financial asset that a buyer or seller may take;

2. Historically, Nasdaq (at one time abbreviated as NASDAQ, standing for "National Association of Securities Dealers Quotations") started as an OTC stock market. Now the stocks traded on the Nasdaq exchange are listed stocks.

- restrictions on market makers; and
- halts to trading that may be imposed by regulators where the financial asset is traded.

Short Selling and Its Importance in Financial Markets

An investor who expects the price of a security to increase can benefit from buying that security. However, suppose that an investor expects the price of a security to decline and wants to benefit if the price actually does decline. What can the investor do? The investor may be able to sell the security without owning it. Various institutional arrangements allow an investor to borrow securities so that the borrowed security can be delivered to satisfy the sale.

This practice of selling securities that are not owned at the time of sale is referred to as **selling short**. The security is purchased subsequently by the investor and returned to the party that lent it. When the security is returned, the investor is said to have "covered the short position." A profit will be realized if the purchase price is less than the price at which the investor sold short the security.

The ability of investors to sell short is an important mechanism in financial markets. In the absence of an effective short-selling mechanism, security prices will tend to be biased toward the view of more optimistic investors, causing a market to depart from the standards of a perfect price-setting situation. In fact, many large and developed securities markets allow short selling, although regulatory bodies tend to monitor this practice more closely than other features of markets. Nonetheless, the prevalence of short selling is clear evidence of its usefulness to the price-setting function of securities markets.

Below we first explain the importance of a having a mechanism for selling short to the functioning of financial markets and then describe the mechanics of short selling.

Theoretical and empirical rationales for short selling Let's first look at the theoretical arguments in favor of short selling. When restrictions are imposed on short selling a security, the price of that security is then set by the most optimistic investors. There are limited trading opportunities for investors who are less optimistic about the issuer's future prospects, which impacts the security's future price. For those investors who are less optimistic about the security's price, in the absence of (or restrictions on) short selling, they would have to sell their holdings. The result is potential overpricing of some securities. The opportunity to short sell such overpriced securities is exploitable only when the overpricing is due to factors that are likely to be revealed in the relatively near future.

Edward Miller builds on this principle by arguing that a substantial divergence of investor opinion about a stock implies a negative expected return.[3] This is because restrictions on short

3. See Edward M. Miller, "Risk, Uncertainty, and Divergence of Opinion," *Journal of Finance* 32 (1977): 1151–1168, and the following two chapters in Frank J. Fabozzi, ed., *Short Selling: Strategies, Risks, and Rewards*

selling prevent unfavorable opinions from being fully reflected in stock prices. Therefore, with restricted short selling, divergence of opinion tends to raise prices, and profits can be improved by avoiding securities with a high divergence of opinion, especially those that analysts disagree about. Miller further demonstrates that because risk correlates with divergence of opinion, the return to risk is less than what investors would otherwise require. This reasoning led Miller to suggest that typical investors should overweight the less risky stocks in their portfolio.

The description of the short selling of common stock in chapter 23 shows that in real-world markets, constraints are imposed on investors who want to sell short. These constraints include transaction costs and the legal and institutional constraints. When such constraints are imposed on certain securities, these securities can be overpriced and thus have low future returns until the overpricing is corrected. Focusing on stocks, Lamont and Jones provide empirical evidence of such overpricing by showing that stocks with high short-sale constraints tend to experience particularly low returns in the future.[4] They also present specific cases where extremely high short-sale constraints led to extremely high prices.

Mechanics of short selling To illustrate short selling with an example, suppose Ms. Stokes believes that Wilson Pharmaceuticals common stock is overpriced at $20 per share and wants to be in a position to benefit if her assessment is correct. Ms. Stokes calls her broker, Mr. Yats, indicating that she wants to sell 100 shares of Wilson Pharmaceuticals. Mr. Yats will do two things: sell 100 shares of Wilson Pharmaceuticals on behalf of Ms. Stokes, and arrange to borrow 100 shares of that stock. Suppose that Mr. Yats is able to sell the stock for $20 per share and arrange to borrow the stock from Mr. Jordan. The shares borrowed from Mr. Jordan will be delivered to the buyer of the 100 shares. The proceeds from the sale (ignoring commissions) will be $2,000. However, the proceeds will not be given to Ms. Stokes, because she has not given her broker the 100 shares.

Now, suppose that one week later, the price of Wilson Pharmaceuticals stock declines to $15 per share. Ms. Stokes may instruct her broker to *buy* 100 shares of Wilson Pharmaceuticals. The cost of buying the shares (once again ignoring commissions) is $1,500.The shares purchased are then delivered to Mr. Jordan, who loaned the original 100 shares to Ms. Stokes. At this point, Ms. Stokes has sold 100 shares and bought 100 shares, so she no longer has any obligation to her broker or to Mr. Jordan—she has "covered her short position". She is entitled to the funds in her account that were generated by the selling and buying activity. She sold the stock for $2,000 and bought it for $1,500. Thus, she realizes a profit of $500 before commissions and fees. The broker's commission and a fee charged by the lender of the stock are then subtracted from the $500. Furthermore, if any dividends

(Hoboken, NJ: John Wiley & Sons, 2004): "Implications of Short Selling and Divergence of Opinion for Investment Strategy" (chapter 5), and "Short Selling and Financial Puzzles" (chapter 6).

4. Charles M. Jones and Owen A. Lamont, "Short Sale Constraints and Stock Returns," *Journal of Financial Economics* 66 (2002): 207–239.

were paid by Wilson Pharmaceuticals while the stock was borrowed, Ms. Stokes must return them to Mr. Jordan, who still owned the stock at the time.

Instead of falling, suppose that the price of Wilson Pharmaceuticals stock rises. Ms. Stokes will realize a loss when she is forced to cover her short position. For example, if the price rises to $27 per share, Ms. Stokes will lose $700, to which must be added commissions and the cost of borrowing the stock.

Note the downside risk for a short seller versus a long buyer. When an investor purchases a stock (i.e., takes a long position), the most that the investor can lose is the purchase price. In contrast, when an investor sells short a stock, the maximum amount of the loss can be significant and not known at the time the stock is sold short. For example, in our illustration, if the price of Wilson Pharmaceutical increases to $50 per share, then loss would be $3,000. A price increase to $100 would result in a loss of $8,000. This is the reason that short selling is a very risky transaction.

Role of Brokers and Dealers in Real Markets

Common occurrences in real markets keep them from meeting the theoretical standards of being perfect. Because of these occurrences, brokers and dealers are necessary to the smooth functioning of a secondary market.

Brokers

One way in which a real market might not meet all the exacting standards of a theoretically perfect market is that many investors may not be present at all times in the marketplace.

Furthermore, a typical investor may not be skilled in the art of the deal or completely informed about every facet of trading in the asset. Clearly, even in smoothly functioning markets, most investors need professional assistance. Investors need someone to receive and keep track of their orders for buying or selling, to find other parties wishing to sell or buy, to negotiate for good prices, to serve as a focal point for trading, and to execute the orders. The broker performs all these functions. Obviously, these functions are more important for complicated trades, such as for exceptionally small or large trades, than for simple transactions or those of typical size.

A broker is an entity that acts on behalf of an investor who wishes to execute orders rather than trading for his or her own account. That is, the risks associated with the transaction (long or short) belong to the client (i.e., the investor), not the broker. These functions are performed by brokers or agents of the investor. It is important to realize that the brokerage activity does not require the broker to buy and sell or hold in inventory the financial asset that is the subject of the trade. (Such activity is termed "taking a position" in the asset, and it is the role of the dealer, another important financial market participant discussed in the following text.) Instead, the broker receives, transmits, and executes investors' orders with other investors. The broker receives an explicit commission for these services, and the commission is a transactions cost of the securities markets. If the broker also provides other services, such as research, recordkeeping, or advising, investors may pay additional charges.

Dealers as Market Makers

A real market might also differ from the perfect market because of the possibly frequent event of a temporary imbalance in the number of buy and sell orders that investors may place for any security at any given time. Such unmatched or unbalanced flow causes two problems. One is that the security's price may change abruptly, even if there has been no shift in either supply or demand for the security. Another problem is that buyers may have to pay higher than market-clearing prices (or sellers accept lower ones) if they want to make their trades immediately.

An example can illustrate these points. Suppose that the consensus price for ABC security is $50, which was determined in several recent trades. Now suppose that a flow of buy orders from investors who suddenly have cash arrives in the market, but there is no accompanying supply of sell orders. This temporary imbalance could be sufficient to push the price of ABC security to, say, $55. Thus, the price has changed sharply, even though nothing has changed in any fundamental financial aspect of the issuer. Buyers who want to buy immediately must pay $55 rather than $50, and this difference can be viewed as the price of **immediacy**. By "immediacy," we mean that buyers and sellers do not want to wait for the arrival of sufficient orders on the other side of the trade, which would bring the price closer to the level of recent transactions.

As explained earlier, the existence of imbalances explains the need for the dealer or market maker, who stands ready and willing to buy a financial asset for its own account (to add to an inventory of the financial asset) or sell from its own account (to reduce the inventory of the financial asset). At a given time, dealers are willing to buy a financial asset at a price (the bid price) that is less than what they are willing to sell the same financial asset for (the ask price). In the 1960s, two economists, George Stigler[5] and Harold Demsetz,[6] analyzed the role of dealers in securities markets. They viewed dealers as the suppliers of immediacy—the ability to trade promptly—to the market. The bid-ask spread can be viewed in turn as the price charged by dealers for supplying immediacy together with short-run price stability (continuity or smoothness) in the presence of short-term order imbalances. Dealers play two other roles: providing reliable price information to market participants, and, in certain market structures, providing the services of an auctioneer in bringing order and fairness to a market.[7]

5. George Stigler, "Public Regulation of Securities Markets," *Journal of Business* 37 (1964): 117–134.

6. Harold Demsetz, "The Cost of Transacting," *Quarterly Journal of Economics* 82 (1968): 35–36.

7. For a more detailed discussion, see chapter 1 in Robert A. Schwartz, *Equity Markets: Structure, Trading, and Performance* (New York: Harper & Row, 1988), 389–397.

The price stabilization role follows from our earlier example of what may happen to the price of a particular transaction in the absence of any intervention when there is a temporary imbalance of orders. By taking the opposite side of a trade when there are no other orders, the dealer prevents the price from materially diverging from the price at which a recent trade was consummated.

Investors are concerned not only with immediacy but also with being able to trade at prices that are reasonable, given prevailing conditions in the market. Although dealers do not know with certainty the true price of a security, they do have a privileged position in some market structures with respect not only to the flow of market orders but also to **limit orders**, which are special orders that can be executed only if the market price of the asset changes in a specified way. (See chapter 23 for more on limit orders.) For example, the dealers of the organized markets, called **specialists** and discussed in chapter 22, have just such a privileged position, from which they get special information about the flow of market orders.

Finally, the dealer acts as an **auctioneer** in some market structures, thereby providing order and fairness in the operations of the market. For example, as explained in chapter 22, the market maker on organized stock exchanges in the United States performs this function by organizing trading to make sure that the exchange rules for the priority of trading are followed.

The role of a market maker in a call market structure is that of an auctioneer. The market maker does not take a position in the traded asset, as a dealer does in a continuous market.

What factors determine the price that dealers should charge for the services they provide? Or equivalently, what factors determine the bid-ask spread? One of the most important is the order processing costs incurred by dealers. The costs of equipment necessary to do business and a dealer's administrative and operations staff are examples. The lower these costs are, the narrower the bid-ask spread will be. With the reduced cost of computing and better-trained personnel, these costs have declined since the 1960s.

Dealers also have to be compensated for bearing risk. A **dealer's position** may involve carrying inventory of a security (a **long position**) or selling a security that is not in inventory (a **short position**). In markets where shorting is common, positions are often referred to as "long only" or "short only." Three types of risks are associated with maintaining a long or short position in a given security. First, there is the uncertainty about the future price of the security. A dealer who has a net long position in the security is concerned that the price will decline in the future; a dealer who is in a net short position is concerned that the price will rise. In short, dealers trade for their own account, while brokers trade for someone else's account, their customer.

The second type of risk has to do with the expected time it will take the dealer to unwind a position and its uncertainty. And this, in turn, depends primarily on the number of buyers and sellers in the market for the security. In a thin market, there is a low number of buyers and sellers seeking transactions in the security, while in thick market there is a large number of buyers and sellers. Finally, even though a dealer may have access to better information about order flows than the general public does, there are some trades where the dealer takes the risk of trading with someone who has better information.[8] This results in the better-informed trader obtaining a better price at the expense of the dealer. Consequently, when establishing the bid-ask spread for a trade, a dealer will assess whether the trader might have better information.[9]

Market Efficiency

The term "efficient capital market" has been used in several contexts to describe the operating characteristics of a capital market. There is a distinction, however, between an **operationally** (or **internally**) **efficient market** and a **pricing** (or **externally**) **efficient capital market**.[10]

Operational Efficiency

In an **operationally efficient market**, investors can obtain transaction services as cheaply as possible, given the costs associated with furnishing those services. The cost of transacting is critical to investors and professional asset managers. Moreover, the SEC has continued to amend the Securities Exchange Act so that investors can obtain the best execution possible. Below we provide a brief explanation of trading costs.[11]

Transaction costs are more than merely brokerage commissions—they consist of commissions, fees, execution costs, and opportunity costs. Commissions are the fees paid to brokers to execute orders, and the commission is negotiable between the investor and the broker. Other types of fees include custodial fees and transfer fees. Custodial fees are the those charged by the financial entity that holds securities in safekeeping for an investor.

Beyond fees, there are hidden costs of trading. **Execution costs** represent the difference between the execution price of a security and the price that would have existed in the absence of the trade. Execution costs can be further decomposed into market (or price) impact and market timing costs. **Market impact cost** (or simply **impact cost**) is the result of the bid-ask spread and a price concession extracted by dealers to mitigate their risk that an investor's demand for liquidity is information motivated. (By a "price concession," we mean the investor will have to pay a higher price when buying and a lower price when selling.) **Market timing cost** arises when an adverse price movement of the security during the time of the transaction can be attributed in part to other activity in the security and is not

8. Walter Bagehot, "The Only Game in Town," *Financial Analysts Journal* 27, no. 2 (1971): 12–14, 22.

9. Some trades that we will discuss in Chapter 18 can be viewed as informationless trades: The dealer knows or believes that a trade is being requested to accomplish an investment objective that is not motivated by the potential future price movement of the security.

10. Richard R. West, "Two Kinds of Market Efficiency," *Financial Analysts Journal* 31, no. 6 (1975): 30–34.

11. Some of this discussion draws from Bruce M. Collins and Frank J. Fabozzi, "A Methodology for Measuring Transactions Costs," *Financial Analysts Journal* 47, no. 2 (1991): 27–36.

the result of a particular transaction. Execution costs, then, are related to both the demand for liquidity and the trading activity on the trade date.

A distinction can be made between **information-motivated trades** and **informationless trades**.[12] Information-motivated trading occurs when investors believe they possess pertinent information not currently reflected in the security's price. This style of trading tends to increase market impact, because it emphasizes the speed of execution, or because the market maker believes a desired trade is driven by information and increases the bid-ask spread to provide some protection. It can involve the sale of one security in favor of another. Informationless trades result from either a reallocation of wealth or the implementation of an investing strategy that depends only on existing public information. An example of the former is a pension fund's decision to invest cash in the stock market. Other examples of informationless trades include portfolio rebalancing, the investment of new money, or liquidations. In these circumstances, the demand for liquidity alone should not lead the market maker to demand the significant price concessions associated with new information.

The problem with measuring execution costs is that the true measure—which is the difference between the price of the security in the absence of the investor's trade and the execution price—is not observable. Furthermore, the execution prices depend on supply and demand conditions at the margin. Thus, the execution price may be influenced by competitive traders who demand immediate execution or on other investors with similar motives for trading. Then the execution price realized by an investor is the consequence of the structure of the market mechanism, the demand for liquidity by the marginal investor, and the competitive forces of investors with similar motivations for trading.

The cost of not transacting represents an **opportunity cost**.[13] Opportunity costs may arise when a desired trade fails to be executed. This component of costs represents the difference in performance between an investor's desired investment and the same investor's actual investment after adjusting for execution costs, commissions, and fees.

Opportunity costs are characterized as the hidden cost of trading. Some analysts suggest that the shortfall in performance of many actively managed portfolios is the consequence of failing to execute all desired trades.[14] Measurement of opportunity costs is subject to the same problems as measurement of execution costs. The true measure of opportunity costs depends on knowing the resulting performance of a security if all desired trades were executed at the desired time across an investment horizon. Because these desired trades were not executed, the benchmark is inherently unobservable.

12. Larry Cuneo and Wayne Wagner, "Reducing the Cost of Stock Trading," *Financial Analysts Journal* 31, no. 6 (1975), pp. 35–43.

13. For a discussion of opportunity cost in the context of costs defined as the implementation shortfall of an investment strategy, see André F. Perold, "The Implementation Shortfall: Paper versus Reality," *Journal of Portfolio Management* 14 (1988): 4–9.

14. For a discussion of the consequences of high opportunity costs, see Jack L. Treynor, "What Does It Take to Win the Trading Game?" *Financial Analysts Journal* 37, no. 1 (1981), pp. 55–60.

Pricing Efficiency

Pricing efficiency refers to a market where prices at all times fully reflect all available information that is relevant to the valuation of securities. That is, relevant information about the security is quickly integrated into the price of securities.

In his seminal review article on pricing efficiency, Eugene Fama pointed out that to test whether a market is price-efficient, two definitions are necessary. First, it is necessary to define what it means that prices "fully reflect" information. Second, the "relevant" set of information that is assumed to be "fully reflected" in prices must be defined.[15] Fama, as well as others, defines "fully reflects" in terms of the expected return from holding a security. The expected return over some holding period is equal to expected cash distributions plus the expected price change, all divided by the initial price. The price formation process defined by Fama and others is that the expected return one period from now is a random variable that already takes into account the "relevant" information set.

When defining the "relevant" information set that prices should reflect, Fama classified the pricing efficiency of a market into three forms: weak, semi-strong, and strong. The distinction between these forms lies in the relevant information that is hypothesized in the price of the security. **Weak efficiency** means that the price of the security reflects the past price and trading history of the security. **Semi-strong efficiency** means that the price of the security fully reflects all public information, which includes but is not limited to historical price and trading patterns. **Strong efficiency** exists in a market where the price of a security reflects all information, regardless of whether it is publicly available.

A price-efficient market carries certain implications for the investment strategy that investors wish to pursue. Throughout this book, we refer to various active strategies employed by investors. In an active strategy, investors seek to capitalize on what they perceive to be the mispricing of a security or securities. In a market that is price efficient, active strategies will not consistently generate an abnormal return after taking into consideration transaction costs and the risks associated with a strategy that is actively managed rather than simply buying and holding securities. In certain markets that empirical evidence suggests are price efficient, investors may pursue a strategy of **indexing**, which simply seeks to match the performance of some financial index. We look at the pricing efficiency of the stock market in chapter 23.

Electronic Trading

Traditionally, securities trading has historically occurred mainly in person (e.g., on stock exchange trading floors) or via the telephone (typically in the bond market, as explained in chapter 26). Currently, however, securities buyers and seller are mainly brought together electronically (that is, through electronic trading platforms), which is referred to as **etrad-**

15. Eugene F. Fama, "Efficient Capital Markets: A Review of Theory and Empirical Work," *Journal of Finance* 25 (1970): 383–417.

ing, Electronic trading provides virtual trading platforms. Often systems for clearing and settlement of trades are integrated in trading systems. This is referred to as **straight-through processing**. There are many types of equity and bond electronic trading systems.

Key Points

- A secondary market in financial assets is one where existing or outstanding assets are traded among investors.
- A secondary market serves several needs of the firm or governmental unit that issues securities in the primary market.
- The secondary market provides the issuer with regular information about the value of its outstanding stocks or bonds, and it encourages investors to buy securities from issuers, because it offers them an ongoing opportunity for liquidating their investments in securities.
- Investors get services from the secondary market, because the market supplies them with liquidity and prices for the assets they are holding or want to buy, and the market brings interested investors together, thereby reducing the costs of searching for other parties and of making trades.
- In general, secondary market structures can be classified as order driven or quote driven, with real-world financial markets using a combination of these market structures.
- Quote-driven markets do not require a dealer, and the prices are determined by the interaction of natural buyers and natural sellers rather than being set by a dealer.
- Order-driven markets can be further classified as continuous order-driven and periodic call auction markets.
- Markets are classified as exchange markets and over-the-counter (OTC) markets.
- Secondary markets may be continuous or call markets or a combination of the two.
- In a continuous market, trading and price determination go on throughout the day as orders to buy and sell reach the market.
- In a call market, prices are determined by executions of batched or grouped orders to buy and sell at a specific time (or times) in the trading day.
- A market can be perfect, in a theoretical sense, only if it meets many conditions regarding number of participants, flow of information, freedom from regulation, and freedom from costs that hinder trading.
- An investor who expects that the price of a security to decline can benefit by selling that security short.
- A mechanism to allow investors to sell short is critical in financial markets, because in the absence of such a mechanism, security prices will tend to be biased toward the view of more optimistic investors.

• Even the most developed and smoothly functioning secondary market falls short of being perfect in the economically theoretical meaning of the term.

• Actual markets tend to have numerous frictions that affect prices and investors' behavior.

• Some key frictions are transactions costs, which include commissions, fees, and execution costs.

• Because of imperfections in actual markets, investors need the services of two types of market participants: dealers and brokers.

• Brokers assist investors by collecting and transmitting orders to the market, bringing willing buyers and sellers together, negotiating prices, and executing orders; the fee for these services is the broker's commission.

• Dealers perform three functions in markets: (1) they provide the opportunity for investors to trade immediately rather than waiting for the arrival of sufficient orders on the other side of the trade (immediacy), and they do this while maintaining short-run price stability (continuity); (2) they offer price information to market participants; and (3) in certain market structures, dealers serve as auctioneers by bringing order and fairness to a market.

• Dealers buy for their own account and maintain inventories of assets, and their profits come from selling assets at higher prices than the prices at which they purchased them.

• A market is operationally efficient if it offers investors reasonably priced services related to buying and selling.

• Execution costs represent the difference between the execution price of a security and the price that would have existed in the absence of the trade; these costs arise out of the demand for immediate execution through both the demand for liquidity and the trading activity on the trade date.

• Opportunity costs arise when a desired trade fails to be executed.

• A market is price efficient if at all times prices fully reflect all available information that is relevant to the valuation of securities.

• Three forms of pricing efficiency are based on the relevant information set: weak form, semi-strong form, and strong form.

• In a price-efficient market, active strategies pursued will not consistently produce superior returns after adjusting for risk and transactions costs.

• Electronic trading (or etrading) brings buyers and sellers together electronically, replacing personal and telephone contact in most markets.

Questions

1. How do secondary markets benefit investors?
2. What is meant by an "OTC market"?

3. How does an order-driven market differ from a quote-driven market?

4. Explain why you agree or disagree with the following statements:

a. “Real-world financial markets can be either a continuous order-driven market or a periodic call auction, but cannot be both.”

b. “The market structure in the OTC market is a periodic call auction.”

5. A market can be perfect, in a theoretical sense, only if it meets certain conditions. What are those conditions?

6. What is meant by the statement that “dealers offer both immediacy and price continuity to investors”?

7. Some years ago, legislators in a state claimed that speculation on land was driving prices to too high a level. They proposed to pass a law that would require the buyer of any piece of land in the state to hold the land for at least three years before he or she could resell it.

a. Analyze this proposal in terms of perfect markets and possible frictions that have been described in this chapter.

b. If that proposal had passed, do you think land prices would have risen or fallen?

8. a. Why would an investor sell short a security?

b. What happens if the price of a security that is sold short rises?

9. What is the role of the broker in a short sale?

10. What might be expected in a financial market that does not allow investors to sell short?

11. What is the difference between a broker and a dealer?

12. How does a dealer make a profit when making a market?

13. What are the risks that a dealer accepts in making a market?

14. The residential real estate market boasts many brokers but very few dealers. What explains this situation?

15. What is meant by the “bid-ask spread”?

16. How does the rate of order flow (or thickness) of a market affect a dealer’s bid-ask spread?

17. What are the benefits that a market derives from the actions of dealers?

18. a. What is meant by an “information-motivated trade”?

b. What is meant by an “informationless trade”?

19. What makes a market operationally or internally efficient?

20. What is the key characteristic of a market that has pricing or external efficiency?

21. What is meant by the “semi-strong form” of market efficiency?

22. Indicate why you agree or disagree with the following statement: “An investor who believes a market is price efficient should pursue an active investment strategy.”

19 The Foreign Exchange Market

CONTENTS

Learning Objectives

After reading this chapter, you will understand:

- what is meant by a foreign exchange rate;
- the different ways that a foreign exchange rate can be quoted (direct versus indirect);
- the conventions for quoting foreign exchange rates;
- what the fundamental determinant of exchange rates is: purchasing power parity;
- what a cross rate is;

- how to calculate a theoretical cross rate;
- what triangular arbitrage is;
- the foreign exchange market structure;
- the composition of the foreign exchange market: spot market and derivatives markets;
- the role of governments in the foreign exchange market;
- the role of dealers in the foreign exchange market;
- the nondealer private participants in the market: importers and exporters (nonfinancial transactions) and financial institutions (financial transactions);
- the dominant role of financing transactions in the foreign exchange market; and
- what foreign exchange risk is.

The fundamental fact of international finance is that different countries issue different currencies, and the relative values of those currencies may change quickly, substantially, and without warning. Moreover, the change may either reflect economic developments or be a response to political events that make no economic sense. As a result, the risk that a currency's value may change adversely, which is called **foreign exchange risk** or **currency risk**, is an important consideration for all participants in the international financial markets. Investors who purchase securities denominated in a currency different from their own must worry about the rate of return on those securities after adjusting for changes in the exchange rate. Firms that issue obligations denominated in a foreign currency face the risk of the uncertain value of the cash payments they owe to investors.

In this chapter, we provide a review of foreign exchange rates and the foreign exchange rate market. The foreign exchange rate market includes the cash market (or spot market) and the derivatives market. The cash market or spot market is the market for settlement of a foreign exchange transaction within two business days. The derivatives market includes currency futures and forward contracts, currency options, and currency swaps. All these derivatives are described in chapter 38.

Foreign Exchange Rates

An **exchange rate** is defined as the amount of one currency that can be exchanged for a unit of another currency. In fact, the foreign exchange (FX) rate is the price of one currency in terms of another currency. And, depending on circumstances, one could define either currency as the price for the other. So FX rates can be quoted "in either direction." For example, the FX rate between the U.S. dollar and the euro could be quoted in one of two ways:

1. The number of U.S. dollars necessary to acquire one euro; this is the dollar price of one euro.
2. The number of euros necessary to acquire one U.S. dollar; this is the euro price of one dollar.

FX Rate Quotation Conventions

FX rate quotations can be either direct or indirect. The difference lies in identifying one currency as a local currency and the other as a foreign currency. For example, from the perspective of a U.S. participant, the local currency would be U.S. dollars, and any other currency, such as the Swiss franc, would be the foreign currency. From the perspective of a Swiss participant, the local currency would be the Swiss franc, and other currencies, such as the U.S. dollar, would be the foreign currency. A **direct quotation** is the number of units of a local currency exchangeable for one unit of a foreign currency.

An **indirect quotation** is the number of units of a foreign currency that can be exchanged for one unit of the local currency. Looking at it from a U.S. participant's perspective, we see that a quotation indicating the number of dollars exchangeable for one unit of a foreign currency is a direct quotation. An indirect quotation from the same participant's perspective would be the number of units of the foreign currency that can be exchanged for one U.S. dollar. Obviously, from the point of view of a non-U.S. participant, the number of U.S. dollars exchangeable for one unit of a non-U.S. currency is an indirect quotation; the number of units of a non-U.S. currency exchangeable for a U.S. dollar is a direct quotation.

Given a direct quotation, we can obtain an indirect quotation (which is simply the reciprocal of the direct quotation) and vice versa. For example, on October 25, 2013, a U.S. investor received a direct quotation of 1.3805 U.S. dollars for one euro. That is, the price of a euro was $1.3805. The reciprocal of the direct quotation is 0.7244, which would have been the indirect quotation for the U.S. investor; that is, one U.S. dollar could be exchanged for $0.7244 euros, which was the euro price of a U.S. dollar.

If the number of units of a foreign currency that can be obtained for one dollar—the price of a dollar in that currency, or the indirect quotation—rises, the dollar is said to appreciate relative to the currency, and the currency is said to depreciate. Thus, appreciation means a decline in the direct quotation.

Although quotations can be either direct or indirect, the problem is defining from whose perspective the quotation is given. FX conventions in fact standardize the ways quotations are given. Because of the importance of the U.S. dollar in the international financial system, currency quotations are all relative to the U.S. dollar. When dealers quote, they either give U.S. dollars per unit of foreign currency (a direct quotation from the U.S. perspective) or the number of units of the foreign currency per U.S. dollar (an indirect quotation from the U.S. perspective). Quoting in terms of U.S. dollars per unit of foreign currency is called **American terms**, whereas quoting in terms of the number of units of the foreign currency per U.S. dollar is called **European terms**. The dealer convention is to use European terms when quoting FX, with a few exceptions. The British pound, the Irish pound, the Australian dollar, and the New Zealand dollar are exceptions that are quoted in American terms.

International Organization for Standardization Currency Code

Currencies are typically identified by reference to their ISO 4217 currency code, as established by the International Organization for Standardization (ISO). The code consists of two parts. The first two characters of the currency code are the country's two-character Internet country code. The third character is the currency unit. The currency code for selected countries is shown in table 19.1. For example, the Internet country codes for the United States, Japan, and the United Kingdom (Great Britain) are US, JP, and GB, respectively, and the currency unit for each is the dollar (D), yen (Y), and pound (P), respectively. Hence the ISO 4217 currency codes for these three countries are USD, JPY, and GBP, respectively. The ISO 4217 currency code for members of the Eurozone is EUR.

FX Rate Determination

Since the early 1970s, exchange rates among major currencies have been free to float, with market forces determining the relative value of a currency. Thus, each day a currency's price relative to that of another freely floating currency may stay the same, increase, or decrease.

A key factor affecting the expectation of changes in a country's exchange rate with another currency is the relative expected inflation rate of the two countries. Spot exchange rates adjust to compensate for the relative inflation rate. This adjustment reflects the so-called **purchasing power parity** relationship, which posits that the exchange rate—the domestic price of the foreign currency—is proportional to the domestic inflation rate and inversely proportional to foreign inflation.

Let's look at what happens when the spot exchange rate changes between two currencies. Suppose that on day 1, the spot exchange rate between the U.S. dollar and country X's currency is $0.7966, and on the next day (day 2), it changes to $0.8011. Consequently, on day 1, one currency unit of country X costs $0.7966. On day 2, it costs more U.S. dollars ($0.8011) to buy one currency unit of country X. Thus, the currency unit of country X *appreciated* relative to the U.S. dollar from day 1 to day 2, or, what amounts to the same thing, the U.S. dollar *depreciated* relative to the currency of country X from day 1 to day 2. Suppose further that on day 3, the spot exchange rate for one currency unit of country X is $0.8000. Relative to day 2, the U.S. dollar appreciated relative to the currency of country X, or, equivalently, the currency of country X depreciated relative to the U.S. dollar.

Cross Rates

Barring any government restrictions, riskless arbitrage will ensure that the exchange rate between two countries will be the same in both countries. The theoretical exchange rate be-

Table 19.1
ISO 4217 currency codes for selected countries.

Country, Currency Unit	ISO 4217 Code	Country, Currency Unit	ISO 4217 Code
Argentina, peso	ARS	Iran, rial	IRR
Australia, dollar	AUD	Iraq, dinar	IQD
Bolivia, boliviano	BOB	Israel, new shekel	ILS
Brazil, real	BRL	Japan, yen	JPY
Britain (United Kingdom), pound	GBP	Korea (North), won	KPW
Bulgaria, lev	BGN	Korea (South), won	KRW
Canada, dollar	CAD	Kuwait, dinar	KWD
Chile, peso	CLP	Latvia, lats	LVL
China, yuan renminbi	CNY	Lebanon, pound	LBP
Colombia, peso	COP	Malaysia, ringgit	MYR
Cyprus, pound	CYP	Mexico, peso	MXN
Czech Republic, koruna	CZK	New Zealand, dollar	NZD
Denmark, krone	DKK	Norway, krone	NOK
Egypt, pound	EGP	Pakistan, rupee	PKR
El Salvador, dollar	SVC	Russia, ruble	RUB
Euro member countries, euro	EUR	Switzerland, franc	CHF
Hong Kong, dollar	HKD	Thailand, baht	THB
Hungarian, forint	HUK	Turkey, new lira	TRY
Iceland, krona	ISK	United Arab Emirates, dirham	AED
India, rupee	INR	United Kingdom, pound	GBP
Indonesia, rupiah	IDR	United States of America, dollar	USD

tween two countries other than the United States can be inferred from their exchange rates with the U.S. dollar. Rates computed in this way are referred to as **theoretical cross rates**. They would be computed as follows for two countries, X and Y:

$$\text{Theoretical cross rate} = \frac{\text{Quote in American terms of currency X}}{\text{Quote in American terms of currency Y}}$$

To illustrate, let's calculate the theoretical cross rate between Japanese yen and British pound on August 11, 2018. The spot exchange rate for the two currencies in American terms was \$1.27691 per British pound and 0.00902 per Japanese yen. Then the number of units of yen (currency Y) per unit of British points (currency X) is

$$\frac{\$1.27691}{\$0.00902} = 141.5643 \text{ yen per British pound.}$$

That is, it would take 141.5643 yen to obtain one British pound. Taking the reciprocal gives the number of British pounds exchangeable for one Japanese yen. In our example, it is 0.0071.

In the real world, it is rare that the theoretical cross rate, as computed from actual dealer dollar exchange rate quotations, will differ from the actual cross rate quoted by dealers. When the discrepancy is large compared to the transaction costs of buying and selling the currencies, a riskless arbitrage opportunity arises. Arbitraging to take advantage of cross-rate mispricing is called **triangular arbitrage**, so named because it involves positions in three currencies—the U.S. dollar and the two foreign currencies. The arbitrage keeps actual cross rates in line with theoretical cross rates.

FX Turnover

Trading volume (or market turnover) statistics for the FX market is reported every three years by the Bank of International Settlements (BIS) in its *Triennial Survey on Foreign Exchange and OTC Derivatives*. The 2016 survey found that the average daily market turnover in the FX market (spot and derivatives) as of April 2016 was US$5.067 trillion. Of that amount, spot market trading was $1.652 trillion per day or 33% of all trading. The balance, $3.415 trillion or 67%, was therefore turnover attributable to FX derivative instruments.

Table 19.2 shows the currency distribution of global FX market turnover as reported in the 2016 survey for the top eight currencies. The dominate role of the U.S. dollar can be seen by its significant share.

The top eight currency pairs turnover from the 2016 BIS survey are shown in table 19.3. As can be seen, the three most heavily traded currency pairs were the U.S. dollar with the euro, the Japanese yen, and the U.K. sterling (British pound). In fact, the data reported by the BIS indicated that these three currency pairs have been the top three since 2001.

Table 19.2
2016 Currency distribution of global FX market turnover, top eight currencies.

Rank	Currency	Share (%)
1	U.S. dollar	88
2	Euro	31
3	Japanese yen	22
4	Sterling	13
5	Australian dollar	7
6	Canadian dollar	5
7	Swiss franc	5
8	China, yuan renminbi	4

Source: Taken from Bank for International Settlements, "Triennial Central Bank Survey: Foreign Exchange Turnover in April 2016" (Basel, Switzerland, 2016), 10, table 2.

Note: Shown are percentage shares of average daily turnover in April 2016. Adjusted for local and cross-border inter-dealer double counting.

Table 19.3
2016 top eight global FX market turnover by currency pair: Daily averages.

Currency Pair	Amount ($ billions)	Share (%)
USD/EUR	1,172	23.1
USD/JPY	901	17.8
USD/GBP	470	9.3
USD/AUD	262	5.2
USD/CAD	218	4.3
USD/CNY	192	3.8
USD/CHF	180	3.6
USD/MXN	90	1.8

Source: Taken from Bank for International Settlements, "Triennial Central Bank Survey: Foreign Exchange Turnover in April 2016" (Basel, Switzerland: 2016), 11, table 3.

Note: Shown are the average daily turnover values in April 2016, in billions of U.S. dollars and percentages.

Market Participants in the FX Market

The FX market is an OTC market that operates 24 hours a day. Market participants in the FX market include the central banks of governments, dealers, nondealer private market entities, and clearinghouses for FX trading.

Central Banks of Governments

Although major currencies are allowed to float, in practice, national monetary authorities can intervene in the foreign market for their currency for a variety of economic reasons. Consequently, the current FX system is sometimes referred to as a "managed" floating-rate system.

In the United States, currency-related activities are the responsibility of the Federal Reserve System and the U.S. Treasury. This is because the primary responsibility for international financial policy was delegated by the U.S. Congress to the U.S. Treasury. However, it is the Federal Reserve Bank of New York (FRBNY) that actually carries out those activities when managing U.S. foreign current reserves. The FRBNY intervenes periodically after monitoring and analyzes market developments throughout the world.

In 1978, the FRBNY formed the Foreign Exchange Committee (FXC). Individuals from financial institutions that are actively involved in the FX markets in global financial markets are members of the FXC. The three objectives that the FXC seeks to accomplish are (1) serving as a working group to discuss best practices and technical issues in the FX market, (2) providing recommendations and guidelines that can be used for risk management in the FX market, and (3) supporting activities that reduce counterparty risk in FX transactions. This last objective involves clearinghouses for the settlement of transactions described later in this section.

Other countries have entities that play the same role as the FXC. For example, in 1973, the United Kingdom formed The London Foreign Exchange Joint Standing Committee, which is chaired and administered by the Bank of England.

Dealers

Because the FX market is an OTC market that operates 24 hours a day, market participants who want to buy or sell a currency must search among different dealers to get the best exchange rate on a specific currency. Alternatively, market participants who want to transact can refer to various widely available bank/broker screens, such as Bloomberg Financial Markets and Reuters. The prices cited on those screens are for indicative pricing only (i.e., a quote which is neither a firm bid nor a binding bid).

FX dealers do not quote one price. Instead, they quote an exchange rate at which they are willing to buy a foreign currency (bid) and one at which they are willing to sell a foreign currency (offer or ask). For example, on September 4, 2017, the following was the bid and offer reported by Reuters for one euro in terms of the U.S. dollar: 1.1883 bid and 1.1884 offer. What this means is that one could exchange one euro for 1.1883 U.S. dollars or pay 1.1884 U.S. dollars to purchase one euro. The bid-offer spread is 0.0001 in terms of euros.

FX dealers are large international banks and other financial institutions that specialize in making markets in FX. Commercial banks dominate the market. There is no organized exchange where foreign currency is traded, but dealers are linked by telephone and cable and by various information transfer services. Consequently, the FX market can best be described as an interbank OTC market. Most transactions between banks are done through FX brokers. Brokers are agents that do not take a position in the foreign currencies involved in the transaction. The normal size of a transaction is $1 million or more.

FX dealers realize revenue from one or more sources: (1) the bid-ask spread (bid-offer), (2) commissions charged on FX transactions, and (3) trading profits (appreciation of the currencies that dealers hold a long position in, depreciation of the currencies that they hold a long position in, or appreciation of the currencies that they have a short position in).

The geographical distribution of FX trading by dealers has been concentrated in the global financial centers in the five countries responsible for 75% of market activity, according to the Triennial Central Bank Surveys. As of 2016, by far the dominant financial center is in the United Kingdom with a share of 36.9%, followed by the United States (19.5%), Singapore (7.9%), Hong Kong (16.7%), and Japan (6.1%).[1]

1. Bank for International Settlements, "Triennial Central Bank Survey: Foreign Exchange Turnover in April 2013" (Basel, Switzerland, 2016), 8.

Nondealer Private Entities

FX dealers in the FX market are acting on behalf of clients for their own accounts. It is the clients who drive the supply and demand for a country's FX. So let's look closely at who these clients are.

Clients can be divided into two categories. The first category includes any entity that imports or exports goods and services and seeks FX to execute the associated transactions. Importers and exporters include businesses and individuals. Importers need the FX of the country from which the products are received. Exporters need to exchange the seller's currency into the domestic currency. Individuals also need a foreign currency when they travel to other countries. The supply and demand for FX by importers and exporters prior to the 1970s were the dominant factors impacting FX rates.

After the 1970s, by far the dominant factor in the determination of FX rates has been financial transactions by institutional investors.[2] Although it is macroeconomic fundamental factors that are the major influence on FX rates, typically, short-term FX rate fluctuations reflect the impact of financial transactions. When a country's FX rate increases (falls) in the short run, it is often due to the belief by investors buying (selling) financial assets denominated in that country's currency expecting a further increase (decrease) in the FX rate.

Appreciation of the U.S. dollar may reflect investors in other countries seeking a safe haven for their investments, which results in non-U.S. investors purchasing the U.S. dollar. A recent example was in the second quarter of 2016, where in general the U.S. dollar had been appreciating relative to other major currencies. Safe haven investing in the United States that quarter resulted from international developments, specifically, the June 23 referendum on the United Kingdom's membership in the European Union. This investing resulted in appreciation of the U.S. dollar.

The shift from nonfinancial participants seeking currency for imports and exports can be seen from the 2016 Triennial Central Bank Survey, which reports currency trading with counterparties. As noted earlier, daily annual turnover as of April 2016 was US$5.067 trillion. Of that amount, about 39% was with reporting dealers, 52% was with other financial institutions, and only 9% was with nonfinancial customers (i.e., exporters and importers).[3]

Settlement in FX Markets

A risk in transactions is the failure of the counterparty to fulfill its commitment. This risk is reduced by the presence of a reliable settlement system. In the case of financial instruments and FX, there are such systems used by banks.

2. According to the Bank for International Settlements, "Triennial Central Bank Survey," in recent years, facilitated by Internet-based trading platforms, retail investors (private individuals trading on their own behalf) have increased their participation in the FX market.

3. As reported in Bank for International Settlements, "Triennial Central Bank Survey," 12, table 4.

The Society for Worldwide Interbank Financial Telecommunications is a cooperative society that is a communications network for international financial market transactions that link financial institutions throughout the world. Owned by a group of banks in North America and Europe, the Society allows the member banks nearly instantaneously to transact via messages among themselves international payments and other communications regarding banking transactions. The speed of communications is important because it allows counterparties to respond instantaneously and settle transactions using one of the electronic clearing houses discussed below.

The major clearinghouses include Clearing House Interbank Payment System (CHIPS) and Clearing House Automated Payment System (CHAPS). CHIPS is owned by the 12 commercial banks constituting the New York Clearing House Association. Started in 1971, CHIPS is the world's largest electronic payment system (including FX transactions) for settlement among banks in New York; that is, there is no need for physical exchange of checks or funds to settle transactions. The funds are then transferred via the Fedwire, a communication network linking more than 7,000 banks to the Federal Reserve Banks. Similar to CHIPS, CHAPS is a mechanism for clearing in London.

FX Risk and Derivative Instruments

Our major focus in this chapter has been on one sector of the FX market: the spot market. Yet, as emphasized in this chapter when describing FX trading activities, transactions in the FX market involve FX derivatives because of the need for market participants to protect against adverse movements in the FX rate. FX derivatives are used to control FX risk. Consequently, to appreciate the need for FX derivatives, we describe FX risk.

Let us consider a financial transaction that needs to control FX risk, because as mentioned, the dominant form of FX transactions is now financial transactions. From the perspective of a U.S. investor, the cash flows of assets denominated in a foreign currency expose the investor to uncertainty as to the actual level of the cash flow measured in U.S. dollars. The actual number of U.S. dollars that the investor eventually receives depends on the exchange rate between the U.S. dollar and the foreign currency at the time the nondollar cash flow is received and exchanged for U.S. dollars. If the foreign currency depreciates (declines in value) relative to the U.S. dollar (i.e., the U.S. dollar appreciates), the dollar value of the cash flows will be proportionately less, leading to FX risk.

Any investor who purchases an asset denominated in a currency that is not the medium of exchange in the investor's country faces FX risk. For example, a French investor who acquires a yen-denominated Japanese bond is exposed to the risk that the Japanese yen will decline in value relative to the euro.

FX risk is a consideration for the issuer, too. Suppose that IBM issues bonds denominated in euros. IBM's FX risk is that, at the time the coupon interest payments must be made and the principal repaid, the U.S. dollar will have depreciated relative to the euro, requiring that IBM pay more dollars to satisfy its obligation.

Key Points

- An FX rate is defined as the amount of one currency that can be exchanged for another currency.
- A direct exchange rate quotation is the domestic price of a foreign currency. An indirect quotation is the foreign price of the domestic currency.
- Exchange rates can be quoted in either American terms (i.e., in terms of U.S. dollars per unit of foreign currency) or European terms (i.e., in terms of the number of units of the foreign currency per U.S. dollar). With a few exceptions, the market convention is to use European terms.
- Currencies are typically identified by reference to their ISO 4217 currency code.
- The spot exchange rate market is the market for settlement of a currency within two business days.
- In developed countries and some developing ones, exchange rates are free to float.
- According to the purchasing power parity relationship, the exchange rate between two countries—the price of the foreign currency in terms of the domestic currency—is proportional to the domestic price level and inversely proportional to the price level in the foreign country.
- The FX market is an OTC market dominated by brokers and institutional investors for financial transactions.
- FX dealers quote one price at which they are willing to buy a foreign currency and one at which they are willing to sell a foreign currency.
- In the FX market, the dominant form of trading is financial transactions.
- An investor or issuer whose cash flows are denominated in a foreign currency is exposed to FX risk.

Questions

1. a. What is the ISO 4237 currency code?

b. What does the following exchange rate mean: CAD/MXN?

2. The following are quotes on August 19, 2016, for four currencies with the quote in terms of U.S. dollars per unit. Complete the values in the second column.

	Currency Unit	Units per U.S. Dollar	U.S. Dollars per Unit
EUR	(euro)	?	1.1325477382
GBP	(British pound)	?	1.3077000000
INR	(Indian rupee)	?	0.0148968912
AUD	(Australian dollar)	?	0.7626350000

3. The following are quotes on August 19, 2016, for four currencies with the quote in terms of units per U.S. dollar. Complete the values in the last column.

	Currency Unit	Units per U.S. Dollar	U.S. Dollars per Unit
MYR	(Malaysian ringgit)	4.0154996681	?
JPY	(Japanese yen)	100.2160000000	?
CNY	(Chinese yuan renminbi)	6.6507000000	?
NZD	(New Zealand dollar)	1.3743059755	?

4. The following spot FX rates were reported on October 25, 2013.

	Japanese Yen	British Pound	Australian Dollar
U.S. dollar	0.010267	1.616500	0.957900

Note: The exchange rates indicate the number of U.S. dollars necessary to purchase one unit of the foreign currency.

a. From the perspective of a U.S. investor, are the preceding FX rates direct or indirect quotations?

b. How much of each of the foreign currencies is needed to buy one U.S. dollar?

5. For the exchange rates in question 4, calculate the theoretical cross rates between:

a. the Australian dollar and the Japanese yen,

b. the Australian dollar and the British pound, and

c. the Japanese yen and the British pound.

6. Below are quotes for FX rates between the euro and other currencies on August 19, 2015, and one year later (August 19, 2016). The quote is in terms of the number of units of the currency per euro.

Currency Code	Currency Name	Units per EUR (August 19, 2015)	Units per EUR (August 19, 2016)
GBP	British pound	0.70712814	0.867300414
INR	Indian rupee	72.09718253	76.04223967
AUD	Australian dollar	1.511989135	1.486415575
CAD	Canadian dollar	1.455905913	1.458507691
SGD	Singapore dollar	1.554966916	1.525800563
CHF	Swiss franc	1.073200586	1.086794982
MYR	Malaysian ringgit	4.539774144	4.548440709
JPY	Japanese yen	137.2743242	113.5447394
CNY	Chinese yuan renminbi	7.075979567	7.53592369
NZD	New Zealand dollar	1.685256522	1.558592403
THB	Thai baht	39.37040071	39.22792237
HUF	Hungarian forint	310.1395155	310.1571238

a. Which of the currencies appreciated relative to the euro?

b. Which of the currencies depreciated relative to the euro?

7. Explain the meaning of triangular arbitrage, and show how it is related to cross rates.

8. Why is the primary factor impacting the short-term movements in FX rates the supply and demand for a currency by importers and exporters?

9. In the second quarter of 2016, the British pound depreciated sharply against the U.S. dollar immediately following the outcome of the U.K. referendum to exit the European Union (nicknamed "Brexit"). This resulted in a 7.3% decline in the British pound–U.S. dollar exchange rate over the second quarter. Why did the U.K. pound depreciate relative to the U.S. dollar?

10. A U.S. life insurance company that buys British government bonds faces FX risk. Specify the nature of that risk in terms of the company's expected return in U.S. dollars.

V GLOBAL GOVERNMENT DEBT MARKETS

20 Sovereign Debt Markets

CONTENTS

Learning Objectives

After reading this chapter, you will understand:

- the benefits for a country to have a well-developed government securities market;
- the two basic types of government securities—discount and coupon securities;

This chapter is coauthored with Steven V. Mann.

- inflation-linked government securities, floating-rate government securities, and exchange-rate-linked government securities;
- The objectives of the structure of the primary market and primary distribution methods of government securities;
- the differences between a single-price auction and a multiple-price auction;
- the functions of a primary dealer;
- the characteristics of a well-developed secondary market;
- the structure of a secondary market—organized exchange versus OTC market;
- how stripping and reconstitution of government coupon securities work; and
- the role of repurchase agreements in government markets.

Sovereign debt refers to the debt issued by the highest level of government in a particular country. Sovereign governments occupy a central place in the financial market. Not only are they among the largest single group of borrowers in most countries, but the marketable debt issued by central governments is considered to be the debt in a country that has the lowest default risk. The reason is that central governments borrow in a currency whose value they control. To pay off their nominal debt, governments can simply print more money to pay off these claims. A notable exception is the European Union, where member nations cede control of monetary policy to the European Central Bank. Table 20.1 shows the amount of central bank debt securities outstanding for 18 countries as of year-end 2016. Of the total amount outstanding of almost US$20.5 trillion, 59% was issued by the U.S. government.

Governments generate revenue to service their debt from two primary sources. First, the government has, more or less, the unlimited power to tax its citizens. This power can be exercised in the short run only. In the long run, for governments that must face an electorate in fair and legitimate elections, the electorate has the final say on the legitimacy of any tax policy. The second source is the perception of unused capacity for additional borrowing. The prospect of additional borrowing depends on the productive capacity of the economy as well as the government's reputation for management of its liabilities.

According to the World Bank, various benefits accrue to a country that has a well-developed securities market.[1] First, a government securities market provides a channel for the transmission and implementation of monetary policy, especially monetary targets and inflation objectives. Second, it provides another avenue to finance budget deficits other than the central bank. Third, the existence of a sovereign debt market can enable authorities to smooth consumption and investment expenditures in response to macroeconomic shocks. Finally, a liquid and well-developed market can almost certainly reduce the interest cost of debt over the medium and long term.

1. World Bank, *Developing a Government Bond Market* (Washington, DC: 2001).

Table 20.1
Central government debt securities outstanding in Billions of U.S. Dollars as of year end, 2016.

	Debt (billions U.S. dollars)				
	Total	Fixed Rate	Floating Rate	Inflation-Linked	Exchange Rate-Linked
All countries	**20,443.4**	**17,080.1**	**827.0**	**2,448.5**	**86.9**
Argentina	74.5	6.1	13.6	13.3	41.4
Australia	333.8	311.0	0.0	22.8	0.0
Belgium	361.8	347.6	5.2	0.0	9.0
Brazil	897.8	319.3	269.8	304.1	4.6
Canada	386.3	353.8	0.0	32.5	0.0
Chile	43.2	17.5	—	25.8	—
Chinese Taipei	171.1	171.1	—	—	—
Colombia	76.8	53.3	0.0	23.5	—
Czech Republic	51.4	43.2	8.2	0.0	0.0
Germany	1,245.7	1,115.1	28.4	72.2	30.1
Hong Kong SAR	13.3	9.0	0.0	4.3	0.0
Hungary	45.1	35.3	6.1	3.6	—
India	—	—	—	—	—
Indonesia	130.2	122.7	6.3	0.0	1.2
Israel	129.7	64.2	11.3	54.1	0.0
Korea	500.4	491.3	—	9.1	—
Malaysia	139.3	139.3	0.0	0.0	0.0
Mexico	247.5	131.3	56.0	60.2	—
Peru	18.8	17.7	0.0	1.1	0.0
Philippines	73.2	71.5	1.1	—	0.5
Poland	138.0	102.3	34.6	1.1	0.0
Russia	64.0	61.2	—	2.9	0.0
Saudi Arabia	56.9	32.4	24.5	—	—
Singapore	69.8	69.8	0.0	0.0	0.0
South Africa	124.9	91.5	0.0	33.4	...
Spain	853.1	819.7	3.1	30.4	0.0
Thailand	112.0	112.0	0.0	0.0	0.0
Turkey	133.2	79.3	23.5	30.3	0.0
United Kingdom	1,860.4	1,383.7	0.0	476.7	0.0
United States	12,090.3	10,508.0	335.1	1,247.2	0.0

Source: BIS Statistical Bulletin (Basel, Switzerland: Bank for International Settlements, September 2017), 191, table C.

Notes: —, data not available. For some reason, BIS did not include the debt of the Japanese government, which was $9 trillion, the second largest issuer of government debt.

Investors can be domiciled in the country where the central government has issued the bond, or they can be foreign investors. In each of these groups, we distinguish between financial entities—banks, contractual savings entities, and collective investment funds—and nonfinancial entities—nonfinancial firms and individual retail investors. Financial entities are key players in the sovereign debt market. Commercial banks invest in government securities for a variety of reasons. They use these securities to meet liquid asset requirements, manage their interest rate risk, and provide collateral for certain transactions (repurchase agreements described later in this chapter). The contractual savings entities include pension funds and life insurance companies. Their mission is to fund a liability structure. Because their liabilities are long term, they are important buyers of longer-term maturity government securities. Collective investment funds—including bond mutual funds and money market funds—are active participants across the entire yield curve.

In this chapter, we describe sovereign debt instruments and the markets in which they trade. We explain who participates in this market and how the securities are distributed to investors in the primary market and the role of primary dealers in the process. Once securities are issued, they trade in the secondary market. We highlight the role of an efficient and liquid secondary market in financing governments. Important markets related to efficient functioning of the sovereign debt market are also covered. Another important aspect of a well-functioning sovereign debt market is interest rate derivative contracts on sovereign bonds. We postpone discussion of these instruments until chapter 37.

Types of Securities Issued

Central governments typically issue marketable and nonmarketable securities. Our focus here is on marketable securities. Most sovereign borrowers issue bonds with a fairly wide range of maturities. By doing so, they move toward a benchmark yield which can aid in the pricing of other debt instruments. Governments routinely issue two types of securities—discount and coupon. A **discount security** pays a single cash flow at the end of its life. The difference between the maturity value and the purchase price is the interest that the investor receives. An example of this type of security is a three-month discount instrument sold by several governments, including the United States and Switzerland. Most sovereign debt issued with an original maturity of one year or less is issued as discount securities. Table 20.2 lists the various maturities routinely issued as short-term securities for selected countries.

In contrast to discount securities, **coupon securities** are issued with a stated rate of interest, make interest payments periodically, and have a terminal payment equal to their principal value. In some countries, such as the United States, the interest payments are made semiannually. In others, such as in many European countries, interest payments are made annually. Sovereign debt with an original maturity of greater than one year is generally issued as coupon securities. For example, securities issued by the government of Singapore with maturities of two years or longer are coupon securities where the interest payments are paid semiannually, and on the maturity date, a principal payment is made. Table 20.3 lists the coupon securities offered by selected countries. As can be seen from table 20.1, the largest sector of the government bond market is that of fixed-rate bonds.

In addition to discount instruments and fixed-rate coupon securities, sovereigns issue two types whose payments are not fixed: inflation-adjusted securities and floating-rate

Table 20.2
Maturities of short-term debt for selected countries.

Country	One-Month	Three-Month	Six-Month	Nine-Month	One-Year	Floating	Inflation
United States	x	x	x		x	Yes	Yes
Canada		x	x		x	No	Yes
Brazil	x	x	x	x	x	Yes	Yes
Mexico	x	x	x	x	x	No	Yes
United Kingdom	x	x	x		x	No	Yes
France	x	x	x	x	x	No	No
Germany	x	x	x	x	x	Yes	Yes
Italy	x	x	x	x	x	No	No
Spain	x	x	x	x	x	Yes	Yes
Portugal		x	x	x	x	No	No
Sweden	x	x	x			No	Yes
Netherlands		x	x	x	x	No	No
Switzerland		x	x		x	No	No
Greece	x	x	x		x	No	Yes
Japan			x		x	No	Yes
Australia	x	x	x		x	No	Yes
New Zealand		x	x		x	No	No
South Korea			x		x	No	Yes

Sources: International Monetary Fund, Bank for International Settlements, and central bank websites.

securities. **Inflation-adjusted securities** adjust the payments (either coupon or principal) to investors for some measure of the country's rate of inflation. **Floating-rate securities** are securities whose interest payments change periodically according to a predetermined coupon formula. The coupon formula includes a reference rate (benchmark interest rate) adjusted with a spread. Developed countries that issue sovereign floating-rate securities include Germany, Spain, Belgium, and the United States. The United States only began issuing floating-rate securities in January 2014. Developing countries that issue floating-rate debt include Brazil, Turkey, Poland, and Indonesia. Two of the largest issuers of sovereign debt, Japan and the United Kingdom, have never issued floating-rate debt. For selected countries, table 20.2 shows whether the government issues floating-rate debt or inflation-indexed bonds. Floating-rate securities and inflation-adjusted securities are described next.

Floating-Rate Securities

Governments around the world issue floating-rate securities. This type of security, also referred to as a "floater," has a coupon rate that resets periodically according to a predetermined formula, known to as the **coupon formula**. The coupon formula for a basic floater consists of two parts: a reference rate and a quoted margin.

Table 20.3
Maturities for coupon debt securities 2–30 years and availability of stripping, selected countries.

Country	2	3	4	5	6	7	8	9	10	15	20	30	Strip
United States	x	x		x		x			x			x	Yes
Canada	x			x					x		x	x	Yes
Brazil	x	x	x	x		x			x		x	x	No
Mexico		x		x		x			x		x	x	Yes
United Kingdom	x	x	x	x	x	x	x	x	x	x	x	x	Yes
France	x	x	x	x	x	x	x	x	x	x	x	x	Yes
Germany	x	x	x	x	x	x	x	x	x	x	x	x	Yes
Italy	x	x	x	x	x	x	x	x	x	x	x	x	Yes
Spain	x	x	x	x	x	x	x	x	x	x	x	x	Yes
Portugal	x	x	x	x	x	x	x	x	x	x	x		No
Sweden	x			x					x			x	No
Netherlands	x	x	x	x	x	x	x	x	x		x	x	No
Switzerland	x	x	x	x	x	x	x	x	x		x	x	No
Greece	x			x					x	x	x	x	Yes
Japan	x	x	x	x	x	x	x	x	x	x	x	x	Yes
Australia	x	x	x	x	x	x	x	x	x	x			No
New Zealand	x			x		x			x				No
South Korea	x	x	x	x					x		x		Yes

Sources: IMF, BIS, and central bank websites.

Note: "Strip" indicates whether the government permits coupon stripping.

A reference rate is some benchmark interest rate, such as 3-month LIBOR. The quoted margin, commonly referred to as the "spread," can be added to the reference rate or subtracted from the reference rate. The quoted margin is a function of the level of rates as well as the floater's risk exposure. For example, a floater's coupon formula could be 3-month LIBOR plus 50 basis points. The reference rate is 3-month LIBOR, and the spread is 50 basis points. So for each period, the coupon rate is reset according to the current level of 3-month LIBOR. In January 2014, the U.S. Treasury issued floating-rate notes for the first time. Interest rates rise and fall on these securities, based on the rate on of 13-week U.S. Treasury bills. The Republic of Argentina issued a floater in 2014 that matures on January 25, 2024, with a coupon formula of BADLAR plus 200 basis points. (BADLAR is the average interest paid by Argentine public or private banks for deposits in excess of $1 million.) Another example is the floater issued by the Polish government in 2014 that matured March 28, 2017, with a coupon formula of 6-month WIBO flat. Flat means that the spread is zero. WIBO is the ACI Polska Poland Warsaw Interbank bid rate.

Inflation-Adjusted Securities

Sovereign governments, as well corporations, offer securities whose interest rate is tied to the rate of inflation. These debt instruments, referred to as **inflation-linked bonds**, or simply "linkers," have been issued by sovereign governments since 1945. The earlier issuers of linkers were the governments of Argentina, Brazil, and Israel. The modern linker is attributed to the U.K. government's index-linked gilt issued in 1981, followed by Australia, Canada, and Sweden.

The United States introduced an inflation-linked security in January 1997, calling those securities **Treasury Inflation Protected Securities** (TIPS). These securities carry the full faith and credit of the U.S. government. Shortly after the introduction of TIPS in 1997, U.S. government-related entities began issuing linkers.

Different designs can be used for linkers. The reference rate that is a proxy for the inflation rate is changed according to some CPI. In the United Kingdom, for example, the index used is the Retail Prices Index (All Items), or RPI. In France, there are two linkers with two different indexes: the French CPI (excluding tobacco) and the Eurozone's Harmonised Index of Consumer Prices (HICP) (excluding tobacco). In the United States, the index used is CPI—Urban, Nonseasonally Adjusted (denoted by CPI-U), as calculated by the U.S. Bureau of Labor Statistics.[2]

Given the reference rate, the design of a linker can be such that over time, the principal or the coupon income is adjusted for inflation between the date of issuance and the payment date of a cash flow. The most commonly used design for a linker today calls for adjusting both the principal and the coupon interest. Before maturity, prices for trades in the secondary market are adjusted similarly. The inflation adjustment is usually done with a lag. This structure is used in the United States for its linker (TIPS), with a three-month lag in the CPI-U.

To highlight the differences between inflation-indexed bonds and traditional bonds, consider two eight-year annual pay bonds—one traditional bond and one inflation-indexed bond. The inflation-indexed bond has a real coupon rate of 2% annually. Inflation is assumed to be a constant 1% per year for the next eight years. The traditional bond has a coupon rate of 3% annually. Both bonds have a principal value of $100. Payments of the two bonds are presented side-by-side in table 20.4. Note that for the traditional bond, the nominal values for principal and coupon payments remain constant, but their real values decline with inflation. To be sure, nominal values are deflated by 1% per year with inflation. For the inflation-indexed bond, just the opposite occurs. The real values remain constant, but the nominal values for the principal and coupon payments increase with inflation. Notice the coupon rate in the inflation-indexed bond remains constant, but the coupon payments increase and coincide with the increase in the inflation-adjusted principal. Nominal values are inflated by 1% per year so as to keep real values constant.

2. The CPI-U is the most widely followed and perhaps the best understood inflation index among alternative choices, such as the GDP deflator and the personal consumption expenditure deflator. Changes in the CPI-U represent the average change in prices facing urban consumers for a fixed basket of goods and services. This group of urban consumers represents about 87% of the total U.S. population. The Treasury reserves the right to substitute an alternative price index under the following circumstances: (1) the CPI-U is discontinued; (2) the CPI-U is altered materially to the detriment of the investor or the security; (3) the CPI-U is altered by legislation or executive order in a manner harmful to the investor or the security.

Table 20.4
Comparison between a traditional bond and an inflation-adjusted bond.

	Traditional Bond				Inflation-Adjusted Bond			
Year	Nominal Principal Value	Real Principal Value	Nominal Coupon Payment	Real Coupon Payment	Nominal Principal Value	Real Principal Value	Nominal Coupon Payment	Real Coupon Payment
1	100	99.010	3	2.970	101.000	100	2.020	2
2	100	98.030	3	2.941	102.010	100	2.040	2
3	100	97.059	3	2.912	103.030	100	2.061	2
4	100	96.098	3	2.883	104.060	100	2.081	2
5	100	95.147	3	2.854	105.101	100	2.102	2
6	100	94.205	3	2.826	106.152	100	2.123	2
7	100	93.272	3	2.798	107.214	100	2.144	2
8	100	92.348	3	2.770	108.286	100	2.166	2

The relationship between nominal interest rates, real interest rates, and expectations of future inflation is thought to be governed by the Fisher hypothesis. As explained in chapter 15, the Fisher hypothesis states that nominal yield is approximately equal to the real yield plus the market's expectation of future inflation. This relationship is an approximation, because it does not include a term for the potential interaction between inflation and the real economy. An implication of this relationship is that the differential maturity-matched yields on nominal Treasury securities and TIPS are often viewed as a proxy for the market's inflationary expectations.

Exhange Rate-Linked Securities

As can be seen from table 20.1, a small part of the central government securities markets is exchange rate-linked government debt, also referred to as principal exchange rate-linked government debt. The structure of this debt instrument is that the principal depends on the exchange rate between the U.S. dollar and some other currency, typically the exchange rate of the issuing country. The two major issuers of this type of bond are Argentina and Germany.

Primary Markets for Sovereign Debt

In chapter 17, we discussed primary markets. In the case of bond issuance, the primary market is the market where securities are issued for the first time. According to the World Bank, the structure of the primary market for government bonds should accomplish the following five objectives: (1) ensure cost effectiveness; (2) encourage participation from a wide range of investors, including foreign institutions; (3) maximize competition; (4)

minimize placement risk; and (5) foster transparency.[3] The infrastructure of the distribution channel must be well designed to meet these objectives.

The two key issues in structuring a primary market are the type of distribution method and whether primary dealers necessary.

Distribution Methods

Various distribution methods are used in the primary sovereign debt markets. The three primary distribution methods are (1) auctions; (2) syndications/underwriting; and (3) tap sales. For countries with well-developed markets, the primary distribution method is an auction. Indeed, auctions have proven to be more transparent and cost effective than other selling methods. In developing markets, other methods, such as syndication, underwriting, and tap sales, are used.

Auctions Many sovereigns use either a **single-price auction** (also called a **uniform-price auction**) or a **multiple-price auction** (also called a "discriminatory auction") for all marketable securities issued. In a multiple-price auction, competitive bidders (e.g., primary dealers) state the amount of the securities desired and the yields they are willing to accept.[4] The yields are then ranked from lowest to highest. This ranking is equivalent to arranging the bids from the highest price to the lowest price. Starting from the lowest yield bid, all competitive bids are accepted until the amount to be distributed to the competitive bidders is completely allocated. The highest yield accepted by the sovereign is called the "stop yield," and bidders at that yield are awarded a percentage of their total tender offer. The single-price auction proceeds in the same fashion, except that all accepted bids are filled at the highest yield of accepted competitive tenders (i.e., the stop yield).

To highlight the differences between these two types of auctions, let us work a simple example. Assume a government has €500 million of 10-year bonds to auction off. Bidders submit bids that include a yield and a quantity. The information on the four bids is presented in the table 20.5. Starting at the lowest yield, bids are accepted until the amount to be distributed is exhausted. In our illustration, bids 1, 2, and 3 shown in table 20.5 would be accepted. Bid 4 is shut out of the market and does not receive any securities. The stop yield is 2.52%, and it is the highest accepted yield (the lowest accepted price). In a multiple-price auction, all accepted bidders would pay the price they bid for the quantity they bid. In contrast, in a single-price auction, all accepted bids will pay the same price at the stop yield, and that price is the lowest accepted bid. In our illustration, the stop yield is 2.62%, so this the price all accepted bidders will pay.

3. World Bank, *Developing a Government Bond Market*.

4. Until the move to single-price auctions in the United States, Treasury securities had been sold using multiple-price auctions since 1929.

Table 20.5
Price auction illustration.

Bid	Yield (%)	Quantity (millions euro)
1	2.60	300
2	2.61	100
3	2.62	100
4	2.64	200

In the United States, the Treasury moved to single-price auctions for all Treasury securities in 1998 after conducting single-price auctions for monthly sales of two- and five-year notes since September 1992. Paul Malvey and Christine Archibald conducted a study of the relative performance of the two auction mechanisms.[5] Their empirical results suggest that single-price auctions broaden participation and accordingly reduce the concentration of securities at issuance. (By "concentration," we mean too many securities owned by too few investors.) Moreover, they also present somewhat weaker evidence that the single-price auctions reduce the Treasury's financing costs. In principle, single-price auctions reduce financing costs by encouraging more aggressive bidding relative to multiple-price auctions. Multiple-price auctions suffer from the so-called winner's curse problem.[6] Conversely, in a single-price auction, all successful bidders pay the same price and have less incentive to bid conservatively. Multiple-price auctions for a given quantity tend to shift the demand curve down and to the left.

The frequency of auctions is a function of the debt management practices of the government and the desire to promote a liquid secondary market. Short-term securities, such as bills, are usually auctioned weekly. In most countries, the day of the week for the auction is fixed. Longer-term coupon securities, such as notes and bonds, are typically auctioned less frequently, usually monthly or quarterly. A well-defined schedule announced in advance is believed to lead to a lower effective borrowing cost.

Syndication In less-well-developed markets with few bidders, auctions may not be the best distribution channel. Instead, governments appoint a group of financial institutions that, for a negotiable fee, will subscribe to the entire bond issue and sell it to other investors. This process is usually referred to as **syndication**. The key advantage of syndication is that it reduces placement risk when demand for the securities is very uncertain. Syndica-

5. Paul F. Malvey and Christine M. Archibald, "Uniform-Price Auctions: Update of the Treasury Experience" (Washington, DC: U.S. Treasury, October 1998).

6. A winner's curse is a phenomenon in auctions with incomplete information where the winner of the auction tends to overpay.

tion also adds value if the government is trying to introduce a new debt instrument. The main disadvantage of syndication is the lack of transparency compared to an auction. Price and fees must be negotiated with the financial institutions that will subscribe to the issue. Auctions are more transparent, because such negotiation is not required.

An alternative method for selling government securities is called **underwriting**. The government establishes a minimum price for a debt issue to be sold. For a commission, the underwriter subscribes to the entire issue at the minimum price. The underwriter can then retain the portion of the issue it desires and sells the rest to other investors.

Tap sales A **tap sale** is a method of distributing securities that allows issuers to sell additional bonds from past issues. The bonds are sold at their current market price but retain their original face value, coupon rate, and maturity. The British and French governments have issued additional securities using this method. Advantages to the issuer include avoiding some of the fixed costs of auctioning off new securities. This method is used for issuing a small principal amount of a security when the cost of a new issue is prohibitive.

Primary Dealers

A key component of the primary market for any government's securities is the participation of a group of primary dealers. A **primary dealer** is a designated intermediary who, in exchange for special status, is obligated to be a meaningful participant in the primary market and an active market maker in the secondary market. A primary dealer is usually designated by the central bank. By "active market maker," we mean a dealer willing and able to quote two-way prices (bids and offers) for some or all securities. The risk of endowing a small group of financial institutions special status is that it might encourage collusion. This prospect is more likely when fewer primary dealers are involved and the markets are less well developed. To preclude this possibility, how primary dealers are selected, organized, and monitored becomes an important policy decision.

In the United States, primary dealers are specially designated banks and investment banks that are selected and regulated by the Federal Reserve. They are invariably large and well capitalized. Being a primary dealer has benefits as well as obligations. Primary dealers have the exclusive right to trade with the Federal Reserve when it is conducting open market operations. Primary dealers are expected to be active participants in the Treasury primary and secondary markets and to quote two-sided markets. The Federal Reserve actively monitors the participation of primary dealers, and if their performance is found to be wanting, the firm risks removal from the primary dealer list.

As another example, Italy established a primary dealer system of 16 dealers or specialists in 1994 under the supervision of the Ministry of Finance. The specialists consist of both investment and commercial banks, including foreign institutions. They are obligated to bid at government securities auctions and quote two-way prices in the secondary market. In exchange, the specialists garner exclusive access to tap sales and buybacks.[7] Specialist status is reviewed every two years.

Secondary Markets

As explained in chapter 18, secondary markets are where previously issued securities are traded among investors. Securities can be traded directly from investor to investor, or through a broker or primary dealer to facilitate the transaction. The major participants in secondary government bond markets globally are large institutional investors and central banks. The presence of retail investors in secondary government securities market is small.

The secondary market for government securities must provide for the immediate purchase and sale of securities. According to the World Bank, transactions in the secondary market should possess the following characteristics: (1) low transaction costs, (2) continuous and widely disseminated price information, (3) immediate execution of trades, (4) a safe and rapid settlement system, and (5) efficient custodial and safekeeping services.

A hallmark of a liquid, well-developed market is how it handles spot transactions. A spot transaction is the immediate purchase and sale of a security. An important gauge of a market's efficiency is the amount of time between trade execution and settlement. The shorter the gap is, the more cash-like securities become. **Settlement** is the process that occurs after the trade is made. The bonds are delivered to the buyer for payment received from the seller. Secondary market settlement for government bonds typically takes place on a T + 1 basis—that is, the day after the transaction date. Cash settlement, in which trading and settlement occur the same day, is standard for most governments in developed secondary markets. Trades clear in either (or both) of the two main clearing systems, Euroclear and Clearstream. Settlement occurs by means of a simultaneous exchange of bonds for cash on the books of the clearing system. An electronic bridge connecting Euroclear and Clearstream allows transfer of bonds from one system to the other.

In Japan, the Bank of Japan oversees the payment and settlement systems and provides settlement accounts on those systems. For securities settlement, the Bank of Japan is responsible for settling all Japanese government bond transactions. Japanese government bond transactions are settled on a real time delivery-versus-payment basis through BOJ-NET JBG Services, an online system for transferring Japanese government bonds between financial institutions.

Secondary markets are mainly structured in one of two ways: as an organized exchange or as an OTC market. An organized exchange provides a place where buyers and sellers

7. Sovereigns occasionally buy back unmatured marketable securities to manage their public debt outstanding. Buybacks are done on an irregular basis.

can meet to arrange their trades. Although buy or sell orders may come from anywhere, the transaction must take place at the exchange according to the rules imposed by the exchange. In contrast, with OTC markets, buy and sell orders initiated from various locations are matched through a communications network. Thus, OTC markets need electronic trading platforms, through which users submit buy and sell orders. Bloomberg Fixed Income Electronic Trading platform is an example of such a platform, through which dealers stand ready to trade in multiple bond markets globally. Although there is some trading of government bonds and very active corporate bonds on many stock exchanges around the world, nearly all bonds are traded in OTC markets.

The secondary market for U.S. Treasuries is an OTC market where a group of U.S. government securities dealers offers continuous bid and ask prices on outstanding Treasuries for a virtual 24-hour trading of Treasury securities. The three primary trading locations are New York, London, and Tokyo. The normal settlement period for Treasury securities is the business day after the transaction day ("next day" settlement).

The most recently auctioned issue of a particular maturity Treasury is referred to as the **on-the-run issue** or the **current issue.** For example, the most recently issued 10-year Treasury notes is called the on-the-run 10-year or the current 10-year. Securities that are replaced by the on-the-run issue are called **off-the-run issues**. Sometimes traders use the terms "one-off-the-run" and "two-off-the-run" to indicate how recently a Treasury was issued. Issues replaced by several on-the-run issues are said to be "well-off-the-run issues."

Despite the huge volume of trading in the secondary market for government securities, the reporting of trades (i.e., the transparency of the market) is not at the level of that of U.S. common stocks. However, the reporting of government securities transactions has made some major strides since 1991. These developments came from the private sector. The prominent example is GovPX. This firm, created in 1990 by primary dealers and interdealer brokers (described below) in the government securities market, provides 24-hour, worldwide distribution of government securities information as transacted by market participants through interdealer brokers. The information reported by GovPX consists of the price and size of the best bid and offer, and current repo rates and volume (intraday updates) for repo transactions. The information reported by this firm is primarily distributed as an optional service through the major market data vendors (Bloomberg, Reuters, and Telerate) and to client sites.

Treasury dealers trade with the investing public and with other dealer firms. When they trade with each other, it is through intermediaries known as **interdealer brokers.** Dealers use interdealer brokers because of the speed and efficiency with which trades can be accomplished. Interdealer brokers do not trade for their own account, keeping the names of the dealers involved in the trades confidential. Interdealer brokers match buyers and sellers of Treasury securities (anonymously) and receive a brokerage fee if a match can be obtained. The quotations provided on the government dealer screens represent prices in the "inside" or "interdealer" market.

Stripping and Reconstitution

Longer-term zero-coupon securities are not typically issued by sovereign governments. Instead, they are created by market participants using a process called "stripping and reconstitution." Market participants have the ability to separate the bond's individual coupon payments and trade them as separate zero-coupon securities. This process is called **stripping**. Moreover, dealers can recombine the appropriate individual zero-coupon securities and reproduce the underlying coupon sovereign debt instrument. To do so, the entity that seeks to reconstitute a security must obtain the appropriate principal strip and all unmatured interest components for the security being reconstituted. This process is called **reconstitution**.

To illustrate this process, consider a 2% coupon U.K. gilt issued by the British government that matures on September 7, 2025. There are two series of gilts that are strippable. The first series, those coupon-paying instruments whose coupon dates are June 7 and December 7, became strippable in December 1997. The second series, those paying coupons on March 7 and September 7, became strippable in April 2002. Only gilt-edged market makers, the British Treasury, and The Bank of England may strip and reconstitute gilts. All stripping and reconstituting of gilts is done through the Gilt Strips Facility.

Table 20.6 is a representation of the 21 remaining payments—20 coupon payments of £10,000 and a maturity value payment of £1,000,000. Each one of these payments can trade separately from the whole as a zero-coupon bond that matures on the day it is due. A distinction is made between zero-coupon securities derived from coupon payments and those derived from principal payments. Zero-coupon securities created from coupon payments are called "coupon strips.' Zero-coupon securities created from principal payments are called "principal strips."

In many countries, a disadvantage of a taxable entity investing in government strips is that accrued interest is taxed each year, even though interest is not paid. Thus, these instruments are negative cash flow instruments until the maturity date. They are negative cash flows, because tax payments on interest earned but not received must be made. One reason for distinguishing between strips created from the principal and those created from the coupon is that some non-U.S. buyers have a preference for strips created from the principal (i.e., principal strips) because of the tax treatment of the interest in their home country. Some country's tax laws treat the interest as a capital gain if the principal strip is purchased. The capital gain receives a preferential tax treatment (i.e., lower rate) compared to ordinary income.

Repurchase Agreements

A **repurchase agreement** (or simply "repo") is the sale of a security with a simultaneous agreement by the seller to buy the same security back at a future date from the purchaser at an agreed-on price.[8] In practical terms, a repurchase agreement can be viewed as a collater-

8. Repurchase agreements can be structured such that the transaction is terminable on demand.

Table 20.6
Total payments of a 2% gilt to be stripped.

3/7/2016 £10,000	9/7/2016 £10,000	3/7/2017 £10,000	9/7/2017 £10,000	3/7/2018 £10,000
9/7/2018 £10,000	3/7/2019 £10,000	9/7/2019 £10,000	3/7/2020 £10,000	9/7/2020 £10,000
3/7/2021 £10,000	9/7/2021 £10,000	3/7/2022 £10,000	9/7/2022 £10,000	3/7/2023 £10,000
9/7/2023 £10,000	3/7/2024 £10,000	9/7/2024 £10,000	3/7/2025 £10,000	9/7/2025 £10,000
9/7/2025 £1 million				

Note: The table entries list the date of payment followed by the amount of the payment.

alized loan where the security sold and subsequently repurchased represents the collateral posted. One party is borrowing money and providing collateral for the loan at an interest rate. The interest rate, referred to as the **repo rate**, is typically lower than the rate on an otherwise similar bank loan. The other party is lending money while accepting a security as collateral for the loan. Therefore, the seller in a repo is effectively a secured lender.

Repos are a common source of funding for dealer firms in many countries around the world. An active market in repos underpins every liquid bond market. Financial and non-financial institutions participate actively in the market as both sellers and buyers of collateral, depending on their circumstances. Central banks are also active users of repurchase agreements in their daily money market operations, to either lend to the market to increase the supply of funds or withdraw surplus funds from the market.

Structure of repo and reverse repurchase agreements Consider a dealer that has a forecast on the direction of interest rates in a country and this forecast is expected to materialize over the next 24 hours. The dealer decides to take a long position in that country's 10-year government security.

How will the dealer finance the position in the government security? Suppose the dealer wants to fund the position overnight and through the next business day. The dealer has two basic choices—use its own funds or borrow the funds. Dealers usually opt to employ leverage to fund the position. The dealer could borrow the money from a bank. However, in these circumstances, the dealer chooses to enter into a repo to fund the position. As noted above, a repo is a collateralized loan where one party is providing collateral and borrowing money and the counterparty is accepting collateral and lending money. A repurchase agreement may be constructed as follows: The dealer sells the 30-year government security to a counterparty for cash today. At the same time, the dealer makes a promise to buy the same 30-year government security on the next business day for an agreed-on price. The price at which the dealer repurchases the gilt is known as the repurchase price. The date when the 30-year government security is repurchased, the next business day in this example, is called the **repurchase date**. When the term of a repurchase agreement is one day, it is called an "overnight repo," which can be rolled over. When the agreement is for more than one day, it is called a **term repo**.

Just as there is no single interest rate, there is no one repo rate. The rate varies from agreement to agreement owing to various factors: quality of the collateral, term of the repo, delivery requirement, availability of the collateral, and the prevailing rates on alternative fund sources. In the United States, the alternative funding sources would be the federal funds rate for some institutions. The repo rate is inversely related to the quality of the collateral. Rates differ by maturity and the current shape of the benchmark yield curve. If delivery of the collateral is required, the repo rate will be lower. The more difficult it is to obtain the collateral, the lower the repo rate will be. The more difficult it is to obtain the collateral, the lower the repo rate will be. To understand why this is so, remember that the borrower (or equivalently, the seller of the collateral) has a security that lenders of cash want, for whatever reason. Such collateral is referred to as **hot collateral** or **special collateral**. Collateral that does not have this characteristic is referred to as **general collateral**. The party that needs the hot collateral will be willing to lend funds at a lower repo rate to obtain the collateral.

In the example above, a dealer is using a repurchase agreement to fund a long position in a 30-year government security. Simply put, the dealer is borrowing money. A repurchase agreement can also be used to borrow securities to establish a short position. In this case, the dealer is lending money and accepting securities the dealer wants as collateral. The counterparty is borrowing money and providing securities as collateral. This transaction is called a **reverse repurchase agreement** or simply a "reverse." In market parlance, what distinguishes a repo from a reverse repo is always viewed from the perspective of the dealer. If the dealer is borrowing money, it is a repo. If the dealer is borrowing securities, it is a reverse. Both types of transaction are otherwise structured the same.

Sovereign Credit Risk

Sovereign debt exposes investors to **credit risk** as varied as that observed in other debt markets discussed in this book. Sovereign ratings are credit ratings for countries as assigned by the credit rating agencies that we described in chapter 5. Specifically, sovereign ratings are assessments of the relative likelihood that a borrower (i.e., a central government) will default on its obligations. Governments seek these credit ratings to increase their access to international capital markets. Sovereign ratings matter to investors, because other things being equal, investors prefer rated issues to unrated ones. They matter to borrowers as well, because the rating agencies are reluctant to assign a credit rating to a lower level of government or corporation that is higher than that of the issuer's home country.

Two sovereign debt ratings are assigned by credit rating agencies: a **local currency debt rating** and a **foreign currency debt rating.** The two general categories of risk analyzed when assigning ratings are **economic risk** and **political risk**. The former category is an assessment of the ability of a government to satisfy its obligations. Both quantitative and qualitative analyses are used when assessing economic risk. Political risk is an assessment of the willingness of a government to satisfy its obligations. A government may have the ability but may be unwilling to pay. Political risk is assessed based on qualitative analysis of the political factors that influence a government's economic policies.

The reason for distinguishing between local debt ratings and foreign currency debt ratings is that historically, the default frequency differs by the currency denomination of the debt. Specifically, defaults have been greater on foreign currency–denominated debt. The reason for the difference in default rates for local currency debt and foreign currency debt is that if a government is willing to raise taxes and control its domestic financial system, it can generate sufficient local currency to meet its local currency debt obligation. This is not the case with foreign currency–denominated debt. A national government must purchase foreign currency to meet a debt obligation in that foreign currency and therefore has less control with respect to its exchange rate. Thus, a significant depreciation of the local currency relative to a foreign currency in which a debt obligation is denominated will impair a national government's ability to satisfy such obligations. This distinction is not observed with the 17 countries of the European Union's Eurozone, where there is only a single credit rating for a sovereign's issues, irrespective of what currency the country is issuing.

Those borrowers perceived to have the lowest default risk receive the coveted AAA/Aaa rating from the three credit rating agencies. As of year-end 2015, only nine sovereign issuers are rated at this (theoretically) risk-free level (Australia, Canada, Denmark, Germany, Luxembourg, Norway, Singapore, Sweden, and Switzerland). The 2007–2009 global financial crisis resulted in many sovereign issuers taking on potentially unsustainable debt loads when they took over the liabilities of their country's failed banks. Subsequently, many sovereigns suffered downgrades from the AAA/Aaa level, including Ireland in 2009 and Spain in 2010. In August 2011, one rating agency, S&P, lowered the AAA credit rating of the United States for the first time since assigning sovereign credit ratings in 1917.

A country whose domestic currency is a liquid currency, and which boasts a sizeable domestic institutional savings base, has the capacity to fund its debt in local currency.[9] However, where there is a demand for it, either from foreign investors or for issues in another currency, a sovereign may also issue in a foreign currency. When this occurs, it will usually swap the proceeds into its local currency. A demand for a particular sovereign name from different investors may cause the issuer to raise debt in a foreign currency; this is common for highly rated borrowers, such as Switzerland, Finland, and Sweden, which issue U.S. dollar and euro debt.

The factors analyzed when assessing the creditworthiness of a national government's local currency debt and foreign currency debt will differ to some extent. When assessing the credit quality of local currency debt, for example, one rating agency, S&P, emphasizes domestic government policies that foster or impede timely debt service.

9. By "liquid currency," we mean a currency that can be bought or sold quickly and cheaply at close to its true value.

When assigning a rating for a country's foreign currency debt, credit analysis by S&P focuses on the interaction of domestic and foreign government policies. S&P analyzes a country's balance of payments and the structure of its external balance sheet. The areas of analysis with respect to its external balance sheet are the net public debt, total net external debt, and net external liabilities.

Moody's, another major rating agency, focuses on the following four factors as the foundation of its sovereign bond ratings methodology: (1) economic strength—wealth, size, diversification, and long-term potential; (2) institutional strength—governance, quality of institutions, and policy predictability; (3) government financial strength—ability to deploy resources to face current and expected liabilities; and (4) susceptibility to event risk—risk of sudden change in risk migration.[10]

Key Points

- Sovereign debt refers to the debt issued by the highest level of government in a particular country.
- There are two types of government securities issued—discount and coupon.
- A discount security pays a single cash flow at the end of its life; the difference between the maturity value and the purchase price is the interest that the investor receives.
- Coupon securities are issued with a stated rate of interest, make interest payments periodically, and have terminal payments equal to their principal value.
- Floating-rate securities are securities whose interest payments change periodically according to a predetermined coupon formula.
- The coupon formula for a basic floater consists of two parts: a reference rate and a quoted margin.
- Inflation-adjusted securities adjust the payments (either coupon or principal) to investors for some measure of the country's rate of inflation.
- The U.S. inflation-linked securities are referred to as Treasury Inflation Protected Securities (TIPS).
- Different designs can be used for inflation-adjusted securities.
- Given the reference rate, the design of an inflation-adjusted security can be such that over time, the principal and/or the coupon income are adjusted for inflation between the date of issuance and the payment date of a cash flow.
- A small part of the central government securities markets is exchange rate–linked government debt. The structure of this debt instrument is that the principal depends on the

10. Moody's, "Sovereign Bond Ratings" (New York: Moody's Investors Service, September 2008).

exchange rate between the U.S. dollar and some other currency, typically that of the issuing country.

- The structure of the primary market for government bonds should accomplish five objectives: (1) ensure cost-effectiveness; (2) encourage participation from a wide range of investors, including foreign institutions; (3) maximize competition; (4) minimize placement risk; and (5) foster transparency.
- The three distribution methods used in the primary sovereign debt markets are (1) auctions; (2) syndications/underwriting; and (3) tap sales.
- For countries with well-developed markets, the primary distribution method is an auction.
- Many sovereigns use either a single-price auction or a multiple-price auction to distribute marketable securities at issue.
- A primary dealer is a designated intermediary who is obligated to be an active participant in both the primary and secondary markets.
- Secondary markets are where previously issued securities are traded among investors.
- The process of breaking apart coupon securities to create zero-coupon securities is called "stripping."
- The process of reassembling coupon securities from a portfolio of strips is called "reconstitution."
- Repurchase agreements (repos) are a primary source of financing for government securities dealers.
- Sovereign ratings are assessments by credit rating agencies of the relative likelihood that a borrower (i.e., a central government) will default on its obligations.
- Two sovereign debt ratings are assigned by credit rating agencies: a local currency debt rating and a foreign currency debt rating.
- The two general categories of risk analyzed by credit rating agencies when assigning ratings are economic risk and political risk.

Questions

1. What are the perceived benefits to a country from developing a viable government securities market?
2. What types of securities do sovereign governments routinely issue?
3. Suppose an investor buys at issuance a 10-year security issued by the Italian government. The par value of the position is €1 million, and the coupon rate is 1.5% paid semiannually. If it is held to maturity, what cash flows can the investor expect to receive?
4. Explain how inflation-indexed securities work.

5. Explain how floating-rate securities work.

6. a. How is the primary market for sovereign debt structured?

b. Ideally, what objectives is this structure trying to accomplish?

7. a. What are the primary distribution methods for government securities?

b. How would the choice of a distribution method be affected by the stage of market development?

8. a. What is/are the salient difference(s) between a single-price and a multiple-price auction?

b. Make a case for and against each method.

9. a. Aside from auctions, what are the alternative methods for distributing government securities?

b. What are the benefits and costs of each method?

10. The excerpt below is from the November 6, 2013, letter to the U.S. Secretary of the Treasury from the Treasury Borrowing Advisory Committee. Explain what this excerpt means.

> As the electronic trading volume of on-the-run Treasury securities increases, it could enhance their liquidity and reduce future Treasury borrowing costs, especially if volumes of electronically traded off-the-run securities increase over time as well.

11. What economic mechanism forces the actual market price of a Treasury security toward its theoretical value based on theoretical spot rates?

12. a. What functions does a primary dealer perform in the primary market?

b. What functions does a primary dealer perform in the secondary market?

13. What are the characteristics of a well-developed secondary government bond market?

14. How do stripping and reconstitution work?

15. What is a repurchase agreement?

16. How does the existence of a viable repo market contribute to the functioning of a sovereign debt market?

17. China is the largest foreign investor in U.S. Treasury securities. Does having a single country that holds a significant portion of another country's debt have any consequences for the functioning of the primary or secondary markets of the debtor country?

18. Congratulations! You have just been appointed minister of finance of Country X. Currently X currently does not have a primary dealer system in place. Your first official task is to make recommendations on whether Country X should adopt a primary dealer system for its sovereign debt market. Make a case for and against.

19. State whether you agree or disagree with the following statements:

a. Sovereign debt issues have the lowest credit risk in a country.

b. Credit rating agencies make a distinction between debt issued in a sovereign's local currency and that issued in a foreign currency.

c. Political risk is an assessment of the willingness of a government to satisfy its obligations.

20. Suppose that £100 million par values of 5-year U.K. gilts with a 4% coupon rate are purchased to create zero-coupon strips. Further suppose that the coupon payment dates are June 30 and December 31. What are the coupon strips and principal strips that can be created from these securities?

21. Mario Draghi, president of the European Central Bank, said in a speech on November 5, 2015, "History teaches us that deflation, although relatively less common, can have consequences just as destabilizing as excessive inflation." What impact does deflation have on the coupon payments and principal of inflation-adjusted securities?

21 Subnational (Municipal) Government Debt Markets

CONTENTS

Learning Objectives

After reading this chapter, you will understand:

- what subnationals are;
- the need for subnationals to obtain financing for large-scale infrastructure projects in developing and developed countries;
- the two types of municipal debt structures: bank lending and bond issuance;
- what a municipal bank is;
- what a municipal bond bank is;
- the role of multilateral financial institutions in the development of a sustainable municipal debt market in developing countries;
- the use of public-private partnerships and project finance initiatives in infrastructure financing for subnationals;
- what green bonds are;
- the types of U.S. municipal bond structures;
- the difference between tax-exempt municipal bonds and taxable municipal bonds;
- the credit risk associated with U.S. municipal securities;
- the factors considered by credit rating agencies when rating U.S. municipal securities;
- what the municipal bankruptcy process is in the United States;
- the secondary market for municipal bonds; and
- the actions taken by the People's Republic of China to create a sustainable municipal bond market.

Subnational governments include states, regions, provinces, counties, and municipalities, as well as local utilities companies either owned or regulated by these entities. In the United States, the SEC has reported that there are about 44,000 state and local entities that issue securities. Dexia reports that the number of subnational governments in the European Union is 90,380, which included 89,149 municipalities, 981 entities referred to as "intermediary entities" (which includes departments and provinces), and 250 regions. For the 27 member countries in the European Union, 80% of the 89,149 municipalities are located in five countries: France (41%), Germany (13%), Spain (9%), Italy (9%), and Czech Republic (7%).

Subnational governments need to obtain proceeds to fulfill their delegated responsibilities. They traditionally derive their revenue from one or more of the following sources: (1) tax revenue (income taxes, property taxes, and sales taxes); (2) share of revenue from the central government; (3) fees and charges on local services provided; (4) asset sales; (5) investment income; and (6) grants from nongovernmental organizations.[1]

To obtain the necessary funding to operate a subnational government, the revenue sources of funding are combined with some debt arrangement (bank borrowing or the issuance of bonds). With the rapid industrialization and urbanization in developing countries has come the need for funding large-scale investments in infrastructure. For developed countries, the aging of its infrastructure will require a substantial commitment of capital. Although in both developed and developing economies, some financing will come from central governments and multilateral financial institutions, the rest must come from the subnationals themselves and any debt funding that they can obtain. Estimates for what the global need will be for infrastructure financing is provided by McKinsey, a consulting firm. McKinsey estimates that between 2012 and 2030, $57 trillion will be needed globally for infrastructure. For this reason, central governments in many countries are seeking ways to improve their municipal debt market.

In this chapter, we describe the issues concerning the development of subnational or municipal debt markets, including the two types of models for obtaining debt. These structures include the bank lending model and the bond issuance model. The first model mentioned has severe limitations, and therefore the major push in many countries is to develop the municipal bond market. Because the U.S. municipal bond market is an example of a well-developed bond issuance market, we describe this market in considerable detail in this chapter.

Central Government Control of Municipal Borrowing

A key issue that arises regarding the raising of funds in the financial markets by subnational governments is whether central governments should regulate subnational borrowing. The argument has been made that such regulation is unnecessary, because investors in financial markets will discipline subnational borrowing. Excessive borrowing as perceived by market participants would be discouraged as borrowing costs rise. Bank borrowing would become too expensive.

This view, however, is based on assumptions that if not true would require central government control over subnational borrowers. The assumptions include (1) lenders have sufficient information about the subnationals that they are providing funding for; (2) local governments respond in an appropriate manner to private market signals, thus avoiding being shut out of the credit market; and (3) lenders believe that there will be a central

1. Otaviano Canuto and Lili Liu, "Subnational Debt: Making It Sustainable," in *The Day after Tomorrow—A Handbook on the Future of Economic Policy in the Developing World,* ed. Otaviano Canuto and Marcelo Giugale (Washington, DC: World Bank, 2010), chapter 13.

government bailout should the subnational default. Given that it is not likely that these assumptions will hold in real world markets, it is argued that the development of a credit market for subnationals would benefit from some central government regulations and control.[2]

Structure of a Municipal Credit Market

Central governments have two models from which to develop their subnational debt markets. The first is via bank lending, and the second is the issuance of municipal bonds. Bank lending to subnationals is the primary source for funding subnationals today in Europe and Asia, but in North America, the primary source is municipal bonds. Of course, a hybrid of the two can be used.

Bank Lending Model

Some banks specialize in lending to subnationals. The largest one is Credit Local de France, which is now part of the Dexia Group. These banks have offered loans for investment projects of from 15 to 30 years. Municipal banks seek to establish a permanent partnership with subnationals. The typical services that they provide to supplement their lending include preparing and structuring budgets, planning and designing investment projects that a subnational is considering financing, managing the subnational's finances, and serving as an intermediary between the subnational and central government in matters related to tax-sharing arrangements and grant allocations.[3]

Municipal banks often are granted certain advantages in performing their role of providing loans for subnationals. The banks in some countries are given a legal monopoly for lending to subnationals. Municipal banks have access to some form of below-market interest rate funds not available to other types of banks. Municipal banks often benefit from laws that require that municipalities deposit accounts with them. The interest paid on those deposits is a below-market interest rate.

The environment has been changing for municipal banks due to financial sector deregulation. Legal monopolies are disappearing, forcing municipal banks to compete with other financial institutions to borrow funds. As a result of financial sector deregulation, municipal banks have lost access to below-market interest rates, again requiring that they complete with financial institutions (in particular, commercial banks). The type of relationship banking that existed when municipal banks dominated has disappeared, and subnationals now

2. For a detailed discussion of controlling local financing by central governments, see the contributed chapters in Bernard Dafflon, ed., *Local Public Finance in Europe: Balancing the Budget and Controlling Debt, Studies in Fiscal Federalism and State-Local Finance* (Cheltenham, UK: Edward Elgar, 2002).

3. George E. Peterson, "Banks or Bonds? Building a Municipal Credit Market" (Washington, DC: Urban Institute, undated). The discussion of municipal banks here draws from this publication. Available at http://www.oecd.org/greengrowth/21559374.pdf.

must compete with corporate and consumer borrowers for available funding. Commercial banks traditionally have been less likely sources for funding long-term infrastructure projects. For this reason, central governments have fostered the development of a municipal bond market.

Bond Issuance Model

Raising funds via the issuance of bonds is quite a different avenue for fund raising than is borrowing from municipal banks. Although investment bankers do seek to establish long-term relationships with a subnational, each time a subnational comes to market with a bond offering, competition among investment bankers dictates who would be the underwriter of that issue. This type of competition, particularly for subnationals who frequently come to market with a bond offering, is likely to result in a lower funding cost.

For small subnationals that do not come to market frequently, the lower-cost funds may not be realized. This can be partially overcome by bond banks that are quasi-government entities. These banks purchase bonds from smaller subnationals that are infrequent issuers in the bond market, pool the bonds to create another bond issue backed by the pooled bonds, and resell them to the public. Because the pooled bonds can be issued at a higher credit rating than that of the bonds issued by individual subnationals, the interest rate that must be paid on pooled bonds will be less than what must be paid for individual subnationals. The benefits of the lower cost can be passed through to the individual subnationals. In the United States, examples of bond banks are the Maine Municipal Bond Bank and the Indiana Bond Bank, both established by their respective states.

The development of the municipal bond market in any country requires the introduction of credit ratings by credit rating agencies (CRAs), the entities that were the subject of chapter 5. As explained later in this chapter, CRAs evaluate various factors pertaining to the entity that they are rating. One of the major factors is the entity's financial condition. A rating will not be assigned if reliable financial information is not available. In the case of rating the bond of a subnational, CRAs need information about its local budget, all financial obligations outstanding, and its arrangements with the central government. These ratings are necessary for certain investors in the country to purchase the subnational bond and, in many countries, a minimum rating is needed before the central government will permit the subnational to issue the bond. Recall from our discussion of CRAs in chapter 5 that because the rating is an issuer-pay model, there is concern that CRAs may give in to economic pressure to give the rating necessary for the subnational to obtain approval from the central government.

The U.S. municipal bond market is the model that has proved to be highly successful in facilitating funding for states, counties, and townships. Later in this chapter, we focus on the U.S. municipal bond market, which is a highly successful municipal debt market.

Multilateral Financial Institution Arrangements

Multilateral financial institutions, which are also referred to as supranationals, include the International Monetary Fund, the World Bank Group, the European Bank for Reconstruction and Development, the European Investment Bank, the Asian Development Bank, and the Global Environmental Fund. It has been argued that the greatest need for infrastructure financing in developing markets is Asia because of its rate of urbanization. The Asian Development Bank estimated that $8 trillion worth of infrastructure projects would be needed in Asia simply to maintain the region's economic growth rates. Recognizing this growing need for infrastructure financing, in 2015 China led the creation of the Asian Infrastructure Investment Bank. This bank has 57 founding member countries that committed $100 billion in capital to fund infrastructure projects in the region. China contributed $30 million. Japan has committed to inject a significant amount.

The experience of multilateral institutions in fostering the development of a sustainable bond municipal debt market is sort of a puzzle. Take the case of Brazil, which has used loans from multilateral institutions for more than 30 years to develop a municipal debt market. Despite the many successes of this type of financing in terms of low rates of nonperforming municipal loans and investment projects that have been successful, market observers believe that Brazil "is as far away as ever from having a functioning local credit market."[4] Brazil's subnationals are not allowed to issue bonds, and because private banks view lending to subnationals as too risky, they do not make intermediate- and long-term loans. To obtain any other type of borrowing, central government approval is required on a case-by-case basis.

To foster infrastructure financing in developing economies, multilateral institutions use public-private partnerships and project finance initiatives, which we discuss next.

Infrastructure Financing via Project Finance and Public-Private Partnerships

The substantial worldwide need for financing infrastructure projects and the constraints on the budgets of subnationals has resulted in some countries turning to the private sector. This is done by either a public-private partnership or direct financing of projects (referred to as **project finance initiatives**).[5] These alternative funding arrangements are attractive, because they typically do not appear as part of a subnational's budget. For this reason, they are referred to as "off-budget" mechanisms.

A **public-private partnership** (PPP) is an agreement between a public agency or government department and a private sector entity (or entities) that calls for the procurement,

4. Peterson, "Banks or Bonds? Building a Municipal Credit Market," 3.

5. For a more detailed described of PPP and PFI, see Frank J. Fabozzi and Carmel F. de Nahik, *Project Financing*, eighth edition (London: Euromoney International Investors, 2012), chapter 30.

building, or development of a facility or service and that shares risks and rewards between the public and private sector partners. This is very often in the form of a concession agreement, which is a contract between a private sector entity and a government entity to operate a specific service within that government entity's jurisdiction, subject to certain restrictions. However, this may sometimes take the form of a privately funded project known as a **private finance initiative** (PFI).[6]

The key distinction between a PPP and a PFI is that a PPP describes the overarching approach used to assist in more efficient procurement or management of projects that may be only partly privatized. Consequently, some or all of the ownership of the project remains in the hands of the government entity that has partnered with the private sector entity, and the project is set up to operate the facilities through a concession agreement. In contrast, PFIs include fund raising for the project and usually a shift in ownership—even if only during the lifetime of the finance—to the private sector. Despite this distinction, sometimes the terms PPP and PFI are used interchangeably.

Although there are many reasons for a subnational using PPP and PFI to finance infrastructure projects, one of the major ones is that these arrangements will lower interest cost compared with the same project financed through the public sector.

The largest PPP in the United States is the $4 billion LaGuardia Airport Terminal B redevelopment project in New York. The partnership is between the LaGuardia Gateway Partners, and the subnational entity is the Port Authority of New York and New Jersey. The purpose of the PPP is to build a new state-of-the art 1.3 million square foot LaGuardia Airport Central Terminal B and manage the terminal operations to better meet the needs of the 15 million passengers who use the terminal each year and the four airlines who use the terminal as their home (American Airlines, United, Southwest, and Air Canada). The LaGuardia Gateway Partners include Vantage Airport Group, Skanska, Meridiam, and JLC Infrastructure, which are responsible for the development of the terminal and providing the equity investment. Vantage Airport Group is responsible for managing the terminal's operations.

Municipal Green Bond Issuance

Green bonds are issued by supranationals, development banks, governments, and corporations. The largest issuers are the European Investment Bank, the International Bank for Reconstruction and Development, the African Development Bank, and the International Finance Corporation.[7]

6. The term PFI is generally considered to have originated in the United Kingdom in 1992 and was defined in a parliamentary research paper dated 2001.

7. RBC Capital Markets, "Green Bonds: Fifty Shades of Green" (Toronto, March 26, 2014).

A "green project" refers to a project or activity that promotes climate or other environmental sustainability goals. **Green bonds** are financial instruments whose proceeds are used solely to finance new and existing green projects. The catalysts for the introduction and growth of the green bond market are the World Bank Group and the European Development Bank.[8] The World Bank has issued green bonds since 2008; through mid-2013, it had 67 transactions in 17 currencies totaling more than $6.4 billion.[9] In 2014, a local government agency in Norway. Kommunalbanken AS, issued a $550 million green bond.

The bonds are issued in response to specific investor demand for a triple-A-rated product that supports projects to mitigate climate change or to help those people affected by climate change adapt to it. The first green bond investors were a group of Scandinavian pension funds seeking "investment opportunities for the fixed income portion of their portfolios that would help them support climate mitigation and adaptation projects."[10]

Voluntary transparency and disclosure guidelines, referred to as the Green Bond Principles, have been formulated for the purpose of promoting the integrity and development of the green bond market.[11] The broad categories of potentially eligible green projects to which the bond proceeds can be applied, as suggested by the Green Bond Principles, include (but are not limited to) renewable energy, energy efficiency (including energy-efficient buildings), sustainable waste management, sustainable land use (including sustainable forestry and agriculture), biodiversity conservation, clean transportation, and clean water or drinking water. Green bonds are classified, mostly by intended use, into four types: green proceeds bonds, green revenue bonds, green project bonds, and green securitized bonds.[12]

U.S. Municipal Securities Market

U.S. municipal securities are issued by state and local governments and by the entities that they establish. All states issue municipal securities. Local governments include cities and counties. Political subdivisions of municipalities that issue securities include school districts and special districts for fire prevention, water, sewer, and other purposes. Public agencies or instrumentalities include authorities and commissions.

8. The two groups in the World Bank Group that were involved in fostering green bonds were the International Bank for Reconstruction and Development and the International Financial Corporation.

9. Heike Reichelt and Alexandra Klöpfer, "Green Bonds Market Tops $20 Billion, Expands to New Issuers, Currencies & Structures" (Washington, DC: World Bank, July 23, 2014), http://blogs.worldbank.org/climatechange/green-bondissuance-tops-20-billion-and-expanding-new-issuers-currencies-products.

10. Reichelt and Klöpfer, "Green Bonds Market Tops $20 Billion."

11. Ceres, "Green Bond Principles, 2014: Voluntary Process Guidelines for Issuing Green Bonds" (Boston: Ceres, January 13, 2014), http://www.ceres.org/resources/reports/green-bond-principles-2014-voluntaryprocess-guidelines-for-issuing-green-bonds.

12. Ceres, "Green Bond Principles, 2014."

Municipal bonds are issued for various purposes. Short-term notes typically are sold in anticipation of the receipt of funds from taxes or proceeds from the sale of a bond issue, for example. The proceeds from the sale of short-term notes permit the issuing municipality to cover seasonal and temporary imbalances between outlays for expenditures and tax inflows. Municipalities issue long-term bonds as the principal means for financing both (1) long-term capital projects (such as the construction of schools, bridges, roads, and airports) and (2) long-term budget deficits that arise from current operations.

The municipal bond market includes two sectors: the tax-exempt bond sector and the taxable bond sector. The attractiveness of tax-exempt municipal securities is due to their tax treatment at the federal income tax level. Most municipal securities are tax exempt, which means that interest on the security is exempt from federal income taxation. The exemption applies to interest income, not capital gains. The exemption may or may not extend to the state and local levels. Each state has its own rules as to how interest on municipal securities is taxed.[13] The taxable municipal bond sector, by far the smaller sector, includes bonds whose interest is taxed at the federal income tax level.

Historically, investors in municipal securities have included retail investors, mutual funds, closed-end funds, exchange-traded funds, bank trust departments, and property and casualty insurance companies. These investors are interested in the tax-exempt feature of municipal securities. Retail investors either directly or indirectly through their ownership of collective investment vehicles (i.e., mutual funds, closed-end funds, or exchange-traded funds) own 75% of the municipal securities outstanding. More recently, hedge funds, arbitrageurs, life insurance companies, and foreign banks have become important participants. These investors are not interested in the tax-exempt feature. Instead, their primary interest is in opportunities to benefit from leveraged strategies that seek to generate capital gains.

Types and Features of Municipal Bonds

The two basic types of municipal security structures are tax-backed debt and revenue bonds. Other securities share characteristics of tax-backed debt and revenue bonds.[14]

Tax-backed debt Debt issued by states, counties, special districts, cities, towns, and school districts and secured by some form of tax revenue is called **tax-backed debt**. This type of debt includes general obligation debt, appropriation-backed obligations, and debt obligations supported by public credit enhancement programs.

13. The tax treatment at the state level is one of the following: (1) exemption of interest from all municipal securities, (2) taxation of interest from all municipal securities, (3) exemption of interest from municipal securities if the issuer is in state but taxation of interest if the issuer is out of state.

14. For a further discussion of these securities, see Sylvan G. Feldstein and Frank J. Fabozzi (eds.), *The Handbook of Municipal Securities* (Hoboken, NJ: John Wiley & Sons, 2008).

The broadest type of tax-backed debt is **general obligation debt**. The two types of general obligation pledges are unlimited and limited. An unlimited tax general obligation debt is the stronger form of general obligation pledge, because it is secured by the issuer's unlimited taxing power. Tax revenue sources include corporate and individual income taxes, sales taxes, and property taxes. Unlimited tax general obligation debt is said to be secured by the full faith and credit of the issuer. A limited tax general obligation debt is a limited tax pledge because of a statutory limit on the tax rates the issuer may levy to service the debt.

Certain general obligation bonds are secured not only by the issuer's general taxing powers to create revenues accumulated in a general fund but also by certain identified fees, grants, and special charges, which provide additional revenues from outside the general fund. Such bonds are considered to be double-barreled in security because of the dual nature of the revenue sources. For example, the debt obligations issued by special purpose service systems may be secured by a pledge of property taxes, a pledge of special fees/operating revenue from the service provided, or a pledge of both property taxes and special fees/operating revenues. In the last case, they are double barreled.

Agencies or authorities of several states issue bonds that carry a potential state liability for making up shortfalls in the issuing entity's obligation. This type of debt is called an **appropriation-backed obligation**. The appropriation of funds from the state's general tax revenue must be approved by the state legislature. However, the state's pledge is not binding. Debt obligations with this nonbinding pledge of tax revenue are called **moral obligation bonds**. Because a moral obligation bond requires legislative approval to appropriate the funds, it is classified as an appropriation-backed obligation. The purpose of the moral obligation pledge is to enhance the creditworthiness of the issuing entity. However, the investor must rely on the best efforts of the state to approve the appropriation. Another type of appropriation-backed obligation is lease-backed debt.

Even though a moral obligation is a form of credit enhancement provided by a state, it is not a legally enforceable or legally binding obligation of the state. Some entities issue debt that carries some form of public credit enhancement that is legally enforceable. This type of credit enhancement occurs when the state or a federal agency guarantees or takes on an obligation to automatically withhold and deploy state aid to pay any defaulted debt service by the issuing entity. Typically, the latter form of public credit enhancement is used for debt obligations of a state's school systems.

Revenue bonds The second basic type of security structure is found in a **revenue bond**. Such bonds are issued for either project or enterprise financing where the bond issuers pledge to the bondholders the revenues generated by the operating projects financed. A feasibility study is performed before the endeavor is undertaken to determine whether it will be self-supporting.

Examples of revenue bonds include airport revenue bonds, college and university revenue bonds, hospital revenue bonds, single-family mortgage revenue bonds, multifamily revenue bonds, public power revenue bonds, resource recovery revenue bonds, seaport revenue bonds, sports complex and convention center revenue bonds, student loan revenue bonds, toll road and gas tax revenue bonds, and water revenue bonds.

Hybrid and special bond structures Some municipal securities create special security structures that share characteristics of tax-backed debt and revenue bonds. They include insured bonds, prerefunded bonds, and structured/asset-based bonds.

Insured bonds, in addition to being secured by the issuer's revenue, are also backed by insurance policies written by commercial insurance companies. Insurance on a municipal bond is an agreement by an insurance company, referred to as a "monoline insurer," to pay the bondholder any bond principal or coupon interest due on a stated maturity date that is not paid by the bond issuer. Once issued, this municipal bond insurance usually extends for the term of the bond issue, and it cannot be canceled by the insurance company. Municipal bond insurance is just one form of credit enhancement used by municipal bond issuers, although the most commonly used form.

Because municipal bond insurance reduces credit risk for the investor, the marketability of certain municipal securities can be greatly expanded. Municipal securities that benefit most from the insurance would include lower-quality bonds; bonds issued by smaller governmental units not widely known in the financial community; bonds that have a sound, though complex and difficult-to-understand security structure; and bonds issued by infrequent local government borrowers who do not have a general market following among investors. Of course, a major factor for an issuer in obtaining bond insurance is that its creditworthiness without the insurance is substantially lower than what it would be with the insurance. That is, the interest cost savings are only of sufficient magnitude to offset the cost of the insurance premium when the underlying creditworthiness of the issuer is lower.

Municipal bond insurance was first introduced in 1971 and until 2008 was a common form of credit enhancement. From 2000 to 2007, more than half of municipal securities issues were insured bonds or had some other form of credit enhancement. As a result of the financial crisis that began in 2007 that resulted in substantial payouts for insured mortgage-backed securities (not municipal securities), the issuance of insured bonds fell dramatically as the credit ratings of the monoline insurers were downgraded. For a monoline insurer to insure a municipal bond so that it receives the highest investment-grade rating, triple A (AAA by S&P and Fitch; Aaa by Moody's), the insurer must have a triple A rating. Because they were all downgraded to below triple A, insured municipal securities ceased. *The Bond Buyer* reports that in 2005, 57% municipal securities were insured, but in 2010 and 2011, that figure was only 5.2% and 6.2%, respectively.[15] In fact, for the years 2009, 2010, and

15. *The Bond Buyer's 2011 in Statistics*, February 13, 2012, available at http://www.bondbuyer.com/pdfs/2012_bb_stats_supp.pdf.

2011, only 17% of municipal securities had some form of private credit enhancement.[16] Although private credit enhancement has declined, public credit enhancement has increased.

Although originally issued as either revenue or general obligation bonds, municipals are sometimes prerefunded and are called **prerefunded municipal securities**. (They are also called **refunded bonds**.) A prerefunding usually occurs when the original bonds are escrowed or collateralized by direct obligations guaranteed by the U.S. government. A portfolio of securities guaranteed by the U.S. government is placed in a trust. The portfolio is assembled so that the cash flows from the securities match the obligations that the issuer must pay. For example, suppose that a municipality has a 5% $100 million issue with 12 years remaining to maturity. The municipality's obligation is to make payments of $2.5 million every 6 months for the next 12 years and $100 million 12 years from now. If the issuer wants to prerefund this issue, it purchases a portfolio of U.S. government obligations with cash flows of $2.5 million every 6 months for the next 12 years and $100 million 12 years from now.

Once this portfolio of securities whose cash flows match those of the municipality's obligation is in place, the prerefunded bonds are no longer secured as either general obligation or revenue bonds. The bonds are now supported by cash flows from the portfolio or securities held in an escrow fund. Such bonds, if escrowed with securities guaranteed by the U.S. government, have little, if any, credit risk. They are the safest municipal securities available.

The escrow fund for a prerefunded municipal bond can be structured so that the bonds to be refunded are to be called at the first possible call date or a subsequent call date established in the original bond indenture. Although prerefunded bonds are usually retired at their first or subsequent call date, some are structured to match the debt obligation to the maturity date. Such bonds are known as **escrowed-to-maturity bonds**.

Some state and local governments issue bonds where the debt service is paid from so-called dedicated revenues, such as sales taxes, tobacco settlement payments, fees, and penalty payments. These structures, referred to as asset-backed securities, will be discussed in chapter 27. Asset-backed securities are also referred to as **dedicated revenue bonds** and **structured bonds**.

Municipal Notes

Municipal securities issued for periods of up to three years are considered to be short term in nature. They include tax anticipation notes, revenue anticipation notes, grant anticipation notes, bond anticipation notes, tax-exempt commercial paper, variable-rate demand obligations, and commercial paper/variable-rate demand obligations.

16. Securities and Exchange Commission, *Report on the Municipal Securities Market* (Washington, DC, 2012), 26.

Tax anticipation notes (TANs), **revenue anticipation notes** (RANs), **grant anticipation notes** (GANs), and **bond anticipation notes** (BANs) are temporary borrowings by states, local governments, and special jurisdictions. Usually the notes are issued for a period of 12 months, although it is not uncommon for notes to be issued for periods as short as three months or as long as three years. TANs and RANs (also known as TRANs) are issued in anticipation of the collection of taxes or other expected revenues. The purpose of these borrowings is to even out irregular flows into the treasuries of the issuing entity. BANs are issued in anticipation of the sale of long-term bonds.

We will discuss commercial paper issued by corporations in chapter 25. **Tax-exempt commercial paper** is used by municipalities to raise funds on a short-term basis ranging from 1 to 270 days. The dealer sets interest rates for various maturity dates, and the investor then selects the desired date. Tax regulations restrict the issuance of tax-exempt commercial paper. Specifically, tax regulations limit the amount of new issuance of municipal obligations that is tax exempt. As a result, every maturity of a tax-exempt municipal issuance is considered a new debt issuance. Consequently, very limited issuance of tax-exempt commercial paper exists. Instead, issuers use one of the next two products to raise short-term funds.

Variable-rate demand obligations (VRDOs) are floating-rate obligations that have a nominal long-term maturity but have a coupon rate that is reset either daily or every 7 days. The investor has an option to put the issue back to the trustee at any time with 7 days' notice. The put price is par plus accrued interest.

The **commercial paper/VRDO hybrid** is customized to meet the cash flow needs of an institutional investor. As with tax-exempt commercial paper, the maturity is flexibly structured, because the remarketing agent establishes interest rates for a range of maturities. Although the instrument may have a long nominal maturity, there is a put provision, as with a VRDO. Put periods can range from one day to more than 360 days. On the put date, the investor can put back the bonds, receiving principal and interest, or the investor can elect to extend the maturity at the new interest rate and put date posted by the remarketing agent at that time. Thus, the investor has two choices when initially purchasing this instrument: the interest rate and the put date.

Default Risk

Investors in municipal securities are exposed to default risk—the risk that the issuer fails to meet its contractual obligations. Default rates are less than for corporate bonds of the same maturity and with the same initial credit rating. For example, a study by Moody's of default rates through 2012 found that the cumulative default rate after 10 years for municipal and corporate bonds was as follows:[17]

17. As reported in Moody's Investors Service, "US Municipal Bond Defaults and Recoveries, 1970–2012," May 7, 2013.

Initial Rating	Municipal Securities (%)	Corporate Bonds (%)
AAA	0.00	0.50
AA	0.01	0.92
A	0.05	2.48
BBB	0.30	4.74

Moody's also looked at the default rate by the different sectors of the municipal market from 1970 to 2012. General obligations had lower default rates than did revenue bonds. The default rate was about 7%. The revenue bond that had the highest default rate was the housing sector with a default rate of 40%, followed by the hospital and health care sector with a 30% default rate.

As will be explained in chapter 26, default rates alone do not indicate a debt obligation's default risk. Moody's reported that for 1970–2012, the ultimate recovery for municipal securities averaged about 62%. In the case of senior unsecured corporate bonds (which provide a better comparison than all corporate bonds), the ultimate recovery rate was much lower (49%) for 1987–2012. The range of recovery rates for municipal securities was from 2% to 100%.

Spiotto provides a history of municipal bond defaults as well as the causes and nature of defaults.[18] These include:

- *Economic conditions:* Defaults are caused by downturns in the economy and high interest rates.
- *Nonessential services:* Revenue bonds were issued for services that are no longer needed.
- *Feasibility of projects and industries:* Revenue bonds are issued after a feasibility study for a project is completed. The feasibility study may have been too optimistic with respect to the demand for the project or the cost of completing the project.
- *Fraud:* Municipal officials fail to comply with the terms of the relevant documents.
- *Mismanagement:* A municipality is unable to successfully manage a project.
- *Unwillingness to pay:* A municipality may simply be unwilling to pay (i.e., repudiation of the debt obligation).
- *Natural disasters:* The impairment of a municipality's budget (reduction in revenue and increase in costs) may be the result of a natural disaster, such as a hurricane.

Bear in mind that a default does not mean a municipal bankruptcy, nor does a bankruptcy mean a default. That is, a municipality can default on an issue but the default may not

18. James E. Spiotto, "A History of Modern Municipal Defaults," chapter 44 in Feldstein and Fabozzi, *The Handbook of Municipal Securities*.

result in a bankruptcy filing; a municipal bankruptcy filing may not result in a default of the municipality on its debt. In fact, historically, very few municipalities that have filed for bankruptcy have actually defaulted.

Factors considered by credit rating agencies when assigning ratings Many institutional investors in the municipal bond market rely on their own in-house municipal credit analysts for determining the creditworthiness of a municipal issue; other investors rely on the CRAs. The assigned rating system is the same as that used for corporate bonds that we will discuss in chapter 26. The credit rating for the central government acts as a ceiling for the rating on the credit rating of its subnationals. Although it is not unprecedented, it is rare to see a subnational with a higher rating than its sovereign.

To evaluate general obligation bonds, the CRAs assess information in four basic categories. The first category includes information on the issuer's debt structure and overall debt burden. The second category relates to the issuer's ability and political discipline to maintain sound budgetary policy. The focus of attention here usually is on the issuer's general operating funds and whether it has maintained balanced budgets over three to five years. The third category involves determining the specific local taxes and intergovernmental revenues available to the issuer, as well as obtaining historical information both on tax collection rates (which are important when looking at property tax levies) and the dependence of local budgets on specific revenue sources. The fourth and last category of information necessary for the credit analysis is an assessment of the issuer's overall socioeconomic environment. The determinants for this category include trends in local employment distribution and composition, population growth, real estate property valuation, and personal income, among other economic factors.

Although numerous security structures can be used for revenue bonds, the underlying principle for rating is whether the project being financed will generate sufficient cash flow to satisfy the obligation due bondholders.

Municipal bankruptcy We have referred to municipal bankruptcy. The provision in the U.S. bankruptcy code dealing with bankruptcy protection for municipalities is Chapter 9. This provision is much like a Chapter 11 bankruptcy in that it provides for a reorganization plan. There is no equivalent for municipalities of what is provided for in a Chapter 7 bankruptcy filing, which pertains to the liquidation of a corporation. This is because a municipality cannot be liquidated, because that would violate the Tenth Amendment of the U.S. Constitution granting states sovereignty over their internal affairs.[19] Effectively, Chapter 9 grants a municipality more power over its creditors than a corporation has over its creditors. A municipality's creditors cannot compel a municipality to liquidate its assets.

19. The Tenth Amendment, ratified in 1791, provides that powers that the Constitution does not either delegate to the federal government or prohibit to the states are reserved to the states or the people.

States are not permitted to file for Chapter 9 bankruptcy. Hence only nonstate municipal entities (cities, counties, townships, school districts, public improvement districts, and authorities of revenue-producing entities) can file. This action is not a simple process, explaining why historically the number of municipal entities filing for Chapter 9 bankruptcy protection is low. For example, according to data from the American Bankruptcy Institute,[20] for the period 1980 through the second quarter of 2011, there were only 159 filings. Chapter 11 bankruptcies for any single year are far greater than that.

Municipality entities must overcome a major obstacle to file for bankruptcy. Title 11 of Chapter 9 of the bankruptcy code requires that the state in which the municipal is located must grant approval to that entity to file for bankruptcy protection. This allows individual states to assess the trade-off of the adverse economic impact of the municipal entity seeking to obtain bankruptcy protection against the needs of the municipality entities that need protection offered by a Chapter 9 filing. Twenty-two states do not allow municipal entities access to Chapter 9 bankruptcy, 16 states impose conditions that must be satisfied by a municipality to file, and the remaining 12 states provide blanket authorization to file.[21]

Because of the Tenth Amendment, a U.S. bankruptcy judge does not have the same power in a municipal bankruptcy as in a corporate bankruptcy. As a result, a U.S. bankruptcy judge is not as active in Chapter 9 bankruptcy filings as he or she is in Chapter 11 bankruptcy. After determination of whether a municipal entity is entitled by state law to file for bankruptcy, a bankruptcy judge is responsible for approving the plan for how the municipal entity is going to pay its creditors and ensuring that the municipal entity executes that plan.

As of 2017, the four largest municipal Chapter 9 bankruptcies are:

- City of Detroit, Michigan, filed in 2013 due to its inability to satisfy unfunded pension obligations: $18 billion.
- Jefferson City, Alabama, filed in 2011 because of a failed investment strategy (bets on interest rate) leading to losses: $4 billion.
- Orange County, California, filed in 1994 due to losses of more than $1 billion on leveraged investments in exotic mortgage-backed security products: $2 billion.
- Stockton, California, filed in 2012 due to difficulties satisfying pension obligations: $1 billion.

Secondary Market for Municipal Bonds

Municipal securities are traded in the OTC market supported by more than 1,500 municipal bond dealers. Markets for the debts of smaller issuers (referred to as **local credits**) are maintained by regional brokerage firms, local banks, and some of the larger Wall Street

20. See http://www.abiworld.org/statcharts/Ch9Filings1980-Current.pdf.

21. See http://archive.news10.net/news/pdf/State-Policies-on-Chapter-9-bankruptcy.pdf.

firms. Markets for the bonds of larger issuers (referred to as **generic names**) are supported by the larger brokerage firms and banks, many of whom have investment banking relationships with these issuers.

In the municipal bond market, an "odd lot" of bonds is $25,000 or less in par value for retail investors. For institutions, anything below $100,000 in par value is considered an odd lot. Dealer spreads depend on several factors. For the retail investor, the spread can range from as low as 0.25 points ($12.50 per $5,000 par value) on large blocks of actively traded bonds to four points ($200 per $5,000 of par value) for odd-lot sales of an inactive issue. For institutional investors, the dealer spread rarely exceeds 0.5 points ($25 per $5,000 of par value). The convention for both corporate and Treasury bonds is to quote prices as a percentage of par value with 100 equal to par. However, municipal securities generally are traded and quoted in terms of yield (yield to maturity or yield to call). The price of the bond in this case is called a "basis price." The exception is certain long-maturity revenue bonds. A bond traded and quoted in dollar prices (actually, as a percentage of par value) is called a **dollar bond**.

As noted earlier, more than 75% of the outstanding principal amount of municipal securities is held directly or indirectly by retail (individual investors). Historically, the market has been viewed as one where investors tended to buy a municipal security and then hold it to maturity. Thus, after the initial sale of a municipal security, there is infrequent trading. However, a significant volume of secondary market trading does occur. According to trade data compiled by the Municipal Securities Rulemaking Board (MSRB), annual trading in municipal securities for the years 2010–2013 averaged $3.4 trillion in principal value; the average number of trades per year over the same period averaged 10.3 million.[22] The number of trades for revenue bonds during those years was approximately double the number for general obligation bonds. For the three years ending 2013, trading in tax-exempt bonds was almost 10 times greater than taxable bonds in terms of the number of trades.

Investors typically have limited access to pretrade information. Generally, municipal bond dealers do not make available firm bid and ask quotations available to the public. Pretrade information might be available to investors from alternative trading systems, such as electronic communication networks made available to municipal bond dealers. Trades are typically executed for customers on a principal basis (i.e., the municipal bond dealer buys and sells from its own inventory). For customer trades not executed in that way, the dealer will either search the OTC market to execute the trade or use an alternative trading system. In general, particularly for retail investors, the cost of transacting is higher than in other investment-grade bond markets due to the lack of market transparency.

Roughly 43% of the trading in the municipal securities in 2012 and 2013 was executed through five bond dealers, according to data compiled by the MSRB.[23] Roughly two-thirds of all trades were executed by 20 bond dealers.

22. The data reported here were computed from several tables in Municipal Securities Rulemaking Board, *2013 Fact Book* (Washington, DC, 2014).

23. Municipal Securities Rulemaking Board, *2013 Fact Book*.

The SEC study of the municipal securities market made several recommendations for improving the secondary market and providing greater investor protection. The two major areas where improvements have been suggested are ongoing disclosure and improving market structure.

Yields on Tax-Exempt Municipal Bonds

Because of the tax-exempt feature of municipal securities, their yield is less than that on Treasuries with the same maturity. The difference in yield between tax-exempt securities and Treasury securities is typically measured not in basis points but in percentage terms. More specifically, it is measured as the percentage of the yield on a municipal security relative to a comparable Treasury security and is called the **yield ratio**. Historically, the yield ratio has varied not just by credit rating and maturity but over time. The range for the yield ratio has been from 0.80 to more than 1.0.

In the municipal bond market, several benchmark curves exist. In general, a benchmark yield curve is constructed for AAA-rated state general obligations. In the Treasury and corporate bond markets, it is not unusual to find at different times shapes for the yield curve described in chapter 16 (see figure 16.1). In general, the municipal yield curve is positively sloped.

Participants in the municipal securities market calculate a yield to approximate what yield would have to be earned on a taxable bond to net the same yield after taxes as buying a taxable bond. That yield is referred to as a taxable-equivalent yield. We described this yield measure and its calculation in chapter 16.

Chinese Municipal Bond Market

The People's Republic of China is making a major push to create a sustainable municipal debt market that has relied on banks to provide infrastructure finance to bond issuance. For example, in 2011, three cities (Beijing, Shanghai, Shenzhen) and the province of Zhejiang were allowed to issue bonds directly to the capital markets. These bonds are issued without a sovereign guarantee. On September 1, 2014, the Chinese parliament passed changes in the budget law that allows local governments to issue bonds directly. Local governments may issue bonds to fund projects that promote the public good (investments in infrastructure) but may not use borrowed money for day-to-day operations. In recent years, the Chinese government has made a major push to develop the country's municipal debt market. Prior to 2010, subnational government entities borrowed through the Urban Development and Investment Corporation, which is the investment and financing platform for subnationals in China. This corporation borrows directly from financial markets, and the subnational is responsible for servicing the debt.

Another important financing vehicle that has been used in China since the global financial crisis is the "local government-backed unit." These units are used to fund infrastructure projects. A local government-backed unit is a state-owned enterprise with a local government as the only shareholder. To create a unit, the local government transfers land, utilities, or infrastructure to the unit in exchange for equity ownership. Just like regular corporations, the local government-backed unit raises capital from bank loans or the sale of debt instruments. Local governments service the debt through the sale of land. They are not permitted to use tax revenue to fund the debt.[24]

Key Points

- Subnational governments include states, regions, provinces, counties, municipalities, as well as local utilities companies either owned or regulated by these entities.
- To obtain the necessary funding to operate a subnational government, revenue sources of funding are combined with some debt arrangement (bank borrowing or the issuance of bonds).
- A major issue faced by subnationals in developing and developed countries is how to obtain debt funding for large-scale investments in infrastructure.
- Although some financing for infrastructure comes from central governments and multilateral financial institutions, the rest must come from the subnationals themselves and any debt funding that they can obtain; for this reason, central governments are seeking to strengthen the debt market for their subnationals.
- Central governments have two models from which to develop their subnational debt markets: bank lending and bond issuance.
- Bank lending is via municipal banks that have been established in a country.
- The development of the municipal bond market in any country requires the introduction of credit ratings by credit rating agencies.
- For small subnationals that are infrequent issuers of bonds, issuance is made possible through municipal bond banks.
- Multilateral financial institutions work with developing countries when seeking to create a sustainable municipal debt market.
- The substantial need for financing throughout the world for infrastructure projects and the constraints on the budgets of subnationals have resulted in some countries turning to the private sector via public-private partnerships and project finance initiatives.
- Funding arrangements via public-private partnerships and project finance initiatives are attractive to subnationals, because they typically do not appear as part of a subnational's budget.

24. Brent Ambrose, Yongheng Deng, and Jing Wu, "Understanding the Risk of China's Local Government Debts and Its Linkage with Property Markets" (Social Science Research Network: January 2015). Available at http://papers.ssrn.com/sol3/papers.cfm?abstract_id=2557031.

- Green bonds are bonds whose proceeds are restricted to fund green projects, which are projects that promote climate or other environmental sustainability goals.
- In the United States, municipal bonds are issued by state and local governments and their authorities.
- Although there are both tax-exempt and taxable municipal bonds in the United States, most municipal securities are of the tax-exempt variety.
- The interest received from a tax-exempt municipal security is exempt from federal income taxation.
- Investors in municipal securities attracted by their tax advantage are retail investors, collective investment vehicles, and property and casualty insurance companies.
- Because of the tax-exempt feature of municipal securities, the yield on tax-exempt municipal securities is less than that on Treasuries with the same maturity.
- The yield ratio measures the yield on a municipal security relative to a comparable Treasury security.
- The two basic types of municipal bond structures are tax-backed debt and revenue bonds.
- Tax-backed debt obligations are instruments issued by states, counties, special districts, cities, towns, and school districts that are secured by some form of tax revenue.
- Tax-backed debt includes general obligation debt (the broadest type of tax-backed debt), appropriation-backed obligations, and debt obligations supported by public credit enhancement programs.
- A general obligation bond is said to be double-barreled when it is secured not only by the issuer's general taxing powers to create revenues accumulated in a general fund but also by certain identified fees, grants, and special charges, which provide additional revenues from outside the general fund.
- Revenue bonds are issued for enterprise financings secured by the revenues generated by the completed projects themselves, or for general public-purpose financings in which the issuers pledge to the bondholders the tax and revenue resources that were previously part of the general fund.
- Prerefunded bonds are no longer secured as either general obligation or revenue bonds but are supported by a portfolio of securities held in an escrow fund. If escrowed with securities guaranteed by the U.S. government, prerefunded bonds are the safest municipal securities available.
- A prerefunded municipal bond is one in which the escrow fund is structured so that the bonds are to be called at the first possible call date or a subsequent call date established in the original bond indenture.
- Municipal securities structured as asset-backed securities are backed by "dedicated" revenues, such as sales taxes and tobacco settlement payments.

- Municipal notes are issued for shorter periods (one to three years) than are municipal securities.
- Investing in municipal securities exposes investors to credit risk and tax risk.
- Default rates are lower and recovery rates are higher for municipal securities compared to otherwise comparable corporate bonds.
- Historically, the causes and nature of defaults have been economic conditions, nonessential services, feasibility of projects and industries, fraud, mismanagement, unwillingness to pay, and natural disasters.
- To evaluate general obligation bonds, the credit rating agencies assess information in four basic categories: (1) issuer's debt structure and overall debt burden, (2) issuer's ability and political discipline to maintain sound budgetary policy, (3) issuer's access to specific local taxes and intergovernmental revenues, and (4) issuer's overall socioeconomic environment.
- The provision in the U.S. bankruptcy code dealing with bankruptcy protection for municipalities is Chapter 9 and provides for a reorganization plan.

Questions

1. Explain why you agree or disagree with the following statement: "Subnationals are free to select the form of debt obtained."

2. Why do subnationals have a substantial need for debt?

3. What are the limitations of municipal banks in establishing a sustainable municipal debt market?

4. What are the prerequisites for a subnational to issue a municipal bond?

5. a. What is a municipal bond bank?

b. Why is it advantageous for a small subnational that is an infrequent issuer to issue via a municipal bond bank?

6. What is the key distinction between a public-private partnership and a project finance initiative?

7. Why are public-private partnerships and project finance initiatives referred to as "off-balance financing"?

8. Why are green bonds issued?

9. Explain why you agree or disagree with the following statement: "All U.S. municipal bonds are exempt from federal income taxes."

10. How does the shape of the Treasury yield curve compare to that of the municipal yield curve?

11. What is the yield ratio, and why is it typically less than 1?

12. In December 2017, the U.S. Congress changed the tax law so as to decrease marginal tax rates. What do you think will happen to the price of municipal securities?

13. What is the major difference between a tax-backed debt and a revenue bond?

14. Why did the downgrading of municipal bond insurers following the financial crisis that began in 2007 basically result in the elimination of the issuance of insured municipal bonds?

15. a. What is a prerefunded bond?

b. Give two reasons an issuing municipality would want to prerefund an outstanding bond.

16. Why does a properly structured prerefunded municipal bond have no credit risk?

17. The following statement appeared in a publication by Idaho's State Treasurer's Office:

> 63-3202. PROCEDURE FOR ISSUANCE OF NOTES. (1) Whenever the state treasurer shall deem it to the best interests of the state of Idaho to issue state of Idaho tax anticipation notes, as provided in section 63-3201, Idaho Code, the state treasurer shall make written application to the state board of examiners, stating the amount of state of Idaho tax anticipation notes the state treasurer deems advisable to issue. Upon approval of the state board of examiners by order or resolution duly entered on the minutes of the state board of examiners, the state treasurer shall issue the tax anticipation notes in accordance with the provisions of this chapter.[25]

What is a tax anticipation note?

18. The four largest tobacco companies in the United States reached a settlement with 46 state attorney generals to pay a total of $206 billion over the following 25 years. States and municipalities, New York City being the first, sold bonds backed by the future payments of tobacco companies. What are these bonds called?

19. Why are municipal bankruptcies (Chapter 9) rare?

20. When describing the development of the Chinese municipal bond market, the following statement appeared on CNBC:

> Foreign investors will still have some lingering concerns, particularly over local government finances, however. Municipalities would need to improve the disclosure of their accounts, and the central government will probably need to impose debt limits as well as authorize the big three U.S. agencies to start rating the municipalities, said ANZ's Li-Gang.[26]

Explain why these actions would be important in the development of China's municipal bond market.

25. Idaho State Treasurer's Office, Title 63, Revenue and Taxation, chapter 32, "Anticipation of Revenue by State." https://legislature.idaho.gov/wp-content/uploads/statutesrules/idstat/Title63/T63CH32.pdf.

26. Mia Tahara-Stubbs, "China's Muni Bond Market Set for Take Off," CNBC online, May 5, 2015. https://www.cnbc.com/2015/05/05/chinas-muni-bond-market-set-to-explode.html.

VI CORPORATE FUNDING MARKETS

22 The Structure and Trading Venues of the Equity Market

CONTENTS

Learning Objectives

After reading this chapter, you will understand:

- the evolution of the stock market;
- how the stock market has become institutionalized;
- electronic trading of stocks;
- regulation of the stock market;
- order-driven markets versus quote-driven markets;
- the venues where stocks are traded in the United States;
- the different types of alternative trading systems;
- why investors use alternative trading systems;
- how orders are executed in the market by brokers;
- the historical background for the current regulatory framework;
- who the federal regulators of the equity market are;
- the federal regulations dealing with market volatility (trading limits and circuit breakers), short selling, and insider trading; and
- what global depository receipts and euro equities are.

Equity securities represent an ownership interest in a corporation. Holders of equity securities are entitled to the earnings of the corporation when those earnings are distributed in the form of dividends. They are also entitled to a pro rata share of the remaining equity if a corporation is liquidated. The two types of equity securities are common stock and preferred stock. The key distinction between these two forms of equity securities lies in the degree to which they may participate in any distribution of earnings and capital and the priority given to each in the distribution of earnings. Typically, preferred stockholders are entitled to a fixed dividend, which they receive before common stockholders may receive dividends, and they also have priority over common stockholders in a claim on assets in a liquidation. We therefore refer to preferred stock as a *senior corporate security*.

In the secondary market for common stock, the opinions of investors about the economic prospect of a company are expressed through the trades they execute. Taken together, these trades establish the market consensus opinion about the price of the stock. In turn, the company's estimated cost of common stock is determined.

In this chapter and the two that follow, we cover the world's equity markets. In this chapter, our focus is on the venues for the secondary trading of equities in the United States. In chapter 23, we describe trading arrangements in the U.S. secondary market, explain the costs of transacting, and review the pricing efficiency of the equities market, along with its implications for equity strategies. In chapter 24, we examine global non-U.S. equity markets.

Evolution of Stock Markets and Their Institutionalization

Stocks throughout the world have traditionally been transacted or traded on venues, or exchanges (bourses), which are physical locations. The nature of stock exchanges, however, has changed considerably since 1980. Table 22.1 summarizes these major changes. (Many of the terms and entities listed in the table are described in this and later chapters.) The table shows the evolution of stock exchanges from a market that was characterized as single country, limited product, mutually owned, floor trading exchanges to international, multiproduct, publicly owned, electronic trading exchanges.

Four general interacting factors contributed to significant changes experienced by the equity markets throughout the world over the past 40 years:

1. institutionalization of the stock market as a result of a shift away from traditional small individual investors to large institutional investors;
2. change in trading from mutual member-owned floor trading exchanges to publicly owned computer-based trading exchanges together with automated trading systems;
3. automation of settlement systems; and
4. changes in government regulation of the market.

The institutionalization of the common stock market has important implications for the design of equity trading systems, because the demands made by institutional investors differ from those made by traditional small investors. Moreover, the role of the equity market in facilitating capital formation for public corporations means designing a market structure that considers not just large corporations but also small corporations and startup companies seeking to raise equity capital, a market sector that we describe in chapter 28.

The nature of equity trading is currently dominated by the use of computers to generate orders as a result of advances in computer technology, through what is referred to as

Table 22.1
Trading stock markets: Then and now.

1980	Current
Exchanges	Exchanges—Publicly Owned
– Mutual organization	– Demutualization
– Member owned: Trading access via "seats" or memberships	– IPOs
	– For-profit organizations
	Automated trading systems
	– Off-exchange trading
	– ECNs
	– Light pool markets
	– Crossing networks
	– Dark pools (no pre-trade transparency)
– NYSE, Nasdaq, American Stock Exchange, regional exchanges[1]	– NYSE Arca, Nasdaq, Better Alternative Trading System (BATS)
Floor Trading	Electronic trading
– Specialists	– High frequency trading
– Floor traders	– Low latency (microseconds)
Manual trading systems	Electronic trading systems
Single country	Multicountry
	– NYSE, Euronext
	– Deutsche Börse, London Stock Exchange
	– Large, multiproduct, international corporations
	– Mergers and acquisitions
Common stocks	Common stocks
	Options: stocks and others
	Exchange traded funds
	Clearing and settlement services

[1]Chicago, Philadelphia, Boston, National (formerly Cincinnati), and Pacific exchanges.

algorithmic trading. Because of this dominance of computer trading, the equity market has been referred to as an *algorithmic marketplace*, in contradistinction to how equity markets previously operated, which is called a *manual market*.[1] These topics are discussed throughout this chapter.

1. This term was used in a speech by the chair of the Securities and Exchange Commission, Mary Jo White, "Enhancing Our Equity Market Structure," June 5, 2014, http://www.sec.gov/News/Speech/Detail/Speech/1370542004312#.U8KHXmcg_IW.

Electronic Trading

Traditionally, equities have been traded globally on "exchanges," which are physical locations at which individual traders conduct transactions with one another. The nature of exchanges has changed considerably over the past few decades in the United States, as summarized in table 22.1. Globally, exchanges have followed similar trends. The current overall approach to equity trading, as summarized in figure 22.1, consists of a combination of exchange trading venues and off-exchange trading systems (called "alternative trading systems" (ATS)) of equities. Consider a recent advance in trading, called **electronic trading**.

Electronic trading is a method of trading securities whereby traders are brought together via electronic trading platforms or networks that create a "virtual marketplace," rather than via a physical trading floor. Electronic trading has to a large extent replaced "floor trading" and telephone trading, as discussed below, wherein traders are brought together physically on a trading floor or by telephone contact, respectively.

Now let us consider U.S. trading venues. Floor trading was used exclusively until recently by the major stock exchange, the New York Stock Exchange (NYSE) described later in this chapter, and is now used only for a small portion of its trading. Nasdaq was formed in 1971 as the world's first electronic stock market.

Electronic trading provides several advantages over floor trading:

- *Lower transaction costs*: Automating the entire process (including trade processing, position keeping, clearing and settlement, referred to as "straight-through processing") has further reduced costs.
- *Increased transparency:* It is easier to track prices that are maintained in an electronic system.
- *Increased liquidity*: By more efficiently connecting all buyers and sellers, the market becomes more liquid.
- *Smaller spreads*: Automation has lowered costs, increased transparency, and increased liquidity, which results in smaller spreads.
- *Expanded trading hours*.

Later we will discuss trading venues in the United States. Of these trading venues, both the NYSE and Nasdaq use electronic trading. The NYSE is an auction market (discussed below), which has a specialist assigned to each stock, although independent floor traders do most of the trades. In addition, NYSE has an electronic Super Designated Order Turnaround system (SuperDOT system) for "small" trades of less than 100,000 shares (with priority given to trades of less than 2,100 shares) and transmits the orders (both market and limit) directly to the specialist for this stock. This system provides more efficient transactions, because the orders go directly to the specialist rather than to a floor trader and then to manually transaction. Executed orders are also reported to the broker through the SuperDOT system. The DOT and SuperDOT systems began in 1976. NYSE's recent Arca market, which is discussed below, is completely electronic.

Regulation of U.S. Equity Markets

The regulation of the securities markets around the globe, including stock exchanges, has three primary objectives: (1) to protect investors, (2) to ensure the smooth functioning of the market, and (3) to reduce systemic risk.

To protect investors, regulation must address informational asymmetries between the issuers of securities and investors. This can be achieved through disclosure regulation. The equities markets in most countries are highly regulated to ensure that investors are protected against fraudulent practices that might be followed by corporations when issuing stock or by brokers and dealers when executing transaction orders by investors. The smooth functioning of the market requires trading and settlement rules to minimize the risk of market disruptions. Systemic risk has been discussed in chapter 10 and touched on in several other chapters in this book.

U.S. Regulatory System

In the United States, there are three types of regulations: federal regulation by the Securities and Exchange Commission, regulation by a self-regulatory organization (the Financial Industry Regulatory Authority), and regulation by state regulators. Here we briefly describe each type.

Securities and Exchange Commission The primary regulator of U.S. securities markets is the **Securities and Exchange Commission** (SEC), created by the Securities Exchange Act of 1934 (the Exchange Act). Two important pieces of legislation were passed by Congress following the stock market crash of October 1929 and the Great Depression that followed. The first was the Securities Act of 1933, which required that investors receive financial information—in the form of a "prospectus"—before going public (the primary market for securities). The second was the Securities Act of 1934, which created the SEC, whose goal was to protect investors and maintain the fair and orderly functioning of the securities markets. Among the SEC's responsibilities are to promote full public disclosure and to protect investors from fraudulent and manipulative markets. Briefly, the Securities Act of 1933 covered the primary markets, and the Securities Exchange Act of 1934 covered the secondary markets for U.S. securities.

The purpose of the Securities Act of 1933 and the Securities Exchange Act of 1934 was to restore the confidence of investors in the stock market. The two ways that Congress sought to do so were by specifying: (1) the information (as well as the timing of that information) that companies offering securities to the public must furnish to investors (the primary markets); and (2) the practices that brokers, dealers, and trading venues must follow when executing orders on behalf of investors (the secondary markets).

The five general areas where the SEC has responsibility are:

- interpreting and enforcing federal securities laws passed by Congress;
- issuing new rules and amending of existing rules;
- overseeing and monitoring the major players in the securities markets (i.e., securities firms, brokers, investment advisers, and ratings agencies);
- overseeing private self-regulatory organizations in the securities, accounting, and auditing fields; and
- coordinating U.S. securities regulation with other federal entities (e.g., Congress, the Department of the Treasury, and the Federal Reserve), state regulators, and foreign authorities.

To carry out its responsibilities, the SEC relies on its five divisions:

- *Division of Corporation Finance:* Executing the SEC's duty for overseeing corporate disclosure of important information to investors when securities are publicly offered is this division's responsibility.
- *Division of Trading and Markets:* This division is responsible for executing the SEC's duty to maintain fair, orderly, and efficient markets.
- *Division of Investment Management:* The responsibility of this division is to provide investor protection and promote capital formation by using its oversight and regulatory authority over the investment management industry.
- *Division of Enforcement:* This division is responsible for law enforcement function by recommending investigations of securities law violations, recommending the SEC bring civil actions in federal court or an administrative proceeding before an administrative law judge, and prosecuting these cases.
- *Division of Economic and Risk Analysis:* This division provides sophisticated and data-driven economic and risk analyses to inform the SEC in its policymaking, rulemaking, enforcement, and examinations.

Financial Industry Regulatory Authority The Financial Industry Regulatory Authority (FINRA) is an independent, not-for-profit organization authorized by Congress with a dual mission objective: to protect investors and to foster market integrity. FINRA is referred to as a self-regulatory organization. Created in 2007 when the National Association of Securities Dealers merged with the regulatory functions of the NYSE, FINRA writes and enforces rules governing the activities of securities firms, examines securities firms for compliance with those rules, and fosters market transparency.

To accomplish its dual mission, FINRA does the following:[2]

1. *Deters misconduct by enforcing the rules.* To safeguard investors against fraud and bad practices, FINRA writes and enforces rules and regulations for all U.S. brokerage firms and brokers, and it examines broker-dealers for compliance with its own rules and also with federal securities laws and rules. FINRA licenses all brokers. FINRA financial examiners perform on-site examinations to assess how brokerage firms are operating, focusing on major risks to the markets and investors.

2. *Disciplines those who break the rules.* If brokers fail to comply with the rules, FINRA may impose a fine or penalty, suspend a violator from the industry for a specified period of time, or bar a violator from the industry.

3. *Detects and prevents wrongdoing.* FINRA monitors trades in the U.S. listed equity market (about six billion shares traded) using data-gathering and analysis technology that has the capability of detecting potential abuses.

4. *Educates and informs investors.* The FINRA website provides investors with tools and resources that can aid them when making investment decisions.

5. *Resolves securities disputes.* Through arbitration and mediation, FINRA resolves securities-related disputes that arise between investors and securities firms or individual brokers.

State regulation In addition to federal securities laws, there are state securities laws. The focus of state laws, referred to as "blue sky laws," is on the issuance of securities and periodic disclosure, as opposed to market regulation. Each state has a regulatory agency responsible for regulating the sale of securities in the state. Every state is a member of the North American Securities Administrators Association, which, although lacking the authority to enforce laws, formulates and recommends model securities laws. What most states use as the basis for their securities laws is the Uniform Securities Act of 1956. Because this act is written broadly, and because the laws may vary from state to state, state securities laws will not be discussed here.

Stock Trading Market Structures

An *exchange* is often defined as a market where intermediaries meet to deliver and execute customer orders. This description, however, also applies to many dealer networks. In the United States, an exchange is an institution that performs this function and is registered with the SEC as an exchange. Some off-exchange markets also perform this function.

There are two overall market models for trading stocks. The first model is order driven, in which buy and sell orders of those public participants who are the holders of the securi-

2. For further discussion, see FINRA's website, www.finra.org/AboutFINRA/WhatWeDo.

ties establish the prices at which other public participants can trade. These orders can be either market orders or limit orders, which we describe in chapter 23. The second model is quote driven, in which intermediaries (i.e., market makers or dealers) quote the prices at which the public participants trade. Market makers provide a bid quote (to buy) and an offer quote (to sell), and they realize revenues from the spread between these quotes. Thus, market makers derive a profit from the spread and the turnover of their stocks.

Order-Driven Markets

Participants in a **pure order-driven market** are referred to as "naturals" (the natural buyers and sellers). No intermediary participates as a trader in a pure order-driven market. Instead, the investors supply the liquidity themselves. That is, the **natural buyers** are the source of liquidity for the **natural sellers**, and vice versa. The naturals can be either buyers or sellers, each using market or limit orders.

Order-driven markets can be structured in two different ways: as a continuous market or as a call auction at a specific point of time. In a **continuous market**, a trade can be made at any moment in continuous time during which a buy order and a sell order meet at a specific time. In this case, trading is a series of bilateral matches. In the **call auction**, orders are batched together for a simultaneous execution in a multilateral trade at a specific point in time. All buy orders at this price and higher and all sell orders at this price and lower are executed.

Continuous trading is better for customers who need immediacy. However, for markets with very low trading volume, an intraday call may focus liquidity at one (or a few) times of the day and permit the trades to occur. In addition, very large orders—block trades—may be facilitated by the feasibility of continuous trading.

Nonintermediated markets involve only naturals; that is, such markets do not require a third party. However, a market may not have sufficient liquidity to function without the participation of intermediaries, who are third parties in addition to the natural buyers and sellers. This leads to the need for intermediaries and quote-driven markets.

Quote-Driven Markets

Quote-driven markets permit intermediaries to provide liquidity. Intermediaries may be **brokers** (who are agents for the naturals); **dealers** or **market makers** (who are principals in the trade); or **specialists**, as on the NYSE (who act as both agents and principals). Dealers are independent, profit-making participants in the process. Dealers operate as principals, not agents. Dealers continually provide bid and offer quotes to buy for or sell from their own accounts and profit from the spread between their bid and offer quotes.

Dealers compete with one another in their bids and offers. Obviously, from the customer's perspective, the "best" market is the highest bid and lowest offer among the dealers. This

Table 22.2
Quote-driven/dealer market.

Stock Alpha				
Bids		Offers		
Dealer	Bid ($)	Dealer	Offer ($)	
A	40.50	C	41.00	Top of the Book:
B	40.35	B	41.10	40.50 (A) / 41.00 (C)
C	40.20	A	41.20	

highest bid/lowest offer combination is referred to as the "inside market" or the "top of the book." For example, assume that dealers A, B, and C have the bids and offers (also called **asking prices**) for hypothetical stock Alpha as shown in table 22.2.

The best (highest) bid is by dealer A of $40.50; the best (lowest) offer is by dealer C of $41.00. Thus, the inside market is the $40.50 bid (by A) and $41.00 offer (by C). Note that A's spread is $40.50 bid and $41.20 offer for a spread (or profit margin) of $0.70. A has the highest bid but not the lowest offer. C has the lowest offer but not the highest bid. B has neither the highest bid nor the lowest offer. For a stock in the U.S. market, the highest bid and lowest offer across all markets is called the **national best bid and offer** (NBBO).

Dealers add value to the transaction process by providing capital for trading and facilitating order handling. With respect to providing capital for trading, they buy and sell for their own accounts at their bid and offer prices, respectively, thereby providing liquidity. With respect to order handling, they provide value in two ways. First, they assist in the price improvement of customer orders; that is, the order is executed within the bid/offer spread. Second, they facilitate the market timing of customer orders to achieve price discovery. Price discovery is a dynamic process that involves customer orders being translated into trades and transaction prices. Because price discovery is not instantaneous, individual participants have an incentive to "market-time" the placement of their orders. Intermediaries may understand the order flow and may assist the customer in this regard. The intermediary may be a person or an electronic system.

The over-the-counter (OTC) markets are quote-driven markets. The OTC markets began during a time when stock quotes were passed over the counter. A customer may choose to buy from or sell to a specific market maker to whom they wish to direct an order. Directing an order to a specific market is referred to as "preferencing."

Order-Driven versus Quote-Driven Markets

Overall, nonintermediated, order-driven markets may be less costly due to the absence of profit-seeking dealers. But the markets for many stocks are not inherently sufficiently liquid to operate in this way. For this reason, intermediated, dealer markets are often necessary for inherently less liquid markets. The dealers provide dealer capital, participate in price discovery, and facilitate market timing.

Because of the different advantages of these two approaches, many equity markets are now **hybrid markets**. For example, the NYSE is primarily a continuous auction order-driven system based on customer orders, but the specialists enhance the liquidity by their market making to maintain a fair and orderly market, and market makers also enhance liquidity. Overall, the NYSE is primarily an auction, order-driven market that has specialists (who often engage in market making), other floor traders, call markets at the open and close, and upstairs dealers who provide proprietary capital to facilitate block transactions. Thus, the NYSE is a hybrid combination of these two models. Another hybrid aspect of the NYSE is that it opens and closes trading with a call auction. The continuous market and call auction market are combined. Thus, the NYSE is a continuous market during the trading day and a call auction market to open and close the market and to reopen after a stop in trading.

Nasdaq, which we describe later in this chapter, began as a descendent of the OTC dealer network and is a dealer quote-driven market. It remains primarily a quote-driven market but has added some order-driven aspects, such as its limit order book, called SuperMontage, which made it a hybrid market.

Figure 22.1 provides an overview of the non-intermediated, auction, order-driven markets and the intermediated, dealer, quote-driven markets in the United States.

Another structural change that has occurred in exchanges is their evolution from membership-owned, floor-traded organizations to publicly owned, electronically traded (that is, no trading floor) organizations. The nature of this evolution (or revolution) was discussed earlier.

U.S. Equity Trading Venues

Broadly speaking, equity trading in the United States occurs mainly through either: (1) national securities exchanges or (2) alternative trading systems. These methods are summarized in figure 22.2. Under the Securities Exchange Act of 1934, a securities exchange must be registered with the SEC under Section 6 of the Act. An **alternative trading system** (ATS), also referred to as an **off-exchange trading venue**, involves the trading of stocks off an exchange which are listed on an exchange, or for the trading of stocks in the after-hours market (when the national exchanges are closed). Under U.S. securities law, an ATS is given the option to register as a registered exchange or as a broker-dealer.[3] For this reason, an ATS can also be classified as a registered securities exchange if it elects to register with the SEC as such.

3. See SEC Release No. 34–40760, http://www.sec.gov/rules/final/34-40760.txt.

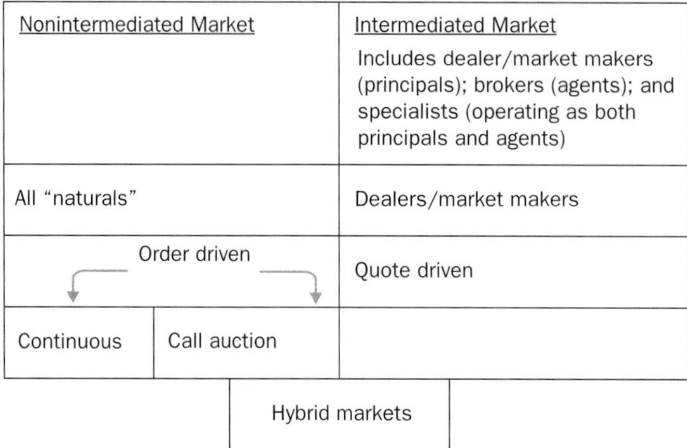

Nonintermediated Market
Intermediated Market
Includes dealer/market makers (principals); brokers (agents); and specialists (operating as both principals and agents)
All "naturals"
Dealers/market makers
Order driven
Quote driven
Continuous
Call auction
Hybrid markets

Figure 22.1
Structure of U.S. stock markets.

In the United States, there are 14 SEC registered securities that trade equities. As explained below, some of the SEC registered exchanges are in fact ATSs that elected to be registered and regulated as national securities exchanges.

When discussing the different types of venues for trading, it is useful to think of the classification of traded stocks in terms of their listing on an exchange. The Securities Exchange Act of 1934 defines two categories of traded stocks. The first is exchange-traded stocks, also called "listed" stocks. The second is what is called OTC stocks, or non-exchange-traded stocks and thus, by inference, "unlisted." We will therefore refer to non-ATS venues as exchanges for trading listed stocks or exchanges for trading unlisted stocks. There is some overlap (and ambiguity) in the use of trading of listed and OTC stocks and the trading of these on exchanges and ATS. Although this is helpful for classifying non-ATS exchanges, it should be pointed out that there are requirements for stocks to be traded on exchanges for unlisted stocks.

Information provided by trading venues is important for market transparency. **Pre-trade transparency** is the disclosure by the trading venue of a stock's supply and demand as measured in terms of bid-ask prices. That information, provided in what is called the **order book**, indicates the liquidity and depth of the market for that stock. **Post-trade transparency** is the disclosure of trades that have been executed on the trading venue.

Transparency is provided by reporting on the Consolidated Quote System and Consolidated Tape System (CTS). Pre-trade transparency is provided by the display of the stock's national best bid and offer (NBBO) on the Consolidated Quote System. The CTS provides

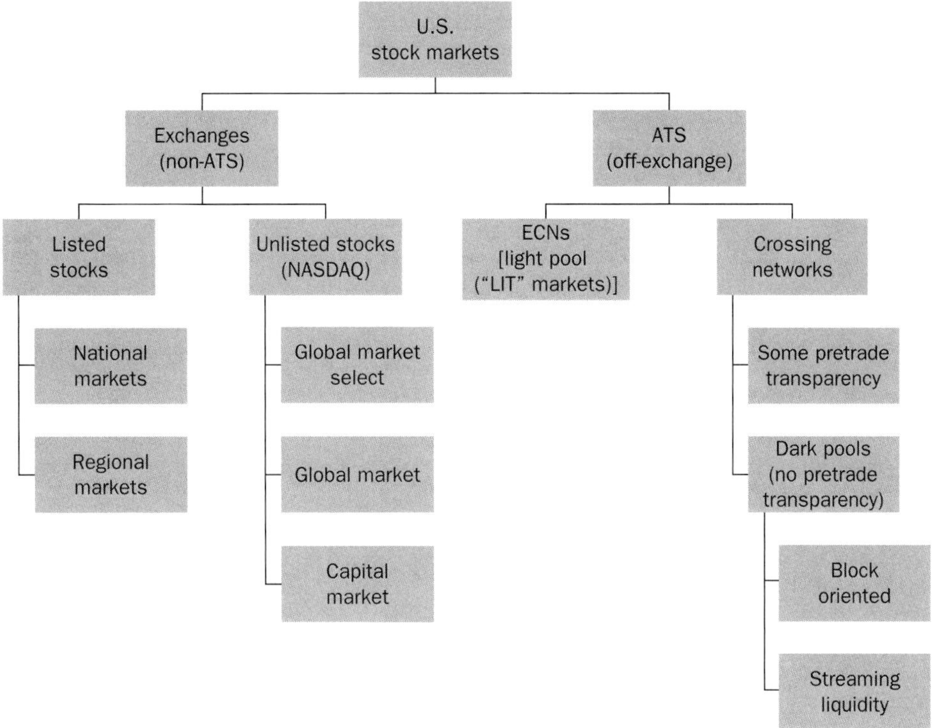

Figure 22.2
U.S. equity trading venues.

post-trade transparency by providing post-trade data, which include the transaction prices and the quantities traded. These topics are considered further below.

Exchange Markets for Listed Stocks

Traditionally, exchange markets have been physical locations that are populated by "members" that use the exchange facilities and systems to exchange or trade listed stocks. Stocks traded on an exchange are said to be listed stocks. To be listed, a company must apply and satisfy requirements established by the exchange for minimum capitalization, shareholder equity, average closing share price, and other criteria. Even after being listed, exchanges may delist a company's stock if it no longer meets the exchange requirements.

Some stocks are traded on regional as well as national stock exchanges. Two kinds of stocks are listed on a regional stock exchange: (1) stocks of companies that either could not qualify for listing on one of the major national exchanges or could qualify for listing but chose not to list there; and (2) stocks, known as **dually listed stocks**, that are also listed on a major national exchange. A company may be motivated to dual list, for example, if a local brokerage firm that purchases a membership on a regional exchange can trade the company's listed stocks without having to purchase a considerably more expensive membership on the national stock exchange where the stock is also listed. Alternatively, a local brokerage firm could use the services of a member of a major national stock exchange to execute an order, but it then gives up part of its commission. The regional stock exchanges compete with the major national exchanges for the execution of smaller trades. Major national brokerage firms route such orders to regional exchanges because of the lower cost they charge for executing orders or better prices.

New York Stock Exchange The major exchange that trades its own listed stocks is the traditional NYSE. A more recent electronic version of the NYSE stock exchange, NYSE Arca, is discussed below. Members trade stocks listed on the traditional NYSE in a centralized continuous auction market at a designated location on the trading floor, called a "post," with brokers representing their customers' buy and sell orders. A single specialist is the market maker for each stock. A member firm may be designated as a specialist for the common stock of more than one company, that is, several stocks can trade at the same post. But only one specialist is designated for the common stock of each listed company.

Prior to 2006, the NYSE was a pure continuous-order market.[4] Such a market is also called a "continuous market" or "continuous auction market." In this type of order-driven market, prices are determined continuously throughout the trading day as buyers and sellers submit orders. The other type of market structure is the order-driven market, characterized by a periodic call auction, or an auction market, in which orders are batched or grouped together for simultaneous execution at preannounced times. Today, the NYSE uses both types of market structures, continuous auction and call auction. More specifically, the NYSE is a continuous auction market during the trading day and a call auction market to open and close the market (as well as to restart trading if a stock has stopped trading). Hence the NYSE can be described as a hybrid market.

A specialist for each stock stands at a trading position around one of the NYSE posts. Each post is essentially an auction site where orders, bids, and offers arrive. In addition to the single specialist market maker on an exchange, member firms of an exchange can trade for themselves or on behalf of their customers. NYSE member firms, which are broker-dealer organizations that serve the investing public, employ brokers on the trading floor who serve as fiduciaries in the execution of customer orders.

4. See the discussion of the equity market structure later in this chapter.

Specialists are required to conduct the auction process and maintain an orderly market in one or more designated stocks. Specialists may act as both a broker (agent) and a dealer (principal). In their role as a broker, or agent, specialists transact customer orders in their assigned stocks, which arrive at their post electronically or are entrusted to them by a floor broker to be executed if and when a stock reaches a price specified by a customer (i.e., a limit or stop order, as discussed in chapter 23). As a dealer or principal, specialists buy and sell shares in their assigned stocks for their own account as necessary to maintain an orderly market. Specialists must always give precedence to public orders over trading for their own account.

Certain types of orders not immediately executed on the trading floor are known as limit orders and stop orders (which are discussed in chapter 23). If the order is a limit or stop order, the member firm's floor broker can wait in the trading crowd or give the order to the specialist in the stock, who enters the order in that specialist's limit order book (or simply the "book") for later execution based on the relationship between the market price and the price specified in the limit or stop order. The book lists the limit and stop orders, arranged by size and nearness to the current market price. The book used to be an actual physical paper book but is now maintained electronically. Traders can see the total limit-order volume at every bid and offer price, allowing for market transparency.

NYSE-assigned specialists have four major roles:

1. As dealers, they trade for their own accounts in any temporary absence of public buyers or sellers, and only after executing all public orders in their possession at the specified price;
2. As agents, they execute market orders entrusted to them by brokers, as well as orders awaiting a specific market price;
3. As catalysts, they help bring buyers and sellers together; and
4. As auctioneers, they quote current bid-ask prices that reflect total supply and demand for each of the stocks assigned to them.

When carrying out their duties, specialists may act as either an agent or a principal. When acting as an agent, the specialist simply fills customer market orders or limit or stop orders (either new orders or orders from the limit order book) by opposite orders (buy or sell). When acting as a principal, the specialist assumes responsibility for maintaining a fair and orderly market. Regulations prohibit specialists from engaging in transactions in securities unless such transactions are necessary to maintain a fair and orderly market. Specialists profit only from those trades in which they are involved; that is, they realize no revenue for trades in which they act as agent.

The term **fair and orderly market** means that a market is characterized by price continuity and reasonable depth. Thus, specialists are required to maintain a reasonable spread between bids and offers and small changes in price between transactions. Specialists are expected to bid and offer for their own account if necessary to promote such a fair and orderly market. They cannot put their own interests ahead of public orders and are obliged to trade on their own account against the market trend to help maintain liquidity and continuity as the price of a stock goes up or down. They may purchase stock for their investment account only if such purchases are necessary to create a fair and orderly market.

Specialists balance buy and sell orders at the opening of the trading day to arrange an equitable opening price for the stock. They participate in the opening of the market only to the extent necessary to balance supply and demand. Although trading throughout the day is conducted as a continuous auction-based system, as explained earlier, the opening is conducted as a single-priced call auction system, as determined by the specialists.

If an imbalance between buy and sell orders either at the opening or during the trading day results in inability to maintain a fair and orderly market, a specialist may, under restricted conditions, close the market in that stock (i.e., discontinue trading) until the specialist is able to determine a price that reestablishes a balance of buy and sell orders. Such closings of trading can occur either during the trading day or at the opening, which is more common, and can last for minutes or days. Closings of a day or more may occur when, for example, one firm acquires another or when a corporation makes an unexpected announcement. (For this reason, many announcements are made after the close of trading.)

NYSE trading officials oversee the activities of the specialist and trading-floor brokers. Approval from these officials must be sought for a delay in trading at the opening or to halt trading during the trading day when unusual trading situations or price disparities develop. Because of their critical public role and the necessity of capital in performing their function as a market maker, specialists are subject to capital requirements imposed by the exchanges.

The description of the NYSE so far might leave the impression that the U.S. market is composed of a specialist-based NYSE; however, the NYSE made considerable strides toward electronic trading by internal development, specifically, the electronic DOT and SuperDOT systems beginning in 1976. But, the greatest changes have been more recent and are due to acquisitions.

The Pacific Exchange was a regional stock exchange based in San Francisco until 2001. In 1999, it became the first U.S. stock exchange to demutualize. Its trading floor in San Francisco was closed in 2002. In 2003, it initiated an electronic options trading platform. In 2005, the Pacific Exchange was bought by Archipelago Holdings, the first all-electronic stock exchange in the United States—this was a significant advancement in stock trading (Archipelago Holdings began in 1996 in Chicago). In February 2006, the NYSE (actually, NYSE Euronext) merged with (through a reverse merger) Archipelago Holdings and changed its name to **NYSE Arca**. (The NYSE demutualized and became the for-profit NYSE Group just before this merger was accomplished.) Thus, NYSE had the first all-electronic stock trading platform in the United States. NYSE Arca is now NYSE's electronic trading platform and has significant trading volume. Arca is owned by the Intercontinental Exchange and is based in Chicago, where Archipelago, its founder, was located. Arca trades options and exchanged-traded funds in addition to stocks.

The NYSE continues to explore new markets. The NYSE is noted for its position with large listed companies and large investors. However, during 2017, it began changing its listing standards and its rule book to attract listings from IPOs by startups. The mechanism for doing this is "direct listing." The large IPO listings they are trying to attract are called "unicorns," which are startups valued $1 billion or more. Direct listings permit companies to trade without raising money (as in the typical IPO), and also no restrictions are imposed regarding when insiders can sell shares.[5]

The NYSE permits unicorns that want to be publicly traded but have sufficient cash to dispense with raising funds, so they do not need an investment banker to do an underwriting.

In a direct listing, a company transfers its shares to an exchange and lets them trade publicly without being underwritten by a Wall Street bank, as is the usual case in an IPO. The approach is often used by companies that are traded in the lightly regulated OTC markets but want to switch to the NYSE or Nasdaq. But it is a rare move for private firms, which typically use IPOs to go public.

Direct listings would allow unicorns to avoid hefty underwriting fees, which can amount to millions of dollars. The listings also could make it easier for existing shareholders of these companies to cash out more quickly. That is because they don't necessarily involve lockup periods, which are rules designed to protect new investors from a deluge of selling by making insiders wait before they can unload shares. Executives can also discuss the company publicly. In a typical IPO, the SEC mandates a quiet period before the offering.

Nasdaq Stock Market: Exchange Market for Unlisted Stocks

An OTC stock market is known as a market for unlisted stocks. There are two such markets. The first is the Nasdaq Stock Market, a national securities exchange registered with the SEC that trades unlisted stocks. The second is the collection of unrelated dealers who make markets in unlisted stocks. With respect to Nasqaq, although this market is referred to as a market for unlisted stocks, certain "listing requirements" must be maintained for a stock to be traded on the Nasdaq Stock Market. Nevertheless, exchange-traded stocks—such as the NYSE stocks—are called **listed,** and stocks traded in the Nasdaq Stock Market are called **unlisted**. Another part of the OTC market, referred to generally as the "third market," is for truly unlisted stocks (i.e., stocks not traded on the Nasdaq Stock Market).

The Nasdaq Stock Market is composed of three market tiers: (1) the Nasdaq Global Select Market; (2) the Nasdaq Global Market; and (3) the Nasdaq Capital Market. Each

5. "'Spotify Rule' Would Benefit the NYSE," *Wall Street Journal*, May 27–29, 2017, p. B1.

market tier has its own financial, liquidity, and corporate governance requirements that must be satisfied to be approved for listing. The corporate governance requirements for all tiers are the same. The most stringent financial and liquidity requirements are for the Nasdaq Global Select Market, the requirements for the Nasdaq Global Market are next, and the requirements for the Nasdaq Capital Market are the least stringent. The market capitalization requirement is such that the Nasdaq Global Select Market includes large market capitalization stocks, the Nasdaq Global Market includes mid-market capitalization stocks, and the Nasdaq Capital Market includes small capitalization stocks.

Nasdaq is essentially a telecommunications network that links thousands of geographically dispersed market-making participants. Its electronic quotation system provides price quotations to market participants on Nasdaq-listed stocks. Although it maintains no central trading floor, Nasdaq functions as an electronic "virtual trading floor." More than 4,100 common stocks trade in the Nasdaq system. More than 500 dealers, known as market makers, representing some of the world's largest securities firms, provide competing bids to buy and offers to sell Nasdaq stocks to investors. Market makers must: (1) continuously post firm two-sided quotes good for most stocks; (2) report trades promptly; (3) be ready for automatic execution against their quotes; (4) integrate customer limit orders into their proprietary quotes; and (5) give precedence to customer limit orders and not place a quote on any system different from their Nasdaq quote unless that system is linked backed into Nasdaq. Many trades are "internalized," which means that a broker-dealer firm acts as market maker when executing on a principal basis the trade of one of its customers. Although not traded on an exchange, these trades must be reported through regular means, as discussed below.

Alternative Trading Systems

As mentioned earlier, ATS are off-exchange trading venues that serve as an alternative to trading on exchanges and for after-hours trading. There are two types of ATSs, electronic communication networks and crossing networks.

Electronic communications networks **Electronic communications networks** (ECNs) display quotes that reflect actual orders and provide members with an anonymous way to enter orders. Essentially, an ECN is a limit order book that is widely disseminated and open for continuous trading to subscribers, who may enter and access orders displayed on the ECN. ECNs offer transparency, anonymity, automated service, and reduced costs; they are therefore effective for handling small orders. Because ECNs provide for pre-trade transparency about orders and post-trade transparency about executed trades, they are referred to as **light pool markets**, as opposed to venues known as dark pools that do not provide pre-trade transparency (we discuss them shortly). It important to note that some ECNs are now going "dark"—that is; they have dark pools. Similarly, some dark pools are being "lit"—they are now providing pre-trade transparency.

ECNs are used to disseminate firm commitments to trade (firm bids or offers) to participants, or subscribers, which typically have either purchased or leased hardware for the operation of the ECN or have built a custom connection to the ECN. In general, ECNs use the Internet to link buyers and sellers, bypassing brokers and trading floors. Examples of ECNs are Bloomberg Tradebook, Track ECN, and LavaFlow.

An ECN's subscribers include institutional and retail investors, market makers, and broker-dealers. In chapter 23, we describe the different types of orders. ECN subscribers can enter such orders into the ECN, and the orders will then be posted by the ECN on the system for other subscribers to view. The listing of the buy and sell orders that subscribers may view is the ECN's order book. The ECN will then electronically match orders to complete the execution. The buyer and seller typically remain anonymous to each other, with the publicly disclosed trade execution reports identifying the ECN as the counterparty to the trade.

The fee structure an ECN charges depends on the type of order. Orders either add to or remove liquidity from the ECN's order book.[6] The fee structure involves a rebate to the party in the transaction that adds liquidity to the ECN's order book and a fee charged to the counterparty. Incentives in the form of higher rebates or lower fees may be offered to subscribers based on trade volume.

Brokers may allow customers direct market access to an ECN, with the fee and the rebate passed through from the broker to the customer.

Crossing networks ATSs allow institutional investors to "cross" trades, typically matching traders directly by computer buyers and sellers.[7] Crossing networks are batch processes that aggregate orders for execution at specified times. Pre-trade transparency varies with the type of crossing network. Crossing networks that do not provide pre-trade transparency are called "dark pools."

For dark pools, post-trade transparency is required, but because the executed transactions are treated as OTC trades, less information is required than for trades on the NYSE. Because there is no pre-trade transparency (i.e., no public displaying of orders), dark pools

6. Later in this chapter, we describe the different types of market orders. An example of an order that adds liquidity to the ECN's order book is a limit order that is not immediately executable (i.e., when for a buy limit order, the limit price is less than the ask price; and for a sell limit order, the limit price is greater than the bid price). When a market order is immediately executable, it removes liquidity from the ECN's order book.

7. The SEC defines crossing networks as "systems that allow participants to enter unpriced orders to buy and sell securities. These orders are crossed at a specified time at a price derived from another market." Securities and Exchange Commission, "Regulation of Exchanges and Alternative Trading Systems," Release Number 34-40760, December 8, 1998, footnote 37.

provide institutional investors with several benefits, including less leakage of information contained in an order, the avoidance of front-running on large orders, and reduced market impact costs (a cost we discuss in chapter 23). With respect to information leakage, the order may be part of a proprietary trading strategy pursued by an intuitional investor, and a displayed order might provide information about such strategies to competitors. There is a concern that other market participants (such as broker-dealers and traders) could front-run the order, with the result that trading costs would be higher than in the absence of a public display of an order.

Some dark pools are either moving in the direction of pre-trade transparency or have done so already. For example, some dark pools use electronic messages to reveal an indication of interest, which is like a firm quotation, to a subset of subscribers.

Dark pools are classified based on the minimum size of transactions that can be traded for each order. **Block-oriented dark pools** set a minimum size for each order, such as 5,000 shares. **Streaming liquidity pools** have no minimum size for any order. Other characteristics of dark pools in addition to trade size are the ownership of the dark pool, who is permitted to trade in a dark pool (i.e., constituencies), price and order discovery, liquidity levels and types, accessibility, and the existence of liquidity partners. Based on the common characteristics of dark pools, Hitesh Mittal has identified five general categories (which are not necessarily mutually exclusive):[8]

- *Public crossing networks:* The traditional dark pools are the public crossing networks started by brokerage firms. Because of the reduction in commissions realized by brokerage firms, these dark pools sought to generate revenue to offset lost commissions. Examples of public crossing networks are POSIT, POSIT Now, BLOCKalert, Liquidnet, NYFIX Millennium, Pipeline, and Instinet CBX. A key feature of public crossing networks that distinguishes them from the other types of dark pools is that there is no proprietary flow from the operator of the dark pool.
- *Internalization pools:* Dark pools that are referred to as "internalization pools" seek primarily to internalize the operator of the dark pool's trade flow. Internalization pools were initially established by the major dealers to generate revenue by executing orders within the trading platform rather than sending those orders to other venues for execution. The constituents of internalization pools are institutional and retail investors and the dark pool operator's trading desk; internalization pools can restrict access to competitors (i.e., other sell-side firms). That is, unlike public crossing networks, not all the liquidity is obtained from external constituents but rather could come from the dark pool operator's market-making arm or its proprietary trading desk. However, because of a concern about the potential lack of liquidity, operators have partnered with other entities to provide liquidity. These

8. Hitesh Mittal, "Are You Playing in a Toxic Dark Pool? A Guide to Preventing Information Leakage," *Journal of Trading* 3, no. 3 (2008): 20–33.

liquidity partners have a special status as constituents that may have an adverse impact on the dark pool's regular customers.[9]

• *Ping destinations:* Two features of ping destinations distinguish them from other dark pools. The first is that if the order placed is not fulfilled immediately, the order is canceled. Such orders are referred to as "immediate or cancel" (IOC) orders and, therefore, unlike in other dark pools, which accept different types of orders, only IOC orders are accepted. The second distinguishing feature is that customers interact only with the dark pool operator's flow. Typically, this type of dark pool is operated by either a hedge fund or an electronic market maker. Customers are typically sell-side firms, not buy-side firms. The decision by the dark pool operator as to whether to accept an IOC order is based on a quantitative model developed by the operator.

• *Exchange-based pools:* Because they are similar in terms of pricing, dark pools classified as exchange-based pools include two types of dark pools. The first are dark pools that are registered with the SEC as national securities exchanges. (Recall that an ATS may elect to be regulated as a national securities exchange or as a broker-dealer.) The second type consists of ECNs and exchanges that create pools of liquidity resulting from hidden orders, where, unlike in other dark pools, the hidden order usually interacts with regular displayed orders. Unlike the other categories of dark pools, which charge a fee on a per share basis, exchange-based pools follow the ECN pricing policy, which provides fees and rebates depending on whether the transacting party is a supplier or a taker of liquidity.

• *Consortium-based pools*: A consortium-based pool is one that is started by several broker-dealers. Unlike an internalization pool operated by one broker-dealer that may not permit access to other sell-side firms (i.e., other broker-dealers), consortium-based pools provide access to their competitors that are sell-side firms. Broker-dealers that are partners in a consortium-based pool typically have an internalization pool for crossing trades so as to generate fee income before they route a trade to the consortium.

Execution of an Order

With the considerable number of venues for the secondary trading of common stock, the processing of an order should be simple. However, that is not at all the case. The large number of alternative venues has created fragmented market making. It is important to understand the process by which an order is executed once it is placed with a broker. The reason is that how the broker ultimately executes the order affects the price at which the trade is executed and therefore the overall effective cost of the trade.

On receiving an order from a customer, a broker must decide how to execute the order. That is, the broker must decide which of the venues described earlier to use to execute the

9. For further discussion of the potential asymmetry of information that may arise, see Mittal, "Are You Playing in a Toxic Dark Pool?" 26–27.

order. When deciding on the venue, the broker has an obligation to find the "best execution" that is reasonably available for customer orders. To do so, the broker considers all customer orders and makes an evaluation of which venue gives the most favorable terms.

When evaluating the alternative venues to obtain the best execution for customer orders, the broker will look for (1) a better price than quoted in the market when the order is placed (referred to as "price improvement"), (2) the likelihood that the order will be executed, and (3) the speed of execution. The speed of execution is important when a market order is placed, because in a fast-moving market, any delays in the execution of an order can result in an inferior price than at the time the order was received. Although the SEC does not set forth any rules that require the execution of an order be completed within a specific time after the order is placed, a brokerage firm that advertises about the speed at which it can execute an order would be expected to execute accordingly.

A customer does have the right to direct the broker to use a particular venue to execute an order, but a cost may be associated with doing so. A fee may be charged by the broker. Assuming that the customer does not specify a venue, the broker's decision as to which venue to direct the order to is as follows. For a stock that is listed on an exchange, the broker has three choices: (1) direct the order to the exchange where the stock is listed, (2) direct the order to a regional exchange, or (3) direct the order to a firm that stands ready to execute the order at publicly quoted prices. For this last alternative, such firms are referred to as **third market makers.** If instead of an exchange-listed stock, the order involves an unlisted stock traded on Nasdaq, the broker may send the order to a market maker on Nasdaq.

To induce brokers to route an order to their venue, regional exchanges, third market makers, and many Nasdaq market makers will pay brokers a fee based on the number of shares directed. This practice is referred to as **payment for order flow**. The broker cannot do this without the approval and knowledge of the customer. When an account is opened, the brokerage firm must inform the customer by written notification whether they receive payment for order flow. This notification must also be provided annually. Moreover, on a trade confirmation, the customer must be told whether the broker received a payment for order flow. If the customer desires, more information about the payment for a trade can be obtained by requesting the information from a broker.

Two other choices are available to a broker for routing an order: (1) a division of the broker's firm that can execute the order or (2) an ECN. When an order is routed internally (i.e., within the brokerage firm), the firm will fulfill the order from its own inventory. This is referred to as **internalization of an order**.

Market Trading Regulation in the United States

Regulation of securities markets, such as the stock market, has three primary objectives: (1) to protect investors, (2) to ensure the smooth functioning of the market, and (3) to reduce systemic risk. When seeking to protect investors, regulation must address information asymmetries between the issuers of securities and investors. This can be achieved through disclosure regulation. The smooth functioning of the market involves trading and settlement rules that minimize the risk of market disruptions. Systemic risk has been discussed in several earlier chapters in this book.

Here our discussion of stock market regulation in the United States focuses on secondary market trading regulation. Recent regulations in this area were the result of financial crises in the stock market that required a major market regulatory overhaul or of high-profile market disruptions that necessitated plugging a regulatory gap. We begin with a brief description of stock market regulation in the United States since the 1960s and then turn to the current regulators. Finally, we look at several key regulations concerned with market volatility. We continue with our review of certain stock market trading regulations in chapter 23, because they require an understanding of trading strategies that regulators have found can cause market disruption.

Regulatory Background

In the 1960s and early 1970s, the U.S. secondary markets for stocks became increasingly fragmented. In a **fragmented market**, some orders for a given stock are handled differently from other orders, as explained earlier in this chapter. Thus, the treatment of the order differs, depending on where it is ultimately executed. A differential treatment of orders may also arise if those orders vary in size, even if they pertain to the same stock and are executed in the same trading venue.

Regulators were concerned that investors did not uniformly receive the best execution, that is, that transactions were not necessarily being executed by a broker on behalf of a customer at the most favorable price available. Another concern with the increased fragmentation of the secondary market for stocks had to do with the growing number of completed transactions in listed stocks that were not reported to the public. This lapse in reporting happened because transactions in the third market and on the regional exchanges were not immediately disclosed on the major national exchange ticker tapes where the stock was listed.

Because of these concerns, Congress enacted the Securities Act of 1975. The most important and relevant provision of this legislation is Section 11A(a)(2), which amended the Securities Exchange Act of 1934 and directed the SEC to "facilitate the establishment of a national market system for securities." The SEC, in its efforts to implement a national market system (NMS), targeted six elements, described as follows by N. S. Posner:[10]

1. A system for public reporting of completed transactions on a consolidated basis (consolidated tape).

10. N. S. Posner, "Restructuring the Stock Markets: A Critical Look at the SEC's National Market System," *New York University Law Review* 56, no. 883 (1981): 916.

2. A composite system for the collection and display of bid and asked quotations (composite quotation system).
3. Systems for transmitting from one market to another both orders to buy and sell securities and reports of completed transactions (market linkage systems).
4. Elimination of restrictions on the ability of exchange members to effect OTC transactions in listed securities (off-board trading rules).
5. Nationwide protection of limit price orders against inferior execution in another market.
6. Rules defining the securities that are qualified to be traded in the NMS.

These six elements required changes in technology, legislative initiative, or both. For example, a consolidated tape, composite quotation system, market linkage system, and system for nationwide protection of limit price orders required changes in technology. The elimination of off-board trading rules and the specification of securities to be included in a national market system required legislative initiative. In fact, changes of both types occurred.

In 2005, various relevant rules were consolidated into Reg. NMS, including the Order Protection Rule (also known as "trade-through rule"), which provides intermarket price priority for quotations that are immediately and automatically accessible (Rule 610). The Order Protection Rule has been controversial, because it requires that trades on a trading venue be transacted at the lowest price rather than on a venue offering the quickest or the most reliable execution.

Reg. NMS is intended to ensure that investors receive the best price executions for their orders by encouraging competition in the markets.

Reg. NMS consists of four different rules:

- "Order Protection Rule" requires trading centers to establish and enforce written policies designed to prevent the execution of trades at prices inferior to protected quotations displayed by automated trading centers;
- "Access Rule" requires fair and nondiscriminatory access to quotations, establishes a limit on access fees to harmonize the pricing of quotations across different trading centers, and requires each national securities exchange and association to adopt and enforce rules that prohibit their members from displaying quotations that lock or cross automated quotations;
- "Sub-Penny Rule" prohibits market participants from accepting, ranking, or displaying orders, quotations, or indications of interest in a pricing increment smaller than a penny, except for orders priced at less than $1.00 per share; and
- "Market Data Rules" update the requirements for consolidating, distributing, and displaying market information.

Overall, the general issue that the SEC has faced is how to design the NMS. Should it be structured as an electronic linkage of existing exchange floors? Or should it be an electronic trading system that is not tied to any existing exchange? After experimenting with several pilot programs, the SEC developed a set of arrangements for listed stocks.

As explained earlier in this chapter, although the market has evolved to an electronic trading platform since 1978, market fragmentation continues.

Market Regulation

Here we describe regulation involving three activities: market volatility, short selling, and insider trading. More on market regulation is provided in the next chapter after we describe the various types of trading arrangements used by investors.

Market volatility rules Market volatility rules involve trading limit rules and circuit breakers.

Trading limit rules **Trading limit** (also referred to as a **price limit**) specifies a minimum price limit below which the market price index level may not decline because of an institutionally mandated termination of trading, at least at prices below the specified price (the price limit), for a specified period of time. For example, suppose that a market index[11] was trading at 11,000 and its price limit was 500 points below that: Then no trades could occur below 10,500. This pause in trading is intended to "give the market a breather" to at least calm emotions. Two different types of price limits are circuit breakers and trading collars. We discuss each here.

Circuit-breaker rules A **circuit breaker** is a temporary halting of trading during a severe market decline. The key to instituting circuit breakers is coordination and infrequency. Coordination across markets is important because of the interrelationship among the stock market, stock index futures market, and stock index options market. We discuss this relationship in chapter 35. The infrequency with which trading was temporarily suspended was emphasized by several government- and exchange-sponsored studies after Black Monday. These studies noted that too frequent halting of trading other than in the case of extreme movements impedes price discovery and does not allow the efficient implementation of portfolio strategies by investors.

Two types of circuit breakers have been adopted to deal with significant market volatility: market-wide circuit breakers and single-stock circuit breakers. The regulations deal with market-wide circuit-breaker rules that would be implemented depending on the level of market volatility. The trading could halt temporarily, or, in the case of extreme market volatility, the market could close before the normal close of the trading session. The stock market indicator selected to measure market volatility for determining trading halts is the S&P 500. The three circuit-breaker thresholds are 7% (Level 1), 13% (Level 2), and 20% (Level 3), with the triggers based on levels that are computed daily from the previous day's

11. We discuss stock market indexes in chapter 23.

closing price of the S&P 500 index. Here is what the three levels mean. If a market decline that is either Level 1 or Level 2 occurs before 3:25 p.m., a market-wide suspension of trading activity will be imposed for 15 minutes; in contrast, if that trigger occurs on or after 3:25 p.m., no market-wide trading halt is required. In the extreme case of a market decline that occurs any time during the trading day triggered by a Level 3 circuit breaker, a market-wide trading halt is required for the balance of the trading day.

Single-stock circuit-breaker rules were adopted by the SEC in response to extreme movements in the prices of many individual stocks that did not result in the triggering of the market-wide circuit breakers. In May 2012, however, the SEC replaced the single-stock circuit-breaker rules with what is referred to as the "limit up–limit down" rule. The previous single-stock circuit-breaker rules were triggered *after* a trade occurred and at times could be triggered by erroneous trades. The intention of the limit up–limit down rule is to prevent trades in individual stocks from being executed outside a specified price band. The price band is established as a percentage level above and below the stock's average price, where the average price is computed over the immediately preceding five-minute trading period. Failure of the price of a stock trading outside the price band to return to a price in the band within 15 seconds results in a five-minute trading halt.

Short selling rules In chapter 18, we described short selling and the mechanism for selling a security short. A short sale is the sale of a security not owned by an investor. The expectation of an investor who shorts a security is that the price will decline, so that the investor can purchase the security at a future date at a price less than the price at which the security was sold. Short selling is illegal only if it done by an investor with an intent to manipulate the market. An example of such a manipulative practice would be an investor entering into a series of transactions with the intent of depressing a security's price so as induce the purchase or sale of the security by others.

Rules adopted by the SEC to deal with short sales include the alternative uptick rule and rules applied to naked short selling. The current short sale price test restriction for stocks, commonly referred to as the **alternative uptick rule**,[12] restricts short selling from further driving down a stock's price that has fallen more than 10% in a single trading day, with the drop being calculated based on the closing price on the previous trading day. If this short-sale-related circuit breaker is triggered, short selling is permitted only if the security's price exceeds the current national best bid.

Although the mechanism for selling short involves borrowing the shorted security to cover the sales, there are short sales where no borrowing occurs or no arrangement is made for borrowing in time for the settlement of the shorted security to the buyer. This is referred to as **naked short selling**. It may result in the short seller not being able to deliver the shorted

12. The reason the rule is referred to as the "alternative" uptick rule is that it replaced a rule for short sales that was part of the Securities Exchange Act of 1934. The alternative uptick rule came into effect in February 2010.

security. A failure to deliver at the required settlement date is referred to as a "fail." Naked short selling is not a violation of SEC regulations. In fact, the practice of short selling may add liquidity to the market. A good example is the liquidity provided by a market maker who stands ready to sell a security continuously throughout the day. The market maker would effectively be pursuing a naked short selling if the market maker did not have the security in inventory and there were no sellers of the security in the market. In its objective of making a market for the security in a fast-moving market, the market maker may not have the time to arrange to cover the security sold through some borrowing arrangement or by the purchase of the security. The SEC adopted rules to deal with the problems associated with failed trades.

Insider trading rules An activity that undermines the confidence that investors have in the fairness and integrity of the stock market is trading in a stock by an insider using material nonpublic information. In general terms, the SEC describes illegal insider trading activity as the trading in a security that is "in breach of a fiduciary duty or other relationship of trust and confidence, while in possession of material, nonpublic information about the security."[13] This is not a legal definition, because the laws dealing with insider trading are shaped by judicial opinions. That is, although Congress gave the SEC responsibility and the enforcement powers (both criminal and civil) to protect investors and maintain the integrity of the market, what constitutes insider trading has been developed on a case-by-case basis under the antifraud provisions of the federal securities laws (principally Section 10(b) of the Securities Exchange Act of 1934, described shortly).

Examples of insiders and illegal insider trading are corporate officers, directors, and employees who trade their corporation's stock following the acquisition of information that is a significant, confidential corporate development. Insider trading violations extend to others who may have received a tip ("tippees") from a person (the "tipper") who had access to material, nonpublic information. Examples of tippees are family members, friends, and business associates of such officers, directors, and employees who trade the securities after receiving such information.[14]

Not all trading by insiders is illegal. That is, corporate insiders can legally buy or sell the stock of their corporation provided the trading activity is not based on material, nonpublic information. Of course, when bringing any legal action against a corporate insider who buys or sells a stock prior to a major movement in the stock, the SEC must demonstrate that the trading activity was based on insider information. Trading their own corporation's stock by corporate insiders must be reported to the SEC within a specified time of the incident.

The federal securities laws covering insider trading are set forth in Section 10(b) of the Securities Exchange Act of 1934, which makes it illegal for individuals

13. See the website http://www.sec.gov/answers/insider.htm.

14. Other noncorporate-related persons who would be treated as insiders include employees of securities firms and government entities who were the recipients of material, nonpublic information as part of their duties.

> to use or employ, in connection with the purchase or sale of any security registered on a national securities exchange or any security not so registered, any manipulative or deceptive device or contrivance in contravention of such rules and regulations as the [SEC] may prescribe.

The SEC adopted Rule 10b-5 to implement Section 10(b). This rule defines when a trade is done on the basis of material nonpublic information. The SEC has two rules that make up Rule 10b-5: Rule 10b-5-1 and Rule 10b-5-2. The former applies to a person who trades on the basis of material nonpublic information if that person at the time of the trade knows that the information in his or her possession is in fact material nonpublic information. Conditions under which permissible trading may be done by an insider are described. For example, an insider is allowed to trade if that information is not a factor in the decision to trade. An example would be an executive who has an established investment plan that specifies the automatic purchase of the corporation's stock at designated time intervals.

The second part of Rule 10b-5, Rule 10b-5-2, applies to nonbusiness relationships' (e.g., family members' and friends') use of material nonpublic information when trading. The rule provides circumstances in which such nonbusiness relationships create what the SEC refers to as a "duty of trust or confidence" that if used by a person would be breached by the disclosure of material nonpublic information and would be considered illegal.[15]

Other Types of Common Stock Trading

Other types of common stock trading vehicles and security types are available to investors.

Offshore Trading

Broker-dealers may trade exchange-listed and Nasdaq equities offshore on foreign exchanges (e.g., the Bermuda Stock Exchange) or OTC through foreign trading desks (e.g., a broker-dealer's London office). In general, such transactions must be reported to a U.S. marketplace (typically the third market) during the next trading day.

Rule 144A Securities

Rule 144A, adopted by the SEC in April 1990, is designed to facilitate secondary market trading in nonfungible unregistered securities among qualified institutional buyers by providing a "safe harbor" from the registration requirements of the Securities Act of 1933. Qualified institutional buyers are institutions with $100 million invested in the securities

15. This rule is based on what the SEC refers to as the misappropriation theory of insider trading, as set forth in Section 10(b). The SEC applies this theory when the disclosing or trading party has no duty to the issuer but "misappropriated" the information from the source of the information, violating a duty of confidentiality to the source of the information.

of issuers not affiliated with the qualified buyer. Basically, Rule 144A permits the issue of nonregistered securities and their purchase by qualified institutions.

American depository receipts (ADRs) are negotiable certificates in registered form, issued in the United States by a U.S. bank, which certify that a specific number of foreign shares have been deposited with an overseas branch of the bank (or another financial institution) that acts as a custodian in the country of origin.

ADRs provide an opportunity for investors who want to invest in the shares of a foreign corporation to buy, hold, and sell their interests in these foreign securities without having to take physical possession of the securities, and while receiving dividends and exercising voting rights conveniently. A holder of an ADR can at any time request the underlying shares. Conversely, ADRs enable foreign corporations with shares that have not been admitted to a U.S. stock exchange to obtain access to the U.S. public capital market. Usually, only shares traded on a recognized foreign stock exchange are represented by ADRs. ADRs are discussed in greater detail below.

When a corporation's equities are traded in a foreign market, they are typically in the form of a **global depository receipt** (GDR), regardless of whether they were issued in the foreign market. GDRs are issued by banks as evidence of ownership of the underlying stock of a foreign corporation that the bank holds in trust. Each GDR may represent ownership of one or more shares of common stock of a corporation. The advantage of the GDR structure to the corporation is that the corporation does not have to comply with all the regulatory issuing requirements of the foreign country where the stock is to be traded. GDRs are typically, but not always, sponsored by the issuing corporation. That is, the issuing corporation works with a bank to offer its common stock in a foreign country through the sale of GDRs.

As an example, consider the U.S. version of the GDR, the ADR, just discussed above. The combination of GDRs and ADRs for a given company is called simply a "depository receipt." The initial success of the ADR structure in the United States resulted in the rise of GDRs throughout the world. ADRs are denominated in U.S. dollars and pay dividends in U.S. dollars, but the basis for these payments is the local currency of the underlying stock. Thus, a change in the exchange rate between the local currency of the underlying corporation and the U.S. dollar will affect the ADR's U.S. dollar price and dividend.

ADRs can be created in one of two ways. First, one or more banks or brokerage firms can assemble a large block of the shares of a foreign corporation and issue ADRs without the participation of the foreign corporation, in which case the ADRs are called **unsponsored ADRs**. The Bank of New York is the leading U.S. depository bank for ADRs. More typically, however, with **sponsored ADRs**, the foreign corporation seeks to have its stock traded in the United States. In these instances, only one depository bank issues the ADRs. Periodic financial reports in English are provided by the issuing corporation to the holders of an ADR.

By construction, ADRs are not a direct holding in the company but a derivative created by a financial institution that holds the underlying securities. The holder of an ADR typically does not have voting or preemptive rights. The decision to treat ADR holders differently from direct stockholders, however, is at the discretion of the company. This distinction sometimes may not be applied.[16]

ADRs can either be traded on one of the exchanges or traded in the OTC market. The unsponsored ADR is typically traded in the OTC market. Because ADRs can be continuously created to meet investor demand, they provide the same trading liquidity as the home market securities they represent.

A U.S. investor who buys an ADR of an international company rather than hold the international stock directly can realize several advantages. First, the investor can trade the stock in a U.S. market (on an exchange or OTC) during U.S. hours and according to U.S. trading practices. Second, the investor makes and receives payments in U.S. dollars rather than foreign currency, although as already mentioned, the investor is subject to foreign exchange risk. Finally, the U.S. investor can use a U.S. custodian rather than a global one, which can be easier and save costs, and in some cases, can avoid some country-specific taxes.

Euro Equity

Corporations may issue equities outside their home market to finance subsidiaries in other countries or to reduce the cost of raising equity capital. In fact, new equity issues may be offered in more than one country simultaneously. The term **euro equity** applies to a stock issue offered simultaneously in several countries by an international syndicate.

U.S. corporations engage in equity offerings that, in addition to the primary U.S. component, include a portion of the issuance reserved for sale in the Euromarkets. This portion of a newly issued stock is referred to as a **euro-equity tranche**. Similarly, European firms offer equity securities with a U.S. tranche. The innovation of the euro-equity markets was not a matter of new equity securities or structures. Instead, the innovation consisted of an efficient international system for selling and distributing equity offerings to various markets in different countries at the same time.

Key Points

- Equity securities represent an ownership interest in a corporation, giving the investor the right to receive the earnings of the corporation when those earnings are distributed in the form of dividends.
- The two types of equity securities are common stock and preferred stock, the latter being a senior corporate security, because it has priority over the common stock in a claim on assets in a liquidation and receives a fixed dividend before common stock holders receive their dividends.

16. Craig Karmin, "ADR Holders Find They Have Unequal Rights," *Wall Street Journal*, March 1, 2001, C1, C15.

- The equity market has changed dramatically over the past 50 years because of (1) the institutionalization of the stock market as a result of a shift away from traditional small investors to large institutional investors, (2) changes in government regulation of the market, and (3) innovation owing largely to advances in computer technology.
- Important consequences of the shifting of the market from one dominated by retail investors to one dominated by institutional investors have included the redesign of equity trading systems to accommodate the types of trading required by institutional investors.
- To ensure that investors are protected against fraudulent practices that might be followed by corporations when issuing stock and by brokers and dealers when executing orders by investors, the equity market is highly regulated.
- Regulation is carried out by the Securities and Exchange Commission (SEC, a federal regulator), the Financial Industry Regulatory Authority (FINRA, a self-regulatory organization), and state regulators.
- The SEC is responsible for (1) interpreting and enforcing federal securities laws; (2) issuing new rules and amending existing rules; (3) overseeing and monitoring market participants; (4) overseeing private self-regulatory organizations involved in the securities field, including accounting and auditing organizations; and (5) coordinating regulation with other federal and state regulators and foreign authorities.
- FINRA is an independent, not-for-profit organization authorized by Congress.
- FINRA's dual objective is to protect investors and to foster market integrity.
- FINRA writes and enforces rules governing the activities of securities firms, examines securities firms for compliance with those rules, and fosters market transparency.
- State securities laws focus on the issuance of securities and periodic disclosure as opposed to market regulation.
- Equity trading in the United States typically occurs either on a national securities exchange or on an alternative trading system.
- The different types of trading venues can be classified in terms of their listing on an exchange: exchange-traded stocks (also called "listed" stocks) and OTC (unlisted) stocks.
- Information provided by trading venues is important for market transparency.
- Disclosure of a stock's supply and demand by a trading venue is referred to as "pre-trade transparency" and is measured by the bid-ask prices for a stock.
- The order book shows a stock's pre-trade transparency information, providing an indication of the liquidity and depth of the market for that stock.
- Pre-trade transparency is provided by the display of the stock's national best bid and offer (NBBO) on the Consolidated Quote System. The Consolidated Tape System provides post-trade transparency by providing post-trade data, including the transaction price and the quantity traded.

• Regional stock exchanges compete with the major national exchanges for the execution of smaller trades. Major national brokerage firms route such orders to regional exchanges because of the lower cost they charge for executing orders or better prices.

• The New York Stock Exchange (NYSE) is the major exchange on which listed stocks are traded.

• On the NYSE, trading is done in a centralized continuous auction market at a designated location by a single specialist who is the market maker for each stock.

• Although at one time, the NYSE was a pure continuous-order market, today it uses both a continuous auction during the trading day and a call auction to open and close the market.

• Specialists are required to conduct the auction process and maintain an orderly market in one or more designated stocks.

• Specialists may act as both a broker (agent) and a dealer (principal).

• A specialist conducts activities so as to maintain a fair and orderly market, which means a market that is characterized by price continuity and reasonable depth.

• The OTC market has two components: (1) the national securities exchange, which is registered with the SEC and trades unlisted stocks, and (2) the third market.

• The national securities exchange registered with the SEC is the Nasdaq Stock Market, which has listing requirements that must be maintained for a stock to be traded on the Nasdaq Stock Market.

• The Nasdaq Stock Market is composed of three market tiers: (1) the Nasdaq Global Select Market, (2) the Nasdaq Global Market, and (3) the Nasdaq Capital Market.

• Nasdaq is essentially a telecommunications network that links thousands of geographically dispersed market-making participants.

• Nasdaq market makers must continuously post firm two-sided quotations good for most stocks.

• Many Nasdaq trades are "internalized," which means that a broker-dealer firm acts as market maker when executing on a principal basis the trade of one of its customers.

• An alternative trading system (ATS) is a trading venue that serves as an alternative to trading on exchanges and for after-hours trading.

• There are two types of ATSs: electronic communication networks (ECNs) and crossing networks.

• ECNs display quotations that reflect actual orders and provide subscribers (which include institutional and retail investors, market makers, and broker-dealers) with an anonymous way to enter orders.

• ECNs provide both pre-trade transparency about orders and post-trade transparency about executed trades and are referred to as "light pool markets."

- The fee structure imposed by an ECN depends on whether the order adds liquidity to or removes liquidity from the ECN's order book.
- Crossing networks are an ATS where orders are aggregated for execution at specified times, with pre-trade transparency varying by crossing network.
- Crossing networks that do not provide pre-trade transparency are called "dark pools." Post-trade transparency is required, but because the executed transactions are treated as OTC trades, less information is required than for a trade on the NYSE.
- When there is no public displaying of orders (i.e., no pre-trade transparency) in crossing networks, dark pools provide institutional investors several benefits: they reduce information leakage contained in an order, avoid front-running of large orders, and lower market-impact costs.
- Dark pools are sorted into five general categories: public crossing networks, internalization pools, ping destinations, exchange-based pools, and consortium-based pools.
- When deciding where to execute a customer's order, a broker has an obligation to find the "best execution" that is reasonably available for customer orders.
- When evaluating alternative trading venues to obtain the best execution, a broker will consider (1) a better price than quoted in the market when the order is placed, (2) the likelihood that the order will be executed, and (3) the speed of execution.
- A broker may route an order to a division of his or her firm for execution. This is referred to as "internalization" of an order.
- Federal regulation of securities markets has three primary objectives: (1) to protect investors, (2) to ensure the smooth functioning of the market, and (3) to reduce systemic risk.
- The U.S. equity market is referred to as a "fragmented market," because some orders for a given stock are handled differently from other orders.
- Trading or price limits specify a minimum price limit, below which the market price index level may not decline because of an institutionally mandated termination of trading, at least at prices below the specified price (the price limit), for a specified period of time.
- A circuit breaker is a condition precipitating a temporary halting of trading during a severe market decline. There are market-wide circuit breakers and single-stock circuit breakers.
- The two rules that the SEC has adopted to deal with short sales are the alternative uptick rule and a rule to deal with naked short selling.
- The purpose of the alternative uptick rule is to restrict short selling from further driving down the price of a stock that has fallen by more than 10% in a single trading day from the closing price on the previous trading day.

• Naked short selling refers to a short sale where no borrowing of the stock occurs or no arrangement with the buyer is made for borrowing in time for the settlement of the shorted security.

• The risk with naked short selling is that the short seller is not able to deliver the shorted security.

• Although there is no legal definition of insider trading, the SEC describes illegal insider trading activity as trading in a security that is "in breach of a fiduciary duty or other relationship of trust and confidence, while in possession of material, nonpublic information about the security."

• What constitutes insider trading has been developed on a case-by-case basis under the antifraud provisions of the federal securities laws.

• Not all trading by corporate insiders is illegal, because they can legally buy or sell the stock of their corporation as long as the trading activity is not based on material nonpublic information.

• The SEC adopted Rule 10b-5-1 and Rule10b-5-2 to implement federal securities law dealing with insider trading.

• Other types of common stock trading vehicles and security types are available to investors: offshore trading, Rule 144A securities, and American depository receipts (ADRs).

• A company may want to list its shares on the exchanges of other countries in order to diversify its sources of capital across national boundaries and tap various funds available globally for investment in new issues. Management may believe that an internationally varied ownership diminishes the prospect of takeover by other domestic concerns, or it may expect foreign listings to boost the company's name awareness and, as a result, the sales of the company's products.

• When a corporation's equities are traded in a foreign market, they are typically in the form of a global depository receipt (GDR), regardless of whether they were issued in the foreign market. GDRs are issued by banks as evidence of ownership of the underlying stock of a foreign corporation that the bank holds in trust.

• The advantage of the GDR structure to the corporation is that the corporation does not have to comply with all the regulatory issuing requirements of the foreign country where the stock is to be traded.

• New equity issues may be offered in more than one country simultaneously. The term "euro equity" is used to describe a new stock offering that is offered simultaneously in several countries by an international syndicate.

Questions

1. "Stocks traded on the Nasdaq are nonlisted stocks." Explain why you agree or disagree with this statement.

2. Explain why the NYSE is described as a "hybrid market."

3. In an alternative trading system, why might only one party to the trade have to pay a transaction fee?

4. "Unlike national securities exchanges, the danger of alternative trading systems is that they are unregulated." Explain why you agree or disagree with this statement.

5. What is the motivation for the use of crossing networks by institutional investors?

6. How does an electronic communications network differ from a crossing network?

7. What is meant by light pool market and dark pool market?

8. What is the difference between a block-oriented dark pool and a streaming liquidity pool?

9. What is meant by the internalization of a trade?

10. a. What is meant by payment for order flow?

b. What are the requirements for a broker to receive a payment for order flow?

c. What is the disadvantage to an investor of requesting a broker to direct an order to a particular venue?

11. a. What are the alternatives available to a broker when executing a trade?

b. What factors must be considered by a broker when determining where to execute a trade?

12. a. What is meant by a circuit-breaker rule?

b. What was the motivation for the adoption of circuit breakers?

13. a. What is the purpose of the alternative uptick rule?

b. What are the risks with naked short selling?

14. "Federal securities law define what illegal insider trading is." Explain whether you agree or disagree with this statement.

15. There is a widespread use of Rule 10b-5-1 trading plans by officers and directors of public companies who regularly possess material nonpublic information but who want to buy or sell stock of their corporation at a time when they are not in possession of material nonpublic information. Usually, a 10b-5-1 trading plan is a contract between the insider and a broker. Why are these plans used by corporate insiders, such as officers and directors?

16. Several academic studies suggest that Rule 10b-5-1 has led to above-market returns. These findings have caught the interest of federal prosecutors and the SEC enforcement staff. Explain why.

17. What is Rule 144A?

18. a. What is a euro-equity issue and a euro-equity tranche?

b. What is the most important innovation that euro equities have achieved?

19. Some stocks are listed on several exchanges around the world. Give three reasons a firm might want its stock to be listed on an exchange in the firm's home country and on exchanges in other countries.

20. What are the differences between a sponsored GDR and an unsponsored GDR?

23 U.S. Common Stock Market: Pricing Efficiency, Trading, and Investment Strategies

CONTENTS

Learning Objectives

After reading this chapter, you will understand:

- equity classes based on market capitalization and style;
- the role played by stock market indexes and how they are constructed;
- the various types of stock market indexes;
- the meaning of market capitalization, large-cap, mid-cap, and small-cap stocks;
- the meaning of growth stocks and value stocks and their definitions;
- what is meant by the pricing efficiency of the stock market and the different forms of pricing efficiency;
- the technical analysis or charting forms of pricing efficiency;
- the difference between the efficient market hypothesis and the random walk hypothesis;
- what macro and micro market efficiency are;
- the evidence on the pricing efficiency of the stock market and the implications for the selection of a common stock strategy (weak, semi-strong, and strong);
- the difference among long-only, long/short, and short strategies;
- the difference between active and passive common stock strategies;
- what is meant by an indexing strategy and a smart beta strategy;
- the advantages of market cap weighting;
- the meaning of fundamental indexing and the definitions and advantages of fundamentally weighted indexes: earnings, book value, and cash flow;
- the Chicago Board Options Exchange Volatility Index;
- the different types of order: market, limit, stop, stop-limit, and market-if-touched, opening, closing, fill-or-kill, good until all answered, and flash orders;

- how margins are calculated: long and short selling;
- the different types of transaction costs: explicit and implicit (impact, timing, and opportunity costs);
- trading mechanisms, such as the types of orders, short selling, and margin transactions;
- the different types of transaction costs beyond brokerage commissions;
- trading arrangements to accommodate institutional traders, such as block trades and program trades; and
- what is meant by high-frequency trading, the different forms of high-frequency trading, and the debate about the impact of high-frequency trading on the stock market.

In chapter 22, we looked at the structure of the U.S. equity market, including trading venues and market regulation. In this chapter, we look at U.S. stock market indexes; the pricing efficiency of the equity market and its implications for common stock investment strategies; and equity trading mechanics, trading costs, and trading strategies.

Equity Asset Classes

As explained in chapter 1, market participants talk about asset classes. Common stock or equity is one of the major asset classes. Based on studies of the performance of different categories of common stock, the market practice is to treat categories of stocks based on market capitalization and style. We discuss each category below.

Asset Classes Based on Market Capitalization

In the second half of the 1970s, many academic studies suggested that simple categorization of stocks should be based on size as measured by market capitalization, because these size categories produced different performance patterns. A company's market capitalization (referred to simply as "market cap") is equal to the total market value of its common stock. It is calculated as follows:

Market cap = Price per share × Number of shares.

The calculation seems straightforward enough, except that "Number of shares" must be defined.

Two methods are used to calculate a company's market cap: the full-market cap method and free-float cap method. In the full market cap method, the number of shares used to calculate a company's market cap is all shares outstanding. In the free-float cap method, the number of shares used is the number of shares available in the market. The reason the number of shares available in the market differs from the free float is that there are shares given to, for example, top management, board members, and key employees. Thus, market cap based on the free-float cap method will produce a lower market cap than that using the full-market cap method.

Many services that calculate market caps for purposes of constructing a stock market index use the free-float market cap method. The reason for using this method to construct a stock market index is that it provides a better indication of the stock market trends, because only those shares available for trade are considered. That is, only the shares of stocks that are available for trading are included.

The following are classified as asset classes for stocks based on market capitalization:

- mega-capitalization stocks (greater than $200 billion),
- large-capitalization stocks ($10 billion to $200 billion),
- mid-capitalization stocks ($1 billion to $10 billion),
- small-capitalization stock ($300 million to $1 billion),
- micro-capitalization stocks ($50 million to $300 million), and
- nano-capitalization stocks (less than $50 million).

Asset Classes Based on Style

In the early 1970s, academic studies found that there were categories of stocks that had similar characteristics and performance patterns. Moreover, the returns of these stock categories performed differently than did those of other categories of stocks. That is, the returns of stocks in a given category were highly correlated, and the returns between different categories of stocks were relatively uncorrelated. Practitioners began to view these categories of stocks with similar performance as a "style" of investing. Today, the notion of an equity investment style is widely accepted in the investment community. The acceptance of equity style investing can also be seen from the proliferation of style indexes published by several vendors, as well as the introduction of futures and options contracts based on some of these style indexes.

There are many ways to classify stocks based on style. The most common is in terms of one or more measures of "growth" and "value." These value/growth style categories have garnered ample empirical support. The most commonly used measure for classifying stocks as growth or value is the price-to-book value per share (P/B) ratio. The use of this measure is justified as follows. A company's earnings growth will increase the book value per share. Assuming that there is no change in the company's P/B ratio, its stock price will increase if earnings grow. Thus, the lower the P/B ratio is, the more the stock looks like a value stock; the higher the P/B ratio is, the more the stock looks like a growth stock.

When classifying stock as value and growth, the notion of "lower P/B" and "higher P/B" is relative. The way in which the stocks comprising a universe of stocks (say, the S&P 500) is placed in one of these two categories is done as follows:

Step 1: Calculate the total market capitalization of all the stocks in the universe.

Step 2: Calculate the P/B ratio for each stock in the universe.

Step 3: Sort the stocks from the lowest P/B ratio to the highest P/B ratio.

Step 4: Calculate the accumulated market capitalization starting from the lowest P/B ratio stock to the highest P/B ratio stock.

Step 5: Select the lowest P/B stocks up to the point where half of the total market capitalization computed in Step 1 is found.

Step 6: Classify the stocks found in Step 5 as value stocks.

Step 7: Classify the remaining stocks from the universe as growth stocks.

Any given growth and value style has a substyle based on some measure of size (market cap), as discussed above. The combinations of style and size are often displayed as in the following grid:

Large value	Large growth
Small value	Small growth

The four cells shown in the above grid have different risk/return combinations. In addition to book value (B), style is often calculated as a ratio to earnings (E); that is, the style ratio is P/E, the price-to-earnings ratio.

Stock Market Indexes

Stock market indexes perform a variety of functions, from serving as benchmarks for evaluating the performance of professional money managers to answering the question, "How did the market do today?" Thus, stock market indexes (or averages) are a part of everyday life. In general, stock market indexes rise and fall in fairly similar patterns. However, the various indexes do not move in exactly the same way at all times. The differences in movement reflect the different methods used for the construction of the indexes. Common stock indexes that are popularly cited in the media, and which are discussed below, are the Dow Jones Industrial Average, the S&P 500 Index, and the Nasdaq Index.

Now let us consider how stock indexes are created. To begin with, every stock index needs a sponsor, whose job it is to define the stocks in the index, collect the prices of these stocks on a daily basis, calculate the index from these prices, and distribute the index to users.

There are two different types of sponsors. The first type of sponsor is the exchange on which the stocks in the index are traded. The New York Stock Exchange Index and the Nasdaq Index are examples of this type of sponsor. The second type is an independent financial organization that defines, calculates, and distributes the index. The Standard & Poor's Indexes and the Dow Jones Industrial Averages are examples of indexes having this type of sponsor.

A sponsor must make three decisions when developing an index from the individual stock prices. The first decision is how to define the general category or universe of the stocks to be included in the index. For example, the S&P 500 is intended to capture large capitalization (cap) U.S. stocks, the Russell 2000 captures small cap U.S. stocks, and the MSCI Developed Country Index captures the non-U.S. stocks from developed countries. Also, among the other categories represented in indexes besides size (large cap and small cap) are style (value and growth) and sector (financial, industrial).

Given the stocks included in the general category, the second decision that must be made is the selection of the specific stocks to be included in the index. The sponsors of some indexes choose the individual stocks in this universe in a transparent, rules-based methodology. The Russell indexes and the MSCI indexes are of this type. For example, the Russell 3000 is composed on an annual basis (on June 30 of each year) of the 3,000 largest stocks (by market cap). Other indexes are chosen by subjective decisions by the organization sponsoring the index. The S&P indexes and the Dow Jones Industrial Average indexes are based on such an ad hoc basis.

The third decision that must be made is the method used for weighting the individual stocks in the overall index, which we discuss next.

Stock Weighting Methods

Three weighting methods have been traditionally used. The first method is **price weighting**; that is, using one share of each stock chosen (or the same number of shares). The second method is **equal weighting**; that is, using equal dollar values (e.g., \$100) of each stock in the index. The third method is market **capitalization weighting** (price multiplied by the number of shares outstanding), that is, equal "cap weighting" values of each stock in the index.

Consider an example where two stocks are chosen to be in an index. Each of these three weighting methods is used to construct a weighted average of these two stock prices. Only the variables used as the weights differ. In our example, we will use two hypothetical stocks, A and B, with prices \$5 and \$25, respectively, and market caps of \$20 billion and \$50 billion, respectively, as shown in table 23.1. The weights calculated according to each method are shown in the table in parentheses. The asset allocations (the percentage of each stock in the index) of A and B for each of the three weighting methods are also shown in the table. These numbers represent the fraction of the index in stocks A and B (i.e., the weight as-

Table 23.1
Stock weights by index weighting methods—hypothetical data.

Stock	Price Weighted	Equal Weighted	Market Cap Weighted
A	16.7% (5/30)	50%	28.6% (20/70)
B	83.3% (25/30)	50%	71.4% (50/70)
Total	100%	100%	100%

Table 23.2
Stock index weighting methods—actual data.

	Price Weight	Equal Weight	Market Cap (in billions)	Earnings (Net Income) (in billions)	Book Value (in billions)
Alphabet	$715.31 (98.2%)	1.00 (50%)	$425.0 (89.0%)	$16.35 (68.9%)	120.33 (80.8%)
Ford	$13.09 (1.8%)	1.00 (50%)	52.4 (11.0%)	7.37 (31.1%)	28.64 (19.2%)
Total	$728.40	2.00	$477.4	$23.72	$148.97
Ratio (Alphabet% / Ford%)	54.6×	1.0×	8.11×	2.2×	4.20×

Note: Index weights are listed in parentheses.

signed to each stock). There is a considerable range of weights for A and B, depending on the weighting method used: from 16.7% (for price weighted) to 50% (for equal weighted) for Stock A.

Table 23.2 provides an example of actual data for calculating these indexes for a stock universe consisting of only two stocks—Alphabet (formerly Google) and Ford Motor—which, let's assume, represent the entire stock market. The data are from May 21, 2016. Again, the three different indexes can be calculated from the data for these two stocks using the three different weighting methods. Note that the weight for Alphabet varies from 98.2% to 89.0% to 50% for the three weighting methods. The weights for Ford Motor vary from 0.098% to 50%. This example shows the very significant changes in the assigned weights for portfolios using these different weighting methods.

Consider the metric for the "size" of a stock that we used in the illustration above—market capitalization. Although other measures of size are considered, the common metric is market capitalization, that is, the number of shares outstanding of the stock times the price of each share.

Historically, the earliest weighting methodology was the price weighted index, adopted for the Dow Jones Industrial Average (DJIA), first published on May 26, 1896. This method involves simply buying one share of each stock in the index. Accordingly, to calculate the value of the index, the index provider simply adds the prices of the stocks and then divides by the number of stocks in the index. This method is still used for the DJIA (it now includes 30 stocks chosen by Dow Jones & Company, not all of which are currently industrials, despite the name given to the index). Thus, the price weighted average index would be tilted toward high priced stocks regardless of their market capitalization.

The equal-weighted method means that an investor selects the same value of each stock in the index. Thus, for an S&P 500 Equal Weighted Index, $1.00 of each of the 500 stocks would be included, for a total portfolio of $500.00 with each stock holding 0.2% (that is, $1.00/$500.00) of the total portfolio. Thus, the biggest and smallest (by market cap) stocks in the S&P 500 would have the same weights in the portfolio, obviously a "tilt" away from large stocks and toward small stocks. There are several equal-weighted S&P 500 mutual funds and exchange-trade funds (ETFs).

Both price weighted and equal-weighted indexes have significant limitations. The only justification for a price weighted index is that when the DJIA was developed in the 1890s, the only data readily available were stock prices. This index remains popular due to its simplicity and history. But the relationship between a stock's price and anything fundamental about the stock is spurious. In this regard, consider the data for ExxonMobil and FedEx on May 20, 2016:

	Price	Market Cap
ExxonMobil	$89.74	$372.12 billion
FedEx	$161.63	$43.39 billion

It seems inappropriate to have an index in which FedEx has a weight 80% higher than that of ExxonMobil ($161.63/$89.74 = 1.80) due simply to the fact that its price is 80% higher and even though ExxonMobil has a market cap that is more than eight times larger than that of FedEx (373.12/43.39 = 8.6).

The equal-weighted index also has a strong small-cap bias, which would cause confounding problems for an investor during a large-cap stock rally. As a result, it is not surprising that most indexes currently employ the third method—the market cap method—as the metric for size, and thus are market cap–weighted indexes.

Let us return to table 23.2, which shows the index weights for Alphabet and Ford Motor for May 21, 2016, for the three weighting methodologies. Note that the resultant weights vary widely for the price weighting, equal weighting, and market cap–weighting calculations. The market cap–weighted index appears to be more reasonable than either the equal-weighted or price-weighted index.

There are also theoretical arguments favoring market cap weighting. First, market cap–weighted portfolios are "macro consistent," meaning that if all investors invested in such a portfolio, all available shares in its universe would be held, and none would be left over, and so the prices would be stable equilibrium prices. With the other weighting methods, it is mathematically impossible for all investors to hold the stocks in this index portfolio at the initial prices. Thus, changes in portfolio holdings would be necessary, and security prices would change for all other weighting methods. Thus, if an investor holds a market cap–weighted portfolio and some market prices change, it is not necessary to rebalance the portfolio weights for the portfolio to continue to replicate the index—that is, the portfolio remains "indexed." Not needing to rebalance to maintain index weights is a major practical and operational advantage of market cap weighting. It also conserves transaction costs. As a result, it is not surprising that most equity portfolio families employ primarily market cap weighting. These families include S&P, Russell, MSCI, and Morningstar.

But there is a major concern about market cap weighting. As mentioned, equal weighting has a small-cap bias. Recently, it has been pointed out that market cap weighting has a large-cap growth bias with, perhaps, some resulting investment disadvantages.

Given its theoretical advantage (macro consistency), operational advantage (no need for rebalancing), intuitive sense that securities should be weighted by size when forming an index, and given that market cap is the common measure of size for equities, it is not surprising that market cap weighting has become the dominant index weighting mechanism.

Recently, however, a limitation of the market cap–weighting method has been recognized. Consider portfolios that were indexed to or just followed generally the S&P 500 index as a benchmark during the tech bubble of 1995 to March 2000. During this period, significant appreciation was realized by large cap growth stocks, primarily due to the technology sector, at the expense of other sectors of the stock market. As this mania for large cap growth technology stocks continued, it became self-propelling because of the indexation process. As investments in large cap growth stocks continued, their prices increased, and as they became a component of the S&P 500 Index, they became overvalued. These investments were funded by the liquidation of large cap value and small cap value stocks. These purchases of larger cap growth stocks occurred due to either strict indexing or using indexing as a general benchmark.

As a result, this process led to large growth stocks becoming more expensive (higher price) due to buying as part of the index, and large and small value stocks becoming cheaper due to their lack of demand (because they were not part of the index). In essence, investors were buying expensive large cap growth technology stocks and selling—or not buying—cheap small cap value stocks. That is, they were "buying high and selling low," hardly an ideal investment strategy. Of course, bubbles always eventually burst, as this one did during 2000–2002. Note in the table below the sharp reversal of the returns of large cap growth and small cap value stocks from 1998, the core of the tech bubble, to 2001 after the bubble burst.

	Returns	
	Large Growth	Small Value
1998	0.3464	−0.0863
2001	−0.1559	0.4024

In the bubble year of 1998, large growth stocks significantly outperformed small value stocks. In the bubble-bursting year of 2001, this pattern reversed.

These results indicate that market cap–weighted index strategies promote overbuying and overselling and thus cause volatile markets. Proponents of this view also proposed an alternative to market cap–weighted indexes. These proponents agree that size is a correct metric for weighting stocks in an index. They assert, however, that market cap is the wrong measure of size. It is the price variable in the market cap metric for size that promotes overbuying and subsequent overselling, basically providing self-fulfilling prophecies. These critics instead assert that the measure of size used should be a "fundamental" variable from corporate financial statements (income statement and balance sheet), rather than a price-based measure. It is the price variable in the size measure that causes the extreme overreactions. These alternate variables include net income, dividends, sales, cash flow, book value, among others. Such indexes weight stock prices by a measure of size, but that measure does not have a self-perpetuating feature, because it does not include the stock price variable. This approach has come to be known as "fundamental indexing." Many mutual funds and ETFs based on fundamental factors have become available. The most common fundamental factors used are net income and dividends. However, market cap–weighted indexes still dominate institutional and individual markets.

Although market cap weighting gives indexes a large-cap and growth bias, weighting by fundamental factors (such as net income and dividends) gives indexes a value tilt.

Major U.S. Stock Market Indexes

As mentioned earlier, stock market indicators can be classified into two groups: those produced by stock exchanges based on all stocks traded on the respective exchange, and those produced by other financial organizations that subjectively select the stocks to be included in an index.

The first group includes the New York Stock Exchange Composite Index, which reflects the market value of all stocks traded on the exchange. The NASDAQ Composite Index also falls into this category, because the index represents all stocks tracked by the Nasdaq system. The second group includes the Dow Jones Composite Index and the S&P's stock indexes, which are produced by other financial organizations.

Some indexes represent a broad segment of the overall stock market, whereas others represent a particular sector, such as technology, energy, or financials. In addition, because the notion of an equity investment style is widely accepted in the investment community, some indexes are based on either of the two equity styles: growth or value. As for growth versus value, growth is the appellation applied to the stock of companies with high earnings growth expectations. That is, the stock is expected to appreciate as the company continues to generate future cash flow increments. In contrast, a value strategy involves investing in stocks that have low expected earnings growth and that the market has somehow undervalued.

Other indexes have separate indexes based on size (that is, on small, medium, or large market capitalization stocks).

NYSE Composite Index The New York Stock Exchange Composite Index includes more than 2,000 stocks, of which approximately 1,600 are from the United States and approximately 360 are foreign. These include American depositary receipts (ADRs), real estate investment trusts (REITs), and foreign listings. The NYSE also provides subindexes on tech/media/telecom, energy, financial, and healthcare. The NYSE uses a free-float market cap–weighting method. These indexes are not widely used in practice.

NASDAQ Composite Index The NASDAQ Composite Index also falls into the second group of stock market indicators. It includes all the stocks traded by Nasdaq. The index includes ADRs, tracking stocks, and limited partnership interests, but is heavily weighted toward information technology stocks. It is market cap weighted. It is one of the most commonly followed indexes in the U.S.

Nasdaq also provides the Nasdaq100 Index, which is based on 100 of the largest nonfinancial companies traded on Nasdaq. Since the tech bubble in 1995–1999, this index has come to be known as the "technology index." Nasdaq also provides less commonly used indexes based on industrials, banks, insurance, other finance, telecommunications, and computers. The Nasdaq100 and other subindexes are modified market cap–weighted indexes (they use rules capping the influence of the largest stocks).

Dow Jones Industrial Average The DJIA originally included 30 large and widely held industrial stocks. The companies included in the average are those selected by Dow Jones & Company, the publisher of the *Wall Street Journal*. The index now also includes technology, financial, and other sector stocks. The company now also provides the Dow Jones Transportation Average (20 stocks) and the Dow Jones Utility Average (15 stocks). The most controversial aspect of the DJIA is that it is price weighted (it is the only major index that is price weighted), most likely due to its early development (in the 19th century). Although price weighted, the price is adjusted for stock splits and other changes.

Standard & Poor's 500 Index Also in the second group, the S&P 500 Index represents 500 large—not necessarily the 500 largest—stocks chosen from the listings of the two major national stock exchanges (NYSE and NASDAQ) and the OTC market. The stocks in the index at any given time are determined by a committee of Standard & Poor's Corporation, which may occasionally add or delete (on no prespecified schedule) individual stocks or the stocks of entire industry groups. The committee has considerable discretion in its choice. A free-float market cap–weighted index is used. (The float is the number of shares available for public trading, not the total number of shares outstanding.)

The S&P 500 is one of the most widely followed U.S. stock indexes and is commonly used as an indicator of the stock market. Standard & Poor's also provides indexes based on size and style. Their size indexes are the Mid-Cap 400 and Small-Cap 600, which along with the large cap S&P 500, provide the S&P Composite 1500, representing the entire stock market. S&P also provides style indexes (growth and value) for each size category. These subindexes are commonly used by investment professionals.

Neither the DJIA nor the S&P indexes have specific rules regarding which stocks must be included in their indexes or the timing of changes; that is, the composition of the indexes is not rules based. Thus, the composition of the indexes is determined by the discretion of the sponsor.

MSCI indexes MSCI Inc., formerly Morgan Stanley Capital International (called "MSCI"), provides a family of U.S. and global stock indexes (as well as fixed income and hedge fund indexes). The U.S. equity indexes are provided in the following categories: Investible Market (2,500 stocks), Prime Market Index (750 stocks), Large-Cap Index (300 stocks), Mid-Cap 450 Index (450 stocks), Small-Cap 1750 Index (1,750 stocks), and Micro-Cap Index.

Russell indexes Another family of nonexchange-sponsored U.S. stock indexes is the Russell Family, Russell Inc. In this family of equity indexes, the broad-based index is the Russell 3000, which is based on the largest 3000 stocks in the United States. The Russell 3000 index is divided into the large cap Russell 1000 and the remaining small cap Russell 2000 Index. These indexes are rebalanced annually, typically scheduled for the closing prices on the last Friday in June. These market caps determine the largest 3,000 stocks and the break-up into the 1,000 and 2,000 stocks. This process is called "reconstitution." This stock selection process is thus completely rules based, unlike the discretionary Standard & Poor's and DJIA processes. There are also growth and value versions of the Russell indexes. These indexes are widely used in practice.

Wilshire indexes The Wilshire 5000 Total Market Index (the Wilshire 5000), sponsored by Wilshire Associates (in Santa Monica, California), is also a market cap–weighted index of most of the common stocks (including REITs) actively traded on the NYSE and Nasdaq. As of year-end 2016, the index had 3,618 stocks. This index has moderate use. Another Wilshire index, the Wilshire 4,500 Completion Index, includes the stocks in the Wilshire 5000 with the stocks in the S&P 500 removed.

In this regard, the number of publicly listed stocks has declined by approximately 50% from 7,322 in 1996 to 3,671 in 2016. The major reasons for this are that the delistings due primarily to mergers, acquisitions, and private equity activity have exceeded initial public offerings.

CBOE Volatility Index Another index which has become very popular in the equity markets is the CBOE Volatility Index (VIX, which stands for "volatility index"). The VIX is not a stock index, but it is a stock-related index. The VIX is a measure of the implied volatility of the S&P 500 index option, which is calculated by the Chicago Board Options Exchange (CBOE) and used by stock traders. The VIX provides a measure of this option's market expectation of the S&P 500 stock market volatility over the next 30-day period. The VIX is quoted as a percentage, which is consistent with its being a volatility. A high VIX measure indicates that the stock market is expected to be very volatile and is regarded as a bearish signal. For this reason, the VIX is regarded as a "fear index." Futures and options contracts on the VIX are available from the CBOE.

Pricing Efficiency of the Stock Market

As explained in chapter 18, a price-efficient market is one in which the security prices at all times fully reflect all available information relevant to their valuation. When a market is price efficient, investment strategies pursued to outperform a broad-based stock market index will not consistently produce superior returns after adjusting for risk and transaction costs.

Numerous studies have examined the pricing efficiency of the stock market. Although it is not our intent in this chapter to provide a comprehensive review of these studies, we can summarize their basic findings and their implications for investment strategies.

Forms of Efficiency

The three different forms of pricing efficiency include (1) a weak form, (2) a semi-strong form, and (3) a strong form. The distinctions among these forms lie in the relevant information assumed to be taken into consideration in the price of the security at all times. **Weak efficiency** means that the price of the security reflects the past price and trading volume of the security. **Semi-strong efficiency** means that the price of the security fully reflects all public information, which includes (but is not limited to) historical price and trading patterns. This information includes, importantly, the financial information provided by the corporation to the SEC. **Strong efficiency** exists in a market where the price of a security reflects all information, whether it is publicly available or is known privately only to insiders, such as the firm's managers or directors. Of course, using inside information may be illegal.

The preponderance of empirical evidence supports the claims that the common stock market is efficient in the weak form. The evidence emerges from sophisticated tests that explore whether historical price movements can be used to project future prices in such a way as to produce returns above what one would expect from market movements and the risk class of the security. Such returns are known as **positive abnormal returns**. The implications are that investors who follow a strategy of selecting stocks solely on the basis of price patterns or trading volume—such investors are often referred to as **technical analysts** or **chartists**—should not expect to do better than the market. In fact, they may fare worse because of higher transaction costs associated with frequent buying and selling of stocks.

The evidence is mixed on whether the stock market is price efficient in the semi-strong form. Some studies support the proposition of efficiency when they suggest that investors who select stocks on the basis of **fundamental security analysis**—which consists of analyzing financial statements, the quality of management, and the economic environment of a company—will not outperform the market. This result is certainly reasonable: so many analysts use the same approach, with the same publicly available data, that the price of the stock remains in line with all the relevant factors that determine value. In contrast, a sizable number of other studies have produced evidence indicating instances and patterns of pricing inefficiency in the stock market over long periods. Economists and financial analysts often label these examples of inefficient pricing **anomalies in the market**, that is, phenomena that cannot be easily explained and often persist. Semi-strong efficiency remains controversial.

Empirical tests of the strong form of pricing efficiency fall into two groups: (1) studies of the performance of professional money managers and (2) studies of the activities of insiders (persons who are company directors, major officers, or major stockholders). Studies of the performance of professional money managers to test the strong form of pricing efficiency are based on the belief that professional managers have access to better information than is available to the general public. Whether this point is true is moot, because the empirical evidence suggests professional managers do not outperform the market consistently. In contrast, evidence based on the activities of insiders generally reveals that this group often achieves higher returns than does the stock market. Of course, insiders could not get those high abnormal returns if the stock prices fully reflected all relevant information about the values of the firms. Thus, the empirical evidence on insider trading argues against the notion that the market is efficient in the strong form sense. This activity is referred to **insider trading** and is not legal.

Efficient market hypothesis and the random walk hypothesis The efficient market hypothesis states that the market incorporates new information completely and quickly. In an efficient market, stock prices behave as if they followed a random walk (sometimes called a "drunken sailor's walk"). According to the random walk hypothesis, at any time, it cannot be determined whether prices will increase or decrease during the next period.

Expressed mathematically, the next period's price, denoted by P_{t+1}, can be expressed as the current period's price, denoted by P_t, plus a random error term denoted by e_{t+1}:

$$P_{t+1} = P_t + e_{t+1}.$$

The serial correlation coefficient is the correlation coefficient between P_{t+1} and P_t. Statistically, the serial correlation coefficient (also called the "autocorrelation coefficient") is the extent to which the price in one period is related to the next period's price.

If the serial correlation coefficient is zero, the returns exhibit a random walk relationship and are random. If the serial correlation is positive or negative, the returns exhibit a relationship and have positive or negative momentum, respectively. Based on annual returns for large cap and small cap stocks, the serial correlation coefficients over the period 1926 to 2016 are both approximately zero (0.02 and 0.06, respectively).[1]

The efficient market hypothesis and the random walk hypothesis are related but not identical. To be efficient, market prices must exhibit a random walk as prices grope toward the efficient level. But prices could exhibit a random walk without being efficient. A pricing model, in addition, is necessary to determine the efficiency of a market. Thus, a random walk is a necessary but not sufficient condition for market efficiency. Calculating the degree of randomness in a series is simple, but determining the efficiency of a market is difficult and remains a controversial topic.

Overall, if a market is highly price efficient, it is impossible to outperform the market consistently and, as a result, a passive strategy is ideal. For active strategies to be appropriate, there must be inefficiencies in market prices that can be exploited. Of course, these active strategies would also have to cover transaction costs to be successful.

Micro versus Macro Stock Market Efficiency

Professor Paul Samuelson, the first winner of the Nobel Prize in Economic Science, made the following comment about stock market efficiency:

> Modern markets show considerable micro efficiency (for the reason that the minority who spot aberrations from micro efficiency can make money from those occurrences and, in doing so, they tend to wipe out any persistent inefficiencies). In no contradiction to the previous sentence, I had hypothesized considerable macro inefficiency, in the sense of long waves in the time series of aggregate indexes of security prices below and above various definitions of fundamental values.[2]

Basically, Samuelson argued that the efficient market hypothesis is likely to work better for individual stocks than for the aggregate stock market. That is, the stock market, according to Samuelson, is "micro efficient" but not necessarily "macro inefficient." This view, referred to as "Samuelson's dictum," has considerable empirical support. Studies have looked for efficiency in the aggregate stock market and in various components of the stock market, such as industries.[3] Inefficiencies in terms of pricing were measured in these studies on the basis of excess volatility (i.e., volatility that should not be excessive in an efficient market).

1. Ibbotson SBBI, *2017 Classic Yearbook* (Chicago: Morningstar, 2017).

2. Cited in Robert J. Shiller, *Irrational Exuberance*, 2nd ed. (New York: Broadway Books, 2001), 243.

3. See, for example, Robert J. Shiller, "Do Stock Prices Move Too Much to Be Justified by Subsequent Changes in Dividends?" *American Economic Review* 71 (1981): 421–436; Stephen F. LeRoy and Richard D. Porter, "The Present Value Relation: Tests Based on Variance Bounds," *Econometrica* 49 (1981): 555–574; John Y. Campbell and Robert J. Shiller, "The Dividend-Price Ratio and Expectations of Future Dividends and Discount Factors," *Review of Financial Studies* 1 (1988): 195–228; John Y. Campbell and Robert J. Shiller, "Stock Prices, Earnings, and Expected Dividends," *Journal of Finance* 43 (1988): 661–676; John Y. Campbell, "A Variance Decomposition for Stock Returns," *Economic Journal* 101 (1991): 157–179; Tuomo Vuolteenaho, "What Drives Firm-Level Stock Returns?" *Journal of Finance* 57 (2002): 233–264; and Jeeman Jung and Robert J. Shiller, "Samuelson's Dictum and the Stock Market," *Economic Inquiry* 43 (April 2005): 221–228.

The studies found that inefficiencies existed at the aggregate stock market level (thereby providing support for macro inefficiency) but not at the industry sector or the individual security level (thereby providing support for micro efficiency).

Implications of Market Efficiency for Investing in Common Stock

Common stock investment strategies can be classified into two general categories: active strategies and passive strategies. **Active investment strategies** attempt to outperform the market by one or more of the following methods: timing the selection of transactions, such as in the case of technical analysis; identifying undervalued or overvalued stocks using fundamental security analysis; and selecting stocks according to market anomalies. Obviously, the decision to pursue an active strategy rests on the belief that some type of gain can be made from such efforts, even after costs, but gains are possible only if pricing inefficiencies exist. The particular strategy chosen depends on what pricing inefficiencies the investor believes are occurring.

Investors who believe that the market is pricing stocks efficiently should accept the implication that attempts to outperform the market cannot be systematically successful, except by luck. This implication does not mean that investors should shun the stock market but instead suggests that they should pursue a **passive investment strategy**, which is one that does not attempt to outperform the market. Is there an optimal investment strategy for someone who holds this belief in the pricing efficiency of the stock market and thereby captures the risk premiums in the stock market? There is. Its theoretical basis is modern portfolio theory and capital market theory, which we discussed in chapter 13. According to modern portfolio theory, the market portfolio offers the highest level of return per unit of risk in a market that is price efficient. A portfolio of financial assets with characteristics similar to those of a portfolio consisting of the entire market—the market portfolio—will capture the pricing efficiency of the market.

But how can such a passive strategy be implemented? More specifically, what is meant by a "market portfolio," and how should that portfolio be constructed? In theory, the **market portfolio** consists of all financial assets, not just common stock. The reason is that investors compare all investment opportunities, not just stock, when committing their capital. Thus, our principles of investing must be based on capital market theory, not just stock market theory. When the theory is applied to the stock market, the market portfolio consists of a large universe of common stocks. But how much of each common stock should be purchased when constructing the market portfolio? Theory states that the chosen portfolio should be an appropriate fraction of the market portfolio; hence the weighting of each stock in the market portfolio should be based on its relative market capitalization. Thus, if the aggregate market capitalization of all stocks included in the market portfolio is \$$T$ and the market capitalization of one of these stocks is \$$A$, then the fraction of this stock that should be held in the market portfolio is \$$A$/\$$T$.

The passive strategy just described is called **indexing**. As evidence mounted about the inability of many investment managers to outperform the stock market on a risk-adjusted basis after transaction costs and fees, the amount of funds managed using an indexing strategy grew substantially. However, index funds still account for a relatively large and still-growing fraction of institutional stock investments.

Traditionally, the benchmarks for indexing strategies have been one of the broad-based market indexes designed around market capitalization weighting, as described earlier in the chapter. However, there has been increasing interest in the use of alternative benchmarks as a low-cost strategy to capture the risk premiums in the stock market. This strategy is referred to as a **smart beta strategy**. The underlying assumption of those who support a smart beta strategy is that, in contrast to indexing, which seeks to replicate the risk premiums embedded in an overall stock market index, a smart beta strategy seeks to capture a risk premium of subsets of the overall stock market by means of a low-cost investment process. To do so, a smart beta strategy requires the identification of systematic risk drivers of stock returns to construct a benchmark (which is referred to as "smart beta") that may offer a better risk/return profile than one of the traditional market cap–weighted stock market indexes.

A hybrid of the pure passive and pure active approaches is the core-satellite strategy, wherein the overall portfolio has a core of large holdings in passive, low-expense holdings in efficient asset classes and satellites around the core consisting of small holdings of more expensive, active noncore holdings.

Common Stock Investment Strategies

Investment strategies pursued by professional money managers can be organized in several different ways. The most common method is to divide strategies into two categories: passive and active, as introduced above.

To begin simply, assume that an investor's portfolio has N stocks, S_1, S_2, …, S_N. The investor wants to develop a portfolio of these N stocks with weights WS_1, WS_2, …, WS_N. Assume also that the investor has selected an index I, which is used as a basis for the portfolio—the index has weights IS_1, IS_2, …, IS_N.

A **passive portfolio**—also called an **index portfolio**—relative to the index I—is one in which: $WS_1 = IS_1$, $WS_2 = IS_2$, …, $WS_N = IS_N$. That is, $WS_i = IS_i$ for all i. The weight of each stock in the portfolio is identical to its weight in the index.

If this is the definition of a passive strategy, what is the definition of an active strategy? The answer is "anything else." That is, at least two of the weights in the portfolio must be different than the weights in the index (obviously, one difference cannot occur alone). As a result, for a given set of N stocks, there is only one passive strategy, but there are an infinite number of active strategies. For $WS_i \neq IS_i$ (for any two or more i), the strategy is active.[4]

4. Note that $\sum_{N}^{i=1} WS_i = \sum_{N}^{i=1} IS_i$ where the WS_i and IS_i are provided as percentages (%) of the whole portfolio.

Note that the return on a pure passive portfolio must equal the return on the index (excluding expenses, which are considered below). Note also that the return on any individual active portfolio may be greater or less than the return on the index; that is, an individual active managed portfolio may outperform or underperform its index, respectively. As stated by William Sharpe, the original findings on this topic are:

> If "active" and "passive" management styles are defined in sensible ways; it *must* be the case that:
>
> (1) before costs, the return on the average actively managed dollar will equal the return on the average passively managed dollar; and
>
> (2) after costs, the return on the average actively managed dollar will be less than the return on the average passively managed dollar.
>
> These assertions hold for any time period.[5]

Basically, "passive" has a singular meeting—it means to match an index exactly, both in composition and weights of the securities therein. But there are many different types of active portfolios.

Traditionally, the two dominant active strategies have been "stock picking" and "market timing." **Stock picking** means overweighting and/or underweighting (including zero weights) some stocks relative to their index. Equity analysts determine which stocks to overweight or underweight by fundamental analysis. **Market timing** refers to shifting between high expected return assets and low expected return assets, depending on the degree of bullish and bearish beliefs of the investor, often shifting between stocks and cash.

Between the polar extremes of passive and active strategies, there are developments on a continuum of strategies based on their "degree of activeness."[6] Some portfolios may deviate from their indexes significantly; others only slightly.

The strategies addressed thus far have had only long positions, that is, where stocks are purchased with cash. These are called "long-only" strategies. Beginning with hedge funds, however, investors have also used short positions. Short positions are achieved by borrowing a company's stock from another party (for example, a broker), selling the stock, and then using the cash from the sale to purchase additional stocks or let it remain in cash. These are called **long-short strategies**. Overall, a long positon is a bullish position; that is, the position profits if the stock price increases. A short position is a bearish position; that is, a short position profits if the stock price decreases. Consequently, long-short strategies

5. William F. Sharpe. "The Arithmetic of Active Management," *Financial Analysts Journal* 47, no. 1 (1991): 7.

6. A recently developed concept, "active share," is a metric that is the percentage difference between the individual holdings of a portfolio and its benchmark; it has been used to measure the degree of difference from the index. For example, an active share of 70% of a portfolio (by market cap) deviates from its index and 30% is consistent with its index. See Antti Petojisto and Martijn Cremers, "How Active Is Your Fund Manager? A New Measure that Predicts Performance," *Review of Financial Studies* 22, no. 9 (2009): 3329–3365.

can be either bullish or bearish, depending on the identities and weights of the long and short positions.[7]

Common Stock Trading Arrangements

Trading arrangements involve the types of orders placed by investors. We begin with the types of orders, margin transactions, trading priority rules, and transaction costs. We then discuss trading arrangements for retail trading and those for institutional investors (block trades and program trades) for coping with the trading needs of institutional investors.

Types of Orders

When an investor wants to buy or sell a share of common stock, the price and conditions under which the order is to be executed must be communicated to a broker. As explained in chapter 18, the simplest type of order is the **market order**, an order to be executed at the best price available in the market. If the stock is listed and traded on an organized exchange, the best price is ensured by the exchange rule that when more than one order on the same side of the buy/sell transaction reaches the market at the same time, the order with the best price is given priority. Thus, buyers bidding a higher price are given priority over those bidding a lower price, and sellers offering a lower price are given priority over those offering a higher price.

Another priority rule of exchange trading is needed to handle the receipt of more than one order at the same price. Most often, the priority in executing such orders is based on the time of arrival of the order—the first orders in are the first orders executed—although higher priority is given to certain types of market participants over other types of market participants seeking to transact at the same price. For example, on exchanges, orders may be classified as either public orders or orders of those member firms dealing for their own accounts (both nonspecialists and specialists). Exchange rules require that public orders be given priority over orders of member firms dealing for their own accounts.

The danger of a market order is that an adverse price movement may take place between the time the investor places the order and the time the order is executed. To avoid this danger, the investor can place a **limit order** that designates a price threshold for the execution of the trade. A **buy limit order** indicates that the stock may be purchased only at the designated price or lower. A **sell limit order** indicates that the stock may be sold at

7. Long-short strategies in general and hedge funds, in particular, comprise a wide variety of strategies of various degrees of activeness. These include, for example: market neutral strategy (long and short positions offset each other completely in market risk), 130% /30% strategy (portfolio includes 130% long positions and 30% short positions), and bear market strategy (short positions more than completely offset the long positions).

the designated price or higher. The key disadvantage of a limit order is that it offers no guarantee that it will be executed at all; the designated price may simply not be obtainable. A limit order that is not executable at the time it reaches the market is recorded in a **limit order book**, as mentioned in the chapter 22.

The limit order is a **conditional order**: It is executed only if the limit price or a better price can be obtained. Another type of conditional order is the **stop order**, which specifies that the order is not to be executed until the market moves to a designated price, at which time it becomes a market order. A **buy stop order** specifies that the order is not to be executed until the market rises to a designated price, that is, until it trades at or above, or is bid at or above, the designated price. A **sell stop order** specifies that the order is not to be executed until the market price falls below a designated price, that is, until it trades at or below, or is offered at or below, the designated price. A stop order is useful when an investor cannot watch the market constantly. Profits can be preserved or losses minimized on a stock position by allowing market movements to trigger a trade. In a sell (buy) stop order, the designated price is lower (higher) than the current market price of the stock. In a sell (buy) limit order, the designated price is higher (lower) than the current market price of the stock. The relationship between the two types of conditional orders, and the market movements that trigger them, appear in table 23.3.

Two dangers are associated with stop orders. Stock prices sometimes exhibit abrupt price changes, so the direction of a change in a stock price may be quite temporary, resulting in the premature trading of a stock. Also, once the designated price is reached, the stop order becomes a market order and is subject to the uncertainty of the execution price noted earlier for market orders.

A **stop-limit order**, a hybrid of a stop order and a limit order, is a stop order that designates a price limit. In contrast to the stop order, which becomes a market order if the stop is reached, the stop-limit order becomes a limit order if the stop is reached. The stop-limit order can be used to cushion the market impact of a stop order. The investor may limit the

Table 23.3
Conditional orders and the direction of triggering security price movements.

Price of Security	Limit Order	Market-If-Touched Order	Stop-Limit Order	Stop Order
Higher than initial price	Price specified for a sell limit order	Price specified for a sell market-if-touched order	Price specified for a buy stop-limit order	Price specified for a buy stop order
Lower than initial price	Price specified for a buy limit order	Price specified for a buy market-if-touched order	Price specified for a sell stop-limit order	Price specified for a sell stop order
Comment	Can be filled only at price or better; does not become a market order until price is reached	Becomes a market order when price is reached	Does not become a market order when price is reached; can be executed only at price or better	Becomes a market order when price is reached

possible execution price after the activation of the stop. As with a limit order, the limit price may never be reached after the order is activated, which therefore defeats one purpose of the stop order—to protect a profit or limit a loss.

An investor may also enter a **market-if-touched order**. This order becomes a market order if a designated price is reached. A market-if-touched order to buy becomes a market order if the market falls to a given price, whereas a stop order to buy becomes a market order if the market price rises to a given price. Similarly, a market-if-touched order to sell becomes a market order if the market rises to a specified price, whereas the stop order to sell becomes a market order if the market falls to a given price. We can think of the stop order as an order designed to get out of an existing position at an acceptable price (without specifying the exact price) and the market-if-touched order as an order designed to get into a position at an acceptable price (also without specifying the exact price).

Orders may be placed to buy or sell at the open or the close of trading for the day. An **opening order** indicates a trade to be executed only in the opening range for the day, and a **closing order** indicates a trade is to be executed only within the closing range for the day.

An investor may enter orders that contain order cancellation provisions. A **fill-or-kill order** must be executed as soon as it reaches the trading floor or it is immediately canceled. Orders may designate the period for which the order is effective—a day, week, or month, or perhaps by a given time within the day. An **open order**, or **good until canceled order**, is good until the investor specifically terminates the order.

An important type of order that is key in a trading strategy discussed later (high-frequency trading) is a **flash order**. With a flash order, the trade must be executed immediately or withdrawn if not executed immediately.

Orders are also classified by their size. One **round lot** is typically 100 shares of a stock. An **odd lot** is defined as less than a round lot. For example, an order of 75 shares of Microsoft is an odd lot order. An order of 350 shares of Microsoft includes an odd lot portion of 50 shares. A **block trade** is defined on the NYSE as an order of 10,000 shares of a given stock or a total market value of $200,000 or more.

Margin Transactions

As explained in chapter 18, investors can borrow cash to buy securities and use the securities themselves as collateral. A transaction in which an investor borrows to buy shares using the shares themselves as collateral is referred to as **buying on margin**. The funds borrowed to buy the additional stock will be provided by the broker, and the broker gets the money from a bank. The **call money rate** or broker loan rate is the interest rate that banks charge brokers for funds for this purpose. The broker charges the borrowing investor the call money rate plus a service charge.

A brokerage firm is not free to lend as much as it wishes to the investor to buy securities. The Securities Exchange Act of 1934 (the "Exchange Act") prohibits brokers from lending more than a specified percentage of the market value of the securities. The initial margin requirement is the proportion of the total market value of the securities that the investor must pay as an equity share, and the remainder is borrowed from the broker. The Exchange Act gives the Board of Governors of the Federal Reserve (the Fed) the responsibility to set initial margin requirements, which it does under Regulations T and U. The Fed changes margin requirements as an instrument of economic policy. The initial margin requirement was previously below 40%; it is 50% as of this writing. Initial margin requirements vary for stocks and bonds.

The Fed also establishes a maintenance margin requirement, which is the minimum proportion of the equity in the investor's margin account to the total market value. If the investor's margin account falls below the minimum maintenance margin (which would happen if the share's price fell), the investor is required to put up additional cash. The investor receives a margin call from the broker specifying the additional cash to be put into the investor's margin account. If the investor fails to put up the additional cash, the broker has the authority to sell the securities for the investor's account.

Let us illustrate maintenance. Assume that an investor buys 100 shares of stock at $60 per share for $6,000 of stock on 50% margin, and the maintenance margin is 25%. By purchasing $6,000 of stock on 50% margin, the investor must put up $3,000 in cash (or other equity) and thus borrows $3,000 (referred to as the **debit balance**). The investor, however, must maintain 25% of margin. To what level must the stock price decline to hit the maintenance margin level? The price is $40. At this price, the stock position has a value of $4,000 ($40 × 100 shares). With a loan of $3,000, the equity in the account is $1,000 ($4,000 – $3,000), or 25% of the account value ($1,000/$4,000 = 25%). If the price of the stock decreases below $40, the investor must deposit more equity to bring the equity level up to 25%. In general, the account level has to decrease to 1.333 times the amount borrowed (the debit balance) to hit the minimum maintenance margin level.

Margin practices also apply in short selling. Let's consider a similar margin example for a short position. An investor shorts (borrows and sells) 100 shares of stock at $60 for a total stock value of $6,000. With an initial margin of 50%, the investor must deposit $3,000 (in addition to leaving the $6,000 from the sale in the account). So the investor has a credit balance of $9,000 (which does not change with the stock price, because it is in cash). However, the investor owes 100 shares of the stock at the current market price. To what level must the stock price increase to hit the maintenance margin level, assumed to be 30% (which is the equity in the account as a percentage of the market value of the stock)? The answer is $69.23, for a total stock value of $6,923. If the stock is worth $6,923, the account contains $2,077 of equity ($9,000 – $6,923), which represents 30% of the market value of the stock ($2,077/$6,923 = 30%). The value of the stock that triggered the maintenance level is calculated by multiplying the credit balance by 10/13 (10/13 × $9,000 = $6,923).

Trading (Transaction) Costs

Investment managers must meet performance standards, which are typically based on the total rate of return of their portfolios. The returns on their portfolios are net of transaction (or trading) costs. One-half of one percentage point in return can substantially affect a manager's record. Therefore, an important aspect of an investment strategy is controlling the transaction costs necessary to implement the strategy. The measurement of trading costs, although important, is difficult.[8]

Institutional investors have developed computer-automated programs to enter trading orders to minimize the costs associated with trading, which we discuss below. The use of computer programs for this purpose is known as **algorithmic trading**. Once an institutional investor makes a decision to buy or sell a large stock position, the program partitions the trade into several smaller orders to minimize transaction costs.

We begin by defining trading costs. Trading costs can be decomposed into two major components: explicit costs and implicit costs. **Explicit trading costs** are the direct costs of trading, such as broker commissions, fees, and taxes. **Implicit trading costs** represent such indirect costs as the price impact of the trade and the opportunity costs of failing to execute in a timely manner or at all. Whereas explicit costs are associated with identifiable accounting charges, no such reporting of implicit costs occurs.

Explicit costs The main explicit cost is the commission paid to the broker for execution. Commission costs are fully negotiable and vary systematically by broker type and market mechanism. The commission may depend on both the price per share and the number of shares in the transaction. In addition to commissions, other explicit costs include custodial fees (the fees charged by an institution that holds securities in safekeeping for an investor) and transfer fees (the fees associated with transferring an asset from one owner to another).

Competition and computer technology have driven down the bid-ask spread for stocks to as little as one penny per share. The decline in explicit trading costs began with the elimination of fixed commissions by the SEC on May 1, 1975, commonly called "May Day." After this date, trading fees were set by market competition. Prior to 2001, stock prices were quotes in increments of one-eighth of a dollar, or 12.5 cents. In 2001, the SEC eliminated this pricing practice and moved to decimalization, which resulted in the spreads declining to as little as one penny per share. In the opinion of some analysts, the impact of decimalization compares to that of the end of fixed commissions.

8. For more on this point, see Bruce M. Collins and Frank J. Fabozzi, "A Methodology for Measuring Transactions Costs," *Financial Analysts Journal* 47, no. 2 (1991): 27–36.

Implicit costs **Implicit trading costs** include impact costs, timing costs, and opportunity costs.

The **impact cost** of a transaction is the change in market price resulting from supply/demand imbalances caused by the presence of the trade. Bid-ask spread estimates, although informative, fail to capture the fact that large trades—those that exceed the number of shares the market maker is willing to trade at the quoted bid and ask prices—may move prices in the direction of the trade. That is, large trades may increase the price for buy orders and decrease the price for sell orders. The resulting market impact or price impact of the transaction can be thought of as the deviation of the transaction price from the "unperturbed price" that would prevail if the trade did not occur. Crossing networks, discussed in chapter 22, are designed to minimize impact costs.

Timing cost is measured as the price change between the time the parties to the implementation process assume responsibility for the trade and the time they complete the trade. Timing costs occur when orders sit on the trading desk of a buy-side firm (e.g., an investment management firm) but are not yet released to the broker, because the trader fears that the trade may swamp the market.

Opportunity cost is the "cost" of securities not traded. This cost results from missed or only partially completed trades. These costs are the natural consequence of the release delays. For example, if the price moves too much before the trade can be completed, the manager will not make the trade. In practice, this cost is measured on shares not traded, based on the difference between the market price at the time of decision and the closing price 30 days later.

Although commissions and impact costs are actual and visible out-of-pocket costs, opportunity costs and timing costs are the costs of forgone opportunities and are invisible. Opportunity costs can arise for two reasons. First, some orders are executed with a delay, during which the price moves against the investor. Second, some orders incur an opportunity cost, because they are only partially filled or are not executed at all.

Research on trading costs Overall, although the trading commission is the most obvious, measurable, and discussed trading cost, it is only one of the four types of trading costs and, in fact, may be the smallest. The implicit trading costs, however, are much more difficult to measure.

Studies about transaction costs allow us to draw several conclusions:

1. Although considerable debate still surrounds how to measure trading costs, the consensus is that implicit trading costs are economically significant relative to explicit costs (and also relative to realized portfolio returns).
2. Equity trading costs vary systematically with trade difficulty and order-placement strategy.
3. Differences in market design, investment style, trading ability, and reputation are important determinants of trading costs.

4. Even after researchers control for trade complexity and trade venue, trading costs vary considerably across managers.

5. The accurate prediction of trading costs requires more detailed data on the entire order-submission process than are available, especially information on pre-trade decision variables.

Trading Arrangements for Institutional Investors

With the increase in trading by institutional investors, trading arrangements more suitable to these investors have developed. Institutional investors' needs include trading in large size and trading groups of stocks, both at a low commission and with low market impact. These requirements resulted in the evolution of special arrangements for the execution of certain types of orders commonly sought by institutional investors: (1) orders requiring the execution of a trade of many shares of a given stock and (2) orders requiring the execution of trades in many different stocks as simultaneously as possible. The former types of trades are called **block trades**; the latter are called **program trades**. An example of a block trade would be a mutual fund that seeks to buy 15,000 shares of Apple Inc. stock. An example of a program trade would be a pension fund that wants to buy shares of 200 companies at the end of a trading day.

The institutional arrangement that accommodates these two types of institutional trades is a network of trading desks of the major securities firms and other institutional investors that communicate with one another by means of electronic display systems and telephones. This network is referred to as the "upstairs market." Participants in the upstairs market play a key role (1) by providing liquidity to the market so that such institutional trades can be executed and (2) through arbitrage activities that help integrate the fragmented stock market.

Block trades On the NYSE, Rule 72 defines a **block** as either trades of at least 10,000 shares of a given stock or trades of shares with a market value of at least $200,000, whichever is less. For institutional investors, because the execution of large numbers of block orders places strains on the specialist system, the NYSE implemented special procedures to handle them. Typically, an institutional customer contacts its salesperson at a brokerage firm, indicating that it wishes to place a block order. The salesperson then gives the order to the brokerage firm's block execution department. It should be noted that the salesperson does not submit the order to be executed to the exchange where the stock might be traded or, in the case of an unlisted stock, try to execute the order on the Nasdaq system.

The sales traders in the block execution department then contact other institutions to attempt to find one or more institutions that would be willing to take the other side of the order. That is, they use the upstairs market in their search to fill the block trade order. If the sales traders cannot find enough institutions to take the entire block (e.g., if the block trade order is for 30,000 shares of Apple Inc., but only 25,000 can be "crossed" with other institutions), then the balance of the block trade order is given to the firm's market maker.

The market maker must then decide how to handle the balance of the block trade order. The brokerage firm can take a position in the stock and buy the shares for its own account. Or the unfilled order can be executed by using the services of competing market makers. In the former case, the brokerage firm is committing its own capital.

NYSE Rule 127 states that if a member firm receives an order for a large block of stock that might not be readily absorbed by the market, the member firm should nevertheless explore the market on the floor, including, where appropriate, consulting the specialist as to the specialist's interest in the security. If a member firm intends to cross a large block of stock for a public account at a price that is outside the current quotation, it should inform the specialist of its intention.

NYSE block volume is facilitated by upstairs traders, but it is not the case that all block trades are facilitated by upstairs trading desks and then brought to the floor to be printed. There is a difference between upstairs-facilitated trades and block trades. A block trade is defined by its size, not by the method of execution. Although negotiation in the informal upstairs market provides better execution than does execution in the downstairs market (i.e., on the NYSE trading floor) for large trades, these differences are economically small.

Program trades **Program trades** involve the buying or selling large numbers of stocks simultaneously. Such trades are also called **basket trades**, because effectively, a "basket" of stock is being traded. The NYSE defines a program trade as any trade involving the purchase or sale of a basket of at least 15 stocks with a total value of $1 million or more.

The two major applications of program trades are asset allocation and index arbitrage. With respect to asset allocation trades, some examples of why an institutional investor may want to use a program trade are to deploy new cash into the stock market; to implement a decision to move funds invested in the bond market to the stock market, or vice versa; and to rebalance the composition of a stock portfolio because of a change in investment strategy. For example, a mutual fund money manager can move funds quickly into or out of the stock market for an entire portfolio of stocks through a single program trade. All these strategies relate to asset allocation.

Program trading is also used for a strategy called **index arbitrage**. In chapter 33, we will discuss futures contracts traded on stock indexes, called "stock index futures." In chapter 35, we will discuss how the price of a futures contract derives from the underlying cash product. In the case of a stock index futures contract, the underlying cash product includes all of the stocks making up the stock index. Specifically, a mathematical relationship exists between the price of the stock index and the value of the stocks included in the index, taking into account transaction costs and the cost of borrowing funds. This relationship establishes bounds for the price of the stock index futures contract. When the price of the stock index futures contract moves outside these bounds, an opportunity arises for riskless profits to be obtained by trading the stocks in the index and the futures contract.

Unfortunately, the popular press often uses the terms "program trading" and "index arbitrage" interchangeably, which is incorrect. One is an investment strategy (index arbitrage), and the other is an institutional trading arrangement (program trading), even though a program trade is necessarily employed to implement an index arbitrage.

Another confusion is worth noting. Because computers are used to execute a program trade, the popular press often wrongly characterizes program trading as computerized trading. Program trading does not have to be, and generally is not, computer initiated. Sometimes computer algorithms facilitate the decision process, and almost always computers help route the trade to each individual stock in the program, but traders make the decisions and implement them.

High-Frequency Trading

One of the most significant market developments in recent years, according to the SEC, is **high-frequency trading** (HFT).[9] HFT is a form of trading that leverages high-speed computing, high-speed communications, tick-by-tick data, and technological advances to execute trades in as little as milliseconds. High-speed trading strategies use computerized quantitative models (i.e., algorithms) that identify which stocks to buy or sell, as well as the quantity, price, timing, and location of the trades. HFT was first applied to the stock market. Today, however, it is also used in the bond market and the derivatives markets. Our focus here is on its use in the stock market. The SEC estimates that HFT is typically more than 50% of the total volume in U.S.-listed equities, concluding that "by any measure, HFT is a dominant component of the current market structure and likely to affect nearly all aspects of its performance."[10]

There is no universally accepted definition of HFT. Martin Wheatley, chief executive officer of the Securities and Futures Commission in Hong Kong and former deputy chief executive of the London Stock Exchange, defines HFT as "the execution of trading strategies based on computer programmes or algorithms to capture opportunities that may be small or exist for a very short period of time."[11] Four characteristics that Wheatley identifies as being associated with HFT are (1) a high volume of trades on a daily basis, with a low level of profits per trade; (2) an extremely short stock holding period; (3) the submission of numerous orders; and (4) no significant open position overnight. How to quantify these characteristics is a matter of debate. One proposed definition is to define high-frequency traders (HFTers) as those traders who hold positions between 10 milliseconds

9. Securities and Exchange Commission, "Concept Release on Equity Market Structure," Securities Exchange Act Release 34–61358, 75 FR 3594, 3606, January 21, 2010.

10. Securities and Exchange Commission, "Concept Release on Equity Market Structure," 45.

11. Martin Wheatley, "We Need Rules to Limit the Risk of Superfast Trades," *Financial Times*, September 20, 2010. Available at http://www.ft.com/cms/s/0/ad7f31f6-c4cd-11df-9134-00144.

and 10 seconds.[12] Execution times are often expressed in microseconds. However, the SEC adopts a somewhat less precise definition, defining HFTers as professionals acting in a proprietary capacity and able to generate many trades per day.

There is considerable controversy over HFT's impact on financial markets in terms of the cost of trading to investors. Two events brought the issue of HFT to the forefront of the investing public's and regulators' attention. The first was the severe market disruption that occurred on May 6, 2010, as a result of HFT, known as the "flash crash." On the afternoon of that trading day, the major stock market indexes (as well as the stock index futures contracts, described in chapter 33) had declined by 4% relative to their closing price on the prior trading day. This decline came about because of the news at the opening of trading about the European debt crisis. In a matter of minutes, the stock market index dropped by 5% to 6%. But that loss was not sustained. Almost as quickly, the market rebounded, ending the trading day with a loss of 3% from the prior trading day.[13] The descriptor "flash" used to describe the crash refers to the fact that the orders placed were flash orders (i.e., orders that are executed immediately or withdrawn if not executed immediately).

The second was the publication in March 2014 of Michael Lewis's book *Flash Boys: A Wall Street Revolt,* dealing with HFT, which concluded that the stock market is rigged by HFT investors. This set off a barrage of criticisms of Lewis and other opponents of HFT because of their failure to understand the wide range of trading activities in which HFT is used. This is not to say that the concerns over certain types of trading strategies used by HFTers were not legitimate. However, a blanket statement about the adverse market impacts of HFT per se reflected a failure to understand the various uses of HFT. As noted by BlackRock Inc., the world's largest asset management firm, in a position paper on HFT, some of these uses are constructive in the market: They have a legitimate purpose and provide benefits to market participants. Other users of HFT deploy it "to manipulate the market or disadvantage end-investors." BlackRock refers to such use as "predatory" HFT, stating that these "practices constitute market abuse and should be treated as such in law."[14]

How does HFT differ from what we referred to as "program trading," discussed earlier? Both use algorithmic trading with no human intervention. The difference lies in the use of algorithmic trading by an institutional investor for orders that are so large that, if executed

12. Michael Kearns, Alex Kulesza, and Yuriy Nevmyvaka, "Empirical Limitations on High Frequency Trading Profitability," faculty paper, University of Pennsylvania, Philadelphia, September 2010. Available at http://www.cis.upenn.edu/~mkearns/papers/hft.pdf.

13. As reported in "Findings Regarding the Market Events of May 6, 2010: Report of the Staffs of the CFTC and SEC to the Joint Advisory Committee on Emerging Regulatory Issues," September 30, 2010. Available at http://www.sec.gov/news/studies/2010/marketevents-report.pdf.

14. Barbara Novick, Richie Prager, Hubert de Jesus, Supurna VedBrat, and Joanne Medero, "Viewpoint: US Equity Market Structure: An Investor Perspective" (New York: BlackRock, April 2014). Available at http://www.blackrock.com/corporate/en-es/literature/whitepaper/viewpoint-us-equity-market-structure-april-2014.pdf.

at one time, they would have an excessive price impact. That is a legitimate use of rapid, algorithmic trading. A computer algorithm in that case merely breaks up the order into many smaller orders, which are fed into the marketplace over time. The SEC recognizes that "these large order algorithms should not be classified as HFT because they typically enable institutional investors to establish or liquidate positions with time horizons far beyond the primarily intraday horizons characteristic of HFT."[15]

HFT is engaged in by a wide variety of entities, including electronic market makers, proprietary desks, hedge funds, and institutional investors. Many of these firms are privately held proprietary trading firms or hedge funds. The biggest players in HFT reportedly include the electronic market makers and the proprietary trading desks of large banks. The technology goal of HFTers is to reduce latency (i.e., delay) in placing, filling, confirming, or canceling orders; the business goal is typically to profit from small arbitrage opportunities present at short time horizons.

The SEC classifies HFT strategies according to strategy:

- *Passive market-making strategy:* A passive market-making strategy primarily involves the submission of orders by electronic market makers that cannot be executed immediately, because the order seeks a price better than that available in the market. Such orders provide liquidity to the marketplace at specified prices. As such, they are quite different from flash orders and do not depend on the direction of the market.
- *Arbitrage strategies:* Arbitrage strategies generally seek to capture pricing disparities between related products or markets. An example is index arbitrage, described earlier, in which an investor seeks to capture pricing discrepancies between the cash equity market and stock index futures market. These strategies depend on the convergence of prices rather than on directional price movements.
- *Structural trading strategies:* Structural trading strategies seek to exploit structural vulnerabilities in the market. An example is a trader who has access to low- to lowest-latency market data and computer algorithms and who can profit by trading with market participants on a trading venue that is offering executions at stale prices.
- *Directional trading strategies:* Such strategies generally entail taking a long or a short position in the market in anticipation of a directional price movement (i.e., either an up or a down movement). There are two types of directional strategies: (1) an order anticipation strategy, which seeks to uncover the existence of large buyers or sellers in the marketplace and then front-run those trades in anticipation that those large orders will move market prices, and (2) a momentum ignition strategy, which seeks to create a rapid price movement by initiating a series of orders and trades.

15. SEC Staff of the Division of Trading and Markets, "Equity Market Structure Literature Review Part II: High Frequency Trading," U.S. Securities and Exchange Commission, March 18, 2014, p. 5.

BlackRock, for example, regards the use of HFT for passive market making a type of HFT that "brings tangible benefits to our clients through tighter spreads and by delivering intermediation in a fragmented trading landscape."[16] In this chapter, we have already described the need for arbitrage activities to maintain an efficient market. The concerns surrounding HFT have mostly to do with directional trading and structural trading strategies. A structural trading strategy in which HFTers use information advantages obtained from special access to market data is the best example of a predatory HFT strategy. Many of the directional trading strategies, as the SEC notes, are not new. Instead, it is the technology that gives HFTers pursuing directional trading strategies the opportunity to better identify and execute trading strategies. Even prior to HFT, front-running (using order-anticipation strategies) and market manipulation (using momentum-ignition strategies) were illegal.

The failure of lawmakers to understand the various types of HFT strategies and program trading strategies has led to proposals to impose regulations to limit the impact of HFT. One such proposal that is most often suggested as an effective way to limit the impact of HFT entails the imposition of a *financial transaction tax*. The problem with such a tax is that by attempting to mitigate the potential impact of predatory HFT, it would significantly reduce trading volume, liquidity, and price discovery, thereby dramatically affecting all market participants. Some have argued that one effective way to reduce the adverse impact of predatory HFT already exists: the use of circuit breakers, which we discussed in chapter 22.

One way to address the speed-advantage issue available to HFTers relative to other investors is by providing access to data centers and co-location at a reasonable cost. Co-location is one of the tools used by proprietary firms that engage in HFT. To further reduce latency, HFTers place their trading servers at the trading venues to be close to the exchange matching engines. This is commonly referred to as "co-location." Carol Clark, a financial markets and payments system risk specialist in the Chicago Federal Reserve's financial market group, remarks that it is estimated that for each 100 miles the server is located away from the matching engine, 1 millisecond of delay is added to the time it takes to transmit trade instructions and execute matched trades or to access the central order book, where information on buy/sell quotations and current market prices is warehoused. A trading venue that operates its own data centers, as well as third parties that host matching engines of trading venues, offer co-location as a service. For example, the NYSE completed a nearly 400,000-square-foot data center facility in Mahwah, New Jersey, to attract in co-location large Wall Street banks, traditional brokerages, and hedge funds. The center's 40 gigabyte per second standard hardware will allow it to handle up to a million messages a second; new trading technology will reduce latency to 10 microseconds. The SEC is undertaking an analysis of the impact of co-location on long-term investors and market quality.

A survey paper by Charles Jones at the Columbia Business School delivered the following conclusion about HFT:

16. Novick et al., "Viewpoint: US Equity Market Structure," 2.

Based on the vast majority of the empirical work to date, HFT and automated, competing markets improve market liquidity, reduce trading costs, and make stock prices more efficient. Better liquidity lowers the cost of equity capital for firms, which is an important positive for the real economy. Minor regulatory tweaks may be in order, but those formulating policy should be especially careful not to reverse the liquidity improvements of the last twenty years.[17]

Key Points

- Common stock is typically classified based on market capitalization; the three most common classes are small, medium, and large market capitalizations.
- In addition to market capitalization, a universe of common stocks can be classified as either value or growth stocks based on their price-to-book value ratio.
- Stock market indexes can be classified into two groups: (1) those produced by stock exchanges and include all stocks to be traded on the exchange, and (2) those for which a committee subjectively selects the stocks to be included in the index.
- Some indexes represent a broad segment of the stock market, whereas others represent a particular sector, such as technology, energy (oil and gas), and financials.
- Three forms of pricing efficiency follow according to what is hypothesized to be the relevant information embodied in the price of a stock at all times: (1) weak form, (2) semi-strong form, and (3) strong form.
- Most of the empirical evidence appears to suggest that markets are efficient in the weak form.
- The evidence for the semi-strong form of market efficiency is mixed because of observed pockets of inefficiency. Empirical tests of strong-form pricing efficiency also produce conflicting results.
- Paul Samuelson's dictum asserts that the stock market is "micro efficient" but not necessarily "macro inefficient."
- Common stock investment strategies can be classified into two general categories: active strategies and passive strategies.
- Active strategies attempt to outperform the market by one or more of the following: timing the selection of transactions, such as in the case of technical analysis; identifying undervalued or overvalued stocks using fundamental security analysis; or selecting stocks according to market anomalies.
- The optimal strategy to pursue when the stock market is perceived to be price efficient is passive indexing, because it allows the investor to capture the efficiency of the market.

17. Charles M. Jones, "What Do We Know about High-Frequency Trading?" Columbia Business School Research Paper 13-11 (New York: Columbia University Business School, March 20, 2013). Available at http://ssrn.com/abstract=2236201 or http://dx.doi.org/10.2139/ssrn.2236201.

- Smart beta is an alternative low-cost passive strategy that has been suggested for capturing the risk premiums in the stock market that cannot be captured by market capitalization–weighted indexes.
- A core-satellite strategy is a hybrid of the pure passive and pure active approaches.
- According to the random walk hypothesis, at any time, it cannot be determined whether prices will increase or decrease during the next period.
- Different types of orders may be submitted to the stock markets.
- The most common type of order is a market order—an order that must be filled immediately at the best price.
- Other types of orders, such as stop and limit orders, are filled only if the market price reaches a price specified in the order.
- For a flash order, the trade must be executed immediately or withdrawn if not executed immediately. These orders are used by certain types of high-frequency traders.
- Several components of costs are associated with trading.
- Although a brokerage commission is the most obvious type of trading cost and the object of competition among broker-dealers for both institutional and retail investors, other types of trading costs may exceed the brokerage commission. Such costs include impact costs and opportunity costs.
- Block trades are trades of 10,000 shares or more of a given stock or trades with a market value of $200,000 or more.
- Program trades, or basket trades, involve the buying or selling of large numbers of names (stocks) simultaneously. The institutional arrangement developed to accommodate these needs is the upstairs market, which is a network of trading desks of the major securities firms and institutional investors that communicate with one another by means of electronic display systems and telephones.
- Buying on margin is a transaction in which an investor borrows to buy shares using the shares themselves as collateral.
- In a margin transaction, the funds borrowed to buy the additional stock are provided by the broker, and the investor is charged the call money rate or broker loan rate to borrow the funds.
- Institutional investors have developed automated computer programs to enter trading orders to minimize the costs associated with trading. The use of computer programs for this purpose is known as algorithmic trading.
- Trading costs can be decomposed into explicit costs and implicit costs.
- Explicit trading costs are the direct costs of trading, such as broker commissions, fees, and taxes.

- Implicit trading costs represent such indirect costs as the price impact of the trade and the opportunity costs of failing to execute in a timely manner or at all.
- The main explicit cost is the commission paid to the broker for execution.
- Implicit trading costs include impact costs, timing costs, and opportunity costs
- The impact cost of a transaction is the change in market price resulting from supply/demand imbalances caused by the trade.
- Timing cost is measured as the price change between the time the parties to the implementation process assume responsibility for the trade and the time they complete the trade; it is the result of orders remaining on the trading desk of an investor that have not yet been released to the broker because the trader fears that the trade may swamp the market.
- Opportunity cost is the "cost" of securities not traded as a result of missed trades or only partially completed trades.
- Explicit trading costs are often the smallest components of trading costs.
- Because of the significant increase in trading by institutional investors, trading arrangements more suitable to these investors developed: block trading and program trades.
- Block trading and program trades allow institutional investors the opportunity to trade in large size and trading groups of stock at a low commission and with low market impact.
- Block trades allow for orders requiring the execution of a trade of many shares of a given stock.
- Program trades allow for orders requiring the execution of trades in many different stocks as simultaneously as possible.
- High-frequency trading (HFT) is a form of trading that leverages high-speed computing, high-speed communications, tick-by-tick data, and technological advances to execute trades in as little as milliseconds using computerized quantitative models (i.e., algorithms) that identify which stocks to buy or sell, as well as the quantity, price, timing, and location of the trades.
- Four characteristics of HFT are (1) a high volume of trades on a daily basis with a low level of profits per trade, (2) an extremely short stock holding period, (3) the submission of numerous orders, and (4) no significant open position overnight.
- There is considerable controversy over HFT's impact on financial markets in terms of the cost of trading to investors.
- The SEC classifies HFT strategies into four categories: passive market-making strategies, arbitrage strategies, structural trading strategies, and directional trading strategies.
- Latency means "speed" and refers to the time it takes to complete an execution. HFTers refer to latency in milliseconds and even microseconds.

Questions

1. Why are stocks categorized in terms of market capitalization?

2. In 2002, a leading sponsor of global indexes shifted to the free-float method for calculating market capitalization. What does this mean?

3. What is the key measure used when classifying stocks as either value or growth stocks?

4. What is the difference between a market value–weighted index and an equally weighted index?

5. What are the main features of the S&P 500 common stock index?

6. "The stocks selected for the S&P 500 are the largest 500 companies in the United States." Indicate whether you agree or disagree with this statement.

7. Some participants and analysts in the stock market are called "chartists" or "technical analysts." What does the theory that the market is weak-form efficient say about these investors' chances of beating the market?

8. Why should an investor who believes that the market is efficient pursue an indexing strategy?

9. Discuss the choice of a trading strategy—active versus passive—depending on the degree of market efficiency of the market being analyzed.

10. Explain what is meant by "fundamental indexing."

11. Proponents of a smart beta strategy believe that it can offer superior returns in the long run over an indexing strategy in which the benchmark is a market capitalization index. Explain why.

12. The following quotation is taken from Wayne H. Wagner:

> When a trader decides how to bring an order to the market, he or she must deal with some very important issues; to me, the most important is: What kind of trade is this? It could be either an active or a passive trade. The type of trade will dictate whether speed of execution is more or less important than cost of execution. In other words, do I want immediate trading (a market order); or am I willing to forgo the immediate trade for the possibility of trading less expensively if I am willing to "give" on the timing of the trade (a limit order)?[18]

a. What is meant by a "market order"?

b. Why would a market order be placed when an investor wants immediate trading?

c. What is meant by a "limit order"?

d. What are the risks associated with a limit order?

13. What is meant by "algorithmic trading"?

18. Wayne H. Wagner, "The Taxonomy of Trading Strategies," in *Trading Strategies and Execution Costs,* ed. Katrina F. Sherrerd (Charlottesville, VA: Institute of Chartered Financial Analysts, 1988).

14. Suppose that Ms. Martinez purchased the stock of XYZ for $90 and that she sets a maximum loss that she will accept on this stock at $85. What type of order can Ms. Martinez place?

15. Why would a block trade or program trade be used by an institutional investor?

16. What is the difference between a block trade and a program trade?

17. How is a program trade used by an institutional investor?

18. The following statements are taken from Greta E. Marshall's article in the proceedings of a conference held in New York City on December 3, 1987:

> There are three components of trading costs. First there are direct costs which may be measured—commissions. Second, there are indirect—or market impact—costs. Finally, there are the undefined costs of not trading.[19]

a. What are market impact costs, and what do you think the "undefined costs of not trading" represent?

> Market impact, unlike broker commissions, is difficult to identify and measure.

b. Why is market impact cost difficult to measure?

19. The following statement appears in a report to the Joint Advisory Committee on Emerging Regulatory Issues, September 30, 2010:

> Generally, a customer has a number of alternatives as to how to execute a large trade. First, a customer may choose to engage an intermediary, who would, in turn, execute a block trade or manage the position. Second, a customer may choose to manually enter orders into the market. Third, a customer can execute a trade via an automated execution algorithm, which can meet the customer's needs by taking price, time or volume into consideration. Effectively, a customer must make a choice as to how much human judgment is involved while executing a trade.[20]

Explain each of these alternatives for executing a large trade.

20. Charles Schwab, chairman of the brokerage firm Charles Schwab Corporation, came out with the following statement in support of the conclusion in Michael Lewis's book *Flash Boys* that markets are rigged because of high-frequency trading: "High-frequency trading is a growing cancer that needs to be addressed." He concluded that HFT "is a technological arms race designed to pick the pockets of legitimate market participants," and "a scam … that [regulators] should simply make illegal." Explain whether you agree or disagree with this statement.

21. In an invited editorial appearing in *The Journal of Portfolio Management*, the founder of Vanguard, John Bogle, made the following two statements about Michael Lewis's book *Flash Boys*.

19. Greta E. Marshall, "Execution Costs: The Plan Sponsor's View," in *Trading Strategies and Execution Costs* (New York: Institute of Chartered Financial Analysts, 1988).

20. "Findings Regarding the Market Events of May 6, 2010."

a. Explain whether you agree or disagree with the following statement.

Flash Boys, by best-selling author Michael Lewis, regaled the financial community with its polemic on the rise of HFT. "The stock market is rigged," Lewis told the huge television audience watching *60 Minutes*, without explaining precisely what that meant. "Wall Street has gone insane," he intoned to the *Guardian*, which described his view that his calling is "a moral crusade." But he seems to have largely ignored the vital role of HFT in reducing the frictional costs of trading to minuscule levels. Lewis is particularly strident on the harm HFT does to ordinary individual investors. But it is here that he seems most clearly wrong. Yes, he sees lots of smoke in HFT, but finds the most fire is where that smoke is virtually absent. Retail investors who trade for themselves are beneficiaries of the new trading environment, with lower trading costs and faster market access.[21]

b. What are the "well-founded concerns" that Mr. Bogle refers to in the following statement?

HFT is a long way from perfection. There are well-founded concerns—and heated arguments pro and con—about front-running by insiders (based largely on knowledge of pending transactions); huge volumes of cancelled orders (from HFT firms, as well as others); those mysterious dark pools; and outlandish profits earned by HFT firms.

21. This and the following statements are from John Bogle, "No Speed Limits: High-Frequency Trading and Flash Boys," *Journal of Portfolio Management* 40, no. 4 (2014): 1.

24 Non-U.S. Equity Markets

CONTENTS

Learning Objectives

After reading this chapter, you will understand:

- the motivation for investors investing outside their domestic stock market;
- what the major changes in global exchanges in the past two decades have been;
- the major non-U.S. stock market indexes;
- the U.K. and European stock market regulatory systems;
- the implications of the United Kingdom's Big Bang;
- the structure and regulation of the Chinese stock market;
- the three major stock exchanges in China—Shanghai, Shenzhen, and Hong Kong—and their differences;
- the role of state-owned enterprises in the development of the Chinese economy and in the Chinese stock market; and
- the differences between A-shares, B-shares, and H-shares traded on the Chinese stock exchanges.

In the previous two chapters, our focus was on the various aspects of the U.S. equity markets. We complete this three-chapter suite with a treatment of the non-U.S. equity markets. This chapter begins with a review of the non-U.S. equity markets—developed, emerging (developing), and frontier (pre-emerging) markets. Because the Chinese equity markets are relatively young but are very large, growing quickly, and quite complicated, we discuss the Chinese equity markets in more detail.

Although non-U.S. equities have become a large component of the investment portfolio of many institutional investors, retail (individual) investors can also invest in these markets. As can be seen in table 24.1 below, North America (the United States and Canada[1]) represented approximately 44% of the Financial Times Stock Exchange (FTSE) Global All Cap Index as of April 30, 2017. Most individual investors do not typically trade non-U.S. stocks directly but instead obtain exposure via collective vehicles that invest in individual countries or regions (such as mutual funds and exchange-traded funds) and depositary receipts (ADRs and GDRs).

Rationale for Investing Outside the Home Equity Market

Investors have a choice of investing solely in their home equity market or expanding their portfolio to include the stocks of companies outside their home market. For example, a French investor can invest solely in stocks of French companies and traded in the French

1. Mexico is not included because it is an emerging equity market as described later in this chapter.

stock market or can invest in not only French companies but also in companies trading in other European countries, Asian companies, and North American companies. Why do investors bother to invest outside their home equity market? There are several reasons for doing do.

The major reason that is often cited is that investing in the companies outside their home market is diversification. Recall our discussion in chapter 13, where we described the Markowitz efficient frontier and how that efficient frontier impacted the correlation between assets. The argument for investing outside the home market is that the stock market return correlations are less than one and therefore, there is the opportunity to "push out" the efficient frontier. "Pushing out the efficient frontier" means that a given level of expected return can be achieved at a lower level of risk. Economists have argued that this is a "free lunch." Whether they are right is an empirical question. Some studies support correlation levels between country stock market returns that can produce this outcome. However, other studies show that as the world has become more integrated, correlations have approached one, particularly during a financial crisis.

The second rationale is that there are different levels of market efficiency in different countries. Hence, although the home equity market may or may not offer the opportunity to obtain superior returns due to market inefficiency, there are countries that may be far less efficient.

However, investing outside one's home market opens an investor to other issues that must be considered, such as liquidity, taxation, and other types of risk (specifically, different credit risks, country risk, and currency risk).

Non-U.S. Equity Markets

Table 24.1 shows the composition of the global equity markets according to a well-known global stock market index, the Financial Times Stock Exchange (FTSE) Global All Cap Index, as of April 30, 2017.

As explained in chapter 1, countries and their equity markets are typically divided into three categories: developed, emerging (developing), and frontier (pre-emerging). The differences among these three types are based mainly on two factors: the development of their economies and the development of their capital markets.[2] Their economic development refers mainly to their per capita income and their potential growth. Developed countries have higher levels of per capita income but lower potential growth. The development of their capital markets refers to the size of their market capitalization, the level of liquidity, and the development of their supporting regulatory and legal bodies. These characteristics affect the growth potential, risk, and liquidity of investments in their markets. Developed

2. "What Is the Difference between a Developed, Emerging, and Frontier Market?" May 11, 2012. http://www.nasdaq.com/article/what-is-the-difference-between-a-developed-emerging-and-frontier-market-cm140649.

Table 24.1
Country composition of the FTSE Global All Cap Index, April 30, 2017.

Country	Share of FTSE Global All Cap Index (%)
Europe	
United Kingdom	6.0
France	3.1
Germany	3.0
Switzerland	2.8
Spain	1.1
Sweden	1.1
Netherlands	1.1
Other	2.7
Subtotal	20.9
Pacific	
Japan	8.0
Australia	2.4
South Korea	1.7
Hong Kong	1.2
Other	0.6
Subtotal	13.9
Emerging Markets	
China	2.2
Taiwan	1.5
India	1.2
Other	4.0
Subtotal	8.9
North America	
United States	53.0
Canada	3.1
Subtotal	56.1
Middle East	0.2

countries are found mostly in North America, Western Europe, and Australasia, including the United States, Canada, Germany, the United Kingdom, Australia, New Zealand, and Japan.

An emerging (developing) market is a country that has some of the characteristics of a developed market but not all of them. Developing countries include the BRICs (Brazil, Russia, India, and China); and the PIIGS (Portugal, Ireland, Italy, Greece, and Spain). As shown in table 24.1, emerging market companies comprise 8.9% of the FTSE Global All Cap Index, with 2.2% in China, 1.5% in Taiwan, 1.2% in India, and 4.0% in other emerging markets. Notice that North America (the United States and Canada) represents 56.1% of the global equity market, the other developed countries (Europe and the Pacific) represent 34.8%, and emerging market countries represent 8.9%. The Middle East represents the final 0.22%.

A frontier or pre-emerging market is one that is too small and undeveloped to be considered an emerging market. These markets are smaller, less liquid, and less accessible than emerging markets, but nevertheless "investable." These markets tend to have high expected long run returns and low correlations with other markets. There are 21 markets that MSCI considers frontier markets, as shown in table 24.2.

Overall, less-developed countries have higher risks and higher potential returns, not an unusual trade-off when investing in financial markets.

There are several methods for classifying stock markets. In this chapter, we use the Morgan Stanley Capital International (MSCI) market classification, which is a family of indexes constructed and maintained by that organization. Its structure and current data are provided in table 24.2.[3] MSCI's broadest index is the MSCI ACWI Index (ACWI stands for "All Country World Index"). As shown, this broad index is divided into the categories of developed markets, emerging markets, frontier markets, and standalone markets. Each is further divided into geographical regions. In general, the emerging market sector has been grouped in several different ways. The most commonly used grouping is the BRIC group. These four countries were thought to be of similar levels of development. Subsequently, South Africa was added to this group to form the BRICS.[4] Interestingly, as of year-end 2017, China was the second largest global stock market but remains a developing market.

Table 24.3 provides basic data on the 20 largest global equity exchanges.. Global equity data on a frequent basis (daily or weekly) are found for many countries, exchanges, and sectors in the *Wall Street Journal*, *Barron's*, *The Economist*, and *Bloomberg*.

Stock Market Indexes

Stock market indexes are provided in all global countries and exchanges. In every country where stock trading takes place, at least one index measures general share price movements on the domestic exchange. If a country has more than one stock exchange, each exchange usually has its own index. Non-exchange financial institutions also provide stock market data as explained in chapter 22 News organizations and financial advisory services create and distribute indexes.

3. https://www.msci.com/market-classification, table 2 results from MSCI's Annual Classification Review, which is communicated every June.

4. Jonathan Lemco, "Are Emerging Markets Still Built on BRICS?" Vanguard, May 2016. https://institutional.vanguard.com/VGApp/iip/site/institutional/researchcommentary/article/InvResEmergingMarketsBRICS.

Table 24.2
Global stock indexes.

MSCI ACWI and Frontier Markets Index

A. Developed Markets

Americas	Europe	Pacific
Canada	Austria	Australia
United States	Belgium	Hong Kong
	Denmark	Japan
	Finland	New Zealand
	France	Singapore
	Germany	
	Ireland	
	Israel	
	Italy	
	Netherlands	
	Norway	
	Portugal	
	Spain	
	Sweden	
	Switzerland	
	United Kingdom	

B. Emerging Markets

Americas	Europe, Middle East, and Africa	Asia
Brazil	Czech Republic	China
Chile	Egypt	India
Colombia	Greece	Indonesia
Mexico	Hungary	Korea
	Qatar	Philippines
	Russia	Taiwan
	South Africa	Thailand
	Turkey	
	United Arab Emirates	

C. Frontier Markets

Americas	Europe and the Commonwealth of Independent States	Africa	Middle East	Asia
Argentina	Croatia	Kenya	Bahrain	Bangladesh
	Estonia	Mauritius	Jordan	Pakistan
	Lithuania	Morocco	Kuwait	Sri Lanka
	Kazakhstan	Nigeria	Lebanon	Vietnam
	Romania	Tunisia	Oman	
	Serbia			
	Slovenia			

D. Standalone Markets

Saudi Arabia	Jamaica	Bosnia Herzegovina	Botswana	Palestine
	Trinidad	Bulgaria	Ghana	
	Tobago	Ukraine	WAEMU	
			Zimbabwe	

Source: "MSCI—Who We Are," https://www.msci.com/market-cap-weighted-indexes.

Table 24.3
Twenty largest global stock exchanges by market capitalization, January 31, 2015.

Rank	Exchange	Economy	Headquarters	Market Cap (billion U.S. $)	Monthly Trade Volume (billion U.S. $)
1	New York Stock Exchange	United States	New York	19,223	1,520
2	Nasdaq	United States	New York	6,831	1,183
3	London Stock Exchange Group	United Kingdom Italy	London	6,187	165
4	Japan Exchange Group—Tokyo	Japan	Tokyo	4,485	402
5	Shanghai Stock Exchange	China	Shanghai	3,986	1,278
6	Hong Kong Stock Ex-change	Hong Kong	Hong Kong	3,325	155
7	Euronext	European Union	Amsterdam Brussels Lisbon London Paris	3,321	184
8	Shenzhen Stock Exchange	China	Shenzhen	2,285	800
9	TMX Group	Canada	Toronto	1,939	120
10	Deutsche Borse	Germany	Frankfurt	1,762	142
11	Bombay Stock Exchange	India	Mumbai	1,682	11.8
12	National Stock Exchange of India	India	Mumbai	1,642	62.2
13	SIX Swiss Exchange	Switzerland	Zurich	1,516	126
14	Australian Securities Exchange	Australia	Sydney	1,272	55.8
15	Korea Exchange	South Korea	Seoul	1,251	136
16	OMX Nordic Exchange	Northern Europe, Armenia	Stockholm	1,212	63.2
17	JSE Limited	South Africa	Johannesburg	951	27.6
18	BME Spanish Exchanges	Spain	Madrid	942	94.0
19	Taiwan Stock Exchange	Taiwan	Taipei	861	54.3
20	BM&F Bovespa	Brazil	São Paulo	824	51.1

Source: World Federation of Exchanges, www.world-exchanges.org/statistics/monthly-reports.

Exchange-Provided Indexes

Here we review exchange-provided stock indexes for four countries: Japan, the United Kingdom, Germany, and France. Chinese stock indexes are described later in this chapter.

Japan has two major stock indexes. The Tokyo Stock Exchange produces the Tokyo Stock Price Index, or TOPIX. This composite index is based on all shares in the Tokyo market's First Section, a designation reserved for established and large companies whose shares are most actively traded and widely held. The TOPIX is computed based on the included firm's market cap. The second major Japanese index is sponsored by the financial information firm, Nihon Keizai Shimbun Inc., which also calculates and publishes the Nikkei 225 Stock Average. This average, computed in the same way as the Dow Jones 30, is based on the prices of 225 of the largest companies in the First Section.

The U.K.'s London Stock Exchange (LSE) is covered by several widely followed indexes, all created by the *Financial Times*. The *Financial Times* is a daily international newspaper based in London and owned by Nikkei Inc. in Tokyo, Japan. The most popular is the Financial Times Stock Exchange 100 Index (FTSE 100 Index), often called the "Footsie," which is a market value index that commonly includes the shares of the largest 100 U.K. firms, whose market value makes up most of the market value of all U.K. equities. The other indexes are the FTSE 350 Index (which combines the 350 largest U.K. firms), the FTSE Small Cap Index, and the FTSE All-Share Index (which is the aggregation of the largest U.K. stocks plus the stocks in the FTSE Small Cap Index).

The primary German stock index is the DAX, which stands for Deutscher Aktienindex, produced by the Frankfurt Stock Exchange. The German name for this exchange is the Frankfurter Wertpapierbörse. Some financial services regularly refer to the exchange by its initials, FWB. The DAX is based on the 30 most actively traded shares listed on the Frankfurt exchange. The FAZ index is another popular German index. Compiled by the *Frankfurter Allgemeine Zeitung,* which is a daily newspaper, the FAZ index is computed from the share prices of the 100 largest companies listed on the Frankfurt exchange.

In France, a national association of stockbrokers and the Paris Bourse produce an index based on the shares of 40 large and prominent firms traded on the exchange. The index is known as the CAC 40 Index after the name of the bourse's electronic trading system. Given the increasing economic integration of Europe, the CAC 40, the FTSE 100, and the DAX are all regarded as reliable indicators of the overall performance of European stocks and markets.

Non-Exchange Sponsors of International Indexes

To meet the increased interest in global equity investing, global non-exchange financial institutions have developed several respected international stock indexes.

The MSCI provides families of U.S. and international stock indexes. The international global equity indexes followed by most institutional investors is the MSCI EAFE (Europe, Australasia, and Far East) Index. The MSCI is divided into the MSCI Global Standard Indexes, MSCI Global Small Cap Indexes, and MSCI Value and Growth Indexes. The components in the MSCI database have been used to create more than 28,000 indexes. The MSCI World Index is a common benchmark for the global stock market. They are market-cap weighted. Table 24.2 lists the equity indexes provided by MSCI, divided into developed markets, emerging markets, frontier markets, and standalone markets. These indexes are widely used by institutional investors. There are also growth and value versions of these indexes.

The *Financial Times* has also created a series of global stock market indices: FTSE All-World Index Series, FTSE Emerging Markets, FTSE Global Equity Index Series, FTSE

Global Sector Index Series, FTSE Global Small Cap Index Series, FTSE Global Style Index Series, FTSE Gold Mines Index Series, FTSE Multinationals Index Series, FTSE Shariah Global Equity Index Series, and FTSE Watch List Index Series. This series of indexes is also widely used.

Regulation of the U.K. and European Stock Markets

It is not possible here to provide a detailed discussion of the regulation of the equity markets in the United Kingdom and Europe. Here we simply provide a brief discussion of the major events and legislation.

Market in Financial Instruments Directive

The Market in Financial Instruments Directive (MiFID), promulgated in November 2007, provided significant changes in the European Union (EU) securities market regulatory infrastructure. Note that during 2007–2009, the period during which the global Great Recession occurred, significant reform also took place in the U.S. equities markets.

There are currently both similarities and differences between the U.S. (described in chapter 22) and EU financial regulations.[5] Both regulatory systems attempt to maintain fair and orderly markets, protect investors, and provide price transparency, although MiFID rules do not apply to dark pools. There are two major differences. First, investor protection rules for the European Union are two-tiered between retail and professional investors; in the United States, the same regulatory scheme protects all investors (with some carve-outs for institutional investors). Second, in the United States, quotes and transaction data reported by the national exchanges are consolidated into a single system and disseminated to market participants. In contrast, in the European Union, quotes and trades are fragmented among multiple trading venues, and no consolidation is required.

On January 3, 2018, the European Union revised its MiFID rules to include MiFID II, which ensures that asset managers obtain value for trade research by unbundling what asset managers pay for investment research. According to these rules, asset managers will either have to pay for the research themselves or charge their customers for the research. U.S. investors who do business in the European Union or the United Kingdom will also be affected. The effects of these changes are projected to be significant.

Competition in the securities markets has increased in the European Union, but trading has become more fragmented, and liquidity has moved from the exchanges, raising the concern of "fragmented liquidity" that led to the adoption of Reg. NMS in the United States, as discussed in chapter 22. In both regions, consolidation among exchanges has increased, and it seems that an increasing share of equity trading has moved to dark pools.

5. Tanja Boskovic, Caroline Cerruti, and Michel Noel, "Comparing European and U.S. Securities Regulations, MiFID versus Corresponding U.S. Regulations," World Bank Working Paper 184 (Washington, DC: World Bank, 2010).

The Big Bang

A strong impetus for regulatory change in Europe was the "Big Bang," which occurred in London in 1986. The Big Bang caused significant permanent changes in the U.K. market structure and mechanics. The changes included terminating fixed commissions and ending the distinction between stockbrokers and stockjobbers. Stockbrokers acted as agents for their clients on a commission basis. Stockjobbers ("jobbers") made markets; that is, they engaged in the purchase and sale of stocks for their own "books" and were, thus, principals in the markets. Jobbers thus provided liquidity to the markets. Prior to this change, brokers and jobbers had to be independent and not be part of a broader financial group. These restrictions were removed by the Big Bang.

These regulatory changes immediately changed the LSE from floor-based, open-outcry markets to screen-based, electronic trading markets. The LSE's rules went into effect on October 27, 1986. A surge in trading activity followed, but quickly thereafter, there was a complete change in market structure regarding electronic trading, and the LSE floor became empty as all the trading moved "upstairs," which means into offices off of the exchange floor. These changes pre-dated similar changes that occurred in many other global exchanges and eventually in the NYSE.

Chinese Equity Markets

The Chinese equity markets are relatively young, and China is not currently considered a developed country, but rather a developing country. The Chinese stock market is very different from most other developed country global stock markets. It is driven by retail rather than institutional investors. According to CNBC, roughly 85% of trades are by retail investors.[6]

Chinese retail investors also tend to be very sensitive to risk—they sell on bad news and buy on good news more quickly than do institutional and retail investors in the United States. Retail investors are often considered to be "noise investors;" that is, they make buy and sell decisions without using fundamental data and often overreact to both good and bad news. Overall, China's retail investors are very active traders/speculators, not long-term investors. In addition, in China, most of the large-cap companies are owned by large state-owned enterprises (SOEs), and the retail investors gravitate to the smaller companies, making these smaller markets even more volatile. These factors account for the Chinese stock market being much more volatile than the U.S. market. For these reasons, market observers refer to the Chinese stock market as a "casino," with the price of companies bearing little connection to their underlying economic fundamentals.[7]

6. Mark Fahey and Eric Chemi, "Three Charts Explaining China's Strange Stock Market," www.cnbc.com/2015/07/09/three-charts-explaining-chinese-strange-stock-market.html, July 9, 2015.

7. "China's Stock Market—A Crazy Casino," *The Economist*, May 26, 2015.

In general, it is commonly regarded that the following are major disadvantages of the Chinese equity markets. The first disadvantage is the short-term, speculative orientation of the investors. This results in substantial volatility of the Chinese equity markets, especially the unlisted markets (as discussed below) and its investors. The second is the absence of financial advisors to counsel retail investors. Retail transactions are conducted by banks, which do not provide financial advice. The third drawback is the lack of longer term institutional investors; that is, there are very few mutual funds (including index funds). Fourth is the opaque nature of the unlisted markets—which adds to volatility. The fifth disadvantage is the poor quality of the accountability-oriented policies for shareholder protection coupled with weak business practices, such as limited financial disclosure and insider transactions. Finally, Chinese government market intervention policies are not well developed and not well understood by investors. With respect to government intervention policies, for example, during the significant Chinese stock market decline of 2015, the major Chinese stock index, the CSI 300 (discussed below), declined from over 5,000 to below 3,000. In response, the Chinese government became more interventionist to contravene declining prices. Among the actions of the Chinese government took were actively encouraging investors to buy stock on margin and prohibiting institutions holding more than 5% stakes in Chinese companies from selling their positions.

On the other hand, among the advantages of the Chinese equity markets are (1) its large size, (2) its rapid growth, and (3) the low correlation of the Chinese equity markets with other international markets. Investors find these advantages compelling.

As the Chinese equity markets mature, the abovementioned disadvantages may moderate. Because the Chinese equity markets are very large, are growing rapidly, and have already have become major parts of many global portfolios, we conclude this chapter with a discussion of these markets.

Chinese Stock Market Structure

The structure and workings of the Chinese equity markets are quite different from those of other international exchanges. This structure is shown in figure 24.1. As shown in the figure, about 30% of Chinese stocks are listed on one of the three stock exchanges (Hong Kong, Shanghai, and Shenzhen exchanges), and 70% are not listed on an exchange. Stocks not listed on any of these exchanges are referred to as "unlisted," that is, not traded on any exchanges and traded only on private markets. The private markets are very active. Of the 30% of listed stocks, about half are government-owned companies, referred to as state-owned enterprises (SOEs), and the other half are private companies. This mix between SOEs and private companies has changed over time. SOEs are discussed further below.

A unique aspect of the Chinese stock market is the SOEs. SOEs are legal entities that are fully or partially owned by the state and conduct commercial activities on behalf of the state. At the birth of the People's Republic of China in 1949, all businesses were SOEs. The

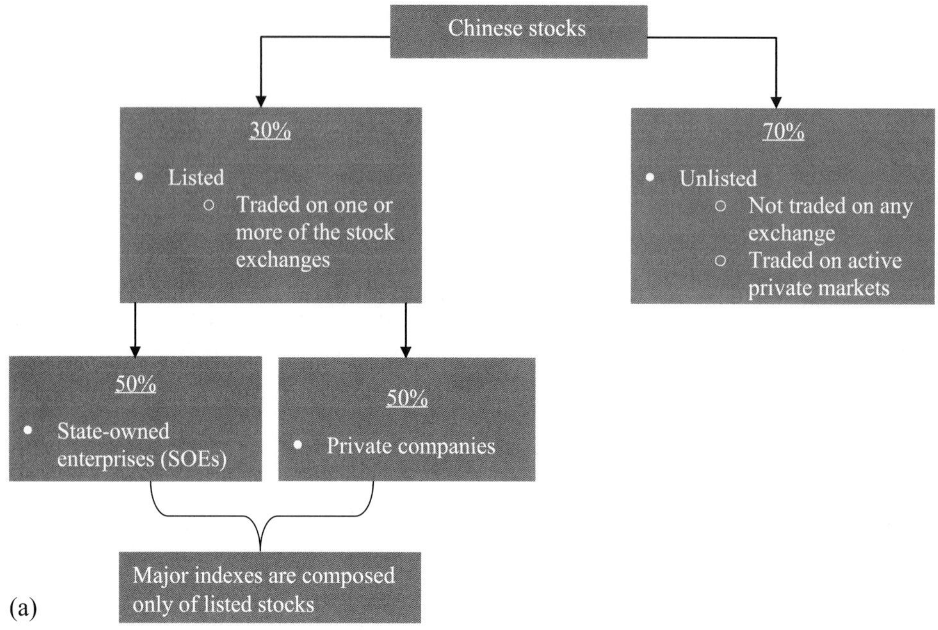

Figure 24.1
The Chinese stock market and exchanges: (a): structure of the Chinese stock market; (b) Chinese stock exchanges; (c) Chinese stock indexes.

Chinese government has sold many of its SOEs since the turn of the century. As of 2011, 35% of business activity and 43% of the profits in the People's Republic of China was due to companies in which the government had a majority ownership.[8] These SOEs are typically extremely large and most are located in Beijing.

SOEs have played an important role in the development of the Chinese economy. In the 1980s, SOEs (the state sector) accounted for 80% of the Chinese economy. However, due to the rapid increase in the private economy, by 2017, SOEs accounted for only 20% of the economy.

The Chinese stock market indexes capture only the listed markets, which are heavily state owned. The unlisted market is very large but is not represented in any of the indexes. This structure causes a concern about transparency.

Table 24.4 shows the Chinese stock exchanges. The Chinese stock exchanges collectively represent the second largest stock market in the world. China's market comprises the fifth, sixth, and eight largest stock exchanges in the world. Stocks traded on these exchanges are referred to as "listed" and "mainstream" stock exchanges.

8. Gabriel Wildau, "China's State Owned Zombie Economy," *Financial Times*, February 29, 2016, available at https://www.ft.com/content/253d7eb0-11e5-84df-70594b99fc47.

Table 24.4
The Chinese Stock Exchanges (as of January 31, 2015).

Exchange	Size (by market cap; billion U.S. $)	World Ranking (in market cap)	Founded	Index
Shanghai Stock Exchange (SSE)	3,986	5	11/26/90	Shanghai Stock Exchange Composite Index (SH Comp)
Hong Kong Stock Exchange (SEHK)	3,325	6	1891/1986	Hang Seng Index (HSI)
Shenzhen Stock Exchange (SZSE)	2,285	8	12/1/90	Shenshen Stock Exchange Component Index (SZSE Component Index)
ChiNext (part of Shenzhen Exchange)	–	–	10/23/09	—

The Shenzhen Stock Exchange (SZSE) also owns a technology exchange, ChiNext, founded on October 23, 2009. The Shanghai Stock Exchange (SSE) is in general considered to be similar to the NYSE, which lists many large stocks, whereas the SZSE specializes in small cap and technology stocks and is considered to be similar to the Nasdaq.

The two mainland exchanges, Shanghai and Shenzhen, opened in 1990 as part of Deng Xiaoping's privatization program. The Hong Kong Stock Exchange (SEHK) was formally set up in 1891, and a number of important developments occurred beginning in 1986. The two mainland Chinese stock exchanges, SSE and the SZSE, were founded in 1990.

The last column in table 24.4 shows the designations for the Chinese stock market indexes, which are discussed below. As explained above, only stock exchange-traded stocks are included in these indexes. This raises a concern about transparency.

Chinese currency China's official currency is called the renminbi (denoted by RMB). Renminbi translates to "the people's currency" in Mandarin. It was first issued in December 1948 with the establishment of the People's Republic of China. Although its official abbreviation is ¥, the common abbreviation is RMB.

The yuan is the base unit of account of the currency, which means that the currency is denominated in 1 yuan, 2 yuan, and so on. The yuan is denoted by ¥. An analogy with the U.S. would be between the unit of value of the Federal Reserve Note (a unit of value akin to the yuan) and the U.S. dollar (a currency akin to the renminbi). Prices are referred to in dollars, not Federal Reserve Notes.

In practice, however, they are fungible. The yuan is commonly used for international applications. The *Wall Street Journal* and the *New York Times* report the Chinese currency versus the U.S. dollar in yuan rather than RMB.

Chinese Stock Market Regulations

The China Securities Regulatory Commission (CSRC) is an institution of the People's Republic of China. It is the main regulator of the securities industry in China. China's Securities Law, which became effective July 1, 1999, was the nation's first securities legislation. The responsibilities of the CSRC are mandated in the Securities Law, the Law of the People's Republic of China on Securities Investment Funds, and a series of related laws that have expanded the duties and powers of the CSRC. Several regulatory reforms have been enacted to support the movement toward a more market-based financial sector.

The CSRC's authorization to implement a centralized and unified regulation of China's securities market to ensure its lawful operation is granted by Chinese law. The CSRC oversees China's nationwide centralized securities supervisory system, with the power to regulate and supervise securities issuers, as well as to investigate and impose penalties for "illegal activities related to securities and futures." Its functions are similar to those of the SEC in the United States.

The CSRC's responsibilities include: (1) formulating policies, laws, and regulations concerning markets in securities and futures contracts; (2) overseeing issuing, trading, custody, and settlement of equity shares, bonds, and investment funds; and (3) supervising listing, trading, and settlement of futures contracts; futures exchanges; and securities and futures firms.

The CSRC performs a unified regulatory function over the securities and futures market of China, maintains an orderly securities and futures market, and ensures a legal operation of the capital market. CSRC is located in Beijing, China.

Split-share-structure reform Prior to April 2005, companies traded on China's stock markets followed a split share structure, whereby one-third of the shares were public stocks, which were freely traded, and two-thirds were SOEs, which were nontradable shares (NTS). The NTS contributed to both significant corporate governance problems and to a lack of incentives and manager responsibilities for the state-ownership structure of many enterprises, which it was believed contributed to the inefficiency and low productivity of the SOEs.[9] These two types of shares had the same dividends and voting rights; they were distinguishable only by whether they could be traded and thus, by their liquidity.

The original reason for the existence of the NTS structure was that the main goal of the Chinese government in forming the stock market was to raise capital for its SOEs and yet retain control of these enterprises. Achieving these goals jointly required secondary market trading. The tradable shares were called "floating" shares; and the nontradable shares were

9. Cheng Wui Wing, "Impact of Split Share Structure Reform of China State-Owned Enterprises on China's Corporate Government Development," Hang Seng Management College, Hong Kong, China, undated, http://wbiconpro.com/308-Andy.pdf.

called "nonfloating," state-owned, or "legal" shares. One-third of the shares were freely traded public stocks, and two-thirds were SOEs, which were not publicly traded.

This so-called split-share structure did not achieve its goals. The NTS did not trade efficiently. So, in April 2005, the CSRC adopted a reform called the "Split Share Structure Reform" (SSSR), whereby all NTS became tradable on the listed stock markets, that is, they became floating shares.

Due to these differences in liquidity, tradable shares had a greater value than the otherwise identical NTS. Thus, before the NTS began trading according to the SSSR, the holders of the tradable shares had to be compensated by the holders of the previous NTS for their differences in value. For this reason, nontradable shareholders negotiated a settlement with tradable shareholders which would apply when the NTS became tradable. Specifically, according to the reform proposal, the shareholders of the NTS compensated the tradable shareholders with approximately three additional shares per ten original shares when all their NTS shares became tradable.

In retrospect, the SSSR has provided a significant positive effect on the Chinese stock market. The quality and dependability of stock market pricing has improved significantly since the implementation of the SSSR. Specifically, an empirical study by the European Central Bank confirmed that the SSST benefited small stocks, stocks issues with poorer governance, and stocks with less liquidity. Neglected stocks also saw an increase in trading volume and prices.[10]

Overall, the SSSR implemented a reform which eliminated the NTS shares typically held by the state or by politically connected institutional investors. China's A-share market efficiency—liquidity and pricing—improved significantly after the SSSR was adopted. These SSSR reforms applied only to A-shares, not B- and H-shares, as discussed below.

Qualified Foreign Institutional Investor Program The Qualified Foreign Institutional Investor (QFII) is a program that permits certain licensed international investors to participate in China's mainland stock exchanges. The QFII program was launched by the People's Republic of China in 2002 to allow foreign investors access to its stock exchanges in Shanghai and Shenzhen. Prior to QFII, foreign investors were not able to buy or sell shares on China's stock exchanges because of China's tight capital controls. With the launch of the QFII program, licensed investors can buy and sell RMB-denominated "A" shares. Foreign access to these shares is limited by specified quotas that determine the amount of money that the licensed foreign investors are permitted to invest in China's capital markets. Thus, foreign investors benefit from an opportunity to invest in onshore China, which is otherwise often insulated from the rest of the world, and are subject to capital controls governing and movement of assets in and out of the country.

10. Andrea Beltratti, Bernardo Bortolotti, and Marianna Caccavaio, "The Stock Market Reaction to the 2005 Non-Tradable Share Reform in China," Working Paper 1339 (Frankfurt: European Central Bank, May 2011), 4.

As of April 2012, the combined quota for the QFII program was set at \$80 billion. The quotas are granted by China's State Administration of Foreign Exchange, and the quotas can be adjusted to reflect and respond to the country's economic and financial situation. The types of investments include listed A-share stocks (excluding foreign-oriented B-shares). To be approved as a licensed investor, certain qualifications must be met (qualifications depend on the type of investor, such as fund management companies and insurance companies). For example, fund management companies are required to have a minimum of five years of experience in assets management and must have managed at least \$5 billion in securities assets.

The QFII program was instrumental in including A-shares in U.S. stock indexes by MSCI, as discussed below. MSCI is moving slowly to include A-shares in its indexes, because an investor has to be part of the QFII program to invest in A-shares, which sets limits on the amount investors can invest.

As indicated, QFII permits foreign investors to invest in China. The obverse of this is the Qualified Domestic Institutional Investor (QDII) program, which permits certain Chinese institutional investors (such as banks, funds, and investment companies) to invest in securities outside China. The QDII program in China was set up to provide the growing number of Chinese investors with a larger market where they could invest their funds. The Chinese stock markets were not always deep enough to provide sufficient investment markets. As an example, an institutional investor could be approved, according to QDII, to invest up to 50% of its net assets into allowable foreign securities, as long as not more than 5% was invested in any single security.

Chinese Stock Exchanges

There are three major exchanges in the Chinese stock market: the Hong Kong Stock Exchange (SEHK), the Shanghai Stock Exchange (SSE), and the Shenzhen Stock Exchange (SZSE). The last two exchanges are often referred to as the "mainland" or "on-shore" stock exchanges. Figure 24.1 provides the designations for the Chinese stock exchanges and their corresponding indexes.

The SEHK is the sixth largest global stock exchange and Asia's third largest stock exchange, after the Tokyo Stock Exchange and Shanghai Stock Exchange. The exchange has been very aggressive in introducing electronic trading. After introducing a computer-assisted trading system in 1986, it introduced its complete system in October 2000. A small physical trading floor still exists, but it accounts for less than 1% of total trading volume. SEHK is entirely open to foreign investors.

The SSE is the fifth largest global stock exchange and the largest stock exchange in mainland China. It is a nonprofit organization operated by the CSRC. Stocks, funds, and bonds are all traded on the exchange, which has listing requirements including that a company must be in business and be earning a profit for at least three years before joining the exchange. SSE was established in 1990. SSE has a total of approximately 870 listed companies, 1,351 listed stocks (A-shares and B-shares) with $2.78 trillion in market capitalization and a $5.22 trillion stock turnover. The trading system is capable of processing and executing 180 million orders for A-share trading and four million orders for B-share trading on a daily basis.

The SZSE is the eighth largest global exchange, the third largest exchange in China, and the fourth largest exchange in Asia. The SZSE lists more than 1,500 companies, most of which are controlled by the Chinese government. The SZSE opened the ChiNext board, a Nasdaq-type exchange for technology start-ups, during October 2009. Founded in 1990, the SZSE operates a Main Board, a Small and Medium-Sized Enterprises Board, a Growth Enterprise Board, and a stock transfer agent system. Recently, there have been 467 companies on the Main Board, 327 companies on the Small and Medium-Sized Enterprises Board, and 36 companies on the Growth Enterprise Board, with market capitalizations of approximately $0.6 trillion, $0.25 trillion, and $24.1 million, respectively.

Chinese Stock Market Share Classes (A, B, and H)

Stock trading in China is often thought to be complicated, mainly due to its multiple classes and the rules for permitted types of investors for each class. Overall, as indicated above, Chinese stock trading occurs on three exchanges, the SEHK, SSE, and the SZSE. In addition, many Chinese stocks are unlisted: They do not trade on the exchanges but are traded on private markets (see figure 24.1). Listed companies (on these exchanges) in China fall into three primary share class categories: A-shares, B-shares, and H-shares.

For every stock listed on either the SSE or the SZSE, two share classes are listed: A-shares and B-shares. In general, A-shares are traded by mainland Chinese investors and B-shares by international investors.

A-shares are traded in yuan (RMB) and are available to all mainland Chinese investors; they are also available to foreign investors but only through a QFII program. A-shares were only available to mainland Chinese investors, but this restriction ended in 2013. Since then, QFII-licensed foreign institutions that have received a special permission by the Chinese government, can also participate in this A-share market, as discussed above.

B-shares are traded mainly among international investors. They are also available to mainland Chinese investors who have a legal foreign currency account. B-shares are quoted in U.S. dollars on the SSE and in Hong Kong dollars on the SZSE. B-shares are based on local Chinese companies. They have a face value in RMB. They are listed for trading primarily by international investors. However, B-shares are also open to domestic investors, provided that these investors set up a foreign currency account. B-shares are traded in U.S. dollars on the SSE and in Hong Kong dollars on the SZSE. Many companies list and trade their shares simultaneously on the SEHK and the mainland Chinese stock exchanges and thus offer two share classes, called "dual listing," as discussed below.

H-shares are shares of companies incorporated in mainland China, which are listed on the SEHK. Although they are regulated by the Chinese legal system, H-shares are denominated in Hong Kong dollars and are traded in the same way as the other stocks on the SEHK. Many companies list their shares on both the SEHK and one of the two mainland Chinese stock exchanges (dual listing), as discussed below.

The top part of table 24.5 summarizes the characteristics of A-, B-, and H-share classes. The bottom part of the table summarizes the availability of the three share classes to Chinese and U.S. investors.

A-Shares versus H-Shares

Prior to 2013, A-shares were available only to mainland Chinese investors and were traded by Chinese investors (on the Shanghai and Shenzhen exchanges). However, since 2013, QFII investors can also trade A-shares. H-shares can be traded freely by anyone (including mainland Chinese investors) with legal foreign currency accounts. Prior to 2007, Chinese investors could trade only A-shares (on the two mainland exchanges), not H-shares, even for stocks for which both A-shares and H-shares were listed.

Since 2007, China has allowed Chinese investors to invest in either A-shares or H-shares of companies that have H-shares listed on the SEHK. Different types of investors can own the A-shares (which trade on the two mainland exchanges) and the H-shares (which trade on the SEHK) of the identical, mainland stocks. As a result, very large price differences may occur between the two markets for two otherwise identical stocks. Spreads of 30%, 80%, and even 100% between the two shares are observed. That is, A-shares may trade at large premiums to H-shares for these dual-listed stocks.

Despite these large spreads, there is no channel for arbitrage between the two markets. Among the reasons for the existences of these spreads are (1) large institutional foreign investors invest in H-shares, and the institutions are better at assessing value and are not as speculative; (2) there is a large imbalance between the supply of and demand for high quality stocks in China due to market segmentation; and (3) restrictions/regulations combined with high demand increase the premiums for A-shares.

The number of dual listings (that is, the same stock being listed on a mainland exchange and on SEHK) is small. There were less than 100 dually listed stocks in early 2017.

Red chips A red chip company is a company based in mainland China that is incorporated internationally and listed on the SEHK. Red chip stocks are expected to maintain the filing and reporting requirements of the SEHK, which makes them a main outlet for foreign investors who wish to participate in the rapid growth of the Chinese economy. Red chips may be issued in addition to A-shares of the same companies, although only Chinese citizens can invest in the A-shares (unless the investor is part of a QFII program).

Table 24.5
Chinese share types.

Summary of Share Types

Shares	Listed Companies	Investors
A	Based on mainland Chinese companies; denominated in Renminbi; traded on Shanghai and Shenzhen Exchanges	Traded mainly by Chinese investors on the Shanghai and Shenzhen exchanges; QFII investors can also trade (since 2013)
B	Based on mainland Chinese companies; denominated in Renminbi; Traded on Shanghai and Hong Kong Stock Exchange or Shenzhen Exchanges.	Traded mainly by international investors: – In U.S. $ on the Shanghai exchange – In H.K. $ on the Shenzhen exchange Mainland Chinese investors can trade with legal foreign currency account.
H	Chinese companies regulated by Chinese law; Companies incorporated on mainland China, and listed on Hong Kong exchange, quoted in H.K. $	Freely tradable by all investors; Quoted in H.K. $ Traded in same way as other stocks on Hong Kong exchange

Share-Types and Types of Investors

	A-Shares	B-Shares	H-Shares
Chinese Investors	Yes (Shanghai and Shenzhen Stock Exchanges)	Only with legal foreign currency account	Yes on Hong Kong exchange (through Stock Connect with either Shanghai or Shenzen)
U.S. Investors	Only through QFII program	Yes	Yes on Hong Kong exchange

Shanghai–Hong Kong Stock Connect Stock Connect is an investment channel that connects SSE and SEHK, so that investors in each market can trade shares on the other's market using their local brokers and clearing houses. This "connection" was the first link between the mainland and Hong Kong for a broad range of investors. This program began in November 2014. A similar link, the Shenzhen–Hong Kong Stock Connect, began in December 2016 and connects SZSE and SEHK. These links are used mostly by institutions. For individuals to use these links they must demonstrate that they are sophisticated investors by having a minimum level of assets and passing a test. It may be necessary, however, for individuals to go to Hong Kong and open an account with a local broker. Only A-shares are included in these stock connects, not B-shares.

Chinese Stock Market Indexes

The Chinese stock market indexes are based entirely on listed stocks, that is, stocks listed on one of the exchanges. The listed stocks are approximately 50% based on SOEs and 50% based on private stocks. Unlisted stocks are traded in very active markets and are not traded on any exchange. The major stock indexes in China are the Hang Seng Index, the Shanghai Composite Index, the Shenzhen Component Index, and the CSI 300 Index.

The Hang Seng Index (HSI) is a free-float-adjusted market capitalization-weighted stock market index traded on the SEHK. The 50 constituent companies of the HSI represent about 58% of the capitalization of the SEHK. The index is used to record and monitor daily changes of the largest companies. The HSI was started in November 1969 and is currently compiled and maintained by Hang Seng Indexes Company Limited, which is a wholly owned subsidiary of Hang Seng Bank. The 50 HSI stocks are also divided into four subindexes: finance, utilities, properties, and commerce and industry

The Shanghai Stock Exchange Composite Index (SSE Comp) is a capitalization-weighted index that tracks the price performance of all the A-shares and B-shares listed on the SSE. The index was developed on December 19, 1990 with a base value of 100.

The Shenzhen Composite Index (SZSE Composite Index), the major index of SZSE, is an index of 500 stocks traded on this exchange. It is a capitalization weighted index that was developed on April 3, 1991.

The CSI 300 is free-float market cap-weighted index of 300 A-share stocks that are listed on the two mainland stock exchanges. The index was established in April 2005. It is compiled by the China Securities Index Company Ltd. It is divided into 10 subindexes: energy, materials, industrials, consumer discretionary, consumer stables, health care, financial, information technology, telecommunications, and utilities.

A recently constructed Chinese stock index is the S&P China 500, which is based on 500 of the largest, most liquid Chinese companies. Its composition approximates the sector composition of the broader Chinese equity market. The Chinese A-share classes and offshore listings are eligible for inclusion. The index is calculated via weighting by the float-adjusted market cap. This index is one of a family of S&P Dow Jones Indexes.

U.S. stock index sponsors are increasingly including stocks traded on Chinese exchanges in their indexes. For example, in July 2017, MSCI began including China A-shares in the relevant MSCI indexes (MSCI China Index, MSCI Emerging Markets Index, and others), which includes A-share stocks listed on the Shanghai-listed and Shenzhen-listed shares in this index. This change added 222 Chinese A-shares from both the Shanghai and Shenzhen exchanges. Prior to this, MSCI Emerging Markets Index and other related indexes included only Chinese stocks which were not A-shares: for example, Alibaba (which trades on the NYSE) and China Mobile (which trades on the Hong Kong exchange). The inclusion of A-shares in the MSCI Indexes supports a greater institutional investor base for these Chinese stocks. To be included in U.S. indexes, non-Chinese investors have to be eligible to buy A-shares by being eligible through the QFII, as discussed above.

Chinese vs U.S. Equity Markets

Let's compare the Chinese equity market to the U.S. equity market. Both have quite a long history. The year each Chinese stock exchange was established is shown in table 24.4. The Shanghai Stock Exchange dates back to the 1860s and the Hong Kong Stock Exchange began in 1891 and then reopened in 1986. In the United States, the New York Stock Exchange was founded in 1792.

A large share of stock trading in the United States is by institutions, while most trading in the Chinese stock market is done by retail traders. As noted earlier, Chinese exchanges are often likened to casinos. While U.S. companies are heavily dependent on equity financing, Chinese companies are much more dependent on bank loans and retained earnings.

The U.S. equity markets are much more open to foreign investors than Chinese equity markets. As discussed earlier, on Chinese equity exchanges A-shares are primarily traded among Chinese investors on the Shanghai and Shenzen exchanges; B-shares are primarily traded by non-Chinese investors; and H-shares are open to both Chinese and non-Chinese investors.

With respect to investor participation, the Chinese equity market structure is much more complicated than the U.S. market structure.

Key Points

- The reasons for investing outside one's domestic market are that it allows for better diversification (a better efficient frontier) and captures attractive returns by investing in less price efficient markets.
- An investor can invest in stock markets in other countries not only by buying individual stocks traded in those countries but also by investing in collective investment vehicles such

closed-end funds, mutual funds, and exchange-traded funds and via depositary receipts (ADRs and GDRs).

• The non-U.S. equity markets represent almost 50% of the global equity markets.

• The non-U.S. equity markets are composed of the European, Pacific, and emerging markets.

• The Big Bang in the United Kingdom made significant changes in equity trading and caused an immediate movement from floor trading to "upstairs" electronic trading.

• The Chinese stock market is the second largest stock market globally and is composed of two mainland stock exchanges (the Shanghai and Shenzhen Stock Exchanges) and the Hong Kong Stock Exchange.

• China's stock exchanges are large. The Shanghai Stock Exchange is the fifth largest globally, the Hong Kong is the sixth largest globally, and the Shenzhen Stock Exchange is the eighth largest.

• The China Securities Regulatory Commission (CSRC) is China's stock regulatory body, the analogue of the U.S. SEC.

• The Chinese stock market is composed mainly of retail, not institutional, investors.

• Because retail investors in the Chinese stock market are very short-term traders, who are very risk-sensitive, the Chinese markets are highly volatile.

• The Chinese stock market is composed of 70% unlisted (that is, not listed on any exchange) stocks and 30% listed, exchange-traded stocks; the latter consist of approximately 50% private companies and 50% government, state-owned enterprises (SOEs).

• There are several stock indexes, some associated with the exchanges and others developed independent of the exchanges.

• The CSI 300 is considered to be the S&P 500 of China.

• The renminbi (denoted by RMB) is the official currency of China. The Chinese yuan is the unit of account for the currency.

• The Qualified Foreign Institutional Investor (QFII) program permits some international investors to invest in China's mainland stock exchanges. Specifically, QFII-licensed international investors can participate in Chinese A-shares.

• China's stock exchanges, among them, list three different share classes: A, B, and H.

• A-shares and B-shares are listed on the Shanghai and Shenzhen Exchanges, whereas H-shares are listed on the Hong Kong Exchange.

• Different types of investors (Chinese and international) can trade different types of the share classes, on different exchanges.

• A-shares are intended for use by Chinese investors; B-shares are intended for use by international investors.

- On the Shanghai exchange, B-shares are denominated in U.S. dollars, whereas on the Shenzhen exchange, they are denominated in Hong Kong dollars.
- A red chip company is one that is based on mainland China, incorporated internationally, and listed on the Hong Kong Stock Exchange.
- The major Chinese Stock Market Indexes are the Hang Seng Index (HSI); Shanghai Composite Index (SH Comp); Shenzhen Component Index (SZSE Component Index); and CSI 300 Index.
- Although the Chinese equity markets have large market capitalizations by international standards, they are relatively young.
- The Chinese equity markets are primarily retail markets in contrast to the U.S. equity market which is institutional.
- Equity financing is less important in China than it is in the United States.

Questions

1. An investor believes that her domestic stock market is highly price efficient but would like to actively manage her portfolio. Explain why this investor may find it beneficial to invest in stock markets outside her own country.

2. A Spanish based investor wishes to develop a portfolio of domestic and non-Spanish stocks. When investing in non-Spanish stocks, what alternative investment choices are available rather than investing directly in stocks in other countries?

3. What issues should investors consider when investing in stocks traded outside their domestic stock market?

4. What are the major stock market indexes for developed, developing, and frontier countries?

5. Emerging market stocks have become much more popular among global investors. What are the considerations of a global institution investor investing in emerging market stocks?

6. Discuss the following categories of emerging market stocks: BRIC, BRICS, PIIGS, and the MSCI categories.

7. a. What is the QFII (Qualified Foreign Institutional Investor) program?

b. What are its effects on global stocks markets? Specifically, what would be its effect on U.S. investors?

8. a. What are MiFID and MiFID II?

b. How does the MiFID structure compare with the U.S. equity regulatory structure?

9. Discuss the structure of the MSCI data for the global stock markets in terms of the various types of stocks and the types of countries included in various categories.

10. Describe the various Chinese stock market share classes and the types of investors they were intended for.

11. a. Which of the Chinese share classes could a U.S. investor invest in?

b. Which of them could a mainland Chinese investor invest in?

12. Describe the relationship between Chinese A-shares and H-shares. Are the prices of these two share classes equal or unequal for two stocks that are the same in every way except their different exchange listings? Explain.

13. a. Describe the workings of the Chinese stock market before the Split Share Structure Reform (SSSR) was introduced in 2005 and the changes this reform had on the Chinese stock market.

b. Has this change been beneficial to the Chinese stock markets?

14. a. Describe the relationship between Chinese A-shares, Chinese B-shares, and Hong Kong H-shares.

b. Discuss the linkages, overlaps, and differences among their users.

15. a. Discuss the differences in the investment approaches of U.S. and Chinese retail investors.

b. What are the implications for the market behaviors of their related stock markets?

16. a. What does "casino markets" mean?

b. How does this relate to the Chinese stock markets?

25 Global Short-Term Funding and Investing Markets

CONTENTS

This chapter is coauthored with Steven V. Mann.

Learning Objectives

After reading this chapter, you will understand:

- what the money market is;
- the different types of private debt instruments traded in the money market;
- the impact of the 2008–2009 financial crisis on the instruments traded in the money market;
- what the interbank funding (lending) market is, its importance, and its future;
- what a repurchase agreement is and how it can be used to finance a security position;
- what eurocurrency is;
- the features of the federal funds market and the federal funds rate;
- the link between the federal funds rate and the London interbank offered rate (LIBOR);
- the calculation of LIBOR and its importance to participants in the global financial market;
- the different unsecured lending rates;
- the factors that influence the interest rate on repurchase agreements;
- what causes repo rates to be negative and what the consequences are;
- what commercial paper is and why it is issued;
- the types of issuers (financial and nonfinancial) and major buyers of commercial paper;
- what eurocommercial paper is and how it differs from commercial paper issued in the United States;
- what a banker's acceptance is and how it is created;
- what a certificate of deposit is and the different types of certificates of deposit;
- the different types of money market funds, and the key role these collective vehicles play in the money market; and
- recent regulatory changes for improving the liquidity and safety of money market funds.

As we have seen, financial markets can be classified in various ways. For example, there is the classification into equity markets versus debt markets according to the nature of the claim of the holder of the financial instrument. The cash market and the derivative markets differ, as explained in earlier chapters. As explained in chapter 1, for debt obligations, a distinction is made based on the maturity of the financial instrument. The two markets based on a maturity classification are the money market and the capital market. Financial instruments that at the time of issuance have a maturity of one year or less are referred to as **money market instruments** and the market they trade in is called the **money market**. In contrast, the capital market is the market where financial instruments with a maturity in excess of one year trade. Because equity has a perpetual maturity, it is part of the capital market.

Our focus in this chapter is on the money market. This market plays the following three vital roles in the financial system. First, it provides investors who want to invest in liquid assets a market where they can do so. Second, it provides those entities in need of liquidity a market where they can borrow. Third, the money market provides central banks globally an avenue through which they can implement monetary policy by influencing the availability and cost of liquidity.

In this chapter, we describe the various private money market instruments traded in the money market. By "private money market instruments," we mean instruments issued by nongovernmental entities: nonfinancial and financial corporations. Private money market instruments include unsecured loans made between banks, repurchase agreements, commercial paper, large-denomination negotiable certificates of deposit, banker's acceptances, and money market funds.

What is important in reviewing private money market instruments is not just the first role cited above—that is, the appeal of the various instruments from the perspective of an investor—but also the last two roles. As we have mentioned frequently in this book, liquidity is an important issue for financial and nonfinancial corporations. When we described in chapter 2 government bailouts during the recent financial crisis as well as historically, the problem encountered by the entity needing assistance was liquidity. Indeed, liquidity was the chief culprit in the financial crisis that began in 2007, which then caused a global recession in 2008–2009. Private money market instruments must be purchased by investors willing to accept the associated credit risk. Since the recent financial crisis, major shifts have occurred in the structure and regulation of the money market. These changes are highlighted in this chapter.

Interbank Funding Market

Prior to the financial crisis that began with the subprime mortgage crisis in 2007, the most immediate liquidity source for banks was the **interbank funding market** (also referred to as the **interbank lending market**). As the name indicates, this is the market where banks lend funds to one another, although there is some participation in this market by nondepository institutions. Two types of lending take place between banks in this market: unsecured and secured lending. In the unsecured sector of the market, lending is done through the federal funds market. In the secured sector, lending is done through repurchase agreements that we describe later in this chapter; this sector is referred to as the **repo market**.

In the financial market, the interbank funding market was the most liquid sector during normal market conditions. Certain events have stressed this market. For example, the terrorist attacks on September 11, 2001, resulted in disruptions in communications and reporting systems such that demand by banks for liquidity increased substantially. However, within a few days, the market had returned to its normal functioning. In contrast, the 2008–2009 global recession caused such disruptions in the interbank funding market that questions arose about the future viability of parts of this market. In fact, one of the key problems that characterized the financial crisis from 2007 on was the problems faced in the interbank funding market. Understanding the reasons for these problems is important for understanding the growing importance of other sectors of the money market (i.e., the private money market instruments) that we describe in this chapter. This is because the entire structure of the money market has changed as a result of the changes in the interbank funding market since the financial crisis.

The **eurocurrency market** is the market for deposits operating under a different regulatory apparatus than for deposits used for making domestic transactions. One prominent example is bank deposits denominated in British pounds sterling in banks outside the United Kingdom. The "euro" in "eurocurrency" is a misnomer. These markets have origins in Europe. Today the term refers to any currency held in deposits offshore. Another example is an **international banking facility**. These facilities allow depository institutions in the United States to provide banking services to nonresidents and are not be subject to the U.S. regulations that restrict the behavior of banks. International banking facilities are free from some Federal Reserve requirements (see chapter 6).

There is a parallel structure in the provision of banking services—onshore and offshore. **Onshore** refers to the traditional domestic market. **Offshore** refers to eurocurrency. As noted, eurocurrency is any currency on deposit in banks outside their country of origin. These deposits are traded in the eurocurrency market. The source of these deposits is large financial institutions and corporations. Interbank interest rates are rates that large financial institutions charge one another for loans.

Interbank Lending Rates

Federal funds rate and central bank interest rates In the United States, transactions of depository institutions with either another depository institution or an eligible nondepository entity that involve one party making an unsecured loan to the other party takes place in the **federal funds market** (or **fed funds market**). The average interest rate at which these fed funds transactions take place in the market is referred to as the **federal funds rate** or **fed funds rate**. Using daily data on federal funds transactions voluntarily supplied by major brokers in the fed funds market to the Federal Reserve Bank of New York (New York Fed), a measure of the overnight fed funds rate is computed each day. This rate is called the **daily federal funds effective rate**.

As explained in chapter 6, banks must maintain reserves at their local Federal Reserve Bank. At one time, no interest was paid by the Federal Reserve Banks on the reserves deposited with them. These deposited reserves have two components. The first is required reserves and the second is excess reserves (i.e., the amount of reserves that exceeds required reserves). In 2008, the Federal Reserve Banks began paying interest on reserves because of the ongoing financial crisis.[1] The Federal Reserve Banks pay a different interest on required reserves and excess reserves. The rate paid on required reserves is called the **interest on reserves**, and the rate paid on excess reserves is called the **interest on excess reserves** (IOER). The Fed's objective in paying interest on reserves was to eliminate the opportunity cost faced by banks when funds were tied up in the form of reserves. The purpose of paying IOER was linked to the Fed's ability to control the daily federal funds effective rate. In the fed funds market, excess reserves are traded (i.e., lent) to those banks that do not have sufficient deposits to satisfy required reserves. Before the payment of IOER by the Federal Reserve Bank, banks with excess reserves could lend those reserves at a market rate. With the Fed paying IOER, it became less appealing for a bank with excess reserves to lend those funds at a rate below the IOER.

The mechanism used by the Fed to influence the overnight fed funds rate so that the rate set in the market was close to the target level for the overnight fed funds rate that was established by the Federal Open Market Committee (FOMC) is as follows. Through open market operations, the Fed changes the supply of reserves in the market and, in combination with IOER, the overnight fed funds rate is affected such that it is within the range of the target level established by the FOMC.

The federal funds reserve rate is the rate the Federal Reserve establishes. Central banks in other countries establish a similar interest rate. Table 25.1 lists the names of various central banks and their interest rates.

Unsecured interbank offered rate benchmarks The U.S. fed funds rate is not a market-determined rate that reflects unsecured borrowing by banks in the interbank funding market. Instead, the fed funds rate is an artificial rate whose target level is determined by the Federal Reserve. In contrast, there is an interbank funding rate at which banks can borrow on an unsecured basis outside the United States in the London money market. That rate is the **London interbank offered rate** (LIBOR).

1. Federal Reserve Banks were directed to pay interest on required reserves and on excess reserves by the Financial Services Regulatory Relief Act of 2006, which specified that the Fed amend Regulation D (Reserve Requirements of Depository Institutions) to do so. The implementation of this mandate was accelerated to October 2008 by the Emergency Economic Stabilization Act of 2008.

Table 25.1
Central bank rates.

Country	Central Bank, Interest Rate
Australia	Reserve Bank of Australia, official cash rate
Brazil	Banco Central do Brasil, Sistema Especial de Liquidacao e Custodia rate
Canada	Bank of Canada, key policy rate
Chile	Banco Central de Chile, monetary policy rate
China	People's Bank of China, base interest rate
Czech Republic	Czech National Bank, two-week repo rate
Denmark	Nationalbanken, lending rate
European Union	European Central Bank, refi rate
Hungary	Magyar Nemzeti Bank, two-week bill rate
India	Reserve Bank of India, key short-term lending rate
Indonesia	Bank Indonesia, Bank Indonesia rate
Israel	Bank of Israel, headline rate of interest
Japan	Bank of Japan, uncollateralized overnight call rate
Mexico	Banco de Mexico, overnight interbank rate
New Zealand	Reserve Bank of New Zealand, official cash rate
Norway	Norges Bank, key policy rate
Poland	Narodowy Bank Polski, reference rate
Russia	Bank of Russia, Central Bank of Russia key rate
Saudi Arabia	Saudi Arabian Monetary Agency, repo rate
South Africa	South African Reserve Bank, repo rate
South Korea	Bank of Korea, base rate
Sweden	Sveriges Riksbank, repo rate
Switzerland	Swiss National Bank, three-month LIBOR CHF
Turkey	Central Bank of the Republic of Turkey, one-week repo rate
United Kingdom	Bank of England, official bank rate
United States	Federal Reserve, federal funds rate

LIBOR is not derived directly from actual unsecured loan transactions in the interbank funding market. Instead, LIBOR is calculated based on responses to a daily market survey by an administrator of this interest rate. Prior to 2014, the British Bankers' Association (BBA) was the administrator of this rate. In early 2014, the responsibility of administrating LIBOR was shifted to the Intercontinental Exchange (ICE) and LIBOR is now referred to as "ICE LIBOR."

To calculating LIBOR, a panel of large banks[2] estimates the interest rate at which it could borrow on the interbank market for seven different maturities: overnight (one day), one week, one month, two months, three months, six months, and 12 months. Moreover, LIBOR is calculated for five different currencies: the U.S. dollar (USD LIBOR), the Brit-

2. The BBA selects the panel banks with assistance from the U.K. Foreign Exchange and Money Markets Committee. For each currency, a panel consists of at least eight and a maximum of 16 banks that are considered to be representative of participants in the London money market.

ish pound sterling (GBP LIBOR), euros (EUR LIBOR or Euribor), the Japanese yen (JPY LIBOR), and the Swiss franc (CHF LIBOR).[3] ICE's official LIBOR values for each maturity and each currency, abbreviated as shown here, are announced by Thomson Reuters once a day.

The **Euro Overnight Index Average** is the average overnight Euribor. It is compiled as an average of rates charged by 35 contributing banks on overnight unsecured loans denominated in euros. The contributing banks include EU banks and large international banks from non-EU countries that are part of the Eurozone.

Understanding how the official LIBOR for each maturity and currency is calculated is important. Every panel bank reports to Thomson Reuters at 11 a.m. London time every working day the interest rate at which it would expect to be able to raise a substantial loan in the interbank money market at that time. Because not every panel bank borrows a substantial amount for each maturity (or any maturity, for that matter) every day, the calculation is not based on actual loan transactions. From the rates reported by the panel banks, Thomson Reuters eliminates the lowest and highest 25% and then averages the remaining reported rates to obtain the official LIBOR for a given maturity and currency.

LIBOR is a key interest rate, because it is used as a reference interest rate for an estimated $360 trillion of derivative contracts. Moreover, it is used to set rates on commercial business loans, consumer loans, and mortgage loans for residential and commercial property. Consequently, LIBOR is viewed as the most important benchmark interest rate in the global financial market. As such, its calculation is extremely important for all participants in the financial market.

The current issue regarding LIBOR is whether this survey-based borrowing cost truly reflects interbank funding costs, particularly during periods of market distress, such as the 2008–2009 financial crisis. During this period, little trading took place in the interbank funding market in London. Consequently, many market participants questioned the official suite of rates reported by the BBA when it was the administrator for LIBOR.

In 2012, several stories in the press reported that some panel banks had submitted false information used to calculate LIBOR. It was alleged that certain panel banks had intentionally underestimated the rate at which they estimated they could borrow funds overnight from other banks. The reason for underestimating the borrowing rate is that had this not been done, it would have increased the cost for overnight loans, signaling that the financial condition of the bank submitting the information was deteriorating. Subsequent investigations of the survey process for computing LIBOR by regulators in several countries confirmed the manipulation of LIBOR by some panel banks. This LIBOR-rigging scandal led to the filing of lawsuits against the panel banks alleged to have been involved. Several banks

3. In 2013, the BBA discontinued LIBOR for five currencies: the Canadian dollar, Australian dollar, New Zealand dollar, Swedish krona, and Danish krone.

have settled these suits.[4] In the United Kingdom, the BBA agreed to transfer oversight of LIBOR to regulators in that country based on the recommendation of an independent review committee headed by Martin Wheatley, managing director of the U.K. Financial Services Authority.

The interest rate on unsecured lending plays an important role in global financial markets. For this reason, the Financial Stability Board (FSB) prepared a report in 2014 titled *Reforming Major Interest Rate Benchmarks*.[5] The report made two recommendations. The first recommendation involved enhancing prevailing interest rate benchmarks for key interbank offered rates in the unsecured lending markets. These key interbank offered rates are referred to as the "IBORs." The second recommendation was for promoting the development and adoption of interest rates that reflected nearly risk-free benchmark rates. In July 2015, the FSB published a report titled *Progress in Reforming Major Interest Rate Benchmarks* as an interim report describing the implementation of the recommendations that were made in the 2014 report.[6] After the July 2015 interim report, the group responsible for IBOR took further steps toward implementing the recommendations in the 2014 FSB report, which was to improve the interest rate benchmarks for unsecured lending. It did so by adopting a methodology to obtain whenever possible rates based on transaction data to avoid the problems discussed earlier with LIBOR.

Future of the interbank funding market During the financial crisis that began with the subprime mortgage crisis in mid-2007, severe disruptions took place in the interbank funding market. Some observers have argued that the market froze, and furthermore, some believe the market will not recover.

The 2008–2009 financial crisis caused an increase in the demand for highly liquid assets. U.S. bank managers preferred to pursue a strategy of maintaining liquid assets that might be needed if the crisis worsened rather than make loans that would be illiquid assets on their balance sheets.[7] In addition, bank management preference shifted to very short-term, high-credit-quality secured loans. The preference for the type of collateral for

4. To settle its role in the manipulation of LIBOR, Barclays in June 2012 agreed to pay a total of $453 million in fines to the U.S. Commodities Future Trading Commission, the U.S. Department of Justice, and the British Financial Services Authority. To settle its role in the LIBOR scandal, UBS agreed in December 2012 to pay a record-setting fine of $1.5 billion to authorities in the United States, the United Kingdom, and Switzerland. For a summary of the lawsuits and potential lawsuits arising from the manipulation of LIBOR, see C. Cowden W. Rayburn, "The LIBOR Scandal and Litigation: How the Manipulation of LIBOR Could Invalidate Financial Contracts," *North Carolina Banking Institute Journal* 17 (2013): 221–247.

5. Financial Stability Board, *Reforming Major Interest Rate Benchmarks*, 2014, www.fsb.org/wp-content/uploads/r_140722.pdf.

6. Financial Stability Board, *Progress in Reforming Major Interest Rate Benchmarks*, 2015, www.fsb.org/wp-content/uploads/OSSG-interest-rate-benchmarks-progress-report-July-2015.pdf.

7. The same occurred in the United Kingdom. See Viral V. Acharya and Ouarda Merrouche, "Precautionary Hoarding of Liquidity and Inter-Bank Markets: Evidence from the Sub-Prime Crisis," Working Paper, World Bank and New York University, Stern School of Business, July 3, 2009; rev. January 2012.

secured loans changed from the pre-crisis period. In lending transactions with other banks and financial institutions, bank management preferred liquid assets. That is, in a lending arrangement such as a repurchase agreement (to be discussed later in the chapter), collateral could be, for example, a short-term financial instrument of high credit quality or a pool of residential mortgage loans to borrowers with impaired credit history. Banks preferred the former types of loans to the latter.

Consequently, the economic and financial conditions resulted in an environment in which banks were conservative in the amount they lent in order to maintain highly liquid assets on their balance sheets, and when secured loans were made, collateral that was of high credit quality with high liquidity was preferred. Moreover, loans with a short maturity were preferred. Because of the reduction in the supply of interbank loans, borrowing costs increased significantly. This resulted in a vicious cycle, leading to further conservative policies by bank management that increased the demand for liquidity, a reduction in the amount of loans, and a further increase in borrowing costs. For example, prior to the month when Lehman Brothers Holdings Inc. filed for bankruptcy protection, loans between U.S. commercial banks reached a peak of $494 billion in September 2008. After the bankruptcy filing, loans between U.S. banks fell to $153 billion.[8] It was not until the federal government took the actions we described in chapter 2 that the cycle was broken, but concerns remained that the interbank funding market might not be relied on to provide liquidity in the future.

Several studies have provided empirical support for the freezing of the interbank funding market globally. For example, Gary Gorton and Andrew Metrick found that in the repo market, bank policies that involved increasing the amount of collateral required effectively caused a run in the repo market, particularly for loans involving low-credit-quality assets.[9] A different conclusion about the survival of the interbank lending market is provided in a study by Gara Afonso, Anna Kovner, and Antoinette Schoar, who investigated the response of the fed funds market to the bankruptcy of Lehman Brothers.[10] They found that the average amount of borrowing was stable, even though the fed funds rate increased significantly and the terms of the lending agreements became more sensitive to the risk characteristics of the borrowing bank. They argue that the market did not freeze, but also that it did not expand to meet the increased demand by banks needing liquidity.

8. Mark Gilbert and Matthew Brown, "Interbank Lending Market 'Died with Lehman' Bankruptcy: Chart of the Day," *Bloomberg News*, June 1, 2010, http://www.bloomberg.com/news/2010-06-01/interbank-lendingmarket-died-with-lehman-bankruptcy-chart-of-the-day.html.

9. Gary Gorton and Andrew Metrick, "Securitized Banking and the Run on Repo," *Journal of Financial Economics* 104, no. 3 (2012): 425–451.

10. Gara Afonso, Anna Kovner, and Antoinette Schoar, "Stressed, Not Frozen: The Federal Funds Market in the Financial Crisis," revised May 2011, Federal Reserve Bank of New York Staff Report 437, http://www.newyorkfed.org/research/staff_reports/sr437.pdf.

Repo Market

A **repurchase agreement** (or simply repo) is the sale of a security with a commitment by the seller to buy the security back from the purchaser at a specified price at a designated future date. Basically, a repurchase agreement is a collateralized loan where the collateral is a security or a pool of assets. The collateral in a repo can be money market instruments, Treasury securities, federal agency securities, mortgage-backed securities, asset-backed securities, or a pool of loans. As noted in our discussion of the interbank funding market, repurchase agreements were used by banks to make loans to other banks.

A repo agreement is best explained with an illustration. Suppose a securities dealer purchases \$10 million of a particular bond issue. Where does the dealer obtain the funds to finance that position? Of course, the dealer can finance the position with its own funds or by borrowing from a bank. Typically, however, the dealer uses the repo market to obtain financing. In the repo market, the dealer can use the \$10 million of the bond issue as collateral for a loan. The term of the loan and the interest rate that the dealer agrees to pay (referred to as the **repo rate**) are specified. When the term of the loan is one day, it is called an **overnight repo**; a loan for more than one day is called a **term repo**.

The transaction is referred to as a repurchase agreement because it calls for the sale of the security and its repurchase at a future date. Both the sale price and the repurchase price are specified in the agreement. The difference between the purchase (repurchase) price and the sale price is the dollar interest cost of the loan.

In our illustration, the dealer needs to finance \$10 million par value of the bond that it purchased and plans to hold overnight. Suppose that a customer of the dealer has excess funds of \$10 million. The dealer would agree to deliver (i.e., sell) \$10 million of the bond to the customer for an amount determined by the repo rate and buy (i.e., repurchase) the same bond from the customer for \$10 million the next day. Suppose that the overnight repo rate is 3.5%.Then (as explained below), the dealer would agree to deliver the bond for \$9,999,027.78 and repurchase the same bond for \$10 million the next day. The \$972.22 difference between the sale price of \$9,999,027.78 and the repurchase price of \$10 million is the dollar interest on the financing. From the customer's perspective, the agreement is called a **reverse repo**.

The following formula is used to calculate the dollar interest on a repo transaction:

$$\text{Dollar interest} = \text{Dollar principal} \times \text{Repo rate} \times \text{Repo term}/360.$$

Notice that the interest is computed on a 360-day basis. In our example, at a repo rate of 3.5% and a repo term of one day (overnight), the dollar interest is \$972.22, derived as follows:

$$\text{Dollar interest} = \$10{,}000{,}000 \times 0.035 \times 1/360 = \$972.22.$$

The advantage to the dealer of using the repo market for borrowing on a short-term basis is that the rate is less than the cost of bank financing. We explain why later in this section.

From the customer's perspective, the repo market offers an attractive yield on a short-term secured transaction that is highly liquid.

The example illustrates financing a dealer's long position in the repo market, but dealers can also use the repo market to cover a short position. For example, suppose a government dealer sold $10 million of Treasury securities two weeks ago and must now cover the position—that is, deliver the securities. The dealer can do a reverse repo (agree to buy the securities and sell them back). Of course, the dealer eventually would have to buy the Treasury security in the market to cover its short position.

A good deal of Wall Street jargon is used to describe repo transactions. To understand it, it is useful to remember that one party is lending money and accepting a security as collateral for the loan; the other party is borrowing money and providing the lender collateral for the loan. When someone lends securities in order to receive cash (i.e., borrows money), that party is said to be "reversing out" securities. A party that lends money with the security as collateral is said to be "reversing in" securities. The expressions "to repo securities" and "to do repo" are also used. The former means that someone is going to finance securities using the security as collateral; the latter means that the party is going to invest in a repo. Finally, the expressions "selling collateral" and "buying collateral" are used to describe a party financing a security with a repo, on one hand, and lending on the basis of collateral on the other.

Credit Risk

Despite the high-quality collateral typically underlying a repo transaction, both parties to the transaction are exposed to credit risk (i.e., counterparty risk). Even prior to the 2008–2009 financial crisis, the failure of a few small government securities dealer firms who were parties to repo transactions in the 1980s made market participants more cautious about the creditworthiness of the counterparty to a repo.[11]

Why does credit risk occur in a repo transaction? Let's consider our illustration in which the dealer uses $10 million of government securities as collateral for this borrowing. If the dealer cannot repurchase the government securities, the customer may keep the collateral. If interest rates on government securities increase subsequent to the repo transaction, the market value of the government securities declines, and the customer owns securities with a market value less than the amount it lent to the dealer firm. If the market value of the security rises instead, the dealer firm will be concerned with the return of the collateral from the counterparty, which then has a market value higher than the loan.

Repos are now more carefully structured to reduce credit risk exposure. The amount lent is less than the market value of the securities used as collateral, which provides the lender

11. Failed firms include Drysdale Government Securities, Lion Capital, RTD Securities Inc., Belvill Bressler & Schulman Inc., and ESM Government Securities Inc.

with some cushion should the market value of the securities decline. The amount by which the market value of the securities used as collateral exceeds the value of the loan is called the "margin" or "haircut." The amount of margin varies with the type of collateral, such as its liquidity and the creditworthiness of the borrower.

Another practice used to limit credit risk is to mark the collateral to market on a regular basis. Recall that the practice of marking to market means recording the value of a position at its market value. When the market value changes by a certain percentage, the repo position is adjusted accordingly. Suppose that a dealer firm borrows $20 million using collateral with a market value of $20.8 million, so that the margin is 4%. Suppose further that the market value of the collateral drops to $20.1 million. A repo agreement can specify either a margin call or repricing of the repo. In the case of a margin call, the dealer firm is required to put up additional collateral with a market value of $700,000 to bring the margin up to $800,000. If repricing is agreed on, the parties to the transaction adjust the amount of the collateral in the transaction to the correct margin level. The dealer then sends the customer sufficient funds so that the loan's new amount is in line with the collateral's market value.

One concern in structuring a repo is delivery of the collateral to the lender. The most obvious procedure is for the borrower to deliver the collateral to the lender. At the end of the repo term, the lender returns the collateral to the borrower in exchange for the principal and interest payment. This procedure may be too costly, though, particularly for short-term repos, because of the costs associated with delivering the collateral.

The cost of delivery is factored into the transaction in the form of a lower repo rate offered by the borrower. The risk of the lender not taking possession of the collateral is that the borrower may sell the security or use the same security as collateral for a repo with another party.

As an alternative to delivering the collateral, the lender may agree to allow the borrower to hold the security in a segregated customer account. Of course, the lender still faces the risk that the borrower may use the collateral fraudulently by offering it as collateral for another repo transaction.

Another method is for the borrower to deliver the collateral to the lender's custodial account at the borrower's clearing bank. The custodian then takes possession of the collateral, which it holds on behalf of the lender. This practice reduces the cost of delivery, because it is merely a transfer within the borrower's clearing bank. If, for example, a dealer enters into an overnight repo with customer A, the next day the collateral is transferred back to the dealer. The dealer can then enter into a repo with customer B for, say, five days without having to redeliver the collateral. The clearing bank simply establishes a custodian account for customer B and holds the collateral in that account. This arrangement is called a **tri-party agreement**.

With this understanding of repos, we can appreciate the run in the repo market that Gorton and Metrick[12] report occurred in the interbank funding market during the 2008–2009 financial crisis. During the crisis, banks raised the amount of the haircut on repos, particularly when the collateral was illiquid, low-credit-quality assets, such as a pool of subprime mort-

12. Gorton and Metrick, "Securitized Banking and the Run on Repo."

gage loans. To see the impact of increasing the haircut, consider once again a dealer firm that borrows $20 million using collateral with a market value of $20.8 million and a margin of 4%. The proceeds received by the borrower come to $20 million. Suppose that at the end of the term, the lender wants a 10% margin rather than 4%. Then for collateral of $20.8 million, the margin or haircut would be $18,909,091 ($20.8 million/1.10) instead of $20 million. That is, $1,090,909 less in proceeds will be received by the dealer firm from the repo agreement. Now suppose that the dealer firm in our illustration is a bank and is using the repo market to obtain funds. Hence, the bank will receive $1,090,909 less in proceeds as a result of a higher haircut, which, as argued by Gorton and Metrick, is effectively a run on the repo market.

Participants in the Market

Because it is used by dealer firms (investment banking firms and money center banks acting as dealers) to finance positions and cover short positions, the repo market represents one of the largest sectors of the money market. Financial and nonfinancial firms participate in the market as both sellers and buyers of collateral, depending on the circumstances they face. Depository institutions (commercial banks and thrifts) are typically net sellers of collateral (i.e., net borrowers of funds); money market funds (MMFs), bank trust departments, municipalities, and corporations are typically net buyers of collateral (i.e., providers of funds).

Even though banks and dealer firms use the repo market as the primary means for financing inventory and covering short positions, they also use the repo market to run a **matched book** by taking on repos and reverse repos with the same maturity. A dealer firm uses a matched book to capture the spread at which it enters into the repo and reverse repo agreements. For example, suppose that a dealer firm enters into a term repo of 10 days with an MMF and a reverse repo with a thrift for 10 days in which the collateral is identical. In this transaction, the dealer firm borrows funds from the MMF and lends money to the thrift. If the repo rate is 3.5% and the reverse repo rate is 3.55%, the dealer firm borrows at 3.5% and lends at 3.55%, locking in a spread of 0.05% (five basis points).

Another participant is the **repo broker.** To understand the role of the repo broker, suppose a dealer firm shorts $50 million of a security. It then surveys its regular customers to determine whether it can borrow by means of a reverse repo the security it shorted. Suppose that it cannot find a customer willing to do a repo transaction (a repo from the customer's point of view, a reverse repo from the dealer's). At that point, the dealer firm uses the services of a repo broker.

The Federal Reserve is also involved in the repo market. The Fed influences short-term interest rates through its open market operations, that is, by the outright purchase or sale of government securities. This practice is not commonly followed by the Fed, however. Instead it uses the repo market to implement monetary policy by purchasing or selling collateral. By buying collateral (i.e., lending funds), the Fed injects money into the financial markets, thereby exerting downward pressure on short-term interest rates. When the Fed buys collateral for its own account, it is called a **system repo**. The Fed also buys collateral on behalf of foreign central banks in repo transactions referred to as **customer repos**. It is primarily through system repos that the Fed attempts to influence short-term rates. By selling securities from its own account, the Fed drains money from the financial markets, thereby exerting upward pressure on short-term interest rates. This transaction is called a **matched sale**.

Note the language used to describe the transactions of the Fed in the repo market. When the Fed lends funds based on collateral, we call it a "system" or "customer repo," not a "reverse repo." Borrowing funds using collateral is called a "matched sale," not a "repo." The jargon is confusing, which is why we used the terms "buying collateral" and "selling collateral" to describe what parties in the market are doing.

Determinants of the Repo Rate

Repo rates vary from transaction to transaction, depending on the following factors:

- *Quality.* The higher the credit quality and liquidity of the collateral are, the lower the repo rate will be.
- *Term of the repo.* The effect of the term of the repo on the rate depends on the shape of the yield curve.
- *Delivery requirement.* As noted earlier, if delivery of the collateral to the lender is required, the repo rate will be lower. If the collateral can be deposited with the bank of the borrower, a higher repo rate is paid.
- *Availability of collateral.* The more difficult it is to obtain the collateral, the lower the repo rate will be. To understand why, remember that the borrower (or equivalently, the seller of the collateral) may have a security that is a hot or special issue. The party that needs the collateral will be willing to lend funds at a lower repo rate to obtain the collateral. Collateral is classified as generic collateral and special collateral. **Generic collateral** refers to collateral that is readily available to borrow in the market. When the collateral is difficult to acquire, it is said to be **special collateral** (or **hot collateral**). The repo rate is less for special collateral than for generic collateral.

Although these factors determine the repo rate on a particular transaction, the federal funds rate determines the general level of repo rates. The repo rate will be below the federal funds rate, because a repo involves collateralized borrowing, whereas a federal funds transaction is unsecured borrowing.

Negative repo rates We discuss negative interest rates in chapter 16. Negative repo rates can occur in so-called normal markets, especially in Europe. When collateral becomes special collateral, this is an indication of exceptionally high borrowing demand in the repo market and, as a result, repo rates can become negative. This is more common in countries where the general level of interest rates is at or near zero. Another set of conditions that can induce negative repo rates is financial distress, which serves as a prime breeding ground for negative repo rates. During episodes of financial distress, even general collateral rates can turn negative due to high demand for these securities as safe havens. A negative repo rate means the cash lender pays repo interest to the cash borrower, because the repurchase price is less than the purchase price.

Suppose a customer has excess cash of €10,000,000 with no immediate use for the funds for two weeks. Also suppose a dealer wants to finance a €10,000,000 par value position in sovereign debt for two weeks. The repo margin is 2%, and the repo rate is –0.25%. The amount lent in this transaction is €10,000,000/1.02 or €9,803,921.57. This value is the purchase price. The repurchase price is the purchase price plus repo interest for two weeks. Repo interest is given by €9,803,921.57 × (–0.0025) × 14/360, or—€953.16. The repurchase price is €9,802,968.41. The following summarizes this repo when there are negative repo rates:

Purchase price	€9,803,921.57 (€10,000,000/1.02)
Purchase date	Day 1
Repurchase date	Day 15
Repurchase price	€9,802,968.41
Repo rate	–0.25
Repo interest	–€953.16 = €9,803,9212.57 × (–0.0025) × 14/360.

When repo rates are positive, there is an incentive for the dealer (i.e., the seller) to deliver collateral on the purchase date. A dealer failing to deliver the collateral will not receive the purchase price until the collateral is delivered. The dealer—regardless of whether the collateral is delivered—is obligated to pay the full amount of the repo interest to the customer (i.e., the buyer) on the repurchase date. Paying interest on cash not available for use provides a strong incentive to deliver the collateral. When repo rates are negative, the incentive to deliver the collateral on the purchase date is gone. In fact, negative repo rates reward failure of delivery, because the repurchase price is less than the purchase price.

Commercial Paper Market

Commercial paper (CP) is a short-term unsecured promissory note issued in the open market that represents the obligation of the issuing corporation. The issuers of CP typically have a high credit rating. Both domestic and foreign corporations issue CP in the United States. CP issued by foreign entities is called a **Yankee CP**. MMFs purchase roughly one-third of all CP issued. Pension funds, state and local governments, and nonfinancial corporations seeking short-term investments purchase the balance. Little secondary trading of CP takes place. Typically, an investor in CP is an entity that plans to hold it until maturity, which is understandable, because an investor can purchase CP in a direct transaction with the issuer, who sells paper with the specific maturity that the investor desires.

The issuance of CP is an alternative to bank borrowing for large corporations with strong credit ratings. It is the largest short-term debt instrument issued in the financial market. The original purpose of CP was to provide short-term funds for seasonal and working capital needs, but companies use this instrument for other purposes. It has been used for bridge financing. For example, suppose that a corporation needs long-term funds to build a plant or acquire equipment. Rather than raising long-term funds immediately, the corporation may elect to postpone the offering until more favorable capital market conditions prevail. The funds raised by issuing CP are used until longer-term securities are sold. In the United States, the maturity of CP is typically less than 270 days, with most maturing in less than 90 days. Several reasons explain this pattern of maturities. First, the Securities Act of 1933 requires that securities be registered with the SEC. Special provisions in the 1933 act exempt CP from registration as long as the maturity does not exceed 270 days. Hence, to avoid the costs associated with registering issues with the SEC, firms rarely issue CP with maturities exceeding 270 days. Another consideration when determining the maturity is whether the CP would be eligible collateral for a bank borrowing from the Federal Reserve Bank's discount window. To be eligible, the maturity of the paper may not exceed 90 days. Because eligible paper trades at a lower cost than paper that is not eligible, firms prefer to issue paper whose maturity does not exceed 90 days.

To pay off holders of maturing CP, issuers generally use the proceeds obtained by selling new CP. This process is often described as "rolling over short-term paper." The risk that the investor in CP faces is that the issuer will be unable to sell new CP at maturity and, as a result, unable to obtain financing to pay off the investors in the maturity CP. This risk is referred to as **rollover risk**. As a safeguard against rollover risk, CP issued in the United States is typically backed by unused bank credit lines. The commitment fee that the bank charges for providing a credit line increases the effective cost of issuing CP.

Credit rating agencies evaluate the credit risk of CP and assign a letter rating based on the likelihood of default. The ratings assigned to CP by Moody's Investors Service, Standard & Poor's, and Fitch are shown in table 25.2.

Table 25.2
Commercial paper ratings.

	Commercial Rating Agency		
Category	Fitch	Moody's	Standard & Poor's
Superior	F1+ or F1	P1	A1+ or A1
Satisfactory	F2	P2	A2
Adequate	F3	P3	A3
Speculative	F4	NP	B or C
Defaulted	F5	NP	D

Issuers in the CP Market

The CP market is categorized by sector according to the type of issuer: financial corporations, nonfinancial corporations, and asset-backed commercial paper (ABCP). As shown in the following table, as of October 2017, in the United States there was U.S. $1,009.5 trillion of CP outstanding, according to the Federal Reserve. The breakdown between the various categories of commercial paper both domestic and foreign was (in billions of U.S. dollars):[13]

Nonfinancial			Financial				
Total	Domestic	Foreign	Total	Domestic	Foreign	Asset-Backed	Other
290.4	228.6	61.8	476.6	213.4	263.2	242.0	0.4

As we can see from the table above, financial entities are the dominant issuers of CP. Three types of financial companies issue CP: bank-related finance companies, captive finance companies, and independent finance companies. A bank holding company may have a subsidiary finance company that provides loans to enable individuals and businesses to acquire a wide range of products. Captive finance companies are subsidiaries of equipment manufacturing companies. Their primary purpose is to secure financing for the customers of the parent company. Independent finance companies are not subsidiaries of equipment manufacturing firms or bank holding companies.

The appendix to this chapter describes the asset-backed commercial paper market.

Although financial entities now dominate the issuance of CP, nonfinancial corporations dominated the CP market in the early years of its development. The major issuers were utility and transportation companies. By 1992, the financial sector dominated the market. At the beginning of the financial crisis, in mid-2007, the financial sector accounted for more than 92% of CP issuance.[14]

Identifying the reasons for the shift in dominance from nonfinancial sector issuers to financial sector issuers has been the focus of several studies. One study found that the shift could be attributed to three factors.[15] The first factor was nonfinancial companies' aggressive pursuit of policies to reduce their holdings in inventory. As holdings declined, there

13. The data are from "Commercial Paper Rates and Outstanding Summary," published by the Board of Governors of the Federal Reserve System, available at https://www.federalreserve.gov/releases/cp/.

14. Marcin Kacperczyk and Philipp Schnabl, "When Safe Proved Risky: Commercial Paper during the Financial Crisis of 2007–2009," *Journal of Economic Perspectives* 24, no. 1 (2010): 29–50.

15. Pu Shen, "Why Has the Nonfinancial Commercial Paper Market Shrunk Recently?" Federal Reserve Bank of Kansas City, *Economic Review* 88, no. 1 (2003): 55–75. Further evidence to support the conclusion in this paper can be found in Richard G. Anderson and Charles S. Gascon, "The Commercial Paper Market, the Fed, and the 2007–2009 Financial Crisis," *Federal Reserve Bank of St. Louis Review* 91, no. 6 (2009): 589–612.

was less need to obtain short-term borrowing (such as CP) to fund inventory positions. The second factor was an increased tendency of nonfinancial companies to take advantage of relatively low interest rates to issue long-term bonds. This corporate management financial strategy removed the uncertainty about the risk of having to refinance at future interest rates that might be higher. Finally, the credit quality of issuers decreased, and the tolerance of investors for credit risk also decreased.

This shift from nonfinancial issuers to financial issuers has important implications, particularly in light of the discussion of the future of the interbank funding market earlier in this chapter. In fact, some now argue that the CP market is the new interbank funding market.

Directly Placed versus Dealer-Placed Paper

CP is classified as either directly placed paper or dealer placed paper. **Directly placed paper** is sold by the issuing firm directly to investors without the help of an agent or an intermediary. (An issuer may set up its own dealer firm to handle sales.) Most issuers of direct paper are financial companies. These entities require continuous funds to enable them to provide loans to customers. As a result, they find it cost effective to establish a sales force to sell their CP directly to investors. General Electric Capital Corporation (GE Capital) is an example of a direct issuer, having issued CP for more than 50 years. GE Capital is the principal financial services arm of General Electric Company and is the largest and most active direct issuer in the United States.

Dealer-placed CP requires the services of an agent to sell an issuer's paper. CP agents are large securities dealer firms and subsidiaries of bank holding companies. Typically, nonfinancial companies and smaller financial companies use this avenue for issuing CP, because the amount and frequency at which they need to borrow cannot justify maintaining a sales force. The agent distributes the paper on a best-efforts underwriting basis (for more on best-efforts underwriting, see chapter 9) by investment banking firms.

Tier 1 and Tier 2 Paper

A major investor in CP is MMFs, which we describe later. The SEC imposes restrictions on the investments made by these entities. Specifically, Rule 2a-7 of the Investment Company Act of 1940 limits the credit risk exposure of money market mutual funds by restricting their investments to "eligible" paper. Eligibility is defined in terms of the CP credit ratings shown in table 25.2. To be eligible paper, the issue must carry one of the two highest ratings (1 or 2) from at least two of the nationally recognized statistical rating organizations. Tier 1 paper is defined as eligible paper that is rated 1 by at least two of the rating organizations; Tier 2 paper security is defined as eligible paper that is not a Tier 1 security.

MMFs may hold no more than 5% of their assets in the Tier 1 paper of any individual issuer and no more than 1% of their assets in the Tier 2 paper of any individual issuer. Furthermore, holdings of Tier 2 paper may not represent more than 5% of the fund's assets.

Defaults in the CP Market

From its beginnings until 1970, the CP market grew continuously, with no real crisis. In June 1970, a major issuer of CP at the time, Penn Central Railroad, with $84 million outstanding, faced financial difficulties, which raised concerns in the CP market. Because of the importance of the CP market, the federal government provided assistance that permitted Penn Central to repay maturing CP. The plan failed, and one year, later Penn Central filed for bankruptcy.

Despite recessionary periods, the years that followed the Penn Central episode saw the market grow in terms of issuance, fostered by the growth in MMFs, which were the major investors in CP. It was not until 1982 that the market saw its first default since Penn Central, the default by Johns Manville Corporation.[16] That was followed by three defaults in 1989 and three more in 1990.[17] The defaults in 1989 prompted federal legislation to tighten the rules for the purchasing of CP by MMFs that we described earlier (i.e., SEC Rule 2a-7). Fast-forward to the fall of 2007: The subprime mortgage crisis in the United States brought down the growth of the ABCP market. As explained in the appendix to this chapter, this sector of the CP market provided funding for the issuance of securitized products, particularly subprime mortgage–backed securities that we describe in chapter 30. Failures in this market by issuers of ABCP closed down this market sector. Another key event in the CP market was the bankruptcy of Lehman Brothers in September 2008. As a result of these events, by fall 2008, market participants were concerned about the ability of the CP market to survive, given the demands placed on it. Investors reallocated their short-term investments from the CP market to MMFs that held only government securities.

Because of the importance of this market, federal programs were enacted by the U.S. Department of the Treasury and the Fed to address two potential problems caused by the failures in the CP market. The first problem was the concern that financial issuers of CP would not make timely payments to investors on their obligation at the maturity date and would thereby extend the maturity date. To deal with this concern, the Fed instituted several lending programs during the financial crisis, but the two principal ones dealing with the CP market were the Commercial Paper Funding Facility and the Asset-Backed Commercial Paper Money Market Fund Liquidity Facility, both created in September 2008. The programs involved the purchase by the Fed of CP, the first time in the Fed's history that it had been a purchaser of this type of asset. The Fed's participation, which began at the end of October 2008, stabilized the CP market. As a result of the Fed's participation, it became the largest single investor in CP by January 2009. The Fed held 22% of outstanding CP at that time, but it subsequently reduced its holdings to 3.4% by October 2009.[18]

16. Mitchell A. Post, "The Evolution of the U.S. Commercial Paper Market Since 1980," *Federal Reserve Bulletin* 78, no. 12 (1992): 880–891.

17. Anderson and Gascon, "The Commercial Paper Market, the Fed, and the 2007–2009 Financial Crisis."

18. Kacperczyk and Schnabl, "When Safe Proved Risky," 20.

The second problem lay in the potential impact on the major holders of commercial MMFs. As explained later, these collective investment vehicles are designed to maintain a net asset value (NAV) of $1. The concern was that these funds would suspend redemption of shares as a consequence of problems with their CP holdings. When we discuss MMFs later in the chapter, we will describe what the federal government did to address the second concern.

Yields on CP

CP may be issued in either a discount form or an interest-bearing form. In a discount form, the investor buys the paper at less than face value and when it matures receives the face value. The difference between the face value and the purchase price is the interest. When the paper is issued in interest-bearing form, it is purchased from the issuer at face value and a specified interest rate. At maturity, the investor receives the face value plus the accrued interest based on the specified interest rate.

The yield offered on CP tracks that of other money market instruments. There are three reasons that the yield on CP is higher than that on short-term U.S. Treasury securities for the same maturity. First, the investor in CP is exposed to credit risk. Second, interest earned from investing in Treasury bills is exempt from state and local income taxes; as a result, CP must offer a higher yield to offset this tax disadvantage relative to Treasury bills. Finally, CP is less liquid than Treasury bills. The liquidity premium demanded may be small, however, because investors typically follow a buy-and-hold strategy with CP and so are less concerned with liquidity.

Non-U.S. CP Markets

Non-U.S. corporations issue CP in the U.S. market, which, as noted earlier, is referred to as "Yankee CP." Other countries have developed their own CP markets for companies domiciled in their country and for foreign companies. For example, in Japan, CP can be issued by Japanese corporations in Japan's domestic market and yen-dominated CP can be issued by non-Japanese entities. The latter CP is referred to as Samurai CP. According to the Asian Development Bank, other Asian countries that issue CP are Malaysia and the Philippines. Although domestic commercial paper has developed in some European countries (especially in France, Spain, and the United Kingdom), the eurocommercial paper (ECP) market is the market of choice for many European CP issuers. ECP is short-term unsecured debt issued in Euromarkets with maturities of 1 to 360 days. As of June 2016, financial ECP was U.S. $325.73 billion, and corporate ECP stood at $21.99 billion, according to the European Central Bank.

ECP is issued and placed outside the jurisdiction of the currency of denomination. U.S. CP and ECP differ with respect to the characteristics of the paper and the structure of the market. First, CP issued in the United States usually has a maturity of less than 270 days, with the most common maturity ranging from 30 to 50 days or less. The maturity of ECP can be considerably longer. The average maturity of ECP is about twice as long as U.S. commercial paper. Second, although an issuer in the United States must have unused bank credit lines, it is possible to issue ECP without such backing in the ECP market. Third, ECP sports a wider distribution of issuer credit quality. Unlike most U.S. CP, most ECP is not rated. Fourth, in the United States, CP can be directly placed or dealer placed, but ECP is almost always dealer placed. ECP is issued on a best-efforts basis through a syndicate of dealers. The fifth distinction is that numerous dealers participate in the ECP market, whereas only a few dealers dominate the market in the United States. Finally, because of the longer maturity of ECP, it is traded more often in the secondary market than is U.S. CP. Investors in CP in the United States typically buy and hold to maturity, and the secondary market is thin and illiquid.

Large-Denomination Negotiable Certificates of Deposit

A **certificate of deposit** (CD) represents a financial obligation issued by a depository institution that indicates a specified sum of money deposited at the issuing depository institution. Depository institutions issue CDs to raise funds for financing their business activities. A CD bears a maturity date and a specified interest rate. It can be issued in any denomination. CDs issued by a depository are insured by the Federal Deposit Insurance Corporation (FDIC), but only for amounts up to $250,000 per account. CDs are not subject to any limit on the maximum maturity, but by Federal Reserve regulations, CDs cannot have a maturity of less than seven days.

A CD may be nonnegotiable or negotiable. In the former case, the initial depositor must wait until the maturity date of the CD to obtain the funds. If the depositor chooses to withdraw funds prior to the maturity date, an early withdrawal penalty is imposed. In contrast, a negotiable CD allows the initial depositor (or any subsequent owner of the CD) to sell the CD in the open market prior to the maturity date. The negotiable CDs purchased by institutional investors are **large-denomination negotiable CDs** that typically have a denomination of $10 million or more.

Our focus here is on the large-denomination negotiable CDs, and we refer to them simply as “CDs.” The largest group of investors in such CDs consists of MMFs.

CD Issuers

CDs can be classified into four categories, according to the issuing institution. First are CDs issued by domestic banks. Second are CDs denominated in U.S. dollars but issued outside the United States. These CDs are called **Eurodollar CDs**, or **euro CDs.** A third category of CD is the **Yankee CD**, a CD denominated in U.S. dollars and issued by a foreign bank with a branch in the United States. Finally, **thrift CDs** are issued by S&Ls and savings banks.

Money center banks and large regional banks are the primary issuers of domestic CDs. Most CDs are issued with a maturity of less than one year. Those issued with a maturity greater than one year are called **term CDs**.

Unlike Treasury bills, commercial paper, and banker's acceptances (discussed later), the yields on domestic CDs are quoted on an interest-bearing basis. CDs with a maturity of one year or less pay interest at maturity. For purposes of calculating interest, a year is treated as having 360 days. Term CDs issued in the United States normally pay interest semiannually, again with a year taken as 360 days.

With a **floating-rate CD**, the interest rate changes periodically in accordance with a predetermined formula that indicates the spread (or margin) above some index at which the rate will reset periodically. Floating-rate CDs may reset the coupon daily, weekly, monthly, quarterly, or semiannually. Typically, floating-rate CDs have maturities of 18 months to five years.

Euro CDs are U.S. dollar-denominated CDs issued primarily in London by U.S., Canadian, European, and Japanese banks.

CD Yields

The yields posted on CDs vary, depending on three factors: (1) the credit rating of the issuing bank, (2) the maturity of the CD, and (3) the supply of and demand for CDs. With respect to the third factor, banks and thrifts issue CDs as part of their liability management strategy, so the supply of CDs will be driven by the demand for bank loans and the cost of alternative sources of capital to fund these loans. Moreover, bank loan demand depends on the cost of alternative funding sources, such as CP. When loan demand is weak, CD rates decline. When demand is strong, the rates rise. The effect of maturity depends on the shape of the yield curve, a topic we covered in chapter 16.

Credit risk is an important consideration, as the amount of the deposit of a large-denomination negotiable CD far exceeds the maximum FDIC insurance. At one time, domestic CDs issued by money center banks traded on a "no-name basis" (i.e., they offered a uniform yield regardless of the issuing money center bank). Recent financial crises in the banking industry, however, caused investors to take a closer look at issuing banks. **Prime CDs** (those issued by highly rated domestic banks) trade at a lower yield than **nonprime CDs** (those issued by lower-rated domestic banks). Because of investors' unfamiliarity with foreign banks, generally Yankee CDs trade at a higher yield than do domestic CDs.

Euro CDs offer a higher yield than domestic CDs for three reasons. First, the Federal Reserve imposes reserve requirements on CDs issued by U.S. banks that do not apply to issuers of euro CDs. The reserve requirement effectively raises the cost of funds to the issuing bank, because it cannot invest all the proceeds it receives from the issuance of a CD, and the amount that must be kept as reserves will not earn a return for the bank. Because it earns less on funds raised by selling domestic CDs, the domestic issuing bank pays less on its domestic CD than on a euro CD. Second, the bank issuing the CD must pay an insurance premium to the FDIC, which again raises the cost of funds. Finally, euro CDs are dollar obligations payable by an entity operating in a foreign jurisdiction, exposing the holders to a risk (referred to as "sovereign risk") that their claim may not be enforced by the foreign jurisdiction. As a result, a portion of the spread between the yield offered on euro CDs and domestic CDs reflects what can be termed a "sovereign risk premium." This premium varies with the degree of confidence in the international banking system.

CD yields are higher than yields on Treasury securities of the same maturity. The spread is due mainly to the credit risk that a CD investor is exposed to and the fact that CDs offer less liquidity. The spread resulting from credit risk varies with both economic conditions and confidence in the banking system, increasing during a "flight to quality" (which means investors shift their funds in significant amounts to debt of high quality or little risk) or a crisis in the banking system.

Banker's Acceptances

A **banker's acceptance** (BA) is a financial instrument created to facilitate commercial trade transactions. This financial instrument is referred to as a BA because the issuing bank accepts the ultimate responsibility to repay a loan to the holder of the financial instrument. The use of BAs to finance a commercial transaction is referred to as **acceptance financing**, and BAs are accordingly sometimes referred to as "acceptances."

The transactions in which BAs are created include (1) the importing of goods into the United States, (2) the exporting of goods from the United States to foreign entities, (3) the storing and shipping of goods between two foreign countries where neither the importer nor the exporter is a U.S. firm,[19] and (4) the storing and shipping of goods between two entities in the United States. As demonstrated in the following illustration, maturities are typically arranged to cover the time required to ship and dispose of the goods being financed.

BAs are sold on a discounted basis, just as Treasury bills and CP are. To calculate the rate to be charged the customer for issuing a BA, a bank determines the rate for which it can sell its BA in the open market. To this rate it adds a commission.

Illustration of the Creation of a BA

The best way to explain the creation of a BA is by an illustration. Several entities are involved in our hypothetical transaction:

19. Banker's acceptances created from these transactions are called "third-country acceptances."

- Car Imports Corporation of American (Car Imports), a firm in New Jersey that sells automobiles;
- Germany Fast Autos Inc. (GFA), a manufacturer of automobiles in Germany;
- First Hoboken Bank (Hoboken Bank), a commercial bank in Hoboken, New Jersey;
- Berlin National Bank (Berlin Bank), a bank in Germany; and
- High-Caliber Money Market Fund, a mutual fund in the United States that invests in money market instruments.

Car Imports and GFA are considering a commercial transaction. Car Imports wants to import 15 cars manufactured by GFA. GFA is concerned with the ability of Car Imports to make payment on the 15 cars when they are received. Acceptance financing is suggested as a means for facilitating the transaction. Car Imports offers $300,000 for the 15 cars. The terms of the sale stipulate payment to be made to GFA 60 days after it ships the 15 cars to Car Imports. GFA determines whether it is willing to accept the $300,000. When considering the offering price, GFA must calculate the present value of the $300,000, because it will not be receiving payment until 60 days after shipment. Suppose that GFA agrees to these terms.

Car Imports arranges with its bank, Hoboken Bank, to issue a letter of credit. The letter of credit indicates that Hoboken Bank will make good on the payment of $300,000 that Car Imports must make to GFA 60 days after shipment. The letter of credit, or time draft, will be sent by Hoboken Bank to GFA's bank, Berlin Bank. On receipt of the letter of credit, Berlin Bank will notify GFA, which will then ship the 15 cars. After the cars are shipped, GFA presents the shipping documents to Berlin Bank and receives the present value of $300,000. GFA is now out of the picture.

Berlin Bank presents the time draft and the shipping documents to Hoboken Bank. The latter will then stamp "accepted" on the time draft. By doing so, Hoboken Bank creates a BA and agrees to pay the holder of this BA $300,000 at the maturity date. Car Imports receives the shipping documents so that it can procure the 15 cars once it signs a note or some other type of financing arrangement with Hoboken Bank.

At this point, the holder of this BA is the Berlin Bank. It has two choices. It can continue to hold the BA as an investment in its loan portfolio, or it can request that Hoboken Bank make a payment of the present value of $300,000. Let's assume that Berlin Bank requests payment of the present value of $300,000.

Now the holder of this BA is Hoboken Bank. It has two choices: retain the BA as an investment as part of its loan portfolio or sell it to an investor. Suppose that Hoboken Bank chooses the latter, and that High-Caliber Money Market Fund is seeking a high-quality investment with the same maturity as that of the BA. Hoboken Bank sells the BA to the MMF at the present value of $300,000. Rather than sell the instrument directly to an investor, Hoboken Bank could sell it to a dealer, who would then resell it to an investor, such as an MMF. In either case, at the maturity date, the MMF presents the BA to Hoboken Bank, receiving $300,000, which the bank in turn recovers from Car Imports.

Accepting Banks

Banks that create BAs are called **accepting banks**. Banker's acceptances can be distributed through a dealer market, which involves 15 to 20 large firms, most of which are headquartered in New York City. The larger regional banks maintain their own sales forces to sell the BAs they create but will use dealers to distribute those they cannot sell.

Eligible BAs

The Board of Governors of the Federal Reserve classifies a BA as either an eligible or an ineligible BA. The classification is important. There are two types of eligible BAs. The first is an eligible BA that a bank uses as collateral for a loan at the Fed's discount window. Regulation A of the Fed sets forth the eligibility requirements. The second type of eligible BA is one that the Federal Open Market Committee is permitted to purchase. Regulation B sets forth the eligibility requirements.

One requirement for eligibility is maturity, which, with a few exceptions, cannot exceed six months. Although the other requirements for eligibility are too detailed to review here, the basic principle is simple.[20] The candidate BA should be financing a self-liquidating commercial transaction.

Eligibility is also important because the Fed imposes a reserve requirement on funds raised by means of BAs that are ineligible. BAs sold by an accepting bank are potential liabilities of the bank, but no reserve requirements are imposed for eligible BAs. Consequently, most BAs satisfy the various eligibility criteria. Finally, the Federal Reserve also imposes a limit on the amount of eligible BAs that may be issued by a bank.

Although the Fed no longer purchases BAs as part of its open market operations, this has not always been the case. There is a history of the Fed's participation in the BA market dating back to the beginning of the creation of the Federal Reserve System in 1916 with the goal of developing this sector of the money market to compete with the banks in London. At that time, the Fed actively discounted BAs and purchased eligible BAs. In fact, during one period in U.S. history, the Fed's open market policy involved the purchase of only BAs.[21]

20. The eligibility requirements are described in William C. Melton and Jean M. Mahr, "Bankers' Acceptances," Federal Reserve Bank of New York, *Quarterly Review* 6, no. 2 (1981): 39–55.

21. See chapter 4 in Allan H. Meltzer, *A History of the Federal Reserve* (Chicago: University of Chicago Press, 2003).

Credit Risk

Investing in BAs exposes the investor to the credit risk that neither the borrower nor the accepting bank will be able to pay the principal due at the maturity date. The market interest rates that BAs offer investors reflect this risk, because BAs have higher yields than risk-free Treasury bills. A yield may also include a premium for relative illiquidity. The yield on a BA has such a premium because its secondary market is far less developed than that of a Treasury bill. Hence, the spread between rates on BAs and rates on Treasury bills represents a combined reward to investors for bearing the higher risk and relative illiquidity of a BA. That spread is not constant over time. The change in the spread reveals shifting investor valuation of the risk and illiquidity differences between the assets.

Money Market Funds

Now that we have described money market instruments, we conclude this chapter by discussing a major institutional investor that participates in the money market: MMFs. In chapter 32, we explain mutual funds (open-end funds), a type of registered investment vehicle and one type of collective investment vehicle. In the category of mutual funds is one type that invests only in financial instruments that have a maturity of one year or less. These mutual funds are called **money market funds** and are approaching $3 trillion under management.

Although we have mentioned the role of MMFs as investors many times throughout this chapter, because MMFs are viewed as cash equivalents, they appeal to retail and institutional investors seeking highly liquid short-term investment vehicles. The portfolio managers of MMFs have an investment objective of obtaining the highest potential return consistent with the restrictions on the types of money market instruments in which they may invest and maintain an NAV of $1 at all times. Historically, it has been the $1 stable NAV objective that MMFs maintain under Rule 2a-7 that has appealed to investors and resulted in the dramatic growth in MMFs. The concern of investors is that the portfolio might include money market instruments whose market value declines significantly such that the NAV declines below $1 (referred to as "breaking the buck"). A typical warning given to potential investors about the risk associated with investing in an MMF which appears in the prospectus of an MMF is: "An investment in a money market fund is not insured or guaranteed by the Federal Deposit Insurance Corporation. The fund seeks to preserve the value of your investment at $1.00 per share. However, it is possible to realize a loss of capital by investing in the fund. This is because interest rate increases can cause the price of money market securities and hence the fund's value to decrease."

MMFs are regulated by the SEC because of their crucial role in the financial system. For example, earlier we described SEC Rule 2a-7, which restricts the types of CP that can be purchased by MMFs. Because of the problems that occurred with MMFs in the 2008–2009 financial crisis, legislation has been adopted and other legislation proposed for regulating MMFs, as we discuss later in this section.

Types of MMFs

MMFs are classified according to the types of money market instruments in which the fund manager may invest. The first classification is based on the tax treatment of the money market instruments that may be included in the portfolio. Taxable MMFs invest in the private money market instruments described earlier in this chapter, as well as in Treasury securities and federal agency securities. Tax-free MMFs invest in the money market instruments issued by state and local governments, which are described in chapter 32.

Taxable and tax-free MMFs are classified further, again based on the types of money market instruments in which they are permitted to invest. Taxable MMFs fall into three categories: those that invest only in Treasury securities, those that invest in Treasury and agency securities, and those that invest in Treasury and agency securities and the private money market instruments described in this chapter.

Taxable MMFs that invest in Treasury securities, agency securities, and the private money market instruments described in this chapter are referred to **as prime money market funds**. With respect to credit risk, prime MMFs carry greater risk than taxable MMFs that invest in Treasury securities only or those that invest in Treasury securities and agency securities. Accordingly, the potential yield is higher for prime MMFs.

Tax-free MMFs are categorized as national municipal MMFs and state municipal MMFs. **National municipal MMFs** invest in high-quality, short-term municipal money market instruments that are typically exempt from federal income taxes. **State municipal MMFs** restrict the holdings to instruments of the designated state.

SEC MMF Rules Adopted and Proposed as a Result of the Financial Crisis

Because of the importance of the money market to the financial market and, in turn, the critical role of MMFs as suppliers of capital to the money market, MMFs are highly regulated by the SEC so as to reduce the interest rate risk, credit risk, and liquidity risk faced by investors in this collective investment vehicle. Before the financial crisis that began in 2007, only one MMF had ever broken the buck (i.e., the NAV fell below \$1). That track record since the development of the MMF made investors confident about the safety of MMFs as a short-term investment vehicle. Events since the financial crisis, coupled with recent reports on how other MMFs would have broken the buck had it not been for support by the MMF's sponsor, prompted further regulation.

In 2008 one prime MMF, the Reserve Primary Fund, a \$65 billion fund, became the second MMF to break the buck. The reason for this was the investment of this fund in CP by Lehman Brothers Holdings Inc. We recall here that reserve funds can invest in CP in addition to Treasury and federal agency financial instruments. Reserve Primary Fund, which had a \$785 million position in Lehman's CP when that firm failed on September 15, 2008, did not have sufficient assets to ensure that holders of their shares could redeem them at \$1 per share. The failure of Lehman Brothers resulted in a share price (NAV) of \$0.97, a loss of 3%. As a result, there were massive redemptions, the equivalent to a run on a bank. To meet the demand for redemptions, the fund's portfolio manager liquidated investments in a money market that was already in a panic mode. The problem faced by the Reserve Primary Fund then spread to other MMFs, resulting in redemptions of about $310 billion from prime MMFs (primarily by institutional investors) during the week of Lehman Brothers' failure.[22]

However, at least two studies have reported that many more MMFs were in danger of breaking the buck were it not for the support of the MMF's sponsors. In a 2012 Staff Report by the Federal Reserve Bank of New York, the authors of the report found that in September and October 2008, the losses for at least 29 MMFs were large enough to cause them to break the buck without the support of the sponsor of the MMF.[23] The average loss would have been 2.2%. They found that at least five MMFs experienced losses of 3% of assets. The Prime Reserve Fund, as noted above, lost 3%. A 2012 study by the Federal Reserve Bank of Boston that examined 341 prime MMFs from 2007 to 2011 found that at least 21 funds were spared breaking the buck because of sponsorship support.[24] Each of the 21 MMFs received support of about 0.5% of the fund's assets to maintain an NAV of $1.

Because of the important role of MMFs as suppliers of capital to financial and nonfinancial corporations, the money market froze, and corporations that relied on the issuance of CP faced funding problems. The rippling impact of the failure of the Reserve Primary Fund on the MMF industry and the money market itself resulted in government intervention. The announcement of the U.S. Department of the Treasury of its Temporary Treasury Money Market Guarantee Program in September 19, 2008, which would temporarily provide a guarantee for all MMFs, halted the run on MMFs.

As a first step to addressing regulatory concerns identified from the financial crisis, the SEC adopted several rule changes for MMFs. The key reforms that were adopted in February 2010 to better protect investors in MMFs during periods of financial distress were

- rules to enhance risk-limiting constraints on MMF portfolios,
- procedures for facilitating the orderly redemption of MMF shares, and
- the imposition of constraints on repo agreements.

The rules to enhance risk-limiting constraints involved tightening credit standards for MMF portfolio holdings, shortening the weighted average maturity of holdings, and adopting

22. Security and Exchange Commission, "Unofficial Transcript: Roundtable on Money Market Funds and Systemic Risk," May 10, 2011, http://www.sec.gov/spotlight/mmf-risk/mmf-risk-transcript-051011.htm.

23. Patrick E. McCabe, Marco Cipriani, Michael Holscher, and Antoine Martin, "The Minimum Balance at Risk: A Proposal to Mitigate the Systemic Risks Posed by Money Market Funds," Federal Reserve Bank of New York Staff Report 564, July 2012.

24. Steffanie A. Brady, Ken E. Anadu, and Nathaniel R. Cooper, "The Stability of Prime Money Market Mutual Funds: Sponsor Support from 2007 to 2011," Federal Reserve Bank of Boston, Risk and Policy Unit, Working Paper RPA 12–13, August 13, 2012.

liquidity requirements. The procedure for orderly redemption was a new rule introduced with the goal of mitigating systemic risk caused by breaking the buck. Under the new rule, the portfolio manager of an MMF that is at risk for breaking the buck is permitted to promptly suspend redemptions and liquidate its portfolio in an orderly manner.

Because of the importance of MMFs in repo agreements, the new rules place more stringent constraints on the type of collateral that can be used. As we noted earlier, in a repo agreement, the collateral can be cash or securities (government securities or private debt instruments). The greater constraints involve repurchase agreements where the collateral is a private debt instrument.

To further improve safeguards for investors in MMFs, the *Report of the President's Working Group on Financial Markets: Money Market Fund Reform Options* (hereafter the PWG report), published on October 21, 2010, identified features of MMFs that made them susceptible to runs and discussed issues related to systemic risk for prime MMFs.[25] Although it endorsed the new rules adopted in February 2010, the PWG report acknowledged that further reforms were needed to prevent the types of market disruptions that had occurred in September 2008. More specifically, the PWG report "undertook a study of possible further reforms that, individually or in combination, might mitigate systemic risk by complementing the SEC's changes to MMF regulation."[26]

The PWG report identified several policy options for further reducing the risks of a run on an MMF, and it sought public comment on these suggestions. The key policy options suggested in the PWG report include the following:

- Allow the NAV to float rather than be maintained at $1 per share. It is the vulnerability to breaking the buck that caused the run on MMFs during the financial crisis.
- Adopt a two-tier system of MMFs: (1) a stable-value NAV MMF and (2) a floating-rate NAV MMF.
- Require that MMFs establish a capital cushion.
- Establish a private emergency liquidity facility.

In July 2014, the SEC adopted its new MMF rules in an 869-page release. The two critical rules are (1) institutional prime and institutional tax-exempt MMFs are required to value their portfolio securities at market value and sell and redeem shares based on a floating NAV, and (2) government MMFs and retail MMFs are permitted to continue to seek to maintain a stable NAV at $1.

25. U.S. Department of the Treasury, *Report of the President's Working Group on Financial Markets: Money Market Fund Reform Options* (Washington, DC: December 21, 2010), available at http://www.treasury.gov/press-center/press-releases/Documents/10.21%20PWG%20Report%20Final.pdf. The President's Working Group consists of the secretary of the Treasury, the chair of the Federal Reserve Board of Governors, the chair of the Securities and Exchange Commission, and the chair of the Commodity Futures Trading Commission.

26. U.S. Department of the Treasury, *Report of the President's Working Group on Financial Markets*, 1.

Key Points

- Money market instruments are debt obligations that at issuance have a maturity of one year or less.
- The interbank funding market (interbank lending market) is the market where unsecured and secured loans are made between banks.
- Unsecured lending in the interbank funding market is done in the federal funds market.
- In the secured sector, lending is done by means of repurchase agreements in the repo market.
- In London, unsecured lending in the interbank funding market is used to estimate the cost of borrowing by banks. The rate in this market is the London interbank offered rate (LIBOR).
- Eurocurrency is any currency on deposit in banks outside their country of origin.
- LIBOR is calculated by the British Bankers' Association based on rates reported by a panel of large banks for actual and estimated borrowings.
- The official LIBOR, reported for seven maturities and five currencies, is the most important global interest rate benchmark because of its use as a reference rate for interest rate derivatives and the setting of business and consumer loan rates.
- Manipulation of LIBOR by the panel banks resulted in investigations by regulators and lawsuits filed by parties that claimed financial damages as a consequence of the manipulation.
- In the federal funds market, depository institutions borrow (buy) and sell (lend) excess reserves held in the form of deposits in a Federal Reserve Bank.
- The interest rate for overnight loans of excess reserves as determined in the fed funds market is the funds rate. The Fed establishes a target level for this rate, and so it is not truly a market-determined rate.
- The Federal Reserve Bank pays interest on required reserves and a higher interest rate on excess reserves.
- Disruptions in the interbank funding market during the financial crisis raised the issue of whether this market will be viable in the future.
- A repurchase agreement (or repo agreement) is a lending transaction in which the borrower uses a security as collateral for the borrowing. The transaction is referred to as a "repurchase agreement," because it specifies the sale of a security and its subsequent repurchase at a future date.
- For a repo agreement, the difference between the purchase (repurchase) price and the sale price is the dollar interest cost of the loan.
- An overnight repo is for one day; a loan for more than one day is called a "term repo."

• The collateral in a repo may be a Treasury security, money market instrument, federal agency security, or mortgage-backed security.

• The parties to a repo are exposed to credit risk, limited by margin and the market-to-market practices included in the repo agreement.

• The Fed uses the repo market to implement monetary policy.

• Factors that determine the repo rate are the federal funds rate, the credit quality and liquidity of the collateral, the term of the repo, the delivery requirement, and the availability of the collateral.

• Repo rates can be negative in times of market stress and in normal conditions when rates are near zero.

• Commercial paper (CP) is a short-term unsecured promissory note issued in the open market that represents the obligation of the issuing entity.

• Generally, CP has a maturity of less than 90 days.

• Financial and nonfinancial corporations issue CP, with most issued by financial corporations.

• Directly placed CP is sold by the issuing firm directly to investors without using an agent as an intermediary. For dealer-placed CP, the issuer uses the services of an agent to sell its paper.

• Asset-backed commercial paper (ABCP) has been used to fund assets using the securitization process. Unlike traditional securitization, the special-purpose vehicle had to roll over the CP issued and was also permitted to obtain additional assets financed by the issuance of additional CP.

• Eurocommercial paper is issued and placed outside the jurisdiction of the currency of denomination; it differs from dollar-denominated paper issued in the United States in several ways.

• Certificates of deposit (CDs) are issued by banks and thrifts to raise funds for financing their business activities. Unlike other bank deposits, CDs are negotiable in the secondary market. CDs can be classified into four types: domestic CDs, Eurodollar CDs (or euro CDs), Yankee CDs, and thrift CDs.

• A banker's acceptance is a vehicle created to facilitate commercial trade transactions, particularly international transactions.

• The term "banker's acceptance" arises because a bank accepts the responsibility to repay a loan to the holder of the vehicle created in a commercial transaction in case the debtor fails to perform.

• Eligible banker's acceptances have an advantage in that they can be used as collateral when borrowing from the Fed at its discount window, and no reserves are required.

• Money market funds (MMFs) are major investors in money market instruments. They are designed to maintain a $1 NAV.

- There are two types of MMFs: taxable and tax-free.
- The three types of taxable MMFs are those that invest in (1) only Treasury securities, (2) Treasury and federal agency securities, and (3) Treasury, federal agency securities, and private money market instruments (these are referred to as “prime MMFs”).
- Tax-free MMFs are categorized as national municipal MMFs and state municipal MMFs.
- The concern with MMFs is that the portfolio selection could result in the NAV falling below $1 per share. Such an occurrence is referred to as “breaking the buck.”
- Because of the importance of MMFs to the financial markets, additional safeguards have been adopted by the SEC to enhance the credit and liquidity of their portfolios.
- New rules adopted by the SEC to improve the safety of MMFs are based on whether the fund is an institutional prime, an institutional tax-exempt, a government, or a retail MMF.
- Institutional prime and institutional tax-exempt MMFs must be valued at a floating-rate NAV. Government and retail MMFs are still required to maintain a constant NAV of $1.

Questions

1. What is the interbank funding market?
2. How does interbank funding by banks using the federal funds market differ from that in the repo market?
3. What problems were encountered in the interbank funding market during the 2008–2009 financial crisis?
4. For each of the following statements, explain whether you agree or disagree:

a. The fed funds rate and LIBOR are interest rates determined in the U.S. interbank funding market based on actual transactions by banks borrowing from other banks.

b. The Federal Reserve Banks pay interest on excess reserves but not on required reserves.

c. The official LIBOR is provided only for the U.S. dollar and only for maturities up to six months.

5. There is a parallel structure in the provision of banking services—onshore and offshore. Explain.
6. a. Why is LIBOR the most important benchmark interest rate in the global financial market?

b. Explain the scandal involving the manipulation of LIBOR.

7. One party in a repo transaction is said to “buy collateral,” the other party is said to “sell collateral.” Why?
8. Why would the lender of funds in a repo transaction be exposed to credit risk?
9. What is meant by a repo dealer running a “matched book”?

10. When a shortage of a specific security occurs in a repo transaction, will the repo rate increase or decrease?

11. a. What is a system repo?

b. What is a customer repo?

12. In a repo transaction, what is meant by a "haircut"?

13. Suppose the dollar principal in a repo transaction is $40 million and the repo rate is 2.9%.

a. What is the dollar interest if the term of the repo is one day?

b. What is the dollar interest if the term of the repo is five days?

14. Negative repo rates of interest introduce perverse incentives to counterparties of a repo contract. Explain.

15. During the 2008–2009 financial crisis:

a. What type of collateral was preferred by banks that were willing to lend in the interbank funding market?

b. Why was an increase in the haircut in a repo transaction like a run in the repo market?

16. Why is commercial paper (CP) an alternative to short-term bank borrowing for a corporation?

17. Explain the following statement: "The CP market is now the key market for liquidity for financial institutions."

18. How does a securitization in which the special-purpose vehicle issues asset-backed CP differ from a traditional securitization?

19. a. Why does CP issued in the United States have a maturity of less than 270 days?

b. Why does CP issued in the United States typically have a maturity of less than 90 days?

20. What is meant by a "large-denomination negotiable certificate of deposit"?

21. What is eurocommercial paper? How does it differ from commercial paper issued in the United States?

22. Why is a bank that creates a banker's acceptance referred to as an "accepting bank"?

23. Why is the "eligibility" of a banker's acceptance important?

24. What is meant by a money market fund (MMF) "breaking the buck"?

25. Why is there greater credit risk with prime MMFs than with other taxable MMFs?

26. Explain whether you agree or disagree with the following statements:

a. In the history of MMFs, the buck has been broken only once.

b. A prime MMF is allowed to invest in any private money market instrument as long as it has a maturity of less than one year.

27. In the SEC release setting forth the new rules adopted in July 2014 requiring a floating NAV for certain types of MMFs, the SEC explained that the intent of the new requirement was not to deter redemptions that constitute "rational risk management by shareholders or that reflect a general incentive to avoid loss." Instead, the SEC said that the purpose of the new rule was to reduce the first-mover advantage inherent in a stable NAV fund by removing the incentive for redemption activity that could result from investors seeking to exploit an opportunity to redeem shares at a stable share price even if the portfolio suffered a loss.

a. What types of MMFs are required to have a floating NAV?

b. Explain what is meant by a "first-mover advantage," and why a floating NAV reduces the likelihood of redemption activity that the SEC indicates is harmful to investors.

Appendix: Asset-Backed Commercial Paper

In chapter 27, we will discuss the securitization process and the asset-backed securities (ABSs) that corporations can use to obtain debt funding. When CP is issued as part of a securitization that has a short-term maturity, then the CP is referred to as ABCP.[27] As in the case of corporate debt obligations, the distinction between ABSs and ABCP is primarily the tenure of the financial instrument. The former is a medium- to long-term asset, whereas the latter has a short-term maturity.

In our description of ABSs in chapter 27, we explain that a pool of short-term receivables (e.g., credit card receivables) can be purchased by a special-purpose vehicle (SPV), and to fund the purchase of that pool of short-term receivables, the SPV will issue ABSs that are medium- to long-term in maturity. In contrast, securitization can be used by an SPV to finance a pool of longer-term receivables by issuing ABCP. The SPV's objective in a securitization by issuing CP to fund the purchase of the receivables pool is to generate a spread between the yield that can be earned on the pool of receivables and the cost of the funds paid to the holders of the ABCP. Effectively, the SPV is employing a leveraged strategy just as a depository institution does when it borrows funds on a short-term basis and seeks to invest those funds to earn more than its fund cost.

A key distinction between the traditional securitization as described in chapter 27 and the use of securitization to fund a pool of receivables using ABCP has to do with ongoing funding and collateral (i.e., the pool of receivables). In a traditional securitization, once the funding is obtained (i.e., the ABSs are issued), there is no further need to obtain funding. That is, the SPV purchased the pool of receivables using the ABSs issued. In contrast, when ABCP is issued in a securitization, not only is it necessary for the SPV to roll over

27. For a more detailed discussion of ABCP, see chapter 9 in Frank J. Fabozzi and Vinod Kothari, *Introduction to Securitization* (Hoboken, NJ: John Wiley & Sons, 2008).

the ABCP to finance the pool of receivables but the securitization structure also involves adding to the receivables pool. That is, the collateral can increase over time.

Banks have been the major issuers of ABCP, maintaining ongoing ABCP programs. These are runs on the balance sheet of an entity established by the bank called an **ABCP conduit**, which is a thinly capitalized SPV. It is the conduit that continues to add more receivables and to fund their purchase by issuing ABCP. Although banks have been the major issuers of ABCP, nonbank entities have also issued CP. ABCP conduits have been classified as either **single-seller ABCP conduits** or **multiple-seller ABCP conduits** based on the number of originators that provided receivables to the pool.

Risks Associated with Investing in ABCP

The rollover risk to the holder of an ABCP is the same as that for investors in CP issued by nonfinancial corporations and financial corporations: the inability to find investors who are willing to purchase newly issued ABCP when the current ABCP matures. And it is for the same reason that liquidity support is needed for ABCP, just as it is for CP issued by nonfinancial corporations and financial corporations. ABCP is classified according to the type of liquidity support and can be either fully supported or partly supported by the bank that sponsors the ABCP program.

The disadvantage of a bank fully supporting its ABCP program is that for regulatory purposes, the assets held by the conduit must be included as part of the bank's assets for the determination of capital requirements. This is a disadvantage in that it raises the funding cost of an ABCP program because of reserves that must be held. Banks have developed variants of fully supported conduits that, although receiving bank support, have not been treated as such for regulatory purposes.

Another key risk is that ABCP conduits may have purchased long-term credit risk assets that are illiquid. More specifically, some ABCP conduits purchased residential mortgage loans made to borrowers with an impaired credit history. As explained in chapter 29, mortgage loans to borrowers with this credit characteristic are called "subprime mortgage loans." Mortgage loans themselves are highly illiquid. Consequently, ABCP conduits funding a pool of subprime mortgage loans may face difficulty in liquidating such loans if funds are needed to redeem maturing ABCP and the conduit cannot roll over its paper. This is indeed what happened in the financial crisis, as discussed in the body of this chapter.

26 Corporate Debt Markets

CONTENTS

Learning Objectives

After reading this chapter, you will understand:

- the debt financing alternatives available to corporations;
- the different forms of credit risk: default risk, credit spread risk, and downgrade risk;
- what event risk and headline risk are;
- the importance of credit ratings;
- the basic provisions in the Bankruptcy Reform Act of 1978;
- the difference between a liquidation and a reorganization;
- the principle of absolute priority in a bankruptcy;
- what a bank loan is and the difference between an investment-grade bank loan and a leveraged bank loan;
- the market for leveraged loans;
- what a syndicated loan is;
- the two ways a syndicated loan can be sold: assignment and participation;
- the basic terms of a loan agreement;
- the key provisions of a corporate bond issue;
- features of corporate bonds and the reason for their inclusion;
- the secondary market for corporate bonds, including the different types of electronic bond trading systems;
- the high-yield bond sector of the corporate bond market;
- the different type of bond structures used in the high-yield bond market;
- the difference between high-yield bonds and leveraged loans;

- the difference between preferred stock, corporate debt, and common stock;
- what a medium-term note is, and the characteristics of a structured note;
- defaults and recoveries on corporate bonds;
- what a lease financing transaction is; and
- the difference between a single-investor lease and a leveraged lease.

Corporate debt obligations include six financial instruments: (1) commercial paper, (2) bank loans market, (3) bonds, (4) medium-term notes, (5) asset-backed securities, and (6) equipment leases. Our focus in this chapter is on the bank loans, bonds, and medium-term notes. Commercial paper was covered in chapter 25, and asset-backed securities will be covered in chapter 27. At the end of this chapter, we discuss the bankruptcy or insolvency laws as they relate to corporate creditors.

Bank Loans

As an alternative to the issuance of securities, a corporation can raise funds by borrowing from a bank.[1] Until recently, in many countries, the dominant form of corporate borrowing was bank loans, because corporate bond markets were not yet well developed.

A corporation may use any of five sourcing alternatives: (1) a domestic bank in the corporation's home country, (2) a subsidiary of a foreign bank established in the corporation's home country, (3) a foreign bank domiciled in a country where the corporation does business, (4) a subsidiary of a domestic bank established in a country where the corporation does business, or (5) an offshore or Eurobank. Loans made by offshore banks are referred to as **eurocurrency loans**.[2]

The market classifies bank loans to corporate borrowers into two categories: investment-grade loans and leveraged loans. An **investment-grade loan** is a bank loan made to corporate borrowers that have an investment-grade rating. These loans are typically originated and held by the originating bank in its portfolio, because these loans are revolving lines of credit. In such a loan arrangement, a bank sets a maximum amount that can be borrowed by a corporation, and the corporation can take down any part of that amount and repay it at any time. Because of the ability of the corporate borrower to repay at any time and the absence of a maturity date for the loan, an investment-grade bank loan is not sold by the originating bank to institutional investors.

In contrast, a **leveraged loan** is a bank loan to a corporation that has a below-investment-grade rating. A leveraged loan has a maturity and the interest rate is floating, the reference

1. Bank debt is widely used as the senior financing for a leveraged buyout, acquisition, or recapitalization. These actions are collectively referred to as "highly leveraged transactions."

2. Such loans can be denominated in a variety of currencies. Loans denominated in U.S. dollars are called "Eurodollar loans."

rate being the LIBOR. In fact, when market participants refer to corporate bank loans, they typically mean a leveraged loan. These loans can be sold to institutional investors. In the next section, we discuss a corporate bond issued by corporations with a below-investment-grade rating called a "high-yield bond." A corporation may have as its debt obligations both leveraged loans and high-yield bonds. Later in this chapter, we discuss the difference between a leveraged loan and a high-yield bond.

Syndicated Bank Loans

A **syndicated bank loan** is one in which a group (or syndicate) of banks provides funds to the borrower. Roughly $2.5 trillion of financing to U.S. companies is provided by syndicated loans, with the size of a syndicated loan ranging from $20 million to more than $2 billion. Consequently, the need for a group of banks arises, because the amount sought by a borrower might be too large for any one bank to be exposed to the borrower's credit risk. Therefore, the syndicated bank loan is used by borrowers who seek to raise a large amount of funds in the bank loan market rather than through the issuance of securities.

The syndication may include using the securitization process to create collateralized loan obligations, discussed in chapter 39, and is therefore an important part of the corporate bank loan market. Another important component of this market is loans that provide short-term or backstop financing for corporations that are seeking funds until a more permanent source of financing can be obtained. Such loans are referred to as **bridge loans** if a loan is provided and **bridge loan commitments** if the agreement is to provide a future loan. Together, bridge loans and bridge loan commitments are referred to as **bridge loan facilities**.

Syndicated bank loans are called **senior bank loan loans** because of their priority position over subordinated lenders (bondholders) with respect to repayment of interest and principal. The interest rate on a syndicated bank loan is a rate that **floats**, which means that the loan rate is based on some reference rate. The loan rate is periodically reset at the reference rate plus a spread. The reference rate is typically LIBOR, although it could be the prime rate (the rate that a bank charges its most creditworthy customers) or the rate on CDs. The term of the loan is fixed. A syndicated loan is typically structured so that it is amortized according to a predetermined schedule, and repayment of principal begins after a specified number of years (typically not longer than five or six years). Structures in which no repayment of the principal is made until the maturity date can be arranged and are referred to as **bullet loans**.

A syndicated loan is arranged by either a bank or a securities house. The arranger then lines up the syndicate. Each bank in the syndicate provides the funds for which it has committed. The banks in the syndicate have the right to sell their parts of the loan subsequently to other banks.

Syndicated loans are distributed by two methods: assignment or participation. Each method has its advantages and disadvantages, with the method of assignment being the more desirable of the two. The holder of a loan that is interested in selling a portion can do so by passing the interest in the loan by the **method of assignment**. In this procedure, the seller transfers all rights completely to the holder of the assignment, now called the **assignee**. The assignee is said to have **privity of contract** with the borrower. Because of the clear path between the borrower and assignee, assignment is the more desirable choice of transfer and ownership. A **participation** involves a holder of a loan "participating out" a portion of the holding in that particular loan. The holder of the participation does not become a party to the loan agreement and has a relationship not with the borrower but with the seller of the participation. Unlike an assignment, a participation does not confer privity of contract on the holder of the participation, although the holder of the participation has the right to vote on certain legal matters concerning amendments to the loan agreement. These matters include changes regarding maturity, interest rate, and issues concerning the loan collateral. Because syndicated loans can be sold in this manner, they are marketable.

In response to the large number of bank loans issued and their strong credit protection, some commercial banks and securities houses are more willing to commit capital and resources to facilitate trading as broker-dealers. Also, these senior bank loans can be securitized through the same innovations discussed in chapter 27 for the securitization of loans and discussed further in chapter 39. Further development of the senior bank loan market will no doubt eventually erode the once-important distinction between a security and a loan: A security has long been seen as a marketable financial asset, whereas a loan has not been marketable. Interestingly, the trading of these loans is not limited to **performing loans**, which are loans whose borrowers are fulfilling contractual commitments. A market also exists for trading nonperforming loans—loans on which the borrowers have defaulted.

Secondary Market for Syndicated Bank Loans

Syndicated bank loans can be traded in the secondary market or securitized to create collateralized loan obligations using the securitization technology that is discussed in chapter 27. The trade association that has been the main advocate of commercial loans as an asset class is the Loan Syndications and Trading Association (LSTA). The LSTA has helped foster the development of a liquid and transparent secondary market for bank loans by establishing market practices and settlement and operational procedures. The LSTA collects quotations on U.S. loans on a daily basis.

In conjunction with Standard & Poor's Leveraged Commentary & Data index, the LSTA has also developed a leveraged loan index to gauge the performance of the different sectors of the syndicated loan market. The S&P/LSTA Leveraged Loan 100 Index is a weekly total return index.

Corporate Bonds

Corporate bonds are classified by the type of issuer. The four general classifications are (1) public utilities, (2) transportation companies, (3) banks/finance companies, and (4) industrial companies.[3] Finer breakdowns are often made to create more homogeneous groupings. For example, public utilities are subdivided into electric power companies, gas distribution companies, water companies, and communications companies. Transportation companies are divided further into airlines, railroads, and trucking companies. Banks/finance companies include money center banks and regional banks, savings and loan institutions, brokerage firms, insurance companies, and finance companies. Industrial companies are the catchall class and the most heterogeneous of the groups with respect to investment characteristics. Industrial companies include manufacturers, mining companies, merchandising companies, retailers, energy companies, and companies in service-related industries.

Classification of the Global Corporate Bond Market

There is no uniform system for classifying the sectors of the global corporate bond market. One possible classification is the one we used in chapter 1 to describe the global financial market. There we said that from the perspective of a given country, the global financial market can be classified into two markets: an internal financial market and an external financial market.

The internal financial market, also called the "national financial market," can be broken into two parts: the domestic financial market and the foreign financial market. The domestic financial market includes the domestic corporate bond market. This market is where issuers domiciled in the country issue bonds and where those bonds are subsequently traded.

The foreign financial market of a country includes the country's foreign corporate bond market. This is the market where bonds of issuers not domiciled in the country are issued and traded. For example, in the United States, the foreign bond market is where bonds are issued by non-U.S. entities and then subsequently traded. Bonds traded in the U.S. foreign bond market are nicknamed "Yankee bonds." In Japan, a yen-denominated bond issued by a British corporation and subsequently traded in Japan's bond market is part of the Japanese foreign bond market. Yen-denominated bonds issued by non-Japanese entities are nicknamed "samurai bonds." Foreign bonds in the United Kingdom are referred to as "bulldog bonds," those in the Netherlands are referred to as "Rembrandt bonds," and those in Spain are called "matador bonds."

3. Traditionally, the Yankee and Canadian bonds are considered part of the corporate bond market. These issues include dollar-denominated bonds issued in the United States by sovereign governments, local governments, and non-U.S. corporations.

Regulatory authorities in the country where the bond is issued impose certain rules governing their issuance. These may include the following:

- restrictions on the bond structures that may be issued (e.g., unsecured debt, zero-coupon bonds, convertible bonds),
- restrictions on the minimum or maximum size of an issue and/or the frequency with which an issuer may come to market,
- a waiting period before an issuer may bring the issue to market (imposed to avoid an oversupply of issues),
- a minimum quality standard (credit rating) for the issue or issuer,
- disclosure and periodic reporting requirements, and
- restrictions on the types of financial institutions permitted to underwrite issues.

In the 1980s, governments generally relaxed or abolished these restrictions to open up bond markets to issuers.

The **external corporate bond market**, also called the **international corporate bond market**, is that part of a country's external financial market that includes bonds with the following distinguishing features:

- they are underwritten by an international syndicate;
- at issuance, they are offered simultaneously to investors in more than one country;
- they are issued outside the jurisdiction of any single country; and
- they are in unregistered form.

Basic Features of a Corporate Bond Issue

The essential features of a corporate bond issue are relatively simple. The corporate issuer promises to pay a specified percentage of par value (known as the coupon payment) on designated dates and to repay par or principal value of the bond at maturity. In some countries, such as the United States, interest payments are made semiannually; in other countries, the interest payments are made annually. Failure to pay either principal or interest when due constitutes legal default, and court proceedings can be instituted to enforce the contract. Bondholders, as creditors, have a prior legal claim over common and preferred stockholders with regard to both income and assets of the corporation for the principal and interest due them.

The promises of corporate bond issuers and the rights of investors who buy their bonds are set forth in great detail in contracts called **bond indentures**. The covenants or restrictions on management are important in the analysis of the credit risk of a corporate bond issue. To determine at a particular time whether the corporate issuer is meeting its obligations, a third party to the contract is used: a corporate trustee. A corporate trustee is a bond or trust company with a corporate trust department and officers who are experts in performing the functions of a trustee. The indenture is made out to the corporate trustee as a representative of the interests of bondholders; that is, the trustee acts in a fiduciary capacity for investors who own the bond issue.

A bond's indenture clearly outlines three important aspects: its maturity, its security, and its provisions for retirement.

Maturity of bonds Most corporate bonds are **term bonds**; that is, they run for a term of years and then become due and payable. Term bonds are often referred to as having **bullet maturity**, or simply, **bullet bonds**. Any amount of the liability not paid off prior to maturity must be paid off at that time. The bond's term may be long or short. Generally, obligations due less than 10 years from the date of issue are called **notes**.[4]

Most corporate borrowings take the form of bonds due in 20 to 30 years. Term bonds may be retired by payment at final maturity or retired prior to maturity if provided for in the indenture. Some corporate bond issues are so arranged that specified principal amounts become due on specified dates prior to maturity. Such issues are called "serial bonds." Equipment trust certificates (discussed later) are structured as serial bonds.

Security for bonds Either real property (using a mortgage) or personal property may be pledged to offer security beyond that of the general credit standing of the issuer. A **mortgage bond** grants the bondholders a lien against the pledged assets. A **lien** is a legal right to sell mortgaged property to satisfy unpaid obligations to bondholders. In practice, the foreclosure and sale of mortgaged property are unusual. If a default occurs, usually a financial reorganization of the issuer makes the provision for settlement of the debt to bondholders. However, the mortgage lien is important, because it gives the mortgage bondholders a strong bargaining position relative to other creditors when determining the terms of a reorganization in a bankruptcy. (We discuss reorganization later in this chapter.)

Some companies do not own fixed assets or other real property, and so they have nothing on which they can give a mortgage lien to secure bondholders. Instead, these firms own securities of other companies and thus are holding companies. The firms whose shares are owned are subsidiaries. To satisfy the desire of bondholders for security, the holding companies pledge stocks, notes, bonds, or whatever other kind of financial instruments they own. These assets are termed "collateral" (or "personal property"), and bonds secured by such assets are called "collateral trust bonds."

4. From our discussion of the various debt instruments in chapter 25, it can be seen that the word "notes" is used to describe a variety of instruments, such as medium-term notes. The use of the term "notes" here is as a market convention distinguishing notes and bonds on the basis of the number of years to maturity at the time the security is issued.

Many years ago, the railway companies developed a way of financing the purchase of cars and locomotives (i.e., rolling stock) that enabled them to borrow at just about the lowest rates in the corporate bond market. Railway rolling stock was for a long time regarded by investors as excellent security for debt. The equipment is sufficiently standardized that it can be used by one railway as well as another. And, of course, it can be readily moved from the tracks of one railroad to those of another. Therefore, generally a good market exists for the lease or sale of cars and locomotives. The railroads take advantage of these characteristics of rolling stock by developing a legal arrangement for giving investors a legal claim on it that is different from, and generally superior to, a mortgage lien.

In this situation, the legal arrangement vests legal title to railway equipment in a trustee. When a railway company orders some cars and locomotives from a manufacturer, the manufacturer transfers legal title to the equipment to that trustee. The trustee in turn leases the equipment to the railroad, and at the same time sells equipment trust certificates to obtain the funds to pay the manufacturer. The trustee collects lease payments from the railroad and uses these receipts to pay interest and principal on the certificates. The principal is therefore paid off on specified dates, a provision that distinguishes a certificate from a term bond.

The general idea of the equipment trust arrangement is also used by companies engaged in providing other kinds of transportation. For example, trucking companies finance the purchase of huge fleets of trucks in the same manner; airlines use this kind of financing to purchase planes; and international oil companies use it to buy huge tankers.

A **debenture bond** is not secured by a specific pledge of property, which does not mean that this type of bond has no claim on the property of issuers or on their earnings. Debenture bondholders hold the claim of general creditors on all assets of the issuer not pledged specifically to secure other debt. Also, holders of debentures can claim pledged assets to the extent that these assets have value greater than that necessary to satisfy secured creditors. A **subordinated debenture bond** is an issue that ranks after secured debt, after debenture bonds, and often after some general creditors in its claim on assets and earnings.

The type of corporate security issued determines the cost to the issuer. For a given corporation, mortgage bonds will cost less than debenture bonds, and debenture bonds will cost less than subordinated debenture bonds. A **guaranteed bond** is an obligation guaranteed by another entity. The safety of a guaranteed bond depends on the financial capability of the guarantor to satisfy the terms of the guarantee, as well as on the financial capability of the issuer. The terms of the guarantee may call for the guarantor to guarantee the payment of interest and/or repayment of the principal.

Note that a superior legal status will not prevent bondholders from suffering financial loss when the issuer's ability to generate cash flow adequate to pay its obligations is seriously eroded.

Provisions for paying off bonds Most corporate issues contain a call provision allowing the issuer the option to buy back all or part of the issue prior to maturity. Some issues carry a

sinking fund provision, which specifies that the issuer must retire a predetermined amount of the issue periodically.

When negotiating the terms of a new bond issue, an important question is whether the issuer has the right to redeem the *entire amount* of bonds outstanding on a date before maturity. Issuers generally want this right, because they recognize that at some time in the future, the general level of interest rates may fall sufficiently below the issue's coupon rate that redeeming the issue and replacing it with another issue carrying a lower coupon rate would be attractive. For reasons discussed later in this chapter, this right represents a disadvantage to the bondholder.

The usual practice is a provision that denies the issuer the right to redeem bonds during the first 5 to 10 years following the date of issue with proceeds received from the sale of lower-cost debt obligations that have an equal or superior rank to the debt to be redeemed. This type of redemption is called **refunding**. Even though most long-term issues carry these refunding restrictions, they may be immediately callable, in whole or in part, if the source of funds is something other than money raised with debt that carries a lower interest cost. Under such a provision, acceptable sources include cash flow from operations, proceeds from a common stock sale, or funds from the sale of property.

Investors often confuse refunding protection with call protection. Call protection is much more comprehensive, because it prohibits the early redemption of the bond *for any reason*. In contrast, refunding restrictions provide protection only against the one type of redemption already mentioned. As a rule, corporate bonds are callable at a premium above par. Generally, the amount of the premium declines as the bond approaches maturity and often reaches zero after some number of years following issuance. The initial amount of the premium may be as much as one year's coupon interest or as little as the coupon interest for half of a year.

If the issuer has the choice to retire all or part of an issue prior to maturity, the buyer of the bond takes the chance that the issue will be called away at a disadvantageous time. This risk is referred to as **call risk** or **timing risk**. Call provisions present two disadvantages from the investor's perspective. First, as explained in chapter 11, a decline in interest rates in the economy increases the price of a debt instrument, although in the case of a callable bond, the price increase is somewhat limited. If and when interest rates decline far enough below the coupon rate to make a call an immediate or prospective danger, the market value of the callable bond will not rise as much as that of noncallable issues that are similar in all other respects. Second, when a bond issue is called as a result of a decline in interest rates, the investor must reinvest the proceeds received at a lower interest rate (unless the investor chooses debt of greater risk).

Corporate bond indentures may require the issuer to retire a specified portion of an issue each year. This sinking fund provision for the repayment of the debt may be designed to liquidate all of a bond issue by the maturity date, or it may call for the liquidation of only a part of the total by the end of the term. If only a part of the outstanding bond is paid before retirement, the remainder is called a **balloon maturity**. The purpose of the sinking fund provision is to reduce credit risk. Generally, the issuer may satisfy the sinking fund requirement by either (1) making a cash payment of the face amount of the bonds to be retired to the corporate trustee, which then calls the bonds for redemption using a lottery, or (2) delivering to the trustee bonds with a total face value equal to the amount that must be retired from bonds purchased in the open market.

Bond Features

Here we look at the different type of bond features that have been used by corporations throughout the world. We discuss unique structures for issuers of high-yield corporate bonds later.

Convertible and exchangeable bonds The conversion provision in a corporate bond issue grants the bondholder the right to convert the bond to a predetermined number of shares of common stock of the issuer. A **convertible bond** is therefore a corporate bond with a call option to buy the common stock of the issuer. An **exchangeable bond** grants the bondholder the right to exchange the bond for the common stock of a firm other than the issuer of the bond. For example, Ford Motor Credit exchangeable bonds are exchangeable for the common stock of its parent company, Ford Motor Company.

Issues of debt with warrants Warrants may be attached as a part of a bond issue. A **warrant** grants the holder the right to purchase a designated security at a specified price from the issuer of the bond. A warrant is simply a call option. It may permit the holder to purchase the common stock of the issuer of the debt or the common stock of a firm other than the issuer's. Or the warrant may grant the holder the right to purchase a debt obligation of the issuer. Generally, warrants can be detached from the bond and sold separately. Typically, when exercising the warrant, an investor may choose either to pay cash or to offer the debt (valued at par) that was part of the offering. A major difference between warrants and convertible or exchangeable bonds is that an investor exercising the option provided by the latter must turn the bond in to the issuer.

Putable bonds A putable bond grants the bondholder the right to sell the issue back to the issuer at par value on designated dates. The advantage to the bondholder is that if interest rates rise after the issue date, thereby reducing the market value of the bond, the bondholder can sell the bond back to the issuer for par.

Zero-coupon bonds Zero-coupon bonds are, just as the name implies, bonds without coupon payments or a stated interest rate. In the Treasury market, the U.S. government does not issue zero-coupon bonds. Dealers strip issues and create these bonds from the cash flow of a coupon Treasury bond. Corporations, however, can and do issue zero-coupon bonds. The first such public offering was in the spring of 1981. From the investor's perspective, the attractiveness of a zero-coupon bond is that the investor who holds the bond to the maturity date will realize a predetermined return on the bond, unlike a coupon bond, where the actual return realized, if the bond is held to maturity, depends on the rate at which coupon payments can be reinvested.

Floating-rate securities The coupon interest on floating-rate securities is reset periodically to follow changes in the level of some predetermined benchmark rate. For example, the coupon rate may be reset every six months to a rate equal to a spread of 100 basis points over the six-month Treasury bill rate.

Floating-rate securities are attractive to some institutional investors, because they allow the purchase of an asset with an income stream that closely matches the floating nature of the income of specific liabilities. Certain floating-rate instruments are viewed by some investors as a passive substitute for short-term investments, particularly that part of a short-term portfolio that is more or less consistently maintained at certain minimum levels. Thus, floating-rate securities save on the costs of constantly rolling over short-term securities as they reach maturity.

Why do corporations issue floating-rate securities? Closer matching of their income flows from variable-rate assets with floating-rate liabilities is of major importance, especially with such lenders as banks, thrifts, and finance companies. Issuers can fix or lock in a spread between the cost of borrowed funds and the rate at which those funds are loaned out. Another reason might be to avoid uncertainties associated with what could be an unreceptive market at some future date. The issuer can tap a new source for intermediate- to long-term funds at short-term rates, thereby making fewer trips to the marketplace and avoiding related issuance costs.

Also, in the presence of inflation, a floating-rate security (rolled over, if needed) may have a lower interest cost than a fixed-rate, long-term security. The reason is that, with inflation, the long rate may incorporate a substantial premium against the uncertainty of future inflation and interest rates. Finally, as noted in our discussion of interest rate swaps in chapter 37, an issuer may find that it can issue a floating-rate security and convert payments into a fixed-rate stream through an interest rate swap agreement. An issuer will elect this approach if the cost of issuing a floating-rate security and then using an interest rate swap results in a lower cost than simply issuing a fixed-rate security.

Other features may be included in a floating-rate issue. For example, many floating-rate issues include a put option. Some issues are exchangeable either automatically at a certain date (often five years after issuance) or at the option of the issuer into fixed-rate securities. A few issues are convertible into the common stock of the issuer. Many floating-rate issues have a ceiling or maximum interest rate for the coupon rate; some have a floor or minimum interest rate for the coupon rate.

Inflation-indexed bonds **Corporate inflation-indexed bonds** have interest or principal linked to a nationally recognized inflation measure, such as the U.S. consumer price index (U.S. CPI) in the United States, the Eurozone's Harmonised Index of Consumer Prices (excluding tobacco), the U.K.'s Retail Price Index, and France's CPI (excluding tobacco). As explained in chapter 20, these issues are referred to as "Treasury inflation protected securities," or TIPS. Outside the United States, bond coupon rates are linked to the rate of inflation and are referred to as **linkers**.

Dual-currency bonds Some issues pay coupon interest in one currency and the principal in a different currency. Such issues are called **dual-currency issues**. For the first type of dual-currency bond, the exchange rate that is used to convert the principal and coupon payments into a specific currency is specified at the time the bond is issued. The second type differs from the first in that the applicable exchange rate is the rate that prevails at the time a cash flow is made (i.e., at the spot exchange rate at the time a payment is made). A third type offers to either the investor or the issuer the choice of currency. These bonds are commonly referred to as **option currency bonds**.

Adjusting Yields for Different Interest Payment Frequencies

For a bond that pays coupon interest, the frequency with which the issuer makes interest payments varies by country. Although yield measures, such as the yield to maturity, are not very useful for assessing the potential return from investing in a bond, market convention is used for calculating yield.

Let's begin with the traditional convention for calculating yield to maturity. In that convention, the benchmark is computing the yield on a bond that pays interest semiannually. The yield to maturity measure is calculated by first determining the interest rate that makes the present value of the semiannual cash flow equal to the price, and then doubles that interest rate. As explained in chapter 16, the yield to maturity calculated in this manner is called the bond-equivalent yield (BEY).

The frequency of corporate bond interest payments can be semiannual or annual payments. Different countries follow a practice of issuing one or the other. In the United States, Canada, the United Kingdom, Japan, and Australia, for example, the frequency of payment of corporate bonds is semiannually. In the Eurobond market and many European countries, the practice is to make coupon interest payments annually. To compare an annual-pay bond to a semiannual-pay bond on BEY basis, the following formula is used:

$$\text{BEY of an annual-pay bond} = 2[(1 + \text{Yield to maturity on an annual pay bond})^{1/2} - 1].$$

This formula computes the semiannual yield for the annual-pay bond and then doubles it. Recall the convention used in calculating the BEY for a semiannual-paying bond. For example, suppose that the yield to maturity of an annual-pay bond is 6%. Then its BEY is

$$2[(1+0.06)^{1/2}-1]=0.0591=5.91\%.$$

Notice that the BEY will always be less than the annual-pay bond's yield to maturity.

To convert the BEY of a semiannual-pay basis so that it can be compared to the yield to maturity of an annual-pay bond, the following formula can be used:

$$\text{Yield to maturity on annual-pay basis} = [1 + (\text{Yield to maturity on a BEY basis}/2)]^2 - 1.$$

For example, suppose that the yield to maturity of a semiannual-pay bond is quoted on a BEY basis is 5.5%.The yield to maturity on an annual-pay basis would then be

$$[(1+0.055/2)^2]-1=0.0558=5.58\%.$$

The yield to maturity on an annual-pay basis is always greater than the yield to maturity on a BEY basis.

High-Yield Sector

As already noted, high-yield bonds are issues with a credit rating below triple B. Bond issues in this sector of the market may have been rated investment grade at the time of issuance and have been downgraded subsequently to noninvestment grade, or they may have been rated noninvestment grade at the time of issuance, called **original-issue, high-yield bonds**.

Downgraded bonds fall into two groups: (1) issues downgraded because the issuer voluntarily significantly increased its debt as a result of a leveraged buyout or a recapitalization, and (2) issues downgraded for other reasons. The latter issues are commonly referred to as **fallen angels**.

Role of high-yield bonds in financial markets The introduction of original-issue, high-yield bonds proved to be an important financial innovation with wide impact throughout the financial system. A common view held that high-default-risk bonds would not be attractive to the investing public, at least at interest rates that would be acceptable to the borrower. The view rested on the skewed nature of the outcomes offered by the instrument: The maximum return that an investor can obtain is capped by the coupon and face value, but the loss could be as large as the principal invested. It was the merit of Drexel Burnham Lambert, and particularly of Michael Milken of that firm, to disprove that view, as evidenced by the explosive growth of this market.

Before the development of the high-yield market, U.S. corporations that could not issue securities in the public debt market would borrow from commercial banks or finance companies on a short- to intermediate-term basis or would be shut off from credit. With the advent of the high-yield bond structure, financing shifted from commercial banks to the public market.

In essence, the high-yield bond market shifts the risk from commercial banks to the investing public in general. Several advantages occur with such a shift. First, when commercial banks lend to high-credit-risk borrowers, that risk is accepted indirectly by all U.S. citizens, who may not wish to accept the risk. The reason is that the commercial bank liabilities are backed by the FDIC and so carry the guarantee of the U.S. government. If high-credit-risk corporations default on their loans, causing an FDIC bailout, all taxpayers eventually may have to pay. The liabilities of other investors (excluding thrifts that have invested in high-yield bonds) are not backed by the U.S. government (and, therefore, not by U.S. citizens). The risks of this investing are taken by the specific investor group willing to accept them.

The second advantage is that commercial bank loans are typically short-term, floating-rate loans, which make debt financing less attractive to corporations. High-yield bond issues give corporations the opportunity to issue long-term, fixed-rate debt. Third, commercial banks set interest rates based on their credit analysis. When high-yield bonds are traded in a public market, the investing public establishes the interest rate. Finally, the high-yield market opens up the possibility of funding for some firms that previously had no means to obtain it.

Corporate bond issuers use the proceeds from a bond sale for various purposes, including working capital, expansion of facilities, refinancing of outstanding debt, and financing takeovers (mergers and acquisitions). In the case of noninvestment-grade bonds, it is the use of the proceeds to finance takeovers (particularly hostile takeovers) that aroused public concern over the excessive use of debt by U.S. corporations.[5]

High-yield bond structures In the early years of the high-yield market, all issues followed a conventional structure: The issues paid a fixed coupon rate and were term bonds. Today, however, more complex bond structures occupy the junk bond space, particularly for bonds issued for leveraged buyout (LBO) financing and recapitalizations producing higher debt.

In an LBO or a recapitalization, the heavy interest payment burden that the corporation assumes places severe cash flow constraints on the firm. To reduce this burden, firms involved in LBOs and recapitalizations issue bonds with deferred coupon structures that permit the issuer to avoid using cash to make interest payments for a period of three to seven years. Deferred coupon structures include (1) deferred-interest bonds, (2) step-up bonds, and (3) payment-in-kind bonds.

Deferred-interest bonds are the most common type of deferred coupon structure. These bonds sell at a deep discount and do not pay interest for an initial period, typically for three to seven years. (Because no interest is paid for an initial period, these bonds are sometimes referred to as "zero-coupon" bonds.) **Step-up bonds** do pay coupon interest, but the coupon rate is low for an initial period and then increases ("steps up") to a higher coupon rate. Finally, **payment-in-kind bonds** give the issuer an option to pay cash at a coupon payment date or give the bondholder a similar bond (i.e., a bond with the same coupon rate and a par value equal to the amount of the coupon payment that would have been paid). The period during which the issuer can make this choice varies from 5 to 10 years.

5. In a hostile takeover, the targeted firm's management resists the merger or acquisition.

As explained earlier in this chapter, **leveraged loans** are bank loans in which the borrower is a noninvestment-grade borrower. Hence, leveraged loans and high-yield bonds are alternative sources of debt for noninvestment-grade borrowers. Here we summarize the distinguishing characteristics of these sources of debt funding.

The coupon rate on high-yield bonds is typically a fixed interest rate. For leveraged loans, it is a floating rate, with the most common reference rate being the three-month LIBOR. High-yield bonds usually have a maturity of 10 years and are noncallable until three or five years after issuance. Leveraged loans are shorter term, usually five to eight years, and offer no call protection: They are callable at any time.

In the capital structure, leveraged loans are the most senior bonds, and high-yield bonds are subordinated to bank loans. With respect to covenants, they are stronger for leveraged loans than for high-yield bonds, which is one of the reasons corporate borrowers prefer to issue bonds. Finally, as we explain below, investors are concerned with the amount that can be recovered in the case of a default. Historically, the average recovery rate for defaulted leveraged loans is much higher than that for defaulted high-yield bonds.

Corporate bond defaults and recovery rates A good deal of published research has investigated corporate bond default rates.[6] Various methodologies are used by CRAs and researchers to measure corporate bond default rates. As expected, all studies indicate that historically, there was a higher percentage of defaults as the credit rating declines. For example, Moody's reports that for 1982 to 2010, virtually no defaults occurred for corporate bonds rated in its top three rating categories (Aaa, Aa1, and Aa2). In contrast, for Moody's Ca-rated corporate bonds, the default rate was about 33%. Looking at default rates for investment-grade and speculative-grade bonds, the average Moody's default rate for the former was less than 1%, whereas for the latter it was 4.8%.[7]

To evaluate the performance of the corporate bond sector, more than just default rates are needed. The reason is that default rates by themselves are not of paramount significance: It

6. See, for example, Edward I. Altman, "Measuring Corporate Bond Mortality and Performance, " *Journal of Finance* 44, no. 4 (1989): 909–922; Edward I. Altman, "Research Update: Mortality Rates and Losses, Bond Rating Drift" (unpublished study prepared for a workshop sponsored by Merrill Lynch Merchant Banking Group, "High Yield Sales and Trading," New York, 1989); Edward I. Altman and Scott A. Nammacher, *Investing in Junk Bonds* (New York: John Wiley & Sons, 1987); Paul Asquith, David W. Mullins, Jr., and Eric D. Wolff, "Original Issue High-Yield Bonds: Aging Analysis of Defaults, Exchanges, and Calls," *Journal of Finance* 44 (1989): 923–952; 1989); Marshall Blume and Donald Keim, "Realized Returns and Defaults on Lower-Grade Bonds," *Financial Analysts Journal*, July/August 1987, 26–33; Bond Investors Association, "Bond Investors Association Issues Definitive Corporate Default Statistics," press release, August 15, 1989; Gregory T. Hradsky and Robert D. Long, " High-Yield Default Losses and the Return Performance of Bankrupt Debt, " *Financial Analysts Journal* 45, no. 4 (1989): 38–49; "Historical Default Rates of Corporate Bond Issuers 1970–1988," *Moody's Special Report,* July 1989; "High-Yield Bond Default Rates," Standard & Poor's *Creditweek*, August 7, 1989, 21–23; David Wyss, Christopher Probyn, and Robert de Angelis, "The Impact of Recession on High-Yield Bonds," mimeo (Washington, DC: Alliance for Capital Access, 1989); and the 1984–1989 issues of *High Yield Market Report: Financing America's Futures* (New York and Beverly Hills: Drexel Burnham Lambert).

7. The default rates cited here are based on the issuer-weighted recovery rates obtained from Exhibit 32 in Moody's Investors Service, "Corporate Default and Recovery Rates, 1982–2010," February 28, 2011.

is perfectly possible for a portfolio of corporate bonds to suffer defaults and to outperform Treasuries at the same time, provided the yield spread of the portfolio is sufficiently high to offset the losses from defaults. Furthermore, because holders of defaulted bonds typically recover a percentage of the face amount of their investment, this is called the **recovery rate**. Therefore, an important measure for studying the performance of the corporate bond sector is the **default loss rate**, which is defined as follows:

$$\text{Default loss rate} = \text{Default rate} \times (100\% - \text{Recovery rate}).$$

For instance, a default rate of 5% and a recovery rate of 30% means a default loss rate of 3.5% (5% × 70%). Therefore, focusing exclusively on default rates merely highlights the worst possible outcome that a diversified portfolio of corporate bonds would suffer, assuming all defaulted bonds would be totally worthless.

As with default rates, different methodologies have been used to compute recovery rates. The annual average recovery rate on defaulted bank loans from 1982 to 2010 as reported by Moody's was 65.8% for first-lien bank loans, 29.1% for second-lien bank loans, and 47.8% for third-lien bank loans. For bonds, the average annual recovery rate by the bond's lien position ranged from 50.8% for senior secured bonds to 24.7% for junior subordinated bonds.[8]

Corporate Issuance in the Eurobond Market

The Eurobond market is divided into sectors depending on the currency in which the issue is denominated. For example, when Eurobonds are denominated in U.S. dollars, they are referred to as **Eurodollar bonds**. Eurobonds denominated in Japanese yen are referred to as **Euroyen bonds**.

It has become increasingly difficult to classify a bond issue as a foreign bond or a Eurobond based on the distinguishing characteristics cited earlier. It is common to refer to a corporate bond as a "Eurobond offering" if it has only one underwriter and its issue is placed primarily outside the national market of both the issuer and the underwriter. Another characteristic of a Eurobond is that it is not regulated by the single country whose currency is used to pay bondholders. In practice, however, only the United States and Canada do not place restrictions on U.S. dollar-denominated or Canadian dollar-denominated issues sold outside the two countries. Regulators of other countries whose currencies are used in Eurobond issues have closely supervised such offerings. Their power to regulate Eurobond offerings comes from their ability to impose foreign exchange or capital restrictions.

Although Eurobonds are typically registered on a national stock exchange (the most common being the Luxembourg, London, or Zurich exchanges), the bulk of all trading is

8. The average corporate debt recovery rates by lien position provided here are based on post-default trading prices and on issuer-weighted recovery rates obtained from Exhibit 7 in Moody's Investors Service, "Corporate Default and Recovery Rates, 1982–2010."

in the over-the-counter (OTC) market. Listing is purely to circumvent restrictions imposed on some institutional investors who are prohibited from purchasing securities that are not listed on an exchange. Some of the stronger issuers privately place issues with international institutional investors.

Asian Corporate Bond Market

The principal market for raising capital in the debt market in Asian countries has been via traditional bank borrowing. Following the global financial crisis, however, corporations have made greater use of the bond market to diversify their funding sources. Measured in terms of the amount of corporate bonds outstanding relative to the size (in terms of GDP) of a country's economy, five countries have outstanding bonds exceeding 50% of GDP and are viewed as having advanced bond markets: Hong Kong, Singapore, South Korea, Malaysia, and Taiwan.[9] China, India, Indonesia, and Thailand are countries in the early stages of development of their corporate bond market, but there are signs that these markets will grow rapidly. For example, China doubled the share of corporate bonds outstanding relative to GDP in 2009–2013, making it the largest regional corporate bond market in terms of U.S. dollars.

The Asian corporate bond market is divided into two sectors, based on whether the currency of denomination of the issue is a foreign currency or the local currency. Corporate bonds denominated in a foreign currency are referred to as the **regional corporate bonds**, whereas corporate bonds denominated in the country's own currency are referred to as **local currency bonds**. The foreign currency for most regional corporate bonds is the U.S. dollar. The corporate issuers in this market are global and top-tier local corporate entities. Approximately 83% of Asian non-financial corporate bonds markets are denominated in their local currencies.[10]

The Secondary Corporate Bond Market and Its Regulation

As with all bonds, the principal secondary market for corporate bonds is the OTC market. The major concern is market transparency.

In the United States, the reporting system and compliance vehicle of the Financial Industry Regulatory Authority (FINRA), the **Trade Reporting and Compliance Engine** (TRACE), requires that all broker-dealers who are members of FINRA must, under a set of rules approved by the SEC, report transactions in corporate bonds (investment grade, high

9. See "Asia's Corporate Bond Markets—Large Differences, Close Cooperation Needed," *Revue-Banque France*, May 19, 2014. Available at http://www.revue-banque.fr/banque-investissement-marches-gestion-actifs/article/asia-corporate-bond-markets-large-differences-c.

10. "Asia's Corporate Bond Markets—Large Differences, Close Cooperation Needed."

yield, and convertible bonds) to TRACE. At the end of each trading day, market aggregate statistics are published on corporate bond market activity. The end-of-day recap information provided includes (1) the number of securities and total par amount traded; (2) advances, declines, and 52-week highs and lows; and (3) the 10 most active investment-grade, high-yield, and convertible bonds for the day.

The European Union has passed various legal acts dealing with financial markets. The legal acts are in the form of what the European Union refers to as "regulations" and "directives."[11] There are EU regulations and directives on various aspects of the financial markets. These legal acts deal with wide-ranging issues and attempt to create a single European financial market that provides greater protection for investors, improved conduct by market participants, stability for the financial system, and market transparency. The key regulations for providing transparency in the secondary bond market (including securitized products) are part of the Markets in Financial Instruments Directive II (MiFID II), Level 1 adopted in April 2014 by the EU Parliament The rules are now applied to bonds and derivatives, whereas the MiFID, referred to as MiFID I, set rules only for equities.

MiFID II introduces a market structure framework that ensures that trading, wherever appropriate, takes place on regulated platforms. The regulation calls for the reporting of post-trade information in as close to real time as possible. Markets in Financial Instruments Regulation allows waivers to the reporting requirements based on certain factors, with the specific rules regarding waivers (as well as delayed reporting) left to the European Securities and Markets Authority to formulate. Improved transparency was established by rules to enhance the effective consolidation and disclosure of trading data. These rules oblige trading venues to make available to market participants pre- and post-trade data at a reasonable cost and to do so by establishing a consolidated tape mechanism for post-trade data.

Electronic bond trading Traditionally, corporate bond trading has been an OTC market conducted by telephone and based on broker-dealer trading desks that take principal positions in corporate bonds to fulfill the buy and sell orders of their customers. There has been a transition away from this traditional form of bond trading and toward electronic trading.

Electronic bond trading makes up about 30% of corporate bond trading. The major advantages of electronic trading over traditional corporate bond trading in the OTC market are (1) the ability to provide liquidity to the markets, (2) enhanced price discovery (particularly for less liquid markets), (3) the use of new technologies, and (4) trading and portfolio management efficiencies. As an example of the advantage, a portfolio manager can load buy and sell orders on a website, trade from these orders, and then clear the orders.

11. As explained on the official website of the European Union, a regulation is a binding legislative act that applies to all EU members. In contrast, a directive establishes a goal for EU member states but leaves to the individual members how to accomplish that goal. For more on the European Union's regulations and directives concerning the bond market, see http://europa.eu/eu-law/decision-making/legal-acts/index_en.htm.

There are five types of electronic corporate bond trading systems. **Auction systems** allow participants with a low market share to conduct electronic auctions of securities offerings for both new issues in the primary market and secondary market offerings. Auction systems are not typically used. **Cross-matching systems** bring dealers and institutional investors together in electronic trading networks that provide real-time or periodic cross-matching sessions. Buy and sell orders are executed automatically when matched. **Interdealer systems** allow dealers to execute transactions electronically with other dealers through the anonymous services of "brokers' brokers." The clients of dealers are not involved in interdealer systems. **Multidealer systems** allow customers with consolidated orders from two or more dealers to execute from among multiple quotes. Multidealer systems, also called **client-to-dealer systems**, typically display to customers the best bid or offer price of those posted by all dealers. The participating dealer usually acts as the principal in the transaction. **Single-dealer systems** permit investors to execute transactions directly with the specific dealer desired; this dealer acts as a principal in the transaction, with investor access to the dealer, which increasingly has been through the Internet. Thus, single-dealer systems simply replace telephone contact between a single dealer and a customer with Internet contact.

Medium-Term Notes

A **medium-term note (MTN)** is a corporate debt instrument with the unique characteristic that such notes are offered continuously to investors by an agent of the issuer. Investors can select from several maturity ranges: nine months to one year, more than one year to 18 months, more than 18 months to two years, and so on, up to 30 years. MTNs are registered with the SEC under Rule 415 (the shelf registration rule), which gives a corporation maximum flexibility for issuing securities on a continuous basis.

The term "medium-term note" to describe this corporate debt instrument is misleading. Traditionally, the term "note" or "medium term" was used to refer to debt issues with a maturity greater than one year but less than 15 years. Certainly, this characteristic is stretched for MTNs, because they have been sold with maturities from nine months to 30 years, and even longer. For example, in July 1993, Walt Disney Corporation issued a security with a 100-year maturity off its medium-term note shelf registration.

In 1982, Rule 415 was adopted, making it easier for issuers to sell registered securities on a continuous basis.

Borrowers have flexibility when designing MTNs to satisfy their own needs. They can issue fixed- or floating-rate debt. The coupon payments can be denominated in U.S dollars or in a foreign currency.

When the treasurer of a corporation contemplates an offering of either MTNs or corporate bonds, two factors affect the decision. The most obvious is the cost of the funds raised after consideration of registration and distribution costs. This cost is referred to as the **all-in-cost of funds**. The second is the flexibility afforded to the issuer in structuring the offering. The growth in the MTN market is evidence of the relative advantage of MTNs with respect to cost and flexibility for some offerings. However, some corporations raise funds by issuing both bonds and MTNs, which would indicate that no absolute advantage can be gained in all instances and market environments.

MTNs are rated by credit rating agencies. About 99% of all MTNs issued receive an investment-grade rating at the time of issuance.

The Primary Market

MTNs differ from corporate bonds in the way that they are distributed to investors when initially sold. Although some investment-grade corporate bond issues are sold on a best-efforts basis, typically they are underwritten by investment bankers. The traditional method of distribution for MTNs is on a best-efforts basis by either an investment banking firm or other broker-dealers acting as agents. Another difference between corporate bonds and MTNs when they are offered is that MTNs are usually sold in relatively small amounts on a continuous or an intermittent basis, whereas corporate bonds are sold in large, discrete offerings.

In the United States, a corporation that wants an MTN program will file a shelf registration with the SEC for the offering of securities. The SEC registration for MTN offerings is between $100 and $1 billion, but once the total is sold, the issuer can file another shelf registration. The registration includes a list of the investment banking firms, usually two to four, that the corporation has engaged to act as agents to distribute the MTNs. The large New York-based investment banking firms dominate the distribution market for MTNs.

The issuer then posts rates over a range of maturities: for example, nine months to one year, one year to 18 months, 18 months to two years, and annually thereafter. Usually, an issuer will post rates as a spread over a Treasury security of comparable maturity. The rate offering schedule can be changed at any time by the issuer either in response to changing market conditions or because the issuer has raised the desired amount of funds at a given maturity. In the latter case, the issuer can either not post a rate for that maturity range or lower the rate. The agents then make the offering rate schedule available to their investor base interested in MTNs. An investor interested in the offering contacts the agent. In turn, the agent contacts the issuer to confirm the terms of the transaction. Because the maturity range in the offering rate schedule does not specify a specific maturity date, the investor can choose the final maturity subject to approval by the issuer. The minimum size an investor can purchase of an MTN offering typically ranges from $1 million to $25 million.

Structured MTNs

It is common today for issuers of MTNs to couple their offerings with transactions in the derivative markets (options, futures/forward contracts, swaps, caps, and floors) so as to create debt obligations with more interesting risk/return features than are available in the corporate bond market. Specifically, an issue may have a floating rate over all or part of the life of the security, and the coupon reset formula may be based on a benchmark interest rate, equity index or individual stock price, a foreign exchange rate, or a commodity index.

Some MTNs even offer coupon reset formulas that vary inversely with a benchmark interest rate; that is, if the benchmark interest rate increases (decreases), the coupon rate decreases (increases). Debt instruments with this coupon characteristic are called **inverse floating-rate securities**.

MTNs created when the issuer simultaneously transacts in the derivative markets are called **structured notes**. The most common derivative instrument used when creating structured notes is a swap—a derivative instrument that we discussed in chapter 37. The motivation for issuing a structured note is that investors are willing to pay a premium for such securities and, as a result, the issuer will realize a lower funding cost than by just issuing a standard MTN or corporate bond.

Lease Financing

The market for lease financing is a segment of the larger market for equipment financing. Any type of equipment that can be purchased with borrowed funds can also be leased. Our interest here is in the leasing of equipment that can be classified as a big-ticket item (i.e., equipment costing more than $5 million). Included in this group are commercial aircraft, large ships, large quantities of production equipment, and energy facilities. A special type of leasing arrangement, known as a leveraged lease, is used when financing such equipment.

Leasing works as follows. The potential equipment user, called the **lessee**, first selects the equipment and the dealer or manufacturer from which the equipment will be purchased. The lessee negotiates such aspects of the transaction as the purchase price, specifications, warranties, and delivery date. When the lessee accepts the terms of the deal, another party, such as a bank or finance company, buys the equipment from the dealer or manufacturer and leases it to the lessee. This party is called the **lessor**. The lease is so arranged that the lessor realizes the tax benefits associated with the ownership of the leased equipment.

Basically, leasing is a vehicle by which tax benefits can be transferred from the user of the equipment (the lessee), which may not have the capacity to take advantage of the tax benefits associated with equipment ownership (e.g., depreciation and any tax credits), to another entity that can utilize them (the lessor). In exchange for these tax benefits, a lessor provides lower-cost financing to the lessee than the lessee could get by purchasing the equipment with borrowed funds. Such leases are referred to as **tax-oriented leases**.

The two ways in which a lessor can finance the purchase of the equipment are, first, to provide all the financing from its own funds and therefore be at risk for 100% of the funds used to purchase the equipment. Such leasing arrangements are referred to as **single-investor** or **direct leases**. Essentially, such leases are two-party agreements (between the lessee and the lessor). The second way is for the lessor to use only a portion of its own funds to purchase the equipment and to borrow the balance from a bank or group of banks. This type of leasing arrangement is called a **leveraged lease**. The three parties to a leveraged lease agreement are the lessee, the lessor, and the lender. The leveraged lease arrangement allows the lessor to realize all the tax benefits from owning the equipment and the tax benefits from borrowing funds—deductible interest payments—while putting up only a portion of its own funds to purchase the equipment. Therefore, leveraged leasing is commonly used in financing big-ticket items.

In a leveraged lease transaction, it is necessary for a party to arrange for the equity and the debt portions of the funding involved. The same party can arrange both. The equity portion is typically provided by one or more institutional investors. The debt portion is arranged with a bank. Because leveraged lease transactions are for large-ticket items, the bank debt is typically arranged as a syndicated bank loan. For example, the financing of aircraft is normally accomplished through leveraged lease financing.

Insolvency Laws

Every country has its own insolvency laws or bankruptcy laws for dealing with corporations having financial difficulties paying off their creditors and the treatment of corporate creditors. We first review the general issues covered by the bankruptcy laws in all countries. However, we cannot provide a description of every country's insolvency laws. Because many countries base their bankruptcy procedures on the U.S. bankruptcy system, we will review this system.

Issues Covered by Insolvency Laws

Insolvency or bankruptcy laws deal with the following issues:

- who can file for bankruptcy;
- the weight that the courts dealing with bankruptcy will give to creditors, equity investors, and other stakeholders;
- whether the company's management will be permitted to continue to manage the enterprise;
- the type of bankruptcy arrangement permitted (liquidation or reorganization); and
- whether there will be an automatic injunction that prevents creditors from recovering their debt when a company files for bankruptcy (referred to as an "automatic stay").

Preconditions must be satisfied for business enterprises to use the country's insolvency laws. If these conditions are satisfied, a business enterprise itself can apply for bankruptcy, referred to a **voluntary bankruptcy**, or its creditors can force it into bankruptcy, referred to an **involuntary bankruptcy**. After analyzing the conditions for bankruptcy for about

42 countries, one study finds that "as a whole, most countries make the inability to pay off debts the basic condition for bankruptcy."[12]

There is a priority of payments to creditors. Most countries follow priority rules for creditors whereby senior creditors paid in full before junior creditors are paid anything. Most countries give priority to secured creditors over employee creditors (i.e., amount due to employees for their compensation owed). This occurs depending on the development of a country's financial market. Countries that give priority to secured creditors over employee creditors do so because in the early stage of economic development, raising capital in the financial market is viewed as being more important than the need for labor.[13]

A common objective of the bankruptcy laws in most countries is the ability to allow the business entity to work out with creditors a financial plan to enable it to satisfy some creditor obligations and remain in business as a new business entity. This is referred to a **reorganization** of the business entity. Bankruptcy rules deal with how reorganization is to take place. Some holders of claims against the bankrupt business entity receive cash in exchange for their claims, others may receive new securities in the new business entity that results from the reorganization, and others may receive a combination of both cash and new securities in the resulting business entity. In contrast to a reorganization is the **liquidation** of a business entity. In a liquidation, all the assets of the bankrupt business entity will be distributed to the holders of claims, and no business entity will come into existence.

The U.S. Bankruptcy System

The law governing bankruptcy in the United States is the Bankruptcy Reform Act of 1978 and its amendments. This act sets forth the rules for a corporation to be either liquidated or reorganized. Another purpose of the bankruptcy act is to give a corporation time to decide whether to reorganize or liquidate, and then the necessary time to formulate a plan to accomplish either decision. The time is allowed because when a corporation files for bankruptcy, the act grants the corporation protection from creditors who seek to collect their claims. The petition for bankruptcy can be filed either by the company itself (i.e., a voluntary bankruptcy) or by its creditors (an involuntary bankruptcy). A company that files for protection under the bankruptcy act generally becomes a "debtor in possession" and continues to operate its business under the supervision of the court.

The bankruptcy act consists of 15 chapters, each chapter covering a particular type of bankruptcy. Of particular interest are Chapter 7 and Chapter 11 bankruptcies. Chapter 7 deals with the liquidation of a company; Chapter 11 deals with the reorganization of a company.

12. Wang Huaiyu, "An International Comparison of Insolvency Laws," in *Legal & Institutional Reforms of Asian Insolvency Systems* (Paris: Organisation for Economic Co-Operation and Development, 2006), available at https://www.oecd.org/china/38182541.pdf.

13. Huaiyu, "An International Comparison of Insolvency Laws."

Priority: Theory and practice When a company is liquidated, creditors receive distribution based on the absolute priority rule to the extent assets are available. The **absolute priority rule** holds that senior creditors are to be paid in full before junior creditors are paid anything. For secured creditors and unsecured creditors, this rule guarantees their seniority to equity holders.

In liquidations, the absolute priority rule generally holds. In contrast, a good body of literature argues that in reorganizations, strict absolute priority is not upheld by the courts or the SEC.[14] Studies of actual reorganizations under Chapter 11 find that the violation of absolute priority is the rule rather than the exception.[15]

Failure of the courts to follow strict absolute priority creates implications for the capital structure decision (i.e., the choice between debt and equity) of a firm. The view of financial economists that the firm is effectively owned by the creditors who sold the shareholders a call option on the firm's assets is not sustainable if the stockholders are not viewed as residual claimants.[16]

Several hypotheses have been suggested as to why, in a reorganization, the distribution made to claimants diverges from that required by the absolute priority principle. The **incentive hypothesis** argues that the longer the negotiation process among the parties continues, the greater will be the bankruptcy costs and the smaller the amount to be distributed to all parties. In a reorganization, a committee representing the various claim holders is appointed for the purpose of formulating a plan of reorganization. To be accepted, a plan of reorganization must be approved by the parties. Consequently, a lengthy bargaining process is expected. The longer the negotiation process among the parties takes, the more likely it is that the company will be operated in a manner not in the best interest of the creditors, and, as a result, the smaller will be the amount to be distributed to all parties. Because all impaired classes, including equity holders, generally must approve the plan of reorganization, creditors often convince equity holders to accept the plan by offering to distribute some value to them.

14. See, for example, William H. Meckling, "Financial Markets, Default, and Bankruptcy," *Law and Contemporary Problems* 41 (1977): 124–177; Merton H. Miller, "The Wealth Transfers of Bankruptcy: Some Illustrative Examples," *Law and Contemporary Problems* 41 (1977): 39–46; Jerold B. Warner, "Bankruptcy, Absolute Priority, and the Pricing of Risky Debt Claims," *Journal of Financial Economics* 4 (1977): 239–276; and Thomas H. Jackson, "Of Liquidation, Continuation, and Delay: An Analysis of Bankruptcy Policy and Nonbankruptcy Rules," *American Bankruptcy Law Journal* 60 (1986): 399–428.

15. See Julian R. Franks and Walter N. Torous, "An Empirical Investigation of U.S. Firms in Reorganization," *Journal of Finance* 44 (1989): 747–769; Lawrence A. Weiss, "Bankruptcy Resolution: Direct Costs and Violation of Priority of Claims," *Journal of Financial Economics* 27 (1990): 285–314; and Frank J. Fabozzi, Jane Tripp Howe, Takashi Makabe, and Toshihide Sudo, "Recent Evidence on the Distribution Patterns in Chapter 11 Reorganizations," *Journal of Fixed Income* 2, no. 4 (1993): 6–23.

16. Fischer Black and Myron Scholes, "The Pricing of Options and Corporate Liabilities," *Journal of Political Economy* 81 (1973): 637–654. Also, in the derivation of the pricing of risky debt, Robert Merton assumes that absolute priority holds; see Robert Merton, "The Pricing of Corporate Debt: The Risk Structure of Interest Rates," *Journal of Finance* 29 (1974): 449–470.

The **recontracting process hypothesis** argues that the violation of absolute priority reflects a recontracting process between stockholders and senior creditors that acknowledges the ability of management to preserve value on behalf of stockholders.[17] According to the **stockholders' influence on reorganization plan hypothesis**, creditors are less informed about the true economic operating conditions of the firm than is management. Because the distribution to creditors in the plan of reorganization is based on the valuation by the firm, creditors without perfect information suffer the loss.[18] According to Karen Hooper Wruck, managers generally have a better understanding than do creditors or stockholders of a firm's internal operations, whereas creditors and stockholders can have better information about industry trends. Management may therefore use its superior knowledge to present the data in a manner that reinforces its position.[19]

The essence of the **strategic bargaining process hypothesis** is that the increasing complexity of firms that declare bankruptcy accentuates the negotiating process and results in an even higher incidence of violation of the absolute priority rule. The likely outcome is further supported by the increased number of official committees in the reorganization process, as well as the increased number of financial and legal advisers.

Some observers have argued that creditors receive a higher value in reorganization than they would in liquidation, in part because of the costs associated with liquidation.[20] Finally, the lack of symmetry in the tax system (negative taxes are not permitted, although loss deductions may be carried forward) results in situations in which the only way to use all current loss deductions is to merge.[21] The tax system may encourage continuance or merger and discourage bankruptcy.

Consequently, although investors in the debt of a corporation may feel that they have priority over the equity owners and priority over other classes of debtors, the actual outcome of a bankruptcy may be far different from what the terms of the debt agreement state.

Fabozzi, Howe, Makabe, and Sudo examined the extent of violation of the absolute priority rule among three broad groups—secured creditors, unsecured creditors, and equity holders—and among various types of debt and equity securities.[22] They also provide evidence on which asset class bears the cost of violations of absolute priority, and an initial estimate of total distributed value relative to liquidation value. Their findings suggest that

17. Douglas G. Baird and Thomas H. Jackson, "Bargaining after the Fall and the Contours of the Absolute Priority Rule," *University of Chicago Law Review* 55 (1988): 738–789.

18. L. A. Bebchuk, "A New Approach to Corporate Reorganizations," *Harvard Law Review* 101 (1988): 775–804.

19. Karen Hooper Wruck, "Financial Distress, Reorganization, and Organizational Efficiency," *Journal of Financial Economics* 27 (1990): 419–444.

20. Michael C. Jensen, "Eclipse of the Public Corporation," *Harvard Business Review* 89 (1989): 61–62; and Wruck, "Financial Distress, Reorganization, and Organizational Efficiency."

21. J. I. Bulow and J. B. Shoven, "The Bankruptcy Decision," *Bell Journal of Economics* 9 (1978): 437–456. For a further discussion of the importance of net operating losses and the current tax law, see Fabozzi et al., "Recent Evidence on the Distribution Patterns in Chapter 11 Reorganizations."

22. Fabozzi et al., "Recent Evidence on the Distribution Patterns in Chapter 11 Reorganizations."

unsecured creditors bear a disproportionate cost of reorganization, senior unsecured creditors may bear a disproportionate cost relative to the junior unsecured creditors, and equity holders often benefit from violations of absolute priority.

Key Points

- Corporate debt obligations include commercial paper, bank loans, bonds, medium-term notes, asset-backed securities, and equipment leases.
- Corporate debt obligations take priority over holders of a corporation's common stock in the case of bankruptcy.
- Corporate bank loans, an alternative to the issuance of securities, are classified as investment-grade loans and leveraged bank loans.
- Leveraged bank loans are sold to institutional investors and traded in a secondary market.
- Although bank loans to corporations include both types of bank loans, it is common in the market to use the terms "bank loan" and "leveraged loan" interchangeably.
- In a syndicated bank loan, a group of banks provides funds to the borrower.
- Corporate bonds are debts obligating a corporation to pay periodic interest, with full repayment by maturity.
- The promises of the corporate bond issuer and the rights of the investors are set forth in the bond indenture.
- Provisions to be specified include call and sinking fund provisions.
- Security for bonds may be real or personal property.
- Debenture bonds are not secured with a specific pledge of property.
- Subordinated debenture bonds are issues that rank after secured debt, after debenture bonds, and often after some general creditors in their claim on assets and earnings.
- Special corporate bond features include convertible and exchangeable bonds, units of debt with warrants, putable bonds, zero-coupon bonds, and floating-rate securities.
- High-yield bonds are issues with a credit rating below triple B.
- There are several complex bond structures in the high-yield bond sector, particularly bonds issued for leveraged buyout (LBO) financing and recapitalizations producing higher levels of debt to equity.
- High-yield bond structures include deferred-coupon bonds (deferred-interest bonds, step-up bonds, and payment-in-kind bonds) and extendable reset bonds.
- Focusing on the default rates of corporate bonds does not provide sufficient insight into the risks and rewards of investing in corporate bonds. An investor must look at both the default rate and the recovery rate.

- The default loss rate is defined as the product of the default rate and (1 – recovery rate).
- Several different methods can be used to compute default rates.
- Secondary trading information for corporate bonds is provided by the Trade Reporting and Compliance Engine (TRACE).
- Electronic corporate bond trading systems are of five types: auction systems, cross-matching systems, interdealer systems, multidealer systems, and single-dealer systems.
- EU regulations and directives deal with a wide range of issues for bonds, with the major legislation focusing on conduct by market participants, stability of the financial system, and market transparency.
- The Markets in Financial Instruments Directive II (MiFID II), Level 1, improves transparency for the secondary bond market with respect to the reporting of post-trade details and pre-trade indicative quotes.
- A medium-term note (MTN) is a corporate debt instrument with the unique characteristic that such notes are offered continuously to investors by an agent of the issuer.
- Investors in an MTN can select from several maturity ranges: nine months to one year, more than one year to 18 months, more than 18 months to two years, and so on up to 30 years.
- MTNs differ from corporate bonds in the manner by which they are initially distributed to investors: Unlike a typical investment-grade corporate bond offering that is underwritten by investment bankers, MTNs are sold on a best-efforts basis.
- Another difference between corporate bonds and MTNs when they are offered is that MTNs are usually sold in relatively small amounts on a continuous or an intermittent basis, whereas corporate bonds are sold in large, discrete offerings.
- In the United States, a corporation that wants an MTN program will file a shelf registration with the SEC for the offering of securities.
- Issuers of MTNs often couple their offerings with transactions in the derivative markets (options, futures/forward contracts, swaps, caps, and floors) so as to create debt obligations with more attractive risk/return features than are available in the corporate bond market; such MTNs are referred to as "structured MTNs."
- Leasing is a form of bank borrowing that is basically a vehicle by which tax benefits can be transferred from the user of the equipment (the lessee), who may not have the capacity to utilize the tax benefits associated with equipment ownership, to another entity that can utilize them.
- A single-investor lease is a two-party agreement involving the lessee and the lessor.
- In a leveraged lease, the lessor uses only a portion of its own funds to purchase the equipment and borrows the balance from a bank or group of banks.
- Insolvency or bankruptcy laws deal with (1) who can file for bankruptcy, (2) the weight that the courts will give to creditors, equity investors, and other stakeholders in a bank-

ruptcy proceeding, (3) whether management will be permitted to continue to manage the enterprise, (4) the type of bankruptcy arrangement permitted (liquidation or reorganization), and (5) whether there will be an automatic injunction that prevents creditors from recovering their debt when a company files for bankruptcy.

- In a voluntary bankruptcy, a business enterprise itself can apply for bankruptcy; in an involuntary bankruptcy, the creditors can force it into bankruptcy.
- Bankruptcy rules deal with how reorganization is to take place.
- In a reorganization, some holders of claims against the bankrupt business entity receive cash in exchange for their claims, others may receive new securities in the new business entity that results from the reorganization, and yet others may receive a combination of both cash and new securities in the resulting business entity.
- In a liquidation of a business entity, all the assets of the bankrupt business entity will be distributed to the holders of claims, and no business entity will come into existence.
- The Bankruptcy Reform Act of 1978 governs the bankruptcy process in the United States.
- Chapter 7 of the bankruptcy act deals with the liquidation of a company; Chapter 11 deals with the reorganization of a company.
- In theory, creditors receive distributions based on the absolute priority rule to the extent that assets are available, meaning that senior creditors are paid in full before junior creditors are paid anything.
- In practice, the absolute priority rule holds in the case of liquidations, but this rule is typically violated in a reorganization.

Questions

1. a. Bank loans are classed into investment-grade and leveraged bank loans. Explain the difference between these two types of loans.

b. Which of the two types of bank loans can be sold and traded in the secondary market?

2. a. What is a syndicated bank loan?

b. What is the reference rate typically used for a syndicated bank loan?

c. What is the difference between an amortized bank loan and a bullet bank loan?

3. Explain the two ways in which a bank can sell its position in a syndicated loan.

4. a. What are the disadvantages of investing in a callable bond?

b. What is the advantage to the issuer of issuing a callable bond?

5. What is the difference between a noncallable bond and a nonrefundable bond?

6. a. What is a sinking fund requirement in a bond issue?

b. "A sinking fund provision in a bond issue benefits the investor." Do you agree with this statement?

7. What is a:

a. serial bond?

b. mortgage bond?

c. equipment trust certificate?

d. collateral bond?

8. What is the difference between a convertible bond and an exchangeable bond?

9. What is the difference between a fallen angel and an original-issue, high-yield bond?

10. What determines the yield that will be offered on a medium-term note?

11. a. What is a structured note?

b. What is the motivation for an issuer to create a structured note?

12. How does the original distribution of a medium-term note differ from that of a corporate bond?

13. When assessing the performance of an investment in high-yield corporate bonds, why is focusing on only default rates of limited value?

14. If the default rate is 5% and the recovery rate is 60%, what is the default loss rate?

15. What is TRACE, and why is it important to market participants in the corporate bond market?

16. With respect to bond transparency, what are the key provisions of the MiFID II, Level 1?

17. a. For a lease financing transaction, who are the lessee and the lessor?

b. Who is entitled to the tax benefits, and what are those tax benefits?

c. If a manufacturing corporation has no taxable income, is it likely to buy equipment or to lease equipment? Why?

18. What is the difference between a single-investor lease and a leveraged lease?

19. a. What is the difference between a liquidation and a reorganization?

b. What is the difference between a Chapter 7 and a Chapter 11 bankruptcy filing?

20. What is meant by a debtor-in-possession?

21. What is meant by the principle of absolute priority?

22. Give three reasons explaining why absolute priority might be violated in a reorganization.

23. What are the major advantages of electronic trading over traditional corporate bond trading in the OTC market?

27 Market for Asset-Backed Securities

CONTENTS

Learning Objectives

After reading this chapter, you will understand:

- how asset-backed securities are created;
- the basic structure of a securitization;
- who the parties to a securitization are;
- how financial markets benefit from securitization;
- what is meant by originate-to-hold and originate-to-distribute approaches pursued by financial institutions;

- the concerns about securitization;
- how corporations can reduce funding costs via securitization;
- the role of the special-purpose vehicle;
- regulation of securitization resulting from the recent global financial crisis;
- the purpose of risk-retention rules in securitization regulation; and
- how corporations can use securitization to manage risks.

In this chapter, we focus on a vehicle used by financial and nonfinancial corporations for raising debt. This financial instrument, referred to as "asset-backed security," is created through a process referred to as **asset securitization** or simply **securitization**. The creation of securitized products was primarily done in the United States until the late 1980s, when it became a technique used in some European countries. One reason for the late development of securitized products outside the United States is that the process requires the establishment of a legal and regulatory framework that allows for the benefits of securitization. Although the major type of securitization that has taken place throughout the world involves the securitization of residential real estate mortgage loans, nonbanks and banks have created products backed by a wide range of non–real estate consumer loans and receivables. For example, banks and subsidiaries of automobile manufacturers have securitized automobile loans and leases.

In this chapter, we explain the securitization process and the types of bonds created by the process, the role of securitization in financial markets, and the public policy issues concerning securitization following the financial crisis of 2008–2009. This chapter provides an overview of securitization used by corporations. In chapter 30, we take a close look at a major sector of the securitization market, the market for securitized bonds backed by U.S. residential mortgage loans issued by a government agency and two government-sponsored enterprises. This market is so large that it warrants its own chapter.

Securitization and the Creation of a Securitized Product

To explain how a securitized product is created and the parties to a securitization, we will use an illustration. Suppose that FAF Lab Equipment Inc. manufactures high-quality equipment used by both medical and clinical laboratories throughout the world. Although the company has cash sales, the bulk of its sales come from installment sales contracts. An installment sale contract is a loan to the buyer of the laboratory equipment (e.g., a dental, medical, or clinical laboratory) wherein the buyer agrees to repay FAF Laboratory Equipment Inc. over a specified period of time for the amount borrowed plus interest. The laboratory equipment purchased is the collateral for the loan. We will assume that the loans are all for five years.

The credit department of FAF Lab Equipment Inc. makes the decision as to whether to extend credit to a customer. That is, the credit department receives a credit application from a potential customer and, based on criteria established by the company, decides whether to make a loan. The criteria for granting a loan are referred to as "underwriting standards." Because FAF Lab Equipment Inc. is granting the loan, the company is referred to as the **originator of the loan**.

Moreover, FAF Lab Equipment Inc. may have a department that is responsible for servicing the loan. **Servicing** involves collecting payments from borrowers, notifying borrowers who may be delinquent, and, when necessary, recovering and disposing of the collateral (the laboratory equipment, in our illustration) if the borrower fails to make the contractual loan payments. Although the servicer of the loans need not be the originator of the loans, in our illustration, FAF Lab Equipment Inc. is the servicer.

Now let's get to how these loans are used in a securitization transaction. We assume that FAF Lab Equipment Inc. has more than $300 million of installment sales contracts. We further assume that FAF Lab Equipment Inc. wants to raise $300 million. Rather than issuing corporate bonds for $300 million, the treasurer of the corporation decides to raise the funds through a securitization. To do so, FAF Lab Equipment Inc. will set up a legal entity referred to as a **special-purpose vehicle** (SPV). At this point we will not explain the purpose of this legal entity, but it will become clear later that the SPV is critical in a securitization transaction.

In our illustration, the SPV that is set up is called "FAF Asset Trust" (FAFAT). FAF Lab Equipment Inc. will then sell to FAFAT $300 million of the loans. FAF Lab Equipment Inc. will receive from FAFAT $300 million in cash, the amount of funds it wanted to raise. FAFAT obtains the $300 million by selling securities that are backed by the $300 million of loans. The securities are the asset-backed securities mentioned above.

In the prospectus for a securitization issued in the United States, these securities are usually referred to as "certificates."

The Parties to a Securitization

Let's clarify the parties to a securitization. In our hypothetical securitization, FAF Lab Equipment Inc. is not the issuer of the securitized product (although it is sometimes referred to as the "issuer," because it is the entity that ultimately raises the funds). Instead, it originated the loans. Hence, in this transaction, FAF Lab Equipment Inc. is referred to by different names: "seller" or "depositor" or "originator." The reason it is referred to as the "seller" is because it sells the receivables to FAFAT. It is referred to as the "depositor," because it deposits the receivables into the pool of loans. And FAF Lab Equipment Inc. may be referred to as the "originator," because it originated the receivables. In practice, FAF Lab Equipment Inc. might have a subsidiary that is a captive finance company whose responsibility is to finance the product of the parent company. In that case, the captive finance company would be the seller, depositor, or originator.

The SPV in a securitization is referred to as the "issuer" or in some countries, the "trust" in the prospectus. In our simple transaction, FAF Lab Equipment Inc. manufactured the lab equipment and originated the loans. The critical role of the SPV will be explained later.

There will be a trustee for the securities issued. The responsibilities of the trustee are to represent the interests of the bond classes by monitoring compliance with covenants and, in the event of default, to enforce remedies as specified in the governing documents.[1]

Securitized Products Created and Transaction Structure

The end result of a securitization is the creation of securities that are generically referred to as **asset-backed securities** (ABSs). In a securitization prospectus, ABSs are referred to as "certificates," "asset-backed notes," and "bond classes." In the market, the terminology often used to describe the securities created is "tranches."

A securitization has transaction structure. This refers to the securities created, the rules that set forth the way in which the losses are to be distributed among the securities in the structure, the rules for the distribution of interest each month among the securities in the structure, and the rules for the distribution of principal repayment among the securities in the structures. The rules are referred to as the structure "waterfall."

Let's look at some different types of structure, starting with a simple one using the FAF Lab Equipment Inc. sale of receivables to FAFAT—the SPV and issuer of the securities. Suppose in the bond structure there are three bond classes, A, B, and C. Recall that the total amount of the receivables in that hypothetical securitization transaction is \$300 million and that the par amount of the bond classes sold is the same amount. Let's assume that the par value of bond class A is \$260 million, bond class B is \$30 million, and bond class C is \$10 million, and that the rules for the distribution of the losses from the pool of receivables backing this securitization are as follows:

- Losses on the pool of receivables are first allocated to bond class C up to \$10 million (the par amount of that bond class).
- Subsequent losses on the pool of receivables are then allocated to bond class B up to \$30 million (the par amount of that bond class) above the \$10 million loss absorbed by bond class C.
- Finally, should losses on the pool of receivables exceed \$40 million, losses are then absorbed by bond class A.

For the distribution of principal when it is paid by the borrowers, the rules are:

- Pay bond class A with all principal received up to the amount of its par value (\$260 million).

1. For further discussion of the role of the trustee in a securitization, see Karen Cook and F. Jim Della Sala, "The Role of the Trustee in Asset-Backed Securities," in *Handbook of Structured Financial Products*, ed. Frank J. Fabozzi (Hoboken, NJ: John Wiley & Sons, 1998), chapter 7.

- Once bond class A is fully repaid its par amount of \$260 million, the principal received is distributed to bond class B up to its par value of \$30 million.
- Finally, after bond class B is paid off, any additional principal is paid to bond class C.

Let's consider what happens under different situations with respect to losses on the pool of receivables. Suppose that the total loss for the pool of receivables over the life of the securities is \$6 million. In this case, bond class A and bond class B will be repaid their par value in full. However, bond class C will absorb the loss of \$6 million and therefore receive only \$4 million of the \$10 million par value. If the total loss for the pool of receivables over the life of the securities is \$28 million, then bond class C receives no principal, and bond class A receives the entire principal. However, bond class B must absorb the loss above \$10 million that is absorbed by bond class C. That amount is \$18 million (\$28 million – \$10 million). Consequently, bond class B will receive only \$12 million of its par value (\$30 million – \$18 million). Finally, let's consider the case where the loss is \$60 million. In this case, neither bond class B nor bond class C will receive any principal, and bond class A must absorb the excess losses that the two other bond classes absorbed. That excess is \$20 million (= \$60 million – \$10 million – \$30 million), and therefore bond class A will receive \$240 in principal rather than its par amount of \$260 million.

Notice what has happened in this structure. Bond class C is providing credit support against losses from the pool of receivables for bond class A and bond class B up to \$10 million. Moreover, bond class B is providing credit support against losses from the pool of receivables for bond class A up to an additional \$30 million above that provided by bond class C. For this reason, we say that bond class B and bond class C are "subordinated" bond classes. Because bond class C is the first to absorb the losses, it is referred to as the "first-loss" piece. We also say that because bond class A is not providing credit support for the other two bond classes, it is the **senior bond class**. The structure itself is a **senior-subordinated structure**.

We discuss the credit risk and the senior-subordinated structure in the next section. Here we note only that each bond class will receive a credit rating. The senior bond class will receive the highest credit rating, and the two subordinated bond classes will receive lower credit ratings. More specifically, bond class B will receive a lower credit rating than bond class A but a higher credit rating than bond class C, because bond class B is being provided credit support by bond class C.

As should be apparent, the purpose of this structure is to redistribute the credit risk associated with the collateral (i.e., pool of receivables). This process is referred to as "credit tranching"—that is, a set of bond classes is created to allow investors a choice in the amount of credit risk they prefer to bear.

Let's add one more wrinkle to the structure. Suppose that the structure is as follows, where bond classes B and C are the subordinated bond classes, as in the previous structure, but there are four senior bond classes, A1, A2, A3, and A4:

Bond Class	Par Value ($ millions)
A1 (senior)	150
A2 (senior)	60
A3 (senior)	30
A4 (senior)	20
B (subordinated)	30
C (subordinated)	10
Total	300

In this structure, the two subordinated bond classes, B and C, provide credit support for all senior bond classes. Once again we see credit tranching. In contrast to the prior structure, however, there is not one senior bond class but four. The rule for the distribution of principal payments to the senior bond classes is as follows:

- All principal is paid to bond class A1 until that bond class is paid its par value of $150 million.
- Once bond class A1 is paid off, then all principal is paid to bond class A2 until that bond class is paid its par value of $60 million.
- Once bond class A2 is paid off, then all principal is paid to bond class A3 until that bond class is paid its par value of $30 million.
- Once bond class A3 is paid off, then all principal is paid to bond class A4 until that bond class is paid its par value of $20 million.

Once all senior bonds are paid off, the rules for the distribution of principal are the same as in the prior structure:

- The principal received is distributed to bond class B up to its par value of $30 million.
- Finally, after bond class B is paid off, any additional principal is paid to bond class C.

In this example, it should be clear that the senior bond classes are not providing credit support for any other senior bond classes. Suppose that at the end of three years, the following situation exists:

1. There are no losses for the pool of receivables through year 3, but in the first month of year 4, the pool suffers a $60 million loss.
2. The principal paid to bond class A1 through year 3 is $70 million.

Thus as of the end of the first month in year 4, the two subordinated bond classes are wiped out (i.e., will not receive any principal). The principal due (before adjustment for the losses) is the same as when the securitization was issued, with the exception that bond class A1 has a par value that is reduced by the $60 million principal paid to that bond class. That is, the par value is $90 million ($150 million – $60 million). So we now have the following situation before the adjustment for the loss of receivables above and beyond what was allocated to the two bond classes:

Bond Class	Par Value ($ millions)
A1 (senior)	90
A2 (senior)	60
A3 (senior)	30
A4 (senior)	20
Total	200

The four senior bond classes must be allocated the loss not absorbed by the two subordinate bond classes. That amount is $20 million: the loss of $60 million minus the $40 million that the two subordinated bond classes absorbed. Because the par value at the beginning of year 4 is $200 for all senior bond classes in total, that means each senior bond class has to be allocated 10% of the loss ($20 million to be allocated divided by $200 million in par value for the senior bonds). So the principal owed to each bond class is as follows:

Bond Class	Par Value ($ millions)
A1 (senior)	81
A2 (senior)	54
A3 (senior)	27
A4 (senior)	18
Total	180

What was accomplished by carving up the senior bond into four bond classes that are paid off sequentially? Effectively, the senior bond class (bond class A) in the prior structure had a certain maturity. With the use of four senior bond classes, bonds with different maturities can be created (we'll see this in more detail in chapter 30). Consequently, carving up a senior bond class is referred to as **time tranching** (i.e., creating bonds with different maturities). Therefore, this structure has both time tranching for the senior bond class (through the creation of bond classes A1, A2, A3, and A4) and credit tranching (through the creation of the senior bond classes and the two subordinate bond classes B and C).

The first-loss piece (i.e., the first bond class to absorb losses from the collateral) is critical in a structure. As we'll see when we discuss the concerns about securitization, investors are concerned that the loans/receivables in the pool be properly underwritten. Because the originator of loans/receivables is not going to hold those assets on its balance sheet but instead will package those assets and distribute them to the public through a securitization, how does one control for this moral hazard problem (i.e., the poor underwriting of loans)?

In the United States and Europe, as explained later in this chapter, there are regulations requiring that originators retain in their portfolio the first-loss piece, for the purpose of placing originators at risk if they underwrite poor credit loans.

Benefits of Securitization to Financial Markets

As we stress throughout this book, some vehicles have been introduced into financial markets to reduce the reliance of borrowers on banks. High-yield corporate bonds, the subject of chapter 26, are one example of such vehicles. Securitized bonds issued through the securitization process are another example.

Just before the onset of the global financial crisis, which can be traced back to the subprime mortgage crisis starting in the early summer of 2007—a crisis allegedly caused in part by securitization—major public officials in the United States were commenting on the critical role of securitization in the financial markets. For example, several months after the beginning of the financial crisis, then–U.S. Secretary of the Treasury Henry M. Paulson, Jr., described securitization in a speech as "a process that has been extremely valuable in extending the availability of credit to millions of homeowners nationwide and lowering their cost of financing."[2]

On June 1, 2008, José Manuel González-Páramo, a member of the executive board of the European Central Bank (the central bank for the Eurozone and the monetary policy administrator of the 17 EU countries), described the benefits of securitization for banks as follows:

> The securitization of their loan portfolios has provided banks with access to an additional funding source and enabled them to mitigate some of the risks intrinsically related to their core business of liquidity transformation. … By allowing banks to transform their illiquid assets into marketable securities and providing an additional source of funding to expand lending, securitization provides an effective mechanism to mitigate such risks and reduces the role in liquidity transformation traditionally performed by depository banks.[3]

2. Henry M. Paulson, Jr., "Current Housing and Mortgage Market Developments," speech, Georgetown University Law Center, Washington, DC, October 16, 2007, HP-612.

3. José Manuel González-Páramo, speech, Global ABS Conference 2008, Cannes, June 1, 2008.

Some observers think that in Asia, securitization will play an even more critical role than in the United States and Europe, for two reasons.[4] First, in contrast to the developed bond markets in the United States and Europe, the Asian bond market is still underdeveloped. Second, funding by Asian companies is still highly dependent on banks. Securitization offers a means for developing the Asian bond and moving countries away from relying solely on the banking system. The same is true in Russia.

Finally, in January 2012, John Walsh, then acting U.S. comptroller of the currency, stated the following about securitization, which drives home the key point about its benefits:

> Securitization is sometimes maligned and frequently misunderstood, and its importance to our nation's economy is often not fully appreciated. Whether in mortgages, credit cards, auto finance, or student loans, meeting the needs of American consumers depends heavily on securitization. It is hard to imagine full recovery of the financial system without the liquidity and funding avenues provided by a well functioning securitization market.[5]

It should be clear at this point that securitization plays a critical role in financial markets. Let's tie this observation into our earlier discussion of the important role of financial intermediation for a financial market, and more specifically, the three economic functions of financial intermediaries, which are (1) to provide maturity intermediation, (2) to reduce risk through diversification, and (3) to reduce the costs of contracting and information processing (see chapter 3). However, securitization is a vehicle for raising funds directly in the public market without the need for a financial intermediary. That is, securitization results in financial disintermediation.

Let's see how securitization can fulfill the three economic roles of financial intermediaries. First, a pool of loans can be used to create ABSs with different maturity ranges. For example, as explained earlier in this chapter, time tranching can be used to create securitized vehicles with maturities that are short, intermediate, and long term. (In chapter 30, we illustrate this principle with a pool of 30-year residential mortgage loans.) Hence, securitization provides maturity intermediation.

Second, diversification within an asset type is accomplished because of the large number of loans in a typical securitization. Hence, securitization reduces risk through diversification.

Finally, the costs of contracting and information processing are provided for in asset securitization. The contracting costs are provided by the originator of the loans. Information processing is provided at two levels. The first is when a loan is originated. The second is when a credit rating agency rates the individual ABSs in the transaction.

4. Eiichi Sekine, Kei Kodachi, and Tetsuya Kamiyama, "The Development and Future of Securitization in Asia," Nomura Institute of Capital Markets Research, paper presented at the Fourth Annual Brookings–Tokyo Club–Wharton Conference, Washington, DC, October 16, 2008.

5. John Walsh, speech delivered at the American Securitization Forum Annual Conference, January 24, 2012, available at http://www.occ.gov/news-issuances/speeches/2012/pub-speech-2012-11.pdf.

The key benefit of securitization to financial markets is that it allows the creation of tradable securities with better liquidity for financial claims that would otherwise have remained in the portfolio of financial intermediaries and would therefore be highly illiquid. For example, very few institutional or individual investors would be willing to invest in residential mortgage loans, automobile loans, or credit card receivables. Yet they would be willing to invest in a security backed by these loan types. By making financial assets tradable in this way, securitization (1) reduces agency costs, thereby making financial markets more efficient, and (2) improves liquidity for the underlying financial claims, thereby reducing liquidity risk in the financial system.

Concerns about Securitization

The major benefits of securitization do not come without a significant potential risk. To understand the major risk, let's look at the traditional approach to lending followed by banks, and then be more specific and consider the process for originating loans to purchase residential property.

First we consider the approach taken by a bank when it originates a loan to purchase a property and, after origination, the bank retains the loan on its balance sheet. The approach is referred to as the "originate-to-hold" approach, with the "hold" meaning that the bank will retain the loan in its portfolio. In this approach, the bank's lending officer reviews an applicant's request for a loan. The applicant provides information about his or her credit history and employment history, as well as information about the property to be purchased. The lending officer retains the services of a competent appraiser (employed by the bank or an independent third party) to assess the property's attributes and obtain an appraised value. Based on the due diligence performed by the lending officer, the loan is either approved or denied. If approved, the loan is held in the bank's portfolio. The performance of the loan portfolio in terms of defaults is closely monitored by bank management, and problem loans in the portfolio are investigated. If it is determined that the lending officer or the appraiser failed to properly assess the credit risk of the loan, then action is taken against the individual or individuals responsible. Because the bank is at risk for the loans, it will exercise the necessary due diligence to minimize that risk.

Now let's consider the case involving securitization. This approach involves what is referred to as the "originate-to-distribute" approach. In this case, a bank may either originate loans with the intent to securitize them or the bank may purchase loans originated by other entities (e.g., acquired from mortgage banking firms that are subsidiaries of the bank). Employees of these other entities who originate loans, as well as the entities themselves, receive compensation from loans that are approved. Because the loans will be sold to a bank, which will then include those loans in a securitization and not hold them in its portfolio, the credit evaluation process breaks down. The entities originating the loans have an incentive to approve as many loans as possible to generate revenue from loans approved and for the bank not to re-underwrite the loans it purchases, because the loans will not be held by the bank. Instead, the bank generates fees associated with a securitization (i.e., earning a higher interest rate on the loans in the pool of loans backing a securitization than it has to pay to the investors in the securitized bonds). The economic incentives to originate as many loans as possible that can eventually be securitized without bearing the credit risk is the major concern that arises in securitization.

Need for the Development of an Accommodating Legal Structure

A market for securitized products cannot efficiently develop until a legal structure is in place that can accommodate securitization. Here we explain the role of the SPV, the entity in a securitization that we have touched on only briefly. Indeed, without a provision equivalent to an SPV in the trust law of a country seeking to develop a market for securitized products, the benefits of securitization by an entity seeking to raise funds would be limited. Law based on case law or precedent is called "common law" and is based on judicial decisions. A trust is a relationship that involves one party holding property on behalf of another party, and it is also based on a common law system. In a securitization, therefore, a trust is created (the SPV), and the treatment of that trust is based on a country's common law system.

Role of the SPV

Let's illustrate this pivotal role of the SPV using our hypothetical case of FAF Lab Equipment Inc., a corporation that has a credit rating obtained from a credit rating agency. For illustrative purposes, let's suppose that the credit rating assigned to FAF Lab Equipment Inc. is single B. Such a credit rating means that FAF Lab Equipment Inc. has a noninvestment-grade rating.

Recall that the treasurer of FAF Lab Equipment Inc. wants to raise $300 million. One alternative is to issue a five-year corporate bond rather than use securitization to issue a securitized bond. A major concern of the firm's treasurer is the cost of borrowing (i.e., the interest rate) that would be paid on the corporate bond. The treasurer's primary objective is to obtain the lowest possible interest rate available. Interest rates or funding costs are measured as a spread over some benchmark. Let's suppose that the benchmark interest rate is the U.S. Treasury rate of the same maturity as the corporate bond that would be issued. Because we are assuming that the treasurer would issue a five-year corporate bond, the interest rate would be the five-year Treasury rate plus a spread, and that spread reflects the compensation investors want in order to be induced to purchase the corporate bond. The rating assigned to the corporate bond issue by the credit rating agency will be the major factor affecting the size of the spread. Another factor that influences the spread arising from credit risk is the collateral that might be used for the bond issue. As explained in chapter 26, a corporate bond that has collateral is a secured bond and would be expected to reduce the credit spread by a small amount compared to the spread on a corporate bond that has no collateral (i.e., an unsecured corporate bond). The treasurer can use the loans as collateral for the secured corporate bond offering. So if FAF Lab Equipment Inc. issues a five-year corporate bond to raise $300 million, then, with its credit rating of single B, the credit spread will reflect its credit rating primarily and the collateral slightly. We'll see why the collateral would have only a slight impact on the credit spread.

Now suppose that instead of using the loans to its customers as collateral for a secured corporate bond issue, the treasurer of FAF Lab Equipment Inc. undertakes a securitization by creating a legal entity and selling the contracts in an arm's-length transaction to that entity, the SPV, which we called "FAFAT" earlier in the chapter. In our illustration of the mechanics of a securitization, after the sale of the receivables by FAF Lab Equipment Inc. to FAFAT is completed, FAFAT legally owns the receivables, not FAF Lab Equipment Inc. As a result, if FAF Lab Equipment Inc. is ever forced into bankruptcy while the receivables sold are still outstanding, FAF Lab Equipment Inc.'s creditors cannot recover the receivables, because they are legally owned by FAFAT.

As a result of securitization, then, when the SPV (FAFAT, in our illustration) issues the securitized bonds that are backed by the cash flow from the pool of loans, investors contemplating the purchase of any bond class in the securitization structure will evaluate the credit risk associated with collecting the payments due on the receivables independent of FAF Lab Equipment Inc.'s credit rating.

The credit ratings will be assigned to the different bond classes created in the securitization and will reflect how the credit rating agencies evaluate the credit risk based on the expected performance of the collateral (i.e., the pool of loans). As a result of the SPV, the quality of the collateral, and the capital structure of the SPV (i.e., the number of senior and subordinated bond classes), a corporation can raise funds through a securitization in which some of the bond classes have a better credit rating than the corporation itself that is seeking to raise funds. And so in the aggregate, the funding cost is less than that of issuing a secured corporate bond. This is the key role of the SPV in a securitization.

It is important to understand why a securitization may have a lower funding cost than a corporate bond secured by the same collateral as the securitization. The reason lies in the treatment of secured creditors in the case of a corporate reorganization in many countries. In the United States, for example, during the liquidation of a corporation, the absolute priority rule dictates how the bankrupt corporation's assets are to be distributed among creditors and stockholders (see chapter 26). The absolute priority rule is the principle that senior creditors are paid in full before junior creditors are paid anything. For secured creditors and unsecured creditors, the absolute priority rule guarantees their seniority to equity holders. In liquidations, the absolute priority rule generally holds. In contrast, it is well documented that in actual reorganizations, the courts have not followed strict absolute priority rules when distributing assets. Consequently, although investors in the debt of a corporation may feel they have priority over the equity owners and priority over other classes of debtholders, in practice, the actual outcome of a bankruptcy may deviate greatly from the terms of the debt agreement. That is, there is no assurance that if a corporate bond has collateral (i.e., is a secured bond), the rights of the debtholders will be respected should a reorganization occur. It is for this reason that the credit spread does not decrease dramatically for a secured bond compared to that for an unsecured bond. In contrast, for a securitization, the courts have no discretion. This is because no bankruptcy takes place. Instead, there are only rules (i.e., the "waterfall," or the rules for distributing losses, interest, and repayment of principal among the securities in a structure) that the trustee must follow when cash flow is received from the pool of loans. Those rules specify how the losses are to be absorbed by each bond class in the securitization's capital structure.

An actual example of the cost reduction benefit of securitization should make this clear. Our example is that of Ford Motor Company, an automobile manufacturer. Beginning in 2000, there were concerns that the credit rating of Ford would be downgraded. The company has a captive finance company, Ford Motor Credit, whose credit rating would also be downgraded. However, the captive finance company had the ability to securitize its auto loans to customers, and it issued a securitized bond. What Ford Motor Credit did was reduce its exposure from $42 billion to $8 billion of standard corporate bond issuance, substituting the sale of securitized automobile loans that carried the highest credit rating, triple A. In fact, from 2000 to mid-2003, Ford Motor Credit increased securitizations to $55 billion (28% of its total funding) from $25 billion (13% of its total funding). Also, even though the credit ratings of not only Ford Motor Company but also the other major auto manufacturers were downgraded in May 2005, the credit ratings on several of the securitization transactions of these automobile manufacturers were not downgraded. In fact, some were upgraded.

Understanding this important decoupling of the credit risk of the entity needing funds and the bond classes issued by the SPV should make it clear that the SPV's legal role is critical. This occurs in the United States because of the treatment of SPVs by the legal system. That is, despite several challenges that have occurred (discussed next), the assets in a properly structured securitization belong to the SPV, not to the entity that sold the assets to the SPV in exchange for funds.

However, other countries may not have the same legal framework as the United States. This is why outside the United States, there have been impediments in some countries with respect to the issuance of securitized bonds created from a securitization, because the concept of trust law does not exist.

Legal Challenge in the United States

The long-standing view is that investors in ABSs are protected from the creditors of the seller of the collateral. That is, when the seller of the collateral transfers it to the trust (the SPV), the transfer represents a "true sale," and therefore, in case of the seller's bankruptcy, the bankruptcy court cannot penetrate the trust to recover the collateral or cash flow from the collateral. However, this issue has never been fully tested. The closest challenge was the bankruptcy of LTV Steel Company. In the bankruptcy, LTV argued that its securitizations were not true sales and therefore it should be entitled to the cash flows it had transferred to the trust. Although the case was settled and the settlement included a summary finding that LTV's securitizations were a true sale, the court's decision to permit LTV to use the cash flows prior to the settlement is a major concern for investors.

Securitization Regulation

The abuses and problems identified by the global financial crisis led to one of the most significant changes in the regulation of financial markets throughout the world. Although the abuses were due to the securitization of real estate loans (which we describe in chapter 30) and collateralized debt obligation (securitization technology applied to the pooling of debt instruments, such as mortgage-backed securities and certain types of ABSs), the postcrisis financial regulations apply to securitization in general.

Steven Schwarcz classifies the regulations dealing with securitization into four categories: increasing disclosure, requiring risk retention, reforming credit rating agencies, and imposing capital requirements.[6] The last category involves rules with respect to risk-backed capital requirement described in chapter 6. Reforming credit rating agencies was included by regulators because of the questionable practices of these entities when rating certain types of mortgage-backed securities.

In the United States, the primary regulation is provided for in the Dodd-Frank Wall Street Reform and Consumer Protection Act of July 2010, which amended the Securities Exchange Act of 1934). This legislation, referred to simply as the "Dodd-Frank Act," deals with more issues than just the regulation of securitizations in the United States. However, we will focus here only on that part of the Dodd-Frank Act dealing with securitization. Although Congress passed the act in mid-2010, implementation of the act's provisions was delegated to various government agencies: the SEC, the three federal banking agencies (the Federal Reserve Board, the Office of the Comptroller of the Currency, and the FDIC), the Federal Housing Finance Agency, and the Department of Housing and Urban Development.

The Dodd-Frank Act refers to the entity that does a securitization as the "securitizer" and defines a securitizer or sponsor of a securitization as "a person who organizes and initiates an asset-backed securities transaction by selling or transferring assets, either directly or indirectly, including through an affiliate, to the issuer." An ABS is generally defined by

6. Steven L. Schwarcz, "Securitization and Post-Crisis Financial Regulation," *Cornell Law Review Online* 101 (2016): 115–139. https://scholarship.law.duke.edu/faculty_scholarship/3558/.

the Securities Exchange Act of 1934 to be "a fixed income or other security collateralized by any type of self-liquidating financial asset (including a loan, lease, mortgage, or other secured or unsecured receivable) that allows the holder of the security to receive payments that depend primarily on cash flow from the asset."

The Dodd-Frank Act requires the SEC to adopt several rules regarding securitization. These rules deal with

- reporting standards and disclosure for a securitization transaction in an ABS prospectus;
- the representations and warranties required to be provided in securitization transactions and the mechanisms for enforcing them; and
- due diligence requirements with respect to the loans underlying the securitization transactions.

The importance of the last rule should be clear from what we discussed in the chapter regarding the need for better underwriting standards when loans are to be distributed through a securitization.

Section 941 of the of the Dodd-Frank Act deals with another key element to mitigate the risks associated with shoddy underwriting of loans and receivables included in a securitization. The basic principle underlying Section 941 is that the issuer should hold enough economic interest in the securitization transaction so that failure to properly perform due diligence on the loans or receivables will have an adverse impact on the securitizer. This is done by having the securitizer hold a meaningful portion of the bond classes issued. The rule addressing this issue is referred to as the "risk retention rule." The rule is designed to ensure that the amount of credit risk retained by the securitizer would be economically meaningful while at the same time reducing the potential for the risk retention rule to adversely affect the availability and cost of credit to consumers and businesses.[7]

The European Parliament and Council proposed regulations in September 2015 that set forth rules dealing with securitization. In addition, this entity created a European framework for simple, transparent, and standardized securitization. There are risk-retention rules under the proposed EU regulations just as in the United States.

Securitization as a Corporate Risk Management Tool

In the previous section, we explained why securitization offers the corporate issuer the potential to reduce funding costs. Moreover, it allows corporate issuers to diversify their

7. There are exemptions to the risk retention rule. Securitizers are not required to retain credit risk when all of the pooled assets are "qualified residential mortgages." The definition of a qualified residential mortgage is left to certain federal banking agencies.

funding sources. As stated by Toyota Motor Credit Corporation, a captive finance subsidiary of Toyota, in its filing with the U.S. SEC: "Asset-backed securitization of our earning asset portfolio provides us with an alternative source of funding."[8]

Beyond the potential funding benefits is another important benefit from securitization: it can be used as a corporate risk management tool. More specifically, it can be used to manage (1) interest rate risk, (2) credit risk, and (3) other risks associated with the collateral.

First let's consider interest rate risk. The loans or receivables backing a securitization are debt obligations or fixed income instruments. Consequently, if the loans or receivables remain on the books of the originator, their value declines if interest rates increase. That is, the originator of the portfolio of loans or receivables is exposed to interest rate risk. However, if that portfolio of loans or receivables is removed from the originator's balance sheet by being used as collateral for a securitization, the originator no longer is exposed to the interest rate risk associated with those loans or receivables.

Second, the credit risk associated with the portfolio of loans and receivables is removed. To understand why, consider once again Ford Motor Company and its captive finance subsidiary, Ford Motor Credit. Since 2000, Ford Motor Credit has used securitization to reduce its portfolio of automobile loans. By doing so, it has reduced its exposure to the credit risk associated with those loans (i.e., the risk that the borrower will default). At the end of 2001, Ford Motor Credit carried $208 million in auto loans and realized first quarter credit losses of $912 million. By 2003, credit losses for the first quarter had declined to $493 million, with loans on the balance sheet down by $28 million to $180 million.

Third, consider managing the other risks associated with a portfolio of loans or receivables. Let's look once again at securitization as done in the automobile industry. As explained later in this chapter, not only are loans used in a securitization, so also are leases (the asset being lease receivables). In an automobile lease, the user of the automobile (referred to as the "lessee") makes payments to the owner of the automobile (called the "lessor") over the term of the lease. At the end of the lease term, the lessee has the option either to buy the automobile at a predetermined fixed price or to return it to the lessor. The market value of the leased automobile at the end of the lease term is referred to as its "residual value." The lessee's decision at the end of the lease term depends on the market value of the automobile compared to the predetermined fixed price set forth in the lease agreement. If the market value is less than the predetermined fixed price, the lessee will return to the automobile to the lessor. The lessor therefore then owns a portfolio of automobiles whose market value is below what was expected when the leases were originated. This risk in a lease transaction from the perspective of the lessor or originator is called "residual risk." This risk is removed when a securitization is created, because the risk is passed on to the investors in the securitized bonds.

8. From p. 50 of Toyota's 2013 Form 10-K, available at http://www.toyotafinancial.com/consumer/ShowBinary/BEA%20Repository/tfs/en_US/document/Fiscal_2013_Form_10K.pdf.

Key Points

- Asset securitization (or simply, "securitization") plays a critical role in the financial markets and the real economy.
- The end result of a securitization is the creation of securities that are generically referred to as asset-backed securities (ABSs) or bond classes or tranches that are backed by a pool of loans or receivables.
- The main parties to a securitization are the seller/originator (the party seeking to raise funds), a special-purpose vehicle (SPV), and the servicer.
- Securitization has resulted in financial disintermediation.
- The motivation for an entity seeking funds to issue ABSs rather than a corporate bond is the potential reduction in funding cost.
- The key to the potentially lower funding cost that may arise from a securitization is the role of the SPV.
- In a securitization, the transaction structure or "waterfall" refers to the securities created, the rules that set forth the way in which the losses are to be distributed among the securities in the structure, the rules for the distribution of interest each month among the securities in the structure, and the rules for the distribution of principal repayment among the securities in the structure.
- ABSs are credit enhanced to provide greater protection to bond classes against defaults.
- In a senior-subordinated structure, the credit support for the senior bonds is provided by the subordinated bonds.
- The senior bond class will receive a higher credit rating than the subordinated bond classes.
- The purpose of the senior-subordinated structure is to redistribute the credit risk associated with the collateral (i.e., pool of receivables); the redistribution is referred to as "credit tranching."
- The senior-subordinated structure allows investors a choice in the amount of credit risk they prefer to bear.
- The senior bond class can be tranched further to create bonds with different maturities, referred to as "time tranching," allowing investors a choice of maturity.
- Securitization plays a critical role in financial markets in terms of the three functions that have historically been provided by financial intermediation: (1) providing maturity intermediation; (2) reducing risk through diversification; and (3) reducing the costs of transacting and information processing.
- Securitization is a fundraising vehicle, with funds raised directly in the public market without the need for a financial intermediary, and hence results in financial disintermediation.

- The key benefit of securitization to financial markets is that it allows the creation of tradable securities with better liquidity for financial claims that would otherwise have remained in the portfolio of financial intermediaries and therefore would be highly illiquid.
- The two approaches that a bank originating loans can follow are originate to hold and originate to distribute.
- Securitization is the originate-to-distribute approach.
- Securitization raises concerns of moral hazard (i.e., poor underwriting standards in loan origination) because originators of loans/receivables are not going to hold those assets on their balance sheet (i.e., originate to hold) but instead will pool them and distribute securities backed by the pool of loans to the public.
- The economic incentives to originate as many loans as possible that can then eventually be securitized without the originator bearing the credit risk is the major concern about securitization.
- Legislation in the United States has sought to mitigate the moral hazard problem in the origination of loans associated with securitization.
- A market for securitized products cannot efficiently develop until a legal structure is in place that can accommodate securitization.
- Without a provision equivalent to an SPV in a country's trust law, the benefits of using securitization by an entity seeking to raise funds are limited.
- The SPV allows decoupling of the credit risk of the entity needing funds and the bond classes issued through the securitization (where the SPV is the issuer).
- Regulations dealing with securitization in the United States and the European Union fall into four categories: increasing disclosure, requiring risk retention, reforming credit rating agencies, and imposing capital requirements.
- The abuses and problems associated with securitization identified by the global financial crisis were addressed in the United States by the Dodd-Frank Wall Street Reform and Consumer Protection Act of 2010, which required the SEC to adopt several rules regarding securitization.
- In addition to the opportunity to raise funds at a lower cost through securitization, securitization offers corporate issuers the ability to diversify funding sources and a vehicle for transferring risk (i.e., it is a corporate risk management tool).

Questions

1. How has asset securitization resulted in financial disintermediation?
2. Why is the entity seeking to raise funds through a securitization referred to as the "seller" or the "originator"?

3. What is a special-purpose vehicle (SPV)?
4. What is meant by the "servicing of loans"?
5. What is meant by the "moral hazard" associated with the securitization of loans?
6. What is meant by a securitization's "waterfall"?
7. In a securitization structure, explain the following:

a. first-loss piece.

b. senior bonds.

8. What is meant by a "senior-subordinated structure"?
9. A financial corporation with a BBB credit rating has a consumer loan portfolio. An investment banker suggests that this corporation consider issuing an ABS where the collateral for the security would the consumer loan portfolio. What would be the advantage of issuing an ABS rather than a corporate bond for which the consumer loan portfolio serves as collateral?
10. In achieving the benefits associated with a securitization, why is the SPV important to the transaction?
11. What is the difference between credit tranching and time tranching, and how are they used to create securities that are more appealing to investors?
12. The following statement appeared in the executive summary of a report by a global joint initiative:

> The securitization and structured credit markets have become critically important to the global capital markets, and thereby also to the world economies. The absence of well-functioning securitization markets negatively impacts consumers, banks, issuers and investors, resulting in lower economic activity and fewer than needed new jobs being created in the future. The price of credit is likely to be higher for the consumer and the availability scarcer. Banks will no longer have a tool to reduce risk and diversify their financing sources to free up capital for other activities. Investors will encounter rising difficulty in gaining exposure to an asset class that has become a significant part of their portfolios.[9]

a. Explain why "securitization and structured credit markets have become critically important to the global capital markets, and thereby also to the world economies."

b. Explain why the "price of credit is likely to be higher for the consumer and the availability scarcer."

c. Explain why banks "will no longer have a tool to reduce risk and diversify their financing sources to free up capital for other activities."

9. Securities Industry and Financial Markets Association, American Securitization Forum, European Securitisation Forum, and Australian Securitisation Forum, "Restoring Confidence in the Securitization Markets," Executive Summary, December 3, 2008.

13. The following appeared in an International Monetary Fund working paper by Miguel Segoviano, Bradley Jones, Peter Lindner, and Johannes Blankenheim:

Securitization, like other forms of financial innovation, has costs and benefits associated with it. There are conditions under which securitization can be a net benefit for the financial system and vice versa. As such, securitization as a concept is neither inherently good nor bad per se—a point underscored by the marked variation in the performance of different classes of securitized assets during and after the global financial crisis (GFC). This point of departure stands in contrast to some of the more polarizing views associated with securitization, which were advanced in the aftermath of the GFC.[10]

What are the costs associated with securitization that the quotation is referring to?

14. In the publication cited in the previous question, the following statement appeared:

The Originate-to-Distribute Model associated with the boom in securitization meant that originators often had little or no economic interest ("skin in the game") in the loans that were written and, therefore, did not always have a strong incentive to originate loans that borrowers could realistically repay, as long as there was a buyer for the loans.

What is meant by the "Originate-to-Distribute Model"?

15. When describing the response of European regulators to the abuses attributable to securitization that caused the financial crisis, Steven Schwarcz wrote: "To avoid a recurrence of the allegedly flawed originate-to-distribute model, the originator or sponsor must retain an unhedged material net economic interest in the securitization of at least 5%."[11] What does this mean?

16. Securitization plays a critical role in financial markets in terms of the functions that have historically been provided by financial intermediation. Explain how securitization:

a. provides maturity intermediation.

b. reduces risk through diversification.

c. reduces the costs of transacting and information processing.

17. The following quotation is from Theodor Baums:

The slowest process of all has been the process of establishing the legal framework for securitization in individual countries. Those countries which have been successful in doing so have found themselves home to many special purpose vehicles issuing securities backed by assets from their own and/or foreign countries. Nevertheless for most countries the process has been slow up to now.[12]

Explain what the author is referring to in the above quotation.

10. Miguel Segoviano, Bradley Jones, Peter Lindner, and Johannes Blankenheim, "Securitization: Lessons Learned and the Road Ahead," IMF Working Paper WP/13/255 (Washington, DC: International Monetary Fund, November 2013), Introduction.

11. Schwarcz, "Securitization and Post-Crisis Financial Regulation."

12. Theodor Baums, "Asset Securitization in Europe," in *Forum International*, volume 20 (Alphen aan den Rijn, Netherlands: Kluwer Law and Taxation Publishers, 1990).

28 Financing Market for Small, Medium-Sized, and Entrepreneurial Enterprises

CONTENTS

Learning Objectives

- the importance of the small and medium-sized enterprises (SMEs) and new ventures to an economy;
- the difficulties of SMEs and new ventures in obtaining funding;
- government programs and initiatives for providing funding for SMEs and new ventures;
- the stages of development and financing for a new business venture;
- the sources of funding for seed stage financing;
- the role of angel investors, angel groups, and super angels in providing seed stage financing;
- the role of equity crowdfunding platforms and seed accelerators in seed stage financing;
- expansion stage financing available from venture capitalists, corporate venture capitalists, and online venture capital funds;
- institutional investor involvement in expansion stage financing;
- the advantages and disadvantages of going public (i.e., issuing stock via an initial public offering); and
- the different types of equity dilutive securities used in new ventures (convertible preferred stock, convertible note, and debt with warrants).

In the market for business financing, much of the focus in financial markets is on the sources for funding publicly traded companies and the characteristics of the financial instruments that they can use. Yet there is considerable evidence that growth of a country's real economy is tied to innovations in its product and service markets. These innovations create jobs. Often, such innovations result from small and medium-sized enterprises (SMEs) and startup companies. In many countries, firms classified as SMEs are a large share of businesses, but a much smaller share of the country's GDP. For example, it is estimated that in the European Union, about 90% of all businesses fall into what would be classified as an SME. In Japan, about 4.69 million enterprises are classified as SMEs, representing 99.7% of all enterprises and employing 70% of the workforce. One of the most successful countries that has transititioned from one the world's poorest countries to twelveth largest economy in terms of GDP is the Republic of Korea, where 99.9% of all companies are SMEs, accounting for 87.7% of all employees.[1]

1. Wonsik Choi, Richard Dobbs, Dongrok Suh, Jan Mischke, Eunjo Chon, Hangjip Cho, Boyoung Kim, and Hyunmin Kim, "Beyond Korean Style: Shaping a New Growth Formula" (New York: McKinsey Global Institute, April 2013).

The specific definition of what an SME is varies from country to country. Although economists have argued that the link between SMEs and a country's economic growth is not a simple one (and, in fact, may be a weak link), governments view SMEs and new ventures as important components of their econonomy and have instituted laws to support financing for these business entities. This view about supporting SMEs is shared by supranationals (such as the World Bank) and central banks.

In this chapter, we describe the markets for financing SMEs and new ventures as well as the financing instruments used by new ventures.

Definition of Small and Medium-Sized Enterprises

There is no universal definition of what an SME is. The definition is important, because it may impact the ability of an enterprise to qualify for access to financing programs in a country and those available from suprantionals. In a country, it may impact an enterprise's tax status and regulatory treatment.

The national governments and international organizations establish their own guidelines for defining an SME. Typically this definition is based one or more of the following metrics: number of employees, level of sales (revenue), or total assets. Table 28.1 shows the definition for an SME in terms of the three metrics for three countries (Australia, Canada, and the United States), the European Union, and three supranationals (the World Bank, the Multilateral Investment Fund of the Inter-American Development Bank, and the African Development Bank). As can be seen, there is considerable variation in how an SME is defined. Moreover, emerging countries have even greater variation in their definitions of an SME.

There are further categorizations of SMEs that might be adopted. The European Union, for example, identifies micro, small, and medium enterprises as follows:

Characteristic	Micro	Small	Medium-Sized
Number of employees	<10	<50	<250
and			
Revenue[2] (in € million)	≤2	≤10	≤50
or			
Balance sheet (in € million)	≤2	≤10	≤43

2. Technically, the metric is "turnover," which is revenue that is adjusted.

Table 28.1
Various definitions of SMEs.

Country	Number of Employees	Annual Revenue/Sales	Asssets	Notes
Australia[1]	≤200	N/A	N/A	
Canada	<200	<C$50 million	N/A	
United States[2]	<500	N/A	N/A	
Region				
European Union[3]	<250	≤€50 million	≤€43 million	Annual revenue or balance sheet total
Supranational institution				
World Bank	≤300	≤US$15 million	≤US$15 million	
Multilateral Investment Fund of the Inter-American Development Bank	≤100	≤US$3 million	N/A	
African Development Bank	≤ 100	N/A	N/A	

Sources: Australia: Government of Australia, Australian Bureau of Statistics, "Definition of Small Business," (Docklands, Australia: Australian Bureau of Statistics, April 3, 2009); Canada: Government of Canada, Industry Canada, *Small Business Quarterly*, February 2010; United States: U.S. International Trade Commission, *Small and Medium-Sized Enterprises: Overview of Participation in U.S. Exports* (Washington, DC: USITC, 2010); European Union: European Commission, Directorate-General for Enterprise and Industry, *The New SME Definition: User Guide and Model Declaration* (Brussels: European Commission, 2005).

Note: N/A, not available.

[1]SME defined for nonfarm enterprises.

[2]SME for all manufacturing firms.

[3]Annual revenue or total assets are used.

Government Programs and Initiatives

It is well known that the financing market available to SMEs is characterized by market failures and market imperfections. The failure of the market system to provide funding for SMEs as a result of the global financial crisis that began in 2008 has highlighted this shortcoming. Market imperfections in this market has resulted in information asymmetries and high transaction costs for the small loan size typically sought by SMEs. These undesirable characteristics of this market leads to a suboptimal allocation of capital. Recognizing the importance of SMEs and new ventures to the growth of their economies, governments and regional bodies have developed policies for making access to financing easier for these enterprises while also protecting investors. The failure of governments to intervene to support SMEs and entrepreneurial ventures in the manufacturing sector, for example, has lead to two adverse impacts. The first is an underinvestment in research and development (R&D) that can impede the creation of new jobs and products. The second is that because

SME manufacturers are less likely than larger firms to implement and adopt new technology and to invest in worker training and education, SME productivity improvements are slower than they would be with government support.

A 2011 report by the Information Technology & Innovation Foundation identified and analyzed support programs and practices for SME manufacturing companies implemented in 11 countries (Argentina, Australia, Austria, Canada, China, Germany, Japan, Korea, Spain, the United Kingdom, and the United States).[3] Focusing on the manufacturing sector, more and more countries have introduced and funded agencies, programs, and policy instruments supporting SME manufacturers to enhance their global competitiveness, productivity, and innovation capacity. According to John Ezell and Robert Atkinson, coauthors of the Information Technology & Innovation Foundation's study, these government initiatives seek to

1. Mentor and train SME manufacturers in continuously improving their processes and operational performance by adopting lean or quality manufacturing principles and new manufacturing process technologies;
2. Promote the diffusion of new technologies and knowledge from universities, national laboratories, or public research institutes to SME manufacturers;
3. Help SME manufacturers innovate new products and services by supporting their R&D and new product development efforts; or
4. Address gaps in SME manufacturers' access to financing for their R&D and innovation activities.[4]

The European Union's "Small Business Act" for Europe is its major policy initiative supporting SMEs, providing a comprehensive framework to promote entrepreneurship and strengthening the competitiveness of European SMEs. The act focuses on three areas: (1) improving access to finance, (2) formulating prudent regulation, and (3) taking advantage of the single market concept that the European Union seeks to establish. To improve SME access to finance, the act deals with financial instruments that can be used to facilitate the raising of venture capital investments and and provides guarantees for lending to SMEs. Furthermore, the European Commission established a permanent SME Finance Forum that brings together representatives of the SME community, banks, and other financial institutions, including the European Investment Bank. The purpose of the SME Finance Forum is to tackle the various obstacles faced by SMEs seeking to obtain credit.

As we discuss the varying funding sources later this chapter, we'll give examples of government programs, agencies, and initiatives.

3. Stephen J. Ezell and Robert D. Atkinson, "International Benchmarking of Countries' Policies and Programs Supporting SME Manufacturers" (Washington, DC: Information Technology & Innovation Foundation, September 2011), available at http://www.nist.gov/mep/data/upload/International_benchmarking.pdf.

4. Ezell and Atkinson, "International Benchmarking of Countries' Policies and Programs Supporting SME Manufacturers," p. 12.

Stages of Development and Financing for a Business Venture

Below we describe the stages of a privately held company in terms of the milestones achieved, according to the American Institute of Certified Public Accountants.[5] This categorization of a business venture is important for understanding the sources of financing available to entrepreneurs.

The American Association of Certified Public Accountants provides the following six stages of development and financing:

- **Stage 1:** In this stage, the venture is typically characterized as follows: founders have an idea, but no product revenue has been generated and possibly product development is in the initial phase. This stage might be best described as the **pre-commercialization stage** or **pre-marketing stage**. In terms of technology, the company is in **early stage technology**: technology that is not yet commercialized and has not been proven beyond the drawing board (i.e., nothing beyond laboratory experiments). In fact, neither the basic research nor the commercial feasibility may have been completed. Every new high-tech product requires an extensive pre-commercialization stage. For some companies, the legal structure may not have been decided on by the founders, because no decision may yet have been made to proceed with the formal formation of a company. Consequently, the founders' financing needs can vary, based on the costs associated with (1) conducting of business feasibility studies, (2) building prototypes, (3) testing and validating the offering, (4) evaluating the market potential, and (5) filing the legal documents to protect the intellectual property developed. Financing is **seed capital financing** at the early phase of this stage and **first round financing** or **series A financing** in the late of phase of this stage.
- **Stage 2:** No product revenue but considerable expenses characterize this stage. Product development has begun, and the founder team is identifying and managing new business challenges as they arise. It is at this stage that venture capitalists provide second- or third-round financing. The founders need further guidance on management strategies for growing the business, so that in addition to capital, the new venture needs expertise and relationship building (partnerships) that can be provided by suppliers of capital, such as venture capitalists.
- **Stage 3:** Typically, the venture is still operating at a loss due to a lack of revenue generation. But it has made significant advances in product development, such as the completion of alpha and beta testing of its offering. The venture is further increasing its value by reaching other key milestones, such as the hiring of a management team.
- **Stage 4:** Although still operating at loss, typically milestones have been reached regarding the product, and there is customer validation in the form of first orders and first shipments. As a result, some revenue has been generated. The new venture can now be viewed

5. *Valuation of Privately-Held-Company Equity Securities Issued as Compensation* (New York: American Institute of Certified Public Accountants, 2004).

as being in the expansion stage, because the venture now has to expand its operations, hopefully improving its production process, improving its product, and investing in more costly marketing efforts. The company has surpassed a sufficient number of key nonfinancial milestones to consider the possibility of an initial public offering (IPO).

- **Stage 5:** The general level of product revenue allows the venture to reach key financial milestones, such as break-even operations, operating profitability, or positive cash flows. It is possible for some type of exit event to occur—possibly an IPO or the sale of the company.
- **Stage 6:** If an exit event has not occurred by this stage, the company has a sufficiently strong financial and operational track record to make it a strong candidate for acquisition.

This general description of the stages of business development and financing is not carved in stone. No two ventures have the same rate of growth of revenue and product development. Therefore they have different capital needs that do not fall neatly into the stages described above. The conventions characterizing the stages in the literature can vary even among venture capitalists. For example, suppose that a new venture's founders do not seek funding for what we described above as seed capital until it has developed a prototype for its product. A venture capitalist that provides financing for this new venture might indeed classify this investment as seed capital; however, another venture capitalist might classify it as early startup financing. What is important is not the specific nomenclature used but understanding what types of financing are needed as the business develops.

For purposes of describing the various funding sources available for new venture financing, prior to the hopeful liquidation of a company resulting from either an acquisition, a merger, or an IPO, we can simplify those six stages into two broader stages of financing: early stage financing and expansion stage financing.

Early stage financing includes Stage 1 of the six stages described above. In turn, this can be divided into two phases: the seed round and first round. In the **seed round**, the founders seek to finance the development of a product or service (i.e., its offerings). Typically, there has not been the commercialization of the intended offerings, and hence, this stage of financing is sometimes referred to as the **pre-commercialization financing stage**. In addition to administrative costs, the major costs incurred are for developing a customer base, developing a prototype of the offering, and market testing. It may be necessary to hire technical staff, such as engineers, scientists, and software developers, particularly for high-tech companies. For investors, this is the stage of a startup that has the greatest risks and therefore should offer the greatest rewards.

Usually, funding in the very early stages comes primarily through the use by the founders of whatever cash they can obtain from personal savings, refinancing a home, using a home as collateral for a second mortgage, cashing out on a life insurance policy, and from a personal bank loan (as opposed to a business bank loan). Some founders will start a business while still employed by other organizations and use their salaries to help fund the new business. Using these sources of funding by founders is referred to as **bootstrap**

financing. Other sources of funding at this stage may come from the personal assets of the family members and friends, the prudent use of credit cards, and the strategic use of vendor financing.

Probably the best-known use of credit card financing was by the founders of Google. While doctoral students in the computer science department at Stanford University in the mid-1990s, the founders of Google, Larry Page and Sergey Brin, financed the company in its first two years of operation with the prudent use of credit cards. Carefully watching spending limits, they used credit cards to purchase used computers and software.[6] Another example is Charles Huang, the designer of "Guitar Hero III: Legends of the Rock," who in 2007 used credit cards to finance his company.[7] Credit card financing is a form of debt financing and has the risks associated with using debt. The advantage of credit card financing is the ease with which founders with a good credit rating can obtain multiple credit cards with generous lines of credit.

The use of suppliers to provide funding for the purchase of equipment, material needed for production, and services needed for production is known as vendor financing or trade credit. The benefit to vendors is that offering attractive trade credit terms can stimulate sales, and vendors do compete on the trade credit terms that they provide. Trade credit works as follows. Suppose the founders of a company make a purchase from a vendor. The vendor might give the founders a specified period to make the payment and if made within the designated period, the founders are permitted to take a discount from the invoice price. The period in which the founders are entitled to take the discount is called the "discount period." Once the discount period passes, the company must pay the full invoice price. If the discount is not taken, vendor financing becomes another form of debt financing, and it, too, comes with a cost, although there is no stated interest rate. Instead, there is an implicit interest rate that should be estimated before using this form of debt financing and compared to alternative forms of financing.

After the above sources are exhausted, management will seek other sources. **First round financing** is commonly referred to as the **Series A round** or simply **A financing**. The milestone that has been reached at this stage is the generation of revenue. Neither break-even operations nor a profit are typically reached at this stage. Although the risk of first round investors is still considerable, it is less than that for investors in the seed round. The most common source of funding at the Series A round is venture capitalists, which we describe later in this chapter.

In the seed stage, it is difficult for founders to obtain debt financing from banks in the form of loans except when the founders have sufficient collateral or assets to provide personal guarantees. Nor has the startup generated sufficient cash flow to justify a business loan. However, once first round financing is obtained from venture capitalists, there are spe-

6. Tom Ehrenfeld, *The Startup Garden: How Growing a Business Grows You* (New York: McGraw-Hill, 2002).

7. "Finance Your Start-up with Credit Cards? Google Did," CreditCards.com, April 27, 2011, http://smallbusiness.foxbusiness.com/finance-accounting/2011/04/26/finance-start-credit-cards-google-did/.

cialty banks and non-bank entities that are willing to provide such loans. These loans are referred to as **venture debt** and contain an equity kicker for the lender in the form of warrants.

Expansion stage financing includes the last five stages of business development and financing described above. It is funding for the purpose of expanding the company's business by expanding production and acquiring customers based on its marketing strategy. Financing here includes bridge loans, second round financing (also called Series B round), third round financing (also called Series C round), and so on. Additional rounds of financing may be necessary if the company does not have a liquidating event after several rounds of financing. As explained later in this chapter, the entry of a new investor group, institutional investors, has allowed ventures to raise funds via an IPO, which provides substantial funds for a company to expand without the need to go public.

Sources for Seed Stage Financing

After the abovementioned sources are exhausted, seed finance can come from one or more of the following: government-supported funding via agencies, programs, and initiatives; angel investors, angel groups, and super angels; and seed accelerators.

Government-Supported Funding Programs

National governments have recognized the need to support SMEs and new venture enterprises for the reasons described earlier in this chapter. The types of government-supported funding programs that have been used by countries make financing more accessible to SMEs and new ventures are loan guarantees, direct credit loans, loan subsidies, grant programs, and preferable tax treatment for lenders to SMEs. In 2008, the World Bank reported the results of a study on bank financing for SMEs in developed and developing countires.[8] One focus of the survey, which included 91 banks, is on the role of government loan programs. The study found that six of the seven developed countries and 32 of the 45 developing countries had government programs to foster financing for SMEs. The study concluded that guarantee programs are the most common government program used by developed and developing countries to support SME financing. The second most popular program in developed programs was interest rate subsidies. In contrast, for developing countries, the second most common program was direct credit programs.

Types of funding arrangements **Loan guarantees** (or **credit guarantees**) are not direct loans by a government to SMEs. Instead, the loans are made by private financial institutions with guarantees from the sponsoring government. The guarantee can cover the entire

8. Thorsten Beck, Asli Demirgüç-Kunt, and María Soledad Martínez Pería, "Bank Financing for SMEs around the World: Drivers, Obstacles, Business Models and Lending Practices," Policy Research Working Paper 4785 (Washington, DC: World Bank, November 2008).

amount borrowed or just a specified portion of it. Because the sponsoring government and the private financial institution share the risk associated with default by borrowers, such programs are referred to as "risk-sharing" or "cost-sharing" programs. This is the SME financing support model used in the United States and the United Kingdom.

Direct credit loans are loans made by the sponsoring government to an SME. The government is at risk for the entire amount of the loan. Canada's SME funding program is primarily a direct credit program. There are also loans with an interest rate subsidy and outright government grant programs.

Preferable tax treatment involves a range of tax reliefs provided for qualified SMEs and new ventures. Tax relief can be in the form of a lower tax rate for qualifying entities or even a tax holiday (i.e., no tax for a designated period) and/or a tax credit which is dollar for dollar in the tax liability.[9] France has a wide range of tax benefits targeting SMEs. Although many countries provide tax credits for various reasons, France has a specified R&D tax credit for SMEs. The credit features a full exemption from the corporate income tax in the first fiscal year. In the United Kingdom, the Seed and Enterprise Investment Schemes provide tax relief in different forms to encourage investors to acquire equity in qualifying early stage companies and small high-risk companies. The United Kingdom's Small Business Rates Relief also provides tax benefits.

Here we describe the government supported-government supplied by some countries.

In the United States, the Small Business Administration (SBA) is an independent agency of the U.S. government created by the Small Business Act of 1953 with the mission to "aid, counsel, assist and protect the interests of small business concerns, to preserve free competitive enterprise and to maintain and strengthen the overall economy of our nation."[10] In the programs available from the SBA, the agency is not the lender. Participating banks and other lenders make the loans with a large portion the loans guaranteed by the SBA.

The Japanese have long recognized the importance of SMEs and have passed legislation and founded agencies aimed at supporting SMEs, backing their efforts to start new enterprises or open new product markets.[11] For example, in 1948, the Small and Medium Enterprise Agency was established. As the Japanese economy grew rapidly in the 1960s, the "SME Basic Act" was passed in 1963 to deal with disparities between SMEs and large corporations. The SME Basic Act was revised in 1999 and 2013.[12] Japan responded by strengthening the financing function of government-affiliated financial institutions, includ-

9. See https://www.gov.uk/government/uploads/system/uploads/attachment_data/file/192088/seed_enterprise_investment_scheme.pdf.

10. U.S. Small Business Administration website, http://www.sba.gov/about-sba/what_we_do/mission.

11. For a discussion of this development, see Teruhiko Yoshimura and Rika Kato, "The Policy Environment for Promoting SMEs in Japan," 2011, pp. 103–127. Available at https://pdfs.semanticscholar.org/5257/03766cc3cefead56278e86c54cbed28b33aa.pdf?_ga=2.166615161.673805255.1534172925-1038845931.1534172925.

12. The 1999 SME Basic Act defined an SME quantitatively by industry (manufacturing and others, wholesale, retail, and services) in terms of capital size and the number of employees.

ing the Japan Finance Corporation for Small and Medium Enterprise established in 1953, the National Life Finance Corporation, and the Shoko Chukin Bank.

As noted at the start of this chapter, the Republic of Korea has made an amazing transition from one of the world's poorest countries with most of the country's employees working in SMEs. To accomplish economic growth, the government supported funding for SMEs, increasing that support during the global financial crisis. The financing framework for Korea includes (1) the central government via its Small & Medium Business Corporation, the Korea Finance Corporation, the Credit Guarantee Fund, and the Korea Technology Credit Guarantee Fund; (2) Bank of Korea; and (3) local governments. For example, the central government uses its Small & Medium Business Corporation to make direct and indirect loans through Korean financial institutions. The local government support is in the form of credit guarantees and interest rate subsidies.

Angel Investors, Angel Groups, and Super Angels

After founders have exhausted funding sources from their personal assets and those of family and friends, and before venture capitalists have stepped up to provide funding, the primary source of funding early-stage funding is so-called **angel investors**. In Europe, angels are referred to as "business angels." The European Business Angel Nework defines business angels as follows:

> A business angel is an individual investor (qualified as defined by some national regulations) that invests directly (or through their personal holding) their own money predominantly in seed or startup companies with no family relationships. Business angels make their own (final) investment decisions and are financially independent, i.e., a possible total loss of their business angel investments will not significantly change the economic situation of their assets. BAs invest with a medium to long term set time-frame and are ready to provide, on top of their individual investment, follow-up strategic support to entrepreneurs from investment to exit.[13]

This definition mentions "qualified as defined by national regulations." In the United States, for example, angel investing is available to individuals who qualify under the SEC's definition of "accredited investors."

The funding vehicles used are typically convertible securities, which we describe later in this chapter. In addition to providing funding, angel investors provide strategic planning advice, assist in team building, and provide contacts for developing key partnerships and further fundraising.

In the United States, there are approximately 270,000 active angel investors.[14] According to *Forbes*, individuals who are the the most active angel investors include Jeff Bezos (founder, president, chief executive officer, and chairman of the board of Amazon.com),

13. European Business Angel Nework, http://www.eban.org/glossary/business-angel-ba/#.Ve75FMxAIT0.

14. Angel Capital Association, http://www.angelcapitalassociation.org/blog/why-is-the-aca-making-a-big-deal-about-the-sec-ruling-on-general-solicitation/.

Paul Buchheit and Paul Graham (partners at Y Combinator, a Silicon Valley-based seed accelerator), Jean-François Clavier (founder and managing partner of SoftTech VC), and David Lee (founder and managing member at SV Angel, LLC). It is estimated that in 2012, angel investors invested about $23 billion in more than 67,000 startup companies, representing nearly 90% of the outside capital for these ventures. Compared to venture capital firms, angel investors provided funding for roughly 20 times more startups, even though venture capital firms invested $27 billion.[15] Although venture capitalists are credited with success stories such as Apple, AOL, Amazon.com, Facebook, and Google, for seed stage financing, these companies all relied on angel financing.

In Europe, it is estimated that there are about 75,000 business angels as of 2010.[16] Business angels are even more important than in the United States because of the absence of venture capitalists in some European countries and the fallout from the 2008 financial crisis, which has resulted in less bank lending and venture capital investment. Consequently, in such countries, business angels are the major source of equity funding for seed and startup enterprises. Compared to angel investing in the United States, European business angel investing is still in its infancy. The amount invested by business angels in the European Union is estimated to be €3–5 billion per year as of 2010 (compared to $20 billion in the United States) and in far fewer companies: 2,800 in the European Union compared to 62,000 in the United States.[17]

Since the mid-1990s, angel investors typically have invested through groups or networks. Some of the groups specialize in particular industries and may restrict their investments to particular regions of the country. Angel investors enjoy four benefits from forming an angel group to collectively evaluate and invest in startups. First, pooling of funds allows for investing in more startups that, at least in theory, provides for risk reduction via diversification. Second, the cost of information gathering and contracting can be shared among members of the group. Third, the diverse expertise of members of the angel group reduce the risk of not taking into account key factors that may lead to potentially good ventures being overlooked. Finally, the greater name recognition of a group of wealthy individuals, as opposed to a single individual, is likely to result in more deals being made. From an angel investor's perspective, a disadvantage of participating in (i.e., becoming a member of) an angel group is the time commitment required. Members must attend events, particularly participation in the screening of deals.

The Angel Capital Association, a trade association that supports the American professional angel community, publishes an annual report on the state of the industry. The report is

15. Angel Capital Association, http://www.angelcapitalassociation.org/blog/why-is-the-aca-making-a-big-deal-about-the-sec-ruling-on-general-solicitation/.

16. European Business Angel Network, *Statistics Compendium 2010* (Brussels: European Business Angel Network, December 2010).

17. Jeffrey Sohl, "The Angel Investor Market in 2010: A Market on the Rebound" (Durham: Center for Venture Research, University of New Hampshire, April 2011).

titled the *Halo Report.* According to the 2017 *Halo Report*, 63% of angel group deals were concentrated in three sectors: software (27%), consumer products and services (21%), and healthcare (15%). While in prior years internet and mobile companies dominated the deals, in 2017 these two sectors dropped from 11.2% to 4.48% of the deals.[18] In addition, this issue of the *Halo Report* states that the median round size was $270,000 with an average size of $637,000. According to the report, the five largest angel groups in 2017 are Keiretsu Forum, Houston Angel Network, Y Combinations, Central Texas Angel Network, and New York Angels. .

Although venture capitalists invest primarily in first round financing, some venture capital firms do provide seed financing. These firms, referred to as **super angels**, are set up as private equity firms. (A description of private equity firms is provided when we describe venture capital firms later in this chapter.) They differ from traditional venture capital firms in that the amount that can be raised from super angels is less.

One study investigated the role of funding for high-growth startup firms by angel investors in terms of the growth, survival, and access to follow-up funding.[19] The four key findings of the study are:

1. The success of a startup is highly correlated to the level of interest that angel investors exhibit during the initial presentation and by the follow-up due diligence performed by angel investors.
2. Startups are more likely to survive at least four years if they have angel funding.
3. Startups are more likely to raise follow-up funding outside the angel group if they obtain funding from angel investors
4. Startup performance and growth is more likely to improve if the startup obtains angel investor funding.

Moreover, the study finds that it may not be access to capital per se that angel groups provide entrepreneurs of startup firms. Instead, it may be the benefits of advising and furnishing business contacts that are of greatest value.

There is disagreement as to whether angel investors earn attractive returns from the ventures in which they invest.[20] As Robert Wiltbank of Willamette University observes:

18. The *Halo Report* documents angel group investment activity and is published each quarter by the Angel Resource Institute in collaboration with Silicon Valley Bank and CB Insights. See http://www.angelresource.org/en/Research/Halo-Report.aspx.

19. William R. Kerr, Josh Lerner, and Antoinette Schoar, "The Consequences of Entrepreneurial Finance: A Regression Discontinuity Analysis," Working Paper 10-086 (Boston: Harvard Business School, 2010).

20. For arguments suggesting why angel investors do not make money, see Andy Racheff, "Why Angel Investors Don't Make Money … And Advice for People Who Are Going to Become Angels Anway," September 20, 2012, available at http://techcrunch.com/2012/09/30/why-angel-investors-dont-make-money-and-advice-for-people-who-are-going-to-become-angels-anyway/.

> The investing world seemed certain that angel investors were rubes. Conventional wisdom dictated that they made reckless investments in very early-stage ventures mostly doomed to fail. And whenever they might come close to succeeding, savvy "professional" investors would just swoop in, cram them down, and win the real returns. In addition, angels were up against a selection problem: All the best entrepreneurs and opportunities would naturally gravitate to the best venture capital funds, leaving only the "scraps" for angel investors.[21]

Wiltbank and Boeker studied the returns to angel investments that were completed by 2007 using the most comprehensive data available.[22] Their findings for returns on group-affiliated angel investments were as follows:

- The average was 2.6 times the return on investment after 3.5 years.
- Almost 48% of the returns on exited investments provided a return that was more than the amount invested by the angel group, or equivalently, 52% resulted in a loss.
- There were returns of more than 10 times the amount invested for 7% of the exited investments.

The above findings are the returns for individual ventures. When looking at angel investor portfolios, they find that only 39% of the portfolios realized a loss (in contrast to 52% of individual investments). Overall findings appear to be comparable to those of venture capitalists that we describe later in this chapter.

Instead of studying actual returns on angel investments, in a study sponsored by the Federal Reserve Bank of Atlanta, DeGennaro and Dwyer investigate the expected returns that drive investments.[23] For their sample of 588 angel investments during 1972–2007, which contains 419 investments that were completed by the end of 2007 (i.e., exited investments),[24] they found that angel investors can expect to earn net returns of 70% in excess of the risk-free rate of return available in the market for an average holding period of 3.67 years. This is roughly the same profile that has been found for venture capitalists.[25]

Equity Crowdfunding Platforms

Crowdfunding is the practice of raising funds for a startup from a large number of investors who invest small sums. Typically, the funds are raised via the Internet. There are two

21. Robert Wiltbank, "Angel Investors Do Make Money, Data Shows 2.5× Returns Overall," October 13, 2012, available at http://techcrunch.com/2012/0/13/angel-investors-make-2-5x-returns-overall/.

22. Robert Wiltbank and Warren Boeker, "Returns to Angel Investors in Groups," November 1, 2007. Available at http://ssrn.com/abstract=1028592.

23. Ramon P. DeGennaro and Gerald P. Dwyer, "Expected Returns to Stock Investments by Angel Investors in Groups," Working Paper 2010–14 (Atlanta: Federal Reserve Bank of Atlanta, August 2010).

24. The data used were from the Angel Investor Performance Project.

25. John H. Campbell, "The Risk and Return of Venture Capital," *Journal of Financial Economics* 75 (2006): 3–52.

types of crowdfunding: reward (donation) crowdfunding and equity crowdfunding.[26] Our focus here is on **equity crowdfunding**, which allows investors to obtain an equity interest in a startup company.

Any startup that is interested in raising equity capital has to comply with its home country's securities regulations. In the United States, for example, startup companies must comply with the general solicitation and advertising as set forth by the SEC. Prior to April 5, 2012, equity crowdfunding was not allowed in the United States. However, provisions in the Jumpstart Our Business Starts Act (JOBS Act) made possible the soliciting of funds by startups, allowing for equity crowdfunding. Since that time, numerous equity crowdfunding platforms have been started.

Seed Accelerators

Seed accelerators provide a vehicle for founders to launch a company in a high-tech industry. They do so by providing seed stage financing in exchange for a small equity stake in the startup. The amount of funding available from accelerators ranges from $20,000 to $100,000 in exchange for 2–10% equity in the company. Funding is in the form of a convertible note, the same instrument used by angel investors and described later in this chapter.

What is key for founders who are considering seed accelerators is the opportunity to gain access not only to needed funding but also to other potential investors, training in a short period of time, temporary office space, and access to a team of experts. By providing mentoring for founders, seed accelerators prepare founders to present their ideas for a product or service to potential venture capitalists. At the conclusion of the program (i.e., on graduation from the program), there is a "demo day," where founders can make presentations to potential investors and the press.

Expansion Financing

Until about 2010, the primary sources for expansion financing have been traditional venture capital firms, corporate venture capital firms, and online venture capital funds. The most recent entrants providing financing for startup companies in the very late stages are institutional investors, such as mutual funds and closed-end investment companies.

26. Tanya Prive, "Crowdfunding: It's Not Just for Startups," *Forbes* February 6, 2013, available at http://www.forbes.com/sites/tanyaprive/2013/02/06/crowdfunding-its-not-just-for-startups/.

Venture Capitalists

According to the National Venture Capital Association (NVCA), venture capital firms are "professional, institutional managers of risk capital that enables and supports the most innovative and promising companies."[27] The funds invested in a startup business are in the form of equity. The investments are typically made in a series or in rounds that typically occur every two years, based on predetermined milestones being reached by the startup company. The equity investments are typically highly illiquid and have little value until the company matures, which is expected to take from five to eight years after the company is launched.

Because venture capital firms typically take equity positions in private companies, how do they differ from private equity firms that invest in private companies? Venture capital firms are often said to be a special type of private equity firm that invests in startup companies.[28] In contrast, the typical private equity firm invests in mature companies that are seeking to go private or are considered to be underperforming and have the potential for highly attractive returns. One important difference in how returns are generated between the investments made by venture capital firms and private equity firms is the use of leverage by the latter.

In 2015, capital venture investments were approximately $59.1 billion, used to finance the following stages as categorized by the NVCA: seeding stage, 2%; early stage, 34%, late stage, 27%, and expansion stage, 37%. Of the $59.1 billion, $42.1 was invested in 2,620 information technology companies, $10.9 billion in 664 medical/health/life science companies, and the balance, $6.1 billion, in 420 non-high-tech companies. Of the nine industry sectors in which investments were made by venture capital firms in 2015, half were to just two industry sectors: the software sector (40%) and biotechnology sector (13%).[29]

According to the NVCA, usually only 10% of the business plans submitted to a venture capital firm for funding are given serious consideration, and only 1% of the submitted business plans are eventually funded.

Because of the long-term investment in a startup company, the partners of a venture capital firm actively engage in various aspects of the company in which they invest. At a minimum, this takes the form of participation in corporate governance by obtaining one or more seats on the board of directors.

27. National Venture Capital Association, "Venture Capital 101: What Is Venture Capital?" Available at www.nvca.org/index.php?option=com_docman&task. From a regulatory perspective, there was some concern that under the Dodd-Frank Act, venture capital funds, hedge funds, and private equity firms would need to supply certain information to the SEC. Fortunately for venture capital firms, the SEC in 2011 provided a definition of a venture capital fund that would avoid this requirement. The SEC defined a venture capital fund as one that invests in "qualifying investments." A qualifying investment is mainly in shares of private companies. However, a capital venture fund is permitted to invest 20% in nonqualifying investments. It may not use significant leverage.

28. Each year, *Forbes* publishes a list of the top 10 venture capital firms in the world and the top 10 venture investors in the world. *Forbes* refers to this list as the "Midas List."

29. The data in this paragraph are from figures 5.0, 6.0, and 7.0 in *National Venture Capital Association Yearbook 2015* (Toronto: Thomas Reuters, 2015).

The process for creating a portfolio of ventures by a venture capital firm is as follows. This portfolio of ventures is referred to as the "VC fund." Typically, a limited partnership is formed by the venture capital firm. A limited partnership has general partners and limited partners. The former manage the investment portfolio of ventures and have unlimited liability, whereas the latter do not participate in the selection of ventures to include in the investment portfolio and have limited liability. For a VC fund, the venture capital firm is the general partner, and the limited partners are the outside investors from whom the venture capital firm obtains commitments to invest in the fund. Thus, an investor does not invest in the capital venture firm or an individual venture but rather in a particular VC fund (i.e., portfolio of ventures).

The investors in the VC funds created by venture capital firms are institutional investors, family offices, and high net worth individuals. Institutional investors include pension funds, insurance companies, endowments, and foundations. Family offices are entities that manage the financial and personal affairs of a wealthy family.

A VC fund is created when the venture capital firm obtains sufficient commitments from investors. As investors provide cash to the venture capital firm, the VC fund's general partners make the investments in ventures that are identified by the firm's analysts. Because there are multiple rounds of financing, a certain amount of reserves are set aside for those future rounds. The VC fund's return is realized when the venture either goes public via an IPO, is acquired by another company, or merges with another company.

An article published in the *Harvard Business Review*,[30] by Diane Mulcathy, a former venture capitalist and a director of private equity for the Ewing Marion Kauffman Foundation,[31] explains myths that she believes exist about venture capitalists. Her motivation for busting the six myths is "to help company founders develop a more realistic sense of the industry and what it offers." Mulcathy's six myths are:

- Myth 1: The primary source of funding for startup companies is venture capitalists.
- Myth 2: A venture capitalist takes a big risk when investing in a startup.
- Myth 3: Valuable advice and mentoring is provided by most venture capitalists.
- Myth 4: The returns generated by venture capital firms are spectacular.
- Myth 5: The larger the venture capital fund, the better.
- Myth 6: Venture capitalists are innovators.

In disputing Myth 1, Mulcathy notes that (1) venture capital funds have provided capital for less than 1% of U.S. companies and (2) in contrast to angel investors, whose numbers

30. Diane Mulcahy, "Six Myths About Venture Capitalists," *Harvard Business Review*, May 1, 2013, available at https://hbr.org/2013/05/six-myths-about-venture-capitalists.

31. This foundation is one of the largest private foundations in the United States with assets of approximately $2 billion.

are growing, the venture capital industry is contracting. Myth 2 is clear: it is the investor in VC funds who takes on the risks associated with investing in startups, not the venture capital firm that is the general partner of a VC fund. Not all venture capital firms commit the same amount of time to advising and mentoring a startup company (Myth 3). Thus, founders must perform due diligence when selecting a venture capital firm so that the anticipated involvement sought will be provided by the firm selected. As for Myth 4 regarding the return performance, we will discuss that below. Suffice it to say here that the empirical evidence does not support the view that VC funds have generated anything near spectacular returns. Empirical evidence also fails to support the view that the larger the VC fund, the better (Myth 5). In particular, the evidence shows that as a VC fund's size increases above $250 million, performance declines. Finally, although venture capitalists may provide funding for founders with innovative ideas that need to be commercialized, management of venture capital firms has not been innovative over the past two decades, according to Mulcathy (Myth 6). She concludes by saying that although venture capitalists will play a significant role in funding startups in the future, it will be less than in the past, because the venture capital industry is contracting as new funding sources become available.

Corporate Venture Capitalists

Corporate venture capitalists are corporations that invest in startups that have the potential for providing a good strategic fit to their company's offerings. Although we have described VC funds as sources for first round financing, they are also involved in the seed phases of early stage financing.

Examples of corporate venture funds include Dell Venture, Google Ventures, Cisco Investments, Lilly Ventures, Johnson & Johnson Development Corporation, Microsoft Ventures, Intel Capital, and Samsung Ventures. A benefit of obtaining funding from corporate venture capitalists is that they provide the founders with access to corporate distribution channels and infrastructure, as well as to potential strategic partners.

Corporate venture funds were an important source of startup funding during the first half of 2011, a time when traditional venture capital firms were finding it difficult to raise investment funds because of the global financial crisis. At that time, corporate venture funds provided 11% of venture capital financing.[32] According to the *Corporate Venture Capital Report*, in the third quarter of 2013, investments by corporate venture funds reached its highest level since 2011 with $2.1 billion spread over 140 investments. Corporate venture funds accounted for 30% of all venture capital financing. The dollar investment that is available from corporate venture funds is greater than that provided by traditional venture capital firms.

32. Josh Lerner, "Corporate Venturing," *Harvard Business Review*, October 2013, pp. 86–94.

The potential benefits to the corporate venture fund's parent company are threefold.[33] First, it may help the parent company respond to technological changes faster than traditional R&D programs. Josh Lerner of the Harvard Business School cites Lilly Ventures as an example of one such corporate venture fund that helped its parent company, the pharmaceutical company Eli Lilly, to "catch up with the rapid advances in bioscience that were threatening to render their chemistry-based expertise irrelevant."[34] Second, potentially attractive financial returns can be realized. Finally, a corporate venture fund has the potential to provide a boost to the parent company's product or services as a result of technological spillover.

Empirical evidence reported by Hyunsung Daniel Kang and Vikram Nanda based on an analysis of technological and financial returns generated by investments by 796 corporate venture funds in the bio-pharmaceutical industry between 1985 and 2006 support this third benefit. They find that the technological advances attributable to investments made by corporate venture funds did increase the parent corporation's value. However, in contrast to the positive spillover effect generated by technology on corporate value, they found that financial returns had a negligible effect.[35]

Online Venture Capital Funds

In May 2012, a platform was launched by FundersClub that allows accredited investors to become equity holders in startup ventures by selecting ventures online.[36] At the time of launch, FundersClub had 5,000 members (i.e., accredited investors). It offers two types of funds to its members: single-company funds and multicompany funds that are managed by FundersClub. For a single-company fund, the member selects from a prescreened list of startup companies whose investment profile is provided. In contrast, for a multicompany funds, an investor is investing in a portfolio of yet to be determined startup companies, where the companies to be selected are based on an investment strategy formulated and then executed by the FundersClub investment committee.[37]

33. These potential benefits are identified in Lerner, "Corporate Venturing."

34. Lerner, "Corporate Venturing," p. 86.

35. Hyunsung Daniel Kang and Vikram K. Nanda, "Technological Spillovers and Financial Returns in Corporate Venture Capital," working paper, Georgia Institute of Technology, March 2011, available at http://www.researchgate.net/publication/256016429_Technological_Spillovers_and_Financial_Returns_in_Corporate_Venture_Capital.

36. The SEC raised a regulatory issue as to whether FundersClub was a broker-dealer and therefore had to be registered with the SEC as such. FundersClub refuted this position, arguing that it was a venture capital advisor that, instead of working offline, was working online. In May 2012, FundersClub received from the SEC a "no-action letter," indicating that it would not recommend enforcement action.

37. The shareholder of record for both types of funds is FundersClub.

Although at the time of launch, 500 of the 5,000 members of FundersClub invested approximately $2.5 million in nine different funds, the investment made by investors typically ranges from $2,500 to $250,000. The startup companies available to invest in, which are early, mid-, and late stage private U.S. technology companies, are prescreened by the FundersClub Investment Committee and FundersClub Panel each week. The startup companies that are screened typically are identified from FundersClub network and partners. According to FundersClub, less than 5% of the ventures vetted are selected to be listed on its website for members to review. Using a web platform, members can browse the prescreened startup companies, review their investment profiles (which include a pitch video by the founders), and sign the legal documents. Members also have the opportunity to query a startup company's founder via a moderated question and answer forum. To keep investors up to date after they invest in a startup company, as well as to potentially get them further involved, the startup company will identify on its profile the manner in which it will communicate with its investors. Several methods of communication are available, such as quarterly email updates or inclusion on an "insider investor distribution list" to inform investors of significant milestones, developments that have been achieved, and video messages from the startup company's founders.

The FundersClub platform might seem like crowdfunding as described earlier in this chapter. However, it is not crowdfunding, because investors in crowdfunding each invest a sum in one company on an individual basis. Instead, FundersClub pools the amount invested by individuals and then creates a VC fund to either invest in a single startup company or a portfolio of startup companies. Hence, this investment approach is no different than what traditional venture capitalists do when creating VC funds and can be correctly described as an "on-line VC fund." To avoid potential conflicts of interest in the selection of startups included in one of the funds, FundersClub does not charge startup companies to be included on its platform.

Institutional Investors: Mutual Funds and Hedge Funds

The latest entrants providing expansion financing for new ventures prior to an IPO, acquisition, or merger are institutional investors. These investors include mutual funds and hedge funds.

Like VC funds, these institutional investors are collective investment vehicles. Investors in these collective investment vehicles own a pro rata share of the fund's portfolio. Several of the sponsors of mutual fund families, such as BlackRock Financial Management, Fidelity Investments, T. Rowe Price, Janus Capital Group, and Wellington Management, have invested in startup technology companies for certain of their funds. According to *CB Insight*, mutual funds and hedge funds invested in $628 million in 11 startup technology companies in 2010. In the following three years, they invested in more than 31 deals.

Because investments in startup companies are referred to as "alternative investments," mutual funds that invest a significant portion of the fund's assets in startup companies are referred to as a "alternative" or "alt" mutual funds. For example, consider New Horizons Fund Inc. According to the fund's prospectus, the fund pursues an "aggressive stock fund seeking long-term capital growth primarily through investments in small, rapidly growing companies." The fund is permitted to invest in privately held companies. This fund's 2013 annual report indicated that early-stage companies accounted for about a third of the portfolio's holdings. An example of this fund's holdings in a startup company is its 2009 investment in Twitter.

An example of mutual fund participation in a startup company is Apptio. Founded in 2007, Apptio develops on-demand, cloud-based business software applications. The company's Series A financing of $7 million was obtained in the summer of 2007 from two venture capital firms and an angel investor. Following two additional rounds of financing, by May 2012, Apptio's existing investors included four venture capital firms. In May 2012, Apptio obtained its fourth round of financing (Series D financing) of $50 million from not only its existing venture capital firms but also from T. Rowe Price, which acquired shares for several of the mutual funds it sponsors. One year later in May 2013, Apptio investors added to its existing investors another mutual fund, Janus Capital, as well as another unnamed institutional investor, in a $45 million Series E round financing.

Late-stage expansion financing rounds prior to an IPO typically have not involved the megadeals or rounds that are now possible from institutional investors, involving amounts that can run into hundreds of millions of dollars. The advantage to the founding teams of a high-tech startup companies is that they can postpone going public (i.e., IPOs), so that they can come to the public market with a better track record regarding growth and brand name. The motivation for these institutional investors is to get in on pre-IPO valuation. For example, in the first quarter of 2014, Airbnb Inc. was said to have raised about $450 million when institutional investors participated. To put this amount in perspective, with the exception of the Twitter IPO, no technology startup company has raised more than that amount when it went public.

Initial Public Offering

As the need for financing increases as the company grows, the founders turn to the general public to meet their needs. Public funding is obtained via an IPO. It has long been viewed that an IPO is the holy grail of exit strategies. But not all founders have as their exit plan strategy an IPO. For some founders, an IPO is a necessary evil to obtain adequate funding that was unavailable from traditional sources (which include angel and venture capital financing). However, as explained above, new players in the market—institutional investors—have made the need to rush to an IPO unnecessary for some firms. Instititutional investors could provide a large injection of funds to allow founders to expand without the need of public funding and, as a result, some companies have delayed going public by several years.

The decision to go public begins with discussions with the company's financial advisor to determine whether the company is a suitable candidate to go public and whether market conditions are right for an IPO. Financial advisors know what investors will consider when acquiring the shares in an IPO. For example, in some industries, a company may be able to go public only by exhibiting a long history of strong financial performance, including revenue and earnings growth. (However, a short history of performance may be acceptable for going public for a companies in certain high-tech industries.) In addition, the founders must determine the trading location for their shares (i.e., an exchange or OTC market). In the case of a company whose stock is listed on an exchange, there are listing requirements that the exchange specifies. With respect to timing, market conditions may be such that IPOs coming to market face low a stock valuation. Such unfavorable conditions would encourage a postponement of an IPO until market conditions improve.

Advantages of going public There are two principal advantages of a company going public. First, publicly traded common stock provides liquidity for the shares owned by founders as well as investors and employees who are shareholders. For some founders who desire to harvest or cash out on the value that they created by building the company, an IPO is allows them to do so.

Second, founders can use shares as a form of currency, allowing them to make acquisitions needed to expand their business as well as to attract key executives by offering stock options. The shares are a form of currency because they have a market price, making it unnecessary in transactions involving an acquisition or the hiring of a key officer to negotiate the value of the shares that are used in an exchange. Management of targeted companies that founders seek to acquire and key officers the founders seek to attract have a clearly defined idea of what is being offered by looking at the market value of the shares.

Two other alleged advantages are cited for going public. The first is that publicly traded companies have greater access to alternative financing sources, such as bank loans and bond financing. The second is that a publicly traded company is viewed as more prestigious than a private company, providing greater exposure of its offerings to the public and suppliers, as well as greater exposure to the public investing community.

Disadvantages of going public Some factors make going public less appealing to founders. First, a publicly traded company must comply with the regulatory requirements for reporting companies. For example, in the United States, SEC regulatory requirements result in the occurrence of ongoing costs beyond the initial costs (legal, accounting, and banker fees) associated with an IPO, as well as listing fees charged by an exchange if that is the trading venue selected. The costs of being a public company have increased in the United States as a result of the Sarbanes-Oxley Act of 2002. Second, there are implicit costs that involve the time spent by founders preparing the information that a reporting company must provide on a periodic basis to public investors.

Another concern is the potential loss of confidentiality, a third disadvantage for some companies of taking a private company public. In the United States, a reporting company in its prospectus in its IPO and in its Form 10-K is required to disclose information that founders might view as highly sensitive to it operations or business strategy. The information that is not required from private companies but is from public ones includes information about products, customers, R&D, and management strategies.

The potential loss of control and flexibility when making business decisions as a result of going public is a fourth disadvantage of going public. When the founders lose controlling interest, major decisions (and even minor ones) may necessitate shareholder approval that require costly proxy voting as well as a considerable time delay while approval is sought from shareholders. The board of directors may no longer be controlled by the founders but by major shareholder groups if more than a majority of the shares are sold to the public. Of course, common stock with limited voting rights can be sold, but this may make the common stock less appealing to investors, resulting in a lower share valuation. Moreover, not all founders will be in a position to issue shares with limited voting rights.

Finally, founders who remain with the company after the IPO will experience pressure to perform as expected by shareholders and the financial community to achieve targeted financial metrics, such as earnings per share and earnings growth per share. This often results in the shifting of focus of founders from building a stronger company to achieving short-term financial targets at the expense of long-term performance.

Equity Dilutive Securities Used for New Ventures

The financial instruments that can be issued to raise funds are classified as either equity or debt. For most publicly traded nonfinancial corporations, equity is the larger component of the capital structure. For startup companies, equity (or equity-type debt) is typically an even larger component of the capital structure—particularly in the early stages of financing—than it is for publicly traded nonfinancial corporations. This decision about its capital structure (i.e., how much should be financed by equity versus debt) is typically forced on the founders because of the limited sources of pure debt financing available. By "pure debt" financing refers to debt where the creditors are not entitled to convert the debt for equity. As a startup enters into its later stages, there are opportunities to issue pure debt.

Here we review the issuance of securities in the United States by new ventures that lead to the issuance of common stock, referred to as **equity dilutive securities**. These securities include convertible preferred stock and convertible debt. Most investors in a startup company prefer equity dilutive securities to common stock for the reasons described in this chapter.

When common stock shares or equity dilutive securities are issued to obtain financing, the founders are concerned about the impact on ownership and control of the company. With respect to ownership, founders will look at how their ownership percentage changes following a round of financing. Control means the flexibility afforded the founders when managing the company in terms of strategic planning and directing the future of the company.

Many startup companies have been moving away from the "one share, one vote" common structure and toward a dual-class stock structure, where each class of stock has different voting rights. The motivation for creating different classes with different voting rights is that it allows the company's founders to retain control of the company by controlling the class of common stock with the largest number of voting rights. Typically in a dual-class structure, the two classes of common stock are referred to as "Class A stock" and "Class B stock." One cannot simply tell which class has the larger number of voting rights from the label. That is, there is no industry rule stating A or B will have the larger number of voting rights.

Historically, founding members of companies have been able to maintain control by owning less than a majority of the shares but by controlling the voting shares. For example, Rupert Murdock, CEO of News Corp., owns less than 1% of the nonvoting stock (which is traded in the market) but controls 40% of the voting stock. In 2004, Google adopted a dual-class structure—Class A and Class B common stock. Each share of Class A common stock has one vote per share, whereas Class B has 10 votes per share. The two founders, Larry Page and Sergey Brin, as well as the then-CEO, held the Class B shares. When Google went public, its Class A shares were sold via a Dutch auction. The dual-class structure gave the founders and CEO control over two-thirds of the voting shares. Facebook has a dual class structure with the same number of votes as Google for its Class A and Class B stock. The CEO and co-founder, Mark Zuckerberg, owned shares of Class B stock that allowed the retention of control after the Class A stock was sold via its IPO in 2012.[38]

Convertible Preferred Stock

Preferred stock is a hybrid security that combines the features of common stock and a debt obligation (such as a bond). Despite its debt-like feature, it is considered a form of equity security and on the balance sheet appears as part of stockholders' equity. Unlike common stockholders, preferred stockholders typically do not have voting rights except under certain circumstances described later. In the early stages of a startup company, preferred stock that allows for such investors as angel investors and venture capitalists to convert the

38. In its filing with the SEC (S-1 filing) before its IPO, Facebook estimated that the Class B shareholders have 70% of the voting power prior to the offering and warned that: "This concentrated control will limit your ability to influence corporate matters for the foreseeable future." (After the IPO, Zuckerberg owned 57% of the voting shares but had only a 28% ownership of the company.)

preferred stock into common stock is the vehicle of choice for investors who seek to benefit from the price appreciation potential for the common stock.

Preferred stock comes with provisions that convey rights, preferences, and privileges to the investors. The holders of a company's preferred stock have a claim on the dividends declared by the corporation's board of directors, and this claim is senior to that of the holders of the company's common stock. Preferred stock has a par value and a dividend rate. However, as with common stock issued by a startup company, investors in preferred stock are typically not paid a dividend due to the need to conserve cash.

We now describe the different features of preferred stock.

Dividends The par value together with the preferred stock dividend rate determines the dollar amount of the dividends that would be paid if there are sufficient earnings to pay preferred stockholders. For example, suppose that a company's preferred stock has a par value of $100 per share and a dividend rate of 6%. Multiplying the par value of $100 by the 6% dividend rate gives the annual dividend amount ($6 in our example) that the company agrees to pay its preferred stockholders.

A company is under no legal obligation to pay preferred stockholders any dividends. However, in such instances, there is typically a provision that imposes restrictions on management when dividends have not been paid. One such provision conveys preferred stockholders voting rights to elect some members to the issuer's board of directors. This feature is called "contingent voting rights," because the voting rights are contingent on a missed dividend payment. Despite this adverse impact, the legal consequences for failing to make a preferred stock dividend payment are not as dire as when a company fails to pay creditors the interest payment due to them. In that case, the company is legally obligated to repay the principal immediately (i.e., pay off the debt obligation), and failure to do so may result in bankruptcy.

If there is a shortfall in the quarterly dividend payment to preferred stockholders, is the company required to make up the shortfall in future quarters? The answer depends on how this situation is provided for in the preferred stock agreement. Preferred stock can be either cumulative or noncumulative preferred stock. For cumulative preferred stock, the dividend payment accrues until it is fully paid, and therefore common stockholders cannot receive any dividends until that is done. In the case of noncumulative preferred stock, any shortfall in a quarterly dividend payment is lost. As noted earlier, dividends are typically not paid by startups. Consequently, preferred stock issued by a startup company typically will be cumulative preferred stock, where the unpaid dividends will be added to the preferred stock's par value.

Liquidation preferences During a liquidating event, the par value is the amount that the holder is entitled to receive before common stockholders can receive any amount of the liquidation proceeds. Typically, a liquidating event is defined broadly in the agreement. It is not limited to the actual liquidation of the company as a result of bankruptcy or dissolution.

Instead, it will typically include the sale of the company and a change of control. In practice, startups often will not have much in proceeds if there is a liquidation event that results in the bankruptcy of the company.

The preference granted to preferred stockholders in the case of a liquidating event is considered to be this type of security's key provision, as well as impacting subsequent rounds of financing. To illustrate the importance of the preference granted, let's consider the case of a liquidating event where a company is sold for $22 million (after all costs associated with the sale) and assume the following for the pre-sale capital structure: par value of preferred stock of $5 million and debt of $2 million. Once creditors are paid their $2 million, the amount available to all equity investors (preferred stockholders and common stockholders) is $20 million. Now the question is how the $20 million is allocated between the preferred stockholders and common stockholders. If the preferred stockholders are not permitted to participate in any proceeds above the amount of their par value when there is a liquidation event, then the preferred stock is said to be "nonparticipating preferred stock" (or "1× liquidation preference").[39] In our illustration, the distribution of proceeds resulting from the sale would be as follows: $5 million to preferred stockholders and $15 million to common stockholders.

Founders seek to negotiate terms such that the preferred stock is nonparticipating. In contrast, preferred stockholders in new ventures will seek to participate in the liquidation proceeds beyond the par value of the preferred stock. If preferred stockholders are entitled to share along with common stockholders any remaining liquidation proceeds, then the preferred stock is said to be "participating preferred stock." Preferred stock that conveys a participating right can have different forms of participation, defined in terms of a multiple of the preferred stock's par value. For example, if preferred stockholders are entitled to receive twice or triple their par value (referred to as "2× liquidation preference" and "3× liquidation preference," respectively), then the distribution would be as follows:

Distribution to	2× liquidation preference	3× liquidation preference
Preferred stockholders:	$10 million	$15 million
Common stockholders:	$10 million	$5 million

A hybrid of the two types of preferred stock just described is one in which participation takes place, but it is capped at a specified amount. This form of preferred stock is referred to as **capped participating preferred stock** or **partially participating preferred stock**. For example, in our previous illustration, suppose that the preferred stockholders are entitled to share equally in liquidation proceeds up to $8 million. Then the preferred stockholders would receive $8 million, and the common stockholders would receive the balance of $12 million.

39. For simplicity, we are ignoring the possibility that the amount due to preferred stockholders would reflect the dividends that may have accumulated since the issuance of the preferred stock.

Conversion provision The optional conversion feature in a preferred stock offering often granted to investors in a startup company typically grants the investor the right to convert to the company's common shares. Restrictions may be imposed on when the conversion must occur. Typically, conversion is mandatory if certain events occur, such as an IPO. There are provisions to protect investors against dilution of their potential equity position.

Convertible Note

A **convertible note** is typically issued to investors in the early stages of financing of a startup prior to a first ("Series A") round of financing. Unlike convertible preferred stock, which is a form of equity, a convertible note is a form of debt. The holder of the convertible note either has the option to exchange the note for an equity position or automatically has the position converted into an equity position if there is a Series A round of financing. The equity position received by the holder of a convertible note is typically preferred stock.

Conversion terms Let's first look at a traditional convertible note issued by a mature corporation. The traditional convertible note gives the investor the right to convert into the issuer's common stock. The number of common stock shares into which the convertible note can be converted is called the "conversion ratio." Typically, the conversion ratio is fixed over the life of the convertible note. If the par value of the convertible note is $1,000 and the conversion ratio is 20:1, then the investor is entitled to convert the note into 20 shares of common stock. Effectively the price that the investor would be paying for each share of common stock by exercising the conversion privilege (i.e., the "conversion price") is $50 per share.

When used for seed financing by a startup, the conversion note differs in two ways. First, the conversion is typically into preferred stock and not common stock as in the case of a traditional convertible note. Moreover, the preferred stock is convertible preferred stock. So the exercise of the conversion privilege gives the investor the right to convert into a security that, in turn, has the right to eventually convert into common stock. Because a convertible debt can ultimately result in the issuance of more common stock, it is a form of an equity dilutive security.

The second difference is the price paid for the preferred stock when conversion occurs. The price that an investor will have to pay for the preferred stock shares if conversion occurs is based on a provision set forth in the convertible note offering. There could be a conversion discount or a conversion valuation cap. As explained below, both these provisions are included for the benefit of convertible note investors to compensate them for the substantial risks that they accepted by being early investors.

Conversion discount Early investors in a startup who purchase the convertible note do so in anticipation of generating an attractive return, if the startup performs well and its common stock price increases. Consequently, there must be provisions in the convertible note offering that allow investors to be compensated for accepting this risk exposure at the early stages of the startup. In addition, that reward should be potentially greater than that given to investors who invest in later financing rounds of the startup. In other words, when later investors (such as venture capitalists) make a determination of the value of the startup to purchase the shares of the preferred stock, investors in the convertible note want to be able to purchase the preferred shares at a lower price, because they were the initial bearers of the high risks associated with a startup company.

The provision that allows convertible note investors to do just that is the conversion discount, which specifies the discount at which convertible note investors can buy the preferred stock shares below what Series A investors pay for their preferred stock shares. Here is an example of how it works, assuming a 25% conversion discount.

Suppose that the convertible note funding is $300,000 with an interest rate of 10%. Two years later, there is a Series A financing by a venture capital fund, where the terms obtained are such that preferred stock could be purchased for $1 per share. The 25% conversion discount means that the convertible note investors would pay $0.75 per share of preferred stock (this is what we referred to earlier as the conversion price). How many shares of preferred stock would the convertible note investors receive? Because the convertible note investor is entitled to convert both the par value ($300,000) plus the accrued interest ($60,000), the amount converted is based on $360,000. Because the convertible note's amount to be converted is $360,000 and each preferred share can be purchased for $0.75 per share, the number of preferred shares would be 480,000 shares ($360,000/$0.75).

The conversion discount need not be fixed over the life of the security. Instead it can be structured so that it increases over time until Series A financing is obtained. One might expect that the longer it takes to obtain Series A financing, the greater will be the risk exposure of the convertible note investor and therefore a higher conversion discount is warranted. This is also an incentive for the founders to seek Series A financing as soon as reasonably possible to avoid further dilution.

A startup company may not necessarily raise all funds via convertible notes at one time. There may be several issues of convertible notes offered at different times. The conversion discount can be different for each offering, depending on what is needed to attract investors at the time of each offering. For example, a conversion discount may be higher for very early investors interested in purchasing convertible notes than for later investors in convertible notes.

Unlike a traditional convertible note, where the investors benefit from a rise in the value of the company, although investors in a startup's convertible note also benefit from an increase in valuation, investors do not want to see it rise that much by the Series A round of financing. The higher the valuation placed by the Series A investors is, the fewer shares of preferred stock will be received.

Conversion valuation cap A conversion valuation cap is the maximum dollar amount that can be used for determining the conversion price that the holder of the convertible note has to pay for the right to convert into preferred stock. The reason that this provision benefits the investor is that a lower price can be paid for the preferred stock than Series A investors pay.

To illustrate, suppose that an investor owns $300,000 par value of a convertible note with a conversion valuation cap of $6 million, and the company is raising funds in a Series A financing. Suppose further that the pre-money valuation (recall that this is the valuation before angel financing) is $8 million in this financing for preferred stock with a par value of $1. At the time of financing, assume that the accrued interest for the convertible note is $60,000. The conversion valuation cap of $6 million means that the conversion price for the convertible noteholders to purchase the preferred stock is adjusted below that paid by the Series A investors. The procedure to obtain the adjustment is found by dividing the conversion valuation cap ($6 million in our example) by the pre-money valuation ($8 million in our illustration). In our illustration, the adjustment is then 75%. Thus the convertible note investors will pay 75% of what is paid by the Series A investors to buy the preferred stock. Because Series A investors pay $1 per share of preferred stock, the convertible note investors pay only $0.75. And so because the convertible note investors are converting $360,000 (principal plus accrued interest), they will receive 480,000 prefer stock shares ($360,000/$0.75).

Debt with Warrants

Another form of debt that is an equity dilutive security is debt with warrants to purchase the company's common stock. A **warrant** is a form of option that grants the warrant holder the right to exercise it and receive a specified security. Often this type of financing is raised in the later stages of a company to obtain financing between rounds of financing (i.e., bridge financing).

For example, a company might issue convertible debt with warrants to purchase up to 15% of the common stock. This is referred to as "convertible debt with 15% warrant coverage." Suppose that the par value of this convertible debt is $5 million. Then investors in this convertible debt with warrants have the right to purchase $750,000 ($0.15 \times \$5$ million) of the issuer's common stock. The exercise price for the warrants is determined by what investors in the next round of financing agree to pay for the common stock. Thus, what is important is that investors are confident that there will be another round of financing to determine the conversion price. This is why such financing is used less often in the very early stages of financing but occurs later on in bridge financing, when the company has already gone through several rounds of financing. However, some observrs have suggested tweaks in the convertible debt with warrant structure to increase its use in certain early stage financing situations.

Key Points

- Every country has its own definition of what a small and medium-sized enterprise (SME) is.
- The governments of different countries and international organizations establish their own guidelines for defining SMEs.
- The metrics used in classifying an enterprise as an SME include the number of employees, level of sales (revenue), and total assets.
- Governments provide various programs and initiatives to increase the funding available to qualified SMEs.
- Early-stage financing includes the seed round and the first round.
- In the seed round, sometimes referred to as the "pre-commercialization financing stage," the founders seek to finance the development of a product or service.
- In very early stage financing, typically the major source of funding is the personal assets of the founders. Such financing is referred to as "bootstrap financing."
- In first round financing (or Series A round financing), the milestone that has been reached is the generation of revenue, even though neither break-even operations nor profits are typically reached at this stage.
- It is typically difficult for founders to obtain bank financing in the seed stage (except when the founders have sufficient collateral or assets to provide personal guarantees), but once first round financing is obtained, specialty banks and nonbank entities are willing to provide venture debt that contains an equity kicker for the lender in the form of warrants.
- Sources for seed-round financing are credit cards, vendors, Small Business Administration (SBA) loans, angel investors and angel groups, super angels, seed accelerators, incubators, and crowdfunding platforms, with the most common source of larger amounts of seed financing being angel investors.
- The types of government-supported funding programs that have been used by countries make financing more accessible to SMEs and new ventures are loan guarantees, direct credit loans, loan subsidies, grant programs, and preferable tax treatment for lenders to SMEs.
- Expansion-stage financing is undertaken to expand the company's business by increasing production and acquiring customers through marketing.
- Expansion-stage financing includes bridge loans, second-round financing (Series B round financing), third-round financing (also called "Series C round financing"), and so on.
- Additional rounds of financing may be necessary if the company does not have a liquidating event after several rounds of financing. The entry of a new investor group—institutional investors—has allowed ventures to raise funds through an IPO by providing substantial funds for a company to expand without the need to go public.

• The primary source of early-stage funding is angel investors, wealthy individuals who typically invest between $150,000 and $2 million and who qualify under the SEC's definition of "accredited investors."

• In addition to providing funding, angel investors provide strategic planning advice, assist in team building, and provide contacts for developing key partnerships and further fundraising. Angel investors typically invest through groups or networks.

• Although venture capitalists invest primarily in first round financing, venture capital firms that do provide seed financing are referred to as "super angels" and are set up as private equity firms.

• Crowdfunding is the practice of raising funds for a startup from a large number of investors who invest small sums, typically over the Internet. Equity crowdfunding, one form of crowdfunding, allows investors to obtain an equity interest in a startup company.

• Seed accelerators offer the opportunity for founders to gain access not only to early stage financing in exchange for equity but also to other potential investors, training in a short period of time, temporary office space, and a team of experts.

• An incubator is another type of program that mentors entrepreneurs and other similar services as a seed accelerator.

• The primary sources for expansion financing have historically been traditional venture capital firms, corporate venture capital firms, and online VC funds.

• Venture capital firms invest in a startup business in the form of equity, with the investments typically made in series or rounds that typically occur every two years, based on predetermined milestones being achieved.

• Venture capital firms are often said to be a special type of private equity firm that invests in startup companies, in contrast to a typical private equity firm, which invests in mature companies seeking to go private or that are viewed to be underperforming and have the potential for highly attractive returns.

• Corporate venture capitalists are corporations that invest in startups that have the potential to provide a good strategic fit with their company's offerings.

• Institutional investors, such as mutual funds and hedge funds, are the latest entrants providing expansion financing for new ventures prior to an IPO, an acquisition, or a merger.

• The provision of funding in large sums for expansion by institutional investors has resulted in new ventures postponing going to the public to raise funds through an IPO or by being acquired.

• The founders of a company can turn to the general public to meet the company's needs through an IPO of its shares, whose issuance is governed by securities laws.

• The two principal advantages of an IPO are (1) publicly traded common stock provides liquidity for the shares owned by founders, as well as those owned by investors and employees who are shareholders, and (2) founders can use shares as a form of currency, allowing them to make the acquisitions necessary to expand their business and to attract key executives by offering stock options.

- The disadvantages of an IPO are that the company must comply with and incur the costs associated with SEC regulatory filing requirements, faces implicit costs in the form of the time devoted by founders to preparing the information that a reporting company must provide on a periodic basis to public investors, faces loss of confidentiality because of required disclosures, and management experiences pressure to perform as expected by shareholders and the financial community to achieve targeted financial metrics, resulting in the founders shifting their focus from building a stronger company to achieving short-term financial targets at the expense of long-term performance.
- In the United States, new ventures issue securities that lead to the issuance of common stock, referred to as to as "equity dilutive securities," because investors in startup companies prefer these securities to a direct investment in common stock.
- Equity dilutive securities include convertible preferred stock and convertible debt.
- Preferred stock is a hybrid security that combines the features of common stock and a debt obligation; unlike common stockholders, preferred stockholders typically do not have voting rights except under certain circumstances.
- In the early stages of a startup company, preferred stock that allows investors to convert preferred stock into common stock is the vehicle of choice for investors.
- Preferred stock comes with provisions that convey rights, preferences, and privileges to the investors in this security.
- The par value of preferred stock is important, because if there is a liquidating event, it typically includes the acquisition or merger of the company and the selling off of most of the company's assets.
- Nonparticipating preferred stock does not permit an investor to participate in any proceeds above the amount of their preference when a liquidation event occurs.
- Participating preferred stock allows investors to share along with common stockholders in some fashion with respect to any remaining liquidation proceeds.
- Capped participating preferred stock (partially participating preferred stock) is a form of preferred stock that allows participation but is capped at a specified amount.
- Convertible preferred stock allows the investor to convert into common stock.
- A convertible note, typically issued to investors in the early stages of financing (prior to a Series A round), is a form of debt.
- Convertible noteholders can have either the option to exchange the note for an equity position or automatically has the position converted into an equity position if there is a Series A round of financing.

Questions

1. How is an SME defined?
2. The following is a quote from the World Bank and FIRST Initiative:

> Access to finance for small and medium enterprises (SMEs) has moved up the global reform agenda and has become a topic of great interest for policy makers, regulators, researchers, market practitioners, and other stakeholders.[40]

Explain why.

3. What are the phases of early-stage financing, and where is funding likely to come from in each phase?
4. a. What are benefits of using credit cards as a source of startup funding?

b. What kind of considerations should be taken into account when turning to credit card financing?

5. a. What is the Small Business Administration (SBA) loan program that is most likely to be used by high-tech startups?

b. What kind of repayment options are available and are not available for this type of loan?

6. What are advantages and disadvantages for an investor of joining an angel group?
7. Besides securing capital, how do startups benefit from the backing of angel investors?
8. Explain whether you agree or disagree with the following statement: "In the expansion-stage financing phase, a company goes through an IPO to raise funds for business expansion."
9. Describe seed accelerators and incubators and the differences between them.
10. You are the advisor to the board of directors of a private company contemplating an IPO. What factors would you explain to the board that would be helpful in making the decision to go public?
11. a. What is the difference between a venture capital firm and a private equity firm?

b. What is the difference between equity crowdfunding and an online venture capital fund?

12. Here is the title of an article: "Mutual Funds Are Bypassing IPOs and Going Straight for the Main Course" by Mark DeCambre in *Quartz* (http://qz.com/199833/mutual-funds-are-bypassing-ipos-and-going-straight-for-the-main-course/). Based on the title of the article, what does this mean?
13. In an article published in the *Wall Street Journal*, the following statement was made:

40. World Bank and FIRST Initiative, *Principles for Public Credit Guarantee Schemes for SMEs* (Washington, DC: World Bank, 2015).

Large institutional investors like Fidelity, T. Rowe Price and BlackRock are an increasingly appearing alongside the venture capital firms that traditionally bet on promising young tech entrepreneurs.[41]

What are the implications of the participation of large institutional investors for how quickly private companies go public?

14. a. What is an equity dilutive security?

b. Why do investors in startup companies prefer equity dilutive security?

15. a. What is the difference between cumulative preferred stgock and noncumulative preferred stock?

b. What is capped participating preferred stock?

16. a. What is a convertible note? (Be sure to include a conversion ratio and conversion price in your answer.)

b. How do conversion terms typically differ when the issuer of convertible notes is a mature company versus a startup company?

41. "Mutual Funds Moonlight as Venture Capitalists: Firms Are Pushing into Silicon Valley at a Record Pace," *Wall Street Journal*, April 20, 2014.

VII REAL ESTATE MARKETS

29 The Residential Mortgage Market

CONTENTS

Learning Objectives

After reading this chapter, you will understand:

- what a mortgage is;
- who the major originators of residential mortgages are;
- the mortgage origination process;
- the borrower and property characteristics considered by a lender when evaluating the credit risk of an applicant for a mortgage loan;
- the risks associated with the origination process for a residential mortgage;
- what the servicing of a residential mortgage loan involves;
- the types of residential mortgage loans based on interest rate type, amortization type, repayment structure, lender's recourse, lien status, credit classification, credit guarantees, and conforming versus nonconforming loans;
- what a prepayment is;
- the cash flow of a mortgage;
- what a prepayment penalty mortgage is;
- the risks associated with investing in mortgages;
- the significance of prepayment risk; and
- the development of the secondary market for residential mortgage loans.

The mortgage market in any country is a collection of markets that includes a primary (or origination) market and a secondary market where mortgages trade. A **mortgage** is a pledge of property to secure payment of a debt. Typically, property refers to real estate. If the property owner/borrower (the mortgagor) fails to pay the lender (the mortgagee), the lender has the right to foreclose the loan and seize the property to ensure that the mortgage is repaid. The types of real estate properties that can be mortgaged are divided into two broad categories: single-family residential properties and commercial properties. The former category includes houses, condominiums, and cooperatives. In the United States, the term of a mortgage (i.e., the number of years to maturity) ranges from 15 to 30 years. For most countries in Europe, a residential mortgage typically has a term between 15 and 40 years, but in some countries (e.g., France and Spain), it can be as long as 50 years. Japan is an extreme case: The term can be 100 years. Commercial properties are income-producing properties and multifamily properties (i.e., apartment buildings), office buildings, industrial properties (including warehouses), shopping centers, hotels, and health care facilities (e.g., senior residential care facilities).

Although our focus in this chapter is on the U.S. residential mortgage markets and the types of mortgage loans available, we do discuss the wide range of mortgage types available in other countries. We also discuss the role of government in the residential mortgage market.

Origination of Residential Mortgage Loans

The original lender is called the **mortgage originator**. The principal originators of residential mortgage loans in the United States are thrifts, commercial banks, and mortgage bankers.

Mortgage originators may generate income from mortgage activity in one or more ways. First, they typically charge an **origination fee**. This fee is expressed in terms of points, where each point represents 1% of the borrowed funds. For example, an origination fee of two points on a $200,000 mortgage is $4,000. Originators also may charge application fees and certain processing fees. The second source of revenue is the profit that might be generated from selling a mortgage at a higher price than it originally cost. This profit is called **secondary market profit**. If mortgage rates rise, an originator will realize a loss when the mortgages are sold in the secondary market.

Although technically, the sources of revenue attributable to the origination function are origination fees and secondary marketing profits, there are two other potential sources. First, mortgage originators may service the mortgages they originate, for which they obtain a **servicing fee**. Servicing of the mortgage involves collecting monthly payments from mortgagors and forwarding proceeds to owners of the loan, sending payment notices to mortgagors, reminding mortgagors when payments are overdue, maintaining records of mortgage balances, furnishing tax information to mortgagors, administering an escrow account for real estate taxes and insurance purposes, and (if necessary) initiating foreclosure proceedings. The servicing fee is a fixed percentage of the outstanding mortgage balance, typically 25 basis points to 100 basis points per year. The mortgage originator may sell the servicing of the mortgage to another party, who would then receive the servicing fee. Second, the mortgage originator may hold the mortgage in its investment portfolio.

Mortgage banking refers to the activity of originating mortgages. Banks and thrifts undertake mortgage banking. However, there are companies not associated with a bank or thrift that are involved in mortgage banking. These mortgage bankers, unlike banks and thrifts, typically do not invest in the mortgages they originate. Instead, they derive their income from the origination fees. Commercial banks derive their income from all three sources.

The Mortgage Origination Process

Someone who wants to borrow funds to purchase a home will apply for a loan from a mortgage originator. The potential homeowner completes an application form, which provides financial information about the applicant, and pays an application fee; then the mortgage originator performs a credit evaluation of the applicant. The requirements specified by the originator to grant the loan are referred to as **underwriting standards**.

The two primary quantitative underwriting standards are (1) the **payment-to-income ratio** (PTI) and (2) the **loan-to-value ratio** (LTV). The first is the ratio of monthly payments to monthly income, which measures the ability of the applicant to make monthly payments (both mortgage and real estate tax payments). The lower this ratio is, the greater the likelihood that the applicant will be able to meet the required payments.

The difference between the purchase price of the property and the amount borrowed is the borrower's down payment. The LTV is the ratio of the amount of the loan to the market (or appraised) value of the property. The lower this ratio is, the greater the protection for the lender if the applicant defaults on the payments and the lender must repossess and resell the property. For example, if an applicant wants to borrow $225,000 on a property with an appraised value of $300,000, the LTV is 75%. Suppose the applicant subsequently defaults on the mortgage. The lender can then repossess the property and sell it to recover the amount owed. But the amount that will be received by the lender depends on the market value of the property. In our example, even if conditions in the housing market are weak, the lender will still be able to recover the proceeds lent if the value of the property declines by $75,000. Suppose instead that the applicant wanted to borrow $270,000 for the same property. The LTV would then be 90%. If the lender had to foreclose on the property and then sell it because the applicant defaulted, there is less protection for the lender.

If the lender decides to lend the funds, it sends a **commitment letter** to the applicant. This letter commits the lender to provide funds to the applicant. The length of time of the commitment varies between 30 and 60 days. At the time of the commitment letter, the lender will require that the applicant pay a commitment fee. It is important to understand that the commitment letter obligates the lender—not the applicant—to perform. The commitment fee that the applicant pays is lost if the applicant decides not to purchase the property or uses an alternative source of funds to purchase the property. Thus, the commitment letter states that, for a fee, the applicant has the right but not the obligation to require the lender to provide funds at a certain interest rate and on certain terms. The lender has effectively granted the applicant an option to borrow the funds, with the commitment fee paid by the applicant being the option price.

Mortgage originators can either (1) hold the mortgage in their portfolios, (2) sell the mortgage to an investor that wishes to hold the mortgage in its portfolio, (3) place the mortgage in a pool of mortgages to be used as collateral for the issuance of a security, or (4) sell the mortgage to another party that will place the mortgage in a pool of mortgages to be used as collateral for a security. When a mortgage is used as collateral for the issuance of a security, the mortgage is said to be a **securitized mortgage**. We discuss the securitization of residential mortgages in chapter 30. An entity that purchases mortgages from mortgage originators for the purpose of using them as collateral in a securitization is said to be a **mortgage conduit**.

Risks Associated with Mortgage Origination

The loan applications being processed and the commitments made by a mortgage originator together are referred to as its *pipeline*. **Pipeline risk** refers to the risks associated with originating mortgages. This risk has two components: price risk and fallout risk.

Price risk refers to the adverse effects on the value of the pipeline if mortgage rates in the market rise. If mortgage rates rise, and if the mortgage originator has made commitments at a lower mortgage rate, it will either have to sell the mortgages when they close at a value below the funds lent to homeowners or retain the mortgages as a portfolio investment earning a below-market mortgage rate. The mortgage originator faces the same risk for mortgage applications in the pipeline on which the applicants have elected to fix the rate at the time the applications were submitted.

Fallout risk is the risk that applicants or those who were issued commitment letters will not close (i.e., complete the transaction by purchasing the property with funds borrowed from the mortgage originator). A major reason potential borrowers may cancel their commitments or withdraw their mortgage applications is that mortgage rates decline sufficiently that it is economic to seek an alternative lender. Fallout risk is the result of the mortgage originator giving the potential borrower the right but not the obligation to close (i.e., the right to cancel the agreement). Reasons other than a decline in mortgage rates may also cause a potential borrower to fall out of the pipeline. The property inspection report may be unfavorable, or the purchase could have been predicated on a change in employment that does not occur.

Mortgage originators have several alternatives to protect themselves against pipeline risk. To protect against price risk, the originator could get a commitment from the entity to whom the mortgage originator plans to sell the mortgage. This sort of commitment is effectively a forward contract, a contract we will discuss in chapter 33. The mortgage originator agrees to deliver a mortgage at a future date, and another party (such as a conduit) agrees to buy the mortgage at that time at a predetermined price (or mortgage rate).

Consider what happens, however, if mortgage rates decline and potential borrowers elect to cancel the agreement. The mortgage originator has agreed to deliver a mortgage with a specified mortgage rate. If the potential borrower does not close and the mortgage originator has made a commitment to deliver the mortgage to a conduit, the mortgage originator cannot back out of the transaction. As a result, the mortgage originator will realize a loss—it must deliver a mortgage at a higher mortgage rate in a lower-mortgage-rate environment. This is fallout risk.

Mortgage originators can protect themselves against fallout risk by entering into an agreement with a conduit for optional rather than mandatory delivery of the mortgage. In such an agreement, the mortgage originator is effectively buying an option that gives it the right, but not the obligation, to deliver a mortgage. (Recall that when the originator issued the commitment letter, it gave the applicant such an option.) The conduit has sold that option to the mortgage originator and therefore charges a fee for allowing optional delivery.

Mortgage Servicers

Every mortgage loan must be serviced. As explained earlier, servicing a mortgage involves collecting monthly payments and forwarding proceeds to owners of the loan, sending payment notices to mortgagors, reminding mortgagors when payments are overdue, maintaining records of principal balances, administering an escrow balance for real estate taxes and insurance purposes, initiating foreclosure proceedings if necessary, and furnishing tax information to mortgagors when applicable.

Mortgage servicers include bank-related entities, thrift-related entities, and mortgage bankers. Four sources of revenue arise from mortgage servicing. The primary source is the servicing fee. This fee is a fixed percentage of the outstanding mortgage balance. Consequently, the revenue from servicing declines over time as the mortgage balance declines over time if the borrower is required to make monthly payments to reduce the mortgage balance. The second source of servicing income arises from the interest that can be earned by the servicer from the escrow balance that a borrower often maintains with a servicer. The third source of revenue is the float earned on the monthly mortgage payment. This opportunity arises because of the delay permitted between the time the servicer receives the payment and the time that the payment must be sent to the investor. Fourth, there are several sources of ancillary income: (1) a late fee collected by the servicer if the mortgage payment is not made on time, (2) commissions from cross-selling the borrowers' insurance products, and (3) fees generated from selling mailing lists.

Types of Residential Mortgage Loans

There are different types of residential mortgages available in countries that have a mortgage market. They can be classified according to the following attributes:

- interest rate type,
- repayment structure,
- treatment of prepayments,
- lender's recourse,
- lien status,
- credit classification,
- credit guarantees, and
- conforming versus nonconforming status.

Interest Rate Type

The interest rate on a mortgage is referred to as the **mortgage rate** or **note rate**. Based on interest rate type, mortgages can be classified as follows:

- fixed-rate mortgage,
- indexed adjustable-rate mortgage,

- reviewable adjustable-rate mortgage,
- rollover (renegotiable) mortgage,
- hybrid mortgage, or
- convertible mortgage.

For a **fixed-rate mortgage** (FRM), the mortgage is unchanged over the term of the mortgage. Mortgages of this type can be found in many countries, including the United States, France, Germany, and Denmark, and they are the most common mortgage type in the first two countries listed. In the early years of the development of the mortgage credit market in those countries, the FRM was the most common type of mortgage. The FRM was the most common type in Denmark until recently and in Italy, Spain, and Greece until the early 1990s. Today the dominant mortgage type in Europe and in most other countries is the one we describe next.

An **adjustable-rate mortgage** (ARM), also referred to as a **variable-rate mortgage**, is one whose rate resets periodically. The frequency at which the mortgage rate resets can be monthly, semiannually, or annually. The major risk of using an ARM from the borrower's perspective is that the mortgage rate may increase so dramatically as a result of conditions in the capital market that it may significantly impair the borrower's ability to meet the mortgage payments. To reduce this risk for borrowers, referred to as "payment shock risk," there is typically a cap on how high the mortgage rate can increase. There may be a periodic rate cap, a lifetime rate cap, or both. A **periodic rate cap** limits the amount that the mortgage rate may increase at the reset date. A **lifetime rate cap** specifies the maximum rate that may be imposed over the mortgage's life. When there is a cap, the lender is sharing the payment shock risk with the borrower. An ARM may also specify a floor below which the mortgage rate cannot be reduced, periodically or over the mortgage's term. The inclusion of a floor in the mortgage reduces the interest rate shock risk faced by the lender.

In the United States, a typical ARM agreement has both types of rate caps. In some countries, any rate cap may be set so high that it does not really reduce the borrower's payment shock risk. Spain is an example. It is not uncommon to find realistic rate caps in EU member countries, where the FRM dominates and the ARM is an alternative mortgage product offered by lenders. This is the situation in France, where the rate cap is set at 200 basis points above the initial mortgage rate.[1]

The method for determining the new mortgage rate at a reset date determines the type of ARM, either index referenced or reviewable. For an **indexed ARM**, referred to as an **index tracker ARM** in the European Union, the mortgage rate at a reset date is set by a formula that links the mortgage rate to an interest rate index. For example, in the United States, an

1. Hans-Joachim Dübel and Marc Rothemund, "A New Mortgage Credit Regime for Europe: Setting the Right Priorities" (Brussels: Centre for European Policy Studies/European Credit Research Institute, June 2011), 68.

index-referenced ARM that resets every year might be linked to the one-year U.S. Treasury bill rate. In Korea and Spain, index-referenced ARMs dominate.[2] When the amount of the adjustment of the mortgage rate at a reset date is at the discretion of the lender, the mortgage is called a **reviewable ARM**. In Australia, Ireland, and the United Kingdom, this is the dominant mortgage type.[3]

As with an ARM, a rollover mortgage (or renegotiable mortgage) and a hybrid mortgage have a fixed mortgage rate that is adjusted after a specified period of time. What distinguishes a rollover mortgage from a hybrid mortgage is the type of mortgage rate after the initial specified period. If after the reset date the mortgage rate is fixed for another period, it is called a **rollover mortgage**. In some countries, the new fixed rate might be for the remainder of the mortgage's life. A rollover mortgage is the dominant form in Canada, Denmark, Germany, the Netherlands, and Switzerland.[4] When the mortgage starts out at a fixed rate and then becomes an ARM after a specified initial term, the mortgage is referred to as a **hybrid mortgage**. For example, a hybrid mortgage might have a fixed rate for the first five years, then after five years it might convert to an indexed ARM that is adjusted every year.

Finally, a **convertible mortgage** starts out with a mortgage rate that for a specified period of time can be either fixed or adjustable. The borrower has the option to convert the mortgage into an FRM or an ARM for the remainder of the mortgage's term. The appeal to borrowers of this type of mortgage is that it mitigates payment shock risk. This type of mortgage is available in the United States and several other countries. Almost half of the mortgages in Japan are convertible.[5]

Repayment Structure

The amount borrowed is referred to the "original mortgage balance." The amount that must be repaid by the end of the mortgage term and the method for doing so are referred to as the **repayment structure**. Typically a mortgage payment is made monthly. If any amount of the monthly mortgage payment exceeds the amount of the interest required for that amount, the excess amount is used to reduce the original mortgage balance. A lender would prefer a mortgage where some principal is repaid over the mortgage's term to reduce the credit risk it faces when lending against the property.

The repayment of the principal borrowed as part of the monthly loan payment is referred to as **amortization**. The mortgage can specify that each monthly payment include amor-

2. Michael Lea, "International Comparison of Mortgage Product Offerings," special report (Washington, DC: Research Institute for Housing America and American Bankers Association, September 2010).

3. Lea, "International Comparison of Mortgage Product Offerings."

4. Lea, "International Comparison of Mortgage Product Offerings."

5. T. Shimizu and Y. Nakada, "Japan's Residential Mortgage Loan Characteristics and Trends: RMBS Outlook for 2009" (New York: Standard & Poor's, July 2009).

tization. That is, the monthly mortgage payment can include the monthly interest based on the mortgage balance at the beginning of the month plus a scheduled principal amount that represents scheduled amortization. A mortgage that specifies a scheduled payment of principal that the borrower must make is referred to as an **amortizing mortgage**. An amortizing mortgage is typical in most countries.

For an amortizing mortgage, the monthly scheduled principal payments can be such that when all scheduled principal payments are added, the total is equal to the original mortgage balance. As a result, when the borrower makes the final monthly mortgage payment, the last payment is enough to cover the outstanding mortgage balance for that month. As a result, no further payments are required by the borrower. For example, suppose a mortgage has an original mortgage balance of $200,000, a mortgage rate of 7.5%, and a term of 30 years. Then the monthly mortgage payment would be $1,398.43. Notice that the monthly mortgage payment is the same over all 360 months. How this monthly mortgage payment is determined is explained in the appendix to this chapter. Assuming that the borrower has made all 360 monthly payments on a timely basis, then it can be shown (see the appendix) that after the last monthly mortgage payment is made, the outstanding mortgage balance is zero (i.e., the mortgage is paid off). This type of amortizing mortgage is referred to as a **fully amortizing mortgage** and is the typical mortgage in the United States.

Although our illustration is for an FRM, an ARM is also typically a fully amortizing mortgage. Because the mortgage rate changes, the monthly mortgage payment has to be recalculated at each reset date so that the new monthly mortgage payments are sufficient to fully amortize the outstanding mortgage balance at the reset date. This determination of the new monthly mortgage payment, explained in the appendix, is referred to as "recasting the mortgage." For example, let's consider once again a $200,000, 30-year mortgage. Assume that the mortgage is an ARM that adjusts annually and that the initial mortgage rate (i.e., the mortgage rate for the first 12 months) is 7.5%. It can be shown that at the end of the 12th month, the outstanding mortgage balance would be $198,156.33. Recasting the mortgage involves computing the monthly mortgage payment that will fully amortize a mortgage of $198,156.33 for 29 years (348 months) because after one year, there are 29 years remaining on the loan. The interest rate used to recast the mortgage is the new mortgage rate at the reset date. Suppose that the reset rate is 8.5%. Then the monthly mortgage payment to fully amortize the mortgage can be shown to be $1,535.26, and that is therefore the monthly mortgage payment for the next 12 months.

An amortizing mortgage can be such that the total of the monthly scheduled principal payments is less than the original mortgage balance. For such amortizing mortgages, referred to as **partial amortizing mortgages**, the amount owed at the end of the mortgage's term is the difference between the original mortgage balance and the total of the scheduled principal payment and any unscheduled principal payment that might have been made. This amount, which must be paid by the borrower to the lender, is referred to as a **balloon payment**.

In countries such as Australia, Denmark, Finland, France, Germany, Greece, Ireland, Korea, the Netherlands, Portugal, Spain, Switzerland, and the United Kingdom, and to a limited extent the United States, mortgages are available that require no monthly scheduled principal payments for a specified period of time.[6] Instead, only the monthly interest is paid for that period, and therefore there is no amortization of the original mortgage balance. This type of mortgage is referred to an **interest-only mortgage**. The period of time during which there is no scheduled principal payment is called the **lockout period**. After the lockout period, the monthly mortgage changes so that the monthly mortgage payments include a scheduled principal amount that is sufficient to fully amortize the original amount of the loan over the remaining term of the loan. A special type of interest-only mortgage is one with no scheduled principal payments over the life of the mortgage. This type of mortgage, referred to as an **interest-only life mortgage** or a **bullet mortgage**, is available in Denmark, the Netherlands, and the United Kingdom. This type of mortgage obviously exposes lenders to greater credit risk than an amortizing mortgage.

Treatment of Prepayments

Borrowers often want the right to repay all or part of their mortgage balance before the scheduled maturity date. This may be desirable for many reasons, but a key reason is that if market interest rates decline and the borrower has the opportunity to refinance at a lower mortgage rate, the economic value of refinancing can be considerable, even after taking into account the costs associated with obtaining a new mortgage.

The amount of the payment made in excess of the monthly mortgage payment is called a **prepayment**. As an example, consider once again the 30-year, $200,000 mortgage with a 7.5% mortgage rate. The monthly mortgage payment is $1,398.43. Suppose the borrower makes a payment of $5,398.43. This payment exceeds the monthly mortgage payment by $4,000. This amount represents a prepayment and reduces the outstanding mortgage balance by $4,000. This type of prepayment, in which the entire mortgage balance is not paid off, is called a **partial prepayment** or **curtailment**. When a curtailment is made, the mortgage is not recast (i.e., the monthly mortgage payment is not changed). Instead, the borrower continues to make the same monthly mortgage payment. The effect of the prepayment is that more of the subsequent monthly mortgage payment is applied to reduce the outstanding mortgage balance. The more common type of prepayment is one in which the entire outstanding mortgage balance is paid off before the mortgage's contractual maturity.

Effectively, the borrower's right to prepay a mortgage in whole or in part without a penalty is a call option. The mortgage that mitigates the borrower's right to prepay is a **prepayment penalty mortgage**. This type of mortgage imposes penalties if the borrower

6. See table 7 in Kathleen Scanlon, Jens Lunde, and Christine Whitehead, "Mortgage Product Innovation in Advanced Economies: More Choice, More Risk," *European Journal of Housing Policy* 8, no. 2 (2008): 109–131.

prepays. The penalties are designed to discourage refinancing activity and require a fee to be paid if the loan is prepaid within a certain amount of time after funding.

Because the major concern for a lender is that the borrower will prepay when interest rates decline, prepayment penalties can be viewed as a form of yield maintenance provision that can be found in callable bonds and (as explained in chapter 31) commercial mortgages. Prepayment penalty mortgages that are available in the United States are typically structured to allow borrowers to partially prepay up to 20% of their loan each year the penalty is in effect, and charge the borrower six months of interest for prepayments on the remaining 80% of their balance. Some penalties are waived if the property is sold and are described as "soft" penalties; hard penalties require the penalty to be paid even if the prepayment occurs as a result of the sale of the property.

The laws and regulations governing the imposition of prepayment penalties are established not only by each country but even by jurisdictions within a country. Laws in European countries typically permit penalties for prepayment, and in fact, prepayment penalty mortgages are common in Europe. In the United States, usually the applicable laws for FRMs are specified at the state level. Some states do not allow prepayment penalties on FRMs. Other states do permit them but restrict the type of penalty. For ARMS, certain federal laws override state laws. Consequently, although the proportion of prepayment penalty mortgages is small in the United States, they do exist in states that permit the imposition of such penalties.

Lender's Recourse

Borrowers do default. When that occurs, the lender has the right to repossess the property and then sell it. However, if the proceeds received from the sale of the property are less than the outstanding mortgage balance, what can the lender do to recover the loss? The answer depends on whether the loan is a recourse or a nonrecourse loan. If the lender is entitled to have a claim against the borrower for the shortfall, the mortgage is said to be a **recourse loan**. Thus, the lender can look to the borrower's other assets to try to recover through the legal system as much of the shortfall as possible. With a **nonrecourse mortgage**, unless there is some claim of fraud, the lender does not have a claim against the borrower. That is, the lender can only look to the property to recover the outstanding mortgage balance.

Whether the lender is entitled to recourse in the case of a default varies by country. In the United States, all mortgages to purchase a residence are nonrecourse mortgages. In European countries and Japan, mortgage lending is on a recourse basis. This is one of the reasons for the higher mortgage default rates in the United States than in European countries and Japan. It is the statutory ban on recourse lending for residential mortgage property in the United States that provides an incentive for borrowers to exercise their option to default when their home values have declined below the outstanding mortgage balance, even if they have sufficient financial resources to make timely mortgage payments. Such a practice by borrowers is referred to as a "strategic default."

Lien Status

The **lien status** of a mortgage indicates the lender's seniority in the event of the forced liquidation of the property owing to the borrower's default. For a mortgage that is a **first lien**, the lender would have first call on the proceeds of the liquidation of the property if it were to be repossessed. A mortgage could also be a **second lien** or **junior lien**, and the claims of the lender on the proceeds in the case of liquidation would come after the lender who had a first lien was paid in full.

Credit Classification

In the United States, a mortgage originated for which the borrower is considered to be of high credit quality (i.e., the borrower has strong employment and credit histories, income sufficient to make the mortgage payments without compromising the borrower's creditworthiness, and substantial equity in the underlying property) is classified as a **prime loan**. A loan originated for which the borrower is of lower credit quality or where the loan is not a first lien on the property is classified as a **subprime loan**. Between the prime and the subprime sector is a somewhat nebulous category referred to as an **alternative-A loan**, or more commonly an **alt-A loan**. These loans are considered to be prime loans (the "A" refers to the A grade assigned by underwriting agencies), but they have some attributes that either increase their perceived credit riskiness or cause them to be difficult to categorize and evaluate.

When assessing the credit quality of a mortgage applicant, lenders look at various measures. The starting point is the applicant's credit score. Several firms collect data on the payment histories of individuals from lending institutions and, using statistical models, evaluate and quantify individual creditworthiness in terms of a credit score. Basically, a credit score is a numerical grade for the credit history of the borrower. The three most popular credit reporting companies that compute credit scores are Experian, Transunion, and Equifax. Although the credit scores are determined using different methods, the scores generically are referred to as **FICO scores**.[7] Typically, a lender will obtain more than one score, to minimize the impact of variations in credit scores across providers. FICO scores range from 350 to 850. The higher the FICO score is, the lower is the credit risk.

The LTV has proved to be a good predictor of default: the higher the LTV, the greater the likelihood of default. By definition, the LTV of the loan in a purchase transaction is a function of both the down payment and the purchase price of the property. Lenders calculate income ratios, such as the PTI, to assess the applicant's ability to pay. These ratios compare the monthly mortgage payment that the applicant would have to pay if the loan is

7. This name is used is because credit-scoring companies generally use a model developed by Fair, Isaacs & Co. The model uses 45 criteria to rank the creditworthiness of an individual.

granted to the applicant's monthly income. The most common measures are the front ratio and the back ratio. The **front ratio** is computed by dividing the total monthly payment (which includes interest and principal on the loan plus property taxes and homeowner insurance) by the applicant's pre-tax monthly income. The **back ratio** is computed in a similar manner. The modification is that the back ratio adds other debt payments, such as auto loan and credit card payments, to the total payments. For a loan to be classified as "prime," the front and back ratios should be no more than 28% and 36%, respectively.

The credit score is the primary attribute used to characterize loans as either prime or subprime. Prime (or A-grade) loans generally are made to borrowers with FICO scores of 660 or higher, front and back ratios with the above-noted maximums of 28% and 36%, and LTVs less than 95%. Alt-A loans may vary in a number of important ways. Although subprime loans typically are associated with borrower FICO scores below 660, the loan programs and grades are highly lender specific. One lender might consider a loan with a 620 FICO score to be a "B-rated loan," whereas another lender could grade the same loan higher or lower, especially if the other attributes of the loan (such as the LTV) are higher or lower than average levels.

Outside the United States, there are loans available to credit-impaired borrowers seeking to obtain a mortgage. For example, in the United Kingdom, such mortgages are referred to as "nonconforming" mortgages and include lending to individuals who had previously declared bankruptcy. Two other countries that make mortgages available to credit-impaired borrowers are Ireland and Spain (where lending is available to immigrants who want to reside in major Spanish cities and who have no or limited credit histories). Europe even has its version of Alt-A lending.[8]

Credit Guarantees

Mortgages can be classified based on whether there is some third-party guaranty. The guaranty can be one provided by the national government, a related entity, or a private entity.

In the United States, loans that are backed by agencies of the federal government are referred to under the generic term of **government loans** and are guaranteed by the full faith and credit of the U.S. government. The Department of Housing and Urban Development oversees two agencies that guarantee government loans. The first is the Federal Housing Administration (FHA), a governmental entity created by Congress in 1934 that became part of the Department of Housing and Urban Development in 1965. **FHA-insured loans** are for those borrowers who can afford only a low down payment and who generally also have relatively low levels of income. The second is the Veterans Administration (VA), which is part of the U.S. Department of Veterans Affairs. **VA-guaranteed loans** are made to eligible veterans

8. Dübel and Rothemund, "A New Mortgage Credit Regime for Europe," 19.

and reservists, allowing them to receive favorable loan terms. Although there is no maximum amount for the loans that are guaranteed, typically the loans are limited to an amount determined by statute, because when the VA sells loans that it originates in the secondary market, these limits become important, as explained later in this chapter and in chapter 30.

In contrast to government loans, other loans have no explicit guaranty from the federal government. Such loans are said to be obtained through "conventional financing" and therefore are referred to in the market as **conventional mortgages**. A conventional mortgage may not be insured when it is originated, but a mortgage may qualify to be insured when it is included in a pool of mortgages that secures a mortgage-backed security (MBS). More specifically, MBSs are securities issued by two government-sponsored enterprises, Freddie Mac (previously the Federal Home Loan Mortgage Corporation) and Fannie Mae (previously the Federal National Mortgage Association), entities we discuss in more detail in chapter 30. Because the guaranties of Freddie Mac and Fannie Mae do not carry the full faith and credit of the U.S. government, they are not classified as government loans.

A conventional loan can be insured by a **private mortgage insurer**. Typically the borrower is required to obtain private mortgage insurance when the down payment is less than 20% of the property's purchase price (i.e., when the LTV is greater than 0.8). Because the insurance comes from a private entity, from an investor's perspective, the guaranty is only as good as the credit rating of the insurer.

Conforming versus Nonconforming Status

As explained in chapter 30, Freddie Mac and Fannie Mae are government-sponsored enterprises (GSEs) whose mission is to provide liquidity and support to the mortgage market. Although they are private corporations, they receive a charter from the federal government. This federal charter allows these GSEs to operate with certain benefits that are unavailable to other corporations. However, the federal charter imposes limits on their business activities.

One of the ways that they fulfill their mission is by buying and selling mortgages.[9] The mortgages they purchase can be held in a portfolio or packaged to create an MBS. The securities they create are the subject of chapter 30. Fannie Mae and Freddie Mac can buy or sell any type of residential mortgage, but the mortgages that are packaged into securities are restricted to government loans and those that satisfy their underwriting guidelines. The conventional loans that qualify are referred to as **conforming loans**. Thus, a conforming loan is simply a conventional loan that meets the underwriting standards of Fannie Mae and Freddie Mac. Conventional loans in the market are referred to as **conforming conventional loans** or **nonconforming conventional loans**.

9. The two GSEs must allocate a specific percentage of the loans made for low- and moderate-income households or properties located in targeted geographic areas as designated by the Department of Housing and Urban Development. Such loans are classified as "affordable housing loans."

One of the underwriting standards is the loan balance at the time of origination. For government loans and the loans guaranteed by Freddie Mac and Fannie Mae, there are limits on the loan balance. The maximum loan size for one- to four-family homes changes every year, based on the percentage change in the average home price (for both new and existing homes) published by the Federal Housing Finance Board. The loan limits for Freddie Mac and Fannie Mae are identical, because they are specified by the same statute. For example, effective January 1, 2013, the conforming limit for residential mortgages was $417,000 and is higher for areas designated as high-cost regions. Loans larger than the conforming limit for a given property type are referred to as **jumbo mortgages**.

Other important underwriting standards that must be satisfied relate to the following:

- the type of property (primary residence, vacation or second home, investment property),
- loan type (e.g., fixed rate, ARM),
- LTV ratio by loan type,
- the borrower's credit history, and
- documentation.

Qualifying for a conforming mortgage is important for both the borrower and the mortgage originator, because the two GSEs are the largest buyers of mortgages in the United States. Hence, mortgages that qualify as conforming loans have a greater probability of being purchased by Fannie Mae and Freddie Mac to be packaged into an MBS. As a result, they are available at lower interest rates than are nonconforming conventional mortgages.

When the term "conforming mortgage" is used in other countries, its meaning may be quite different. We mentioned in our discussion of the credit classification of mortgages that in the United Kingdom, the term used for mortgage loans made to credit-impaired borrowers is "nonconforming" mortgage loans. In the United States, such a mortgage would probably be classified as a subprime mortgage. A mortgage in the United Kingdom provided to a creditworthy borrower (however that might be defined in that country) is referred to as a "conforming mortgage." The important point here is that in other countries, the terms "conforming mortgage" and "nonconforming mortgage" have nothing to do with how the terms are used in the United States, where they simply (and exclusively) denote whether a mortgage satisfies the requirements of the two GSEs.

Investment Risks

The principal investors in mortgage loans include thrifts and commercial banks. Pension funds and life insurance companies also invest in these loans, but their ownership is small compared to that of the banks and thrifts. Investors face four main risks when they invest in residential mortgage loans: (1) credit risk, (2) liquidity risk, (3) price risk, and (4) prepayment risk.

Credit Risk

Credit risk is the risk that the homeowner/borrower will default. For FHA- and VA-insured mortgages, this risk is minimal. For privately insured mortgages, the risk can be gauged by the credit rating of the private insurance company that has insured the mortgage. For conventional mortgages that are uninsured, the credit risk depends on the credit quality of the borrower. The LTV ratio provides a useful measure of the risk of loss of principal in case of default. When the LTV ratio is high, default is more likely, because the borrower has little equity in the property.

Liquidity Risk

Although there is a secondary market for residential mortgages, which we discuss in chapter 30, the bid-ask spreads are nonetheless large compared to those of other debt instruments. That is, mortgages tend to be rather illiquid, because they are large and indivisible.

Price Risk

The price of a fixed-income instrument will move in the opposite direction from market interest rates. Thus, a rise in interest rates will decrease the price of a mortgage loan.

Prepayment Risk

The three components of the monthly cash flow are (1) interest, (2) principal repayment (scheduled principal payment or amortization), and (3) any prepayment.

Prepayment risk is the risk associated with a mortgage's cash flow stemming from prepayments. More specifically, investors are concerned that borrowers will pay off a mortgage when prevailing mortgage rates fall below the borrower's mortgage rate. For example, if the borrower's mortgage rate on a mortgage originated five years ago is 6% and the prevailing mortgage rate (i.e., the rate at which a new mortgage can be obtained) is 3.5%, then there is an incentive for the borrower to refinance the mortgage. The decision to refinance will depend on several factors, but the single most important one is the prevailing mortgage rate compared to the borrower's mortgage rate.

The disadvantage to the investor is that the proceeds received from the repayment of the loan must be reinvested at a lower interest rate than that currently earned on the proceeds lent to the borrower. This risk is the same as that faced by an investor in a callable bond. However, unlike a callable bond, there is no premium that may have to be paid by the borrower in the case of a residential mortgage loan except possibly for a prepayment penalty mortgage. Any principal repaid in advance of the scheduled due date is paid at par value.

Development of the Secondary Mortgage Market

The foundations for the secondary mortgage market can be traced back to the Great Depression and the legislation that followed. The response by Congress to the Great Depression and its effects on financial markets was to establish several public-purpose agencies. The Federal Reserve provided increased liquidity for commercial banks through the Federal Reserve discount window. Liquidity for thrifts was provided by the creation of the Federal Home Loan Banks, which were granted the right to borrow from the Treasury. The purpose of creating the Federal Home Loan Banks was to construct a reserve credit system to support housing finance and provide relief for both homeowners and lending institutions impacted by the Great Depression.

Another creation of Congress to help the housing finance market was the FHA, intended to address the problems presented by the mortgage loans used in housing finance at that time. This government agency developed and promoted the fixed-rate, level-payment, fully amortized mortgage. The FHA also reduced credit risk for investors by offering insurance against mortgage defaults. Not all loans could be insured, however—the mortgage applicant had to satisfy FHA underwriting standards, which made the FHA the first organization to standardize mortgage terms. Although we may take standardization for granted today, it was the basis for the development of a secondary mortgage market. In 1944, the VA began insuring qualified loans.

But who was going to invest in these loans? Thrifts could do so, especially with the inducement provided by several tax and regulatory advantages at the time. But the investment would be illiquid in the absence of a market for trading mortgages. Congress thought of that, too. In 1938, it created a federal government agency, the Federal National Mortgage Association. This agency, now officially known as Fannie Mae, was charged with the creating a liquid secondary market for FHA- and VA-insured loans, which it tried to accomplish by buying loans. Fannie Mae needed a funding source in case it faced a liquidity squeeze. Congress provided it by giving Fannie Mae a credit line with the Treasury.

In 1954, legislation transformed Fannie Mae from a government agency into a GSE. Despite the creation of Fannie Mae, the secondary mortgage market did not develop to any significant extent. During periods of tight money, Fannie Mae could do little to mitigate a housing crisis. In 1968, Congress divided Fannie Mae into two organizations: (1) the current Fannie Mae, and (2) the Government National Mortgage Association, popularly known as Ginnie Mae. Ginnie Mae's function is to use the "full faith and credit of the U.S. government" to support the FHA and VA mortgage market. Two years later, in 1970, Congress authorized Fannie Mae to purchase conventional loans (i.e., those not insured by the FHA or VA) and created the Federal Home Loan Mortgage Corporation (popularly known as Freddie Mac) to provide support for FHA- and VA-insured mortgages and conventional mortgages.

Ginnie Mae accomplished its objective by guaranteeing securities issued by private entities that pooled loans together and then used these loans as collateral for the security sold.

Freddie Mac and Fannie Mae purchased loans, pooled them, and issued securities, using the pool of loans as collateral. The securities created are called "mortgage pass-through securities" and are described in chapter 30. They are purchased by many types of investors (domestic and foreign) who previously shunned investment in the mortgage market.

The driving force in the development of a strong secondary market for residential mortgage loans was a financial innovation that involved the packaging (or "pooling") of loans and the issuance of securities collateralized by these loans. As we explained in chapter 27, this process, called "asset securitization," is radically different from the traditional system for financing the acquisition of assets. The traditional system calls for one financial intermediary (such as a commercial bank, thrift, or insurance company) to (1) originate a loan; (2) retain the loan in its portfolio of assets, thereby accepting the credit risk associated with the loan; (3) service the loan by collecting payments and providing tax or other information to the borrower; and (4) obtain funds from the public with which to finance its assets (except for the small amount representing the institution's equity).

By using asset securitization, more than one institution may be involved in lending capital. In the case of mortgage activities, a lending scenario can look like this:

1. A thrift or commercial bank originates a loan.
2. The thrift or commercial bank sells its mortgages to an investment banking firm that creates a security backed by the pool of loans.
3. The investment banker obtains credit risk insurance for the pool of loans from a private insurance company.
4. The investment banker sells the right to service the loans to another thrift or a company specializing in servicing loans.
5. The investment banking firm sells the securities to individuals and institutional investors.

Besides the original bank or thrift, participants include an investment bank, an insurance company, another thrift, an individual, and other institutional investors. The bank or thrift in this case does not have to absorb the credit risk, service the mortgage, or provide the funding.

In 1970, Ginnie Mae pioneered and issued the first MBS. The following year, Freddie Mac issued its first MBS; and in 1981, Fannie Mae issued its first MBS. In the 1980s, private issuers of MBSs that did not use the backing of the three agencies but instead some form of private credit enhancement (described in chapter 30) began issuing MBSs backed by conventional residential mortgage loans.

The major setback to the market and to the future of Fannie Mae and Freddie Mac was the crisis in the subprime MBS market that began in the summer of 2007. We describe the crisis in chapter 30 and explain how it led to the placing of Fannie Mae and Freddie Mac under the conservatorship of the Federal Housing Finance Agency in September 2008. In addition, we discuss proposals to terminate the existence of Fannie Mae and Freddie Mac.

Key Points

- The mortgage market in any country is a collection of markets that includes a primary (or origination) market and a secondary market where mortgages trade.
- A mortgage is a pledge of property to secure payment of a debt with the property, typically a form of real estate.
- The types of real estate properties that can be mortgaged are divided into two broad categories: single-family residential properties and commercial properties. The former category includes houses, condominiums, and cooperatives.
- Commercial properties are income-producing properties: multifamily properties (i.e., apartment buildings), office buildings, industrial properties (including warehouses), shopping centers, hotels, and health care facilities (e.g., senior residential care facilities).
- Mortgage originators (i.e., the original lenders) include thrifts, commercial banks, and mortgage bankers.
- Mortgage originators charge an origination fee and may generate additional income in other ways.
- The two government-sponsored enterprises (GSEs), Fannie Mae and Freddie Mac, can purchase any type of loan; however, the only conventional loans they can securitize to create a mortgage-backed security (MBS) are conforming loans, that is, conventional loans that satisfy their underwriting standards.
- For a mortgage originator, "pipeline risk" refers to the risks associated with originating mortgages. This risk has two components, price risk and fallout risk.
- "Price risk refers" to the adverse effects on the value of the pipeline if mortgage rates in the market rise.
- Fallout risk is the risk that applicants or those who were issued commitment letters will not close (i.e., complete the transaction by purchasing the property with funds borrowed from the mortgage originator).
- The two primary quantitative underwriting standards used by lenders when determining whether to grant a loan are the payment-to-income (PTI) ratio and the loan-to-value (LTV) ratio.
- The PTI ratio is the ratio of monthly payments to monthly income and measures the ability of the applicant to make monthly payments (both mortgage and real estate tax payments). The lower this ratio is, the greater the likelihood that the applicant will be able to meet the required payments.
- The LTV ratio is the ratio of the amount of the loan to the market (or appraised) value of the property. The lower this ratio is, the greater the protection will be for the lender if the applicant defaults on the payments and the lender must repossess and sell the property.

• Every mortgage loan must be serviced. Servicing of a mortgage involves collecting monthly payments and forwarding proceeds to owners of the loan, sending payment notices to mortgagors, reminding mortgagors when payments are overdue, maintaining records of principal balances, administering an escrow balance for real estate taxes and insurance purposes, initiating foreclosure proceedings if necessary, and furnishing tax information to mortgagors when applicable.

• The different types of residential mortgages available in countries that have a mortgage market are classified according to the following attributes: interest rate type, repayment structure, treatment of prepayments, lender's recourse, lien status, credit classification, credit guarantees, and conforming versus nonconforming status.

• The interest rate on a mortgage determines the type of mortgage: a fixed-rate mortgage, an indexed adjustable-rate mortgage, a reviewable adjustable-rate mortgage, a rollover (renegotiable) mortgage, a hybrid mortgage, or a convertible mortgage.

• The method for repaying the principal over time is called the "repayment structure" and is typically paid monthly.

• A lender would prefer a mortgage where some principal is repaid over the mortgage's term in order to reduce the credit risk it faces when lending against the property.

• "Amortization" refers to the repayment of the principal borrowed as part of the monthly loan payment.

• An amortizing mortgage specifies a scheduled payment of principal that the borrower must make and is typical in most countries.

• With a fully amortizing mortgage, the monthly scheduled principal payments are such that when all scheduled principal payments are added up, the total is equal to the original mortgage balance.

• A partial amortizing mortgage is such that the total of the monthly scheduled principal payments is less than the original mortgage balance. A balloon payment must then be made at the end of the loan's term equal to the difference between the amount owed and the total principal payments.

• A prepayment is the amount of the payment made in excess of the monthly mortgage payment.

• A prepayment penalty mortgage mitigates the borrower's right to prepay by imposing a penalty for prepaying.

• With a recourse loan, the lender is entitled to have a claim against the borrower for the shortfall if a default occurs; with a nonrecourse mortgage, unless there is some claim of fraud, the lender does not have a claim against the borrower.

• Whether the lender is entitled to recourse in the case of a shortfall (default) varies by country. In the United States, all mortgages to purchase a residence are nonrecourse mortgages.

- The lien status of a mortgage indicates the lender's seniority in the event of the forced liquidation of the property as a result of the borrower's default.
- For a mortgage that is a first lien, the lender has a first call on the proceeds of the liquidation of the property if it were to be repossessed, whereas for a second lien or junior lien, the lender's claim on the proceeds in the case of liquidation comes after the first lien lenders are paid in full.
- In the United States, loans are classified by the creditworthiness of the borrower: a prime loan is one made to a borrower considered to be of high credit quality; a subprime loan is one made to a borrower of lower credit quality or where the loan is not a first lien on the property; and an Alternative-A loan (Alt-A loan) is made to a borrower considered to be of prime creditworthiness but with some attributes that either increase the borrower's perceived credit riskiness or cause the borrower to be difficult to categorize and evaluate.
- The applicant's credit score is the primary measure used to characterize loans as either prime or subprime.
- Mortgages can be classified based on whether there is a third-party guaranty. The guaranty can be one provided by the national government, a related entity, or a private entity.
- In the United States, loans that are backed by agencies of the federal government are referred to under the generic term "government loans" and are guaranteed by the full faith and credit of the U.S. government.
- Loans that have no explicit guaranty from the federal government are said to be "conventional mortgages."
- A conventional loan can be insured by a private mortgage insurer.
- A conforming loan is one that qualifies for purchase by Fannie Mae and Freddie Mac so that it can be included in an MBS security that they issue.
- When investing in residential mortgage loans, investors are exposed to credit risk, liquidity risk, price risk, and prepayment risk.
- The three components of the monthly cash flow from a mortgage are (1) interest, (2) principal repayment (scheduled principal payment or amortization), and (3) any prepayment.
- Prepayment risk is the risk associated with a mortgage's cash flow as a result of prepayments.
- Prepayment risk arises because the proceeds received from the repayment of the loan might have to be reinvested at a lower interest rate than that currently earned on the proceeds lent to the borrower.
- Prepayment risk is the same risk faced by an investor in a callable bond. However, unlike a callable bond, no premium has to be paid by the borrower in the case of a residential mortgage loan unless it is a prepayment penalty mortgage.

- The driving force in the development of a strong secondary market for residential mortgage loans was asset securitization: the packaging (or pooling) of loans and the issuance of securities collateralized by these loans.

Questions

1. What are the sources of revenue arising from mortgage origination?

2. What are the risks associated with the mortgage origination process?

3. a. What can mortgage originators do with a mortgage after originating it?

b. When selling a mortgage loan for future delivery, what is the advantage of obtaining an optional rather than a mandatory delivery agreement?

c. What is the disadvantage of optional delivery?

4. What are the sources of revenue for mortgage servicers?

5. What are the two primary factors that determine whether funds will be lent to an applicant for a residential mortgage?

6. What is the purpose of a mortgage rate cap? A mortgage rate floor?

7. What is meant by "recasting a mortgage"?

8. What is the difference between an indexed ARM and a reviewable ARM?

9. What is the difference between a rollover (renegotiable) mortgage and a hybrid mortgage?

10. What is the advantage of a prepayment penalty mortgage from the perspective of the lender?

11. What is the risk from the lender's perspective of an interest-only mortgage?

12. All other factors being constant, explain why the higher the LTV ratio is, the greater will be the credit risk to which the lender is exposed.

13. What are the front ratio and the back ratio, and how do they differ?

14. What is the difference between a prime loan and a subprime loan?

15. What is an Alternative-A loan?

16. How are FICO scores used when classifying a borrower's creditworthiness?

17. a. What is an FHA-insured loan?

b. What is a conventional loan?

18. a. What is meant by conforming limits?

b. What is a jumbo mortgage?

19. a. When a prepayment is made that is less than the full amount needed to completely pay off the mortgage, what happens to future monthly mortgage payments for a fixed-rate mortgage loan?

b. What is the impact of a prepayment that is less than the amount required to completely pay off a loan?

20. Explain why, in a fixed-rate mortgage, the amount of the mortgage payment applied to interest declines over time, but the amount applied to the repayment of principal increases.

21. Why is the cash flow of a residential mortgage loan unknown?

22. In what sense has the investor in a residential mortgage loan granted the borrower an option, and how does that option differ from that for a callable bond?

23. The following are excerpts from a paper by Hans-Joachim Dübel and Marc Rothemund.[10] For each excerpt, answer each question that follows it.

a. "Borrower selection policies have been generally less aggressive in Europe compared to the US; however, the claim that there have been no subprime practices in some European market would be incorrect" (p. 16). Explain why the statement is correct.

b. "In Ireland, typical first-time buyer LTVs prior to the house price collapse were 95%, based on highly inflated house prices" (p. 17). What does this mean, and why would you expect these values to lead to higher defaults in Ireland?

c. "The quantitatively most relevant risk feature in Europe beyond the classic risk layering is the high empirical relevance of ARM lending outside the core of France, Germany, Belgium and the Netherlands, which carries large potential payment shock risk" (pp. 20–21). What does this mean?

d. "The index tracker boom of the 2000s has profoundly changed ARM markets, including in countries such as the UK and Ireland that primarily had used reviewable-rate ARM allowing lenders to control the variations and smooth the interest rate cycle. By 2007, those were almost entirely replaced by index trackers with extremely low spreads" (p. 21). What does this mean?

24. Using information in the appendix to this chapter, consider the following fixed-rate, level-payment mortgage:

Maturity = 360 months.

Amount borrowed = $100,000.

Annual mortgage rate = 10%.

a. Construct an amortization schedule for the first 10 months.

b. What will the mortgage balance be at the end of the 360th month, assuming no prepayments?

c. Without constructing an amortization schedule, what is the mortgage balance at the end of month 270, assuming no prepayments?

10. Dübel and Rothemund, "A New Mortgage Credit Regime for Europe," various pages.

d. Without constructing an amortization schedule, what is the scheduled principal payment at the end of month 270, assuming no prepayments?

Appendix: Mortgage Mathematics

The amount of the monthly loan payment that represents the repayment of the principal borrowed is called the **amortization**. Traditionally, both FRMs and ARMs were **fully amortizing loans**. What this means is that the monthly mortgage payments made by the borrower are such that they not only provide the lender with the contractual interest but also are sufficient to completely repay the amount borrowed when the last monthly mortgage payment is made. Thus, for example, for a fully amortizing 30-year loan, at the end of the 360th month, the last mortgage payment is sufficient to pay off any loan balance, so that after that last payment, the amount owed is zero.

Fully Amortizing Fixed-Rate Loans

Fully amortizing fixed-rate loans have a payment that is constant over the life of the loan. For example, suppose a loan has an original balance of $200,000, a note rate of 7.5%, and a term of 30 years. Then the monthly mortgage payment would be $1,398.43. The formula for calculating the monthly mortgage payment is

$$MP = MB_0\left[\frac{i(1+i)^n}{(1+i)^n - 1}\right],$$

where MP = monthly mortgage payment ($),

MB_0 = original mortgage balance ($),

i = note rate divided by 12 (in decimal),

n = number of months of the mortgage loan.

For example, suppose that
$MB_0 = \$200{,}000$, $i = 0.075/12 = 0.00625$, and $n = 360$.
Then the monthly payment is

$$MP = \$200{,}000\left[\frac{0.00625(1.00625)^{360}}{(1.00625)^{360} - 1}\right] = \$1{,}398.43.$$

To calculate the remaining mortgage balance at the end of any month, the following formula is used:

$$MB_t = MB_0\left[\frac{(1+i)^n - (1+i)^t}{(1+i)^n - 1}\right],$$

where MB_t = mortgage balance after t months.

For example, suppose that for month 12 (t = 12) we have:

MB_0 = \$200,000; i = 0.00625; and n = 360.

The mortgage balance at the end of month 12 is

$$MB_t = \$200{,}000\left[\frac{(1.00625)^{360}-(1.00625)^{12}}{(1.00625)^{360}-1}\right] = \$198{,}156.33.$$

To calculate the portion of the monthly mortgage payment that is the scheduled principal payment for a month, the following formula is used:

$$SP_t = MB_0\left[\frac{i(1+i)^{t-1}}{(1+i)^n-1}\right],$$

where SP_t = scheduled principal repayment for month t.

For example, suppose that for month 12 (t = 12) we have:

MB_0 = \$200,000; i = 0.00625; n = 360.

Then the schedule principal repayment for month 12 is

$$SP_{12} = \$200{,}000\left[\frac{0.00625(1.00625)^{12-1}}{(1.00625)^{360}-1}\right] = \$158.95.$$

Assuming that the borrower has made all monthly payments on a timely basis, then, after the last monthly mortgage payment is made, the outstanding balance is zero (i.e., the loan is paid off). This can be seen in the schedule shown in table A29.1, which is referred to as an **amortization schedule**. (Not all 360 months are shown, to conserve space.) The column labeled "Principal Repayment" is the monthly amortization of the loan. Notice that in the 360th month, the ending balance is zero. Also note that in each month, the amount of the monthly mortgage payment applied to interest declines. This is because the amount of the outstanding balance declines each month.

Adjustable-Rate Mortgage

In the case of an ARM, the monthly mortgage payment adjusts periodically. Thus, the monthly mortgage payments must be recalculated at each reset date. This process of resetting the mortgage loan payment is referred to as **recasting the loan**. For example, consider once again a \$200,000, 30-year loan. Assume that the loan adjusts annually and that the initial note rate (i.e., the note rate for the first 12 months) is 7.5%. How much of the loan will be outstanding at the end of one year? We can determine this from table A29.1 by looking at the last column ("Ending Balance") for month 12. That amount is \$198,156.33.

Table A29.1
Amortization schedule.

Original balance:	$200,000.00
Note rate:	7.50%
Term:	30 years
Monthly payment:	$1,398.43

Month	Beginning Balance ($)	Interest ($)	Principal Repayment ($)	Ending Balance ($)
1	200,000.00	1,250.00	148.43	199,851.57
2	199,851.57	1,249.07	149.36	199,702.21
3	199,702.21	1,248.14	150.29	199,551.92
4	199,551.92	1,247.20	151.23	199,400.69
5	199,400.69	1,246.25	152.17	199,248.52
6	199,248.52	1,245.30	153.13	199,095.39
7	199,095.39	1,244.35	154.08	198,941.31
8	198,941.31	1,243.38	155.05	198,786.27
9	198,786.27	1,242.41	156.01	198,630.25
10	198,630.25	1,241.44	156.99	198,473.26
11	198,473.26	1,240.46	157.97	198,315.29
12	198,315.29	1,239.47	158.96	198,156.33
13	198,156.33	1,238.48	159.95	197,996.38
14	197,996.38	1,237.48	160.95	197,835.43
...	...	...	...	...
89	182,656.63	1,141.60	256.83	182,399.81
90	182,399.81	1,140.00	258.43	182,141.37
91	182,141.37	1,138.38	260.05	181,881.33
...	...	...	...	...
145	165,499.78	1,034.37	364.06	165,135.73
146	165,135.73	1,032.10	366.33	164,769.40
147	164,769.40	1,029.81	368.62	164,400.77
...	...	...	...	...
173	154,397.69	964.99	433.44	153,964.24
174	153,964.24	962.28	436.15	153,528.09
175	153,528.09	959.55	438.88	153,089.21
...	...	...	...	...
210	136,417.23	852.61	545.82	135,871.40
211	135,871.40	849.20	549.23	135,322.17
212	135,322.17	845.76	552.67	134,769.51
...	...	...	...	...
290	79,987.35	499.92	898.51	79,088.84
291	79,088.84	494.31	904.12	78,184.71
292	78,184.71	488.65	909.77	77,274.94
...	...	...	...	...
358	4,143.39	25.90	1,372.53	2,770.85
359	2,770.85	17.32	1,381.11	1,389.74
360	1,389.74	8.69	1,389.74	0.00

(Alternatively, the formula given above can be used.) Now recasting the loan involves computing the monthly mortgage payment that will fully amortize a loan of \$198,156.33 for 29 years (348 months), because after one year there are 29 years remaining on the loan. The note rate used is the reset rate. Suppose that the reset rate is 8.5%. Then the monthly mortgage payment to fully amortize the loan is \$1,535.26, which is the monthly mortgage payment for the next 12 months.

Interest-Only Mortgage

A mortgage that involves the payment of only interest and no principal for part of the life of the mortgage is an interest-only mortgage. With this type of loan, only interest is paid for a predetermined period, called the **lockout period**. After the lockout period, the loan is recast such that the monthly mortgage payments will be sufficient to fully amortize the original amount of the loan over the remaining term of the loan. The interest-only product can be an FRM, an ARM, or a hybrid ARM.

For example, consider a \$200,000, 30-year interest-only loan with a lockout period of five years and a note rate of 7.5% (i.e., an FRM). For the first 60 months, the monthly mortgage payment is only the monthly interest, which is \$1,250 (7.5% × \$200,000/12). In the 61st month, the monthly mortgage payment must include both interest and amortization (principal repayment). The monthly mortgage payment for the remaining life of the mortgage loan is the payment necessary to fully amortize a \$200,000 25-year loan with a note rate of 7.5%. That monthly mortgage payment is \$1,477.98.

Note that if the mortgage had been a 30-year fixed-rate loan at 7.5%, the monthly mortgage payment for the first five years would have been \$1,398.43 instead of \$1,200 for the interest-only loan. This is the appealing feature of the interest-only loan. The homeowner can purchase a more expensive home using an interest-only loan. The disadvantage for the homeowner is that for the remaining term of the loan, the interest-only mortgage requires a higher monthly mortgage payment (\$1,477.98) than would a 30-year fully amortizing loan (\$1,398.43). However, if the homeowner anticipates a rise in income, this could more than offset the impact of the higher monthly mortgage payment. From the lender's perspective, however, there is greater credit risk. This is because at the end of five years, the lender's exposure remains at \$200,000 rather than being reduced by the amortization over the lockout period.

30 Residential Mortgage-Backed Securities Market

CONTENTS

Learning Objectives

After reading this chapter, you will understand:

- the process of securitizing residential mortgage loans;
- what is meant by prepayment risk, and how prepayments are measured;
- the different sectors in the residential mortgage-backed securities market: agency and private label;
- the different types of agency mortgage-backed securities and their investment characteristics: pass-through securities, collateralized mortgage obligations, and stripped mortgage-backed securities;
- the motivation for the creation of collateralized mortgage obligations and the different types of tranches/bond classes;
- how tranches with different prepayment risks are created in a collateralized mortgage obligation;
- the difference between prime and subprime residential mortgage-backed securities;
- the subprime crisis in 2007.

As explained in chapter 29, investing in residential mortgage loans exposes the investor to default risk, price risk, liquidity risk, and prepayment risk. A more efficient way to participate in this market is to invest in a security that is backed by a pool of these loans. This type of security is created by applying the same securitization technology described in chapter 27 for creating an asset-backed security (ABS). A residential mortgage loan used as collateral to create the security is said to be "securitized." The general term for a security created through the securitization technology process where the security is backed by a real-estate related mortgage loan is called a **mortgage-backed security** (MBS). More specifically, an MBS is a security created when one or more holders of mortgage loans form a collection (pool) of loans and sell shares or participation certificates in the pool. A pool may consist of several thousand loans or only a few. Risk-averse investors prefer investing in a pool to investing in a single mortgage, partly because a mortgage pass-through security is considerably more liquid than for an individual mortgage.

Two sectors are classified in the MBS market, based on whether the loan securities are for residential mortgage loans or for commercial mortgage loans. We discussed residential mortgage loans in chapter 29, and we describe commercial mortgage loans in chapter 31. An MBS backed by residential mortgage loans is called a **residential mortgage-backed security** (RMBS), and this market is the subject of this chapter. An MBS backed by commercial mortgage loans is called a **commercial mortgage-backed security** (CMBS) and is covered in chapter 31, where we describe the commercial real-estate market.

As explained in chapter 29, the residential mortgage market can be divided into two subsectors based on the credit quality of the borrower: the prime mortgage market and the subprime mortgage market. The former sector includes (1) loans that satisfy the underwriting standards of the Government National Mortgage Association (known as "Ginnie Mae"), Fannie Mae, and Freddie Mac (i.e., conforming loans) and (2) those that fail to conform for a reason other than credit quality, or if the loan is not a first lien on the property. The subprime mortgage sector is the market for loans provided to borrowers with an impaired credit rating or for whom the loan is a second lien.

The RMBS market is divided into two sectors based on the characteristics of the loan. As explained in chapter 29, a conforming loan is one that satisfies the underwriting standard of the agencies. An RMBS that uses conforming loans is called an **agency RMBS**. Nonconforming loans can also be used to create an RMBS, and a security using such loans is referred to as a **private-label RMBS** or a **nonagency RMBS**. In turn, the private-label RMBS historically has been further classified on whether the collateral for the security is composed of prime residential mortgage loans or subprime residential mortgage loans, which we described in chapter 29. An RMBS backed by the latter are referred to as a **subprime RMBS**.

This chapter is divided into two major sections. The first is the agency RMBS market, and the second is the private-label RMBS market.

Agency RMBS Market

The agency RMBS market is the largest sector of the U.S. investment-grade market. That is, of all securities that have an investment-grade rating (a category that includes U.S. Treasury securities), the agency RMBS market has been the largest sector. The size of this sector has varied from 35% to 45% of the investment-grade market since 2000.

The agency MBS market includes three types of securities: agency mortgage pass-through securities, agency collateralized mortgage obligations (CMOs), and agency stripped MBS. As we explain below, agency stripped MBS and agency CMOs are created from mortgage pass-through securities. Agency MBSs are the subject of this section.

Agency Pass-Through Securities

The cash flow of a mortgage pass-through security depends on the cash flow of the underlying mortgage loans. As explained in chapter 29, the cash flow consists of monthly mortgage payments representing interest, the scheduled repayment of principal, and any prepayments.

Payments are made to security holders each month. The amounts and the timing of the cash flow from the pool of mortgages and the cash flow passed through to investors, however, are not identical. The monthly cash flow for a pass-through security is less than the monthly cash flow of the underlying mortgages by an amount equal to the servicing and other fees. The other fees are those charged by the issuer or guarantor of the pass-through security for guaranteeing the issue (discussed later).

The timing of the cash flow also differs. The monthly mortgage payment is due from each mortgagor on the first day of each month, but a delay affects the passing through of

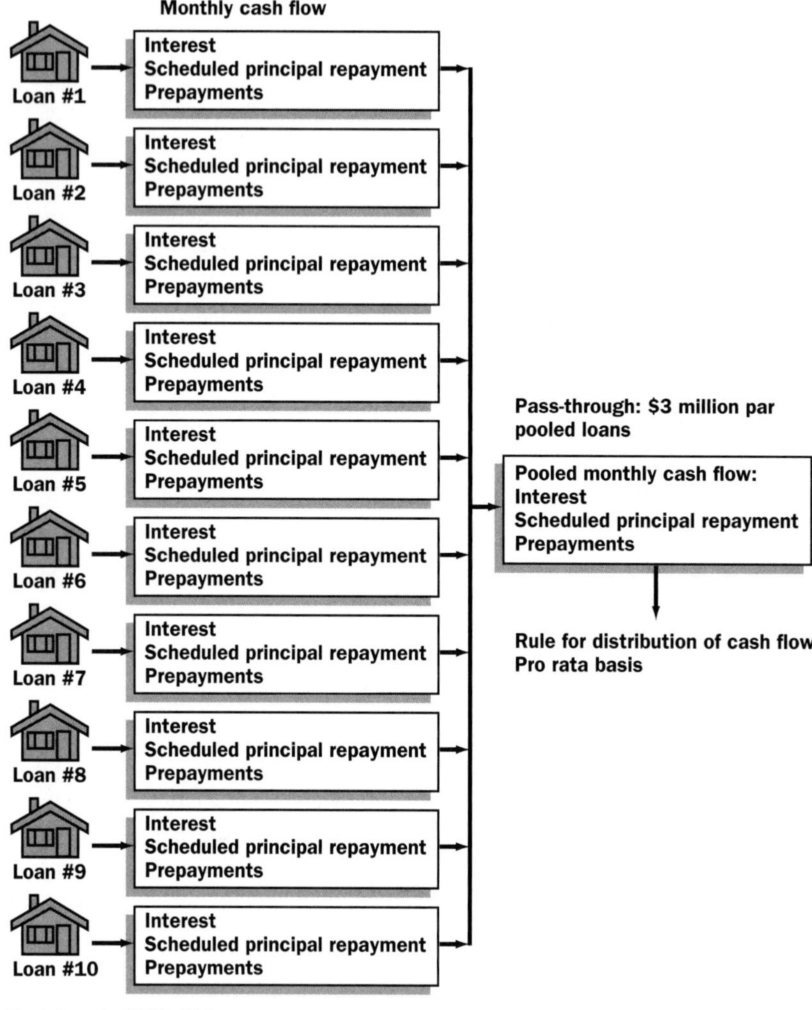

Figure 30.1
Creation of a mortgage pass-through security.

the corresponding monthly cash flow to the security holders. The length of the delay varies by the type of pass-through security.

Figure 30.1 illustrates the process of creating a mortgage pass-through security.

Issuers of agency pass-through securities Agency pass-through securities are issued by Ginnie Mae, Fannie Mae, and Freddie Mac. These three entities were created by Congress to increase the supply of capital to the residential mortgage market and to provide support for an active secondary market.

Ginnie Mae Ginnie Mae is a federally related institution, because it is part of the Department of Housing and Urban Development. As a result, the pass-through securities that it guarantees carry the full faith and credit of the U.S. government with respect to timely payment of both interest and principal. That is, the interest and principal are paid when due even if mortgagors fail to make their monthly mortgage payment. The security guaranteed by Ginnie Mae is an MBS.

Although Ginnie Mae provides the guarantee, it is not the issuer. Pass-through securities that carry its guarantee and bear its name are issued by lenders it approves, such as thrifts, commercial banks, and mortgage bankers. These lenders receive approval only if the underlying loans satisfy the underwriting standards established by Ginnie Mae. When it guarantees securities issued by approved lenders, Ginnie Mae permits these lenders to convert illiquid individual loans into liquid securities backed by the U.S. government. In the process, Ginnie Mae accomplishes its goal of supplying funds to the residential mortgage market and providing an active secondary market. For the guarantee, Ginnie Mae receives a fee, called the "guaranty fee."

Fannie Mae and Freddie Mac As explained at the end of chapter 29, the mission of these two government-sponsored enterprises (GSEs) is to support the liquidity and stability of the mortgage market. They accomplish this by (1) buying and selling mortgages, (2) creating pass-through securities and guaranteeing them, and (3) buying MBSs. The mortgages purchased and held as investments by Fannie Mae and Freddie Mac are held in a portfolio referred to as the **retained portfolio**. However, the MBSs that they issue are not guaranteed by the full faith and credit of the U.S. government. Instead, the payments to investors in the MBSs are secured first by the cash flow from the underlying pool of loans and then by a corporate guarantee. That corporate guarantee, however, is the same as the corporate guarantee to the other creditors of the two GSEs. As with Ginnie Mae, the two GSEs receive a guaranty fee for taking on the credit risk associated with borrowers failing to satisfy their loan obligations.

Although the securities issued by Fannie Mae and Freddie Mac are referred to in this chapter as "agency MBSs," they are also referred to as "conventional pass-through securities." This is because the collateral is typically conventional loans that conform to the underwriting standards of these two GSEs, as explained in chapter 29.

The pass-through securities issued by Fannie Mae are referred to as "MBSs"; Freddie Mac uses the term **participation certificate** (PC) to describe its pass-through security. All Fannie Mae MBSs are guaranteed with respect to the timely payment of interest and principal. Although the PCs that Freddie Mac now issues carry the same guarantee, there are some outstanding PCs that guarantee the timely payment of interest but the eventual return of principal within one year of the due date.

Prepayment risks associated with pass-through securities An investor who owns pass-through securities does not know what the cash flow will be, because the cash flow depends on prepayments. The risk associated with prepayments is called **prepayment risk**.

To understand prepayment risk, consider the following example. Suppose an investor buys a 7.5% coupon Ginnie Mae at a time when the mortgage rates are 7.5%. What will happen to prepayments if mortgage rates decline to, say, 5.5%? Homeowners will have the incentive to prepay all or part of their loan. Thus, the investor must reinvest the proceeds received at a lower interest rate. The second adverse consequence is that appreciation potential of the pass-through security is limited. With a decline in interest rates, the price of an option-free bond (such as a Treasury bond) will rise. In the case of a pass-through security, the rise in price will not be as large as that of an option-free bond because a fall in interest rates increases the probability that the market rate will fall below the rate at which the borrower is paying. This fall in rates gives the borrower an incentive to prepay the loan and refinance the debt at a lower rate. To the extent that this happens, the security holder will be repaid not at a price incorporating the premium but at par value. The holder risks capital loss, which reflects the fact that the anticipated reimbursements at par will not yield the initial cash flow.

The adverse consequences when mortgage rates decline are the same as those faced by holders of callable corporate and municipal bonds. As in the case of those instruments, the upside price potential of a pass-through security is truncated because of prepayments. This result should not be surprising, because a mortgage loan effectively grants the borrower the right to call the loan at par value. The adverse consequence when mortgage rates decline is referred to as **contraction risk**.

Now let's look at what happens if mortgage rates rise to 9.5%. The price of the pass-through, like the price of any bond, will decline. But again, it will decline more, because the higher rates will tend to slow down the rate of prepayment, in effect increasing the amount invested at the coupon rate, which is lower than the market rate. Prepayments will slow down, because homeowners will not refinance or partially prepay their mortgages when mortgage rates are higher than the contractual rate of 7.5%. Of course, it is just the time when investors want prepayments to speed up, so that they can reinvest the prepayments at the higher market interest rate. This adverse consequence of rising mortgage rates is called **extension risk**.

Therefore, prepayment risk encompasses contraction risk and extension risk. Prepayment risk makes pass-throughs unattractive for certain financial institutions to hold from an asset/liability perspective. Let's look at why particular institutional investors may find pass-throughs unattractive:

1. Thrifts and commercial banks, as explained in chapter 4, want to lock in a spread over their cost of funds. Their funds are raised on a short-term basis. If they invest in fixed-rate pass-through securities, they mismatch, because a pass-through is a longer-term security. In particular, depository institutions are exposed to extension risk when they invest in pass-through securities.

2. To satisfy certain obligations of insurance companies, pass-through securities may be unattractive. More specifically, let's consider a life insurance company that has issued a four-year guaranteed investment contract. The uncertainty about the cash flow from a pass-through security, and the likelihood that slow prepayments will result in the instrument being long term, make it an unappealing investment vehicle for such accounts. In such instances, a pass-through security exposes the insurance company to extension risk.

3. A pension fund may want to fund a 15-year liability. Buying a pass-through security exposes the pension fund to the risk that prepayments will speed up and that the maturity of the investment will shorten to considerably less than 15 years. Prepayments speed up when interest rates decline, thereby forcing reinvestment of the prepaid amounts at a lower interest rate. In this case, the pension fund is open to contraction risk.

We can see that some institutional investors are concerned with extension risk and others with contraction risk when they purchase a pass-through security. Altering the cash flow of a pass-through so as to reduce the contraction risk and extension risk for institutional investors is explained later in this chapter when we cover CMOs.

Prepayment conventions The only way to project a cash flow is to make some assumption about the prepayment rate over the life of the underlying mortgage pool. The prepayment rate assumed is called the **prepayment speed**, or simply, **speed**.

The **conditional prepayment rate** (CPR) assumes that some fraction of the remaining principal in the pool is prepaid each year for the remaining term of the mortgage. The prepayment rate assumed for a pool is based on the characteristics of the pool (including its historical prepayment experience) and the current and expected future economic environment. It is referred to as a "conditional rate," because it is conditional on the remaining mortgage balance.

The CPR is an annual prepayment rate. To estimate monthly prepayments, the CPR must be converted into a monthly prepayment rate, commonly referred to as the **single-monthly mortality rate** (SMM). The following formula can be used to determine the SMM for a given CPR:

$$\text{SMM} = 1 - (1 - \text{CPR})^{1/12}. \tag{30.1}$$

Suppose that the CPR used to estimate prepayments is 6%. The corresponding SMM is

$$\begin{aligned}\text{SMM} &= 1 - (1 - 0.06)^{1/12} \\ &= 1 - (0.94)^{0.08333} = 0.005143.\end{aligned}$$

An SMM of w% means that approximately w% of the remaining mortgage balance at the beginning of the month, less the scheduled principal payment, will prepay that month. That is,

Prepayment for month t = SMM × (Beginning mortgage balance for month t − Scheduled principal payment for month t). (30.2)

For example, suppose that an investor owns a pass-through in which the remaining mortgage balance at the beginning of some month is $290 million. Assuming that the SMM is

0.5143% and the scheduled principal payment is \$3 million, the estimated prepayment for the month is

$$0.005143 \times (\$290{,}000{,}000 - \$3{,}000{,}000) = \$1{,}476{,}041.$$

The Public Securities Association (PSA) prepayment benchmark is expressed as a monthly series of annual prepayment rates. The PSA benchmark assumes that prepayment rates are low for newly originated mortgages and then speed up as the mortgages become seasoned.

The PSA benchmark assumes the following CPRs for 30-year mortgages:

1. A CPR of 0.2% for the first month, increased by 0.2% per year per month for the next 30 months, when it reaches 6% per year.
2. A 6% CPR for the remaining years.

This benchmark, referred to as "100% PSA," or simply, "100 PSA," is graphically depicted in figure 30.2. Mathematically, 100 PSA can be expressed as follows:

if $t \leq 30$, then CPR = 6% (t/30),
if $t > 30$, then CPR = 6%,

where t is the number of months since the mortgage originated.

Slower or faster speeds are then referred to as some percentage of PSA. For example, "50 PSA" means one-half the CPR of the PSA benchmark prepayment rate; "150 PSA" means one and a half times the CPR of the PSA benchmark prepayment rate; "300 PSA"

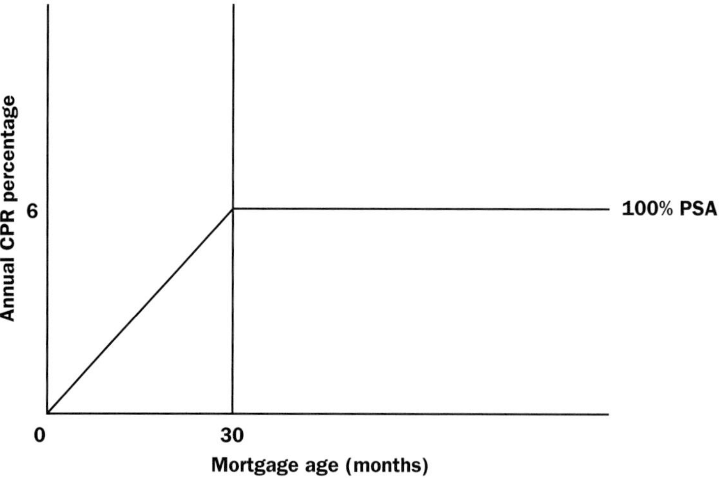

Figure 30.2
Graphical depiction of 100 PSA.

means three times the CPR of the benchmark prepayment rate. A prepayment rate of 0 PSA means that no prepayments are assumed.

The CPR is converted to an SMM using equation (30.1). For example, the SMMs for month 5, month 20, and months 31 through 360 assuming 100 PSA are calculated as follows:

For month 5:

$$\begin{aligned}\text{CPR} &= 6\%(5/30) = 1\% = 0.01,\\ \text{SMM} &= 1-(1-0.01)^{1/12}\\ &= 1-(0.99)^{0.083333} = 0.000837.\end{aligned}$$

For month 20:

$$\begin{aligned}\text{CPR} &= 6\%(20/30) = 4\% = 0.04,\\ \text{SMM} &= 1-(1-0.04)^{1/12}\\ &= 1-(0.96)^{0.083333} = 0.003396.\end{aligned}$$

For months 31 to 360:

$$\begin{aligned}\text{CPR} &= 6\%,\\ \text{SMM} &= 1-(1-0.06)^{1/12}\\ &= 1-(0.9835)^{0.083333} = 0.001386.\end{aligned}$$

Assuming 165 PSA, the SMMs for month 5, month 20, and months 31 through 360 are computed as follows:

For month 5:

$$\begin{aligned}\text{CPR} &= 6\%(5/30) = 1\% = 0.01,\\ 165\ \text{PSA} &= 1.65(0.01) = 0.0165,\\ \text{SMM} &= 1-(1-0.0165)^{1/12}\\ &= 1-(0.9835)^{0.083333} = 0.001386.\end{aligned}$$

For month 20:

$$\begin{aligned}\text{CPR} &= 6\%(20/30) = 4\% = 0.04,\\ 165\ \text{PSA} &= 1.65(0.04) = 0.066,\\ \text{SMM} &= 1-(1-0.066)^{1/12}\\ &= 1-(0.934)^{0.083333} = 0.005674.\end{aligned}$$

For months 31 to 360:

$$\begin{aligned}\text{CPR} &= 6\%,\\ 165\ \text{PSA} &= 1.65(0.06) = 0.099,\\ \text{SMM} &= 1-(1-0.099)^{1/12}\\ &= 1-(0.901)^{0.083333} = 0.00865.\end{aligned}$$

Notice that the SMM assuming 165 PSA is not just 1.65 times the SMM assuming 100 PSA. It is the CPR that is a multiple of the CPR assuming 100 PSA.

Illustration of monthly cash flow construction We now show how to construct a monthly cash flow for a hypothetical pass-through given a PSA assumption. For the purpose of this illustration, the underlying mortgages for this hypothetical pass-through are assumed to be fixed-rate, level-payment mortgages, and the pass-through rate is assumed to be 7.5%. Furthermore, it is assumed that the weighted average maturity (WAM) of the pool of mortgages is 357 months.[1]

Table 30.1 shows the cash flow for selected months assuming 100 PSA. The cash flow breaks down into three components: (1) interest (based on the pass-through rate), (2) the regularly scheduled principal repayment, and (3) prepayments based on 100 PSA.

Let's walk through table 30.1 column by column:

- Column 1 ("Month"): This indicates the month.
- Column 2 ("Outstanding Balance"): The outstanding mortgage balance at the beginning of the month equals the outstanding balance at the beginning of the previous month reduced by the total principal payment in the previous month.
- Column 3 ("SMM," Single-Monthly Mortality): The SMM for 100 PSA changes, based on the assumptions for the CPR. Two aspects of this column should be noted. First, for month 1, the SMM is for a pass-through that has seasoned three months; that is, the CPR is 0.8%, because the WAM is 357. Second, from month 27 on, the SMM is 0.00514, which corresponds to a CPR of 6%.
- Column 4 ("Mortgage Payment"): The total monthly mortgage payment declines over time as prepayments reduce the mortgage balance outstanding. A formula determines what the monthly balance will be for each month given prepayments.[2]
- Column 5 ("Net Interest"): The monthly interest paid to the pass-through investor is determined by multiplying the outstanding mortgage balance at the beginning of the month by the pass-through rate of 7.5% and dividing by 12.
- Column 6 ("Scheduled Principal"): The regularly scheduled principal repayment is the difference between the total monthly mortgage payment (the amount shown in column 4) and the gross coupon interest for the month. The gross coupon interest is 8.125% multiplied by the outstanding mortgage balance at the beginning of the month, then divided by 12.
- Column 7 ("Prepayment"): The prepayment for the month is found by using equation (30.2). So, for example, in month 100, the beginning mortgage balance is $231,249,776,

1. It is necessary to calculate a WAM for a pool of mortgages, because not all mortgages have the same number of months remaining to maturity.

2. The formula is presented in Frank J. Fabozzi, *Fixed Income Mathematics: Analytical and Statistical Techniques* (New York: McGraw-Hill, 2006), chapter 21.

Table 30.1
Monthly cash flow for a $400 million pass-through security (assuming 100 PSA).

Month	Outstanding Balance ($)	SMM	Mortgage Payment ($)	Net Interest ($)	Scheduled Principal ($)	Prepay-ment	Total Principal ($)	Total Cash ($)
1	400,000,000	0.00067	2,975,868	2,500,000	267,535	267,470	535,005	3,035,005
2	399,464,995	0.00084	2,973,877	2,496,656	269,166	334,198	603,364	3,100,020
3	398,861,631	0.00101	2,971,387	2,492,885	270,762	400,800	671,562	3,164,447
4	398,190,069	0.00117	2,968,399	2,488,688	272,321	467,243	739,564	3,228,252
5	397,450,505	0.00134	2,964,914	2,484,066	273,843	533,493	807,335	3,291,401
6	396,643,170	0.00151	2,960,931	2,479,020	275,327	599,514	874,841	3,353,860
7	395,768,329	0.00168	2,956,453	2,473,552	276,772	665,273	942,045	3,415,597
8	394,826,284	0.00185	2,951,480	2,467,664	278,177	730,736	1,008,913	3,476,577
9	393,817,371	0.00202	2,946,013	2,461,359	279,542	795,869	1,075,410	3,536,769
10	392,741,961	0.00219	2,940,056	2,454,637	280,865	860,637	1,141,502	3,596,140
11	391,600,459	0.00236	2,933,608	2,447,503	282,147	925,008	1,207,155	3,654,658
12	390,393,304	0.00254	2,926,674	2,439,958	283,386	988,948	1,272,333	3,712,291
13	389,120,971	0.00271	2,919,254	2,432,006	284,581	1,052,423	1,337,004	3,769,010
14	387,783,966	0.00288	2,911,353	2,423,650	285,733	1,115,402	1,401,134	3,824,784
15	386,382,832	0.00305	2,902,973	2,414,893	286,839	1,177,851	1,464,690	3,879,583
16	384,918,142	0.00322	2,894,117	2,405,738	287,900	1,239,739	1,527,639	3,933,378
17	383,390,502	0.00340	2,884,789	2,396,191	288,915	1,301,033	1,589,949	3,986,139
18	381,800,553	0.00357	2,874,992	2,386,253	289,884	1,361,703	1,651,587	4,037,840
19	380,148,966	0.00374	2,864,730	2,375,931	290,805	1,421,717	1,712,522	4,088,453
20	378,436,444	0.00392	2,854,008	2,365,228	291,678	1,481,046	1,772,724	4,137,952
21	376,663,720	0.00409	2,842,830	2,354,148	292,503	1,539,658	1,832,161	4,186,309
22	374,831,559	0.00427	2,831,201	2,342,697	293,279	1,597,525	1,890,804	4,233,501
23	372,940,755	0.00444	2,819,125	2,330,880	294,005	1,654,618	1,948,623	4,279,503
24	370,992,132	0.00462	2,806,607	2,318,701	294,681	1,710,908	2,005,589	4,324,290
25	368,986,543	0.00479	2,793,654	2,306,166	295,307	1,766,368	2,061,675	4,367,841
26	366,924,868	0.00497	2,780,270	2,293,280	295,883	1,820,970	2,116,852	4,410,133
27	364,808,016	0.00514	2,766,461	2,280,050	296,406	1,874,688	2,171,094	4,451,144
28	362,636,921	0.00514	2,752,233	2,266,481	296,879	1,863,519	2,160,398	4,426,879
29	360,476,523	0.00514	2,738,078	2,252,978	297,351	1,852,406	2,149,578	4,402,736
30	358,326,766	0.00514	2,723,996	2,239,542	297,825	1,841,347	2,139,173	4,378,715
100	231,249,776	0.00514	1,898,682	1,445,311	332,928	1,187,608	1,520,537	2,965,848
101	229,729,239	0.00514	1,888,917	1,435,808	333,459	1,179,785	1,513,244	2,949,052
102	228,215,995	0.00514	1,879,202	1,426,350	333,990	1,172,000	1,505,990	2,932,340
103	226,710,004	0.00514	1,869,538	1,416,938	334,522	1,164,252	1,498,774	2,915,712
104	225,211,230	0.00514	1,859,923	1,407,570	335,055	1,156,541	1,491,596	2,899,166
105	223,719,634	0.00514	1,850,357	1,398,248	335,589	1,148,867	1,484,456	2,882,703
200	109,791,339	0.00514	1,133,751	686,196	390,372	562,651	953,023	1,639,219
201	108,838,316	0.00514	1,127,920	680,239	390,994	557,746	948,740	1,628,980
202	107,889,576	0.00514	1,122,119	674,310	391,617	552,863	944,480	1,618,790
203	106,945,096	0.00514	1,116,348	668,407	392,241	548,003	940,243	1,608,650
204	106,004,852	0.00514	1,110,607	662,530	392,866	543,164	936,029	1,598,560
205	105,068,823	0.00514	1,104,895	656,680	393,491	538,347	931,838	1,588,518
300	32,383,611	0.00514	676,991	202,398	457,727	164,195	621,923	824,320
301	31,761,689	0.00514	673,510	198,511	458,457	160,993	619,449	817,960

(continued)

Table 30.1 (*continued*)

Month	Outstanding Balance ($)	SMM	Mortgage Payment ($)	Net Interest ($)	Scheduled Principal ($)	Prepay-ment	Total Principal ($)	Total Cash ($)
302	31,142,239	0.00514	670,046	194,639	459,187	157,803	616,990	811,629
303	30,525,249	0.00514	666,600	190,783	459,918	154,626	614,545	805,328
304	29,910,704	0.00514	663,171	186,942	460,651	151,462	612,113	799,055
305	29,298,591	0.00514	659,761	183,116	461,385	148,310	609,695	792,811
350	4,060,411	0.00514	523,138	25,378	495,645	18,334	513,979	539,356
351	3,546,432	0.00514	520,447	22,165	496,435	15,686	512,121	534,286
352	3,034,311	0.00514	517,770	18,964	497,226	13,048	510,274	529,238
353	2,524,037	0.00514	515,107	15,775	498,018	10,420	508,437	524,213
354	2,015,600	0.00514	512,458	12,597	498,811	7,801	506,612	519,209
355	1,508,988	0.00514	509,823	9,431	499,606	5,191	504,797	514,228
356	1,004,191	0.00514	507,201	6,276	500,401	2,591	502,992	509,269
357	501,199	0.00514	504,592	3,132	501,199	0	501,199	504,331

Note: Pass-through rate = 7.5%; WAC = 8.125%; WAM = 357 months.

the scheduled principal payment is \$332,298, and the SMM at 100 PSA is 0.00514301 (only 0.00514 is shown in the table, to save space), so the prepayment is 0.00514301(\$231,249,776 − \$332,928) = \$1,187,608.

• Column 8 ("Total Principal"): The total principal payment combines the scheduled principal payment and the prepayment amounts from columns 6 and 7.

• Column 9 ("Total Cash Flow"): The projected monthly cash flow for this pass-through is the sum of the interest paid to the pass-through investor in column 5 and the total principal payments for the month in column 8.

Table 30.2 shows selected monthly cash flows for the same pass-through but assuming 165 PSA.

Average Life The stated maturity of a mortgage pass-through security is an inappropriate measure of the security's life because of prepayments. Instead, market participants commonly use the security's average life. The **average life** of an MBS is the average time to receipt of principal payments (scheduled principal payments and projected prepayments), weighted by the amount of principal expected. Mathematically, the average life is expressed as follows:

$$\text{Average life} = \sum_{t=1}^{T} \frac{t \times \text{Principal received at time } t}{12(\text{Total principal})},$$

where T is the number of months.

Table 30.2
Monthly cash flow for a $400 million pass-through security (assuming 165 PSA).

Month	Outstanding Balance ($)	SMM	Mortgage Payment ($)	Net Interest ($)	Scheduled Principal ($)	Prepayment ($)	Total Principal ($)	TotalCash Flow ($)
1	400,000,000	0.00111	2,975,868	2,500,000	267,535	442,389	709,923	3,209,923
2	399,290,077	0.00139	2,972,575	2,495,563	269,048	552,847	821,896	3,317,459
3	398,468,181	0.00167	2,968,456	2,490,426	270,495	663,065	933,560	3,423,986
4	397,534,621	0.00195	2,963,513	2,484,591	271,873	772,949	1,044,822	3,529,413
5	396,489,799	0.00223	2,957,747	2,478,061	273,181	882,405	1,155,586	3,633,647
6	395,334,213	0.00251	2,951,160	2,470,839	274,418	991,341	1,265,759	3,736,598
7	394,068,454	0.00279	2,943,755	2,462,928	275,583	1,099,664	1,375,246	3,838,174
8	392,693,208	0.00308	2,935,534	2,454,333	276,674	1,207,280	1,483,954	3,938,287
9	391,209,254	0.00336	2,926,503	2,445,058	277,690	1,314,099	1,591,789	4,036,847
10	389,617,464	0.00365	2,916,666	2,435,109	278,631	1,420,029	1,698,659	4,133,769
11	387,918,805	0.00393	2,906,028	2,424,493	279,494	1,524,979	1,804,473	4,228,965
12	386,114,332	0.00422	2,894,595	2,413,215	280,280	1,628,859	1,909,139	4,322,353
13	384,205,194	0.00451	2,882,375	2,401,282	280,986	1,731,581	2,012,567	4,413,850
14	382,192,626	0.00480	2,869,375	2,388,704	281,613	1,833,058	2,114,670	4,503,374
15	380,077,956	0.00509	2,855,603	2,375,487	282,159	1,933,203	2,215,361	4,590,848
16	377,862,595	0.00538	2,841,068	2,361,641	282,623	2,031,931	2,314,554	4,676,195
17	375,548,041	0.00567	2,825,779	2,347,175	283,006	2,129,159	2,412,164	4,759,339
18	373,135,877	0.00597	2,809,746	2,332,099	283,305	2,224,805	2,508,110	4,840,210
19	370,627,766	0.00626	2,792,980	2,316,424	283,521	2,318,790	2,602,312	4,918,735
20	368,025,455	0.00656	2,775,493	2,300,159	283,654	2,411,036	2,694,690	4,994,849
21	365,330,765	0.00685	2,757,296	2,283,317	283,702	2,501,466	2,785,169	5,068,486
22	362,545,596	0.00715	2,738,402	2,265,910	283,666	2,590,008	2,873,674	5,139,584
23	359,671,922	0.00745	2,718,823	2,247,950	283,545	2,676,588	2,960,133	5,208,083
24	356,711,789	0.00775	2,698,575	2,229,449	283,338	2,761,139	3,044,477	5,273,926
25	353,667,312	0.00805	2,677,670	2,210,421	283,047	2,843,593	3,126,640	5,337,061
26	350,540,672	0.00835	2,656,123	2,190,879	282,671	2,923,885	3,206,556	5,397,435
27	347,334,116	0.00865	2,633,950	2,170,838	282,209	3,001,955	3,284,164	5,455,022
28	344,049,952	0.00865	2,611,167	2,150,312	281,662	2,973,553	3,255,215	5,405,527
29	340,794,737	0.00865	2,588,581	2,129,967	281,116	2,945,400	3,226,516	5,356,483
30	337,568,221	0.00865	2,566,190	2,109,801	280,572	2,917,496	3,198,067	5,307,869
100	170,142,350	0.00865	1,396,958	1,063,390	244,953	1,469,591	1,714,544	2,777,933
101	168,427,806	0.00865	1,384,875	1,052,674	244,478	1,454,765	1,699,243	2,751,916
102	166,728,563	0.00865	1,372,896	1,042,054	244,004	1,440,071	1,684,075	2,726,128
103	165,044,489	0.00865	1,361,020	1,031,528	243,531	1,425,508	1,669,039	2,700,567
104	163,375,450	0.00865	1,349,248	1,021,097	243,060	1,411,075	1,654,134	2,675,231
105	161,721,315	0.00865	1,337,577	1,010,758	242,589	1,396,771	1,639,359	2,650,118
200	56,746,664	0.00865	585,990	354,667	201,767	489,106	690,874	1,045,540
201	56,055,790	0.00865	580,921	350,349	201,377	483,134	684,510	1,034,859
202	55,371,280	0.00865	575,896	346,070	200,986	477,216	678,202	1,024,273
203	54,693,077	0.00865	570,915	341,832	200,597	471,353	671,950	1,013,782
204	54,021,127	0.00865	565,976	337,632	200,208	465,544	665,752	1,003,384
205	53,355,375	0.00865	561,081	333,471	199,820	459,789	659,609	993,080
300	11,758,141	0.00865	245,808	73,488	166,196	100,269	266,456	339,953
301	11,491,677	0.00865	243,682	71,823	165,874	97,967	263,841	335,664
302	11,227,836	0.00865	241,574	70,174	165,552	95,687	261,240	331,414

(continued)

Table 30.2 *(continued)*

Month	Outstanding Balance ($)	SMM	Mortgage Payment ($)	Net Interest ($)	Scheduled Principal ($)	Prepay-ment ($)	Total Principal ($)	TotalCash Flow ($)
303	10,966,596	0.00865	239,485	68,541	165,232	93,430	258,662	327,203
304	10,707,934	0.00865	237,413	66,925	164,912	91,196	256,107	323,032
305	10,451,827	0.00865	235,360	65,324	164,592	88,983	253,575	318,899
350	1,235,674	0.00865	159,202	7,723	150,836	9,384	160,220	167,943
351	1,075,454	0.00865	157,825	6,722	150,544	8,000	158,544	165,266
352	916,910	0.00865	156,460	5,731	150,252	6,631	156,883	162,614
353	760,027	0.00865	155,107	4,750	149,961	5,277	155,238	159,988
354	604,789	0.00865	153,765	3,780	149,670	3,937	153,607	157,387
355	451,182	0.00865	152,435	2,820	149,380	2,611	151,991	154,811
356	299,191	0.00865	151,117	1,870	149,091	1,298	150,398	152,259
357	148,802	0.00865	149,809	930	148,802	0	148,802	149,732

Note: Pass-through rate = 7.5%; WAC = 8.125%; WAM = 357 months.

The average life of a pass-through depends on the PSA prepayment assumption. To see this, the average life (in years) is shown below for different prepayment speeds for the pass-through used to illustrate the cash flow for 100 PSA and 165 PSA in table 30.1 and table 30.2:

PSA speed	50	100	165	200	300	400	500	600	700
Average life	15.11	11.66	8.76	7.68	5.63	4.44	3.68	3.16	2.78

U.S. Agency CMOs

Some institutional investors are concerned with extension risk and others with contraction risk when they invest in a pass-through. This problem can be mitigated by redirecting the cash flows of mortgage pass-through securities to different bond classes, called **tranches**, so as to create securities that have different exposure to prepayment risk and, therefore, risk/return patterns that differ from those of the pass-through securities from which the tranches were created.

When the cash flows of pools of mortgage pass-through securities are redistributed to different bond classes, the resulting securities are called **agency collateralized mortgage obligations**. The creation of an agency CMO cannot eliminate prepayment risk; it can only distribute the various forms of this risk among different classes of bondholders. The CMO's major financial innovation is that the securities created more closely satisfy the asset/liability needs of institutional investors and thus broaden the appeal of mortgage-backed products to traditional bond investors.

Rather than list the different types of tranches that can be created in a CMO structure, we show how the tranches can be created as an illustration of financial engineering. Although many different types of CMOs have been created, we look at just three of the key innovations in the CMO market: sequential-pay tranches, accrual tranches, and planned amortization class tranches. Two other important tranches that are not illustrated here are the floating-rate tranche and the inverse floating-rate tranche.

Sequential-pay tranches The first CMO was created in 1983 and was structured so that each class of bond would be retired sequentially. Such structures are referred to as **sequential-pay CMOs**. To illustrate a sequential-pay CMO, we discuss CMO-1, a hypothetical deal made up to illustrate the basic features of the structure. The collateral for this hypothetical CMO is a pass-through with a total par value of $400 million and the following characteristics: (1) the pass-through coupon rate is 7.5%, (2) the WAC is 8.125%, and (3) the WAM is 357 months. We used this same pass-through earlier in the chapter to describe the cash flow of a pass-through based on some PSA assumptions.

From this $400 million of collateral, four bond classes or tranches are created. Their characteristics are summarized in table 30.3. The total par value of the four tranches is equal to the par value of the collateral (i.e., the pass-through security). In this simple structure, the coupon rate is the same for each tranche and is also the same as the coupon rate on the collateral. In reality, the coupon rate typically varies by tranche.

We recall here that a CMO is created by redistributing the cash flow—interest and principal—to the different tranches based on a set of payment rules. The payment rules in the note at the bottom of table 30.3 describe how the cash flow from the pass-through (i.e., collateral) is to be distributed to the four tranches. Separate rules determine the payment of the coupon interest and the payment of the principal, the principal being the total of the regularly scheduled principal payment and any prepayments.

Table 30.3
CMO-1: Hypothetical four-tranche, sequential-pay structure.

Tranche	Par Amount ($)	Coupon Rate (%)
A	194,500,000	7.5
B	36,000,000	7.5
C	96,500,000	7.5
D	73,000,000	7.5
Total	400,000,000	

Notes: The payment rules are as follows. 1. For payment of periodic coupon interest: Disburse periodic coupon interest to each tranche based on the amount of principal outstanding at the beginning of the period. 2. For disbursement of principal payments: Disburse principal payments to tranche A until it is completely paid off. After tranche A is completely paid off, disburse principal payments to tranche B until it is completely paid off. After tranche B is completely paid off, disburse principal payments to tranche C until it is completely paid off. After tranche C is completely paid off, disburse principal payments to tranche D until it is completely paid off.

In CMO-1, each tranche receives periodic coupon interest payments based on the amount of the outstanding balance at the beginning of the month. The disbursement of the principal, however, is made in a special way. A tranche is not entitled to receive principal until the entire principal of the tranche before it in the priority structure is paid off. More specifically, tranche A receives all the principal payments until the entire principal amount owed to that bond class, $194,500,000, is paid off; then tranche B begins to receive principal and continues to do so until it is paid the entire $36,000,000. Tranche C then receives principal, and when it is paid off, tranche D starts receiving principal payments.

Although the priority rules for the disbursement of the principal payments are known, the precise amount of the principal in each period is not. This amount depends on the cash flow and therefore on the principal payments of the collateral, which depend on the actual prepayment rate of the collateral. An assumed PSA speed allows the cash flow to be projected. Table 30.2 shows the cash flow (interest, regularly scheduled principal repayment, and prepayments) assuming 165 PSA. Assuming that the collateral does prepay at 165 PSA, the cash flow available to all four tranches in CMO-1 will be precisely the cash flow shown in table 30.2.

To demonstrate how the priority rules for CMO-1 work, table 30.4 shows the cash flow for selected months, assuming the collateral prepays at 165 PSA. For each tranche, the table shows (1) the balance at the end of the month, (2) the principal paid down (regularly scheduled principal repayment plus prepayments), and (3) interest. In month 1, the cash flow for the collateral consists of a principal payment of $709,923 and an interest payment of $2.5 million (0.075 × $400 million/12). The interest payment is distributed to the four tranches based on the amount of the par value outstanding. So, for example, tranche A receives $1,215,625 (0.075 × $194,500,000/12) of the $2.5 million. The principal, however, is all distributed to tranche A. Therefore, the cash flow for tranche A in month 1 is $1,925,548. The principal balance at the end of month 1 for tranche A is $193,790,076 (Original principal balance of $194,500,000 − Principal payment of $709,923). No principal payment is distributed to the three other tranches, because a principal balance is still outstanding for tranche A. This scenario will be true for months 2 through 80.

After month 81, the principal balance will be zero for tranche A. For the collateral, the cash flow in month 81 is $3,318,521, consisting of a principal payment of $2,032,196 and an interest payment of $1,286,325. At the beginning of month 81 (end of month 80), the principal balance for tranche A is $311,926. Therefore, $311,926 of the $2,032,196 of the principal payment from the collateral will be disbursed to tranche A. After this payment is made, no additional principal payments are made to this tranche, because the principal balance is zero. The remaining principal payment from the collateral, $1,720,271, is disbursed to tranche B. According to the assumed prepayment speed of 165 PSA, tranche B then begins receiving principal payments in month 81.

Table 30.4 shows that tranche B is fully paid off by month 100, which is when tranche C begins to receive principal payments. Tranche C is not fully paid off until month 178, at which time tranche D begins receiving the remaining principal payments. The maturity (i.e., the time until the principal is fully paid off) for these four tranches assuming 165 PSA would be 81 months for tranche A, 100 months for tranche B, 178 months for tranche C, and 357 months for tranche D.

Let's look at what has been accomplished by creating the CMO. First, as shown earlier in this chapter, the average life for the pass-through is 8.76 years, assuming a prepayment speed of 165 PSA. Table 30.5 reports the average life of the collateral and the four tranches, assuming different prepayment speeds. Notice that the four tranches have average lives that are both shorter and longer than the collateral, thereby attracting investors who have a preference for an average life different from that of the collateral.

A major problem remains: The average life for the tranches varies considerably. We see how this issue can be tackled later in this chapter. However, some protection is provided for each tranche against prepayment risk. Prioritizing the distribution of principal (i.e., establishing the payment rules for principal) effectively protects the shorter-term tranche A in this structure against extension risk. This protection must come from somewhere, so it comes from the three other tranches. Similarly, tranches C and D provide protection against extension risk for tranches A and B. At the same time, tranches C and D benefit, because they are provided protection against contraction risk, the protection coming from tranches A and B.

Accrual tranches In CMO-1, the payment rules for interest provide for all tranches to be paid interest each month. In many sequential-pay CMO structures, at least one tranche does not receive current interest. Instead, the interest for that tranche would accrue and be added to the principal balance. Such a bond class is commonly referred to as an **accrual tranche**, or a **Z bond** (because the bond is similar to a zero-coupon bond). The interest that would have been paid to the accrual bond class is then used to accelerate paying down the principal balance of earlier bond classes.

To see this process, consider CMO-2, a hypothetical CMO structure with the same collateral as CMO-1 and with four tranches, each with a coupon rate of 7.5%. The structure is shown in table 30.6. The difference is in the last tranche, Z, which is an accrual bond.

Let's look at month 1 and compare it to month 1 in table 30.4, based on 165 PSA. The principal payment from the collateral is $709,923. In CMO-1, this amount is the principal paydown for tranche A. In CMO-2, the interest for tranche Z, $456,250 (see table 30.4), is not paid to that tranche but instead is used to pay down the principal of tranche A. So the principal payment to tranche A is $1,166,173, which is obtained from the collateral's principal payment of $709,923 (see table 30.2) plus the interest of $456,250 (see table 30.4) that was diverted from tranche Z.

The inclusion of the accrual tranche results in a shortening of the expected final maturity for tranches A, B, and C. It turns out that the final payout for tranche A is 64 months rather than 81 months, for tranche B it is 77 months rather than 100 months, and for tranche C it is 112 rather than 178 months.

Table 30.4
Monthly cash flow for selected months for CMO-1 (assuming 165 PSA).

	Tranche A			Tranche B		
Month	Balance ($)	Principal ($)	Interest ($)	Balance ($)	Principal ($)	Interest ($)
1	194,500,000	709,923	1,215,625	36,000,000	0	225,000
2	193,790,077	821,896	1,211,188	36,000,000	0	255,000
3	192,968,181	933,560	1,206,051	36,000,000	0	225,000
4	192,034,621	1,044,822	1,200,216	36,000,000	0	225,000
5	190,989,799	1,155,586	1,193,686	36,000,000	0	225,000
6	189,834,213	1,265,759	1,186,464	36,000,000	0	225,000
7	188,568,454	1,375,246	1,178,553	36,000,000	0	225,000
8	187,193,208	1,483,954	1,169,958	36,000,000	0	225,000
9	185,709,254	1,591,789	1,160,683	36,000,000	0	225,000
10	184,117,464	1,698,659	1,150,734	36,000,000	0	225,000
11	182,418,805	1,804,473	1,140,118	36,000,000	0	225,000
12	180,614,332	1,909,139	1,128,840	36,000,000	0	225,000
75	12,893,479	2,143,974	80,584	36,000,000	0	225,000
76	10,749,504	2,124,935	67,184	36,000,000	0	225,000
77	8,624,569	2,106,062	53,904	36,000,000	0	225,000
78	6,518,507	2,087,353	40,741	36,000,000	0	225,000
79	4,431,154	2,068,807	27,695	36,000,000	0	225,000
80	2,362,347	2,050,422	14,765	36,000,000	0	225,000
81	311,926	311,926	1,950	36,000,000	1,720,271	225,000
82	0	0	0	34,279,729	2,014,130	214,248
83	0	0	0	32,265,599	1,996,221	201,660
84	0	0	0	30,269,378	1,978,468	189,184
85	0	0	0	28,290,911	1,960,869	176,818
95	0	0	0	9,449,331	1,793,089	59,058
96	0	0	0	7,656,242	1,777,104	47,852
97	0	0	0	5,879,138	1,761,258	36,745
98	0	0	0	4,117,880	1,745,550	25,737
99	0	0	0	2,372,329	1,729,979	14,827
100	0	0	0	642,350	642,350	4,015
101	0	0	0	0	0	0
102	0	0	0	0	0	0
103	0	0	0	0	0	0
104	0	0	0	0	0	0
105	0	0	0	0	0	0
1	96,500,000	0	603,125	73,000,000	0	456,250
2	96,500,000	0	603,125	73,000,000	0	456,250
3	95,500,000	0	603,125	73,000,000	0	456,250
4	96,500,000	0	603,125	73,000,000	0	456,250
5	96,500,000	0	603,125	73,000,000	0	456,250
6	96,500,000	0	603,125	73,000,000	0	456,250
7	96,500,000	0	603,125	73,000,000	0	456,250
8	96,500,000	0	603,125	73,000,000	0	456,250
9	96,500,000	0	603,125	73,000,000	0	456,250
10	96,500,000	0	603,125	73,000,000	0	456,250

Table 30.4 *(continued)*

	Tranche A			Tranche B		
Month	Balance ($)	Principal ($)	Interest ($)	Balance ($)	Principal ($)	Interest ($)
11	96,500,000	0	603,125	73,000,000	0	456,250
12	96,500,000	0	603,125	73,000,000	0	456,250
95	96,500,000	0	603,125	73,000,000	0	456,250
96	96,500,000	0	603,125	73,000,000	0	456,250
97	96,500,000	0	603,125	73,000,000	0	456,250
98	96,500,000	0	603,125	73,000,000	0	456,250
99	95,500,000	0	603,125	73,000,000	0	456,250
100	96,500,000	1,072,194	603,125	73,000,000	0	456,250
101	95,427,806	1,699,243	596,424	73,000,000	0	456,250
102	93,728,563	1,684,075	585,804	73,000,000	0	456,250
103	92,044,489	1,669,039	575,278	73,000,000	0	456,250
104	90,375,450	1,654,134	564,847	73,000,000	0	456,250
105	88,721,315	1,639,359	554,508	73,000,000	0	456,250
175	3,260,287	869,602	20,377	73,000,000	0	456,250
176	2,390,685	861,673	14,942	73,000,000	0	456,250
177	1,529,013	853,813	9,556	73,000,000	0	456,250
178	675,199	675,199	4,220	73,000,000	170,824	456,250
179	0	0	0	72,829,176	838,300	455,182
180	0	0	0	71,990,876	830,646	449,943
181	0	0	0	71,160,230	823,058	444,751
182	0	0	0	70,337,173	815,536	439,607
183	0	0	0	69,521,637	808,081	434,510
184	0	0	0	68,713,556	800,690	429,460
185	0	0	0	67,912,866	793,365	424,455
350	0	0	0	1,235,674	160,220	7,723
351	0	0	0	1,075,454	158,544	6,722
352	0	0	0	916,910	156,883	5,731
353	0	0	0	760,027	155,238	4,750
354	0	0	0	604,789	153,607	3,780
355	0	0	0	451,182	151,991	2,820
356	0	0	0	299,191	150,389	1,870
357	$0	$0	$0	148,802	148,802	930

Table 30.5
Average life for the collateral and the four tranches of CMO-1 (years).

	Average Life				
Prepayment Speed (PSA)	Collateral	Tranche A	Tranche B	Tranche C	Tranche D
50	15.11	7.48	15.98	21.08	27.24
100	11.66	4.90	10.86	15.78	24.58
165	8.76	3.48	7.49	11.19	20.27
200	7.68	3.05	6.42	9.60	18.11
300	5.63	2.32	4.64	6.81	13.36
400	4.44	1.94	3.70	5.31	10.34
500	3.68	1.69	3.12	4.38	8.35
600	3.16	1.51	2.74	3.75	6.96
700	2.78	1.38	2.47	3.30	5.95

Table 30.6
CMO-2: Hypothetical four-tranche sequential-pay structure with an accrual bond class.

Tranche	Par Amount ($)	Coupon Rate (%)
A	194,500,000	7.5
B	36,000,000	7.5
C	96,500,000	7.5
Z (Accrual)	73,000,000	7.5
Total	400,000,000	

Notes: Payment rules: 1. For payment of periodic coupon interest: Disburse periodic coupon interest to tranches A, B, and C based on the amount of principal outstanding at the beginning of the period. For tranche Z, accrue the interest based on the principal plus accrued interest in the previous period. The interest for tranche Z is to be paid to the earlier tranches as a principal paydown. 2. For disbursement of principal payments: Disburse principal payments to tranche A until it is completely paid off. After tranche A is completely paid off, disburse principal payments to tranche B until it is completely paid off. After tranche B is completely paid off, disburse principal payments to tranche C until it is completely paid off. After tranche C is completely paid off, disburse principal payments to tranche Z until the original principal balance plus accrued interest is completely paid off.

The average lives for tranches A, B, and C are shorter in CMO-2 compared to CMO-1 because of the inclusion of the accrual bond. For example, at 165 PSA, the average lives (in years) are as follows:

Structure	Tranche A	Tranche B	Tranche C
CMO-2	2.90	5.86	7.87
CMO-1	3.48	7.49	11.19

The reason for the shortening of the nonaccrual tranches is that the interest that would be paid to the accrual bond is being allocated to the other tranches. Tranche Z in CMO-2 will have a longer average life than tranche D in CMO-1.

Thus, shorter-term tranches and a longer-term tranche are created by including an accrual bond. The accrual bond appeals to investors who are concerned with reinvestment risk. The lack of coupon payments that must be reinvested eliminates reinvestment risk until all the other tranches are paid off.

Planned amortization class tranches In the 1980s, many investors were still concerned about investing in an instrument they continued to perceive as posing significant prepayment risk because of the substantial average life variability, despite the innovations designed to reduce prepayment risk. Traditional corporate bond buyers sought a structure with both the characteristics of a corporate bond (either a bullet maturity or a sinking fund type of schedule for principal repayment) and high credit quality. Although CMOs satisfied the second condition, they did not satisfy the first.

In 1987, CMO issuers began issuing bonds with the characteristic that if prepayments are in a specified range, the cash flow pattern is known. The greater predictability of the cash flow for these classes of bonds, referred to as **planned amortization class (PAC) bonds**, occurs because of a principal repayment schedule that must be satisfied. PAC bond-holders take priority over all other classes in the CMO issue in receiving principal payments from the underlying collateral. The greater certainty of the cash flow for the PAC bonds comes at the expense of the non-PAC classes, called the **support** or **companion bonds**. These bonds absorb the prepayment risk. Because PAC bonds have protection against both extension risk and contraction risk, they are said to provide **two-sided prepayment protection**.

To illustrate how to create a PAC bond, we use as collateral the $400 million pass-through with a coupon rate of 7.5%, a WAC of 8.125%, and a WAM of 357 months. The second column of table 30.7 shows the principal payment (regularly scheduled principal repayment plus prepayments) for selected months assuming a prepayment speed of 90 PSA. The next column shows the principal payments for selected months, assuming that the pass-through prepays at 300 PSA.

The last column of table 30.7 gives the *minimum* principal payment if the collateral speed is 90 PSA or 300 PSA for months 1 to 349. (After month 346, the outstanding principal balance will be paid off if the prepayment speed is between 90 PSA and 300 PSA.) For example, in the first month, the principal payment would be $508,169.52 if the collateral prepays at 90 PSA and $1,075,931.20 if the collateral prepays at 300 PSA. Thus, the minimum principal payment is $508,169.52, as reported in the last column of table 30.7. In month 103, the minimum principal payment is also the amount if the prepayment speed is 90 PSA, $1,446,761, compared to $1,458,618.04 for 300 PSA. In month 104, however, a prepayment speed of 300 PSA would produce a principal payment of $1,433,539.23, which is less than the principal payment of $1,440,825.55 assuming 90 PSA. So, $1,433,539.23

is reported in the last column of table 30.7. In fact, from month 104 on, the minimum principal payment is the one that would result assuming a prepayment speed of 300 PSA.

In fact, if the collateral prepays at any speed between 90 PSA and 300 PSA, the minimum principal payment would be the amount reported in the last column of table 30.7. For example, if we had included principal payment figures assuming a prepayment speed of 200 PSA, the minimum principal payment would not change: from month 11 through month 103, the minimum principal payment is that generated from 90 PSA, but from month 104 on, the minimum principal payment is that generated from 300 PSA.

This characteristic of the collateral allows for the creation of a PAC bond, assuming that the collateral prepays over its life at a constant speed between 90 PSA and 300 PSA. A schedule is specified of principal repayments that the PAC bondholders are entitled to receive before any other bond class in the CMO. The monthly schedule of principal repayments is as specified in the last column of table 30.7, which shows the minimum principal payment. Although collateral prepayment between these two speeds cannot be guaranteed, a PAC bond can be structured to assume that it is.

Table 30.8 shows a CMO structure, CMO-3, created from the $400 million, 7.5% coupon pass-through with a WAC of 8.125% and a WAM of 357 months.

The two bond classes in this structure are a 7.5% coupon PAC bond created assuming 90 to 300 PSA with a par value of $243.8 million, and a support bond with a par value of $156.2 million.

Table 30.9 reports the average life for the PAC bond and the support bond in CMO-3, assuming various *actual* prepayment speeds. Notice that between 90 PSA and 300 PSA, the average life for the PAC bond is stable at 7.26 years. However, at slower or faster PSA speeds, the schedule is broken, and the average life changes, lengthening when the prepayment speed is less than 90 PSA and shortening when it is greater than 300 PSA. Even so, much greater variability characterizes the average life of the support bond, which is substantial.

U.S. Agency Stripped MBSs

Agency stripped mortgage-backed securities, introduced by Fannie Mae in 1986, are another example of derivative mortgage securities. A mortgage pass-through security divides the cash flow from the underlying pool of mortgages on a pro rata basis to the security holders. A stripped MBS is created by altering that distribution of principal and interest from a pro rata distribution to an unequal distribution. As a result, some of the securities created demonstrate a price/yield relationship different from that of the underlying mortgage pool. Stripped MBSs, if properly used, provide a means by which investors can hedge prepayment risk.

The first generation of stripped MBSs were partially stripped, and among them were securities issued by Fannie Mae in mid-1986. The Class B stripped MBSs were backed by

Table 30.7
Monthly principal payment for $400 million, 7.5% coupon pass-through (assuming prepayment rates of 90 PSA and 300 PSA).

Month	At 90 PSA ($)	At 300 PSA ($)	Minimum Principal Payment—PAC Schedule ($)
1	508,169.52	1,075,931.20	508,169.52
2	569,843.43	1,279,412.11	569,843.43
3	631,377.11	1,482,194.45	631,377.11
4	692,741.89	1,683,966.17	692,741.89
5	753,909.12	1,884,414.62	753,909.12
6	814,850.22	2,083,227.31	814,850.22
7	875,536.68	2,280,092.68	875,536.68
8	935,940.10	2,474,700.92	935,940.10
9	996,032.19	2,666,744.77	996,032.19
10	1,055,784.82	2,855,920.32	1,055,784.82
11	1,115,170.01	3,041,927.81	1,115,170.01
12	1,174,160.00	3,224,472.44	1,174,160.00
13	1,232,727.22	3,403,265.17	1,232,727.22
14	1,290,844.32	3,578,023.49	1,290,844.32
15	1,348,484.24	3,748,472.23	1,348,484.24
16	1,405,620.17	3,914,344.26	1,405,620.17
17	1,462,225.60	4,075,381.29	1,462,225.60
18	1,518,274.36	4,231,334.57	1,518,274.36
101	1,458,719.34	1,510,072.17	1,458,719.34
102	1,452,725.55	1,484,126.59	1,452,725.55
103	1,446,761.00	1,458,618.04	1,446,761.00
104	1,440,825.55	1,433,539.23	1,433,539.23
105	1,434,919.07	1,408,883.01	1,408,883.01
211	949,482.58	213,309.00	213,309.00
212	946,033.34	209,409.09	209,409.09
213	942,601.99	205,577.05	205,577.05
346	618,684.59	13,269.17	13,269.17
347	617,071.58	12,944.51	12,944.51
348	615,468.65	12,626.21	12,626.21
349	613,875.77	12,314.16	3,432.32
350	612,292.88	12,008.25	0
351	610,719.96	11,708.38	0
352	609,156.96	11,414.42	0
353	607,603.84	11,126.28	0
354	606,060.57	10,843.85	0
355	604,527.09	10,567.02	0
356	603,003.38	10,295.70	0
357	601,489.39	10,029.78	0

Note: Pass-through rate = 7.5%; WAC = 8.125%; WAM = 357 months.

Table 30.8
CMO-3 structure with one PAC bond and one support bond.

Tranche	Par Amount ($)	Coupon Rate (%)
P (PAC)	243,800,000	7.5
S (Support)	156,200,000	7.5
Total	400,000,000	

Note: Payment rules: 1. For payment of periodic coupon interest: Disburse periodic coupon interest to each tranche based on the amount of principal outstanding at the beginning of the period. 2. For disbursement of principal payments: Disburse principal payments to tranche P based on its schedule of principal repayments. Tranche P has priority with respect to current and future principal payments to satisfy the schedule. Any excess principal payments in a month over the amount necessary to satisfy the schedule for tranche P are paid to tranche S. When tranche S is completely paid off, all principal payments are to be made to tranche P regardless of the schedule.

Table 30.9
Average life for PAC bond and support bond in CMO-3, assuming various prepayment speeds (years).

Prepayment Rate (PSA)	PAC Bond (P)	Support Bond (S)
0	15.97	27.26
50	9.44	24.00
90	7.26	18.56
100	7.26	18.56
150	7.26	12.57
165	7.26	11.16
200	7.26	8.38
250	7.26	5.37
300	7.26	3.13
350	6.56	2.51
400	5.92	2.17
450	5.38	1.94
500	4.93	1.77
700	3.70	1.37

Fannie Mae (FNMA) pass-through securities with a 9% coupon. The mortgage payments from the underlying mortgage pool were distributed to Class B-1 and Class B-2, so that both classes received an equal amount of the principal, but Class B-1 received one-third of the interest payments, whereas Class B-2 received two-thirds.

In a subsequent issue, Fannie Mae distributed the cash flow from the underlying mortgage pool in a far different way. Using Fannie Mae 11% coupon pools, Fannie Mae created Class A-1 and Class A-2. Class A-1 was given 4.95% of the 11% coupon interest, and Class A-2 received the other 6.05%. Class A-1 was given almost all the principal payments (99%), whereas Class A-2 was allotted only 1% of the principal payments.

In early 1987, stripped MBSs began to be issued that allocated all the interest to one class (called the *interest-only* or IO class) and all the principal to the other class (called the *principal-only* or PO class). The IO class receives no principal payments. IO and PO securities are also referred to as **mortgage strips**.

The PO security is purchased at a substantial discount from par value. The yield an investor realizes depends on the speed at which prepayments are made. The faster the prepayments are made, the higher the investor's yield will be. For example, suppose a mortgage pool consists of only 30-year mortgages, with $400 million in principal, and that investors can purchase POs backed by this mortgage pool for $175 million. The dollar return on this investment will be $225 million. How quickly that dollar return is recovered by PO investors determines the yield realized. In the extreme case, if all home owners in the underlying mortgage pool decide to prepay their loans immediately, PO investors will realize the $225 million immediately. At the other extreme, if all home owners decide to remain in their homes for 30 years and make no prepayments, the $225 million will be spread out over 30 years, which would result in a lower yield for PO investors.

The price of a PO security rises when interest rates decline, and it falls when interest rates rise. This price/interest relationship is typical of all the bonds discussed thus far in this book. A characteristic of a PO security is that its price is sensitive to changes in interest rates.

An IO security has no par value. In contrast to the PO investor, the IO investor wants prepayments to be slow, because the IO investor receives interest only on the amount of the principal outstanding. When prepayments are made, less dollar interest will be received as the outstanding principal declines. In fact, if prepayments are too fast, the IO investor may not recover the amount paid for the IO security. The unique aspect of an IO security is that its price changes in the *same* direction as the change in interest rates. Moreover, as in the case of the PO security, its price is highly responsive to a change in interest rates.

Because of these price volatility characteristics of stripped MBSs, institutional investors use them to control the risk of a portfolio of MBSs by creating a risk/return pattern that better fits their needs.

Private-Label RMBSs

Private-label RMBSs (also referred to as "nonagency RMBSs") are RMBSs issued by entities other than Ginnie Mae, Fannie Mae, and Freddie Mac. Private-label RMBS are issued through the conduits of (1) commercial banks (e.g., Citigroup's CitiMortgage), (2) investment banking firms, and (3) entities not associated with either commercial banks or investment banking firms.

At one time, the private-label RMBS market was classified into two sectors, the prime sector and the subprime sector. The distinction was based on the type of borrowers in the pool of mortgage loans. As explained in chapter 29, mortgage loans can be classified as prime loans and subprime loans. The latter are loans made to borrowers with an impaired credit history or when the loan is not a first lien on the property. The convention in the

RMBS market was to classify prime deals as private-label RMBSs but subprime deals as consumer loans, referred to as mortgage-related ABSs. Subprime deals include home equity loans and manufactured housing loans. After the meltdown of the subprime mortgage market in 2007, which we describe shortly, there has been little issuance of subprime deals, and the market tends not to distinguish between prime and subprime deals.

For agency mortgage-related securities described in the previous section, we noted that there are pass-through securities, CMOs, and stripped MBSs. Typically, the structure that is used for a private-label RMBS is the CMO structure. The creation of a private-label CMO is different from that of an agency CMO. When describing agency CMOs, we said that the process first involves pooling loans to create an agency pass-through security. Then a pool of agency pass-through securities is pooled to create an agency CMO. In a private-label CMO, the loans are pooled and used to create different bond classes (tranches).

Before 2007, deals could include all forms of credit enhancement described that we described chapter 27. When sizing the credit enhancement, subprime deals required considerably more credit enhancement than did prime deals. In retrospect, it has been argued that the collapse of the subprime mortgage market can be attributed to insufficient credit enhancement.

Credit Enhancement

Unlike agency RMBSs, private-label CMOs are rated by one or more of the credit rating agencies. Because there is no government or GSE guarantee, to receive an investment-grade rating, these securities must be structured with additional credit support. The credit support is needed to absorb expected losses from the underlying loan pool due to defaults. As explained in chapter 27, this additional credit support is referred to as a **credit enhancement**. Credit enhancements come in different forms: (1) senior-subordinate structure, (2) excess spread, (3) overcollateralization, and (4) monoline insurance. We describe these forms briefly here. These same forms of credit enhancement are used by corporations in the creation of ABS structures to obtain funding, as covered in chapter 27.

When commercial rating agencies assign a rating to the tranches in a private-label CMO, they look at the credit risk associated with a tranche. Basically, that analysis begins by looking at the credit quality of the underlying pool of mortgage loans. For example, a pool of loans can consist of prime borrowers or subprime borrowers. Obviously, one would expect that a pool consisting of prime borrowers would have fewer expected losses as a percentage of the dollar amount of the loan pool compared to a pool consisting of subprime borrowers. Given the credit quality of the borrowers in the pool and other factors (such as the structure of the transaction), a rating agency will determine the dollar amount of the credit enhancement needed for a particular tranche to receive a specific credit rating. The process by which the rating agencies determine the amount of credit enhancement needed is referred to as "sizing the transaction."

There are standard mechanisms for providing credit enhancement in private-label CMOs. We describe these mechanisms below.

Senior-subordinate structure In a **senior-subordinate structure**, two general categories of tranches are created: a senior tranche and subordinate tranches. For example, consider the following hypothetical private-label CMO structure consisting of $400 million of collateral:

Notice that there are seven tranches in this transaction. The tranche with the highest rating is referred to as the **senior tranche**. The **subordinate tranches** are those below the senior tranche.

Tranche	Principal Amount	Credit Rating
X1	$350 million	AAA
X2	$20 million	AA
X3	$10 million	A
X4	$5 million	BBB
X5	$5 million	BB
X6	$5 million	B
X7	$5 million	Not rated

The rules for the distribution of the cash flow (interest and principal) among the tranches as well as how losses are to be distributed are explained in the prospectus. These rules are referred to as the deal's **waterfall**. Basically, the losses are distributed based on the tranche's position in the structure. Losses run from the bottom (the lowest or unrated tranche) to the senior tranche. For example, if over the life of this private-label CMO, the losses are less than $5 million, only tranche X7 will realize a loss. If the loss is, say, $15 million, tranches X7, X6, and X5 will realize total losses and the other tranches no losses.

Note a few points about this structure. First, the credit enhancement for tranches is being provided by other tranches in the structure. For example, the senior tranche, X1, is being protected against losses up to $50 million. This is because it is only when $50 million of losses are realized that tranche X1 will realize a loss. Tranche X4 has credit enhancement of $15 million, because the collateral can realize $15 million in losses before tranche X4 realizes a loss.

Second, compare what is being done to distribute credit risk in this private-label CMO compared to an agency CMO. In an agency CMO, there is no credit risk. What is being done when creating the different tranches is the redistribution of prepayment risk. In contrast, in a private-label CMO, there is both credit risk and prepayment risk. By creating the senior-subordinate tranches, credit risk is being redistributed among the tranches in the structure. Hence, what is being done is **credit tranching**. Can prepayment risk also be redistributed? This is typically done in private-label CMOs but only at the senior tranche level. That is, the $350 million of senior tranches in our hypothetical private-label CMO structure can be carved up to create senior tranches with different exposures to prepayment risk.

Finally, when the tranches are sold in the market, they are sold at different yields. Obviously, the lower the credit rating of a tranche is, the higher is the yield at which it must be offered.

Excess spread **Excess spread** is basically the interest from the collateral that is not being used to satisfy the liabilities (i.e., the interest payments to the tranches in the structure) and the fees (such as mortgage servicing and administrative fees). The excess spread can be used to help offset any losses. If the excess spread is retained in the structure rather than paid out, it can be accumulated in a reserve account and used to pay not only current losses experienced by the collateral but also future losses. Hence, excess spread is a form of credit enhancement. Because the loan rate on subprime loans is greater than that on prime loans and because the expected losses are greater for subprime loans, excess spread is an important source of credit enhancement for subprime RMBS.

Overcollateralization In our hypothetical nonagency CMO, the liabilities are $400 million and are assumed to match the amount of the collateral. Suppose instead that the collateral has a par value of $405 million. In this case, the assets exceed the liabilities by $5 million. This excess collateral is referred to as **overcollateralization** and can be used to absorb losses. Hence, it is a form of credit enhancement.

Overcollateralization is more commonly used as a form of credit enhancement in subprime deals than in prime deals. This is one of the aspects that makes subprime deals more complicated, because a series of tests is built into the structure to determine when collateral can be released.

Monoline insurance In Chapter 8, we discussed life insurance and property and casualty insurance companies. Some insurance companies, by charter, provide only financial guarantees. These insurance companies are called **monoline insurance companies**. These companies provide the guaranty for insured municipal bonds in the United States. For RMBSs, they provide the same function, and therefore this is viewed as a form of credit enhancement.

The Subprime Mortgage Crisis and Securitization

In the summer of 2007 the subprime mortgage market experienced a crisis, which led to a credit and liquidity crisis that had a ripple effect on other sectors of the credit and equity markets. This episode in the history of financial markets is referred to as the **subprime mortgage crisis**.

In keeping with the history of financial innovation bashing, there have been overreactions, misinformation, and widely differing viewpoints regarding this crisis. Some market observers saw it as the inevitable bursting of the "housing bubble" that had characterized the housing market in prior years. Others viewed it as the product of unsavory practices by mortgage lenders who deceived subprime borrowers into purchasing homes they could not afford. Moreover, specific mortgage designs, such as hybrid loans, which made it possible for a subprime borrower to obtain a loan, could have been expected to cause financial difficulties in the future when loan rates were adjusted upward as part of the loan agreement.

Of course, mortgage lenders blamed borrowers for misleading them. Others laid the blame at the feet of Wall Street bankers who packaged subprime loans into bonds and sold them to investors, citing the arguments described earlier in this chapter regarding the originate-to-distribute approach pursued by financial institutions.

Whatever the precise cause, it is hard to deny that securitization—the financial framework that allowed Wall Street to package these loans into MBSs—is of enormous benefit to the economy. Securitization has increased the supply of credit to homeowners and reduced the cost of borrowing. It also spreads the risk among a larger pool of investors rather than concentrating it in a small group of banks and thrifts, and it makes credit available to a wider group of borrowers. Critics of securitization argue that such borrowers may not be suitable candidates for loans. These critics claim that the only reason a lender would make such loans is because it does not hold the loans on its balance sheet; instead, it sells them in the market, either to a conduit that will securitize the loans or by securitizing them itself.

Although it can be argued that not all those who were shut out from the market prior to securitization were in fact weak borrowers, the empirical evidence discussed earlier about the underwriting practice associated with the securitization of subprime loans appears to support the position that standards may have been lax. However, that is an attack on underwriting standards for the mortgage sector and not a reason for attacking securitization in general. As we stated earlier in this chapter, securitization is an important and legitimate way for the financial markets to function more efficiently today than in the past. It is not a smoke-and-mirrors financial structure that fraudulent companies have used to hide the true nature of their operations. Although sometimes complex, real securitization generally takes place in regulated debt markets and with the participation of sophisticated parties—such as underwriters, loan servicers, institutional investors, rating agencies, and monoline insurance companies—that provide financial guarantees. Each of these entities has a unique role to play that helps produce a balanced—but not a riskless—result.

Credit rating agencies (CRAs) were also viewed by some market observers as having contributed in a major way to the crisis. To aid investors when comparing the relative credit risk of securities, issuers generally ask one or more CRAs to assign a credit rating to the securitization. Although no one, not even the rating agencies, can always accurately predict the performance of a bond over time, the agencies' long-term track record is solid. As explained in chapter 5 credit ratings are opinions about future performance. CRAs are not asset managers. They provide an initial screening for asset managers to help determine which bond classes might be suitable candidates for further credit analysis. Credit ratings are not a substitute for the due diligence that should be exercised by investors who claim to be experts on fixed-income securities.

What is surprising to many is why the crisis occurred in July 2007. There was no new information in the market at the time. Investors knew well before that time all about the potential defaults. Moreover, since 2005, the CRAs had taken actions that were transparent to the market. Specifically, the CRAs adjusted their criteria and assumptions regarding how they were rating subprime RMBS transactions, they downgraded some issues, and they publicly commented on their concerns about the subprime sector.

The impact of the subprime mortgage crisis on the financial markets was devastating. But the suggestion that securitization caused the subsequent global financial crisis would be wrong. In a speech by Robert Steel, then undersecretary of the U.S. Department of the Treasury, before the American Securitization Forum on February 5, 2008, Steel stated:

> The securitization market is an example of how this incredible pace of innovation has changed financial markets. Secretary Paulson and I have been very clear—we believe that the benefits of securitization are significant. It enables investors to improve their risk management, achieve better risk adjusted returns and access more liquidity.[3]

Key Points

- The residential mortgage-backed securities (RMBS) market is divided into two sectors, agency MBS and private-label MBS.
- MBSs issued by Ginnie Mae, Fannie Mae, and Freddie Mac are included in the agency MBS sector.
- The loans used as collateral in agency MBSs are conforming loans.
- Agency MBSs include pass-through securities, collateralized mortgage obligations (CDOs), and stripped MBSs.
- To project the cash flow of a pool of mortgages, it is necessary to make some assumption about the prepayment rate over the life of the mortgage pool.
- The conditional prepayment rate (CPR) assumes that some fraction of the remaining principal in the pool is prepaid each year for the remaining term of the mortgage.
- A prepayment model is estimated based on the characteristics of the pool (including its historical prepayment experience) and the current and expected future economic environment.
- To estimate monthly prepayments, the CPR (an annual rate) must be converted into a monthly prepayment rate, commonly referred to as the single-monthly mortality rate (SMM).

3. Robert Steel, speech delivered at the American Securitization Forum Annual Conference, Las Vegas, February 5, 2008, http://www.ustreas.gov/press/releases/hp808.htm.

- The Public Securities Association (PSA) prepayment benchmark is a monthly series of CPRs that assumes that prepayment rates are low for newly originated mortgages and then speed up as the mortgages become seasoned; slower or faster speeds are then referred to as some percentage of the PSA benchmark.
- The average life of an MBS is the average time to receipt of principal payments (scheduled principal payments and projected prepayments) weighted by the amount of principal expected.
- A mortgage pass-through security is created when one or more holders of loans form a collection (pool) of loans and sell shares or participation certificates in the pool.
- Collateralized mortgage obligations (CMOs) are created from pass-through securities to address the prepayment risks associated with investing in pass-through securities: contraction risk and extension risk.
- A CMO sets forth rules for the distribution of interest and principal repayment to the different bond classes in the structure.
- CMO tranches are created to meet the different needs of institutional investors.
- Agency CMOs are an example of time tranching.
- Like a CMO, a stripped MBS is created from a pass-through security.
- The purpose of creating a stripped MBS is to provide an instrument that can be used to control the risk of a portfolio of mortgage-related securities.
- The private-label RMBS market was at one time classified into prime RMBS and subprime RMBS sectors, according to the credit quality of the borrowers.
- Subprime RMBS structures are more complicated and require more credit enhancement than prime RMBS structures.
- The subprime mortgage meltdown began in the summer of 2007 and has been attributed to the collapse of the subprime housing finance market.

Questions

1. What is a mortgage pass-through security?
2. Describe the cash flow of a mortgage pass-through security.
3. What are the different types of agency pass-through securities?
4. What is meant by "prepayment risk," "contraction risk," and "extension risk"?
5. Why would a pass-through security be an unattractive investment for a savings and loan association?
6. What is meant by the "average life" of a pass-through security?
7. Why is an assumed prepayment speed necessary to project the cash flow of a pass-through security?

8. A cash flow for a pass-through security is typically based on some prepayment benchmark. Describe the benchmark.

9. What does a conditional prepayment rate of 8% mean?

10. What does "250 PSA" mean?

11. Why is a sequential-pay bond class an example of time tranching?

12. How does a collateralized mortgage obligation (CMO) alter the cash flow from mortgages so as to shift the prepayment risk across various classes of bondholders?

13. "The creation of a CMO eliminates the prepayment risk associated with the underlying mortgages." Explain why you agree or disagree with this statement.

14. Explain the effect of including an accrual tranche in a CMO structure on the average lives of the sequential-pay structures.

15. What types of investor would be attracted to an accrual bond?

16. What was the motivation for the creation of PAC bonds?

17. Describe how the schedule for a PAC tranche is created.

18. a. Why is it necessary for a private-label RMBS to have credit enhancement?

b. Who determines the amount of credit enhancement needed?

19. a. What is meant by a "senior-subordinate structure"?

b. Why is the senior-subordinate structure a form of credit enhancement?

20. How can excess spread be a form of credit enhancement?

31 Commercial Real Estate Markets

CONTENTS

Learning Objectives

After reading this chapter, you will understand:

- what commercial property is and the different types of commercial property;
- the four categories of commercial real estate: private commercial real estate equity; public commercial real estate equity, private commercial real estate debt, and public commercial real estate debt;
- the primary reasons for investing in commercial real estate;
- the major commercial property indexes;
- the various vehicles for investing in private commercial real estate equity;
- the structuring of public commercial real estate as real estate trusts and real estate operating companies;
- the different types of real estate investment trusts (REITs);
- the ways in which private commercial real estate debt are held;
- what commercial loans are and how they are structured;
- how commercial mortgage loans differ from residential mortgage loans;
- the two indicators of performance used for evaluating commercial mortgage loans—debt-to-service coverage ratio and loan-to-value ratio;
- the ways of investing in public commercial real estate debt: commercial mortgage-backed securities and REITs that invest in mortgage debt;
- what a commercial mortgage-backed security (CMBS) is;
- the structural features of a CMBS deal; and
- the investors in the commercial real estate market.

The real estate market includes residential properties and commercial properties. **Residential real estate** includes one- to four-family properties and is the subject of chapter 30. **Commercial real estate** is income-producing properties. The major commercial property types are multifamily housing, apartment buildings, office buildings, industrial properties (including warehouses), shopping centers, hotels, health care facilities (e.g., senior housing care facilities), and timberlands. In this chapter, we discuss the commercial real estate market.

Categories of the Commercial Real Estate Market

Prior to the introduction of the securitization of real estate–related equity and debt, real estate was defined to include only investments in private commercial real estate equity and private commercial real estate debt. Insurance companies traditionally constructed portfolios composed of individual private real estate mortgages. Pension funds and wealthy families held direct investments in individual buildings and in commingled funds. Given the absence of a secondary market for real estate debt and equity, investors followed a buy-to-hold strategy.

With the advent of securitization in the 1960s, the definition of commercial real estate investments has broadened. Today commercial real estate investments include the following four categories:[1]

1. private commercial real estate equity,
2. public commercial real estate equity,
3. private commercial real estate debt, and
4. public commercial real estate debt.

Regardless of what category a commercial real estate investment falls into, its return is responsive to a common set of factors. But there are unique factors that impact real estate investments for specific categories. Thus, the rationale for broadening the definition of real estate investment beyond its historical definition of private debt and equity is that the factors driving real estate returns for the two private categories are reflected, to a greater or lesser degree, in the returns for the two public categories.

Investors are often explicitly or implicitly invested in all four categories, and therefore are exposed to real estate behaviors in each category. Consequently, when examining the reasons for commercial real estate investing, we should consider the categories rather than accepting the traditional reasons for the role of commercial real estate. These traditional reasons were historically based only on the private equity and ignore not only the other three categories available to investors but also the factors that affect returns.

Primary Reasons Offered for Investing in Commercial Real Estate

The five primary reasons that have been offered for considering commercial real estate as part of a portfolio are to:

1. reduce portfolio risk by combining asset classes that respond in different ways to expected and unexpected events.
2. generate absolute returns that well exceed the risk-free rate.
3. hedge against unexpected inflation or deflation.

1. These four categories were suggested by Jacques Gordon, "The Real Estate Capital Markets Matrix: A Paradigm Approach," *Real Estate Finance* 11, no. 3 (1994): 7–15; Susan Hudson-Wilson, Susan Guenther, and Daniel P. Guenther, "The Four Quadrants: Diversification Benefits for Investors in Real Estate—A Second Look," *Real Estate Finance* 12, no. 2 (1995): 82–99.

4. build a part of a portfolio that is a reasonable reflection of the overall investment universe.
5. generate strong cash flows to the portfolio.[2]

Several studies have attempted to determine whether these reasons offered for investing in real estate can be supported empirically.[3] Investigating these alleged reasons empirically has been difficult. Even what is a simple part of the empirical investigation—calculating market returns for equities and fixed income securities—is controversial in the real estate market. Moreover, research has to examine each of the four quadrants rather than treat real estate as one asset class.

Below we summarize some of the studies dealing with the alleged primary reasons for investment in real estate.

Portfolio Diversifier and Risk Reducer

Several studies find that the correlations between real estate and stocks, real estate and bonds, and real estate and cash suggest that real estate can play a significant role in a mixed-asset portfolio.[4] Recall the underlying principle of portfolio diversification and risk reduction as set forth by Markowitz and explained in chapter 13. When two imperfectly related assets (i.e., having a correlation coefficient less than 1.0) are included in a portfolio, there is an opportunity to construct a portfolio that has a higher expected return at each level of risk, or equivalently, to reduce risk for a given level of expected return. The risk is the portfolio's standard deviation. When the expected return to an asset class is high enough, or the risk is low enough, or the correlation of returns reflects a sufficiently different pattern of returns, an allocation should be made to that asset class in the portfolio for at least a portion of the return-risk spectrum. Commercial real estate satisfies these requirements; therefore, some allocation should be made to it in a well-diversified mixed-asset portfolio.

Absolute Returns or Risk-Adjusted Returns

The second reason for investing in commercial real estate is that this asset class can potentially generate high absolute returns or risk-adjusted returns to a portfolio. One study reports that, on average, real estate did not outperform stocks and bonds in absolute terms

2. These are arguments are given in Susan Hudson-Wilson, Frank J. Fabozzi, and Jacques N. Gordon, "Why Real Estate?" *Journal of Portfolio Management* 29, no. 5 (Special Issue, 2003): 12–25.

3. Hudson-Wilson, Fabozzi, and Gordon, "Why Real Estate?"; Susan Hudson-Wilson, Jacques N. Gordon, Frank J. Fabozzi, Mark J. P. Anson, and S. Michael Giliberto, "Why Real Estate? And How? Where? And When?" *Journal of Portfolio Management* 31, no. 5 (Special Issue, 2005): 12–31.

4. Hudson-Wilson, Fabozzi, and Gordon, "Why Real Estate?"; Hudson-Wilson et al., "Why Real Estate? And How? Where? And When?"

from 1987 to 2004.[5] However, in terms of total return per unit of risk, real estate outperformed both stocks and bonds. Moreover, the study finds that real estate outperforms both stocks and bonds on a risk-adjusted basis using the Sharpe ratio, a reward-risk ratio described in chapter 13.

The same study also offers evidence that provides justification for including real estate in a portfolio from the perspective of risk-adjusted returns. However, the authors of the study argue that it is not immediately justifiable to include real estate for the sole reason of bringing high absolute returns to the portfolio, because real estate is not reliable as a producer of the highest absolute returns.

Inflation Hedge

Real estate is considered by some observers to be an inflation hedge for the following reason: If the inflation rate exceeds the expected inflation rate, then the returns on real estate will compensate for the surprise, helping offset the negative response to excess inflation of other assets in the portfolio. The question is whether this reason can be empirically supported.

Let's begin with the relationship of real estate returns. The relationship is a complicated one, because the response to inflation differs for the four major property types (i.e., offices, warehouses, retail, and apartments). A return is composed of an income and price change component. Inflation impacts the income and value components of the return in a different way for each property type.

After discussing the impact on different property types and reviewing the empirical evidence, one study concludes that although private equity real estate is a very useful partial inflation hedge, the degree of inflation-hedging capacity is not uniform across property types.[6] For publicly traded forms of equity real estate, some benefits of the inflation hedge will be captured but are less successful transmitters of this value than is private equity. The reason is that the links to the stock market, which is generally adversely impacted by inflation, are less successful in transmitting this value. However, recent findings suggest that the returns on real estate investment trusts (REITs) have become less highly correlated with stock market returns, which could result in better inflation hedging by REITs.

Not surprisingly, the study does not find that the inflation-hedging reason for investing in real estate applies to the two debt quadrants. As is the case with most debt, real estate debt is not a good inflation hedge, because unexpected inflation and concomitant increases in nominal interest rates negatively impact the value of outstanding fixed-income securities (mortgages and commercial mortgage-backed securities (CMBSs)).

5. Hudson-Wilson et al., "Why Real Estate? And How? Where? And When?"

6. Hudson-Wilson et al., "Why Real Estate? And How? Where? And When?"

Reasonable Reflection of the Investment Universe

It is argued that real estate belongs in a balanced investment portfolio, because this asset class is an important part of the investment universe. The omission of real estate from a portfolio is fundamentally an investor's view that real estate will perform less well than is implied by the market-driven relative prices. Even if some allocation is made to real estate, capital market theory suggests that any allocation that is less than real estate's overall share in the investment universe implies a different view by the investor from that of an indexed portfolio. Consequently, any underallocation to real estate must be justified.

Strong Cash Flows

Investor needs vary for regular distributions of cash. Investors whose objective is the maximization of total return relative to a benchmark return find the need for strong cash flows to be less important than do investors who need cash to satisfy current and near-term liabilities. For the latter investors, the appeal of an asset class that exhibits strong cash flows is important. The question is whether real estate fits the bill.

One study analyzes the relative income returns on real estate and compares them with those of bonds and stocks.[7] This study finds that real estate is a far superior producer of steady income for investors. For investors who seek to earn a higher proportion of their total portfolio return in the form of realized income rather than unrealized capital appreciation, real estate offers a far greater chance of accomplishing this. This conclusion applies to all four categories of real estate in terms of better production of cash flows compared to stocks and bonds.

Private Commercial Real Estate Equity

Private commercial real estate equity is held by investors as individual assets or in commingled vehicles. Individual investors can invest in private commercial real estate equity via different investment vehicles. Historically, efforts were made to design structures to allow individuals to participate in the private real estate market. The most notable attempt is the limited partnership syndications of the late 1970s and early 1980s. However, in the United States, these design structures were short lived, because the tax benefits were typically dependent on certain tax advantages. When the tax law that allowed for such tax advantages was eliminated with the passage of the Tax Reform Act of 1986, these tax-oriented design structures disappeared.

The usual way that individual investors have obtained exposure to commercial property has been through their pension plans. As explained in chapter 3, in the United States there

7. Hudson-Wilson et al., "Why Real Estate? And How? Where? And When?"

are two types of pension plans: defined benefit plans and defined contribution plans. The former plans have had sizeable allocations to real estate.

The difficulties with the collective investment vehicles that can be used by individual investors to obtain exposure to private equity real estate are twofold: the daily pricing of the portfolio holdings of real estate properties and the liquidity requirement for defined contribution plans. Dealing with the liquidity problem is addressed by the asset manager of the fund by allocating more to cash than would be allocated in a traditional real estate portfolio or a REIT. The major obstacle is the daily pricing in an industry where pricing is typically done on a quarterly basis. The approaches that have been suggested to deal with this difficulty include one or a combination of the following: (1) rotating the appraisal of portfolio properties throughout the quarter, (2) using a mark-to-model approach on a daily basis between appraisals for each property, and (3) using regular quarterly appraisals but also monitoring and revaluing properties any time an event of economic significance occurs. Esrig, Kolasa, and Cerreta discuss how target date funds can better satisfy the daily pricing and liquidity needs of investors than can other types of private equity real estate.

Two more ways for individual investors to participate in the private commercial real estate market are via private REITs and crowdfunded real estate projects. In the United States, the shares of **private REIT**s are not traded on an exchange; nor are they registered with the SEC. Instead, they are issued under one or more of several exemptions to the securities laws. More specifically, private REITs are issued under two rules set forth under Regulation D. The first rule allows an issuer to sell securities to "accredited investors," and the second (Rule 144A) exempts securities issued to qualified institutional buyers. With respect to crowdfunding (discussed in chapter 28), using one of various online crowdfunding platforms, individual investors can search for potential real estate investments. The funds from individual investors are then pooled to finance that real estate project. Effectively, individuals participating in a real estate project are limited partners. In 2014, it is estimated that $1 billion was raised via real estate crowdfunding.[8]

Commercial Property Indexes

With the increased interest in commercial real estate as an institutional asset class came the development of commercial property indexes. Most countries have property indexes. There are numerous commercial property indexes, but we discuss only a few of the major ones here.

For the United States, the National Council of Real Estate Investment Fiduciaries produces a family of property indexes (NPIs) that includes, in addition to the national index, indexes for five property types (apartment, industrial, office, retail, and hotel), as well as for four main regions of the country. Appraised values are used to construct the NPI. Three

8. Vanessa Grout, "With $1 Billion Invested and $100 Entry Points, Real Estate Crowdfunding Grows Up." Forbes.com, March 24, 2015, available at http://www.forbes.com/sites/vanessagrout.

types of return indexes are created for each index: (1) total return; (2) income return; and (3) capital appreciation return.

The Investment Property Databank (IPD) provides information about commercial real estate in the United Kingdom and worldwide. Now a member of the MSCI group, the IPD family of indexes includes the prices of the properties based on appraised values. The IPD UK index, for example, is based on about 21,175 properties held by U.K. institutions, trusts, partnerships and listed property companies.

The NPI and IPD indexes are calculated based on appraised values, but the Moody's/Real Capital Analytics Commercial Property Price Indices are based on real estate transactions that measure property prices at a national level for U.S. apartment, retail, office, and industrial properties. There are indexes for the main properties types and for select metropolitan statistical areas.

Public Commercial Real Estate Equity

Public commercial real estate equity is structured as REITs or as **real estate operating companies** (REOCs). REITs can invest in both equity and debt, the former being a form of public real estate equity. We describe REITs in more detail in chapter 32, which covers collective investment vehicles.

Both REITs and REOCs invest in real estate and issue shares to the public that are traded on an exchange. However, there are two differences between a REOC and a REIT. First, a REOC is afforded more flexibility than a REIT as to the types of real estate investments in which they may invest. Second, a REOC reinvests its earnings in the company rather than distributing earnings to shareholders as a REIT does.

Equity REITs can be classified as diversified REITs, sector REITs, and specialty REITs. As the name suggests, a **diversified REIT** invests in a mix of property types. **Sector REITs** are restricted to holdings of specific major sectors of the real estate market, such as office REITs, industrial REITs, retail REITs, lodging REITs, residential REITs, health care REITs, self-storage REITs, and timberland REITs. **Specialty REITs** invest in a unique mix of property types that are not included in the major REIT sectors, such gas stations, golf courses, race tracks, and movie theaters.

Many developed and developing countries have legislation allowing for the creation of a REIT. Here are a few examples:

- **United Kingdom.** Prior to 2006, in the United Kingdom the vehicle by which investors obtained exposure to commercial real estate market was via **listed property companies**. The Finance Act of 2006 (effective January 2007) allowed for the creation of REITs in the United Kingdom, requiring that they be set up as investment trusts listed on a stock exchange approved by the U.K. Financial Services Authority. As in the United States, U.K. REITs are required to distribute 90% of their income to investors. Because there were tax advantages to investors available from REITs that were not available from listed property companies, nine major listed property companies that were members of the major U.K. equity market index, the FTSE 100, converted to REITs. To provide investors with greater transparency and information about U.K. REITs, "Reita" was created by the Quoted Property Group, set up by several commercial property and financial services companies.

- **Germany.** Germany is the largest European real estate market, split almost evenly between commercial and residential properties. Given the large size of the real estate market, the development of an investment vehicle, such as a REIT, was critical. In 2007, the law allowing REITs was approved by the Ministry of Finance, with the first REIT being the *altria Office REIT-AG* in April 2007. German REITs also have the 90% distribution rule and the requirement of the stock being traded on an exchange.
- **Japan.** Legislation allowing for the creation of REITs was passed in 2001. Japanese REITs are traded on the Tokyo Stock Exchange. Japan's first two REITs, both listed in 2001, were the Nippon Nippon Building Fund Inc. and the Japan Real Estate Investment Corporation. The Japanese REIT market was initially dominated by office properties. In recent years, REITs have diversified and include a wider range of properties from the major sectors.
- **Singapore.** Regulated as a collective investment vehicle under the Monetary Authority of Singapore's Code on Collective Investment or as a business trusts, the REIT was set up in July 2002. REITs in Singapore can invest in a wide range of property sectors in China, Hong Kong, Japan, Indonesia, and Hong Kong. Distribution of at least 90% of its annual income is required. The appealing tax benefit of REITs in Singapore is not being taxed twice: income is taxed only at the investor level and not at the REITs level.
- **Brazil.** Referred to in Brazil as *Fundos de Investimento Imobiliário*, REITs in Brazil were first introduced via legislation in 1993. In 2006, the dividends paid by these REITs have been free of taxes for individual investors (not companies), provided the fund has at least 50 investors and is publicly traded on a stock market.

In countries with REITs, indexes have been developed to evaluate their performance. For example, in the United States, the most popular REIT indexes are the MSCI US REIT index, the Dow Jones U.S. Real Estate Index, and the Dow Jones U.S. Select REIT Index. Three indexes are based on German REITs that have been developed by the Deutsche Borse (Germany's major stock exchange): RX REIT All Share Index, which includes all German REITs listed on the Prime Standard and the General Standard; the RX Real Estate Index, which contains up to 30 REITs and real estate companies from the General Standard; and the RX REIT Index, which contains up to 20 of the largest and most liquid REITs from Prime Standard. (The "Prime Standard" is the group of stocks on the Frankfort Stock Exchange that lists those German companies that comply with international transparency standards.)

The FTSE EPRA/NAREIT Global Real Estate Index Series covers global, developed and emerging indexes, as well the United Kingdom's AIM market.

A family of indexes produced jointly by the European Public Real Estate Association (EPRA), the FTSE, and the National Association of Real Estate Trusts (NAREIT) for the global listed sector is available. The index series covers global (with and without the United Kingdom and the United States), regional (Europe, the Eurozone, and Asia Pacific with and without Japan), developed (the Americas), and emerging real estate equities markets.

Another way for investors to invest in public equity commercial real estate is via exchange-traded funds (ETFs), a collective investment vehicle described in chapter 32. Three examples are the Vanguard REIT Index ETF, iShares Dow Jones U.S. Real Estate, and Schwab U.S. REIT ETF. The Vanguard REIT Index ETF which tracks the MSCI US REIT index, invests in equity REITs with a bias towards large ETFs. As of April 30, 2016, this ETF had a position in 150 REITs, with a quarter of the portfolio's holdings being in the retail REIT sector. As the name indicates, iShares Dow Jones U.S. Real Estate has as its benchmark the Dow Jones U.S. Real Estate Index, whereas the Schwab U.S. REIT ETF tracks the Dow Jones U.S. Select REIT Index.

Public Nontraded REITs

The most popular type of REIT is publicly traded on an exchange and falls into the quadrant of public commercial real estate equity. However, there are **public nontraded REITs** structured in the same way as traditional REITs (and subject to the same investment and payout constraints) but not traded on a public exchange, with the investment generally tied up for 7 to 10 years until a liquidity event (e.g., sale or listing) allows return of any proceeds to investors. Nontraded REITs, typically marketed to "mom and pop" investors, are part of the private commercial real estate equity available to individuals. According to the Investment Program Association, from 2000 to 2014, nontraded REITs raised $124 billion of capital, including $21.1 billion in 2014 alone. The sponsors of nontraded REITs have been criticized for the high fees and sometimes misleading statements by brokers who aggressively sell this investment vehicle. The U.S. SEC identifies the following issues associated with investing in nontraded REITs:

- **Lack of liquidity.** Nontraded REITs are illiquid investments, which mean that they cannot be sold readily in the market. Instead, investors generally must wait until the non-traded REIT lists its shares on an exchange or liquidates its assets to achieve liquidity. These liquidity events, however, might not occur until more than 10 years after your investment.
- Nontraded REITs usually offer investors' opportunities to redeem their shares early but these share redemption programs are typically subject to significant limitations and may be discontinued at the discretion of the REIT without notice. Redemption programs also may require that shares be redeemed at a discount, meaning investors lose part of their investment if they redeem their shares.

- **High fees.** Nontraded REITs typically charge high upfront fees to compensate a firm or individual selling the investment and to lower their offering and organizational costs.... In addition to the high upfront fees, nontraded REITs may have significant transaction costs, such as property acquisition fees and asset management fees.
- **Distributions may come from principal.** Investors may be attracted to nontraded REITs by their high distributions, which may be referred to as dividend yields, compared to other investment options, including publicly traded REITs. However, the initial distributions may not represent earnings from operations since nontraded REITs often declare these distributions prior to acquiring significant assets....
- **Lack of share value transparency.** Because nontraded REITs are not publicly traded, there is no market price readily available. Consequently, it can be difficult to determine the value of a share of a nontraded REIT or the performance of your investment. In addition, any share valuation will be based on periodic or annual appraisals of the properties owned by the nontraded REIT, and therefore may not be accurate or timely.[9]

Private Commercial Real Estate Debt

Private commercial real estate debt is held as directly issued commercial mortgages held in funds, commingled vehicles or whole loans (i.e., a single commercial mortgage that has not been securitized), or both. Commercial mortgage loans are mortgage loans for income-producing properties. A commercial mortgage loan is originated either to finance a commercial purchase or to refinance a prior mortgage obligation. The whole loan market, which is largely dominated by insurance companies and banks, is focused on loans between \$10 and \$50 million issued on traditional property types (multifamily, retail, office, and industrial).

A commercial mortgage loan exposes the lender to credit risk. For commercial mortgage loans, the lender relies on the ability of the borrower to repay and has no recourse from the borrower if the payment terms are not satisfied. That is, commercial mortgage loans are nonrecourse loans. As a result, the lender can look only to the income-producing property backing the loan for interest and principal repayment. Because of the credit risk, lenders rely on various measures to assess the credit risk. The two most commonly used measures of potential credit risk are the debt-to-service coverage ratio and the loan-to-value ratio.

The **debt-to-service coverage ratio (DSCR)** measures the ability of the property to generate income to service the loan's obligations relative to the amount of the debt service required. More specifically, this ratio is equal to a property's net operating income (NOI) divided by the debt service. The NOI is equal to the projected rental income reduced

9. SEC, "Investor Bulletin: Non-traded REITs," August 31, 2015, available at http://www.sec.gov/oiea/investor-alerts-bulletins/ib_nontradedreits.html.

by cash operating expenses (adjusted for a replacement reserve). A DCSR that exceeds 1 means that the NOI is sufficient to cover the debt servicing required by the loan. The higher the DSCR, the more likely it is that the borrower will be able to meet debt servicing from the property's cash flow.

As with residential mortgage loans described in chapter 29, the **loan-to-value ratio** (LTV ratio) is a measure of the amount of the loan to the value of the property being financed by the loan. For residential mortgage loans, "value" is either market value or appraised value. For commercial properties, the value of the property is based on the fundamental principles of valuation that we have mentioned throughout this book. The value of an asset is the present value of its expected cash flow. Valuation requires projecting an asset's cash flow and discounting at an appropriate interest rate. For valuing commercial property, the cash flow is the future NOI. A discount rate (a single rate), referred to as the "capitalization rate" and reflecting the risks associated with the cash flow, is then used to compute the present value of the future NOI. Consequently, considerable variation in the estimates of NOI and the appropriate capitalization rate can occur when estimating a property's market value. Thus, investors are often skeptical about estimates of market value and the resulting LTV ratios reported for properties.

For residential mortgage loans, only prepayment penalty mortgages provide some protection for the lender against prepayments. For commercial mortgage loans, call protection can take the following forms: a prepayment lockout, prepayment penalty points, yield maintenance charges, and defeasance.

A **prepayment lockout** is a contractual agreement that prohibits any prepayments during a specified time, called the **lockout period**. The lockout period can be from two to 10 years. After the lockout period, call protection usually comes in the form of either prepayment penalty points or yield maintenance charges.

Prepayment penalty points are predetermined penalties that must be paid by the borrower if the borrower wishes to refinance. For example, 5–4–3–2–1 is a common prepayment penalty point structure. That is, if the borrower wishes to prepay during the first year, the borrower must pay a 5% penalty; in the second year, a 4% penalty would apply, and so on.

A **yield maintenance** charge is designed to make the lender indifferent as to the timing of prepayments. The yield maintenance charge, also called the "make-whole charge," makes it uneconomical to refinance solely to get a lower mortgage rate. The simplest and most restrictive form of yield maintenance charge ("Treasury flat yield maintenance") penalizes the borrower based on the difference between the mortgage coupon and the prevailing Treasury rate.

With **defeasance**, the borrower provides sufficient funds for the servicer to invest in a portfolio of Treasury securities that replicates the cash flows that would exist in the absence of prepayments.

Another feature of commercial mortgage loans is that they are typically **balloon loans, r**equiring substantial principal payment at the end of the loan's term. If the borrower fails to make the balloon payment, the borrower is in default. The lender may extend the loan and in so doing will typically modify the original loan terms. During the workout period for the loan, a higher interest rate will be charged—the default interest rate. The risk that a borrower will not be able to make the balloon payment because the borrower either cannot arrange for refinancing at the balloon payment date or cannot sell the property to generate sufficient funds to pay off the balloon balance is called **balloon risk**. Because the term of the loan will be extended by the lender during the workout period, balloon risk is also referred to as **extension risk**.

Public Commercial Real Estate Debt

Public commercial real estate debt includes such structures as CMBSs and REITs that invest in mortgage debt. The latter are discussed in chapter 32, where we explain that REITs that invest in mortgage debt constitute a small part of the REIT market. Below we describe CMBSs.

In discussions about the CMBS market, participants distinguish between the types of CMBSs issued (i.e., the structure of the transactions, as described below). The pre-global financial crisis is referred to as "CMBS 1.0" and the years to follow as "CMBS 2.0."

Commercial Mortgage-Backed Securities

Many types of commercial loans can be sold by the loan's originator as a commercial whole loan or structured into a CMBS transaction. A CMBS is a security backed by one or more commercial mortgage loans described earlier in this chapter. In CMBSs, loans of virtually any size (from as small as $1 million to single property transactions as large as $200 million) can be securitized.

In the United States, CMBSs, like residential MBSs described in chapter 30, can be issued by Ginnie Mae, Fannie Mae, Freddie Mac, and private entities. All securities issued by Ginnie Mae, Fannie Mae, and Freddie Mac are consistent with their mission of providing funding for residential housing. This includes securities backed by nursing home projects and health care facilities. Securities issued by Ginnie Mae are backed by the FHA—that is, they are insured multifamily housing loans. These loans are called **project loans**. From these loans, Ginnie Mae creates project loan pass-through securities. The securities can be backed by a single project loan on a completed project or by multiple project loans. Freddie Mac and Fannie Mae purchase multifamily housing loans from approved lenders and either retain them in their portfolio or use them for collateral for a security. This is no different from what these two entities do with the single-family housing mortgage loans that they acquire. Although securities backed by Ginnie Mae, Fannie Mac, and Freddie Mac constitute the largest sector of the RMBS market, it is the securities issued by private entities that constitute by far the largest sector of the CMBS market.

CMBSs are backed by either newly originated or seasoned commercial mortgage loans. Most CMBSs are backed by newly originated loans. CMBSs can be classified by the type of loan pool. The first type of CMBS consists of loans backed by a single borrower. Usually such CMBSs are backed by large properties, such as regional malls or office buildings. The investors in this type of CMBS are insurance companies. The second type of CMBS consists of those backed by loans to multiple borrowers. This is the most common type of CMBS and is backed by a variety of property types. The most prevalent form of deal backed by commercial mortgage loans to multiple borrowers is the **conduit deal**. These deals are created by investment banking firms that establish a conduit arrangement with mortgage bankers to originate commercial mortgage loans specifically for the purpose of securitizing them (i.e., of creating CMBSs). The mortgage bankers originate and underwrite loans using the capital provided by the investment banking firm. There are multiple-borrower CMBS deals that combine loans that are included in conduit deals with a large or "mega" loan. These CMBS deals are called **fusion deals** or **hybrid deals**. Fusion deals dominate the U.S. CMBS market and are an important but not dominant sector outside the United States.

In Europe, one of the consequences of the global financial crisis has been the simplification of the transactions by only including a single large commercial loan rather than multiple commercial loans of varying size. An example of a single large loan backing a CMBS is the £263 million issued in July 2013 backed by the retail stores of Toys R Us, a privately owned retailer. (This company declared bankruptcy in September 2017.) The problem in Europe is that a single large loan CMBS is not sustainable, given that there may not be enough issuers of sufficient size to back a CMBS.

CMBS structure We explained in chapter 30 how private-label RMBS transactions are structured to redistribute credit risk. The structure of a CMBS deal is much the same. Different bond classes or tranches are created, and waterfall rules are in place for the distribution of interest, principal, and losses. The structure of a CMBS transaction is the same as for a private-label RMBS in that most structures have multiple bond classes (tranches) with different ratings, and rules exist for the distribution of interest and principal to the bond classes. However, three major differences arise from the features of the underlying loans.[10]

First, as explained earlier when discussing private commercial real estate debt, prepayment terms for commercial mortgages differ significantly from those for residential mortgages. The former imposes prepayment penalties or restrictions on prepayments. Although some residential mortgages have prepayment penalties, they make up a small fraction of the market. When structuring a CMBS, there are rules for the allocation of any prepayment

10. David P. Jacob, James M. Manzi, and Frank J. Fabozzi, "The Impact of Structuring on CMBS Bond Class Performance," in *The Handbook of Mortgage-Backed Securities*, ed. Frank J. Fabozzi, 6th edition (New York: McGraw-Hill, 2006), chapter 6.

penalties among the bondholders. In addition, if defeasance occurs, the credit risk of a CMBS virtually disappears, because it is then backed by U.S. Treasury securities.

The second difference in structuring stems from the significant difference between commercial and residential mortgages with respect to the role of the servicer when a default occurs. With commercial mortgages, the loan can be transferred by the servicer to the "special servicer" when the borrower is in default, in imminent default, or in violation of covenants. The key here is that the loan can be transferred when a default is imminent. The special servicer has the responsibility of modifying the loan terms in the case of an imminent default to reduce the likelihood of default. There is no equivalent feature for a residential mortgage in the case of an imminent default. The particular choice of action that may be taken by the special servicer in a commercial mortgage will generally have different effects on the various bond classes in a CMBS structure. Moreover, a default can occur as a result of failure to make the balloon payment at the end of the loan term, and different loans may have different mechanisms for dealing with such a default. Thus, balloon risk must be taken into account when structuring a CMBS transaction, because the significant size of the balloon payment can have a considerable impact on the cash flow of the structure. Balloon risk is not something that has to be dealt with when structuring an RMBS.

The third difference in structuring between CMBSs and RMBSs has to do with the role of the buyers when the structure is being created. Specifically, for a CMBS, typically potential buyers of the junior bond classes are first sought by the issuer before the deal is structured. The potential buyers review the proposed pool of mortgage loans and in the review process, depending on market demand for CMBS products, may request the removal of some loans from the pool. This phase in the structuring process, which one does not find in RMBS transactions, provides an additional layer of security for the senior buyers, particularly because some of the buyers of the junior classes have tended to be knowledgeable real estate investors.

Illustration of a CMBS deal In chapter 30, we discussed how an agency CMO and a private-label CMO are created. The structure of a CMBS deal is much the same. There are different bond classes or tranches, and there are rules for the distribution of interest, principal, and losses.

Table 31.1 shows the bond classes of a CMBS deal, Banc of America Commercial Mortgage Trust 2006-1. Only the bond classes offered to the public are identified. The credit rating for each bond class is shown. For the bond classes offered, the senior certificates in this CMBS deal are Class A-1, Class A-2, Class A-3A, Class A-3B, Class A-4, Class A-1A, and Class XP Certificates. The junior certificates are Class A-M, Class A-J, Class B, Class C, and Class D. The subordination (credit support), priority of payment, and order of loss allocation as set forth in the prospectus supplement are reproduced in figure 31.1.

The mortgage pool consists of 192 loans. A loan may be for more than one property. The offering documents for the bond classes will disclose the number of mortgage properties

Table 31.1
CMBS deal: Banc of America Commercial Mortgage Trust 2006-1.

Class	Balance ($)	Coupon Rate (%)	Moody/S&P Rating
A-1	81,500,000	5.219	Aaa/AAA
A-2	84,400,000	5.334	Aaa/AAA
A-3A	130,100,000	5.447	Aaa/AAA
A-3B	25,000,000	5.447	Aaa/AAA
A-4	616,500,000	5.372[1]	Aaa/AAA
A-1A	355,399,000	5.378[1]	Aaa/AAA
A-M	203,766,000	5.421[1]	Aaa/AAA
A-J	142,637,000	5.46[1]	Aaa/AAA
XP	1,989,427,000	0.3406[2]	Aaa/AAA
B	20,377,000	5.49[1]	Aa1/AA+
C	22,924,000	5.509[1]	Aa2/AA
D	20,376,000	5.6424[3]	Aa3/AA–

Source: Prospectus Supplement.
[1]The Class A-4, Class A-1A, Class A-M, Class A-J, Class B, and Class C certificates will each accrue interest at a fixed rate subject to a cap at the weighted average net mortgage rate.
[2]The Class D certificates will accrue interest at the weighted average net mortgage rate minus 0.134%.
[3]The Class XP certificates will accrue interest on their related notional amount as described in the prospectus supplement.

by type, as well as the 10 largest loans in the mortgage pool with their LTV ratio and debt-to-service ratio at the time of issuance.

How CMBSs trade in the market One might think that because CMBSs and RMBSs are backed by mortgage loans, they would trade in a similar manner in the marketplace. That is not the case. The primary reason has to do with the greater prepayment protection given to investors in CMBSs compared to RMBSs. We described that protection at the loan level. At the structure level (i.e., when the commercial mortgage loans are pooled to create a CMBS), certain bond classes can be created that give even greater prepayment protection. We described how this is done for certain RMBS tranches in collateralized mortgage obligations. As a result, CMBSs trade much like corporate bonds than RMBS.

Investors in the Commercial Real Estate Market

The 1980s witnessed increased interest in commercial real estate as an asset class by institutional investors. However, the difficulties arising from the crash of property values in the early 1990s led to a massive retreat by institutional investors from this asset class. It took many years to persuade institutional investors that real estate would not fall apart in every recession. With any class asset, there are two components to returns: a cyclical component and a secular component. It was the downturn in the market—a cyclical component—that

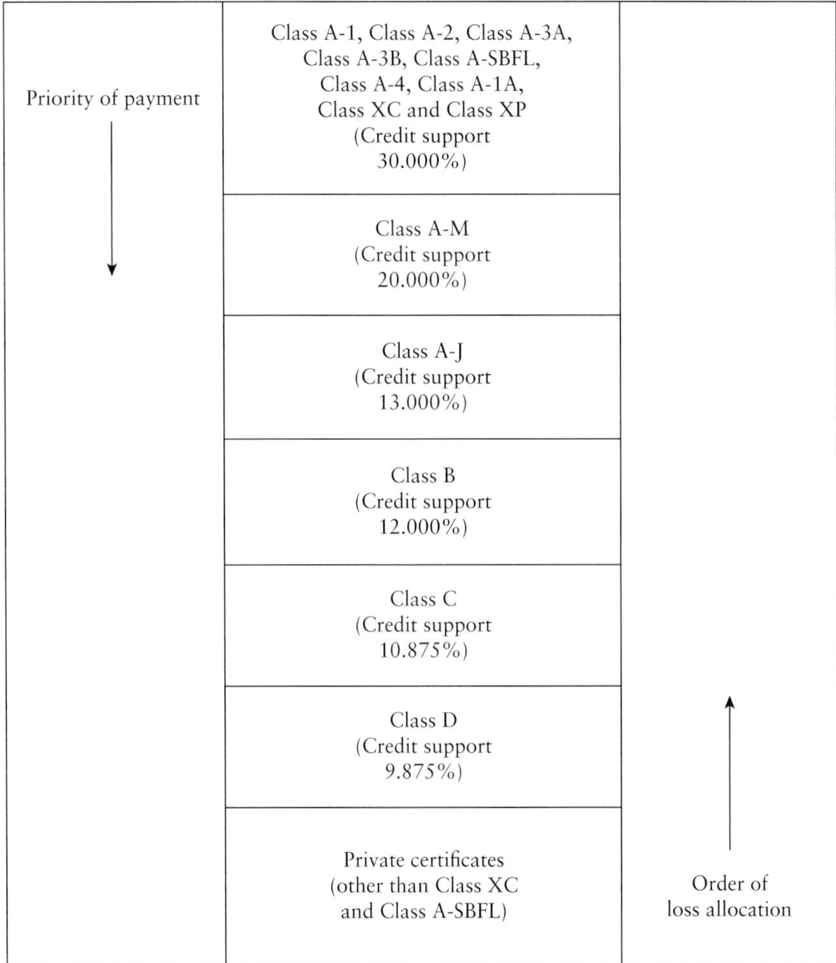

Figure 31.1
Subordination (credit support), priority of payment, and order of loss allocation for Banc of America Commercial Mortgage Trust 2006-1.

scared off institutional investors, resulting in a decline in the allocation to commercial real estate.

Even following the 2008–2009 global financial crisis, institutional investors have not abandoned the asset class due to the acceptance of several of the reasons for investing in commercial real estate discussed earlier in this chapter. In fact, because of the low interest rate environment pursued by governments throughout the world, commercial real estate has become more attractive as a source of relatively steady returns. According to the 2015 investor report by the Pension Real Estate Association, as of year-end 2014, the average allocation to real estate by institutional investors was 8.4% of total assets, representing a slight increase from 2013. The Pension Real Estate Association report notes that allocations substantially higher than the 8.4% are not uncommon for some institutional investors.

Commercial real estate falls into the alternative asset class, along with hedge funds and private equity. According to Towers Watson in its "Global Alternatives Survey 2015," for the top 100 asset managers of alternative assets, real estate constitutes one-third of the total assets under management, making it the largest component of the alternative asset class. Consequently, real estate has now become the "mainstream alternative" alternative asset class.

It has been argued that the pattern of institutional investor commitments to the commercial real estate market is different from that in past cycles.[11] The reasons for the change in the expected pattern of institutional investors' commitment to the global commercial real estate market are due to how investors have behaved and how the underlying fundamentals have behaved. The changes from past cycles in the real estate market reflect new trends that are likely to continue and accelerate in the future.

In the years that followed the global financial crisis, the commercial real estate market has attracted significant inflows of capital from two major sources. Motivated by low interest rates available in global market, pension funds, foundations, and endowments, the first source was traditional institutional investors in real estate, who in their search for yield, have increased their allocation to real estate. The second major source is the entrance into the real estate market of nontraditional institutional investors. Some of these new institutional investors have already become important participants in the market, exerting a significant impact on commercial property values and real estate returns. Although other nontraditional institutional investors are now participating in the real estate market, they are still in the early stages of participation. Yet these new market participants may potentially have a major impact on the market.

A particularly important investor that is relatively new to real estate is that of sovereign wealth funds (SWFs). SWFs represent a large and rapidly growing capital pool. According to data from Preqin (a company providing alterative asset data),[12] as well one study by the International Monetary Fund,[13] overall assets under management have increased from $3.07 trillion at the end of 2008 to $6.31 trillion in May 2015. According to Preqin, 59% of SWFs invest in the real estate market. However, for the larger SWFs, the percentage is much higher, with 100% of SWFs larger than $100 billion investing in real estate. SWFs

11. See Jim Clayton, Frank J. Fabozzi, S. Michael Giliberto, Jacques N. Gordon, Youguo Liang, Greg MacKinnon, and Asieh Mansour, "New Horizons and Familiar Landscapes: New Capital Sources Confront Shifting Real Estate Fundamentals," *Journal of Portfolio Management* 41, no. 5 (Special Real Estate Issue, 2015): 11–20.

12. Preqin, "2015 Preqin Global Real Estate Report," 2015.

13. A. Al-Hassan, M. Papaioannon, M. Skanke, and C. C. Sung, "Sovereign Wealth Funds: Aspects of Governance Structures and Investment Management," IMF Working Paper 13-231 (Washington, DC: International Monetary Fund, 2013).

have been investors in real estate markets globally, and they have made their presence felt in a major way. The attraction of the real estate market for SWFs is that they typically have long-term wealth preservation as an investment objective and have few near-term liabilities. As a result, certain types of real estate are a good match for their investment objectives. Because of both the large capital pool and the long investment horizons of SWFs, it is felt that their participation in the market will greatly impact the real estate market.

Another major change in the real estate market is the growth in cross-border transactions. In dollar volume, cross-border transactions have increased steadily since 2009. In 2014, there were $327 billion of cross-border real estate transactions. This level of cross-border transactions represented 46% of total volume for 2014. The increase in cross-border capital flows can have an important impact on markets. It has been argued that the influx of foreign capital has increased property values in major real estate markets throughout the world, resulting in lower returns.[14]

Our discussion thus far has been on the impact on the real estate market of the participation of nontraditional institutional investors as new sources of capital that is likely to continue to grow in influence. However, some market observers believe it may be small investors who will create the largest changes in the commercial property market. Individual (retail) investors are able to access the private market for private equity real estate via one or more of collective vehicles described in chapter 32. These alternatives for individual investors are relatively new. It is argued that because individual investors may have different investment objectives and constraints (such as liquidity) for their real estate investments than traditional institutional investors, individual investors could alter not only the demand for real estate but also the characteristics of the market in the long term.

Key Points

- Commercial mortgage loans are nonrecourse loans for the purchase of income-producing properties.
- The major commercial property types are multifamily housing, apartment buildings, office buildings, industrial properties (including warehouses), shopping centers, hotels, health care facilities (e.g., senior housing care facilities), and timberlands.
- Today commercial real estate investments include four categories: (1) private commercial real estate equity, (2) public commercial real estate equity, (2) private commercial real estate debt, and (4) public commercial real estate debt.
- The primary reasons that have been offered for considering commercial real estate as part of a portfolio are to (1) reduce portfolio risk in a diversified portfolio, (2) generate absolute

14. The first study empirically supporting this view for the office sector is Patrick McAllister and Anupam Nanda, "Does Foreign Investment Affect U.S. Office Real Estate Prices?" *Journal of Portfolio Management* 41, no. 5 (Special Real Estate Issue, 2015): 38–47.

returns in excess of the risk-free rate, (3) hedge against unexpected inflation or deflation, (4) constitute a part of a portfolio that is a reasonable reflection of the overall investment universe, and (5) generate strong cash flows to the portfolio.

- Studies that have examined whether commercial real estate provides high absolute returns or high risk-adjusted returns do not support this reason for investing in this asset class.
- Private commercial real estate equity is held by investors as individual assets or in commingled vehicles, such as private REITs.
- Most countries have one or more property indexes.
- Public commercial real estate equity is structured as real estate investment trusts or real estate operating companies, both entities issuing shares to the public that are traded on an exchange.
- Many developed and developing countries have legislation allowing for the creation of a REIT.
- Equity REITs can be classified as diversified REITs, sector REITs, and specialty REITs.
- Public nontraded REITs are structured in the same way as traditional REITs but are not traded on a public exchange and have the following issues: lack of liquidity, high fees, and lack of share value transparency.
- Private commercial real estate debt is held as directly issued commercial mortgages held in funds, commingled vehicles or whole loans (i.e., single commercial mortgage that has not been securitized), or both.
- Commercial mortgage loans are nonrecourse mortgage loans for income-producing properties that expose the lender to credit risk.
- The two measures that have been found to be key indicators of the potential credit performance of a commercial mortgage loan are the debt-to-service ratio and the LTV ratio.
- Call protection for commercial mortgage loans includes prepayment lockout, defeasance, prepayment penalty points, and yield maintenance charges.
- Public commercial real estate debt includes such structures as CMBSs and REITs that invest in mortgage debt.
- CMBSs are backed by commercial mortgage loans with the deal backed by either loans to a single borrower, loans to multiple borrowers (called "conduit deals"), or a combination of loans that are included in conduit deals with a large or "mega" loan (called "fusion" or "hybrid" deals).
- Fusion-type deals dominate the U.S. CMBS market; in Europe, CMBSs are predominately backed by a single large commercial loan.
- CMBSs are structured to redistribute the credit risk among the bond classes in the deal.

- Despite the 2008–2009 global financial crisis, allocation of institutional investor portfolios to the commercial real estate market has increased, with new entrants, such as sovereign wealth funds, entering the market.
- Commercial real estate is the largest type of alternative asset in which institutional investors allocate funds.

Questions

1. What is the rationale for categorizing the commercial real estate market into four categories?

2. The following quote is taken from a September 2011 report by Morningstar regarding the performance of commercial real estate through publicly traded equity REITs and private equity real estate funds:

> The actual performance records now available reveal that publicly traded equity REITs provide a significant investment return premium compared with private equity real estate funds, as well as other public market attributes of liquidity, transparency, monitoring and access to public debt and equity financing.[15]

Explain what is meant by "as well as other public attributes."

3. The following statement is taken from a June 2012 Merrill Lynch publication:

> Real estate has historically displayed low or negative correlations to other major asset classes, providing investors with valuable diversification benefits that can work to improve an investor's efficient frontier.[16]

Explain this quote.

4. The following statement is from an online article by Rick Ferri:

> REITs have a positive real expected return due to a combination of rental income and income growth. Landlords pass inflation increases to tenants based on a general level of price increases and this gives real estate owners a built-in inflation hedge. The value of real estate eventually reflects higher rents through higher prices.[17]

Explain whether you agree or disagree with this statement.

5. Explain how retail investors can obtain exposure to the commercial real estate equity market.

6. How does a real estate operating company differ from a REIT?

15. "Commercial Real Estate Investment: REITs and Private Equity Real Estate Funds," Morningstar, September 2011.

16. James D. Bowden and Michael R. Smith, "Commercial Real Estate," Merrill Lynch, June 2012.

17. Rick Ferri, "REITS and Your Portfolio," *Forbes,* January 7, 2014. https://www.forbes.com/sites/rickferri/2014/01/07/reits-and-your-portfolio/#1cc300a771ac.

7. What is a commercial mortgage loan?

8. How is the net operating income of a commercial property determined?

9. Why might an investor be skeptical about the LTV ratio for a commercial mortgage loan?

10. What types of prepayment protection provisions result in a prepayment premium being paid if a borrower prepays?

11. Why is balloon risk referred to as "extension risk"?

12. What are the major differences in structuring CMBS and RMBS transactions?

13. How does the typical CMBS in the United States differ from that in Europe?

14. Why do CMBSs trade in the market more like corporate bonds than RMBSs?

15. The following quote is from Jim Clayton et al.:

> Although the continued and increased commitment to real estate of the traditional institutional investor base has contributed to capital flows, helping propel property values, perhaps even more important for the future of the asset class has been the rising importance over the last several years of the second major source of capital inflows: capital sources that have not traditionally been involved in real estate.[18]

a. What institutional investors comprise the traditional investors in the commercial real estate market?

b. What is the second source of commercial real estate investors?

16. Why does the pattern of institutional investor commitments to the commercial real estate market differ now from that in past real estate cycles?

17. Some observers believe it may be individual (retail) investors who in the future may create the largest changes in the commercial property market. Why?

18. Jim Clayton, Frank J. Fabozzi, S. Michael Giliberto, Jacques N. Gordon, Youguo Liang, Greg MacKinnon, and Asieh Mansour, "New Horizons and Familiar Landscapes: New Capital Sources Confront Shifting Real Estate Fundamentals," *Journal of Portfolio Management* 41, no. 6 (Special Real Estate Issue, 2015): 12.

VIII COLLECTIVE INVESTMENT VEHICLES AND FINANCIAL DERIVATIVES MARKETS

32 Market for Collective Investment Vehicles

CONTENTS

Learning Objectives

After reading this chapter, you will understand:

- the benefits of collective investment vehicles;
- what an investment company is, and the different types of investment companies that are registered investment vehicles: open-end funds (mutual funds) and closed-end funds;
- how net asset value is calculated;
- how the share prices of investment companies are determined;
- how investment companies differ depending on their investment objectives;
- what exchange-traded funds (ETFs) are;
- the similarities of and differences between ETFs and closed-end funds;
- how ETF shares are created and redeemed;
- the use of ETF shares by investors;
- what a hedge fund is, and the different types of hedge funds;
- the attributes of hedge funds;
- concerns about hedge funds;
- the three types of REITs: equity, mortgage, and hybrid;
- the tax advantages of REITs;
- what a venture capital firm is, and the role it plays for startup companies;
- the stages involved in a venture capital firm creating a venture capital fund; and
- the capital commitment made by investors in a venture capital fund.

Collective investment vehicles are products that are managed by asset management firms. These investment vehicles involve the pooling of funds by investors and the investment of those funds in certain financial assets. The investors then have an equity interest in the net assets (i.e., assets minus liabilities) of the fund's portfolio. In general, the advantages associated with investing by means of pooled funds rather than directly in financial assets are obtaining superior portfolio diversification, achieving better liquidity, and acquiring the expertise of professional asset management. Asset management firms receive compensation in the form of a management fee and, with some collective investment vehicles, additional compensation based on performance, which is referred to as an "incentive fee."

The major collective investment vehicles covered in this chapter are investment company shares, exchange-traded funds, hedge funds, real estate investment trusts (REITs), and venture capital funds.

Investment Company Shares

Investment companies are financial intermediaries that sell shares to the public and invest the proceeds in a diversified portfolio of financial assets. Each share represents a proportional interest in the net assets in which the funds are invested.

The primary U.S. regulator of investment companies is the Securities and Exchange Commission (SEC), and the Investment Company Act of 1940 is the primary legislation governing their regulation. The definition of what constitutes an investment company given in the 1940 act is "as an issuer which is or holds itself out as being engaged primarily, or proposes to engage primarily, in the business of investing, reinvesting or trading in 'securities.'" Pooled investment vehicles satisfying the definition of an investment company under the federal securities law must be registered. Hence investment companies are technically called **registered investment companies** (RICs).

The 1940 act classifies investment companies as management companies, unit investment trusts, or face amount of certificate companies. Our focus in this chapter is on management companies. This category of investment company is typically structured as either a corporation or a trust, with a board of directors (or trustees) to monitor the management of the investment company. The operation of the management company is undertaken by an investment adviser, which is typically a separate entity that is registered with the SEC.

Management companies are divided into open-end companies and closed-end companies. They are more commonly referred to as open-end and closed-end "funds." Although both types of management companies are popularly referred to as "mutual funds," technically, only open-end funds are mutual funds.

Open-End Funds

Open-end funds, commonly referred to simply as **mutual funds**, are portfolios of securities—mainly stocks, bonds, and money market instruments. Investors in mutual funds own a pro rata share of the overall portfolio, which is managed by the fund's investment manager, who buys and sells securities.

Additionally, the value or price of each share of the portfolio, called the **net asset value** (NAV), equals the market value of the portfolio minus the liabilities of the mutual fund divided by the number of shares owned by the fund's investors:

$$\text{NAV} = \frac{\text{Market value of portfolio} - \text{Liabilities}}{\text{Number of shares outstanding}}.$$

For example, suppose that a mutual fund with 10 million shares outstanding has a portfolio with a market value of \$215 million and liabilities of \$15 million. The NAV is

$$\text{NAV} = \frac{\$215{,}000{,}000 - \$15{,}000{,}000}{10{,}000{,}000} = \$20.00.$$

The mutual fund's NAV or price of the fund is determined only once each day, at the close of the day. For example, the NAV for a stock mutual fund is determined from the closing stock prices for the day. Finally, all new investments into the mutual fund or withdrawals from the fund during the day are priced at the closing NAV (investments made after the end of the day or on a nonbusiness day are priced at the next day's closing NAV).

The total number of shares in a mutual fund increases if more investments than withdrawals are made during the day. For example, assume that at the beginning of a day, the market value of a mutual fund's portfolio is $1 million, with no liabilities, and 10,000 shares are outstanding. Thus, the NAV for this mutual fund is $100. Assume that during the day, investors deposit $5,000 into the fund and withdraw $1,000 from it, and the prices of all the securities in the portfolio remain constant. These transactions mean that 50 shares were issued for the $5,000 deposited (because each share is valued at $100), and 10 shares were redeemed for $1,000. The net number of new shares issued equals 40. Therefore, at the end of the day the fund contains 10,040 shares, with a market value for the portfolio of $1,004,000. The NAV remains $100.

If instead the prices of the securities in the portfolio change, both the total market value of the portfolio and, therefore, the NAV will change. In the previous example, assume that during the day, the market value of the portfolio doubles to $2 million. Because deposits and withdrawals are priced at the end-of-day NAV, which is now $200 (after the doubling of the portfolio's market value), the $5,000 deposit will purchase 25 shares ($5,000/$200), and the $1,000 withdrawn will reduce the number of shares outstanding by 5 shares ($1,000/$200). Thus, at the end of the day, the mutual fund has 10,020 shares outstanding (10,000 shares initially + 25 shares − 5 shares) with an NAV of $200, and the market value of the portfolio is $2,004,000. (Note that 10,020 shares × $200 NAV = $2,004,000, the portfolio value.)

Overall, a mutual fund's NAV increases or decreases as a result of an increase or decrease in the price of the securities in the portfolio. The number of shares issued increases or decreases as a result of the net deposits into and withdrawals from the fund. The market value of the fund's portfolio will increase or decrease for both reasons.

Closed-End Funds

The shares of a **closed-end fund** (CEF) are similar to those of common stock of a corporation. The new shares of a CEF are initially issued by an underwriter, and after their issuance, the number of shares remains constant. That is, after the initial issue, no sales or purchases of CEF shares are made by the fund's portfolio manager as with open-end mutual funds. Instead, the shares are traded on a secondary market, either on an exchange or in the over-the-counter market.

Investors can buy shares at the time of the initial issue or on the secondary market. Shares are sold only on the secondary market. The price of a share of a CEF is determined by the supply and demand in the market in which the fund shares are traded. Thus, investors who transact CEF shares must pay a brokerage commission at the time of purchase and at the time of sale.

The NAV of CEFs is calculated in the same way as for mutual funds. However, the price of a share in a CEF is determined by supply and demand, so the price can fall below or rise above the NAV per share. Shares selling below NAV are said to be "trading at a discount," whereas shares trading above NAV are trading at a premium.

Consequently, two important attributes distinguish open-end mutual funds from CEFs. First, the number of shares of a mutual fund varies, because the fund sponsor sells new shares to investors and buys existing shares from shareholders. Second, consequently, the share price is always the mutual fund's NAV. In contrast, a CEF has a constant number of shares outstanding, because the fund sponsor does not redeem shares and sell new shares to investors except at the time of a new underwriting. Thus, supply and demand in the market determine the price of the CEF shares, which may be greater than or less than the NAV.

Although the divergence of the share price from the NAV is often puzzling, in some cases, the reasons for the premium or discount are easily understood. For example, a share's price may be below the NAV because of the CEF's large built-in tax liabilities and because investors discount the share's price for that future tax liability. (This tax liability issue is discussed later in the chapter.) A CEF's leverage and resulting risk may be another reason for the share price of a CEF to trade below NAV. A fund's shares may trade at a premium to the NAV, because the fund offers relatively cheap access to, and professional management of, stocks of another country, about which information is not readily available to small investors.

The relatively new exchange-traded funds (ETFs), which are discussed later in this chapter, pose a threat to the growth of both open-end mutual funds and CEFs. ETFs are essentially hybrid CEFs that trade on exchanges but typically trade very close to NAV. Because CEF shares are traded like stocks, the cost to any investor of buying or selling a CEF is the same as that of buying or selling a stock. The obvious charge is the stockbroker's commission. The bid-ask spread of the market in which the stock is traded is also a cost.

Fund Sales Charges and Annual Operating Expenses

Investors in mutual funds bear two types of costs. The first is the **shareholder fee**, usually called the **sales charge**. This cost is a "one-time" charge debited to the investor for a specific transaction, such as a purchase, redemption, or exchange. The type of charge is related to the way the fund is sold or distributed. The second cost is the annual fund operating expense, usually called the **expense ratio**, which covers the fund's expenses, the largest of which is for investment management. This charge is imposed annually and occurs for all funds and for all types of distribution.

Sales charge Sales charges on open-end mutual funds are related to their method of distribution. The two types of distribution are through a sales force (or wholesale) and direct.

Sales force (wholesale) distribution occurs through an intermediary, such as an agent, a stockbroker, an insurance agent, or other entity providing investment advice and incentive to the client. Such an entity actively "makes the sale" and provides subsequent service. The other approach is **direct distribution**, or distribution from the mutual fund company to the investor. The client approaches the mutual fund company (most likely by a toll-free telephone number or website) in response to media advertisements or general information and opens the account. Little or no investment counsel or service is provided either initially or subsequently.

For the service provided in the sales force distribution method, the customer bears a sales charge paid to the agent. The sales charge is called a **load**. The traditional type of load is called a **front-end load**, because the load is deducted at the time the purchase is made, or "up front." That is, the load is subtracted from the amount invested by the client and paid to the agent/distributor. Directly purchased mutual funds require no intermediary sales agent and therefore infrequently carry a sales charge. Funds with no sales charge are called **no-load mutual funds**.

Recent adaptations of the sales load are back-end loads and level loads. Front-end loads are imposed at the time of the purchase of the fund, but the **back-end load** is imposed at the time fund shares are sold or redeemed. **Level loads** are assessed uniformly each year. These two alternative methods both provide ways to compensate the agent. However, unlike the front-end load, both of these distribution mechanisms permit the client to buy a fund at NAV, that is, not have any of the initial investment debited as a sales charge before it is invested in the shareholder's account. The most common type of back-end load currently is the **contingent deferred sales charge**. In this approach, a gradually declining load is imposed on withdrawals. For example, a common 3–3–2–2–1–1–0 contingent deferred sales charge approach imposes a 3% load on the amount withdrawn after one year, a 3% load on the amount withdrawn after the second year, a 2% on the amount withdrawn after the third year, and so on. No sales charge for withdrawals applies after the seventh year.

Another type of load is neither a front-end load at the time of investment nor a (gradually declining) back-end load at the time of withdrawal but a constant load each year (e.g., a 1% load every year).This approach is called a **level load**. This type of load appeals to financial planners who charge annual fees rather than commissions, such as sales charges.

Many mutual fund families offer their funds with all three types of loads—that is, front-end loads (these fund shares are usually called "A shares"), back-end loads (called "B shares"), and level loads ("C shares")—and permit the distributor and its client, the investor, to select the type of load they prefer.

The sales charge is, in effect, paid by the client to the distributor. How does the fund family (typically called the "sponsor" or "manufacturer" of the fund) cover its costs and make a profit? This second type of cost to the investor covers the fund's annual operating expenses.

Annual operating expenses (expense ratio) The **operating expense**, also called the **expense ratio**, is debited annually from the investor's fund balance by the fund sponsor. The three main categories of annual operating expenses are the management fee, the distribution fee, and other expenses.

The **management fee**, also called the **investment advisory fee**, is charged by the investment adviser for managing a fund's portfolio. If the investment adviser works for a company that is separate from the fund sponsor, some or all of this investment advisory fee is passed on to the investment adviser by the fund sponsor. In this case, the fund manager is called a **subadviser**. The management fee varies by the type of fund, and specifically with the difficulty of managing the fund.

The management fee is typically a fixed fee based solely on the market value of the fund's assets. The fee structure for managing some mutual funds is on a sliding scale, with the fee declining with the market value of the fund's assets. A few mutual funds have adopted performance-based fees, which specify that if the quarterly performance is good, the fund manager receives a fee, and if it is not, the fee is waived for the quarter.

In 1980, the SEC approved the imposition of a fixed annual fee, called the **12b-1 fee**, which is, in general, intended to cover distribution costs, including continuing agent compensation and manufacturer marketing and advertising expenses. Such 12b-1 fees are now imposed by many mutual funds. By law, 12b-1 fees cannot exceed 1% of the fund's assets per year. The 12b-1 fee may include a service fee of up to 0.25% of assets per year to compensate sales professionals for providing services or maintaining shareholder accounts. The major rationale for the component of the 12b-1 fee that accrues to the selling agent is to provide an incentive to selling agents to continue to service their accounts after they receive a transaction-based fee, such as a front-end load. As a result, a 12b-1 fee of this type is consistent with sales-force-sold load funds, not with no-load funds sold directly to the investor. The rationale for the component of the 12b-1 fee that accrues to the manufacturer of the fund is to provide incentive and compensate for continuing advertising and marketing costs.

Other expenses include primarily the costs of (1) custody (holding the cash and securities of the fund), (2) the transfer agent's activities (transferring cash and securities among buyers and sellers of the securities, making fund distributions, etc.), (3) the independent public accountant's fees, and (4) directors' fees.

The sum of the annual management fee, the annual distribution fee, and other annual expenses is called the "expense ratio." All the cost information on a fund, including sales charges and annual expenses, are included in the fund's prospectus.

Economic Motivation for Funds

In chapter 3, we noted that financial intermediaries obtain funds by issuing financial claims against themselves and then investing these funds. An investment company is a financial intermediary in that it pools the funds of individual investors and uses these funds to buy portfolios of securities. We also noted the special role in financial markets played by financial intermediaries. Financial intermediaries provide some or all of the following six economic functions: (1) risk reduction through diversification, (2) lower costs of contracting and processing information, (3) professional portfolio management, (4) liquidity, (5) variety, and (6) a payments mechanism. Let's consider these economic functions as provided by mutual funds.

First is the function of risk reduction through diversification. By investing in a fund, an investor can obtain broad-based ownership of a sufficient number of securities to reduce portfolio risk. (We are more specific about the type of risk that is reduced in chapter 10.) Although an individual investor may be able to acquire a broad-based portfolio of securities, the degree of diversification will be limited by the amount available to invest. By investing in an investment company, however, an investor can effectively achieve the benefits of diversification at a lower cost, even if the amount of money available to invest is not large.

The second economic function is the reduced cost of contracting and processing information, because an investor purchases the services of a presumably skilled financial adviser at less cost than if the investor were to directly and individually negotiate with such an adviser. The advisory fee is lower because of the larger size of assets managed, as well as the reduced costs of searching for an investment manager and obtaining information about the securities. Also, the costs of transacting in the securities are reduced, because a fund is better able to negotiate transaction costs, and custodial fees and record-keeping costs are less for a fund than for an individual investor. For these reasons, investment management enjoys economies of scale relative to those benefits that can accrue to individual investors.

Third, and related to the first two advantages, is the advantage of professional management of the mutual fund. The fourth advantage is liquidity. Mutual funds can be bought or liquidated any day at the closing NAV. The fifth advantage is the variety of funds available in general, and even in one particular family of funds. Finally, money market funds and some other types of funds provide payment services by allowing investors to write checks drawn on the fund, although this facility may be limited in various ways.

Types of Funds by Investment Objective

Mutual funds developed out of a need to satisfy the various investment objectives of investors. In general, in the main categories—stock funds, bond funds, money market funds, and others—several subcategories of funds exist. Other funds are U.S. only, international (no U.S. securities), or global (both U.S. and international securities). Still other funds are considered passive or active funds. **Passive** (or **indexed**) **funds** are designed to replicate an index, such as the S&P 500 stock index, the Barclays Capital Aggregate Bond Index, or the Morgan Stanley Capital International EAFE (Europe, Australasia, and Far East) Index. These funds are **beta products**. In contrast, **Active funds** attempt to outperform an index and other funds by actively trading the fund portfolio and are therefore alpha products. The objective of numerous other categories of funds is stated in the specific fund's prospectus, as required by the SEC and the Investment Company Act of 1940.

Stock funds differ in the following ways:

- the average market capitalization ("market cap": divided into large, mid, and small) of the stocks in the portfolio;
- style (growth, value, blend, and other); and
- sector specialization, such as technology, health care, or utilities.

With respect to style, stocks with high price-to-book and price-to-earnings ratios are considered growth stocks, and stocks with low price-to-value and price-to-earnings ratios are considered value stocks, although other variables are also considered. Some styles can be considered blend stocks.

Bond funds differ by the creditworthiness of the issuers of the bonds in the portfolio (e.g., U.S. government, investment-grade corporate, high-yield corporate) and by the maturity (or duration) of the bonds (long, intermediate, short). Another category of bond funds, called "municipal bond funds," offers tax-exempt coupon interest. These funds may also be single-state bond funds (i.e., all the bonds in the portfolio were issued by issuers in the same state) or multistate.

Asset allocation, hybrid, or balanced funds all hold both stocks and bonds. Convertible bond funds provide another option for investors.

A category of money market funds with maturities of one year or less provides protection against interest rate fluctuations. These funds may have some degree of credit risk, except for the U.S. government money market category. Most of these funds offer check-writing privileges. In addition to taxable money market funds, tax-exempt municipal money market funds are available as well.

Among the other fund offerings are index funds and funds of funds. Index funds, as already discussed, attempt to passively replicate an index. A **fund of funds** invests in other mutual funds in the same fund family.

Several organizations provide data on mutual funds. The most popular ones are Morningstar and Lipper, which provide data on fund expenses, portfolio managers, fund sizes, and fund holdings. But, perhaps most important, they provide performance (i.e., rate of return) data and fund rankings based on performance and other factors. To compare fund performance on an "apples-to-apples" basis, these firms divide mutual funds into several categories intended to be fairly homogeneous by investment objective. The categories provided by Morningstar and Lipper are similar but not identical. Mutual fund data are also provided by the Investment Company Institute, the national association for mutual funds.

The Concept of a Family of Funds

A concept that revolutionized the fund industry and benefited many investors is what the mutual fund industry calls a **family of funds**, a group of funds or a complex of funds. Many fund management companies offer investors a choice of numerous funds with different investment objectives in the same fund family. In many cases, with a phone call, investors may move their assets from one fund to another in the family at little or no cost. Of course, if these funds are in a taxable account, tax consequences may accompany the sale. Although the same policies regarding loads and other costs may apply to all members of the family, a management company may have different fee structures for transfers among different funds under its control.

Large fund families usually include money market funds; U.S. bond funds of several types; global stock and bond funds; broadly diversified U.S. stock funds; U.S. stock funds that specialize by market capitalization and style; and stock funds devoted to particular sectors, such as health care, technology, or precious minerals companies. According to Morningstar, the 10 largest mutual fund families are American Funds, BlackRock Inc., Columbia Management, Fidelity Investments, Franklin Templeton Investments, Oppenheimer Funds, Pacific Investment Management Co. (PIMCO), T. Rowe Price, J.P. Morgan, and the Vanguard Group. Fund families may also use external investment advisers along with internal advisers in their fund families.

Taxation of RICs RICs must distribute at least 90% of their net investment income earned (bond coupons and stock dividends) exclusive of realized capital gains or losses to shareholders (along with meeting other criteria) to qualify as a RIC; as such, they are not required to pay taxes at the fund level prior to distributions to shareholders. Consequently, funds make these distributions. Taxes on distributions are paid only at the investor level, not the fund level. Even though many investors in RICs choose to reinvest these distributions, the distributions are taxable to the investor, either as ordinary income or as capital gains (long term or short term), whichever is relevant.

Capital gains distributions must occur annually, and typically occur late in the calendar year. The capital gains distributions may be either long- or short-term capital gains, depending on whether the fund held the security for a year or more. Investors have no control over the size of these distributions, and as a result, the timing and amount of taxes paid on their fund holdings are largely out of their control. In particular, withdrawals by some investors may necessitate sales in the fund, which in turn cause realized capital gains and a tax liability to accrue to investors who maintain their holdings.

New investors in the fund may assume a tax liability even though they realize no gains. All shareholders as of the record date receive a full year's worth of dividends and capital gains distributions, even if they have owned shares for only one day. This lack of control over capital gains taxes is regarded as a major limitation of investing in RICs. In fact, this adverse tax consequence is one of the reasons suggested for a CEF's price falling below par value. Also, this adverse tax consequence is one reason for the popularity of ETFs, discussed next.

Of course, the investor must also pay ordinary income taxes on distributions of income. Finally, when investors in the fund sell their shares, they realize long- or short-term capital gains or losses, depending on whether they have held the fund for at least a year.

ETFs

Open-end mutual funds are often criticized for three reasons. First, the fund shares are priced at, and can be transacted only at, the end-of-day or closing price. Specifically, transactions—purchases and sales—cannot be made at intraday prices but only at closing prices. The second criticism relates to taxes and the investors' control over taxes. As noted earlier, withdrawals by some fund shareholders may cause taxable realized capital gains for shareholders who maintain their positions. Finally, it has been argued that the fees charged by asset managers are excessive.

In 1993, a new investment vehicle with many of the same features as open-end mutual funds but that responded to two of the three criticisms was introduced.[1] This investment vehicle, called an **exchange-traded fund**, is a fund that is similar to mutual funds but that trades like stocks on an exchange. ETFs are, in a sense, similar to CEFs, which have small premiums or discounts from their NAVs. They offer investors beta (passive) instruments for obtaining exposure to asset classes and market sectors that previously could not be accessed easily. As of August 25, 2017, Morningstar tracked ETFs that had total market assets of about $3 trillion. By far the largest asset class for ETFs was for equity, which was almost $2.4 trillion.

Every ETF is based on a benchmark index. For the first generation of ETFs, the portfolio manager responsible for the ETF sought to match the performance of the benchmark index by purchasing securities and using the derivative instruments described in chapter 23. Thus, the portfolio manager of the ETF seeks the same total return for the ETF as the that for the index. The second generation of ETFs—and by far a smaller segment of ETF market—consists of actively managed ETFs, where the investment objective of the ETF's portfolio manager is to outperform the benchmark index.

Because ETFs are traded on an exchange, an ETF's share price is determined by the market forces of supply and demand. ETF shares can be purchased on margin, can be sold short, and use the types of orders that are available for taking a position in stocks (such as stop orders and limit orders). There are even derivative futures and options for which an ETF is the underlying instrument. (We discuss these in chapter 33.)

As with a CEF, the forces of supply and demand can cause the ETF's market price to deviate from its NAV. If executed properly, deviations between the ETF's NAV and its market price will be small. This is because arbitrageurs, referred to as **authorized participants**, can create or redeem large blocks of shares on any day at NAV, significantly limiting the deviations. We'll describe the key role of authorized participants shortly.

A second major distinction between open-end mutual funds and ETFs relates to taxation. For both open-end mutual funds and ETFs, dividend income and capital gains realized when the mutual fund or ETF is sold are taxable to the investor. But, in addition, in the case

1. Although in this chapter, we are treating an ETF as a different investment vehicle from an open-end mutual fund, technically an ETF is considered a RIC under the federal securities law.

of redemptions, open-end mutual funds may have to sell securities (if the cash position is not sufficient to fund the redemptions), thus causing a capital gain or loss for those who held their shares. In contrast, ETFs do not have to sell portfolio securities, because redemptions are effected by an in-kind exchange of the ETF shares for a basket of the underlying portfolio securities. This exchange is not a taxable event to investors under the U.S. tax code. Therefore, investors in ETFs are subject to significant capital gains taxes only when they sell their ETF shares (at a price above the original purchase price). However, ETFs do distribute cash dividends and may distribute a limited amount of realized capital gains, and these distributions are taxable. Overall, ETFs, like index mutual funds, avoid realized capital gains and the taxation thereof through their low portfolio turnover. But unlike index mutual funds (or other funds, for that matter), they do not cause potentially large capital gains tax liabilities that accrue to those who held their positions to meet shareholder redemptions because of the unique way in which they are redeemed.

Finally, the expense ratio for an ETF is generally less than that for a CEF or open-end mutual fund that has the same benchmark index. This is because ETFs are passively managed, unlike most CEFs and open-end mutual funds. Moreover, because of their low portfolio turnover (because most are passively managed), ETFs typically have lower portfolio trading costs than do CEFs or mutual funds.

Types of ETFs and ETF Sponsors

When ETFs were first introduced into the U.S. financial market, in 1993, and for several years thereafter, the types of ETFs available were all based on U.S. stock indexes and international stock market indexes.[2] The first ETF in the United States was the Standard & Poor's Depositary Receipts (SPDRs, pronounced "spiders"), an index fund that was designed to track the performance of the S&P 500 stock index. An ETF that followed was designed to track subsectors of the S&P 500, the Mid-Cap SPDRs. Other ETFs based on other U.S. stock indexes were then introduced. These included Diamonds, which track the Dow Jones Industrial Average and is sponsored by State Street Global Investors, and QQQs, designed to track the NASDAQ 100 index.

Today, there are numerous ETF products designed to track not only stock market indexes but also customized stock market benchmarks and indexes for other asset classes. In fact, Yahoo Finance maintains a website dedicated to ETFs, called the "ETF Center."[3] The ETF Center allows an investor to search for ETFs based on different criteria and by fund family.[4]

2. The first ETFs were the Toronto Stock Exchange Index Participations, listed on the Toronto Stock Exchange, which were designed to track the TSE 35 Index and later to track the TSE 100 Index.

3. See the web page http://finance.yahoo.com/etf.

4. See the web page http://finance.yahoo.com/etf/lists/?mod_id=mediaquotesetf & tab=tab5rcnt=50.

As with open-end mutual funds and CEFs, there are actively and passively managed ETFs. Most mutual funds and CEFs are actively managed. In contrast, in the ETF world, most are passively managed. Obviously, the ETFs that are actively managed have a higher cost structure. Consequently, ETFs provide investors with alpha products.

The Process of Creating and Redeeming ETF Shares

The objective of an ETF is for the performance of the portfolio of securities to be as close as possible to that of the target index. That is, the ETF portfolio's NAV should deviate as little as possible from that of its market price. This can only be accomplished with the intervention of a third party that is charged with the responsibility of arbitraging any discrepancy between the ETF's NAV and the share price.

The following is an explanation of the arbitrage process that the agent follows in two different scenarios:

1. Scenario 1: The ETF's share price exceeds the ETF portfolio's NAV (i.e., the ETF share price is relatively expensive). The action taken by the agent in this scenario to generate an arbitrage process would be to buy the underlying ETF portfolio and sell the ETF shares.
2. Scenario 2: The ETF's share price is below that of the ETF portfolio's NAV (i.e., the ETF share price is relatively cheap). In this scenario, the agent would purchase the ETF shares and sell the underlying portfolio at NAV.

The result of the action of the agent in both scenarios would be the generation of a profitable arbitrage. Moreover, the action by the agent to capture the potential arbitrage would tend to cause the ETF's share price to trade very close (or equal) to that of the ETF portfolio's NAV.

We referred to the third party as an agent. Actually, there are many agents, all large institutional investors selected by the ETF's sponsor. Because these agents perform the arbitrage, they are called **arbitrageurs**. And because they are retained by the ETF sponsor to take the action described above to bring about equality of the ETF share price and the ETF's portfolio NAV by creating and redeeming ETF shares, they are referred to as **authorized participants** (usually denoted by "AP").

Only an agent is authorized to create ETF shares by providing the ETF sponsor with a specified basket of securities, in exchange for which the agent receives ETF shares, called **creation units**. These units can be transacted only in large, specified quantities. In scenario 1 above, the action taken by the agent (the authorized professional) results in creation units. When the authorized professional delivers a specified number of ETF shares to the ETF sponsor in exchange for a specific basket of securities, the ETF shares exchanged are referred to as **redemption units**. In scenario 2 above, the action by the authorized professional results in redemption units.

The arbitrage process just described becomes more difficult for an actively managed ETF. The reason is that the authorized professional does not know what the underlying portfolio is, because the portfolio is permitted to deviate from the benchmark index.

Tracking the Performance of ETFs

The task of the authorized professional is critical and may seem simple enough. However, a fundamental requirement must be met for the arbitrage process to work: The composition and the NAV of the ETF portfolio must be known accurately, and the securities in the portfolio must be continuously traded throughout the trading day. An obvious example of such a portfolio would be the S&P 500 index portfolio. The 500 stocks in the index are very liquid, and their prices and the value of the index are quoted continuously throughout the trading day.

A study by Buetow and Henderson analyzed a broad sample of ETFs traded on U.S. exchanges.[5] Their sample included all U.S. ETFs for which they were able to identify a benchmark index from the prospectus and to collect return series for both the ETF and the benchmark index.

They found that daily returns for the majority of the ETFs in their study closely tracked returns for the respective indexes and exhibited high correlations with the index. However, some ETFs did exhibit significant tracking error and had lower correlations with the returns of their benchmark index. This poorer performance in terms of tracking error and correlation with index returns tended to be larger when the benchmark index for an ETF was composed of less liquid assets.

Uses of ETFs

In this book, we describe different asset classes and different investment strategies. ETFs provide a cost-effective means for retail and institutional investors to gain exposure to asset classes and sectors through either passively or actively managed ETFs.

ETFs can be used to alter exposure to asset classes of the U.S. market. Similarly, by using ETFs that have a non-U.S. benchmark index, the investor can avoid the custodian and transaction costs associated with creating an exposure to non-U.S. markets. An active portfolio manager who wants to alter exposure to a sector of the market can do so by using an ETF that is passively managed. For example, consider an active equity portfolio manager who is seeking to outperform the S&P 500 index and wants to do so by increasing exposure to a sector of the equity market that he or she believes will outperform the other sectors. That is, the manager wants to overweight exposure to that sector. This can be done by using an appropriate ETF. To make the example more concrete, suppose that the portfolio

5. Gerald W. Buetow and Brian J. Henderson, "An Empirical Analysis of Exchange-Traded Funds," *Journal of Portfolio Management* 30, no. 3 (2012): 112–127.

manager wants to overweight the telecommunications sector of the S&P 500 index. This can be done by purchasing shares of, say, the Vanguard Telecom Services ETF. Shorting that ETF would reduce exposure to the telecommunications sector.

Hedge Funds

It would be nice to be able to define what a hedge fund is by, say, pointing to its definition in the federal securities law. However, no such legal definition exists; nor is there any universally accepted definition to describe the 9,000 privately pooled investment entities in the United States called "hedge funds," which in aggregate, invest more than $1.3 trillion in assets.

The term *hedge fund* was first used by *Fortune* magazine in 1966 to describe the private investment fund of Alfred Winslow Jones. When managing the portfolio, Jones sought to "hedge" the market risk of the fund by creating a portfolio that was long and short the stock market by an equal amount. (As explained in chapter 18, shorting the stock market means selling stock that is not owned, with the expectation that the price will decline in the future. A portfolio constructed in this way is said to be "hedged" against stock market risk.) Moreover, Jones determined that under U.S. securities law, his private investment partnership would not be regulated by the SEC if the investors were "accredited investors." The securities law defines an accredited investor as an investor who does not need the protection offered other investors by filings with the SEC.[6]

And that is the way federal securities law treated hedge funds until the passage of the Dodd-Frank Wall Street Reform and Consumer Protection Act of 2010. This act changed the registration of hedge funds that had previously been granted exemption because they were "private advisers," replacing the exemption with several narrower exemptions for such advisers as venture capital funds, discussed later in this chapter. Not only did the act set forth regulatory changes regarding the registration of hedge funds, it also imposed reporting and record-keeping requirements. More specifically, the act gave the SEC the authority to collect data from hedge funds. The requirements were put in place not only to protect investors but also to allow the information mandated to be used by the Financial Stability Oversight Council (discussed in chapter 2) to assess the systemic risk that might be posed by large hedge funds.

Attributes of Hedge Funds

Let's look at some definitions of hedge funds that have been proposed based on their attributes. George Soros is the chairman of Soros Fund Management. His firm advises a privately owned group of hedge funds, the Quantum Group of Funds. He defines a hedge fund as follows:

6. The Securities Act of 1933 sets forth much more specific criteria for an investor to be classified as an accredited investor. The details are not important to the present discussion.

Hedge funds engage in a variety of investment activities. They cater to sophisticated investors and are not subject to the regulations that apply to mutual funds geared toward the general public. Fund managers are compensated on the basis of performance rather than as a fixed percentage of assets. "Performance funds" would be a more accurate description.[7]

The President's Working Group on Financial Markets, a group created by then president Ronald Reagan and consisting of the secretary of the Treasury and the chairs of the Board of Governors of the Federal Reserve Board, the SEC, and the Commodity Futures Trading Commission, provides the following definition:

The term "hedge fund" is commonly used to describe a variety of different types of investment vehicles that share some common characteristics. Although it is not statutorily defined, the term encompasses any pooled investment vehicle that is privately organized, administered by professional money managers, and not widely available to the public.[8]

A useful definition based on the characteristics of hedge funds is the following, provided by the United Kingdom's Financial Services Authority, the regulatory body of all providers of financial services in that country:

The term can also be defined by considering the characteristics most commonly associated with hedge funds. Usually, hedge funds:

- are organised as private investment partnerships or offshore investment corporations;
- use a wide variety of trading strategies involving position-taking in a range of markets;
- employ an assortment of trading techniques and instruments, often including short-selling, derivatives and leverage;
- pay performance fees to their managers; and
- have an investor base comprising wealthy individuals and institutions and a relatively high minimum investment limit (set at US$100,000 or higher for most funds).[9]

From the above definitions, we can take away the following about hedge funds. First, the word "hedge" in hedge funds is misleading. Although the word may have been appropriate for characterizing the fund managed by Alfred Winslow Jones, it is not a characteristic of hedge funds today.

Second, hedge funds use a wide range of trading strategies and techniques in an attempt to earn superior returns. The strategies used by a hedge fund can include one or more of the following:

7. George Soros, *Open Society: Reforming Global Capitalism* (New York: PublicAffairs, 2000), 100.

8. President's Working Group on Financial Markets, *Hedge Funds, Leverage, and the Lessons of Long-Term Capital Management: Report of the President's Working Group on Financial Markets* (Washington, DC: Department of the Treasury et al., April 1999), 1, available at http://www.treasury.gov/resource-center/fin-mkts/Documents/hedgfund.pdf.

9. Financial Services Authority, "Hedge Funds and the FSA," Discussion Paper 16 (London: Financial Services Authority, 2002), 8.

- leverage, or the use of borrowed funds;
- short selling, or the sale of a financial instrument not owned in anticipation of a decline in that financial instrument's price;
- arbitrage, or the simultaneous buying and selling of related financial instruments to realize a profit from the temporary misalignment of their prices; and
- risk control, or the use of financial instruments (such as derivatives) to reduce the risk of loss.

Risk control is more general than hedging. In a hedge, one often thinks about eliminating a risk. Risk control means that a risk is mitigated to the degree desired by the investor. Very few hedge funds employ hedging in the sense of eliminating all risks.

Third, hedge funds operate in all the financial markets described in this book: the cash market for stocks, bonds, and currencies and the derivatives markets.

Fourth, the management fee structure for hedge funds is a combination of a fixed fee based on the market value of assets managed plus a share of the positive return. The latter is a performance-based compensation referred to as an **incentive fee**.

Finally, when evaluating hedge funds, investors are interested in the absolute return generated by the asset manager, not the relative return. **Absolute return** on a portfolio is simply the return realized. The **relative return** is the difference between the absolute return and the return on some benchmark or index. The use of absolute return rather than relative return for evaluating an asset manager's performance managing a hedge fund is quite different from the criteria used to evaluate the performance of an asset manager managing the other types of portfolios discussed in this chapter.

Types of Hedge Funds

The different types of hedge funds can be categorized in various ways. Mark Anson uses the following four broad categories: market directional, corporate restructuring, convergence trading, and opportunistic.[10]

A **market directional hedge fund** is one in which the asset manager retains some exposure to "systematic risk." In the category of market directional hedge funds are those funds that pursue the following strategies: equity long/short strategies, equity market timing, and short selling.

A **corporate restructuring hedge fund** is one whose asset manager positions the portfolio to capitalize on the anticipated impact of a significant corporate event. These events include a merger, an acquisition, or bankruptcy.

The strategy of **convergence trading hedge funds** involves the identification of potential misalignments of prices and/or yields that are expected to move back to or "converge"

10. Mark J. P. Anson, *Handbook of Alternative Assets*, 2nd ed. (Hoboken, NJ: John Wiley & Sons, 2006).

to the expected relationship. The asset manager positions the portfolio to benefit from the convergence.

Opportunistic hedge funds have the broadest mandate of the four hedge fund categories. Asset managers of opportunistic hedge funds can make specific bets on stocks or currencies, or they can have well-diversified portfolios. Two groups of hedge funds fall into this category: global macro hedge funds and funds of funds. **Global macro hedge funds** are hedge funds that invest opportunistically based on macroeconomic considerations in any market in the world. Probably the best-known hedge fund that falls into this group is the Quantum Hedge Fund. Here are two well-documented strategies that the asset managers of this hedge fund employed that produced significant profits. Based on macroeconomic conditions in 1992 in the United Kingdom, the hedge fund bet on the devaluation of the British currency, the pound sterling. The British government did in fact devalue the pound. In 1997, the hedge fund's macroeconomic analysis indicated that the currency of Thailand, the baht, was overvalued and would be devalued by the government of Thailand. The bet it made on the currency was right. The government of Thailand did devalue the baht.

As we explained earlier in this chapter, there are funds of funds that invest in mutual funds. Similarly, there are funds of funds that invest in other hedge funds. That is, that portfolio of a fund of funds consists of interests in other hedge funds.

Concerns about Hedge Funds in Financial Markets

There is considerable debate over the role of hedge funds in financial markets because of their size and the impact they have on financial markets as a result of their investment strategies. On the positive side, it has been argued that they provide liquidity to the market. A Federal Reserve Bank study found that market participants described hedge funds "as a significant stability force" in the interest rate options markets.[11] (We describe interest rate options in chapters 34 and 37.) In addition, hedge funds have provided liquidity by participating in the municipal bond market.

The concern, however, is the risk of a severe financial crisis (i.e., systemic risk) as a result of the activities and investment strategies of hedge funds, most notably the employment of excess leverage. The best-known example is the collapse of Long-Term Capital Management (LTCM) in September 1998. Studies of LTCM indicate that it used a leverage of 50. That is, for every \$1 million of capital provided by investors, LTCM was able to borrow \$50 million. The reason LTCM was able to borrow such a large amount was because lenders did not understand or ignored the huge risks associated with that hedge fund's investment strategies. The loss of LTCM because of bad bets is not a concern per se, because the investors in that hedge fund were sophisticated investors who took their

11. Federal Reserve Board, *Concentration and Risk in the OTC Markets for U.S. Dollar Interest Rate Options* (Washington, DC: Department of the Treasury, Board of Governors of the Federal Reserve System, March 2005), 3.

chances in the hope of reaping substantial returns. Instead, the problem was that the real losers of that hedge fund's activities were major commercial banks and investment banking firms that lent funds to LTCM. In the view of the Federal Reserve, there were potential dire consequences from the potential failure of LTCM, and the Federal Reserve reacted by organizing a rescue plan for that hedge fund.

More recently, in June 2007, two hedge funds sponsored by the investment banking firm Bear Stearns collapsed: the High-Grade Structured Credit Strategies Enhanced Leverage Fund and the High-Grade Structured Credit Strategies Fund. These failures required the sponsor, Bear Stearns, to bail out the hedge funds.[12]

As a result of the LTCM failure, the President's Working Group on Financial Markets made several recommendations for improving the functioning of hedge funds in financial markets. The major recommendation was that commercial banks and investment banks that lend to hedge funds improve their credit risk management practices.

REITs

Real estate investment trusts (REITs) are stocks that represent an interest in an underlying pool of real estate properties. They are similar to closed-end funds, because the stock is publicly traded and the market price can differ from that of the REIT's NAV. In the case of REITs, the investments in the portfolio are real estate properties. The principal advantage of REITs is that they allow investors access to an illiquid asset class that would be difficult for an individual investor to invest in directly. Moreover, because a REIT has a large number of properties in its portfolio, individual investors obtain better diversification than by directly investing in real estate properties.

Moreover, tax advantages are granted to a company that qualifies as a REIT. Specifically, under the U.S. federal tax code, dividends paid by a corporation cannot be taken as a tax deduction when determining taxable income. As a result, there is double taxation of corporate income: taxes are paid at the corporate level, and income is then taxed again when distributed to shareholders. The corporate tax treatment for a REIT is different. A REIT is allowed to deduct the dividends paid to its shareholders when determining its corporate taxable income. It is only when the dividends are paid to shareholders that the income is taxed at the individual level, not at the corporate level. Most states apply the same tax treatment to the income of REITs. As a result, to avoid double taxation of income, most REITs follow a dividend distribution policy whereby all their taxable income is distributed to their shareholders, and therefore no corporate taxes are paid.

To obtain the favorable tax treatment granted to a REIT, a company must satisfy requirements set forth by the federal tax code. The bulk of its invested assets must be in real

12. The funds primarily invested in subprime mortgages. The subprime mortgage meltdown in the summer of 2007 is discussed in chapter 30. In March 2008, the Federal Reserve had to institute a plan to rescue Bear Stearns.

estate–related investments. As for the income generated, the source must come from primarily real estate investments, and at least 90% of a REIT's taxable income must be distributed to shareholders annually in the form of dividends.

Investors in REITs include retail (individual) investors and institutional investors. Retail investors invest through their nonretirement savings, IRAs, or defined contribution plans. Institutional investors, such as defined benefit plans and endowment funds, invest in REITs to obtain exposure to the commercial real estate market.

REIT ETFs are traded based on various REIT indexes.

Types of REITs

There are three types of REITs: equity REITs, mortgage REITs, and hybrid REITs.

In an **equity REIT**, the manager purchases real estate property. That is, the REIT portfolio consists of real estate properties that are owned by the REIT. In addition, the REIT manager may also manage, renovate, and develop real estate properties. Income generated for the investors in an equity REIT is derived from rental and lease payments from the properties owned and any price appreciation. About 90% of the REITs traded are equity REITs.

A diversified equity REIT invests in more than one type of property. Typically, however, equity REITs specialize in one type of property. The National Association of Real Estate Investment Trusts (NAREIT), the leading organization representing the REIT industry, categorizes equity trusts by the type of properties in which they specialize. The categories are:

- industrial and office trusts specializing in industrial and/or office properties;
- retail REITs, specializing in strip malls, larger malls, and other types of retail properties;
- residential REITs, specializing in multifamily apartments and/or developments for manufactured housing;
- REITs specializing in lodging and resorts, holding ownership in hotels, motels, and resort properties;
- REITs specializing in ownership and management of self-storage units; and
- health care REITs, specializing in hospitals and other health care facilities.

Other equity REITs do not fall into one of the categories above because they own such properties as golf courses, timberland, or prisons.

A much smaller sector of the REIT market is the **mortgage REIT**. This second kind of REIT originates and holds various types of real estate debt that are used to purchase real estate. Thus, the portfolio of a mortgage REIT includes investment vehicles that represent financing to owners, developers, and purchasers of real estate. Mortgage REITs do not own real estate. The returns for investors are generated from the interest earned on the financing they provide.

There are two types of mortgage REITs, based on the type of real estate property: residential or commercial property. Residential property includes single-family homes. Commercial property includes the other types of real estate properties mentioned above when categorizing equity REITs. Thus, mortgage REITs are categorized as either residential mortgage REITs or commercial mortgage REITs. A **residential mortgage REIT** primarily originates and acquires loans that are used for the acquisition of single-family homes. There are only about 30 such REITs in the United States. **Commercial mortgage REITs** invest primarily in loans and securities backed by commercial properties. The securities that commercial mortgage REITs invest in are commercial mortgage-backed securities, which we discussed in chapter 31. In the REIT universe, only about 10% are mortgage REITs.

A REIT that invests in both the equity interests and the debt interests in real estate properties is called a **hybrid REIT**. Hybrid REITs provide lending for the acquisition and development of real estate properties, as a mortgage REIT does, and also purchase and develop real estate properties themselves, as an equity REIT does. Some hybrid REITs specify in their prospectus what allocation between equity ownership and mortgage financing they will pursue. Other hybrid REITs do not fix the allocation between ownership and financing but rather allow flexibility, so that management can capitalize on perceived opportunities in the market.

Benchmark indexes are available to assess the performance of REITs. The most popular index is the FTSE NAREIT US Real Estate Index series, which includes both equity and mortgage REITs. (For the purpose of the index construction, hybrid REITs are classified as either equity or mortgage REITs.) Subindexes are available to measure the different specialized categories discussed above (equity REITs and mortgage REITs), as well as the different categories of equity REITs. Other REIT indexes focusing on U.S. REITs are the MSCI US REIT Index, the Wilshire Real Estate Securities Index, and the S&P US REIT Index.

Venture Capital Funds

An important participant in the real economy is the entrepreneur who develops new products and services. Entrepreneurs who want to move from their business plan and any prototype that they develop to the formation of a company to implement their business plan need varying amounts of capital. Startup companies typically lack tangible assets that can be used as collateral for a loan and are unlikely to produce positive earnings for several years.

The stages of a startup firm are (1) the early stage, (2) the expansion stage, and (3) the acquisition/buyout stage. In the very early stage, funds are typically obtained from the entrepreneur's own resources, loans or investments from family and friends, and bank loans collateralized by the entrepreneur's personal assets. As the company expands, an entrepreneur may seek funding from an angel investor. An **angel investor** is a wealthy individual who invests his or her own funds in startup companies for amounts ranging from $150,000 to $2 million. The investment is in the form of either equity ownership or convertible debt (i.e., debt that can be converted into equity). The reality show on the ABC television network, *Shark Tank*, shows entrepreneurs pitching their venture to some well-known entrepreneurs, such as Mark Cuban. To better research and evaluate startups, angel investors have formed groups or networks. There are more than 330 angel groups in North America, according to the Angel Capital Association.

Entrepreneurs needing funds far in excess of what can be raised from loans and angel investors turn to venture capital firms. In turn, these firms create venture capital funds, which are pooled investment funds.

Venture Capital Firms

A **venture capital firm** is an institutional management firm that provides equity financing to startup companies that do not have a sufficient track record to attract investment capital from traditional sources (e.g., the public markets or lending institutions). Venture capital firms typically specialize in one or more stages of a startup firm's business and by economic sector. Venture capital firms typically specialize in industries.

The ultimate goal (the "exit strategy") for a venture capital firm is to sell its equity interest in its portfolio companies through an acquisition or an initial public offering (IPO). After they invest in a company, venture capital firms are not passive investors. Instead, they take an active role either in an advisory capacity or by way of representation on the company's board of directors. The company's progress is monitored, the incentive plans for the entrepreneurs and the management team are designed and implemented, and the startup company's financial goals are established. In addition to providing guidance to the companies in which they invest, venture capital firms often have the right to hire and fire key managers, including the original entrepreneur.

Investing in a Venture Capital Fund

To obtain the funds to invest in startup companies, venture capital firms raise capital from individual and institutional investors. An investor does not invest in the venture capital firm but in a particular fund managed by the firm and referred to as a **venture capital fund**.

A venture capital fund is typically structured as a limited partnership.[13] A **limited partnership** has general partners (the venture capital firm in the case of a venture capital fund) and limited partners, who are the investors. The fund's income and capital gains are not taxed at the partnership level but instead are passed through to the investors, who are then taxed. The general partners are responsible for managing the fund, which means evaluating

13. The other type of legal structure used is a limited liability company.

and selecting the portfolio of companies in which the venture capital fund invests. All the fund's partners will commit to a specific investment amount at the formation of the limited partnership. The venture capital firm receives the cash to invest as investors fulfill the terms of their commitment agreement. Unlike investors in the other collective investment vehicles discussed in this chapter, an investor in a venture capital fund must commit funds for a long period of time, typically at least 10 years. No cash contributions are made by the limited partners until they are called on by the general partner to do so. This is referred to as "taking down" the commitment and is done by the general partner making a "capital call." The general partner will make a capital call when startup companies are identified in which the venture capital fund's management team wants to invest. Capital is committed not only by the limited partners but also by the general partner, the venture capital firm. By committing its own capital, the venture capital firm aligns its interests with those of the investors and the firm; that is, principal-agent problems are reduced.

The fees received by a venture capital firm when managing a venture capital fund are the management fee and the profit-sharing or incentive fee. The management fee for most venture capital funds is in the 2% to 2.5% range and is used to pay the expenses of the venture capital firm. The profit-sharing or incentive fee, the primary source of revenue for a venture capital firm, provides the firm with a share of the profits generated by the fund and typically is 20%, although incentive fees as high as 35% exist.

Stages of a Venture Capital Fund

Here are the stages that a venture capital firm goes through in setting up a venture capital fund. Fundraising from outside investors is the first stage. Although the duration of this stage varies with the reputation of the venture capital firm and the state of the economy, fundraising typically takes from six months to a year.

Once the funds are raised, the fund is said to be "closed," and the second stage begins. This stage involves the firm's management team performing due diligence to assess the potential attractiveness of candidate startup firms in which to invest. This stage can take up to five years, during which time no profits are generated by the venture capital fund. Instead, losses are realized owing to the management fees that must be paid based on the amount committed by the limited partners.

The third stage involves the beginning of investment in the startup companies. The venture capital firm's team of managers determines how much capital to commit to each startup company and what form the investment should take. An investment is typically in the form of convertible preferred shares or convertible debentures. It is at this stage that the general partner (the venture capital firm) will make capital calls to the venture capital fund's limited partners (the outside investors) to draw down on the capital commitment. In this third stage, there is still no income generated.

The investing of funds to create the portfolio of companies is the fourth stage, a stage that lasts almost to the end of the fund's term. During this time, the venture capital management team continues to operate, because it may be involved in several activities discussed earlier in this section. Moreover, it is during this period that the fund will hopefully begin to generate income.

The venture capital fund's final stage is its windup and liquidation stage. By the time this stage is reached, all committed capital has been invested, and the venture capital fund is now reaping the financial rewards from its portfolio of companies. Each portfolio company is sold, brought to the public markets through an IPO, or liquidated through a legal bankruptcy liquidation process. The limited partners and the venture capital firm (i.e., the general partner) are allocated their share of the profits (the incentive fee, in the case of the venture capital firm).

Key Points

- Collective investment vehicles are products created through the pooling of funds and the management (investment) of those fund by an asset management firm, which receives compensation through a management fee and possibly an incentive fee.
- Retail and institutional investors invest in pooled funds and thereby have an equity interest in the fund's net assets.
- The advantages of collective investment vehicles compared to direct investment in financial assets are better portfolio diversification, better liquidity, professional management expertise, and possibly favorable tax treatment.
- Investment companies sell shares to the public and invest the proceeds in a diversified portfolio of securities, with each share representing a proportionate interest in the underlying portfolio of securities.
- Investment companies must be registered with the SEC and are therefore referred to as "registered investment companies."
- One type of investment company as classified by federal securities law is a management company, which is created as either a corporation or a trust.
- Management companies are further classified as open-end funds (also called "mutual funds") and closed-end funds.
- A wide range of funds with many different investment objectives is available. Securities law requires that a fund clearly set forth its investment objective in its prospectus, and the objective identifies the types of assets the fund will purchase and hold.
- Open-end mutual funds and closed-end funds provide two crucial economic functions associated with financial intermediaries: risk reduction through diversification and lower costs of contracting and information processing. Money market funds allow shareholders

to write checks against their shares, thus providing a payment mechanism, another economic function of financial intermediaries.

• Investment companies are extensively regulated, with most of that regulation occurring at the federal level. The key legislation is the Investment Company Act of 1940.

• The most important feature regarding regulation is that the funds are exempt from taxation on their gains if the gains are distributed to investors in a relatively short time. Even allowing for that special tax-free status, it is necessary to recognize that regulations apply to many features of the funds' administration, including sales fees, asset management, degree of diversification, distributions, and advertising.

• Exchange-traded funds (ETFs) overcome two major drawbacks of open-end mutual funds, namely, the pricing of mutual fund transactions only at the end of the trading day and tax inefficiencies.

• ETFs are similar to open-end mutual funds in that they trade based on NAV, but unlike open-end funds, they trade like stocks.

• An ETF has a sponsor. The asset manager of an ETF is responsible for managing the portfolio so as to replicate as closely as possible the return of the benchmark index.

• Although there are no universally accepted definitions of the private investment entities called "hedge funds," these entities have in common the use of leverage, short selling, arbitrage, and risk control when seeking to generate superior returns.

• Despite the term "hedge" in describing these entities, they do not completely hedge their positions.

• The Dodd-Frank Act of 2010 requires hedge funds to be registered with the SEC and imposes certain reporting requirements on them.

• Hedge funds can be categorized as market directional, corporate restructuring, convergence trading, and opportunistic.

• The public policy concern with hedge funds has been the excessive use of leverage.

• Real estate investment trusts (REITs) are publicly traded stocks that represent an interest in an underlying pool of real estate properties. Just as with closed-end funds, the market price can differ from the NAV.

• The three types of REITs are equity REITs, mortgage REITs, and hybrid REITs. About 90% of REITs are equity REITs.

• The manager of an equity REIT purchases real estate property as well as renovates and develops real estate properties. Income for this type of REIT is obtained from rental and lease payments and any price appreciation.

• The different categories of equity REITs are based on the type of property purchased for the portfolio. For example, there are industrial and office REITs, retail REITs, residential REITs, lodging and resort REITs, and health care REITs.

- Mortgage REITs provide financing for properties either by the origination or through the acquisition of loans and investing in mortgage-related securities.
- Hybrid REITs both invest in real estate properties and provide financing.
- Venture capital firms provide financing for startup companies. They specialize by sector and the stage of financing of a startup.
- Venture capital firms create venture capital funds, for which they seek investors. Investors in a venture capital fund commit to a specific investment amount but only have to provide cash when the venture capital firm makes a capital call.
- Capital for a venture capital fund is committed not only by outside investors but also by the venture capital firm itself, thereby aligning the interests of the outside investors and the venture capital firm.
- A venture capital fund's final stage is its windup and liquidation stage. Each portfolio company is sold, brought to the public market through an IPO, or liquidated through a legal bankruptcy liquidation process. Profits are distributed to all investors, and the incentive fee is paid to the venture capital firm.

Questions

1. An investment company has $1.05 million in assets, $50,000 in liabilities, and 10,000 shares outstanding.

a. What is its NAV?

b. Suppose the fund pays off its liabilities while at the same time, the value of its assets doubles. How many shares will an investor who invests $5,000 receive?

2. a. "The NAV of an open-end fund is determined continuously throughout the trading day." Explain why you agree or disagree with this statement.

b. "A closed-end fund will always trade at its NAV." Explain why you agree or disagree with this statement.

3. Why might the price of a share of a closed-end fund diverge from its NAV?

4. a. Describe the following: front-end load, back-end load, level load, 12b-1 fee, management fee.

b. Why do mutual funds have different classes of shares?

5. What is a fund of funds?

6. What costs are incurred by a mutual fund?

7. Why might the investor in a mutual fund be faced with a potential tax liability arising from capital gains, even though the investor did not benefit from such a gain?

8. Does an investment company provide any economic function that individual investors cannot provide for themselves on their own? Explain your answer.

9. What is an exchange-traded fund (ETF)?

10. What are the advantages of an ETF relative to open-end and closed-end investment companies?

11. What is the role played by an ETF's authorized participants?

12. a. Why is the term "hedge," as used in the term "hedge funds," misleading?

b. Where is the term "hedge fund" described in the U.S. securities law?

13. How does the management fee structure of the asset manager of a hedge fund, a venture capital fund, or a real estate investment trust (REIT) differ from that of an asset manager of a mutual fund?

14. How has the Dodd-Frank Act affected the regulation of hedge funds?

15. Some hedge funds refer to their strategies as "arbitrage strategies." Why would this claim be misleading?

16. What is meant by a "convergence traded hedge fund"?

17. What was the major recommendation of the President's Working Group on Financial Markets regarding hedge funds?

18. Two investors are arguing about the types of investment made by REITs. One investor believes that REITs are investors in real estate properties. The other investor believes that REITs provide financing for the purchase of real estate properties. The two investors ask you who is right. How would you respond to these investors?

19. What are the two types of mortgage REITs?

20. A capital venture firm does more than provide financing for startup companies. Explain what other activities the firm's management team performs.

21. How does the raising of funds for a venture capital fund differ from that of other collective investment vehicles?

22. a. When a capital venture fund is structured as a partner, who are the limited partners and who are the general partners?

b. What does it mean for a venture capital fund's general partner to make a capital call on the limited partners?

23. What is a venture capital fund's exit strategy?

33 Financial Futures Markets

CONTENTS

Learning Objectives

After reading this chapter, you will understand:

- what a derivative contract is;
- the types of derivatives;
- what a futures contract is;
- the basic economic function of a futures contract;
- the differences between futures and forward contracts;
- the role of the clearinghouse;
- the mark-to-market and margin requirements of a futures contract;
- what is meant by a "risk-sharing arrangement" for a derivative;
- what is meant by an "insurance arrangement" for a derivative;
- contract specifications of U.S. stock index futures contracts, single stock futures contracts, and narrow-based stock index futures contracts;
- contract specifications of major interest rate futures contracts;
- currency forward and futures contracts; and
- the role of futures markets in the financial markets.

In the last seven chapters in this section of the book, we cover financial instruments known as **financial derivatives** or simply **derivatives**. The price or value of a derivative is derived from the value of some underlying asset, reference rate, or index. We shall simply refer to the underlying asset, reference rate, or index as the "underlying." The economic purpose of derivatives is to provide efficient vehicles for controlling some risk by transferring risk to another party willing to accept the unwanted risk. For this reason, derivatives are referred to as "risk transfer vehicles." The development of the derivatives markets throughout the world was a response to the need for an efficient risk-transference mechanism as a result of stock price and interest rate volatility. As we will see when discussing derivatives in this section of the book, some derivatives provide for a *risk-sharing* type of arrangement, whereas others are a type of *insurance* arrangement.

Derivatives are classified as futures, forwards, options, and swaps. Our focus in this chapter and the next is on futures and forward contracts. Here we provide the fundamentals, some of the more important financial futures contracts, and their role in financial markets. We postpone a description of the pricing of futures and their applications to chapters 35 and 36, respectively.

Futures contracts can be classified as either commodities or financial futures contracts. Commodities futures include agricultural commodities (such as grain and livestock), imported foodstuffs (such as coffee, cocoa, and sugar), and industrial commodities. Futures contracts based on a financial instrument or a financial index are known as financial futures. Financial futures can be classified as (1) stock index futures, (2) interest rate futures, and (3) currency futures.

The three major derivatives exchanges in the world are Chicago Mercantile Exchange, the NYSE Euronext Liffe, and the Euroex. Historically, the trading of futures contracts has been via an open outcry environment, where traders and brokers shout out bids and offers in a trading pit or ring. Although open outcry has been the primary method of trading certain types of futures contracts, since 2004, trading in many financial futures in the United States has moved to an electronic trading platform, where market participants post their bids and offers on a computerized trading system. The trading of futures contracts outside the United States takes place on an electronic platform.

Futures Contracts

A **futures contract** is an agreement between a buyer and a seller, in which

1. the buyer agrees to take delivery of something at a specified price at the end of a designated period, and
2. the seller agrees to make delivery of something at a specified price at the end of a designated period.

No one buys or sells anything when entering into a futures contract. Instead, the parties to the contract agree to buy or sell a specific amount of a specific item at a specified future date. When we speak of the "buyer" or the "seller" of a contract, we are simply adopting the jargon of the futures market, which refers to parties of the contract in terms of the future obligation they are committing themselves to.

Let's look closely at the key elements of this contract. The price at which the parties agree to transact in the future is called the **futures price**. The designated date at which the parties must transact is the **settlement date** or **delivery date**. The "something" that the parties agree to exchange is the **underlying**.

To illustrate, suppose a futures contract is traded on an exchange where the underlying to be bought or sold is Asset XYZ, and the settlement date is three months from now. Assume further that Bob buys this futures contract, and Sally sells this futures contract, and the price at which they agree to transact in the future is $100. Then $100 is the futures price. At the settlement date, Sally will deliver Asset XYZ to Bob. Bob will give Sally $100, the futures price.

When an investor takes a position in the market by buying a futures contract (or agreeing to buy at the future date), the investor is said to be in a **long position** or to be **long futures**. If, instead, the investor's opening position is the sale of a futures contract (which means the contractual obligation to sell something in the future), the investor is said to be in a **short position** or to be **short futures**.

The buyer of a futures contract will realize a profit if the futures price increases; the seller of a futures contract will realize a profit if the futures price decreases. For example, suppose that one month after Bob and Sally take their positions in the futures contract, the futures price of Asset XYZ increases to $120. Bob, the buyer of the futures contract, could then sell the futures contract and realize a profit of $20. Effectively, he has agreed to buy at the settlement date Asset XYZ for $100 and to sell Asset XYZ for $120. Sally, the seller of the futures contract, will realize a loss of $20.

If the futures price falls to $40 and Sally buys the contract, she realizes a profit of $60 because she agreed to sell Asset XYZ for $100, and now can buy it for $40. Bob would realize a loss of $60. Thus, if the futures price decreases, the buyer of the futures contract realizes a loss, and the seller of the futures contract realizes a profit.

Liquidating a Position

Depending on the contract, there is a predetermined time in the contract settlement month that the contract stops trading, and a price is determined by the exchange for settlement of the contract. The contract with the closest settlement date is called the **nearby futures contract**. The next futures contract is the one that settles just after the nearby contract. The contract farthest away in time from settlement is called the **most distant (**or **deferred)** futures contract.

A party to a futures contract has two choices on liquidation of the position. First, the position can be liquidated prior to the settlement date. For this purpose, the party must take an offsetting position in the same contract. For the buyer of a futures contract, this means selling the same number of identical futures contracts; for the seller of a futures contract, this means buying the same number of identical futures contracts.

The alternative is to wait until the settlement date. At that time, the party purchasing a futures contract accepts delivery of the underlying; the party that sells a futures contract liquidates the position by delivering the underlying at the agreed-on price. For some futures contracts that we shall describe later in this chapter, settlement is made in cash only. Such contracts are referred to as **cash settlement contracts**.

A useful statistic measuring the liquidity of a contract is the number of contracts that have been entered into but not yet liquidated. This figure is called the contract's **open interest**.

An open interest figure is reported by an exchange for all futures contracts traded on the exchange.

Role of the Clearinghouse

Associated with every futures exchange is a **clearinghouse**, which performs several functions. One of these functions is to guarantee that the two parties to the transaction will perform according to the contract. To see the importance of this function, consider potential problems in the futures transaction described earlier from the perspective of the two parties—Bob the buyer and Sally the seller. Each must be concerned with the other's ability to fulfill the obligation at the settlement date. Suppose that at the settlement date, the price of Asset XYZ in the cash market is \$70. Sally can buy Asset XYZ for \$70 and deliver it to Bob, who in turn must pay her \$100. If Bob does not have the capacity to pay \$100 or refuses to pay, however, Sally has lost the opportunity to realize a profit of \$30. Suppose, instead, that the price of Asset XYZ in the cash market is \$150 at the settlement date. In this case, Bob is ready and willing to accept delivery of Asset XYZ and pay the agreed-on price of \$100. If Sally cannot deliver or refuses to deliver Asset XYZ, Bob has lost the opportunity to realize a profit of \$50.

The clearinghouse exists to eliminate this problem. When someone takes a position in the futures market, the clearinghouse takes the opposite position and agrees to satisfy the terms set forth in the contract. Because of the clearinghouse, the two parties need not worry about the financial strength and integrity of the party taking the opposite side of the contract. After initial execution of an order, the relationship between the two parties ends. The clearinghouse interposes itself as the buyer for every sale and the seller for every purchase. Thus, the two parties are then free to liquidate their positions without involving the other party in the original contract, and without worry that the other party may default. This function is referred to as the **guarantee function**.

Besides its guarantee function, the clearinghouse makes it simple for parties to a futures contract to unwind (i.e., reverse) their positions prior to the settlement date. Suppose that Bob wants to get out of his futures position. He will not have to seek out Sally and work out an agreement with her to terminate the original contract. Instead, Bob can unwind his position by selling an identical futures contract. As far as the clearinghouse is concerned, its records will show that Bob has bought and sold an identical futures contract. At the settlement date, Sally will not deliver Asset XYZ to Bob but will be instructed by the clearinghouse to deliver to someone who bought and still has an open futures position. In the same way, if Sally wants to unwind her position prior to the settlement date, she can buy an identical futures contract.

The importance of a clearinghouse to the success of a derivatives market in general cannot be overemphasized. As explained in chapter 37, some derivatives have provoked increasing concerns about counterparty risk, particularly following the recent financial crisis and the failure of Lehman Brothers. As a result, international agreements have sought to ensure that an effective clearinghouse mechanism is implemented.

Margin Requirements

When a position is first taken in a futures contract, the investor must deposit a minimum dollar amount per contract as specified by the exchange. This amount, called **initial margin**, is required as a deposit for the contract. Individual brokerage firms are free to set margin requirements above the minimum established by the exchange. The initial margin may be in the form of an interest-bearing security. As the price of the futures contract fluctuates each trading day, the value of the investor's equity in the position changes. The **equity** in a futures account is the sum of all margins posted and all daily gains less all daily losses to the account. We develop this important concept throughout this section.

At the end of each trading day, the exchange determines the settlement price for the futures contract. The settlement price is different from the closing price, which many people know from the stock market and which is the price of the security in the final trade of the day (whenever that trade occurred during the day). In contrast, the **settlement price** is the value that the exchange considers to be representative of trading at the end of the day. The representative price may in fact be the price in the day's last trade. But, if there is a flurry of trading at the end of the day, the exchange looks at all trades in the last few minutes and identifies a median or average price among those trades. The exchange uses the settlement price to mark to market the investor's position, so that any gain or loss from the position is quickly reflected in the investor's equity account.

Maintenance margin is the minimum level (specified by the exchange) to which an investor's equity position may fall as a result of an unfavorable price movement before the investor is required to deposit additional margin. The additional margin deposited is called **variation margin**, and it is the amount necessary to bring the equity in the account back to its initial margin level. Unlike initial margin, the variation margin must be in cash rather than in interest-bearing instruments. Any excess margin in the account may be withdrawn by the investor. If a party to a futures contract who is required to deposit variation margin fails to do so within 24 hours, the exchange closes the futures position out.

Although there are initial and maintenance margin requirements for buying securities on margin, the concept of margin differs for securities and futures. When securities are acquired on margin, the difference between the price of the security and the initial margin is borrowed from the broker. The security purchased serves as collateral for the loan, and the investor pays interest. For futures contracts, the initial margin, in effect, serves as good faith money, an indication that the investor will satisfy the obligation of the contract. Normally, no money is borrowed by the investor who takes a futures position.

To illustrate the mark-to-market procedure, let's assume the following margin requirements for Asset XYZ: (1) initial margin of $7 per contract and (2) maintenance margin of $4 per contract. Let's assume that Bob buys 500 contracts at a futures price of $100, and Sally sells the same number of contracts at the same futures price. The initial margin for both Bob and Sally is $3,500, which is determined by multiplying the initial margin of $7 by the number of contracts, which is 500. Bob and Sally must put up $3,500 in cash or Treasury bills or other acceptable collateral. At this time, $3,500 is also called the "equity in the account." The maintenance margin for the two positions is $2,000 (the maintenance margin per contract of $4 multiplied by 500 contracts). The equity in the account may not fall below $2,000. If it does, the party whose equity falls below the maintenance margin must put up additional margin, which is the variation margin. Two points are worth noting here. First, the variation margin must be cash. Second, the amount of variation margin required is the amount needed to bring the equity up to the initial margin, not to the maintenance margin.

To illustrate the mark-to-market procedure, assume the following settlement prices at the end of several trading days after the transaction was entered into:

Trading Day	Settlement Price
1	$99
2	$97
3	$98
4	$95

First, consider Bob's position. At the end of trading day 1, Bob realizes a loss of $1 per contract, or $500 for the 500 contracts he bought. Bob's initial equity of $3,500 is reduced by $500 to $3,000. No action is taken by the clearinghouse, because Bob's equity is still above the maintenance margin of $2,000. At the end of the second day, Bob realizes a further loss as the price of the futures contract has declined another $2 to $97, resulting in an additional reduction in his equity position by $1,000. Bob's equity is then $2,000: the equity at the end of trading day 1 of $3,000 minus the loss on trading day 2 of $1,000. Despite the loss, no action is taken by the clearinghouse, because the equity still meets the $2,000 maintenance requirement. At the end of trading day 3, Bob realizes a profit from the previous trading day of $1 per contract or $500. Bob's equity increases to $2,500. The drop in price from $98 to $95 at the end of trading day 4 results in a loss for the 500 contracts of $1,500 and consequent reduction of Bob's equity to $1,000. As Bob's equity is now below the $2,000 maintenance margin, Bob is required to put up additional margin of $2,500 (variation margin) to bring the equity up to the initial margin of $3,500. If Bob cannot put up the variation margin his position will be liquidated.

Now, let's look at Sally's position. Sally as the seller of the futures contract benefits if the price of the futures contract declines. As a result, her equity increases at the end of the first two trading days. In fact, at the end of trading day 1, she realizes a profit of $500, which increases her equity to $4,000. She is entitled to take out the $500 profit and use these funds elsewhere. Suppose she does, and her equity, therefore, remains at $3,500 at the end of trading day 1. At the end of trading day 2, she realizes an additional profit of $1,000 that she also withdraws. At the end of trading day 3, she realizes a loss of $500 with the increase of the price from $97 to $98. This results in a reduction of her equity to $3,000. Finally, on trading day 4, she realizes a profit of $1,000, making her equity $4,000. She can withdraw $500.

Leveraging Aspect of Futures

A party taking a position in a futures contract need not put up the entire amount of the investment. Instead, the exchange or clearinghouse requires only the initial margin to be put up. To see the crucial consequences of this fact, suppose Bob has $100 and wants to invest in Asset XYZ, because he believes its price will appreciate. If Asset XYZ is selling for $100, he can buy one unit of the asset. His payoff will then be based on the price action of one unit of Asset XYZ.

Suppose further that the exchange where the futures contract for Asset XYZ is traded requires an initial margin of only 5%, which in this case, would be $5. This means Bob can purchase 20 contracts with his $100 investment. (We ignore the fact that Bob may need funds for variation margin.) His payoff will then depend on the price action of 20 units of Asset XYZ. Thus, he can leverage the use of his funds. (The degree of leverage equals 1/margin rate. In this case, the degree of leverage equals 1/0.05, or 20.) Although the degree of leverage available in the futures market varies from contract to contract, as the initial margin requirement varies, the leverage attainable is considerably greater than in the cash market.

At first, the leverage available in the futures market may suggest that the market benefits mainly those who want to speculate on price movements. As we shall see in chapter 35, however, futures markets can also be used to reduce price risk. Without the leverage possible in futures transactions, the cost of reducing price risk using futures would be too high for many market participants.

Daily Price Limits

The exchange has the right to impose a limit on the daily price movement of a futures contract from the previous day's closing price. A **daily price limit** sets the minimum and maximum price at which the futures contract may trade that day. When a daily price limit is reached, trading does not stop but rather continues at a price that does not violate the minimum or maximum price.

The rationale offered for the imposition of daily price limits is that they provide stability to the market at times when new information may cause the futures price to exhibit extreme fluctuations. Those who support daily price limits argue that giving market participants time to digest or reassess such information if price is restricted when price limits would be violated gives them greater confidence in the market. Not all economists agree with this rationale. The question of the role of daily price limits and whether they are necessary remains the subject of extensive debate.

Futures versus Forward Contracts

A **forward contract**, just like a futures contract, is an agreement for the future delivery of the underlying at a specified price at the end of a designated period. Futures contracts are standardized agreements as to the delivery date (or month) and quality of the deliverable, and they are traded on organized exchanges. A forward contract is usually nonstandardized, because the terms of each contract are negotiated individually between buyer and seller. Also, there is no clearinghouse for trading forward contracts, and secondary markets are often nonexistent or extremely thin. Unlike a futures contract, which is an exchange-traded product, a forward contract is an over-the-counter (OTC) instrument.

Although both futures and forward contracts set forth terms of delivery, futures contracts are not intended to be settled by delivery. In fact, generally fewer than 2% of outstanding futures contracts are settled by delivery. In contrast, forward contracts are intended for delivery.

Futures contracts are marked to market at the end of each trading day. Consequently, futures contracts are subject to interim cash flows, as additional margin may be required in the case of adverse price movements, or as an investor who has experienced favorable price movements withdraws any cash that exceeds the account's margin requirement. A forward contract may or may not be marked to market, depending on the wishes of the two parties. For a forward contract that is not marked to market, there are no interim cash flow effects, because no additional margin is required.

Finally, the parties in a forward contract are exposed to credit risk, because either party may default on the obligation. Credit risk is minimal in the case of futures contracts, because the clearinghouse associated with the exchange guarantees the other side of any transaction.

Other than these differences, which reflect the institutional arrangements in the two markets, most of what we say about futures contracts applies equally to forward contracts.

Risk-Sharing versus Insurance Arrangements

As mentioned at the outset of this chapter, derivatives allow for the transfer of risk. The two types of risk transfer arrangements are risk-sharing and insurance arrangements.

Risk-Sharing Arrangements

Futures and forward contracts are risk-sharing arrangements because of the nature of the payoff of futures contracts. For simplicity, let us consider a commodity futures contract rather than a financial futures contract.

Consider a producer of crude oil and a manufacturing firm that uses crude oil. Both are concerned about the price of crude oil in the future. The former is concerned that after the crude oil is produced, the future price of crude oil will decline below its current market price; the latter is concerned that when crude oil is needed in the future, its price will be higher than the current market price. Both parties are concerned with price risk. A futures contract allows both parties to manage this risk.

A straightforward way to manage risk is for the two parties to agree to a fixed price at which to transact (buy and sell) at some specified future date. For example, suppose the crude oil producer and the manufacturing firm agree to exchange X barrels of crude oil three months from now at a fixed price of $101 per barrel. By doing so, both parties have eliminated price risk for crude oil three months from now. Both have also given up the opportunity to benefit from a favorable movement in the price of crude oil three months from now. Because both parties are sharing the price risk, a futures contract is said to be a "risk-sharing arrangement."

Given this arrangement, let's consider what happens for every $1 per barrel change in the market price of crude oil three months from now. For every $1 per barrel decrease in the price, the crude oil producer realizes a gain by having agreed to sell crude oil for $101 per barrel when its market price is $100. The gain from the agreement offsets the loss of having to sell a barrel of crude oil in the market three months from now for $100 per barrel. The manufacturing firm realizes a loss of $1 per barrel, but that loss is offset by the firm's being able to buy crude oil in the market for $1 less. Similarly, if the market price of crude oil increases three months from now, the crude oil producer realizes a loss on the agreement, but that loss is offset by the producer's being able to sell crude oil at a higher price. Similarly, the manufacturing firm realizes a gain on the arrangement, but that gain is offset by the higher cost of purchasing crude oil in the market.

This payoff pattern is referred to as a **symmetric payoff**. Because in such a payoff, every $1 change in the price of the underlying results in an identical gain or loss for the two parties, this type of arrangement is also referred to as a **linear payoff derivative**.

Interest rate and equity swaps are other types of derivatives that are risk-sharing arrangements.

Insurance Arrangements

Now that we understand what a risk-sharing arrangement for transferring price risk is, let's look at another way of managing the price risk faced by the two parties in our illustration and introduce a solution from the perspective of the manufacturing firm. By doing so, we will clarify the concept of an insurance arrangement.

Suppose that some third party is willing to ensure that the manufacturing firm will not have to pay more than $101 per barrel for crude oil three months from now. Basically, this would be an insurance contract that the third party would provide. It would specify that for a fee, which is effectively an insurance premium, the manufacturing firm is guaranteed not to have to pay more than $101 per barrel for crude oil three months from now. Let's assume that the insurance premium is $1.50 per barrel.

Effectively, the manufacturing firm is establishing a maximum price for crude oil of $102.50 per barrel, the price of $101 under the insurance contract plus the insurance premium of $1.50. Suppose that the price of crude oil increases to more than $101 per barrel three months from now. Then the manufacturing firm will require the insurer to sell the manufacturing firm crude oil for $101 per barrel. The manufacturing firm effectively pays $102.50 and avoids the higher price. Now suppose the price of crude oil declines to $98 per barrel. The manufacturing firm then just walks away from the agreement (remember, the contract allows but does not require the manufacturing firm to buy the crude oil), losing only the $1.50 insurance premium.

Effectively, the manufacturing firm pays $99.50 per barrel ($98 + $1.50). In this way, the manufacturing firm benefits from a favorable price movement for crude oil but limits the loss to the insurance premium. From the third party's perspective (effectively, the insurer's), there is considerable downside risk, and the upside potential is limited to the insurance premium. This type of payoff is referred to as a "nonlinear payoff," and hence, derivatives with this attribute are referred to as **nonlinear payoff derivatives** or **asymmetric payoff derivatives**.

This type of payoff occurs, because unlike the case of a linear payoff derivative, where both parties are required to act, with a nonlinear payoff derivative, only one party is required to perform: the party providing the insurance. In terms of their economic function, nonlinear payoff derivatives are equivalent to insurance, so they are often referred to as **insurance arrangements**.

What type of derivative has this type of payoff? As we will see in the chapter 34, options fall into this category of derivatives.

Stock-Related Contracts

In this section, we describe major stock-related futures contracts. Stock-related futures contracts include broad-based stock index futures, narrow-based stock index futures, and single-stock futures. Another type of equity-related futures contract is one where the underlying is some measure of stock market volatility.

Broad-Based Stock Index Futures

Seeking to accommodate institutional investors' need for financial instruments to control risk for portfolios, in 1982, exchanges offered some broad-based stock index futures contracts that covered U.S. and non-U.S. equity markets.

In the United States, the securities law defines a broad-based stock index as a basket of securities for which the weight of any single constituent does not exceeds 30% and the weight of the five largest components does not exceed 60% of the index. All other indexes are said to be "narrow-based" indexes and stock index futures, which we discuss in the next section.

The distinction between broad-based and narrow-based indexes is important, because it determines which U.S. government entity regulates the stock-related futures contract: the SEC or the Commodities Futures Trading Commission (CFTC).[1] The former regulates stock index futures contracts where the underlying is a broad-based index, and the latter regulates stock index futures contracts where the underlying is a narrow-based index.

Regardless of the stock index futures contract, its dollar value is the product of the futures price and the contract's multiple:

$$\text{Dollar value of a stock index futures contract} = \text{Futures price} \times \text{Contract multiple.}$$

For example, the contract multiple for the S&P 500 futures contract is \$250. For some indexes, there is a "mini contract." The introduction of mini contracts was to allow for their use by retail (as opposed to institutional) investors. Consequently, when referring to contracts that have a corresponding mini contract, the larger contract is referred to as the "full contract." For example, in the case of the S&P 500 futures contact, the contract multiple for full contract is \$250. The mini contract is one-fifth of the S&P 500 futures contract, so the contract multiple is \$50.

To illustrate the formula, if the futures price for the S&P 500 futures contract is 2,160.00, then the dollar value of the full contract is $2160.00 \times \$250 = \$540{,}000$, and for the mini contract it is $2160.00 \times \$50 = \$108{,}000$.

Now that we know how the value of a stock index futures contract is determined, let's see how an investor gains or loses when the futures price changes. Once again, consider the S&P 500 full futures contract. Suppose an investor buys (takes a long position in) an S&P 500 full futures contract at 2160 and sells it at 2,190. The investor realizes a profit of 30 points times \$250, or \$7,500. If the futures contract is sold instead for 2140, the investor realizes a loss of 20 points times \$250, or \$5,000.

As indicated, the S&P500 futures contract at the CME is based on \$250 times the value of the S&P500 (1). So, if the S&P500 was at 3,000, the futures contract would have a value of \$750,000. This large size and the resulting volatility made it too large a trading exposure for many individual investors (and speculators). As a result, in September 1997 the CME listed a smaller futures contract on the S&P500 index. It was valued at \$50 times the S&P500, one fifth the size of the full-sized contract. The other contract specifications were the same. This contract was traded electronically, not floor traded as were the original contacts. Due to its electronic trading, it was able to be kept open for longer trading hours (Sunday to Friday, 5:00 p.m. to 4:00 p.m. central daylight time). It is closed for one hour a day for maintenance. Thus, it provides almost 24-hour-per-day market access. The small size, low margins, and long trading hours make it ideal for active speculators. This contract has become one of the largest futures contact in the world. This contract, due to its

1. The regulator of stock-related futures contract is determined by the agreement between the SEC and CFTC known as the Shad-Johnson Accord.

specifications, is called an “E-Mini” contract. Stock index futures contracts such as on the Nasdaq 100 and the S&P MidCap 400 were also added. These E- mini futures prices are continuously available and are covered widely in the press.

Stock index futures contracts are cash settlement contracts. Therefore, at the settlement date, cash will be exchanged to settle the contract. As explained earlier, futures contracts come with margin requirements (initial, maintenance, and variation). Margin requirements are revised periodically. The exchanges classify users of contracts as hedgers or speculators, with the margin for the former being less than that for the latter. Futures positions are marked to market at the end of each trading day.

Narrow-Based Stock Index Futures

Futures exchanges have found that there are investors who want to take long and short positions in the stock market for a group of stocks and do so by paying for only one trade. Hence only one brokerage commission is paid to trade the group of stocks. These futures contracts are referred to as **narrow-based stock index futures**.

In the United States, securities law defines a narrow-based stock index as an index in which (1) the index has nine or fewer component securities, (2) a component security comprises more than 30% of the index’s weighting, (3) the five highest weighted component securities in the aggregate comprise more than 60% of the index’s weighting, or (4) the lowest weighted component securities comprise, in the aggregate, 25% of the index’s weighting, have an aggregate dollar value of average daily trading volume of less than $50 million (or in the case of an index with 15 or more component securities, $30 million). Futures on security indexes that are not narrow-based indexes are not subject to the jurisdiction of the SEC.

The unit of trading for these indexes is the notional value of the index divided by 1,000. That is, the market value for each component of the index is multiplied by its number of shares specified in the contract. The sum of all the market values of the components is then computed, and the total market value is divided by 1,000.

Single-Stock Futures

There are single-stock futures on selected stocks: futures in which the underlying is the stock of an individual company. The contracts are for 100 shares of the underlying stock. At the settlement date, physical delivery of the stock is required. Although single-stock futures are traded in several countries outside the United States, trading in these contracts was banned until late 2000.[2] It was not until November 2002 that they began trading in the United States. Single-stock futures contracts can be used by portfolio managers as a substitute for long and

2. This ban was to the result of an earlier regulatory dispute between the SEC and CFTC as to which regulatory body should have control over single-stock futures. The dispute resulted in the 1984 Johnson-Shad Accord ban-

short positions in the underlying stocks. As of 2016, on the Eurex Exchange there were more than 1,100 single stock futures from 20 different global markets, including emerging markets.

Stock Market Volatility Futures

A key risk factor for equity investors is stock market volatility. Several indexes have been developed for gauging stock market volatility. These indexes are forward-looking measures of stock market volatility that investors might expect to see over some period of time. The volatility measure used is the implied volatility of the options traded on a specific broad-based market index. Thus, the underlying cannot be purchased in the cash market. When we describe options in chapter 34 and the pricing of options in chapter 35, the concept of implied volatility of an option will be explained.

The first stock market volatility index that has been commercialized is the Chicago Board Options Exchange (CBOE) Market Volatility Index (VIX), dubbed the "investor fear index." The VIX is based on the S&P 500 index options with 30 days to expiration. Hence, the VIX is a measure of the forward-looking volatility of the S&P 500 over the next 30 days. The methodology developed for the construction of the VIX has been used by the CBOE to create a market volatility index for the Dow Jones Industrial Average (VXD), the NASDAQ 100 (VXN), and the Russell 2000 (RVX). The NYSE Euronext has created market volatility indexes for several European countries: the AEX (an index of 25 stocks traded in Amsterdam), the BEL20 (an index of 20 Belgium stocks), and the CAC40 (an index of 40 French stocks).

Interest Rate Futures Contracts

Interest rate futures contracts were first introduced in the United States in October 1975. Today, numerous types of interest rate futures contracts are traded, and the number continues to grow. In the United States, the two major exchanges where interest rate futures contracts are traded are the Chicago Mercantile Exchange Group (CME) and the NYSE Euronext Global Derivatives exchanges.

Both exchanges provide short-term interest rate futures products that allow exposure to U.S. short-term LIBOR (Eurodollar futures) and short-term euro interest rates (euribor futures). In addition, the exchanges already offer or plan to offer other short-term interest rate products that allow exposure to short-term interest rates outside the United States. For example, the NYSE Liffe trades short gilt futures and Euroswiss futures, allowing exposure to U.K. and Swiss short-term rates, respectively.

Both exchanges offer U.S. Treasury futures, including two-year, five-year, and 10-year Treasury notes, 30-year Treasury bonds, and ultra Treasury bond futures. The ultra Treasury bond futures is a contract created for managing long-term interest rates.

---

ning single-stock futures. The Commodity Futures Modernization Act of 2002 repealed the ban on single-stock futures, clearing the path for trading of this product in the United States.

Each futures contract specifies what is permissible to deliver (deliverable grades), price quotations system, tick size (i.e., the smallest price increment in which a financial instrument's price can be quoted), contract months, last trading day, last delivery day, and delivery method. For the futures contracts mentioned above, information is available from the website of each exchange. Here we discuss the two short-term interest rate futures traded on both exchanges (the Eurodollar futures and euribor futures) and the U.S. Treasury futures contracts (Treasury bond, Treasury note, and Treasury ultra bond futures).

Outside the United States, there are exchanges that list interest rate futures with short-, intermediate-, and long-term maturities. For example, the Eurex Exchange includes short-term interest rate futures traded on the euribor and the Euro Over Night Index Average. The government bond futures traded on the Euro Exchange, for example, include four German debt maturities: Euro-Schatz futures (short-term debt instrument with a term of 1.75 to 2.25 years), Euro-Bobl futures (medium-term debt instrument with a term of 4.5 to 5 years), Euro-Bund (long-term debt instrument with a term of 8.5 to 10.5 years), and Euro-Buxl (long-term debt instrument with a term of 24 to 35 years).

Below we briefly describe the U.S. interest rate futures contracts.

Eurodollar Futures

One of the most heavily traded futures contracts in the world, the Eurodollar futures contract, is frequently used to trade the short end of the yield curve, and many hedgers have found this contract to be the best hedging vehicle for a wide range of hedging situations.

A Eurodollar futures contract represents a commitment to pay/receive a quarterly interest payment determined by the level of the three-month LIBOR. The dollar amount paid is based on a notional principal of $1 million on the settlement date. Various quarterly settlement dates for Eurodollar futures contracts are available—March, June, September, and December—that extend out 10 years. The Eurodollar futures contract is a cash settlement contract. That is, the parties settle in cash for the value of the contract based on LIBOR on the settlement date.

This contract is traded on an index-price basis. The index-price basis on which the contract is quoted is equal to 100 minus the annualized futures LIBOR. For example, a Eurodollar futures price of 97.00 means a futures three-month LIBOR of 3%.

The minimum price fluctuation (tick) for this contract is 0.01 (or 0.0001 in terms of LIBOR). As a result, the price value of a basis point for this contract is $25, found as follows. The simple interest on $1 million for 90 days is equal to

$$\$1{,}000{,}000 \times (\text{LIBOR} \times 90/360).$$

If LIBOR changes by one basis point (0.0001), then $\$1{,}000{,}000 \times (0.0001 \times 90/360) = \$25$.

Euribor Futures

The euro interbank offered rate (euribor) is a reference rate at which banks in the eurozone lend unsecured funds to one another. As with LIBOR, this reference rate is an interbank rate. The contract represents a commitment to pay/receive a quarterly interest payment determined by the level of three-month euribor. The amount paid is based on a notional principal of €1 million on the settlement date. The contract is a cash settlement contract.

As with Eurodollar futures, the contract is quoted on an index-price basis, as follows: 100 minus the annualized futures reference rate, where the reference rate is based on euribor rather than on LIBOR. For example, a euribor futures price of 97.00 means a futures three-month euribor of 3%. The minimum price fluctuation (tick) for this contract is 0.005 (or 0.00005 in terms of euribor). Thus the price value of a basis point for this contract is €12.50.

U.S. Treasury Bond Futures

The underlying instrument for a U.S. Treasury bond futures contract is $100,000 par value of a hypothetical 20-year, 6% coupon bond. The futures price is quoted in terms of par being 100. Quotes are in 32nds of 1%. Thus, a quotation for a Treasury bond futures contract of 97–16 means 97 and 16/32, or 97.50. So, if a buyer and seller agree on a futures price of 97–16, the buyer agrees to accept delivery of the hypothetical underlying Treasury bond and pay 97.50% of par value, and the seller agrees to accept 97.50% of par value. Because the par value is $100,000, the futures price that the buyer and seller agree to pay for this hypothetical Treasury bond is $97,500.

As mentioned, the minimum price fluctuation for the Treasury bond futures contract is a 32nd of 1%. The dollar value of a 32nd for a $100,000 par value (the par value for the underlying Treasury bond) is $31.25. Thus, the minimum price fluctuation is $31.25 for this contract.

We have been referring to the underlying as a hypothetical Treasury bond. That reference does not mean that the contract is a cash settlement contract. The seller of Treasury bond futures who decides to make delivery rather than liquidate the position by buying back the contract prior to the settlement date must deliver some Treasury bond. But what Treasury bond? The exchange where the contract is traded allows the seller to deliver one of several Treasury bonds that the exchange declares is acceptable for delivery. The specific Treasury bond issues that the seller may deliver are published by the exchange prior to the initial trading of a futures contract with a specific settlement date.

The delivery process for the Treasury bond futures contract makes the contract interesting. At the settlement date, the seller of a futures contract (the short) is required to deliver to the buyer (the long) $100,000 par value of a 6%, 20-year Treasury bond. Because no such bond exists, the seller must choose from one of the acceptable deliverable Treasury bonds that the exchange has specified. Suppose the seller is entitled to deliver $100,000 of a 4%,

20-year Treasury bond to settle the futures contract. The value of this bond, of course, is less than the value of a 6%, 20-year Treasury bond. Delivery of a 4%, 20-year Treasury bond would be unfair to the buyer of the futures contract, who contracted to receive $100,000 of a 6%, 20-year Treasury bond. Alternatively, suppose the seller delivers $100,000 of a 10%, 20-year Treasury bond. The value of a 10%, 20-year Treasury bond is greater than that of a 6%, 20-year Treasury bond, which would be a disadvantage to the seller.

To make delivery equitable to both parties, the exchange provides conversion factors for determining the invoice price of each acceptable deliverable Treasury issue against the Treasury bond futures contract. The conversion factor is determined by the exchange before a contract with a specific settlement date begins trading and is constant throughout the trading period of the futures contract for a given settlement month. The short must notify the long of the actual bond that will be delivered one day before the delivery date.

The invoice price for the Treasury bond futures contract is the futures price plus accrued interest. However, as just noted, the seller can deliver one of several acceptable Treasury issues, and to make delivery fair to both parties, the invoice price must be adjusted based on the actual Treasury issue delivered. The conversion factors are used to adjust the invoice price as follows:

$$\text{Invoice price} = \text{Contract size} \times \text{Futures contract settlement price} \times \text{Conversion factor} + \text{Accrued interest}.$$

Suppose the Treasury bond futures contract settles at 94–08, and the short elects to deliver a Treasury bond issue with a conversion factor of 1.20. The futures contract settlement price of 94–08 means 94.25% of par value. As the contract size is $100,000, the invoice price that the buyer pays the seller is

$$\$100{,}000 \times 0.9425 \times 1.20 + \text{Accrued interest} = \$113{,}100 + \text{Accrued interest}.$$

When selecting the issue to be delivered, the short will select from all the deliverable issues the one that is cheapest to deliver. This issue is referred to as the **cheapest-to-deliver issue** and plays a key role in the pricing of a futures contract. The cheapest-to-deliver issue is determined by participants in the market as follows. For each of the acceptable Treasury issues from which the seller can select, the seller calculates the return that can be earned by buying that issue and delivering it at the settlement date. Note that the seller can calculate the return based on the known price of the Treasury issue now and the futures price agreed to for delivery of the issue. The return so calculated is called the **implied repo rate**. The cheapest-to-deliver issue is then the one issue among all acceptable Treasury issues with the highest implied repo rate, because it is the issue that would give the seller of the futures contract the highest return by buying and then delivering the issue.

In addition to the choice of which acceptable Treasury issue to deliver—sometimes referred to as the **quality option** or **swap option**—the short position has two more options granted under the exchange delivery guidelines. The short position is permitted to decide when in the delivery month the delivery will actually take place, which is called the **timing option**. The other option is the right of the short position to give notice of intent to deliver up to 8:00 p.m. Chicago time after the closing of the exchange (3:15 p.m. Chicago time) on the date when the futures settlement price has been fixed. This option is referred to as the **wild card option**. The quality option, the timing option, and the wild card option (in sum referred to as the **delivery options**) mean that the long position can never be sure which Treasury bond will be delivered or when it will be delivered.

The contract specification for the Treasury bond futures has been used in other countries to design a futures contract on their government bonds.

Treasury Note Futures

There are three U.S. Treasury note futures contracts: 10-year, five-year, and two-year. All three contracts are modeled after the Treasury bond futures contract and are traded on the exchange. The underlying instrument for the 10-year Treasury note futures contract is $100,000 par value of a hypothetical 10-year, 6% Treasury note. Several acceptable Treasury issues may be delivered by the short. An issue is acceptable if the maturity is not less than 6.5 years and not greater than 10 years from the first day of the delivery month. Delivery options are granted to the short position.

For the five-year Treasury note futures contract, the underlying is $100,000 par value of a 6% notional coupon U.S. Treasury note that satisfies the following conditions: (1) an original maturity of not more than five years and three months, (2) a remaining maturity no greater than five years and three months, and (3) a remaining maturity not less than four years and two months. The underlying for the two-year Treasury note futures contract is $200,000 par value of a 6% notional coupon U.S. Treasury note with a remaining maturity of not more than two years and not less than one year and nine months. Moreover, the original maturity of the note delivered to satisfy the two-year futures cannot be more than five years and three months.

Ultra Treasury Bond Futures

For the U.S. Treasury bond futures, the rule beginning with the March 2011 contract was that acceptable deliverable bond issues had to have a maturity of at least 15 years but no more than 25 years. The deliverable specification for the ultra Treasury bond futures contract calls for the acceptable deliverable bonds to have at least 25 years to maturity. All other specifications for the contract are the same as for the Treasury bond futures contract.

By modifying the Treasury bond futures contract to limit maturity for deliverable bond issues to less than 25 years and requiring the ultra Treasury bond futures contract's deliverable bond issues to have at least 25 years to maturity, the exchange allowed market participants to manage the longer end of the yield curve more effectively. The Treasury bond futures contract is effectively a short-maturity bond futures contract, and the ultra Treasury bond futures contract is effectively a long-maturity bond futures contract that is better suited for managing the interest rate risk for portfolios of long-term bonds.

Currency Forward and Futures Contracts

Both forward and futures contracts are available to market participants to control foreign exchange-rate risk.

Currency Forward Contracts

Most currency forward contracts have a maturity of less than two years. Longer-dated forward contracts have relatively large bid-ask spreads; that is, the size of the bid-ask spread for a given currency increases with the maturity of the contract. Consequently, forward contracts are not attractive for hedging long-dated foreign currency exposure. In chapter 38, we will discuss a derivative instrument (a currency swap) that can be used for this purpose.

Futures contracts, which are creations of an exchange, have certain advantages over forward contracts in many cases, such as stock indexes and government securities. In contrast, the forward market is the market of choice for foreign exchange, and trading there is much larger than trading on exchanges. However, because the foreign exchange forward market is an interbank market, reliable information on the number of contracts outstanding at any time, or open interest, is not publicly available.

Currency Futures Contracts

As explained earlier, futures contracts are exchange-traded products, as opposed to forward contracts, which are OTC contracts. In the case of currency futures contracts, the major exchange is the CME. The exchange rates traded are those between the U.S. dollar and the currencies of the following countries: Australia, Belgium, Canada, Japan, New Zealand, Norway, Switzerland, the United Kingdom, and Sweden.

In addition, there are futures contracts in which the underlying is a cross-rate pair (i.e., an exchange rate that does involve the local currency). For example, for a U.S. investor, the exchange rate between the euro and Japanese yen would be a cross-rate pair. Futures contracts are available on the following cross-rates: the Swiss franc/Japanese yen exchange rate, the euro/Canadian dollar exchange rate, and the British pound/Japanese yen exchange rate.

Futures contracts are also available for emerging market currency pairs with the U.S. dollar and the following four currencies: the Brazilian real, the Czech koruna, the Israeli shekel, and the Hungarian forint. Cross-rate pairs are also available with the euro.

The amount of each foreign currency that must be delivered for a contract varies by currency. For example, the British pound futures contract calls for delivery of 62,500 pounds, the Japanese yen futures contract calls for delivery of 12.5 million yen, and the euro futures contract calls for delivery of €125,000. There are "E-micro" contracts that provide for one-tenth of the contract size. The maturity cycle for currency futures is March, June, September, and December. The longest maturity is one year. Consequently, as in the case of a currency forward contract, currency futures do not provide a good vehicle for hedging long-dated foreign exchange-rate risk exposure.

Role of Futures Contracts in Financial Markets

In the absence of futures contracts, investors would have only one trading location to alter portfolio positions when they get new information that is expected to influence the value of assets—the cash market. If economic news that is expected to have an adverse impact on the value of an asset is received, investors can reduce their price-risk exposure to that asset. The opposite is true if the new information is expected to have a favorable impact on the value of that asset: an investor would increase price-risk exposure to that asset. Of course, transaction costs are associated with altering exposure to an asset: explicit costs (commissions) and hidden or execution costs (bid-ask spreads and market impact costs).[3]

Futures markets provide another market that investors can use to alter their risk exposure to an asset when new information is acquired. But which market—cash or futures—should the investor employ to alter a position quickly on the receipt of new information? The answer is simple: the one that is more efficient to use to achieve the objective. The factors to consider are liquidity (including speed of execution), transaction costs, and leverage. In well-developed futures markets, it is the futures market and not the cash market that offers better liquidity, far lower transaction costs, and has embedded leverage (a property of futures described earlier in this chapter).

The market that investors feel is the one that is more efficient to use to achieve their investment objectives should be the one where prices will be established that reflect the new economic information. That is, it will be the market where price discovery takes place. Price information is then transmitted to the other market. In many of the markets that we discuss in this book, it is easier and less costly to alter a portfolio position in the futures market. Therefore, the futures market will be the market of choice and will serve as the price discovery market. It is in the futures market that investors send a collective message about how any new information is expected to impact the cash market.

How is this message sent to the cash market? We will see in chapter 35 how the theoretical futures price is determined. That chapter discusses how the futures price and the cash market price are tied together in a specific way and shows that if the actual futures market price deviates from the theoretical futures market price, arbitrageurs (attempting to obtain

3. These costs are discussed in chapter 25.

arbitrage profits) would pursue a strategy to bring them back into line. Arbitrage brings the cash market price into line with the futures price. This mechanism ensures that the cash market price will reflect the information collected in the futures market.

Is it possible for the futures market to take on a life of its own, so that the futures price does not reflect the economic value of the contract's underlying instrument? It could be, if no mechanism were available to bring futures prices and cash market prices in line. This mechanism is the arbitrage we just mentioned and will be explained chapter 34.

Effect of Futures on the Volatility of the Underlying Asset

A criticism that has been frequently raised by some investors and the popular press is that the introduction of futures markets has increased the volatility of prices of the underlying asset. This criticism is referred to as the "destabilization hypothesis."[4] Two variants of the destabilization hypothesis are the liquidity variant and the populist variant.

According to the liquidity variant, large transactions that are too difficult to accommodate in the cash market will be executed first in the futures market because of better liquidity. The increased volatility that may occur in the futures market is only temporary, because volatility will return to its normal level once the liquidity problem is resolved. The implication is that no long-term impact on the volatility of the underlying cash market asset will occur.

In contrast, the populist variant asserts that as a result of speculative trading in the futures market, the cash market instrument does not reflect fundamental economic value. The implication here is that the asset price would better reflect economic value in the absence of a futures market.

It is an empirical question as to whether the introduction of a futures market destabilizes prices.[5] However, regardless of whether the introduction of futures or swaps contracts increases cash market price volatility, we might ask whether greater volatility inflicts negative effects on markets. At first glance, it might seem that volatility adversely affects allocative efficiency and market participation.

Actually, some analysts point out that this inference may not be justified if, say, the introduction of new markets lets prices respond more promptly to changes in fundamentals, and if the fundamentals themselves are subject to large shocks.[6] Thus the greater volatility resulting from an innovation may simply more faithfully reflect the actual variability of

4. Lawrence Harris, "S&P 500 Futures and Cash Stock Price Volatility," unpublished manuscript, University of Southern California, Los Angeles, 1987.

5. The following study concluded that, in general, it would take a substantial number of "irrational" speculators to destabilize cash markets: Jerome L. Stein, "Real Effects of Futures Speculation: Rational Expectations and Diverse Opinions," Working Paper 88 (New York: Center for the Study of Futures Markets, Columbia University, 1984).

6. Eugene F. Fama, "Perspectives on October 1987, or What Did We Learn from the Crash?" in *Black Monday and the Future of Financial Markets*, ed. Robert J. Barro, Robert W. Kamphuis, Roger C. Kormendi, and J. W. Henry Watson. (Homewood, IL: Dow Jones-Irwin, 1989), 72.

fundamental values. In this case, more asset volatility need not be a bad artifact but instead may be a manifestation of a well-functioning market. Of course, to say that more volatility need not be bad does not mean that it is good. Clearly, price volatility greater than what can be justified by relevant new information or fundamentals (or by standard asset pricing models) is undesirable. By definition, it makes prices inefficient and is referred to as "excess volatility."[7]

No one has been able to test whether recent financial innovations actually increased or decreased excess volatility. Moreover, as Franklin Edwards has pointed out, "Too little volatility is equally bad, although this concept does not seem to have generated enough interest to have been given the label of 'deficient volatility.'"[8]

A Closer Look at the Benefits of Stock Index Futures

Above we have focused on futures markets in general. Let's look more specifically at stock index futures and the evidence regarding several of the issues identified as associated with the existence of futures markets.

First, a comparison of transaction costs indicates that these costs are substantially lower in the stock index futures market than in the cash market. Typically, transaction costs in this market are between 5% and 10% of transaction costs in the cash market.

Second, the speed at which orders can be executed also gives the advantage to the futures market. The estimated time to sell a block of stock at a reasonable price is about two to three minutes, whereas a futures transaction can be accomplished in 30 seconds or less. The advantage is also on the side of the stock index futures market when it comes to the amount of money that must be put up in a transaction (i.e., leverage). As explained in chapter 23, margin requirements for transactions in the stock market are considerably higher than in the stock index futures market. Thus, a study by the SEC's Division of Market Regulation concludes:

> [Institutions can] sell portions of their equity positions in a faster, less expensive manner by using index futures than by selling directly on stock exchanges.
>
> Futures are used instead of stocks because of the increased speed and reduced transaction costs entailed in trading a single product in the futures market.... As a result of the futures market's liquidity, investors can execute large transactions with much smaller market effects than is possible in the separate stocks.

Which market do investors select to alter their stock market risk exposure? John Merrick found that before 1985, the cash market dominated the price discovery process, relative

7. Franklin R. Edwards, "Futures Trading and Cash Market Volatility: Stock Index and Interest Rate Futures," *Journal of Futures Markets* 8, no. 4 (1988): 423.

8. Edwards, "Futures Trading and Cash Market Volatility," 423.

to the stock index futures market.[9] Since 1985, however, the S&P 500 futures market has played the dominant price discovery role. This reversal of the dominant market was not an accident. It followed the pattern of trading volume. When trading volume in the futures market surpassed that on the cash market, the futures market dominated.

How does the existence of competing markets with the attributes described previously affect the stock market? In her testimony before Congress on July 23, 1987, Susan Phillips, then the chairperson of the Commodity Futures Trading Commission, stated: "The depth and liquidity of the futures markets facilitate the absorption of new fundamental information quickly, thus improving the efficiency of the stock markets."[10]

Critics of stock index futures point to program trading and index arbitrage when a substantial decline in the cash market or increased stock price volatility occurs. As we explained in chapter 23, program trading is a technique for trading lists of stocks as close in time as possible. It is not, as is often stated in the popular press, a trading strategy. Program trades typically are implemented electronically using the automated order-execution facilities of the exchanges that allow orders to be transmitted simultaneously for execution. Why is it important for an institution to execute a list of orders as close in time as possible? Several investment strategies depend on the timing of trades: indexing and index arbitrage. The question is whether either of these strategies that rely on program trading and stock index futures is disruptive to the stock market. We'll describe index arbitrage in chapter 34 and how it ties together cash market prices and futures. Here we just discuss indexing.

Indexing, a strategy explained in chapter 23, is not a strategy that attempts to trade on information. Theory tells us that indexing is a strategy that investors should employ in an efficient market to capture the efficiency embodied in the market. Yet the theory tells us nothing about how to implement the strategy. To manage an indexed portfolio, an asset manager first constructs an initial portfolio to replicate the performance of the market. The asset manager must rebalance the portfolio, however, as new monies are added to or withdrawn from an indexed portfolio. Program trading is used so that all stocks in the portfolio can be sold or purchased by simultaneous order at the closing prices, so that the performance of the indexed portfolio will do a good job of tracking the index. Therefore, indexing should not be a disruptive market force.

Finally, let's look at the issue of the effect of stock index futures on price volatility on the stock market. Several studies empirically investigated the effect of the introduction of stock index futures trading on stock price volatility. In the case of stock index futures, one study concludes:

9. John J. Merrick, Jr., "Price Discovery in the Stock Market," Working Paper 87-4 (Philadelphia: Federal Reserve Bank of Philadelphia, March 1987).

10. *Hearings before the Subcommittee on Telecommunications and Finance, Committee on Energy and Commerce, U.S. House of Representatives,* 100th Cong. (July 23, 1987) (testimony of Susan M. Phillips, chairwoman, Commodity Futures Trading Commission), 1.

> Investors are concerned about the present and future value of their investments (and wealth). Greater volatility leads to a perception of greater risk, which threatens investors' assets and wealth. When the stock market takes a sharp nose-dive, investors see the value of their assets rapidly dissipating. They are not consoled by being told that there is no social cost associated with this price change, only a redistribution of wealth. Even more fundamental, when asset prices exhibit significant volatility over very short periods of time (such as a day), investors "lose confidence in the market." They begin to see financial markets as the province of the speculator and the insider, not the rational.[11]

A fair conclusion that can be drawn from all these studies is that the introduction of stock index futures (as well as stock index options described in chapter 34 and index-related strategies) did not increase stock price volatility except possibly during periods when stock index futures settled and stock index options expired.

Key Points

- The economic function of derivatives is to allow market participants to control risk, and so derivatives are referred to as "risk transfer vehicles."
- The key role of derivatives is that, in a well-functioning futures market, these contracts provide a more efficient means for investors to alter their risk exposure to an asset.
- Futures contracts are classified as commodity futures and financial futures.
- Futures contracts are creations of exchanges.
- A futures contract is an agreement between a buyer and a seller in which the buyer agrees to take delivery of something at the futures price at the settlement date and the seller agrees to make delivery.
- A party to a futures contract can liquidate a position prior to the settlement date by taking an offsetting position in the same contract.
- Associated with every futures exchange is a clearinghouse, which provides a guarantee function.
- Parties to a futures contract must satisfy margin requirements (initial, maintenance, and variation), and futures contracts are marked to market at the end of each trading day.
- Because only initial margin is required when an investor takes a futures position, futures markets provide investors with substantial leverage for the money invested.
- A buyer (seller) of a futures contract realizes a profit if the futures price increases (decreases); the buyer (seller) of a futures contract realizes a loss if the futures price decreases (increases).
- A forward contract is an OTC derivative product.

11. Franklin R. Edwards, "Does Futures Trading Increase Stock Price Volatility?" *Financial Analysts Journal* 44, no. 1 (1988): 64.

• A forward contract differs from a futures contract in that the parties to a forward contract are exposed to the risk of nonperformance by the counterparty and unwinding a position in a forward contract may be difficult.

• Although there is no requirement that the parties to a forward contract mark positions to market, this is typically done to mitigate counterparty risk.

• Financial derivatives can be either a risk-sharing arrangement or an insurance arrangement.

• The type of transfer arrangement depends on the type of payoff: symmetric versus asymmetric.

• Symmetric payoff derivatives (or linear payoff derivatives) are risk-sharing arrangements; asymmetric payoff derivatives (or nonlinear payoff derivatives) are insurance arrangements.

• Futures and forward contracts are risk-sharing types of derivatives.

• With a linear payoff derivative, both parties are required to perform; nonlinear payoff derivatives (asymmetric payoff derivatives) have their specific payoff pattern because only one party to the agreement is obligated to perform, whereas the other party pays a fee to enter into the agreement.

• Options are insurance type derivatives.

• Stock-related futures contracts include broad-based stock index futures, narrow-based stock index futures, single-stock futures, and stock market volatility futures.

• The dollar value of a stock index futures contract is determined by the product of the futures price and the contract's multiple.

• Futures on volatility indexes can be used to manage or speculate on future market volatility.

• Eurodollar futures and euribor futures are the most popular short-term interest rate futures contracts. Both contracts are cash settlement contracts.

• There are two types of U.S. Treasury bond futures contracts: (1) Treasury bond futures, in which the acceptable deliverable bond issues must have at least 15 years to maturity but less than 25 years, and (2) the ultra Treasury bond futures, in which the acceptable deliverable bond issues must have at least 25 years to maturity.

• The Treasury bond and note futures contracts give the short several delivery options, including the quality or swap option, the timing option, and the wild card option.

• There are currency forward and futures contracts.

• Because of the short-term maturity of currency and futures contracts, they are limited with respect to providing market participants with the ability to control foreign-exchange rate risk.

- Futures contracts on major currency pairs with the U.S. dollar, select cross-rate currency pairings, and select emerging market currencies paired with the U.S. dollar and the euro are available.
- Futures markets are often the market of choice for altering asset positions and therefore represent the price discovery market because of the lower transactions costs involved and the greater speed with which orders can be executed compared to the case markets.
- The actions of arbitrageurs ensure that price discovery in the futures markets will be transmitted to the cash market.
- Critics of the futures market believe these markets are the source of greater price volatility in the cash market for the underlying asset.
- Although the destabilization hypothesis regarding the introduction of futures markets is an empirical question, even if price volatility in the cash market were greater, it does not necessarily follow that greater volatility is bad for the economy.

Questions

1. The chief financial officer of the corporation you work for recently told you that he had a strong preference to use forward contracts rather than futures contracts to contracts: "You can get contracts tailor-made to suit your needs."

a. Comment on the chief financial officer's statement.

b. What other factors influence the decision to use futures or forward contracts?

2. Explain the functions of a clearinghouse associated with a futures exchange.

3. Suppose you bought a stock index futures contract for 200 and were required to put up initial margin of $10,000. The value of the contract is 200 times the $500 multiple, or $100,000. On the next three days, the contract's settlement price was at these levels: day 1, 205; day 2, 197; day 3, 190.

a. Calculate the value of your margin account on each day.

b. If the maintenance margin for the contract is $7,000, how much variation margin did the exchange require you to put up at the end of the third day?

c. If you had failed to put up that much, what would the exchange have done?

4. How do margin requirements in the futures market differ from margin requirements in the cash market?

5. Forward contracts are not marked to market derivatives. Explain why you agree or disagree.

6. a. What is meant by "open interest"?

b. Why is open interest important to an investor?

7. a. Why is a futures contract referred to as a "risk-sharing arrangement" for transferring risk?

b. Why is a futures contract a symmetric payoff contract?

8. You work as part of a portfolio management team at an asset management firm. A junior portfolio manager on the team has asked you what type of derivative to use to protect against price risk. She states that insurance type risk transfer derivatives are always the best, because the potential upside benefits do not have to be shared with the counterparty. Comment on the junior portfolio manager's position.

9. What is meant by a "cash settlement futures contract"?

10. What may be an alternative for an investor who wants to short the stock of a particular company instead of shorting in the cash market?

11. a. What was the motivation for the creation of a narrow-based stock index futures contract?

b. How are the component stocks of a narrow-based stock index futures contract selected?

12. On September 1, you sold 100 S&P 500 futures contracts at 1,800 with multiples of $250, expiration date in three months, and an initial margin of 10%. After that date, the index fell steadily, and you were not required to post any additional margin, but you also did not withdraw any of the cash profits you were earning. On November 1, the futures price of the contract was 1,620, and you reversed your position by buying 100 contracts.

a. How much money did you make (ignoring taxes and commissions)?

b. What was the rate of return on your invested funds?

c. In those two months, the S&P 500 futures price fell 10%. Explain why your rate of return is so much higher than this level.

13. "The futures market is where price discovery takes place." Do you agree with this statement? If so, why? If not, why not?

14. What is the underlying instrument for the Eurodollar futures contract?

15. If the index price of a Eurodollar futures contract is 92.40, what is the annualized futures LIBOR contract?

16. What is a euribor futures contract?

17. a. What is the underlying instrument for the Treasury bond futures contract and ultra Treasury bond futures contract?

b. What is the purpose of the conversion factors for the U.S. Treasury bond futures contract?

18. Explain why the implied repo rate is important when determining the cheapest-to-deliver issue.

19. a. For a U.S. Treasury futures contract, there are choices or options granted to one of the parties to the contract. Which party has these choices, the buyer or seller?

b. What are the options that are granted to the party?

20. Currency forward contracts are typically superior to currency futures contracts for controlling long-term foreign exchange-rate risk. Comment on this statement.

21. A U.S. General Accounting Office study discusses the importance of derivatives for market participants. Page 6 of the report states:

> Derivatives serve an important function of the global financial marketplace, providing end-users with opportunities to better manage financial risks associated with their business transactions. The rapid growth and increasing complexity of derivatives reflect both the increased demand from end-users for better ways to manage their financial risks and the innovative capacity of the financial services industry to respond to market demands.[12]

Explain whether you agree or disagree with the conclusions of the report.

12. U.S. General Accountability Office, *Financial Derivatives: Actions Needed to Protect the Financial System* (Washington, DC: U.S. General Accountability Office, May 1994), 6.

34 Options Markets

CONTENTS

Learning Objectives

After reading this chapter, you will understand:

- what an option contract is, and the basic features of an option;
- the difference between a call option and a put option;
- why an option is a derivative instrument;
- the different types of exercise styles for an option (American, European, Bermuda);
- the difference between an exchange-traded option and an over-the-counter option;
- the difference between a futures contract and an option contract;
- the risk/return characteristics of call and put options for both the seller and the buyer of the options;
- the hedging role of options in financial markets;
- the extensive role that organized exchanges play in standardizing and guaranteeing options contracts traded on exchanges;
- how stock options can change the risk/return profile of a portfolio;
- the basic features of stock index options;
- the basic features of interest rate options;
- what an exotic option is;
- some key aspects of non-U.S. options markets; and
- the basic features of options on futures or futures options.

In chapter 33, we introduced a derivative instrument, a futures contract. In this chapter, we introduce another derivative contract, an options contract, and we discuss the differences between the two. In particular, in chapter 33, we explained how derivatives transfer risk by either a risk-sharing arrangement or an insurance arrangement. Unlike futures contracts, which are risk-sharing arrangements, options contracts are insurance arrangements. In chapter 35, we show how to determine the price of an option, and in chapter 36, we explain how market participants can use these contracts.

Options Contracts

There are two parties to an options contract: the buyer and the **writer** (also called the "seller"). In an options contract, the writer of the option grants the buyer of the option the right, but not the obligation, to purchase from or sell to the writer something at a specified price in a specified period of time (or on a specified date). The writer grants this right to the buyer in exchange for a certain sum of money, which is called the **option price** or **option**

premium. The price at which the underlying (that is, the asset or commodity) may be bought or sold is called the **exercise price** or **strike price**. The date after which an option is void is called the **expiration date** or **maturity date**. Our focus in this chapter is on options for which the underlying is a financial instrument or financial index.

When an option grants the buyer the right to purchase the underlying from the writer (seller), it is referred to as a **call option**, or simply, a **call**. When the option buyer has the right to sell the underlying to the writer, the option is called a **put option**, or simply, a **put**.

The timing of the possible exercise of an option is an important characteristic of the contract. This feature of an option is referred to as its **exercise style**. Some options may be exercised at any time up to and including the expiration date. Such options are referred to as **American options**. Other options may be exercised only at the expiration date; these are called **European options**. A **Bermuda option**, also referred to as an **Atlantic option**, can be exercised only on specified dates.

Let's use an illustration to demonstrate the fundamental options contract. Suppose that Jack buys a call option for $3 (the option price) with the following terms:

1. The underlying is one unit of Asset XYZ.
2. The exercise price is $100.
3. The expiration date is three months from now, and the option can be exercised any time up to and including the expiration date (that is, it is an American option).

At any time up to and including the expiration date, Jack can decide to buy from the writer (seller) of this option one unit of Asset XYZ, for which he will pay a price of $100. If it is not beneficial for Jack to exercise the option, he will not, and we'll explain shortly how he decides whether it will be beneficial. Regardless of whether Jack exercises the option, the $3 he paid for the option will be kept by the option writer. If Jack buys a put option rather than a call option, then he would be able to sell Asset XYZ to the option writer for a price of $100.

The maximum amount that an option buyer can lose is the option price. The maximum profit that the option writer (seller) can realize is the option price. The option buyer has substantial upside return potential, whereas the option writer has substantial downside risk. We will investigate the risk/reward relationship for option positions later in this chapter.

There are no margin requirements for the buyer of an option once the option price has been paid in full. Because the option price is the maximum amount that the investor can lose, no matter how adverse the price movement of the underlying, no margin is needed. Because the writer (seller) of an option has agreed to accept all of the risk (and none of the reward) of the position in the underlying, the writer is generally required to put up the option price received as margin. In addition, as price changes occur that adversely affect the writer's position, the writer is required to deposit additional margin (with some exceptions) as the position is marked to market.

Options, like other financial instruments, may be traded either on an organized exchange or in the over-the-counter (OTC) market. **Exchange-traded options** have three advantages. The first is standardization of the exercise price, the quantity of the underlying, and the expiration date of the contract. Second, as in the case of futures contracts, the direct link between buyer and seller is severed after the order is executed because of the interchangeability of exchange-traded options. The clearinghouse associated with the exchange where the option trades performs the same function in the options market it does in the futures market. Finally, the transactions costs are lower for exchange-traded options than for OTC options.

The higher cost of an OTC option reflects the cost of customizing the option for the common situation where an institutional investor needs to have a tailor-made option because the standardized exchange-traded option does not satisfy its investment objectives. Investment banking firms and commercial banks act as principals as well as brokers in the OTC options market. Most institutional investors are not concerned that an OTC option is less liquid than an exchange-traded option because they use OTC options as part of an asset/liability strategy in which they intend to hold them to expiration.

Differences between Options and Futures Contracts

One distinction between futures and options contracts is that one party to an option contract is not obligated to transact at a later date. Specifically, the option buyer has the right but not the obligation to exercise the option. However, the option writer (seller) does have the obligation to perform, if the buyer of the option insists on exercising it. In the case of a futures contract, both buyer and seller are obligated to perform. Of course, a futures buyer does not pay the seller to accept the obligation, whereas an options buyer pays the seller an option price.

Consequently, the risk/reward characteristics of the two contracts are also different. In the case of a futures contract, the buyer of the contract realizes a dollar-for-dollar gain when the price of the futures contract increases and suffers a dollar-for-dollar loss when its price drops. The opposite occurs for the seller of a futures contract. Options do not provide this symmetric risk/reward relationship. The most that the buyer of an option can lose is the option price. Although the buyer of an option retains all the potential benefits, the gain is always reduced by the amount of the option price. The maximum profit that the writer (seller) may realize is the option price; this is offset against substantial downside risk. This difference between options and futures is extremely important, because as we shall see in subsequent chapters, investors can use futures to protect against symmetric risk and options to protect against asymmetric risk.

Now we can see why options are derivatives that have an insurance type arrangement for transferring risk. Unlike a risk-sharing derivative (such as a futures contract) where both parties are required to act, with an options contract, only one party is required to perform: the party providing the insurance. Moreover, options contracts have a nonsymmetric payoff and are therefore nonlinear payoff derivatives.

We will return to the difference between options and futures later in this chapter when we discuss the application of these contracts to hedging.

Risk and Return Characteristics of Options

Here we illustrate the risk and return characteristics of the four basic option positions: buying a call option (which market participants refer to as being **long a call option**), selling a call option (**short a call option**), buying a put option (**long a put option**), and selling a put option (**short a put option**). The illustrations assume that each option position is held to the expiration date and is not exercised early. To simplify the illustrations, we ignore transactions costs.

Buying Call Options

Assume that there is a call option on Asset XYZ that expires in one month and has a strike price of $100. The option price is $3. Suppose that the current price of Asset XYZ is $100. What is the profit or loss for the investor who purchases this call option and holds it to the expiration date?

The profit and loss from the strategy will depend on the price of Asset XYZ at the expiration date. Several outcomes are possible:

1. If Asset XYZ's price at the expiration date is less than $100, the investor will not exercise the option. It would be foolish to pay the option writer $100 when Asset XYZ can be purchased in the market at a lower price. In this case, the option buyer loses the entire, original option price of $3. Notice, however, that this is the maximum loss that the option buyer will realize regardless of how low Asset XYZ's price declines.

2. If Asset XYZ's price is equal to $100 at the expiration date, again, there is no economic value in exercising the option. As in the case where the price is less than $100, the buyer of the call option will lose the entire option price, $3.

3. If Asset XYZ's price is more than $100 but less than $103 at the expiration date, the option buyer will exercise the option. By exercising, the option buyer can purchase Asset XYZ for $100 (the strike price) and sell it in the market for the higher price. Suppose, for example, that Asset XYZ's price is $102 at the expiration date. The buyer of the call option will realize a $2 gain by exercising the option. Of course, the cost of purchasing the call option was $3, so $1 is lost on this position. By failing to exercise the option, the investor loses $3 instead of only $1.

Table 34.1
Profit/loss profile for a long call position.

Assumptions:
Option price = $3
Strike price = $100
Time to expiration = 1 month

Price of Asset XYZ at Expiration Date ($)	Net Profit/ Loss[1] ($)	Price of Asset XYZ at Expiration Date ($)	Net Profit/ Loss[1] ($)
150	47	100	–3
140	37	99	–3
130	27	98	–3
120	17	97	–3
115	12	96	–3
114	11	95	–3
113	10	94	–3
112	9	93	–3
111	8	92	–3
110	7	91	–3
109	6	90	–3
108	5	89	–3
107	4	88	–3
106	3	87	–3
105	2	86	–3
104	1	85	–3
103	0	80	–3
102	–1	70	–3
101	–2	60	–3

Note: Maximum loss = $3.
[1]Price at expiration is –$100 – $3.

4. If Asset XYZ's price is equal to $103 at the expiration date, the investor will exercise the option. In this case, the investor breaks even, realizing a gain of $3 that offsets the cost of the option, $3.

5. If Asset XYZ's price is more than $103 at the expiration date, the investor will exercise the option and realize a profit. For example, if the price is $113, exercising the option will generate a profit on Asset XYZ of $13. Reducing this gain by the cost of the option ($3), the investor will realize a net profit of $10 from this position.

Table 34.1 shows the profit and loss for the buyer of the hypothetical call option in tabular form, and figure 34.1 graphically portrays the result. Although the break-even point and the size of the loss depend on the option price and the strike price, the profile shown in figure 34.1 holds for all buyers of call options. The shape indicates that the maximum loss is the option price and that there is substantial upside potential.

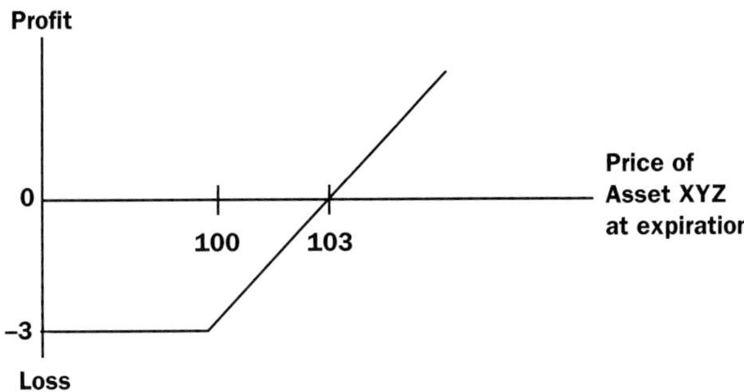

Figure 34.1
Profit/loss profile for a long call position.

It is worthwhile to compare the profit and loss profile of the call option buyer to that of someone taking a long position in one unit of Asset XYZ. The payoff from the position depends on Asset XYZ's price at the expiration date. Consider again the five price outcomes given above (and again ignore transactions costs):

1. If Asset XYZ's price at the expiration date is less than $100, the investor in the call option loses the entire option price of $3. In contrast, a long position in Asset XYZ will have one of three possible losses:

a. If Asset XYZ's price is less than $100 but greater than $97, the loss on the long position in Asset XYZ will be less than $3.

b. If Asset XYZ's price is $97, the loss on the long position in Asset XYZ will be $3.

c. If Asset XYZ's price is less than $97, the loss on the long position in Asset XYZ will be greater than $3. For example, if the price at the expiration date is $80, the long position in Asset XYZ will result in a loss of $20.

2. If Asset XYZ's price is equal to $100, the buyer of the call option will realize a loss of $3 (option price). Similarly, there will be no gain or loss on the long position in Asset XYZ.

3. If Asset XYZ's price is more than $100 but less than $103, the option buyer will realize a loss of less than $3, and the long position in Asset XYZ will realize a profit.

4. If the price of Asset XYZ at the expiration date is equal to $103, there will be no loss or gain from buying the call option. However, the long position in Asset XYZ will produce a gain of $3.

5. If Asset XYZ's price at the expiration date is greater than $103, both the call option buyer and the long position in Asset XYZ will post a profit. However, the profit for the buyer of the call option will be $3 less than that for the long position. For example, if Asset XYZ's price is $113, the profit from the call position is $10, whereas the profit from the long position in Asset XYZ is $13.

Table 34.2
Comparison of long call position and long asset position.

Assumptions:
Initial price of Asset XYZ = $100
Option price = $3
Strike price = $100
Time to expiration = 1 month

	Net Profit/Loss			Net Profit/Loss	
Price of Asset XYZ at Expiration Date ($)	Long Call[1] ($)	Long Asset XYZ[2] ($)	Price of Asset XYZ at Expiration Date ($)	Long Call[1] ($)	Long Asset XYZ[2] ($)
150	47	50	100	−3	0
140	37	40	99	−3	−1
130	27	30	98	−3	−2
120	17	20	97	−3	−3
115	12	15	96	−3	−4
114	11	14	95	−3	−5
113	10	13	94	−3	−6
112	9	12	93	−3	−7
111	8	11	92	−3	−8
110	7	10	91	−3	−9
109	6	9	90	−3	−10
108	5	8	89	−3	−11
107	4	7	88	−3	−12
106	3	6	87	−3	−13
105	2	5	86	−3	−14
104	1	4	85	−3	−15
103	0	3	80	−3	−20
102	−1	2	70	−3	−30
101	−2	1	60	−3	−40

Note: Maximum loss = $3.
[1]Calculated as Price at expiration − $100
[2]Calculated as Price of Asset XYZ − $100

Table 34.2 compares the long call strategy and the long position in Asset XYZ. This comparison clearly demonstrates the way in which an option can change the risk/return profile for investors. An investor who takes a long position in Asset XYZ realizes a profit of $1 for every $1 increase in Asset XYZ's price. However, as Asset XYZ's price falls, the investor loses dollar-for-dollar. If the price drops by more than $3, the long position in Asset XYZ results in a loss of more than $3. In contrast, the long call strategy limits the loss to only the option price of $3 but retains the upside potential, which will be $3 less than for the long position in Asset XYZ.

Which alternative is better, buying the call option or buying the asset? The answer depends on what the investor is attempting to achieve. This will become clearer in chapter 36, where we explain various strategies using either option positions or cash market positions.

This hypothetical example demonstrates another important feature of options: their speculative appeal. Suppose an investor has strong expectations that Asset XYZ's price will rise in one month. At an option price of $3, the speculator can purchase 33.33 call options for each $100 invested. If Asset XYZ's price rises, the investor realizes the price appreciation associated with 33.33 units of Asset XYZ, whereas with the same $100, the investor could have bought only one unit of Asset XYZ selling at $100, realizing the appreciation associated with only one unit if Asset XYZ's price increases. For example, suppose that in one month the price of Asset XYZ rises to $120. The long call position will result in a profit of $566.66 [($20×33.33)−$100] or a return of 566.66% on the $100 investment in the call option. By comparison, a $100 investment in the long position in Asset XYZ results in a profit of $20, for only a 20% return on $100.

It is this greater leverage that attracts investors to options when they wish to speculate on price movements. Leverage does have some drawbacks, however. Suppose that Asset XYZ's price is unchanged at $100 at the expiration date. In this case, the long call position (33.33 options) results in a loss of the entire investment of $100, and the long position in Asset XYZ produces neither a gain nor a loss.

Writing (Selling) Call Options

To illustrate the option seller's (writer's) position, we use the same call option as in the example of buying a call option. The profit and loss profile of the short call position (that is, the position of the call option writer) is the mirror image of the profit and loss profile of the long call position (the position of the call option buyer). Consequently, the profit of the short call position for any given price of Asset XYZ at the expiration date is the same as the loss of the long call position. Furthermore, the maximum profit that the short call position can produce is the option price. The maximum loss is not limited, because it is the highest price reached by Asset XYZ on or before the expiration date, less the option price; this price can be indefinitely high. These relationships can be seen in figure 34.2, which shows the profit/loss profile for a short call position.

Buying Put Options

To illustrate the position of the buyer of a put option, we assume a hypothetical put option on one unit of Asset XYZ with one month to maturity and a strike price of $100. Assume that the put option is selling for $2 and that the current price of Asset XYZ is $100. The profit or loss for this position at the expiration date depends on the market price of Asset XYZ. The possible outcomes are:

1. If Asset XYZ's price is greater than $100, the buyer of the put option will not exercise it, because exercising would mean selling Asset XYZ to the writer for a price that is less than

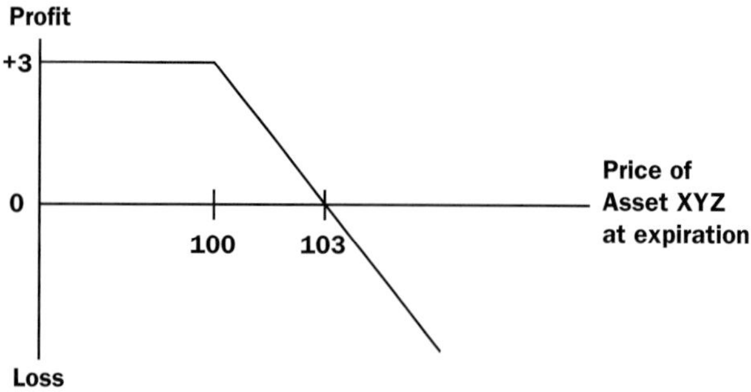

Figure 34.2
Profit/loss profile for a short call position.

the market price. In this case, a loss of $2 (the original price of the option) will result from buying the put option. Once again, the option price represents the maximum loss to which the buyer of the put option is exposed.

2. If Asset XYZ's price at expiration is equal to $100, the put will not be exercised, leaving the put buyer with a loss equal to the option price of $2.

3. If Asset XYZ's price is less than $100 but greater than $98, the option buyer will experience a net loss on the position; however, exercising the put option limits the loss to less than the option price of $2. For example, suppose that the price is $99 at the expiration date. By exercising the option, the option buyer will realize a loss of only $1. This is because the buyer of the put option can sell Asset XYZ, purchased in the market for $99, to the writer for $100, realizing a gain of $1. Deducting the $2 cost of the option results in a net loss of $1 to the position.

4. If Asset XYZ's price is $98 at the expiration date, the put buyer will break even. The investor will realize a gain of $2 by selling Asset XYZ to the writer of the option for $100, and this gain exactly offsets the cost of the option ($2).

5. If Asset XYZ's price is below $98 at the expiration date, the long put position (the put buyer) will realize a profit. For example, suppose the price falls at expiration to $80. The long put position will produce a profit of $18: a gain of $20 for exercising the put option less the $2 option price.

The profit and loss profile for the long put position is shown in tabular form in the second column of table 34.3 and in graphical form in figure 34.3. As with all long option positions, the loss is limited to the option price. The profit potential, however, is substantial: the theoretical maximum profit is generated if Asset XYZ's price falls to zero. Contrast this profit potential with that of the buyer of a call option. The theoretical maximum profit for a call buyer cannot be determined beforehand, because it depends on the highest price that can be reached by Asset XYZ before or at the option expiration date, a price that is indeterminate.

Table 34.3
Profit/loss profile for a long put position compared to a short asset position.

Assumptions:
Initial price of Asset XYZ = $100
Option price = $2
Strike price = $100
Time to expiration = 1 month

	Net Profit/Loss			Net Profit/Loss	
Price of Asset XYZ at Expiration Date ($)	Long Put[1] ($)	Short Asset XYZ[2] ($)	Price of Asset XYZ at Expiration Date ($)	Long Put[1] ($)	Short Asset XYZ[2] ($)
150	−2	−50	91	7	9
140	−2	−40	90	8	10
130	−2	−30	89	9	11
120	−2	−20	88	10	12
115	−2	−15	87	11	13
110	−2	−10	86	12	14
105	−2	−5	85	13	15
100	−2	0	84	14	16
99	−1	1	83	15	17
98	0	2	82	16	18
97	1	3	81	17	19
96	2	4	80	18	20
95	3	5	75	23	25
94	4	6	70	28	30
93	5	7	65	33	35
92	6	8	60	38	40

Note: Maximum loss = $2.
[1]Calculated as $100 − Price at expiration.
[2]Calculated as $100 − Price of Asset XYZ.

To see how an option alters the risk/return profile for an investor, we again compare it to a position in Asset XYZ. The long put position is compared to taking a short position in Asset XYZ, because this is the position that would realize a profit if the price of the asset falls.[1] Suppose an investor sells Asset XYZ short for $100. The short position in Asset XYZ would produce the following profit or loss compared to the long put position (without considering transactions costs):

1. If Asset XYZ's price rises above $100, the long put option results in a loss of $2, but the short position in Asset XYZ realizes one of the following:

a. If the price of Asset XYZ is less than $102, there will be a loss of less than $2, which is the loss to the long put position.

1. See chapter18 for more detail on selling short in a securities market.

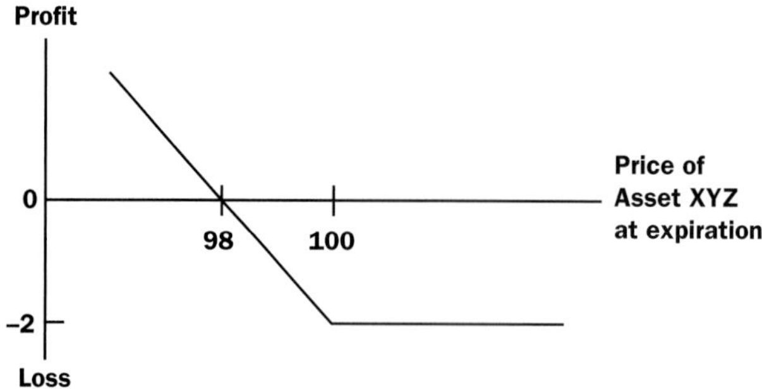

Figure 34.3
Profit/loss profile for a long put position.

b. If the price of Asset XYZ is equal to $102, the loss will be $2, the same as the maximum loss of the long put position.

c. If the price of Asset XYZ is greater than $102, the loss will be greater than $2. For example, if the price is $125, the short position will realize a loss of $25, because the short seller must now pay $125 for Asset XYZ that the seller sold short at $100.

2. If Asset XYZ's price at expiration is equal to $100, the long put position will realize a $2 loss, while there will be no profit or loss on the short position in Asset XYZ.

3. If Asset XYZ's price is less than $100 but greater than $98, the long put position will experience a loss of less than $2, but the short position will realize a profit. For example, a price of $99 at the expiration date will result in a loss of $1 for the long put position but a profit of $1 for the short position.

4. If Asset XYZ's price is $98 at the expiration date, the long put position will break even, but the short position in Asset XYZ will generate a $2 profit.

5. If Asset XYZ's price is below $98, both positions will generate a profit; however, the profit for the long put position will always be $2 less than that for the short position.

Table 34.3 presents a detailed account of this comparison of the profit and loss profiles for the long put position and short position in Asset XYZ. Although the investor who takes a short position in Asset XYZ faces all the downside risk as well as the upside potential, the long put position limits the downside risk to the option price while still maintaining upside potential (reduced only by an amount equal to the option price).

Writing (Selling) Put Options

The profit/loss profile for a short put option is the mirror image of that for the long put option. The maximum profit from this position is the option price. The theoretical maximum loss can be substantial should the price of the underlying asset fall; however, if the price

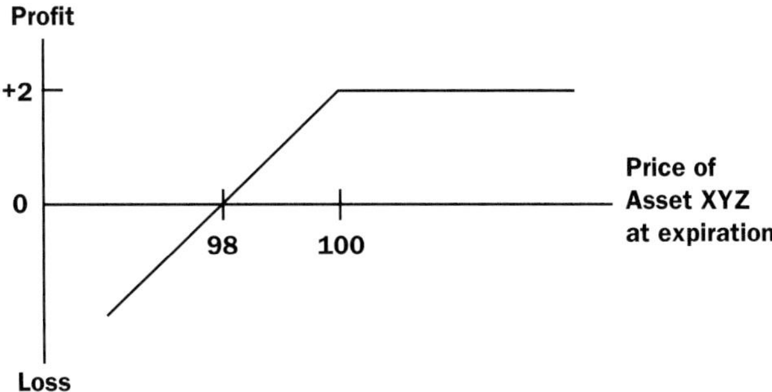

Figure 34.4
Profit/loss profile for a short put position.

were to fall all the way to zero, the loss would be as large as the strike price less the option price. Figure 34.4 graphically depicts this profit and loss profile.

To summarize these illustrations of the four option positions, we can say the following: Buying calls or selling puts allows the investor to gain if the price of the underlying asset rises; and selling calls and buying puts allows the investor to gain if the price of the underlying asset falls.

Considering the Time Value of Money

Our illustrations of the four option positions do not take into account the time value of money. Specifically, the buyer of an option must pay the seller the option price at the time the option is purchased. Thus, the buyer must finance the purchase price of the option, or (assuming the purchase price does not have to be borrowed) the buyer loses the income that can be earned by investing the amount of the option price until the option is sold or exercised. In contrast, assuming that the seller does not have to use the option price amount as margin for the short position or can use an interest-earning asset as security, the seller has the opportunity to earn income from the proceeds of the option sale.

The time value of money changes the profit/loss profile of the option positions we have discussed. The breakeven price for the buyer and the seller of an option will not be the same as in our illustrations. The breakeven price for the underlying asset at the expiration date is higher for the buyer of the option; for the seller, it is lower.

Our comparisons of the option position with long and short positions in the underlying asset also ignore the time value of money. We have not considered the fact that the underlying asset may generate interim cash flows (dividends in the case of common stock, interest in the case of bonds). The buyer of a call option is not entitled to any interim cash flows generated by the underlying asset. However, the buyer of the underlying asset would receive any interim cash flows and would have the opportunity to reinvest them. A complete comparison of the long call option position and the long position in the underlying asset must take into account the additional dollars from reinvesting any interim cash flows. Moreover, any effect on the price of the underlying asset as a result of the distribution of cash must be considered. This occurs, for example, when the underlying asset is common stock and, as a result of a dividend payment, the stock declines in price.

Economic Role of the Options Markets

Futures contracts allow investors to hedge the risks associated with adverse price movements. Hedging with futures lets a market participant lock in a price and thereby eliminates price risk. In the process, however, the investor gives up the opportunity to benefit from a favorable price movement. In other words, hedging with futures involves trading off the benefits of a favorable price movement for protection against an adverse price movement.

Hedging with options has a variety of potential benefits, which we discuss in chapter 36. For now, we provide an overview of how options can be used for hedging and how the outcomes of hedging with options differ from those of hedging with futures. A good way to show the hedging uses of options is to return to the initial illustration in this chapter where the underlying for the option is Asset XYZ.

Let's consider an investor who owns Asset XYZ, currently selling for $100, which she expects to sell one month from now. The investor's concern is that, one month from now, Asset XYZ's price may decline below $100. One alternative available to this investor is to sell Asset XYZ now. However, suppose that the investor does not want to sell this asset now, because either some restrictions prevent this or she thinks that the price may rise during the month. Suppose also that an insurance company offers to sell the investor an insurance policy providing that, if at the end of one month, Asset XYZ's price is less than $100, the insurance company will make up the difference between $100 and the market price. For example, if one month from now Asset XYZ's price is $80, the insurance company will pay the investor $20.

The insurance company naturally charges the investor a premium to write this policy. Let's suppose that the premium is $2. Holding aside the cost of the insurance policy, the payoff that this investor then faces is as follows. The minimum price for Asset XYZ that the investor can receive is $100, because if the price is less, the insurance company will make up the difference. However, if Asset XYZ's price is greater than $100, the investor will receive the higher price. The premium of $2 that is required to purchase this insurance policy effectively assures the investor of a minimum price of $98 ($100 minus $2), but if the price is above $100, the investor realizes the benefits of a higher price (reduced always by the $2 for the insurance policy). In buying this policy, the investor has purchased protection against an adverse price movement while maintaining the opportunity to benefit from a favorable price movement.

Insurance companies do not offer such policies, but we have described an option strategy that provides the same protection. Consider the put option on Asset XYZ with one month to expiration, a strike price of $100, and an option price of $2 discussed earlier in this chapter. The payoff to a long position in this put is identical to the insurance policy. The option price resembles the hypothetical insurance premium; this is the reason the option price is referred to as the option "premium." Thus, a put option can be used to hedge against a decline in the price of the underlying instrument.

The long put's payoff is quite different from that of a futures contract. Suppose that a futures contract with Asset XYZ as the underlying instrument has a futures price equal to $100 and a settlement date of one month from now. By selling this futures contract, the investor would be agreeing to sell Asset XYZ for $100 one month from now. If Asset XYZ's price falls below $100, the investor is protected, because she will receive $100 on delivery of the asset to satisfy the futures contract. If Asset XYZ's price rises above $100, however, the investor will not realize the price appreciation, because she must deliver the asset for an agreed-on amount of $100. By selling the futures contract, the investor has locked in a price of $100 and fails to realize a gain if the price rises while avoiding a loss if the price declines.

Call options are also useful for hedging. A call option can be used to protect against a rise in the price of the underlying instrument while maintaining the opportunity to benefit from a decline in the price of the underlying instrument. For example, suppose that an investor expects to receive $100 one month from now and plans to use that money to purchase Asset XYZ, which is selling currently for $100. The risk that the investor faces is that Asset XYZ's price will rise above $100 one month from now. Let us further suppose there is a call option such as that described earlier in the chapter. The option costs $3 and has a strike price of $100 and one month to expiration. By purchasing that call option, the investor has hedged the risk of a rise in the price of Asset XYZ.

The hedge outcome is as follows. If the price rises above $100 one month from now, the investor would exercise the call option and realize the difference between the market price of Asset XYZ and $100. Thus, ignoring the cost of the option for the moment, we can see that the investor is ensuring that the maximum price she will have to pay for Asset XYZ is $100. Should the asset's price fall below $100, the call option expires worthless, but the investor benefits by being able to purchase Asset XYZ at a price less than $100. Once the $3 cost of the option is considered, the payoff is as follows. Regardless of the eventual price of the asset, the maximum price that the investor will have to pay for Asset XYZ is $103 (the strike price plus the option price). If the price of the asset declines below $100, the investor will benefit by the amount of the price decline less $3.

Compare this situation to a futures contract where Asset XYZ is the underlying instrument, the settlement is in one month, and the futures price is $100. Suppose that the investor buys this futures contract. If one month from now the price of Asset XYZ rises above $100, the investor has contracted to buy the asset for $100, thereby eliminating the risk of a price rise. However, if the price falls below $100, the investor cannot benefit, because she has contracted to pay $100 for the asset.

It should be clear now how hedging with options differs from hedging with futures. This difference cannot be overemphasized—options and futures are not interchangeable instruments.

Although our focus has been on hedging price risk, options also allow investors an efficient way to expand the range of return characteristics available. That is, investors can use options to "shape" a return distribution for a portfolio to fit particular investment objectives.[2]

U.S. Options Markets

There are a variety of options traded throughout the world. Here we provide a survey of the major ones, focusing on the United States but also mentioning other markets.

Stock Options

In the United States, exchange-traded stock options are for 100 shares of a designated common stock. The major U.S. exchanges where options are traded are the Chicago Board Options Exchange (CBOE), the New York Stock Exchange (NYSE), and the Nasdaq.

The Office of the Comptroller of the Currency (OCC) has established standard strike price guidelines for listed options. For stocks with a price above $100, option strike prices are set at $10 intervals; for stocks with a price below $100 and above $30, strike prices are set at $5 intervals; and for stocks priced between $10 and $30 the interval is $2.50. Although the strike price of exchange-traded options is not changed because of cash dividends paid to common stockholders, the strike price is adjusted for stock splits, stock dividends, reorganization, and other recapitalizations affecting the value of the underlying stock.

All exchange-traded stock options in the United States may be exercised any time before the expiration date; that is, they are American options. They expire at 11:59 p.m. Eastern Standard Time on the Saturday following the third Friday of the expiration month. Exchange rules require that investors wishing to exercise an expiring option must instruct a broker about the exercise no later than 5:30 p.m. Eastern time on the business day immediately preceding the expiration date. Notices to exercise a nonexpiring option on a date other than the expiration date must be made between 10:00 a.m. and 8:00 p.m. Eastern Standard Time. When a nonexpiring option is exercised, the OCC assigns the obligation the next day to someone who has an outstanding short position in an option of the same exercise price, expiration date, and underlying stock. This assignment is on a random basis.

2. See Stephen A. Ross, "Options and Efficiency," *Quarterly Journal of Economics* 90, no. 1 (1976): 75–89; Fred Arditti and Kose John, "Spanning the State Space with Options," *Journal of Financial and Quantitative Analysis* 25, no. 1(1980): 1–9.

Options are designated by the name of the underlying common stock, the expiration month, the strike price, and the type of option (put or call). Thus, an exchange-traded stock call option on Apple Inc. (APPL ticker symbol) with a strike price of $115 expiring June 16, 2017, is referred to as the "APPL June 2017 115 call."

The expiration dates are standardized. Each stock is assigned an option cycle, the three option cycles being January, February, and March. The expiration months for each option cycle are as follows:

Option Cycle	Expiration Months
January	January, April, July, October
February	February, May, August, November
March	March, June, September, December

In addition, the practice is to trade options with an expiration date of the current calendar month, the next calendar month, and the next two expiration months in the cycle. For example, suppose a stock is assigned the January option cycle. In February, options with the following expiration months would be traded: February (the current calendar month), March (the next calendar month), April (the next expiration month in the January option cycle), and July (the last option cycle month in the January option cycle). In May, the following expiration months would be traded for a stock assigned to the January option cycle: May (the current calendar month), April (the next calendar month), July (the next expiration month in the January option cycle), and October (the last option cycle month in the January option cycle).

Stock Index Options

In March 1983, a revolution in stock options and investments in general occurred. At that time, trading an option whose underlying instrument was a stock index, the S&P 100 (originally called the "CBOE 100"), began on the CBOE. Reflecting the trading needs of global investors for tools to more efficiently manage portfolios, the number of stock index options traded throughout the world exploded. There are currently options on all the major stock market indexes and on narrow sectors in those indexes.

In the United States, the most popular stock index options in terms of trading volume are the S&P 500 Index Option (ticker symbol SPX), the S&P 100 Index Option (ticker symbol OEX), the NASDAQ 100 Index Option (NDX), the Dow Jones Industrial Average (ticker symbol DJX), and the Russell 2000 Index Option (RUT). All these contracts are listed on the CBOE. Index options can have a European exercise style and are cash settled because of the difficulty of delivering a basket of stocks. All stock index options have a multiple. For the popular stock index options, the multiple is $100. To give an individual investor and smaller institutional investors the opportunity to use stock index products, the exchanges have created mini versions of some of the contracts, in which the underlying is one-tenth of the multiple used for the index. Since the multiple for the stock indexes described above is $100, the mini version's multiple is $10. Specifically, CME also added options on E-mini S&P500 futures contracts on both the standard $250 sizes and mini $50 sizes. American quarterly options and also European weekly and EOM (end of month) options are offered. Moreover, as explained for stock options, there are long-term equity anticipation securities, weeklies, and Flex versions of the contract.

For the S&P 500 Index Option the underlying is of course the S&P 500. The underlying for the S&P 100 Index Option is a market capitalization–weighted index of 100 stocks from a broad range of industries in the S&P 500. The underlying index for the NASDAQ 100 Index Option is a modified market capitalization–weighted index composed of the 100 largest nonfinancial stocks listed on the Nasdaq stock market. The Russell 2000 Index is composed of the small-capitalization segment of the U.S. equity universe in the Russell 2000 Index. In addition to U.S. stock market indexes, there are global stock indexes and country-specific stock market indexes on which options are traded. An example of the former is the Euro STOXX 50 Index option (OESX), which covers global and regional stock market indexes.

There are also stock index options for components of the major broad-based stock market indexes, selected industries, and selected sectors. For example, the CBOE lists the Dow Jones Transportation Average Index Option, Dow Jones Utility Average Index Option, Dow Jones Internet Commerce Index Option, Dow Jones Equity REIT Index Option, CBOE Internet Index Option, CBOE Oil Index Option, CBOE Technology Index Option, and Morgan Stanley Retail Index Option. There are stock index options based on some attribute of the components of an index other than industry or sector. For example, the CBOE lists stock index options based on a classification of the component stock of the Russell 3000 in terms of value and growth. The Russell 1000 Growth Index Option and Russell 1000 Value Index Option include the 1,000 largest stocks in terms of market capitalization in the Russell 3000 that are classified as growth and value, respectively. The underlying for the Dow 10 Index Option includes the top 10 dividend-yielding stocks in the Dow Jones Industrial Average, with each component stock equally weighted in the index.

There are also stock index options based on the exercise style and the length of the expiration period. For example, the S&P 100 Index Option is available in American and European exercise style.

If a stock option is exercised, a stock must be delivered. It would be complicated, to say the least, to settle a stock index option by delivering all the stocks that make up the index. Instead, stock index options are **cash settlement contracts**. That is, if the option is exercised, the exchange-assigned option writer pays cash to the option buyer. No stock is delivered.

The dollar value of the stock index underlying an index option is equal to the current cash index value multiplied by the contract's multiple:

Dollar value of underlying index = Cash index value × Contract multiple.

Each stock index option has a contract multiple. For example, for the S&P 100 Stock Index the multiple is $100. So, if the cash index value for the S&P 100 is 1,000, then the dollar value of the S&P 100 contract is 1,000 × $100 = $100,000.

For a stock option, the price at which the buyer of the option can buy or sell the stock is the strike price. For an index option, the strike index is the index value at which the buyer of the option can buy or sell the underlying stock index. The strike index is converted into a dollar value by multiplying the strike index by the multiple for the contract. For example, if the strike index is 1,750 for an S&P 100 Index option, the strike value is $175,000 (1,750 × $100). If an investor purchases a call option on the S&P 100 with a strike index of 1,750 and exercises the option when the index value is 1,800, then the investor has the right to purchase the index for $175,000 when the dollar value of the index is $180,000. The buyer of the call option would then receive $5,000 (= $180,000—$175,000) from the option writer.

Long-Term Equity Anticipation Securities

For an individual stock and a stock index, only the next two expiration months are traded on an exchange. Consequently, the longest time before expiration of a standard exchange-traded option is six months. **Long-term equity anticipation securities** (LEAPS) are options contracts designed to offer longer maturities. These contracts are available on individual stocks and some indexes. Stock option LEAPS are comparable to standard stock options except that the maturities can range up to 39 months from the origination date. Index options LEAPS differ in size compared with standard index options, having a multiplier of 10 rather than 100.

Interest Rate Options

Interest rate options can be written on cash instruments or futures. At one time, several exchange-traded options contracts were available whose underlying instrument was a debt instrument. These contracts are referred to as **options on physicals**. For reasons explained later, options on futures that are based on debt instruments have been far more popular than options on physicals.

Market participants have made increasingly greater use of OTC options on Treasury, agency debentures, and mortgage-backed securities.[3] Certain institutional investors who

3. For a more detailed discussion of OTC options, see Mark Pitts and Frank J. Fabozzi, *Interest Rate Futures and Options* (Chicago: Probus Publishing, 1989), chapter 2.

want to purchase an option on a specific Treasury security or a Ginnie Mae pass-through can do so on an OTC basis. There are government and mortgage-backed securities dealers who make a market in options on specific securities. Typically, the maturity of the option coincides with the period over which the buyer of the option wants to hedge, so the buyer is not concerned with the option's liquidity.

Besides options on fixed-income securities, investors can obtain OTC options on a yield spread (such as the spread between mortgage pass-through securities and Treasuries or between double-A corporates and Treasuries).

FLEX Options

A **FLEX option**[4] is an option contract with some terms that have been customized. It is traded on an options exchange and cleared and guaranteed by the associated clearinghouse for the exchange. The need for customization of certain terms is a result of the wide range of portfolio strategy needs of institutional investors that cannot be satisfied by standard exchange-traded options.

A FLEX option can be created for individual stocks, stock indexes, and Treasury securities. The value of FLEX options is the ability to customize the terms of the contract along four dimensions: underlying, strike price, expiration date, and settlement style (i.e., American versus European). Moreover, the exchange provides a secondary market to offset or alter positions and an independent daily marking of prices.

The development of the FLEX option is a response to the growing OTC market. The exchanges seek to make the FLEX option attractive by providing price discovery through a competitive auction market, an active secondary market, daily price valuations, and the virtual elimination of counterparty risk. The FLEX option represents a link between listed options and OTC products.

Exotic Options

OTC options can be customized in any manner sought by an institutional investor. Basically, if a dealer can reasonably hedge the risk associated with the opposite side of the option sought, it will create the option desired by a customer. OTC options are not limited to European or American types. An option can be created in which the option can be exercised at several specified dates as well as the expiration date of the option. As noted earlier, such options are referred to as "Bermuda options."

The more complex options created are called **exotic options**. Here are just two types of such exotic options: alternative options and outperformance options. An **alternative option**,

4. For a more detailed description of FLEX options, see James J. Angel, Gary L. Gastineau, and Clifford J. Weber, *Equity FLEX Options* (Hoboken, NJ: John Wiley & Sons, 1999).

also called an **either-or option**, has a payoff that is the best independent payoff of two distinct assets. For example, suppose that Donna buys an alternative call option with the following terms:

1. The underlying is one unit of Asset M or one unit of Asset N.
2. The strike price for Asset M is $80.
3. The strike price for Asset N is $110.
4. The expiration date is three months from now.
5. The option can only be exercised three months from now (i.e., it is a European option).

At the expiration date, Donna can decide to buy from the writer of this option *either* one unit of Asset M at $80 or one unit of Asset N at $110. Donna will buy the asset with the larger payoff. So, for example, if Asset M and Asset N at the expiration date are $84 and $140, respectively, then the payoff would be $4 if Donna elects to exercise to buy Asset M but $30 if she elects to exercise to buy Asset N. Thus, she will choose to buy Asset N. If the price for both assets at the expiration date is below their strike prices, Donna will let the option expire worthless.

An **outperformance option** is an option whose payoff is based on the relative payoff of two assets at the expiration date. For example, consider the following outperformance call option purchased:

1. Portfolio A consists of the stock of 50 public utility companies with a market value of $1 million.
2. Portfolio B consists of the stock of 50 financial services companies with a market value of $1 million.
3. The expiration date is six months from now and is a European option.
4. The strike is equal to

Market value of Portfolio B – Market value of Portfolio A.

At the expiration date, if the market value of Portfolio A is greater than the market value of Portfolio B, then there is no value to this option, and it will expire worthless. The option will be exercised if the market value of Portfolio B exceeds the market value of Portfolio A at the expiration date.

Futures Options

An option on a futures contract, commonly referred to as a **futures option**, gives the buyer the right to buy from or sell to the writer a designated futures contract at a designated price at any time during the life of the option. If the futures option is a call option, the buyer has the right to purchase one designated futures contract at the exercise price. That is, the buyer has the right to acquire a long futures position in the designated futures contract. If the buyer exercises the call option, the writer (seller) acquires a corresponding short position in the futures contract.

A put option on a futures contract grants the buyer the right to sell one designated futures contract to the writer at the exercise price. That is, the option buyer has the right to acquire a short position in the designated futures contract. If the put option is exercised, the writer acquires a corresponding long position in the designated futures contract.

There are futures options on all the interest rate futures contracts reviewed in chapter 34.

Mechanics of Trading Futures Options

The parties to the futures option will realize a position in a futures contract when the option is exercised. The question is: What will the futures price be? That is, at what price will the long be required to pay for the instrument underlying the futures contract, and at what price will the short be required to sell the instrument underlying the futures contract?

On exercise, the futures price for the futures contract will be set equal to the exercise price. The position of the two parties is then immediately marked to market based on the then-current futures price. Thus, the futures position of the two parties will be at the prevailing futures price. At the same time, the option writer or seller must pay the option buyer the economic benefit from exercising. In the case of a call futures option, the option writer must pay the difference between the current futures price and the exercise price to the buyer of the option. In the case of a put futures option, the option writer must pay the option buyer the difference between the exercise price and the current futures price.

For example, suppose an investor buys a call option on some futures contract in which the exercise price is 85. Assume also that the futures price is 95 and that the buyer exercises the call option. On exercise, the call buyer is given a long position in the futures contract at 85, and the call writer is assigned the corresponding short position in the futures contract at 85. The futures position of the buyer and the writer is immediately marked to market by the exchange. Because the prevailing futures price is 95 and the exercise price is 85, the long futures position (the position of the call buyer) realizes a gain of 10, whereas the short futures position (the position of the call writer) realizes a loss of 10. The call writer pays the exchange 10, and the call buyer receives 10 from the exchange. The call buyer, who now has a long futures position at 95, can either liquidate the futures position at 95 or maintain a long futures position. If the former course of action is taken, the call buyer sells a futures contract at the prevailing futures price of 95. There is no gain or loss from liquidating the position. Overall, the call buyer realizes a gain of 10. If the call buyer elects to hold the long futures position, then he or she will face the same risk and reward of holding such a position. But the call buyer still has realized a gain of 10 from the exercise of the call option.

Suppose, instead, that the futures option is a put rather than a call, and the current futures price is 60 rather than 95. If the buyer of this put option exercises it, the buyer would have a short position in the futures contract at 85; the option writer would have a long position in the futures contract at 85. The exchange then marks the position to market at the then-current futures price of 60, resulting in a gain to the put buyer of 25 and a loss to the put writer of the same amount. The put buyer, now having a short futures position at 60, can either maintain that position or liquidate it by buying a futures contract at the prevailing futures price of 60. In either case, the put buyer realizes a gain of 25 from exercising the put option.

The exchange imposes no margin requirements for the buyer of a futures option once the option price has been paid in full. Because the maximum amount the buyer can lose is the option price, regardless of how adverse the price movement of the underlying instrument, there is no need for margin.

Because the writer (seller) of an option has agreed to accept all the risk (and none of the reward) of the position in the underlying instrument, the writer (seller) is required to deposit not only the margin required on the interest rate futures contract position if that is the underlying instrument, but also (with certain exceptions) the option price that is received for writing the option. In addition, if prices for the underlying futures contract adversely affect the writer's position, the writer would be required to deposit variation margin as it is marked to market.

Reasons for the Popularity of Futures Options

Futures options on fixed-income securities have largely supplanted options on physicals as the options vehicle used by institutional investors for three reasons.[5] First, unlike options on fixed-income securities, futures options on Treasury coupon futures do not require payments to be made for accrued interest. Consequently, when a futures option is exercised, the call buyer and the put writer need not compensate the other party for accrued interest.

Second, futures options are believed to be "cleaner" instruments because of the reduced likelihood of delivery squeezes. Market participants who must deliver an instrument are concerned that the instrument to be delivered will be in short supply at the time of delivery, resulting in a higher price to acquire it. As the deliverable supply of futures contracts is more than adequate for futures options currently traded, there is no concern about a delivery squeeze.

Finally, to price any option, it is imperative to know at all times the price of the underlying instrument. As mentioned in our discussions of the various bond markets, current bond prices are not easily available. In contrast, futures prices are readily available.

5. Laurie Goodman, "Introduction to Debt Options," in *Winning the Interest Rate Game: A Guide to Debt Options*, ed. Frank J. Fabozzi (Chicago: Probus Publishing, 1985), chapter 1, 13–14.

Key Points

- An option is a contract in which the writer of the option grants the buyer the right, but not the obligation, to purchase from or sell to the writer something at the exercise (or strike) price in a specified period of time (until the expiration date).
- The price paid by the option buyer is called the "option price" or "option premium."
- A call option grants the option buyer the right to buy something from the option writer, and a put option grants the option buyer the right to sell something to the option writer.
- The maximum amount that an option buyer can lose is the option price, while the maximum profit that the option writer can realize is the option price; the option buyer has substantial upside return potential, whereas the option writer has substantial downside risk.
- The option contract specifies the exercise style (American, European, Bermuda).
- Options may be traded either on an organized exchange or in the OTC market.
- Unlike a futures contract, only one party to an option contract is obligated to transact at a later date: the option writer.
- Futures have a symmetric risk/reward relationship, whereas options do not, because the buyer of an option retains all the potential benefits, but the gain is always reduced by the amount of the option price.
- Futures are risk-sharing arrangements, but options are insurance arrangements.
- There are four basic option positions: buying a call option, selling a call option, buying a put option, and selling a put option.
- An option can be used to alter the risk/reward relationship from that of a position in the underlying.
- The buyer of a call option benefits if the price of the underlying rises; the writer (seller) of a call option benefits if the price of the underlying is unchanged or falls.
- The buyer of a put option benefits if the price of the underlying falls; the writer (seller) of a put option benefits if the price of the underlying is unchanged or rises.
- When determining the payoff from an option, the time value of money as a result of having to finance the option price must be considered.
- Some options are traded on individual shares of common stock, and some options are traded on common stock indexes.
- The dollar value of a stock index option contract is equal to the index value multiplied by the contract's multiple.
- There are interest rate options in which the underlying is a debt instrument (called an "option on a physical") and a futures contract (called a "futures option").

- Exchange-traded options on futures that are based on debt instruments have been far more popular than exchange-traded options on physicals.
- A futures option gives the buyer the right to buy from or sell to the writer a designated futures contract at a designated price at any time during the life of the option.
- If the buyer of the futures option exercises, the futures price for the futures contract will be set equal to the exercise price, but the position of the two parties is then immediately marked to market based on the then-current futures price.
- For several reasons, futures options on fixed-income securities have been used more by institutional investors than have options on physicals.
- There has been increased use by institutional investors of OTC options on Treasury and mortgage-backed securities.
- Complex OTC options are called "exotic options," two examples being alternative options and outperformance options.

Questions

1. Identify and explain the key features of an options contract.
2. What is the difference between a put option and a call option?
3. What is the difference between an American option and a European option?
4. Why does an option writer need to post margin?
5. Identify two important ways in which an exchange-traded option differs from a typical OTC option.
6. a. What are the main ways in which an option differs from a futures contract?

b. Why are options and futures called "derivative securities"?

7. Explain how this statement can be true: "A long call position offers potentially unlimited gains, if the underlying asset's price rises, but a fixed, maximum loss if the underlying asset's price drops to zero."
8. Suppose a call option on a stock has an exercise price of $70 and a cost of $2, and suppose you buy the call. Identify the profit to your investment, at the call's expiration, for each of these values of the underlying stock: $25, $70, $100, $400.
9. Consider again the situation in question 8. Suppose you had sold the call option. What would your profit be, at expiration, for each of the stock prices?
10. Explain why you agree or disagree with this statement: "Buying a put is just like short selling the underlying asset. You gain the same thing from either position, if the underlying asset's price falls. If the price goes up, you have the same loss."
11. Why do stock index options involve cash settlement rather than delivery of the underlying stocks?

12. Suppose you bought an index call option for $5.50 that has a strike price of 200 and that, at expiration, you exercised it. Also suppose that at the time you exercised the call option, the index has a value of 240.

a. If the index option has a multiple of $100, how much money does the writer of this option pay you?

b. What profit did you realize from buying this call option?

13. How do LEAPS differ from standard stock options and standard index options?

14. a. What are the terms that can be customized in a FLEX option?

b. Why was the FLEX option introduced by exchanges?

15. Suppose that you buy an alternative call option with the following terms:

- The underlying asset is one unit of Asset G or one unit of Asset H.
- The strike price for Asset G is $100.
- The strike price for Asset H is $115.
- The expiration date is four months from now.
- The option can only be exercised at the expiration date.

a. What is the payoff from this option if at the expiration date, the price of Asset G is $125 and the price of Asset H is $135?

b. What is the payoff from this option if at the expiration date, the price of Asset G is $90 and the price of Asset H is $125?

c. What is the payoff from this option if at the expiration date, the price of Asset G is $90 and the price of Asset H is $105?

16. Suppose that you buy an outperformance call option with the following terms:

- Portfolio X consists of bonds with a market value of $5 million.
- Portfolio Y consists of stocks with a market value of $5 million.
- The expiration date is nine months from now and is a European option.
- The strike price is equal to

Market value of Portfolio X − Market value of Portfolio Y.

What is the payoff of this option if at the expiration date, the market value of Portfolio X is $10 million and the market value of Portfolio Y is $12 million?

17. Suppose you have a long position in a call option on a futures contract, and the strike price is $80. The futures contract price is now $87, and you want to exercise your option. Identify the gains from exercise, specifying any cash inflow and the futures position you get (and the price of the futures contract).

35 Pricing Futures and Options Contracts

CONTENTS

Learning Objectives

After reading this chapter, you will understand:

- the theory of pricing a futures contract;
- how arbitrage between the futures market and the cash or spot market links the prices of those markets;
- the meaning of the terms "cost of carry" and "net financing cost";
- the convergence of the futures and cash prices for a particular asset at the settlement date of the futures contract;
- why the actual futures price may differ from the theoretical futures price;
- how the market price of an option can be broken down into an intrinsic value and a time premium;
- why arbitrage ensures that the prices of calls and puts on the same underlying asset with the same exercise price and expiration date have a certain relationship to each other;
- the factors that affect the price of an option: the underlying asset's current price and expected price volatility, the contract's expiration date and exercise price, the short-term rate of interest, and any cash flows from the underlying asset; and
- the principles of the binomial option pricing model and how the model is derived.

In chapters 33 and 34, we described the various types of futures and options contracts. In this chapter, we explain how to determine the theoretical price of these contracts using arbitrage arguments. A close examination of the underlying assumptions necessary to derive the theoretical price indicates how it must be modified to price the specific contracts described in the previous two chapters.

Pricing of Futures Contracts

To understand what determines the futures price, consider once again the futures contract in chapter 33, whose underlying instrument is Asset XYZ. We make several assumptions:

1. Asset XYZ is selling for $100 in the cash market.
2. Asset XYZ pays the holder (with certainty) $12 per year in four quarterly payments of $3, and the next quarterly payment is exactly three months from now.

3. The futures contract requires delivery three months from now.
4. The current three-month interest rate at which funds can be lent or borrowed is 8% per year.

What should the price of this futures contract be? Suppose the price of the futures contract is \$107. Consider this strategy:

Sell the futures contract at \$107.

Purchase Asset XYZ in the cash market for \$100.

Borrow \$100 for three months at 8% per year.

The borrowed funds are used to purchase Asset XYZ, resulting in no initial cash outlay for this strategy. At the end of three months, \$3 will be received from holding Asset XYZ. Three months from now, Asset XYZ must be delivered to settle the futures contract, and the loan must be repaid. This strategy produces an outcome as follows:

1.	From settlement of the futures contract:	
	Proceeds from sale of Asset XYZ to settle the futures contract	= \$107
	Payment received from investing in Asset XYZ for three months	= 3
	Total proceeds	= \$110
2.	From the loan:	
	Repayment of the loan principal	= \$100
	Interest on loan (2% for three months)	= 2
	Total outlay	= \$102
3.	Profit:	\$8

Notice that this strategy guarantees a profit of \$8. Moreover, this profit is generated with no investment outlay: The funds needed to buy Asset XYZ were borrowed. The profit is realized regardless of what the futures price at the settlement date is. In financial terms, the profit arises from a riskless arbitrage between the price of Asset XYZ in the cash or spot market and the price of Asset XYZ in the futures market. Obviously, in a well-functioning market, arbitrageurs who could get this riskless gain for a zero investment would sell the futures and buy Asset XYZ, forcing the futures price down and bidding up Asset XYZ's price so as to eliminate this profit.

This strategy, which resulted in the capturing of the arbitrage profit, is referred to as a **cash and carry trade**. The reason for this name is that it involves borrowing cash to purchase a security and "carrying" that security to the futures settlement date.

Suppose instead that the futures price is $92 and not $107. Let's consider this strategy:

Buy the futures contract at $92.

Sell (short) Asset XYZ for $100.

Invest (lend) $100 for three months at 8% per year.[1]

Once again, no initial cash outlay is needed for the strategy: The cost of the long position in the futures contract is zero, and there is no cost to selling the asset short and lending the money. Three months from now, Asset XYZ must be purchased to settle the long position in the futures contract. Asset XYZ accepted for delivery will then be used to cover the short position—to cover the short sale of Asset XYZ in the cash market. Shorting Asset XYZ requires the short seller to pay the lender of Asset XYZ the proceeds that the lender would have earned for the quarter. Therefore, the strategy requires a payment of $3 to the lender of Asset XYZ. The outcome in three months would be as follows:

1.	From settlement of the futures contract:	
	Price paid for purchase of Asset XYZ to settle futures contract	= $92
	Proceeds to lender of Asset XYZ to borrow the asset	= 3
	Total outlay	= $95
2.	From the loan:	
	Principal from maturing of investment	= $100
	Interest earned on loan ($2 for three months)	= 2
	Total proceeds	= $102
3.	Profit	= $7

The $7 profit from this strategy is also a riskless arbitrage profit. This strategy requires no initial cash outlay but will generate a profit regardless of the price of Asset XYZ at the settlement date. Clearly, this opportunity would lead arbitrageurs to buy futures and short Asset XYZ, and the effect of these two actions would be to raise the futures price and lower the cash price until the profit again disappeared.

1. Consider the first strategy (cash and carry trade), which had these elements: Technically, a short seller may not be entitled to the full use of the proceeds resulting from the sale. We will discuss this later in this section.

This strategy that resulted in the capturing of the arbitrage profit is referred to as a **reverse cash and carry trade**. That is, with this strategy, a security is sold short, and the proceeds received from the short sale are invested.

At what futures price would the arbitraging stop? Another way to ask this question is this: Is there a futures price that would prevent the opportunity for the riskless arbitrage profit? Yes, there is. There will be no arbitrage profit if the futures price is $99. Let's look at what happens if the two previous strategies (cash and carry trade and reverse cash and carry trade) are followed, now assuming a futures price of $99.

Consider the first strategy (cash and carry), which has these elements:

Sell the futures contract at $99.

Purchase Asset XYZ in the cash market for $100.

Borrow $100 for three months at 8% per year.

In three months, the outcome will be as follows:

1.	From settlement of the futures contract:	
	Price paid for purchase of Asset XYZ to settle futures contract	= $99
	Proceeds to lender of Asset XYZ to borrow the asset	= 3
	Total outlay	= $102
2.	From the loan:	
	Principal from maturing of investment	= $100
	Interest earned on loan ($2 for three months)	= 2
	Total proceeds	= $102
3.	Profit:	= $0

If the futures price is $99, the arbitrage profit has disappeared.

Next, consider the strategy consisting of these actions:

Buy the futures contract at $99.

Sell (short) Asset XYZ for $100.

Invest (lend) $100 for three months at 8% per year.

The outcome in three months would be as follows:

1.	From settlement of the futures contract:	
	Price paid for purchase of Asset XYZ to settle futures contract	= $99
	Proceeds to lender of Asset XYZ to borrow the asset	= 3
	Total outlay	= $102
2.	From the loan:	
	Principal from maturing of investment	= $100
	Interest earned on loan ($2 for three months)	= 2
	Total proceeds	= $102
3.	Profit:	= $0

Thus, if the futures price were $99, neither strategy would result in an arbitrage profit. Hence, a futures price of $99 is the equilibrium price, because any higher or lower futures price will permit riskless arbitrage profits.

Theoretical Futures Price Based on Arbitrage Model

According to the arbitrage arguments we have just presented, we see that the equilibrium or theoretical futures price can be determined based on the following information:

1. The price of the asset in the cash market.
2. The cash yield earned on the asset until the settlement date. In our example, the cash yield on Asset XYZ is $3 on a $100 investment or 3% quarterly (12% annual cash yield).
3. The **financing cost**, which is the interest rate for borrowing and lending until the settlement date. In our example, the financing cost is 2% for the three months.

To develop a theory of futures pricing, we will use the following notation:

F = Futures price ($)

P = Cash market price ($)

r = Financing cost (%)

y = Cash yield (%)

Now, consider the cash and carry trade:

Sell (or take a short position in) the futures contract at F.

Purchase Asset XYZ for P.

Borrow P at a rate of r until the settlement date.

The outcome at the settlement date would be:

1.	From settlement of the futures contract:	
	Proceeds from sale of Asset XYZ to settle the futures contract	$=F$
	Payment received from investing in Asset XYZ	$=yP$
	Total proceeds	$=F+yP$
2.	From the loan:	
	Repayment of principal of loan	$=P$
	Interest on loan	$=rP$
	Total outlay	$=P+rP$

The profit will equal

Profit = Total proceeds − Total outlay,
Profit $=F+yP-(P+rP)$.

The equilibrium futures price is the price that ensures that the profit from this arbitrage strategy is zero. Thus, equilibrium requires that

$$0=F+yP-(P+rP).$$

Solving for the theoretical futures price gives this equation:

$$F=P+P(r-y)$$

In other words, the equilibrium futures price is simply a function of the cash price, the financing cost, and the cash yield on the asset.

Alternatively, let us consider the reverse cash and carry trade illustrated in our example above, which looks like this:

Buy the futures contract at F.

Sell (short) Asset XYZ for P.

Invest (lend) P at a rate of r until the settlement date.

The outcome at the settlement date would be

1.	From settlement of the futures contract:	
	Price paid for purchase of asset to settle futures contract	$=F$
	Payment to lender of asset to borrow the asset	$=yP$
	Total outlay	$=F+yP$
2.	From the loan:	
	Principal from maturing of investment	$=P$
	Interest earned on loan	$=rP$
	Total proceeds	$=P+rP$

The profit will equal

Profit = Total proceeds − Total outlay,
$\text{Profit}=P+rP-(F+yP)$.

Setting the profit equal to zero, so that there will be no arbitrage profit, and solving for the futures price, we obtain the same equation for the futures price as derived earlier:

$$F=P+P(r-y).$$

It is instructive to apply this equation to our previous example to determine the theoretical futures price. In that example, the key variables have these values:

$r=0.02$
$y=0.03$
$P=\$100$

Then the theoretical futures price is

$$F=\$100-\$100(0.03-0.02)$$
$$=\$100-\$1=\$99.$$

This agrees with the equilibrium futures price we proposed earlier.

The theoretical futures price may be at a premium to the cash market price (higher than the cash market price) or at a discount from the cash market price (lower than the cash market price), depending on the value of $P(r-y)$. The term $r-y$, which reflects the difference between the cost of financing and the asset's cash yield, is called the **net financing cost**. The net financing cost is more commonly called the **cost of carry**, or simply, **carry**. **Positive carry** means that the yield earned is greater than the financing cost; **negative carry** means that the financing cost exceeds the yield earned. We can summarize the effect of carry on the difference between the futures price and the cash market price in this way:

Carry	Futures Price
Positive ($y>r$)	Will sell at a discount to cash price ($F<P$)
Negative ($y<r$)	Will sell at a premium to cash price ($F>P$)
Zero ($r=y$)	Will be equal to the cash price ($F=P$)

Price Convergence at the Delivery Date

At the delivery date, which is when the futures contract settles, the futures price must equal the cash market price, because a futures contract with no time left until delivery is equivalent to a cash market transaction. Thus, as the delivery date approaches, the futures price will converge to the cash market price. This fact is evident from the equation for the theoretical futures price. As the delivery date approaches, the financing cost approaches zero, and the yield that can be earned by holding the investment approaches zero. Hence, the cost of carry approaches zero, and the futures price will approach the cash market price.

A Closer Look at the Theoretical Futures Price

To derive the theoretical futures price using the arbitrage argument, we made several assumptions. When the assumptions are violated, the actual futures price will diverge from the theoretical futures price. That is, the difference between the two prices will differ from the value of carry. Next, we examine those assumptions and identify practical reasons for the tendency of actual prices of all financial futures contracts to deviate from their theoretical prices.

Interim Cash Flows

Our theoretical analysis assumes that no interim cash flows arise because of changes in futures prices and the variation margin of the organized exchanges on which futures are traded. In addition, our approach assumes implicitly that any dividends or coupon interest payments are paid at the delivery date rather than at some time between initiation of the cash position and expiration of the futures contract. However, we know that interim cash flows of either type can and do occur in practice.

In the case of stock index futures, incorporating interim dividend payments into the pricing model is necessary, because a cash position in a set of 100 or 500 stocks (the number of stocks underlying an index) generates cash flows in the form of dividends from the stocks. The dividend rate and the pattern of dividend payments are not known with certainty. They must be projected from the historical dividend payments of the companies in the index.

Once the dividend payments are projected, they can be incorporated into the pricing model. The only problem is that the value of the dividend payments at the settlement date will depend on the interest rate at which the dividend payments can be reinvested from the time they are projected to be received until the settlement date. The lower the dividend is, and the closer the dividend payments are to the settlement date of the futures contract, the less important the reinvestment income is when determining the futures price.

It is important to note that, in the absence of initial and variation margins, the theoretical price for the contract is technically the theoretical price for a forward contract, not the theoretical price for a futures contract. This is because, unlike a futures contract, a forward contract is not marked to market at the end of each trading day, and therefore does not require variation margin and does not generate cash inflows from gains or outflows from losses.

Differences between Lending and Borrowing Rates

When deriving the theoretical futures price, we assumed that the investor's borrowing and lending rates are equal. Typically, however, the borrowing rate is higher than the lending rate. The impact of this inequality is important and easy to identify. We begin by adopting these symbols for the two rates:

r_B = Borrowing rate,
r_L = Lending rate.

Now, consider the cash and carry trade:

Sell the futures contract at F.

Purchase the asset for P.

Borrow P at r_B until the settlement date.

Clearly, the futures price that would produce no arbitrage profit is

$$F = P + P(r_B - y).$$

Recall that the reverse cash and carry trade is

Buy the futures contract at F.

Sell (short) the asset for P.

Invest (lend) P at r_L until the settlement date.

The futures price that would prevent a riskless profit is

$$F = P + P(r_L - y).$$

These two equations together provide boundaries between which the futures price will be in equilibrium. The first equation establishes the upper boundary, and the second equation the lower boundary. For example, assume that the borrowing rate is 8% per year, or 2% for three months, and the lending rate is 6% per year, or 1.5% for three months. According to the first equation, the upper boundary is

$$F\text{ (upper boundary)} = \$100 + \$100(0.02 - 0.03) = \$99.$$

The lower boundary according to the second equation is

$$F\text{ (lower boundary)} = \$100 + \$100(0.015 - 0.03) = \$98.50.$$

Thus, equilibrium is achieved if the futures price takes on any value between the two boundaries. In other words, equilibrium requires that $\$98.50 \leq F \leq \$99$.

Transaction Costs

When deriving the theoretical futures price, we ignored transaction costs of the elements in the arbitrage strategies. In reality, the costs of entering into and closing the cash position as well as round-trip transaction costs for the futures contract do affect the futures price. It is easy to show, as we did previously for borrowing and lending rates, that transaction costs widen the boundaries for the equilibrium futures price. The details need not concern us here.

Short Selling

In the strategy involving short selling of Asset XYZ when the futures price is below its theoretical value, we explicitly assumed in the reverse cash and carry trade that the proceeds from the short sale are received and reinvested. In practice, for individual investors, the proceeds are not received, and, in fact, the individual investor is required to put up margin (securities margin, not futures margin) to short sell. For institutional investors, the asset may be borrowed, but there is a cost to borrowing. This cost of borrowing can be incorporated into the model by reducing the yield on the asset.

For strategies applied to stock index futures, a short sale of the stocks in the index means that all stocks in the index must be sold simultaneously. The stock exchange rule for the short selling of stock, which we explained in chapter 23, may prevent an investor from implementing the arbitrage strategy. The short selling rule for stocks specifies that a short sale can be made only at a price that is higher than the previous trade (referred to as an "uptick"), or at a price that is equal to the previous trade (referred to as a "zero tick") but higher than the last trade at a different price. If the arbitrage requires selling the stocks in the index simultaneously, and the last transaction for some of the stocks is not an uptick, then the stocks cannot be shorted simultaneously. Thus, an institutional rule may in effect keep arbitrageurs from bringing the actual futures price in line with the theoretical futures price.

Known Deliverable Asset and Settlement Date

Our example illustrating arbitrage strategies assumes that (1) only one asset is deliverable, and (2) the settlement date occurs at a known, fixed point in the future. Neither assumption is consistent with the delivery rules for some futures contracts. The case of U.S. Treasury bond and note futures contracts illustrates the point: An investor in a long position cannot know either the specific Treasury bond to be delivered or the specific date in the contract month when it might be delivered. This substantial uncertainty is a result of the delivery options that the short position in a futures contract has. As a reflection of the short positions' options and advantages, the actual futures price will be less than the theoretical futures price for the Treasury bond and note futures contracts.

The Deliverable Is a Basket of Securities

Some futures contracts involve a single asset, but other contracts apply to a basket of assets or an index. Stock index futures and municipal bond index futures contracts are examples. The problem in arbitraging these two futures contracts is that it is too expensive to buy or sell every security included in the index. Instead, a portfolio containing a smaller number of assets may be constructed to track the index (which means having price movements that are very similar to changes in the index). Nonetheless, arbitrage based on this tracking portfolio is no longer risk-free, because of the risk that the portfolio will not track the index exactly. Clearly, then, the actual price of futures based on baskets of assets may diverge from the theoretical price because of transactions costs as well as uncertainty about the outcome of the arbitrage.

Different Tax Treatment of Cash and Futures Transactions

The basic arbitrage model presented in this chapter ignores not only taxes but also different tax treatment of cash market transactions and futures transactions. Obviously, these factors can keep the actual futures price from being equal to the theoretical price.

Pricing of Options

The theoretical price of an option is also derived from arbitrage arguments. However, the pricing of options is not as simple as the pricing of futures contracts.

Basic Components of the Option Price

The option price is the sum of the option's **intrinsic value** and a premium over intrinsic value that is often referred to as the "time value" or "time premium." Although the former term is more common, we will use the term **time premium** to avoid confusion between the time value of money and the time value of the option.

Intrinsic Value

The intrinsic value of an option at any time is its economic value if it is exercised immediately. If no positive economic value would result from exercising immediately, the intrinsic value is zero.

Computationally, the intrinsic value of a call option is the difference between the current price of the underlying asset and the strike price. If that difference is positive, then the intrinsic value equals that difference; if the difference is zero or negative, then the intrinsic value is set equal to zero. For example, if the strike price for a call option is \$100 and the current asset price is \$105, the intrinsic value is \$5. That is, an option buyer exercising the option and simultaneously selling the underlying asset would realize \$105 from the sale of the asset, which would be covered by acquiring the asset from the option writer for \$100, thereby, netting a \$5 gain.

When an option has intrinsic value, it is said to be **in the money**. When the strike price of a call option exceeds the current asset price, the call option is said to be **out of the money**; it has no intrinsic value. An option for which the strike price is equal to the current asset price is said to be **at the money**. Both at-the-money and out-of-the-money options have intrinsic values of zero, because it is not profitable to exercise them. Our call option with a strike price of \$100 would be: (1) in the money when the current asset price is more than \$100, (2) out of the money when the current asset price is less than \$100, and (3) at the money when the current asset price is equal to \$100.

For a put option, the intrinsic value is equal to the amount by which the current asset price is below the strike price. For example, if the strike price of a put option is \$100, and the current asset price is \$92, the intrinsic value is \$8. That is, the buyer of the put option who simultaneously buys the underlying asset and exercises the put option will net \$8 by exercising. The asset will be sold to the writer for \$100 and purchased in the market for \$92. For our put option with a strike price of \$100, the option would be: (1) in the money when the current asset price is less than \$100, (2) out of the money when the current asset price exceeds \$100, and (3) at the money when the current asset price is equal to \$100.

Time Premium

The time premium of an option is the amount by which the option's market price exceeds its intrinsic value. The option buyer hopes that, at some time prior to expiration, changes in the market price of the underlying asset will increase the value of the rights conveyed by the option. For this prospect, the option buyer is willing to pay a premium above the intrinsic value. For example, if the price of a call option with a strike price of \$100 is \$9 when the current asset price is $105, then the time premium of this option is $4 ($9 minus its intrinsic value of $5). Had the current asset price been $90 instead of $105, then the time premium of this option would be the entire $9, because the option has no intrinsic value. Clearly, other things being equal, the time premium of an option will increase with the amount of time remaining to expiration.

An option buyer has two ways to realize the value of a position taken in the option. The first way is to exercise the option. The second way is to sell the call option for its market price. In the first example above, selling the call for $9 is preferable to exercising, because the exercise will realize a gain of only $5 but the sale will realize a gain of $9. As this example shows, exercise causes the immediate loss of any time premium. It is important to note that in some circumstances, an option may be exercised prior to the expiration date. These circumstances depend on whether the total proceeds at the expiration date would be greater by holding the option or exercising and reinvesting any received cash proceeds until the expiration date.

Put–Call Parity Relationship

An important relationship holds between the price of a call option and the price of a put option on the same underlying instrument, with the same strike price and the same expiration date. An example can illustrate this relationship, which is commonly referred to as the **put–call parity relationship**.

Our example comes from the previous chapter and assumes that a put option and a call option are available on the same underlying asset (Asset XYZ), and that both options have one month to expiration and a strike price of $100. The example assumes that the price of the underlying asset is $100. The call and put prices are assumed to be $3 and $2, respectively.

To see whether the two prices have the right relationship, consider what happens if an investor pursues this strategy:

Buy Asset XYZ at a price of $100.

Sell a call option at a price of $3.

Buy a put option at a price of $2.

This strategy generates these positions:

Long Asset XYZ

Short the call option

Long the put option

Table 35.1 shows the profit/loss profile at the expiration date for this strategy. Notice that, no matter what Asset XYZ's price is at the expiration date, the strategy will produce

Table 35.1
Profit/loss profile for a strategy involving a long position in Asset XYZ, short call option position, and long put option position.

Assumptions:
Price of Asset XYZ: $100
Call option price: $3
Put option price: $2
Strike price 5: 100
Time to expiration: 1 month

Price of Asset XYZ at Expiration Date ($)	Profit from Asset XYZ[1] ($)	Price Received for Call ($)	Price Paid for Put ($)	Overall Profit ($)
150	0	3	−2	1
140	0	3	−2	1
130	0	3	−2	1
120	0	3	−2	1
115	0	3	−2	1
110	0	3	−2	1
105	0	3	−2	1
100	0	3	−2	1
95	0	3	−2	1
90	0	3	−2	1
85	0	3	−2	1
80	0	3	−2	1
75	0	3	−2	1
70	0	3	−2	1
65	0	3	−2	1
60	0	3	−2	1

[1]There is no profit, because at a price above $100, Asset XYZ will be called from the investor at a price of $100, and at a price below $100, Asset XYZ will be put by the investor at a price of $100.

a profit of $1. The net cost of creating this position is the cost of purchasing Asset XYZ ($100) plus the cost of buying the put ($2) less the price received from selling the call ($3), which is $99. Suppose that the net cost of creating the position for one month is less than $1. Then, by borrowing $99 to create the position so that no investment outlay is made by the investor, this strategy will produce a net profit of $1 (as shown in the last column of table 34.1) less the cost of borrowing $99, which is assumed to be less than $1. This situation cannot exist in an efficient market. As market participants implement the strategy to capture the $1 profit, their actions will have one or more of the following consequences, which will tend to eliminate the $1 profit: (1) the price of Asset XYZ will increase, (2) the call option price will drop, or (3) the put option price will rise.

Our example clearly implies that if Asset XYZ's price does not change, the call price and the put price must tend toward equality. But our example ignores the time value of money (financing and opportunity costs, cash payments, and reinvestment income). Also, our example does not consider the possibility of early exercise of the options. Thus, we have been considering a put–call parity relationship only for European options.

It can be shown that the put–call parity relationship for options when the underlying asset makes cash distributions and the time value of money is recognized is

Put option price − Call option price = Present value of strike price + Present value of cash distribution − Price of underlying asset.

Once more, note that this relationship is actually the put–call parity relationship for European options. However, the values of puts and calls that are American options do conform approximately to this relationship. If this relationship does not hold, arbitrage opportunities exist. That is, investors will be able to construct portfolios consisting of long and short positions in the asset and related options that will provide an extra return with (practical) certainty.

Factors That Influence the Option Price

Six factors influence the price of an option:

1. Current price of the underlying asset,
2. Strike price,
3. Time to expiration of the option,
4. Expected price volatility of the underlying asset over the life of the option,
5. Short-term, risk-free interest rate over the life of the option, and
6. Anticipated cash payments on the underlying asset over the life of the option.

The impact of each of these factors may depend on whether (1) the option is a call or a put, and (2) the option is an American option or a European option. A summary of the effect of each factor on put and call option prices is presented in table 35.2. Here we briefly explain why the factors have the indicated effects.

Current Price of the Underlying Asset

The option price will change as the price of the underlying asset changes. For a call option, as the price of the underlying asset increases (all other factors constant), the option price increases. The opposite holds for a put option: As the price of the underlying asset increases, the price of a put option decreases.

Table 35.2
Summary of factors that affect the price of an option.

	Effect of an Increase of Factor on	
Factor	Call Price	Put Price
Current price of underlying asset	Increase	Decrease
Strike price	Decrease	Increase
Time to expiration of option	Increase	Increase
Expected price volatility	Increase	Increase
Short-term interest rate	Increase	Decrease
Anticipated cash payments	Decrease	Increase

Strike Price

The strike price is fixed for the life of the option. All other factors equal, the lower the strike price is, the higher will be the price for a call option. For put options, the higher the exercise price is, the higher will be the option price. Table 35.3 shows this for the price of Apple Inc. (APPL) call and put options on August 15, 2016, expiring on March 17, 2017. Option prices shown in this way are referred to as an "option chain." On August 15, 2016, the closing price for Apple Inc. (traded on the Nasdaq) was $109.48.

Time to Expiration of the Option

An option is a **wasting asset**. That is, after the expiration date, the option has no value. All other factors equal, the longer the time to expiration of the option is, the higher the option

Table 35.3
Option chain on August 15, 2016, for Apple Inc (APPL) put and call option expiring on March 17, 2017 (APPL Price = $109.48).

	Call			Put	
Strike	Last Sale	Open Interest	Strike	Last Sale	Open Interest
100	13.05	13,539	100	4.15	4,360
105	9.85	6,218	105	5.88	1,088
110	7.12	7,211	110	8.10	576
115	4.90	10,823	115	11.06	657
120	3.35	8,060	120	15.00	248

Source: Prices obtained from Nasdaq.

Note: Last Sale is the most recent trade. Open Interest is the total number of derivatives contracts traded that have not yet been liquidated either by an offsetting derivative transaction or by delivery.

Table 35.4
Option chain on August 14, 2016, for Apple Inc (APPL) put and call options with a strike price of 105 for different expiration dates.

Expiration Date	Call Price	Put Price
September 2, 2016	4.65	0.33
October 21, 2016	6.40	1.75
November 18, 2016	7.39	3.09
December 16, 2016	7.92	3.65
January 20, 2017	8.70	4.35
March 17, 2017	9.85	5.88
April 21, 2017	10.35	6.43
June 16, 2017	11.40	7.71
November 17, 2017	13.69	10.95
January 19, 2018	14.53	11.10

Source: Prices obtained from Nasdaq.

price will be. This is because, as the time to expiration decreases, less time remains for the underlying asset's price to rise (for a call buyer) or fall (for a put buyer), and therefore the probability of a favorable price movement decreases. Consequently, for American options, as the time remaining until expiration decreases, the option price approaches its intrinsic value. This can be seen in table 35.4, which shows the price of Apple options on August 15, 2016, with different expiration dates.

Expected Price Volatility of the Underlying Asset over the Life of the Option

All other factors equal, the greater is the expected volatility (as measured by the standard deviation or variance) of the price of the underlying asset, the more an investor will be willing to pay for the option, and the more an option writer will demand for it. This occurs because the greater the volatility is, the greater the probability that the price of the underlying asset will move in favor of the option buyer at some time before expiration.

Notice that it is the standard deviation or variance, not the systematic risk as measured by beta, as described in chapter 14, that is relevant in the pricing of options.

Short-Term, Risk-Free Interest Rate over the Life of the Option

Buying the underlying asset ties up one's money. Buying an option on the same quantity of the underlying asset makes the difference between the asset price and the option price available for investment at an interest rate at least as high as the risk-free rate. Consequently, all other factors held constant, the higher the short-term, risk-free interest rate is, the greater will be the cost of buying the underlying asset and carrying it to the expiration date of the call option. Hence, the higher the short-term, risk-free interest rate is, the more attractive the call option will be relative to the direct purchase of the underlying asset. As a result, a higher short-term, risk-free interest rate results in a higher price for a call option.

Anticipated Cash Payments on the Underlying Asset over the Life of the Option

Cash payments on the underlying asset tend to decrease the price of a call option, because the cash payments make it more attractive to hold the underlying asset than to hold the option. For put options, cash payments on the underlying asset tend to increase the price.

Option Pricing Models

We have shown that the theoretical price of a futures contract can be determined by using arbitrage arguments. An option pricing model uses a set of assumptions and arbitrage arguments to derive a theoretical price for an option. As we shall see in the following text, deriving a theoretical option price is much more complicated than deriving a theoretical futures price, because the option price depends on the expected price volatility of the underlying asset over the life of the option.

Several models have been developed to determine the theoretical value of an option. The most popular one was developed by Fischer Black and Myron Scholes in 1973 for valuing European call options.[2] Some modifications were subsequently made to their model. We use another pricing model called the **binomial option pricing model** to see how arbitrage arguments can be used to determine a fair value for a call option.[3]

Basically, the idea behind the arbitrage argument is that if the payoff from owning a call option can be replicated by (1) purchasing the asset underlying the call option and (2) borrowing funds, the price of the option is then (at most) the cost of creating the replicating strategy.

Deriving the Binomial Option Pricing Model

To derive a one-period binomial option pricing model for a call option, we begin by constructing a portfolio consisting of (1) a long position in a certain amount of the asset and (2) a short call position in the underlying asset. The amount of the underlying asset purchased

2. Fischer Black and Myron Scholes, "The Pricing of Corporate Liabilities," *Journal of Political Economy* 81 (1973): 637–659.

3. John C. Cox, Stephen A. Ross, and Mark Rubinstein, "Option Pricing: A Simplified Approach," *Journal of Financial Economics* 7 (1979): 229–263; Richard J. Rendleman and Brit J. Bartter, "Two-State Option Pricing," *Journal of Finance* 34 (1979): 1093–1110; William F. Sharpe, *Investments* (Englewood Cliffs, NJ: Prentice Hall, 1981), chapter 16.

is such that the position will be hedged against any change in the price of the asset at the expiration date of the option. That is, the portfolio consisting of the long position in the asset and the short position in the call option is riskless and will produce a return that equals the risk-free interest rate. A portfolio constructed in this way is called a **hedged portfolio**.

We can show how this process works with an extended illustration. Let us assume first that an asset has a current market price of $80 and that only two possible future states can occur one year from now. Each state is associated with one of only two possible values for the asset, and they can be summarized in this way:

State	Price ($)
1	100
2	70

We assume further that there is a call option on this asset with a strike price of $80 (the same as the current market price) and that it expires in one year. Let us suppose an investor forms a hedged portfolio by acquiring two-thirds of a unit of the asset and selling one call option. The two-thirds of a unit of the asset is the so-called hedge ratio (how we derive the hedge ratio is explained later). Consider the outcomes for this hedged portfolio corresponding to the two possible outcomes for the asset.

If the price of the asset one year from now is $100, the buyer of the call option will exercise it. Then the investor will have to deliver one unit of the asset in exchange for the strike price, $80. As the investor has only two-thirds of a unit of the asset, she has to buy one-third at a cost of $100/3 (the market price divided by 3). Consequently, the outcome will equal the strike price of $80 received, minus the $100/3 cost to acquire the one-third unit of the asset to deliver, plus whatever price the investor initially sold the call option for. That is, the outcome will be

$$80 - 100/3 + \text{Call option price} = 46\tfrac{2}{3} + \text{Call option price}.$$

If instead the price of the asset one year from now is $70, the buyer of the call option will not exercise it. Consequently, the investor will own two-thirds of a unit of the asset. At the price of $70, the value of two-thirds of a unit is $46⅔. The outcome in this case is then the value of the asset plus whatever price the investor received when she initially sold the call option. That is, the outcome will be

$$46\tfrac{2}{3} + \text{Call option price}.$$

It is apparent that, given the possible asset prices, the portfolio consisting of a short position in the call option and two-thirds of a unit of the asset will generate an outcome that hedges changes in the price of the asset; hence, the hedged portfolio is riskless. Furthermore, this riskless hedge will hold regardless of the price of the call, which affects only the magnitude of the outcome.

Deriving the Hedge Ratio

To show how to calculate the hedge ratio, we use the following notation:

S = current asset price,

u = 1 plus the percentage change in the asset's price if the price goes up in the next period,

d = 1 plus the percentage change in the asset's price if the price goes down in the next period,

r = a risk-free one-period interest rate (the risk-free rate until the expiration date),

C = current price of a call option,

C_u = intrinsic value of the call option if the asset price goes up,

C_d = intrinsic value of the call option if the asset price goes down,

E = strike price of the call option,

H = hedge ratio (that is, the amount of the asset purchased per call sold).

In our illustration, u and d are

$u = 1.250$ ($100/$80),

$d = 0.875$ ($70/$80),

Furthermore, State 1 in our illustration means that the asset's price goes up, and State 2 means that the asset's price goes down.

The investment made in the hedged portfolio is equal to the cost of buying H amount of the asset minus the price received from selling the call option. Therefore, because

Amount invested in the asset $= HS$,

then

Cost of the hedged portfolio $= HS - C$.

The payoff of the hedged portfolio at the end of one period is equal to the value of the HS amount of the asset purchased minus the call option price. The payoffs of the hedged portfolio for the two possible states are defined in this way:

State 1, if the asset's price goes up: $uHS - C_u$,

State 2, if the asset's price goes down: $dHS - C_d$.

In our illustration, we have these payoffs:

If the asset's price goes up: $1.250H$ \$80 – C_u, or \$100$H – C_u$;
If the asset's price falls: 0.875 H \$80 – C_d, or \$70$H – C_d$.

If the hedge is riskless, the payoffs must be the same. Thus,

$$uHS - C_u = dHS - C_d. \tag{35.1}$$

Solving equation (35.1) for the hedge ratio H, we have

$$H = \frac{C_u - C_d}{(u-d)S}. \tag{35.2}$$

To determine the value of the hedge ratio H, we must know Cu and Cd. These two values are equal to the difference between the price of the asset and the strike price in the two possible states. Of course, the minimum value of the call option in any state is zero. Mathematically, the differences can be expressed as follows:

If the asset's price goes up: $C_u = \text{Max}\,[0, (uS - E)]$;
If the asset's price goes down: $C_d = \text{Max}\,[0, (dS - E)]$.

As the strike price in our illustration is \$80, the value of uS is \$100, and the value of dS is \$70. Then,

If the asset's price goes up: $C_u = \text{Max}\,[0, (\$100 - \$80)] = \$20$;
If the asset's price goes down: $C_d = \text{Max}\,[0, (\$70 - \$80)] = \$0$.

To continue with our illustration, we substitute the values of u, d, S, C_u, and C_d into equation (35.2) to obtain the hedge ratio's value:

$$H = \frac{\$20 - \$0}{(1.25 - 0.875)\$80} = \tfrac{2}{3}.$$

This value for H agrees with the amount of the asset purchased when we introduced this illustration.

Now we can derive a formula for the call option price. Figure 35.1 diagrams the situation. The top left half of the figure shows the current price of the asset for the current period and at the expiration date. The lower left portion of the figure does the same thing using the notation above. The upper right side of the figure gives the current price of the call option and the value of the call option at the expiration date; the lower right side does the same thing using our notation. Figure 35.2 uses the values in our illustration to construct the outcomes for the asset and the call option.

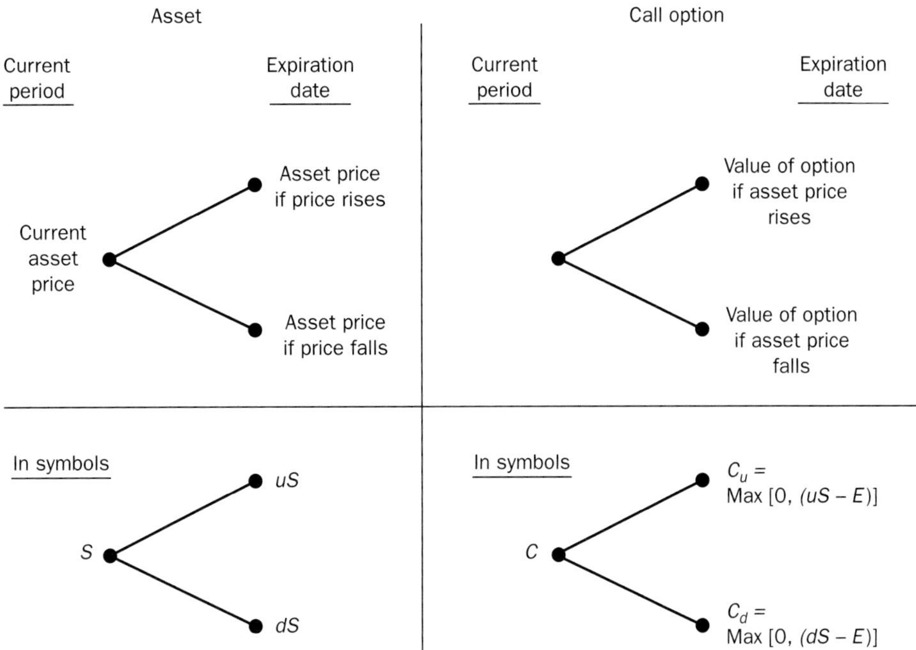

Figure 35.1
One-period option pricing model.

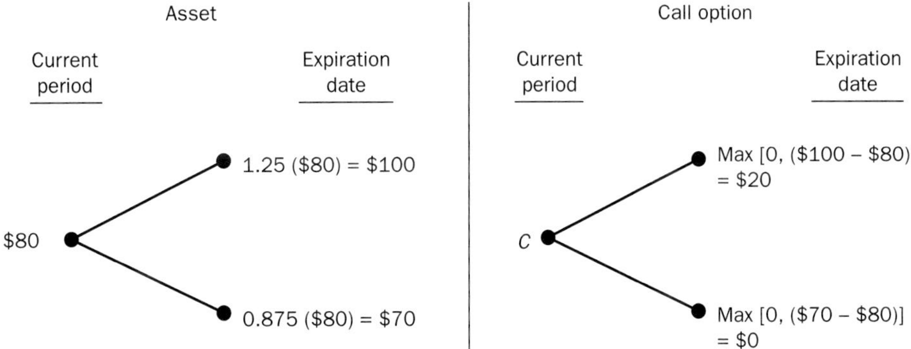

Figure 35.2
One-period option pricing model illustration.

Deriving the Price of a Call Option

To derive the price of a call option, we can rely on the basic principle that the hedged portfolio, being riskless, must have a return equal to the risk-free rate of interest. Given that the amount invested in the hedged portfolio is $HS-C$, the amount that should be generated one period from now is

$$(1+r)(HS-C). \tag{35.3}$$

We also know what the payoff will be for the hedged portfolio if the asset's price goes up or down. Because the payoff of the hedged portfolio will be the same whether the asset's price rises or falls, we can use the payoff if it goes up, which is

$$uHS-C_u.$$

The payoff of the hedged portfolio given above should be the same as the initial cost of the portfolio given by equation (35.3). Equating the two, we have

$$(1+r)(HS-C)=uHS—C_u. \tag{35.4}$$

Substituting equation (35.2) for H into equation (35.4) and solving for the call option price C, we find

$$C=\left(\frac{1+r-d}{u-d}\right)\left(\frac{C_u}{1+r}\right)+\left(\frac{u-1-r}{u-d}\right)\left(\frac{C_d}{1+r}\right). \tag{35.5}$$

Equation (35.5) is the formula for the one-period binomial option pricing model. We would have derived the same formula if we had used the payoff for a decline in the price of the underlying asset. This derivation is left as an exercise for the reader.

Applying equation (35.5) to our illustration, where

$u=1.250$,

$d=0.875$,

$r=0.10$,

$C_u=\$20$,

$C_d=\$0$,

we get

$$\begin{aligned}C&=\left(\frac{1+0.10-0.875}{1.25-0.875}\right)\left(\frac{\$20}{1+0.10}\right)+\left(\frac{1.25-1-0.10}{1.25-0.875}\right)\left(\frac{\$0}{1+0.10}\right).\\&=\$10.90\end{aligned}$$

The approach we present for pricing options may seem oversimplified, given that we assume only two possible future states for the price of the underlying asset. In fact, we can extend the procedure by making the period shorter and shorter, and in that way calculate a fair value for an option. Note that extended and comprehensive versions of the binomial pricing model are in wide use throughout the world of finance. Moreover, the other popular option pricing model, the Black-Scholes model mentioned earlier, is in reality the mathematical equivalent of the binomial approach as the periods become very short. Thus, the approach we have described in detail here provides the conceptual framework for much of the analysis of option prices that today's financial market participants regularly perform.

Fixed-Income Option Pricing Models

Because of the assumptions required for the binomial model described above, such models may have limited applicability to the pricing of options on fixed-income securities. More specifically, the binomial model assumes that (1) the price of the security can take on any positive value with some probability—no matter how small, (2) the short-term interest rate is constant over the life of the option, and (3) the volatility of the price of the security is constant over the life of the option.

These assumptions are unreasonable for an option on a fixed-income security. First, the price of a fixed-income security cannot exceed the undiscounted value of the cash flow. Any possibility that the price can go higher than this value implies that interest rates can be negative. Second, the price of an interest rate option will change as interest rates change. A change in the short-term interest rate changes the rates along the yield curve. Therefore, to assume that the short-term rate will be constant is inappropriate for interest rate options. The third assumption (that the variance of prices is constant over the life of the option) is inappropriate, because as a bond moves closer to maturity, its price volatility declines.

Fortunately, it is possible to avoid the problem of negative interest rates. We can develop a binomial option pricing model that is based on the distribution of interest rates rather than on prices. Once a binomial interest rate tree is constructed, it can be converted into a binomial price tree by using its interest rates to determine the prices of the bond at the end of the period. We can apply to these prices the same procedure described earlier to calculate the option price by working backward from the value of the call option at the expiration date.

Although the binomial option pricing model based on yields is superior to models based on prices, it still has a theoretical drawback. All theoretically valid option pricing models must satisfy the put–call parity relationship. The problem with the binomial model based on yields is that it does not satisfy this relationship. It violates the relationship, because it fails to take into consideration the yield curve, thereby allowing arbitrage opportunities.

The most elaborate models that take the yield curve into consideration, and as a result eliminate arbitrage opportunities, are called **yield curve option pricing models** or **arbitrage-free option pricing models**. These models can incorporate different volatility assumptions along the yield curve. They are theoretically superior to the other models we have described.[4]

Key Points

- The equilibrium or theoretical futures price can be determined through arbitrage arguments.
- The strategy that can be used to capture the arbitrage profit for an overpriced futures contract is the cash and carry trade; the strategy that can be used to capture the arbitrage profit for an underpriced futures contract is the reverse cash and carry trade.
- The theoretical futures price depends on the price of the underlying asset in the cash market, the cost of financing a position in the underlying asset, and the cash yield on the underlying asset.
- The ability of market participants to implement cash and carry trades and reverse cash and carry trades (or arbitrage strategies) results in the theoretical futures price being equal to the cash market price plus the cost of carry.
- At the delivery date, the price of a futures contract converges to the cash market price.
- The cost of carry is the net financing cost, that is, the difference between the financing rate and the cash yield on the underlying asset.
- The theoretical futures price will be less than the cash market price if the cost of carry is positive, equal to the cash market price if the cost of carry is zero, and more than the cash market price if the cost of carry is negative.
- Developing the theoretical futures price with arbitrage arguments requires certain assumptions; if these assumptions are violated for a specific futures contract, the theoretical futures price must be modified.
- The actual futures price will diverge from the theoretical futures price because of interim cash flows, differences between lending and borrowing rates, transaction costs, restrictions on short selling, and uncertainty about the deliverable asset and the date it will be delivered.
- Because of the difference between borrowing and lending rates and because of transaction costs, there is not one theoretical futures price but instead a boundary around the theoretical futures price. So long as the actual futures price remains within this boundary, arbitrage profits cannot be realized.
- The price of an option consists of two components: the intrinsic value and the time premium.
- The intrinsic value is the economic value of the option if it is exercised immediately.

4. For a discussion of yield curve or arbitrage-free option pricing models, see Mark Pitts and Frank J. Fabozzi, *Interest Rate Futures and Options* (Chicago: Probus Publishing, 1989), chapter 9.

- If no positive economic value results from exercising immediately, the intrinsic value of the option is zero.
- The time premium is the amount by which the option price exceeds the intrinsic value.
- Six factors influence the option price: (1) the current price of the underlying asset; (2) the strike price of the option; (3) the time remaining to the expiration of the option; (4) the expected price volatility of the underlying asset; (5) the short-term, risk-free interest rate over the life of the option; and (6) the anticipated cash payments on the underlying asset.
- The put–call parity relationship is the relationship between the price of a call option and the price of a put option on the same underlying instrument, with the same strike price and the same expiration date.
- The theoretical price of an option can be determined on the basis of arbitrage arguments; it is much more complicated to determine than the theoretical price of a futures contract, because the option price depends on the expected price volatility of the underlying asset over the life of the option.
- Several models have been developed to determine the theoretical value of an option.
- The value of an option is equal to the cost of creating a replicating hedge portfolio.
- The theoretical option price can be calculated with the binomial option pricing model, which also employs arbitrage arguments.
- Application of the binomial model to the pricing of options on fixed-income securities poses problems because of the model's underlying assumptions.

Questions

1. Models for pricing futures and options are said to be based on arbitrage arguments.

a. What does arbitrage mean?

b. What is the investor's incentive to engage in arbitrage?

2. Suppose that financial Asset ABC is the underlying asset for a futures contract with settlement six months from now. You know the following about this financial asset and the futures contract:

(i) In the cash market, ABC is selling for $80.

(ii) ABC pays $8 per year in two semiannual payments of $4, and the next semiannual payment is due exactly six months from now.

(iii) The current six-month interest rate at which funds can be loaned or borrowed is 6%.

a. What is the theoretical (or equilibrium) futures price?

b. What action would you take if the futures price is $83?

c. What action would you take if the futures price is $76?

d. Suppose that ABC pays interest quarterly instead of semiannually. If you know that you can reinvest any funds you receive three months from now at 1% for three months, what would be the theoretical futures price for six-month settlement?

e. Suppose that the borrowing rate and lending rate are not equal. Instead, suppose that the current six-month borrowing rate is 8% and the six-month lending rate is 6%. What are the boundaries for the theoretical futures price?

3. a. Explain why restrictions on short selling of stocks would cause the actual price of a stock index futures contract to diverge from its theoretical price.

b. Explain why creating a portfolio of stocks in which the number of stocks is less than the number of stocks in the index underlying a stock index futures contract would result in an arbitrage that is not riskless.

4. Why do the delivery options in a Treasury bond futures contract cause the actual futures price to diverge from its theoretical price?

5. "Of course, the futures are more expensive than the cash price—there's positive carry." Do you agree with this statement? Explain your answer.

6. Consider the following call option with three months to expiration:

Strike price = $72,

Current price of underlying assets = $87,

Market price of option = $6.

a. What is the intrinsic value for this call option?

b. What is the time premium for this call option?

7. Suppose the option in the previous question is a put option rather than a call option.

a. What is the intrinsic value for this put option?

b. What is the time premium for this put option?

8. You obtain the following price quotes for call options on Asset ABC. It is now December, with the near contract maturing in one month's time. Asset ABC's price is currently trading at $50.

Strike Price ($)	March Quote ($)	January Quote ($)	June Quote ($)
40	11	12	11.50
50	6	7	8.50
60	7	8	9.00

Glancing at the figures, you note that two of these quotes seem to violate some of the rules you learned regarding options pricing.

a. What are these discrepancies?

b. How could you take advantage of the discrepancies? What is the minimum profit you would realize by arbitraging based on these discrepancies?

9. Explain why you agree or disagree with the following statements:

a. "To determine the theoretical value of an option, we will need some measure of the price volatility of the underlying asset. Because financial theorists tell us that the appropriate measure of risk is beta (that is, systematic risk), then we should use this value."

b. "If the expected price volatility of an option increases, the theoretical value of an option decreases."

c. "It does not make sense that the price of a call option should rise in value if the price of the underlying asset falls."

10. Consider two options with the same expiration date and for the same underlying asset. The two options differ only in the strike price. Option 1's strike price is greater than that of Option 2.

a. If the two options are call options, which option will have a higher price?

b. If the two options are put options, which option will have a higher price?

11. Consider two options with the same strike price and for the same underlying asset. The two options differ only with respect to the time to expiration. Option A expires in three months, and Option B expires in six months.

a. If the two options are call options, which option will have the higher intrinsic value (assuming the options are in the money)?

b. If the two options are call options, which option will have a higher time premium?

c. Would your answers to (a) and (b) be different if the option is a put rather than a call?

12. In an option pricing model, what statistical measure is used as a measure of the price volatility of the underlying asset?

13. For an asset that does not make cash distributions over the life of an option, it does not pay to exercise a call option prior to the expiration date. Why?

14. Consider two strategies:

Strategy 1: Purchase one unit of Asset M currently selling for \$103. A distribution of \$10 is expected one year from now.

Strategy 2: (a) Purchase a call option on Asset M with an expiration date one year from now and a strike price of \$100; and (b) place sufficient funds in a 10% interest-bearing bank account to exercise the option at expiration (\$100) and to pay the cash distribution that would be paid by Asset M (\$10).

a. What is the investment required under Strategy 2?

b. Give the payoffs of Strategy 1 and Strategy 2, assuming that the price of Asset M one year from now is

(i) \$120,

(ii) \$103,

(iii) \$100,

(iv) \$80.

c. For the four prices of Asset M one year from now listed in part (b), demonstrate that the following relationship holds: Call option price ≥ Max [0, (Price of underlying asset – Present value of strike price – resent value of cash distribution)].

15. What is meant by a hedge ratio in developing an option pricing model?

16. a. Calculate the option value for a two-period European call option with the following terms:

Current price of underlying asset = \$100,

Strike price = \$10,

One-period, risk-free rate = 5%.

The stock price can either go up or down by 10% at the end of one period.

b. Recalculate the value for the option when the stock price can move either up or down by 50% at the end of one period. Compare your answer with the calculated value in part (a).

17. What is the problem with applying the binomial pricing model to the pricing of options on fixed-income securities?

36 Applications of Futures and Options Contracts

CONTENTS

Learning Objectives

After reading this chapter, you will understand:

- how participants use stock index futures to control a stock portfolio's risk and other portfolio applications;
- how investors in fixed-income securities employ interest rate futures to control the interest rate risk of a portfolio and other portfolio applications;
- how and under what circumstances futures can be used to enhance portfolio returns;
- how futures can be used to alter the allocation of a portfolio between equities and bonds;
- the differences between hedging with futures and options;
- how stock options and stock index options allow investors to protect the values of their stock portfolios;
- how interest rate options enable fixed-income investors to hedge against adverse changes in interest rates;
- what is meant by the "basis" and that the basis can change over time;
- that hedging with futures eliminates price risk but exposes the hedged position to basis risk;
- what is meant by cross-hedging and the risks associated with cross-hedging; and
- the difference between the long or buy hedge and the short or sell hedge, both in direct hedging and cross-hedging.

In chapters 33–35, we focused on the general properties of financial futures and options contracts, the specific contracts available, and how they are priced. Although we have alluded to various applications of these contracts, particularly their use in hedging, we did not cite specific applications. In this chapter, we provide an overview of how market participants can and do employ derivative instruments. The appendix to this chapter explains the general principles of hedging with futures contracts.

Applications of Futures Contracts

We begin with the various ways in which market participants can use stock index futures and interest rate futures.

Stock Index Futures

Institutional investors can use stock index futures for seven distinct investment strategies. We describe these strategies in the following text.

Speculating on the movement of the stock market Prior to the development of stock index futures, an investor who wanted to speculate on the future course of aggregate stock prices had to buy or short individual stocks. Now, a stock index can be bought or sold in the futures market. However, making speculation easier for investors is not the main function of stock index futures contracts. The other strategies discussed in the following text show how institutional investors can use stock index futures effectively to meet investment objectives.

Controlling the risk of a stock portfolio An institution that wishes to alter its exposure to the market can do so by revising the portfolio's beta. This can be done by rebalancing the portfolio with stocks that will produce the target beta, but there are transaction costs associated with rebalancing a portfolio. Because of the leverage embedded in futures, institutions can use stock index futures to achieve a target beta at a considerably lower transaction cost than is possible by rebalancing. Buying stock index futures will increase a portfolio's beta, and selling futures will reduce it.

Hedging against adverse stock price movements Hedging is a special case of controlling a stock portfolio's exposure to adverse price changes. In a hedge, the objective is to alter a current or anticipated stock portfolio position so that its beta is zero. A portfolio with a beta of zero should generate a risk-free interest rate. Such a return from a zero-beta portfolio is consistent with the capital asset pricing model discussed in chapter 14 and is also consistent with our discussion of the pricing of futures contracts in chapter 35.

Remember that using stock index futures for hedging locks in a price, and that the hedger cannot then benefit from a favorable movement in the portfolio's value. (As we explain later, using stock index options has downside protection but retains the upside potential reduced by the cost of the option.)

Two examples of how investment banking firms can use stock index futures to hedge their activities became known shortly after stock index futures began trading. In June 1982, International Harvester traded its stock portfolio to Goldman Sachs in exchange for a bond portfolio.[1] As recipient of the stock portfolio, Goldman Sachs was exposed to market risk. To protect itself against a decline in the value of the stock portfolio, Goldman Sachs placed a hedge on a "significant" portion of the stock portfolio, using all three stock index futures trading at the time to implement the hedge.

The second example involves Salomon Brothers, which used stock index futures to protect itself against a decline in stock prices in a transaction involving $400 million of stock. In that transaction, the New York City Pension Fund switched $400 million of funds that were being managed by Alliance Capital to Bankers Trust so that the latter could manage the funds with an indexing approach. Salomon Brothers guaranteed prices at which the

1. Kimberly Blanton, "Index Futures Contracts Hedge Big Block Trades," *Pension & Investments Age*, July 19, 1982: 1, 38.

Pension Fund and Bankers Trust could purchase or sell the stocks in the portfolio being transferred. To do this, Salomon Brothers used options on individual stocks to protect against price changes in certain stocks, but it also used stock index futures to protect itself against broad market movements that would decrease the value of the stocks in the portfolio.

Constructing indexed portfolios As explained in chapter 23, an increasing number of institutional equity funds are indexed to some broad-based stock market index. Creating a portfolio that replicates a targeted stock index requires outlays for management fees and transaction costs. The higher these costs are, the greater the divergence will be between the performance of the indexed portfolio and the target index. To control costs, many fund managers creating an indexed portfolio will not purchase all the stocks that comprise the index but instead will purchase a group that "tracks the targeted index" or moves in much the same way as the index. As a result, the indexed portfolio produces **tracking error risk**, which is the chance that its movements will not precisely follow those of the index. To avoid the problems of using the cash market to construct an indexed portfolio, the manager can use stock index futures.

However, note that index fund managers can use stock index futures to create an index fund only if stock index futures contracts are fairly priced or cheap. If the futures price is less than the theoretical futures price (that is, the futures contracts are cheap), the index fund manager can enhance the indexed portfolio's return by buying the futures and buying the Treasury bills. That is, the return on the futures/Treasury bill portfolio will be greater than that on the underlying index when the position is held to the settlement date. In this case, the stock index futures contracts offer yet another advantage to the manager.

Index arbitrage Opportunities to enhance returns as a result of the mispricing of the futures contract are not restricted to index fund management. Money managers and arbitrageurs monitor the cash and futures market to see when the differences between the theoretical futures price and actual futures price are sufficiently large to generate an arbitrage profit. These investors respond to those opportunities by selling the futures index if it is expensive and buying stocks, or buying the futures index if it is cheap and selling the stocks. **Index arbitrage** plays an important role in linking futures prices and cash prices. Program trading is used to execute the buy and sell orders.[2]

Creating portfolio insurance As explained in chapter 35, a put option can protect the value of an asset. At the expiration date of the put option, the minimum value for the asset will be the strike price minus the cost of the put option. Put options on stock indexes can do the same for a diversified portfolio of stocks.

2. Program trading is discussed in chapter 23.

Alternatively, an institutional investor can create a put option synthetically by using either (1) stock index futures or (2) stocks and a riskless asset. Of course, as market conditions change, the portfolio manager must change the allocation of the portfolio's funds to stock index futures or between stocks and a riskless asset.[3] A strategy that seeks to insure the value of a portfolio through the use of a synthetic put option strategy is called **dynamic hedging**.

Given that put options on stock indexes are available to portfolio managers, why should they bother with dynamic hedging? There are four reasons. First, the size of the market for options on stock indexes is not as large as that for stock index futures and therefore may not easily accommodate a large portfolio insurance program without moving the price of the option substantially. Second, exchanges impose limits on the number of contracts in which an investor can have a position. Institutions wishing to protect large equity portfolios may find that position limits effectively prevent them from using exchange-traded index options to protect their portfolio. Third, existing exchange-traded index options contracts are of shorter maturity than the period over which some investors seek protection. Finally, the cost of a put option may be higher than the transaction costs associated with dynamic hedging.

In one way, however, hedging with put options does offer an advantage. Although the cost of a put option is known (and is determined by expected price volatility), the cost of creating portfolio insurance by using stock index futures or stocks will be determined by actual price volatility in the market. The greater the market's price volatility is, the more rebalancing of the portfolio will be necessary and the higher will be the cost of creating portfolio insurance.

Asset Allocation

The decision on how to divide funds across the major asset classes (for example, equities, bonds, foreign securities, real estate) is referred to as the **asset allocation decision**. Futures and options can be used to implement an asset allocation decision more effectively than transacting in the cash markets would.

For example, suppose that a pension fund sponsor with assets of $1 billion has allocated $300 million to the bond market and $700 million to the stock market. Suppose further that the sponsor has decided to alter that bond/stock mix to $600 million in bonds and $400 million in stock. Liquidation of $300 million in stock will involve significant transaction costs—both commissions and execution (market impact) costs.[4] Moreover, the external money managers who are managing the stock portfolios will face disruption as funds are withdrawn by the sponsor. Rather than liquidating the stock portfolio immediately, the sponsor can sell an appropriate number of stock index futures contracts. This action effectively

3. For a more detailed explanation of this strategy, see Mark Rubinstein and Hayne Leland, "Replicating Options with Positions in Stock and Cash," *Financial Analysts Journal* 37, no. 4 (1981): 63–72.

4. These costs are described in chapter 23.

decreases the exposure of the pension fund to the stock market. To increase the fund's exposure to the bond market, the sponsor can buy interest rate futures contracts.

Interest Rate Futures

Market participants can employ interest rate futures in various ways, which we now discuss.

Speculating on the movement of interest rates The price of a futures contract moves in the opposite direction from interest rates: When rates rise (fall), the futures price will fall (rise). An investor who wants to speculate that interest rates will rise (fall) can sell (buy) interest rate futures. Before interest rate futures were available, investors who wanted to speculate on interest rates did so with the long-term Treasury bond: shorting it if they expected interest rates to rise, and buying it if they expected interest rates to fall.

Three advantages result from using interest rate futures instead of the cash market (trading long-term Treasuries themselves). First, the transaction costs of using futures are lower than those in the corresponding cash market. Second, margin requirements are lower for futures than for Treasury securities; using futures thus permits greater leverage. Finally, it is easier to take a short position in the futures market than to sell short in the Treasuries market. As we remarked when discussing the use of stock index futures to speculate on stock price movements: Making speculation easier for investors is not the function of interest rate futures contracts.

Controlling the interest rate risk of a portfolio Stock index futures can be used to change the market risk of a diversified stock portfolio, that is, to alter the beta of a portfolio. Likewise, interest rate futures can be used to alter the interest rate sensitivity of a portfolio. As explained in chapter 11, duration is a measure of interest rate sensitivity.

Investment managers with strong expectations about the direction of the future course of interest rates will adjust the durations of their portfolios so as to capitalize on their expectations. Specifically, a manager expecting rates to increase will reduce the interest rate sensitivity of a portfolio. A manager expecting rates to decrease will raise the interest rate sensitivity of the portfolio. Although investment managers can alter the interest rate sensitivity of their portfolios with cash market instruments, a quick and inexpensive means for doing so (on either a temporary or permanent basis) is to use futures contracts.

Hedging against adverse interest rate movements Interest rate futures can be used to hedge against adverse interest rate movements by locking in either a price or an interest rate. Some examples of hedging with interest rate futures will illustrate the basic concepts.

1. Suppose that a pension fund manager knows that bonds must be liquidated in 40 days to make a $5 million payment to the beneficiaries of the pension fund. If interest rates rise

in 40 days, more bonds will have to be liquidated to realize proceeds of $5 million. The pension fund manager can hedge by selling in the futures market to lock in a selling price.

2. A pension fund manager who is expecting substantial cash contributions that must be invested but is concerned that interest rates may fall can hedge against declining returns by buying interest rate futures. Also, a money manager who knows that bonds are maturing in the near future and who expects that interest rates will be lower at the time of reinvestment can buy interest rate futures. In both cases, interest rate futures are used to hedge against a fall in interest rates that would cause cash flows to be reinvested at a lower interest rate.

3. A corporation planning to sell long-term bonds two months from now can protect itself against a rise in interest rates by selling or taking a short position in interest rate futures now.

4. A thrift or commercial bank can hedge its cost of funds by locking in a rate using the Eurodollar futures contract.

5. A corporation that plans to sell commercial paper one month from now can use Treasury bill futures or Eurodollar futures to lock in a commercial paper rate.

6. Investment banking firms can use interest rate futures to protect both the value of positions held by their trading desks and positions assumed by the underwriting of new bond issues. An example of the latter is a 1979 Salomon Brothers underwriting of $1 billion of IBM bonds. To protect itself against a rise in interest rates, which would reduce the value of the IBM bonds, Salomon Brothers sold (shorted) Treasury futures. In October 1979, interest rates rose when the Federal Reserve Board announced that it was allowing interest rates more flexibility to move. Although the value of the IBM bonds held by Salomon Brothers declined in value, so did the Treasury bond futures contracts. Because Salomon Brothers had sold these futures, it realized a gain and thus reduced the loss on the IBM bonds it underwrote.

Enhancing returns when futures are mispriced In our earlier discussion of stock index futures, we explained that institutional investors look for mispricing of stock index futures to create arbitrage profits and thereby enhance portfolio returns. We referred to this strategy as "index arbitrage," because it involves a stock index. If interest rate futures are mispriced (even after considering the pricing problems discussed in chapter 35), institutional investors can enhance returns in the same way that they do in equities.

Asset Allocation

As noted earlier, interest rate futures and stock index futures are quick, cheap, and effective ways to change the composition of a portfolio between bonds and stocks.

Applications of Options Contracts

Stock Options and Stock Index Options

Stock options can be used to take advantage of the anticipated price movement of individual stocks. Alternatively, they can help protect current or anticipated positions in individual stocks. For example, an investor can protect against a decline in the price of a stock in her portfolio by buying a put option on that stock. The put guarantees a minimum price equal to the strike price minus the cost of buying the option. This strategy is called a **protective put buying strategy**. Also, if an investor anticipates buying a stock in the future but fears that the stock price will rise over that time, she can buy a call option on the stock. This strategy guarantees that the maximum price that will be paid in the future is the strike price plus the option price.

Now consider an institutional investor that holds a portfolio consisting of a large number of stock issues. Using stock options to protect against an adverse price movement in the portfolio's value, the institutional investor would have to buy a put on every stock in the portfolio, which would be quite costly. By taking an appropriate position in a suitable stock index option, the institutional investor can create a protective put for the entire diversified portfolio. For example, suppose that an institutional investor, who holds a diversified portfolio of common stock that is highly correlated with the S&P 100, is concerned that the stock market will decline in value over the next three months. Suppose, too, that a three-month put option on the S&P 100 is available. Because the put option buyer gains when the price of the underlying stock index declines, purchasing a put option will offset any adverse movements in the portfolio's value due to a decline in the stock market. This protective put-buying strategy obviously offers a cheap, effective, and flexible alternative to either buying puts on the various stocks or liquidating the entire portfolio and converting holdings into cash.

When stock options or stock index options are used to protect an existing or anticipated position, the investor need not exercise the option if the prices of the held stocks move in the direction that the investor wants. This freedom not to exercise makes options more suited than futures to the task of protecting a cash position. An institutional investor can obtain downside protection using options at a cost equal to the option price, but can also preserve upside potential (reduced by the option price).

Interest Rate Options

An institutional investor can use interest rate options or options on interest rate futures to speculate on fixed-income security price movements based on expectations of interest rate changes. Because a call option increases in price if interest rates decline, an investor can buy call options if he expects interest rates to move in that direction. Alternatively, because the writer of a put option will benefit if the price increases, an investor who expects interest rates to fall can write put options. Purchasing put options and/or selling call options would be appropriate for an investor who expects interest rates to rise. Remember that, unlike interest rate futures, interest rate options limit downside risk and permit upside potential that is reduced only by the amount of the option price.

As noted, institutional investors can use interest rate options to hedge against adverse interest rate movements but still let the investor benefit from a favorable interest rate movement. It is important to recognize that hedging in this way can basically set a floor or ceiling on an institution's targeted interest rate. We will use the illustrations given earlier for interest rate futures to explain how this works using options.

1. Suppose that a pension fund manager knows that bonds must be liquidated in 40 days to make a $5 million payment to the beneficiaries of the pension fund. If interest rates rise in 40 days, more bonds will have to be liquidated to realize $5 million. The hedger will buy put options (that is, follow a protective put buying strategy). If interest rates rise, the value of the bonds to be sold will decline, but the put options purchased will rise in value. For a transaction that is properly structured, the gain on the put options will offset the loss on the bonds. The cost of the safety bought by this strategy will then be the option price paid. If, instead, interest rates decline, the value of the bonds will rise. The pension fund manager will not exercise the put option. A gain equal to the rise in the bond value minus the put option price will be realized.

2. Suppose that a pension fund manager knows there will be substantial cash contributions flowing into the fund and is concerned that interest rates may fall. Or suppose that a money manager knows that bonds are maturing in the near future and expects interest rates to fall. In both cases, proceeds will be reinvested at a lower interest rate. Call options can be purchased in this situation. If interest rates fall, the call options will increase in value, offsetting the loss in interest income that will result when the proceeds must be invested at a lower interest rate. The cost of this hedge strategy is the call option price. If interest rates rise instead, the proceeds can be invested at a higher rate. The benefit of the higher rate will be reduced by the cost of the call option, which expires worthless.

3. A corporation plans to issue long-term bonds two months from now. To protect itself against a rise in interest rates, the corporation can buy put options. If interest rates rise, the interest cost of the bonds issued two months from now will be higher, but the put option will have increased in value. Buying an appropriate number of put options yields a gain on the put options sufficient to offset the higher interest cost of the bond issue. Again, the cost of this strategy is the price of the put options. If interest rates decline instead, the corporation will benefit from a lower interest cost when the bonds are issued, a benefit that is reduced by the cost of the put options.

4. A thrift or commercial bank wants to make sure that the cost of its funds will not exceed a certain level. This can be done by buying put options on Eurodollar futures.

5. A corporation plans to sell commercial paper one month from now. Buying put options on Treasury bill futures or Eurodollar futures lets the corporation set a ceiling on the interest cost of its commercial paper.

Key Points

- Investors can use stock index futures to speculate on stock prices, control a portfolio's price risk exposure, hedge against adverse stock price movements, construct indexed portfolios, engage in index arbitrage, and create a synthetic put option.
- Market participants can employ interest rate futures to speculate on interest rate movements, control a portfolio's risk exposure to interest rate changes, hedge against adverse interest rate movements, and enhance returns when futures are mispriced.
- Because futures are highly leveraged and transaction costs are less than in the cash market, market participants can alter their risk exposure to a market (stock or bond) more efficiently in the futures market.
- Buying a futures contract increases a market participant's exposure to a market; selling a futures contract decreases a market participant's exposure to a market.
- A money manager can use both stock index futures and interest rate futures to more efficiently allocate funds between the stock market and the bond market.
- Market participants can obtain downside protection using options at a cost equal to the option price and also preserve upside potential (reduced by the option price).
- A protective put buying strategy can be used to reduce the risk exposure of a stock portfolio to a decline in stock prices, guaranteeing a minimum price equal to the strike price minus the cost of buying the put option.
- The purchase of a call option can be used to guarantee that the maximum price that will be paid in the future is the strike price plus the option price.
- By taking an appropriate position in a suitable stock index option, an institutional investor can create a protective put for a diversified portfolio.
- Interest rate options or options on interest rate futures can be used by investors and issuers to hedge against adverse interest rate movements but still benefit from a favorable interest rate movement.
- When contracts are mispriced, a market participant can capitalize on this opportunity by enhancing returns (in the case of an investor) or reducing the cost of issuing an obligation (in the case of an issuer of securities).

Questions

1. a. If a stock portfolio's indicator of volatility is its beta, explain how stock index futures can be used to change the portfolio's volatility.

b. Suppose an institutional investor wants to increase the beta of a portfolio of stocks. Should this investor buy or sell S&P 500 futures contracts?

2. a. What is the difference between an index arbitrage strategy and an indexing strategy?

b. Why would a portfolio manager find it advantageous to use stock index futures in an indexing strategy?

3. Suppose a corporation plans to issue bonds three months from now and wants to protect against a rise in interest rates. Should the corporation buy or sell interest rate futures contracts?

4. a. What is meant by a "synthetic put option"?

b. What is meant by "dynamic hedging"?

5. Assume that you own an asset and there are both futures contracts and options contracts on that asset. Provide a clear account of the difference between hedging against a price decline with futures and hedging with options. Direct your analysis to the potential gains from options and the nature of losses from a futures position.

6. a. What is the basis of a futures contract?

b. Explain why hedging with futures contracts substitutes basis risk for price risk.

7. Under what conditions would a perfect hedge occur?

8. a. Why is a short futures hedge called a "sell hedge"?

b. Why is a long futures hedge called a "buy hedge"?

9. In a publication by the Commodity Futures Trading Commission, the following statement appears:

> Many people think that futures markets are just about speculating or "gambling." While it is true that futures markets can be used for speculating, that is not the primary reason for their existence. Futures markets are actually designed as vehicles for hedging and risk management, that is, to help people avoid "gambling" when they don't want to.[5]

Explain how futures markets help investors manage risk.

10. The following two quotations are from an article in the *Wall Street Journal*:

> Brokerage firms in the business, which tiptoed back into program trading after the post-crash furor died down, argue that such strategies as stock-index arbitrage—rapid trading between stock index futures and stocks to capture fleeting price differences—link two related markets and thus benefit both.

The second quotation in the article is from a senior vice president at Twenty-First Securities Corp:

> Program trading is a product that is here, links markets, and it is not going to disappear. It is a function of the computerization of Wall Street.[6]

5. Commodity Futures Trading Commission, "The Economic Purpose of Futures Markets" (Washington, DC: Commodity Futures Trading Commission, February 3, 2006).

6. Both quotes are from "Program Trading Spreads from Just Wall Street Firms," *Wall Street Journal*, August 18, 1989.

Do you agree with these statements?

11. This quotation is from *Business Week*:

> The idea sounds almost un-American. Instead of using your smarts to pick stocks that will reach the sky, you put money in a fund that merely tracks a broad market index. But that is precisely what institutional investors are doing.... Indexing is a new force in the stock market.... But the impact of index-funds reaches far beyond stock prices.[7]

Discuss how indexing may have contributed to the growth of the stock index derivatives markets.

12. This quotation appeared in the December 1988 issue of *Euromoney*:

> The proliferation of futures and options markets has created new opportunities for international investors. It is now possible to change investment exposure from one country to another through the use of derivative instruments, augmented by a limited number of individual securities. Asset allocation in most major markets is now feasible using futures and options.[8]

Discuss the quotation and the reasons for using derivatives rather than cash instruments to facilitate asset allocation decisions.

13. What are the risks associated with cross-hedging?

14. Donald Singleton is an investment banker for a regional firm. One of his clients, Dolby Manufacturing Inc., is a private company that will be making an initial public offering of 20 million shares of common stock. Mr. Singleton's firm will buy the issue at $10 per share. He has suggested to the managing director of the firm, John Wilson, that the firm should hedge the position using stock index futures contracts. What should Mr. Wilson's response be?

15. a. Explain why you agree or disagree with the following statement by Gary Gastineau:

> Stock index futures and options were introduced in the early 1980s. Their introduction was partly a response to institutional portfolio managers' preference for trading portfolios rather than individual stocks and partly a way of reducing transaction costs in the implementation of asset-allocation and market-timing decisions.

b. In the same article, Gary Gastineau made the following statement:

> Long positions in stock index futures combined with short-term fixed income securities are an almost perfect substitute for a stock index portfolio. Conversely, selling futures contracts against a portfolio of stocks is a low-cost way to reduce market exposure.[9]

Explain the conditions that must hold for this statement to be true.

16. An associate who is not an expert in financial futures has been reviewing a publication describing the three-year and 10-year Moscow City bonds published by the Russian Trading System Stock Exchange. In the publication, the following appears:

7. *Business Week*, June 8, 1987.

8. *Euromoney*, December 1988.

9. Both quotes are from Gary Gastineau, "A Short History of Program Trading," *Financial Analysts Journal* 47, no. 5 (1991): 4–7.

Futures on the 3Y and 10Y Moscow City bonds are standard long-term contracts. The underlying asset—the basket of bonds issued by the Government of Moscow—is the benchmark Russian fixed-income market instrument. Futures on the bond basket allow investors to hedge not only risks associated with Moscow City bonds but also risks related to bonds issued by other entities.

The publication goes on to say:

Futures on the 3Y and 10Y Moscow City bonds provide fixed-income traders with the following additional advantages:

- portfolio risk management
- short-selling abilities
- bond margin trading abilities
- the ability to create synthetic "short-term" bonds
- portfolio duration management abilities
- reduction in transaction costs
- using the spreads between the short-term and long-term interest rates without using the underlying assets
- using the spreads between the hard currency-denominated and ruble-denominated interest rates without using the underlying assets
- arbitrage possibilities.

Your associate has asked you to explain the following advantages from using these contracts:

a. Hedging "not only risks associated with Moscow City bonds but also risks related to bonds issued by other entities."

b. "Short-selling abilities."

c. "Portfolio duration management abilities"

d. "Reduction in transaction costs."

e. "Using the spreads between the short-term and long-term interest rates without using the underlying assets."

Appendix: General Principles of Hedging with Futures

The major function of futures markets is to transfer price risk from hedgers to speculators. That is, risk is transferred from those willing to pay to avoid risk to those wanting to assume the risk in the hope of gain. **Hedging** in this case is the employment of a futures transaction as a temporary substitute for a transaction to be made in the cash market. The hedge position locks in a value for the cash position. As long as cash and futures prices move together, any loss realized on one position (whether cash or futures) will be offset by a profit on the other position. When the profit and loss are equal, the hedge is called a **perfect hedge**. In a market where the futures contract is correctly priced, a perfect hedge should provide a return equal to the risk-free rate.

Risks Associated with Hedging

In practice, hedging is not that simple. The amount of the loss or profit on a hedge will be determined by the relationship between the cash price and the futures price when a hedge is placed and when it is lifted. The difference between the cash price and the futures price is called the **basis**. That is,

Basis = Cash price – Futures price.

As we explained earlier, if a futures contract is priced according to its theoretical value, the difference between the cash price and the futures price should be equal to the cost of carry. The risk that the hedger takes is that the basis will change, which is called **basis risk**. Therefore, hedging involves the substitution of basis risk for price risk, that is, the substitution of the risk that the basis will change for the risk that the cash price will change.

When a futures contract is used to hedge a position where either the portfolio or the individual financial instrument is not identical to the instrument underlying the futures, it is called **cross-hedging**. Cross-hedging is common in asset/liability and portfolio management, because no futures contracts are typically available on specific common stock shares and bonds. Cross-hedging introduces another risk—the risk that the price movement of the underlying instrument of the futures contract may not accurately track the price movement of the portfolio or financial instrument to be hedged. This risk is called **cross-hedging risk**. Therefore, the effectiveness of a cross-hedge will be determined by:

1. The relationship between the cash price of the underlying instrument and its futures price when a hedge is placed and when it is lifted.
2. The relationship between the market (cash) value of the portfolio and the cash price of the instrument underlying the futures contract when the hedge is placed and when it is lifted.

Short Hedge and Long Hedge

A **short hedge** is used to protect against a decline in the future cash price of a financial instrument or portfolio. To execute a short hedge, the hedger sells a futures contract (agrees to make delivery). Consequently, a short hedge is also known as a **sell hedge**. By establishing a short hedge, the hedger has fixed the future cash price and transferred the price risk of ownership to the buyer of the futures contract.

A **long hedge** is undertaken to protect against an increase in the price of a financial instrument or portfolio to be purchased in the cash market at some future time. In a long hedge, the hedger buys a futures contract (agrees to accept delivery). A long hedge is also known as a **buy hedge**.

Illustrations of Hedging

Although our focus in this chapter is on financial derivatives, to illustrate hedging, we present several numerical examples from the traditional commodities markets. It is better to start with traditional commodities, because they are simpler than most financial futures contracts. The principles illustrated are equally applicable to financial futures contracts, but it is easier to grasp the sense of the commodities product example without getting into the nuances of financial contracts.

Assume that a mining company expects to sell 1,000 ounces of palladium one week from now and that the management of a manufacturing company plans to purchase 1,000 ounces of palladium one week from now. The managers of both the mining company and the manufacturing company want to lock in a price—that is, they both want to eliminate the price risk associated with palladium one week from now. The cash price for palladium is currently $352.40 per ounce. The cash price is also called the **spot price**. The futures price for palladium is currently $397.80 per ounce. Each futures contract is for 100 (troy) ounces of palladium.

Because the mining company seeks protection against a decline in the price of palladium, the company will place a short hedge. That is, the mining company will promise to make delivery of palladium at the current futures price. The mining company will sell 10 futures contracts.

The management of the manufacturing company seeks protection against an increase in the price of palladium. Consequently, it will place a long hedge. That is, it will agree to accept delivery of palladium at the futures price. Because it is seeking protection against a price increase for 1,000 ounces of palladium, it will buy 10 contracts.

Let's look at what happens under various scenarios for the cash price and futures price of palladium one week from now when the hedge is lifted.

Perfect Hedge

Suppose that at the time the hedge is lifted, the cash price has declined to $304.20 and the futures price has declined to $349.60. Notice what has happened to the basis under this scenario. At the time the hedge is placed, the basis is –$45.40 ($352.40 – $397.80). When the hedge is lifted, the basis is still –$45.40 ($304.20 – $349.60).

The mining company wanted to lock in a price of $352.40 per ounce of palladium, or $352,400 for 1,000 ounces. The company sold 10 futures contracts at a price of $397.80 per ounce, or $397,800 for 1,000 ounces. When the hedge is lifted, the value of 1,000 ounces of palladium is $304,200 ($304.20 × 1,000). The palladium mining company realizes a decline in the cash market in the value of its palladium of $48,200. However, the futures price has declined to $349.60, or $349,600 for 1,000 ounces. The mining company thus realizes a $48,200 gain in the futures market. The net result is that the gain in the futures market matches the loss in the cash market. Consequently, the mining company does not realize an overall gain or loss. This example of a perfect hedge is summarized in table A36.1.

The outcome for the manufacturing company of its long hedge is also summarized in table A36.1. Because of the decline in the cash price, the manufacturing company realizes a gain in the cash market equal to $48,200 but realizes a loss of the same amount in the futures market. Therefore the long hedge is also a perfect hedge.

This scenario illustrates two important points. First, both participants incur no overall gain or loss, because the basis did not change when the hedge was lifted. Consequently, if the basis does not change, the effective purchase or sale price ends up being the cash

Table A36.1
A hedge that locks in the current price of palladium: Cash price decreases.

Assumptions:
Cash price at time hedge is placed: $352.40 per oz
Futures price at time hedge is placed: $397.80 per oz
Cash price at time hedge is lifted: $304.20 per oz
Futures price at time hedge is lifted: $349.60 per oz
Number of ounces to be hedged: 1,000
Number of ounces per futures contract: 100
Number of futures contracts used in hedge: 10

Cash Market	Futures Market	Basis
Short (Sell) Hedge by Mining Company		
At time hedge is placed:		
Value of 1,000 oz: 1,000 × $352.40 = $352,400	Sell 10 contracts: 10 × 100 × $397.80 = $397,800	–$45.40 per oz
At time hedge is lifted:		
Value of 1,000 oz: 1,000 × $304.20 = $304,200 Loss in cash market = $48,200	Buy 10 contracts: 10 × 100 × $349.60 = $349,600 Gain in futures market = $48,200 Overall gain or loss = $0	–$45.40 per oz
Long (Buy) Hedge by Manufacturing Company		
At time hedge is placed:		
Value of 1,000 oz: 1,000 × $352.40 = $352,400	Buy 10 contracts: 10 × 100 × $397.80 = $397,800	–$45.40 per oz
At time hedge is lifted:		
Value of 1,000 oz: 1,000 × $304.20 = $304,200 Gain in cash market = $48,200	Sell 10 contracts: 10 × 100 × $349.60 = $349,600 Loss in futures market = $48,200 Overall gain or loss = $0	–$45.40 per oz

price on the day the hedge is set. Second, note that the management of the manufacturing company would have been better off had it not hedged. The cost of the palladium would have been $48,200 less. This result, however, should not be interpreted as a sign of a bad decision. Managers are usually not in the business of speculating on the price of palladium, and hedging is the standard practice used to protect against an increase in the cost of doing business in the future. The "price" of obtaining this protection is the potential windfall that one gives up.

Suppose that when the hedge is lifted, the cash price of palladium has increased to $392.50 and the futures price has increased to $437.90. Notice that the basis is unchanged at –$45.40. Because the basis is unchanged, the effective purchase and sale price will equal

Table A36.2
A hedge that locks in the current price of palladium: Cash price increases.

Assumptions:
Cash price at time hedge is placed: $352.40 per oz
Futures price at time hedge is placed: $397.80 per oz
Cash price at time hedge is lifted: $392.50 per oz
Futures price at time hedge is lifted: $437.90 per oz
Number of ounces to be hedged: 1,000
Number of ounces per futures contract: 100
Number of futures contracts used in hedge: 10

Cash Market	Futures Market	Basis
Short (Sell) Hedge by Mining Company		
At time hedge is placed:		
Value of 1,000 oz:	Sell 10 contracts:	–$45.40 per oz
1,000 × $352.40 = $352,400	10 × 100 × $397.80 = $397,800	
At time hedge is lifted:		
Value of 1,000 oz:	Buy 10 contracts:	–$45.40 per oz
1,000 × $392.50 = $392,500	10 × 100 × $437.90 = $437,900	
Gain in cash market = $40,100	Loss in futures market = $40,100	
	Overall gain or loss = $0	
Long (Buy) Hedge by Manufacturing Company		
At time hedge is placed:		
Value of 1,000 oz:	Buy 10 contracts:	–$45.40 per oz
1,000 × $352.40 = $352,400	10 × 100 × $397.80 = $397,800	
At time hedge is lifted:		
Value of 1,000 oz:	Sell 10 contracts:	–$45.40 per oz
1,000 × $392.50 = $392,500	10 × 100 × $437.90 = $437,900	
Loss in cash market = $40,100	Gain in futures market = $40,100	
	Overall gain or loss = $0	

the price of palladium at the time the hedge is placed. The mining company will gain in the cash market, because the value of 1,000 ounces of palladium is $392,500 ($392.50 × 1,000) and represents a $40,100 gain compared to the cash value at the time the hedge was placed. However, the mining company must liquidate its position in the futures market by buying 10 futures contracts at a total price of $437,900, which is $40,100 more than the price when the contracts were sold. The loss in the futures market offsets the gain in the cash market. The results of this hedge are summarized in table A36.2.

The manufacturing company realizes a $40,100 gain in the futures market but will have to pay $40,100 more in the cash market to acquire 1,000 ounces of palladium. The results of this hedge are also summarized in table A36.2.

Notice that in this scenario, the management of the manufacturing company saved $40,100 by employing a hedge. In contrast, the mining company would have been better off had it not hedged and simply sold its product on the market one week later. However, it must be emphasized that the management of the mining company, just like the management of the manufacturing company, employed a hedge to protect against unforeseen adverse price changes in the cash market, and the price of this protection is that one forgoes the favorable price changes enjoyed by those who do not hedge.

Basis Risk

In the two previous scenarios, we assumed that the basis does not change. In the real world, however, the basis frequently changes between the time a hedge is placed and the time it is lifted.

Assume that the cash price of palladium decreases to $304.20, just as in the first scenario; however, assume further that the futures price decreases to $385.80 rather than $349.60. The basis has now declined from –$45.40 to –$81.60 ($304.20 – $385.80). The results are summarized in table A36.3. For the short hedge, the $48,200 loss in the cash market is only partially offset by the $12,000 gain realized in the futures market. Consequently, the hedge resulted in an overall loss of $36,200.

Several points are pertinent here. First, if the mining company did not hedge, the loss would have been $48,200, because the value of its 1,000 ounces of palladium is $304,200 compared to the value $352,400 just one week earlier. Although the hedge is not perfect, the loss of $36,200 is less than the loss of $48,200 that would have occurred without the hedge, which is what we meant earlier by stating that hedging substitutes basis risk for price risk. Second, the management of the manufacturing company faces the same problem from the opposite perspective. An unexpected gain for one participant results in an unexpected loss of equal dollar value for the other. That is, the participants face a zero-sum game, because they hold identically opposite cash and futures positions. Consequently, the manufacturing company would realize an overall gain of $36,200 from its long (buy) hedge.

Table A36.3
Hedge: Cash price decreases and basis widens.

Assumptions
Cash price at time hedge is placed: $352.40 per oz
Futures price at time hedge is placed: $397.80 per oz
Cash price at time hedge is lifted: $304.20 per oz
Futures price at time hedge is lifted: $385.80 per oz
Number of ounces to be hedged: 1,000
Number of ounces per futures contract: 100
Number of futures contracts used in hedge: 10

Cash Market	Futures Market	Basis
Short (Sell) Hedge by Mining Company		
At time hedge is placed:		
Value of 1,000 oz: 1,000 × $352.40 = $352,400	Sell 10 contracts: 10 × 100 × $397.80 = $397,800	–$45.40 per oz
At time hedge is lifted:		
Value of 1,000 oz: 1,000 × $304.20 = $304,200 Loss in cash market = $48,200	Buy 10 contracts: 10 × 100 × $385.80 = $385,800 Gain in futures market = $12,000 Overall loss = $36,200	–$81.60 per oz
Long (Buy) Hedge by Manufacturing Company		
At time hedge is placed:		
Value of 1,000 oz: 1,000 × $352.40 = $352,400	Buy 10 contracts: 10 × 100 × $397.80 = $397,800	–$45.40 per oz
At time hedge is lifted:		
Value of 1,000 oz: 1,000 × $304.20 = $304,200 Gain in cash market = $48,200	Sell 10 contracts: 10 × 100 × $385.80 = $385,800 Loss in futures market = $12,000 Overall gain $36,200	–$81.60 per oz

This gain represents a gain in the cash market of $48,200 and a realized loss in the futures market of $12,000.

Suppose that the cash price increases to $392.50 per ounce, just as in the second scenario, but that the basis widens to –$81.60. That is, at the time the hedge is lifted, the futures price has increased to $474.10. The results of this hedge are summarized in table A36.4.

As a result of the long hedge, the manufacturing company realizes a gain of $76,300 in the futures market but only a $40,100 loss in the cash market, for an overall gain of $36,200. For the mining company, the overall loss is $36,200.

In the two previous scenarios, it was assumed that the basis widened. It can be demonstrated that if the basis narrowed, the outcome will not be a perfect hedge.

Table A36.4
Hedge: Cash price increases and basis widens.

Assumptions:
Cash price at time hedge is placed: $352.40 per oz
Futures price at time hedge is placed: $397.80 per oz
Cash price at time hedge is lifted: $392.50 per oz
Futures price at time hedge is lifted: $474.10 per oz
Number of ounces to be hedged: 1,000
Number of ounces per futures contract: 100
Number of futures contracts used in hedge: 10

Cash Market	Futures Market	Basis
Short (Sell) Hedge by Mining Company		
At time hedge is placed:		
Value of 1,000 oz: 1,000 × $352.40 = $352,400	Sell 10 contracts: 10 × 100 × $397.80 = $397,800	–$45.40 per oz
At time hedge is lifted:		
Value of 1,000 oz: 1,000 × $392.50 = $392,500 Gain in cash market = $40,100	Buy 10 contracts: 10 × 100 × $474.10 = $474,100 Loss in futures market = $76,300 Overall loss = $36,200	–$81.60 per oz
Long (Buy) Hedge by Manufacturing Company		
At time hedge is placed:		
Value of 1,000 oz: 1,000 × $352.40 = $352,400	Buy 10 contracts: 10 × 100 × $397.80 = $397,800	–$45.40 per oz
At time hedge is lifted:		
Value of 1,000 oz: 1,000 × $392.50 = $392,500 Loss in cash market = $40,100	Sell 10 contracts: 10 × 100 × $474.10 = $474,100 Gain in futures market = $76,300 Overall gain = $36,200	–$81.60 per oz

Cross-Hedging

Suppose that a mining company on a faraway planet plans to sell 2,500 ounces of kryptonite one week from now, and that a manufacturing company plans to purchase the same amount of kryptonite in one week. Both parties want to hedge against price risk.[10] However, kryptonite futures contracts are not currently traded. Both parties believe a close relationship exists between the price of kryptonite and the price of palladium. Specifically, both parties believe that the cash price of kryptonite will remain at 40% of the cash price of palladium. The cash price of kryptonite is currently $140.96 per ounce, and the cash price

10. We will ignore interplanetary exchange rate risk in our illustrations.

of palladium is currently $352.40 per ounce. The futures price of palladium is currently $397.80 per ounce.

We shall examine various scenarios to see how effective the cross-hedge will be. In each scenario, the palladium basis is held constant at –$45.40. We make this assumption so that we can focus on the importance of the relationship between the two cash prices at the two points in time.

Before proceeding, we must first determine how many palladium futures contracts should be used in the cross-hedge. The value of 2,500 ounces of kryptonite at the cash price of $140.96 per ounce is $352,400. To protect the value of the kryptonite using palladium futures, the cash value of 1,000 ounces of palladium ($352,400/$352.40) must be hedged. Because each palladium futures contract covers 100 ounces, 10 palladium futures contracts will be used.

Suppose that the cash prices of kryptonite and palladium decrease to $121.68 and $304.20 per ounce, respectively, and that the futures price of palladium decreases to $349.60 per ounce. The relationship between the cash price of kryptonite and the cash price of palladium when the cross-hedge was placed holds when the cross-hedge is lifted. That is, the cash price of kryptonite is 40% of the cash price of palladium. The palladium basis stays constant at –$45.40. The outcome for the short and long cross-hedge is summarized in table A36.5.

The short cross-hedge produces a gain of $48,200 in the futures market and an exactly offsetting loss in the cash market. The opposite occurs for the long cross-hedge. Neither an overall gain nor a loss from the cross-hedge accrues for either hedger in this scenario. The same would occur if the cash prices of both commodities increase by the same percentage and the basis does not change.

Suppose that the cash price of both commodities decreases, but the cash price of kryptonite falls by a greater percentage than that of palladium. For example, suppose that the cash price of kryptonite falls to $112.00 per ounce, and the cash price of palladium falls to $304.20 per ounce. The futures price of palladium falls to $349.60, so that the basis is not changed. The cash price of kryptonite at the time the cross-hedge is lifted is 37% of the cash price of palladium, rather than the 40% when the cross-hedge was constructed. The outcomes for the long and short cross-hedge are shown in table A36.6.

For the short cross-hedge, the loss in the cash market exceeds the realized gain in the futures market by $24,200. For the long cross-hedge, the opposite is true. An overall gain of $24,200 results from the cross-hedge.

If the cash price of kryptonite had fallen by a smaller percentage amount than the cash price of palladium, the short cross-hedge would have produced an overall gain, whereas the long cross-hedge would have generated an overall loss.

Suppose that the cash price of kryptonite falls to $121.68 per ounce, whereas the cash price and futures price of palladium rise to $392.50 and $437.90, respectively. The results of the cross-hedge are shown in table A36.7.

Table A36.5
Cross-hedge: Cash price of kryptonite to be hedged and price of futures used decreased by same percentage.

Assumptions:
Price of kryptonite:
Cash price at time hedge is placed: \$140.96 per oz
Cash price at time hedge is lifted: \$121.68 per oz
Price of palladium:
Cash price at time hedge is placed: \$352.40 per oz
Futures price at time hedge is placed: \$397.80 per oz
Cash price at time hedge is lifted: \$304.20 per oz
Futures price at time hedge is lifted: \$349.60 per oz
Number of ounces of kryptonite to be hedged: 2,500
Number of ounces of palladium to be hedged, assuming ratio of cash price of kryptonite to palladium is 0.4: 1,000
Number of ounces per futures contract for palladium: 100
Number of palladium futures contracts used in hedge: 10

Cash Market	Futures Market	Palladium Basis
Short (Sell) Cross-Hedge by Kryptonite Mining Company		
Value of 2,500 oz: 2,500 × \$140.96 = \$352,400	Sell 10 contracts: 10 × 100 × \$397.80 = \$397,800	−\$45.40 per oz
At time hedge is lifted:		
Value of 2,500 oz: 2,500 × \$121.68 = \$304,200 Loss in cash market = \$48,200	Buy 10 contracts: 10 × 100 × \$349.60 = \$349,600 Gain in futures market = \$48,200 Overall gain or loss = \$0	−\$45.40 per oz
Long (Buy) Cross-Hedge by Manufacturing Company ***At time hedge is placed:***		
Value of 2,500 oz: 2,500 × \$140.96 = \$352,400	Buy 10 contracts: 10 × 100 × \$397.80 = \$397,800	−\$45.40 per oz
At time hedge is lifted:		
Value of 2,500 oz: 2,500 × \$121.68 = \$304,200 Gain in cash market = \$48,200	Sell 10 contracts: 10 × 100 × \$349.60 = \$349,600 Loss in futures market = \$48,200 Overall gain or loss = \$0	−\$45.40 per oz

Table A36.6
Cross-hedge: Cash price of kryptonite to be hedged falls by a greater percentage than the futures used for the hedge.

Assumptions:

Price of kryptonite

Cash price at time hedge is placed: $140.96 per oz

Cash price at time hedge is lifted: $112.00 per oz

Price of palladium

Cash price at time hedge is placed: $352.40 per oz

Futures price at time hedge is placed: $397.80 per oz

Cash price at time hedge is lifted: $304.20 per oz

Futures price at time hedge is lifted: $349.60 per oz

Number of ounces of kryptonite to be hedged: 2,500

Number of ounces of palladium to be hedged, assuming ratio of cash price of kryptonite to palladium is 0.4: 1,000

Number of ounces per futures contract for palladium: 100

Number of palladium futures contracts used in hedge: 10

Cash Market	Futures Market	Basis
Short (Sell) Cross-Hedge by Kryptonite Mining Company		
At time hedge is placed:		
Value of 2,500 oz: 2,500 × $140.96 = $352,400	Sell 10 contracts: 10 × 100 × $397.80 = $397,800	–$45.40 per oz
At time hedge is lifted:		
Value of 2,500 oz: 2,500 × $112.00 = $280,000 Loss in cash market = $72,400	Buy 10 contracts: 10 × 100 × $349.60 = $349,600 Gain in futures market = $48,200 Overall loss = $24,200	–$45.40 per oz
Long (Buy) Cross-Hedge by Manufacturing Company		
At time hedge is placed:		
Value of 2,500 oz: 2,500 × $140.96 = $352,400	Buy 10 contracts: 10 × 100 × $397.80 = $397,800	–$45.40 per oz
At time hedge is lifted:		
Value of 2,500 oz: 2,500 × $112.00 = $280,000 Gain in cash market = $72,400	Sell 10 contracts: 10 × 100 × $349.60 = $349,600 Loss in futures market = $48,200 Overall gain = $24,200	–$45.40 per oz

Table A36.7
Cross-hedge: Cash price of kryptonite to be hedged falls and the price of futures used for the hedge rises.

Assumptions:
Price of kryptonite
Cash price at time hedge is placed: $140.68 per oz
Cash price at time hedge is lifted: $121.68 per oz
Price of palladium
Cash price at time hedge is placed: $352.40 per oz
Futures price at time hedge is placed: $397.80 per oz
Cash price at time hedge is lifted: $392.50 per oz
Futures price at time hedge is lifted: $437.90 per oz
Number of ounces of kryptonite to be hedged: 2,500
Number of ounces of palladium to be hedged, assuming ratio of cash price of kryptonite to palladium is 0.4: 1,000
Number of ounces per futures contract for palladium: 100
Number of palladium futures contracts used in hedge: 10

Cash Market	Futures Market	Palladium Basis
Short (Sell) Cross-Hedge by Kryptonite Mining Company		
At time hedge is placed:		
Value of 2,500 oz:	Sell 10 contracts:	
2,500 × $140.96 = $352,400	10 × 100 × $397.80 = $397,800	–$45.40 per oz
At time hedge is lifted:		
Value of 2,500 oz:	Buy 10 contracts:	
2,500 × $121.68 = $304,200	10 × 100 × $437.90 = $437,900	–45.40 per oz
Loss in cash market = $48,200	Loss in futures market = $40,100	
	Overall loss = $88,300	
Long (Buy) Cross-Hedge by Manufacturing Company		
At time hedge is placed:		
Value of 2,500 oz:	Buy 10 contracts:	
2,500 × $140.96 = $352,400	10 × 100 × $397.80 = $397,800	–$45.40 per oz
At time hedge is lifted:		
Value of 2,500 oz:	Sell 10 contracts:	
2,500 × $121.68 = $304,200	10 × 100 × $437.90 = $437,900	–$45.40 per oz
Gain in cash market = $48,200	Gain in futures market = $40,100	
	Overall gain = $88,300	

The short cross-hedge results in a loss in both the cash market and the futures market. The overall loss is $88,300. Had the kryptonite mining company not used the cross-hedge, its loss would have been limited to the decline in the cash price—$48,200, in this instance. In contrast, the long hedger realizes a gain in both the cash and futures market, and therefore an overall gain.

If instead the cash price of kryptonite increases to $189.10 per ounce, and the cash and futures price of palladium decline to $304.20 and $349.60, respectively, it can be demonstrated that the long cross-hedge results in a loss in both the cash and futures markets. The total loss is $168,550. The loss would have been only $120,350 (that is, the loss in the cash market), had the management of the manufacturing company not cross-hedged with palladium.

These illustrations demonstrate the risks associated with cross-hedging.

37 Over-the-Counter Interest Rate Derivatives: Forward Rate Agreements, Swaps, Caps, and Floors

CONTENTS

Learning Objectives

After reading this chapter, you will understand:

- what a forward rate agreement is;
- what an interest rate swap is;
- how an interest rate swap can be used by institutional investors and corporate borrowers;
- why the interest rate swap market has grown so rapidly;
- the risk/return characteristics of an interest rate swap;
- two ways to interpret an interest rate swap;
- the reasons for the development of an interest rate swap market;
- the determinants of the swap spread;
- what a swaption is;
- what a forward start swap is;
- what an interest rate/equity swap is;
- what an interest rate cap and floor is;
- how interest rate caps and floors and forward rate agreements can be used by institutional investors and corporate borrowers;
- the relationship between an interest rate cap and floor and an option; and
- how an interest rate collar can be created.

Interest rate futures and options can be used to control interest rate risk. Commercial banks and investment banks also customize other contracts useful for controlling interest rate risk for their clients. These include interest rate swaps, interest rate caps and floors, and forward rate agreements. According to a survey by the Bank for International Settlements (BIS), trading in over-the-counter (OTC) interest rate derivatives markets dominates the OTC derivatives market.[1] As of year end 2017, the gross market value of OTC interest rate derivatives was $7.6 trillion. In this chapter, we review each type of OTC interest rate derivative and explain how borrowers and institutional investors use them.

Forward Rate Agreements

A **forward rate agreement** (FRA) is the OTC equivalent of the exchange-traded futures contracts on short-term rates. Typically, the short-term rate is the London Interbank Offered Rate (LIBOR).

1. Bank for International Settlement, *Statistical Release: OTC Derivatives Statistics at End-December 2017* (Basel, Switzerland: Bank for International Settlement, May 2018), https://www.bis.org/publ/otc_hy1805.htm.

The elements of an FRA are the contract rate, reference rate, settlement rate, notional amount, and settlement date. The parties to an FRA agree to buy and sell funds on the settlement date. The FRA's **contract rate** is the rate specified in the FRA at which the buyer of the FRA agrees to pay for funds and the seller of the FRA agrees to receive for investing funds. The **reference rate** is the interest rate used. For example, the reference rate could be the three-month or six-month LIBOR. The benchmark from which the interest payments are to be calculated is specified in the FRA and is called the **notional amount** (or "notional principal amount"). This amount is not exchanged between the two parties. The **settlement rate** is the value of the reference rate at the FRA's settlement date. The source for determining the settlement rate is specified in the FRA.

The buyer of the FRA is agreeing to pay the contract rate, or equivalently, to buy funds at the settlement date at the contract rate; the seller of the FRA is agreeing to receive the contract rate, or equivalently, to sell funds at the settlement date at the contract rate. So, for example, if the FRA has a contract rate of 5% for the three-month LIBOR (the reference rate) and the notional amount is for $10 million, the buyer is agreeing to pay 5% to buy or borrow $10 million at the settlement date and the seller is agreeing to receive 5% to sell or lend $10 million at the settlement date.

If at the settlement date, the settlement rate is greater than the contract rate, the FRA buyer benefits, because the buyer can borrow funds at a below-market rate. If the settlement rate is less than the contract rate, this benefits the seller, who can lend funds at an above-market rate. If the settlement rate is the same as the contract rate, neither party benefits. This is summarized as follows:

FRA buyer benefits if Settlement rate > Contract rate,
FRA seller benefits if Contract rate > Settlement rate,
Neither party benefits if Settlement rate = Contract rate.

As with the Eurodollar futures contract, FRAs are cash settlement contracts. At the settlement date, the party that benefits based on the contract rate and settlement rate must be compensated by the other. Assuming the settlement rate is not equal to the contract rate, then

Buyer receives compensation if Settlement rate > Contract rate,
Seller receives compensation if Contract rate > Settlement rate.

To determine the amount one party must compensate the other, the following is first calculated assuming a 360-day count convention:

If Settlement rate > Contract rate:

$$\text{Interest differential} = (\text{Settlement rate} - \text{Contract rate}) \times (\text{Days in contract period}/360) \times \text{Notional amount}.$$

If Contract rate > Settlement rate:

$$\text{Interest differential} = (\text{Contract rate} - \text{Settlement rate}) \times (\text{Days in contract period}/360) \times \text{Notional amount}.$$

The amount that must be exchanged at the settlement date is not the interest differential. Instead, the present value of the interest differential is exchanged. The discount rate used to calculate the present value of the interest differential is the settlement rate. Thus, the compensation is determined as follows:

$$\text{Compensation} = \frac{\text{Interest differential}}{[1 + \text{Settlement rate} \times (\text{Days in contract period}/360)]}.$$

To illustrate, assume the following terms for an FRA: Reference rate is the three-month LIBOR, the contract rate is 5%, the notional amount is for \$10 million, and the number of days to settlement is 91 days. Suppose the settlement rate is 5.5%. In this case, the buyer benefits, because the buyer can borrow at 5% (the contract rate) when the market rate (the settlement rate) is 5.5%. The interest differential is

$$\text{Interest differential} = (0.055 - 0.05) \times (91/360) \times \$10{,}000{,}000 = \$12{,}638.89.$$

The compensation or payment that the seller must make to the buyer is

$$\text{Compensation} = \frac{\$12{,}638.89}{[1 + 0.055 \times 91/360]} = \frac{\$12{,}638.89}{1.0139027} = \$12{,}465.58.$$

It is important to note the difference in who benefits when interest rates move in an FRA and an interest rate futures contract. The buyer of an FRA benefits if the reference rate increases, and the seller benefits if the reference rate decreases. In a futures contract, the buyer benefits from a falling rate, whereas the seller benefits from a rising rate. This is summarized in table 37.1. The different parties benefit under different conditions, because the underlying for each of the two contracts is different. In the case of an FRA, the underlying is a rate. The buyer gains if the rate increases and loses if the rate decreases. In contrast,

Table 37.1
Effect of rate changes on parties to an FRA and an interest rate futures contract.

	Interest Rates			
	Decrease		Increase	
Party	FRA	Futures	FRA	Futures
Buyer	Loses	Gains	Gains	Loses
Seller	Gains	Loses	Loses	Gains

Table 37.5
Cash flow for the purchase of a five-year, floating-rate bond financed by borrowing on a fixed-rate basis.

Transaction: Purchase for \$50 million a five-year, floating-rate bond:
floating rate = LIBOR, semiannual pay
Borrow \$50 million for five years: fixed rate = 10% semiannual payments

	Cash Flow (in millions of dollars) from:		
Six-Month Period	Floating-Rate Bond	Borrowing Cost	Net
0	\$50.0	+\$50.0	\$0
1	$+(LIBOR_1/2)\times 50$	− 2.5	$+(LIBOR_1/2)\times 50–2.5$
2	$(LIBOR_2/2)\times 50$	2.5	$(LIBOR_2/2)\times 50–2.5$
3	$(LIBOR_3/2)\times 50$	2.5	$(LIBOR_3/2)\times 50–2.5$
4	$(LIBOR_4/2)\times 50$	2.5	$(LIBOR_4/2)\times 50–2.5$
5	$(LIBOR_5/2)\times 50$	2.5	$(LIBOR_5/2)\times 50–2.5$
6	$(LIBOR_6/2)\times 50$	2.5	$(LIBOR_6/2)\times 50–2.5$
7	$(LIBOR_7/2)\times 50$	2.5	$(LIBOR_7/2)\times 50–2.5$
8	$(LIBOR_8/2)\times 50$	2.5	$(LIBOR_8/2)\times 50–2.5$
9	$(LIBOR_9/2)\times 50$	2.5	$(LIBOR_9/2)\times 50–2.5$
10	$+(LIBOR_{10}/2)\times 50+50$	52.5	$+(LIBOR_{10}/2)\times 50–2.5$

Note: The subscript on *LIBOR* indicates the six-month LIBOR as per the terms of the floating-rate bond at a specific time.

as to provide a better match between assets and liabilities. The two institutions are a commercial bank and a life insurance company.

Suppose a bank has a portfolio consisting of five-year term commercial loans with a fixed interest rate. The principal value of the portfolio is \$50 million, and the interest rate on all the loans in the portfolio is 10%. The loans are interest only loans; interest is paid semiannually, and the entire principal is paid at the end of five years. That is, assuming no default on the loans, the cash flow from the loan portfolio is \$2.5 million every six months for the next five years and \$50 million at the end of five years. To fund its loan portfolio, assume that the bank is relying on the issuance of six-month CDs. The interest rate that the bank plans to pay on its six-month CDs is the six-month Treasury bill rate plus 40 basis points (bps).

The risk that the bank faces is that the six-month Treasury bill rate will be 9.6% or greater. To understand why, remember that the bank is earning 10% annually on its commercial loan portfolio. If the six-month Treasury bill rate is 9.6%, it will have to pay 9.6% plus 40 bps to depositors for six-month funds, or 10%, and there will be no spread income. Worse, if the six-month Treasury bill rate rises above 9.6%, there will be a loss; that is, the cost of funds will exceed the interest rate earned on the loan portfolio. The bank's objective is to lock in a spread over the cost of its funds.

The other party in this illustration is a life insurance company that has committed itself to paying a 9% rate for the next five years on a guaranteed investment contract (GIC) it has issued. The amount of the GIC is $50 million. Suppose that the life insurance company has the opportunity to invest $50 million in what it considers an attractive five-year, floating-rate instrument in a private placement transaction. The interest rate on this instrument is the six-month Treasury bill rate plus 160 bps. The coupon rate is set every six months.

The risk that the life insurance company faces is that the six-month interest rate will fall, so that the company will not earn enough to realize a spread over the 9% rate that it has guaranteed to the GIC holders. If the six-month Treasury bill rate falls to 7.4% or less, no spread income will be generated. To understand why, suppose that at the date the floating-rate instrument resets its coupon, the six-month Treasury bill rate is 7.4%. Then the coupon rate for the next six months will be 9% (7.4% plus 160 bps). Because the life insurance company has agreed to pay 9% on the GIC policy, there will be no spread income. If the six-month Treasury bill rate falls below 7.4%, then the life insurance company will incur a loss.

We can summarize the asset/liability problem of the bank and life insurance company as follows:

Bank:

1. Has lent long-term and borrowed short-term;
2. If the six-month Treasury bill rate rises, spread income declines.

Life insurance company:

3. Has effectively lent short-term and borrowed long-term;
4. If the six-month Treasury bill rate falls, spread income declines.

Now let's suppose that an intermediary offers a five-year interest rate swap with a notional principal amount of $50 million to both the bank and life insurance company. The terms offered to the bank are:

1. Every six months, the bank will pay 10% (annual rate) to the intermediary.
2. Every six months, the intermediary will pay the six-month Treasury bill rate plus 155 bps to the bank.

The terms offered to the insurance company are:

1. Every six months, the life insurance company will pay the six-month Treasury bill rate plus 160 bps per year to the intermediary.
2. Every six months, the intermediary will pay the insurance company 10% (annual rate).

What has this interest rate contract done for the bank and the life insurance company? Consider first the bank. For every six-month period during the life of the swap agreement, the interest rate spread will be as follows:

Annual Interest Rate Received:	
From commercial loan portfolio	= 10%
From interest rate swap	= 6-month T-bill rate + 155 bps.
Total	= 11.55% + 6-month T-bill rate
Annual Interest Rate Paid:	
To CD depositors	= 6-month T-bill rate + 40 bps.
On interest rate swap	= 10%
Total	= 10.40% + 6-month T-bill rate
Outcome:	
To be received	= 11.55% + 6-month T-bill rate
To be paid	= 10.40% + 6-month T-bill rate
Spread income	= 1.15% or 115 bps.

Thus, regardless of what happens to the six-month Treasury bill rate, the bank locks in a spread of 115 bps.

Now let's look at the effect of the interest rate swap on the life insurance company:

Annual Interest Rate Received:		
From floating-rate instrument	=	6-month T-bill rate + 160 bps
From interest rate swap	=	10%
Total	=	11.6% + 6-month T-bill rate
Annual Interest Rate Paid:		
To GIC policyholders	=	9%
On interest rate swap	=	6-month T-bill rate + 160 bps
Total	=	10.6% + 6-month T-bill rate
Outcome:		
To be received	=	11.6% + 6-month T-bill rate
To be paid	=	10.6% + 6-month T-bill rate
Spread income	=	1.0% or 100 bps

Regardless of what happens to the six-month Treasury bill rate, the life insurance company locks in a spread of 100 bps.

The interest rate swap has allowed each party to accomplish its asset/liability objective of locking in a spread.[2] The swap permits each financial institution to alter the cash flow characteristics of its assets: from fixed to floating in the case of the bank, and from floating to fixed in the case of the life insurance company. This type of transaction is referred to as an **asset swap**. The bank and the life insurance company could have used the swap market instead to change the cash flow nature of their liabilities. Such a swap is called a **liability swap**. Although we used a bank in our illustration, an interest rate swap obviously would be appropriate for savings and loan associations that, because of regulation, borrow short term on a floating-rate basis and lend long term on fixed-rate mortgages.

Of course, the two institutions could have chosen other ways to match the cash flow characteristics of their assets and liabilities. The bank might refuse to make fixed-rate commercial loans and insist only on floating-rate loans. This approach has a major pitfall: If borrowers can find another source willing to lend on a fixed-rate basis, the bank would lose these customers. The life insurance company might refuse to purchase a floating-rate instrument. But suppose that the terms offered on the private placement instrument were more attractive than what would have been offered on a floating-rate instrument of comparable credit risk. Thus, by using the swap market, the life insurance company can earn a yield higher than what it would earn if it had invested directly in a five-year, fixed-rate security. For example, suppose the life insurance company can invest in a comparable credit risk five-year, fixed-rate security with a yield of 9.8%. Given the funding through the GIC with a 9% rate, this investment would result in spread income of 80 bps—less than the 100-bp spread income that the life insurance company achieved by purchasing the floating-rate instrument and entering into the swap.

Consequently, an interest rate swap performs two important functions: (1) It can change the risk of a financial position by altering the cash flow characteristics of assets or liabilities, and (2) under certain circumstances, it also can be used to enhance returns. Obviously, this second function arises only if there are market imperfections.

A final point can be made in this illustration. Look at the floating-rate payments that the life insurance company makes to the intermediary and the floating-rate payments that the intermediary makes to the bank. The life insurance company pays the six-month Treasury bill rate plus 160 bps, but the intermediary pays the bank the six-month Treasury bill rate plus only 155 bps. The difference of 5 bps represents the fee to the intermediary for the services of intermediation.

Application to debt issuance Our second illustration considers two U.S. entities, a triple-A rated commercial bank and a triple-B rated nonfinancial corporation: Each wants to raise \$100 million for 10 years. For various reasons, the bank wants to raise floating-rate funds,

2. Whether the size of the spread is adequate is not relevant for us in this illustration.

whereas the nonfinancial corporation wants to raise fixed-rate funds. The interest rates available to the two entities in the U.S. bond market are:

Bank: Floating rate = Six-month LIBOR + 30 bps,
Nonfinancial corporation: Fixed rate = 12%.

Suppose also that both entities could issue securities in the Eurodollar bond market, if they wanted to. Let us assume that the following terms are available in the Eurodollar bond market for 10-year securities for these two entities:

Bank: Fixed rate = 10.5%,
Nonfinancial corporation: Floating rate = Six-month LIBOR + 80 bps.

Notice that we indicate the terms that the bank could obtain on fixed-rate financing and that the nonfinancial corporation could obtain on floating-rate securities. You will shortly see why we did this. First, let us summarize the situation for the two entities in the U.S. domestic and Eurodollar bond markets:

Floating-Rate Securities

Entity	Bond Market	Rate
Bank	U.S. domestic	6-month LIBOR + 30 bps
Nonfinancial corporation	Eurodollar	6-month LIBOR + 80 bps
		Quality spread = 50 bps

Fixed-Rate Securities

Entity	Bond Market	Rate
Bank	Eurodollar	10.5%
Nonfinancial corporation	U.S. domestic	12.0%
		Quality spread = 150 bps

In this table, we use the term **quality spread**. This term simply means the differential borrowing costs that reflect the difference in the creditworthiness of the two entities.

Notice that the quality spread for floating-rate securities (50 bps) is narrower than the quality spread for fixed-rate securities (150 bps). This difference in spreads provides an opportunity for both entities to reduce the cost of raising funds. To see how, suppose each entity issued securities in the Eurodollar bond market, and then simultaneously entered into the following 10-year interest rate swap with a $100 million notional principal amount offered by an intermediary:

Bank:

Pay floating rate of 6-month LIBOR + 70 bps
Receive fixed rate of 11.3%

Nonfinancial Corporation:

Pay fixed rate of 11.3%
Receive floating rate of 6-month LIBOR + 45 bps

Interest Paid:

On fixed-rate Eurodollar bonds issued	= 10.5%
On interest rate swap	= six-month LIBOR + 70 bps
Total	= 11.2% + 6-month LIBOR

Interest Received:

On interest rate swap	= 11.3%

Net Cost:

Interest paid	= 11.2% + six-month LIBOR
Interest received	= 11.3%
Total	= six-month LIBOR − 10 bps

Interest Paid:

On floating-rate Eurodollar bonds issued	= six-month LIBOR + 80 bps
On interest rate swap	= 11.3%
Total	= 12.1% + six-month LIBOR

Interest Received:

On interest rate swap	= six-month LIBOR + 45 bps

Net Cost:

Interest paid	= 12.1% + six-month LIBOR
Interest received	= six-month LIBOR + 45 bps
Total	= 11.65%

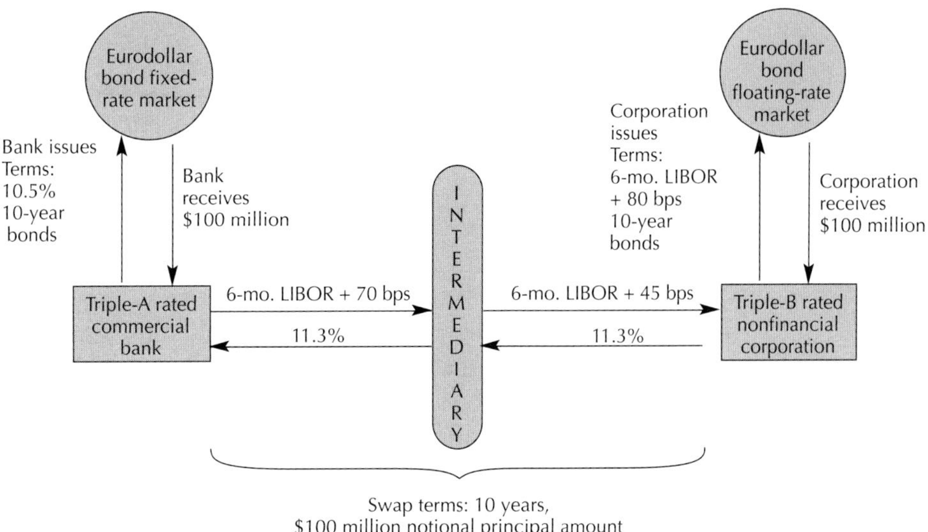

Figure 37.1
Interest rate swap for debt issuance.

The transactions are diagrammed in figure 37.1. By issuing securities in the Eurodollar bond market and using the interest rate swap, both entities are able to reduce their cost of issuing securities. The bank was able to issue floating-rate securities for six-month LIBOR minus 10 bps rather than issue floating-rate securities in the U.S. domestic bond market for six-month LIBOR plus 30 bps, thereby saving 40 bps. The nonfinancial corporation saved 35 bps (11.65% versus 12%) by issuing floating-rate bonds in the Eurodollar bond market and using the interest rate swap.

The point of this illustration is to show that, if differences in quality spreads exist in different sectors of the bond markets, borrowers can use the interest rate swap to arbitrage the inconsistency. Whether these differences do exist is another question, which we address below.

Finally, look once again at the intermediary in this transaction. The intermediary pays a floating rate of six-month LIBOR plus 45 bps to the nonfinancial corporation, and it receives six-month LIBOR plus 70 bps from the bank, realizing 25 bps for its intermediary services.

Reasons for the Development of the Interest Rate Swap Market

According to the BIS, the interest rate swap market, which began in late 1981, is the largest component of the OTC interest rate derivatives market. The interest rate swap market has grown rapidly since its inception. What is behind this rapid growth? As our two illustrations have demonstrated, an interest rate swap is a quick way for institutional investors and corporate borrowers to change the nature of assets and liabilities or to exploit any perceived capital market imperfection.

The initial motivation for the interest rate swap market was borrower exploitation of what were perceived to be **credit arbitrage** opportunities. These opportunities were attributed to the fact that quality spreads (i.e., the difference in yields between lower- and higher-rated credits) were frequently not the same in the fixed-rate market as in the floating-rate market, and often the quality spreads were not the same in the U.S. debt markets as in the Eurodollar bond markets. Note that our second illustration assumes a spread of 50 bps in the floating-rate markets and 150 bps in the fixed-rate markets. Publications by dealer firms[3] and academic research have suggested this credit arbitrage motivation.[4]

Basically, this argument for swaps rested on the well-known economic principle of comparative advantage, which was developed in international economics. The argument takes the following form. Even though a high credit-rated issuer could borrow at a lower cost in both the fixed-rate and floating-rate markets (that is, have an absolute advantage in both), it will have a comparative advantage relative to a lower credit-rated issuer in one of the markets (and a comparative disadvantage in the other). Under these conditions, each borrower could benefit from issuing securities in the market in which it has a comparative advantage and then swapping obligations for the desired type of financing. The swap market developed as the vehicle for swapping obligations.

Several observers have challenged the notion that credit arbitrage opportunities exist. They insist that the comparative advantage argument, although based on arbitrage, does not rely on irrational mispricing but on assumptions of equilibrium in segmented markets. That is, two completely separate markets can be perfectly competitive unto themselves but can set different prices for risk. An economic agent transacting simultaneously in both markets would see an imperfectly competitive market and an opportunity to make money.

Those who challenge the credit arbitrage notion argue that the differences in quality spreads in the fixed-rate and floating-rate markets represent differences in the risks that lenders face in these two markets. Let us consider short- and long-term markets in this regard. The interest rate for a floating-rate note effectively represents a short-term interest rate; therefore, the quality spread on floating-rate notes is a spread in the short-term market. In contrast, the quality spread on fixed-rate medium- and long-term notes represents the spread in that maturity sector. There is no reason for the quality spreads across those two markets to be the same.[5]

Some observers attribute the difference in quality spreads among markets to differences in regulations among countries. Similarly, differences in tax treatment across countries also cre-

3. See, for example, T. Lipsky and S. Elhalaski, "Swap-Driven Primary Issuance in the International Bond Market" (New York: Salomon Brothers, January 1986).

4. See, for example, James Bicksler and Andrew Chen, "An Economic Analysis of Interest Rate Swaps," *Journal of Finance* 41 (1986): 645–655.

5. Two researchers demonstrate that differences in quality spreads between the fixed-rate and floating-rate markets are consistent with option-pricing theory. See Ian Cooper and Antonio Mello, "Default Spreads in the Fixed and in the Floating Rate Markets: A Contingent Claims Approach," *Advances in Futures and Options Research* 3 (1988): 269–290.

ate differences in the price of risk and in expected returns.[6] Thus, swaps can be used for regulatory or tax arbitrage and may be explained by such differences among national markets.

Finally, another argument suggested for the growth of the interest rate swap market is the increased volatility of interest rates that has led borrowers and lenders to hedge or manage their exposure. Even though risk/return characteristics can be replicated by a package of forward contracts, interest rate forward contracts are not as liquid as interest rate swaps. And entering into or liquidating swap transactions has been facilitated by the standardization of documentation published by the International Swap Dealers Association in early 1987. Moreover, a swap to hedge or manage a position costs less than a package of interest rate forward contracts.

Consequently, we can say that the swap market originally developed for the purpose of exploiting real or perceived imperfections in the capital market, but it eventually evolved into a transactionally efficient market for accomplishing asset/liability objectives.

Role of the Intermediary

The role of the intermediary in an interest rate swap sheds some light on the evolution of the market. Intermediaries in these transactions have been commercial banks and investment banks, who, in the early stages of the market, sought out end users of swaps. That is, commercial banks and investment banking firms found in their client bases those entities that needed swaps to accomplish funding or investing objectives, and they matched the two entities. In essence, the intermediary in this type of transaction performed the function of a broker.

In the early years of this market, the only time that the intermediary would take the opposite side of a swap (that is, would act as a principal) was when it had to do so to balance out the transaction. For example, if an intermediary had two clients that were willing to do a swap but one wanted the notional principal amount to be $100 million and the other wanted it to be $85 million, the intermediary might become the counterparty to the extent of $15 million. That is, the intermediary would warehouse or take a position as a principal to the transaction to make up the $15 million difference between the clients' objectives. To protect itself against an adverse interest rate movement, the intermediary would hedge its position.

To explain how the intermediary's role developed over time, we need to address an important feature of the swap that we have not yet discussed. The parties to the swaps we have described had to be concerned that the other party would default on its obligation. Although a default would not mean any principal was lost (because the notional principal amount had not been exchanged), it would mean that the objective for which the swap was entered into would be impaired. As the early transactions involved a higher and a lower credit-rated entity, the former would be concerned with the potential for default of the latter. To reduce

6. This is especially relevant to currency swaps, which we discuss in chapter 38. Several examples of the way swaps can be used to exploit differences in taxes are given in Clifford W. Smith, Charles W. Smithson, and Lee MacDonald Wakeman, "The Evolving Market for Swaps," *Midland Corporate Finance Journal* 3 (1986): 20–32.

the risk of default, many early swap transactions required that the lower credit-rated entity obtain a guarantee from a highly rated commercial bank. Often, the intermediary in the swap was a bank of this type. Involvement as insurer or guarantor in this way led banks to accept the role of dealer or counterparty.

As the frequency and size of the transactions increased, many intermediaries became comfortable with swap transactions and became principals instead of simply acting as brokers. As long as an intermediary had one entity willing to enter into a swap, the intermediary was willing to be the counterparty. Consequently, interest rate swaps became part of an intermediary's inventory of products. Advances in quantitative techniques and futures products for hedging complex positions (such as swaps) made the protection of large inventory positions feasible.

Yet another development encouraged intermediaries to become principals rather than brokers in swaps. As more intermediaries entered the swap market, bid-ask spreads on swaps narrowed sharply. To make money in the swaps market, intermediaries had to do a sufficient volume of business, which was possible only if they had (1) an extensive client base willing to use swaps and (2) a large inventory of swaps. Accomplishing these objectives required the intermediaries to act as principals. A survey by *Euromoney* asked 150 multinationals and supranationals to identify the characteristics that make a swap house efficient.[7] The results indicated that the speed at which a swap could be arranged for a client was the most important criterion. That speed depends on client base and inventory. The same survey also revealed clients to be less interested in brokered deals than in transactions in which the intermediary is a principal.

Market Quotes

The convention that has evolved for quoting swaps levels is for a swap dealer to set the floating rate equal to the index and then quote the fixed rate that will apply. To illustrate this convention, we use the swap in our second example of the application of swaps. The terms for that 10-year swap are as follows:

Bank:

Pay floating rate of 6-month LIBOR + 70 bps.

Receive fixed rate of 11.3%.

Nonfinancial Corporation:

Pay fixed rate of 11.3%.

Receive floating rate of 6-month LIBOR + 45 bps.

The offer price that the dealer would quote to the nonfinancial corporation (the fixed-rate payer) would be to pay 10.85% and receive LIBOR flat. (The term *flat* means with no spread.) The 10.85% is obtained by subtracting from the fixed rate of 11.3% the 45-basis

7. "Special Supplement on Swaps," *Euromoney*, July 1987, 14.

point spread over LIBOR. The bid price that the dealer would quote to the commercial bank would be to pay LIBOR flat and receive 10.6%. The 10.6% represents the payment to be received of 11.3% minus the 70-basis point spread over LIBOR.

The dealer determines or sets the quoted fixed rate by adding some spread to the Treasury yield curve with the same term to maturity as the swap. We refer to this spread as the **swap spread**. In our illustration, suppose that the 10-year Treasury yield is 10.35%. In this case, the offer price that the dealer would quote to the fixed-rate payer is the 10-year Treasury rate plus 50 bps versus receiving LIBOR flat. For the floating-rate payer, the bid price quoted would be LIBOR flat versus the 10-year Treasury rate plus 40 bps. In the terminology of the market, the dealer would actually quote this particular swap as "40–50." This swap spread means that the dealer is willing to enter into a swap on either side: to receive LIBOR and pay a fixed rate equal to the 10-year Treasury rate plus 40 bps, or to pay LIBOR and receive a fixed rate equal to the 10-year Treasury rate plus 50 bps. The difference between the fixed rate paid and received is the bid-offer spread, which is 40 bps.

Primary Determinants of Swap Spreads

Earlier we provided two interpretations of a swap: (1) a package of futures/forward contracts, and (2) a package of cash market instruments.[8] The swap spread is defined as the difference between the swap's fixed rate and the rate on a Treasury whose maturity matches the swap's maturity. Although a discussion of the valuation of interest rate swaps is beyond the scope of this chapter, it can be shown that they are valued using no-arbitrage relationships relative to instruments (funding or investment vehicles) that produce the same cash flows under the same circumstances.[9]

The swap spread is determined by the same factors that drive the spread over Treasuries on instruments that replicate a swap's cash flows (i.e., produce a similar return or funding profile). As discussed below, the swap spread's key determinant for swaps with maturities of five years or less is the cost of hedging in the Eurodollar futures market.[10] For swaps with a longer maturity, the swap spread is largely driven by credit spreads in the corporate bond market.[11] Specifically, longer-dated swaps are priced relative to rates paid by investment-grade credits in traditional fixed- and floating-rate markets.

8. The discussion in this section is adapted from Frank J. Fabozzi and Steven V. Mann, *Floating-Rate Securities* (New Hope, PA: Frank J. Fabozzi Associates, 2000), chapter 6.

9. For an explanation of the valuation of swaps, see Jeffrey Buetow and Frank J. Fabozzi, *Valuation of Interest Rate Swaps* (New Hope, PA: Frank J. Fabozzi Associates, 2001).

10. Naturally, this observation presupposes that the reference rate for the swap is LIBOR. Furthermore, part of the swap spread is attributable simply to the fact that LIBOR for a given maturity is higher than the rate of a comparable-maturity U.S. Treasury. For a discussion of non-LIBOR swaps and their valuation, see Buetow and Fabozzi, *Valuation of Interest Rate Swaps*.

11. The default risk component of a swap spread will be smaller than for a comparable bond credit spread for two reasons. First, because only net interest payments are exchanged rather than both principal and coupon interest

Given that a swap is a package of futures and forward contracts, the shorter-term swap spreads respond directly to fluctuations in Eurodollar futures prices. A Eurodollar futures contract is an instrument in which a fixed dollar payment (i.e., the futures price) is exchanged for the three-month LIBOR. There is a liquid market for Eurodollar futures contracts with maturities every three months for five years. A market participant can create a synthetic fixed-rate security or a fixed-rate funding vehicle of up to five years by taking a position in a bundle of Eurodollar futures contracts (i.e., a position in every three-month Eurodollar futures contract up to the desired maturity date).

For example, consider a financial institution that has fixed-rate assets and floating-rate liabilities. Both the assets and liabilities have a maturity of three years. The interest rate on the liabilities resets every three months based on the three-month LIBOR. This financial institution can hedge this mismatched asset/liability position by buying a three-year bundle of Eurodollar futures contracts. By doing so, the financial institution is receiving the LIBOR over the three-year period and paying a fixed dollar amount (i.e., the futures price). The financial institution is now hedged, because the assets are fixed rate and the bundle of long Eurodollar futures synthetically creates a fixed-rate funding arrangement. From the fixed dollar amount over the three years, an effective fixed rate that the financial institution pays can be computed. Alternatively, the financial institution can synthetically create a fixed-rate funding arrangement by entering into a three-year swap, in which it pays fixed and receives the three-month LIBOR. Other factors being equal, the financial institution will use the vehicle that delivers the lowest cost of hedging the mismatched position. That is, the financial institution will compare the synthetic fixed rate (expressed as a percentage over U.S. Treasuries) to the three-year swap spread. The difference between the synthetic spread and the swap spread should be within a few basis points under normal circumstances.

Swaps with maturities greater than five years cannot rely on the Eurodollar futures, because liquid markets do not exist for these contracts at longer maturities. Instead, longer-dated swaps are priced using rates available to investment-grade corporate borrowers in fixed-rate and floating-rate debt markets. Because a swap can be interpreted as a package of long and short positions in a fixed-rate bond and a floating-rate bond, it is the credit spreads in those two market sectors that will determine the swap spread. Empirically, the swap rate for a given maturity is greater than the yield on U.S. Treasury securities and less than the yield for AA-rated banks.[12] Swap fixed rates are lower than AA-rated bond yields because of their lower credit, which stems from netting and offsetting of swap positions.

In addition, other technical factors influence the level of swap spreads. Although the impact of some of these factors is ephemeral, their influence can be considerable in the short

---

payments, the total cash flow at risk is lower. Second, the probability of default depends jointly on the probability of the counterparty defaulting and whether the swap has a positive value. See John C. Hull, *Introduction to Futures and Options Markets*, 3rd edition (Upper Saddle River, NJ: Prentice Hall, 1998).

12. For a discussion of this point, see Andrew R. Young, *A Morgan Stanley Guide to Fixed Income Analysis* (New York: Morgan Stanley, 1997).

run. Included among these factors are (1) the level and shape of the Treasury yield curve, (2) the relative supply of fixed- and floating-rate payers in the interest rate swap market, (3) the level of asset-based swap activity, and (4) technical factors that affect swap dealers.[13]

Secondary Market for Swaps

Three general types of transactions take place in the secondary market for swaps: a swap reversal, a swap sale (or assignment), and a swap buyback (or close-out or cancellation).

In a **swap reversal**, the party that wants out of the transaction will arrange for an additional swap in which (1) the maturity on the new swap is equal to the time remaining of the original swap, (2) the reference rate is the same, and (3) the notional principal amount is the same. For example, suppose party X enters into a five-year swap with a notional principal amount of $50 million, in which it pays 10% and receives LIBOR, but that two years later, X wants out of the swap. In a swap reversal, X would enter into a three-year interest rate swap with a counterparty different from the original counterparty (let's say Z), in which the notional principal amount is $50 million, and X pays LIBOR and receives a fixed rate. The fixed rate that X receives from Z will depend on prevailing swap terms for floating-rate receivers at the initiation of the three-year swap.

Although party X has effectively terminated the original swap in economic terms, this approach has a major drawback: Party X is still liable to original counterparty Y, as well as to the new counterparty Z. That is, party X now has two offsetting interest rate swaps on its books instead of one, and as a result, it has increased its default risk exposure.

The **swap sale** or **swap assignment** overcomes this drawback. In this secondary market transaction, the party that wishes to close out the original swap finds another party that is willing to accept its obligations under the swap. In our illustration, X finds another party (say, A) that will agree to pay 10% to Y and receive LIBOR from Y for the next three years. Party A might have to be compensated to accept the position of X, or A might be willing to compensate X. Who will receive compensation depends on the swap terms at the time. For example, if interest rates have risen so that, to receive LIBOR for three years, a fixed-rate payer would have to pay 12%, then A would have to compensate X, because A has to pay only 10% to receive LIBOR. The compensation would be equal to the present value of a three-year annuity of 2% times the notional principal amount. If, instead, interest rates have fallen so that, to receive LIBOR for three years, a fixed-rate payer would have to pay 6%, then X would have to compensate A. The compensation would be equal to the present value of a three-year annuity of 4% times the notional principal amount. Once the transaction is completed, it is then A, not X, that is obligated to perform under the swap terms. (Of course, an intermediary could act as principal and become party A.)

13. For a further discussion of these technical factors, see Fabozzi and Mann, *Floating-Rate Securities*.

To accomplish a swap sale, the original counterparty (Y in our example) must agree to the sale. A key factor in whether Y will agree is whether it is willing to accept the credit of A. For example, if A's credit rating is triple B and X's is double A, Y would be unlikely to accept A as a counterparty.

A **buyback** or **close-out sale** (or **cancellation**) involves the sale of the swap to the original counterparty. As in the case of a swap sale, one party might have to compensate the other, depending on how interest rates and credit spreads have changed since the inception of the swap.

Beyond the Plain Vanilla Swap

Thus far we have described the plain vanilla or generic interest rate swap. Nongeneric or individualized swaps have evolved as a result of the asset/liability needs of borrowers and lenders. These include swaps in which the notional principal changes in a predetermined way over the life of the swap and those in which both counterparties pay a floating rate. There are complex swap structures, such as options on swaps (called "swaptions"), and swaps that do not begin until some future time (called "forward start swaps"). We discuss these swaps below. It may be difficult to fully appreciate the importance of these swap structures as a tool for managing the interest rate risk of a financial institution in this book, because of our limited coverage of risk management. What is important to appreciate is that these swap structures are not just "bells and whistles" added to the plain vanilla swap to make them more complicated: They are features that managers need to control interest rate risk.

Swaps that vary the notional principal amount In a generic or plain vanilla swap, the notional principal amount does not vary over the life of the swap. This type of swap is sometimes referred to as a **bullet swap**. In contrast, for amortizing, accreting, and roller-coaster swaps, the notional principal amount varies over the life of the swap.

An **amortizing swap** is one in which the notional principal amount decreases in a predetermined way over the life of the swap. Such a swap would be used when the principal of the asset that is being hedged with the swap amortizes over time. For example, in our illustration of the asset/liability problem faced by the bank, the commercial loans are assumed to pay only interest every six months and repay principal at the end of the loan term. However, what if the commercial loan is a typical term loan (that is, a loan that amortizes)? Or, suppose that it is a typical mortgage loan that amortizes. In such circumstances, the outstanding principal for the loans would decline, and the bank would need a swap in which the notional principal amount amortizes in the same way as the loans.

Less common than the amortizing swap are the **accreting swap** and the **roller-coaster swap**. An accreting swap is one in which the notional principal amount increases in a predetermined way over time. In a roller-coaster swap, the notional principal amount can rise or fall from period to period.

Basis swaps and constant maturity swaps The terms of a generic interest rate swap call for the exchange of fixed- and floating-rate payments. In a **basis rate swap**, both parties exchange floating-rate payments based on a different reference rate. As an example, assume a commercial bank has a portfolio of loans in which the lending rate is based on the prime rate, but the bank's cost of funds is based on the LIBOR. The risk the bank faces is that the spread between the prime rate and LIBOR will change. This is referred to as "basis risk." The bank can use a basis rate swap to make floating-rate payments based on the prime rate (because that is the reference rate that determines how much the bank is receiving on the loans) and receive floating-rate payments based on the LIBOR (because that is the reference rate that determines the bank's funding cost).

Another popular swap is to have the floating leg tied to a longer-term rate, such as the two-year Treasury note, rather than on a money market rate. For example, one of the parties to the swap would pay the two-year Treasury rate, and the counterparty would pay the LIBOR. Such a swap is called a **constant maturity swap**. The reference rate for determining the yield on the constant maturity Treasury in a constant maturity swap is typically the Constant Maturity Treasury rate published by the Federal Reserve. Consequently, a constant maturity swap tied to this rate is called a **Constant Maturity Treasury swap**.

Swaptions Options on interest rate swaps are called **swaptions** and grant the option buyer the right to enter into an interest rate swap at a future date. The time until expiration of the swap, the term of the swap, and the swap rate are specified. The swap rate is the strike rate for the swaption. The swaption can have any exercise style—American, European, and Bermuda.

There are two types of swaptions—a payer swaption and a receiver swaption. A **payer swaption** entitles the option buyer to enter into an interest rate swap in which the buyer of the option pays a fixed rate and receives a floating rate. For example, suppose that the strike rate is 7%, the term of the swap is three years, and the swaption expires in two years. Also, assume that it has a European-type exercise provision. Then at the end of two years, the buyer of this swaption has the right to enter into a three-year interest rate swap in which the buyer pays 7% (the swap rate, which is equal to the strike rate) and receives the reference rate.

In a **receiver swaption**, the buyer of the swaption has the right to enter into an interest rate swap that requires paying a floating rate and receiving a fixed rate. For example, if the strike rate is 6.25%, the swap term is five years, and the option expires in one year, the buyer of this receiver swaption has the right when the option expires in one year (assuming it is a European-type exercise provision) to enter into a four-year interest rate swap in which the buyer receives a swap rate of 6.25% (i.e., the strike rate) and pays the reference rate.

How is a swaption used? We can see its usefulness for managing interest rate risk if we return to the bank–insurance company example. The bank makes fixed-rate payments on the interest rate swap (10%) using the interest rate it is earning on the commercial loans (10%). Suppose that the commercial loan borrowers default on their obligations. The bank will not receive from the commercial loans the 10% to make its swap payments. This problem can be addressed at the outset of the initial swap transaction by the bank entering into a swaption that effectively gives it the right to terminate or cancel the swap. That is, the bank will enter into a receiver swaption, receiving fixed of 10% so as to offset the fixed rate it is obligated to pay under the initial swap. In fact, the borrowers do not have to fail for the swap to have an adverse impact on the bank. Suppose that the commercial loans can be prepaid. Then the bank has a similar problem to that of having borrowers default. For example, suppose rates on commercial loans decline to 7% and the borrowers prepay. Then the bank would be obligated to make the 10% payments under the terms of the swap. With the proceeds received from the prepayment of the commercial loans, the bank may only be able to invest in similar loans at 7%, for example, a rate that is less than the bank's obligations.

Forward start swaps A **forward start swap** is a swap wherein the swap does not begin until some future date that is specified in the swap agreement. Thus, the swap has a beginning date at some time in the future and a maturity date. A forward start swap will also specify the swap rate at which the counterparties agree to exchange payments commencing at the start date.

Interest Rate/Equity Swaps

In addition to interest rate swaps, there are currency and foreign exchange swaps and **interest rate/equity swaps**. We will discuss the former in chapter 38. Here we explain interest rate/equity swaps.

To illustrate this swap, consider the following swap agreement:

- The counterparties to this swap agreement are the Brotherhood of Basket Weavers (a pension sponsor) and the Reliable Investment Management Corporation (a money management firm).
- The notional principal amount is $50 million.
- Every year for the next five years, the Brotherhood agrees to pay Reliable Investment Management Corporation the return realized on the S&P 500 stock index for the year minus 200 bps.
- Every year for the next five years, Reliable Investment Management Corporation agrees to pay the pension sponsor 10%.

For example, if over the past year, the return on the S&P 500 stock index is 14%, then the pension sponsor pays Reliable Investment Management Corporation 12% (14% minus 2%) of $50 million, or $6 million, and the money management firm agrees to pay the pension sponsor $5 million (10% times $50 million).

Application to Creation of a Security

Swaps can be used by investment bankers to create a security. To see how this is done, suppose the following. The Universal Information Technology Company (UIT) seeks to raise \$100 million for the next five years on a fixed-rate basis. UIT's investment banker, Credit Suisse, indicates that if bonds with a maturity of five years are issued, the interest rate on the issue would have to be 8%. At the same time, some institutional investors are seeking to purchase bonds but are interested in making a play on the stock market. These investors are willing to purchase a bond whose annual interest rate is based on the actual performance of the S&P 500 stock market index.

Credit Suisse recommends to UIT's management that it consider issuing a five-year bond whose annual interest rate is based on the actual performance of the S&P 500. The risk with issuing such a bond is that UIT's annual interest cost is uncertain, because the cost depends on the performance of the S&P 500. However, suppose that the following two transactions are entered into:

1. On January 1, UIT agrees to issue, using Credit Suisse as the underwriter, a \$100 million, five-year bond issue whose annual interest rate is the actual performance of the S&P 500 that year minus 300 bps. The minimum interest rate, however, is set at zero. The annual interest payments are made on December 31.

2. UIT enters into a five-year, \$100 million notional principal amount interest rate/equity swap with Credit Suisse in which each year for the next five years, UIT agrees to pay 7.9% to Credit Suisse and Credit Suisse agrees to pay the actual performance of the S&P 500 that year minus 300 bps. The terms of the swap call for the payments to be made on December 31 of each year. Thus, the swap payments coincide with the payments that must be made on the bond issue. Also, as part of the swap agreement, if the S&P 500 minus 300 bps results in a negative value, Credit Suisse pays nothing to UIT.

Let's look at what has been accomplished with these two transactions from the perspective of UIT. Specifically, focus on the payments that must be made by UIT on the bond issue and the swap, and the payments that it will receive from the swap:

Interest payments on bond issue:	S&P 500 return − 300 bps
Swap payment from Credit Suisse:	S&P 500 return + 300 bps
Swap payment to Credit Suisse:	7.9%
Net interest cost:	7.9%

Thus, the net interest cost is a fixed rate despite the bond issue paying an interest rate tied to the S&P 500. This transformation was accomplished by using an interest rate/equity swap.

Several questions should be addressed. First, what was the advantage to UIT of entering into this transaction? Recall that if UIT issued a bond, Credit Suisse estimated that UIT would have to pay 8% annually. Thus, UIT has saved 10 bps (8% minus 7.9%) per year. Second, why would investors purchase this bond issue? As explained in previous chapters, restrictions are imposed on institutional investors as to types of investment. For example, a depository institution may not be entitled to purchase common stock; however, it may be permitted to purchase a bond of an issuer such as UIT, even though the interest rate is tied to the performance of common stocks. Third, isn't Credit Suisse exposed to the risk of the performance of the S&P 500? Although it is difficult to demonstrate here, there are ways that Credit Suisse can protect itself.

Although this may seem like a far-fetched application, it is not. In fact, it is quite common. Debt instruments created by using swaps are commonly referred to as "structured notes," which we discussed in chapter 26.

Interest Rate Caps and Floors

An interest rate cap and floor is an agreement between two parties in which one party, for an upfront premium, agrees to compensate the other if a designated interest rate (called the **reference rate**) is different from a predetermined level. When one party agrees to pay the other if the reference rate exceeds a predetermined level, the agreement is referred to as an **interest rate cap** or **ceiling**. The agreement is referred to as an **interest rate floor** when one party agrees to pay the other if the reference rate falls below a predetermined level. The predetermined level of the reference interest rate is called the **strike rate**. The terms of an interest rate agreement include:

1. The reference rate,
2. The strike rate that sets the ceiling or floor,
3. The length of the agreement,
4. The frequency of settlement, and
5. The notional principal amount.

For example, suppose that C buys an interest rate cap from D with terms as follows:

1. The reference rate is the six-month LIBOR.
2. The strike rate is 8%.
3. The agreement is for seven years.
4. Settlement is every six months.
5. The notional principal amount is $20 million.

Under this agreement, every six months for the next seven years, D will pay C whenever six-month LIBOR exceeds 8%. The payment will equal the dollar value of the difference between the six-month LIBOR and 8% times the notional principal amount divided by two. For example, if six months from now, the six-month LIBOR is 11%, then D will pay C 3% (11% minus 8%) times $20 million divided by 2, or $300,000. If six-month LIBOR is 8% or less, D does not have to pay anything to C.

As an example of an interest rate floor, assume the same terms as the interest rate cap we just illustrated. In this case, if the six-month LIBOR is 11%, C receives nothing from D, but if the six-month LIBOR is less than 8%, D compensates C for the difference. For example, if the six-month LIBOR is 7%, D will pay C $100,000 (8% minus 7%, times $20 million divided by 2).

Interest rate caps and floors can be combined to create an **interest rate collar**. This is done by buying an interest rate cap and selling an interest rate floor. Some commercial banks and investment banking firms now write options on interest rate agreements for customers. Options on caps are called **captions**, and options on floors are called **flotions**.

Risk/Return Characteristics

In an interest rate cap and floor, the buyer pays an upfront fee, which represents the maximum amount the buyer can lose and the maximum amount the writer of the agreement can gain. The only party that is required to perform is the writer of the interest rate agreement. The buyer of an interest rate cap benefits if the underlying interest rate rises above the strike rate, because the seller (writer) must compensate the buyer. The buyer of an interest rate floor benefits if the interest rate falls below the strike rate, because the seller (writer) must compensate the buyer.

How can we better understand interest rate caps and interest rate floors? In essence, these contracts are equivalent to a package of interest rate options. The question is: What types of options package make up a cap and what types make up a floor? Recall from our earlier discussion of the relationship between futures, FRAs, and swaps that the relationship depends on whether the underlying is an interest rate or a fixed-income instrument. The same applies to call options, put options, caps, and floors.

If the underlying is considered a fixed-income instrument, its value changes inversely with interest rates. Therefore,

For a Call Option on a Fixed-Income Instrument:

1. Interest rates increase → fixed-income instrument's price decreases → call option's value decreases;

2. Interest rates decrease → fixed-income instrument's price increases → call option's value increases.

For a Put Option on a Fixed-Income Instrument:

3. Interest rates increase → fixed-income instrument's price decreases → put option's value increases;

4. Interest rates decrease → fixed-income instrument's price increases → put option's value decreases.

To summarize,

	When Interest Rates:	
Value of:	Increase	Decrease
Long call	Decrease	Increase
Short call	Increase	Decrease
Long put	Increase	Decrease
Short put	Decrease	Increase

For a cap and floor, the situation is as follows:

	When Interest Rates:	
Value of:	Increase	Decrease
Short cap	Decrease	Increase
Long cap	Increase	Decrease
Short floor	Increase	Decrease
Long floor	Decrease	Increase

Therefore, buying a cap (long cap) is equivalent to buying a package of puts on a fixed-income instrument, and buying a floor (long floor) is equivalent to buying a package of calls on a fixed-income instrument.

In contrast, if an option is viewed as an option on an interest rate (underlying), then buying a cap (long cap) is equivalent to buying a package of calls on interest rates. Buying a floor (long floor) is equivalent to buying a package of puts on interest rates.

Note that, once again, a complex contract can be seen to be a package of basic contracts, or options in the case of interest rate agreements.

Applications

To see how interest rate agreements can be used for asset/liability management, consider the problems faced by the commercial bank and the life insurance company in the example discussed earlier in this chapter.

Recall that the bank's objective is to lock in an interest rate spread over its cost of funds. Yet, because it raises funds through a variable-rate instrument and is basically borrowing short term, the bank's cost of funds is uncertain. The bank may be able to purchase a cap so that the cap rate plus the cost of purchasing the cap is less than the rate it is earning on its fixed-rate commercial loans. If short-term rates decline, the bank does not benefit from the cap, but its cost of funds declines. The cap, therefore, allows the bank to impose a ceiling on its cost of funds but retains the opportunity to benefit from a decline in rates. This use of a cap is consistent with the view of an interest rate cap as simply a package of call options.

The bank can reduce the cost of purchasing the cap by also selling a floor. In this case, the bank agrees to pay the buyer of the floor if the underlying rate falls below the strike rate. The bank receives a fee for selling the floor, but it has sold off its opportunity to benefit from a decline in rates below the strike rate. By buying a cap and selling a floor, the bank has created a range (i.e., a collar) for its cost of funds.

Consider again from that same example of the application of interest rate swaps the problem of the life insurance company that has guaranteed a 9% rate on a GIC for the next five years and is considering the purchase of an attractive floating-rate instrument in a private placement transaction. The risk that the company faces is that interest rates will fall, so that it will not earn enough to realize the 9% guaranteed rate plus a spread. The life insurance company may be able to purchase a floor to set a lower bound on its investment return, yet retain the opportunity to benefit should rates increase. To reduce the cost of purchasing the floor, the life insurance company can sell an interest rate cap. By doing so, however, it gives up the opportunity of benefiting from an increase in the six-month Treasury bill rate above the strike rate of the interest rate cap.

Key Points

- A forward rate agreement (FRA) is the OTC equivalent of the exchange-traded futures contracts on short-term rates and is a cash settlement contract in which the short-term reference rate is typically the LIBOR.
- The elements of an FRA are the contract rate, reference rate, settlement rate, notional amount, and settlement date.
- The buyer of the FRA agrees to pay the contract rate and the seller of the FRA agrees to receive the contract rate. The amount that must be exchanged at the settlement date is the present value of the interest differential.

- An interest rate swap is an agreement whereby two counterparties agree to exchange periodic interest payments based on a notional principal amount.
- A position in an interest rate swap can be interpreted as a position in a package of forward contracts or a package of cash flows from buying and selling cash market instruments.
- Although the initial motivation for the swap market was borrower exploitation of what were perceived to be credit arbitrage opportunities, such opportunities are limited and depend on the presence of market imperfections.
- The swap market has evolved into a transactionally efficient market for accomplishing asset/liability objectives to alter the cash flow characteristics of assets (an asset swap) or liabilities (a liability swap).
- Commercial bank and investment banking firms take positions in swaps rather than act simply as intermediaries.
- For swaps with maturities of less than five years, the swap spread is driven by rates in the Eurodollar futures market, but for swaps with maturities greater than five years, the spread is determined primarily by the credit spreads in the corporate bond market.
- In addition to the generic swap structure where one party pays fixed and the other floating, there are swaps with varying notional principal amounts, basis swaps (floating payments made by both parties), constant maturity swaps, swaptions, and forward start swaps.
- An interest rate cap and floor allows one party the right to receive compensation from the writer of the agreement for an upfront premium if a designated interest rate is different from a predetermined level.
- An interest rate cap calls for one party to receive a payment if a designated interest rate is above the predetermined level. An interest rate floor lets one party receive a payment if a designated interest rate is below the predetermined level.
- An interest rate cap can be used to establish a ceiling on the cost of funding; an interest rate floor can be used to establish a minimum return.
- A collar is created by buying an interest rate cap and selling an interest rate floor.
- An interest rate floor can be used by a depository institution to lock in an interest rate spread over its cost of funds but maintain the opportunity to benefit if rates decline.
- The buyer of a floating-rate asset can use an interest rate floor to establish a lower bound on its investment return, yet retain the opportunity to benefit should rates increase.

Questions

1. Hieber Manufacturing Corporation purchased the following FRA from the First Commercial Bank Corporation: (1) reference rate is the three-month LIBOR, (2) contract rate is 6% (3) notional amount is for $20 million, and (4) number of days to settlement is 91 days.

a. Suppose the settlement rate is 6.5%. Which party must compensate the other at the settlement date?

b. If the settlement rate is 6.5%, how much will the compensation be?

2. Explain whether you agree or disagree with the following statement: "Both the buyers of an interest rate futures contract and FRA benefit if interest rates decline."

3. At any time in the life of the interest rate swap, does the notional principal become a cash flow to either party or to the intermediary?

4. Consider a swap with these features: Maturity is five years, notional principal is $100 million, payments occur every six months, the fixed-rate payer pays a rate of 9.05% and receives the LIBOR, whereas the floating-rate payer pays LIBOR and receives 9%. Now suppose that at a payment date, the LIBOR is at 6.5%. What is each party's payment and receipt at that date?

5. A bank borrows funds by issuing CDs that carry a variable rate equal to the yield of the six-month Treasury bill plus 50 bps. The bank gets the chance to invest in a seven-year loan that will pay a fixed rate of 7%. So, the bank wants to engage in an interest rate swap designed to lock in an interest spread of 75 bps. Give the outlines of two possible swaps: one designed to change the asset's cash flow into a variable rate, and the other designed to change the liability's cash flow into a fixed rate.

6. Identify two factors that have contributed to the growth of the interest rate swap market.

7. a. Describe the role of the intermediary in a swap.

b. What are the two factors that led swap brokers/intermediaries to act as principals or dealers?

8. Suppose a dealer quotes these terms on a five-year swap: fixed-rate payer to pay 9.5% for the LIBOR flat, and floating-rate payer to pay the LIBOR flat for 9.2%.

a. What is the dealer's bid-ask spread?

b. How would the dealer quote the terms by reference to the yield on five-year Treasury notes, assuming this yield is 9%?

9. Explain the three major ways in which a party to a swap can reverse that position in the secondary market for swaps.

10. Why can a fixed-rate payer in an interest rate swap be viewed as being short the bond market, and the floating-rate payer be viewed as being long the bond market?

11. a. Why would a depository institution use an interest rate swap?

b. Why would a corporation that plans to raise funds in the debt market use an interest rate swap?

12. Suppose that a life insurance company has issued a three-year GIC with a fixed rate of 10%. Under what circumstances might it be feasible for the life insurance company to

invest the funds in a floating-rate security and enter into a three-year interest rate swap in which it pays a floating rate and receives a fixed rate?

13. A portfolio manager buys a swaption with a strike rate of 6.5% that entitles the portfolio manager to enter into an interest rate swap to pay a fixed rate and receive a floating rate. The term of the swaption is five years.

a. Is this swaption a payer swaption or a receiver swaption? Explain why.

b. What does the strike rate of 6.5% mean?

14. The manager of a savings and loan association is considering the use of a swap as part of the association's asset/liability strategy. The swap would be used to convert the payments of its portfolio of fixed-rate residential mortgage loans into a floating payment.

a. What is the risk of using a plain vanilla or generic interest rate swap?

b. Why might a manager consider using an interest rate swap in which the notional principal amount declines over time?

c. Why might a manager consider buying a swaption?

15. Suppose that a corporation is considering using an interest rate swap in conjunction with the offering of a floating-rate bond issue. That is, the corporation wants to use the swap to change the funding arrangement from a floating rate to a fixed rate.

a. Would the corporation enter into a swap in which it pays or receives a fixed rate?

b. Suppose that the corporation does not plan to issue the bond for one year. What type of swap can the firm's management enter into in order to set the terms of the swap today?

16. The Window Wipers Union (a pension sponsor) and the All-Purpose Asset Management Corporation (a money management firm) entered into a four-year swap with a notional principal amount of $150 million with the following terms: Every year for the next four years, the Window Wipers Union agrees to pay All-Purpose Asset Management the return realized on the S&P 500 for the year minus 400 bps and receive from All-Purpose Asset Management 9%.

a. What type of swap is this?

b. In the first year when payments are to be exchanged, suppose that the return on the S&P 500 is 7%. What is the amount of the payment that the two parties must make to each other?

17. Several depository institutions offer CDs where the interest rate paid is based on the performance of the S&P 500.

a. What is the risk that a depository institution encounters by offering such CDs?

b. How can a depository institution protect itself against the risk you identified in part (a)?

18. Suppose a savings and loan association buys an interest rate cap that has these terms: The reference rate is the six-month Treasury bill rate, the cap will last for five years, payment is semiannual, the strike rate is 5.5%, and the notional principal amount is $10 mil-

lion. Suppose further that at the end of some six-month period, the six-month Treasury bill rate is 6.1%.

a. What is the amount of the payment that the savings and loan association will receive?

b. What would the writer of this cap pay if the six-month Treasury rate were 5.45% instead of 6.1%?

19. What is the relationship between an interest rate agreement and an interest rate option?

20. How can an interest rate collar be created?

21. Acme Insurance Company has purchased a five-year bond whose interest rate floats with the LIBOR. Specifically, in a given year, the interest rate is equal to the LIBOR plus 200 bps. At the same time the insurance company purchases this bond, it enters into a floor agreement with Goldman Sachs in which the notional principal amount is $35 million with a strike rate of 6%. The premium Acme Insurance Company agrees to pay Goldman Sachs each year is $300,000.

a. Suppose that when it is necessary to determine whether a payment must be made by Goldman Sachs, the LIBOR is 9%. How much must Goldman Sachs pay Acme Insurance Company?

b. Suppose that when it is necessary to determine whether a payment must be made by Goldman Sachs, the LIBOR is 3%. How much must Goldman Sachs pay Acme Insurance Company?

c. What is the minimum interest rate that Acme Insurance Company has locked in each year for the next five years by entering into this floor agreement and buying the five-year bond, ignoring the premium that Acme Insurance Company must make each year?

38 Market for Foreign Exchange Derivatives

CONTENTS

Learning Objectives

After reading this chapter, you will understand:

- the different instruments for hedging foreign exchange (FX) risk: forward contracts, futures contracts, options, and swaps;
- the limitations of forward contracts and futures contracts for hedging long-dated FX risk;
- how a forward exchange rate is determined;
- what interest rate parity is;
- what is covered interest arbitrage is;

- what an FX swap is;
- what a currency swap is; and
- the motivation for using swaps.

The foreign exchange (FX) market includes the spot (cash) market and the derivatives market. Two facts about FX markets highlighted in chapter 19 are worth repeating here. First, more than half of the transactions in the FX market are in the derivatives sector of the market. Second, the major motivation for trades in the FX market is financial transactions by investors.

Chapter 19 covered the FX spot market. FX derivatives are the subject of this chapter. These instruments include forward contracts, futures contracts, options, and swaps. An important theoretical relationship, referred to as "interest rate parity," explains how the spot exchange rate and the interest rates in two countries determine the forward exchange rate of their currencies. We do not review here FX risk, because this topic was covered at the end of chapter 19.

FX Forward Contracts

As explained in chapter 33, forward contracts require one party to buy the underlying and the counterparty agreeing to sell that underlying for a specific price at a designated date in the future. Here we consider forward contracts in which the underlying is FX. In the FX market, such forward contracts are also referred to as **outright forwards**. In chapter 34, we explained that unlike a futures contract, which is traded on an exchange, a forward contract is an over-the-counter (OTC) derivative.

In general, forward contracts involve physical delivery if the contract is not closed out prior to the settlement date. In the FX market, there are **nondeliverable forwards**, for which only a cash settlement takes place at the settlement date. These contracts are typically used for emerging markets because of the absence of liquidity for FX forward contracts, but they are now increasingly used for major currencies.

Most FX forward contracts have a maturity of less than two years. Longer-dated forward contracts have relatively large bid-ask spreads; that is, the size of the bid-ask spread for a given currency increases with the maturity of the contract. Consequently, forward contracts are not attractive for hedging long-dated FX exposure.

As chapter 33 emphasizes, both forward contracts and futures contracts can be used to lock in a certain price, which in this case would be the FX rate. By locking in a rate and eliminating downside risk, the user forgoes the opportunity to benefit from any advantageous FX rate movement. Futures contracts, which are creations of an exchange, have certain advantages over forward contracts in many cases, such as stock indexes and Treasury securities. In contrast, for FX, the forward market is the market of choice, and trading there is much larger than trading on exchanges. However, because the FX forward market is an

Table 38.1
Global FX derivative daily turnover, 2016 (billions of U.S. dollars).

Type of FX Transaction	Daily Turnover
All FX transactions	5,067
Spot transactions	1,652
Outright forwards	600
FX swaps	2,378
Currency swaps	82
FX Options	254

interbank market, reliable information on the number of open contracts (commitments) outstanding at any time, or open interest, is not publicly available.

As explained in chapter 19, the Bank for International Settlements publishes the results of its survey of FX market transactions every three years. The latest survey as of this writing, the publication, 2016 Triennial Central Bank Survey, provides a breakdown of cash and derivatives turnover. The results of the 2016 survey are shown in table 38.1. We discussed the average daily trading for the FX spot market in chapter 19.

Pricing FX Forward Contracts

In chapter 35, we showed the relationship between spot prices and forward prices and explained how arbitrage ensures that the relationship holds. We now apply similar considerations to the pricing of FX futures contracts on the basis of the spot exchange rate using an extended example.

Consider a U.S. investor with a one-year investment horizon who has two choices:

Alternative 1: Deposit \$100,000 in a U.S. bank that pays 7% compounded annually for one year.

Alternative 2: Deposit in a bank in country X the U.S. dollar equivalent of \$100,000 in country X's currency that pays 9% compounded annually for one year.

The two alternatives and their outcomes one year from now are depicted in figure 38.1. Which is the better alternative? It will be the alternative that produces the most U.S. dollars one year from now. Ignoring U.S. and country X's taxes on interest income or any other taxes, we need to know two things in order to determine the better alternative: (1) the spot exchange rate between U.S. dollars and country X's currency and (2) the spot exchange rate one year from now between U.S. dollars and country X's currency. The former is known; the latter is not.

However, we can determine the spot rate one year from now between U.S. dollars and country X's currency that will make the investor indifferent between the two alternatives.

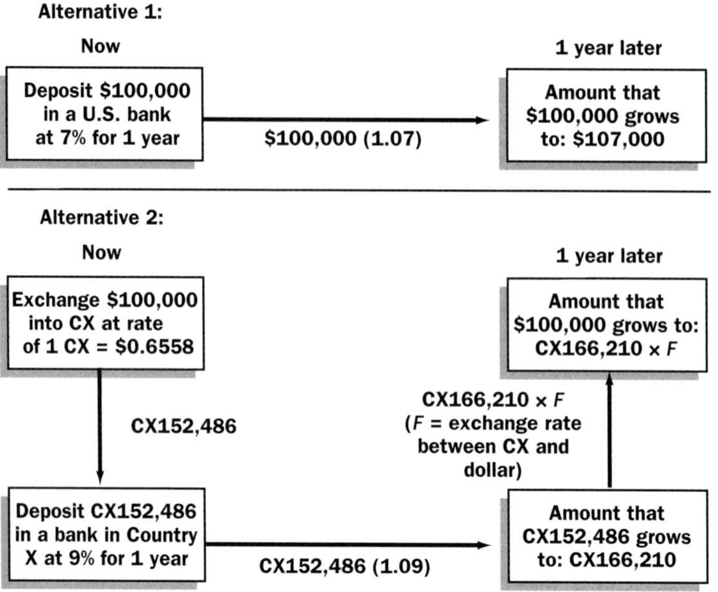

Figure 38.1
Outcome of two alternatives: determination of theoretical forward rate.
Note: CX, unit of currency for Country X.

Alternative 1: The amount of U.S. dollars available one year from now would be \$107,000 (\$100,000 × 1.07).

Alternative 2: Assume that the spot rate is \$0.6558 for one unit of country X's currency at this time. We denote country X's currency by CX. Then, ignoring commissions, \$100,000 can be exchanged for CX 152,486 (\$100,000/6,558). The amount of country X's currency available at the end of one year would be CX 166,210 (CX 152,476 × 1.09).

The number of U.S. dollars for which CX 166,210 can be exchanged depends on the exchange rate one year from now. Let F denote the exchange rate between these two currencies one year from now. Specifically, F denotes the number of U.S. dollars that can be exchanged for one CX. Thus, the number of U.S. dollars at the end of one year from the second alternative is:

Amount in U.S. dollars one year from now = CX 166,210 × F.

The investor will be indifferent between the two alternatives if the number of U.S. dollars is \$107,000:

\$107,000 = CX 166,210 × F.

Solving, we find that F is equal to \$0.6438. Thus, if one year from now, the spot exchange rate is \$0.6438 for one unit of country X's currency, then the two alternatives will produce the same number of U.S. dollars. If more than \$0.6438 can be exchanged for one unit of country X's currency, then the investor receives more than \$107,000 at the end of one year. An exchange rate of \$0.6500 for one unit of country X's currency, for example, would produce \$108,037 (CX 166,210 × \$0.6500). The opposite is true if less than \$0.6438 can be exchanged for one unit of country X's currency. For example, if the future exchange rate is \$0.6400, the investor would receive \$106,374 (CX 166,210 × \$0.6400).

Let us now look at this situation from the perspective of an investor in country X. Suppose that an investor in country X with a one-year investment horizon has two alternatives:

Alternative 1: Deposit CX 152,486 in a bank in country X that pays 9% compounded annually for one year.

Alternative 2: Deposit the equivalent of CX 152,486 in U.S. dollars in a U.S. bank that pays 7% compounded annually for one year.

Once again, assume that the spot exchange rate is \$0.6558 for one unit of country X's currency. The investor in country X will select the alternative that generates the most CX at the end of one year. The first alternative would generate CX 166,210 (CX 152,486 × 1.09). The second alternative requires that CX be exchanged for U.S. dollars at the spot exchange rate at this time. Given the spot exchange rate assumed, CX 152,486 can be exchanged for \$100,000 (CX 152,486 × \$0.6558). At the end of one year, the second alternative would generate \$107,000 (\$100,000 × 1.07). Letting F continue to denote the number of U.S. dollars in country X, following alternative 2 would realize the following amount of country X's currency one year from now:

Amount of country X's currency one year from now = \$107,000/F.

The investor will be indifferent between the two alternatives if

\$107,000/F = CX 166,210.

The equation yields a value for F of \$0.6438, the same exchange rate that we found when we sought the exchange rate one year from now that would make the U.S. investor indifferent between the two alternatives facing that investor.

Now suppose that a dealer quotes a one-year forward exchange rate between the two currencies. The one-year forward exchange rate fixes today the exchange rate one year from now. Thus, if the one-year forward exchange rate quoted is \$0.6438 for one unit of country X's currency, investing in the bank in country X will provide no arbitrage opportunity for the U.S. investor. If the one-year forward rate quoted is more than \$0.6438 for one unit of country X's currency, the U.S. investor can arbitrage the situation by selling country X's currency forward (and buying U.S. dollars forward for CX).

To see how this arbitrage opportunity can be exploited, suppose that the one-year forward exchange rate is \$0.6500 for one unit of country X's currency. Also, assume that the borrowing and the lending rates in each currency's country are the same. Suppose that the

U.S. investor borrows $100,000 for one year at 7% compounded annually and enters into a forward contract agreeing to deliver CX 166,210 1 year from now at $0.6500 per CX. That is, one year from now, the investor agrees to deliver CX 166,210 in exchange for $108,037 (CX 166,210 × $0.6500).

The $100,000 that was borrowed can be exchanged for CX 152,486 at the spot rate of $0.6558 to one unit of country X's currency, which can be invested in country X at 9%. One year from now, the U.S. investor will have CX 166,210 from the investment in country X, which can be delivered against the forward contract. The U.S. investor will receive $108,037 and repay $107,000 to satisfy the bank loan, netting $1,037. Assuming that the counterparty to the forward contract does not default, this riskless arbitrage situation results in a $1,037 profit generated with no initial investment. This riskless profit will prompt many arbitrageurs to follow this strategy and will, obviously, result in the U.S. dollar rising relative to country X's currency in the forward exchange-rate market, or possibly some other adjustment.[1]

However, if the one-year forward exchange rate quoted is less than $0.6438, an investor in country X can arbitrage the situation by buying CX forward (and by selling U.S. dollars forward). This riskless arbitrage again leads arbitrageurs to act, with the result that the forward exchange rate of U.S. dollars relative to CX falls.[2] The conclusion of this argument is that the one-year forward exchange rate must be $0.6438, because any other forward exchange rate would result in an arbitrage opportunity for either the U.S. investor or the investor in country X.

Thus, the spot exchange rate and the interest rates in two countries determine the forward exchange rate of their currencies. The relationship among the spot exchange rate, the interest rates in two countries, and the forward rate is called **interest rate parity**. The parity relationship implies that an investor, by hedging in the forward exchange-rate market, realizes the same domestic return whether investing domestically or in a foreign country. The arbitrage process that forces interest rate parity is called **covered interest arbitrage**.

Mathematically, interest rate parity between the currencies of two countries, A and B, can be expressed in this way:

Let

I = amount of A's currency to be invested for a time period of length t,

S = spot exchange rate: the price of foreign currency in terms of domestic currency (units of domestic currency per unit of foreign currency),

1. Actually, a combination of things may occur when U.S. investors attempt to exploit this situation: (1) the spot exchange rate of U.S. dollars relative to country X's currency will fall as U.S. investors sell dollars and buy CX; (2) U.S. interest rates will rise in the United States as investors borrow in the United States and invest in country X; (3) country X's interest rates will fall as more is invested in country X; and (4) the one-year forward rate of U.S. dollars relative to the CX will fall. In practice, the last effect will dominate.

2. A combination of things may occur when country X investors attempt to exploit this situation: (1) the spot exchange rate of U.S. dollars relative to CX will rise as country X investors buy dollars and sell CX; (2) country X's interest rates will fall as more is invested in the United States; and (3) the one-year forward rate of U.S. dollars relative to the CX will rise. In practice, the last effect will dominate.

$F = t$-period forward rate: the price of foreign currency t periods from now,

$i_{\mathrm{A}} =$ interest rate on an investment maturing at time t in country A,

$i_{\mathrm{B}} =$ interest rate on an investment maturing at time t in country B.

Then

$$I(1+i_{\mathrm{A}}) = (I/S)(1+i_{\mathrm{B}})F.$$

To illustrate, let country A be the United States and country B represent country X. In our example, we have:

$I = \$100{,}000$ for one year,

$S = \$0.6558$,

$F = \$0.6438$,

$i_{\mathrm{A}} = 0.07$,

$i_{\mathrm{B}} = 0.09$.

Then, according to interest rate parity, this relationship holds:

$$\$100{,}000(1.07) = (\$100{,}000/\$0.6558)(1.09)(\$0.6438),$$
$$\$107{,}000 = \$107{,}005,$$

where the \$5 difference is due to rounding.

Interest rate parity can also be expressed as:

$$(1+i_{\mathrm{A}}) = (F/S)(1+i_{\mathrm{B}}).$$

Rewriting the equation, we obtain the theoretical forward rate implied by the interest rates and spot exchange rate:

$$F = S\left(\frac{1+i_A}{1+i_B}\right).$$

Although we have referred so far to investors, we could use borrowers as well to illustrate interest rate parity. A borrower has the choice of obtaining funds in a domestic or foreign market. Interest rate parity ensures that a borrower who hedges in the forward exchange-rate market realizes the same domestic borrowing rate whether borrowing domestically or in a foreign country.

To derive the theoretical forward exchange rate using the arbitrage argument, we made several assumptions. When the assumptions are violated, the actual forward exchange rate may deviate from the theoretical forward exchange rate. First, when deriving the theoretical forward exchange rate, we assumed that the investor faced no commissions or bid-ask spread when exchanging in the spot market today and at the end of the investment horizon.

In practice, investors incur such costs, which cause the actual forward exchange rate to be plus or minus a small amount of the theoretical rate.

Second, we assumed that the borrowing and lending rates in each currency are the same. Dropping this unrealistic assumption eliminates the possibility of a single theoretical forward exchange rate and instead implies a band around a level reflecting borrowing and lending rates. The actual rate should be within this band.

Third, we ignored taxes. In fact, the divergence between actual and theoretical forward exchange rates can be the result of the different tax structures of the two countries. Finally, we assumed that arbitrageurs can borrow and invest in another country as much as they want to exploit mispricing in the exchange market. It should be noted, however, that any restrictions on foreign investing or borrowing in each country impede arbitrage and may cause a divergence between actual and theoretical forward exchange rates.

Link between Eurocurrency Market and Forward Prices

To derive the interest rate parity, we looked at the interest rates in both countries. In fact, market participants in most countries look to one interest rate to perform covered interest arbitrage, and that is the interest rate in the Eurocurrency market. The **Eurocurrency market** is the name of the unregulated and informal market for bank deposits and bank loans denominated in a currency other than that of the country where the bank initiating the transaction is located. Examples of transactions in the Eurocurrency market are a British bank in London that lends U.S. dollars to a French corporation, and a Japanese corporation that deposits Swiss francs in a German bank. An investor seeking covered interest arbitrage will accomplish it with short-term borrowing and lending in the Eurocurrency market.

The largest sector of the Eurocurrency market involves bank deposits and bank loans in U.S. dollars and is called the "Eurodollar market." The seed for the Eurocurrency market was, in fact, the Eurodollar market. As international capital market transactions increased, the market for bank deposits and bank loans in other currencies developed.

FX Futures Contracts

As explained in chapter 35, futures contracts are exchange-traded products, as opposed to forward contracts, which are OTC contracts. In the case of FX futures contracts, the major exchange is the Chicago Mercantile Exchange (CME). The FX rates traded are those between the U.S. dollar and the currencies of the following countries: Australia, Belgium, Canada, Japan, New Zealand, Norway, Switzerland, the United Kingdom, and Sweden. In addition, there are futures contracts in which the underlying is a cross-rate pair (i.e., an FX rate that does involve the local currency). For example, for a U.S. investor, the FX rate between the euro and Japanese yen would be a cross-rate pair. There are futures contracts on the following cross-rates: the Swiss franc/Japanese yen exchange rate, the euro/

Canadian dollar exchange rate, and the British pound/Japanese yen exchange rate. Futures contracts are also available for emerging market currency pairs with the U.S. dollar and the following four currencies: the Brazilian real, the Czech koruna, the Israeli shekel, and the Hungarian forint. Cross-rate pairs are also available with the euro.

The amount of each foreign currency that must be delivered for a contract varies by currency. For example, the British pound futures contract calls for delivery of 62,500 pounds, the Japanese yen futures contract calls for delivery of 12.5 million yen, and the euro futures contract calls for delivery of €125,000. "E-micro" contracts provide for one-tenth of the contract size. The maturity cycle for currency futures is March, June, September, and December. The longest maturity is one year. Consequently, as in the case of a currency forward contract, currency futures do not provide a good vehicle for hedging long-dated FX risk exposure.

Currency Option Contracts

In contrast to a forward or futures contract, an option gives the option buyer the opportunity to benefit from favorable exchange-rate movements but establishes a maximum loss. The option price is the cost of arranging such a risk/return profile.

The two types of foreign currency options are options on the foreign currency and futures options. The latter are options to enter into FX futures contracts. (We describe the features of futures options in chapter 34.) Futures options are traded on the CME, the trading location of the FX futures contracts.

Options on foreign currencies have been traded on the Nasdaq QMX. The foreign currency pairs that are currently traded are the U.S. dollar and the following: Australian dollar, British pound, Canadian dollar, euro, Japanese yen, Swiss franc, and New Zealand dollar. The exercise style is European (i.e., the option buyer can only exercise at the expiration date). The number of units of foreign currency underlying each option contract is 10,000 units of the currency except for the Japanese yen, for which it is JPY one million.

The factors that affect the price of any option are discussed in chapter 35. One key factor is the expected volatility of the underlying over the life of the option. In the case of currency options, the underlying is the foreign currency specified by the option contract. So, the volatility that affects the option's value is the expected volatility of the exchange rate between the two currencies from the present time to the expiration of the option. The strike price also is an exchange rate, and it affects the option's value: the higher the strike price is, the lower the value of a call will be, and the higher the value of a put. Another factor that influences the option price is the relative risk-free interest rate in the two countries.[3]

3. To understand why, recall the portfolio we created in chapter 35 to replicate the payoff of a call option on an asset. A portion of the asset is purchased with borrowed funds. In the case of a currency option, it involves purchasing a portion of the foreign currency underlying the option. However, the foreign currency acquired can be

FX Swaps and Currency Swaps

In chapter 37 we discussed interest rate swaps—a transaction in which two counterparties agree to exchange interest payments with no exchange of principal. The FX market has two types of swaps: FX swaps and currency swaps. As can be seen from table 38.1, currency swaps are a small part of the derivatives market. In contrast, FX swaps are the largest part of the derivatives market. Moreover, FX swap transactions exceed spot transactions in number.

FX Swaps

To see how a company may use an FX swap, assume the following:

- A U.S. manufacturing firm operating primarily in the United States has generated revenue of €1 million.
- The company's management needs the revenue generated in euros for its U.S. operations to be paid in U.S. dollars.
- The company's management knows that four months from now, it will need to pay suppliers of material in Europe €1 million.

Because of the second assumption, management cannot simply hold euros for the four months. Consider two of the possible alternatives available to management for dealing with the €1 million that must be paid four months from now:

Alternative 1: Sell €1 million today in exchange for U.S. dollars. The number of U.S. dollars received will be based on the spot FX rate. In four months, purchase €1 million at the spot FX rate for euro/U.S. dollar at that time.

Alternative 2: Sell to a bank €1 million today in exchange for U.S. dollars at the spot FX rate and simultaneously agree to repurchase from the bank €1 million at today's forward FX rate.

Let's look at the FX risk associated with alternative 1. In four months when the company must acquire €1 million, the FX rate between euros and U.S. dollars is unknown. More specifically, if the U.S. dollar depreciates relative to the euro, it will cost the company more U.S. dollars to acquire euros. With alternative 2, FX risk has been eliminated, because the company has locked in a specific FX rate by agreeing to purchase €1 million at the forward rate at the time the transaction is entered into.

Let's take a closer look at these two alternatives. Alternative 1 involves two transactions at spot rates, which is what results in the FX risk. In contrast, alternative 2 involves

invested at a risk-free interest rate in the foreign country. Consequently, the pricing of a currency option is similar to the pricing of an option on an income-earning asset, such as a dividend-paying stock or an interest-paying bond. At the same time, the amount that must be set aside to meet the strike price depends on the domestic rate. Thus, the option price, just like interest rate parity, reflects both rates.

two simultaneous transactions, one at the spot rate and the other at the forward rate. Consequently, alternative 2 is effectively an arrangement for hedging FX risk. However, the transaction involves two transaction costs.

Suppose that the company can enter into one agreement that covers both transactions in alternative 2. Well there is such an agreement: That is precisely what an FX swap is. Given our understanding of alternative 2, we can now define an FX swap: It is an agreement whereby one party agrees to sell to a counterparty a specified amount of a currency based on the current FX spot rate and simultaneously agrees at a specified future date to buy the same amount of that currency at the current FX forward rate.

Note that an FX swap still involves risk, because we are dealing with an OTC derivative. That is, although the FX risk may be hedged, there is counterparty risk.

Currency Swaps

In a **currency swap**, both interest and principal are exchanged. The best way to explain a currency swap is with an illustration.

Assume that two companies, a U.S. company and a Swiss company, each seek to borrow for 10 years in its domestic currency. The U.S. company seeks U.S. $100 million debt, and the Swiss company seeks debt in the amount of CHF 127 million. For reasons that we explore later, let's suppose that each wants to issue 10-year bonds in the bond market of the other country, and those bonds are denominated in the other country's currency. That is, the U.S. company wants to issue the Swiss franc equivalent of U.S. $100 million in Switzerland, and the Swiss company wants to issue the U.S. dollar equivalent of CHF 127 million in the United States.

Let's also assume the following:

1. At the time when both companies want to issue their 10-year bonds, the spot exchange rate between the U.S. dollar and CHF is one U.S. dollar for 1.27 Swiss francs.
2. The coupon rate that the U.S. company would have to pay on the 10-year, Swiss franc–denominated bonds issued in Switzerland is 6%.
3. The coupon rate that the Swiss company would have to pay on the 10-year, U.S. dollar–denominated bonds issued in the United States is 11%.

By the first assumption, if the U.S. company issues the bonds in Switzerland, it can exchange the CHF 127 million for U.S. $100 million. By issuing U.S. $100 million of bonds in the United States, the Swiss company can exchange the proceeds for CHF 127 million. Therefore, both get the amount of financing they seek. Assuming the coupon rates given by the last two assumptions, and assuming for purposes of this illustration that coupon payments are made annually, the cash outlays that the companies must make for the next 10 years are summarized as follows:

Year	U.S. Company (in CHF)	Swiss Company (in U.S. $)
1–10	7,620,000	11,000,000
10	127,000,000	100,000,000

Each issuer faces the risk that, at the time a payment on its liability must be made, its domestic currency will have depreciated relative to the other currency. Such a depreciation would require a greater outlay of the domestic currency to satisfy the liability. That is, both firms are exposed to FX risk.

In a currency swap, the two companies issue bonds in the other's bond market and enter into an agreement requiring that:

1. The two parties exchange the proceeds received from the sale of the bonds.
2. The two parties make the coupon payments to service the debt of the other party.
3. At the termination date of the currency swap (which coincides with the maturity of the bonds), both parties agree to exchange the par value of the bonds.

In our illustration, these arrangements result in the following:

1. The U.S. company issues 10-year, 6% coupon bonds with a par value of CHF 127 million in Switzerland and gives the proceeds to the Swiss company. At the same time, the Swiss company issues 10-year, 11% bonds with a par value of U.S. $100 million in the United States and gives the proceeds to the U.S. company.
2. The U.S. company agrees to service the coupon payments to the Swiss company by paying the U.S. $11,000,000 per year for the next 10 years to the Swiss company: the Swiss company agrees to service the coupon payments of the U.S. company by paying CHF 7,620,000 for the next 10 years to the U.S. company.
3. At the end of 10 years (the termination date of this currency swap and the maturity of the two bond issues), the U.S. company would pay U.S. $100 million to the Swiss company, and the Swiss company would pay CHF 127 million to the U.S. company.

This complex agreement is diagrammed in figure 38.2.

Now let's assess what this transaction accomplishes. Each party received the amount of financing it sought. The U.S. company's coupon payments are in dollars, not Swiss francs; the Swiss company's coupon payments are in Swiss francs, not U.S. dollars. At the termination date, both parties will receive an amount sufficient in their local currency to pay off the holders of their bonds. With the coupon payments and the principal repayment in their local currency, neither party faces FX risk.

In practice, the two companies would not deal directly with each other. Instead, either a commercial bank or an investment banking firm would function as an intermediary (as

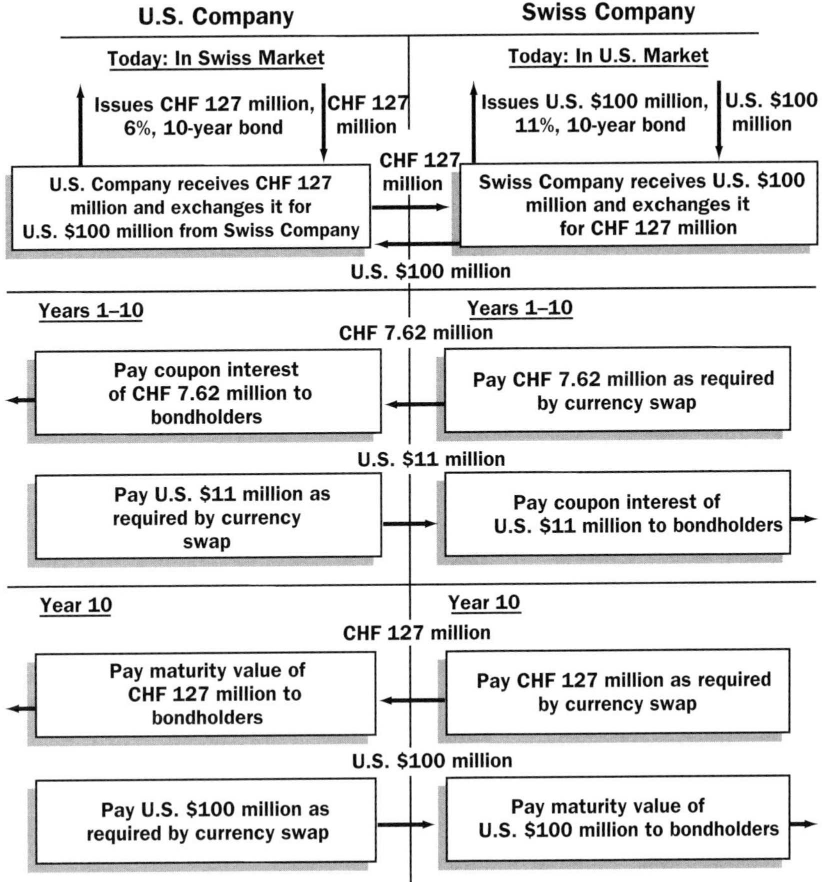

Figure 38.2
A currency swap example.

either a broker or dealer) in the transaction. As a broker, the intermediary would simply bring the two parties together, receiving a fee for the service. If instead the intermediary served as a dealer, it would not only bring the two parties together but would also guarantee payment to both parties. Thus, if one party were to default, the counterparty would continue to receive its payments from the dealer. Of course, in this arrangement, both parties are concerned with the credit risk of the dealer. When the currency swap market started, transactions were typically brokered. The more prevalent arrangement today is that the intermediary acts as a dealer.

As we explained in chapter 37, an interest rate swap is nothing more than a package of forward contracts. The same is true for a currency swap: It is simply a package of currency forward contracts.

Currency coupon swap In our illustration, we assumed that both parties made fixed cash flow payments. Suppose instead that one of the parties sought floating-rate rather than fixed-rate financing. Returning to the same illustration, let's assume that instead of fixed-rate financing, the Swiss company wanted LIBOR-based financing. In this case, the U.S. company would issue floating-rate bonds in Switzerland. Suppose that it could do so at a rate of LIBOR plus 50 basis points. Because the currency swap would call for the Swiss company to service the coupon payments of the U.S. company, the Swiss company would make annual payments of LIBOR plus 50 basis points. The U.S. company would still make fixed-rate payments in U.S. dollars to service the debt obligation of the Swiss company in the United States. Now, however, the Swiss company would make floating-rate payments (LIBOR + 50 basis points) in Swiss francs to service the debt obligation of the U.S. company in Switzerland.

Currency swaps in which one of the parties pays a fixed rate and the counterparty pays a floating rate are called **currency coupon swaps**.

Reasons for development of the currency swap market Why would companies find a currency swap beneficial? In a global financial market without the market imperfections of regulations, taxes, and transaction costs, the cost of borrowing should be the same whether the issuer raises funds domestically or in any foreign capital market. In a world with market imperfections, it may be possible for an issuer to reduce its borrowing cost by borrowing funds denominated in a foreign currency and hedging the associated exchange-rate risk, also known as an arbitrage opportunity. The currency swap allows borrowers to capitalize on any such arbitrage opportunities.

Prior to the establishment of the currency swap market, capitalizing on such arbitrage opportunities required use of the currency forward market. The market for long-dated forward exchange-rate contracts is thin, however, which increases the cost of eliminating FX risk. Eliminating FX risk in our U.S.-Swiss illustration would have required each issuer to enter 10 currency forward contracts (one for each yearly cash payment that the issuer was committed to make in the foreign currency). The currency swap provides a more transactionally efficient means for protecting against FX risk when an issuer (or its investment banker) identifies an arbitrage opportunity and seeks to benefit from it.

As the currency swap market developed, the arbitrage opportunities for reduced funding costs that were available in the early days of the swap market became less common. In fact, it was the development of the swap market that reduced arbitrage opportunities. When these opportunities do arise, they last for only a short time, usually less than a day.

As another motivation for currency swaps, some companies seek to raise funds in foreign countries as a means of increasing their recognition by foreign investors, even though the cost of funding is the same as in the United States. The U.S. company in our illustration might be seeking to expand its potential sources of future funding by issuing bonds today in Switzerland.

Key Points

- FX derivative instruments include forward contracts (outright forward contracts), futures contracts, options, and swaps.
- Nondeliverable forwards are cash settlement at the settlement date rather than physical delivery.
- Most FX forward contracts have a maturity of less than two years.
- Longer-dated forward contracts have relatively large bid-ask spreads, and therefore, forward contracts are not attractive for hedging long-dated FX exposure.
- Interest rate parity determines the relationship among the spot exchange rate, the interest rates in two countries, and the forward rate.
- Interest rate party is ensured by the application of covered interest arbitrage.
- Interest rate parity implies that investors and borrowers who hedge in the forward exchange-rate market will realize the same domestic return or face the same domestic borrowing rate whether investing or borrowing domestically or in a foreign country.
- Futures contracts on major currency pairs with the U.S. dollar, select cross-rate currency pairings, and select emerging market currencies paired with the U.S. dollar and the euro are available.
- Options and futures options are available on currency pairings with the U.S. dollar.
- There are two types of swap derivatives in the FX market: FX swaps and currency swaps.
- An FX swap is an agreement whereby one party agrees to sell to a counterparty a specified amount of a currency based on the current FX spot rate and simultaneously agrees at a specified future date to buy the same amount of that currency at the current FX forward rate.
- A currency swap is effectively a package of currency forward contracts, with the advantage that it allows hedging of long-dated FX risk and is more transactionally efficient than futures or forward contracts.
- Currency swaps are used to arbitrage the increasingly rare opportunities in the global financial market for raising funds at less cost than in the domestic market.
- Currency coupon swaps are a type of currency swap in which one of the parties pays a fixed rate and the counterparty pays a floating rate.

Questions

1. "With the exception of FX futures, all FX derivatives are OTC instruments." Explain whether you agree or disagree with this statement.
2. "Hedging with FX derivatives eliminates all risks." Explain whether you agree or disagree with this statement.

3. "The FX forward rate is determined solely by the market's expected change in the FX rate in the future." Explain whether you agree or disagree with this statement.

4. Suppose that the spot exchange rate today between the U.S. dollar and the currency of country W is U.S. $1.9905 per unit of currency of country W, and that for the U.S. dollar and the currency of country V is U.S. $0.00779 per unit of country V. The following forward rates are also quoted today:

	Country W Currency	Country V Currency
30 days	1.9908	0.007774
60 days	1.9597	0.007754
90 days	1.9337	0.007736

a. Explain what someone who enters into a 30-day forward contract to deliver the currency of country W is agreeing to do.

b. Explain what someone who enters into a 90-day forward contract to buy the currency of country V is agreeing to do.

c. What can you infer about the relationship between U.S. and country W's short-term interest rates and U.S. and country V's short-term interest rates?

5. What is the drawback of using FX outright forward contracts for hedging long-dated positions?

6. What is the rationale for nondeliverable forward contracts when the underlying is an emerging market currency?

7. How does covered interest arbitrage relate to interest rate parity?

8. Why are the interest rates in the Eurocurrency market important in covered interest arbitrage?

9. Suppose you know the following items: you can borrow and lend $500,000 at the one-year interest rate in the United States of 7.5%; in country A both the borrowing and lending rates are 9.2%; the spot exchange rate between the U.S. dollar and country A's currency is now $0.1725 per unit of currency of country A; and the one-year forward exchange rate is $0.2 per unit of currency of country W.

a. Explain how you could make a profit without risk and without investing any of your own money. (Assume commissions, fees, etc., to be equal to zero.)

b. Aside from assuming commissions, fees, and so on, to be zero, several unrealistic assumptions must be made in answering part (a). What are they?

c. Even if we incorporated realistic considerations regarding commissions and so on, the interest rate and exchange-rate numbers in this question would probably produce a profit of some size. Why do you think opportunities like the one in this question are unlikely to come along often in the real world?

10. If the one-year borrowing and lending rates are 3% in country ABC and 4% in the United States, and if the forward exchange rate between dollars and the currency of country ABC is $0.007576 per unit of currency of country ABC (i.e., $1 could buy 131.99 units of country ABC's currency), then what should the spot exchange rate of dollars for the currency of country ABC be?

11. Explain why you agree or disagree with the following statement: "FX futures contracts are only available between major currencies and the U.S. dollar, and there are no contracts for emerging market currencies."

12. "FX outright forward contracts are the most common type of FX derivative." Explain whether you agree or disagree with this statement.

13. The following excerpt appeared in the January 14, 1991, *Wall Street Letter:*

The Philadelphia Stock Exchange plans to list the first nondollar denominated options to trade in the United States, according to sources at the exchange. The Phlx will list cross-currency options based on the relationships between the Deutsche mark and the Japanese yen, as well as British pound/yen and pound/mark options, a spokesman confirmed....

The exchange currently lists currency options that are based on the relationship between that currency and the dollar, one Phlx member explained. "If you're not American," he added, "then the dollar doesn't do it for you." The three new cross-currency options should be attractive to the same banks and broker-dealers that currently trade dollar-based currency options, as well as non-U.S. entities that have interests in other currencies.

Cross-currency options are "a very big part of international trade and international capital markets," and are big over-the-counter products, but none currently trades on an exchange. The advantage of exchange-traded options, the Phlx member said, is that "99% of the customers don't have the credit" to trade such a product over-the-counter with a big bank.

a. Explain what the representative of the Phlx means by saying, "If you're not American, then the dollar doesn't do it for you."

b. Why is the credit of customers critical in the OTC market but not for an exchange-traded contract?

c. When the Philadelphia Stock Exchange filed with the SEC to list cross-currency options, the exchange indicated that the demand for this product has been "spawned by recent large fluctuations and dramatic increases in volatility levels for cross-rate options." Why would this increase the demand for cross-currency options?

14. What is the major difference between a currency swap and an interest rate swap?

15. Assume the following:

• A French manufacturing firm operating primarily in France has generated revenue of U.S. $1 million from sales in the United States.

• The company's management needs the sales proceeds generated in U.S. dollars for its French operations to be paid in euros and therefore the company cannot simply hold U.S. dollars for the six months.

• The company's management knows that six months from now, it will need to pay suppliers of material in the United States $1 million.

The company is considering the following two alternatives:

Alternative I: Sell U.S. $1 million today in exchange for euros. The number of euros received will be based on the spot FX rate. In six months, purchase U.S. $1 million at the spot FX rate for euro/U.S. dollar at that time.

Alternative II: Sell to a bank U.S. $1 million today in exchange for U.S. dollars at the spot FX rate and simultaneously agree to repurchase from the bank U.S. $1 million at today's forward FX rate.

a. Which of these two alternatives involves two spot rate transactions?

b. Which of these two alternatives exposes the company to FX risk and why?

c. Which of these two alternatives hedges FX risk and why?

d. What type of FX derivative can be used instead of entering the transactions required for alternative II?

16. How does an FX swap differ from a currency swap?

39 Market for Credit Risk Transfer Vehicles

CONTENTS

Learning Objectives

After reading this chapter, you will understand:

- what a credit risk transfer vehicle is;
- what a credit derivative is;
- the purpose of a credit derivative;
- types and classification of credit derivatives;
- how a credit event can be defined;
- what a credit default swap is;
- the different types of credit default swaps: single-name credit default swap, basket default swap, and credit default swap index;
- what is meant by a collateralized debt obligation, collateralized bond obligation, and collateralized loan obligation;
- the difference between a collateralized debt obligation and an asset-backed security;
- the structure of a collateralized debt obligation;
- the difference between an arbitrage and a balance sheet transaction;
- the economics underlying an arbitrage transaction;
- the motivation for a balance sheet transaction;
- what a synthetic collateralized debt obligation is and the motivation for its creation;
- what a credit-linked note is; and
- concerns with the new credit risk transfer vehicles.

The development of the derivatives markets prior to the turn of the twenty-first century provided participants in financial markets with efficient vehicles for the transfer of interest rate, price, and currency risks, as well as for enhancing the liquidity of the underlying assets. However, the market for the efficient transfer of credit risk has developed only recently. As explained in chapter 10, credit risk is the risk that a debt instrument will decline in value as a result of the borrower's inability (real or perceived) to satisfy the contractual terms of its borrowing arrangement. In the case of corporate debt obligations, credit risk encompasses default, credit spread, and rating downgrade risks.

The most obvious way for a financial institution, such as a bank, to transfer the credit risk of a loan it has originated is to sell it to another party. Loan covenants typically require that the borrower be informed of the sale. The drawback of a sale in the case of bank loans (more specifically, leveraged loans) is the potential impairment of the originating financial institution's relationship with the corporate borrower whose loan is sold. As explained in chapter 26, syndicated loans overcome the drawback of an outright sale, because banks in the syndicate may sell their loan shares in the secondary market. The sale may be through an assignment or through participation. Although the assignment mechanism for a syndicated loan requires the approval of the borrower, participation does not, because the payments are merely passed through to the purchaser and therefore the borrower need not know about the sale.

Another form of credit risk transfer (CRT) vehicle developed in the 1980s is securitization. In a securitization, a financial institution that originates loans and receivables pools them and sells them to a special-purpose vehicle (SPV). The SPV obtains funds to acquire the pool of loans by issuing securities. Payment of interest and principal on the securities issued by the SPV is obtained from the cash flow of the pool of loans. Although the financial institution employing securitization retains some of the credit risk associated with the pool of loans and receivables, as determined by the risk retention requirements described in chapter 27, the majority of the credit risk is transferred to the holders of the securities issued by the SPV.

Two relatively recent CRT vehicles are credit derivatives and collateralized debt obligations (CDOs). For financial institutions, **credit derivatives**, particularly credit default swaps (CDSs), allow the transfer of credit risk to another party without the sale of the loan. A CDO is an application of the securitization technology, but we will explain how it differs from the types of securitization discussed in chapter 27. Credit derivatives can be used to create CRT products. The two most common products employing CDSs are synthetic CDOs and credit-linked notes. In this chapter, we describe all these CRT products: credit derivatives, CDOs, synthetic CDOs, and credit-linked notes.

Although our focus in this chapter is on the transfer of corporate credit risk, credit derivatives and CDOs also have been used to transfer sovereign credit risk and municipal credit risk.[1]

Credit Derivatives

Credit derivatives are used by institutional portfolio managers in the normal course of activities to more efficiently control the credit risk of a portfolio or the balance sheet of a financial institution and to transact more efficiently than by transacting in the cash market. For example, credit derivatives provide a mechanism for portfolio managers to more efficiently short a credit-risky security than by shorting in the cash market, which is often difficult to do. For traders and hedge fund managers, credit derivatives provide a means for leveraging an exposure in the credit market.

Credit derivatives can be characterized in several ways. One such categorization is shown in figure 39.1. Some of the derivatives identified in the figure are not true credit

1. For a discussion of the use of credit derivatives in the municipal bond market, see Frank J. Fabozzi, "Municipal Credit Default Swaps," in *The Handbook of Municipal Bonds*, ed. Sylvan G. Feldstein and Frank J. Fabozzi (Hoboken, NJ: John Wiley & Sons, 2008), chapter 40. The creation of CDOs backed by municipal bonds is discussed in Rebecca Manning, Douglas J. Lucas, Laurie S. Goodman, and Frank J. Fabozzi, "Municipal Collateralized Debt Obligations," in Feldstein and Fabozzi, *The Handbook of Municipal Bonds*, chapter 41.

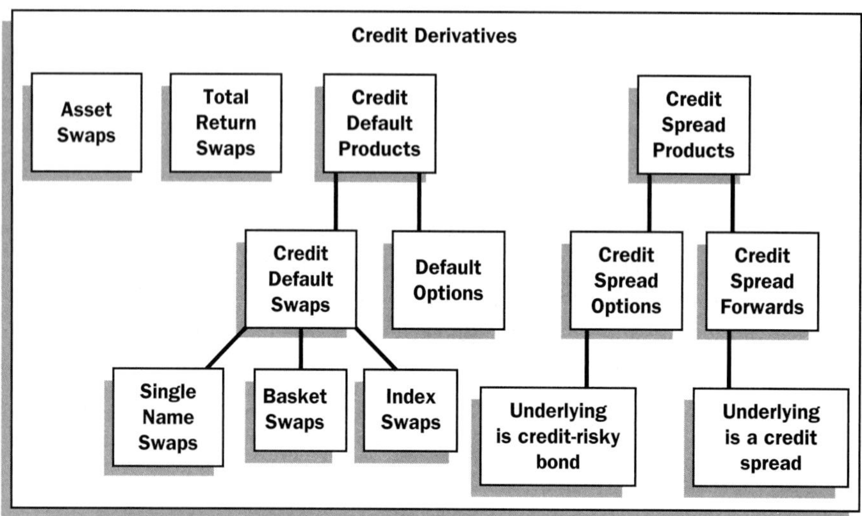

Figure 39.1
Categorization of credit derivatives.

derivatives in that they do not provide protection against credit risk only. Instead, they provide protection against both interest rate risk and credit risk.

By far the most popular type of credit derivative is the **credit default swap** (CDS). Not only is this form of credit derivative the most commonly used stand-alone product, it is also used extensively in products known as **structured credit products**. A CDS is probably the simplest form of CRT vehicle among all credit derivatives, and according to the British Bankers' Association, it is the dominant form of credit derivative. We will look at the different types of CDSs later in the chapter. In this section, we discuss an important market development that fostered the growth of this market: the standardized documentation for the contract.

ISDA Documentation

Prior to 1998, the development of the credit derivatives market was hindered by the lack of standardization of legal documentation. Every trade (i.e., the buying and selling of a credit derivative contract) had to be customized. In 1998, the **International Swap and Derivatives Association** (ISDA) developed a standardized contract that could be used by parties to trades of a credit derivatives contract. **ISDA documentation** is primarily designed for CDSs, but the contract form is sufficiently flexible that it can be used for other types of credit derivatives.

Reference entity and reference obligation The documentation identifies the reference entity and the reference obligation. The **reference entity** is the issuer of the debt instrument and hence is also referred to as the **reference issuer**. It could be a corporation or a sovereign government. The **reference obligation**, also referred to as the **reference asset**, is the particular debt issue for which the credit protection is being sought. For example, a reference entity could be Ford Motor Credit Company. The reference obligation would be a specific Ford Motor Credit Company bond issue.

Credit events Credit derivative products have a payout that is contingent on a **credit event** occurring. The ISDA provides definitions of credit events. The *1999 ISDA Credit Derivatives Definitions* (referred to as the "1999 Definitions") provides a list of eight credit events: (1) bankruptcy, (2) credit event on merger, (3) cross acceleration, (4) cross default, (5) downgrade, (6) failure to pay, (7) repudiation/moratorium, and (8) restructuring. These eight event categories attempt to capture every type of situation that could cause the credit quality of the reference entity to deteriorate or the value of the reference obligation to decline.

Bankruptcy is defined as a variety of acts that are associated with bankruptcy or insolvency laws. **Failure to pay** results when a reference entity fails to make one or more required payments when due. When a reference entity breaches a covenant, it has defaulted on its obligation.

When a default occurs, the obligation becomes due and payable prior to the scheduled due date had the reference entity not defaulted. This is referred to as an **obligation acceleration**. A reference entity may disaffirm or challenge the validity of its obligation. This is a credit event that is covered by **repudiation/moratorium**.

The most controversial credit event that may be included in a credit derivative product is restructuring of an obligation. A **restructuring** occurs when the terms of the obligation are altered so as to make the new terms less attractive to the debtholder than the original terms. The changes would typically include, but are not limited to, one or more of the following: (1) a reduction in the interest rate, (2) a reduction in the principal, (3) a rescheduling of the principal repayment schedule (e.g., lengthening the maturity of the obligation) or the postponement of an interest payment, or (4) a change in the level of seniority of the obligation in the reference entity's debt structure.

The reason restructuring is so controversial is that a protection buyer benefits from the inclusion of restructuring as a credit event and feels that eliminating restructuring as a credit event will erode its credit protection. The protection seller, in contrast, would prefer not to include restructuring, because even routine modifications of obligations that occur in lending arrangements would trigger a payout to the protection buyer. Moreover, if the reference obligation is a loan and the protection buyer is the lender, there is a dual benefit for the protection buyer to restructure a loan. The first benefit is that the protection buyer receives a payment from the protection seller. The second benefit is that accommodating restructuring fosters a relationship between the lender (who is the protection buyer) and its customer (the corporate entity that is the obligor of the reference obligation).

Because of this problem, the *Restructuring Supplement to the 1999 ISDA Credit Derivatives Definitions* (the "Supplement Definition"), issued in April 2001, provided a modified definition for restructuring. There is a provision for limiting the reference obligations in connection with the restructuring of loans made by the protection buyer to the borrower that is the obligor of the reference obligation. This provision requires the following conditions to qualify for a restructuring: (1) there must be four or more holders of the reference obligation, and (2) there must be a consent to the restructuring of the reference obligation by a supermajority (66⅔%). In addition, the supplement limits the maturity of reference obligations that are physically deliverable when restructuring results in a payout triggered by the protection buyer.

As the credit derivatives market developed, market participants learned a great deal about how to better define credit events, particularly with the record level of high-yield corporate bond default rates in 2002 and the sovereign defaults, especially the experience with the 2001–2002 Argentina debt crisis. In January 2003, the ISDA published its revised credit events definitions in the *2003 ISDA Credit Derivative Definitions.* The revised definitions reflected amendments to several of the definitions for credit events set forth in the 1999 Definitions. Specifically, there were amendments for bankruptcy, repudiation, and restructuring.

The major change was to restructuring, whereby the ISDA allows parties to a given trade to select from among the following four definitions: (1) **no restructuring**, (2) **full** or **old restructuring**, which is based on the 1999 Definitions, (3) **modified restructuring**, which is based on the Supplement Definition, and (4) **modified modified restructuring**. The last choice is new and was included to address issues that arose in the European market.

Credit Default Swaps

CDSs are used to shift credit exposure to a credit protection seller. Their primary purpose is to hedge the credit exposure to a particular asset or issuer. A CDS in which there is one reference entity is called a **single-name CDS**. When there are multiple reference entities (e.g., 10 high-yield corporate bonds of 10 different issuers), it is referred to as a **basket CDS**. A **CDS index** has multiple entities, as in a basket CDS. However, unlike a basket CDS, there is a standardized basket of reference entities.

In a CDS, the protection buyer pays a fee to the protection seller in return for the right to receive a payment conditional on the occurrence of a credit event by the reference obligation or the reference entity. Should a credit event occur, the protection seller must make a payment to the protection buyer.

The interdealer market has evolved to where single-name CDSs for corporate and sovereign reference entities are standardized. Although trades between dealers have been standardized, nonetheless, occasional trades in the interdealer market use a customized agreement. For portfolio managers seeking credit protection, dealers are willing to create customized products. The tenor, or length of time of a CDS, is typically five years.

Portfolio managers can have a dealer create a tenor equal to the maturity of the reference obligation or construct one for a shorter period to match the manager's investment horizon.

CDSs can be settled in cash or physically. Physical delivery means that if a credit event as defined by the documentation occurs, the reference obligation is delivered by the protection buyer to the protection seller in exchange for a cash payment. Because physical delivery does not rely on obtaining market prices for the reference obligation when determining the amount of the payment in a single-name CDS, this method of delivery is more efficient.

The payment by the credit protection seller if a credit event occurs may be a predetermined fixed amount, or it may be determined by the decline in value of the reference obligation. When the reference entity is a corporate bond or a sovereign bond, the standard single-name CDS is fixed based on a notional amount. When the cash payment is based on the amount of asset value deterioration, this amount is typically determined by a poll of several dealers. If no credit event has occurred by the maturity date of the swap, both sides terminate the swap agreement, and no further obligations are incurred.

The methods used to determine the amount of the payment obligated of the protection seller under the swap agreement can vary greatly. For instance, a CDS can specify the exact amount of payment that will be made at the contract date by the protection seller should a credit event occur. Conversely, the CDS can be structured so that the amount of the swap payment by the seller is determined after the credit event has occurred. Under these circumstances, the amount payable by the protection seller is determined based on the observed prices of similar debt obligations of the reference entity in the market.

In a typical CDS, the protection buyer pays for the protection premium over several settlement dates rather than up front. A standard CDS specifies quarterly payments.

Single-Name CDSs

Let's work through the mechanics of a single-name CDS. Assume that the reference entity is XYX Corporation and the underlying is \$10 million par value of XYZ bonds. The \$10 million is the notional amount of the contract. The **swap premium**—the payment made by the protection buyer to the protection seller—is 200 basis points.

The standard contract for a single-name CDS calls for a quarterly payment of the swap premium. The quarterly payment is determined using one of the day count conventions in the bond market. The day count convention used for CDSs is actual/360, the same convention used in the interest rate swap market. A day convention of actual/360 means that to determine the payment in a quarter, the actual number of days in the quarter is used and 360 days are assumed for the year. Consequently, the swap premium payment for a quarter is given by the following:

$$\text{Quarterly swap premium payment} = \text{Notional amount} \times \text{swap rate (in decimal)} \times (\text{Actual no. of days in quarter}/360).$$

For example, assume a hypothetical CDS where the notional amount is \$10 million and there are 92 actual days in a quarter. Because the swap premium is 200 basis points (0.02), the quarterly swap premium payment made by the protection buyer would be

$$\$10{,}000{,}000 \times (0.02) \times (92/360) = \$51{,}111.11.$$

In the absence of a credit event, the protection buyer will make a quarterly swap premium payment over the life of the swap. If a credit event occurs, two things happen. First, no further payments of the swap premium are made by the protection buyer to the protection seller. Second, a **termination value** is determined for the swap. The procedure for computing the termination value depends on the settlement terms provided for by the swap. This will be either physical settlement or cash settlement. The market practice for settlement for single-name CDSs is physical delivery.

With **physical settlement**, the protection buyer delivers a specified amount of the face value of bonds of the reference entity to the protection seller. The protection seller pays the protection buyer the face value of the bonds. Because all reference entities that are the subject of CDSs have many issues outstanding, there will be alternative issues of the reference entity that the protection buyer can deliver to the protection seller. These issues are known as **deliverable obligations**. The swap documentation will set forth the characteristics necessary for an issue to qualify as a deliverable obligation. Recall that for Treasury bond and note futures contracts, the short has the choice of which Treasury issue to deliver from among those the exchange specifies as acceptable for delivery. The short will select the issue cheapest to deliver, and the choice granted to the short is effectively an embedded option. The same is true for physical settlement of a single-name CDS. From the list of deliverable obligations, the protection buyer will select for delivery to the protection seller the cheapest-to-deliver issue.

Figure 39.2 shows the mechanics of a single-name CDS. The cash flows are shown before and after a credit event occurs. It is assumed in the figure that there is physical settlement.

Single-name CDSs can be used in the following ways by portfolio managers:

- The liquidity of the swap market compared to the corporate bond market makes it more efficient to obtain exposure to a reference entity by taking a position in the swap market rather than in the cash market. To obtain exposure to a reference entity, a portfolio manager would sell protection and thereby receive the swap premium.
- Conditions in the corporate bond market may be such that it is difficult for a portfolio manager to sell the current holding of a corporate bond of an issuer for which it has a credit concern. Rather than selling the current holding, the portfolio manager can buy protection in the swap market.
- If a portfolio manager expects that an issuer will have difficulties in the future and wants to take a position based on that expectation, it will short the bond of that issuer. However,

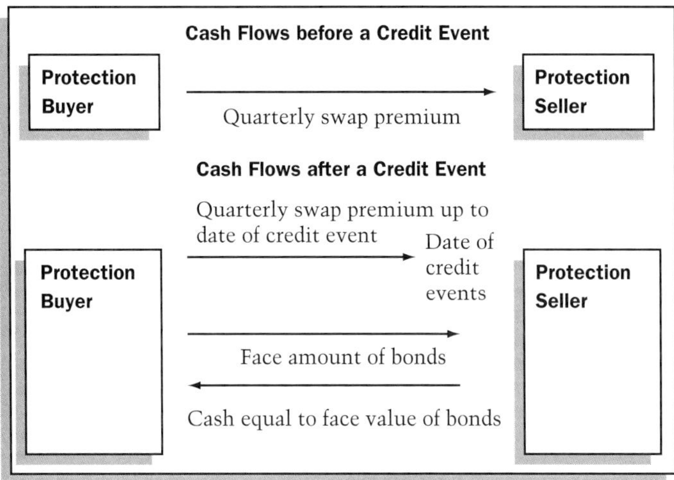

Figure 39.2
Mechanics of a single-name credit default swap with physical delivery.

shorting bonds in the corporate bond market is difficult. The equivalent position can be obtained by entering into a swap as the protection buyer.

- A portfolio manager seeking a leveraged position in a corporate bond can do this in the swap market. The economic position of a protection buyer is equivalent to a leveraged position in a corporate bond.

Basket CDSs

With a basket CDS, or simply "basket default swaps," the time when a payout must be made needs to be specified. For example, if a basket credit default swap has 10 reference obligations, does a credit event for just one of the 10 reference obligations result in the triggering of a payment by the protection seller? It depends. Basket default swaps can be structured in different ways.

In the simplest case, if any one of the reference obligations defaults, there is a payout and then termination of the swap. This type of swap is referred to as a **first-to-default basket swap**. Similarly, if a payout is triggered only after two reference obligations default, the swap is referred to as a **second-to-default basket swap**. In general, if it takes k reference obligations to trigger a payout, the swap is referred to as a ***k*-to-default basket swap**.

Unlike that for a single-name CDS, the preferred settlement term for a basket CDS is cash settlement. With **cash settlement**, the termination value is equal to the difference between the nominal amount of the reference obligation for which a credit event has occurred and its market value at the time of the credit event. The termination value is then the amount of the payment made by the protection seller to the protection buyer. No bonds are delivered by the protection buyer to the protection seller. The documentation for the basket CDS will set forth how the market value at the time of the credit event is determined.

CDS Index

In a **CDS index**, the credit risk of a standardized basket of reference entities is transferred between the protection buyer and protection seller. For North America, the only standardized indexes are those compiled and managed by Dow Jones. For the corporate bond indexes, there are separate indexes for investment-grade and high-grade names. The most actively traded contract is the one based on the North American Investment Grade Index (denoted by DJ.CDX.NA.IG). As the name suggests, the reference entities in this index are those with an investment-grade rating. The index includes 125 corporate names in North America. The index is an equally weighted index. That is, each corporate name (i.e., reference entity) in the index has a weight of 0.8%. The index is updated semiannually by Dow Jones.

The mechanics of a CDS index are slightly different from those of a single-name CDS. As with a single-name CDS, a swap premium is paid. However, if a credit event occurs, the swap premium payment ceases in the case of a single-name CDS. In contrast, for a CDS index, the swap payment continues to be made by the protection buyer. However, the amount of the quarterly swap premium payment is reduced. This is because the notional amount is reduced as result of a credit event for a reference entity.

For example, suppose that a portfolio manager is the protection buyer for a DJ.CDX.NA.IG, and the notional amount is $200 million. Using the following formula for computing the quarterly swap premium payment, the payment before a credit event occurs would be:

$\$200{,}000{,}000 \times \text{Swap rate (in decimal)} \times (\text{Actual no. of days in quarter}/360).$

After a credit event occurs for one reference entity, the notional amount declines from $200 million to $199,840,000. The new notional amount is equal to 99.2% of the $200 million, because each reference entity for the DJ.CDX.NA.IG is weighted by 0.8%. Thus, the revised quarterly swap premium payment until the maturity date or until another credit event occurs for one of the other 124 reference entities is

$\$199{,}840{,}000 \times \text{Swap rate (in decimal)} \times (\text{Actual no. of days in quarter}/360).$

As of this writing, the settlement term for a CDS index is physical settlement. However, the market is considering moving to cash settlement. The reason is because of the cost of delivering an odd lot of the bonds of the reference entity in the case of a credit event. For example, in our hypothetical CDS index, if a credit event occurs, the protection buyer would have to deliver to the protection seller bonds of the reference entity with a face value of $160,000. Neither the protection buyer nor the protection seller would like to deal with such a small position.

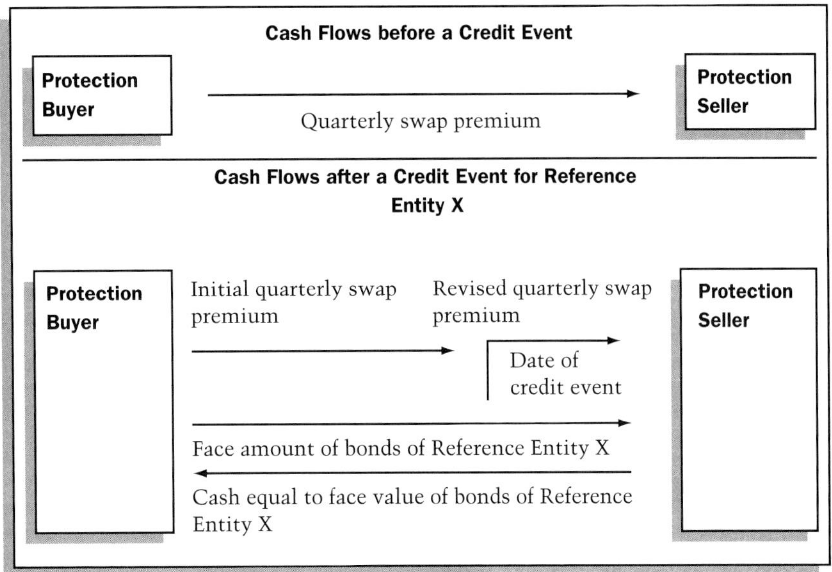

Figure 39.3
Mechanics of a credit default swap index with physical delivery.

Figure 39.3 shows the cash flow for a generic CDS index after a credit event for one reference entity.

Because a CDS index, such as the DJ.CDX.NA.IG, provides exposure to a diversified basket of credits, it can be used by a portfolio manager to help adjust a portfolio's exposure to the credit sector of a bond market index. By entering into a CDS index as the protection seller, a portfolio manager increases exposure to the credit sector. Exposure to the credit sector is reduced by a portfolio manager being the protection buyer.

Collateralized Debt Obligations

A **collateralized debt obligation** is a security backed by a diversified pool of one or more of the following types of debt obligations:

- U.S. domestic investment-grade and high-yield corporate bonds,
- U.S. domestic bank loans,
- emerging market bonds,
- special situation loans and distressed debt,
- foreign bank loans,

- asset-backed securities, and
- residential and commercial mortgage–backed securities.

When the underlying pool of debt obligations consists of bond-type instruments (corporate and emerging market bonds), a CDO is referred to as a **collateralized bond obligation**. When the underlying pool of debt obligations is bank loans, a CDO is referred to as a **collateralized loan obligation** (CLO).

A CDO is an important CRT vehicle used by financial institutions and portfolio managers. In this section, we explain the basic CDO structure, the reason CDOs are created, and the types of CDOs.[2] The creation of these structures requires the use of derivative instruments, specifically, interest rate swaps (covered in chapter 37) or CDSs (particularly those discussed earlier in this chapter).

After the subprime mortgage crisis in the United States, which started in the summer of 2007, and the global credit crunch that followed, CDO performance, particularly of CDOs that invested in nonagency residential mortgage–backed securities (RMBSs), led to considerable losses by investors.[3] According to the Securities Industry and Financial Markets Association, in 2007 the global issuance of CDOs was $482 billion. By January 2009, participants in the CDO market had written down $218 billion in losses from their holdings of CDOs that were backed by asset-backed securities (ABSs). As a result, global CDO issuance in 2009 fell by about 99% from its 2007 level, to only $4 billion. However, because of the low interest rate environment since 2007 and the potential to invest in better-structured CDO deals, by early 2013, institutional investors showed renewed interest in CDOs that invested in commercial mortgage–backed securities (CMBSs). For example, an issuance of a CDO backed by a diversified portfolio of CMBS took place in January 2013, the first such offering since the credit crunch that began in 2008. Unlike CDOs backed by nonagency RMBSs and CMBSs, there were offerings in CLOs. CDOs are now subject to the provisions of the Dodd-Frank Wall Street Reform and Consumer Protection Act of 2010, which we described earlier in this book.

Structure of a CDO

In a CDO structure, a **collateral manager** is responsible for managing the portfolio of debt obligations. The portfolio of debt obligations in which the collateral manager invests is referred to as the "collateral." The individual issues held that make up the collateral are referred to as the "collateral assets."

The funds to purchase the collateral assets are obtained from the issuance of debt obligations. These debt obligations are referred to as "tranches" or "bond classes." The tranches include senior tranches, possibly mezzanine tranches, and subordinated/equity tranches.

2. For a more detailed discussion of CDOs, see Douglas J. Lucas, Laurie S. Goodman, and Frank J. Fabozzi, *Collateralized Debt Obligations: Structures and Analysis*, 2nd edition (Hoboken, NJ: John Wiley & Sons, 2006).

3. These securitized products are described in chapter 27.

A rating will be sought for all but the subordinate/equity tranche. For the senior tranches, at least an A rating is typically sought. For the mezzanine tranches, a rating of BBB, but no less than B, is sought. The subordinated/equity tranche receives the residual cash flow; hence, no rating is sought for this tranche. There are restrictions imposed on what the collateral manager may do, and certain tests must be satisfied for the CDO to maintain the credit rating assigned at the time of issuance.

The ability of the collateral manager to make the interest payments to the tranches and to pay off the tranches as they mature depends on the performance of the collateral. The proceeds to meet the obligations to the CDO tranches (interest and principal repayment) can come from the following: (1) coupon interest payments from the collateral assets, (2) maturing of collateral assets, or (3) the sale of collateral assets.

In a typical structure, one or more of the tranches has a floating rate. With the exception of deals backed by bank loans that pay a floating rate, the collateral manager invests in fixed-rate bonds. Now, that presents a problem—paying tranche investors a floating rate and investing in assets with a fixed rate. To deal with this problem, the collateral manager uses interest rate swaps to be able to convert a portion of the fixed-rate payments from the assets into floating-rate cash flows to pay floating-rate tranches. As explained in chapter 37, an interest rate swap allows a market participant to swap fixed-rate payments for floating-rate payments or vice versa. A credit rating agency (CRA) will require the use of swaps to eliminate any cash flow mismatches.

CDOs are categorized based on the motivation of the sponsor of the transaction. If the sponsor's motivation is to earn the spread between the yield offered on the collateral and the payments made to the various tranches in the structure, then the transaction is referred to as an **arbitrage transaction**. If the motivation of the sponsor is to remove debt instruments (primarily loans) from its balance sheet, then the transaction is referred to as a **balance sheet transaction**. Sponsors of balance sheet transactions are typically financial institutions (such as banks) seeking to reduce their capital requirements specified by bank regulators by removing loans from their balance sheet.

Future of CDO Products

As noted earlier, participants in the CDO market have realized significant losses. A study by the CRA Fitch found that a little more than half the value of the CDOs that were issued throughout the world from 2000 to 2011 has been or will eventually be lost.[4] Most disconcerting was that a large portion of the losses was realized on bond classes that carried a triple-A credit rating (i.e., the highest investment-grade rating). Because of investors' loss of confidence in this product, global CDO issuance has declined dramatically. So the question that is being asked is whether the CDO market will recover and remain a tool for CRT by financial institutions.

4. Fitch Ratings, "Global Structured Finance Losses, 2000–2011 Issuance," October 22, 2012, http://www.fitchratings.com/creditdesk/reports/report_frame.cfm?rpt_id=695352.

Some believe that despite the adverse publicity, the CDO market received as a result of the losses, CDOs are not an inherently flawed financial instrument, and market participants have learned their lesson when participating in the CDO market. As noted by Kent Smetters, a professor at the Wharton School, in an interview published on April 19, 2013:

> CDOs and CLOs (collateralized loan obligations) are not going to go away, because in principle they are powerful risk management devices. They allow for diversifying of risk that otherwise would be quite concentrated. … But during the crisis, CDOs were being created for their own sake. … The motivation was not risk management. Now, CDOs are more in tune with their actual purpose, which is "risk diversification," not risk amplification.[5]

As for what investors learned, Smetters stated in the interview, "The hope now is that there are going to be smarter and more informed buyers out there."

The CRAs have been attacked for failing to properly assess the credit risks associated with CDOs, particularly those backed by subprime RMBSs. Critics of CRAs argue that these commercial enterprises had an economic interest in providing higher ratings than warranted to drum up business for the rating of future CDOs issued. One of the problems during the crisis is that investors failed to understand that credit ratings are opinions that provide an initial screening for CDO creditworthiness, not the sole metric to be used for selecting CDOs in which to invest. Hopefully, that lesson has been learned. CDOs offer institutional investors the opportunity to earn attractive returns, but suitable credit analysis must be performed by investors beyond sole reliance on a CDO's credit rating.

The Dodd-Frank Act should also provide some comfort to investors. CDOs are subject to the risk retention rules. This means that unlike the CDOs issued prior to the act, CDO sponsors must accept exposure to CDOs, and that exposure cannot directly or indirectly be hedged away.

Finally, it should be remembered that CDOs are backed by different types of collateral. The CDOs that caused the major losses were those backed by private-label RMBSs. Most market observers believe that this sector of the CDO market is not likely to be revived in the near future. Instead, other sectors, such as CDOs backed by CMBSs, will be viable, as deals are more carefully underwritten.

Credit-Linked Notes

A **credit-linked note** (CLN) is a security issued by an investment banking firm or another issuer (typically an SPV) that has credit risk to a second issuer (called the "reference issuer"), and the return is linked to the credit performance of the reference issuer. Embedded in a CLN is a credit derivative, typically a CDS.

5. Kent Smetters, "CDOs Are Back: Will They Lead to Another Financial Crisis?" April 9, 2013, Knowledge@Wharton, http://knowledge.wharton.upenn.edu/article/cdos-are-back-will-they-lead-to-another-financial-crisis.

A CLN can be quite complicated, so we will focus on the basic structure only. The issuer of a CLN is the credit protection buyer; the investor in the CLN is the credit protection seller. The basic CLN is just like a standard bond: It has a coupon rate (fixed or floating), a maturity date, and a maturity value. However, in contrast to a standard bond, the maturity value depends on the performance of the reference issuer. Specifically, if a credit event occurs with respect to the reference issuer, then (1) the bond is paid off, and (2) the maturity value is adjusted down. How the adjustment is made is described in the prospectus. The compensation for the investor accepting the credit risk of the reference issuer is an enhanced coupon payment.

Typically, CLNs have a maturity of anywhere from three months to several years, with one to three years being the most likely term of credit exposure. The short maturity of CLNs reflects the desire of investors to take a credit view for such a time period.

Concerns about CRT Vehicles

As with any new complex financial product introduced by financial institutions, there are regulatory and supervisory concerns.[6] The introduction of CRT vehicles, such as cash CDOs and credit derivatives that are employed to create synthetic CDOs, has elicited the same cautious response from overseers of the global banking system. Many of these concerns are the same as those identified for other derivatives, such as interest rate and equity derivatives, and securitized products, such as ABSs, RMBSs, and CMBSs.

Prior to the 2007 crisis, five studies had identified regulatory and supervisory concerns with CRT vehicles, such as credit derivatives and CDOs. The first is a study by the Financial Stability Forum of the Joint Forum (the Joint Forum).[7] The Joint Forum consists of the Basel Committee on Banking Supervision, the International Organization of Securities Commissions, and the International Association of Insurance Supervisors. The second study was conducted by the European Central Bank (ECB) and was a market survey based on interviews with more than 100 banks from 15 EU banks, five large internationally active non-EU banks, and securities houses operating in London.[8] The last three studies are by CRAs, two by Fitch Ratings[9] and one by Standard & Poor's.[10] From the five studies, the following four general issues were identified:

6. This section draws on Douglas J. Lucas, Laurie S. Goodman, and Frank J. Fabozzi, "Collateralized Debt Obligations and Credit Risk Transfer," *Journal of Financial Transformation* 20 (2007): 47–59.

7. Joint Forum, "Credit Risk Transfer" (Basel, Switzerland: Bank for International Settlements, 2005).

8. European Central Bank, "Credit Risk Transfer by ECU Banks: Activities, Risk and Risk Management" (Frankfurt: European Central Bank, May 2004).

9. Fitch Ratings, "Global Credit Derivatives: A Qualified Success" (New York: Fitch Ratings, September 24, 2003), and "Global Credit Derivatives Survey: Single-Name CDS Fuel Growth" (New York: Fitch Ratings, September 7, 2004).

10. Standard & Poor's, "Demystifying Banks' Use of Credit Derivatives" (New York: Standard & Peer's, December 2003).

- the transfer of risk may not be clean,
- market participants may fail to understand the associated risks,
- the concentration of risk is potentially high, and
- adverse selection may occur.

We discuss each below.

Transfer of Risk May Not Be Clean

As CRTs have developed, increasing the market liquidity for corporate debt (such as bonds and bank loans), the nature of the risks faced by market participants has changed in several ways. At one time, the focus of an investor in a corporate debt was on the ability of the corporation to meet its obligations. The issue with new CRTs is whether a "clean" transfer of credit risk takes place.

There are concerns with credit derivatives, and therefore with synthetic CDOs being used as CRT vehicles. First is a concern about counterparty risk—the failure of the counter-party selling credit protection would result in the buyer of credit protection maintaining the credit exposure that it thought it had eliminated. With respect to this concern, studies have noted that standard procedures are available in risk management that can be employed to reduce counterparty risk. These risk management tools are equally applicable to over-the-counter derivatives used to manage interest rate and currency risk by regulated financial entities.

Second, although the development of standard documentation for credit derivative trades by the ISDA fostered the growth of that market, there remains a concern about legal risks that may arise from a transaction. The legal risk is the risk that a credit derivative contract will not be enforceable or legally binding on the counterparty to the trade or may contain ambiguous provisions that result in a failure of the contract to fulfill its intent. The most prominent example is what the credit derivatives market faced early in its life dealing with the issue of whether a credit event had occurred and, in particular, with controversial credit events, such as restructuring. The 2004 survey of financial institutions by Fitch investigated the frequency of disputed credit events and found that about 14% of the credit events captured in the survey were reported to have involved some form of dispute. As for the resolution of those disputes, Fitch found that at the time, nearly all had been or were being resolved without the involvement of the court system. Another example of legal risk is whether the counterparty has the authority to enter into a credit derivative transaction. This is not unique to credit derivatives but has been the subject of litigation in other derivatives markets. For example, interest rate swaps between various dealers and local U.K. authorities were voided in 1991, because it was ruled that the latter did not have the legal authority to enter into the contracts in the first place.

Market Participants May Fail to Understand the Risks

The development of any market vehicle raises concerns that market participants will not understand the associated risks. For example, evidence in the interest rate swap market suggests that corporate entities failed to understand these risks; the two best-known legal cases are probably those of Gibson Greetings and Procter & Gamble. The same is true for collateralized mortgage obligations. Both instruments have been important financial innovations, but some users/investors experienced financial difficulties or fiascoes, because product innovation may have run far ahead of product education.

In the case of a financial institution that seeks to make a market in CRT vehicles, the concern is that when selling more complex products, such as CDOs, they may not be properly hedging their positions and may therefore be increasing the institution's risk. There is modeling risk. For example, in the case of a single-tranche CDO, the dealer will have an imbalanced position in CDSs and will try to hedge that position by hedging.[11] The risk is that the dealer has not hedged properly.

With respect to this issue, the recommendations of the report of the Joint Forum concentrated on the need for market participants to continue "improving risk management capabilities and for supervisors and regulators to continue improving their understanding of the associated issues." Given this focus, the report sets forth recommendations for market participants and supervisors in three areas: risk management, disclosure, and supervisory approaches, with particular emphasis on reporting and disclosure.

Concentration of Risk Is Potentially High

A CRT vehicle can result in the transfer of credit risk either from one bank to another or from a bank to a nonbank entity. In the banking system, the concern is whether credit risk has become too concentrated. For credit risk transferred out of the banking system, there is concern over the extent to which credit risk is being transferred to nonbanks, such as monoline or multiline insurance companies and hedge funds. The overall concern is with the impact on the financial system resulting from a failure of one or a few major participants in the CRT market.

The two studies by Fitch Ratings reported the number of banks (North American and European) and insurance companies active in the CRT market and the relative size of each. In its 2003 market survey, Fitch surveyed about 200 financial institutions (banks, securities firms, and insurance companies), focusing on those it classified as protection sellers. Fitch found that through credit derivatives, the global banking system transferred U.S. $229 billion of credit risk outside the banking system. Most of this was to the insurance industry

11. See Douglas J. Lucas, Laurie S. Goodman, Frank J. Fabozzi, and Rebecca Manning, *Developments in the Collateralized Debt Obligations Markets: New Products and Insights* (Hoboken, NJ: John Wiley & Sons, 2007).

(monoline insurance companies/financial guarantors, reinsurance, and insurance companies). The insurance industry itself is the largest seller of credit protection. Fitch estimated that the insurance industry sold $381 billion of net credit protection (i.e., credit protection sold less credit protection purchased). Of that amount, insurance companies provided $303 billion in credit protection through the credit derivatives market and the balance, $78 billion, in credit protection through their participation in the cash CDO market. In the insurance industry, the largest seller of credit protection is financial guarantors, insuring the senior tranches in synthetic CDO deals. Fitch concluded that bank buying of credit protection through credit derivatives has resulted in considerable improvement in secondary credit market liquidity which, in turn, allows market participants to efficiently transfer risk to other sectors of the financial market that lack the ability to originate credit. There was a relatively high concentration of credit protection buying by larger, more sophisticated banks. Smaller and regional banks were net sellers of credit protection, even though banks were net buyers of credit protection in the aggregate.

With respect to counterparty concentration, Fitch reported that the market was concentrated among the top 10 global banks and broker-dealers. Although having investment-grade ratings, the risk is that the withdrawal of one or more of these firms from the market for financial or strategic reasons could undermine the confidence in the CRT market. This was one of the major concerns of the Federal Reserve in early 2008 when justifying the bailout of the investment banking firm Bear Stearns.

In its 2003 survey, Fitch attempted to collect information on hedge fund activities by writing to the 50 largest hedge funds in the world. None responded. In its 2004 survey, Fitch included questions for the major intermediaries as to their dealings with hedge funds. Fitch found that hedge funds represented 20% to 30% of their overall CDS index trading. Ultimately, counterparty risk exposure to hedge funds depends on the extent of the collateralization of the trades. Although most of the intermediaries in the survey responded that their positions with hedge funds were fully collateralized, some stated that it was less than 100% collateralized.

Fitch also found a high concentration in the corporations that were the reference obligations in CDSs. Settlement problems could occur if one of these reference entities experienced a credit event, leading to a major market disruption. Moreover, because of the higher correlation of default that exists for counterparties and corporate references in the CRT market compared with other derivative markets, there is a concern about the market facing multiple defaults. The ECB report concluded that the potential for disruption of the new CRT vehicles was generally small.

Adverse Selection May Occur

The ability of originators to transfer credit risk through credit derivatives, CDOs, or securitization has raised concerns that a lending culture based on origination volume rather than prudent lending practices may be inadvertently adopted by banks. This is a concern about securitization in general that we described in chapter 11 and that the Dodd-Frank Act sought to address with its risk retention rules.

Key Points

- Credit derivatives can be used to alter the credit risk exposure of a balance sheet, individual security, or a portfolio.
- The ISDA has standardized documentation for credit derivative contracts, and the documents define potential credit events.
- The most controversial credit event is restructuring.
- The credit risk transfer (CRT) market makes it possible to transfer large amounts of corporate credit risk exposure among banks, as well as from the financial sector to the nonfinancial sector through credit derivatives and collateralized debt obligations (CDOs).
- By far the most dominant type of credit derivative is the credit default swap (CDS), in which the protection buyer makes a payment of the swap premium to the protection seller; however, the protection buyer receives a payment from the protection seller only if a credit event occurs.
- There are single-name CDSs, basket CDSs, and CDS indexes.
- A CDO is a security backed by a diversified pool of one or more debt obligations.
- A CDO in which the collateral assets are bond-type instruments is called a "collateralized bond obligation." A collateralized loan obligation is a CDO in which the collateral assets are bank loans.
- A CDO uses securitization technology to create different bond classes with different degrees of credit risk.
- A collateral manager is responsible for managing the collateral, subject to restrictions imposed regarding the composition of the collateral.
- There are CDOs backed by nonagency RMBSs and CMBSs. The dismal performance of the CDOs backed by the former type of collateral since 2007 has resulted in a major decline in the global offering of CDOs.
- CDO sponsors must comply with rules of securitization set forth in the Dodd-Frank Wall Street Reform and Consumer Protection Act of 2010.
- The funds to purchase collateral assets come from the issuance of debt obligations. These debt obligations include senior tranches, mezzanine tranches, and a subordinate/equity tranche.
- The ability of the collateral manager to make the interest payments to the tranches and pay off the tranches as they mature depends on the performance of the collateral selected.
- CDOs are categorized as either arbitrage transactions or balance sheet transactions, the categorization depending on the motivation of the transaction's sponsor.

- In an arbitrage transaction, the sponsor seeks to earn the spread between the yield offered on the collateral assets and the payments made to the various tranches in the structure.
- In a balance sheet transaction, the sponsor's motivation is to remove debt instruments from its balance sheet.
- Interest rate swaps are often used in CDO structures because of the mismatch between the characteristics of the collateral cash flow and some of the liabilities.
- One variety of CDO is the synthetic CDO, in which credit risk exposure is transferred through credit risk transfer rather than by transferring ownership of CDOs.
- CDSs can be embedded in a bond structure to create a credit-linked note.
- Regulators have raised concerns regarding CDOs and CDSs. These concerns include the clean transfer of risk, the failure of market participants to understand the associated risks, a potentially high concentration of risk, and adverse selection.

Questions

1. What is the primary purpose of a credit derivative?
2. In a CDS, what is meant by:

a. A reference entity?

b. A reference obligation?

3. What authoritative source is used for defining a credit event?
4. Why is restructuring the most controversial credit event?
5. Why does a CDS have an option-type payoff?
6. a. What is a basket CDS?

b. When does the protection seller have to make a payment to the protection buyer in a basket default swap?

7. For a CDS with the following terms, calculate the quarterly premium payment.

Swap Premium	Notional Amount ($)	Days in Quarter	Quarterly Premium Payment
a. 600 bps	15,000,000	90	
b. 450 bps	8,000,000	91	
c. 720 bps	15,000,000	92	

8. All other factors constant, for a given reference obligation and a given scheduled term, explain whether a CDS using full (or old) restructuring or modified restructuring would be more expensive.

9. a. For a single-name CDS, what is the difference between physical settlement and cash settlement?

b. In a physical settlement, why is there a cheapest-to-deliver issue?

10. How do the cash flows for a CDS index differ from that of a single-name CDS?

11. a. Explain how a single-name CDS can be used by a portfolio manager who wants to short a reference entity.

b. Explain how a single-name CDS can be used by a portfolio manager who is having difficulty acquiring the bonds of a particular corporation in the cash market.

12. How are CDS indexes used by portfolio managers?

13. What is a CLO?

14. What is meant by a balance sheet transaction CDO?

15. How does a CDO use the securitization technology?

16. How does a CDO differ from an ABS?

17. Why is the subordinate/equity tranche of a CDO not rated?

18. What are the sources of funds that are used in a CDO to pay bondholders?

19. What was the type of CDO collateral that caused the major losses realized by institutional investors during the financial crisis?

20. "The problem with a CLO issued by a bank is that the issuer does not necessarily have any risk exposure to the transaction." Comment.

21. In a basic credit-linked note, how does the maturity value differ compared to a standard bond structure?

Index

Note: Footnote information is indicated with n and note number following the page number.